Real-Time Rendering
Fourth Edition

Real-Time Rendering
Fourth Edition

Tomas Akenine-Möller

Eric Haines

Naty Hoffman

Angelo Pesce

Michał Iwanicki

Sébastien Hillaire

CRC Press
Taylor & Francis Group
Boca Raton London New York

CRC Press is an imprint of the
Taylor & Francis Group, an **informa** business

A BALKEMA BOOK

CRC Press
Taylor & Francis Group
6000 Broken Sound Parkway NW, Suite 300
Boca Raton, FL 33487-2742

First issued in hardback 2019

ISBN-13: 978-1-1386-2700-0 (hbk)

Library of Congress Cataloging-in-Publication Data

Names: Möller, Tomas, 1971- author.
Title: Real-time rendering / Tomas Akenine-Möller, Eric Haines, Naty Hoffman, Angelo Pesce, Michał Iwanicki, Sébastien Hillaire
Description: Fourth edition. | Boca Raton : Taylor & Francis, CRC Press, 2018.
Identifiers: LCCN 2018009546 | ISBN 9781138627000 (hardback : alk. paper)
Subjects: LCSH: Computer graphics. | Real-time data processing. | Rendering (Computer graphics)
Classification: LCC T385 .M635 2018 | DDC 006.6/773--dc23
LC record available at https://lccn.loc.gov/2018009546

**Visit the Taylor & Francis Web site at
http://www.taylorandfrancis.com**

**and the CRC Press Web site at
http://www.crcpress.com**

Printed and bound in Great Britain by Bell & Bain Ltd, Glasgow

Dedicated to Eva, Felix, and Elina
T. A-M.

Dedicated to Cathy, Ryan, and Evan
E. H.

Dedicated to Dorit, Karen, and Daniel
N. H.

Dedicated to Fei, Clelia, and Alberto
A. P.

Dedicated to Aneta and Weronika
M. I.

Dedicated to Stéphanie and Svea
S. H.

Contents

Preface   xiii

1   Introduction   1
   1.1   Contents Overview   3
   1.2   Notation and Definitions   5

2   The Graphics Rendering Pipeline   11
   2.1   Architecture   12
   2.2   The Application Stage   13
   2.3   Geometry Processing   14
   2.4   Rasterization   21
   2.5   Pixel Processing   22
   2.6   Through the Pipeline   25

3   The Graphics Processing Unit   29
   3.1   Data-Parallel Architectures   30
   3.2   GPU Pipeline Overview   34
   3.3   The Programmable Shader Stage   35
   3.4   The Evolution of Programmable Shading and APIs   37
   3.5   The Vertex Shader   42
   3.6   The Tessellation Stage   44
   3.7   The Geometry Shader   47
   3.8   The Pixel Shader   49
   3.9   The Merging Stage   53
   3.10   The Compute Shader   54

4   Transforms   57
   4.1   Basic Transforms   58
   4.2   Special Matrix Transforms and Operations   70
   4.3   Quaternions   76
   4.4   Vertex Blending   84
   4.5   Morphing   87
   4.6   Geometry Cache Playback   92
   4.7   Projections   92

5   Shading Basics   103
    5.1   Shading Models   103
    5.2   Light Sources   106
    5.3   Implementing Shading Models   117
    5.4   Aliasing and Antialiasing   130
    5.5   Transparency, Alpha, and Compositing   148
    5.6   Display Encoding   160

6   Texturing   167
    6.1   The Texturing Pipeline   169
    6.2   Image Texturing   176
    6.3   Procedural Texturing   198
    6.4   Texture Animation   200
    6.5   Material Mapping   201
    6.6   Alpha Mapping   202
    6.7   Bump Mapping   208
    6.8   Parallax Mapping   214
    6.9   Textured Lights   221

7   Shadows   223
    7.1   Planar Shadows   225
    7.2   Shadows on Curved Surfaces   229
    7.3   Shadow Volumes   230
    7.4   Shadow Maps   234
    7.5   Percentage-Closer Filtering   247
    7.6   Percentage-Closer Soft Shadows   250
    7.7   Filtered Shadow Maps   252
    7.8   Volumetric Shadow Techniques   257
    7.9   Irregular Z-Buffer Shadows   259
    7.10   Other Applications   262

8   Light and Color   267
    8.1   Light Quantities   267
    8.2   Scene to Screen   281

9   Physically Based Shading   293
    9.1   Physics of Light   293
    9.2   The Camera   307
    9.3   The BRDF   308
    9.4   Illumination   315
    9.5   Fresnel Reflectance   316
    9.6   Microgeometry   327
    9.7   Microfacet Theory   331

9.8   BRDF Models for Surface Reflection 336
9.9   BRDF Models for Subsurface Scattering 347
9.10   BRDF Models for Cloth 356
9.11   Wave Optics BRDF Models 359
9.12   Layered Materials 363
9.13   Blending and Filtering Materials 365

10 Local Illumination   375
10.1   Area Light Sources 377
10.2   Environment Lighting 391
10.3   Spherical and Hemispherical Functions 392
10.4   Environment Mapping 404
10.5   Specular Image-Based Lighting 414
10.6   Irradiance Environment Mapping 424
10.7   Sources of Error 433

11 Global Illumination   437
11.1   The Rendering Equation 437
11.2   General Global Illumination 441
11.3   Ambient Occlusion 446
11.4   Directional Occlusion 465
11.5   Diffuse Global Illumination 472
11.6   Specular Global Illumination 497
11.7   Unified Approaches 509

12 Image-Space Effects   513
12.1   Image Processing 513
12.2   Reprojection Techniques 522
12.3   Lens Flare and Bloom 524
12.4   Depth of Field 527
12.5   Motion Blur 536

13 Beyond Polygons   545
13.1   The Rendering Spectrum 545
13.2   Fixed-View Effects 546
13.3   Skyboxes 547
13.4   Light Field Rendering 549
13.5   Sprites and Layers 550
13.6   Billboarding 551
13.7   Displacement Techniques 564
13.8   Particle Systems 567
13.9   Point Rendering 572
13.10 Voxels 578

14 Volumetric and Translucency Rendering   589
    14.1   Light Scattering Theory   589
    14.2   Specialized Volumetric Rendering   600
    14.3   General Volumetric Rendering   605
    14.4   Sky Rendering   613
    14.5   Translucent Surfaces   623
    14.6   Subsurface Scattering   632
    14.7   Hair and Fur   640
    14.8   Unified Approaches   648

15 Non-Photorealistic Rendering   651
    15.1   Toon Shading   652
    15.2   Outline Rendering   654
    15.3   Stroke Surface Stylization   669
    15.4   Lines   673
    15.5   Text Rendering   675

16 Polygonal Techniques   681
    16.1   Sources of Three-Dimensional Data   682
    16.2   Tessellation and Triangulation   683
    16.3   Consolidation   690
    16.4   Triangle Fans, Strips, and Meshes   696
    16.5   Simplification   706
    16.6   Compression and Precision   712

17 Curves and Curved Surfaces   717
    17.1   Parametric Curves   718
    17.2   Parametric Curved Surfaces   734
    17.3   Implicit Surfaces   749
    17.4   Subdivision Curves   753
    17.5   Subdivision Surfaces   756
    17.6   Efficient Tessellation   767

18 Pipeline Optimization   783
    18.1   Profiling and Debugging Tools   784
    18.2   Locating the Bottleneck   786
    18.3   Performance Measurements   788
    18.4   Optimization   790
    18.5   Multiprocessing   805

19 Acceleration Algorithms   817
   19.1   Spatial Data Structures   818
   19.2   Culling Techniques   830
   19.3   Backface Culling   831
   19.4   View Frustum Culling   835
   19.5   Portal Culling   837
   19.6   Detail and Small Triangle Culling   839
   19.7   Occlusion Culling   840
   19.8   Culling Systems   850
   19.9   Level of Detail   852
   19.10 Rendering Large Scenes   866

20 Efficient Shading   881
   20.1   Deferred Shading   883
   20.2   Decal Rendering   888
   20.3   Tiled Shading   892
   20.4   Clustered Shading   898
   20.5   Deferred Texturing   905
   20.6   Object- and Texture-Space Shading   908

21 Virtual and Augmented Reality   915
   21.1   Equipment and Systems Overview   916
   21.2   Physical Elements   919
   21.3   APIs and Hardware   924
   21.4   Rendering Techniques   932

22 Intersection Test Methods   941
   22.1   GPU-Accelerated Picking   942
   22.2   Definitions and Tools   943
   22.3   Bounding Volume Creation   948
   22.4   Geometric Probability   953
   22.5   Rules of Thumb   954
   22.6   Ray/Sphere Intersection   955
   22.7   Ray/Box Intersection   959
   22.8   Ray/Triangle Intersection   962
   22.9   Ray/Polygon Intersection   966
   22.10 Plane/Box Intersection   970
   22.11 Triangle/Triangle Intersection   972
   22.12 Triangle/Box Intersection   974
   22.13 Bounding-Volume/Bounding-Volume Intersection   976
   22.14 View Frustum Intersection   981
   22.15 Line/Line Intersection   987
   22.16 Intersection between Three Planes   990

23 Graphics Hardware   **993**
  23.1   Rasterization 993
  23.2   Massive Compute and Scheduling 1002
  23.3   Latency and Occupancy 1004
  23.4   Memory Architecture and Buses 1006
  23.5   Caching and Compression 1007
  23.6   Color Buffering 1009
  23.7   Depth Culling, Testing, and Buffering 1014
  23.8   Texturing 1017
  23.9   Architecture 1019
  23.10 Case Studies 1024
  23.11 Ray Tracing Architectures 1039

24 The Future   **1041**
  24.1   Everything Else 1042
  24.2   You 1046

Bibliography   **1051**

Index   **1155**

Preface

"Things have not changed *that* much in the past eight years," was our thought entering into this fourth edition. "How hard could it be to update the book?" A year and a half later, and with three more experts recruited, our task is done. We could probably spend another year editing and elaborating, at which time there would be easily a hundred more articles and presentations to fold in. As a data point, we made a Google Doc of references that is more than 170 pages long, with about 20 references and related notes on each page. Some references we cite could and do each take up a full section in some other book. A few of our chapters, such as that on shadows, have entire books dedicated to their subjects. While creating more work for us, this wealth of information is good news for practitioners. We will often point to these primary sources, as they offer much more detail than appropriate here.

This book is about algorithms that create synthetic images fast enough that the viewer can interact with a virtual environment. We have focused on three-dimensional rendering and, to a limited extent, on the mechanics of user interaction. Modeling, animation, and many other areas are important to the process of making a real-time application, but these topics are beyond the scope of this book.

We expect you to have some basic understanding of computer graphics before reading this book, as well as knowledge of computer science and programming. We also focus on algorithms, not APIs. Many texts are available on these other subjects. If some section does lose you, skim on through or look at the references. We believe that the most valuable service we can provide you is a realization of what you yet do not know about—a basic kernel of an idea, a sense of what others have discovered about it, and ways to learn more, if you wish.

We make a point of referencing relevant material as possible, as well as providing a summary of further reading and resources at the end of most chapters. In prior editions we cited nearly everything we felt had relevant information. Here we are more a guidebook than an encyclopedia, as the field has far outgrown exhaustive (and exhausting) lists of all possible variations of a given technique. We believe you are better served by describing only a few representative schemes of many, by replacing original sources with newer, broader overviews, and by relying on you, the reader, to pursue more information from the references cited.

Most of these sources are but a mouse click away; see realtimerendering.com for the list of links to references in the bibliography. Even if you have only a passing interest in a topic, consider taking a little time to look at the related references, if for nothing else than to see some of the fantastic images presented. Our website also contains links to resources, tutorials, demonstration programs, code samples, software libraries, book corrections, and more.

Our true goal and guiding light while writing this book was simple. We wanted to write a book that we wished we had owned when we had started out, a book that both was unified yet also included details and references not found in introductory texts. We hope that you will find this book, our view of the world, of use in your travels.

Acknowledgments for the Fourth Edition

We are not experts in everything, by any stretch of the imagination, nor perfect writers. Many, many people's responses and reviews improved this edition immeasurably, saving us from our own ignorance or inattention. As but one example, when we asked around for advice on what to cover in the area of virtual reality, Johannes Van Waveren (who did not know any of us) instantly responded with a wonderfully detailed outline of topics, which formed the basis for that chapter. These kind acts by computer graphics professionals were some of the great pleasures in writing this book. One person is of particular note: Patrick Cozzi did a yeoman's job, reviewing every chapter in the book. We are grateful to the many people who helped us along the way with this edition. We could write a sentence or three about everyone who helped us along the way, but this would push us further past our book-breaking page limit.

To all the rest, in our hearts we give our appreciation and thanks to you: Sebastian Aaltonen, Johan Andersson, Magnus Andersson, Ulf Assarsson, Dan Baker, Chad Barb, Rasmus Barringer, Michal Bastien, Louis Bavoil, Michael Beale, Adrian Bentley, Ashwin Bhat, Antoine Bouthors, Wade Brainerd, Waylon Brinck, Ryan Brucks, Eric Bruneton, Valentin de Bruyn, Ben Burbank, Brent Burley, Ignacio Castaño, Cem Cebenoyan, Mark Cerny, Matthaeus Chajdas, Danny Chan, Rob Cook, Jean-Luc Corenthin, Adrian Courrèges, Cyril Crassin, Zhihao Cui, Kuba Cupisz, Robert Cupisz, Michal Drobot, Wolfgang Engel, Eugene d'Eon, Matej Drame, Michal Drobot, Alex Evans, Cass Everitt, Kayvon Fatahalian, Adam Finkelstein, Kurt Fleischer, Tim Foley, Tom Forsyth, Guillaume François, Daniel Girardeau-Montaut, Olga Gocmen, Marcin Gollent, Ben Golus, Carlos Gonzalez-Ochoa, Judah Graham, Simon Green, Dirk Gregorius, Larry Gritz, Andrew Hamilton, Earl Hammon, Jr., Jon Harada, Jon Hasselgren, Aaron Hertzmann, Stephen Hill, Rama Hoetzlein, Nicolas Holzschuch, Liwen Hu, John "Spike" Hughes, Ben Humberston, Warren Hunt, Andrew Hurley, John Hutchinson, Milan Ikits, Jon Jansen, Jorge Jimenez, Anton Kaplanyan, Gökhan Karadayi, Brian Karis, Nicolas Kasyan, Alexander Keller, Brano Kemen, Emmett Kilgariff, Byumjin Kim, Chris King, Joe Michael Kniss, Manuel Kraemer, Anders Wang Kristensen, Christopher Kulla, Edan Kwan, Chris Landreth, David Larsson, Andrew Lauritzen, Aaron Lefohn, Eric Lengyel, David Li, Ulrik Lindahl, Edward Liu, Ignacio Llamas, Dulce Isis Segarra López, David Luebke, Patrick Lundell, Miles Macklin, Dzmitry Malyshau, Sam Martin, Morgan McGuire, Brian McIntyre, James McLaren, Mariano Merchante, Arne Meyer, Sergiy Migdalskiy, Kenny Mitchell, Gregory Mitrano, Adam Moravanszky, Jacob Munkberg, Kensaku Nakata, Srinivasa G. Narasimhan, David Neubelt, Fabrice Neyret, Jane Ng, Kasper Høy Nielsen, Matthias

Nießner, Jim Nilsson, Reza Nourai, Chris Oat, Ola Olsson, Rafael Orozco, Bryan Pardilla, Steve Parker, Ankit Patel, Jasmin Patry, Jan Pechenik, Emil Persson, Marc Petit, Matt Pettineo, Agnieszka Piechnik, Jerome Platteaux, Aras Pranckevičius, Elinor Quittner, Silvia Rasheva, Nathaniel Reed, Philip Rideout, Jon Rocatis, Robert Runesson, Marco Salvi, Nicolas Savva, Andrew Schneider, Michael Schneider, Markus Schuetz, Jeremy Selan, Tarek Sherif, Peter Shirley, Peter Sikachev, Peter-Pike Sloan, Ashley Vaughan Smith, Rys Sommefeldt, Edvard Sørgård, Tiago Sousa, Tomasz Stachowiak, Nick Stam, Lee Stemkoski, Jonathan Stone, Kier Storey, Jacob Ström, Filip Strugar, Pierre Terdiman, Aaron Thibault, Nicolas Thibieroz, Robert Toth, Thatcher Ulrich, Mauricio Vives, Alex Vlachos, Evan Wallace, Ian Webster, Nick Whiting, Brandon Whitley, Mattias Widmark, Graham Wihlidal, Michael Wimmer, Daniel Wright, Bart Wroński, Chris Wyman, Ke Xu, Cem Yuksel, and Egor Yusov. We thank you for your time and effort, selflessly offered and gratefully received.

Finally, we want to thank the people at Taylor & Francis for all their efforts, in particular Rick Adams, for getting us going and guiding us along the way, Jessica Vega and Michele Dimont, for their efficient editorial work, and Charlotte Byrnes, for her superb copyediting.

Tomas Akenine-Möller
Eric Haines
Naty Hoffman
Angelo Pesce
Michał Iwanicki
Sébastien Hillaire
February 2018

Acknowledgments for the Third Edition

Special thanks go out to a number of people who went out of their way to provide us with help. First, our graphics architecture case studies would not have been anywhere as good without the extensive and generous cooperation we received from the companies making the hardware. Many thanks to Edvard Sørgard, Borgar Ljosland, Dave Shreiner, and Jørn Nystad at ARM for providing details about their Mali 200 architecture. Thanks also to Michael Dougherty at Microsoft, who provided extremely valuable help with the Xbox 360 section. Masaaki Oka at Sony Computer Entertainment provided his own technical review of the PLAYSTATION® 3 system case study, while also serving as the liaison with the Cell Broadband Engine™ and RSX® developers for their reviews.

In answering a seemingly endless stream of questions, fact-checking numerous passages, and providing many screenshots, Natalya Tatarchuk of ATI/AMD went well beyond the call of duty in helping us out. In addition to responding to our usual requests for information and clarification, Wolfgang Engel was extremely helpful in providing us with articles from the upcoming *ShaderX*^{6} book and copies of the difficult-to-obtain *ShaderX²* books [427, 428], now available online for free. Ignacio Castaño at NVIDIA provided us with valuable support and contacts, going so far as to rework a refractory demo so we could get just the right screenshot.

The chapter reviewers provided an invaluable service to us. They suggested numerous improvements and provided additional insights, helping us immeasurably. In alphabetical order they are: Michael Ashikhmin, Dan Baker, Willem de Boer, Ben Diamand, Ben Discoe, Amir Ebrahimi, Christer Ericson, Michael Gleicher, Manny Ko, Wallace Lages, Thomas Larsson, Grégory Massal, Ville Miettinen, Mike Ramsey, Scott Schaefer, Vincent Scheib, Peter Shirley, K.R. Subramanian, Mauricio Vives, and Hector Yee.

We also had a number of reviewers help us on specific sections. Our thanks go out to Matt Bronder, Christine DeNezza, Frank Fox, Jon Hasselgren, Pete Isensee, Andrew Lauritzen, Morgan McGuire, Jacob Munkberg, Manuel M. Oliveira, Aurelio Reis, Peter-Pike Sloan, Jim Tilander, and Scott Whitman.

We particularly thank Rex Crowle, Kareem Ettouney, and Francis Pang from Media Molecule for their considerable help in providing fantastic imagery and layout concepts for the cover design.

Many people helped us out in other ways, such as answering questions and providing screenshots. Many gave significant amounts of time and effort, for which we thank you. Listed alphabetically: Paulo Abreu, Timo Aila, Johan Andersson, Andreas Bærentzen, Louis Bavoil, Jim Blinn, Jaime Borasi, Per Christensen, Patrick Conran, Rob Cook, Erwin Coumans, Leo Cubbin, Richard Daniels, Mark DeLoura, Tony DeRose, Andreas Dietrich, Michael Dougherty, Bryan Dudash, Alex Evans, Cass Everitt, Randy Fernando, Jim Ferwerda, Chris Ford, Tom Forsyth, Sam Glassenberg, Robin Green, Ned Greene, Larry Gritz, Joakim Grundwall, Mark Harris, Ted Himlan, Jack Hoxley, John "Spike" Hughes, Ladislav Kavan, Alicia Kim, Gary King, Chris Lambert, Jeff Lander, Daniel Leaver, Eric Lengyel, Jennifer Liu, Brandon Lloyd, Charles Loop, David Luebke, Jonathan Maïm, Jason Mitchell, Martin Mittring, Nathan Monteleone, Gabe Newell, Hubert Nguyen, Petri Nordlund, Mike Pan, Ivan Pedersen, Matt Pharr, Fabio Policarpo, Aras Pranckevičius, Siobhan Reddy, Dirk Reiners, Christof Rezk-Salama, Eric Risser, Marcus Roth, Holly Rushmeier, Elan Ruskin, Marco Salvi, Daniel Scherzer, Kyle Shubel, Philipp Slusallek, Torbjörn Söderman, Tim Sweeney, Ben Trumbore, Michal Valient, Mark Valledor, Carsten Wenzel, Steve Westin, Chris Wyman, Cem Yuksel, Billy Zelsnack, Fan Zhang, and Renaldas Zioma.

We also thank many others who responded to our queries on public forums such as GD Algorithms. Readers who took the time to send us corrections have also been a great help. It is this supportive attitude that is one of the pleasures of working in this field.

As we have come to expect, the cheerful competence of the people at A K Peters made the publishing part of the process much easier. For this wonderful support, we thank you all.

On a personal note, Tomas would like to thank his son Felix and daughter Elina for making him understand (again) just how fun it can be to play computer games (on the Wii), instead of just looking at the graphics, and needless to say, his beautiful wife Eva. . .

Eric would also like to thank his sons Ryan and Evan for their tireless efforts in finding cool game demos and screenshots, and his wife Cathy for helping him survive it all.

Naty would like to thank his daughter Karen and son Daniel for their forbearance when writing took precedence over piggyback rides, and his wife Dorit for her constant encouragement and support.

Tomas Akenine-Möller
Eric Haines
Naty Hoffman
March 2008

Acknowledgments for the Second Edition

One of the most agreeable aspects of writing this second edition has been working with people and receiving their help. Despite their own pressing deadlines and concerns, many people gave us significant amounts of their time to improve this book. We would particularly like to thank the major reviewers. They are, listed alphabetically: Michael Abrash, Ian Ashdown, Ulf Assarsson, Chris Brennan, Sébastien Dominé, David Eberly, Cass Everitt, Tommy Fortes, Evan Hart, Greg James, Jan Kautz, Alexander Keller, Mark Kilgard, Adam Lake, Paul Lalonde, Thomas Larsson, Dean Macri, Carl Marshall, Jason L. Mitchell, Kasper Høy Nielsen, Jon Paul Schelter, Jacob Ström, Nick Triantos, Joe Warren, Michael Wimmer, and Peter Wonka. Of these, we wish to single out Cass Everitt at NVIDIA and Jason L. Mitchell at ATI Technologies for spending large amounts of time and effort in getting us the resources we needed. Our thanks also go out to Wolfgang Engel for freely sharing the contents of his upcoming book, *ShaderX* [426], so that we could make this edition as current as possible.

From discussing their work with us, to providing images or other resources, to writing reviews of sections of the book, many others helped in creating this edition. They all have our gratitude. These people include: Jason Ang, Haim Barad, Jules Bloomenthal, Jonathan Blow, Chas. Boyd, John Brooks, Cem Cebenoyan, Per Christensen, Hamilton Chu, Michael Cohen, Daniel Cohen-Or, Matt Craighead, Paul Debevec, Joe Demers, Walt Donovan, Howard Dortch, Mark Duchaineau, Phil Dutré, Dave Eberle, Gerald Farin, Simon Fenney, Randy Fernando, Jim Ferwerda, Nickson Fong, Tom Forsyth, Piero Foscari, Laura Fryer, Markus Giegl, Peter Glaskowsky, Andrew Glassner, Amy Gooch, Bruce Gooch, Simon Green, Ned Greene, Larry Gritz, Joakim Grundwall, Juan Guardado, Pat Hanrahan, Mark Harris, Michael Herf, Carsten Hess, Rich Hilmer, Kenneth Hoff III, Naty Hoffman, Nick Holliman, Hugues Hoppe, Heather Horne, Tom Hubina, Richard Huddy, Adam James, Kaveh Kardan, Paul Keller, David

Kirk, Alex Klimovitski, Jason Knipe, Jeff Lander, Marc Levoy, J.P. Lewis, Ming Lin, Adrian Lopez, Michael McCool, Doug McNabb, Stan Melax, Ville Miettinen, Kenny Mitchell, Steve Morein, Henry Moreton, Jerris Mungai, Jim Napier, George Ngo, Hubert Nguyen, Tito Pagán, Jörg Peters, Tom Porter, Emil Praun, Kekoa Proudfoot, Bernd Raabe, Ravi Ramamoorthi, Ashutosh Rege, Szymon Rusinkiewicz, Chris Seitz, Carlo Séquin, Jonathan Shade, Brian Smits, John Spitzer, Wolfgang Straßer, Wolfgang Stürzlinger, Philip Taylor, Pierre Terdiman, Nicolas Thibieroz, Jack Tumblin, Fredrik Ulfves, Thatcher Ulrich, Steve Upstill, Alex Vlachos, Ingo Wald, Ben Watson, Steve Westin, Dan Wexler, Matthias Wloka, Peter Woytiuk, David Wu, Garrett Young, Borut Zalik, Harold Zatz, Hansong Zhang, and Denis Zorin. We also wish to thank the journal *ACM Transactions on Graphics* for providing a mirror website for this book.

Alice and Klaus Peters, our production manager Ariel Jaffee, our editor Heather Holcombe, our copyeditor Michelle M. Richards, and the rest of the staff at A K Peters have done a wonderful job making this book the best possible. Our thanks to all of you.

Finally, and most importantly, our deepest thanks go to our families for giving us the huge amounts of quiet time we have needed to complete this edition. Honestly, we never thought it would take this long!

Tomas Akenine-Möller
Eric Haines
May 2002

Acknowledgments for the First Edition

Many people helped in making this book. Some of the greatest contributions were made by those who reviewed parts of it. The reviewers willingly gave the benefit of their expertise, helping to significantly improve both content and style. We wish to thank (in alphabetical order) Thomas Barregren, Michael Cohen, Walt Donovan, Angus Dorbie, Michael Garland, Stefan Gottschalk, Ned Greene, Ming C. Lin, Jason L. Mitchell, Liang Peng, Keith Rule, Ken Shoemake, John Stone, Phil Taylor, Ben Trumbore, Jorrit Tyberghein, and Nick Wilt. We cannot thank you enough.

Many other people contributed their time and labor to this project. Some let us use images, others provided models, still others pointed out important resources or connected us with people who could help. In addition to the people listed above, we wish to acknowledge the help of Tony Barkans, Daniel Baum, Nelson Beebe, Curtis Beeson, Tor Berg, David Blythe, Chas. Boyd, Don Brittain, Ian Bullard, Javier Castellar, Satyan Coorg, Jason Della Rocca, Paul Diefenbach, Alyssa Donovan, Dave Eberly, Kells Elmquist, Stuart Feldman, Fred Fisher, Tom Forsyth, Marty Franz, Thomas Funkhouser, Andrew Glassner, Bruce Gooch, Larry Gritz, Robert Grzeszczuk, Paul Haeberli, Evan Hart, Paul Heckbert, Chris Hecker, Joachim Helenklaken, Hugues Hoppe, John Jack, Mark Kilgard, David Kirk, James Klosowski, Subodh Kumar, André LaMothe, Jeff Lander, Jens Larsson, Jed Lengyel, Fredrik Liliegren, David Luebke, Thomas Lundqvist, Tom McReynolds, Stan Melax, Don Mitchell, André Möller,

Steve Molnar, Scott R. Nelson, Hubert Nguyen, Doug Rogers, Holly Rushmeier, Gernot Schaufler, Jonas Skeppstedt, Stephen Spencer, Per Stenström, Jacob Ström, Filippo Tampieri, Gary Tarolli, Ken Turkowski, Turner Whitted, Agata and Andrzej Wojaczek, Andrew Woo, Steve Worley, Brian Yen, Hans-Philip Zachau, Gabriel Zachmann, and Al Zimmerman. We also wish to thank the journal *ACM Transactions on Graphics* for providing a stable website for this book.

Alice and Klaus Peters and the staff at AK Peters, particularly Carolyn Artin and Sarah Gillis, have been instrumental in making this book a reality. To all of you, thanks.

Finally, our deepest thanks go to our families and friends for providing support throughout this incredible, sometimes grueling, often exhilarating process.

Tomas Möller
Eric Haines
March 1999

Chapter 1
Introduction

Real-time rendering is concerned with rapidly making images on the computer. It is the most highly interactive area of computer graphics. An image appears on the screen, the viewer acts or reacts, and this feedback affects what is generated next. This cycle of reaction and rendering happens at a rapid enough rate that the viewer does not see individual images, but rather becomes immersed in a dynamic process.

The rate at which images are displayed is measured in frames per second (FPS) or Hertz (Hz). At one frame per second, there is little sense of interactivity; the user is painfully aware of the arrival of each new image. At around 6 FPS, a sense of interactivity starts to grow. Video games aim for 30, 60, 72, or higher FPS; at these speeds the user focuses on action and reaction.

Movie projectors show frames at 24 FPS but use a shutter system to display each frame two to four times to avoid flicker. This *refresh rate* is separate from the display rate and is expressed in Hertz (Hz). A shutter that illuminates the frame three times has a 72 Hz refresh rate. LCD monitors also separate refresh rate from display rate.

Watching images appear on a screen at 24 FPS might be acceptable, but a higher rate is important for minimizing response time. As little as 15 milliseconds of temporal delay can slow and interfere with interaction [1849]. As an example, head-mounted displays for virtual reality often require 90 FPS to minimize latency.

There is more to real-time rendering than interactivity. If speed was the only criterion, any application that rapidly responded to user commands and drew anything on the screen would qualify. Rendering in real time normally means producing three-dimensional images.

Interactivity and some sense of connection to three-dimensional space are sufficient conditions for real-time rendering, but a third element has become a part of its definition: graphics acceleration hardware. Many consider the introduction of the 3Dfx Voodoo 1 card in 1996 the real beginning of consumer-level three-dimensional graphics [408]. With the rapid advances in this market, every computer, tablet, and mobile phone now comes with a graphics processor built in. Some excellent examples of the results of real-time rendering made possible by hardware acceleration are shown in Figures 1.1 and 1.2.

Figure 1.1. A shot from *Forza Motorsport 7*. *(Image courtesy of Turn 10 Studios, Microsoft.)*

Figure 1.2. The city of Beauclair rendered in *The Witcher 3*. *(CD PROJEKT®, The Witcher® are registered trademarks of CD PROJEKT Capital Group. The Witcher game © CD PROJEKT S.A. Developed by CD PROJEKT S.A. All rights reserved. The Witcher game is based on the prose of Andrzej Sapkowski. All other copyrights and trademarks are the property of their respective owners.)*

Advances in graphics hardware have fueled an explosion of research in the field of interactive computer graphics. We will focus on providing methods to increase speed and improve image quality, while also describing the features and limitations of acceleration algorithms and graphics APIs. We will not be able to cover every topic in depth, so our goal is to present key concepts and terminology, explain the most robust and practical algorithms in the field, and provide pointers to the best places to go for more information. We hope our attempts to provide you with tools for understanding this field prove to be worth the time and effort you spend with our book.

1.1 Contents Overview

What follows is a brief overview of the chapters ahead.

Chapter 2, The Graphics Rendering Pipeline. The heart of real-time rendering is the set of steps that takes a scene description and converts it into something we can see.

Chapter 3, The Graphics Processing Unit. The modern GPU implements the stages of the rendering pipeline using a combination of fixed-function and programmable units.

Chapter 4, Transforms. Transforms are the basic tools for manipulating the position, orientation, size, and shape of objects and the location and view of the camera.

Chapter 5, Shading Basics. Discussion begins on the definition of materials and lights and their use in achieving the desired surface appearance, whether realistic or stylized. Other appearance-related topics are introduced, such as providing higher image quality through the use of antialiasing, transparency, and gamma correction.

Chapter 6, Texturing. One of the most powerful tools for real-time rendering is the ability to rapidly access and display images on surfaces. This process is called texturing, and there are a wide variety of methods for applying it.

Chapter 7, Shadows. Adding shadows to a scene increases both realism and comprehension. The more popular algorithms for computing shadows rapidly are presented.

Chapter 8, Light and Color. Before we perform physically based rendering, we first need to understand how to quantify light and color. And after our physical rendering process is done, we need to transform the resulting quantities into values for the display, accounting for the properties of the screen and viewing environment. Both topics are covered in this chapter.

Chapter 9, Physically Based Shading. We build an understanding of physically based shading models from the ground up. The chapter starts with the underlying physical phenomena, covers models for a variety of rendered materials, and ends with methods for blending materials together and filtering them to avoid aliasing and preserve surface appearance.

Chapter 10, Local Illumination. Algorithms for portraying more elaborate light sources are explored. Surface shading takes into account that light is emitted by physical objects, which have characteristic shapes.

Chapter 11, Global Illumination. Algorithms that simulate multiple interactions between the light and the scene further increase the realism of an image. We discuss ambient and directional occlusion and methods for rendering global illumination effects on diffuse and specular surfaces, as well as some promising unified approaches.

Chapter 12, Image-Space Effects. Graphics hardware is adept at performing image processing at rapid speeds. Image filtering and reprojection techniques are discussed first, then we survey several popular post-processing effects: lens flares, motion blur, and depth of field.

Chapter 13, Beyond Polygons.   Triangles are not always the fastest or most realistic way to describe objects. Alternate representations based on using images, point clouds, voxels, and other sets of samples each have their advantages.

Chapter 14, Volumetric and Translucency Rendering.   The focus here is the theory and practice of volumetric material representations and their interactions with light sources. The simulated phenomena range from large-scale atmospheric effects down to light scattering within thin hair fibers.

Chapter 15, Non-Photorealistic Rendering.   Attempting to make a scene look realistic is only one way of rendering it. Other styles, such as cartoon shading and watercolor effects, are surveyed. Line and text generation techniques are also discussed.

Chapter 16, Polygonal Techniques.   Geometric data comes from a wide range of sources, and sometimes requires modification to be rendered rapidly and well. The many facets of polygonal data representation and compression are presented.

Chapter 17, Curves and Curved Surfaces.   More complex surface representations offer advantages such as being able to trade off between quality and rendering speed, more compact representation, and smooth surface generation.

Chapter 18, Pipeline Optimization.   Once an application is running and uses efficient algorithms, it can be made even faster using various optimization techniques. Finding the bottleneck and deciding what to do about it is the theme here. Multiprocessing is also discussed.

Chapter 19, Acceleration Algorithms.   After you make it go, make it go fast. Various forms of culling and level of detail rendering are covered.

Chapter 20, Efficient Shading.   A large number of lights in a scene can slow performance considerably. Fully shading surface fragments before they are known to be visible is another source of wasted cycles. We explore a wide range of approaches to tackle these and other forms of inefficiency while shading.

Chapter 21, Virtual and Augmented Reality.   These fields have particular challenges and techniques for efficiently producing realistic images at rapid and consistent rates.

Chapter 22, Intersection Test Methods.   Intersection testing is important for rendering, user interaction, and collision detection. In-depth coverage is provided here for a wide range of the most efficient algorithms for common geometric intersection tests.

Chapter 23, Graphics Hardware.   The focus here is on components such as color depth, framebuffers, and basic architecture types. A case study of representative GPUs is provided.

Chapter 24, The Future.   Take a guess (we do).

Due to space constraints, we have made a chapter about Collision Detection free for download at realtimerendering.com, along with appendices on linear algebra and trigonometry.

1.2 Notation and Definitions

First, we shall explain the mathematical notation used in this book. For a more thorough explanation of many of the terms used in this section, and throughout this book, get our linear algebra appendix at realtimerendering.com.

1.2.1 Mathematical Notation

Table 1.1 summarizes most of the mathematical notation we will use. Some of the concepts will be described at some length here.

Note that there are some exceptions to the rules in the table, primarily shading equations using notation that is extremely well established in the literature, e.g., L for radiance, E for irradiance, and σ_s for scattering coefficient.

The angles and the scalars are taken from $\mathbb{R}$, i.e., they are real numbers. Vectors and points are denoted by bold lowercase letters, and the components are accessed as

$$\mathbf{v} = \begin{pmatrix} v_x \\ v_y \\ v_z \end{pmatrix},$$

that is, in column vector format, which is commonly used in the computer graphics world. At some places in the text we use (v_x, v_y, v_z) instead of the formally more correct $(v_x \ v_y \ v_z)^T$, since the former is easier to read.

Type	Notation	Examples
angle	lowercase Greek	$\alpha_i, \phi, \rho, \eta, \gamma_{242}, \theta$
scalar	lowercase italic	a, b, t, u_k, v, w_{ij}
vector or point	lowercase bold	$\mathbf{a}, \mathbf{u}, \mathbf{v}_s \ \mathbf{h}(\rho), \mathbf{h}_z$
matrix	capital bold	$\mathbf{T(t)}, \mathbf{X}, \mathbf{R}_x(\rho)$
plane	π: a vector and a scalar	$\pi : \mathbf{n} \cdot \mathbf{x} + d = 0,$ $\pi_1 : \mathbf{n}_1 \cdot \mathbf{x} + d_1 = 0$
triangle	$\triangle$ 3 points	$\triangle \mathbf{v}_0 \mathbf{v}_1 \mathbf{v}_2, \triangle \mathbf{cba}$
line segment	two points	$\mathbf{uv}, \mathbf{a}_i \mathbf{b}_j$
geometric entity	capital italic	A_{OBB}, T, B_{AABB}

Table 1.1. Summary of the notation used in this book.

Using homogeneous notation, a coordinate is represented by four values $\mathbf{v} = (v_x \quad v_y \quad v_z \quad v_w)^T$, where a vector is $\mathbf{v} = (v_x \quad v_y \quad v_z \quad 0)^T$ and a point is $\mathbf{v} = (v_x \quad v_y \quad v_z \quad 1)^T$. Sometimes we use only three-element vectors and points, but we try to avoid any ambiguity as to which type is being used. For matrix manipulations, it is extremely advantageous to have the same notation for vectors as for points. For more information, see Chapter 4 on transforms. In some algorithms, it will be convenient to use numeric indices instead of x, y, and z, for example $\mathbf{v} = (v_0 \quad v_1 \quad v_2)^T$. All these rules for vectors and points also hold for two-element vectors; in that case, we simply skip the last component of a three-element vector.

The matrix deserves a bit more explanation. The common sizes that will be used are 2×2, 3×3, and 4×4. We will review the manner of accessing a 3×3 matrix $\mathbf{M}$, and it is simple to extend this process to the other sizes. The (scalar) elements of $\mathbf{M}$ are denoted m_{ij}, $0 \leq (i,j) \leq 2$, where i denotes the row and j the column, as in Equation 1.1:

$$\mathbf{M} = \begin{pmatrix} m_{00} & m_{01} & m_{02} \\ m_{10} & m_{11} & m_{12} \\ m_{20} & m_{21} & m_{22} \end{pmatrix}. \tag{1.1}$$

The following notation, shown in Equation 1.2 for a 3×3 matrix, is used to isolate vectors from the matrix $\mathbf{M}$: $\mathbf{m}_{,j}$ represents the jth column vector and $\mathbf{m}_{i,}$ represents the ith row vector (in column vector form). As with vectors and points, indexing the column vectors can also be done with x, y, z, and sometimes w, if that is more convenient:

$$\mathbf{M} = \begin{pmatrix} \mathbf{m}_{,0} & \mathbf{m}_{,1} & \mathbf{m}_{,2} \end{pmatrix} = \begin{pmatrix} \mathbf{m}_x & \mathbf{m}_y & \mathbf{m}_z \end{pmatrix} = \begin{pmatrix} \mathbf{m}_{0,}^T \\ \mathbf{m}_{1,}^T \\ \mathbf{m}_{2,}^T \end{pmatrix}. \tag{1.2}$$

A plane is denoted $\pi : \mathbf{n} \cdot \mathbf{x} + d = 0$ and contains its mathematical formula, the plane normal $\mathbf{n}$ and the scalar d. The normal is a vector describing what direction the plane faces. More generally (e.g., for curved surfaces), a normal describes this direction for a particular point on the surface. For a plane the same normal happens to apply to all its points. π is the common mathematical notation for a plane. The plane π is said to divide the space into a *positive half-space*, where $\mathbf{n} \cdot \mathbf{x} + d > 0$, and a *negative half-space*, where $\mathbf{n} \cdot \mathbf{x} + d < 0$. All other points are said to lie in the plane.

A triangle can be defined by three points $\mathbf{v}_0$, $\mathbf{v}_1$, and $\mathbf{v}_2$ and is denoted by $\triangle \mathbf{v}_0 \mathbf{v}_1 \mathbf{v}_2$.

Table 1.2 presents some additional mathematical operators and their notation. The dot, cross, determinant, and length operators are explained in our downloadable linear algebra appendix at realtimerendering.com. The transpose operator turns a column vector into a row vector and vice versa. Thus a column vector can be written in compressed form in a block of text as $\mathbf{v} = (v_x \quad v_y \quad v_z)^T$. Operator 4, introduced in *Graphics Gems IV* [735], is a unary operator on a two-dimensional vector. Letting

	Operator	Description
1:	$\cdot$	dot product
2:	$\times$	cross product
3:	$\mathbf{v}^T$	transpose of the vector $\mathbf{v}$
4:	$\perp$	the unary, perp dot product operator
5:	$\lvert \cdot \rvert$	determinant of a matrix
6:	$\lvert \cdot \rvert$	absolute value of a scalar
7:	$\lVert \cdot \rVert$	length (or norm) of argument
8:	x^+	clamping x to 0
9:	$x^{\overline{+}}$	clamping x between 0 and 1
10:	$n!$	factorial
11:	$\binom{n}{k}$	binomial coefficients

Table 1.2. Notation for some mathematical operators.

this operator work on a vector $\mathbf{v} = (v_x \ v_y)^T$ gives a vector that is perpendicular to $\mathbf{v}$, i.e., $\mathbf{v}^\perp = (-v_y \ v_x)^T$. We use $|a|$ to denote the absolute value of the scalar a, while $|\mathbf{A}|$ means the determinant of the matrix $\mathbf{A}$. Sometimes, we also use $|\mathbf{A}| = |\mathbf{a} \ \mathbf{b} \ \mathbf{c}| = \det(\mathbf{a}, \mathbf{b}, \mathbf{c})$, where $\mathbf{a}$, $\mathbf{b}$, and $\mathbf{c}$ are column vectors of the matrix $\mathbf{A}$.

Operators 8 and 9 are clamping operators, commonly used in shading calculations. Operator 8 clamps negative values to 0:

$$x^+ = \begin{cases} x, & \text{if } x > 0, \\ 0, & \text{otherwise,} \end{cases} \tag{1.3}$$

and operator 9 clamps values between 0 and 1:

$$x^{\overline{+}} = \begin{cases} 1, & \text{if } x \geq 1, \\ x, & \text{if } 0 < x < 1, \\ 0, & \text{otherwise.} \end{cases} \tag{1.4}$$

The tenth operator, factorial, is defined as shown below, and note that $0! = 1$:

$$n! = n(n-1)(n-2)\cdots 3 \cdot 2 \cdot 1. \tag{1.5}$$

The eleventh operator, the binomial factor, is defined as shown in Equation 1.6:

$$\binom{n}{k} = \frac{n!}{k!(n-k)!}. \tag{1.6}$$

	Function	**Description**
1:	atan2(y, x)	two-value arctangent
2:	$\log(n)$	natural logarithm of n

Table 1.3. Notation for some specialized mathematical functions.

Further on, we call the common planes $x = 0$, $y = 0$, and $z = 0$ the *coordinate planes* or *axis-aligned planes*. The axes $\mathbf{e}_x = (1 \quad 0 \quad 0)^T$, $\mathbf{e}_y = (0 \quad 1 \quad 0)^T$, and $\mathbf{e}_z = (0 \quad 0 \quad 1)^T$ are called *main axes* or *main directions* and individually called the x-axis, y-axis, and z-axis. This set of axes is often called the *standard basis*. Unless otherwise noted, we will use orthonormal bases (consisting of mutually perpendicular unit vectors).

The notation for a range that includes both a and b, and all numbers in between, is $[a, b]$. If we want all number between a and b, but not a and b themselves, then we write (a, b). Combinations of these can also be made, e.g., $[a, b)$ means all numbers between a and b including a but not b.

The C-math function atan2(y,x) is often used in this text, and so deserves some attention. It is an extension of the mathematical function $\arctan(x)$. The main differences between them are that $-\frac{\pi}{2} < \arctan(x) < \frac{\pi}{2}$, that $0 \leq$ atan2(y, x) $< 2\pi$, and that an extra argument has been added to the latter function. A common use for arctan is to compute $\arctan(y/x)$, but when $x = 0$, division by zero results. The extra argument for atan2(y,x) avoids this.

In this volume the notation $\log(n)$ always means the natural logarithm, $\log_e(n)$, not the base-10 logarithm, $\log_{10}(n)$.

We use a right-hand coordinate system since this is the standard system for three-dimensional geometry in the field of computer graphics.

Colors are represented by a three-element vector, such as (*red, green, blue*), where each element has the range $[0, 1]$.

1.2.2   Geometrical Definitions

The basic rendering primitives (also called *drawing primitives*) used by almost all graphics hardware are points, lines, and triangles.[1]

Throughout this book, we will refer to a collection of geometric entities as either a *model* or an *object*. A *scene* is a collection of models comprising everything that is included in the environment to be rendered. A scene can also include material descriptions, lighting, and viewing specifications.

Examples of objects are a car, a building, and even a line. In practice, an object often consists of a set of drawing primitives, but this may not always be the case; an object may have a higher kind of geometrical representation, such as Bézier curves or

---

[1]The only exceptions we know of are Pixel-Planes [502], which could draw spheres, and the NVIDIA NV1 chip, which could draw ellipsoids.

surfaces, or subdivision surfaces. Also, objects can consist of other objects, e.g., a car object includes four door objects, four wheel objects, and so on.

1.2.3 Shading

Following well-established computer graphics usage, in this book terms derived from "shading," "shader," and related words are used to refer to two distinct but related concepts: computer-generated visual appearance (e.g., "shading model," "shading equation," "toon shading") or a programmable component of a rendering system (e.g., "vertex shader," "shading language"). In both cases, the intended meaning should be clear from the context.

Further Reading and Resources

The most important resource we can refer you to is the website for this book: realtimerendering.com. It contains links to the latest information and websites relevant to each chapter. The field of real-time rendering is changing with real-time speed. In the book we have attempted to focus on concepts that are fundamental and techniques that are unlikely to go out of style. On the website we have the opportunity to present information that is relevant to today's software developer, and we have the ability to keep it up-to-date.

Chapter 2
The Graphics
Rendering Pipeline

"A chain is no stronger than its weakest link."
—Anonymous

This chapter presents the core component of real-time graphics, namely the *graphics rendering pipeline*, also known simply as "the pipeline." The main function of the pipeline is to generate, or *render*, a two-dimensional image, given a virtual camera, three-dimensional objects, light sources, and more. The rendering pipeline is thus the underlying tool for real-time rendering. The process of using the pipeline is depicted in Figure 2.1. The locations and shapes of the objects in the image are determined by their geometry, the characteristics of the environment, and the placement of the camera in that environment. The appearance of the objects is affected by material properties, light sources, textures (images applied to surfaces), and shading equations.

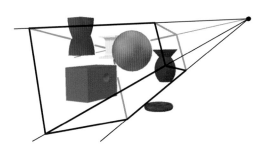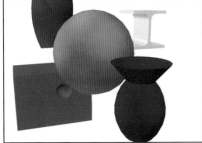

Figure 2.1. In the left image, a virtual camera is located at the tip of the pyramid (where four lines converge). Only the primitives inside the view volume are rendered. For an image that is rendered in perspective (as is the case here), the view volume is a *frustum* (plural: *frusta*), i.e., a truncated pyramid with a rectangular base. The right image shows what the camera "sees." Note that the red donut shape in the left image is not in the rendering to the right because it is located outside the view frustum. Also, the twisted blue prism in the left image is clipped against the top plane of the frustum.

We will explain the different stages of the rendering pipeline, with a focus on function rather than implementation. Relevant details for applying these stages will be covered in later chapters.

2.1 Architecture

In the physical world, the pipeline concept manifests itself in many different forms, from factory assembly lines to fast food kitchens. It also applies to graphics rendering. A pipeline consists of several stages [715], each of which performs part of a larger task.

The pipeline stages execute in parallel, with each stage dependent upon the result of the previous stage. Ideally, a nonpipelined system that is then divided into n pipelined stages could give a speedup of a factor of n. This increase in performance is the main reason to use pipelining. For example, a large number of sandwiches can be prepared quickly by a series of people—one preparing the bread, another adding meat, another adding toppings. Each passes the result to the next person in line and immediately starts work on the next sandwich. If each person takes twenty seconds to perform their task, a maximum rate of one sandwich every twenty seconds, three a minute, is possible. The pipeline stages execute in parallel, but they are stalled until the slowest stage has finished its task. For example, say the meat addition stage becomes more involved, taking thirty seconds. Now the best rate that can be achieved is two sandwiches a minute. For this particular pipeline, the meat stage is the *bottleneck*, since it determines the speed of the entire production. The toppings stage is said to be *starved* (and the customer, too) during the time it waits for the meat stage to be done.

This kind of pipeline construction is also found in the context of real-time computer graphics. A coarse division of the real-time rendering pipeline into four main stages—*application, geometry processing, rasterization,* and *pixel processing*—is shown in Figure 2.2. This structure is the core—the engine of the rendering pipeline—which is used in real-time computer graphics applications and is thus an essential base for

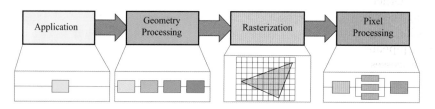

Figure 2.2. The basic construction of the rendering pipeline, consisting of four stages: application, geometry processing, rasterization, and pixel processing. Each of these stages may be a pipeline in itself, as illustrated below the geometry processing stage, or a stage may be (partly) parallelized, as shown below the pixel processing stage. In this illustration, the application stage is a single process, but this stage could also be pipelined or parallelized. Note that rasterization finds the pixels inside a primitive, e.g., a triangle.

discussion in subsequent chapters. Each of these stages is usually a pipeline in itself, which means that it consists of several substages. We differentiate between the functional stages shown here and the structure of their implementation. A functional stage has a certain task to perform but does not specify the way that task is executed in the pipeline. A given implementation may combine two functional stages into one unit or execute using programmable cores, while it divides another, more time-consuming, functional stage into several hardware units.

The rendering speed may be expressed in *frames per second* (FPS), that is, the number of images rendered per second. It can also be represented using *Hertz* (Hz), which is simply the notation for $1/seconds$, i.e., the frequency of update. It is also common to just state the time, in milliseconds (ms), that it takes to render an image. The time to generate an image usually varies, depending on the complexity of the computations performed during each frame. Frames per second is used to express either the rate for a particular frame, or the average performance over some duration of use. Hertz is used for hardware, such as a display, which is set to a fixed rate.

As the name implies, the *application* stage is driven by the application and is therefore typically implemented in software running on general-purpose CPUs. These CPUs commonly include multiple cores that are capable of processing multiple *threads of execution* in parallel. This enables the CPUs to efficiently run the large variety of tasks that are the responsibility of the application stage. Some of the tasks traditionally performed on the CPU include collision detection, global acceleration algorithms, animation, physics simulation, and many others, depending on the type of application. The next main stage is *geometry processing*, which deals with transforms, projections, and all other types of geometry handling. This stage computes what is to be drawn, how it should be drawn, and where it should be drawn. The geometry stage is typically performed on a graphics processing unit (GPU) that contains many programmable cores as well as fixed-operation hardware. The *rasterization* stage typically takes as input three vertices, forming a triangle, and finds all pixels that are considered inside that triangle, then forwards these to the next stage. Finally, the *pixel processing* stage executes a program per pixel to determine its color and may perform depth testing to see whether it is visible or not. It may also perform per-pixel operations such as blending the newly computed color with a previous color. The rasterization and pixel processing stages are also processed entirely on the GPU. All these stages and their internal pipelines will be discussed in the next four sections. More details on how the GPU processes these stages are given in Chapter 3.

2.2 The Application Stage

The developer has full control over what happens in the application stage, since it usually executes on the CPU. Therefore, the developer can entirely determine the implementation and can later modify it in order to improve performance. Changes here can also affect the performance of subsequent stages. For example, an application stage algorithm or setting could decrease the number of triangles to be rendered.

All this said, some application work can be performed by the GPU, using a separate mode called a *compute shader*. This mode treats the GPU as a highly parallel general processor, ignoring its special functionality meant specifically for rendering graphics.

At the end of the application stage, the geometry to be rendered is fed to the geometry processing stage. These are the *rendering primitives*, i.e., points, lines, and triangles, that might eventually end up on the screen (or whatever output device is being used). This is the most important task of the application stage.

A consequence of the software-based implementation of this stage is that it is not divided into substages, as are the geometry processing, rasterization, and pixel processing stages.[1] However, to increase performance, this stage is often executed in parallel on several processor cores. In CPU design, this is called a *superscalar* construction, since it is able to execute several processes at the same time in the same stage. Section 18.5 presents various methods for using multiple processor cores.

One process commonly implemented in this stage is *collision detection*. After a collision is detected between two objects, a response may be generated and sent back to the colliding objects, as well as to a force feedback device. The application stage is also the place to take care of input from other sources, such as the keyboard, the mouse, or a head-mounted display. Depending on this input, several different kinds of actions may be taken. Acceleration algorithms, such as particular culling algorithms (Chapter 19), are also implemented here, along with whatever else the rest of the pipeline cannot handle.

2.3   Geometry Processing

The geometry processing stage on the GPU is responsible for most of the per-triangle and per-vertex operations. This stage is further divided into the following functional stages: vertex shading, projection, clipping, and screen mapping (Figure 2.3).

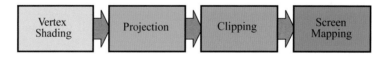

Figure 2.3. The geometry processing stage divided into a pipeline of functional stages.

---

[1]Since a CPU itself is pipelined on a much smaller scale, you could say that the application stage is further subdivided into several pipeline stages, but this is not relevant here.

2.3.1 Vertex Shading

There are two main tasks of vertex shading, namely, to compute the position for a vertex and to evaluate whatever the programmer may like to have as vertex output data, such as a normal and texture coordinates. Traditionally much of the shade of an object was computed by applying lights to each vertex's location and normal and storing only the resulting color at the vertex. These colors were then interpolated across the triangle. For this reason, this programmable vertex processing unit was named the vertex shader [1049]. With the advent of the modern GPU, along with some or all of the shading taking place per pixel, this vertex shading stage is more general and may not evaluate any shading equations at all, depending on the programmer's intent. The vertex shader is now a more general unit dedicated to setting up the data associated with each vertex. As an example, the vertex shader can animate an object using the methods in Sections 4.4 and 4.5.

We start by describing how the vertex position is computed, a set of coordinates that is always required. On its way to the screen, a model is transformed into several different *spaces* or *coordinate systems*. Originally, a model resides in its own *model space*, which simply means that it has not been transformed at all. Each model can be associated with a *model transform* so that it can be positioned and oriented. It is possible to have several model transforms associated with a single model. This allows several copies (called *instances*) of the same model to have different locations, orientations, and sizes in the same scene, without requiring replication of the basic geometry.

It is the vertices and the normals of the model that are transformed by the model transform. The coordinates of an object are called *model coordinates*, and after the model transform has been applied to these coordinates, the model is said to be located in *world coordinates* or in *world space*. The world space is unique, and after the models have been transformed with their respective model transforms, all models exist in this same space.

As mentioned previously, only the models that the camera (or observer) sees are rendered. The camera has a location in world space and a direction, which are used to place and aim the camera. To facilitate projection and clipping, the camera and all the models are transformed with the *view transform*. The purpose of the view transform is to place the camera at the origin and aim it, to make it look in the direction of the negative z-axis, with the y-axis pointing upward and the x-axis pointing to the right. We use the $-z$-axis convention; some texts prefer looking down the $+z$-axis. The difference is mostly semantic, as transform between one and the other is simple. The actual position and direction after the view transform has been applied are dependent on the underlying application programming interface (API). The space thus delineated is called *camera space*, or more commonly, *view space* or *eye space*. An example of the way in which the view transform affects the camera and the models is shown in Figure 2.4. Both the model transform and the view transform may be implemented as 4×4 matrices, which is the topic of Chapter 4. However, it is important to realize that

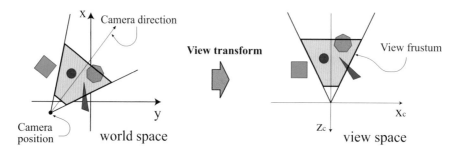

Figure 2.4. In the left illustration, a top-down view shows the camera located and oriented as the user wants it to be, in a world where the $+z$-axis is up. The view transform reorients the world so that the camera is at the origin, looking along its negative z-axis, with the camera's $+y$-axis up, as shown on the right. This is done to make the clipping and projection operations simpler and faster. The light blue area is the view volume. Here, perspective viewing is assumed, since the view volume is a frustum. Similar techniques apply to any kind of projection.

the position and normal of a vertex can be computed in whatever way the programmer prefers.

Next, we describe the second type of output from vertex shading. To produce a realistic scene, it is not sufficient to render the shape and position of objects, but their appearance must be modeled as well. This description includes each object's material, as well as the effect of any light sources shining on the object. Materials and lights can be modeled in any number of ways, from simple colors to elaborate representations of physical descriptions.

This operation of determining the effect of a light on a material is known as *shading*. It involves computing a *shading equation* at various points on the object. Typically, some of these computations are performed during geometry processing on a model's vertices, and others may be performed during per-pixel processing. A variety of material data can be stored at each vertex, such as the point's location, a normal, a color, or any other numerical information that is needed to evaluate the shading equation. Vertex shading results (which can be colors, vectors, texture coordinates, along with any other kind of shading data) are then sent to the rasterization and pixel processing stages to be interpolated and used to compute the shading of the surface.

Vertex shading in the form of the GPU vertex shader is discussed in more depth throughout this book and most specifically in Chapters 3 and 5.

As part of vertex shading, rendering systems perform *projection* and then clipping, which transforms the view volume into a unit cube with its extreme points at $(-1, -1, -1)$ and $(1, 1, 1)$. Different ranges defining the same volume can and are used, for example, $0 \leq z \leq 1$. The unit cube is called the *canonical view volume*. Projection is done first, and on the GPU it is done by the vertex shader. There are two commonly used projection methods, namely *orthographic* (also called *parallel*)

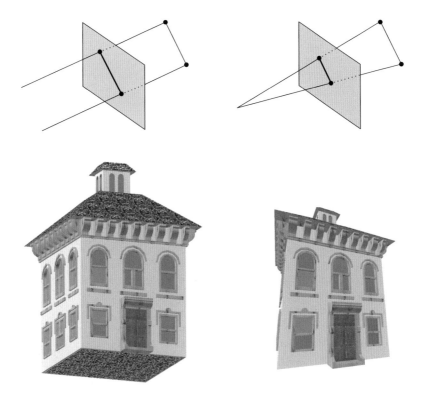

Figure 2.5. On the left is an orthographic, or parallel, projection; on the right is a perspective projection.

and *perspective* projection. See Figure 2.5. In truth, orthographic is just one type of parallel projection. Several others find use, particularly in the field of architecture, such as oblique and axonometric projections. The old arcade game *Zaxxon* is named from the latter.

Note that projection is expressed as a matrix (Section 4.7) and so it may sometimes be concatenated with the rest of the geometry transform.

The view volume of orthographic viewing is normally a rectangular box, and the orthographic projection transforms this view volume into the unit cube. The main characteristic of orthographic projection is that parallel lines remain parallel after the transform. This transformation is a combination of a translation and a scaling.

The perspective projection is a bit more complex. In this type of projection, the farther away an object lies from the camera, the smaller it appears after projection. In addition, parallel lines may converge at the horizon. The perspective transform thus mimics the way we perceive objects' size. Geometrically, the view volume, called a *frustum*, is a truncated pyramid with rectangular base. The frustum is transformed into the unit cube as well. Both orthographic and perspective transforms can be constructed with 4×4 matrices (Chapter 4), and after either transform, the models are said to be in *clip coordinates*. These are in fact homogeneous coordinates, discussed in Chapter 4, and so this occurs before division by w. The GPU's vertex shader must always output coordinates of this type in order for the next functional stage, clipping, to work correctly.

Although these matrices transform one volume into another, they are called projections because after display, the z-coordinate is not stored in the image generated but is stored in a z-buffer, described in Section 2.5. In this way, the models are projected from three to two dimensions.

2.3.2 Optional Vertex Processing

Every pipeline has the vertex processing just described. Once this processing is done, there are a few optional stages that can take place on the GPU, in this order: tessellation, geometry shading, and stream output. Their use depends both on the capabilities of the hardware—not all GPUs have them—and the desires of the programmer. They are independent of each other, and in general they are not commonly used. More will be said about each in Chapter 3.

The first optional stage is *tessellation*. Imagine you have a bouncing ball object. If you represent it with a single set of triangles, you can run into problems with quality or performance. Your ball may look good from 5 meters away, but up close the individual triangles, especially along the silhouette, become visible. If you make the ball with more triangles to improve quality, you may waste considerable processing time and memory when the ball is far away and covers only a few pixels on the screen. With tessellation, a curved surface can be generated with an appropriate number of triangles.

We have talked a bit about triangles, but up to this point in the pipeline we have just processed vertices. These could be used to represent points, lines, triangles, or other objects. Vertices can be used to describe a curved surface, such as a ball. Such surfaces can be specified by a set of patches, and each patch is made of a set of vertices. The tessellation stage consists of a series of stages itself—hull shader, tessellator, and domain shader—that converts these sets of patch vertices into (normally) larger sets of vertices that are then used to make new sets of triangles. The camera for the scene can be used to determine how many triangles are generated: many when the patch is close, few when it is far away.

The next optional stage is the *geometry shader*. This shader predates the tessellation shader and so is more commonly found on GPUs. It is like the tessellation shader in that it takes in primitives of various sorts and can produce new vertices. It is a much simpler stage in that this creation is limited in scope and the types of output primitives are much more limited. Geometry shaders have several uses, with one of the most popular being particle generation. Imagine simulating a fireworks explosion.

Each fireball could be represented by a point, a single vertex. The geometry shader can take each point and turn it into a square (made of two triangles) that faces the viewer and covers several pixels, so providing a more convincing primitive for us to shade.

The last optional stage is called *stream output*. This stage lets us use the GPU as a geometry engine. Instead of sending our processed vertices down the rest of the pipeline to be rendered to the screen, at this point we can optionally output these to an array for further processing. These data can be used by the CPU, or the GPU itself, in a later pass. This stage is typically used for particle simulations, such as our fireworks example.

These three stages are performed in this order—tessellation, geometry shading, and stream output—and each is optional. Regardless of which (if any) options are used, if we continue down the pipeline we have a set of vertices with homogeneous coordinates that will be checked for whether the camera views them.

2.3.3 Clipping

Only the primitives wholly or partially inside the view volume need to be passed on to the rasterization stage (and the subsequent pixel processing stage), which then draws them on the screen. A primitive that lies fully inside the view volume will be passed on to the next stage as is. Primitives entirely outside the view volume are not passed on further, since they are not rendered. It is the primitives that are partially inside the view volume that require clipping. For example, a line that has one vertex outside and one inside the view volume should be clipped against the view volume, so that the vertex that is outside is replaced by a new vertex that is located at the intersection between the line and the view volume. The use of a projection matrix means that the transformed primitives are clipped against the unit cube. The advantage of performing the view transformation and projection before clipping is that it makes the clipping problem consistent; primitives are always clipped against the unit cube.

The clipping process is depicted in Figure 2.6. In addition to the six clipping planes of the view volume, the user can define additional clipping planes to visibly chop objects. An image showing this type of visualization, called *sectioning*, is shown in Figure 19.1 on page 818.

The clipping step uses the 4-value homogeneous coordinates produced by projection to perform clipping. Values do not normally interpolate linearly across a triangle in perspective space. The fourth coordinate is needed so that data are properly interpolated and clipped when a perspective projection is used. Finally, *perspective division* is performed, which places the resulting triangles' positions into three-dimensional *normalized device coordinates*. As mentioned earlier, this view volume ranges from $(-1, -1, -1)$ to $(1, 1, 1)$. The last step in the geometry stage is to convert from this space to window coordinates.

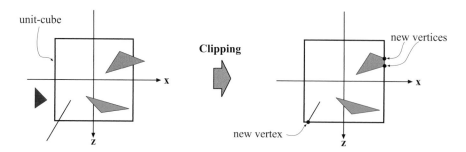

Figure 2.6. After the projection transform, only the primitives inside the unit cube (which correspond to primitives inside the view frustum) are needed for continued processing. Therefore, the primitives outside the unit cube are discarded, and primitives fully inside are kept. Primitives intersecting with the unit cube are clipped against the unit cube, and thus new vertices are generated and old ones are discarded.

2.3.4 Screen Mapping

Only the (clipped) primitives inside the view volume are passed on to the screen mapping stage, and the coordinates are still three-dimensional when entering this stage. The x- and y-coordinates of each primitive are transformed to form *screen coordinates*. Screen coordinates together with the z-coordinates are also called *window coordinates*. Assume that the scene should be rendered into a window with the minimum corner at (x_1, y_1) and the maximum corner at (x_2, y_2), where $x_1 < x_2$ and $y_1 < y_2$. Then the screen mapping is a translation followed by a scaling operation. The new x- and y- coordinates are said to be screen coordinates. The z-coordinate ($[-1, +1]$ for OpenGL and $[0, 1]$ for DirectX) is also mapped to $[z_1, z_2]$, with $z_1 = 0$ and $z_2 = 1$ as the default values. These can be changed with the API, however. The window coordinates along with this remapped z-value are passed on to the rasterizer stage. The screen mapping process is depicted in Figure 2.7.

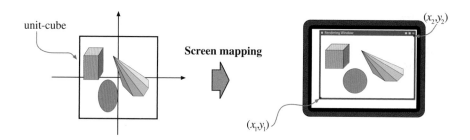

Figure 2.7. The primitives lie in the unit cube after the projection transform, and the screen mapping procedure takes care of finding the coordinates on the screen.

Next, we describe how integer and floating point values relate to pixels (and texture coordinates). Given a horizontal array of pixels and using Cartesian coordinates, the left edge of the leftmost pixel is 0.0 in floating point coordinates. OpenGL has always used this scheme, and DirectX 10 and its successors use it. The center of this pixel is at 0.5. So, a range of pixels $[0, 9]$ cover a span from $[0.0, 10.0)$. The conversions are simply

$$d = \texttt{floor(c)}, \tag{2.1}$$

$$c = d + 0.5, \tag{2.2}$$

where d is the discrete (integer) index of the pixel and c is the continuous (floating point) value within the pixel.

While all APIs have pixel location values that increase going from left to right, the location of zero for the top and bottom edges is inconsistent in some cases between OpenGL and DirectX.[2] OpenGL favors the Cartesian system throughout, treating the lower left corner as the lowest-valued element, while DirectX sometimes defines the upper left corner as this element, depending on the context. There is a logic to each, and no right answer exists where they differ. As an example, $(0, 0)$ is located at the lower left corner of an image in OpenGL, while it is upper left for DirectX. This difference is important to take into account when moving from one API to the other.

2.4 Rasterization

Given the transformed and projected vertices with their associated shading data (all from geometry processing), the goal of the next stage is to find all pixels—short for *picture elements*—that are inside the primitive, e.g., a triangle, being rendered. We call this process *rasterization*, and it is split up into two functional substages: triangle setup (also called primitive assembly) and triangle traversal. These are shown to the left in Figure 2.8. Note that these can handle points and lines as well, but since triangles are most common, the substages have "triangle" in their names. Rasterization, also called *scan conversion*, is thus the conversion from two-dimensional vertices in screen space—each with a z-value (depth value) and various shading information associated with each vertex—into pixels on the screen. Rasterization can also be thought of as a synchronization point between geometry processing and pixel processing, since it is here that triangles are formed from three vertices and eventually sent down to pixel processing.

Whether the triangle is considered to overlap the pixel depends on how you have set up the GPU's pipeline. For example, you may use point sampling to determine

---

[2] "Direct3D" is the three-dimensional graphics API component of DirectX. DirectX includes other API elements, such an input and audio control. Rather than differentiate between writing "DirectX" when specifying a particular release and "Direct3D" when discussing this particular API, we follow common usage by writing "DirectX" throughout.

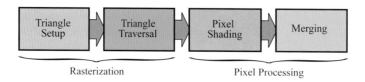

Figure 2.8. Left: rasterization split into two functional stages, called triangle setup and triangle traversal. Right: pixel processing split into two functional stages, namely, pixel processing and merging.

"insideness." The simplest case uses a single point sample in the center of each pixel, and so if that center point is inside the triangle then the corresponding pixel is considered inside the triangle as well. You may also use more than one sample per pixel using supersampling or multisampling antialiasing techniques (Section 5.4.2). Yet another way is to use conservative rasterization, where the definition is that a pixel is "inside" the triangle if at least part of the pixel overlaps with the triangle (Section 23.1.2).

2.4.1   Triangle Setup

In this stage the differentials, edge equations, and other data for the triangle are computed. These data may be used for triangle traversal (Section 2.4.2), as well as for interpolation of the various shading data produced by the geometry stage. Fixed-function hardware is used for this task.

2.4.2   Triangle Traversal

Here is where each pixel that has its center (or a sample) covered by the triangle is checked and a *fragment* generated for the part of the pixel that overlaps the triangle. More elaborate sampling methods can be found in Section 5.4. Finding which samples or pixels are inside a triangle is often called *triangle traversal*. Each triangle fragment's properties are generated using data interpolated among the three triangle vertices (Chapter 5). These properties include the fragment's depth, as well as any shading data from the geometry stage. McCormack et al. [1162] offer more information on triangle traversal. It is also here that perspective-correct interpolation over the triangles is performed [694] (Section 23.1.1). All pixels or samples that are inside a primitive are then sent to the pixel processing stage, described next.

2.5   Pixel Processing

At this point, all the pixels that are considered inside a triangle or other primitive have been found as a consequence of the combination of all the previous stages. The pixel processing stage is divided into *pixel shading* and *merging*, shown to the right in Figure 2.8. Pixel processing is the stage where per-pixel or per-sample computations and operations are performed on pixels or samples that are inside a primitive.

2.5.1 Pixel Shading

Any per-pixel shading computations are performed here, using the interpolated shading data as input. The end result is one or more colors to be passed on to the next stage. Unlike the triangle setup and traversal stages, which are usually performed by dedicated, hardwired silicon, the pixel shading stage is executed by programmable GPU cores. To that end, the programmer supplies a program for the pixel shader (or fragment shader, as it is known in OpenGL), which can contain any desired computations. A large variety of techniques can be employed here, one of the most important of which is *texturing*. Texturing is treated in more detail in Chapter 6. Simply put, texturing an object means "gluing" one or more images onto that object, for a variety of purposes. A simple example of this process is depicted in Figure 2.9. The image may be one-, two-, or three-dimensional, with two-dimensional images being the most common. At its simplest, the end product is a color value for each fragment, and these are passed on to the next substage.

Figure 2.9. A dragon model without textures is shown in the upper left. The pieces in the image texture are "glued" onto the dragon, and the result is shown in the lower left.

2.5.2 Merging

The information for each pixel is stored in the *color buffer*, which is a rectangular array of colors (a red, a green, and a blue component for each color). It is the responsibility of the merging stage to combine the fragment color produced by the pixel shading stage with the color currently stored in the buffer. This stage is also called ROP, standing for "raster operations (pipeline)" or "render output unit," depending on who you ask. Unlike the shading stage, the GPU subunit that performs this stage is typically not fully programmable. However, it is highly configurable, enabling various effects.

This stage is also responsible for resolving visibility. This means that when the whole scene has been rendered, the color buffer should contain the colors of the primitives in the scene that are visible from the point of view of the camera. For most or even all graphics hardware, this is done with the z-buffer (also called *depth buffer*) algorithm [238]. A z-buffer is the same size and shape as the color buffer, and for each pixel it stores the z-value to the currently closest primitive. This means that when a primitive is being rendered to a certain pixel, the z-value on that primitive at that pixel is being computed and compared to the contents of the z-buffer at the same pixel. If the new z-value is smaller than the z-value in the z-buffer, then the primitive that is being rendered is closer to the camera than the primitive that was previously closest to the camera at that pixel. Therefore, the z-value and the color of that pixel are updated with the z-value and color from the primitive that is being drawn. If the computed z-value is greater than the z-value in the z-buffer, then the color buffer and the z-buffer are left untouched. The z-buffer algorithm is simple, has $O(n)$ convergence (where n is the number of primitives being rendered), and works for any drawing primitive for which a z-value can be computed for each (relevant) pixel. Also note that this algorithm allows most primitives to be rendered in any order, which is another reason for its popularity. However, the z-buffer stores only a single depth at each point on the screen, so it cannot be used for partially transparent primitives. These must be rendered after all opaque primitives, and in back-to-front order, or using a separate order-independent algorithm (Section 5.5). Transparency is one of the major weaknesses of the basic z-buffer.

We have mentioned that the color buffer is used to store colors and that the z-buffer stores z-values for each pixel. However, there are other channels and buffers that can be used to filter and capture fragment information. The *alpha channel* is associated with the color buffer and stores a related opacity value for each pixel (Section 5.5). In older APIs, the alpha channel was also used to discard pixels selectively via the alpha test feature. Nowadays a discard operation can be inserted into the pixel shader program and any type of computation can be used to trigger a discard. This type of test can be used to ensure that fully transparent fragments do not affect the z-buffer (Section 6.6).

The *stencil buffer* is an offscreen buffer used to record the locations of the rendered primitive. It typically contains 8 bits per pixel. Primitives can be rendered into the stencil buffer using various functions, and the buffer's contents can then be used to control rendering into the color buffer and *z*-buffer. As an example, assume that a filled circle has been drawn into the stencil buffer. This can be combined with an operator that allows rendering of subsequent primitives into the color buffer only where the circle is present. The stencil buffer can be a powerful tool for generating some special effects. All these functions at the end of the pipeline are called *raster operations* (ROP) or *blend operations*. It is possible to mix the color currently in the color buffer with the color of the pixel being processed inside a triangle. This can enable effects such as transparency or the accumulation of color samples. As mentioned, blending is typically configurable using the API and not fully programmable. However, some APIs have support for raster order views, also called pixel shader ordering, which enable programmable blending capabilities.

The *framebuffer* generally consists of all the buffers on a system.

When the primitives have reached and passed the rasterizer stage, those that are visible from the point of view of the camera are displayed on screen. The screen displays the contents of the color buffer. To avoid allowing the human viewer to see the primitives as they are being rasterized and sent to the screen, *double buffering* is used. This means that the rendering of a scene takes place off screen, in a *back buffer*. Once the scene has been rendered in the back buffer, the contents of the back buffer are swapped with the contents of the *front buffer* that was previously displayed on the screen. The swapping often occurs during *vertical retrace*, a time when it is safe to do so.

For more information on different buffers and buffering methods, see Sections 5.4.2, 23.6, and 23.7.

2.6 Through the Pipeline

Points, lines, and triangles are the rendering primitives from which a model or an object is built. Imagine that the application is an interactive *computer aided design* (CAD) application, and that the user is examining a design for a waffle maker. Here we will follow this model through the entire graphics rendering pipeline, consisting of the four major stages: application, geometry, rasterization, and pixel processing. The scene is rendered with perspective into a window on the screen. In this simple example, the waffle maker model includes both lines (to show the edges of parts) and triangles (to show the surfaces). The waffle maker has a lid that can be opened. Some of the triangles are textured by a two-dimensional image with the manufacturer's logo. For this example, surface shading is computed completely in the geometry stage, except for application of the texture, which occurs in the rasterization stage.

Application

CAD applications allow the user to select and move parts of the model. For example, the user might select the lid and then move the mouse to open it. The application stage must translate the mouse move to a corresponding rotation matrix, then see to it that this matrix is properly applied to the lid when it is rendered. Another example: An animation is played that moves the camera along a predefined path to show the waffle maker from different views. The camera parameters, such as position and view direction, must then be updated by the application, dependent upon time. For each frame to be rendered, the application stage feeds the camera position, lighting, and primitives of the model to the next major stage in the pipeline—the geometry stage.

Geometry Processing

For perspective viewing, we assume here that the application has supplied a projection matrix. Also, for each object, the application has computed a matrix that describes both the view transform and the location and orientation of the object in itself. In our example, the waffle maker's base would have one matrix, the lid another. In the geometry stage the vertices and normals of the object are transformed with this matrix, putting the object into view space. Then shading or other calculations at the vertices may be computed, using material and light source properties. Projection is then performed using a separate user-supplied projection matrix, transforming the object into a unit cube's space that represents what the eye sees. All primitives outside the cube are discarded. All primitives intersecting this unit cube are clipped against the cube in order to obtain a set of primitives that lies entirely inside the unit cube. The vertices then are mapped into the window on the screen. After all these per-triangle and per-vertex operations have been performed, the resulting data are passed on to the rasterization stage.

Rasterization

All the primitives that survive clipping in the previous stage are then rasterized, which means that all pixels that are inside a primitive are found and sent further down the pipeline to pixel processing.

Pixel Processing

The goal here is to compute the color of each pixel of each visible primitive. Those triangles that have been associated with any textures (images) are rendered with these images applied to them as desired. Visibility is resolved via the z-buffer algorithm, along with optional discard and stencil tests. Each object is processed in turn, and the final image is then displayed on the screen.

Conclusion

This pipeline resulted from decades of API and graphics hardware evolution targeted to real-time rendering applications. It is important to note that this is not the only possible rendering pipeline; offline rendering pipelines have undergone different evolutionary paths. Rendering for film production was often done with *micropolygon* pipelines [289, 1734], but ray tracing and path tracing have taken over lately. These techniques, covered in Section 11.2.2, may also be used in architectural and design previsualization.

For many years, the only way for application developers to use the process described here was through a *fixed-function pipeline* defined by the graphics API in use. The fixed-function pipeline is so named because the graphics hardware that implements it consists of elements that cannot be programmed in a flexible way. The last example of a major fixed-function machine is Nintendo's Wii, introduced in 2006. Programmable GPUs, on the other hand, make it possible to determine exactly what operations are applied in various sub-stages throughout the pipeline. For the fourth edition of the book, we assume that all development is done using programmable GPUs.

Further Reading and Resources

Blinn's book *A Trip Down the Graphics Pipeline* [165] is an older book about writing a software renderer from scratch. It is a good resource for learning about some of the subtleties of implementing a rendering pipeline, explaining key algorithms such as clipping and perspective interpolation. The venerable (yet frequently updated) *OpenGL Programming Guide* (a.k.a. the "Red Book") [885] provides a thorough description of the graphics pipeline and algorithms related to its use. Our book's website, realtimerendering.com, gives links to a variety of pipeline diagrams, rendering engine implementations, and more.

Chapter 3
The Graphics Processing Unit

"The display is the computer."
—Jen-Hsun Huang

Historically, graphics acceleration started with interpolating colors on each pixel scanline overlapping a triangle and then displaying these values. Including the ability to access image data allowed textures to be applied to surfaces. Adding hardware for interpolating and testing z-depths provided built-in visibility checking. Because of their frequent use, such processes were committed to dedicated hardware to increase performance. More parts of the rendering pipeline, and much more functionality for each, were added in successive generations. Dedicated graphics hardware's only computational advantage over the CPU is speed, but speed is critical.

Over the past two decades, graphics hardware has undergone an incredible transformation. The first consumer graphics chip to include hardware vertex processing (NVIDIA's GeForce256) shipped in 1999. NVIDIA coined the term *graphics processing unit* (GPU) to differentiate the GeForce 256 from the previously available rasterization-only chips, and it stuck. During the next few years, the GPU evolved from configurable implementations of a complex fixed-function pipeline to highly programmable blank slates where developers could implement their own algorithms. Programmable *shaders* of various kinds are the primary means by which the GPU is controlled. For efficiency, some parts of the pipeline remain configurable, not programmable, but the trend is toward programmability and flexibility [175].

GPUs gain their great speed from a focus on a narrow set of highly parallelizable tasks. They have custom silicon dedicated to implementing the z-buffer, to rapidly accessing texture images and other buffers, and to finding which pixels are covered by a triangle, for example. How these elements perform their functions is covered in Chapter 23. More important to know early on is how the GPU achieves parallelism for its programmable shaders.

Section 3.3 explains how shaders function. For now, what you need to know is that a shader core is a small processor that does some relatively isolated task, such as transforming a vertex from its location in the world to a screen coordinate, or computing the color of a pixel covered by a triangle. With thousands or millions of triangles being sent to the screen each frame, every second there can be billions of *shader invocations*, that is, separate instances where shader programs are run.

To begin with, *latency* is a concern that all processors face. Accessing data takes some amount of time. A basic way to think about latency is that the farther away the information is from the processor, the longer the wait. Section 23.3 covers latency in more detail. Information stored in memory chips will take longer to access than that in local registers. Section 18.4.1 discusses memory access in more depth. The key point is that waiting for data to be retrieved means the processor is stalled, which reduces performance.

3.1 Data-Parallel Architectures

Various strategies are used by different processor architectures to avoid stalls. A CPU is optimized to handle a wide variety of data structures and large code bases. CPUs can have multiple processors, but each runs code in a mostly serial fashion, limited SIMD vector processing being the minor exception. To minimize the effect of latency, much of a CPU's chip consists of fast local caches, memory that is filled with data likely to be needed next. CPUs also avoid stalls by using clever techniques such as branch prediction, instruction reordering, register renaming, and cache prefetching [715]

GPUs take a different approach. Much of a GPU's chip area is dedicated to a large set of processors, called *shader cores*, often numbering in the thousands. The GPU is a stream processor, in which ordered sets of similar data are processed in turn. Because of this similarity—a set of vertices or pixels, for example—the GPU can process these data in a massively parallel fashion. One other important element is that these invocations are as independent as possible, such that they have no need for information from neighboring invocations and do not share writable memory locations. This rule is sometimes broken to allow new and useful functionality, but such exceptions come at a price of potential delays, as one processor may wait on another processor to finish its work.

The GPU is optimized for *throughput*, defined as the maximum rate at which data can be processed. However, this rapid processing has a cost. With less chip area dedicated to cache memory and control logic, latency for each shader core is generally considerably higher than what a CPU processor encounters [462].

Say a mesh is rasterized and two thousand pixels have fragments to be processed; a pixel shader program is to be invoked two thousand times. Imagine there is only a single shader processor, the world's weakest GPU. It starts to execute the shader program for the first fragment of the two thousand. The shader processor performs a few arithmetic operations on values in registers. Registers are local and quick to access, so no stall occurs. The shader processor then comes to an instruction such as a texture access; e.g., for a given surface location the program needs to know the pixel color of the image applied to the mesh. A texture is an entirely separate resource, not a part of the pixel program's local memory, and texture access can be somewhat involved. A memory fetch can take hundreds to thousands of clock cycles, during which time the GPU processor is doing nothing. At this point the shader processor would stall, waiting for the texture's color value to be returned.

To make this terrible GPU into something considerably better, give each fragment a little storage space for its local registers. Now, instead of stalling on a texture fetch, the shader processor is allowed to switch and execute another fragment, number two of two thousand. This switch is extremely fast, nothing in the first or second fragment is affected other than noting which instruction was executing on the first. Now the second fragment is executed. Same as with the first, a few arithmetic functions are performed, then a texture fetch is again encountered. The shader core now switches to another fragment, number three. Eventually all two thousand fragments are processed in this way. At this point the shader processor returns to fragment number one. By this time the texture color has been fetched and is available for use, so the shader program can then continue executing. The processor proceeds in the same fashion until another instruction that is known to stall execution is encountered, or the program completes. A single fragment will take longer to execute than if the shader processor stayed focused on it, but overall execution time for the fragments as a whole is dramatically reduced.

In this architecture, latency is hidden by having the GPU stay busy by switching to another fragment. GPUs take this design a step further by separating the instruction execution logic from the data. Called *single instruction, multiple data* (SIMD), this arrangement executes the same command in lock-step on a fixed number of shader programs. The advantage of SIMD is that considerably less silicon (and power) needs to be dedicated to processing data and switching, compared to using an individual logic and dispatch unit to run each program. Translating our two-thousand-fragment example into modern GPU terms, each pixel shader invocation for a fragment is called a *thread*. This type of thread is unlike a CPU thread. It consists of a bit of memory for the input values to the shader, along with any register space needed for the shader's execution. Threads that use the same shader program are bundled into groups, called *warps* by NVIDIA and *wavefronts* by AMD. A warp/wavefront is scheduled for execution by some number GPU shader cores, anywhere from 8 to 64, using SIMD-processing. Each thread is mapped to a *SIMD lane*.

Say we have two thousand threads to be executed. Warps on NVIDIA GPUs contain 32 threads. This yields $2000/32 = 62.5$ warps, which means that 63 warps are allocated, one warp being half empty. A warp's execution is similar to our single GPU processor example. The shader program is executed in lock-step on all 32 processors. When a memory fetch is encountered, all threads encounter it at the same time, because the same instruction is executed for all. The fetch signals that this warp of threads will stall, all waiting for their (different) results. Instead of stalling, the warp is swapped out for a different warp of 32 threads, which is then executed by the 32 cores. This swapping is just as fast as with our single processor system, as no data within each thread is touched when a warp is swapped in or out. Each thread has its own registers, and each warp keeps track of which instruction it is executing. Swapping in a new warp is just a matter of pointing the set of cores at a different set of threads to execute; there is no other overhead. Warps execute or swap out until all are completed. See Figure 3.1.

In our simple example the latency of a memory fetch for a texture can cause a warp to swap out. In reality warps could be swapped out for shorter delays, since the cost of swapping is so low. There are several other techniques used to optimize execution [945], but warp-swapping is the major latency-hiding mechanism used by all GPUs. Several factors are involved in how efficiently this process works. For example, if there are few threads, then few warps can be created, making latency hiding problematic.

The shader program's structure is an important characteristic that influences efficiency. A major factor is the amount of register use for each thread. In our example we assume that two thousand threads can all be resident on the GPU at one time. The more registers needed by the shader program associated with each thread, the fewer threads, and thus the fewer warps, can be resident in the GPU. A shortage of warps can mean that a stall cannot be mitigated by swapping. Warps that are resident are said to be "in flight," and this number is called the *occupancy*. High occupancy means that there are many warps available for processing, so that idle processors are less likely. Low occupancy will often lead to poor performance. The frequency of memory fetches also affects how much latency hiding is needed. Lauritzen [993] outlines how occupancy is affected by the number of registers and the shared memory that a shader uses. Wronski [1911, 1914] discusses how the ideal occupancy rate can vary depending on the type of operations a shader performs.

Another factor affecting overall efficiency is dynamic branching, caused by "if" statements and loops. Say an "if" statement is encountered in a shader program. If all the threads evaluate and take the same branch, the warp can continue without any concern about the other branch. However, if some threads, or even one thread, take the alternate path, then the warp must execute both branches, throwing away the results not needed by each particular thread [530, 945]. This problem is called *thread divergence*, where a few threads may need to execute a loop iteration or perform an "if" path that the other threads in the warp do not, leaving them idle during this time.

All GPUs implement these architectural ideas, resulting in systems with strict limitations but massive amounts of compute power per watt. Understanding how this system operates will help you as a programmer make more efficient use of the power it provides. In the sections that follow we discuss how the GPU implements the rendering pipeline, how programmable shaders operate, and the evolution and function of each GPU stage.

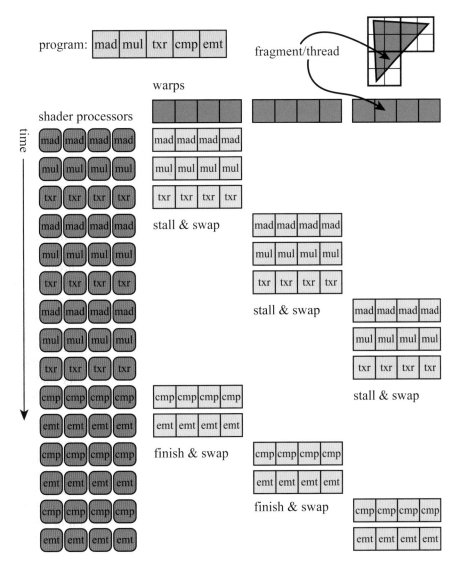

Figure 3.1. Simplified shader execution example. A triangle's fragments, called threads, are gathered into warps. Each warp is shown as four threads but have 32 threads in reality. The shader program to be executed is five instructions long. The set of four GPU shader processors executes these instructions for the first warp until a stall condition is detected on the "txr" command, which needs time to fetch its data. The second warp is swapped in and the shader program's first three instructions are applied to it, until a stall is again detected. After the third warp is swapped in and stalls, execution continues by swapping in the first warp and continuing execution. If its "txr" command's data are not yet returned at this point, execution truly stalls until these data are available. Each warp finishes in turn.

Figure 3.2. GPU implementation of the rendering pipeline. The stages are color coded according to the degree of user control over their operation. Green stages are fully programmable. Dashed lines show optional stages. Yellow stages are configurable but not programmable, e.g., various blend modes can be set for the merge stage. Blue stages are completely fixed in their function.

3.2 GPU Pipeline Overview

The GPU implements the conceptual geometry processing, rasterization, and pixel processing pipeline stages described in Chapter 2. These are divided into several hardware stages with varying degrees of configurability or programmability. Figure 3.2 shows the various stages color coded according to how programmable or configurable they are. Note that these physical stages are split up somewhat differently than the functional stages presented in Chapter 2.

We describe here the *logical model* of the GPU, the one that is exposed to you as a programmer by an API. As Chapters 18 and 23 discuss, the implementation of this logical pipeline, the *physical model*, is up to the hardware vendor. A stage that is fixed-function in the logical model may be executed on the GPU by adding commands to an adjacent programmable stage. A single program in the pipeline may be split into elements executed by separate sub-units, or be executed by a separate pass entirely. The logical model can help you reason about what affects performance, but it should not be mistaken for the way the GPU actually implements the pipeline.

The vertex shader is a fully programmable stage that is used to implement the geometry processing stage. The geometry shader is a fully programmable stage that operates on the vertices of a primitive (point, line, or triangle). It can be used to perform per-primitive shading operations, to destroy primitives, or to create new ones. The tessellation stage and geometry shader are both optional, and not all GPUs support them, especially on mobile devices.

The clipping, triangle setup, and triangle traversal stages are implemented by fixed-function hardware. Screen mapping is affected by window and viewport settings, internally forming a simple scale and repositioning. The pixel shader stage is fully programmable. Although the merger stage is not programmable, it is highly configurable and can be set to perform a wide variety of operations. It implements the "merging" functional stage, in charge of modifying the color, z-buffer, blend, stencil, and any other output-related buffers. The pixel shader execution together with the merger stage form the conceptual pixel processing stage presented in Chapter 2.

Over time, the GPU pipeline has evolved away from hard-coded operation and toward increasing flexibility and control. The introduction of programmable shader stages was the most important step in this evolution. The next section describes the features common to the various programmable stages.

3.3   The Programmable Shader Stage

Modern shader programs use a unified shader design. This means that the vertex, pixel, geometry, and tessellation-related shaders share a common programming model. Internally they have the same *instruction set architecture* (ISA). A processor that implements this model is called a *common-shader core* in DirectX, and a GPU with such cores is said to have a unified shader architecture. The idea behind this type of architecture is that shader processors are usable in a variety of roles, and the GPU can allocate these as it sees fit. For example, a set of meshes with tiny triangles will need more vertex shader processing than large squares each made of two triangles. A GPU with separate pools of vertex and pixel shader cores means that the ideal work distribution to keep all the cores busy is rigidly predetermined. With unified shader cores, the GPU can decide how to balance this load.

Describing the entire shader programming model is well beyond the scope of this book, and there are many documents, books, and websites that already do so. Shaders are programmed using C-like *shading languages* such as DirectX's *High-Level Shading Language* (HLSL) and the *OpenGL Shading Language* (GLSL). DirectX's HLSL can be compiled to virtual machine bytecode, also called the *intermediate language* (IL or DXIL), to provide hardware independence. An intermediate representation can also allow shader programs to be compiled and stored offline. This intermediate language is converted to the ISA of the specific GPU by the driver. Console programming usually avoids the intermediate language step, since there is then only one ISA for the system.

The basic data types are 32-bit single-precision floating point scalars and vectors, though vectors are only part of the shader code and are not supported in hardware as outlined above. On modern GPUs 32-bit integers and 64-bit floats are also supported natively. Floating point vectors typically contain data such as positions ($xyzw$), normals, matrix rows, colors ($rgba$), or texture coordinates ($uvwq$). Integers are most often used to represent counters, indices, or bitmasks. Aggregate data types such as structures, arrays, and matrices are also supported.

A *draw call* invokes the graphics API to draw a group of primitives, so causing the graphics pipeline to execute and run its shaders. Each programmable shader stage has two types of inputs: *uniform* inputs, with values that remain constant throughout a draw call (but can be changed between draw calls), and *varying* inputs, data that come from the triangle's vertices or from rasterization. For example, a pixel shader may provide the color of a light source as a uniform value, and the triangle surface's location changes per pixel and so is varying. A texture is a special kind of uniform input that once was always a color image applied to a surface, but that now can be thought of as any large array of data.

The underlying virtual machine provides special registers for the different types of inputs and outputs. The number of available *constant registers* for uniforms is much larger than those registers available for varying inputs or outputs. This happens because the varying inputs and outputs need to be stored separately for each vertex

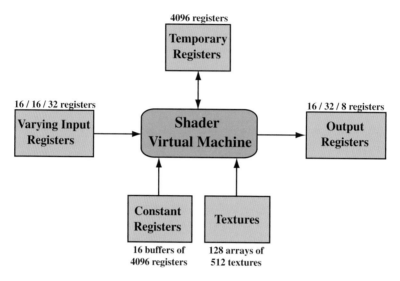

Figure 3.3. Unified virtual machine architecture and register layout, under Shader Model 4.0. The maximum available number is indicated next to each resource. Three numbers separated by slashes refer to the limits for vertex, geometry, and pixel shaders (from left to right).

or pixel, so there is a natural limit as to how many are needed. The uniform inputs are stored once and reused across all the vertices or pixels in the draw call. The virtual machine also has general-purpose *temporary registers*, which are used for scratch space. All types of registers can be array-indexed using integer values in temporary registers. The inputs and outputs of the shader virtual machine can be seen in Figure 3.3.

Operations that are common in graphics computations are efficiently executed on modern GPUs. Shading languages expose the most common of these operations (such as additions and multiplications) via operators such as * and +. The rest are exposed through *intrinsic functions*, e.g., atan(), sqrt(), log(), and many others, optimized for the GPU. Functions also exist for more complex operations, such as vector normalization and reflection, the cross product, and matrix transpose and determinant computations.

The term *flow control* refers to the use of branching instructions to change the flow of code execution. Instructions related to flow control are used to implement high-level language constructs such as "if" and "case" statements, as well as various types of loops. Shaders support two types of flow control. *Static flow control* branches are based on the values of uniform inputs. This means that the flow of the code is constant over the draw call. The primary benefit of static flow control is to allow the same shader to be used in a variety of different situations (e.g., a varying numbers of lights). There is no thread divergence, since all invocations take the same code path. *Dynamic flow control* is based on the values of varying inputs, meaning that each fragment can execute the code differently. This is much more powerful than static flow control but can cost performance, especially if the code flow changes erratically between shader invocations.

3.4   The Evolution of Programmable Shading and APIs

The idea of a framework for programmable shading dates back to 1984 with Cook's *shade trees* [287]. A simple shader and its corresponding shade tree are shown in Figure 3.4. The RenderMan Shading Language [63, 1804] was developed from this idea in the late 1980s. It is still used today for film production rendering, along with other evolving specifications, such as the *Open Shading Language* (OSL) project [608].

Consumer-level graphics hardware was first successfully introduced by 3dfx Interactive on October 1, 1996. See Figure 3.5 for a timeline from this year. Their Voodoo graphics card's ability to render the game *Quake* with high quality and performance led to its quick adoption. This hardware implemented a fixed-function pipeline throughout. Before GPUs supported programmable shaders natively, there were several attempts to implement programmable shading operations in real time via multiple rendering passes. The *Quake III: Arena* scripting language was the first widespread

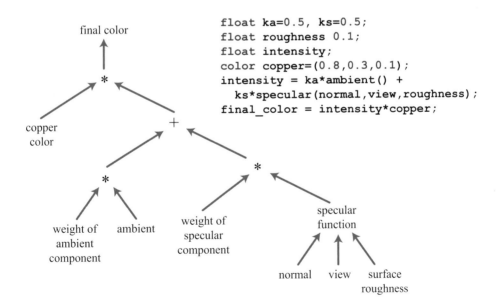

Figure 3.4. Shade tree for a simple copper shader, and its corresponding shader language program. *(After Cook [287].)*

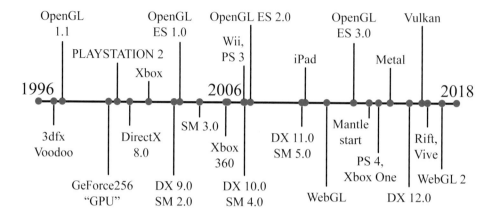

Figure 3.5. A timeline of some API and graphics hardware releases.

commercial success in this area in 1999. As mentioned at the beginning of the chapter, NVIDIA's GeForce256 was the first hardware to be called a GPU, but it was not programmable. However, it was configurable.

In early 2001, NVIDIA's GeForce 3 was the first GPU to support programmable vertex shaders [1049], exposed through DirectX 8.0 and extensions to OpenGL. These shaders were programmed in an assembly-like language that was converted by the drivers into microcode on the fly. Pixel shaders were also included in DirectX 8.0, but pixel shaders fell short of actual programmability—the limited "programs" supported were converted into texture blending states by the driver, which in turn wired together hardware "register combiners." These "programs" were not only limited in length (12 instructions or less) but also lacked important functionality. Dependent texture reads and floating point data were identified by Peercy et al. [1363] as crucial to true programmability, from their study of RenderMan.

Shaders at this time did not allow for flow control (branching), so conditionals had to be emulated by computing both terms and selecting or interpolating between the results. DirectX defined the concept of a *Shader Model* (SM) to distinguish hardware with different shader capabilities. The year 2002 saw the release of DirectX 9.0 including Shader Model 2.0, which featured truly programmable vertex and pixel shaders. Similar functionality was also exposed under OpenGL using various extensions. Support for arbitrary dependent texture reads and storage of 16-bit floating point values was added, finally completing the set of requirements identified by Peercy et al. Limits on shader resources such as instructions, textures, and registers were increased, so shaders became capable of more complex effects. Support for flow control was also added. The growing length and complexity of shaders made the assembly programming model increasingly cumbersome. Fortunately, DirectX 9.0

also included HLSL. This shading language was developed by Microsoft in collaboration with NVIDIA. Around the same time, the OpenGL ARB (Architecture Review Board) released GLSL, a fairly similar language for OpenGL [885]. These languages were heavily influenced by the syntax and design philosophy of the C programming language and included elements from the RenderMan Shading Language.

Shader Model 3.0 was introduced in 2004 and added dynamic flow control, making shaders considerably more powerful. It also turned optional features into requirements, further increased resource limits and added limited support for texture reads in vertex shaders. When a new generation of game consoles was introduced in late 2005 (Microsoft's Xbox 360) and late 2006 (Sony Computer Entertainment's PLAYSTATION 3 system), they were equipped with Shader Model 3.0–level GPUs. Nintendo's Wii console was one of the last notable fixed-function GPUs, which initially shipped in late 2006. The purely fixed-function pipeline is long gone at this point. Shader languages have evolved to a point where a variety of tools are used to create and manage them. A screenshot of one such tool, using Cook's shade tree concept, is shown in Figure 3.6.

The next large step in programmability also came near the end of 2006. Shader Model 4.0, included in DirectX 10.0 [175], introduced several major features, such as the geometry shader and stream output. Shader Model 4.0 included a uniform

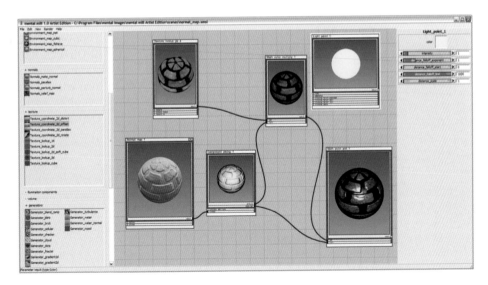

Figure 3.6. A visual shader graph system for shader design. Various operations are encapsulated in function boxes, selectable on the left. When selected, each function box has adjustable parameters, shown on the right. Inputs and outputs for each function box are linked to each other to form the final result, shown in the lower right of the center frame. *(Screenshot from "mental mill," mental images inc.)*

programming model for all shaders (vertex, pixel, and geometry), the unified shader design described earlier. Resource limits were further increased, and support for integer data types (including bitwise operations) was added. The introduction of GLSL 3.30 in OpenGL 3.3 provided a similar shader model.

In 2009 DirectX 11 and Shader Model 5.0 were released, adding the tessellation stage shaders and the compute shader, also called DirectCompute. The release also focused on supporting CPU multiprocessing more effectively, a topic discussed in Section 18.5. OpenGL added tessellation in version 4.0 and compute shaders in 4.3. DirectX and OpenGL evolve differently. Both set a certain level of hardware support needed for a particular version release. Microsoft controls the DirectX API and so works directly with independent hardware vendors (IHVs) such as AMD, NVIDIA, and Intel, as well as game developers and computer-aided design software firms, to determine what features to expose. OpenGL is developed by a consortium of hardware and software vendors, managed by the nonprofit Khronos Group. Because of the number of companies involved, the API features often appear in a release of OpenGL some time after their introduction in DirectX. However, OpenGL allows *extensions*, vendor-specific or more general, that allow the latest GPU functions to be used before official support in a release.

The next significant change in APIs was led by AMD's introduction of the Mantle API in 2013. Developed in partnership with video game developer DICE, the idea of Mantle was to strip out much of the graphics driver's overhead and give this control directly to the developer. Alongside this refactoring was further support for effective CPU multiprocessing. This new class of APIs focuses on vastly reducing the time the CPU spends in the driver, along with more efficient CPU multiprocessor support (Chapter 18). The ideas pioneered in Mantle were picked up by Microsoft and released as DirectX 12 in 2015. Note that DirectX 12 is not focused on exposing new GPU functionality—DirectX 11.3 exposed the same hardware features. Both APIs can be used to send graphics to virtual reality systems such as the Oculus Rift and HTC Vive. However, DirectX 12 is a radical redesign of the API, one that better maps to modern GPU architectures. Low-overhead drivers are useful for applications where the CPU driver cost is causing a bottleneck, or where using more CPU processors for graphics could benefit performance [946]. Porting from earlier APIs can be difficult, and a naive implementation can result in lower performance [249, 699, 1438].

Apple released its own low-overhead API called Metal in 2014. Metal was first available on mobile devices such as the iPhone 5S and iPad Air, with newer Macintoshes given access a year later through OS X El Capitan. Beyond efficiency, reducing CPU usage saves power, an important factor on mobile devices. This API has its own shading language, meant for both graphics and GPU compute programs.

AMD donated its Mantle work to the Khronos Group, which released its own new API in early 2016, called Vulkan. As with OpenGL, Vulkan works on multiple operating systems. Vulkan uses a new high-level intermediate language called SPIR-V, which is used for both shader representation and for general GPU computing. Precompiled shaders are portable and so can be used on any GPU supporting the capabilities needed [885]. Vulkan can also be used for non-graphical GPU computation, as it does not need a display window [946]. One notable difference of Vulkan from other low-overhead drivers is that it is meant to work with a wide range of systems, from workstations to mobile devices.

On mobile devices the norm has been to use OpenGL ES. "ES" stands for Embedded Systems, as this API was developed with mobile devices in mind. Standard OpenGL at the time was rather bulky and slow in some of its call structures, as well as requiring support for rarely used functionality. Released in 2003, OpenGL ES 1.0 was a stripped-down version of OpenGL 1.3, describing a fixed-function pipeline. While releases of DirectX are timed with those of graphics hardware that support them, developing graphics support for mobile devices did not proceed in the same fashion. For example, the first iPad, released in 2010, implemented OpenGL ES 1.1. In 2007 the OpenGL ES 2.0 specification was released, providing programmable shading. It was based on OpenGL 2.0, but without the fixed-function component, and so was not backward-compatible with OpenGL ES 1.1. OpenGL ES 3.0 was released in 2012, providing functionality such as multiple render targets, texture compression, transform feedback, instancing, and a much wider range of texture formats and modes, as well as shader language improvements. OpenGL ES 3.1 adds compute shaders, and 3.2 adds geometry and tessellation shaders, among other features. Chapter 23 discusses mobile device architectures in more detail.

An offshoot of OpenGL ES is the browser-based API WebGL, called through JavaScript. Released in 2011, the first version of this API is usable on most mobile devices, as it is equivalent to OpenGL ES 2.0 in functionality. As with OpenGL, extensions give access to more advanced GPU features. WebGL 2 assumes OpenGL ES 3.0 support.

WebGL is particularly well suited for experimenting with features or use in the classroom:

- It is cross-platform, working on all personal computers and almost all mobile devices.

- Driver approval is handled by the browsers. Even if one browser does not support a particular GPU or extension, often another browser does.

- Code is interpreted, not compiled, and only a text editor is needed for development.

- A debugger is built in to most browsers, and code running at any website can be examined.

- Programs can be deployed by uploading them to a website or Github, for example.

Higher-level scene-graph and effects libraries such as three.js [218] give easy access to code for a variety of more involved effects such as shadow algorithms, post-processing effects, physically based shading, and deferred rendering.

3.5   The Vertex Shader

The vertex shader is the first stage in the functional pipeline shown in Figure 3.2. While this is the first stage directly under programmer control, it is worth noting that some data manipulation happens before this stage. In what DirectX calls the *input assembler* [175, 530, 1208], several streams of data can be woven together to form the sets of vertices and primitives sent down the pipeline. For example, an object could be represented by one array of positions and one array of colors. The input assembler would create this object's triangles (or lines or points) by creating vertices with positions and colors. A second object could use the same array of positions (along with a different model transform matrix) and a different array of colors for its representation. Data representation is discussed in detail in Section 16.4.5. There is also support in the input assembler to perform *instancing*. This allows an object to be drawn several times with some varying data per instance, all with a single draw call. The use of instancing is covered in Section 18.4.2.

A triangle mesh is represented by a set of vertices, each associated with a specific position on the model surface. Besides position, there are other optional properties associated with each vertex, such as a color or texture coordinates. Surface normals are defined at mesh vertices as well, which may seem like an odd choice. Mathematically, each triangle has a well-defined surface normal, and it may seem to make more sense to use the triangle's normal directly for shading. However, when rendering, triangle meshes are often used to represent an underlying curved surface, and vertex normals are used to represent the orientation of this surface, rather than that of the triangle mesh itself. Section 16.3.4 will discuss methods to compute vertex normals. Figure 3.7 shows side views of two triangle meshes that represent curved surfaces, one smooth and one with a sharp crease.

The vertex shader is the first stage to process the triangle mesh. The data describing what triangles are formed is unavailable to the vertex shader. As its name implies, it deals exclusively with the incoming vertices. The vertex shader provides a way

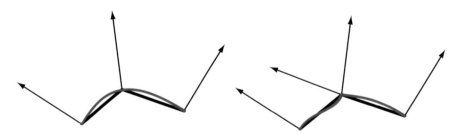

Figure 3.7. Side views of triangle meshes (in black, with vertex normals) representing curved surfaces (in red). On the left smoothed vertex normals are used to represent a smooth surface. On the right the middle vertex has been duplicated and given two normals, representing a crease.

to modify, create, or ignore values associated with each triangle's vertex, such as its color, normal, texture coordinates, and position. Normally the vertex shader program transforms vertices from model space to homogeneous clip space (Section 4.7). At a minimum, a vertex shader must always output this location.

A vertex shader is much the same as the unified shader described earlier. Every vertex passed in is processed by the vertex shader program, which then outputs a number of values that are interpolated across a triangle or line. The vertex shader can neither create nor destroy vertices, and results generated by one vertex cannot be passed on to another vertex. Since each vertex is treated independently, any number of shader processors on the GPU can be applied in parallel to the incoming stream of vertices.

Input assembly is usually presented as a process that happens before the vertex shader is executed. This is an example where the physical model often differs from the logical. Physically, the fetching of data to create a vertex might happen in the vertex shader and the driver will quietly prepend every shader with the appropriate instructions, invisible to the programmer.

Chapters that follow explain several vertex shader effects, such as vertex blending for animating joints, and silhouette rendering. Other uses for the vertex shader include:

- Object generation, by creating a mesh only once and having it be deformed by the vertex shader.

- Animating character's bodies and faces using skinning and morphing techniques.

- Procedural deformations, such as the movement of flags, cloth, or water [802, 943].

- Particle creation, by sending degenerate (no area) meshes down the pipeline and having these be given an area as needed.

- Lens distortion, heat haze, water ripples, page curls, and other effects, by using the entire framebuffer's contents as a texture on a screen-aligned mesh undergoing procedural deformation.

- Applying terrain height fields by using vertex texture fetch [40, 1227].

Some deformations done using a vertex shader are shown in Figure 3.8.

The output of the vertex shader can be consumed in several different ways. The usual path is for each instance's primitives, e.g., triangles, to then be generated and rasterized, and the individual pixel fragments produced to be sent to the pixel shader program for continued processing. On some GPUs the data can also be sent to the tessellation stage or the geometry shader or be stored in memory. These optional stages are discussed in the following sections.

Figure 3.8. On the left, a normal teapot. A simple shear operation performed by a vertex shader program produces the middle image. On the right, a noise function creates a field that distorts the model. *(Images produced by FX Composer 2, courtesy of NVIDIA Corporation.)*

3.6 The Tessellation Stage

The tessellation stage allows us to render curved surfaces. The GPU's task is to take each surface description and turn it into a representative set of triangles. This stage is an optional GPU feature that first became available in (and is required by) DirectX 11. It is also supported in OpenGL 4.0 and OpenGL ES 3.2.

There are several advantages to using the tessellation stage. The curved surface description is often more compact than providing the corresponding triangles themselves. Beyond memory savings, this feature can keep the bus between CPU and GPU from becoming the bottleneck for an animated character or object whose shape is changing each frame. The surfaces can be rendered efficiently by having an appropriate number of triangles generated for the given view. For example, if a ball is far from the camera, only a few triangles are needed. Up close, it may look best represented with thousands of triangles. This ability to control the *level of detail* can also allow an application to control its performance, e.g., using a lower-quality mesh on weaker GPUs in order to maintain frame rate. Models normally represented by flat surfaces can be converted to fine meshes of triangles and then warped as desired [1493], or they can be tessellated in order to perform expensive shading computations less frequently [225].

The tessellation stage always consists of three elements. Using DirectX's terminology, these are the *hull shader*, *tessellator*, and *domain shader*. In OpenGL the hull shader is the *tessellation control shader* and the domain shader the *tessellation evaluation shader*, which are a bit more descriptive, though verbose. The fixed-function tessellator is called the *primitive generator* in OpenGL, and as will be seen, that is indeed what it does.

How to specify and tessellate curves and surfaces is discussed at length in Chapter 17. Here we give a brief summary of each tessellation stage's purpose. To begin, the input to the hull shader is a special *patch* primitive. This consists of several control points defining a subdivision surface, Bézier patch, or other type of curved element. The hull shader has two functions. First, it tells the tessellator how many triangles should be generated, and in what configuration. Second, it performs processing on each of the control points. Also, optionally, the hull shader can modify the incoming

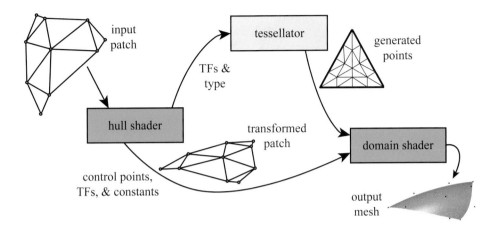

Figure 3.9. The tessellation stage. The hull shader takes in a patch defined by control points. It sends the tessellation factors (TFs) and type to the fixed-function tessellator. The control point set is transformed as desired by the hull shader and sent on to the domain shader, along with TFs and related patch constants. The tessellator creates the set of vertices along with their barycentric coordinates. These are then processed by the domain shader, producing the triangle mesh (control points shown for reference).

patch description, adding or removing control points as desired. The hull shader outputs its set of control points, along with the tessellation control data, to the domain shader. See Figure 3.9.

The tessellator is a fixed-function stage in the pipeline, only used with tessellation shaders. It has the task of adding several new vertices for the domain shader to process. The hull shader sends the tessellator information about what type of tessellation surface is desired: triangle, quadrilateral, or isoline. Isolines are sets of line strips, sometimes used for hair rendering [1954]. The other important values sent by the hull shader are the tessellation factors (*tessellation levels* in OpenGL). These are of two types: inner and outer edge. The two inner factors determine how much tessellation occurs inside the triangle or quadrilateral. The outer factors determine how much each exterior edge is split (Section 17.6). An example of increasing tessellation factors is shown in Figure 3.10. By allowing separate controls, we can have adjacent curved surfaces' edges match in tessellation, regardless of how the interiors are tessellated. Matching edges avoids cracks or other shading artifacts where patches meet. The vertices are assigned barycentric coordinates (Section 22.8), which are values that specify a relative location for each point on the desired surface.

The hull shader always outputs a patch, a set of control point locations. However, it can signal that a patch is to be discarded by sending the tessellator an outer tessellation level of zero or less (or not-a-number, NaN). Otherwise, the tessellator generates a mesh and sends it to the domain shader. The control points for the curved surface from the hull shader are used by each invocation of the domain shader to compute the

Figure 3.10. The effect of varying the tessellation factors. The Utah teapot is made of 32 patches. Inner and outer tessellation factors, from left to right, are 1, 2, 4, and 8. *(Images generated by demo from Rideout and Van Gelder [1493].)*

output values for each vertex. The domain shader has a data flow pattern like that of a vertex shader, with each input vertex from the tessellator being processed and generating a corresponding output vertex. The triangles formed are then passed on down the pipeline.

While this system sounds complex, it is structured this way for efficiency, and each shader can be fairly simple. The patch passed into a hull shader will often undergo little or no modification. This shader may also use the patch's estimated distance or screen size to compute tessellation factors on the fly, as for terrain rendering [466]. Alternately, the hull shader may simply pass on a fixed set of values for all patches that the application computes and provides. The tessellator performs an involved but fixed-function process of generating the vertices, giving them positions, and specifying what triangles or lines they form. This data amplification step is performed outside of a shader for computational efficiency [530]. The domain shader takes the barycentric coordinates generated for each point and uses these in the patch's evaluation equation to generate the position, normal, texture coordinates, and other vertex information desired. See Figure 3.11 for an example.

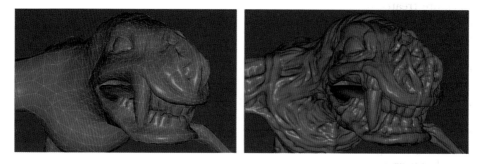

Figure 3.11. On the left is the underlying mesh of about 6000 triangles. On the right, each triangle is tessellated and displaced using PN triangle subdivision. *(Images from NVIDIA SDK 11 [1301] samples, courtesy of NVIDIA Corporation, model from Metro 2033 by 4A Games.)*

Figure 3.12. Geometry shader input for a geometry shader program is of some single type: point, line segment, triangle. The two rightmost primitives include vertices adjacent to the line and triangle objects. More elaborate patch types are possible.

3.7   The Geometry Shader

The geometry shader can turn primitives into other primitives, something the tessellation stage cannot do. For example, a triangle mesh could be transformed to a wireframe view by having each triangle create line edges. Alternately, the lines could be replaced by quadrilaterals facing the viewer, so making a wireframe rendering with thicker edges [1492]. The geometry shader was added to the hardware-accelerated graphics pipeline with the release of DirectX 10, in late 2006. It is located after the tessellation shader in the pipeline, and its use is optional. While a required part of Shader Model 4.0, it is not used in earlier shader models. OpenGL 3.2 and OpenGL ES 3.2 support this type of shader as well.

The input to the geometry shader is a single object and its associated vertices. The object typically consists of triangles in a strip, a line segment, or simply a point. Extended primitives can be defined and processed by the geometry shader. In particular, three additional vertices outside of a triangle can be passed in, and the two adjacent vertices on a polyline can be used. See Figure 3.12. With DirectX 11 and Shader Model 5.0, you can pass in more elaborate patches, with up to 32 control points. That said, the tessellation stage is more efficient for patch generation [175].

The geometry shader processes this primitive and outputs zero or more vertices, which are treated as points, polylines, or strips of triangles. Note that no output at all can be generated by the geometry shader. In this way, a mesh can be selectively modified by editing vertices, adding new primitives, and removing others.

The geometry shader is designed for modifying incoming data or making a limited number of copies. For example, one use is to generate six transformed copies of data to simultaneously render the six faces of a cube map; see Section 10.4.3. It can also be used to efficiently create cascaded shadow maps for high-quality shadow generation. Other algorithms that take advantage of the geometry shader include creating variable-sized particles from point data, extruding fins along silhouettes for fur rendering, and finding object edges for shadow algorithms. See Figure 3.13 for more examples. These and other uses are discussed throughout the rest of the book.

DirectX 11 added the ability for the geometry shader to use instancing, where the geometry shader can be run a set number of times on any given primitive [530, 1971]. In

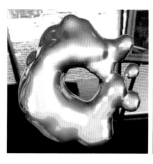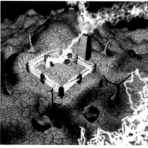

Figure 3.13. Some uses of the geometry shader (GS). On the left, metaball isosurface tessellation is performed on the fly using the GS. In the middle, fractal subdivision of line segments is done using the GS and stream out, and billboards are generated by the GS for display of the lightning. On the right, cloth simulation is performed by using the vertex and geometry shader with stream out. *(Images from NVIDIA SDK 10 [1300] samples, courtesy of NVIDIA Corporation.)*

OpenGL 4.0 this is specified with an invocation count. The geometry shader can also output up to four *streams*. One stream can be sent on down the rendering pipeline for further processing. All these streams can optionally be sent to stream output render targets.

The geometry shader is guaranteed to output results from primitives in the same order that they are input. This affects performance, because if several shader cores run in parallel, results must be saved and ordered. This and other factors work against the geometry shader being used to replicate or create a large amount of geometry in a single call [175, 530].

After a draw call is issued, there are only three places in the pipeline where work can be created on the GPU: rasterization, the tessellation stage, and the geometry shader. Of these, the geometry shader's behavior is the least predictable when considering resources and memory needed, since it is fully programmable. In practice the geometry shader usually sees little use, as it does not map well to the GPU's strengths. On some mobile devices it is implemented in software, so its use is actively discouraged there [69].

3.7.1 Stream Output

The standard use of the GPU's pipeline is to send data through the vertex shader, then rasterize the resulting triangles and process these in the pixel shader. It used to be that the data always passed through the pipeline and intermediate results could not be accessed. The idea of *stream output* was introduced in Shader Model 4.0. After vertices are processed by the vertex shader (and, optionally, the tessellation and geometry shaders), these can be output in a stream, i.e., an ordered array, in addition to being sent on to the rasterization stage. Rasterization could, in fact, be turned off entirely and the pipeline then used purely as a non-graphical stream processor. Data processed in this way can be sent back through the pipeline, thus allowing iterative processing. This type of operation can be useful for simulating flowing water or other particle effects, as discussed in Section 13.8. It could also be used to skin a model and then have these vertices available for reuse (Section 4.4).

Stream output returns data only in the form of floating point numbers, so it can have a noticeable memory cost. Stream output works on primitives, not directly on vertices. If meshes are sent down the pipeline, each triangle generates its own set of three output vertices. Any vertex sharing in the original mesh is lost. For this reason a more typical use is to send just the vertices through the pipeline as a point set primitive. In OpenGL the stream output stage is called *transform feedback*, since the focus of much of its use is transforming vertices and returning them for further processing. Primitives are guaranteed to be sent to the stream output target in the order that they were input, meaning the vertex order will be maintained [530].

3.8 The Pixel Shader

After the vertex, tessellation, and geometry shaders perform their operations, the primitive is clipped and set up for rasterization, as explained in the previous chapter. This section of the pipeline is relatively fixed in its processing steps, i.e., not programmable but somewhat configurable. Each triangle is traversed to determine which pixels it covers. The rasterizer may also roughly calculate how much the triangle covers each pixel's cell area (Section 5.4.2). This piece of a triangle partially or fully overlapping the pixel is called a *fragment*.

The values at the triangle's vertices, including the z-value used in the z-buffer, are interpolated across the triangle's surface for each pixel. These values are passed to the *pixel shader*, which then processes the fragment. In OpenGL the pixel shader is known as the *fragment shader*, which is perhaps a better name. We use "pixel shader" throughout this book for consistency. Point and line primitives sent down the pipeline also create fragments for the pixels covered.

The type of interpolation performed across the triangle is specified by the pixel shader program. Normally we use perspective-correct interpolation, so that the world-space distances between pixel surface locations increase as an object recedes in the distance. An example is rendering railroad tracks extending to the horizon. Railroad ties are more closely spaced where the rails are farther away, as more distance is traveled for each successive pixel approaching the horizon. Other interpolation options are available, such as screen-space interpolation, where perspective projection is not taken into account. DirectX 11 gives further control over when and how interpolation is performed [530].

In programming terms, the vertex shader program's outputs, interpolated across the triangle (or line), effectively become the pixel shader program's inputs. As the GPU has evolved, other inputs have been exposed. For example, the screen position of the fragment is available to the pixel shader in Shader Model 3.0 and beyond. Also,

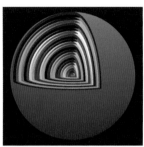

Figure 3.14. User-defined clipping planes. On the left, a single horizontal clipping plane slices the object. In the middle, the nested spheres are clipped by three planes. On the right, the spheres' surfaces are clipped only if they are outside all three clip planes. *(From the three.js examples webgl_clipping and webgl_clipping_intersection [218].)*

which side of a triangle is visible is an input flag. This knowledge is important for rendering a different material on the front versus back of each triangle in a single pass.

With inputs in hand, typically the pixel shader computes and outputs a fragment's color. It can also possibly produce an opacity value and optionally modify its z-depth. During merging, these values are used to modify what is stored at the pixel. The depth value generated in the rasterization stage can also be modified by the pixel shader. The stencil buffer value is usually not modifiable, but rather it is passed through to the merge stage. DirectX 11.3 allows the shader to change this value. Operations such as fog computation and alpha testing have moved from being merge operations to being pixel shader computations in SM 4.0 [175].

A pixel shader also has the unique ability to discard an incoming fragment, i.e., generate no output. One example of how fragment discard can be used is shown in Figure 3.14. Clip plane functionality used to be a configurable element in the fixed-function pipeline and was later specified in the vertex shader. With fragment discard available, this functionality could then be implemented in any way desired in the pixel shader, such as deciding whether clipping volumes should be AND'ed or OR'ed together.

Initially the pixel shader could output to only the merging stage, for eventual display. The number of instructions a pixel shader can execute has grown considerably over time. This increase gave rise to the idea of *multiple render targets* (MRT). Instead of sending results of a pixel shader's program to just the color and z-buffer, multiple sets of values could be generated for each fragment and saved to different buffers, each called a *render target*. Render targets generally have the same x- and y-dimensions; some APIs allow different sizes, but the rendered area will be the smallest of these. Some architectures require render targets to each have the same bit depth, and possibly even identical data formats. Depending on the GPU, the number of render targets available is four or eight.

Even with these limitations, MRT functionality is a powerful aid in performing rendering algorithms more efficiently. A single rendering pass could generate a color image in one target, object identifiers in another, and world-space distances in a third. This ability has also given rise to a different type of rendering pipeline, called *deferred shading*, where visibility and shading are done in separate passes. The first pass stores data about an object's location and material at each pixel. Successive passes can then efficiently apply illumination and other effects. This class of rendering methods is described in Section 20.1.

The pixel shader's limitation is that it can normally write to a render target at only the fragment location handed to it, and cannot read current results from neighboring pixels. That is, when a pixel shader program executes, it cannot send its output directly to neighboring pixels, nor can it access others' recent changes. Rather, it computes results that affect only its own pixel. However, this limitation is not as severe as it sounds. An output image created in one pass can have any of its data accessed by a pixel shader in a later pass. Neighboring pixels can be processed using image processing techniques, described in Section 12.1.

There are exceptions to the rule that a pixel shader cannot know or affect neighboring pixels' results. One is that the pixel shader can immediately access information for adjacent fragments (albeit indirectly) during the computation of gradient or derivative information. The pixel shader is provided with the amounts by which any interpolated value changes per pixel along the x and y screen axes. Such values are useful for various computations and texture addressing. These gradients are particularly important for operations such as texture filtering (Section 6.2.2), where we want to know how much of an image covers a pixel. All modern GPUs implement this feature by processing fragments in groups of 2×2, called a *quad*. When the pixel shader requests a gradient value, the difference between adjacent fragments is returned. See Figure 3.15. A unified core has this capability to access neighboring data—kept in different threads on the same warp—and so can compute gradients for use in the pixel shader. One consequence of this implementation is that gradient information cannot be accessed in parts of the shader affected by dynamic flow control, i.e., an "if" statement or loop with a variable number of iterations. All the fragments in a group must be processed using the same set of instructions so that all four pixels' results are meaningful for computing gradients. This is a fundamental limitation that exists even in offline rendering systems [64].

DirectX 11 introduced a buffer type that allows write access to any location, the *unordered access view* (UAV). Originally for only pixel and compute shaders, access to UAVs was extended to all shaders in DirectX 11.1 [146]. OpenGL 4.3 calls this a *shader storage buffer object* (SSBO). Both names are descriptive in their own way. Pixel shaders are run in parallel, in an arbitrary order, and this storage buffer is shared among them.

Often some mechanism is needed to avoid a *data race condition* (a.k.a. a *data hazard*), where both shader programs are "racing" to influence the same value, possibly

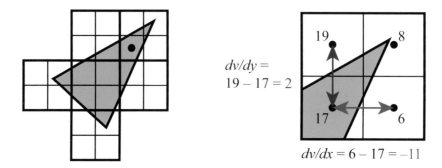

Figure 3.15. On the left, a triangle is rasterized into quads, sets of 2×2 pixels. The gradient computations for the pixel marked with a black dot is then shown on the right. The value for v is shown for each of the four pixel locations in the quad. Note how three of the pixels are not covered by the triangle, yet they are still processed by the GPU so that the gradients can be found. The gradients in the x and y screen directions are computed for the lower left pixel by using its two quad neighbors.

leading to arbitrary results. As an example, an error could occur if two invocations of a pixel shader tried to, say, add to the same retrieved value at about the same time. Both would retrieve the original value, both would modify it locally, but then whichever invocation wrote its result last would wipe out the contribution of the other invocation—only one addition would occur. GPUs avoid this problem by having dedicated atomic units that the shader can access [530]. However, atomics mean that some shaders may stall as they wait to access a memory location undergoing read/modify/write by another shader.

While atomics avoid data hazards, many algorithms require a specific order of execution. For example, you may want to draw a more distant transparent blue triangle before overlaying it with a red transparent triangle, blending the red atop the blue. It is possible for a pixel to have two pixel shader invocations for a pixel, one for each triangle, executing in such a way that the red triangle's shader completes before the blue's. In the standard pipeline, the fragment results are sorted in the merger stage before being processed. *Rasterizer order views* (ROVs) were introduced in DirectX 11.3 to enforce an order of execution. These are like UAVs; they can be read and written by shaders in the same fashion. The key difference is that ROVs guarantee that the data are accessed in the proper order. This increases the usefulness of these shader-accessible buffers considerably [327, 328]. For example, ROVs make it possible for the pixel shader to write its own blending methods, since it can directly access and write to any location in the ROV, and thus no merging stage is needed [176]. The price is that, if an out-of-order access is detected, a pixel shader invocation may stall until triangles drawn earlier are processed.

3.9 The Merging Stage

As discussed in Section 2.5.2, the merging stage is where the depths and colors of the individual fragments (generated in the pixel shader) are combined with the framebuffer. DirectX calls this stage the *output merger*; OpenGL refers to it as *per-sample operations*. On most traditional pipeline diagrams (including our own), this stage is where stencil-buffer and z-buffer operations occur. If the fragment is visible, another operation that takes place in this stage is color blending. For opaque surfaces there is no real blending involved, as the fragment's color simply replaces the previously stored color. Actual blending of the fragment and stored color is commonly used for transparency and compositing operations (Section 5.5).

Imagine that a fragment generated by rasterization is run through the pixel shader and then is found to be hidden by some previously rendered fragment when the z-buffer is applied. All the processing done in the pixel shader was then unnecessary. To avoid this waste, many GPUs perform some merge testing before the pixel shader is executed [530]. The fragment's z-depth (and whatever else is in use, such as the stencil buffer or scissoring) is used for testing visibility. The fragment is culled if hidden. This functionality is called *early-z* [1220, 1542]. The pixel shader has the ability to change the z-depth of the fragment or to discard the fragment entirely. If either type of operation is found to exist in a pixel shader program, early-z then generally cannot be used and is turned off, usually making the pipeline less efficient. DirectX 11 and OpenGL 4.2 allow the pixel shader to force early-z testing to be on, though with a number of limitations [530]. See Section 23.7 for more about early-z and other z-buffer optimizations. Using early-z effectively can have a large effect on performance, which is discussed in detail in Section 18.4.5.

The merging stage occupies the middle ground between fixed-function stages, such as triangle setup, and the fully programmable shader stages. Although it is not programmable, its operation is highly configurable. Color blending in particular can be set up to perform a large number of different operations. The most common are combinations of multiplication, addition, and subtraction involving the color and alpha values, but other operations are possible, such as minimum and maximum, as well as bitwise logic operations. DirectX 10 added the capability to blend two colors from the pixel shader with the framebuffer color. This capability is called *dual source-color blending* and cannot be used in conjunction with multiple render targets. MRT does otherwise support blending, and DirectX 10.1 introduced the capability to perform different blend operations on each separate buffer.

As mentioned at the end of the previous section, DirectX 11.3 provided a way to make blending programmable through ROVs, though at a price in performance. ROVs and the merging stage both guarantee draw order, a.k.a. output invariance. Regardless of the order in which pixel shader results are generated, it is an API requirement that results are sorted and sent to the merging stage in the order in which they are input, object by object and triangle by triangle.

3.10 The Compute Shader

The GPU can be used for more than implementing the traditional graphics pipeline. There are many non-graphical uses in fields as varied as computing the estimated value of stock options and training neural nets for deep learning. Using hardware in this way is called *GPU computing*. Platforms such as CUDA and OpenCL are used to control the GPU as a massive parallel processor, with no real need or access to graphics-specific functionality. These frameworks often use languages such as C or C++ with extensions, along with libraries made for the GPU.

Introduced in DirectX 11, the *compute shader* is a form of GPU computing, in that it is a shader that is not locked into a location in the graphics pipeline. It is closely tied to the process of rendering in that it is invoked by the graphics API. It is used alongside vertex, pixel, and other shaders. It draws upon the same pool of unified shader processors as those used in the pipeline. It is a shader like the others, in that it has some set of input data and can access buffers (such as textures) for input and output. Warps and threads are more visible in a compute shader. For example, each invocation gets a thread index that it can access. There is also the concept of a *thread group*, which consists of 1 to 1024 threads in DirectX 11. These thread groups are specified by x-, y-, and z-coordinates, mostly for simplicity of use in shader code. Each thread group has a small amount of memory that is shared among threads. In DirectX 11, this amounts to 32 kB. Compute shaders are executed by thread group, so that all threads in the group are guaranteed to run concurrently [1971].

One important advantage of compute shaders is that they can access data generated on the GPU. Sending data from the GPU to the CPU incurs a delay, so performance can be improved if processing and results can be kept resident on the GPU [1403]. Post-processing, where a rendered image is modified in some way, is a common use of compute shaders. The shared memory means that intermediate results from sampling image pixels can be shared with neighboring threads. Using a compute shader to determine the distribution or average luminance of an image, for example, has been found to run twice as fast as performing this operation on a pixel shader [530].

Compute shaders are also useful for particle systems, mesh processing such as facial animation [134], culling [1883, 1884], image filtering [1102, 1710], improving depth precision [991], shadows [865], depth of field [764], and any other tasks where a set of GPU processors can be brought to bear. Wihlidal [1884] discusses how compute shaders can be more efficient than tessellation hull shaders. See Figure 3.16 for other uses.

This ends our review of the GPU's implementation of the rendering pipeline. There are many ways in which the GPUs functions can be used and combined to perform various rendering-related processes. Relevant theory and algorithms tuned to take advantage of these capabilities are the central subjects of this book. Our focus now moves on to transforms and shading.

Figure 3.16. Compute shader examples. On the left, a compute shader is used to simulate hair affected by wind, with the hair itself rendered using the tessellation stage. In the middle, a compute shader performs a rapid blur operation. On the right, ocean waves are simulated. *(Images from NVIDIA SDK 11 [1301] samples, courtesy of NVIDIA Corporation.)*

Further Reading and Resources

Giesen's tour of the graphics pipeline [530] discusses many facets of the GPU at length, explaining why elements work the way they do. The course by Fatahalian and Bryant [462] discusses GPU parallelism in a series of detailed lecture slide sets. While focused on GPU computing using CUDA, the introductory part of Kirk and Hwa's book [903] discusses the evolution and design philosophy for the GPU.

To learn the formal aspects of shader programming takes some work. Books such as the *OpenGL Superbible* [1606] and *OpenGL Programming Guide* [885] include material on shader programming. The older book *OpenGL Shading Language* [1512] does not cover more recent shader stages, such as the geometry and tessellation shaders, but does focus specifically on shader-related algorithms. See this book's website, realtimerendering.com, for recent and recommended books.

Chapter 4

Transforms

"What if angry vectors veer
Round your sleeping head, and form.
There's never need to fear
Violence of the poor world's abstract storm."
—Robert Penn Warren

A *transform* is an operation that takes entities such as points, vectors, or colors and converts them in some way. For the computer graphics practitioner, it is extremely important to master transforms. With them, you can position, reshape, and animate objects, lights, and cameras. You can also ensure that all computations are carried out in the same coordinate system, and project objects onto a plane in different ways. These are only a few of the operations that can be performed with transforms, but they are sufficient to demonstrate the importance of the transform's role in real-time graphics, or, for that matter, in any kind of computer graphics.

A *linear transform* is one that preserves vector addition and scalar multiplication. Specifically,

$$\mathbf{f}(\mathbf{x}) + \mathbf{f}(\mathbf{y}) = \mathbf{f}(\mathbf{x} + \mathbf{y}), \tag{4.1}$$

$$k\mathbf{f}(\mathbf{x}) = \mathbf{f}(k\mathbf{x}). \tag{4.2}$$

As an example, $\mathbf{f}(\mathbf{x}) = 5\mathbf{x}$ is a transform that takes a vector and multiplies each element by five. To prove that this is linear, the two conditions (Equations 4.1 and 4.2) need to be fulfilled. The first condition holds since any two vectors multiplied by five and then added will be the same as adding the vectors and then multiplying. The scalar multiplication condition (Equation 4.2) is clearly fulfilled. This function is called a scaling transform, as it changes the scale (size) of an object. The rotation transform is another linear transform that rotates a vector about the origin. Scaling and rotation transforms, in fact all linear transforms for three-element vectors, can be represented using a 3×3 matrix.

However, this size of matrix is usually not large enough. A function for a three-element vector $\mathbf{x}$ such as $\mathbf{f}(\mathbf{x}) = \mathbf{x} + (7, 3, 2)$ is not linear. Performing this function on two separate vectors will add each value of $(7, 3, 2)$ twice to form the result. Adding a fixed vector to another vector performs a translation, e.g., it moves all locations by the same amount. This is a useful type of transform, and we would like to combine various transforms, e.g., scale an object to be half as large, then move it to a different location. Keeping functions in the simple forms used so far makes it difficult to easily combine them.

Combining linear transforms and translations can be done using an *affine transform*, typically stored as a 4×4 matrix. An affine transform is one that performs a linear transform and then a translation. To represent four-element vectors we use *homogeneous notation*, denoting points and directions in the same way (using bold lowercase letters). A direction vector is represented as $\mathbf{v} = (v_x \quad v_y \quad v_z \quad 0)^T$ and a point as $\mathbf{v} = (v_x \quad v_y \quad v_z \quad 1)^T$. Throughout the chapter, we will make extensive use of the terminology and operations explained in the downloadable linear algebra appendix, found on realtimerendering.com.

All translation, rotation, scaling, reflection, and shearing matrices are affine. The main characteristic of an affine matrix is that it preserves the parallelism of lines, but not necessarily lengths and angles. An affine transform may also be any sequence of concatenations of individual affine transforms.

This chapter will begin with the most essential, basic affine transforms. This section can be seen as a "reference manual" for simple transforms. More specialized matrices are then described, followed by a discussion and description of quaternions, a powerful transform tool. Then follows vertex blending and morphing, which are two simple but effective ways of expressing animations of meshes. Finally, projection matrices are described. Most of these transforms, their notations, functions, and properties are summarized in Table 4.1, where an orthogonal matrix is one whose inverse is the transpose.

Transforms are a basic tool for manipulating geometry. Most graphics application programming interfaces let the user set arbitrary matrices, and sometimes a library may be used with matrix operations that implement many of the transforms discussed in this chapter. However, it is still worthwhile to understand the real matrices and their interaction behind the function calls. Knowing what the matrix does after such a function call is a start, but understanding the properties of the matrix itself will take you further. For example, such an understanding enables you to discern when you are dealing with an orthogonal matrix, whose inverse is its transpose, making for faster matrix inversions. Knowledge like this can lead to accelerated code.

4.1 Basic Transforms

This section describes the most basic transforms, such as translation, rotation, scaling, shearing, transform concatenation, the rigid-body transform, normal transform (which is not so normal), and computation of inverses. For the experienced reader, this can be used as a reference manual for simple transforms, and for the novice, it can serve as an introduction to the subject. This material is necessary background for the rest of this chapter and for other chapters in this book. We start with the simplest of transforms—the translation.

Notation	Name	Characteristics
$\mathbf{T}(\mathbf{t})$	translation matrix	Moves a point. Affine.
$\mathbf{R}_x(\rho)$	rotation matrix	Rotates ρ radians around the x-axis. Similar notation for the y- and z-axes. Orthogonal & affine.
$\mathbf{R}$	rotation matrix	Any rotation matrix. Orthogonal & affine.
$\mathbf{S}(\mathbf{s})$	scaling matrix	Scales along all x-, y-, and z-axes according to $\mathbf{s}$. Affine.
$\mathbf{H}_{ij}(s)$	shear matrix	Shears component i by a factor s, with respect to component j. $i, j \in \{x, y, z\}$. Affine.
$\mathbf{E}(h, p, r)$	Euler transform	Orientation matrix given by the Euler angles head (yaw), pitch, roll. Orthogonal & affine.
$\mathbf{P}_o(s)$	orthographic projection	Parallel projects onto some plane or to a volume. Affine.
$\mathbf{P}_p(s)$	perspective projection	Projects with perspective onto a plane or to a volume.
$\mathtt{slerp}(\hat{\mathbf{q}}, \hat{\mathbf{r}}, t)$	slerp transform	Creates an interpolated quaternion with respect to the quaternions $\hat{\mathbf{q}}$ and $\hat{\mathbf{r}}$, and the parameter t.

Table 4.1. Summary of most of the transforms discussed in this chapter.

4.1.1 Translation

A change from one location to another is represented by a translation matrix, $\mathbf{T}$. This matrix translates an entity by a vector $\mathbf{t} = (t_x, t_y, t_z)$. $\mathbf{T}$ is given below by Equation 4.3:

$$\mathbf{T}(\mathbf{t}) = \mathbf{T}(t_x, t_y, t_z) = \begin{pmatrix} 1 & 0 & 0 & t_x \\ 0 & 1 & 0 & t_y \\ 0 & 0 & 1 & t_z \\ 0 & 0 & 0 & 1 \end{pmatrix}. \tag{4.3}$$

An example of the effect of the translation transform is shown in Figure 4.1. It is easily shown that the multiplication of a point $\mathbf{p} = (p_x, p_y, p_z, 1)$ with $\mathbf{T}(\mathbf{t})$ yields a new point $\mathbf{p}' = (p_x + t_x, p_y + t_y, p_z + t_z, 1)$, which is clearly a translation. Notice that a vector $\mathbf{v} = (v_x, v_y, v_z, 0)$ is left unaffected by a multiplication by $\mathbf{T}$, because a direction vector cannot be translated. In contrast, both points and vectors are affected by the rest of the affine transforms. The inverse of a translation matrix is $\mathbf{T}^{-1}(\mathbf{t}) = \mathbf{T}(-\mathbf{t})$, that is, the vector $\mathbf{t}$ is negated.

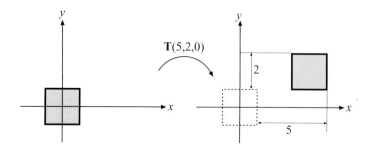

Figure 4.1. The square on the left is transformed with a translation matrix $\mathbf{T}(5, 2, 0)$, whereby the square is moved 5 distance units to the right and 2 upward.

We should mention at this point that another valid notational scheme sometimes seen in computer graphics uses matrices with translation vectors in the bottom row. For example, DirectX uses this form. In this scheme, the order of matrices would be reversed, i.e., the order of application would read from left to right. Vectors and matrices in this notation are said to be in *row-major* form since the vectors are rows. In this book, we use *column-major* form. Whichever is used, this is purely a notational difference. When the matrix is stored in memory, the last four values of the sixteen are the three translation values followed by a one.

4.1.2 Rotation

A rotation transform rotates a vector (position or direction) by a given angle around a given axis passing through the origin. Like a translation matrix, it is a *rigid-body transform*, i.e., it preserves the distances between points transformed, and preserves handedness (i.e., it never causes left and right to swap sides). These two types of transforms are clearly useful in computer graphics for positioning and orienting objects. An *orientation matrix* is a rotation matrix associated with a camera view or object that defines its orientation in space, i.e., its directions for up and forward.

In two dimensions, the rotation matrix is simple to derive. Assume that we have a vector, $\mathbf{v} = (v_x, v_y)$, which we parameterize as $\mathbf{v} = (v_x, v_y) = (r\cos\theta, r\sin\theta)$. If we were to rotate that vector by ϕ radians (counterclockwise), then we would get $\mathbf{u} = (r\cos(\theta + \phi), r\sin(\theta + \phi))$. This can be rewritten as

$$\mathbf{u} = \begin{pmatrix} r\cos(\theta + \phi) \\ r\sin(\theta + \phi) \end{pmatrix} = \begin{pmatrix} r(\cos\theta\cos\phi - \sin\theta\sin\phi) \\ r(\sin\theta\cos\phi + \cos\theta\sin\phi) \end{pmatrix}$$
$$= \underbrace{\begin{pmatrix} \cos\phi & -\sin\phi \\ \sin\phi & \cos\phi \end{pmatrix}}_{\mathbf{R}(\phi)} \underbrace{\begin{pmatrix} r\cos\theta \\ r\sin\theta \end{pmatrix}}_{\mathbf{v}} = \mathbf{R}(\phi)\mathbf{v}, \tag{4.4}$$

where we used the angle sum relation to expand $\cos(\theta + \phi)$ and $\sin(\theta + \phi)$. In three dimensions, commonly used rotation matrices are $\mathbf{R}_x(\phi)$, $\mathbf{R}_y(\phi)$, and $\mathbf{R}_z(\phi)$, which rotate an entity ϕ radians around the x-, y-, and z-axes, respectively. They are given by Equations 4.5–4.7:

$$\mathbf{R}_x(\phi) = \begin{pmatrix} 1 & 0 & 0 & 0 \\ 0 & \cos\phi & -\sin\phi & 0 \\ 0 & \sin\phi & \cos\phi & 0 \\ 0 & 0 & 0 & 1 \end{pmatrix}, \tag{4.5}$$

$$\mathbf{R}_y(\phi) = \begin{pmatrix} \cos\phi & 0 & \sin\phi & 0 \\ 0 & 1 & 0 & 0 \\ -\sin\phi & 0 & \cos\phi & 0 \\ 0 & 0 & 0 & 1 \end{pmatrix}, \tag{4.6}$$

$$\mathbf{R}_z(\phi) = \begin{pmatrix} \cos\phi & -\sin\phi & 0 & 0 \\ \sin\phi & \cos\phi & 0 & 0 \\ 0 & 0 & 1 & 0 \\ 0 & 0 & 0 & 1 \end{pmatrix}. \tag{4.7}$$

If the bottom row and rightmost column are deleted from a 4×4 matrix, a 3×3 matrix is obtained. For every 3×3 rotation matrix, $\mathbf{R}$, that rotates ϕ radians around any axis, the trace (which is the sum of the diagonal elements in a matrix) is constant independent of the axis, and is computed as [997]:

$$\mathrm{tr}(\mathbf{R}) = 1 + 2\cos\phi. \tag{4.8}$$

The effect of a rotation matrix may be seen in Figure 4.4 on page 65. What characterizes a rotation matrix, $\mathbf{R}_i(\phi)$, besides the fact that it rotates ϕ radians around axis i, is that it leaves all points on the rotation axis, i, unchanged. Note that $\mathbf{R}$ will also be used to denote a rotation matrix around any axis. The axis rotation matrices given above can be used in a series of three transforms to perform any arbitrary axis rotation. This procedure is discussed in Section 4.2.1. Performing a rotation around an arbitrary axis directly is covered in Section 4.2.4.

All rotation matrices have a determinant of one and are orthogonal. This also holds for concatenations of any number of these transforms. There is another way to obtain the inverse: $\mathbf{R}_i^{-1}(\phi) = \mathbf{R}_i(-\phi)$, i.e., rotate in the opposite direction around the same axis.

EXAMPLE: ROTATION AROUND A POINT. Assume that we want to rotate an object by ϕ radians around the z-axis, with the center of rotation being a certain point, $\mathbf{p}$. What is the transform? This scenario is depicted in Figure 4.2. Since a rotation around a point is characterized by the fact that the point itself is unaffected by the rotation, the transform starts by translating the object so that $\mathbf{p}$ coincides with the origin, which is done with $\mathbf{T}(-\mathbf{p})$. Thereafter follows the actual rotation: $\mathbf{R}_z(\phi)$. Finally, the object has to be translated back to its original position using $\mathbf{T}(\mathbf{p})$. The resulting transform, $\mathbf{X}$, is then given by

$$\mathbf{X} = \mathbf{T}(\mathbf{p})\mathbf{R}_z(\phi)\mathbf{T}(-\mathbf{p}). \tag{4.9}$$

Note the order of the matrices above. $\qquad\qquad\qquad\qquad\qquad\qquad\qquad\qquad\quad\square$

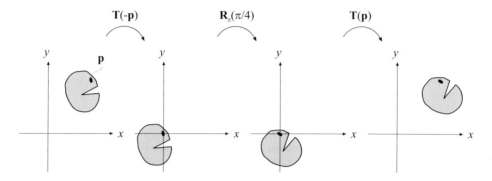

Figure 4.2. Example of rotation around a specific point **p**.

4.1.3 Scaling

A scaling matrix, $\mathbf{S}(\mathbf{s}) = \mathbf{S}(s_x, s_y, s_z)$, scales an entity with factors s_x, s_y, and s_z along the x-, y-, and z-directions, respectively. This means that a scaling matrix can be used to enlarge or diminish an object. The larger the s_i, $i \in \{x, y, z\}$, the larger the scaled entity gets in that direction. Setting any of the components of $\mathbf{s}$ to 1 naturally avoids a change in scaling in that direction. Equation 4.10 shows $\mathbf{S}$:

$$\mathbf{S}(\mathbf{s}) = \begin{pmatrix} s_x & 0 & 0 & 0 \\ 0 & s_y & 0 & 0 \\ 0 & 0 & s_z & 0 \\ 0 & 0 & 0 & 1 \end{pmatrix}. \tag{4.10}$$

Figure 4.4 on page 65 illustrates the effect of a scaling matrix. The scaling operation is called *uniform* if $s_x = s_y = s_z$ and *nonuniform* otherwise. Sometimes the terms *isotropic* and *anisotropic* scaling are used instead of uniform and nonuniform. The inverse is $\mathbf{S}^{-1}(\mathbf{s}) = \mathbf{S}(1/s_x, 1/s_y, 1/s_z)$.

Using homogeneous coordinates, another valid way to create a uniform scaling matrix is by manipulating matrix element at position $(3,3)$, i.e., the element at the lower right corner. This value affects the w-component of the homogeneous coordinate, and so scales every coordinate of a point (not direction vectors) transformed by the matrix. For example, to scale uniformly by a factor of 5, the elements at $(0,0)$, $(1,1)$, and $(2,2)$ in the scaling matrix can be set to 5, or the element at $(3,3)$ can be set to $1/5$. The two different matrices for performing this are shown below:

$$\mathbf{S} = \begin{pmatrix} 5 & 0 & 0 & 0 \\ 0 & 5 & 0 & 0 \\ 0 & 0 & 5 & 0 \\ 0 & 0 & 0 & 1 \end{pmatrix}, \qquad \mathbf{S}' = \begin{pmatrix} 1 & 0 & 0 & 0 \\ 0 & 1 & 0 & 0 \\ 0 & 0 & 1 & 0 \\ 0 & 0 & 0 & 1/5 \end{pmatrix}. \tag{4.11}$$

In contrast to using $\mathbf{S}$ for uniform scaling, using $\mathbf{S}'$ must always be followed by ho-mogenization. This may be inefficient, since it involves divides in the homogenization process; if the element at the lower right (position $(3,3)$) is 1, no divides are necessary. Of course, if the system always does this division without testing for 1, then there is no extra cost.

A negative value on one or three of the components of **s** gives a type of *reflection matrix*, also called a *mirror matrix*. If only two scale factors are -1, then we will rotate π radians. It should be noted that a rotation matrix concatenated with a reflection matrix is also a reflection matrix. Hence, the following is a reflection matrix:

$$\underbrace{\begin{pmatrix} \cos(\pi/2) & \sin(\pi/2) \\ -\sin(\pi/2) & \cos(\pi/2) \end{pmatrix}}_{\text{rotation}} \underbrace{\begin{pmatrix} 1 & 0 \\ 0 & -1 \end{pmatrix}}_{\text{reflection}} = \begin{pmatrix} 0 & -1 \\ -1 & 0 \end{pmatrix}. \tag{4.12}$$

Reflection matrices usually require special treatment when detected. For example, a triangle with vertices in a counterclockwise order will get a clockwise order when transformed by a reflection matrix. This order change can cause incorrect lighting and backface culling to occur. To detect whether a given matrix reflects in some manner, compute the determinant of the upper left 3×3 elements of the matrix. If the value is negative, the matrix is reflective. For example, the determinant of the matrix in Equation 4.12 is $0 \cdot 0 - (-1) \cdot (-1) = -1$.

EXAMPLE: SCALING IN A CERTAIN DIRECTION. The scaling matrix **S** scales along only the x-, y-, and z-axes. If scaling should be performed in other directions, a compound transform is needed. Assume that scaling should be done along the axes of the orthonormal, right-oriented vectors $\mathbf{f}^x$, $\mathbf{f}^y$, and $\mathbf{f}^z$. First, construct the matrix **F**, to change the basis, as below:

$$\mathbf{F} = \begin{pmatrix} \mathbf{f}^x & \mathbf{f}^y & \mathbf{f}^z & \mathbf{0} \\ 0 & 0 & 0 & 1 \end{pmatrix}. \tag{4.13}$$

The idea is to make the coordinate system given by the three axes coincide with the standard axes, then use the standard scaling matrix, and then transform back. The first step is carried out by multiplying with the transpose, i.e., the inverse, of **F**. Then the actual scaling is done, followed by a transform back. The transform is shown in Equation 4.14:

$$\mathbf{X} = \mathbf{F}\mathbf{S}(\mathbf{s})\mathbf{F}^T. \tag{4.14}$$

$\square$

4.1.4 Shearing

Another class of transforms is the set of shearing matrices. These can, for example, be used in games to distort an entire scene to create a psychedelic effect or otherwise warp a model's appearance. There are six basic shearing matrices, and they are denoted $\mathbf{H}_{xy}(s)$, $\mathbf{H}_{xz}(s)$, $\mathbf{H}_{yx}(s)$, $\mathbf{H}_{yz}(s)$, $\mathbf{H}_{zx}(s)$, and $\mathbf{H}_{zy}(s)$. The first subscript is used to denote which coordinate is being changed by the shear matrix, while the second

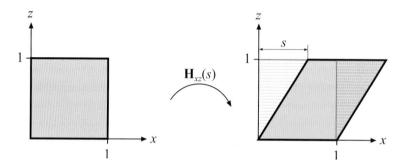

Figure 4.3. The effect of shearing the unit square with $\mathbf{H}_{xz}(s)$. Both the y- and z-values are unaffected by the transform, while the x-value is the sum of the old x-value and s multiplied by the z-value, causing the square to become slanted. This transform is area-preserving, which can be seen in that the dashed areas are the same.

subscript indicates the coordinate which does the shearing. An example of a shear matrix, $\mathbf{H}_{xz}(s)$, is shown in Equation 4.15. Observe that the subscript can be used to find the position of the parameter s in the matrix below; the x (whose numeric index is 0) identifies row zero, and the z (whose numeric index is 2) identifies column two, and so the s is located there:

$$\mathbf{H}_{xz}(s) = \begin{pmatrix} 1 & 0 & s & 0 \\ 0 & 1 & 0 & 0 \\ 0 & 0 & 1 & 0 \\ 0 & 0 & 0 & 1 \end{pmatrix}. \tag{4.15}$$

The effect of multiplying this matrix with a point $\mathbf{p}$ yields a point: $(p_x + sp_z \ \ p_y \ \ p_z)^T$. Graphically, this is shown for the unit square in Figure 4.3. The inverse of $\mathbf{H}_{ij}(s)$ (shearing the ith coordinate with respect to the jth coordinate, where $i \neq j$), is generated by shearing in the opposite direction, that is, $\mathbf{H}_{ij}^{-1}(s) = \mathbf{H}_{ij}(-s)$.

You can also use a slightly different kind of shear matrix:

$$\mathbf{H}'_{xy}(s,t) = \begin{pmatrix} 1 & 0 & s & 0 \\ 0 & 1 & t & 0 \\ 0 & 0 & 1 & 0 \\ 0 & 0 & 0 & 1 \end{pmatrix}. \tag{4.16}$$

Here, however, both subscripts are used to denote that these coordinates are to be sheared by the third coordinate. The connection between these two different kinds of descriptions is $\mathbf{H}'_{ij}(s,t) = \mathbf{H}_{ik}(s)\mathbf{H}_{jk}(t)$, where k is used as an index to the third coordinate. The right matrix to use is a matter of taste. Finally, it should be noted that since the determinant of any shear matrix $|\mathbf{H}| = 1$, this is a volume-preserving transformation, which also is illustrated in Figure 4.3.

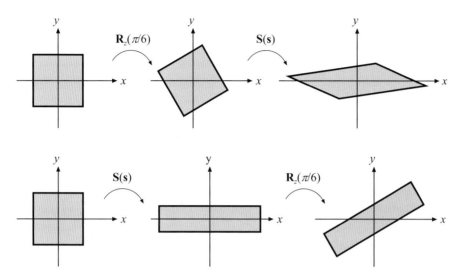

Figure 4.4. This illustrates the order dependency when multiplying matrices. In the top row, the rotation matrix $\mathbf{R}_z(\pi/6)$ is applied followed by a scaling, $\mathbf{S}(\mathbf{s})$, where $\mathbf{s} = (2, 0.5, 1)$. The composite matrix is then $\mathbf{S}(\mathbf{s})\mathbf{R}_z(\pi/6)$. In the bottom row, the matrices are applied in the reverse order, yielding $\mathbf{R}_z(\pi/6)\mathbf{S}(\mathbf{s})$. The results are clearly different. It generally holds that $\mathbf{MN} \neq \mathbf{NM}$, for arbitrary matrices $\mathbf{M}$ and $\mathbf{N}$.

4.1.5 Concatenation of Transforms

Due to the noncommutativity of the multiplication operation on matrices, the order in which the matrices occur matters. Concatenation of transforms is therefore said to be order-dependent.

As an example of order dependency, consider two matrices, $\mathbf{S}$ and $\mathbf{R}$. $\mathbf{S}(2, 0.5, 1)$ scales the x-component by a factor two and the y-component by a factor 0.5. $\mathbf{R}_z(\pi/6)$ rotates $\pi/6$ radians counterclockwise around the z-axis (which points outward from page of this book in a right-handed coordinate system). These matrices can be multiplied in two ways, with the results being entirely different. The two cases are shown in Figure 4.4.

The obvious reason to concatenate a sequence of matrices into a single one is to gain efficiency. For example, imagine that you have a game scene that has several million vertices, and that all objects in the scene must be scaled, rotated, and finally translated. Now, instead of multiplying all vertices with each of the three matrices, the three matrices are concatenated into a single matrix. This single matrix is then applied to the vertices. This composite matrix is $\mathbf{C} = \mathbf{TRS}$. Note the order here. The scaling matrix, $\mathbf{S}$, should be applied to the vertices first, and therefore appears to the right in the composition. This ordering implies that $\mathbf{TRSp} = (\mathbf{T}(\mathbf{R}(\mathbf{Sp})))$, where $\mathbf{p}$ is a point to be transformed. Incidentally, $\mathbf{TRS}$ is the order commonly used by scene graph systems.

It is worth noting that while matrix concatenation is order-dependent, the matrices can be grouped as desired. For example, say that with $\mathbf{TRSp}$ you would like to compute the rigid-body motion transform $\mathbf{TR}$ once. It is valid to group these two matrices together, $(\mathbf{TR})(\mathbf{Sp})$, and replace with the intermediate result. Thus, matrix concatenation is *associative*.

4.1.6 The Rigid-Body Transform

When a person grabs a solid object, say a pen from a table, and moves it to another location, perhaps to a shirt pocket, only the object's orientation and location change, while the shape of the object generally is not affected. Such a transform, consisting of concatenations of only translations and rotations, is called a rigid-body transform. It has the characteristic of preserving lengths, angles, and handedness.

Any rigid-body matrix, $\mathbf{X}$, can be written as the concatenation of a translation matrix, $\mathbf{T}(\mathbf{t})$, and a rotation matrix, $\mathbf{R}$. Thus, $\mathbf{X}$ has the appearance of the matrix in Equation 4.17:

$$\mathbf{X} = \mathbf{T}(\mathbf{t})\mathbf{R} = \begin{pmatrix} r_{00} & r_{01} & r_{02} & t_x \\ r_{10} & r_{11} & r_{12} & t_y \\ r_{20} & r_{21} & r_{22} & t_z \\ 0 & 0 & 0 & 1 \end{pmatrix}. \tag{4.17}$$

The inverse of $\mathbf{X}$ is computed as $\mathbf{X}^{-1} = (\mathbf{T}(\mathbf{t})\mathbf{R})^{-1} = \mathbf{R}^{-1}\mathbf{T}(\mathbf{t})^{-1} = \mathbf{R}^T\mathbf{T}(-\mathbf{t})$. Thus, to compute the inverse, the upper left 3×3 matrix of $\mathbf{R}$ is transposed, and the translation values of $\mathbf{T}$ change sign. These two new matrices are multiplied together in opposite order to obtain the inverse. Another way to compute the inverse of $\mathbf{X}$ is to consider $\mathbf{R}$ (making $\mathbf{R}$ appear as 3×3 matrix) and $\mathbf{X}$ in the following notation (notation described on page 6 with Equation 1.2):

$$\bar{\mathbf{R}} = \begin{pmatrix} \mathbf{r}_{,0} & \mathbf{r}_{,1} & \mathbf{r}_{,2} \end{pmatrix} = \begin{pmatrix} \mathbf{r}_{0,}^T \\ \mathbf{r}_{1,}^T \\ \mathbf{r}_{2,}^T \end{pmatrix},$$

$$\mathbf{X} = \begin{pmatrix} \overrightarrow{\bar{\mathbf{R}}} & \mathbf{t} \\ \mathbf{0}^T & 1 \end{pmatrix}, \tag{4.18}$$

where $\mathbf{r}_{,0}$ means the first column of the rotation matrix (i.e., the comma indicates any value from 0 to 2, while the second subscript is 0) and $\mathbf{r}_{0,}^T$ is the first row of the column matrix. Note that $\mathbf{0}$ is a 3×1 column vector filled with zeros. Some calculations yield the inverse in the expression shown in Equation 4.19:

$$\mathbf{X}^{-1} = \begin{pmatrix} \mathbf{r}_{0,} & \mathbf{r}_{1,} & \mathbf{r}_{2,} & -\bar{\mathbf{R}}^T\mathbf{t} \\ 0 & 0 & 0 & 1 \end{pmatrix}. \tag{4.19}$$

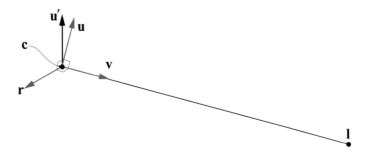

Figure 4.5. The geometry involved in computing a transform that orients the camera at $\mathbf{c}$, with up vector $\mathbf{u}'$, to look at the point $\mathbf{l}$. For that purpose, we need to compute $\mathbf{r}$, $\mathbf{u}$, and $\mathbf{v}$.

EXAMPLE: ORIENTING THE CAMERA. A common task in graphics is to orient the camera so that it looks at a certain position. Here we will present what `gluLookAt()` (from the OpenGL Utility Library, GLU for short) does. Even though this function call itself is not used much nowadays, the task remains common. Assume that the camera is located at $\mathbf{c}$, that we want the camera to look at a target $\mathbf{l}$, and that a given up direction of the camera is $\mathbf{u}'$, as illustrated in Figure 4.5. We want to compute a basis consisting of three vectors, $\{\mathbf{r}, \mathbf{u}, \mathbf{v}\}$. We start by computing the view vector as $\mathbf{v} = (\mathbf{c} - \mathbf{l})/\|\mathbf{c} - \mathbf{l}\|$, i.e., the normalized vector from the target to the camera position. A vector looking to the "right" can then be computed as $\mathbf{r} = -(\mathbf{v} \times \mathbf{u}')/\|\mathbf{v} \times \mathbf{u}'\|$. The $\mathbf{u}'$ vector is often not guaranteed to be pointing precisely up, so the final up vector is another cross product, $\mathbf{u} = \mathbf{v} \times \mathbf{r}$, which is guaranteed to be normalized since both $\mathbf{v}$ and $\mathbf{r}$ are normalized and perpendicular by construction. In the camera transform matrix, $\mathbf{M}$, that we will construct, the idea is to first translate everything so the camera position is at the origin, $(0, 0, 0)$, and then change the basis so that $\mathbf{r}$ is aligned with $(1, 0, 0)$, $\mathbf{u}$ with $(0, 1, 0)$, and $\mathbf{v}$ with $(0, 0, 1)$. This is done by

$$\mathbf{M} = \underbrace{\begin{pmatrix} r_x & r_y & r_z & 0 \\ u_x & u_y & u_z & 0 \\ v_x & v_y & v_z & 0 \\ 0 & 0 & 0 & 1 \end{pmatrix}}_{\text{change of basis}} \underbrace{\begin{pmatrix} 1 & 0 & 0 & -t_x \\ 0 & 1 & 0 & -t_y \\ 0 & 0 & 1 & -t_z \\ 0 & 0 & 0 & 1 \end{pmatrix}}_{\text{translation}} = \begin{pmatrix} r_x & r_y & r_z & -\mathbf{t} \cdot \mathbf{r} \\ u_x & u_y & u_z & -\mathbf{t} \cdot \mathbf{u} \\ v_x & v_y & v_z & -\mathbf{t} \cdot \mathbf{v} \\ 0 & 0 & 0 & 1 \end{pmatrix}. \qquad (4.20)$$

Note that when concatenating the translation matrix with the change of basis matrix, the translation $-\mathbf{t}$ is to the right since it should be applied first. One way to remember where to put the components of $\mathbf{r}$, $\mathbf{u}$, and $\mathbf{v}$ is the following. We want $\mathbf{r}$ to become $(1, 0, 0)$, so when multiplying a change of basis matrix with $(1, 0, 0)$, we can see that the first row in the matrix must be the elements of $\mathbf{r}$, since $\mathbf{r} \cdot \mathbf{r} = 1$. Furthermore, the second row and the third row must consist of vectors that are perpendicular to $\mathbf{r}$, i.e., $\mathbf{r} \cdot \mathbf{x} = 0$. When applying the same thinking also to $\mathbf{u}$ and $\mathbf{v}$, we arrive at the change of basis matrix above. □

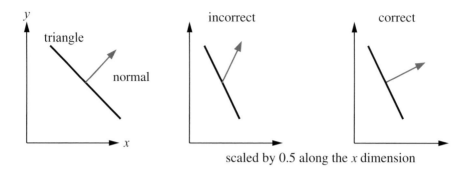

scaled by 0.5 along the x dimension

Figure 4.6. On the left is the original geometry, a triangle and its normal shown from the side. The middle illustration shows what happens if the model is scaled along the x- axis by 0.5 and the normal uses the same matrix. The right figure shows the proper transform of the normal.

4.1.7 Normal Transform

A single matrix can be used to consistently transform points, lines, triangles, and other geometry. The same matrix can also transform tangent vectors following along these lines or on the surfaces of triangles. However, this matrix cannot always be used to transform one important geometric property, the surface normal (and the vertex lighting normal). Figure 4.6 shows what can happen if this same matrix is used.

Instead of multiplying by the matrix itself, the proper method is to use the transpose of the matrix's adjoint [227]. Computation of the adjoint is described in our online linear algebra appendix. The adjoint is always guaranteed to exist. The normal is not guaranteed to be of unit length after being transformed, so typically needs to be normalized.

The traditional answer for transforming the normal is that the transpose of the inverse is computed [1794]. This method normally works. The full inverse is not necessary, however, and occasionally cannot be created. The inverse is the adjoint divided by the original matrix's determinant. If this determinant is zero, the matrix is singular, and the inverse does not exist.

Even computing just the adjoint for a full 4×4 matrix can be expensive, and is usually not necessary. Since the normal is a vector, translation will not affect it. Furthermore, most modeling transforms are affine. They do not change the w-component of the homogeneous coordinate passed in, i.e., they do not perform projection. Under these (common) circumstances, all that is needed for normal transformation is to compute the adjoint of the upper left 3×3 components.

Often even this adjoint computation is not needed. Say we know the transform matrix is composed entirely of a concatenation of translations, rotations, and uniform scaling operations (no stretching or squashing). Translations do not affect the normal. The uniform scaling factors simply change the length of the normal. What is left is a series of rotations, which always yields a net rotation of some sort, nothing more.

The transpose of the inverse can be used to transform normals. A rotation matrix is defined by the fact that its transpose is its inverse. Substituting to get the normal transform, two transposes (or two inverses) give the original rotation matrix. Putting it all together, the original transform itself can also be used directly to transform normals under these circumstances.

Finally, fully renormalizing the normal produced is not always necessary. If only translations and rotations are concatenated together, the normal will not change length when transformed by the matrix, so no renormalizing is needed. If uniform scalings are also concatenated, the overall scale factor (if known, or extracted—Section 4.2.3) can be used to directly normalize the normals produced. For example, if we know that a series of scalings were applied that makes the object 5.2 times larger, then normals transformed directly by this matrix are renormalized by dividing them by 5.2. Alternately, to create a normal transform matrix that would produce normalized results, the original matrix's 3×3 upper left could be divided by this scale factor once.

Note that normal transforms are not an issue in systems where, after transformation, the surface normal is derived from the triangle (e.g., using the cross product of the triangle's edges). Tangent vectors are different than normals in nature, and are always directly transformed by the original matrix.

4.1.8 Computation of Inverses

Inverses are needed in many cases, for example, when changing back and forth between coordinate systems. Depending on the available information about a transform, one of the following three methods of computing the inverse of a matrix can be used:

- If the matrix is a single transform or a sequence of simple transforms with given parameters, then the matrix can be computed easily by "inverting the parameters" and the matrix order. For example, if $\mathbf{M} = \mathbf{T}(\mathbf{t})\mathbf{R}(\phi)$, then $\mathbf{M}^{-1} = \mathbf{R}(-\phi)\mathbf{T}(-\mathbf{t})$. This is simple and preserves the accuracy of the transform, which is important when rendering huge worlds [1381].

- If the matrix is known to be orthogonal, then $\mathbf{M}^{-1} = \mathbf{M}^T$, i.e., the transpose is the inverse. Any sequence of rotations is a rotation, and so is orthogonal.

- If nothing is known, then the adjoint method, Cramer's rule, LU decomposition, or Gaussian elimination could be used to compute the inverse. Cramer's rule and the adjoint method are generally preferable, as they have fewer branch operations; "if" tests are good to avoid on modern architectures. See Section 4.1.7 on how to use the adjoint to invert transform normals.

The purpose of the inverse computation can also be taken into account when optimizing. For example, if the inverse is to be used for transforming vectors, then only the 3×3 upper left part of the matrix normally needs to be inverted (see the previous section).

4.2   Special Matrix Transforms and Operations

In this section, several matrix transforms and operations that are essential to real-time graphics will be introduced and derived. First, we present the Euler transform (along with its extraction of parameters), which is an intuitive way to describe orientations. Then we touch upon retrieving a set of basic transforms from a single matrix. Finally, a method is derived that rotates an entity around an arbitrary axis.

4.2.1   The Euler Transform

This transform is an intuitive way to construct a matrix to orient yourself (i.e., the camera) or any other entity in a certain direction. Its name comes from the great Swiss mathematician Leonhard Euler (1707–1783).

First, some kind of default view direction must be established. Most often it lies along the negative z-axis with the head oriented along the y-axis, as depicted in Figure 4.7. The Euler transform is the multiplication of three matrices, namely the rotations shown in the figure. More formally, the transform, denoted $\mathbf{E}$, is given by Equation 4.21:

$$\mathbf{E}(h, p, r) = \mathbf{R}_z(r)\mathbf{R}_x(p)\mathbf{R}_y(h). \tag{4.21}$$

The order of the matrices can be chosen in 24 different ways [1636]; we present this one because it is commonly used. Since $\mathbf{E}$ is a concatenation of rotations, it is also clearly orthogonal. Therefore its inverse can be expressed as $\mathbf{E}^{-1} = \mathbf{E}^T = (\mathbf{R}_z\mathbf{R}_x\mathbf{R}_y)^T = \mathbf{R}_y^T\mathbf{R}_x^T\mathbf{R}_z^T$, although it is, of course, easier to use the transpose of $\mathbf{E}$ directly.

The Euler angles h, p, and r represent in which order and how much the head, pitch, and roll should rotate around their respective axes. Sometimes the angles are all called "rolls," e.g., our "head" is the "y-roll" and our "pitch" is the "x-roll." Also, "head" is sometimes known as "yaw," such as in flight simulation.

This transform is intuitive and therefore easy to discuss in layperson's language. For example, changing the head angle makes the viewer shake their head "no," changing the pitch makes them nod, and rolling makes them tilt their head sideways. Rather than talking about rotations around the x-, y-, and z-axes, we talk about altering the head, pitch, and roll. Note that this transform can orient not only the camera, but also any object or entity as well. These transforms can be performed using the global axes of the world space or relative to a local frame of reference.

It is important to note that some presentations of Euler angles give the z-axis as the initial up direction. This difference is purely a notational change, though a potentially confusing one. In computer graphics there is a division in how the world is regarded and thus how content is formed: y-up or z-up. Most manufacturing processes, including 3D printing, consider the z-direction to be up in world space; aviation and sea vehicles consider $-z$ to be up. Architecture and GIS normally use z-up, as a building plan or map is two-dimensional, x and y. Media-related modeling systems often consider the y-direction as up in world coordinates, matching how we always describe a camera's screen up direction in computer graphics. The difference between

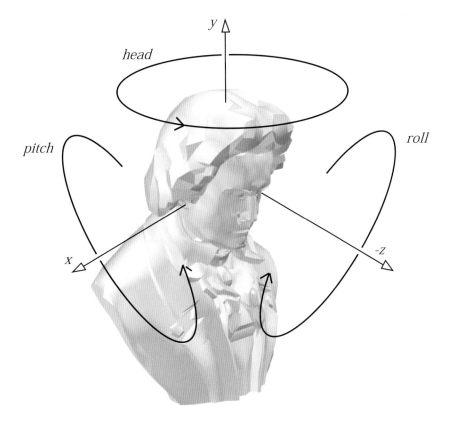

Figure 4.7. The Euler transform and how it relates to the way you change the *head*, *pitch*, and *roll* angles. The default view direction is shown, looking along the negative z-axis with the up direction along the y-axis.

these two world up vector choices is just a 90° rotation (and possibly a reflection) away, but not knowing which is assumed can lead to problems. In this volume we use a world direction of y-up unless otherwise noted.

We also want to point out that the camera's up direction in its view space has nothing in particular to do with the world's up direction. Roll your head and the view is tilted, with its world-space up direction differing from the world's. As another example, say the world uses y-up and our camera looks straight down at the terrain below, a bird's eye view. This orientation means the camera has pitched 90° forward, so that its up direction in world space is $(0, 0, -1)$. In this orientation the camera has no y-component and instead considers $-z$ to be up in world space, but "y is up" remains true in view space, by definition.

While useful for small angle changes or viewer orientation, Euler angles have some other serious limitations. It is difficult to work with two sets of Euler angles in combination. For example, interpolation between one set and another is not a simple matter of interpolating each angle. In fact, two different sets of Euler angles can give the same orientation, so any interpolation should not rotate the object at all. These are some of the reasons that using alternate orientation representations such as quaternions, discussed later in this chapter, are worth pursuing. With Euler angles, you can also get something called gimbal lock, which will be explained next in Section 4.2.2.

4.2.2 Extracting Parameters from the Euler Transform

In some situations, it is useful to have a procedure that extracts the Euler parameters, h, p, and r, from an orthogonal matrix. This procedure is shown in Equation 4.22:

$$\mathbf{E}(h,p,r) = \begin{pmatrix} e_{00} & e_{01} & e_{02} \\ e_{10} & e_{11} & e_{12} \\ e_{20} & e_{21} & e_{22} \end{pmatrix} = \mathbf{R}_z(r)\mathbf{R}_x(p)\mathbf{R}_y(h). \tag{4.22}$$

Here we abandoned the 4×4 matrices for 3×3 matrices, since the latter provide all the necessary information for a rotation matrix. That is, the rest of the equivalent 4×4 matrix always contains zeros and a one in the lower right position.

Concatenating the three rotation matrices in Equation 4.22 yields

$$\mathbf{E} = \begin{pmatrix} \cos r\cos h-\sin r\sin p\sin h & -\sin r\cos p & \cos r\sin h+\sin r\sin p\cos h \\ \sin r\cos h+\cos r\sin p\sin h & \cos r\cos p & \sin r\sin h-\cos r\sin p\cos h \\ -\cos p\sin h & \sin p & \cos p\cos h \end{pmatrix}. \tag{4.23}$$

From this it is apparent that the pitch parameter is given by $\sin p = e_{21}$. Also, dividing e_{01} by e_{11}, and similarly dividing e_{20} by e_{22}, gives rise to the following extraction equations for the head and roll parameters:

$$\frac{e_{01}}{e_{11}} = \frac{-\sin r}{\cos r} = -\tan r \quad \text{and} \quad \frac{e_{20}}{e_{22}} = \frac{-\sin h}{\cos h} = -\tan h. \tag{4.24}$$

Thus, the Euler parameters h (head), p (pitch), and r (roll) are extracted from a matrix $\mathbf{E}$ using the function $\texttt{atan2(y,x)}$ (see page 8 in Chapter 1) as in Equation 4.25:

$$\begin{aligned} h &= \texttt{atan2}(-e_{20}, e_{22}), \\ p &= \arcsin(e_{21}), \\ r &= \texttt{atan2}(-e_{01}, e_{11}). \end{aligned} \tag{4.25}$$

However, there is a special case we need to handle. If $\cos p = 0$, we have gimbal lock (Section 4.2.2) and rotation angles r and h will rotate around the same axis (though possibly in different directions, depending on whether the p rotation angle was $-\pi/2$ or $\pi/2$), so only one angle needs to be derived. If we arbitrarily set $h = 0$ [1769], we get

$$\mathbf{E} = \begin{pmatrix} \cos r & \sin r\cos p & \sin r\sin p \\ \sin r & \cos r\cos p & -\cos r\sin p \\ 0 & \sin p & \cos p \end{pmatrix}. \tag{4.26}$$

Since p does not affect the values in the first column, when $\cos p = 0$ we can use $\sin r / \cos r = \tan r = e_{10}/e_{00}$, which gives $r = \texttt{atan2}(e_{10}, e_{00})$.

Note that from the definition of arcsin, $-\pi/2 \leq p \leq \pi/2$, which means that if $\mathbf{E}$ was created with a value of p outside this interval, the original parameter cannot be extracted. That h, p, and r are not unique means that more than one set of the Euler parameters can be used to yield the same transform. More about Euler angle conversion can be found in Shoemake's 1994 article [1636]. The simple method outlined above can result in problems with numerical instability, which is avoidable at some cost in speed [1362].

When you use Euler transforms, something called *gimbal lock* may occur [499, 1633]. This happens when rotations are made so that one degree of freedom is lost. For example, say the order of transforms is $x/y/z$. Consider a rotation of $\pi/2$ around just the y-axis, the second rotation performed. Doing so rotates the local z-axis to be aligned with the original x-axis, so that the final rotation around z is redundant.

Mathematically, we have already seen gimbal lock in Equation 4.26, where we assumed $\cos p = 0$, i.e., $p = \pm\pi/2 + 2\pi k$, where k is an integer. With such a value of p, we have lost one degree of freedom since the matrix only depends on one angle, $r + h$ or $r - h$ (but not both at the same time).

While Euler angles are commonly presented as being in $x/y/z$ order in modeling systems, a rotation around each local axis, other orderings are feasible. For example, $z/x/y$ is used in animation and $z/x/z$ in both animation and physics. All are valid ways of specifying three separate rotations. This last ordering, $z/x/z$, can be superior for some applications, as only when rotating π radians around x (a half-rotation) does gimbal lock occur. There is no perfect sequence that avoids gimbal lock. Euler angles nonetheless are commonly used, as animators prefer curve editors to specify how angles change over time [499].

EXAMPLE: CONSTRAINING A TRANSFORM. Imagine you are holding a (virtual) wrench that is gripping a bolt. To get the bolt into place, you have to rotate the wrench around the x-axis. Now assume that your input device (mouse, VR gloves, space-ball, etc.) gives you a rotation matrix, i.e., a rotation, for the movement of the wrench. The problem is that it is likely to be wrong to apply this transform to the wrench, which should rotate around only the x-axis. To restrict the input transform, called $\mathbf{P}$, to be a rotation around the x-axis, simply extract the Euler angles, h, p, and r, using the method described in this section, and then create a new matrix $\mathbf{R}_x(p)$. This is then the sought-after transform that will rotate the wrench around the x-axis (if $\mathbf{P}$ now contains such a movement). $\square$

4.2.3 Matrix Decomposition

Up to this point we have been working under the assumption that we know the origin and history of the transformation matrix we are using. This is often not the case.

For example, nothing more than a concatenated matrix may be associated with some transformed object. The task of retrieving various transforms from a concatenated matrix is called *matrix decomposition.*

There are many reasons to retrieve a set of transformations. Uses include:

- Extracting just the scaling factors for an object.

- Finding transforms needed by a particular system. (For example, some systems may not allow the use of an arbitrary 4×4 matrix.)

- Determining whether a model has undergone only rigid-body transforms.

- Interpolating between keyframes in an animation where only the matrix for the object is available.

- Removing shears from a rotation matrix.

We have already presented two decompositions, those of deriving the translation and rotation matrix for a rigid-body transformation (Section 4.1.6) and deriving the Euler angles from an orthogonal matrix (Section 4.2.2).

As we have seen, it is trivial to retrieve the translation matrix, as we simply need the elements in the last column of the 4×4 matrix. We can also determine if a reflection has occurred by checking whether the determinant of the matrix is negative. To separate out the rotation, scaling, and shears takes more determined effort.

Fortunately, there are several articles on this topic, as well as code available online. Thomas [1769] and Goldman [552, 553] each present somewhat different methods for various classes of transformations. Shoemake [1635] improves upon their techniques for affine matrices, as his algorithm is independent of frame of reference and attempts to decompose the matrix to obtain rigid-body transforms.

4.2.4 Rotation about an Arbitrary Axis

Sometimes it is convenient to have a procedure that rotates an entity by some angle around an arbitrary axis. Assume that the rotation axis, $\mathbf{r}$, is normalized and that a transform should be created that rotates α radians around $\mathbf{r}$.

To do this, we first transform to a space where the axis around which we want to rotate is the x-axis. This is done with a rotation matrix, called $\mathbf{M}$. Then the actual rotation is performed, and we transform back using $\mathbf{M}^{-1}$ [314]. This procedure is illustrated in Figure 4.8.

To compute $\mathbf{M}$, we need to find two axes that are orthonormal both to $\mathbf{r}$ and to each other. We concentrate on finding the second axis, $\mathbf{s}$, knowing that the third axis, $\mathbf{t}$, will be the cross product of the first and the second axis, $\mathbf{t} = \mathbf{r} \times \mathbf{s}$. A numerically stable way to do this is to find the smallest component (in absolute value) of $\mathbf{r}$, and set it to 0. Swap the two remaining components, and then negate the first of them

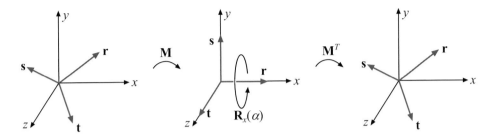

Figure 4.8. Rotation about an arbitrary axis, **r**, is accomplished by finding an orthonormal basis formed by **r**, **s**, and **t**. We then align this basis with the standard basis so that **r** is aligned with the x-axis. The rotation around the x-axis is performed there, and finally we transform back.

(in fact, either of the nonzero components could be negated). Mathematically, this is expressed as [784]:

$$\bar{\mathbf{s}} = \begin{cases} (0, -r_z, r_y), & \text{if } |r_x| \leq |r_y| \text{ and } |r_x| \leq |r_z|, \\ (-r_z, 0, r_x), & \text{if } |r_y| \leq |r_x| \text{ and } |r_y| \leq |r_z|, \\ (-r_y, r_x, 0), & \text{if } |r_z| \leq |r_x| \text{ and } |r_z| \leq |r_y|, \end{cases}$$

$$\mathbf{s} = \bar{\mathbf{s}}/\|\bar{\mathbf{s}}\|,$$

$$\mathbf{t} = \mathbf{r} \times \mathbf{s}.$$

(4.27)

This guarantees that $\bar{\mathbf{s}}$ is orthogonal (perpendicular) to **r**, and that $(\mathbf{r}, \mathbf{s}, \mathbf{t})$ is an orthonormal basis. Frisvad [496] presents a method without any branches in the code, which is faster but has lower accuracy. Max [1147] and Duff et al. [388] improve the accuracy of Frisvad's method. Whichever technique is employed, these three vectors are used to create a rotation matrix:

$$\mathbf{M} = \begin{pmatrix} \mathbf{r}^T \\ \mathbf{s}^T \\ \mathbf{t}^T \end{pmatrix}.$$

(4.28)

This matrix transforms the vector **r** into the x-axis, **s** into the y-axis, and **t** into the z-axis. So, the final transform for rotating α radians around the normalized vector **r** is then

$$\mathbf{X} = \mathbf{M}^T \mathbf{R}_x(\alpha)\mathbf{M}.$$

(4.29)

In words, this means that first we transform so that **r** is the x-axis (using **M**), then we rotate α radians around this x-axis (using $\mathbf{R}_x(\alpha)$), and then we transform back using the inverse of **M**, which in this case is $\mathbf{M}^T$ because **M** is orthogonal.

Another method for rotating around an arbitrary, normalized axis **r** by ϕ radians has been presented by Goldman [550]. Here, we simply present his transform:

$$\mathbf{R} =$$

$$\begin{pmatrix} \cos\phi + (1-\cos\phi)r_x^2 & (1-\cos\phi)r_x r_y - r_z\sin\phi & (1-\cos\phi)r_x r_z + r_y\sin\phi \\ (1-\cos\phi)r_x r_y + r_z\sin\phi & \cos\phi + (1-\cos\phi)r_y^2 & (1-\cos\phi)r_y r_z - r_x\sin\phi \\ (1-\cos\phi)r_x r_z - r_y\sin\phi & (1-\cos\phi)r_y r_z + r_x\sin\phi & \cos\phi + (1-\cos\phi)r_z^2 \end{pmatrix}.$$

(4.30)

In Section 4.3.2, we present yet another method for solving this problem, using quaternions. Also in that section are more efficient algorithms for related problems, such as rotation from one vector to another.

4.3 Quaternions

Although quaternions were invented back in 1843 by Sir William Rowan Hamilton as an extension to the complex numbers, it was not until 1985 that Shoemake [1633] introduced them to the field of computer graphics.[1] Quaternions are used to represent rotations and orientations. They are superior to both Euler angles and matrices in several ways. Any three-dimensional orientation can be expressed as a single rotation around a particular axis. Given this axis & angle representation, translating to or from a quaternion is straightforward, while Euler angle conversion in either direction is challenging. Quaternions can be used for stable and constant interpolation of orientations, something that cannot be done well with Euler angles.

A complex number has a real and an imaginary part. Each is represented by two real numbers, the second real number being multiplied by $\sqrt{-1}$. Similarly, quaternions have four parts. The first three values are closely related to axis of rotation, with the angle of rotation affecting all four parts (more about this in Section 4.3.2). Each quaternion is represented by four real numbers, each associated with a different part. Since quaternions have four components, we choose to represent them as vectors, but to differentiate them, we put a hat on them: $\hat{q}$. We begin with some mathematical background on quaternions, which is then used to construct a variety of useful transforms.

4.3.1 Mathematical Background

We start with the definition of a quaternion.

Definition. A quaternion $\hat{q}$ can be defined in the following ways, all equivalent.

$$\hat{q} = (\mathbf{q}_v, q_w) = iq_x + jq_y + kq_z + q_w = \mathbf{q}_v + q_w,$$
$$\mathbf{q}_v = iq_x + jq_y + kq_z = (q_x, q_y, q_z), \tag{4.31}$$
$$i^2 = j^2 = k^2 = -1, \ jk = -kj = i, \ ki = -ik = j, \ ij = -ji = k.$$

The variable q_w is called the real part of a quaternion, $\hat{q}$. The imaginary part is $\mathbf{q}_v$, and i, j, and k are called imaginary units.   □

For the imaginary part, $\mathbf{q}_v$, we can use all the normal vector operations, such as addition, scaling, dot product, cross product, and more. Using the definition of the quaternion, the multiplication operation between two quaternions, $\hat{q}$ and $\hat{r}$, is derived

---

[1]In fairness, Robinson [1502] used quaternions in 1958 for rigid-body simulations.

as shown below. Note that the multiplication of the imaginary units is noncommutative.

Multiplication: $\hat{\mathbf{q}}\hat{\mathbf{r}} = (iq_x + jq_y + kq_z + q_w)(ir_x + jr_y + kr_z + r_w)$

$$= i(q_y r_z - q_z r_y + r_w q_x + q_w r_x)$$
$$+ \ j(q_z r_x - q_x r_z + r_w q_y + q_w r_y) \qquad (4.32)$$
$$+ \ k(q_x r_y - q_y r_x + r_w q_z + q_w r_z)$$
$$+ \ q_w r_w - q_x r_x - q_y r_y - q_z r_z$$
$$= (\mathbf{q}_v \times \mathbf{r}_v + r_w \mathbf{q}_v + q_w \mathbf{r}_v, \ q_w r_w - \mathbf{q}_v \cdot \mathbf{r}_v).$$

As can be seen in this equation, we use both the cross product and the dot product to compute the multiplication of two quaternions.

Along with the definition of the quaternion, the definitions of addition, conjugate, norm, and an identity are needed:

Addition: $\qquad \hat{\mathbf{q}} + \hat{\mathbf{r}} = (\mathbf{q}_v, q_w) + (\mathbf{r}_v, r_w) = (\mathbf{q}_v + \mathbf{r}_v, q_w + r_w).$

Conjugate: $\qquad \hat{\mathbf{q}}^* = (\mathbf{q}_v, q_w)^* = (-\mathbf{q}_v, q_w).$

Norm: $\qquad n(\hat{\mathbf{q}}) = \sqrt{\hat{\mathbf{q}}\hat{\mathbf{q}}^*} = \sqrt{\hat{\mathbf{q}}^*\hat{\mathbf{q}}} = \sqrt{\mathbf{q}_v \cdot \mathbf{q}_v + q_w^2} \qquad (4.33)$

$$= \sqrt{q_x^2 + q_y^2 + q_z^2 + q_w^2}.$$

Identity: $\qquad \hat{\mathbf{i}} = (\mathbf{0}, 1).$

When $n(\hat{\mathbf{q}}) = \sqrt{\hat{\mathbf{q}}\hat{\mathbf{q}}^*}$ is simplified (result shown above), the imaginary parts cancel out and only a real part remains. The norm is sometimes denoted $||\hat{\mathbf{q}}|| = n(\hat{\mathbf{q}})$ [1105]. A consequence of the above is that a multiplicative inverse, denoted by $\hat{\mathbf{q}}^{-1}$, can be derived. The equation $\hat{\mathbf{q}}^{-1}\hat{\mathbf{q}} = \hat{\mathbf{q}}\hat{\mathbf{q}}^{-1} = 1$ must hold for the inverse (as is common for a multiplicative inverse). We derive a formula from the definition of the norm:

$$n(\hat{\mathbf{q}})^2 = \hat{\mathbf{q}}\hat{\mathbf{q}}^* \iff \frac{\hat{\mathbf{q}}\hat{\mathbf{q}}^*}{n(\hat{\mathbf{q}})^2} = 1. \qquad (4.34)$$

This gives the multiplicative inverse as shown below:

Inverse: $\qquad \hat{\mathbf{q}}^{-1} = \dfrac{1}{n(\hat{\mathbf{q}})^2}\hat{\mathbf{q}}^*. \qquad (4.35)$

The formula for the inverse uses scalar multiplication, which is an operation derived from the multiplication seen in Equation 4.3.1: $s\hat{\mathbf{q}} = (\mathbf{0}, s)(\mathbf{q}_v, q_w) = (s\mathbf{q}_v, sq_w)$, and $\hat{\mathbf{q}}s = (\mathbf{q}_v, q_w)(\mathbf{0}, s) = (s\mathbf{q}_v, sq_w)$, which means that scalar multiplication is commutative: $s\hat{\mathbf{q}} = \hat{\mathbf{q}}s = (s\mathbf{q}_v, sq_w).$

The following collection of rules are simple to derive from the definitions:

Conjugate rules:
$$(\hat{\mathbf{q}}^*)^* = \hat{\mathbf{q}},$$

$$(\hat{\mathbf{q}} + \hat{\mathbf{r}})^* = \hat{\mathbf{q}}^* + \hat{\mathbf{r}}^*, \tag{4.36}$$

$$(\hat{\mathbf{q}}\hat{\mathbf{r}})^* = \hat{\mathbf{r}}^*\hat{\mathbf{q}}^*.$$

Norm rules:
$$n(\hat{\mathbf{q}}^*) = n(\hat{\mathbf{q}}),$$
$$n(\hat{\mathbf{q}}\hat{\mathbf{r}}) = n(\hat{\mathbf{q}})n(\hat{\mathbf{r}}). \tag{4.37}$$

Laws of Multiplication:

Linearity:
$$\hat{\mathbf{p}}(s\hat{\mathbf{q}} + t\hat{\mathbf{r}}) = s\hat{\mathbf{p}}\hat{\mathbf{q}} + t\hat{\mathbf{p}}\hat{\mathbf{r}},$$
$$(s\hat{\mathbf{p}} + t\hat{\mathbf{q}})\hat{\mathbf{r}} = s\hat{\mathbf{p}}\hat{\mathbf{r}} + t\hat{\mathbf{q}}\hat{\mathbf{r}}. \tag{4.38}$$

Associativity:
$$\hat{\mathbf{p}}(\hat{\mathbf{q}}\hat{\mathbf{r}}) = (\hat{\mathbf{p}}\hat{\mathbf{q}})\hat{\mathbf{r}}.$$

A unit quaternion, $\hat{\mathbf{q}} = (\mathbf{q}_v,\ q_w)$, is such that $n(\hat{\mathbf{q}}) = 1$. From this it follows that $\hat{\mathbf{q}}$ may be written as

$$\hat{\mathbf{q}} = (\sin\phi\mathbf{u}_q,\ \cos\phi) = \sin\phi\mathbf{u}_q + \cos\phi, \tag{4.39}$$

for some three-dimensional vector $\mathbf{u}_q$, such that $||\mathbf{u}_q|| = 1$, because

$$n(\hat{\mathbf{q}}) = n(\sin\phi\mathbf{u}_q,\ \cos\phi) = \sqrt{\sin^2\phi(\mathbf{u}_q \cdot \mathbf{u}_q) + \cos^2\phi}$$
$$= \sqrt{\sin^2\phi + \cos^2\phi} = 1 \tag{4.40}$$

if and only if $\mathbf{u}_q \cdot \mathbf{u}_q = 1 = ||\mathbf{u}_q||^2$. As will be seen in the next section, unit quaternions are perfectly suited for creating rotations and orientations in a most efficient way. But before that, some extra operations will be introduced for unit quaternions.

For complex numbers, a two-dimensional unit vector can be written as $\cos\phi + i\sin\phi = e^{i\phi}$. The equivalent for quaternions is

$$\hat{\mathbf{q}} = \sin\phi\mathbf{u}_q + \cos\phi = e^{\phi\mathbf{u}_q}. \tag{4.41}$$

The log and the power functions for unit quaternions follow from Equation 4.41:

Logarithm:
$$\log(\hat{\mathbf{q}}) = \log(e^{\phi\mathbf{u}_q}) = \phi\mathbf{u}_q,$$

$$\tag{4.42}$$

Power:
$$\hat{\mathbf{q}}^t = (\sin\phi\mathbf{u}_q + \cos\phi)^t = e^{\phi t\mathbf{u}_q} = \sin(\phi t)\mathbf{u}_q + \cos(\phi t).$$

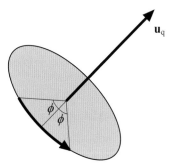

Figure 4.9. Illustration of the rotation transform represented by a unit quaternion, $\hat{\mathbf{q}} = (\sin\phi\mathbf{u}_q,\ \cos\phi)$. The transform rotates 2ϕ radians around the axis $\mathbf{u}_q$.

4.3.2 Quaternion Transforms

We will now study a subclass of the quaternion set, namely those of unit length, called *unit quaternions*. The most important fact about unit quaternions is that they can represent any three-dimensional rotation, and that this representation is extremely compact and simple.

Now we will describe what makes unit quaternions so useful for rotations and orientations. First, put the four coordinates of a point or vector $\mathbf{p} = (p_x\ p_y\ p_z\ p_w)^T$ into the components of a quaternion $\hat{\mathbf{p}}$, and assume that we have a unit quaternion $\hat{\mathbf{q}} = (\sin\phi\mathbf{u}_q,\ \cos\phi)$. One can prove that

$$\hat{\mathbf{q}}\hat{\mathbf{p}}\hat{\mathbf{q}}^{-1} \tag{4.43}$$

rotates $\hat{\mathbf{p}}$ (and thus the point $\mathbf{p}$) around the axis $\mathbf{u}_q$ by an angle 2ϕ. Note that since $\hat{\mathbf{q}}$ is a unit quaternion, $\hat{\mathbf{q}}^{-1} = \hat{\mathbf{q}}^*$. See Figure 4.9.

Any nonzero real multiple of $\hat{\mathbf{q}}$ also represents the same transform, which means that $\hat{\mathbf{q}}$ and $-\hat{\mathbf{q}}$ represent the same rotation. That is, negating the axis, $\mathbf{u}_q$, and the real part, q_w, creates a quaternion that rotates exactly as the original quaternion does. It also means that the extraction of a quaternion from a matrix can return either $\hat{\mathbf{q}}$ or $-\hat{\mathbf{q}}$.

Given two unit quaternions, $\hat{\mathbf{q}}$ and $\hat{\mathbf{r}}$, the concatenation of first applying $\hat{\mathbf{q}}$ and then $\hat{\mathbf{r}}$ to a quaternion, $\hat{\mathbf{p}}$ (which can be interpreted as a point $\mathbf{p}$), is given by Equation 4.44:

$$\hat{\mathbf{r}}(\hat{\mathbf{q}}\hat{\mathbf{p}}\hat{\mathbf{q}}^*)\hat{\mathbf{r}}^* = (\hat{\mathbf{r}}\hat{\mathbf{q}})\hat{\mathbf{p}}(\hat{\mathbf{r}}\hat{\mathbf{q}})^* = \hat{\mathbf{c}}\hat{\mathbf{p}}\hat{\mathbf{c}}^*. \tag{4.44}$$

Here, $\hat{\mathbf{c}} = \hat{\mathbf{r}}\hat{\mathbf{q}}$ is the unit quaternion representing the concatenation of the unit quaternions $\hat{\mathbf{q}}$ and $\hat{\mathbf{r}}$.

Matrix Conversion

Since one often needs to combine several different transforms, and most of them are in matrix form, a method is needed to convert Equation 4.43 into a matrix. A quaternion,

$\hat{\mathbf{q}}$, can be converted into a matrix $\mathbf{M}^q$, as expressed in Equation 4.45 [1633, 1634]:

$$\mathbf{M}^q = \begin{pmatrix} 1 - s(q_y^2 + q_z^2) & s(q_x q_y - q_w q_z) & s(q_x q_z + q_w q_y) & 0 \\ s(q_x q_y + q_w q_z) & 1 - s(q_x^2 + q_z^2) & s(q_y q_z - q_w q_x) & 0 \\ s(q_x q_z - q_w q_y) & s(q_y q_z + q_w q_x) & 1 - s(q_x^2 + q_y^2) & 0 \\ 0 & 0 & 0 & 1 \end{pmatrix}. \tag{4.45}$$

Here, the scalar is $s = 2/(n(\hat{\mathbf{q}}))^2$. For unit quaternions, this simplifies to

$$\mathbf{M}^q = \begin{pmatrix} 1 - 2(q_y^2 + q_z^2) & 2(q_x q_y - q_w q_z) & 2(q_x q_z + q_w q_y) & 0 \\ 2(q_x q_y + q_w q_z) & 1 - 2(q_x^2 + q_z^2) & 2(q_y q_z - q_w q_x) & 0 \\ 2(q_x q_z - q_w q_y) & 2(q_y q_z + q_w q_x) & 1 - 2(q_x^2 + q_y^2) & 0 \\ 0 & 0 & 0 & 1 \end{pmatrix}. \tag{4.46}$$

Once the quaternion is constructed, *no* trigonometric functions need to be computed, so the conversion process is efficient in practice.

The reverse conversion, from an orthogonal matrix, $\mathbf{M}^q$, into a unit quaternion, $\hat{\mathbf{q}}$, is a bit more involved. Key to this process are the following differences made from the matrix in Equation 4.46:

$$\begin{aligned} m_{21}^q - m_{12}^q &= 4 q_w q_x, \\ m_{02}^q - m_{20}^q &= 4 q_w q_y, \\ m_{10}^q - m_{01}^q &= 4 q_w q_z. \end{aligned} \tag{4.47}$$

The implication of these equations is that if q_w is known, the values of the vector $\mathbf{v}_q$ can be computed, and thus $\hat{\mathbf{q}}$ derived. The trace of $\mathbf{M}^q$ is calculated by

$$\mathrm{tr}(\mathbf{M}^q) = 4 - 2s(q_x^2 + q_y^2 + q_z^2) = 4 \left(1 - \frac{q_x^2 + q_y^2 + q_z^2}{q_x^2 + q_y^2 + q_z^2 + q_w^2} \right) \tag{4.48}$$

$$= \frac{4 q_w^2}{q_x^2 + q_y^2 + q_z^2 + q_w^2} = \frac{4 q_w^2}{(n(\hat{\mathbf{q}}))^2}.$$

This result yields the following conversion for a unit quaternion:

$$q_w = \frac{1}{2}\sqrt{\mathrm{tr}(\mathbf{M}^q)}, \qquad q_x = \frac{m_{21}^q - m_{12}^q}{4 q_w},$$

$$q_y = \frac{m_{02}^q - m_{20}^q}{4 q_w}, \qquad q_z = \frac{m_{10}^q - m_{01}^q}{4 q_w}. \tag{4.49}$$

To have a numerically stable routine [1634], divisions by small numbers should be avoided. Therefore, first set $t = q_w^2 - q_x^2 - q_y^2 - q_z^2$, from which it follows that

$$\begin{aligned} m_{00} &= t + 2q_x^2, \\ m_{11} &= t + 2q_y^2, \\ m_{22} &= t + 2q_z^2, \\ u = m_{00} + m_{11} + m_{22} &= t + 2q_w^2, \end{aligned} \tag{4.50}$$

which in turn implies that the largest of m_{00}, m_{11}, m_{22}, and u determine which of q_x, q_y, q_z, and q_w is largest. If q_w is largest, then Equation 4.49 is used to derive the quaternion. Otherwise, we note that the following holds:

$$\begin{aligned}
4q_x^2 &= +m_{00} - m_{11} - m_{22} + m_{33}, \\
4q_y^2 &= -m_{00} + m_{11} - m_{22} + m_{33}, \\
4q_z^2 &= -m_{00} - m_{11} + m_{22} + m_{33}, \\
4q_w^2 &= \mathrm{tr}(\mathbf{M}^q).
\end{aligned} \tag{4.51}$$

The appropriate equation of the ones above is then used to compute the largest of q_x, q_y, and q_z, after which Equation 4.47 is used to calculate the remaining components of $\hat{\mathbf{q}}$. Schüler [1588] presents a variant that is branchless but uses four square roots instead.

Spherical Linear Interpolation

Spherical linear interpolation is an operation that, given two unit quaternions, $\hat{\mathbf{q}}$ and $\hat{\mathbf{r}}$, and a parameter $t \in [0,1]$, computes an interpolated quaternion. This is useful for animating objects, for example. It is not as useful for interpolating camera orientations, as the camera's "up" vector can become tilted during the interpolation, usually a disturbing effect.

The algebraic form of this operation is expressed by the composite quaternion, $\hat{\mathbf{s}}$, below:

$$\hat{\mathbf{s}}(\hat{\mathbf{q}}, \hat{\mathbf{r}}, t) = (\hat{\mathbf{r}}\hat{\mathbf{q}}^{-1})^t \hat{\mathbf{q}}. \tag{4.52}$$

However, for software implementations, the following form, where *slerp* stands for spherical linear interpolation, is much more appropriate:

$$\hat{\mathbf{s}}(\hat{\mathbf{q}}, \hat{\mathbf{r}}, t) = \mathtt{slerp}(\hat{\mathbf{q}}, \hat{\mathbf{r}}, t) = \frac{\sin(\phi(1-t))}{\sin\phi}\hat{\mathbf{q}} + \frac{\sin(\phi t)}{\sin\phi}\hat{\mathbf{r}}. \tag{4.53}$$

To compute ϕ, which is needed in this equation, the following fact can be used: $\cos\phi = q_x r_x + q_y r_y + q_z r_z + q_w r_w$ [325]. For $t \in [0,1]$, the slerp function computes (unique[2]) interpolated quaternions that together constitute the shortest arc on a four-dimensional unit sphere from $\hat{\mathbf{q}}$ ($t = 0$) to $\hat{\mathbf{r}}$ ($t = 1$). The arc is located on the circle that is formed from the intersection between the plane given by $\hat{\mathbf{q}}$, $\hat{\mathbf{r}}$, and the origin, and the four-dimensional unit sphere. This is illustrated in Figure 4.10. The computed rotation quaternion rotates around a fixed axis at constant speed. A curve such as this, that has constant speed and thus zero acceleration, is called a *geodesic* curve [229]. A *great circle* on the sphere is generated as the intersection of a plane through the origin and the sphere, and part of such a circle is called a *great arc*.

The slerp function is perfectly suited for interpolating between two orientations and it behaves well (fixed axis, constant speed). This is not the case with when

---

[2]If and only if $\hat{\mathbf{q}}$ and $\hat{\mathbf{r}}$ are not opposite.

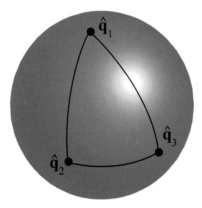

Figure 4.10. Unit quaternions are represented as points on the unit sphere. The function slerp is used to interpolate between the quaternions, and the interpolated path is a great arc on the sphere. Note that interpolating from $\hat{\mathbf{q}}_1$ to $\hat{\mathbf{q}}_2$ and interpolating from $\hat{\mathbf{q}}_1$ to $\hat{\mathbf{q}}_3$ to $\hat{\mathbf{q}}_2$ are not the same thing, even though they arrive at the same orientation.

interpolating using several Euler angles. In practice, computing a slerp directly is an expensive operation involving calling trigonometric functions. Malyshau [1114] discusses integrating quaternions into the rendering pipeline. He notes that the error in the orientation of a triangle is a maximum of 4 degrees for a 90 degree angle when, instead of using slerp, simply normalizing the quaternion in the pixel shader. This error rate can be acceptable when rasterizing a triangle. Li [1039, 1040] provides much faster incremental methods to compute slerps that do not sacrifice any accuracy. Eberly [406] presents a fast technique for computing slerps using just additions and multiplications.

When more than two orientations, say $\hat{\mathbf{q}}_0, \hat{\mathbf{q}}_1, \ldots, \hat{\mathbf{q}}_{n-1}$, are available, and we want to interpolate from $\hat{\mathbf{q}}_0$ to $\hat{\mathbf{q}}_1$ to $\hat{\mathbf{q}}_2$, and so on until $\hat{\mathbf{q}}_{n-1}$, slerp could be used in a straightforward fashion. Now, when we approach, say, $\hat{\mathbf{q}}_i$, we would use $\hat{\mathbf{q}}_{i-1}$ and $\hat{\mathbf{q}}_i$ as arguments to slerp. After passing through $\hat{\mathbf{q}}_i$, we would then use $\hat{\mathbf{q}}_i$ and $\hat{\mathbf{q}}_{i+1}$ as arguments to slerp. This will cause sudden jerks to appear in the orientation interpolation, which can be seen in Figure 4.10. This is similar to what happens when points are linearly interpolated; see the upper right part of Figure 17.3 on page 720. Some readers may wish to revisit the following paragraph after reading about splines in Chapter 17.

A better way to interpolate is to use some sort of spline. We introduce quaternions $\hat{\mathbf{a}}_i$ and $\hat{\mathbf{a}}_{i+1}$ between $\hat{\mathbf{q}}_i$ and $\hat{\mathbf{q}}_{i+1}$. Spherical cubic interpolation can be defined within the set of quaternions $\hat{\mathbf{q}}_i$, $\hat{\mathbf{a}}_i$, $\hat{\mathbf{a}}_{i+1}$, and $\hat{\mathbf{q}}_{i+1}$. Surprisingly, these extra quaternions are computed as shown below [404][3]:

$$\hat{\mathbf{a}}_i = \hat{\mathbf{q}}_i \exp\left[-\frac{\log(\hat{\mathbf{q}}_i^{-1}\hat{\mathbf{q}}_{i-1}) + \log(\hat{\mathbf{q}}_i^{-1}\hat{\mathbf{q}}_{i+1})}{4}\right]. \tag{4.54}$$

---

[3]Shoemake [1633] gives another derivation.

The $\hat{\mathbf{q}}_i$, and $\hat{\mathbf{a}}_i$ will be used to spherically interpolate the quaternions using a smooth cubic spline, as shown in Equation 4.55:

$$\begin{aligned} \texttt{squad}(\hat{\mathbf{q}}_i, \hat{\mathbf{q}}_{i+1}, \hat{\mathbf{a}}_i, \hat{\mathbf{a}}_{i+1}, t) = \\ \texttt{slerp}(\texttt{slerp}(\hat{\mathbf{q}}_i, \hat{\mathbf{q}}_{i+1}, t), \texttt{slerp}(\hat{\mathbf{a}}_i, \hat{\mathbf{a}}_{i+1}, t), 2t(1-t)). \end{aligned} \tag{4.55}$$

As can be seen above, the `squad` function is constructed from repeated spherical interpolation using slerp (Section 17.1.1 for information on repeated linear interpolation for points). The interpolation will pass through the initial orientations $\hat{\mathbf{q}}_i$, $i \in [0, \dots, n-1]$, but not through $\hat{\mathbf{a}}_i$—these are used to indicate the tangent orientations at the initial orientations.

Rotation from One Vector to Another

A common operation is transforming from one direction $\mathbf{s}$ to another direction $\mathbf{t}$ via the shortest path possible. The mathematics of quaternions simplifies this procedure greatly, and shows the close relationship the quaternion has with this representation. First, normalize $\mathbf{s}$ and $\mathbf{t}$. Then compute the unit rotation axis, called $\mathbf{u}$, which is computed as $\mathbf{u} = (\mathbf{s} \times \mathbf{t})/\|\mathbf{s} \times \mathbf{t}\|$. Next, $e = \mathbf{s} \cdot \mathbf{t} = \cos(2\phi)$ and $\|\mathbf{s} \times \mathbf{t}\| = \sin(2\phi)$, where 2ϕ is the angle between $\mathbf{s}$ and $\mathbf{t}$. The quaternion that represents the rotation from $\mathbf{s}$ to $\mathbf{t}$ is then $\hat{\mathbf{q}} = (\sin\phi\mathbf{u}, \cos\phi)$. In fact, simplifying $\hat{\mathbf{q}} = (\frac{\sin\phi}{\sin 2\phi}(\mathbf{s} \times \mathbf{t}), \cos\phi)$, using the half-angle relations and the trigonometric identity, gives [1197]

$$\hat{\mathbf{q}} = (\mathbf{q}_v, q_w) = \left(\frac{1}{\sqrt{2(1+e)}}(\mathbf{s} \times \mathbf{t}), \frac{\sqrt{2(1+e)}}{2} \right). \tag{4.56}$$

Directly generating the quaternion in this fashion (versus normalizing the cross product $\mathbf{s} \times \mathbf{t}$) avoids numerical instability when $\mathbf{s}$ and $\mathbf{t}$ point in nearly the same direction [1197]. Stability problems appear for both methods when $\mathbf{s}$ and $\mathbf{t}$ point in opposite directions, as a division by zero occurs. When this special case is detected, any axis of rotation perpendicular to $\mathbf{s}$ can be used to rotate to $\mathbf{t}$.

Sometimes we need the matrix representation of a rotation from $\mathbf{s}$ to $\mathbf{t}$. After some algebraic and trigonometric simplification of Equation 4.46, the rotation matrix becomes [1233]

$$\mathbf{R}(\mathbf{s}, \mathbf{t}) = \begin{pmatrix} e + hv_x^2 & hv_xv_y - v_z & hv_xv_z + v_y & 0 \\ hv_xv_y + v_z & e + hv_y^2 & hv_yv_z - v_x & 0 \\ hv_xv_z - v_y & hv_yv_z + v_x & e + hv_z^2 & 0 \\ 0 & 0 & 0 & 1 \end{pmatrix}. \tag{4.57}$$

In this equation, we have used the following intermediate calculations:

$$\begin{aligned} \mathbf{v} &= \mathbf{s} \times \mathbf{t}, \\ e &= \cos(2\phi) = \mathbf{s} \cdot \mathbf{t}, \\ h &= \frac{1 - \cos(2\phi)}{\sin^2(2\phi)} = \frac{1 - e}{\mathbf{v} \cdot \mathbf{v}} = \frac{1}{1 + e}. \end{aligned} \tag{4.58}$$

As can be seen, all square roots and trigonometric functions have disappeared due to the simplifications, and so this is an efficient way to create the matrix. Note that the structure of Equation 4.57 is like that of Equation 4.30, and note how this latter form does not need trigonometric functions.

Note that care must be taken when $\mathbf{s}$ and $\mathbf{t}$ are parallel or near parallel, because then $||\mathbf{s} \times \mathbf{t}|| \approx 0$. If $\phi \approx 0$, then we can return the identity matrix. However, if $2\phi \approx \pi$, then we can rotate π radians around *any* axis. This axis can be found as the cross product between $\mathbf{s}$ and any other vector that is not parallel to $\mathbf{s}$ (Section 4.2.4). Möller and Hughes use Householder matrices to handle this special case in a different way [1233].

4.4 Vertex Blending

Imagine that an arm of a digital character is animated using two parts, a forearm and an upper arm, as shown to the left in Figure 4.11. This model could be animated using rigid-body transforms (Section 4.1.6). However, then the joint between these two parts will not resemble a real elbow. This is because two separate objects are used, and therefore, the joint consists of overlapping parts from these two separate objects. Clearly, it would be better to use just one single object. However, static model parts do not address the problem of making the joint flexible.

Vertex blending is one popular solution to this problem [1037, 1903]. This technique has several other names, such as *linear-blend skinning*, *enveloping*, or *skeleton-subspace*

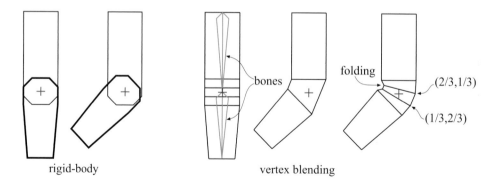

Figure 4.11. An arm consisting of a forearm and an upper arm is animated using rigid-body transforms of two separate objects to the left. The elbow does not appear realistic. To the right, vertex blending is used on one single object. The next-to-rightmost arm illustrates what happens when a simple skin directly joins the two parts to cover the elbow. The rightmost arm illustrates what happens when vertex blending is used, and some vertices are blended with different weights: $(2/3, 1/3)$ means that the vertex weighs the transform from the upper arm by $2/3$ and from the forearm by $1/3$. This figure also shows a drawback of vertex blending in the rightmost illustration. Here, folding in the inner part of the elbow is visible. Better results can be achieved with more bones, and with more carefully selected weights.

deformation. While the exact origin of the algorithm presented here is unclear, defining bones and having skin react to changes is an old concept in computer animation [1100]. In its simplest form, the forearm and the upper arm are animated separately as before, but at the joint, the two parts are connected through an elastic "skin." So, this elastic part will have one set of vertices that are transformed by the forearm matrix and another set that are transformed by the matrix of the upper arm. This results in triangles whose vertices may be transformed by different matrices, in contrast to using a single matrix per triangle. See Figure 4.11.

By taking this one step further, one can allow a single vertex to be transformed by several different matrices, with the resulting locations weighted and blended together. This is done by having a skeleton of bones for the animated object, where each bone's transform may influence each vertex by a user-defined weight. Since the entire arm may be "elastic," i.e., all vertices may be affected by more than one matrix, the entire mesh is often called a *skin* (over the bones). See Figure 4.12. Many commercial modeling systems have this same sort of skeleton-bone modeling feature. Despite their name, bones do not need to necessarily be rigid. For example, Mohr and Gleicher [1230] present the idea of adding additional joints to enable effects such as muscle bulge. James and Twigg [813] discuss animation skinning using bones that can squash and stretch.

Mathematically, this is expressed in Equation 4.59, where $\mathbf{p}$ is the original vertex, and $\mathbf{u}(t)$ is the transformed vertex whose position depends on time t:

$$\mathbf{u}(t) = \sum_{i=0}^{n-1} w_i \mathbf{B}_i(t) \mathbf{M}_i^{-1} \mathbf{p}, \quad \text{where} \quad \sum_{i=0}^{n-1} w_i = 1, \quad w_i \geq 0. \tag{4.59}$$

There are n bones influencing the position of $\mathbf{p}$, which is expressed in world coordinates. The value w_i is the weight of bone i for vertex $\mathbf{p}$. The matrix $\mathbf{M}_i$ transforms from the initial bone's coordinate system to world coordinates. Typically a bone has its controlling joint at the origin of its coordinate system. For example, a forearm bone would move its elbow joint to the origin, with an animated rotation matrix moving this part of the arm around the joint. The $\mathbf{B}_i(t)$ matrix is the ith bone's world transform that changes with time to animate the object, and is typically a concatenation of several matrices, such as the hierarchy of previous bone transforms and the local animation matrix.

One method of maintaining and updating the $\mathbf{B}_i(t)$ matrix animation functions is discussed in depth by Woodland [1903]. Each bone transforms a vertex to a location with respect to its own frame of reference, and the final location is interpolated from the set of computed points. The matrix $\mathbf{M}_i$ is not explicitly shown in some discussions of skinning, but rather is considered as being a part of $\mathbf{B}_i(t)$. We present it here as it is a useful matrix that is almost always a part of the matrix concatenation process.

In practice, the matrices $\mathbf{B}_i(t)$ and $\mathbf{M}_i^{-1}$ are concatenated for each bone for each frame of animation, and each resulting matrix is used to transform the vertices. The vertex $\mathbf{p}$ is transformed by the different bones' concatenated matrices, and then

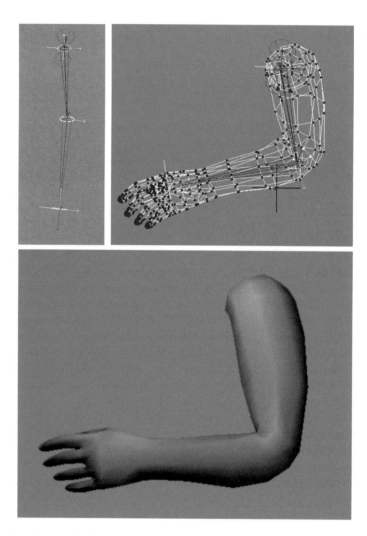

Figure 4.12. A real example of vertex blending. The top left image shows the two bones of an arm, in an extended position. On the top right, the mesh is shown, with color denoting which bone owns each vertex. Bottom: the shaded mesh of the arm in a slightly different position. *(Images courtesy of Jeff Lander [968].)*

blended using the weights w_i—thus the name *vertex blending*. The weights are non-negative and sum to one, so what is occurring is that the vertex is transformed to a few positions and then interpolated among them. As such, the transformed point $\mathbf{u}$ will lie in the convex hull of the set of points $\mathbf{B}_i(t)\mathbf{M}_i^{-1}\mathbf{p}$, for all $i = 0 \ldots n - 1$ (fixed t). The normals usually can also be transformed using Equation 4.59. Depending on the transforms used (e.g., if a bone is stretched or squished a considerable amount), the transpose of the inverse of the $\mathbf{B}_i(t)\mathbf{M}_i^{-1}$ may be needed instead, as discussed in Section 4.1.7.

Vertex blending is well suited for use on the GPU. The set of vertices in the mesh can be placed in a static buffer that is sent to the GPU one time and reused. In each frame, only the bone matrices change, with a vertex shader computing their effect on the stored mesh. In this way, the amount of data processed on and transferred from the CPU is minimized, allowing the GPU to efficiently render the mesh. It is easiest if the model's whole set of bone matrices can be used together; otherwise the model must be split up and some bones replicated. Alternately the bone transforms can be stored in textures that the vertices access, which avoids hitting register storage limits. Each transform can be stored in just two textures by using quaternions to represent rotation [1639]. If available, unordered access view storage allows the reuse of skinning results [146].

It is possible to specify sets of weights that are outside the range $[0, 1]$ or do not sum to one. However, this makes sense only if some other blending algorithm, such as *morph targets* (Section 4.5), is being used.

One drawback of basic vertex blending is that unwanted folding, twisting, and self-intersection can occur [1037]. See Figure 4.13. A better solution is to use *dual quaternions* [872, 873]. This technique to perform skinning helps to preserve the rigidity of the original transforms, so avoiding "candy wrapper" twists in limbs. Computation is less than $1.5\times$ the cost for linear skin blending and the results are good, which has led to rapid adoption of this technique. However, dual quaternion skinning can lead to bulging effects, and Le and Hodgins [1001] present center-of-rotation skinning as a better alternative. They rely on the assumptions that local transforms should be rigid-body and that vertices with similar weights, w_i, should have similar transforms. Centers of rotation are precomputed for each vertex while orthogonal (rigid body) constraints are imposed to prevent elbow collapse and candy wrapper twist artifacts. At runtime, the algorithm is similar to linear blend skinning in that a GPU implementation performs linear blend skinning on the centers of rotation followed by a quaternion blending step.

4.5 Morphing

Morphing from one three-dimensional model to another can be useful when performing animations [28, 883, 1000, 1005]. Imagine that one model is displayed at time t_0 and we wish it to change into another model by time t_1. For all times between t_0 and t_1, a continuous "mixed" model is obtained, using some kind of interpolation. An example of morphing is shown in Figure 4.14.

Morphing involves solving two major problems, namely, the *vertex correspondence* problem and the *interpolation* problem. Given two arbitrary models, which may have different topologies, different number of vertices, and different mesh connectivity, one usually has to begin by setting up these vertex correspondences. This is a difficult

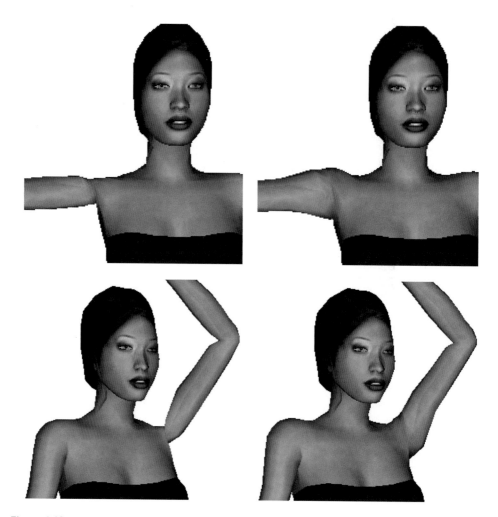

Figure 4.13. The left side shows problems at the joints when using linear blend skinning. On the right, blending using dual quaternions improves the appearance. *(Images courtesy of Ladislav Kavan et al., model by Paul Steed [1693].)*

problem, and there has been much research in this field. We refer the interested reader to Alexa's survey [28].

However, if there already is a one-to-one vertex correspondence between the two models, then interpolation can be done on a per-vertex basis. That is, for each vertex in the first model, there must exist only one vertex in the second model, and vice versa. This makes interpolation an easy task. For example, linear interpolation can be used directly on the vertices (Section 17.1 for other ways of doing interpolation). To

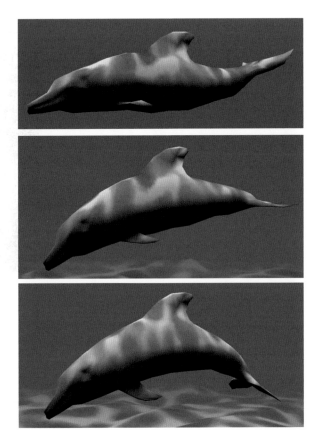

Figure 4.14. Vertex morphing. Two locations and normals are defined for every vertex. In each frame, the intermediate location and normal are linearly interpolated by the vertex shader. *(Images courtesy of NVIDIA Corporation.)*

compute a morphed vertex for time $t \in [t_0, t_1]$, we first compute $s = (t - t_0)/(t_1 - t_0)$, and then the linear vertex blend,

$$\mathbf{m} = (1 - s)\mathbf{p}_0 + s\mathbf{p}_1, \tag{4.60}$$

where $\mathbf{p}_0$ and $\mathbf{p}_1$ correspond to the same vertex but at different times, t_0 and t_1.

A variant of morphing where the user has more intuitive control is referred to as *morph targets* or *blend shapes* [907]. The basic idea can be explained using Figure 4.15. We start out with a neutral model, which in this case is a face. Let us denote this model by $\mathcal{N}$. In addition, we also have a set of different face poses. In the example illustration, there is only one pose, which is a smiling face. In general, we can allow $k \geq 1$ different poses, which are denoted $\mathcal{P}_i$, $i \in [1, \dots, k]$. As a preprocess, the

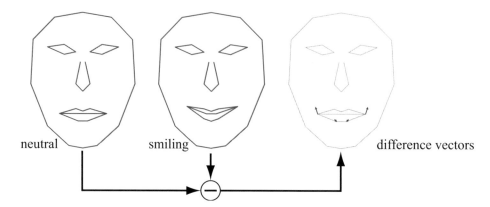

Figure 4.15. Given two mouth poses, a set of difference vectors is computed to control interpolation, or even extrapolation. In morph targets, the difference vectors are used to "add" movements onto the neutral face. With positive weights for the difference vectors, we get a smiling mouth, while negative weights can give the opposite effect.

"difference faces" are computed as: $\mathcal{D}_i = \mathcal{P}_i - \mathcal{N}$, i.e., the neutral model is subtracted from each pose.

At this point, we have a neutral model, $\mathcal{N}$, and a set of difference poses, $\mathcal{D}_i$. A morphed model $\mathcal{M}$ can then be obtained using the following formula:

$$\mathcal{M} = \mathcal{N} + \sum_{i=1}^{k} w_i \mathcal{D}_i. \tag{4.61}$$

This is the neutral model, and on top of that we add the features of the different poses as desired, using the weights, w_i. For Figure 4.15, setting $w_1 = 1$ gives us exactly the smiling face in the middle of the illustration. Using $w_1 = 0.5$ gives us a half-smiling face, and so on. One can also use negative weights and weights greater than one.

For this simple face model, we could add another face having "sad" eyebrows. Using a negative weight for the eyebrows could then create "happy" eyebrows. Since displacements are additive, this eyebrow pose could be used in conjunction with the pose for a smiling mouth.

Morph targets are a powerful technique that provides the animator with much control, since different features of a model can be manipulated independently of the others. Lewis et al. [1037] introduce *pose-space deformation*, which combines vertex blending and morph targets. Senior [1608] uses precomputed vertex textures to store and retrieve displacements between target poses. Hardware supporting stream-out and the ID of each vertex allow many more targets to be used in a single model and the effects to be computed exclusively on the GPU [841, 1074]. Using a low-resolution mesh and then generating a high-resolution mesh via the tessellation stage and displacement mapping avoids the cost of skinning every vertex in a highly detailed model [1971].

Figure 4.16. The Delsin character's face, in *inFAMOUS Second Son*, is animated using blend shapes. The same resting pose face is used for all of these shots, and then different weights are modified to make the face appear differently. *(Images provided courtesy of Naughty Dog LLC. inFAMOUS Second Son © 2014 Sony Interactive Entertainment LLC. inFAMOUS Second Son is a trademark of Sony Interactive Entertainment LLC. Developed by Sucker Punch Productions LLC.)*

A real example of using both skinning and morphing is shown in Figure 4.16. Weronko and Andreason [1872] used skinning and morphing in *The Order: 1886*.

4.6 Geometry Cache Playback

In cut scenes, it may be desirable to use extremely high-quality animations, e.g., for movements that cannot be represented using any of the methods above. A naive approach is to store all the vertices for all frames, reading them from disk and updating the mesh. However, this can amount to 50 MB/s for a simple model of 30,000 vertices used in a short animation. Gneiting [545] presents several ways to reduce memory costs down to about 10%.

First, quantization is used. For example, positions and texture coordinates are stored using 16-bit integers for each coordinate. This step is lossy in the sense that one cannot recover the original data after compression is performed. To reduce data further, spatial and temporal predictions are made and the differences encoded. For spatial compression, parallelogram prediction can be used [800]. For a triangle strip, the next vertex's predicted position is simply the current triangle reflected in the triangle's plane around the current triangle edge, which forms a parallelogram. The differences from this new position is then encoded. With good predictions, most values will be close to zero, which is ideal for many commonly used compression schemes. Similar to MPEG compression, prediction is also done in the temporal dimension. That is, every n frames, spatial compression is performed. In between, predictions are done in the temporal dimension, e.g., if a certain vertex moved by delta vector from frame $n-1$ to frame n, then it is likely to move by a similar amount to frame $n+1$. These techniques reduced storage sufficiently so this system could be used for streaming data in real time.

4.7 Projections

Before one can actually render a scene, all relevant objects in the scene must be projected onto some kind of plane or into some type of simple volume. After that, clipping and rendering are performed (Section 2.3).

The transforms seen so far in this chapter have left the fourth coordinate, the w-component, unaffected. That is, points and vectors have retained their types after the transform. Also, the bottom row in the 4×4 matrices has always been $(0 \ 0 \ 0 \ 1)$. *Perspective projection matrices* are exceptions to both of these properties: The bottom row contains vector and point manipulating numbers, and the homogenization process is often needed. That is, w is often not 1, so a division by w is needed to obtain the nonhomogeneous point. *Orthographic projection*, which is dealt with first in this section, is a simpler kind of projection that is also commonly used. It does not affect the w-component.

In this section, it is assumed that the viewer is looking along the camera's negative z-axis, with the y-axis pointing up and the x-axis to the right. This is a right-handed coordinate system. Some texts and software, e.g., DirectX, use a left-handed system in which the viewer looks along the camera's positive z-axis. Both systems are equally valid, and in the end, the same effect is achieved.

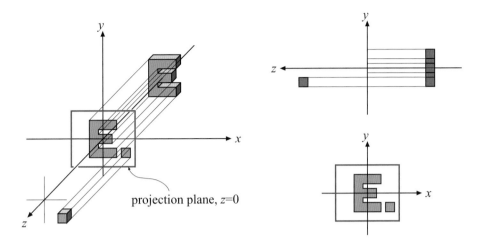

Figure 4.17. Three different views of the simple orthographic projection generated by Equation 4.62. This projection can be seen as the viewer is looking along the negative z-axis, which means that the projection simply skips (or sets to zero) the z-coordinate while keeping the x- and y-coordinates. Note that objects on both sides of $z = 0$ are projected onto the projection plane.

4.7.1 Orthographic Projection

A characteristic of an orthographic projection is that parallel lines remain parallel after the projection. When orthographic projection is used for viewing a scene, objects maintain the same size regardless of distance to the camera. Matrix $\mathbf{P}_o$, shown below, is a simple orthographic projection matrix that leaves the x- and y-components of a point unchanged, while setting the z-component to zero, i.e., it orthographically projects onto the plane $z = 0$:

$$\mathbf{P}_o = \begin{pmatrix} 1 & 0 & 0 & 0 \\ 0 & 1 & 0 & 0 \\ 0 & 0 & 0 & 0 \\ 0 & 0 & 0 & 1 \end{pmatrix}. \tag{4.62}$$

The effect of this projection is illustrated in Figure 4.17. Clearly, $\mathbf{P}_o$ is non-invertible, since its determinant $|\mathbf{P}_o| = 0$. In other words, the transform drops from three to two dimensions, and there is no way to retrieve the dropped dimension. A problem with using this kind of orthographic projection for viewing is that it projects both points with positive and points with negative z-values onto the projection plane. It is usually useful to restrict the z-values (and the x- and y-values) to a certain interval, from, say n (near plane) to f (far plane).[4] This is the purpose of the next transformation.

A more common matrix for performing orthographic projection is expressed by the six-tuple, (l, r, b, t, n, f), denoting the left, right, bottom, top, near, and far planes. This matrix scales and translates the *axis-aligned bounding box* (AABB; see the definition in Section 22.2) formed by these planes into an axis-aligned cube centered around

---

[4]The near plane is also called the *front plane* or *hither*; the far plane is also the *back plane* or *yon*.

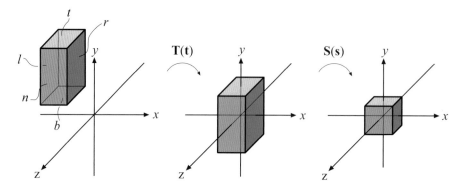

Figure 4.18. Transforming an axis-aligned box on the canonical view volume. The box on the left is first translated, making its center coincide with the origin. Then it is scaled to get the size of the canonical view volume, shown at the right.

the origin. The minimum corner of the AABB is (l, b, n) and the maximum corner is (r, t, f). It is important to realize that $n > f$, because we are looking down the negative z-axis at this volume of space. Our common sense says that the near value should be a lower number than the far, so one may let the user supply them as such, and then internally negate them.

In OpenGL the axis-aligned cube has a minimum corner of $(-1, -1, -1)$ and a maximum corner of $(1, 1, 1)$; in DirectX the bounds are $(-1, -1, 0)$ to $(1, 1, 1)$. This cube is called the *canonical view volume* and the coordinates in this volume are called *normalized device coordinates*. The transformation procedure is shown in Figure 4.18. The reason for transforming into the canonical view volume is that clipping is more efficiently performed there.

After the transformation into the canonical view volume, vertices of the geometry to be rendered are clipped against this cube. The geometry not outside the cube is finally rendered by mapping the remaining unit square to the screen. This orthographic transform is shown here:

$$
\mathbf{P}_o = \mathbf{S}(\mathbf{s})\mathbf{T}(\mathbf{t}) =
\begin{pmatrix}
\dfrac{2}{r - l} & 0 & 0 & 0 \\
0 & \dfrac{2}{t - b} & 0 & 0 \\
0 & 0 & \dfrac{2}{f - n} & 0 \\
0 & 0 & 0 & 1
\end{pmatrix}
\begin{pmatrix}
1 & 0 & 0 & -\dfrac{l + r}{2} \\
0 & 1 & 0 & -\dfrac{t + b}{2} \\
0 & 0 & 1 & -\dfrac{f + n}{2} \\
0 & 0 & 0 & 1
\end{pmatrix}
$$

$$
=
\begin{pmatrix}
\dfrac{2}{r - l} & 0 & 0 & -\dfrac{r + l}{r - l} \\
0 & \dfrac{2}{t - b} & 0 & -\dfrac{t + b}{t - b} \\
0 & 0 & \dfrac{2}{f - n} & -\dfrac{f + n}{f - n} \\
0 & 0 & 0 & 1
\end{pmatrix}.
$$

$$(4.63)$$

As suggested by this equation, $\mathbf{P}_o$ can be written as the concatenation of a translation, $\mathbf{T}(\mathbf{t})$, followed by a scaling matrix, $\mathbf{S}(\mathbf{s})$, where $\mathbf{s} = (2/(r-l), 2/(t-b), 2/(f-n))$, and $\mathbf{t} = (-(r+l)/2, -(t+b)/2, -(f+n)/2)$. This matrix is invertible,[5] i.e., $\mathbf{P}_o^{-1} = \mathbf{T}(-\mathbf{t})\mathbf{S}((r-l)/2, (t-b)/2, (f-n)/2)$.

In computer graphics, a left-hand coordinate system is most often used after projection—i.e., for the viewport, the x-axis goes to the right, y-axis goes up, and the z-axis goes into the viewport. Because the far value is less than the near value for the way we defined our AABB, the orthographic transform will always include a mirroring transform. To see this, say the original AABBs is the same size as the goal, the canonical view volume. Then the AABB's coordinates are $(-1, -1, 1)$ for (l, b, n) and $(1, 1, -1)$ for (r, t, f). Applying that to Equation 4.63 gives us

$$\mathbf{P}_o = \begin{pmatrix} 1 & 0 & 0 & 0 \\ 0 & 1 & 0 & 0 \\ 0 & 0 & -1 & 0 \\ 0 & 0 & 0 & 1 \end{pmatrix}, \tag{4.64}$$

which is a mirroring matrix. It is this mirroring that converts from the right-handed viewing coordinate system (looking down the negative z-axis) to left-handed normalized device coordinates.

DirectX maps the z-depths to the range $[0, 1]$ instead of OpenGL's $[-1, 1]$. This can be accomplished by applying a simple scaling and translation matrix applied after the orthographic matrix, that is,

$$\mathbf{M}_{st} = \begin{pmatrix} 1 & 0 & 0 & 0 \\ 0 & 1 & 0 & 0 \\ 0 & 0 & 0.5 & 0.5 \\ 0 & 0 & 0 & 1 \end{pmatrix}. \tag{4.65}$$

So, the orthographic matrix used in DirectX is

$$\mathbf{P}_{o[0,1]} = \begin{pmatrix} \dfrac{2}{r-l} & 0 & 0 & -\dfrac{r+l}{r-l} \\ 0 & \dfrac{2}{t-b} & 0 & -\dfrac{t+b}{t-b} \\ 0 & 0 & \dfrac{1}{f-n} & -\dfrac{n}{f-n} \\ 0 & 0 & 0 & 1 \end{pmatrix}. \tag{4.66}$$

which is normally presented in transposed form, as DirectX uses a row-major form for writing matrices.

---

[5]If and only if $n \neq f$, $l \neq r$, and $t \neq b$; otherwise, no inverse exists.

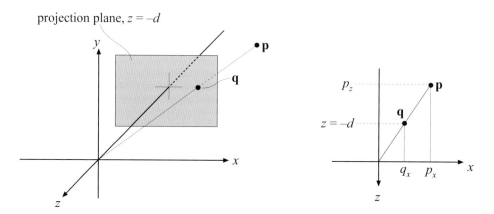

Figure 4.19. The notation used for deriving a perspective projection matrix. The point **p** is projected onto the plane $z = -d$, $d > 0$, which yields the projected point **q**. The projection is performed from the perspective of the camera's location, which in this case is the origin. The similar triangle used in the derivation is shown for the x-component at the right.

4.7.2 Perspective Projection

A more complex transform than orthographic projection is perspective projection, which is commonly used in most computer graphics applications. Here, parallel lines are generally not parallel after projection; rather, they may converge to a single point at their extreme. Perspective more closely matches how we perceive the world, i.e., objects farther away are smaller.

First, we shall present an instructive derivation for a perspective projection matrix that projects onto a plane $z = -d$, $d > 0$. We derive from world space to simplify understanding of how the world-to-view conversion proceeds. This derivation is followed by the more conventional matrices used in, for example, OpenGL [885].

Assume that the camera (viewpoint) is located at the origin, and that we want to project a point, **p**, onto the plane $z = -d$, $d > 0$, yielding a new point $\mathbf{q} = (q_x, q_y, -d)$. This scenario is depicted in Figure 4.19. From the similar triangles shown in this figure, the following derivation, for the x-component of **q**, is obtained:

$$\frac{q_x}{p_x} = \frac{-d}{p_z} \quad \Longleftrightarrow \quad q_x = -d\frac{p_x}{p_z}. \tag{4.67}$$

The expressions for the other components of **q** are $q_y = -dp_y/p_z$ (obtained similarly to q_x), and $q_z = -d$. Together with the above formula, these give us the perspective projection matrix, $\mathbf{P}_p$, as shown here:

$$\mathbf{P}_p = \begin{pmatrix} 1 & 0 & 0 & 0 \\ 0 & 1 & 0 & 0 \\ 0 & 0 & 1 & 0 \\ 0 & 0 & -1/d & 0 \end{pmatrix}. \tag{4.68}$$

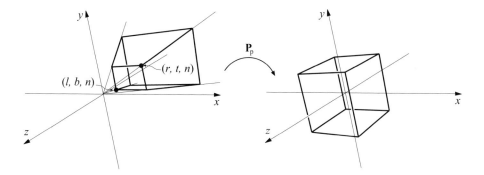

Figure 4.20. The matrix $\mathbf{P}_p$ transforms the view frustum into the unit cube, which is called the canonical view volume.

That this matrix yields the correct perspective projection is confirmed by

$$\mathbf{q} = \mathbf{P}_p\mathbf{p} = \begin{pmatrix} 1 & 0 & 0 & 0 \\ 0 & 1 & 0 & 0 \\ 0 & 0 & 1 & 0 \\ 0 & 0 & -1/d & 0 \end{pmatrix} \begin{pmatrix} p_x \\ p_y \\ p_z \\ 1 \end{pmatrix} = \begin{pmatrix} p_x \\ p_y \\ p_z \\ -p_z/d \end{pmatrix} \Rightarrow \begin{pmatrix} -dp_x/p_z \\ -dp_y/p_z \\ -d \\ 1 \end{pmatrix}. \quad (4.69)$$

The last step comes from the fact that the whole vector is divided by the w-component (in this case $-p_z/d$), to get a 1 in the last position. The resulting z value is always $-d$ since we are projecting onto this plane.

Intuitively, it is easy to understand why homogeneous coordinates allow for projection. One geometrical interpretation of the homogenization process is that it projects the point (p_x, p_y, p_z) onto the plane $w = 1$.

As with the orthographic transformation, there is also a perspective transform that, rather than actually projecting onto a plane (which is noninvertible), transforms the view frustum into the canonical view volume described previously. Here the view frustum is assumed to start at $z = n$ and end at $z = f$, with $0 > n > f$. The rectangle at $z = n$ has the minimum corner at (l, b, n) and the maximum corner at (r, t, n). This is shown in Figure 4.20.

The parameters (l, r, b, t, n, f) determine the view frustum of the camera. The horizontal field of view is determined by the angle between the left and the right planes (determined by l and r) of the frustum. In the same manner, the vertical field of view is determined by the angle between the top and the bottom planes (determined by t and b). The greater the field of view, the more the camera "sees." Asymmetric frusta can be created by $r \neq -l$ or $t \neq -b$. Asymmetric frusta are, for example, used for stereo viewing and for virtual reality (Section 21.2.3).

The field of view is an important factor in providing a sense of the scene. The eye itself has a physical field of view compared to the computer screen. This relationship is

$$\phi = 2\arctan(w/(2d)), \quad (4.70)$$

where ϕ is the field of view, w is the width of the object perpendicular to the line of sight, and d is the distance to the object. For example, a 25-inch monitor is about 22 inches wide. At 12 inches away, the horizontal field of view is 85 degrees; at 20 inches, it is 58 degrees; at 30 inches, 40 degrees. This same formula can be used to convert from camera lens size to field of view, e.g., a standard 50mm lens for a 35mm camera (which has a 36mm wide frame size) gives $\phi = 2\arctan(36/(2 \cdot 50)) = 39.6$ degrees.

Using a narrower field of view compared to the physical setup will lessen the perspective effect, as the viewer will be zoomed in on the scene. Setting a wider field of view will make objects appear distorted (like using a wide angle camera lens), especially near the screen's edges, and will exaggerate the scale of nearby objects. However, a wider field of view gives the viewer a sense that objects are larger and more impressive, and has the advantage of giving the user more information about the surroundings.

The perspective transform matrix that transforms the frustum into a unit cube is given by Equation 4.71:

$$\mathbf{P}_p = \begin{pmatrix} \dfrac{2n}{r-l} & 0 & -\dfrac{r+l}{r-l} & 0 \\ 0 & \dfrac{2n}{t-b} & -\dfrac{t+b}{t-b} & 0 \\ 0 & 0 & \dfrac{f+n}{f-n} & -\dfrac{2fn}{f-n} \\ 0 & 0 & 1 & 0 \end{pmatrix}. \tag{4.71}$$

After applying this transform to a point, we will get another point $\mathbf{q} = (q_x, q_y, q_z, q_w)^T$. The w-component, q_w, of this point will (most often) be nonzero and not equal to one. To get the projected point, $\mathbf{p}$, we need to divide by q_w, i.e.,

$$\mathbf{p} = (q_x/q_w, q_y/q_w, q_z/q_w, 1). \tag{4.72}$$

The matrix $\mathbf{P}_p$ always sees to it that $z = f$ maps to $+1$ and $z = n$ maps to -1.

Objects beyond the far plane will be clipped and so will not appear in the scene. The perspective projection can handle a far plane taken to infinity, which makes Equation 4.71 become

$$\mathbf{P}_p = \begin{pmatrix} \dfrac{2n}{r-l} & 0 & -\dfrac{r+l}{r-l} & 0 \\ 0 & \dfrac{2n}{t-b} & -\dfrac{t+b}{t-b} & 0 \\ 0 & 0 & 1 & -2n \\ 0 & 0 & 1 & 0 \end{pmatrix}. \tag{4.73}$$

To sum up, the perspective transform (in any form), $\mathbf{P}_p$, is applied, followed by clipping and homogenization (division by w), which results in normalized device coordinates.

To get the perspective transform used in OpenGL, first multiply with $\mathbf{S}(1, 1, -1, 1)$, for the same reasons as for the orthographic transform. This simply negates the values in the third column of Equation 4.71. After this mirroring transform has been applied, the near and far values are entered as positive values, with $0 < n' < f'$, as they would traditionally be presented to the user. However, they still represent distances along the world's negative z-axis, which is the direction of view. For reference purposes, here is the OpenGL equation:

$$\mathbf{P}_{\text{OpenGL}} = \begin{pmatrix} \dfrac{2n'}{r-l} & 0 & \dfrac{r+l}{r-l} & 0 \\ 0 & \dfrac{2n'}{t-b} & \dfrac{t+b}{t-b} & 0 \\ 0 & 0 & -\dfrac{f'+n'}{f'-n'} & -\dfrac{2f'n'}{f'-n'} \\ 0 & 0 & -1 & 0 \end{pmatrix}. \tag{4.74}$$

A simpler setup is to provide just the vertical field of view, ϕ, the aspect ratio $a = w/h$ (where $w \times h$ is the screen resolution), n', and f'. This results in

$$\mathbf{P}_{\text{OpenGL}} = \begin{pmatrix} c/a & 0 & 0 & 0 \\ 0 & c & 0 & 0 \\ 0 & 0 & -\dfrac{f'+n'}{f'-n'} & -\dfrac{2f'n'}{f'-n'} \\ 0 & 0 & -1 & 0 \end{pmatrix}, \tag{4.75}$$

where $c = 1.0/\tan(\phi/2)$. This matrix does exactly what the old `gluPerspective()` did, which is part of the OpenGL Utility Library (GLU).

Some APIs (e.g., DirectX) map the near plane to $z = 0$ (instead of $z = -1$) and the far plane to $z = 1$. In addition, DirectX uses a left-handed coordinate system to define its projection matrix. This means DirectX looks along the positive z-axis and presents the near and far values as positive numbers. Here is the DirectX equation:

$$\mathbf{P}_{p[0,1]} = \begin{pmatrix} \dfrac{2n'}{r-l} & 0 & -\dfrac{r+l}{r-l} & 0 \\ 0 & \dfrac{2n'}{t-b} & -\dfrac{t+b}{t-b} & 0 \\ 0 & 0 & \dfrac{f'}{f'-n'} & -\dfrac{f'n'}{f'-n'} \\ 0 & 0 & 1 & 0 \end{pmatrix}. \tag{4.76}$$

DirectX uses row-major form in its documentation, so this matrix is normally presented in transposed form.

One effect of using a perspective transformation is that the computed depth value does not vary linearly with the input p_z value. Using any of Equations 4.74–4.76 to

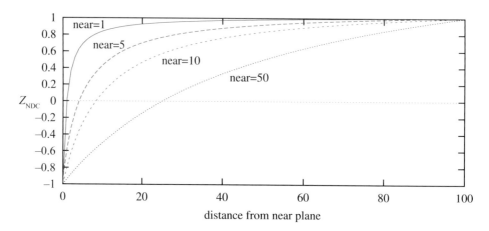

Figure 4.21. The effect of varying the distance of the near plane from the origin. The distance $f' - n'$ is kept constant at 100. As the near plane becomes closer to the origin, points nearer the far plane use a smaller range of the normalized device coordinate (NDC) depth space. This has the effect of making the z-buffer less accurate at greater distances.

multiply with a point $\mathbf{p}$, we can see that

$$\mathbf{v} = \mathbf{Pp} = \begin{pmatrix} \cdots \\ \cdots \\ dp_z + e \\ \pm p_z \end{pmatrix}, \tag{4.77}$$

where the details of v_x and v_y have been omitted, and the constants d and f depend on the chosen matrix. If we use Equation 4.74, for example, then $d = -(f'+n')/(f'-n')$, $e = -2f'n'/(f'-n')$, and $v_x = -p_z$. To obtain the depth in normalized device coordinates (NDC), we need to divide by the w-component, which results in

$$z_{\text{NDC}} = \frac{dp_z + e}{-p_z} = d - \frac{e}{p_z}, \tag{4.78}$$

where $z_{\text{NDC}} \in [-1, +1]$ for the OpenGL projection. As can be seen, the output depth z_{NDC} is inversely proportional to the input depth, p_z.

For example, if $n' = 10$ and $f' = 110$ (using the OpenGL terminology), when p_z is 60 units down the negative z-axis (i.e., the halfway point) the normalized device coordinate depth value is 0.833, not 0. Figure 4.21 shows the effect of varying the distance of the near plane from the origin. Placement of the near and far planes affects the precision of the z-buffer. This effect is discussed further in Section 23.7.

There are several ways to increase the depth precision. A common method, which we call *reversed z*, is to store $1.0 - z_{\text{NDC}}$ [978] either with floating point depth or with integers. A comparison is shown in Figure 4.22. Reed [1472] shows with simulations

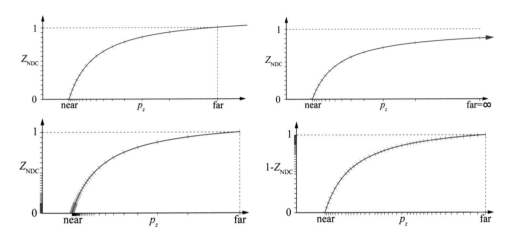

Figure 4.22. Different ways to set up the depth buffer with the DirectX transform, i.e., $z_{\mathrm{NDC}} \in [0, +1]$. Top left: standard integer depth buffer, shown here with 4 bits of precision (hence the 16 marks on the y-axis). Top right: the far plane set to ∞, the small shifts on both axes showing that one does not lose much precision by doing so. Bottom left: with 3 exponent bits and 3 mantissa bits for floating point depth. Notice how the distribution is nonlinear on the y-axis, which makes it even worse on the x-axis. Bottom right: reversed floating point depth, i.e., $1 - z_{\mathrm{NDC}}$, with a much better distribution as a result. *(Illustrations courtesy of Nathan Reed.)*

that using a floating point buffer with reversed z provides the best accuracy, and this is also the preferred method for integer depth buffers (which usually have 24 bits per depth). For the standard mapping (i.e., non-reversed z), separating the projection matrix in the transform decreases the error rate, as suggested by Upchurch and Desbrun [1803]. For example, it can be better to use $\mathbf{P}(\mathbf{Mp})$ than $\mathbf{Tp}$, where $\mathbf{T} = \mathbf{PM}$. Also, in the range of $[0.5, 1.0]$, fp32 and int24 are quite similar in accuracy, since fp32 has a 23-bit mantissa. The reason for having z_{NDC} proportional to $1/p_z$ is that it makes hardware simpler and compression of depth more successful, which is discussed more in Section 23.7.

Lloyd [1063] proposed to use a logarithm of the depth values to improve precision for shadow maps. Lauritzen et al. [991] use the previous frame's z-buffer to determine a maximum near plane and minimum far plane. For screen-space depth, Kemen [881] proposes to use the following remapping per vertex:

$$
\begin{aligned}
z &= w \left(\log_2 \left(\max(10^{-6}, 1 + w) \right) f_c - 1 \right), & \text{[OpenGL]} \\
z &= w \log_2 \left(\max(10^{-6}, 1 + w) \right) f_c/2, & \text{[DirectX]}
\end{aligned}
\tag{4.79}
$$

where w is the w-value of the vertex after the projection matrix, and z is the output z from the vertex shader. The constant f_c is $f_c = 2/\log_2(f + 1)$, where f is the far plane. When this transform is applied in the vertex shader only, depth will still be interpolated linearly over the triangle by the GPU in between the nonlinearly transformed depths at vertices (Equation 4.79). Since the logarithm is a monotonic function, occlusion culling hardware and depth compression techniques will still work as long as the difference between the piecewise linear interpolation and the accurate nonlinearly transformed depth value is small. That's true for most cases with sufficient geometry tessellation. However, it is also possible to apply the transform per fragment. This is done by outputting a per-vertex value of $e = 1 + w$, which is then interpolated by the GPU over the triangle. The pixel shader then modifies the fragment depth as $\log_2(e_i)f_c/2$, where e_i is the interpolated value of e. This method is a good alternative when there is no floating point depth in the GPU and when rendering using large distances in depth.

Cozzi [1605] proposes to use multiple frusta, which can improve accuracy to effectively any desired rate. The view frustum is divided in the depth direction into several non-overlapping smaller sub-frusta whose union is exactly the frustum. The sub-frusta are rendered to in back-to-front order. First, both the color and depth buffers are cleared, and all objects to be rendered are sorted into each sub-frusta that they overlap. For each sub-frusta, its projection matrix is set up, the depth buffer is cleared, and then the objects that overlap the sub-frusta are rendered.

Further Reading and Resources

The *immersive linear algebra* site [1718] provides an interactive book about the basics of this subject, helping build intuition by encouraging you to manipulate the figures. Other interactive learning tools and transform code libraries are linked from realtimerendering.com.

One of the best books for building up one's intuition about matrices in a painless fashion is Farin and Hansford's *The Geometry Toolbox* [461]. Another useful work is Lengyel's *Mathematics for 3D Game Programming and Computer Graphics* [1025]. For a different perspective, many computer graphics texts, such as Hearn and Baker [689], Marschner and Shirley [1129], and Hughes et al. [785] also cover matrix basics. The course by Ochiai et al. [1310] introduces the matrix foundations as well as the exponential and logarithm of matrices, with uses for computer graphics. The *Graphics Gems* series [72, 540, 695, 902, 1344] presents various transform-related algorithms and has code available online for many of these. Golub and Van Loan's *Matrix Computations* [556] is the place to start for a serious study of matrix techniques in general. More on skeleton-subspace deformation/vertex blending and shape interpolation can be read in Lewis et al.'s SIGGRAPH paper [1037].

Hart et al. [674] and Hanson [663] provide visualizations of quaternions. Pletinckx [1421] and Schlag [1566] present different ways of interpolating smoothly between a set of quaternions. Vlachos and Isidoro [1820] derive formulae for C^2 interpolation of quaternions. Related to quaternion interpolation is the problem of computing a consistent coordinate system along a curve. This is treated by Dougan [374].

Alexa [28] and Lazarus and Verroust [1000] present surveys on many different morphing techniques. Parent's book [1354] is an excellent source for techniques about computer animation.

Chapter 5
Shading Basics

"A good picture is equivalent to a good deed."
—Vincent Van Gogh

When you render images of three-dimensional objects, the models should not only have the proper geometrical shape, they should also have the desired visual appearance. Depending on the application, this can range from photorealism—an appearance nearly identical to photographs of real objects—to various types of stylized appearance chosen for creative reasons. See Figure 5.1 for examples of both.

This chapter will discuss those aspects of shading that are equally applicable to photorealistic and stylized rendering. Chapter 15 is dedicated specifically to stylized rendering, and a significant part of the book, Chapters 9 through 14, focuses on physically based approaches commonly used for photorealistic rendering.

5.1 Shading Models

The first step in determining the appearance of a rendered object is to choose a *shading model* to describe how the object's color should vary based on factors such as surface orientation, view direction, and lighting.

As an example, we will use a variation on the *Gooch shading model* [561]. This is a form of non-photorealistic rendering, the subject of Chapter 15. The Gooch shading model was designed to increase legibility of details in technical illustrations.

The basic idea behind Gooch shading is to compare the surface normal to the light's location. If the normal points toward the light, a warmer tone is used to color the surface; if it points away, a cooler tone is used. Angles in between interpolate between these tones, which are based on a user-supplied surface color. In this example, we add a stylized "highlight" effect to the model to give the surface a shiny appearance. Figure 5.2 shows the shading model in action.

Shading models often have properties used to control appearance variation. Setting the values of these properties is the next step in determining object appearance. Our example model has just one property, surface color, as shown in the bottom image of Figure 5.2.

Figure 5.1. The top image is from a realistic landscape scene rendered using the Unreal Engine. The bottom image is from the game *Firewatch* by Campo Santo, which was designed with a illustrative art style. *(Upper image courtesy of Gökhan Karadayi, lower image courtesy of Campo Santo.)*

Like most shading models, this example is affected by the surface orientation relative to the view and lighting directions. For shading purposes, these directions are commonly expressed as normalized (unit-length) vectors, as illustrated in Figure 5.3.

Now that we have defined all the inputs to our shading model, we can look at the mathematical definition of the model itself:

$$\mathbf{c}_{\text{shaded}} = s\,\mathbf{c}_{\text{highlight}} + (1 - s)\left(t\,\mathbf{c}_{\text{warm}} + (1 - t)\,\mathbf{c}_{\text{cool}}\right). \tag{5.1}$$

Figure 5.2. A stylized shading model combining Gooch shading with a highlight effect. The top image shows a complex object with a neutral surface color. The bottom image shows spheres with various different surface colors. *(Chinese Dragon mesh from Computer Graphics Archive [1172], original model from Stanford 3D Scanning Repository.)*

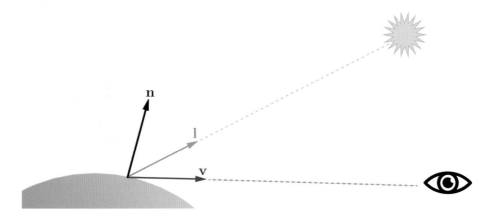

Figure 5.3. Unit-length vector inputs to the example shading model (and most others): surface normal **n**, view vector **v**, and light direction **l**.

In this equation, we have used the following intermediate calculations:

$$\mathbf{c}_{\text{cool}} = (0, 0, 0.55) + 0.25\,\mathbf{c}_{\text{surface}},$$
$$\mathbf{c}_{\text{warm}} = (0.3, 0.3, 0) + 0.25\,\mathbf{c}_{\text{surface}},$$
$$\mathbf{c}_{\text{highlight}} = (1, 1, 1),$$
$$t = \frac{(\mathbf{n} \cdot \mathbf{l}) + 1}{2}, \tag{5.2}$$
$$\mathbf{r} = 2\,(\mathbf{n} \cdot \mathbf{l})\mathbf{n} - \mathbf{l},$$
$$s = \left(100\,(\mathbf{r} \cdot \mathbf{v}) - 97\right)^{\overline{\mp}}.$$

Several of the mathematical expressions in this definition are often found in other shading models as well. Clamping operations, typically clamping to 0 or clamping between 0 and 1, are common in shading. Here we use the $x^{\overline{\mp}}$ notation, introduced in Section 1.2, for the clamp between 0 and 1 used in the computation of the highlight blend factor s. The dot product operator appears three times, in each case between two unit-length vectors; this is an extremely common pattern. The dot product of two vectors is the product of their lengths and the cosine of the angle between them. So, the dot product of two unit-length vectors is simply the cosine, which is a useful measure of the degree to which two vectors are aligned with each other. Simple functions composed of cosines are often the most pleasing and accurate mathematical expressions to account for the relationship between two directions, e.g., light direction and surface normal, in a shading model.

Another common shading operation is to interpolate linearly between two colors based on a scalar value between 0 and 1. This operation takes the form $t\mathbf{c}_{\text{a}} + (1 - t)\mathbf{c}_{\text{b}}$ that interpolates between $\mathbf{c}_{\text{a}}$ and $\mathbf{c}_{\text{b}}$ as the value of t moves between 1 and 0, respectively. This pattern appears twice in this shading model, first to interpolate between $\mathbf{c}_{\text{warm}}$ and $\mathbf{c}_{\text{cool}}$ and second to interpolate between the result of the previous interpolation and $\mathbf{c}_{\text{highlight}}$. Linear interpolation appears so often in shaders that it is a built-in function, called `lerp` or `mix`, in every shading language we have seen.

The line "$\mathbf{r} = 2\,(\mathbf{n} \cdot \mathbf{l})\mathbf{n} - \mathbf{l}$" computes the reflected light vector, reflecting $\mathbf{l}$ about $\mathbf{n}$. While not quite as common as the previous two operations, this is common enough for most shading languages to have a built-in `reflect` function as well.

By combining such operations in different ways with various mathematical expressions and shading parameters, shading models can be defined for a huge variety of stylized and realistic appearances.

5.2 Light Sources

The impact of lighting on our example shading model was quite simple; it provided a dominant direction for shading. Of course, lighting in the real world can be quite complex. There can be multiple light sources each with its own size, shape, color, and intensity; indirect lighting adds even more variation. As we will see in Chapter 9, physically based, photorealistic shading models need to take all these parameters into account.

In contrast, stylized shading models may use lighting in many different ways, depending on the needs of the application and visual style. Some highly stylized models may have no concept of lighting at all, or (like our Gooch shading example) may only use it to provide some simple directionality.

The next step in lighting complexity is for the shading model to react to the presence or absence of light in a binary way. A surface shaded with such a model would have one appearance when lit and a different appearance when unaffected by light. This implies some criteria for distinguishing the two cases: distance from light sources, shadowing (which will be discussed in Chapter 7), whether the surface is facing away from the light source (i.e., the angle between the surface normal $\mathbf{n}$ and the light vector $\mathbf{l}$ is greater than $90°$), or some combination of these factors.

It is a small step from the binary presence or absence of light to a continuous scale of light intensities. This could be expressed as a simple interpolation between absence and full presence, which implies a bounded range for the intensity, perhaps 0 to 1, or as an unbounded quantity that affects the shading in some other way. A common option for the latter is to factor the shading model into lit and unlit parts, with the light intensity k_{light} linearly scaling the lit part:

$$\mathbf{c}_{\text{shaded}} = f_{\text{unlit}}(\mathbf{n}, \mathbf{v}) + k_{\text{light}} f_{\text{lit}}(\mathbf{l}, \mathbf{n}, \mathbf{v}). \qquad (5.3)$$

This easily extends to an RGB light color $\mathbf{c}_{\text{light}}$,

$$\mathbf{c}_{\text{shaded}} = f_{\text{unlit}}(\mathbf{n}, \mathbf{v}) + \mathbf{c}_{\text{light}} f_{\text{lit}}(\mathbf{l}, \mathbf{n}, \mathbf{v}), \qquad (5.4)$$

and to multiple light sources,

$$\mathbf{c}_{\text{shaded}} = f_{\text{unlit}}(\mathbf{n}, \mathbf{v}) + \sum_{i=1}^{n} \mathbf{c}_{\text{light}_i} f_{\text{lit}}(\mathbf{l}_i, \mathbf{n}, \mathbf{v}). \qquad (5.5)$$

The unlit part $f_{\text{unlit}}(\mathbf{n}, \mathbf{v})$ corresponds to the "appearance when unaffected by light" of shading models that treat light as a binary. It can have various forms, depending on the desired visual style and the needs of the application. For example, $f_{\text{unlit}}() = (0, 0, 0)$ will cause any surface unaffected by a light source to be colored pure black. Alternately, the unlit part could express some form of stylized appearance for unlit objects, similar to the Gooch model's cool color for surfaces facing away from light. Often, this part of the shading model expresses some form of lighting that does not come directly from explicitly placed light sources, such as light from the sky or light bounced from surrounding objects. These other forms of lighting will be discussed in Chapters 10 and 11.

We mentioned earlier that a light source does not affect a surface point if the light direction $\mathbf{l}$ is more than $90°$ from the surface normal $\mathbf{n}$, in effect coming from

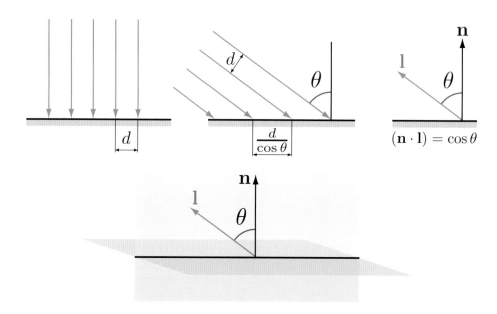

Figure 5.4. The upper row of drawings shows a cross-section view of light on a surface. On the left the light rays hit the surface straight on, in the center they hit the surface at an angle, and on the right we see the use of vector dot products to compute the angle cosine. The bottom drawing shows the cross-section plane (which includes the light and view vectors) in relation to the full surface.

underneath the surface. This can be thought of as a special case of a more general relationship between the light's direction, relative to the surface, and its effect on shading. Although physically based, this relationship can be derived from simple geometrical principles and is useful for many types of non-physically based, stylized shading models as well.

The effect of light on a surface can be visualized as a set of rays, with the density of rays hitting the surface corresponding to the light intensity for surface shading purposes. See Figure 5.4, which shows a cross section of a lit surface. The spacing between light rays hitting the surface along that cross section is inversely proportional to the cosine of the angle between $\mathbf{l}$ and $\mathbf{n}$. So, the overall density of light rays hitting the surface is proportional to the cosine of the angle between $\mathbf{l}$ and $\mathbf{n}$, which, as we have seen earlier, is equal to the dot product between those two unit-length vectors. Here we see why it is convenient to define the light vector $\mathbf{l}$ opposite to the light's direction of travel; otherwise we would have to negate it before performing the dot product.

More precisely, the ray density (and thus the light's contribution to shading) is proportional to the dot product when it is positive. Negative values correspond to light rays coming from behind the surface, which have no effect. So, before multiplying the light's shading by the lighting dot product, we need to first clamp the dot product to 0. Using the x^+ notation introduced in Section 1.2, which means clamping negative values to zero, we have

$$\mathbf{c}_{\text{shaded}} = f_{\text{unlit}}(\mathbf{n}, \mathbf{v}) + \sum_{i=1}^{n} (\mathbf{l}_i \cdot \mathbf{n})^+ \mathbf{c}_{\text{light}_i} f_{\text{lit}}(\mathbf{l}_i, \mathbf{n}, \mathbf{v}). \tag{5.6}$$

Shading models that support multiple light sources will typically use one of the structures from Equation 5.5, which is more general, or Equation 5.6, which is required for physically based models. It can be advantageous for stylized models as well, since it helps ensure an overall consistency to the lighting, especially for surfaces that are facing away from the light or are shadowed. However, some models are not a good fit for that structure; such models would use the structure in Equation 5.5.

The simplest possible choice for the function $f_{\text{lit}}()$ is to make it a constant color,

$$f_{\text{lit}}() = \mathbf{c}_{\text{surface}}, \tag{5.7}$$

which results in the following shading model:

$$\mathbf{c}_{\text{shaded}} = f_{\text{unlit}}(\mathbf{n}, \mathbf{v}) + \sum_{i=1}^{n} (\mathbf{l}_i \cdot \mathbf{n})^+ \mathbf{c}_{\text{light}_i} \mathbf{c}_{\text{surface}}. \tag{5.8}$$

The lit part of this model corresponds to the *Lambertian* shading model, after Johann Heinrich Lambert [967], who published it in 1760! This model works in the context of ideal diffusely reflecting surfaces, i.e., surfaces that are perfectly matte. We present here a somewhat simplified explanation of Lambert's model, which will be covered with more rigor in Chapter 9. The Lambertian model can be used by itself for simple shading, and it is a key building block in many shading models.

We can see from Equations 5.3–5.6 that a light source interacts with the shading model via two parameters: the vector $\mathbf{l}$ pointing toward the light and the light color $\mathbf{c}_{\text{light}}$. There are various different types of light sources, which differ primarily in how these two parameters vary over the scene.

We will next discuss several popular types of light sources, which have one thing in common: At a given surface location, each light source illuminates the surface from only one direction $\mathbf{l}$. In other words, the light source, as seen from the shaded surface location, is an infinitesimally small point. This is not strictly true for real-world lights, but most light sources are small relative to their distance from illuminated surfaces, making this a reasonable approximation. In Sections 7.1.2 and 10.1, we will discuss light sources that illuminate a surface location from a range of directions, i.e., "area lights."

5.2.1 Directional Lights

Directional light is the simplest model of a light source. Both $\mathbf{l}$ and $\mathbf{c}_{\text{light}}$ are constant over the scene, except that $\mathbf{c}_{\text{light}}$ may be attenuated by shadowing. Directional lights have no location. Of course, actual light sources do have specific locations in space. Directional lights are abstractions, which work well when the distance to the light is large relative to the scene size. For example, a floodlight 20 feet away illuminating a small tabletop diorama could be represented as a directional light. Another example is pretty much any scene lit by the sun, unless the scene in question is something such as the inner planets of the solar system.

The concept of a directional light can be somewhat extended to allow varying the value of $\mathbf{c}_{light}$ while the light direction $\mathbf{l}$ remains constant. This is most often done to bound the effect of the light to a particular part of the scene for performance or creative reasons. For example, a region could be defined with two nested (one inside the other) box-shaped volumes, where $\mathbf{c}_{light}$ is equal to $(0,0,0)$ (pure black) outside the outer box, is equal to some constant value inside the inner box, and smoothly interpolates between those extremes in the region between the two boxes.

5.2.2 Punctual Lights

A *punctual light* is not one that is on time for its appointments, but rather a light that has a location, unlike directional lights. Such lights also have no dimensions to them, no shape or size, unlike real-world light sources. We use the term "punctual," from the Latin *punctus* meaning "point," for the class consisting of all sources of illumination that originate from a single, local position. We use the term "point light" to mean a specific kind of emitter, one that shines light equally in all directions. So, point and spotlight are two different forms of punctual lights. The light direction vector $\mathbf{l}$ varies depending on the location of the currently shaded surface point $\mathbf{p}_0$ relative to the punctual light's position $\mathbf{p}_{light}$:

$$\mathbf{l} = \frac{\mathbf{p}_{light} - \mathbf{p}_0}{\|\mathbf{p}_{light} - \mathbf{p}_0\|}. \tag{5.9}$$

This equation is an example of vector normalization: dividing a vector by its length to produce a unit-length vector pointing in the same direction. This is another common shading operation, and, like the shading operations we have seen in the previous section, it is a built-in function in most shading languages. However, sometimes an intermediate result from this operation is needed, which requires performing the normalization explicitly, in multiple steps, using more basic operations. Applying this to the punctual light direction computation gives us the following:

$$\begin{aligned} \mathbf{d} &= \mathbf{p}_{light} - \mathbf{p}_0, \\ r &= \sqrt{\mathbf{d} \cdot \mathbf{d}}, \\ \mathbf{l} &= \frac{\mathbf{d}}{r}. \end{aligned} \tag{5.10}$$

Since the dot product of two vectors is equal to the product of the two vector's lengths with the cosine of the angle between them, and the cosine of $0°$ is 1.0, the dot product of a vector with itself is the square of its length. So, to find the length of any vector, we just dot it with itself and take the square root of the result.

The intermediate value that we need is r, the distance between the punctual light source and the currently shaded point. Besides its use in normalizing the light vector, the value of r is also needed to compute the attenuation (darkening) of the light color $\mathbf{c}_{\text{light}}$ as a function of distance. This will be discussed further in the following section.

Point/Omni Lights

Punctual lights that emit light uniformly in all directions are known as *point lights* or *omni lights*. For point lights, $\mathbf{c}_{\text{light}}$ varies as a function of the distance r, with the only source of variation being the distance attenuation mentioned above. Figure 5.5 shows why this darkening occurs, using similar geometric reasoning as the demonstration of the cosine factor in Figure 5.4. At a given surface, the spacing between rays from a point light is proportional to the distance from the surface to the light. Unlike the cosine factor in Figure 5.4, this spacing increase happens along both dimensions of the surface, so the ray density (and thus the light color $\mathbf{c}_{\text{light}}$) is proportional to the inverse square distance $1/r^2$. This enables us to specify the spatial variation in $\mathbf{c}_{\text{light}}$ with a single light property, $\mathbf{c}_{\text{light}_0}$, which is defined as the value of $\mathbf{c}_{\text{light}}$ at a fixed reference distance r_0:

$$\mathbf{c}_{\text{light}}(r) = \mathbf{c}_{\text{light}_0} \left(\frac{r_0}{r} \right)^2. \tag{5.11}$$

Equation 5.11 is often referred to as *inverse-square light attenuation*. Although technically the correct distance attenuation for a point light, there are some issues that make this equation less than ideal for practical shading use.

The first issue occurs at relatively small distances. As the value of r tends to 0, the value of $\mathbf{c}_{\text{light}}$ will increase in an unbounded manner. When r reaches 0, we will have a divide-by-zero singularity. To address this, one common modification is to add a small value ϵ to the denominator [861]:

$$\mathbf{c}_{\text{light}}(r) = \mathbf{c}_{\text{light}_0} \frac{r_0^2}{r^2 + \epsilon}. \tag{5.12}$$

The exact value used for ϵ depends on the application; for example, the Unreal game engine uses $\epsilon = 1$ cm [861].

An alternative modification, used in the CryEngine [1591] and Frostbite [960] game engines, is to clamp r to a minimum value r_{min}:

$$\mathbf{c}_{\text{light}}(r) = \mathbf{c}_{\text{light}_0} \left(\frac{r_0}{\max(r, r_{\text{min}})} \right)^2. \tag{5.13}$$

Unlike the somewhat arbitrary ϵ value used in the previous method, the value of r_{min} has a physical interpretation: the radius of the physical object emitting the light. Values of r smaller than r_{min} correspond to the shaded surface penetrating inside the physical light source, which is impossible.

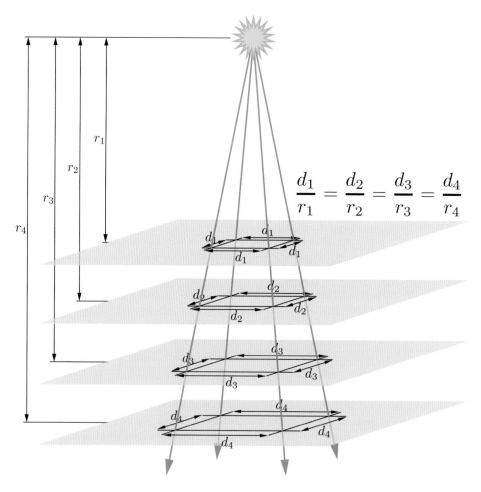

Figure 5.5. The spacing between light rays from a point light increases proportionally to the distance r. Since the spacing increase occurs in two dimensions, the density of rays (and thus the light intensity) decreases proportionally to $1/r^2$.

In contrast, the second issue with inverse-square attenuation occurs at relatively large distances. The problem is not with visuals but with performance. Although light intensity keeps decreasing with distance it never goes to 0. For efficient rendering, it is desirable for lights to reach 0 intensity at some finite distance (Chapter 20). There are many different ways in which the inverse-square equation could be modified to achieve this. Ideally the modification should introduce as little change as possible. To avoid a sharp cutoff at the boundary of the light's influence, it is also preferable for the derivative and value of the modified function to reach 0 at the same distance. One solution is to multiply the inverse-square equation by a *windowing function* with the

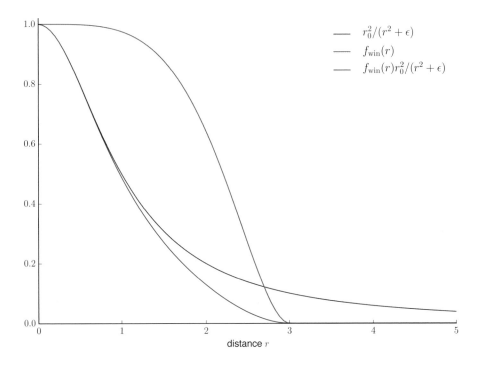

Figure 5.6. This graph shows an inverse-square curve (using the ϵ method to avoid singularities, with an ϵ value of 1), the windowing function described in Equation 5.14 (with r_{max} set to 3), and the windowed curve.

desired properties. One such function [860] is used by both the Unreal Engine [861] and Frostbite [960] game engines:

$$f_{\text{win}}(r) = \left(1 - \left(\frac{r}{r_{\text{max}}} \right)^4 \right)^{+2} . \tag{5.14}$$

The $+2$ means to clamp the value, if negative, to 0 before squaring it. Figure 5.6 shows an example inverse-square curve, the windowing function from Equation 5.14, and the result of multiplying the two.

Application requirements will affect the choice of method used. For example, having the derivative equal to 0 at r_{max} is particularly important when the distance attenuation function is sampled at a relatively low spatial frequency (e.g., in light maps or per-vertex). CryEngine does not use light maps or vertex lighting, so it employs a simpler adjustment, switching to linear falloff in the range between $0.8r_{\text{max}}$ and r_{max} [1591].

For some applications, matching the inverse-square curve is not a priority, so some other function entirely is used. This effectively generalizes Equations 5.11–5.14 to the following:

$$\mathbf{c}_{\text{light}}(r) = \mathbf{c}_{\text{light}_0} f_{\text{dist}}(r),\tag{5.15}$$

where $f_{\text{dist}}(r)$ is some function of distance. Such functions are called *distance falloff functions*. In some cases, the use of non-inverse-square falloff functions is driven by performance constraints. For example, the game *Just Cause 2* needed lights that were extremely inexpensive to compute. This dictated a falloff function that was simple to compute, while also being smooth enough to avoid per-vertex lighting artifacts [1379]:

$$f_{\text{dist}}(r) = \left(1 - \left(\frac{r}{r_{\text{max}}}\right)^2\right)^{+2}.\tag{5.16}$$

In other cases, the choice of falloff function may be driven by creative considerations. For example, the Unreal Engine, used for both realistic and stylized games, has two modes for light falloff: an inverse-square mode, as described in Equation 5.12, and an exponential falloff mode that can be tweaked to create a variety of attenuation curves [1802]. The developers of the game *Tomb Raider* (2013) used spline-editing tools to author falloff curves [953], allowing for even greater control over the curve shape.

Spotlights

Unlike point lights, illumination from nearly all real-world light sources varies by direction as well as distance. This variation can be expressed as a directional falloff function $f_{\text{dir}}(\mathbf{l})$, which combines with the distance falloff function to define the overall spatial variation in light intensity:

$$\mathbf{c}_{\text{light}} = \mathbf{c}_{\text{light}_0} f_{\text{dist}}(r) f_{\text{dir}}(\mathbf{l}).\tag{5.17}$$

Different choices of $f_{\text{dir}}(\mathbf{l})$ can produce various lighting effects. One important type of effect is the *spotlight*, which projects light in a circular cone. A spotlight's directional falloff function has rotational symmetry around a spotlight direction vector $\mathbf{s}$, and thus can be expressed as a function of the angle θ_s between $\mathbf{s}$ and the reversed light vector $-\mathbf{l}$ to the surface. The light vector needs to be reversed because we define $\mathbf{l}$ at the surface as pointing toward the light, and here we need the vector pointing away from the light.

Most spotlight functions use expressions composed of the cosine of θ_s, which (as we have seen earlier) is the most common form for angles in shading. Spotlights typically have an *umbra angle* θ_u, which bounds the light such that $f_{\text{dir}}(\mathbf{l}) = 0$ for all $\theta_s \geq \theta_u$. This angle can be used for culling in a similar manner to the maximum falloff distance r_{max} seen earlier. It is also common for spotlights to have a *penumbra angle* θ_p, which defines an inner cone where the light is at its full intensity. See Figure 5.7.

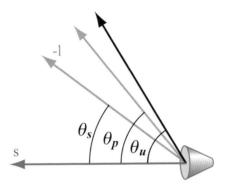

Figure 5.7. A spotlight: θ_s is the angle from the light's defined direction $\mathbf{s}$ to the vector $-\mathbf{l}$, the direction to the surface; θ_p shows the penumbra; and θ_u shows the umbra angles defined for the light.

Various directional falloff functions are used for spotlights, but they tend to be roughly similar. For example, the function $f_{\mathrm{dir_F}}(\mathbf{l})$ is used in the Frostbite game engine [960], and the function $f_{\mathrm{dir_T}}(\mathbf{l})$ is used in the three.js browser graphics library [218]:

$$
\begin{aligned}
t &= \left(\frac{\cos\theta_s - \cos\theta_u}{\cos\theta_p - \cos\theta_u} \right)^{\overline{+}}, \\
f_{\mathrm{dir_F}}(\mathbf{l}) &= t^2, \\
f_{\mathrm{dir_T}}(\mathbf{l}) &= \mathrm{smoothstep}(t) = t^2(3 - 2t).
\end{aligned}
\tag{5.18}
$$

Recall that $x^{\overline{+}}$ is our notation for clamping x between 0 and 1, as introduced in Section 1.2. The smoothstep function is a cubic polynomial that is often used for smooth interpolation in shading. It is a built-in function in most shading languages.

Figure 5.8 shows some of the light types we have discussed so far.

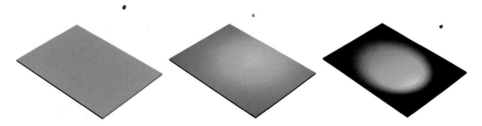

Figure 5.8. Some types of lights. From left to right: directional, point light with no falloff, and spotlight with a smooth transition. Note that the point light dims toward the edges due to the changing angle between the light and the surface.

Other Punctual Lights

There are many other ways in which the $\mathbf{c}_{\text{light}}$ value of a punctual light can vary.

The $f_{\text{dir}}(\mathbf{l})$ function is not limited to the simple spotlight falloff functions discussed above; it can represent any type of directional variation, including complex tabulated patterns measured from real-world light sources. The Illuminating Engineering Society (IES) have defined a standard file format for such measurements. IES profiles are available from many lighting manufacturers and have been used in the game *Killzone: Shadow Fall* [379, 380], as well as the Unreal [861] and Frostbite [960] game engines, among others. Lagarde gives a good summary [961] of issues relating to parsing and using this file format.

The game *Tomb Raider* (2013) [953] has a type of punctual light that applies independent falloff functions for distance along the x, y, and z world axes. In *Tomb Raider* curves can also be applied to vary light intensity over time, e.g., to produce a flickering torch.

In Section 6.9 we will discuss how light intensity and color can be varied via the use of textures.

5.2.3   Other Light Types

Directional and punctual lights are primarily characterized by how the light direction $\mathbf{l}$ is computed. Different types of lights can be defined by using other methods to compute the light direction. For example, in addition to the light types mentioned earlier, *Tomb Raider* also has capsule lights that use a line segment as the source instead of a point [953]. For each shaded pixel, the direction to the closest point on the line segment is used as the light direction $\mathbf{l}$.

As long as the shader has $\mathbf{l}$ and $\mathbf{c}_{\text{light}}$ values for use in evaluating the shading equation, any method can be used to compute those values.

The types of light discussed so far are abstractions. In reality, light sources have size and shape, and they illuminate surface points from multiple directions. In rendering, such lights are called *area lights*, and their use in real-time applications is steadily increasing. Area-light rendering techniques fall into two categories: those that simulate the softening of shadow edges that results from the area light being partially occluded (Section 7.1.2) and those that simulate the effect of the area light on surface shading (Section 10.1). This second category of lighting is most noticeable for smooth, mirror-like surfaces, where the light's shape and size can be clearly discerned in its reflection. Directional and punctual lights are unlikely to fall into disuse, though they are no longer as ubiquitous as in the past. Approximations accounting for a light's area have been developed that are relatively inexpensive to implement, and so are seeing wider use. Increased GPU performance also allows for more elaborate techniques than in the past.

5.3 Implementing Shading Models

To be useful, these shading and lighting equations must of course be implemented in code. In this section we will go over some key considerations for designing and writing such implementations. We will also walk through a simple implementation example.

5.3.1 Frequency of Evaluation

When designing a shading implementation, the computations need to be divided according to their *frequency of evaluation*. First, determine whether the result of a given computation is always constant over an entire draw call. In this case, the computation can be performed by the application, typically on the CPU, though a GPU compute shader could be used for especially costly computations. The results are passed to the graphics API via uniform shader inputs.

Even within this category, there is a broad range of possible frequencies of evaluation, starting from "once ever." The simplest such case would be a constant subexpression in the shading equation, but this could apply to any computation based on rarely changing factors such as the hardware configuration and installation options. Such shading computations might be resolved when the shader is compiled, in which case there is no need to even set a uniform shader input. Alternatively, the computation might be performed in an offline precomputation pass, at installation time, or when the application is loaded.

Another case is when the result of a shading computation changes over an application run, but so slowly that updating it every frame is not necessary. For example, lighting factors that depend on the time of day in a virtual game world. If the computation is costly, it may be worthwhile to amortize it over multiple frames.

Other cases include computations that are performed once per frame, such as concatenating the view and perspective matrices; or once per model, such as updating model lighting parameters that depend on location; or once per draw call, e.g., updating parameters for each material within a model. Grouping uniform shader inputs by frequency of evaluation is useful for application efficiency, and can also help GPU performance by minimizing constant updates [1165].

If the result of a shading computation changes within a draw call, it cannot be passed to the shader through a uniform shader input. Instead, it must be computed by one of the programmable shader stages described in Chapter 3 and, if needed, passed to other stages via varying shader inputs. In theory, shading computations can be performed on any of the programmable stages, each one corresponding to a different evaluation frequency:

- Vertex shader—Evaluation per pre-tessellation vertex.

- Hull shader—Evaluation per surface patch.

- Domain shader—Evaluation per post-tessellation vertex.

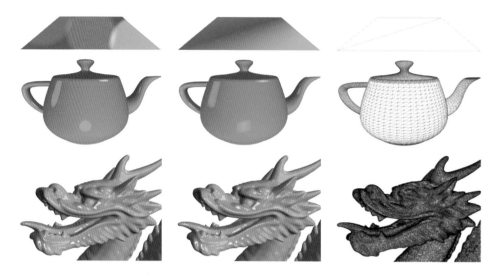

Figure 5.9. A comparison of per-pixel and per-vertex evaluations for the example shading model from Equation 5.19, shown on three models of varying vertex density. The left column shows the results of per-pixel evaluation, the middle column shows per-vertex evaluation, and the right column presents wireframe renderings of each model to show vertex density. *(Chinese Dragon mesh from Computer Graphics Archive [1172], original model from Stanford 3D Scanning Repository.)*

- Geometry shader—Evaluation per primitive.

- Pixel shader—Evaluation per pixel.

In practice most shading computations are performed per pixel. While these are typically implemented in the pixel shader, compute shader implementations are increasingly common; several examples will be discussed in Chapter 20. The other stages are primarily used for geometric operations such as transformation and deformation. To understand why this is the case, we will compare the results of per-vertex and per-pixel shading evaluations. In older texts, these are sometimes referred to as *Gouraud shading* [578] and *Phong shading* [1414], respectively, though those terms are not often used today. This comparison uses a shading model somewhat similar to the one in Equation 5.1, but modified to work with multiple light sources. The full model will be given a bit later, when we cover an example implementation in detail.

Figure 5.9 shows the results of per-pixel and per-vertex shading on models with a wide range of vertex densities. For the dragon, an extremely dense mesh, the difference between the two is small. But on the teapot, vertex shading evaluation causes visible errors such as angularly shaped highlights, and on the two-triangle plane the vertex-shaded version is clearly incorrect. The cause of these errors is that parts of the shading equation, the highlight in particular, have values that vary nonlinearly over

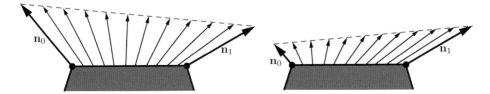

Figure 5.10. On the left, we see that linear interpolation of unit normals across a surface results in interpolated vectors with lengths less than one. On the right, we see that linear interpolation of normals with significantly different lengths results in interpolated directions that are skewed toward the longer of the two normals.

the mesh surface. This makes them a poor fit for the vertex shader, the results of which are interpolated linearly over the triangle before being fed to the pixel shader.

In principle, it would be possible to compute only the *specular highlight* part of the shading model in the pixel shader, and calculate the rest in the vertex shader. This would likely not result in visual artifacts and in theory would save some computation. In practice, this kind of hybrid implementation is often not optimal. The linearly varying parts of the shading model tend to be the least computationally costly, and splitting up the shading computation in this way tends to add enough overhead, such as duplicated computations and additional varying inputs, to outweigh any benefit.

As we mentioned earlier, in most implementations the vertex shader is responsible for non-shading operations such as geometry transformation and deformation. The resulting geometric surface properties, transformed into the appropriate coordinate system, are written out by the vertex shader, linearly interpolated over the triangle, and passed into the pixel shader as varying shader inputs. These properties typically include the position of the surface, the surface normal, and optionally surface tangent vectors, if needed for normal mapping.

Note that even if the vertex shader always generates unit-length surface normals, interpolation can change their length. See the left side of Figure 5.10. For this reason the normals need to be renormalized (scaled to length 1) in the pixel shader. However, the length of the normals generated by the vertex shader still matters. If the normal length varies significantly between vertices, e.g., as a side effect of vertex blending, this will skew the interpolation. This can be seen in the right side of Figure 5.10. Due to these two effects, implementations often normalize interpolated vectors before and after interpolation, i.e., in both the vertex and pixel shaders.

Unlike the surface normals, vectors that point toward specific locations, such as the view vector and the light vector for punctual lights, are typically not interpolated. Instead, the interpolated surface position is used to compute these vectors in the pixel shader. Other than the normalization, which as we have seen needs to be performed in the pixel shader in any case, each of these vectors is computed with a vector subtraction, which is quick. If for some reason it is necessary to interpolate these

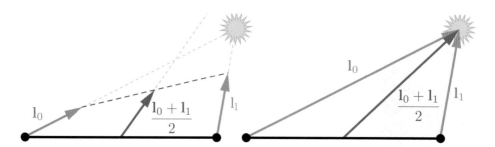

Figure 5.11. Interpolation between two light vectors. On the left, normalizing them before interpolation causes the direction to be incorrect after interpolation. On the right, interpolating the non-normalized vectors yields correct results.

vectors, do not normalize them beforehand. This will yield incorrect results, as shown in Figure 5.11.

Earlier we mentioned that the vertex shader transforms the surface geometry into "the appropriate coordinate system." The camera and light positions, passed to the pixel shader through uniform variables, are typically transformed by the application into the same coordinate system. This minimizes work done by the pixel shader to bring all the shading model vectors into the same coordinate space. But which coordinate system is the "appropriate" one? Possibilities include the global world space as well as the local coordinate system of the camera or, more rarely, that of the currently rendered model. The choice is typically made for the rendering system as a whole, based on systemic considerations such as performance, flexibility, and simplicity. For example, if rendered scenes are expected to include huge numbers of lights, world space might be chosen to avoid transforming the light positions. Alternately, camera space might be preferred, to better optimize pixel shader operations relating to the view vector and to possibly improve precision (Section 16.6).

Although most shader implementations, including the example implementation we are about to discuss, follow the general outline described above, there are certainly exceptions. For example, some applications choose the faceted appearance of per-primitive shading evaluation for stylistic reasons. This style is often referred to as *flat shading*. Two examples are shown in Figure 5.12.

In principle, flat shading could be performed in the geometry shader, but recent implementations typically use the vertex shader. This is done by associating each primitive's properties with its first vertex and disabling vertex value interpolation. Disabling interpolation (which can be done for each vertex value separately) causes the value from the first vertex to be passed to all pixels in the primitive.

5.3.2 Implementation Example

We will now present an example shading model implementation. As mentioned earlier, the shading model we are implementing is similar to the extended Gooch model from

Figure 5.12. Two games that use flat shading as a stylistic choice: *Kentucky Route Zero*, top, and *That Dragon, Cancer*, bottom. *(Upper image courtesy of Cardboard Computer, lower courtesy of Numinous Games.)*

Equation 5.1, but modified to work with multiple light sources. It is described by

$$\mathbf{c}_{\text{shaded}} = \frac{1}{2}\mathbf{c}_{\text{cool}} + \sum_{i=1}^{n}(\mathbf{l}_i \cdot \mathbf{n})^+ \mathbf{c}_{\text{light}_i}\big(s_i\,\mathbf{c}_{\text{highlight}} + (1-s_i)\,\mathbf{c}_{\text{warm}}\big), \qquad (5.19)$$

with the following intermediate calculations:

$$
\begin{aligned}
\mathbf{c}_{\text{cool}} &= (0, 0, 0.55) + 0.25\,\mathbf{c}_{\text{surface}}, \\
\mathbf{c}_{\text{warm}} &= (0.3, 0.3, 0) + 0.25\,\mathbf{c}_{\text{surface}}, \\
\mathbf{c}_{\text{highlight}} &= (2, 2, 2), \\
\mathbf{r}_i &= 2\,(\mathbf{n} \cdot \mathbf{l}_i)\mathbf{n} - \mathbf{l}_i, \\
s_i &= \left(100\,(\mathbf{r}_i \cdot \mathbf{v}) - 97\right)^{\overline{+}}.
\end{aligned}
\tag{5.20}
$$

This formulation fits the multi-light structure in Equation 5.6, repeated here for convenience:

$$
\mathbf{c}_{\text{shaded}} = f_{\text{unlit}}(\mathbf{n}, \mathbf{v}) + \sum_{i=1}^{n}(\mathbf{l}_i \cdot \mathbf{n})^{+}\mathbf{c}_{\text{light}_i}\,f_{\text{lit}}(\mathbf{l}_i, \mathbf{n}, \mathbf{v}).
$$

The lit and unlit terms in this case are

$$
\begin{aligned}
f_{\text{unlit}}(\mathbf{n}, \mathbf{v}) &= \frac{1}{2}\mathbf{c}_{\text{cool}}, \\
f_{\text{lit}}(\mathbf{l}_i, \mathbf{n}, \mathbf{v}) &= s_i\,\mathbf{c}_{\text{highlight}} + (1 - s_i)\,\mathbf{c}_{\text{warm}},
\end{aligned}
\tag{5.21}
$$

with the cool color's unlit contribution adjusted to make results look more like the original equation.

In most typical rendering applications, varying values for material properties such as $\mathbf{c}_{\text{surface}}$ would be stored in vertex data or, more commonly, in textures (Chapter 6). However, to keep this example implementation simple, we will assume that $\mathbf{c}_{\text{surface}}$ is constant across the model.

This implementation will use the shader's dynamic branching capabilities to loop over all light sources. While this straightforward approach can work well for reasonably simple scenes, it does not scale well to large and geometrically complex scenes with many light sources. Rendering techniques to efficiently handle large light counts will be covered in Chapter 20. Also, in the interest of simplicity, we will only support one type of light source: point lights. Although the implementation is quite simple, it follows the best practices covered earlier.

Shading models are not implemented in isolation, but in the context of a larger rendering framework. This example is implemented inside a simple WebGL 2 application, modified from the "Phong-shaded Cube" WebGL 2 sample by Tarek Sherif [1623], but the same principles apply to more complex frameworks as well.

We will be discussing some samples of GLSL shader code and JavaScript WebGL calls from the application. The intent is not to teach the specifics of the WebGL API but to show general implementation principles. We will go through the implementation in "inside out" order, starting with the pixel shader, then the vertex shader, and finally the application-side graphics API calls.

Before the shader code proper, the shader source includes definitions of the shader inputs and outputs. As discussed earlier in Section 3.3, using GLSL terminology, shader inputs fall into two categories. One is the set of *uniform* inputs, which have values set by the application and which remain constant over a draw call. The second type consists of *varying* inputs, which have values that can change between shader invocations (pixels or vertices). Here we see the definitions of the pixel shader's varying inputs, which in GLSL are marked `in`, as well as its outputs:

```
in vec3 vPos;
in vec3 vNormal;
out vec4 outColor;
```

This pixel shader has a single output, which is the final shaded color. The pixel shader inputs match the vertex shader outputs, which are interpolated over the triangle before being fed into the pixel shader. This pixel shader has two varying inputs: surface position and surface normal, both in the application's world-space coordinate system. The number of uniform inputs is much larger, so for brevity we will only show the definitions of two, both related to light sources:

```
struct Light {
    vec4 position;
    vec4 color;
};
uniform LightUBlock {
    Light uLights[MAXLIGHTS];
};

uniform uint uLightCount;
```

Since these are point lights, the definition for each one includes a position and a color. These are defined as `vec4` instead of `vec3` to conform to the restrictions of the GLSL `std140` data layout standard. Although, as in this case, the `std140` layout can lead to some wasted space, it simplifies the task of ensuring consistent data layout between CPU and GPU, which is why we use it in this sample. The array of `Light` structs is defined inside a named uniform block, which is a GLSL feature for binding a group of uniform variables to a buffer object for faster data transfer. The array length is defined to be equal to the maximum number of lights that the application allows in a single draw call. As we will see later, the application replaces the `MAXLIGHTS` string in the shader source with the correct value (10 in this case) before shader compilation. The uniform integer `uLightCount` is the actual number of active lights in the draw call.

Next, we will take a look at the pixel shader code:

```
vec3 lit(vec3 l, vec3 n, vec3 v) {
    vec3 r_l = reflect(-l, n);
    float s = clamp(100.0 * dot(r_l, v) - 97.0, 0.0, 1.0);
    vec3 highlightColor = vec3(2,2,2);
    return mix(uWarmColor, highlightColor, s);
}

void main() {
    vec3 n = normalize(vNormal);
    vec3 v = normalize(uEyePosition.xyz - vPos);
```

```
outColor = vec4(uFUnlit, 1.0);

for (uint i = 0u; i < uLightCount; i++) {
    vec3 l = normalize(uLights[i].position.xyz - vPos);
    float NdL = clamp(dot(n, l), 0.0, 1.0);
    outColor.rgb += NdL * uLights[i].color.rgb * lit(l,n,v);
}
}
```

We have a function definition for the `lit` term, which is called by the `main()` function. Overall, this is a straightforward GLSL implementation of Equations 5.20 and 5.21. Note that the values of $f_{\text{unlit}}()$ and $\mathbf{c}_{\text{warm}}$ are passed in as uniform variables. Since these are constant over the entire draw call, the application can compute these values, saving some GPU cycles.

This pixel shader uses several built-in GLSL functions. The `reflect()` function reflects one vector, in this case the light vector, in the plane defined by a second vector, in this case the surface normal. Since we want both the light vector and reflected vector to point away from the surface, we need to negate the former before passing it into `reflect()`. The `clamp()` function has three inputs. Two of them define a range to which the third input is clamped. The special case of clamping to the range between 0 and 1 (which corresponds to the HLSL `saturate()` function) is quick, often effectively free, on most GPUs. This is why we use it here, although we only need to clamp the value to 0, as we know it will not exceed 1. The function `mix()` also has three inputs and linearly interpolates between two of them, the warm color and the highlight color in this case, based on the value of the third, a mixing parameter between 0 and 1. In HLSL this function is called `lerp()`, for "linear interpolation." Finally, `normalize()` divides a vector by its length, scaling it to a length of 1.

Now let us look at the vertex shader. We will not show any of its uniform definitions since we already saw some example uniform definitions for the pixel shader, but the varying input and output definitions are worth examining:

```
layout(location=0) in vec4 position;
layout(location=1) in vec4 normal;
out vec3 vPos;
out vec3 vNormal;
```

Note that, as mentioned earlier, the vertex shader outputs match the pixel shader varying inputs. The inputs include directives that specify how the data are laid out in the vertex array. The vertex shader code comes next:

```
void main() {
    vec4 worldPosition = uModel * position;
    vPos = worldPosition.xyz;
    vNormal = (uModel * normal).xyz;
    gl_Position = viewProj * worldPosition;
}
```

These are common operations for a vertex shader. The shader transforms the surface position and normal into world space and passes them to the pixel shader for use in shading. Finally, the surface position is transformed into clip space and passed into gl_Position, a special system-defined variable used by the rasterizer. The gl_Position variable is the one required output from any vertex shader.

Note that the normal vectors are not normalized in the vertex shader. They do not need to be normalized since they have a length of 1 in the original mesh data and this application does not perform any operations, such as vertex blending or nonuniform scaling, that could change their length unevenly. The model matrix could have a uniform scale factor, but that would change the length of all normals proportionally and thus not result in the problem shown on the right side of Figure 5.10.

The application uses the WebGL API for various rendering and shader setup. Each of the programmable shader stages are set up individually, and then they are all bound to a program object. Here is the pixel shader setup code:

```
var fSource = document.getElementById("fragment").text.trim();

var maxLights = 10;
fSource = fSource.replace(/MAXLIGHTS/g, maxLights.toString());

var fragmentShader = gl.createShader(gl.FRAGMENT_SHADER);
gl.shaderSource(fragmentShader, fSource);
gl.compileShader(fragmentShader);
```

Note the "fragment shader" references. This term is used by WebGL (and OpenGL, on which it is based). As noted earlier in this book, although "pixel shader" is less precise in some ways, it is the more common usage, which we follow in this book. This code is also where the MAXLIGHTS string is replaced with the appropriate numerical value. Most rendering frameworks perform similar pre-compilation shader manipulations.

There is more application-side code for setting uniforms, initializing vertex arrays, clearing, drawing, and so on, which you can view in the program [1623] and which are explained by numerous API guides. Our goal here is to give a sense of how shaders are treated as separate processors, with their own programming environment. We thus end our walkthrough at this point.

5.3.3 Material Systems

Rendering frameworks rarely implement just a single shader, as in our simple example. Typically, a dedicated system is needed to handle the variety of materials, shading models, and shaders used by the application.

As explained in earlier chapters, a shader is a program for one of the GPU's programmable shader stages. As such, it is a low-level graphics API resource and not something with which artists would interact directly. In contrast, a *material* is an artist-facing encapsulation of the visual appearance of a surface. Materials sometimes also describe non-visual aspects, such as collision properties, which we will not discuss further because they are outside the scope of this book.

While materials are implemented via shaders, this is not a simple one-to-one correspondence. In different rendering situations, the same material may use different shaders. A shader can also be shared by multiple materials. The most common case is parameterized materials. In its simplest form, material parameterization requires two types of material entities: *material templates* and *material instances*. Each material template describes a class of materials and has a set of parameters that can be assigned numerical, color, or texture values depending on the parameter type. Each material instance corresponds to a material template plus a specific set of values for all of its parameters. Some rendering frameworks such as the Unreal Engine [1802] allow for a more complex, hierarchical structure, with material templates deriving from other templates at multiple levels.

Parameters may be resolved at runtime, by passing uniform inputs to the shader program, or at compile time, by substituting values before the shader is compiled. A common type of compile-time parameter is a boolean switch that controls the activation of a given material feature. This can be set by artists via a checkbox in the material user interface or procedurally by the material system, e.g., to reduce shader cost for distant objects where the visual effect of the feature is negligible.

While the material parameters may correspond one-to-one with the parameters of the shading model, this is not always the case. A material may fix the value of a given shading model parameter, such as the surface color, to a constant value. Alternately, a shading model parameter may be computed as the result of a complex series of operations taking multiple material parameters, as well as interpolated vertex or texture values, as inputs. In some cases, parameters such as surface position, surface orientation, and even time may also factor into the calculation. Shading based on surface position and orientation is especially common in terrain materials. For example, the height and surface normal can be used to control a snow effect, blending in a white surface color on high-altitude horizontal and almost-horizontal surfaces. Time-based shading is common in animated materials, such as a flickering neon sign.

One of the most important tasks of a material system is dividing various shader functions into separate elements and controlling how these are combined. There are many cases where this type of composition is useful, including the following:

- Composing surface shading with geometric processing, such as rigid transforms, vertex blending, morphing, tessellation, instancing, and clipping. These bits of functionality vary independently: Surface shading depends on the material, and geometry processing depends on the mesh. So, it is convenient to author them separately and have the material system compose them as needed.

- Composing surface shading with compositing operations such as pixel discard and blending. This is particularly relevant to mobile GPUs, where blending is typically performed in the pixel shader. It is often desirable to select these operations independently of the material used for surface shading.

- Composing the operations used to compute the shading model parameters with the computation of the shading model itself. This allows authoring the shading model implementation once and reusing it in combination with various different methods for computing the shading model parameters.

- Composing individually selectable material features with each other, the selection logic, and the rest of the shader. This enables writing the implementation of each feature separately.

- Composing the shading model and computation of its parameters with light source evaluation: computing the values of $\mathbf{c}_{\text{light}}$ and $\mathbf{l}$ at the shaded point for each light source. Techniques such as deferred rendering (discussed in Chapter 20) change the structure of this composition. In rendering frameworks that support multiple such techniques, this adds an additional layer of complexity.

It would be convenient if the graphics API provided this type of shader code modularity as a core feature. Sadly, unlike CPU code, GPU shaders do not allow for post-compilation linking of code fragments. The program for each shader stage is compiled as a unit. The separation between shader stages does offer some limited modularity, which somewhat fits the first item on our list: composing surface shading (typically performed in the pixel shader) with geometric processing (typically performed in other shader stages). But the fit is not perfect, since each shader performs other operations as well, and the other types of composition still need to be handled. Given these limitations, the only way that the material system can implement all these types of composition is at the source-code level. This primarily involves string operations such as concatenation and replacement, often performed via C-style preprocessing directives such as `#include`, `#if`, and `#define`.

Early rendering systems had a relatively small number of shader variants, and often each one was written manually. This has some benefits. For example, each variant can be optimized with full knowledge of the final shader program. However, this approach quickly becomes impractical as the number of variants grows. When taking all the different parts and options into account, the number of possible different shader variants is huge. This is why modularity and composability are so crucial.

The first question to be resolved when designing a system for handling shader variants is whether selection between different options is performed at runtime via dynamic branching, or at compile time via conditional preprocessing. On older hardware, dynamic branching was often impossible or extremely slow, so runtime selection was not an option. Variants were then all handled at compile time, including all possible combinations of counts of the different light types [1193].

In contrast, current GPUs handle dynamic branching quite well, especially when the branch behaves the same for all pixels in a draw call. Today much of the functionality variation, such as the number of lights, is handled at runtime. However, adding a large amount of functional variation to a shader incurs a different cost: an increase in register count and a corresponding reduction in occupancy, and thus performance.

See Section 18.4.5 for more details. So, compile-time variation is still valuable. It avoids including complex logic that will never be executed.

As an example, let us imagine an application that supports three different types of lights. Two light types are simple: point and directional. The third type is a generalized spotlight that supports tabulated illumination patterns and other complex features, requiring a significant amount of shader code to implement. However, say the generalized spotlight is used relatively rarely, with less than 5% of the lights in the application being this type. In the past, a separate shader variant would be compiled for each possible combination of counts of the three light types, to avoid dynamic branching. While this would not be needed today, it may still be beneficial to compile two separate variants, one for the case when the count of generalized spotlights is equal to or greater than 1, and one for the case where the count of such lights is exactly 0. Due to its simpler code, the second variant (which is most commonly used) is likely to have lower register occupancy and thus higher performance.

Modern material systems employ both runtime and compile-time shader variation. Even though the full burden is no longer handled only at compile time, the overall complexity and number of variations keep increasing, so a large number of shader variants still need to be compiled. For example, in some areas of the game *Destiny: The Taken King*, over 9000 compiled shader variations were used in a single frame [1750]. The number of possible variations can be much larger, e.g., the Unity rendering system has shaders with close to 100 billion possible variants. Only the variants that are actually used are compiled, but the shader compilation system had to be redesigned to handle the huge number of possible variants [1439].

Material-system designers employ different strategies to address these design goals. Although these are sometimes presented as mutually exclusive system architectures [342], these strategies can be—and usually are—combined in the same system. These strategies include the following:

- Code reuse—Implementing functions in shared files, using `#include` preprocessor directives to access those functions from any shader that needs them.

- Subtractive—A shader, often referred to as an *übershader* or *supershader* [1170, 1784], that aggregates a large set of functionality, using a combination of compile-time preprocessor conditionals and dynamic branching to remove unused parts and to switch between mutually exclusive alternatives.

- Additive—Various bits of functionality are defined as nodes with input and output connectors, and these are composed together. This is similar to the code reuse strategy but is more structured. The composition of nodes can be done via text [342] or a visual graph editor. The latter is intended to make it easier for non-engineers, such as technical artists, to author new material templates [1750, 1802]. Typically only part of the shader is accessible to visual graph authoring. For example, in the Unreal Engine the graph editor can only affect the computation of shading model inputs [1802]. See Figure 5.13.

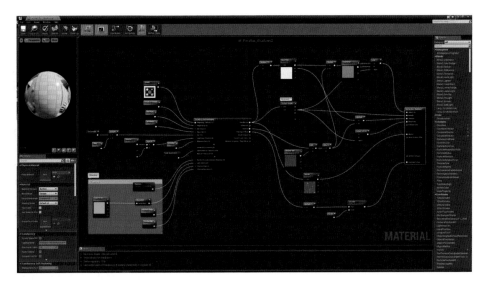

Figure 5.13. The Unreal Engine material editor. Note the tall node on the right side of the node graph. The input connectors of this node correspond to various shading inputs used by the rendering engine, including all the shading model parameters. *(Material sample courtesy of Epic Games.)*

- Template-based—An interface is defined, into which different implementations can be plugged as long as they conform to that interface. This is a bit more formal than the additive strategy and is typically used for larger chunks of functionality. A common example for such an interface is the separation between the calculation of shading model parameters and the computation of the shading model itself. The Unreal Engine [1802] has different "material domains," including the Surface domain for computing shading model parameters and the Light Function domain for computing a scalar value that modulates c_{light} for a given light source. A similar "surface shader" structure also exists in Unity [1437]. Note that deferred shading techniques (discussed in Chapter 20) enforce a similar structure, with the G-buffer serving as the interface.

For more specific examples, several chapters in the (now free) book *WebGL Insights* [301] discuss how a variety of engines control their shader pipelines. Besides composition, there are several other important design considerations for modern material systems, such as the need to support multiple platforms with minimal duplication of shader code. This includes variations in functionality to account for performance and capability differences among platforms, shading languages, and APIs. The *Destiny* shader system [1750] is a representative solution to this type of problem. It uses a proprietary preprocessor layer that takes shaders written in a custom shading language dialect. This allows writing platform-independent materials with automatic translation to different shading languages and implementations. The Unreal Engine [1802] and Unity [1436] have similar systems.

The material system also needs to ensure good performance. Besides specialized compilation of shading variants, there are a few other common optimizations the material system can perform. The *Destiny* shader system and the Unreal Engine automatically detect computations that are constant across a draw call (such as the warm and cool color computation in the earlier implementation example) and move it outside of the shader. Another example is the scoping system used in *Destiny* to differentiate between constants that are updated at different frequencies (e.g., once per frame, once per light, once per object) and update each set of constants at the appropriate times to reduce API overhead.

As we have seen, implementing a shading equation is a matter of deciding what parts can be simplified, how frequently to compute various expressions, and how the user is able to modify and control the appearance. The ultimate output of the rendering pipeline is a color and blend value. The remaining sections on antialiasing, transparency, and image display detail how these values are combined and modified for display.

5.4 Aliasing and Antialiasing

Imagine a large black triangle moving slowly across a white background. As a screen grid cell is covered by the triangle, the pixel value representing this cell should smoothly drop in intensity. What typically happens in basic renderers of all sorts is that the moment the grid cell's center is covered, the pixel color immediately goes from white to black. Standard GPU rendering is no exception. See the leftmost column of Figure 5.14.

Triangles show up in pixels as either there or not there. Lines drawn have a similar problem. The edges have a jagged look because of this, and so this visual artifact is called "the jaggies," which turn into "the crawlies" when animated. More formally, this problem is called *aliasing*, and efforts to avoid it are called *antialiasing* techniques.

The subject of sampling theory and digital filtering is large enough to fill its own book [559, 1447, 1729]. As this is a key area of rendering, the basic theory of sampling and filtering will be presented. We will then focus on what currently can be done in real time to alleviate aliasing artifacts.

5.4.1 Sampling and Filtering Theory

The process of rendering images is inherently a sampling task. This is so since the generation of an image is the process of sampling a three-dimensional scene in order to obtain color values for each pixel in the image (an array of discrete pixels). To use texture mapping (Chapter 6), texels have to be resampled to get good results under varying conditions. To generate a sequence of images in an animation, the animation is often sampled at uniform time intervals. This section is an introduction to the topic of sampling, reconstruction, and filtering. For simplicity, most material will be

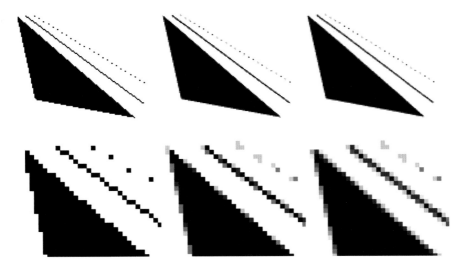

Figure 5.14. The upper row shows three images with different levels of antialiasing of a triangle, a line, and some points. The lower row images are magnifications of the upper row. The leftmost column uses only one sample per pixel, which means that no antialiasing is used. The middle column images were rendered with four samples per pixel (in a grid pattern), and the right column used eight samples per pixel (in a 4 × 4 checkerboard, half the squares sampled).

presented in one dimension. These concepts extend naturally to two dimensions as well, and can thus be used when handling two-dimensional images.

Figure 5.15 shows how a continuous signal is being sampled at uniformly spaced intervals, that is, discretized. The goal of this *sampling* process is

to represent information digitally. In doing so, the amount of information is reduced. However, the sampled signal needs to be *reconstructed* to recover the original signal. This is done by *filtering* the sampled signal.

Whenever sampling is done, aliasing may occur. This is an unwanted artifact, and we need to battle aliasing to generate pleasing images. A classic example of aliasing seen in old Westerns is a spinning wagon wheel filmed by a movie camera. Because

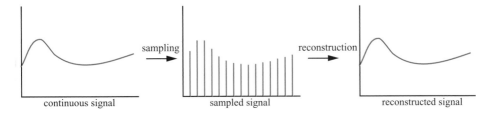

Figure 5.15. A continuous signal (left) is sampled (middle), and then the original signal is recovered by reconstruction (right).

Figure 5.16. The top row shows a spinning wheel (original signal). This is inadequately sampled in second row, making it appear to move in the opposite direction. This is an example of aliasing due to a too low sampling rate. In the third row, the sampling rate is exactly two samples per revolution, and we cannot determine in which direction the wheel is spinning. This is the Nyquist limit. In the fourth row, the sampling rate is higher than two samples per revolution, and we suddenly can see that the wheel spins in the right direction.

the spokes move much faster than the camera records images, the wheel may appear to be spinning slowly (backward or forward), or may even look like it is not rotating at all. This can be seen in Figure 5.16. The effect occurs because the images of the wheel are taken in a series of time steps, and is called *temporal aliasing*.

Common examples of aliasing in computer graphics are the "jaggies" of a rasterized line or triangle edge, flickering highlights known as "fireflies", and when a texture with a checker pattern is minified (Section 6.2.2).

Aliasing occurs when a signal is being sampled at too low a frequency. The sampled signal then appears to be a signal of lower frequency than the original. This is illustrated in Figure 5.17. For a signal to be sampled properly (i.e., so that it is possible to reconstruct the original signal from the samples), the sampling frequency

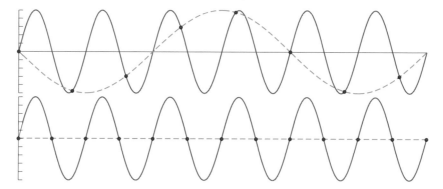

Figure 5.17. The solid blue line is the original signal, the red circles indicate uniformly spaced sample points, and the green dashed line is the reconstructed signal. The top figure shows a too low sample rate. Therefore, the reconstructed signal appears to be of lower frequency, i.e., an alias of the original signal. The bottom shows a sampling rate of exactly twice the frequency of the original signal, and the reconstructed signal is here a horizontal line. It can be proven that if the sampling rate is increased ever so slightly, perfect reconstruction is possible.

has to be more than twice the maximum frequency of the signal to be sampled. This is often called the *sampling theorem*, and the sampling frequency is called the *Nyquist rate* [1447] or *Nyquist limit*, after Harry Nyquist (1889–1976), a Swedish scientist who discovered this in 1928. The Nyquist limit is also illustrated in Figure 5.16. The fact that the theorem uses the term "maximum frequency" implies that the signal has to be *band-limited*, which just means that there are not any frequencies above a certain limit. Put another way, the signal has to be smooth enough relative to the spacing between neighboring samples.

A three-dimensional scene is normally never band-limited when rendered with point samples. Edges of triangles, shadow boundaries, and other phenomena produce a signal that changes discontinuously and so produces frequencies that are infinite [252]. Also, no matter how closely packed the samples are, objects can still be small enough that they do not get sampled at all. Thus, it is impossible to entirely avoid aliasing problems when using point samples to render a scene, and we almost always use point sampling. However, at times it is possible to know when a signal is band-limited. One example is when a texture is applied to a surface. It is possible to compute the frequency of the texture samples compared to the sampling rate of the pixel. If this frequency is lower than the Nyquist limit, then no special action is needed to properly sample the texture. If the frequency is too high, then a variety of algorithms are used to band-limit the texture (Section 6.2.2).

Reconstruction

Given a band-limited sampled signal, we will now discuss how the original signal can be reconstructed from the sampled signal. To do this, a filter must be used. Three commonly used filters are shown in Figure 5.18. Note that the area of the filter should always be one, otherwise the reconstructed signal can appear to grow or shrink.

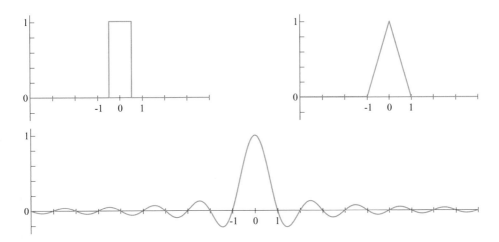

Figure 5.18. The top left shows the box filter, and the top right the tent filter. The bottom shows the sinc filter (which has been clamped on the x-axis here).

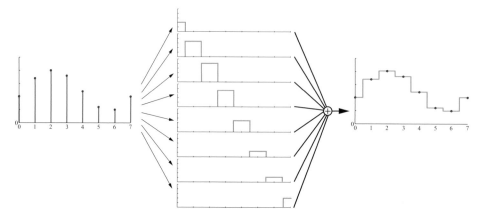

Figure 5.19. The sampled signal (left) is reconstructed using the box filter. This is done by placing the box filter over each sample point, and scaling it in the y-direction so that the height of the filter is the same as the sample point. The sum is the reconstruction signal (right).

In Figure 5.19, the box filter (nearest neighbor) is used to reconstruct a sampled signal. This is the worst filter to use, as the resulting signal is a noncontinuous stair case. Still, it is often used in computer graphics because of its simplicity. As can be seen in the illustration, the box filter is placed over each sample point, and then scaled so that the topmost point of the filter coincides with the sample point. The sum of all these scaled and translated box functions is the reconstructed signal shown to the right.

The box filter can be replaced with any other filter. In Figure 5.20, the tent filter, also called the triangle filter, is used to reconstruct a sampled signal. Note that this

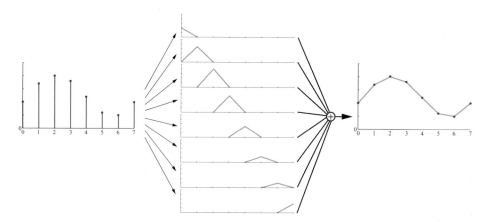

Figure 5.20. The sampled signal (left) is reconstructed using the tent filter. The reconstructed signal is shown to the right.

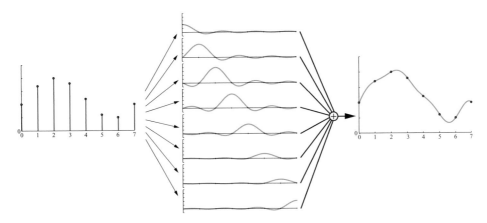

Figure 5.21. Here, the sinc filter is used to reconstruct the signal. The sinc filter is the ideal low-pass filter.

filter implements linear interpolation between neighboring sample points, and so it is better than the box filter, as the reconstructed signal now is continuous.

However, the smoothness of the reconstructed signal using a tent filter is poor; there are sudden slope changes at the sample points. This has to do with the fact that the tent filter is not a perfect reconstruction filter. To get perfect reconstruction the ideal *low-pass filter* has to be used. A frequency component of a signal is a sine wave: $\sin(2\pi f)$, where f is the frequency of that component. Given this, a low-pass filter removes all frequency components with frequencies higher than a certain frequency defined by the filter. Intuitively, the low-pass filter removes sharp features of the signal, i.e., the filter blurs it. The ideal low-pass filter is the sinc filter (Figure 5.18 bottom):

$$\mathrm{sinc}(x) = \frac{\sin(\pi x)}{\pi x}. \tag{5.22}$$

The theory of Fourier analysis [1447] explains why the sinc filter is the ideal low-pass filter. Briefly, the reasoning is as follows. The ideal low-pass filter is a box filter in the frequency domain, which removes all frequencies above the filter width when it is multiplied with the signal. Transforming the box filter from the frequency domain to the spatial domain gives a sinc function. At the same time, the multiplication operation is transformed into the *convolution* function, which is what we have been using in this section, without actually describing the term.

Using the sinc filter to reconstruct the signal gives a smoother result, as shown in Figure 5.21. The sampling process introduces high-frequency components (abrupt changes) in the signal, and the task of the low-pass filter is to remove these. In fact, the sinc filter eliminates all sine waves with frequencies higher than $1/2$ the sampling rate. The sinc function, as presented in Equation 5.22, is the perfect reconstruction filter when the sampling frequency is 1.0 (i.e., the maximum frequency of the sampled signal must be smaller than $1/2$). More generally, assume the sampling frequency is f_s, that is, the interval between neighboring samples is $1/f_s$. For such a case, the perfect reconstruction filter is $\mathrm{sinc}(f_s x)$, and it eliminates all frequencies higher than $f_s/2$. This is useful when resampling the signal (next section). However, the filter width of the sinc is infinite and is negative in some areas, so it is rarely useful in practice.

There is a useful middle ground between the low-quality box and tent filters on one hand, and the impractical sinc filter on the other. Most widely used filter functions [1214, 1289, 1413, 1793] are between these extremes. All these filter functions have some approximation to the sinc function, but with a limit on how many pixels they influence. The filters that most closely approximate the sinc function have negative values over part of their domain. For applications where negative filter values are undesirable or impractical, filters with no negative lobes (often referred to generically as Gaussian filters, since they either derive from or resemble a Gaussian curve) are typically used [1402]. Section 12.1 discusses filter functions and their use in more detail.

After using any filter, a continuous signal is obtained. However, in computer graphics we cannot display continuous signals directly, but we can use them to resample the continuous signal to another size, i.e., either enlarging the signal, or diminishing it. This topic is discussed next.

Resampling

Resampling is used to magnify or minify a sampled signal. Assume that the original sample points are located at integer coordinates $(0, 1, 2, \dots)$, that is, with unit intervals between samples. Furthermore, assume that after resampling we want the new sample points to be located uniformly with an interval a between samples. For $a > 1$, minification (downsampling) takes place, and for $a < 1$, magnification (upsampling) occurs.

Magnification is the simpler case of the two, so let us start with that. Assume the sampled signal is reconstructed as shown in the previous section. Intuitively, since the signal now is perfectly reconstructed and continuous, all that is needed is to resample the reconstructed signal at the desired intervals. This process can be seen in Figure 5.22.

However, this technique does not work when minification occurs. The frequency of the original signal is too high for the sampling rate to avoid aliasing. Instead it has been shown that a filter using $\mathrm{sinc}(x/a)$ should be used to create a continuous signal from the sampled one [1447, 1661]. After that, resampling at the desired intervals can take place. This can be seen in Figure 5.23. Said another way, by using $\mathrm{sinc}(x/a)$ as a filter here, the width of the low-pass filter is increased, so that more of the signal's higher frequency content is removed. As shown in the figure, the filter width (of the individual sinc's) is doubled to decrease the resampling rate to half the original sampling rate. Relating this to a digital image, this is similar to first blurring it (to remove high frequencies) and then resampling the image at a lower resolution.

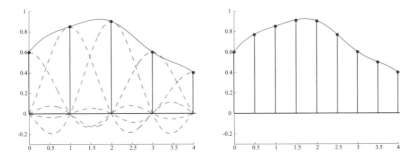

Figure 5.22. On the left is the sampled signal, and the reconstructed signal. On the right, the reconstructed signal has been resampled at double the sample rate, that is, magnification has taken place.

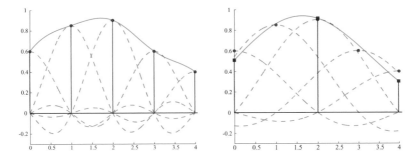

Figure 5.23. On the left is the sampled signal, and the reconstructed signal. On the right, the filter width has doubled in order to double the interval between the samples, that is, minification has taken place.

With the theory of sampling and filtering available as a framework, the various algorithms used in real-time rendering to reduce aliasing are now discussed.

5.4.2 Screen-Based Antialiasing

Edges of triangles produce noticeable artifacts if not sampled and filtered well. Shadow boundaries, specular highlights, and other phenomena where the color is changing rapidly can cause similar problems. The algorithms discussed in this section help improve the rendering quality for these cases. They have the common thread that they are screen based, i.e., that they operate only on the output samples of the pipeline. There is no one best antialiasing technique, as each has different advantages in terms of quality, ability to capture sharp details or other phenomena, appearance during movement, memory cost, GPU requirements, and speed.

In the black triangle example in Figure 5.14, one problem is the low sampling rate. A single sample is taken at the center of each pixel's grid cell, so the most that is

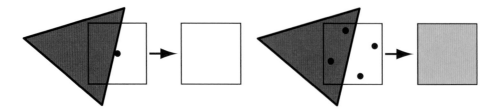

Figure 5.24. On the left, a red triangle is rendered with one sample at the center of the pixel. Since the triangle does not cover the sample, the pixel will be white, even though a substantial part of the pixel is covered by the red triangle. On the right, four samples are used per pixel, and as can be seen, two of these are covered by the red triangle, which results in a pink pixel color.

known about the cell is whether or not the center is covered by the triangle. By using more samples per screen grid cell and blending these in some fashion, a better pixel color can be computed. This is illustrated in Figure 5.24.

The general strategy of screen-based antialiasing schemes is to use a sampling pattern for the screen and then weight and sum the samples to produce a pixel color, **p**:

$$\mathbf{p}(x, y) = \sum_{i=1}^{n} w_i \mathbf{c}(i, x, y), \qquad (5.23)$$

where n is the number of samples taken for a pixel. The function $\mathbf{c}(i, x, y)$ is a sample color and w_i is a weight, in the range $[0, 1]$, that the sample will contribute to the overall pixel color. The sample position is taken based on which sample it is in the series $1, \ldots, n$, and the function optionally also uses the integer part of the pixel location (x, y). In other words, where the sample is taken on the screen grid is different for each sample, and optionally the sampling pattern can vary from pixel to pixel. Samples are normally point samples in real-time rendering systems (and most other rendering systems, for that matter). So, the function $\mathbf{c}$ can be thought of as two functions. First, a function $\mathbf{f}(i, n)$ retrieves the floating point (x_f, y_f) location on the screen where a sample is needed. This location on the screen is then sampled, i.e., the color at that precise point is retrieved. The sampling scheme is chosen and the rendering pipeline configured to compute the samples at particular subpixel locations, typically based on a per-frame (or per-application) setting.

The other variable in antialiasing is w_i, the weight of each sample. These weights sum to one. Most methods used in real-time rendering systems give a uniform weight to their samples, i.e., $w_i = \frac{1}{n}$. The default mode for graphics hardware, a single sample at the center of the pixel, is the simplest case of the antialiasing equation above. There is only one term, the weight of this term is one, and the sampling function $\mathbf{f}$ always returns the center of the pixel being sampled.

Antialiasing algorithms that compute more than one full sample per pixel are called *supersampling* (or *oversampling*) methods. Conceptually simplest, *full-scene antialiasing* (FSAA), also known as "supersampling antialiasing" (SSAA), renders the scene at a higher resolution and then filters neighboring samples to create an image. For example, say an image of 1280×1024 pixels is desired. If you render an image of 2560×2048 offscreen and then average each 2×2 pixel area on the screen, the desired image is generated with four samples per pixel, filtered using a box filter. Note that this corresponds to 2×2 grid sampling in Figure 5.25. This method is costly, as all subsamples must be fully shaded and filled, with a z-buffer depth per sample. FSAA's main advantage is simplicity. Other, lower-quality versions of this method sample at twice the rate on only one screen axis, and so are called 1×2 or 2×1 supersampling. Typically, powers-of-two resolution and a box filter are used for simplicity. NVIDIA's *dynamic super resolution* feature is a more elaborate form of supersampling, where the scene is rendered at some higher resolution and a 13-sample Gaussian filter is used to generate the displayed image [1848].

A sampling method related to supersampling is based on the idea of the *accumulation buffer* [637, 1115]. Instead of one large offscreen buffer, this method uses a buffer that has the same resolution as the desired image, but with more bits of color per channel. To obtain a 2×2 sampling of a scene, four images are generated, with the view moved half a pixel in the screen x- or y-direction as needed. Each image generated is based on a different sample position within the grid cell. The additional costs of having to re-render the scene a few times per frame and copy the result to the screen makes this algorithm costly for real-time rendering systems. It is useful for generating higher-quality images when performance is not critical, since any number of samples, placed anywhere, can be used per pixel [1679]. The accumulation buffer used to be a separate piece of hardware. It was supported directly in the OpenGL API, but was deprecated in version 3.0. On modern GPUs the accumulation buffer concept can be implemented in a pixel shader by using a higher-precision color format for the output buffer.

Additional samples are needed when phenomena such as object edges, specular highlights, and sharp shadows cause abrupt color changes. Shadows can often be made softer and highlights smoother to avoid aliasing. Particular object types can be increased in size, such as electrical wires, so that they are guaranteed to cover at least one pixel at each location along their length [1384]. Aliasing of object edges still remains as a major sampling problem. It is possible to use analytical methods, where object edges are detected during rendering and their influence is factored in, but these are often more expensive and less robust than simply taking more samples. However, GPU features such as conservative rasterization and rasterizer order views have opened up new possibilities [327].

Techniques such as supersampling and accumulation buffering work by generating samples that are fully specified with individually computed shades and depths. The overall gains are relatively low and the cost is high, as each sample has to run through a pixel shader.

Multisampling antialiasing (MSAA) lessens the high computational costs by computing the surface's shade once per pixel and sharing this result among the samples. Pixels may have, say, four (x, y) sample locations per fragment, each with their own

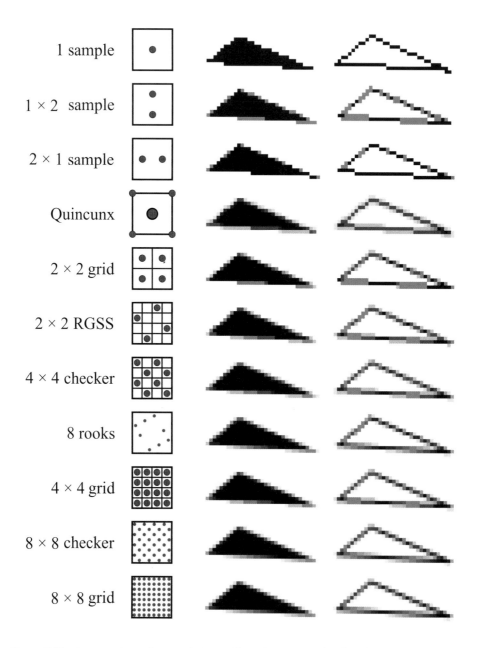

Figure 5.25. A comparison of some pixel sampling schemes, ranging from least to most samples per pixel. Quincunx shares the corner samples and weights its center sample to be worth half of the pixel's final color. The 2×2 rotated grid captures more gray levels for the nearly horizontal edge than a straight 2×2 grid. Similarly, the 8 rooks pattern captures more gray levels for such lines than a 4×4 grid, despite using fewer samples.

MSAA:

#	color & z
0	
1	
2	
3	

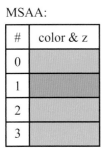 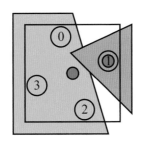 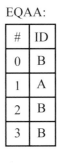

EQAA:

#	ID
0	B
1	A
2	B
3	B

ID	color & z
A	
B	

Figure 5.26. In the middle, a pixel with two objects overlapping it. The red object covers three samples, the blue just one. Pixel shader evaluation locations are shown in green. Since the red triangle covers the center of the pixel, this location is used for shader evaluation. The pixel shader for the blue object is evaluated at the sample's location. For MSAA, a separate color and depth is stored at all four locations. On the right the 2f4x mode for EQAA is shown. The four samples now have four ID values, which index a table of the two colors and depths stored.

color and z-depth, but the pixel shader is evaluated only once for each object fragment applied to the pixel. If all MSAA positional samples are covered by the fragment, the shading sample is evaluated at the center of the pixel. If instead the fragment covers fewer positional samples, the shading sample's position can be shifted to better represent the positions covered. Doing so avoids shade sampling off the edge of a texture, for example. This position adjustment is called *centroid sampling* or *centroid interpolation* and is done automatically by the GPU, if enabled. Centroid sampling avoids off-triangle problems but can cause derivative computations to return incorrect values [530, 1041]. See Figure 5.26.

MSAA is faster than a pure supersampling scheme because the fragment is shaded only once. It focuses effort on sampling the fragment's pixel coverage at a higher rate and sharing the computed shade. It is possible to save more memory by further decoupling sampling and coverage, which in turn can make antialiasing faster still—the less memory touched, the quicker the render. NVIDIA introduced *coverage sampling antialiasing* (CSAA) in 2006, and AMD followed suit with *enhanced quality antialiasing* (EQAA). These techniques work by storing only the coverage for the fragment at a higher sampling rate. For example, EQAA's "2f4x" mode stores two color and depth values, shared among four sample locations. The colors and depths are no longer stored for particular locations but rather saved in a table. Each of the four samples then needs just one bit to specify which of the two stored values is associated with its location. See Figure 5.26. The coverage samples specify the contribution of each fragment to the final pixel color. If the number of colors stored is exceeded, a stored color is evicted and its samples are marked as unknown. These samples do not contribute to the final color [382, 383]. For most scenes there are relatively few pixels containing three or more visible opaque fragments that are radically different in shade, so this scheme performs well in practice [1405]. However, for highest quality, the game *Forza Horizon 2* went with 4× MSAA, though EQAA had a performance benefit [1002].

Once all geometry has been rendered to a multiple-sample buffer, a *resolve* operation is then performed. This procedure averages the sample colors together to determine the color for the pixel. It is worth noting that a problem can arise when using multisampling with high dynamic range color values. In such cases, to avoid artifacts you normally need to tone-map the values before the resolve [1375]. This can be expensive, so a simpler approximation to the tone map function or other methods can be used [862, 1405].

By default, MSAA is resolved with a box filter. In 2007 ATI introduced *custom filter antialiasing* (CFAA) [1625], with the capabilities of using narrow and wide tent filters that extend slightly into other pixel cells. This mode has since been supplanted by EQAA support. On modern GPUs pixel or compute shaders can access the MSAA samples and use whatever reconstruction filter is desired, including one that samples from the surrounding pixels' samples. A wider filter can reduce aliasing, though at the loss of sharp details. Pettineo [1402, 1405] found that the cubic smoothstep and B-spline filters with a filter width of 2 or 3 pixels gave the best results overall. There is also a performance cost, as even emulating the default box filter resolve will take longer with a custom shader, and a wider filter kernel means increased sample access costs.

NVIDIA's built-in TXAA support similarly uses a better reconstruction filter over a wider area than a single pixel to give a better result. It and the newer MFAA (multi-frame antialiasing) scheme both also use *temporal antialiasing* (TAA), a general class of techniques that use results from previous frames to improve the image. In part such techniques are made possible due to functionality that lets the programmer set the MSAA sampling pattern per frame [1406]. Such techniques can attack aliasing problems such as the spinning wagon wheel and can also improve edge rendering quality.

Imagine performing a sampling pattern "manually" by generating a series of images where each render uses a different location within the pixel for where the sample is taken. This offsetting is done by appending a tiny translation on to the projection matrix [1938]. The more images that are generated and averaged together, the better the result. This concept of using multiple offset images is used in temporal antialiasing algorithms. A single image is generated, possibly with MSAA or another method, and the previous images are blended in. Usually just two to four frames are used [382, 836, 1405]. Older images may be given exponentially less weight [862], though this can have the effect of the frame shimmering if the viewer and scene do not move, so often equal weighting of just the last and current frame is done. With each frame's samples in a different subpixel location, the weighted sum of these samples gives a better coverage estimate of the edge than a single frame does. So, a system using the latest two frames averaged together can give a better result. No additional samples are needed for each frame, which is what makes this type of approach so appealing. It is even possible to use temporal sampling to allow generation of a lower-resolution image that is upscaled to the display's resolution [1110]. In addition, illumination methods or other techniques that require many samples for a good result can instead use fewer samples each frame, since the results will be blended over several frames [1938].

While providing antialiasing for static scenes at no additional sampling cost, this type of algorithm has a few problems when used for temporal antialiasing. If the frames are not weighted equally, objects in a static scene can exhibit a shimmer. Rapidly moving objects or quick camera moves can cause ghosting, i.e., trails left behind the object due to the contributions of previous frames. One solution to ghosting is to perform such antialiasing on only slow-moving objects [1110]. Another important approach is to use *reprojection* (Section 12.2) to better correlate the previous and current frames' objects. In such schemes, objects generate motion vectors that are stored in a separate "velocity buffer" (Section 12.5). These vectors are used to correlate the previous frame with the current one, i.e., the vector is subtracted from the current pixel location to find the previous frame's color pixel for that object's surface location. Samples unlikely to be part of the surface in the current frame are discarded [1912]. Because no extra samples, and so relatively little extra work, are needed for temporal antialiasing, there has been a strong interest and wider adoption of this type of algorithm in recent years. Some of this attention has been because deferred shading techniques (Section 20.1) are not compatible with MSAA and other multisampling support [1486]. Approaches vary and, depending on the application's content and goals, a range of techniques for avoiding artifacts and improving quality have been developed [836, 1154, 1405, 1533, 1938]. Wihlidal's presentation [1885], for example, shows how EQAA, temporal antialiasing, and various filtering techniques applied to a checkerboard sampling pattern can combine to maintain quality while lowering the number of pixel shader invocations. Iglesias-Guitian et al. [796] summarize previous work and present their scheme to use pixel history and prediction to minimize filtering artifacts. Patney et al. [1357] extend TAA work by Karis and Lottes on the Unreal Engine 4 implementation [862] for use in virtual reality applications, adding variable-sized sampling along with compensation for eye movement (Section 21.3.2).

Sampling Patterns

Effective sampling patterns are a key element in reducing aliasing, temporal and otherwise. Naiman [1257] shows that humans are most disturbed by aliasing on near-horizontal and near-vertical edges. Edges with near 45 degrees slope are next most disturbing. *Rotated grid supersampling* (RGSS) uses a rotated square pattern to give more vertical and horizontal resolution within the pixel. Figure 5.25 shows an example of this pattern.

The RGSS pattern is a form of *Latin hypercube* or *N-rooks sampling*, in which n samples are placed in an $n \times n$ grid, with one sample per row and column [1626]. With RGSS, the four samples are each in a separate row and column of the 4×4 subpixel grid. Such patterns are particularly good for capturing nearly horizontal and vertical edges compared to a regular 2×2 sampling pattern, where such edges are likely to cover an even number of samples, so giving fewer effective levels.

N-rooks is a start at creating a good sampling pattern, but it is not sufficient. For example, the samples could all be places along the diagonal of a subpixel grid and so give a poor result for edges that are nearly parallel to this diagonal. See Figure 5.27.

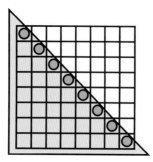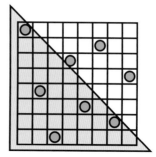

Figure 5.27. *N*-rooks sampling. On the left is a legal *N*-rooks pattern, but it performs poorly in capturing triangle edges that are diagonal along its line, as all sample locations will be either inside or outside the triangle as this triangle shifts. On the right is a pattern that will capture this and other edges more effectively.

For better sampling we want to avoid putting two samples near each other. We also want a uniform distribution, spreading samples evenly over the area. To form such patterns, *stratified sampling* techniques such as Latin hypercube sampling are combined with other methods such as jittering, Halton sequences, and Poisson disk sampling [1413, 1758].

In practice GPU manufacturers usually hard-wire such sampling patterns into their hardware for multisampling antialiasing. Figure 5.28 shows some MSAA patterns used in practice. For temporal antialiasing, the coverage pattern is whatever the programmer wants, as the sample locations can be varied frame to frame. For example, Karis [862] finds that a basic *Halton sequence* works better than any MSAA pattern provided by the GPU. A Halton sequence generates samples in space that appear random but have low discrepancy, that is, they are well distributed over the space and none are clustered [1413, 1938].

While a subpixel grid pattern results in a better approximation of how each triangle covers a grid cell, it is not ideal. A scene can be made of objects that are arbitrarily

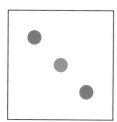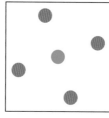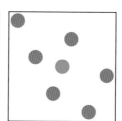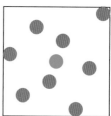

Figure 5.28. MSAA sampling patterns for AMD and NVIDIA graphics accelerators. The green square is the location of the shading sample, and the red squares are the positional samples computed and saved. From left to right: 2×, 4×, 6× (AMD), and 8× (NVIDIA) sampling. *(Generated by the D3D FSAA Viewer.)*

small on the screen, meaning that no sampling rate can ever perfectly capture them. If these tiny objects or features form a pattern, sampling at constant intervals can result in Moiré fringes and other interference patterns. The grid pattern used in supersampling is particularly likely to alias.

One solution is to use *stochastic sampling*, which gives a more randomized pattern. Patterns such as those in Figure 5.28 certainly qualify. Imagine a fine-toothed comb at a distance, with a few teeth covering each pixel. A regular pattern can give severe artifacts as the sampling pattern goes in and out of phase with the tooth frequency. Having a less ordered sampling pattern can break up these patterns. The randomization tends to replace repetitive aliasing effects with noise, to which the human visual system is much more forgiving [1413]. A pattern with less structure helps, but it can still exhibit aliasing when repeated pixel to pixel. One solution is use a different sampling pattern at each pixel, or to change each sampling location over time. *Interleaved sampling*indexsampling!interleaved, where each pixel of a set has a different sampling pattern, has occasionally been supported in hardware over the past decades. For example, ATI's SMOOTHVISION allowed up to 16 samples per pixel and up to 16 different user-defined sampling patterns that could be intermingled in a repeating pattern (e.g., in a 4×4 pixel tile). Molnar [1234], as well as Keller and Heidrich [880], found that using interleaved stochastic sampling minimizes the aliasing artifacts formed when using the same pattern for every pixel.

A few other GPU-supported algorithms are worth noting. One real-time antialiasing scheme that lets samples affect more than one pixel is NVIDIA's older Quincunx method [365]. "Quincunx" means an arrangement of five objects, four in a square and the fifth in the center, such as the pattern of five dots on a six-sided die. Quincunx multisampling antialiasing uses this pattern, putting the four outer samples at the corners of the pixel. See Figure 5.25. Each corner sample value is distributed to its four neighboring pixels. Instead of weighting each sample equally (as most other real-time schemes do), the center sample is given a weight of $\frac{1}{2}$, and each corner sample has a weight of $\frac{1}{8}$. Because of this sharing, an average of only two samples are needed per pixel, and the results are considerably better than two-sample FSAA methods [1678]. This pattern approximates a two-dimensional tent filter, which, as discussed in the previous section, is superior to the box filter.

Quincunx sampling can also be applied to temporal antialiasing by using a single sample per pixel [836, 1677]. Each frame is offset half a pixel in each axis from the frame before, with the offset direction alternating between frames. The previous frame provides the pixel corner samples, and bilinear interpolation is used to rapidly compute the contribution per pixel. The result is averaged with the current frame. Equal weighting of each frame means there are no shimmer artifacts for a static view. The issue of aligning moving objects is still present, but the scheme itself is simple to code and gives a much better look while using only one sample per pixel per frame.

When used in a single frame, Quincunx has a low cost of only two samples by sharing samples at the pixel boundaries. The RGSS pattern is better at capturing more gradations of nearly horizontal and vertical edges. First developed for mobile

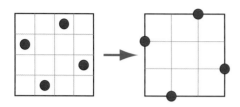 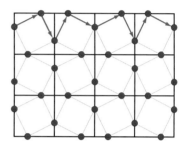

Figure 5.29. To the left, the RGSS sampling pattern is shown. This costs four samples per pixel. By moving these locations out to the pixel edges, sample sharing can occur across edges. However, for this to work out, every other pixel must have a reflected sample pattern, as shown on the right. The resulting sample pattern is called FLIPQUAD and costs two samples per pixel.

graphics, the FLIPQUAD pattern combines both of these desirable features [22]. Its advantages are that the cost is only two samples per pixel, and the quality is similar to RGSS (which costs four samples per pixel). This sampling pattern is shown in Figure 5.29. Other inexpensive sampling patterns that exploit sample sharing are explored by Hasselgren et al. [677].

Like Quincunx, the two-sample FLIPQUAD pattern can also be used with temporal antialiasing and spread over two frames. Drobot [382, 383, 1154] tackles the question of which two-sample pattern is best in his *hybrid reconstruction antialiasing* (HRAA) work. He explores different sampling patterns for temporal antialiasing, finding the FLIPQUAD pattern to be the best of the five tested. A checkerboard pattern has also seen use with temporal antialiasing. El Mansouri [415] discusses using two-sample MSAA to create a checkerboard render to reduce shader costs while addressing aliasing issues. Jimenez [836] uses SMAA, temporal antialiasing, and a variety of other techniques to provide a solution where antialiasing quality can be changed in response to rendering engine load. Carpentier and Ishiyama [231] sample on edges, rotating the sampling grid by 45°. They combine this temporal antialiasing scheme with FXAA (discussed later) to efficiently render on higher-resolution displays.

Morphological Methods

Aliasing often results from edges, such as those formed by geometry, sharp shadows, or bright highlights. The knowledge that aliasing has a structure associated with it can be exploited to give a better antialiased result. In 2009 Reshetov [1483] presented an algorithm along these lines, calling it *morphological antialiasing* (MLAA). "Morphological" means "relating to structure or shape." Earlier work had been done in this area [830], as far back as 1983 by Bloomenthal [170]. Reshetov's paper reinvigorated research into alternatives to multisampling approaches, emphasizing searching for and reconstructing edges [1486].

This form of antialiasing is performed as a post-process. That is, rendering is done in the usual fashion, then the results are fed to a process that generates the

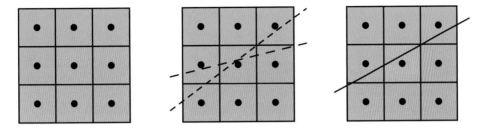

Figure 5.30. Morphological antialiasing. On the left is the aliased image. The goal is to determine the likely orientation of the edge that formed it. In the middle, the algorithm notes the likelihood of an edge by examining neighbors. Given the samples, two possible edge locations are shown. On the right, a best-guess edge is used to blend neighboring colors into the center pixel in proportion to the estimated coverage. This process is repeated for every pixel in the image.

antialiased result. A wide range of techniques have been developed since 2009. Those that rely on additional buffers such as depths and normals can provide better results, such as *subpixel reconstruction antialiasing* (SRAA) [43, 829], but are then applicable for antialiasing only geometric edges. Analytical approaches, such as *geometry buffer antialiasing* (GBAA) and *distance-to-edge antialiasing* (DEAA), have the renderer compute additional information about where triangle edges are located, e.g., how far the edge is from the center of the pixel [829].

The most general schemes need only the color buffer, meaning they can also improve edges from shadows, highlights, or various previously applied post-processing techniques, such as silhouette edge rendering (Section 15.2.3). For example, *directionally localized antialiasing* (DLAA) [52, 829] is based on the observation that an edge which is nearly vertical should be blurred horizontally, and likewise nearly horizontal edges should be blurred vertically with their neighbors.

More elaborate forms of edge detection attempt to find pixels likely to contain an edge at any angle and determine its coverage. The neighborhoods around potential edges are examined, with the goal of reconstructing as possible where the original edge was located. The edge's effect on the pixel can then be used to blend in neighboring pixels' colors. See Figure 5.30 for a conceptual view of the process.

Iourcha et al. [798] improve edge-finding by examine the MSAA samples in pixels to compute a better result. Note that edge prediction and blending can give a higher-precision result than sample-based algorithms. For example, a technique that uses four samples per pixel can give only five levels of blending for an object's edge: no samples covered, one covered, two, three, and four. The estimated edge location can have more locations and so provide better results.

There are several ways image-based algorithms can go astray. First, the edge may not be detected if the color difference between two objects is lower than the algorithm's threshold. Pixels where there are three or more distinct surfaces overlapping are difficult to interpret. Surfaces with high-contrast or high-frequency elements, where the color is changing rapidly from pixel to pixel, can cause algorithms to miss edges. In particular, text quality usually suffers when morphological antialiasing is applied to it. Object corners can be a challenge, with some algorithms giving them a rounded appearance. Curved lines can also be adversely affected by the assumption that edges are straight. A single pixel change can cause a large shift in how the edge is reconstructed, which can create noticeable artifacts frame to frame. One approach to ameliorate this problem is to use MSAA coverage masks to improve edge determination [1484].

Morphological antialiasing schemes use only the information that is provided. For example, an object thinner than a pixel in width, such as an electrical wire or rope, will have gaps on the screen wherever it does not happen to cover the center location of a pixel. Taking more samples can improve the quality in such situations; image-based antialiasing alone cannot. In addition, execution time can be variable depending on what content is viewed. For example, a view of a field of grass can take three times as long to antialias as a view of the sky [231].

All this said, image-based methods can provide antialiasing support for modest memory and processing costs, so they are used in many applications. The color-only versions are also decoupled from the rendering pipeline, making them easy to modify or disable, and can even be exposed as GPU driver options. The two most popular algorithms are *fast approximate antialiasing* (FXAA) [1079, 1080, 1084], and *subpixel morphological antialiasing* (SMAA) [828, 830, 834], in part because both provide solid (and free) source code implementations for a variety of machines. Both algorithms use color-only input, with SMAA having the advantage of being able to access MSAA samples. Each has its own variety of settings available, trading off between speed and quality. Costs are generally in the range of 1 to 2 milliseconds per frame, mainly because that is what video games are willing to spend. Finally, both algorithms can also take advantage of temporal antialiasing [1812]. Jimenez [836] presents an improved SMAA implementation, faster than FXAA, and describes a temporal antialiasing scheme. To conclude, we recommend the reader to the wide-ranging review by Reshetov and Jimenez [1486] of morphological techniques and their use in video games.

5.5 Transparency, Alpha, and Compositing

There are many different ways in which semitransparent objects can allow light to pass through them. For rendering algorithms, these can be roughly divided into light-based and view-based effects. Light-based effects are those in which the object causes light to be attenuated or diverted, causing other objects in the scene to be lit and rendered differently. View-based effects are those in which the semitransparent object itself is being rendered.

In this section we will deal with the simplest form of view-based transparency, in which the semitransparent object acts as an attenuator of the colors of the objects behind it. More elaborate view- and light-based effects such as frosted glass, the bending of light (refraction), attenuation of light due to the thickness of the transparent object, and reflectivity and transmission changes due to the viewing angle are discussed in later chapters.

One method for giving the illusion of transparency is called *screen-door transparency* [1244]. The idea is to render the transparent triangle with a pixel-aligned checkerboard fill pattern. That is, every other pixel of the triangle is rendered, thereby leaving the object behind it partially visible. Usually the pixels on the screen are close enough together that the checkerboard pattern itself is not visible. A major drawback of this method is that often only one transparent object can be convincingly rendered on one area of the screen. For example, if a transparent red object and transparent green object are rendered atop a blue object, only two of the three colors can appear on the checkerboard pattern. Also, the 50% checkerboard is limiting. Other larger pixel masks could be used to give other percentages, but these tend to create detectable patterns [1245].

That said, one advantage of this technique is its simplicity. Transparent objects can be rendered at any time, in any order, and no special hardware is needed. The transparency problem goes away by making all objects opaque at the pixels they cover. This same idea is used for antialiasing edges of cutout textures, but at a subpixel level, using a feature called *alpha to coverage* (Section 6.6).

Introduced by Enderton et al. [423], *stochastic transparency* uses subpixel screen-door masks combined with stochastic sampling. A reasonable, though noisy, image is created by using random stipple patterns to represent the alpha coverage of the fragment. See Figure 5.31. A large number of samples per pixel is needed for the result to look reasonable, as well as a sizable amount of memory for all the subpixel samples. What is appealing is that no blending is needed, and antialiasing, transparency, and any other phenomena that creates partially covered pixels are covered by a single mechanism.

Most transparency algorithms blend the transparent object's color with the color of the object behind it. For this, the concept of *alpha blending* is needed [199, 387, 1429]. When an object is rendered on the screen, an RGB color and a z-buffer depth are associated with each pixel. Another component, called alpha (α), can also be defined for each pixel the object covers. Alpha is a value describing the degree of opacity and coverage of an object fragment for a given pixel. An alpha of 1.0 means the object is opaque and entirely covers the pixel's area of interest; 0.0 means the pixel is not obscured at all, i.e., the fragment is entirely transparent.

A pixel's alpha can represent either opacity, coverage, or both, depending on the circumstances. For example, the edge of a soap bubble may cover three-quarters of the pixel, 0.75, and may be nearly transparent, letting nine-tenths of the light through to the eye, so it is one-tenth opaque, 0.1. Its alpha would then be $0.75 \times 0.1 = 0.075$. However, if we were using MSAA or similar antialiasing schemes, the coverage would be taken into account by the samples themselves. Three-quarters of the samples would be affected by the soap bubble. At each of these samples we would then use the 0.1 opacity value as the alpha.

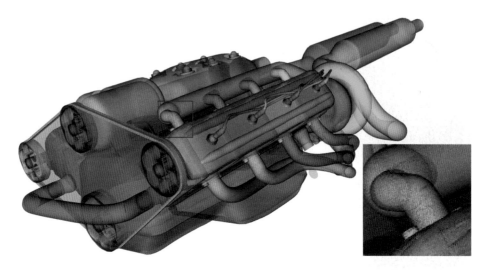

Figure 5.31. Stochastic transparency. The noise produced is displayed in the magnified area. *(Images from NVIDIA SDK 11 [1301] samples, courtesy of NVIDIA Corporation.)*

5.5.1 Blending Order

To make an object appear transparent, it is rendered on top of the existing scene with an alpha of less than 1.0. Each pixel covered by the object will receive a resulting RGBα (also called RGBA) from the pixel shader. Blending this fragment's value with the original pixel color is usually done using the **over** operator, as follows:

$$\mathbf{c}_o = \alpha_s \mathbf{c}_s + (1 - \alpha_s)\mathbf{c}_d \quad [\textbf{over operator}], \tag{5.24}$$

where $\mathbf{c}_s$ is the color of the transparent object (called the *source*), α_s is the object's alpha, $\mathbf{c}_d$ is the pixel color before blending (called the *destination*), and $\mathbf{c}_o$ is the resulting color due to placing the transparent object **over** the existing scene. In the case of the rendering pipeline sending in $\mathbf{c}_s$ and α_s, the pixel's original color $\mathbf{c}_d$ gets replaced by the result $\mathbf{c}_o$. If the incoming RGBα is, in fact, opaque ($\alpha_s = 1.0$), the equation simplifies to the full replacement of the pixel's color by the object's color.

EXAMPLE: BLENDING. A red semitransparent object is rendered onto a blue background. Say that at some pixel the RGB shade of the object is $(0.9, 0.2, 0.1)$, the background is $(0.1, 0.1, 0.9)$, and the object's opacity is set at 0.6. The blend of these two colors is then

$$0.6(0.9, 0.2, 0.1) + (1 - 0.6)(0.1, 0.1, 0.9),$$

which gives a color of $(0.58, 0.16, 0.42)$. $\qquad\qquad\qquad\qquad\qquad\qquad\qquad\square$

The **over** operator gives a semitransparent look to the object being rendered. Transparency done this way works, in the sense that we perceive something as transparent whenever the objects behind can be seen through it [754]. Using **over** simulates

Figure 5.32. A red gauzy square of fabric and a red plastic filter, giving different transparency effects. Note how the shadows also differ. *(Photograph courtesy of Morgan McGuire.)*

the real-world effect of a gauzy fabric. The view of the objects behind the fabric are partially obscured—the fabric's threads are opaque. In practice, loose fabric has an alpha coverage that varies with angle [386]. Our point here is that alpha simulates how much the material covers the pixel.

The **over** operator is less convincing simulating other transparent effects, most notably viewing through colored glass or plastic. A red filter held in front of a blue object in the real world usually makes the blue object look dark, as this object reflects little light that can pass through the red filter. See Figure 5.32. When **over** is used for blending, the result is a portion of the red and the blue added together. It would be better to multiply the two colors together, as well as adding in any reflection off the transparent object itself. This type of physical transmittance is discussed in Sections 14.5.1 and 14.5.2.

Of the basic blend stage operators, **over** is the one commonly used for a transparency effect [199, 1429]. Another operation that sees some use is *additive blending*, where pixel values are simply summed. That is,

$$\mathbf{c}_o = \alpha_s \mathbf{c}_s + \mathbf{c}_d. \tag{5.25}$$

This blending mode can work well for glowing effects such as lightning or sparks that do not attenuate the pixels behind but instead only brighten them [1813]. However, this mode does not look correct for transparency, as the opaque surfaces do not appear

Figure 5.33. On the left the model is rendered with transparency using the z-buffer. Rendering the mesh in an arbitrary order creates serious errors. On the right, depth peeling provides the correct appearance, at the cost of additional passes. *(Images courtesy of NVIDIA Corporation.)*

filtered [1192]. For several layered semitransparent surfaces, such as smoke or fire, additive blending has the effect of saturating the colors of the phenomenon [1273].

To render transparent objects properly, we need to draw them after the opaque objects. This is done by rendering all opaque objects first with blending off, then rendering the transparent objects with **over** turned on. In theory we could always have **over** on, since an opaque alpha of 1.0 would give the source color and hide the destination color, but doing so is more expensive, for no real gain.

A limitation of the z-buffer is that only one object is stored per pixel. If several transparent objects overlap the same pixel, the z-buffer alone cannot hold and later resolve the effect of all the visible objects. When using **over** the transparent surfaces at any given pixel generally need to be rendered in back-to-front order. Not doing so can give incorrect perceptual cues. One way to achieve this ordering is to sort individual objects by, say, the distance of their centroids along the view direction. This rough sorting can work reasonably well, but has a number of problems under various circumstances. First, the order is just an approximation, so objects classified as more distant may be in front of objects considered nearer. Objects that interpenetrate are impossible to resolve on a per-mesh basis for all view angles, short of breaking each mesh into separate pieces. See the left image in Figure 5.33 for an example. Even a single mesh with concavities can exhibit sorting problems for view directions where it overlaps itself on the screen.

Nonetheless, because of its simplicity and speed, as well as needing no additional memory or special GPU support, performing a rough sort for transparency is still commonly used. If implemented, it is usually best to turn off z-depth replacement when performing transparency. That is, the z-buffer is still tested normally, but surviving surfaces do not change the z-depth stored; the closest opaque surface's depth is left intact. In this way, all transparent objects will at least appear in some form, versus suddenly appearing or disappearing when a camera rotation changes the sort order. Other techniques can also help improve the appearance, such as drawing each transparent mesh twice as you go, first rendering backfaces and then frontfaces [1192, 1255].

The **over** equation can also be modified so that blending front to back gives the same result. This blending mode is called the **under** operator:

$$\mathbf{c}_o = \alpha_d \mathbf{c}_d + (1 - \alpha_d)\alpha_s \mathbf{c}_s \quad [\textbf{under operator}],$$
$$\mathbf{a}_o = \alpha_s(1 - \alpha_d) + \alpha_d = \alpha_s - \alpha_s\alpha_d + \alpha_d. \tag{5.26}$$

Note that **under** requires the destination to maintain an alpha value, which **over** does not. In other words, the destination—the closer transparent surface being blended under—is not opaque and so needs to have an alpha value. The **under** formulation is like **over**, but with source and destination swapped. Also, notice that the formula for computing alpha is order-independent, in that the source and destination alphas can be swapped, with the same final alpha being the result.

The equation for alpha comes from considering the fragment's alphas as coverages. Porter and Duff [1429] note that since we do not know the shape of the coverage area for either fragment, we assume that each fragment covers the other in proportion to its alpha. For example, if $\alpha_s = 0.7$, the pixel is somehow divided into two areas, with 0.7 covered by the source fragment and 0.3 not. Barring any other knowledge, the destination fragment covering, say, $\alpha_d = 0.6$ will be proportionally overlapped by the source fragment. This formula has a geometric interpretation, shown in Figure 5.34.

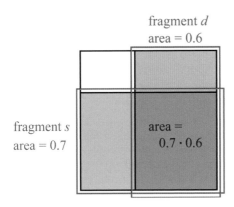

Given two fragments of areas (alphas) 0.7 and 0.6, total area covered = $0.7 - 0.7 \cdot 0.6 + 0.6 = 0.88$

Figure 5.34. A pixel and two fragments, s and d. By aligning the two fragments along different axes, each fragment covers a proportional amount of the other, i.e., they are uncorrelated. The area covered by the two fragments is equivalent to the **under** output alpha value $\alpha_s - \alpha_s\alpha_d + \alpha_d$. This translates to adding the two areas, then subtracting the area where they overlap.

Figure 5.35. Each depth peel pass draws one of the transparent layers. On the left is the first pass, showing the layer directly visible to the eye. The second layer, shown in the middle, displays the second-closest transparent surface at each pixel, in this case the backfaces of objects. The third layer, on the right, is the set of third-closest transparent surfaces. Final results can be found in Figure 14.33 on page 624. *(Images courtesy of Louis Bavoil.)*

5.5.2 Order-Independent Transparency

The **under** equations are used by drawing all transparent objects to a separate color buffer, then merging this color buffer atop the opaque view of the scene using **over**. Another use of the **under** operator is for performing an *order-independent transparency* (OIT) algorithm known as *depth peeling* [449, 1115]. Order-independent means that the application does not need to perform sorting. The idea behind depth peeling is to use two z-buffers and multiple passes. First, a rendering pass is made so that all surfaces' z-depths, including transparent surfaces, are in the first z-buffer. In the second pass all transparent objects are rendered. If the z-depth of an object matches the value in the first z-buffer, we know this is the closest transparent object and save its RGBα to a separate color buffer. We also "peel" this layer away by saving the z-depth of whichever transparent object, if any, is beyond the first z-depth and is closest. This z-depth is the distance of the second-closest transparent object. Successive passes continue to peel and add transparent layers using **under**. We stop after some number of passes and then blend the transparent image atop the opaque image. See Figure 5.35.

Several variants on this scheme have been developed. For example, Thibieroz [1763] gives an algorithm that works back to front, which has the advantage of being able to blend the transparent values immediately, meaning that no separate alpha channel is needed. One problem with depth peeling is knowing how many passes are sufficient to capture all the transparent layers. One hardware solution is to provide a pixel draw counter, which tells how many pixels were written during rendering; when no pixels are rendered by a pass, rendering is done. The advantage of using **under** is that the most important transparent layers—those the eye first sees—are rendered early on. Each transparent surface always increases the alpha value of the pixel it covers. If the alpha value for a pixel nears 1.0, the blended contributions have made the pixel almost opaque, and so more distant objects will have a negligible effect [394]. Front-to-back peeling can be cut short when the number of pixels rendered by a pass falls below some minimum, or a fixed number of passes can be specified. This does not work as well with back-to-front peeling, as the closest (and usually most important) layers are drawn last and so may be lost by early termination.

While depth peeling is effective, it can be slow, as each layer peeled is a separate rendering pass of all transparent objects. Bavoil and Myers [118] presented dual depth peeling, where two depth peel layers, the closest and the farthest remaining, are stripped off in each pass, thus cutting the number of rendering passes in half. Liu et al. [1056] explore a bucket sort method that captures up to 32 layers in a single pass. One drawback of this type of approach is that it needs considerable memory to keep a sorted order for all layers. Antialiasing via MSAA or similar would increase the costs astronomically.

The problem of blending transparent objects together properly at interactive rates is not one in which we are lacking algorithms, it is one of efficiently mapping those algorithms to the GPU. In 1984 Carpenter presented the *A-buffer* [230], another form of multisampling. In the *A*-buffer, each triangle rendered creates a *coverage mask* for each screen grid cell it fully or partially covers. Each pixel stores a list of all relevant fragments. Opaque fragments can cull out fragments behind them, similar to the *z*-buffer. All the fragments are stored for transparent surfaces. Once all lists are formed, a final result is produced by walking through the fragments and resolving each sample.

The idea of creating linked lists of fragments on the GPU was made possible through new functionality exposed in DirectX 11 [611, 1765]. The features used include unordered access views (UAVs) and atomic operations, described in Section 3.8. Antialiasing via MSAA is enabled by the ability to access the coverage mask and to evaluate the pixel shader at every sample. This algorithm works by rasterizing each transparent surface and inserting the fragments generated in a long array. Along with the colors and depths, a separate pointer structure is generated that links each fragment to the previous fragment stored for the pixel. A separate pass is then performed, where a screen-filling quadrilateral is rendered so that a pixel shader is evaluated at every pixel. This shader retrieves all the transparent fragments at each pixel by following the links. Each fragment retrieved is sorted in turn with the previous fragments. This sorted list is then blended back to front to give the final pixel color. Because blending is performed by the pixel shader, different blend modes can be specified per pixel, if desired. Continuing evolution of the GPU and APIs have improved performance by reducing the cost of using atomic operators [914].

The *A*-buffer has the advantage that only the fragments needed for each pixel are allocated, as does the linked list implementation on the GPU. This in a sense can also be a disadvantage, as the amount of storage required is not known before rendering of a frame begins. A scene with hair, smoke, or other objects with a potential for many overlapping transparent surfaces can produce a huge number of fragments.

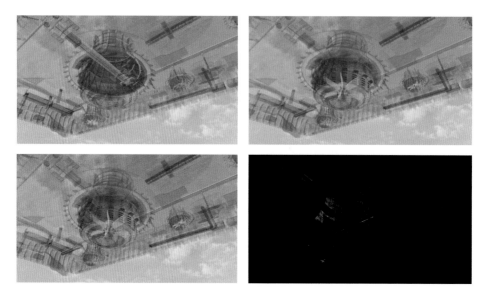

Figure 5.36. In the upper left, traditional back-to-front alpha blending is performed, leading to rendering errors due to incorrect sort order. In the upper right, the A-buffer is used to give a perfect, non-interactive result. The lower left presents the rendering with multi-layer alpha blending. The lower right shows the differences between the A-buffer and multi-layer images, multiplied by 4 for visibility [1532]. *(Images courtesy of Marco Salvi and Karthik Vaidyanathan, Intel Corporation.)*

Andersson [46] notes that, for complex game scenes, up to 50 transparent meshes of objects such as foliage and up to 200 semitransparent particles may overlap.

GPUs normally have memory resources such as buffers and arrays allocated in advance, and linked-list approaches are no exception. Users need to decide how much memory is enough, and running out of memory causes noticeable artifacts. Salvi and Vaidyanathan [1532] present an approach tackling this problem, *multi-layer alpha blending*, using a GPU feature introduced by Intel called pixel synchronization. See Figure 5.36. This capability provides programmable blending with less overhead than atomics. Their approach reformulates storage and blending so that it gracefully degrades if memory runs out. A rough sort order can benefit their scheme. DirectX 11.3 introduced rasterizer order views (Section 3.8), a type of buffer that allows this transparency method to be implemented on any GPU supporting this feature [327, 328]. Mobile devices have a similar technology called *tile local storage* that permits them to implement multi-layer alpha blending [153]. Such mechanisms have a performance cost, however, so this type of algorithm can be expensive [1931].

This approach builds on the idea of the k-buffer, introduced by Bavoil et al. [115], where the first few visible layers are saved and sorted as possible, with deeper layers discarded and merged as possible. Maule et al. [1142] use a k-buffer and account for these more distant deep layers by using *weighted averaging*. Weighted sum [1202] and

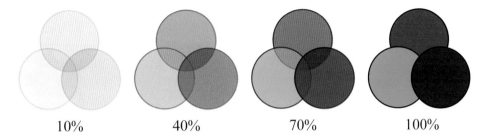

Figure 5.37. The object order becomes more important as opacity increases. *(Images after Dunn [394].)*

weighted average [118] transparency techniques are order-independent, are single-pass, and run on almost every GPU. The problem is that they do not take into account the ordering of the objects. So, for example, using alpha to represent coverage, a gauzy red scarf atop a gauzy blue scarf gives a violet color, versus properly seeing a red scarf with a little blue showing through. While nearly opaque objects give poor results, this class of algorithms is useful for visualization and works well for highly transparent surfaces and particles. See Figure 5.37.

In weighted sum transparency the formula is

$$\mathbf{c}_o = \sum_{i=1}^{n}(\alpha_i \mathbf{c}_i) + \mathbf{c}_d \left(1 - \sum_{i=1}^{n} \alpha_i\right), \tag{5.27}$$

where n is the number of transparent surfaces, $\mathbf{c}_i$ and α_i represent the set of transparency values, and $\mathbf{c}_d$ is the color of the opaque portion of the scene. The two sums are accumulated and stored separately as transparent surfaces are rendered, and at the end of the transparency pass, the equation is evaluated at each pixel. Problems with this method are that the first sum saturates, i.e., generates color values greater than $(1.0, 1.0, 1.0)$, and that the background color can have a negative effect, since the sum of the alphas can surpass 1.0.

The weighted average equation is usually preferred because it avoids these problems:

$$\mathbf{c}_{\text{sum}} = \sum_{i=1}^{n}(\alpha_i \mathbf{c}_i), \quad \alpha_{\text{sum}} = \sum_{i=1}^{n} \alpha_i,$$

$$\mathbf{c}_{\text{wavg}} = \frac{\mathbf{c}_{\text{sum}}}{\alpha_{\text{sum}}}, \quad \alpha_{\text{avg}} = \frac{\alpha_{\text{sum}}}{n}, \tag{5.28}$$

$$u = (1 - \alpha_{\text{avg}})^n,$$

$$\mathbf{c}_o = (1 - u)\mathbf{c}_{\text{wavg}} + u\mathbf{c}_d.$$

The first line represents the results in the two separate buffers generated during transparency rendering. Each surface contributing to $\mathbf{c}_{\text{sum}}$ is given an influence weighted by

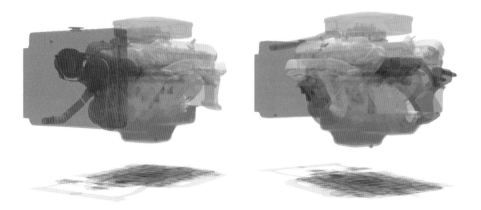

Figure 5.38. Two different camera locations viewing the same engine model, both rendered with weighted blended order-independent transparency. Weighting by distance helps clarify which surfaces are closer to the viewer [1185]. *(Images courtesy of Morgan McGuire.)*

its alpha; nearly opaque surfaces contribute more of their color, and nearly transparent surfaces have little influence. By dividing $\mathbf{c}_{\mathrm{sum}}$ by α_{sum} we get a weighted average transparency color. The value α_{avg} is the average of all alpha values. The value u is the estimated visibility of the destination (the opaque scene) after this average alpha is applied n times, for n transparent surfaces. The final line is effectively the **over** operator, with $(1 - u)$ representing the source's alpha.

One limitation with weighted average is that, for identical alphas, it blends all colors equally, regardless of order. McGuire and Bavoil [1176, 1180] introduced weighted blended order-independent transparency to give a more convincing result. In their formulation, the distance to the surface also affects the weight, with closer surfaces given more influence. Also, rather than averaging the alphas, u is computed by multiplying the terms $(1 - \alpha_i)$ together and subtracting from one, giving the true alpha coverage of the set of surfaces. This method produces more visually convincing results, as seen in Figure 5.38.

A drawback is that objects close to one another in a large environment can have nearly equal weightings from distance, making the result little different than the weighted average. Also, as the camera's distance to the transparent objects changes, the depth weightings may then vary in effect, but this change is gradual.

McGuire and Mara [1181, 1185] extend this method to include a plausible transmission color effect. As noted earlier, all the transparency algorithms discussed in this section blend various colors instead of filtering them, mimicking pixel coverage. To give a color filter effect, the opaque scene is read by the pixel shader and each transparent surface multiplies the pixels it covers in this scene by its color, saving the result to a third buffer. This buffer, in which the opaque objects are now tinted by the transparent ones, is then used in place of the opaque scene when resolving the transparency buffers. This method works because, unlike transparency due to coverage, colored transmission is order-independent.

There are yet other algorithms that use elements from several of the techniques presented here. For example, Wyman [1931] categorizes previous work by memory requirements, insertion and merge methods, whether alpha or geometric coverage is used, and how discarded fragments are treated. He presents two new methods found by looking for gaps in previous research. His stochastic layered alpha blending method uses k-buffers, weighted average, and stochastic transparency. His other algorithm is a variant on Salvi and Vaidyanathan's method, using coverage masks instead of alpha.

Given the wide variety of types of transparent content, rendering methods, and GPU capabilities, there is no perfect solution for rendering transparent objects. We refer the interested reader to Wyman's paper [1931] and Maule et al.'s more detailed survey [1141] of algorithms for interactive transparency. McGuire's presentation [1182] gives a wider view of the field, running through other related phenomena such as volumetric lighting, colored transmission, and refraction, which are discussed in greater depth later in this book.

5.5.3 Premultiplied Alphas and Compositing

The **over** operator is also used for blending together photographs or synthetic renderings of objects. This process is called *compositing* [199, 1662]. In such cases, the alpha value at each pixel is stored along with the RGB color value for the object. The image formed by the alpha channel is sometimes called the *matte*. It shows the silhouette shape of the object. See Figure 6.27 on page 203 for an example. This RGBα image can then be used to blend it with other such elements or against a background.

One way to use synthetic RGBα data is with *premultiplied alphas* (also known as *associated alphas*). That is, the RGB values are multiplied by the alpha value before being used. This makes the compositing **over** equation more efficient:

$$\mathbf{c}_o = \mathbf{c}'_s + (1 - \alpha_s)\mathbf{c}_d, \qquad (5.29)$$

where $\mathbf{c}'_s$ is the premultiplied source channel, replacing $\alpha_s\mathbf{c}_s$ in Equation 5.25. Premultiplied alpha also makes it possible to use **over** and additive blending without changing the blend state, since the source color is now added in during blending [394]. Note that with premultiplied RGBα values, the RGB components are normally not greater than the alpha value, though they can be made so to create a particularly bright semitransparent value.

Rendering synthetic images dovetails naturally with premultiplied alphas. An antialiased opaque object rendered over a black background provides premultiplied values by default. Say a white $(1, 1, 1)$ triangle covers 40% of some pixel along its edge. With (extremely precise) antialiasing, the pixel value would be set to a gray of 0.4, i.e., we would save the color $(0.4, 0.4, 0.4)$ for this pixel. The alpha value, if stored, would also be 0.4, since this is the area the triangle covered. The RGBα value would be $(0.4, 0.4, 0.4, 0.4)$, which is a premultiplied value.

Another way images are stored is with *unmultiplied alphas*, also known as *unassociated alphas* or even as the mind-bending term *nonpremultiplied alphas*. An unmultiplied alpha is just what it says: The RGB value is not multiplied by the alpha value. For the white triangle example, the unmultiplied color would be $(1, 1, 1, 0.4)$. This representation has the advantage of storing the triangle's original color, but this color always needs to be multiplied by the stored alpha before being display. It is best to use premultiplied data whenever filtering and blending is performed, as operations such as linear interpolation do not work correctly using unmultiplied alphas [108, 164]. Artifacts such as black fringes around the edges of objects can result [295, 648]. See the end of Section 6.6 for further discussion. Premultiplied alphas also allow cleaner theoretical treatment [1662].

For image-manipulation applications, an unassociated alpha is useful to mask a photograph without affecting the underlying image's original data. Also, an unassociated alpha means that the full precision range of the color channels can be used. That said, care must be taken to properly convert unmultiplied RGBα values to and from the linear space used for computer graphics computations. For example, no browsers do this properly, nor are they ever likely to do so, since the incorrect behavior is now expected [649]. Image file formats that support alpha include PNG (unassociated alpha only), OpenEXR (associated only), and TIFF (both types of alpha).

A concept related to the alpha channel is *chroma-keying* [199]. This is a term from video production, in which actors are filmed against a green or blue screen and blended with a background. In the film industry this process is called *green-screening* or *blue-screening*. The idea here is that a particular color hue (for film work) or precise value (for computer graphics) is designated to be considered transparent; the background is displayed whenever it is detected. This allows images to be given an outline shape by using just RGB colors; no alpha needs to be stored. One drawback of this scheme is that the object is either entirely opaque or transparent at any pixel, i.e., alpha is effectively only 1.0 or 0.0. As an example, the GIF format allows one color to be designated as transparent.

5.6   Display Encoding

When we calculate the effect of lighting, texturing, or other operations, the values used are assumed to be *linear*. Informally, this means that addition and multiplication work as expected. However, to avoid a variety of visual artifacts, display buffers and textures use nonlinear encodings that we must take into account. The short and sloppy answer is as follows: Take shader output colors in the range $[0, 1]$ and raise them by a power of $1/2.2$, performing what is called *gamma correction*. Do the opposite for incoming textures and colors. In most cases you can tell the GPU to do these things for you. This section explains the how and why of that quick summary.

We begin with the *cathode-ray tube* (CRT). In the early years of digital imaging, CRT displays were the norm. These devices exhibit a power law relationship between input voltage and display radiance. As the energy level applied to a pixel is increased, the radiance emitted does not grow linearly but (surprisingly) rises proportional to that level raised to a power greater than one. For example, imagine the power is 2. A pixel set to 50% will emit a quarter the amount of light, $0.5^2 = 0.25$, as a pixel that is set to 1.0 [607]. Although LCDs and other display technologies have different intrinsic tone response curves than CRTs, they are manufactured with conversion circuitry that causes them to mimic the CRT response.

This power function nearly matches the inverse of the lightness sensitivity of human vision [1431]. The consequence of this fortunate coincidence is that the encoding is roughly *perceptually uniform*. That is, the perceived difference between a pair of encoded values N and $N+1$ is roughly constant over the displayable range. Measured as *threshold contrast*, we can detect a difference in lightness of about 1% over a wide range of conditions. This near-optimal distribution of values minimizes *banding* artifacts when colors are stored in limited-precision display buffers (Section 23.6). The same benefit also applies to textures, which commonly use the same encoding.

The *display transfer function* describes the relationship between the digital values in the display buffer and the radiance levels emitted from the display. For this reason it is also called the *electrical optical transfer function* (EOTF). The display transfer function is part of the hardware, and there are different standards for computer monitors, televisions, and film projectors. There is also a standard transfer function for the other end of the process, image and video capture devices, called the *optical electric transfer function* (OETF) [672].

When encoding linear color values for display, our goal is to cancel out the effect of the display transfer function, so that whatever value we compute will emit a corresponding radiance level. For example, if our computed value is doubled, we want the output radiance to be doubled. To maintain this connection, we apply the inverse of the display transfer function to cancel out its nonlinear effect. This process of nullifying the display's response curve is also called *gamma correction*, for reasons that will become clear shortly. When decoding texture values, we need to apply the display transfer function to generate a linear value for use in shading. Figure 5.39 shows the use of decoding and encoding in the display process.

The standard transfer function for personal computer displays is defined by a color-space specification called *sRGB*. Most APIs controlling GPUs can be set to automatically apply the proper sRGB conversion when values are read from textures or written to the color buffer [491]. As discussed in Section 6.2.2, mipmap generation will also take sRGB encoding into account. Bilinear interpolation among texture values will work correctly, by first converting to linear values and then performing the interpolation. Alpha blending is done correctly by decoding the stored value back into linear values, blending in the new value, and then encoding the result.

It is important to apply the conversion at the final stage of rendering, when the values are written to the framebuffer for the display. If post-processing is applied after

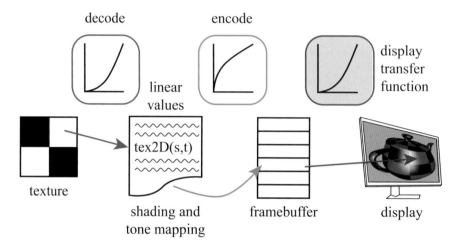

Figure 5.39. On the left, a PNG color texture is accessed by a GPU shader, and its nonlinearly encoded value is converted (blue) to a linear value. After shading and tone mapping (Section 8.2.2), the final computed value is encoded (green) and stored in the framebuffer. This value and the display transfer function determine the amount of radiance emitted (red). The green and red functions combined cancel out, so that the radiance emitted is proportional to the linear computed value.

display encoding, such effects will be computed on nonlinear values, which is usually incorrect and will often cause artifacts. Display encoding can be thought of as a form of compression, one that best preserves the value's perceptual effect [491]. A good way to think about this area is that there are linear values that we use to perform physical computations, and whenever we want to display results or access displayable images such as color textures, we need to move data to or from its display-encoded form, using the proper encode or decode transform.

If you do need to apply sRGB manually, there is a standard conversion equation or a few simplified versions that can be used. In practical terms the display is controlled by a number of bits per color channel, e.g., 8 for consumer-level monitors, giving a set of levels in the range $[0, 255]$. Here we express the display-encoded levels as a range $[0.0, 1.0]$, ignoring the number of bits. The linear values are also in the range $[0.0, 1.0]$, representing floating point numbers. We denote these linear values by x and the nonlinearly encoded values stored in the framebuffer by y. To convert linear values to sRGB nonlinear encoded values, we apply the inverse of the sRGB display transfer function:

$$y = f_{\text{sRGB}}^{-1}(x) = \begin{cases} 1.055x^{1/2.4} - 0.055, & \text{where } x > 0.0031308, \\ 12.92x, & \text{where } x \leq 0.0031308, \end{cases} \quad (5.30)$$

with x representing a channel of the linear RGB triplet. The equation is applied to each channel, and these three generated values drive the display. Be careful if you apply conversion functions manually. One source of error is using an encoded color instead of its linear form, and another is decoding or encoding a color twice.

The bottom of the two transform expressions is a simple multiply, which arises from a need by digital hardware to make the transform perfectly invertible [1431]. The top expression, involving raising the value to a power, applies to almost the whole range $[0.0, 1.0]$ of input values x. With the offset and scale taken into account, this function closely approximates a simpler formula [491]:

$$y = f_{\text{display}}^{-1}(x) = x^{1/\gamma}, \qquad (5.31)$$

with $\gamma = 2.2$. The Greek letter γ is the basis for the name "gamma correction."

Just as computed values must be encoded for display, images captured by still or video cameras must be converted to linear values before being used in calculations. Any color you see on a monitor or television has some display-encoded RGB triplet that you can obtain from a screen capture or color picker. These values are what are stored in file formats such as PNG, JPEG, and GIF, formats that can be directly sent to a framebuffer for display on the screen without conversion. In other words, whatever you see on the screen is by definition display-encoded data. Before using these colors in shading calculations, we must convert from this encoded form back to linear values. The sRGB transformation we need from display encoding to linear values is

$$x = f_{\text{sRGB}}(y) = \begin{cases} \left(\dfrac{y + 0.055}{1.055} \right)^{2.4}, & \text{where } y > 0.04045, \\[2mm] \dfrac{y}{12.92}, & \text{where } y \le 0.04045, \end{cases} \qquad (5.32)$$

with y representing a normalized displayed channel value, i.e., what is stored in an image or framebuffer, expressed as a value in the range $[0.0, 1.0]$. This decode function is the inverse of our previous sRGB formula. This means that if a texture is accessed by a shader and output without change, it will appear the same as before being processed, as expected. The decode function is the same as the display transfer function because the values stored in a texture have been encoded to display correctly. Instead of converting to give a linear-response display, we are converting to give linear values.

The simpler gamma display transfer function is the inverse of Equation 5.31:

$$x = f_{\text{display}}(y) = y^{\gamma}. \qquad (5.33)$$

Sometimes you will see a conversion pair that is simpler still, particularly on mobile and browser apps [1666]:

$$y = f_{\text{simpl}}^{-1}(x) = \sqrt{x},$$
$$x = f_{\text{simpl}}(y) = y^2; \qquad (5.34)$$

that is, take the square root of the linear value for conversion for display, and just multiply the value by itself for the inverse. While a rough approximation, this conversion is better than ignoring the problem altogether.

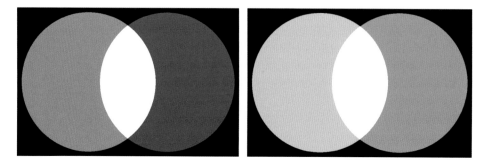

Figure 5.40. Two overlapping spotlights illuminating a plane. In the left image, gamma correction is not performed after adding the light values of 0.6 and 0.4. The addition is effectively performed on nonlinear values, causing errors. Note how the left light looks considerably brighter than the right, and the overlap appears unrealistically bright. In the right image, the values are gamma corrected after addition. The lights themselves are proportionally brighter, and they combine properly where they overlap.

If we do not pay attention to gamma, lower linear values will appear too dim on the screen. A related error is that the hue of some colors can shift if no gamma correction is performed. Say our $\gamma = 2.2$. We want to emit a radiance from the displayed pixel proportional to the linear, computed value, which means that we must raise the linear value to the $(1/2.2)$ power. A linear value of 0.1 gives 0.351, 0.2 gives 0.481, and 0.5 gives 0.730. If not encoded, these values used as is will cause the display to emit less radiance than needed. Note that 0.0 and 1.0 are always unchanged by any of these transforms. Before gamma correction was used, dark surface colors would often be artificially boosted by the person modeling the scene, folding in the inverse display transform.

Another problem with neglecting gamma correction is that shading computations that are correct for physically linear radiance values are performed on nonlinear values. An example of this can be seen in Figure 5.40.

Ignoring gamma correction also affects the quality of antialiased edges. For example, say a triangle edge covers four screen grid cells (Figure 5.41). The triangle's

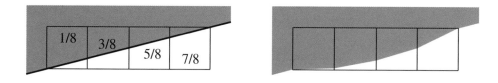

Figure 5.41. On the left, four pixels covered by the edge of a white triangle on a black (shown as gray) background, with true area coverage shown. If gamma correction is not performed, the darkening of midtones will cause the perception of the edge to be distorted, as seen on the right.

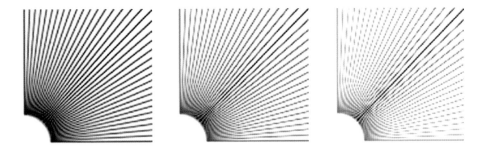

Figure 5.42. On the left, the set of antialiased lines are gamma-corrected; in the middle, the set is partially corrected; on the right, there is no gamma correction. *(Images courtesy of Scott R. Nelson.)*

normalized radiance is 1 (white); the background's is 0 (black). Left to right, the cells are covered $\frac{1}{8}$, $\frac{3}{8}$, $\frac{5}{8}$, and $\frac{7}{8}$. So, if we are using a box filter, we want to represent the normalized linear radiance of the pixels as 0.125, 0.375, 0.625, and 0.875. The correct approach is to perform antialiasing on linear values, applying the encoding function to the four resulting values. If this is not done, the represented radiance for the pixels will be too dark, resulting in a perceived deformation of the edge as seen in the right side of the figure. This artifact is called *roping*, because the edge looks somewhat like a twisted rope [167, 1265]. Figure 5.42 shows this effect.

The sRGB standard was created in 1996 and has become the norm for most computer monitors. However, display technology has evolved since that time. Monitors that are brighter and that can display a wider range of colors have been developed. Color display and brightness are discussed in Section 8.1.3, and display encoding for high dynamic range displays is presented in Section 8.2.1. Hart's article [672] is a particularly thorough source for more information about advanced displays.

Further Reading and Resources

Pharr et al. [1413] discuss sampling patterns and antialiasing in more depth. Teschner's course notes [1758] show various sampling pattern generation methods. Drobot [382, 383] runs through previous research on real-time antialiasing, explaining the attributes and performance of a variety of techniques. Information on a wide variety of morphological antialiasing methods can be found in the notes for the related SIGGRAPH course [829]. Reshetov and Jimenez [1486] provide an updated retrospective of morphological and related temporal antialiasing work used in games.

For transparency research we again refer the interested reader to McGuire's presentation [1182] and Wyman's work [1931]. Blinn's article "What Is a Pixel?" [169] provides an excellent tour of several areas of computer graphics while discussing different definitions. Blinn's *Dirty Pixels* and *Notation, Notation, Notation* books [166, 168] include some introductory articles on filtering and antialiasing, as well as articles on alpha, compositing, and gamma correction. Jimenez's presentation [836] gives a detailed treatment of state-of-the-art techniques used for antialiasing.

Gritz and d'Eon [607] have an excellent summary of gamma correction issues. Poynton's book [1431] gives solid coverage of gamma correction in various media, as well as other color-related topics. Selan's white paper [1602] is a newer source, explaining display encoding and its use in the film industry, along with much other related information.

Chapter 6
Texturing

"All it takes is for the rendered image to look right."
—Jim Blinn

A surface's texture is its look and feel—just think of the texture of an oil painting. In computer graphics, texturing is a process that takes a surface and modifies its appearance at each location using some image, function, or other data source. As an example, instead of precisely representing the geometry of a brick wall, a color image of a brick wall is applied to a rectangle, consisting of two triangles. When the rectangle is viewed, the color image appears where the rectangle is located. Unless the viewer gets close to the wall, the lack of geometric detail will not be noticeable.

However, some textured brick walls can be unconvincing for reasons other than lack of geometry. For example, if the mortar is supposed to be matte, whereas the bricks are glossy, the viewer will notice that the roughness is the same for both materials. To produce a more convincing experience, a second image texture can be applied to the surface. Instead of changing the surface's color, this texture changes the wall's roughness, depending on location on the surface. Now the bricks and mortar have a color from the image texture and a roughness value from this new texture.

The viewer may see that now all the bricks are glossy and the mortar is not, but notice that each brick face appears to be perfectly flat. This does not look right, as bricks normally have some irregularity to their surfaces. By applying *bump mapping*, the shading normals of the bricks may be varied so that when they are rendered, they do not appear to be perfectly smooth. This sort of texture wobbles the direction of the rectangle's original surface normal for purposes of computing lighting.

From a shallow viewing angle, this illusion of bumpiness can break down. The bricks should stick out above the mortar, obscuring it from view. Even from a straight-on view, the bricks should cast shadows onto the mortar. *Parallax mapping* uses a texture to appear to deform a flat surface when rendering it, and *parallax occlusion mapping* casts rays against a heightfield texture for improved realism. *Displacement mapping* truly displaces the surface by modifying triangle heights forming the model. Figure 6.1 shows an example with color texturing and bump mapping.

Figure 6.1. Texturing. Color and bump maps were applied to this fish to increase its visual level of detail. *(Image courtesy of Elinor Quittner.)*

These are examples of the types of problems that can be solved with textures, using more and more elaborate algorithms. In this chapter, texturing techniques are covered in detail. First, a general framework of the texturing process is presented. Next, we focus on using images to texture surfaces, since this is the most popular form of texturing used in real-time work. Procedural textures are briefly discussed, and then some common methods of having textures affect the surface are explained.

6.1 The Texturing Pipeline

Texturing is a technique for efficiently modeling variations in a surface's material and finish. One way to think about texturing is to consider what happens for a single shaded pixel. As seen in the previous chapter, the shade is computed by taking into account the color of the material and the lights, among other factors. If present, transparency also affects the sample. Texturing works by modifying the values used in the shading equation. The way these values are changed is normally based on the position on the surface. So, for the brick wall example, the color at any point on the surface is replaced by a corresponding color in the image of a brick wall, based on the surface location. The pixels in the image texture are often called *texels*, to differentiate them from the pixels on the screen. The roughness texture modifies the roughness value, and the bump texture changes the direction of the shading normal, so each of these change the result of the shading equation.

Texturing can be described by a generalized texture pipeline. Much terminology will be introduced in a moment, but take heart: Each piece of the pipeline will be described in detail.

A location in space is the starting point for the texturing process. This location can be in world space, but is more often in the model's frame of reference, so that as the model moves, the texture moves along with it. Using Kershaw's terminology [884], this point in space then has a *projector* function applied to it to obtain a set of numbers, called *texture coordinates*, that will be used for accessing the texture. This process is called *mapping*, which leads to the phrase *texture mapping*. Sometimes the texture image itself is called the *texture map*, though this is not strictly correct.

Before these new values may be used to access the texture, one or more *corresponder* functions can be used to transform the texture coordinates to texture space. These texture-space locations are used to obtain values from the texture, e.g., they may be array indices into an image texture to retrieve a pixel. The retrieved values are then potentially transformed yet again by a *value transform* function, and finally these new values are used to modify some property of the surface, such as the material or shading normal. Figure 6.2 shows this process in detail for the application of a single texture. The reason for the complexity of the pipeline is that each step provides the user with a useful control. It should be noted that not all steps need to be activated at all times.

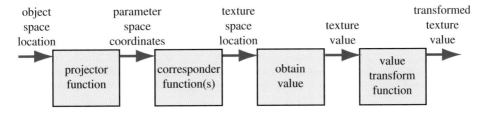

Figure 6.2. The generalized texture pipeline for a single texture.

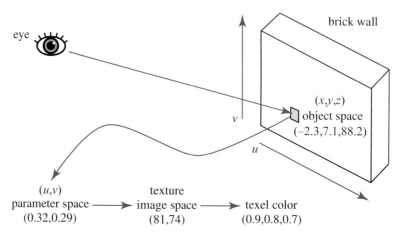

Figure 6.3. Pipeline for a brick wall.

Using this pipeline, this is what happens when a triangle has a brick wall texture and a sample is generated on its surface (see Figure 6.3). The (x, y, z) position in the object's local frame of reference is found; say it is $(-2.3, 7.1, 88.2)$. A projector function is then applied to this position. Just as a map of the world is a projection of a three-dimensional object into two dimensions, the projector function here typically changes the (x, y, z) vector into a two-element vector (u, v). The projector function used for this example is equivalent to an orthographic projection (Section 2.3.1), acting something like a slide projector shining the brick wall image onto the triangle's surface. To return to the wall, a point on its surface could be transformed into a pair of values ranging from 0 to 1. Say the values obtained are $(0.32, 0.29)$. These texture coordinates are to be used to find what the color of the image is at this location. The resolution of our brick texture is, say, 256×256, so the corresponder function multiplies the (u, v) by 256 each, giving $(81.92, 74.24)$. Dropping the fractions, pixel $(81, 74)$ is found in the brick wall image, and is of color $(0.9, 0.8, 0.7)$. The texture color is in sRGB color space, so if the color is to be used in shading equations, it is converted to linear space, giving $(0.787, 0.604, 0.448)$ (Section 5.6).

6.1.1   The Projector Function

The first step in the texture process is obtaining the surface's location and projecting it into texture coordinate space, usually two-dimensional (u, v) space. Modeling packages typically allow artists to define (u, v)-coordinates per vertex. These may be initialized from projector functions or from mesh unwrapping algorithms. Artists can edit (u, v)-coordinates in the same way they edit vertex positions. Projector functions typically work by converting a three-dimensional point in space into texture coordinates. Functions commonly used in modeling programs include spherical, cylindrical, and planar projections [141, 884, 970].

Figure 6.4. Different texture projections. Spherical, cylindrical, planar, and natural (u, v) projections are shown, left to right. The bottom row shows each of these projections applied to a single object (which has no natural projection).

Other inputs can be used to a projector function. For example, the surface normal can be used to choose which of six planar projection directions is used for the surface. Problems in matching textures occur at the seams where the faces meet; Geiss [521, 522] discusses a technique of blending among them. Tarini et al. [1740] describe *polycube maps*, where a model is mapped to a set of cube projections, with different volumes of space mapping to different cubes.

Other projector functions are not projections at all, but are an implicit part of surface creation and tessellation. For example, parametric curved surfaces have a natural set of (u, v) values as part of their definition. See Figure 6.4. The texture coordinates could also be generated from all sorts of different parameters, such as the view direction, temperature of the surface, or anything else imaginable. The goal of the projector function is to generate texture coordinates. Deriving these as a function of position is just one way to do it.

Non-interactive renderers often call these projector functions as part of the rendering process itself. A single projector function may suffice for the whole model, but often the artist has to use tools to subdivide the model and apply various projector functions separately [1345]. See Figure 6.5.

In real-time work, projector functions are usually applied at the modeling stage, and the results of the projection are stored at the vertices. This is not always the case; sometimes it is advantageous to apply the projection function in the vertex or pixel shader. Doing so can increase precision, and helps enable various effects, including animation (Section 6.4). Some rendering methods, such as *environment mapping*

 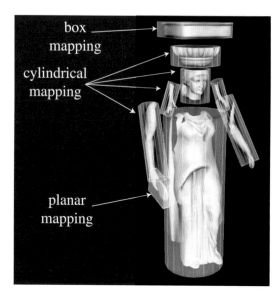

Figure 6.5. How various texture projections are used on a single model. Box mapping consists of six planar mappings, one for each box face. *(Images courtesy of Tito Pagán.)*

(Section 10.4), have specialized projector functions of their own that are evaluated per pixel.

The spherical projection (on the left in Figure 6.4) casts points onto an imaginary sphere centered around some point. This projection is the same as used in Blinn and Newell's environment mapping scheme (Section 10.4.1), so Equation 10.30 on page 407 describes this function. This projection method suffers from the same problems of vertex interpolation described in that section.

Cylindrical projection computes the u texture coordinate the same as spherical projection, with the v texture coordinate computed as the distance along the cylinder's axis. This projection is useful for objects that have a natural axis, such as surfaces of revolution. Distortion occurs when surfaces are near-perpendicular to the cylinder's axis.

The planar projection is like an x-ray beam, projecting in parallel along a direction and applying the texture to all surfaces. It uses orthographic projection (Section 4.7.1). This type of projection is useful for applying decals, for example (Section 20.2).

As there is severe distortion for surfaces that are edge-on to the projection direction, the artist often must manually decompose the model into near-planar pieces. There are also tools that help minimize distortion by unwrapping the mesh, or creating a near-optimal set of planar projections, or that otherwise aid this process. The goal is to have each polygon be given a fairer share of a texture's area, while also maintaining as much mesh connectivity as possible. Connectivity is important in that sampling artifacts can appear along edges where separate parts of a texture meet. A

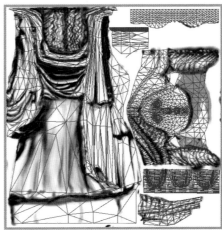

Figure 6.6. Several smaller textures for the statue model, saved in two larger textures. The right figure shows how the triangle mesh is unwrapped and displayed on the texture to aid in its creation. *(Images courtesy of Tito Pagán.)*

mesh with a good unwrapping also eases the artist's work [970, 1345]. Section 16.2.1 discusses how texture distortion can adversely affect rendering. Figure 6.6 shows the workspace used to create the statue in Figure 6.5. This unwrapping process is one facet of a larger field of study, *mesh parameterization*. The interested reader is referred to the SIGGRAPH course notes by Hormann et al. [774].

The texture coordinate space is not always a two-dimensional plane; sometimes it is a three-dimensional volume. In this case, the texture coordinates are presented as a three-element vector, (u, v, w), with w being depth along the projection direction. Other systems use up to four coordinates, often designated (s, t, r, q) [885]; q is used as the fourth value in a homogeneous coordinate. It acts like a movie or slide projector, with the size of the projected texture increasing with distance. As an example, it is useful for projecting a decorative spotlight pattern, called a *gobo*, onto a stage or other surface [1597].

Another important type of texture coordinate space is directional, where each point in the space is accessed by an input direction. One way to visualize such a space is as points on a unit sphere, the normal at each point representing the direction used to access the texture at that location. The most common type of texture using a directional parameterization is the *cube map* (Section 6.2.4).

It is also worth noting that one-dimensional texture images and functions have their uses. For example, on a terrain model the coloration can be determined by altitude, e.g., the lowlands are green; the mountain peaks are white. Lines can also be textured; one use of this is to render rain as a set of long lines textured with a semitransparent image. Such textures are also useful for converting from one value to another, i.e., as a lookup table.

Since multiple textures can be applied to a surface, multiple sets of texture coordinates may need to be defined. However the coordinate values are applied, the idea is the same: These texture coordinates are interpolated across the surface and used to retrieve texture values. Before being interpolated, however, these texture coordinates are transformed by corresponder functions.

6.1.2   The Corresponder Function

Corresponder functions convert texture coordinates to texture-space locations. They provide flexibility in applying textures to surfaces. One example of a corresponder function is to use the API to select a portion of an existing texture for display; only this subimage will be used in subsequent operations.

Another type of corresponder is a matrix transformation, which can be applied in the vertex or pixel shader. This enables to translating, rotating, scaling, shearing, or projecting the texture on the surface. As discussed in Section 4.1.5, the order of transforms matters. Surprisingly, the order of transforms for textures must be the reverse of the order one would expect. This is because texture transforms actually affect the space that determines where the image is seen. The image itself is not an object being transformed; the space defining the image's location is being changed.

Another class of corresponder functions controls the way an image is applied. We know that an image will appear on the surface where (u, v) are in the $[0, 1]$ range. But what happens outside of this range? Corresponder functions determine the behavior. In OpenGL, this type of corresponder function is called the "wrapping mode"; in DirectX, it is called the "texture addressing mode." Common corresponder functions of this type are:

- **wrap** (DirectX), **repeat** (OpenGL), or **tile**—The image repeats itself across the surface; algorithmically, the integer part of the texture coordinates is dropped. This function is useful for having an image of a material repeatedly cover a surface, and is often the default.

- **mirror**—The image repeats itself across the surface, but is mirrored (flipped) on every other repetition. For example, the image appears normally going from 0 to 1, then is reversed between 1 and 2, then is normal between 2 and 3, then is reversed, and so on. This provides some continuity along the edges of the texture.

- **clamp** (DirectX) or **clamp to edge** (OpenGL)—Values outside the range $[0, 1]$ are clamped to this range. This results in the repetition of the edges of the image texture. This function is useful for avoiding accidentally taking samples from the opposite edge of a texture when bilinear interpolation happens near a texture's edge [885].

- **border** (DirectX) or **clamp to border** (OpenGL)—Texture coordinates outside $[0, 1]$ are rendered with a separately defined border color. This function can

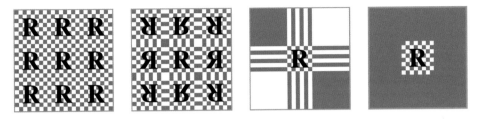

Figure 6.7. Image texture repeat, mirror, clamp, and border functions in action.

be good for rendering decals onto single-color surfaces, for example, as the edge of the texture will blend smoothly with the border color.

See Figure 6.7. These corresponder functions can be assigned differently for each texture axis, e.g., the texture could repeat along the u-axis and be clamped on the v-axis. In DirectX there is also a **mirror once** mode that mirrors a texture once along the zero value for the texture coordinate, then clamps, which is useful for symmetric decals.

Repeated tiling of a texture is an inexpensive way of adding more visual detail to a scene. However, this technique often looks unconvincing after about three repetitions of the texture, as the eye picks out the pattern. A common solution to avoid such *periodicity* problems is to combine the texture values with another, non-tiled, texture. This approach can be considerably extended, as seen in the commercial terrain rendering system described by Andersson [40]. In this system, multiple textures are combined based on terrain type, altitude, slope, and other factors. Texture images are also tied to where geometric models, such as bushes and rocks, are placed within the scene.

Another option to avoid periodicity is to use shader programs to implement specialized corresponder functions that randomly recombine texture patterns or tiles. *Wang tiles* are one example of this approach. A Wang tile set is a small set of square tiles with matching edges. Tiles are selected randomly during the texturing process [1860]. Lefebvre and Neyret [1016] implement a similar type of corresponder function using dependent texture reads and tables to avoid pattern repetition.

The last corresponder function applied is implicit, and is derived from the image's size. A texture is normally applied within the range $[0, 1]$ for u and v. As shown in the brick wall example, by multiplying texture coordinates in this range by the resolution of the image, one may obtain the pixel location. The advantage of being able to specify (u, v) values in a range of $[0, 1]$ is that image textures with different resolutions can be swapped in without having to change the values stored at the vertices of the model.

6.1.3 Texture Values

After the corresponder functions are used to produce texture-space coordinates, the coordinates are used to obtain texture values. For image textures, this is done by accessing the texture to retrieve texel information from the image. This process is dealt with extensively in Section 6.2. Image texturing constitutes the vast majority of texture use in real-time work, but procedural functions can also be used. In the case of procedural texturing, the process of obtaining a texture value from a texture-space location does not involve a memory lookup, but rather the computation of a function. Procedural texturing is further described in Section 6.3.

The most straightforward texture value is an RGB triplet that is used to replace or modify the surface colors; similarly, a single grayscale value could be returned. Another type of data to return is RGBα, as described in Section 5.5. The α (alpha) value is normally the opacity of the color, which determines the extent to which the color may affect the pixel. That said, any other value could be stored, such as surface roughness. There are many other types of data that can be stored in image textures, as will be seen when bump mapping is discussed in detail (Section 6.7).

The values returned from the texture are optionally transformed before use. These transformations may be performed in the shader program. One common example is the remapping of data from an unsigned range (0.0 to 1.0) to a signed range (-1.0 to 1.0), which is used for shading normals stored in a color texture.

6.2   Image Texturing

In image texturing, a two-dimensional image is effectively glued onto the surface of one or more triangles. We have walked through the process of computing a texture-space location; now we will address the issues and algorithms for obtaining a texture value from the image texture, given that location. For the rest of this chapter, the image texture will be referred to simply as the *texture*. In addition, when we refer to a pixel's *cell* here, we mean the screen grid cell surrounding that pixel. As discussed in Section 5.4.1, a *pixel* is actually a displayed color value that can (and should, for better quality) be affected by samples outside of its associated grid cell.

In this section we particularly focus on methods to rapidly sample and filter textured images. Section 5.4.2 discussed the problem of aliasing, especially with respect to rendering edges of objects. Textures can also have sampling problems, but they occur within the interiors of the triangles being rendered.

The pixel shader accesses textures by passing in texture coordinate values to a call such as `texture2D`. These values are in (u, v) texture coordinates, mapped by a corresponder function to a range $[0.0, 1.0]$. The GPU takes care of converting this value to texel coordinates. There are two main differences among texture coordinate systems in different APIs. In DirectX the upper left corner of the texture is $(0, 0)$ and the lower right is $(1, 1)$. This matches how many image types store their data, the top row being the first one in the file. In OpenGL the texel $(0, 0)$ is located in the lower left, a y-axis flip from DirectX. Texels have integer coordinates, but we often want to access a location between texels and blend among them. This brings up the question of what the floating point coordinates of the center of a pixel are. Heckbert [692] discusses how there are two systems possible: truncating and rounding. DirectX 9 defined each center at $(0.0, 0.0)$—this uses rounding. This system was somewhat confusing, as the upper left corner of the upper left pixel, at DirectX's origin, then had the value $(-0.5, -0.5)$. DirectX 10 onward changes to OpenGL's system, where the center of a texel has the fractional values $(0.5, 0.5)$—truncation, or more accurately, flooring, where the fraction is dropped. Flooring is a more natural system that maps well to language, in that pixel $(5, 9)$, for example, defines a range from 5.0 to 6.0 for the u-coordinate and 9.0 to 10.0 for the v.

One term worth explaining at this point is *dependent texture read*, which has two definitions. The first applies to mobile devices in particular. When accessing a texture via `texture2D` or similar, a dependent texture read occurs whenever the pixel shader calculates texture coordinates instead of using the unmodified texture coordinates passed in from the vertex shader [66]. Note that this means any change at all to the incoming texture coordinates, even such simple actions as swapping the u and v values. Older mobile GPUs, those that do not support OpenGL ES 3.0, run more efficiently when the shader has no dependent texture reads, as the texel data can then be prefetched. The other, older, definition of this term was particularly important for early desktop GPUs. In this context a dependent texture read occurs when one texture's coordinates are dependent on the result of some previous texture's values. For example, one texture might change the shading normal, which in turn changes the coordinates used to access a cube map. Such functionality was limited or even non-existent on early GPUs. Today such reads can have an impact on performance, depending on the number of pixels being computed in a batch, among other factors. See Section 23.8 for more information.

The texture image size used in GPUs is usually $2^m \times 2^n$ texels, where m and n are non-negative integers. These are referred to as *power-of-two* (POT) textures. Modern GPUs can handle *non-power-of-two* (NPOT) textures of arbitrary size, which allows a generated image to be treated as a texture. However, some older mobile GPUs may not support mipmapping (Section 6.2.2) for NPOT textures. Graphics accelerators have different upper limits on texture size. DirectX 12 allows a maximum of 16384^2 texels, for example.

Assume that we have a texture of size 256×256 texels and that we want to use it as a texture on a square. As long as the projected square on the screen is roughly the same size as the texture, the texture on the square looks almost like the original image. But what happens if the projected square covers ten times as many pixels as the original image contains (called *magnification*), or if the projected square covers only a small part of the screen (*minification*)? The answer is that it depends on what kind of sampling and filtering methods you decide to use for these two separate cases.

The image sampling and filtering methods discussed in this chapter are applied to the values read from each texture. However, the desired result is to prevent aliasing in the final rendered image, which in theory requires sampling and filtering the final pixel colors. The distinction here is between filtering the inputs to the shading equation, or filtering its output. As long as the inputs and output are linearly related (which is true for inputs such as colors), then filtering the individual texture values is equivalent to filtering the final colors. However, many shader input values stored in textures, such as surface normals and roughness values, have a nonlinear relationship to the output. Standard texture filtering methods may not work well for these textures, resulting in aliasing. Improved methods for filtering such textures are discussed in Section 9.13.

6.2.1 Magnification

In Figure 6.8, a texture of size 48×48 texels is textured onto a square, and the square is viewed rather closely with respect to the texture size, so the underlying graphics system has to magnify the texture. The most common filtering techniques for magnification are *nearest neighbor* (the actual filter is called a box filter—see Section 5.4.1) and *bilinear interpolation*. There is also *cubic convolution*, which uses the weighted sum of a 4×4 or 5×5 array of texels. This enables much higher magnification quality. Although native hardware support for cubic convolution (also called *bicubic interpolation*) is currently not commonly available, it can be performed in a shader program.

In the left part of Figure 6.8, the nearest neighbor method is used. One characteristic of this magnification technique is that the individual texels may become apparent. This effect is called *pixelation* and occurs because the method takes the value of the nearest texel to each pixel center when magnifying, resulting in a blocky appearance. While the quality of this method is sometimes poor, it requires only one texel to be fetched per pixel.

In the middle image of the same figure, bilinear interpolation (sometimes called *linear interpolation*) is used. For each pixel, this kind of filtering finds the four neighboring texels and linearly interpolates in two dimensions to find a blended value for the pixel. The result is blurrier, and much of the jaggedness from using the nearest neighbor method has disappeared. As an experiment, try looking at the left image

Figure 6.8. Texture magnification of a 48×48 image onto 320×320 pixels. Left: nearest neighbor filtering, where the nearest texel is chosen per pixel. Middle: bilinear filtering using a weighted average of the four nearest texels. Right: cubic filtering using a weighted average of the 5×5 nearest texels.

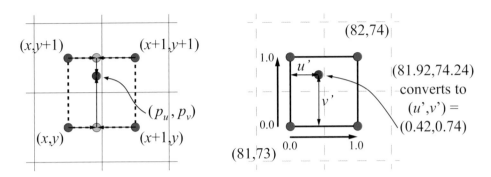

Figure 6.9. Bilinear interpolation. The four texels involved are illustrated by the four squares on the left, texel centers in blue. On the right is the coordinate system formed by the centers of the four texels.

while squinting, as this has approximately the same effect as a low-pass filter and reveals the face a bit more.

Returning to the brick texture example on page 170: Without dropping the fractions, we obtained $(p_u, p_v) = (81.92, 74.24)$. We use OpenGL's lower left origin texel coordinate system here, since it matches the standard Cartesian system. Our goal is to interpolate among the four closest texels, defining a texel-sized coordinate system using their texel centers. See Figure 6.9. To find the four nearest pixels, we subtract the pixel center fraction $(0.5, 0.5)$ from our sample location, giving $(81.42, 73.74)$. Dropping the fractions, the four closest pixels range from $(x, y) = (81, 73)$ to $(x+1, y+1) = (82, 74)$. The fractional part, $(0.42, 0.74)$ for our example, is the location of the sample relative to the coordinate system formed by the four texel centers. We denote this location as (u', v').

Define the texture access function as $\mathbf{t}(x, y)$, where x and y are integers and the color of the texel is returned. The bilinearly interpolated color for any location (u', v') can be computed as a two-step process. First, the bottom texels, $\mathbf{t}(x, y)$ and $\mathbf{t}(x+1, y)$, are interpolated horizontally (using u'), and similarly for the topmost two texels, $\mathbf{t}(x, y+1)$ and $\mathbf{t}(x+1, y+1)$. For the bottom texels, we obtain $(1 - u')\mathbf{t}(x, y) + u'\mathbf{t}(x+1, y)$ (bottom green circle in Figure 6.9), and for the top, $(1 - u')\mathbf{t}(x, y+1) + u'\mathbf{t}(x+1, y+1)$ (top green circle). These two values are then interpolated vertically (using v'), so the bilinearly interpolated color $\mathbf{b}$ at (p_u, p_v) is

$$
\begin{aligned}
\mathbf{b}(p_u, p_v) &= (1 - v')\big((1 - u')\mathbf{t}(x, y) + u'\mathbf{t}(x + 1, y)\big) \\
&\quad + v'\big((1 - u')\mathbf{t}(x, y + 1) + u'\mathbf{t}(x + 1, y + 1)\big) \\
&= (1 - u')(1 - v')\mathbf{t}(x, y) + u'(1 - v')\mathbf{t}(x + 1, y) \\
&\quad + (1 - u')v'\mathbf{t}(x, y + 1) + u'v'\mathbf{t}(x + 1, y + 1).
\end{aligned}
\tag{6.1}
$$

Intuitively, a texel closer to our sample location will influence its final value more. This is indeed what we see in this equation. The upper right texel at $(x+1, y+1)$ has

Figure 6.10. Nearest neighbor, bilinear interpolation, and part way in between by remapping, using the same 2×2 checkerboard texture. Note how nearest neighbor sampling gives slightly different square sizes, since the texture and the image grid do not match perfectly.

an influence of $u'v'$. Note the symmetry: The upper right's influence is equal to the area of the rectangle formed by the lower left corner and the sample point. Returning to our example, this means that the value retrieved from this texel will be multiplied by 0.42×0.74, specifically 0.3108. Clockwise from this texel the other multipliers are 0.42×0.26, 0.58×0.26, and 0.58×0.74, all four of these weights summing to 1.0.

A common solution to the blurriness that accompanies magnification is to use *detail textures*. These are textures that represent fine surface details, from scratches on a cellphone to bushes on terrain. Such detail is overlaid onto the magnified texture as a separate texture, at a different scale. The high-frequency repetitive pattern of the detail texture, combined with the low-frequency magnified texture, has a visual effect similar to the use of a single high-resolution texture.

Bilinear interpolation interpolates linearly in two directions. However, a linear interpolation is not required. Say a texture consists of black and white pixels in a checkerboard pattern. Using bilinear interpolation gives varying grayscale samples across the texture. By remapping so that, say, all grays lower than 0.4 are black, all grays higher than 0.6 are white, and those in between are stretched to fill the gap, the texture looks more like a checkerboard again, while also giving some blend between texels. See Figure 6.10.

Using a higher-resolution texture would have a similar effect. For example, imagine each checker square consists of 4×4 texels instead of being 1×1. Around the center of each checker, the interpolated color would be fully black or white.

To the right in Figure 6.8, a bicubic filter has been used, and the remaining blockiness is largely removed. It should be noted that bicubic filters are more expensive than bilinear filters. However, many higher-order filters can be expressed as repeated linear interpolations [1518] (see also Section 17.1.1). As a result, the GPU hardware for linear interpolation in the texture unit can be exploited with several lookups.

If bicubic filters are considered too expensive, Quílez [1451] proposes a simple technique using a smooth curve to interpolate in between a set of 2×2 texels. We first describe the curves and then the technique. Two commonly used curves are the

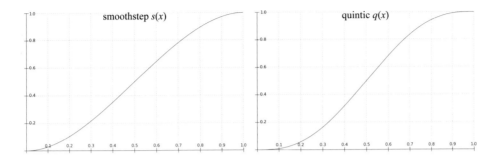

Figure 6.11. The smoothstep curve $s(x)$ (left) and a quintic curve $q(x)$ (right).

smoothstep curve and the quintic curve [1372]:

$$\underbrace{s(x) = x^2(3 - 2x)}_{\text{smoothstep}} \quad \text{and} \quad \underbrace{q(x) = x^3(6x^2 - 15x + 10)}_{\text{quintic}}. \tag{6.2}$$

These are useful for many other situations where you want to smoothly interpolate from one value to another. The smoothstep curve has the property that $s'(0) = s'(1) = 0$, and it is smooth between 0 and 1. The quintic curve has the same properties, but also $q''(0) = q''(1) = 0$, i.e., the second derivatives are also 0 at the start and end of the curve. The two curves are shown in Figure 6.11.

The technique starts by computing (u', v') (same as used in Equation 6.1 and in Figure 6.9) by first multiplying the sample by the texture dimensions and adding 0.5. The integer parts are kept for later, and the fractions are stored in u' and v', which are in the range of $[0, 1]$. The (u', v') are then transformed as $(t_u, t_v) = (q(u'), q(v'))$, still in the range of $[0, 1]$. Finally, 0.5 is subtracted and the integer parts are added back in; the resulting u-coordinate is then divided by the texture width, and similarly for v. At this point, the new texture coordinates are used with the bilinear interpolation lookup provided by the GPU. Note that this method will give plateaus at each texel, which means that if the texels are located on a plane in RGB space, for example, then this type of interpolation will give a smooth, but still staircased, look, which may not always be desired. See Figure 6.12.

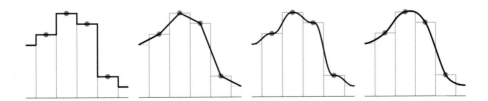

Figure 6.12. Four different ways to magnify a one-dimensional texture. The orange circles indicate the centers of the texels as well as the texel values (height). From left to right: nearest neighbor, linear, using a quintic curve between each pair of neighboring texels, and using cubic interpolation.

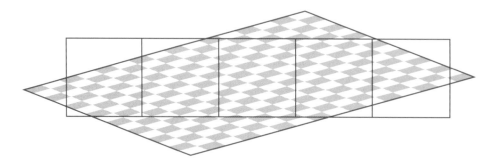

Figure 6.13. Minification: A view of a checkerboard-textured square through a row of pixel cells, showing roughly how a number of texels affect each pixel.

6.2.2 Minification

When a texture is minimized, several texels may cover a pixel's cell, as shown in Figure 6.13. To get a correct color value for each pixel, you should integrate the effect of the texels influencing the pixel. However, it is difficult to determine precisely the exact influence of all texels near a particular pixel, and it is effectively impossible to do so perfectly in real time.

Because of this limitation, several different methods are used on GPUs. One method is to use the nearest neighbor, which works exactly as the corresponding magnification filter does, i.e., it selects the texel that is visible at the center of the pixel's cell. This filter may cause severe aliasing problems. In Figure 6.14, nearest neighbor is used in the top figure. Toward the horizon, artifacts appear because only one of the many texels influencing a pixel is chosen to represent the surface. Such artifacts are even more noticeable as the surface moves with respect to the viewer, and are one manifestation of what is called *temporal aliasing*.

Another filter often available is bilinear interpolation, again working exactly as in the magnification filter. This filter is only slightly better than the nearest neighbor approach for minification. It blends four texels instead of using just one, but when a pixel is influenced by more than four texels, the filter soon fails and produces aliasing.

Better solutions are possible. As discussed in Section 5.4.1, the problem of aliasing can be addressed by sampling and filtering techniques. The signal frequency of a texture depends upon how closely spaced its texels are on the screen. Due to the Nyquist limit, we need to make sure that the texture's signal frequency is no greater than half the sample frequency. For example, say an image is composed of alternating black and white lines, a texel apart. The wavelength is then two texels wide (from black line to black line), so the frequency is $\frac{1}{2}$. To properly display this texture on a screen, the frequency must then be at least $2 \times \frac{1}{2}$, i.e., at least one pixel per texel. So, for textures in general, there should be at most one texel per pixel to avoid aliasing.

To achieve this goal, either the pixel's sampling frequency has to increase or the texture frequency has to decrease. The antialiasing methods discussed in the previous

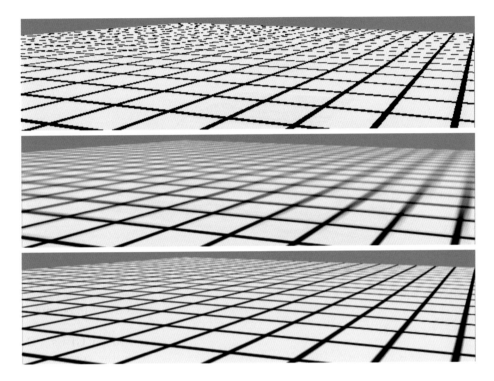

Figure 6.14. The top image was rendered with point sampling (nearest neighbor), the center with mipmapping, and the bottom with summed area tables.

chapter give ways to increase the pixel sampling rate. However, these give only a limited increase in sampling frequency. To more fully address this problem, various texture minification algorithms have been developed.

The basic idea behind all texture antialiasing algorithms is the same: to preprocess the texture and create data structures that will help compute a quick approximation of the effect of a set of texels on a pixel. For real-time work, these algorithms have the characteristic of using a fixed amount of time and resources for execution. In this way, a fixed number of samples are taken per pixel and combined to compute the effect of a (potentially huge) number of texels.

Mipmapping

The most popular method of antialiasing for textures is called *mipmapping* [1889]. It is implemented in some form on all graphics accelerators now produced. "Mip" stands for *multum in parvo*, Latin for "many things in a small place"—a good name for a process in which the original texture is filtered down repeatedly into smaller images.

When the mipmapping minimization filter is used, the original texture is augmented with a set of smaller versions of the texture before the actual rendering takes

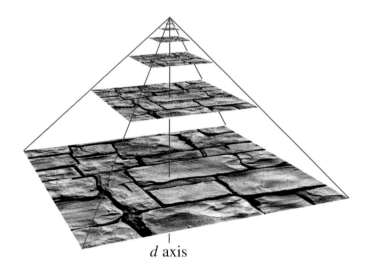

d axis

Figure 6.15. A mipmap is formed by taking the original image (level 0), at the base of the pyramid, and averaging each 2×2 area into a texel value on the next level up. The vertical axis is the third texture coordinate, d. In this figure, d is not linear; it is a measure of which two texture levels a sample uses for interpolation.

place. The texture (at level zero) is downsampled to a quarter of the original area, with each new texel value often computed as the average of four neighbor texels in the original texture. The new, level-one texture is sometimes called a *subtexture* of the original texture. The reduction is performed recursively until one or both of the dimensions of the texture equals one texel. This process is illustrated in Figure 6.15. The set of images as a whole is often called a *mipmap chain*.

Two important elements in forming high-quality mipmaps are good filtering and gamma correction. The common way to form a mipmap level is to take each 2×2 set of texels and average them to get the mip texel value. The filter used is then a box filter, one of the worst filters possible. This can result in poor quality, as it has the effect of blurring low frequencies unnecessarily, while keeping some high frequencies that cause aliasing [172]. It is better to use a Gaussian, Lanczos, Kaiser, or similar filter; fast, free source code exists for the task [172, 1592], and some APIs support better filtering on the GPU itself. Near the edges of textures, care must be taken during filtering as to whether the texture repeats or is a single copy.

For textures encoded in a nonlinear space (such as most color textures), ignoring gamma correction when filtering will modify the perceived brightness of the mipmap levels [173, 607]. As you get farther away from the object and the uncorrected mipmaps get used, the object can look darker overall, and contrast and details can also be affected. For this reason, it is important to convert such textures from sRGB to linear space (Section 5.6), perform all mipmap filtering in that space, and convert the final

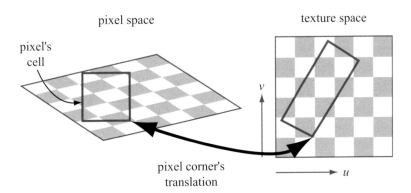

Figure 6.16. On the left is a square pixel cell and its view of a texture. On the right is the projection of the pixel cell onto the texture itself.

results back into sRGB color space for storage. Most APIs have support for sRGB textures, and so will generate mipmaps correctly in linear space and store the results in sRGB. When sRGB textures are accessed, their values are first converted to linear space so that magnification and minification are performed properly.

As mentioned earlier, some textures have a fundamentally nonlinear relationship to the final shaded color. Although this poses a problem for filtering in general, mipmap generation is particularly sensitive to this issue, since many hundred or thousands of pixels are being filtered. Specialized mipmap generation methods are often needed for the best results. Such methods are detailed in Section 9.13.

The basic process of accessing this structure while texturing is straightforward. A screen pixel encloses an area on the texture itself. When the pixel's area is projected onto the texture (Figure 6.16), it includes one or more texels. Using the pixel's cell boundaries is not strictly correct, but is used here to simplify the presentation. Texels outside of the cell can influence the pixel's color; see Section 5.4.1. The goal is to determine roughly how much of the texture influences the pixel. There are two common measures used to compute d (which OpenGL calls λ, and which is also known as the *texture level of detail*). One is to use the longer edge of the quadrilateral formed by the pixel's cell to approximate the pixel's coverage [1889]; another is to use as a measure the largest absolute value of the four differentials $\partial u/\partial x$, $\partial v/\partial x$, $\partial u/\partial y$, and $\partial v/\partial y$ [901, 1411]. Each differential is a measure of the amount of change in the texture coordinate with respect to a screen axis. For example, $\partial u/\partial x$ is the amount of change in the u texture value along the x-screen-axis for one pixel. See Williams's original article [1889] or the articles by Flavell [473] or Pharr [1411] for more about these equations. McCormack et al. [1160] discuss the introduction of aliasing by the largest absolute value method, and they present an alternate formula. Ewins et al. [454] analyze the hardware costs of several algorithms of comparable quality.

These gradient values are available to pixel shader programs using Shader Model 3.0 or newer. Since they are based on the differences between values in adjacent pixels, they are not accessible in sections of the pixel shader affected by dynamic flow control (Section 3.8). For texture reads to be performed in such a section (e.g., inside a loop), the derivatives must be computed earlier. Note that since vertex shaders cannot access gradient information, the gradients or the level of detail need to be computed in the vertex shader itself and supplied to the GPU when using vertex texturing.

The intent of computing the coordinate d is to determine where to sample along the mipmap's pyramid axis. See Figure 6.15. The goal is a pixel-to-texel ratio of at least $1 : 1$ to achieve the Nyquist rate. The important principle here is that as the pixel cell comes to include more texels and d increases, a smaller, blurrier version of the texture is accessed. The (u, v, d) triplet is used to access the mipmap. The value d is analogous to a texture level, but instead of an integer value, d has the fractional value of the distance between levels. The texture level above and the level below the d location is sampled. The (u, v) location is used to retrieve a bilinearly interpolated sample from each of these two texture levels. The resulting sample is then linearly interpolated, depending on the distance from each texture level to d. This entire process is called *trilinear interpolation* and is performed per pixel.

One user control on the d-coordinate is the *level of detail bias (LOD bias)*. This is a value added to d, and so it affects the relative perceived sharpness of a texture. If we move further up the pyramid to start (increasing d), the texture will look blurrier. A good LOD bias for any given texture will vary with the image type and with the way it is used. For example, images that are somewhat blurry to begin with could use a negative bias, while poorly filtered (aliased) synthetic images used for texturing could use a positive bias. The bias can be specified for the texture as a whole, or per-pixel in the pixel shader. For finer control, the d-coordinate or the derivatives used to compute it can be supplied by the user.

The benefit of mipmapping is that, instead of trying to sum all the texels that affect a pixel individually, precombined sets of texels are accessed and interpolated. This process takes a fixed amount of time, no matter what the amount of minification. However, mipmapping has several flaws [473]. A major one is *overblurring*. Imagine a pixel cell that covers a large number of texels in the u-direction and only a few in the v-direction. This case commonly occurs when a viewer looks along a textured surface nearly edge-on. In fact, it is possible to need minification along one axis of the texture and magnification along the other. The effect of accessing the mipmap is that square areas on the texture are retrieved; retrieving rectangular areas is not possible. To avoid aliasing, we choose the largest measure of the approximate coverage of the pixel cell on the texture. This results in the retrieved sample often being relatively blurry. This effect can be seen in the mipmap image in Figure 6.14. The lines moving into the distance on the right show overblurring.

Summed-Area Table

Another method to avoid overblurring is the *summed-area table* (SAT) [312]. To use this method, one first creates an array that is the size of the texture but contains more bits of precision for the color stored (e.g., 16 bits or more for each of red, green, and

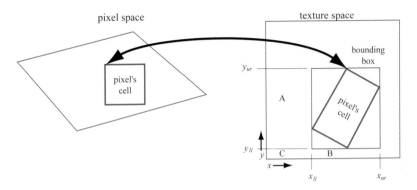

Figure 6.17. The pixel cell is back-projected onto the texture, bound by a rectangle; the four corners of the rectangle are used to access the summed-area table.

blue). At each location in this array, one must compute and store the sum of all the corresponding texture's texels in the rectangle formed by this location and texel $(0,0)$ (the origin). During texturing, the pixel cell's projection onto the texture is bound by a rectangle. The summed-area table is then accessed to determine the average color of this rectangle, which is passed back as the texture's color for the pixel. The average is computed using the texture coordinates of the rectangle shown in Figure 6.17. This is done using the formula given in Equation 6.3:

$$\mathbf{c} = \frac{\mathbf{s}[x_{ur}, y_{ur}] - \mathbf{s}[x_{ur}, y_{ll}] - \mathbf{s}[x_{ll}, y_{ur}] + \mathbf{s}[x_{ll}, y_{ll}]}{(x_{ur} - x_{ll})(y_{ur} - y_{ll})}. \tag{6.3}$$

Here, x and y are the texel coordinates of the rectangle and $\mathbf{s}[x, y]$ is the summed-area value for that texel. This equation works by taking the sum of the entire area from the upper right corner to the origin, then subtracting off areas A and B by subtracting the neighboring corners' contributions. Area C has been subtracted twice, so it is added back in by the lower left corner. Note that (x_{ll}, y_{ll}) is the upper right corner of area C, i.e., $(x_{ll} + 1, y_{ll} + 1)$ is the lower left corner of the bounding box.

The results of using a summed-area table are shown in Figure 6.14. The lines going to the horizon are sharper near the right edge, but the diagonally crossing lines in the middle are still overblurred. The problem is that when a texture is viewed along its diagonal, a large rectangle is generated, with many of the texels situated nowhere near the pixel being computed. For example, imagine a long, thin rectangle representing the pixel cell's back-projection lying diagonally across the entire texture in Figure 6.17. The whole texture rectangle's average will be returned, rather than just the average within the pixel cell.

The summed-area table is an example of what are called *anisotropic filtering* algorithms [691]. Such algorithms retrieve texel values over areas that are not square. However, SAT is able to do this most effectively in primarily horizontal and vertical

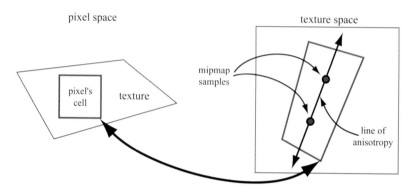

Figure 6.18. Anisotropic filtering. The back-projection of the pixel cell creates a quadrilateral. A line of anisotropy is formed between the longer sides.

directions. Note also that summed-area tables take at least two times as much memory for textures of size 16×16 or less, with more precision needed for larger textures.

Summed area tables, which give higher quality at a reasonable overall memory cost, can be implemented on modern GPUs [585]. Improved filtering can be critical to the quality of advanced rendering techniques. For example, Hensley et al. [718, 719] provide an efficient implementation and show how summed area sampling improves glossy reflections. Other algorithms in which area sampling is used can be improved by SAT, such as depth of field [585, 719], shadow maps [988], and blurry reflections [718].

Unconstrained Anisotropic Filtering

For current graphics hardware, the most common method to further improve texture filtering is to reuse existing mipmap hardware. The basic idea is that the pixel cell is back-projected, this quadrilateral (quad) on the texture is then sampled several times, and the samples are combined. As outlined above, each mipmap sample has a location and a squarish area associated with it. Instead of using a single mipmap sample to approximate this quad's coverage, the algorithm uses several squares to cover the quad. The shorter side of the quad can be used to determine d (unlike in mipmapping, where the longer side is often used); this makes the averaged area smaller (and so less blurred) for each mipmap sample. The quad's longer side is used to create a *line of anisotropy* parallel to the longer side and through the middle of the quad. When the amount of anisotropy is between $1 : 1$ and $2 : 1$, two samples are taken along this line (see Figure 6.18). At higher ratios of anisotropy, more samples are taken along the axis.

This scheme allows the line of anisotropy to run in any direction, and so does not have the limitations of summed-area tables. It also requires no more texture memory than mipmaps do, since it uses the mipmap algorithm to do its sampling. An example of anisotropic filtering is shown in Figure 6.19.

Figure 6.19. Mipmap versus anisotropic filtering. Trilinear mipmapping has been done on the left, and 16 : 1 anisotropic filtering on the right. Toward the horizon, anisotropic filtering provides a sharper result, with minimal aliasing. *(Image from three.js example webgl_materials_texture_anisotropy [218].)*

This idea of sampling along an axis was first introduced by Schilling et al. with their Texram dynamic memory device [1564]. Barkans describes the algorithm's use in the Talisman system [103]. A similar system called *Feline* is presented by McCormack et al. [1161]. Texram's original formulation has the samples along the anisotropic axis (also known as *probes*) given equal weights. Talisman gives half weight to the two probes at opposite ends of the axis. Feline uses a Gaussian filter kernel to weight the set of probes. These algorithms approach the high quality of software sampling algorithms such as the *Elliptical Weighted Average* (EWA) filter, which transforms the pixel's area of influence into an ellipse on the texture and weights the texels inside the ellipse by a filter kernel [691]. Mavridis and Papaioannou present several methods to implement EWA filtering with shader code on the GPU [1143].

6.2.3 Volume Textures

A direct extension of image textures is three-dimensional image data that is accessed by (u, v, w) (or (s, t, r) values). For example, medical imaging data can be generated as a three-dimensional grid; by moving a polygon through this grid, one may view two-dimensional slices of these data. A related idea is to represent volumetric lights in this form. The illumination on a point on a surface is found by finding the value for its location inside this volume, combined with a direction for the light.

Most GPUs support mipmapping for volume textures. Since filtering inside a single mipmap level of a volume texture involves trilinear interpolation, filtering between mipmap levels requires *quadrilinear interpolation*. Since this involves averaging the results from 16 texels, precision problems may result, which can be solved by using a higher-precision volume texture. Sigg and Hadwiger [1638] discuss this and other problems relevant to volume textures and provide efficient methods to perform filtering and other operations.

Although volume textures have significantly higher storage requirements and are more expensive to filter, they do have some unique advantages. The complex process of finding a good two-dimensional parameterization for the three-dimensional mesh can be skipped, since three-dimensional locations can be used directly as texture coordinates. This avoids the distortion and seam problems that commonly occur with two-dimensional parameterizations. A volume texture can also be used to represent the volumetric structure of a material such as wood or marble. A model textured with such a texture will appear to be carved from this material.

Using volume textures for surface texturing is extremely inefficient, since the vast majority of samples are not used. Benson and Davis [133] and DeBry et al. [334] discuss storing texture data in a sparse octree structure. This scheme fits well with interactive three-dimensional painting systems, as the surface does not need explicit texture coordinates assigned to it at the time of creation, and the octree can hold texture detail down to any level desired. Lefebvre et al. [1017] discuss the details of implementing octree textures on the modern GPU. Lefebvre and Hoppe [1018] discuss a method of packing sparse volume data into a significantly smaller texture.

6.2.4 Cube Maps

Another type of texture is the *cube texture* or *cube map*, which has six square textures, each of which is associated with one face of a cube. A cube map is accessed with a three-component texture coordinate vector that specifies the direction of a ray pointing from the center of the cube outward. The point where the ray intersects the cube is found as follows. The texture coordinate with the largest magnitude selects the corresponding face (e.g., the vector $(-3.2, 5.1, -8.4)$ selects the $-z$ face). The remaining two coordinates are divided by the absolute value of the largest magnitude coordinate, i.e., 8.4. They now range from -1 to 1, and are simply remapped to $[0, 1]$ in order to compute the texture coordinates. For example, the coordinates $(-3.2, 5.1)$ are mapped to $((-3.2/8.4 + 1)/2, (5.1/8.4 + 1)/2) \approx (0.31, 0.80)$. Cube maps are useful for representing values which are a function of direction; they are most commonly used for environment mapping (Section 10.4.3).

6.2.5 Texture Representation

There are several ways to improve performance when handling many textures in an application. Texture compression is described in Section 6.2.6, while the focus of this section is on texture atlases, texture arrays, and bindless textures, all of which aim to avoid the costs of changing textures while rendering. In Sections 19.10.1 and 19.10.2, texture streaming and transcoding are described.

To be able to batch up as much work as possible for the GPU, it is generally preferred to change state as little as possible (Section 18.4.2). To that end, one may put several images into a single larger texture, called a *texture atlas*. This is illustrated to the left in Figure 6.20. Note that the shapes of the subtextures can be arbitrary,

Figure 6.20. Left: a texture atlas where nine smaller images have been composited into a single large texture. Right: a more modern approach is to set up the smaller images as an array of textures, which is a concept found in most APIs.

as shown in Figure 6.6. Optimization of subtexture placement atlases is described by Nöll and Stricker [1286]. Care also needs to be taken with mipmap generation and access, since the upper levels of the mipmap may encompass several separate, unrelated shapes. Manson and Schaefer [1119] presented a method to optimize mipmap creation by taking into account the parameterization of the surface, which can generate substantially better results. Burley and Lacewell [213] presented a system called *Ptex*, where each quad in a subdivision surface had its own small texture. The advantages are that this avoids assignment of unique texture coordinates over a mesh and that there are no artifacts over seams of disconnected parts of a texture atlas. To be able to filter across quads, Ptex uses an adjacency data structure. While the initial target was production rendering, Hillesland [746] presents *packed Ptex*, which puts the subtexture of each face into a texture atlas and uses padding from adjacent faces to avoid indirection when filtering. Yuksel [1955] presents *mesh color textures*, which improve upon Ptex. Toth [1780] provides high-quality filtering across faces for Ptex-like systems by implementing a method where filter taps are discarded if they are outside the range of $[0,1]^2$.

One difficulty with using an atlas is wrapping/repeat and mirror modes, which will not properly affect a subtexture but only the texture as a whole. Another problem can occur when generating mipmaps for an atlas, where one subtexture can bleed into another. However, this can be avoided by generating the mipmap hierarchy for each subtexture separately before placing them into a large texture atlas and using power-of-two resolutions for the subtextures [1293].

A simpler solution to these issues is to use an API construction called *texture arrays*, which completely avoids any problems with mipmapping and repeat modes [452]. See the right part of Figure 6.20. All subtextures in a texture array need to have the same dimensions, format, mipmap hierarchy, and MSAA settings. Like a texture atlas, setup is only done once for a texture array, and then any array element can be accessed using an index in the shader. This can be 5× faster than binding each subtexture [452].

A feature that can also help avoid state change costs is API support for *bindless textures* [1407]. Without bindless textures, a texture is bound to a specific texture unit using the API. One problem is the upper limit on the number of texture units, which complicates matters for the programmer. The driver makes sure that the texture is resident on the GPU side. With bindless textures, there is no upper bound on the number of textures, because each texture is associated by just a 64-bit pointer, sometimes called a *handle*, to its data structure. These handles can be accessed in many different ways, e.g., through uniforms, through varying data, from other textures, or from a shader storage buffer object (SSBO). The application needs to ensure that the textures are resident on the GPU side. Bindless textures avoid any type of binding cost in the driver, which makes rendering faster.

6.2.6 Texture Compression

One solution that directly attacks memory and bandwidth problems and caching concerns is fixed-rate *texture compression* [127]. By having the GPU decode compressed textures on the fly, a texture can require less texture memory and so increase the effective cache size. At least as significant, such textures are more efficient to use, as they consume less memory bandwidth when accessed. A related but different use case is to add compression in order to afford larger textures. For example, a non-compressed texture using 3 bytes per texel at 512^2 resolution would occupy 768 kB. Using texture compression, with a compression ratio of $6 : 1$, a 1024^2 texture would occupy only 512 kB.

There are a variety of image compression methods used in image file formats such as JPEG and PNG, but it is costly to implement decoding for these in hardware (though see Section 19.10.1 for information about texture transcoding). S3 developed a scheme called *S3 Texture Compression* (S3TC) [1524], which was chosen as a standard for DirectX and called *DXTC*—in DirectX 10 it is called *BC* (for Block Compression). Furthermore, it is the de facto standard in OpenGL, since almost all GPUs support it. It has the advantages of creating a compressed image that is fixed in size, has independently encoded pieces, and is simple (and therefore fast) to decode. Each compressed part of the image can be dealt with independently from the others. There are no shared lookup tables or other dependencies, which simplifies decoding.

There are seven variants of the DXTC/BC compression scheme, and they share some common properties. Encoding is done on 4×4 texel blocks, also called *tiles*. Each block is encoded separately. The encoding is based on interpolation. For each encoded quantity, two reference values (e.g., colors) are stored. An interpolation factor is saved for each of the 16 texels in the block. It selects a value along the line between the two reference values, e.g., a color equal to or interpolated from the two stored

Name(s)	Storage	Ref colors	Indices	Alpha	Comment
BC1/DXT1	8 B/4 bpt	RGB565×2	2 bpt	–	1 line
BC2/DXT3	16 B/8 bpt	RGB565×2	2 bpt	4 bpt raw	color same as BC1
BC3/DXT5	16 B/8 bpt	RGB565×2	2 bpt	3 bpt interp.	color same as BC1
BC4	8 B/4 bpt	R8×2	3 bpt	–	1 channel
BC5	16 B/8 bpt	RG88×2	2 × 3 bpt	–	2× BC4
BC6H	16 B/8 bpt	see text	see text		For HDR; 1–2 lines
BC7	8 B/4 bpt	see text	see text	optional	1–3 lines

Table 6.1. Texture compression formats. All of these compress blocks of 4×4 texels. The storage column show the number of bytes (B) per block and the number of bits per texel (bpt). The notation for the reference colors is first the channels and then the number of bits for each channel. For example, RGB565 means 5 bits for red and blue while the green channel has 6 bits.

colors. The compression comes from storing only two colors along with a short index value per pixel.

The exact encoding varies between the seven variants, which are summarized in Table 6.1. Note that "DXT" indicates the names in DirectX 9 and "BC" the names in DirectX 10 and beyond. As can be read in the table, BC1 has two 16-bit reference RGB values (5 bits red, 6 green, 5 blue), and each texel has a 2-bit interpolation factor to select from one of the reference values or two intermediate values.[1] This represents a 6 : 1 texture compression ratio, compared to an uncompressed 24-bit RGB texture. BC2 encodes colors in the same way as BC1, but adds 4 bits per texel (bpt) for quantized (raw) alpha. For BC3, each block has RGB data encoded in the same way as a DXT1 block. In addition, alpha data are encoded using two 8-bit reference values and a per-texel 3-bit interpolation factor. Each texel can select either one of the reference alpha values or one of six intermediate values. BC4 has a single channel, encoded as alpha in BC3. BC5 contains two channels, where each is encoded as in BC3.

BC6H is for high dynamic range (HDR) textures, where each texel initially has 16-bit floating point value per R, G, and B channel. This mode uses 16 bytes, which results in 8 bpt. It has one mode for a single line (similar to the techniques above) and another for two lines where each block can select from a small set of partitions. Two reference colors can also be delta-encoded for better precision and can also have different accuracy depending on which mode is being used. In BC7, each block can have between one and three lines and stores 8 bpt. The target is high-quality texture compression of 8-bit RGB and RGBA textures. It shares many properties with BC6H, but is a format for LDR textures, while BC6H is for HDR. Note that BC6H and BC7 are called `BPTC_FLOAT` and `BPTC`, respectively, in OpenGL. These compression techniques can be applied to cube or volume textures, as well as two-dimensional textures.

---

[1] An alternate DXT1 mode reserves one of the four possible interpolation factors for transparent pixels, restricting the number of interpolated values to three—the two reference values and their average.

base color   luminance   decompressed   original

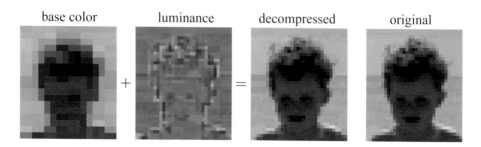

Figure 6.21. ETC (Ericsson texture compression) encodes the color of a block of pixels and then modifies the luminance per pixel to create the final texel color. *(Images compressed by Jacob Ström.)*

The main drawback of these compression schemes is that they are *lossy*. That is, the original image usually cannot be retrieved from the compressed version. In the case of BC1–BC5, only four or eight interpolated values are used to represent 16 pixels. If a tile has a larger number of distinct values in it, there will be some loss. In practice, these compression schemes generally give acceptable image fidelity if correctly used.

One of the problems with BC1–BC5 is that all the colors used for a block lie on a straight line in RGB space. For example, the colors red, green, and blue cannot be represented in a single block. BC6H and BC7 support more lines and so can provide higher quality.

For OpenGL ES, another compression algorithm, called *Ericsson texture compression* (ETC) [1714] was chosen for inclusion in the API. This scheme has the same features as S3TC, namely, fast decoding, random access, no indirect lookups, and fixed rate. It encodes a block of 4×4 texels into 64 bits, i.e., 4 bits per texel are used. The basic idea is illustrated in Figure 6.21. Each 2×4 block (or 4×2, depending on which gives best quality) stores a base color. Each block also selects a set of four constants from a small static lookup table, and each texel in a block can select to add one of the values in this table. This modifies the luminance per pixel. The image quality is on par with DXTC.

In ETC2 [1715], included in OpenGL ES 3.0, unused bit combinations were used to add more modes to the original ETC algorithm. An unused bit combination is the compressed representation (e.g., 64 bits) that decompresses to the same image as another compressed representation. For example, in BC1 it is useless to set both reference colors to be identical, since this will indicate a constant color block, which in turn can be obtained as long as one reference color contains that constant color. In ETC, one color can also be delta encoded from a first color with a signed number, and hence that computation can overflow or underflow. Such cases were used to signal other compression modes. ETC2 added two new modes with four colors, derived differently, per block, and a final mode that is a plane in RGB space intended to handle smooth transitions. *Ericsson alpha compression* (EAC) [1868] compresses an image with one component (e.g, alpha). This compression is like basic ETC compression but for only one component, and the resulting image stores 4 bits per texel. It can optionally be

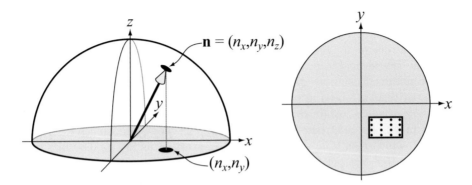

Figure 6.22. Left: the unit normal on a sphere only needs to encode the x- and y-components. Right: for BC4/3Dc, a box in the xy-plane encloses the normals, and 8×8 normals inside this box can be used per 4×4 block of normals (for clarity, only 4×4 normals are shown here).

combined with ETC2, and in addition two EAC channels can be used to compress normals (more on this topic below). All of ETC1, ETC2, and EAC are part of the OpenGL 4.0 core profile, OpenGL ES 3.0, Vulkan, and Metal.

Compression of normal maps (discussed in Section 6.7.2) requires some care. Compressed formats that were designed for RGB colors usually do not work well for normal xyz data. Most approaches take advantage of the fact that the normal is known to be unit length, and further assume that its z-component is positive (a reasonable assumption for tangent-space normals). This allows for only storing the x- and y-components of a normal. The z-component is derived on the fly as

$$n_z = \sqrt{1 - n_x^2 - n_y^2}. \tag{6.4}$$

This in itself results in a modest amount of compression, since only two components are stored, instead of three. Since most GPUs do not natively support three-component textures, this also avoids the possibility of wasting a component (or having to pack another quantity in the fourth component). Further compression is usually achieved by storing the x- and y-components in a BC5/3Dc-format texture. See Figure 6.22. Since the reference values for each block demarcate the minimum and maximum x- and y-component values, they can be seen as defining a bounding box on the xy-plane. The three-bit interpolation factors allow for the selection of eight values on each axis, so the bounding box is divided into an 8×8 grid of possible normals. Alternatively, two channels of EAC (for x and y) can be used, followed by computation of z as defined above.

On hardware that does not support the BC5/3Dc or the EAC format, a common fallback [1227] is to use a DXT5-format texture and store the two components in the green and alpha components (since those are stored with the highest precision). The other two components are unused.

PVRTC [465] is a texture compression format available on Imagination Technologies' hardware called *PowerVR*, and its most widespread use is for iPhones and iPads. It provides a scheme for both 2 and 4 bits per texel and compresses blocks of 4×4 texels. The key idea is to provide two low-frequency (smooth) signals of the image, which are obtained using neighboring blocks of texel data and interpolation. Then 1 or 2 bits per texel are used in interpolate between the two signals over the image.

Adaptive scalable texture compression (ASTC) [1302] is different in that it compresses a block of $n \times m$ texels into 128 bits. The block size ranges from 4×4 up to 12×12, which results in different bit rates, starting as low as 0.89 bits per texel and going up to 8 bits per texel. ASTC uses a wide range of tricks for compact index representation, and the numbers of lines and endpoint encoding can be chosen per block. In addition, ASTC can handle anything from 1–4 channels per texture and both LDR and HDR textures. ASTC is part of OpenGL ES 3.2 and beyond.

All the texture compression schemes presented above are lossy, and when compressing a texture, one can spend different amounts of time on this process. Spending seconds or even minutes on compression, one can obtain substantially higher quality; therefore, this is often done as an offline preprocess and is stored for later use. Alternatively, one can spend only a few milliseconds, with lower quality as a result, but the texture can be compressed in near real-time and used immediately. An example is a skybox (Section 13.3) that is regenerated every other second or so, when the clouds may have moved slightly. Decompression is extremely fast since it is done using fixed-function hardware. This difference is called *data compression asymmetry*, where compression can and does take a considerably longer time than decompression.

Kaplanyan [856] presents several methods that can improve the quality of the compressed textures. For both textures containing colors and normal maps, it is recommended that the maps are authored with 16 bits per component. For color textures, one then performs a *histogram renormalization* (on these 16 bits), the effect of which is then inverted using a scale and bias constant (per texture) in the shader. Histogram normalization is a technique that spreads out the values used in an image to span the entire range, which effectively is a type of contrast enhancement. Using 16 bits per component makes sure that there are no unused slots in the histogram after renormalization, which reduces banding artifacts that many texture compression schemes may introduce. This is shown in Figure 6.23. In addition, Kaplanyan recommends using a linear color space for the texture if 75% of the pixels are above 116/255, and otherwise storing the texture in sRGB. For normal maps, he also notes that BC5/3Dc often compresses x independently from y, which means that the best normal is not always found. Instead, he proposes to use the following error metric for normals:

$$e = \arccos \left(\frac{\mathbf{n} \cdot \mathbf{n}_c}{||\mathbf{n}|| \, ||\mathbf{n}_c||} \right), \tag{6.5}$$

where $\mathbf{n}$ is the original normal and $\mathbf{n}_c$ is the same normal compressed, and then decompressed.

Figure 6.23. The effect of using 16 bits per component versus 8 bits during texture compression. From left to right: original texture, DXT1 compressed from 8 bits per component, and DXT1 compressed from 16 bits per component with renormalization done in the shader. The texture has been rendered with strong lighting in order to more clearly show the effect. *(Images appear courtesy of Anton Kaplanyan.)*

It should be noted that it is also possible to compress textures in a different color space, which can be used to speed up texture compression. A commonly used transform is RGB→YCoCg [1112]:

$$\begin{pmatrix} Y \\ C_o \\ C_g \end{pmatrix} = \begin{pmatrix} 1/4 & 1/2 & 1/4 \\ 1/2 & 0 & -1/2 \\ -1/4 & 1/2 & -1/4 \end{pmatrix} \begin{pmatrix} R \\ G \\ B \end{pmatrix}, \qquad (6.6)$$

where Y is a luminance term and C_o and C_g are chrominance terms. The inverse transform is also inexpensive:

$$G = (Y + C_g), \quad t = (Y - C_g), \quad R = t + C_o, \quad B = t - C_o, \qquad (6.7)$$

which amounts to a handful of additions. These two transforms are linear, which can be seen in that Equation 6.6 is a matrix-vector multiplication, which is linear (see Equations 4.1 and 4.2) in itself. This is of importance since, instead of storing RGB in a texture, it is possible to store YCoCg; the texturing hardware can still perform filtering in the YCoCg space, and then the pixel shader can convert back to RGB as needed. It should be noted that this transform is lossy in itself, which may or may not matter.

There is another reversible RGB→YCoCg transform, which is summarized as

$$\begin{cases} C_o = R - B \\ \quad t = B + (C_o \gg 1) \\ C_g = G - t \\ \quad Y = t + (C_g \gg 1) \end{cases} \Longleftrightarrow \begin{cases} t = Y - (C_g \gg 1) \\ G = C_g + t \\ B = t - (C_o \gg 1) \\ R = B + C_o \end{cases}, \qquad (6.8)$$

where $\gg$ shifts right. This means that it is possible to transform back and forth between, say, a 24-bit RGB color and the corresponding YCoCg representation without any loss. It should be noted that if each component in RGB has n bits then both C_o and C_g have $n + 1$ bits each to guarantee a reversible transform; Y needs only n bits though. Van Waveren and Castaño [1852] use the lossy YCoCg transform to implement fast compression to DXT5/BC3 on either the CPU or the GPU. They store Y in the alpha channel (since it has the highest accuracy), while C_o and C_g are stored in the first two components of RGB. Compression becomes fast since Y is stored and compressed separately. For the C_o- and C_g-components, they find a two-dimensional bounding box and select the box diagonal that produces the best results. Note that for textures that are dynamically created on the CPU, it may be better to compress the textures on the CPU as well. When textures are created through rendering on the GPU, it is usually best to compress the textures on the GPU as well. The YCoCg transform and other luminance-chrominance transforms are often used for image compression, where the chrominance components are averaged over 2×2 pixels. This reduces storage by 50% and often works fine since chrominance tends to vary slowly. Lee-Steere and Harmon [1015] take this a step further by converting to hue-saturation-value (HSV), downsampling both hue and saturation by a factor of 4 in x and y, and storing value as a single channel DXT1 texture. Van Waveren and Castaño also describe fast methods for compression of normal maps [1853].

A study by Griffin and Olano [601] shows that when several textures are applied to a geometrical model with a complex shading model, the quality of textures can often be low without any perceivable differences. So, depending on the use case, a reduction in quality may be acceptable. Fauconneau [463] presents a SIMD implementation of DirectX 11 texture compression formats.

6.3 Procedural Texturing

Given a texture-space location, performing an image lookup is one way of generating texture values. Another is to evaluate a function, thus defining a *procedural texture*.

Although procedural textures are commonly used in offline rendering applications, image textures are far more common in real-time rendering. This is due to the extremely high efficiency of the image texturing hardware in modern GPUs, which can perform many billions of texture accesses in a second. However, GPU architectures are evolving toward less expensive computation and (relatively) more costly memory access. These trends have made procedural textures find greater use in real-time applications.

Volume textures are a particularly attractive application for procedural texturing, given the high storage costs of volume image textures. Such textures can be synthesized by a variety of techniques. One of the most common is using one or more noise functions to generate values [407, 1370, 1371, 1372]. See Figure 6.24. A noise function is often sampled at successive powers-of-two frequencies, called *octaves*. Each octave is given a weight, usually falling as the frequency increases, and the sum of these weighted samples is called a *turbulence* function.

Figure 6.24. Two examples of real-time procedural texturing using a volume texture. The marble on the left is a semitransparent volume texture rendered using ray marching. On the right, the object is a synthetic image generated with a complex procedural wood shader [1054] and composited atop a real-world environment. *(Left image from the shadertoy "Playing marble," courtesy of Stéphane Guillitte. Right image courtesy of Nicolas Savva, Autodesk, Inc.)*

Because of the cost of evaluating the noise function, the lattice points in the three-dimensional array are often precomputed and used to interpolate texture values. There are various methods that use color buffer blending to rapidly generate these arrays [1192]. Perlin [1373] presents a rapid, practical method for sampling this noise function and shows some uses. Olano [1319] provides noise generation algorithms that permit trade-offs between storing textures and performing computations. McEwan et al. [1168] develop methods for computing classic noise as well as simplex noise in the shader without any lookups, and source code is available. Parberry [1353] uses dynamic programming to amortize computations over several pixels to speed up noise computations. Green [587] gives a higher-quality method, but one that is meant more for near-interactive applications, as it uses 50 pixel shader instructions for a single lookup. The original noise function presented by Perlin [1370, 1371, 1372] can be improved upon. Cook and DeRose [290] present an alternate representation, called wavelet noise, which avoids aliasing problems with only a small increase in evaluation cost. Liu et al. [1054] use a variety of noise functions to simulate different wood textures and surface finishes. We also recommend the state-of-the-art report by Lagae et al. [956] on this topic.

Other procedural methods are possible. For example, a *cellular texture* is formed by measuring distances from each location to a set of "feature points" scattered through space. Mapping the resulting closest distances in various ways, e.g., changing the color or shading normal, creates patterns that look like cells, flagstones, lizard skin, and other natural textures. Griffiths [602] discusses how to efficiently find the closest neighbors and generate cellular textures on the GPU.

Another type of procedural texture is the result of a physical simulation or some other interactive process, such as water ripples or spreading cracks. In such cases, procedural textures can produce effectively infinite variability in reaction to dynamic conditions.

When generating a procedural two-dimensional texture, parameterization issues can pose even more difficulties than for authored textures, where stretching or seam artifacts can be manually touched up or worked around. One solution is to avoid parameterization completely by synthesizing textures directly onto the surface. Performing this operation on complex surfaces is technically challenging and is an active area of research. See Wei et al. [1861] for an overview of this field.

Antialiasing procedural textures is both harder and easier than antialiasing image textures. On one hand, precomputation methods such as mipmapping are not available, putting the burden on the programmer. On the other, the procedural texture author has "inside information" about the texture content and so can tailor it to avoid aliasing. This is particularly true for procedural textures created by summing multiple noise functions. The frequency of each noise function is known, so any frequencies that would cause aliasing can be discarded, actually making the computation less costly. There are a variety of techniques for antialiasing other types of procedural textures [407, 605, 1392, 1512]. Dorn et al. [371] discuss previous work and present some processes for reformulating texture functions to avoid high frequencies, i.e., to be *band-limited*.

6.4 Texture Animation

The image applied to a surface does not have to be static. For example, a video source can be used as a texture that changes from frame to frame.

The texture coordinates need not be static, either. The application designer can explicitly change the texture coordinates from frame to frame, either in the mesh's data itself or via functions applied in the vertex or pixel shader. Imagine that a waterfall has been modeled and that it has been textured with an image that looks like falling water. Say the v-coordinate is the direction of flow. To make the water move, one must subtract an amount from the v-coordinates on each successive frame. Subtraction from the texture coordinates has the effect of making the texture itself appear to move forward.

More elaborate effects can be created by applying a matrix to the texture coordinates. In addition to translation, this allows for linear transformations such as zoom, rotation, and shearing [1192, 1904], image warping and morphing transforms [1729], and generalized projections [638]. Many more elaborate effects can be created by applying functions on the CPU or in shaders.

By using texture blending techniques, one can realize other animated effects. For example, by starting with a marble texture and fading in a flesh texture, one can make a statue come to life [1215].

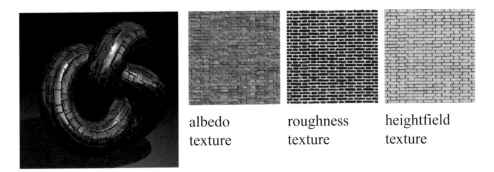

albedo texture   roughness texture   heightfield texture

Figure 6.25. Metallic bricks and mortar. On the right are the textures for surface color, roughness (lighter is rougher), and bump map height (lighter is higher). *(Image from three.js example webgl_tonemapping [218].)*

6.5 Material Mapping

A common use of a texture is to modify a material property affecting the shading equation. Real-world objects usually have material properties that vary over their surface. To simulate such objects, the pixel shader can read values from textures and use them to modify the material parameters before evaluating the shading equation. The parameter that is most often modified by a texture is the surface color. This texture is known as an *albedo color map* or *diffuse color map*. However, any parameter can be modified by a texture: replacing it, multiplying it, or changing it in some other way. For example, in Figure 6.25 three different textures are applied to a surface, replacing the constant values.

The use of textures in materials can be taken further. Instead of modifying a parameter in an equation, a texture can be used to control the flow and function of the pixel shader itself. Two or more materials with different shading equations and parameters could be applied to a surface by having one texture specify which areas of the surface have which material, causing different code to be executed for each. As an example, a metallic surface with some rusty regions can use a texture to indicate where the rust is located, conditionally executing the rusty part of the shader based on that texture lookup and otherwise executing the shiny metal shader (Section 9.5.2).

Shading model inputs such as surface color have a linear relationship to the final color output from the shader. Thus, textures containing such inputs can be filtered with standard techniques, and aliasing is avoided. Textures containing nonlinear shading inputs, such as roughness or bump mapping (Section 6.7), require a bit more care to avoid aliasing. Filtering techniques that take account of the shading equation can improve results for such textures. These techniques are discussed in Section 9.13.

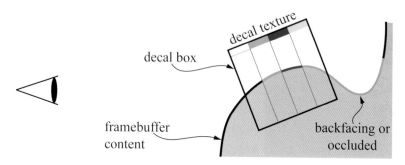

Figure 6.26. One way to implement decals. The framebuffer is first rendered with a scene, and then a box is rendered and for all points that are inside the box, the decal texture is projected to the framebuffer contents. The leftmost texel is fully transparent so it does not affect the framebuffer. The yellow texel is not visible since it would be projected onto a hidden part of the surface.

6.6 Alpha Mapping

The alpha value can be employed for many effects using alpha blending or alpha testing, such as efficiently rendering foliage, explosions, and distant objects, to name but a few. This section discusses the use of textures with alphas, noting various limitations and solutions along the way.

One texture-related effect is *decaling*. As an example, say you wish to put a picture of a flower on a teapot. You do not want the whole picture, but just the parts where the flower is present. By assigning an alpha of 0 to a texel, you make it transparent, so that it has no effect. So, by properly setting the decal texture's alpha, you can replace or blend the underlying surface with the decal. Typically, a clamp corresponder function is used with a transparent border to apply a single copy of the decal (versus a repeating texture) to the surface. An example of how decaling can be implemented is visualized in Figure 6.26. See Section 20.2 for more information about decals.

A similar application of alpha is in making cutouts. Say you make a decal image of a bush and apply it to a rectangle in the scene. The principle is the same as for decals, except that instead of being flush with an underlying surface, the bush will be drawn on top of whatever geometry is behind it. In this way, using a single rectangle you can render an object with a complex silhouette.

In the case of the bush, if you rotate the viewer around it, the illusion fails, since the bush has no thickness. One answer is to copy this bush rectangle and rotate it 90 degrees along the trunk. The two rectangles form an inexpensive three-dimensional bush, sometimes called a "cross tree" [1204], and the illusion is fairly effective when viewed from ground level. See Figure 6.27. Pelzer [1367] discusses a similar configuration using three cutouts to represent grass. In Section 13.6, we discuss a method called *billboarding*, which is used to reduce such rendering to a single rectangle. If the viewer moves above ground level, the illusion breaks down as the bush is seen from above to be

Figure 6.27. On the left, the bush texture map and the 1-bit alpha channel map below it. On the right, the bush rendered on a single rectangle; by adding a second copy of the rectangle rotated 90 degrees, we form an inexpensive three-dimensional bush.

two cutouts. See Figure 6.28. To combat this, more cutouts can be added in different ways—slices, branches, layers—to provide a more convincing model. Section 13.6.5 discusses one approach for generating such models; Figure 19.31 on page 857 shows another. See the images on pages 2 and 1049 for examples of final results.

Combining alpha maps and texture animation can produce convincing special effects, such as flickering torches, plant growth, explosions, and atmospheric effects.

There are several options for rendering objects with alpha maps. Alpha blending (Section 5.5) allows for fractional transparency values, which enables antialiasing the object edges, as well as partially transparent objects. However, alpha blending requires rendering the blended triangles after the opaque ones, and in back-to-front order. A simple cross-tree is an example of two cutout textures where no rendering order is correct, since each quadrilateral is in front of a part of the other. Even when it is theoretically possible to sort and get the correct order, it is usually inefficient to do so. For example, a field may have tens of thousands of blades of grass represented by

Figure 6.28. Looking at the "cross-tree" bush from a bit off ground level, then further up, where the illusion breaks down.

cutouts. Each mesh object may be made of many individual blades. Explicitly sorting each blade is wildly impractical.

This problem can be ameliorated in several different ways when rendering. One is to use alpha testing, which is the process of conditionally discarding fragments with alpha values below a given threshold in the pixel shader. This is done as

$$\text{if (texture.a < alphaThreshold) discard;} \qquad (6.9)$$

where `texture.a` is the alpha value from the texture lookup, and the parameter `alphaThreshold` is a user-supplied threshold value that determines which fragments will get discarded. This binary visibility test enables triangles to be rendered in any order because transparent fragments are discarded. We normally want to do this for any fragment with an alpha of 0.0. Discarding fully transparent fragments has the additional benefit of saving further shader processing and costs for merging, as well as avoiding incorrectly marking pixels in the z-buffer as visible [394]. For cutouts we often set the threshold value higher than 0.0, say, 0.5 or higher, and take the further step of then ignoring the alpha value altogether, not using it for blending. Doing so avoids out-of-order artifacts. However, the quality is low because only two levels of transparency (fully opaque and fully transparent) are available. Another solution is to perform two passes for each model—one for solid cutouts, which are written to the z-buffer, and the other for semitransparent samples, which are not.

There are two other problems with alpha testing, namely too much magnification [1374] and too much minification [234, 557]. When alpha testing is used with mipmapping, the effect can be unconvincing if not handled differently. An example is shown in the top of Figure 6.29, where the leaves of the trees have become more transparent than intended. This can be explained with an example. Assume we have a one-dimensional texture with four alpha values, namely, $(0.0, 1.0, 1.0, 0.0)$. With averaging, the next mipmap level becomes $(0.5, 0.5)$, and then the top level is (0.5). Now, assume we use $\alpha_t = 0.75$. When accessing mipmap level 0, one can show that 1.5 texels out of 4 will survive the discard test. However, when accessing the next two levels, everything will be discarded since $0.5 < 0.75$. See Figure 6.30 for another example.

Castaño [234] presents a simple solution done during mipmap creation that works well. For mipmap level k, the coverage c_k is defined as

$$c_k = \frac{1}{n_k} \sum_i \left(\alpha(k, i) > \alpha_t \right), \qquad (6.10)$$

where n_k is the number of texels in mipmap level k, $\alpha(k, i)$ is the alpha value from mipmap level k at pixel i, and α_t is the user-supplied alpha threshold in Equation 6.9. Here, we assume that the result of $\alpha(k, i) > \alpha_t$ is 1 if it is true, and 0 otherwise. Note that $k = 0$ indicates the lowest mipmap level, i.e., the original image. For each mipmap level, we then find a new mipmap threshold value α_k, instead of using α_t, such that c_k is equal to c_0 (or as close as possible). This can be done using a binary

Figure 6.29. Top: alpha testing with mipmapping without any correction. Bottom: alpha testing with alpha values rescaled according to coverage. *(Images from "The Witness," courtesy of Ignacio Castaño.)*

search. Finally, the alpha values of all texels in mipmap level k are scaled by α_t/α_k. This method was used in the bottom part of Figure 6.29, and there is support for this in NVIDIA's texture tools. Golus [557] gives a variant where the mipmap is not modified, but instead the alpha is scaled up in the shader as the mipmap level increases.

Figure 6.30. On the top are the different mipmap levels for a leaf pattern with blending, with the higher levels zoomed for visibility. On the bottom the mipmap is displayed as it would be treated with an alpha test of 0.5, showing how the object has fewer pixels as it recedes. *(Images courtesy of Ben Golus [557].)*

Wyman and McGuire [1933] present a different solution, where the line of code in Equation 6.9 is, in theory, replaced with

$$\text{if (texture.a < random()) discard;} \qquad (6.11)$$

The random function returns a uniform value in $[0, 1]$, which means that on average this will result in the correct result. For example, if the alpha value of the texture lookup is 0.3, the fragment will be discarded with a 30% chance. This is a form of stochastic transparency with a single sample per pixel [423]. In practice, the random function is replaced with a hash function to avoid temporal and spatial high-frequency noise:

$$\text{float hash2D(x,y) \{ return fract(1.0e4*sin(17.0*x+0.1*y) *}$$
$$\text{(0.1+abs(sin(13.0*y+x)))); \}} \qquad (6.12)$$

A three-dimensional hash is formed by nested calls to the above function, i.e., `float hash3D(x,y,z) { return hash2D(hash2D(x,y),z); }`, which returns a number in $[0, 1)$. The input to the hash is object-space coordinates divided by the maximum screen-space derivatives (x and y) of the object-space coordinates, followed by clamping. Further care is needed to obtain stability for movements in the z-direction, and the method is best combined with temporal antialiasing techniques. This technique is faded in with distance, so that close up we do not get any stochastic effect at all. The advantage of this method is that every fragment is correct on average, while Castaño's method [234] creates a single α_k for each mipmap level. However, this value likely varies over each mipmap level, which may reduce quality and require artist intervention.

Alpha testing displays ripple artifacts under magnification, which can be avoided by precomputing the alpha map as a distance field [580] (see also the discussion on page 677).

Figure 6.31. Different rendering techniques of leaf textures with partial alpha coverage for the edges. From left to right: alpha test, alpha blend, alpha to coverage, and alpha to coverage with sharpened edges. *(Images courtesy of Ben Golus [557].)*

Alpha to coverage, and the similar feature *transparency adaptive antialiasing*, take the transparency value of the fragment and convert this into how many samples inside a pixel are covered [1250]. This idea is like screen-door transparency, described in Section 5.5, but at a subpixel level. Imagine that each pixel has four sample locations, and that a fragment covers a pixel, but is 25% transparent (75% opaque), due to the cutout texture. The alpha to coverage mode makes the fragment become fully opaque but has it cover only three of the four samples. This mode is useful for cutout textures for overlapping grassy fronds, for example [887, 1876]. Since each sample drawn is fully opaque, the closest frond will hide objects behind it in a consistent way along its edges. No sorting is needed to correctly blend semitransparent edge pixels, since alpha blending is turned off.

Alpha to coverage is good for antialiasing alpha testing, but can show artifacts when alpha blending. For example, two alpha-blended fragments with the same alpha coverage percentage will use the same subpixel pattern, meaning that one fragment will entirely cover the other instead of blending with it. Golus [557] discusses using the `fwidth()` shader instruction to give content a crisper edge. See Figure 6.31.

For any use of alpha mapping, it is important to understand how bilinear interpolation affects the color values. Imagine two texels neighboring each other: $rgb\alpha = (255, 0, 0, 255)$ is a solid red, and its neighbor, $rgb\alpha = (0, 0, 0, 2)$, is black and almost entirely transparent. What is the $rgb\alpha$ for a location exactly midway between the two texels? Simple interpolation gives $(127, 0, 0, 128)$, with the resulting rgb value alone a "dimmer" red. However, this result is not actually dimmer, it is a full red that has been premultiplied by its alpha. If you interpolate alpha values, for correct interpolation you need to ensure that the colors being interpolated are already premultiplied by alpha before interpolation. As an example, imagine the almost-transparent neighbor is instead set to $rgb\alpha = (0, 255, 0, 2)$, giving a minuscule tinge of green. This color is not premultiplied by alpha and would give the result $(127, 127, 0, 128)$ when interpolated—the tiny tinge of green suddenly shifts the result to be a (premultiplied) yellow sample. The premultiplied version of this neighbor texel is $(0, 2, 0, 2)$, which gives the proper premultiplied result of $(127, 1, 0, 128)$. This result makes more sense, with the resulting premultiplied color being mostly red with an imperceptible tinge of green.

Ignoring that the result of bilinear interpolation gives a premultiplied result can lead to black edges around decals and cutout objects. The "dimmer" red result gets treated as an unmultiplied color by the rest of the pipeline and the fringes go to black. This effect can also be visible even if using alpha testing. The best strategy is to premultiply before bilinear interpolation is done [490, 648, 1166, 1813]. The WebGL API supports this, since compositing is important for webpages. However, bilinear interpolation is normally performed by the GPU, and operations on texel values cannot be done by the shader before this operation is performed. Images are not premultiplied in file formats such as PNG, as doing so would lose color precision. These two factors combine to cause black fringing by default when using alpha mapping. One common workaround is to preprocess cutout images, painting the transparent, "black" texels with a color derived from nearby opaque texels [490, 685]. All transparent areas often need to be repainted in this way, by hand or automatically, so that the mipmap levels also avoid fringing problems [295]. It is also worth noting that premultiplied values should be used when forming mipmaps with alpha values [1933].

6.7 Bump Mapping

This section describes a large family of small-scale detail representation techniques that we collectively call *bump mapping*. All these methods are typically implemented by modifying the per-pixel shading routine. They give a more three-dimensional appearance than texture mapping alone, but without adding any additional geometry.

Detail on an object can be classified into three scales: macro-features that cover many pixels, meso-features that are a few pixels across, and micro-features that are substantially smaller than a pixel. These categories are somewhat fluid, since the viewer may observe the same object at many distances during an animation or interactive session.

Macrogeometry is represented by vertices and triangles, or other geometric primitives. When creating a three-dimensional character, the limbs and head are typically modeled at a macroscale. Microgeometry is encapsulated in the shading model, which is commonly implemented in a pixel shader and uses texture maps as parameters. The shading model used simulates the interaction of a surface's microscopic geometry, e.g., shiny objects are microscopically smooth, and diffuse surfaces are microscopically rough. The skin and clothes of a character appear to have different materials because they use different shaders, or at least different parameters in those shaders.

Meso-geometry describes everything between these two scales. It contains detail that is too complex to efficiently render using individual triangles, but that is large enough for the viewer to distinguish individual changes in surface curvature over a few pixels. The wrinkles on a character's face, musculature details, and folds and seams in their clothing, are all mesoscale. A family of methods collectively known as bump mapping techniques are commonly used for mesoscale modeling. These adjust the shading parameters at the pixel level in such a way that the viewer perceives small perturbations away from the base geometry, which actually remains flat. The main distinctions between the different kinds of bump mapping are how they represent the detail features. Variables include the level of realism and complexity of the detail features. For example, it is common for a digital artist to carve details into a model, then use software to convert these geometric elements into one or more textures, such as a bump texture and perhaps a crevice-darkening texture.

Blinn introduced the idea of encoding mesoscale detail in a texture in 1978 [160]. He observed that a surface appears to have small-scale detail if, during shading, we substitute a slightly perturbed surface normal for the true one. He stored the data describing the perturbation to the surface normal in the array.

The key idea is that, instead of using a texture to change a color component in the illumination equation, we access a texture to modify the surface normal. The geometric normal of the surface remains the same; we merely modify the normal used in the lighting equation. This operation has no physical equivalent; we perform changes on the surface normal, but the surface itself remains smooth in the geometric sense. Just as having a normal per vertex gives the illusion that the surface is smooth between triangles, modifying the normal per pixel changes the perception of the triangle surface itself, without modifying its geometry.

For bump mapping, the normal must change direction with respect to some frame of reference. To do so, a *tangent frame*, also called a *tangent-space basis*, is stored at each vertex. This frame of reference is used to transform the lights to a surface location's space (or vice versa) to compute the effect of perturbing the normal. With a polygonal surface that has a normal map applied to it, in addition to a vertex normal, we also store what are called the *tangent* and *bitangent vectors*. The bitangent vector is also incorrectly referred to as the *binormal vector* [1025].

The tangent and bitangent vectors represent the axes of the normal map itself in the object's space, since the goal is to transform the light to be relative to the map. See Figure 6.32.

These three vectors, normal $\mathbf{n}$, tangent $\mathbf{t}$, and bitangent $\mathbf{b}$, form a basis matrix:

$$\begin{pmatrix} t_x & t_y & t_z & 0 \\ b_x & b_y & b_z & 0 \\ n_x & n_y & n_z & 0 \\ 0 & 0 & 0 & 1 \end{pmatrix}. \tag{6.13}$$

This matrix, sometimes abbreviated as *TBN*, transforms a light's direction (for the given vertex) from world space to tangent space. These vectors do not have to be truly perpendicular to each other, since the normal map itself may be distorted to fit the surface. However, a non-orthogonal basis introduces skewing to the texture, which can mean more storage is needed and also can have performance implications, i.e., the matrix cannot then be inverted by a simple transpose [494]. One method of saving memory is to store just the tangent and bitangent at the vertex and take their cross product to compute the normal. However, this technique works only if the handedness

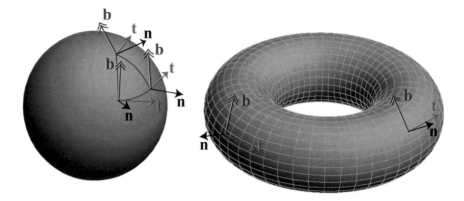

Figure 6.32. A spherical triangle is shown, with its tangent frame shown at each corner. Shapes like a sphere and torus have a natural tangent-space basis, as the latitude and longitude lines on the torus show.

of the matrix is always the same [1226]. Frequently a model is symmetric: an airplane, a human, a file cabinet, and many other objects. Because textures consume a large amount of memory, they are often mirrored onto symmetric models. Thus, only one side of an object's texture is stored, but the texture mapping places it onto both sides of the model. In this case, the handedness of the tangent space will be different on the two sides, and cannot be assumed. It is still possible to avoid storing the normal in this case if an extra bit of information is stored at each vertex to indicate the handedness. If set, this bit is used to negate the cross product of the tangent and bitangent to produce the correct normal. If the tangent frame is orthogonal, it is also possible to store the basis as a quaternion (Section 4.3), which both is more space efficient and can save some calculations per pixel [494, 1114, 1154, 1381, 1639]. A minor loss in quality is possible, though in practice is rarely seen.

The idea of tangent space is important for other algorithms. As discussed in the next chapter, many shading equations rely on only the surface's normal direction. However, materials such as brushed aluminum or velvet also need to know the relative direction of the viewer and lighting compared to the surface. The tangent frame is useful to define the orientation of the material on the surface. Articles by Lengyel [1025] and Mittring [1226] provide extensive coverage of this area. Schüler [1584] presents a method of computing the tangent-space basis on the fly in the pixel shader, with no need to store a precomputed tangent frame per vertex. Mikkelsen [1209] improves upon this technique, and derives a method that does not need any parameterization but instead uses the derivatives of the surface position and derivatives of a height field to compute the perturbed normal. However, such techniques can lead to considerably less displayed detail than using standard tangent-space mapping, as well as possibly creating art workflow issues [1639].

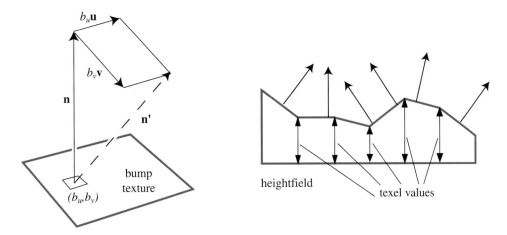

Figure 6.33. On the left, a normal vector **n** is modified in the **u**- and **v**-directions by the (b_u, b_v) values taken from the bump texture, giving **n′** (which is unnormalized). On the right, a heightfield and its effect on shading normals is shown. These normals could instead be interpolated between heights for a smoother look.

6.7.1 Blinn's Methods

Blinn's original bump mapping method stores two signed values, b_u and b_v, at each texel in a texture. These two values correspond to the amount to vary the normal along the **u** and **v** image axes. That is, these texture values, which typically are bilinearly interpolated, are used to scale two vectors that are perpendicular to the normal. These two vectors are added to the normal to change its direction. The two values b_u and b_v describe which way the surface faces at the point. See Figure 6.33. This type of bump map texture is called an *offset vector bump map* or *offset map*.

Another way to represent bumps is to use a *heightfield* to modify the surface normal's direction. Each monochrome texture value represents a height, so in the texture, white is a high area and black a low one (or vice versa). See Figure 6.34 for an example. This is a common format used when first creating or scanning a bump map, and it was also introduced by Blinn in 1978. The heightfield is used to derive u and v signed values similar to those used in the first method. This is done by taking the differences between neighboring columns to get the slopes for u, and between neighboring rows for v [1567]. A variant is to use a Sobel filter, which gives a greater weight to the directly adjacent neighbors [535].

6.7.2 Normal Mapping

A common method for bump mapping is to directly store a *normal map*. The algorithms and results are mathematically identical to Blinn's methods; only the storage format and pixel shader computations change.

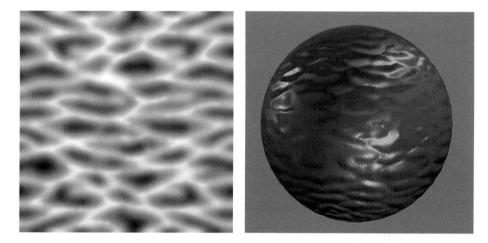

Figure 6.34. A wavy heightfield bump image and its use on a sphere.

The normal map encodes (x, y, z) mapped to $[-1, 1]$, e.g., for an 8-bit texture the x-axis value 0 represents -1.0 and 255 represents 1.0. An example is shown in Figure 6.35. The color $[128, 128, 255]$, a light blue, would represent a flat surface for the color mapping shown, i.e., a normal of $[0, 0, 1]$.

The normal map representation was originally introduced as a world-space normal map [274, 891], which is rarely used in practice. For that type of mapping, the perturbation is straightforward: At each pixel, retrieve the normal from the map and

Figure 6.35. Bump mapping with a normal map. Each color channel is actually a surface normal coordinate. The red channel is the x deviation; the more red, the more the normal points to the right. Green is the y deviation, and blue is z. At the right is an image produced using the normal map. Note the flattened look on the top of the cube. *(Images courtesy of Manuel M. Oliveira and Fabio Policarpo.)*

Figure 6.36. An example of normal map bump mapping used in a game-like scene. Top left: the two normals maps to the right are not applied. Bottom left: normal maps applied. Right: the normal maps. *(3D model and normal maps courtesy of Dulce Isis Segarra López.)*

use it directly, along with a light's direction, to compute the shade at that location on the surface. Normal maps can also be defined in object space, so that the model could be rotated and the normals would then still be valid. However, both world- and object-space representations bind the texture to specific geometry in a particular orientation, which limits texture reuse.

Instead, the perturbed normal is usually retrieved in tangent space, i.e., relative to the surface itself. This allows for deformation of the surface, as well as maximal reuse of the normal texture. Tangent-space normal maps also can compress nicely, since the sign of the z-component (the one aligned with the unperturbed surface normal) can usually be assumed to be positive.

Normal mapping can be used to good effect to increase realism—see Figure 6.36.

Filtering normal maps is a difficult problem, compared to filtering color textures. In general, the relationship between the normal and the shaded color is not linear, so standard filtering methods may result in objectionable aliasing. Imagine looking at stairs made of blocks of shiny white marble. At some angles, the tops or sides of the stairs catch the light and reflect a bright specular highlight. However, the average normal for the stairs is at, say, a 45 degree angle; it will capture highlights from entirely different directions than the original stairs. When bump maps with sharp specular highlights are rendered without correct filtering, a distracting sparkle effect can occur as highlights wink in and out by the luck of where samples fall.

Lambertian surfaces are a special case where the normal map has an almost linear effect on shading. Lambertian shading is almost entirely a dot product, which is a linear operation. Averaging a group of normals and performing a dot product with the result is equivalent to averaging individual dot products with the normals:

$$\mathbf{l} \cdot \left(\frac{\sum_{j=1}^{n} \mathbf{n}_j}{n} \right) = \frac{\sum_{j=1}^{n} (\mathbf{l} \cdot \mathbf{n}_j)}{n}. \tag{6.14}$$

Note that the average vector is not normalized before use. Equation 6.14 shows that standard filtering and mipmaps *almost* produce the right result for Lambertian surfaces. The result is not quite correct because the Lambertian shading equation is not a dot product; it is a *clamped* dot product—$\max(\mathbf{l} \cdot \mathbf{n}, 0)$. The clamping operation makes it nonlinear. This will overly darken the surface for glancing light directions, but in practice this is usually not objectionable [891]. One caveat is that some texture compression methods typically used for normal maps (such as reconstructing the z-component from the other two) do not support non-unit-length normals, so using non-normalized normal maps may pose compression difficulties.

In the case of non-Lambertian surfaces, it is possible to produce better results by filtering the inputs to the shading equation as a group, rather than filtering the normal map in isolation. Techniques for doing so are discussed in Section 9.13.

Finally, it may be useful to derive a normal map from a height map, $h(x, y)$. This is done as follows [405]. First, approximations to derivatives in the x- and the y-directions are computed using centered differences as

$$h_x(x, y) = \frac{h(x+1, y) - h(x-1, y)}{2}, \quad h_y(x, y) = \frac{h(x, y+1) - h(x, y-1)}{2}. \tag{6.15}$$

The unnormalized normal at texel (x, y) is then

$$\mathbf{n}(x, y) = (-h_x(x, y), -h_x(x, y), 1). \tag{6.16}$$

Care has to be taken at the boundaries of the texture.

Horizon mapping [1027] can be used to further enhance normal maps by having the bumps be able to cast shadows onto their own surfaces. This is done by precomputing additional textures, with each texture associated with a direction along the surface's plane, and storing the angle of the horizon in that direction, for each texel. See Section 11.4 for more information.

6.8 Parallax Mapping

A problem with bump and normal mapping is that the bumps never shift location with the view angle, nor ever block each other. If you look along a real brick wall, for example, at some angle you will not see the mortar between the bricks. A bump

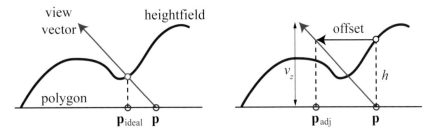

Figure 6.37. On the left is the goal: The actual position on the surface is found from where the view vector pierces the heightfield. Parallax mapping does a first-order approximation by taking the height at the location on the rectangle and using it to find a new location $\mathbf{p}_{\mathrm{adj}}$. *(After Welsh [1866].)*

map of the wall will never show this type of occlusion, as it merely varies the normal. It would be better to have the bumps actually affect which location on the surface is rendered at each pixel.

The idea of *parallax mapping* was introduced in 2001 by Kaneko [851] and refined and popularized by Welsh [1866]. *Parallax* refers to the idea that the positions of objects move relative to one another as the observer moves. As the viewer moves, the bumps should appear to have heights. The key idea of parallax mapping is to take an educated guess of what should be seen in a pixel by examining the height of what was found to be visible.

For parallax mapping, the bumps are stored in a heightfield texture. When viewing the surface at a given pixel, the heightfield value is retrieved at that location and used to shift the texture coordinates to retrieve a different part of the surface. The amount to shift is based on the height retrieved and the angle of the eye to the surface. See Figure 6.37. The heightfield values are either stored in a separate texture, or packed in an unused color or alpha channel of some other texture (care must be taken when packing unrelated textures together, since this can negatively impact compression quality). The heightfield values are scaled and biased before being used to shift the coordinates. The scale determines how high the heightfield is meant to extend above or below the surface, and the bias gives the "sea-level" height at which no shift takes place. Given a texture-coordinate location $\mathbf{p}$, an adjusted heightfield height h, and a normalized view vector $\mathbf{v}$ with a height value v_z and horizontal component $\mathbf{v}_{xy}$, the new parallax-adjusted texture coordinate $\mathbf{p}_{\mathrm{adj}}$ is

$$\mathbf{p}_{\mathrm{adj}} = \mathbf{p} + \frac{h \cdot \mathbf{v}_{xy}}{v_z}. \tag{6.17}$$

Note that unlike most shading equations, here the space in which the computation is performed matters—the view vector needs to be in tangent space.

Though a simple approximation, this shifting works fairly well in practice if the bump heights change relatively slowly [1171]. Nearby neighboring texels then have about the same heights, so the idea of using the original location's height as an estimate

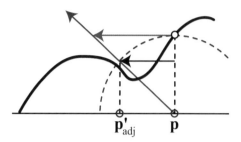 

Figure 6.38. In parallax offset limiting, the offset moves at most the amount of the height away from the original location, shown as a dashed circular arc. The gray offset shows the original result, the black the limited result. On the right is a wall rendered with the technique. *(Image courtesy of Terry Welsh.)*

of the new location's height is reasonable. However, this method falls apart at shallow viewing angles. When the view vector is near the surface's horizon, a small height change results in a large texture coordinate shift. The approximation fails, as the new location retrieved has little or no height correlation to the original surface location.

To ameliorate this problem, Welsh [1866] introduced the idea of offset limiting. The idea is to limit the amount of shifting to never be larger than the retrieved height. The equation is then

$$\mathbf{p}'_{\mathrm{adj}} = \mathbf{p} + h \cdot \mathbf{v}_{xy}. \tag{6.18}$$

Note that this equation is faster to compute than the original. Geometrically, the interpretation is that the height defines a radius beyond which the position cannot shift. This is shown in Figure 6.38.

At steep (face-on) angles, this equation is almost the same as the original, since v_z is nearly 1. At shallow angles, the offset becomes limited in its effect. Visually, this makes the bumpiness lessen at shallow angles, but this is much better than random sampling of the texture. Problems also remain with texture swimming as the view changes, or for stereo rendering, where the viewer simultaneously perceives two viewpoints that must give consistent depth cues [1171]. Even with these drawbacks, parallax mapping with offset limiting costs just a few additional pixel shader program instructions and gives a considerable image quality improvement over basic normal mapping. Shishkovtsov [1631] improves shadows for parallax occlusion by moving the estimated position in the direction of the bump map normal.

6.8.1 Parallax Occlusion Mapping

Bump mapping does not modify texture coordinates based on the heightfield; it varies only the shading normal at a location. Parallax mapping provides a simple approximation of the effect of the heightfield, working on the assumption that the height at a pixel is about the same as the heights of its neighbors. This assumption can quickly

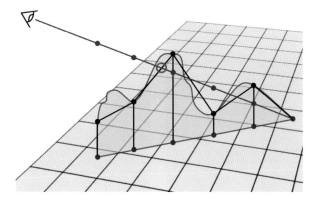

Figure 6.39. The green eye ray is projected onto the surface plane, which is sampled at regular intervals (the violet dots) and the heights are retrieved. The algorithm finds the first intersection of the eye ray with the black line segments approximating the curved height field.

break down. Bumps can also never occlude one another, nor cast shadows. What we want is what is visible at the pixel, i.e., where the view vector first intersects the heightfield.

To solve this in a better way, several researchers have proposed to use ray marching along the view vector until an (approximate) intersection point is found. This work can be done in the pixel shader where height data can be accessed as textures. We lump the research on these methods into a subset of parallax mapping techniques, which exploit ray marching in one way or another [192, 1171, 1361, 1424, 1742, 1743].

These types of algorithms are called *parallax occlusion mapping* (POM) or *relief mapping* methods, among other names. The key idea is to first test a fixed number of heightfield texture samples along the projected vector. More samples are usually generated for view rays at grazing angles, so that the closest intersection point is not missed [1742, 1743]. Each three-dimensional location along the ray is retrieved, transformed into texture space, and processed to determine if it is above or below the heightfield. Once a sample below the heightfield is found, the amount it is below, and the amount the previous sample is above, are used to find an intersection location. See Figure 6.39. The location is then used to shade the surface, using the attached normal map, color map, and any other textures. Multiple layered heightfields can be used to produce overhangs, independent overlapping surfaces, and two-sided relief-mapped impostors; see Section 13.7. The heightfield tracing approach can also be used to have the bumpy surface cast shadows onto itself, both hard [1171, 1424] and soft [1742, 1743]. See Figure 6.40 for a comparison.

There is a wealth of literature on this topic. While all these methods march along a ray, there are several differences. One can use a simple texture to retrieve heights, but it is also possible to use a more advanced data structure and more advanced root-finding methods. Some techniques may involve the shader discarding pixels or writing

Figure 6.40. Parallax mapping without ray marching (left) compared to with ray marching (right). On the top of the cube there is flattening when ray marching is not used. With ray marching, self-shadowing effects are also generated. *(Images courtesy of Manuel M. Oliveira and Fabio Policarpo.)*

to the depth buffer, which can hurt performance. Below we summarize a large set of methods, but remember that as GPUs evolve, so does the best method. This "best" method depends on content and the number of steps done during ray marching.

The problem of determining the actual intersection point between the two regular samples is a root-finding problem. In practice the heightfield is treated more as a depthfield, with the rectangle's plane defining the upper limit of the surface. In this way, the initial point on the plane is above the heightfield. After finding the last point above, and first point below, the heightfield's surface, Tatarchuk [1742, 1743] uses a single step of the secant method to find an approximate solution. Policarpo et al. [1424] use a binary search between the two points found to hone in on a closer intersection. Risser et al. [1497] speed convergence by iterating using a secant method. The trade-off is that regular sampling can be done in parallel, while iterative methods need fewer overall texture accesses but must wait for results and perform slower dependent texture fetches. Brute-force methods seem to perform well overall [1911].

It is critical to sample the heightfield frequently enough. McGuire and McGuire [1171] propose biasing the mipmap lookup and using anisotropic mipmaps to ensure correct sampling for high-frequency heightfields, such as those representing spikes or hair. One can also store the heightfield texture at higher resolution than the normal map. Finally, some rendering systems do not even store a normal map, preferring to derive the normal on the fly from the heightfield using a cross filter [40]. Equation 16.1 on page 696 shows the method.

Another approach to increasing both performance and sampling accuracy is to not initially sample the heightfield at a regular interval, but instead to try to skip intervening empty space. Donnelly [367] preprocesses the height field into a set of voxels, storing in each voxel how far away it is from the heightfield surface. In this

Figure 6.41. Normal mapping and relief mapping. No self-occlusion occurs with normal mapping. Relief mapping has problems with silhouettes for repeating textures, as the rectangle is more of a view into the heightfield than a true boundary definition. *(Images courtesy of NVIDIA Corporation.)*

way, intervening space can be rapidly skipped, at the cost of higher storage for each heightfield. Wang et al. [1844] use a five-dimensional displacement mapping scheme to hold distances to the surface from all directions and locations. This allows complex curved surfaces, self-shadowing, and other effects, at the expense of considerably larger amounts of memory. Mehra and Kumar [1195] use directional distance maps for similar purposes. Dummer [393] introduces, and Policarpo and Oliveira [1426] improve upon, the idea of *cone step mapping*. The concept here is to also store for each heightfield location a *cone radius*. This radius defines an interval on the ray in which there is at most one intersection with the heightfield. This property allows rapid skipping along the ray without missing any possible intersections, though at the cost of needing dependent texture reads. Another drawback is the precomputation needed to create the cone step map, making the method unusable for dynamically changing heightfields. Schroders and Gulik [1581] present *quadtree relief mapping*, a hierarchical method to skip over volumes during traversal. Tevs et al. [1760] use "maximum mipmaps" to allow skipping while minimizing precomputation costs. Drobot [377] also uses a quadtree-like structure stored in mipmaps to speed up traversal, and presents a method to blend between different heightfields, where one terrain type transitions to another.

One problem with all the methods above is that the illusion breaks down along the silhouette edges of objects, which will show the original surface's smooth outlines. See Figure 6.41. The key idea is that the triangles rendered define which pixels should be evaluated by the pixel shader program, not where the surface actually is located. In addition, for curved surfaces, the problem of silhouettes becomes more involved. One approach is described and developed by Oliveira and Policarpo [1325, 1850], which uses a quadratic silhouette approximation technique. Jeschke et al. [824] and Dachsbacher et al. [323] both give a more general and robust method (and review previous work) for dealing with silhouettes and curved surfaces correctly. First explored by Hirche [750], the general idea is to extrude each triangle in the mesh outward and form a prism. Rendering this prism forces evaluation of all pixels in which the heightfield could possibly appear. This type of approach is called *shell mapping*, as the expanded mesh forms a separate shell over the original model. By preserving the nonlinear nature of prisms when intersecting them with rays, artifact-free rendering of heightfields becomes possible, though expensive to compute. An impressive use of this type of technique is shown in Figure 6.42.

Figure 6.42. Parallax occlusion mapping, a.k.a. relief mapping, used on a path to make the stones look more realistic. The ground is actually a simple set of triangles with a heightfield applied. *(Image from "Crysis," courtesy of Crytek.)*

Figure 6.43. Projective textured light. The texture is projected onto the teapot and ground plane and used to modulate the light's contribution within the projection frustum (it is set to 0 outside the frustum). *(Image courtesy of NVIDIA Corporation.)*

6.9 Textured Lights

Textures can also be used to add visual richness to light sources and allow for complex intensity distribution or spotlight functions. For lights that have all their illumination limited to a cone or frustum, projective textures can be used to modulate the light intensity [1192, 1597, 1904]. This allows for shaped spotlights, patterned lights, and even "slide projector" effects (Figure 6.43). These lights are often called *gobo* or *cookie* lights, after the terms for the cutouts used in professional theater and film lighting. See Section 7.2 for a discussion of projective mapping being used in a similar way to cast shadows.

For lights that are not limited to a frustum but illuminate in all directions, a cube map can be used to modulate the intensity, instead of a two-dimensional projective texture. One-dimensional textures can be used to define arbitrary distance falloff functions. Combined with a two-dimensional angular attenuation map, this can allow for complex volumetric lighting patterns [353]. A more general possibility is to use three-dimensional (volume) textures to control the light's falloff [353, 535, 1192]. This allows for arbitrary volumes of effect, including light beams. This technique is memory intensive (as are all volume textures). If the light's volume of effect is symmetrical along the three axes, the memory footprint can be reduced eightfold by mirroring the data into each octant.

Textures can be added to any light type to enable additional visual effects. Textured lights allow for easy control of the illumination by artists, who can simply edit the texture used.

Further Reading and Resources

Heckbert has written a good survey of the theory of texture mapping [690] and a more in-depth report on the topic [691]. Szirmay-Kalos and Umenhoffer [1731] have an excellent, thorough survey of parallax occlusion mapping and displacement methods. More information about normal representation can be found in the work by Cigolle et al. [269] and by Meyer et al. [1205].

The book *Advanced Graphics Programming Using OpenGL* [1192] has extensive coverage of various visualization techniques using texturing algorithms. For extensive coverage of three-dimensional procedural textures, see *Texturing and Modeling: A Procedural Approach* [407]. The book *Advanced Game Development with Programmable Graphics Hardware* [1850] has many details about implementing parallax occlusion mapping techniques, as do Tatarchuk's presentations [1742, 1743] and Szirmay-Kalos and Umenhoffer's survey [1731].

For procedural texturing (and modeling), our favorite site on the Internet is Shadertoy. There are many worthwhile and fascinating procedural texturing functions on display, and you can easily modify any example and see the results.

Visit this book's website, realtimerendering.com, for many other resources.

Chapter 7
Shadows

Shadows are important for creating realistic images and in providing the user with visual cues about object placement. This chapter focuses on the basic principles of computing shadows, and describes the most important and popular real-time algorithms for doing so. We also briefly discuss approaches that are less popular but embody important principles. We do not spend time in this chapter covering all options and approaches, as there are two comprehensive books that study the field of shadows in great depth [412, 1902]. Instead, we focus on surveying articles and presentations that have appeared since their publication, with a bias toward battle-tested techniques.

The terminology used throughout this chapter is illustrated in Figure 7.1, where *occluders* are objects that cast shadows onto *receivers*. Punctual light sources, i.e., those with no area, generate only fully shadowed regions, sometimes called *hard shadows*. If

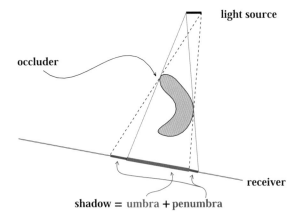

Figure 7.1. Shadow terminology: light source, occluder, receiver, shadow, umbra, and penumbra.

Figure 7.2. A mix of hard and soft shadows. Shadows from the crate are sharp, as the occluder is near the receiver. The person's shadow is sharp at the point of contact, softening as the distance to the occluder increases. The distant tree branches give soft shadows [1711]. *(Image from "Tom Clancy's The Division," courtesy of Ubisoft.)*

area or volume light sources are used, then soft shadows are produced. Each shadow can then have a fully shadowed region, called the *umbra*, and a partially shadowed region, called the *penumbra*. Soft shadows are recognized by their fuzzy shadow edges. However, it is important to note that they generally cannot be rendered correctly by just blurring the edges of a hard shadow with a low-pass filter. As can be seen in Figure 7.2, a correct soft shadow is sharper the closer the shadow-casting geometry is to the receiver. The umbra region of a soft shadow is not equivalent to a hard shadow generated by a punctual light source. Instead, the umbra region of a soft shadow decreases in size as the light source grows larger, and it might even disappear, given a large enough light source and a receiver far enough from the occluder. Soft shadows are generally preferable because the penumbrae edges let the viewer know that the shadow is indeed a shadow. Hard-edged shadows usually look less realistic and can sometimes be misinterpreted as actual geometric features, such as a crease in a surface. However, hard shadows are faster to render than soft shadows.

More important than having a penumbra is having any shadow at all. Without some shadow as a visual cue, scenes are often unconvincing and more difficult to perceive. As Wanger shows [1846], it is usually better to have an inaccurate shadow than none at all, as the eye is fairly forgiving about the shadow's shape. For example, a blurred black circle applied as a texture on the floor can anchor a character to the ground.

In the following sections, we will go beyond these simple modeled shadows and present methods that compute shadows automatically in real time from the occluders in a scene. The first section handles the special case of shadows cast on planar surfaces, and the second section covers more general shadow algorithms, i.e., casting shadows onto arbitrary surfaces. Both hard and soft shadows will be covered. To conclude, some optimization techniques are presented that apply to various shadow algorithms.

7.1 Planar Shadows

A simple case of shadowing occurs when objects cast shadows onto a planar surface. A few types of algorithms for planar shadows are presented in this section, each with variations in the softness and realism of the shadows.

7.1.1 Projection Shadows

In this scheme, the three-dimensional object is rendered a second time to create a shadow. A matrix can be derived that projects the vertices of an object onto a plane [162, 1759]. Consider the situation in Figure 7.3, where the light source is located at $\mathbf{l}$, the vertex to be projected is at $\mathbf{v}$, and the projected vertex is at $\mathbf{p}$. We will derive the projection matrix for the special case where the shadowed plane is $y = 0$, and then this result will be generalized to work with any plane.

We start by deriving the projection for the x-coordinate. From the similar triangles in the left part of Figure 7.3, we get

$$\frac{p_x - l_x}{v_x - l_x} = \frac{l_y}{l_y - v_y} \quad \Longleftrightarrow \quad p_x = \frac{l_y v_x - l_x v_y}{l_y - v_y}. \tag{7.1}$$

The z-coordinate is obtained in the same way: $p_z = (l_y v_z - l_z v_y)/(l_y - v_y)$, while the y-coordinate is zero. Now these equations can be converted into the projection matrix $\mathbf{M}$:

$$\mathbf{M} = \begin{pmatrix} l_y & -l_x & 0 & 0 \\ 0 & 0 & 0 & 0 \\ 0 & -l_z & l_y & 0 \\ 0 & -1 & 0 & l_y \end{pmatrix}. \tag{7.2}$$

It is straightforward to verify that $\mathbf{Mv} = \mathbf{p}$, which means that $\mathbf{M}$ is indeed the projection matrix.

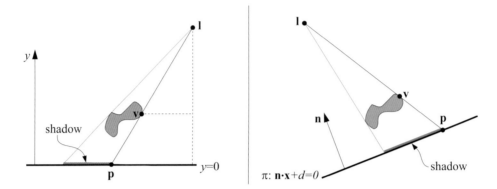

Figure 7.3. Left: A light source, located at **l**, casts a shadow onto the plane $y = 0$. The vertex **v** is projected onto the plane. The projected point is called **p**. The similar triangles are used for the derivation of the projection matrix. Right: The shadow is being cast onto a plane, $\pi : \mathbf{n} \cdot \mathbf{x} + d = 0$.

In the general case, the plane onto which the shadows should be cast is not the plane $y = 0$, but instead $\pi : \mathbf{n} \cdot \mathbf{x} + d = 0$. This case is depicted in the right part of Figure 7.3. The goal is again to find a matrix that projects **v** down to **p**. To this end, the ray emanating at **l**, which goes through **v**, is intersected by the plane π. This yields the projected point **p**:

$$\mathbf{p} = \mathbf{l} - \frac{d + \mathbf{n} \cdot \mathbf{l}}{\mathbf{n} \cdot (\mathbf{v} - \mathbf{l})} (\mathbf{v} - \mathbf{l}). \tag{7.3}$$

This equation can also be converted into a projection matrix, shown in Equation 7.4, which satisfies $\mathbf{Mv} = \mathbf{p}$:

$$\mathbf{M} = \begin{pmatrix} \mathbf{n} \cdot \mathbf{l} + d - l_x n_x & -l_x n_y & -l_x n_z & -l_x d \\ -l_y n_x & \mathbf{n} \cdot \mathbf{l} + d - l_y n_y & -l_y n_z & -l_y d \\ -l_z n_x & -l_z n_y & \mathbf{n} \cdot \mathbf{l} + d - l_z n_z & -l_z d \\ -n_x & -n_y & -n_z & \mathbf{n} \cdot \mathbf{l} \end{pmatrix}. \tag{7.4}$$

As expected, this matrix turns into the matrix in Equation 7.2 if the plane is $y = 0$, that is, $\mathbf{n} = (0, 1, 0)$ and $d = 0$.

To render the shadow, simply apply this matrix to the objects that should cast shadows on the plane π, and render this projected object with a dark color and no illumination. In practice, you have to take measures to avoid allowing the projected triangles to be rendered beneath the surface receiving them. One method is to add some bias to the plane we project upon, so that the shadow triangles are always rendered in front of the surface.

A safer method is to draw the ground plane first, then draw the projected triangles with the z-buffer off, then render the rest of the geometry as usual. The projected

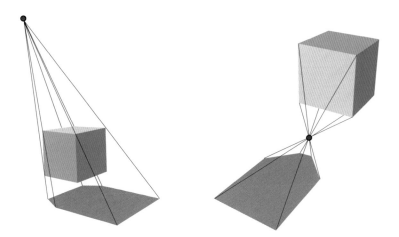

Figure 7.4. At the left, a correct shadow is shown, while in the figure on the right, an antishadow appears, since the light source is below the topmost vertex of the object.

triangles are then always drawn on top of the ground plane, as no depth comparisons are made.

If the ground plane has a limit, e.g., it is a rectangle, the projected shadows may fall outside of it, breaking the illusion. To solve this problem, we can use a stencil buffer. First, draw the receiver to the screen and to the stencil buffer. Then, with the z-buffer off, draw the projected triangles only where the receiver was drawn, then render the rest of the scene normally.

Another shadow algorithm is to render the triangles into a texture, which is then applied to the ground plane. This texture is a type of *light map*, a texture that modulates the intensity of the underlying surface (Section 11.5.1). As will be seen, this idea of rendering the shadow projection to a texture also allows penumbrae and shadows on curved surfaces. One drawback of this technique is that the texture can become magnified, with a single texel covering multiple pixels, breaking the illusion.

If the shadow situation does not change from frame to frame, i.e., the light and shadow casters do not move relative to each other, this texture can be reused. Most shadow techniques can benefit from reusing intermediate computed results from frame to frame if no change has occurred.

All shadow casters must be between the light and the ground-plane receiver. If the light source is below the topmost point on the object, an *antishadow* [162] is generated, since each vertex is projected through the point of the light source. Correct shadows and antishadows are shown in Figure 7.4. An error will also occur if we project an object that is below the receiving plane, since it too should cast no shadow.

It is certainly possible to explicitly cull and trim shadow triangles to avoid such artifacts. A simpler method, presented next, is to use the existing GPU pipeline to perform projection with clipping.

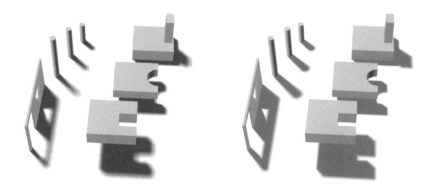

Figure 7.5. On the left, a rendering using Heckbert and Herf's method, using 256 passes. On the right, Haines' method in one pass. The umbrae are too large with Haines' method, which is particularly noticeable around the doorway and window.

7.1.2 Soft Shadows

Projective shadows can also be made soft, by using a variety of techniques. Here, we describe an algorithm from Heckbert and Herf [697, 722] that produces soft shadows. The algorithm's goal is to generate a texture on a ground plane that shows a soft shadow. We then describe less accurate, faster methods.

Soft shadows appear whenever a light source has an area. One way to approximate the effect of an area light is to sample it by using several punctual lights placed on its surface. For each of these punctual light sources, an image is rendered and accumulated into a buffer. The average of these images is then an image with soft shadows. Note that, in theory, any algorithm that generates hard shadows can be used along with this accumulation technique to produce penumbrae. In practice, doing so at interactive rates is usually untenable because of the execution time that would be involved.

Heckbert and Herf use a frustum-based method to produce their shadows. The idea is to treat the light as the viewer, and the ground plane forms the far clipping plane of the frustum. The frustum is made wide enough to encompass the occluders.

A soft shadow texture is formed by generating a series of ground-plane textures. The area light source is sampled over its surface, with each location used to shade the image representing the ground plane, then to project the shadow-casting objects onto this image. All these images are summed and averaged to produce a ground-plane shadow texture. See the left side of Figure 7.5 for an example.

A problem with the sampled area-light method is that it tends to look like what it is: several overlapping shadows from punctual light sources. Also, for n shadow passes, only $n + 1$ distinct shades can be generated. A large number of passes gives an accurate result, but at an excessive cost. The method is useful for obtaining a (literally) "ground-truth" image for testing the quality of other, faster algorithms.

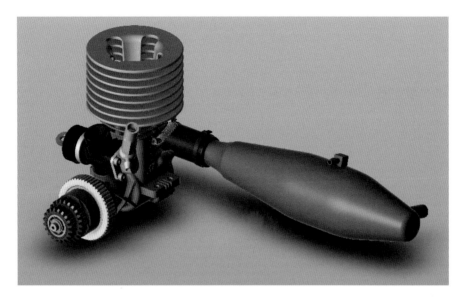

Figure 7.6. Drop shadow. A shadow texture is generated by rendering the shadow casters from above and then blurring the image and rendering it on the ground plane. *(Image generated in Autodesk's A360 viewer, model from Autodesk's Inventor samples.)*

A more efficient approach is to use convolution, i.e., filtering. Blurring a hard shadow generated from a single point can be sufficient in some cases and can produce a semitransparent texture that can be composited with real-world content. See Figure 7.6. However, a uniform blur can be unconvincing near where the object makes contact with the ground.

There are many other methods that give a better approximation, at additional cost. For example, Haines [644] starts with a projected hard shadow and then renders the silhouette edges with gradients that go from dark in the center to white on the edges to create plausible penumbrae. See the right side of Figure 7.5. However, these penumbrae are not physically correct, as they should also extend to areas inside the silhouette edges. Iwanicki [356, 806] draws on ideas from spherical harmonics and approximates occluding characters with ellipsoids to give soft shadows. All such methods have various approximations and drawbacks, but are considerably more efficient than averaging a large set of drop-shadow images.

7.2 Shadows on Curved Surfaces

One simple way to extend the idea of planar shadows to curved surfaces is to use a generated shadow image as a projective texture [1192, 1254, 1272, 1597]. Think of shadows from the light's point of view. Whatever the light sees is illuminated; what it does not see is in shadow. Say the occluder is rendered in black from the light's viewpoint into an otherwise white texture. This texture can then be projected onto the surfaces that are to receive the shadow. Effectively, each vertex on the receivers has a (u, v) texture coordinate computed for it and has the texture applied to it. These texture coordinates can be computed explicitly by the application. This differs a bit from the ground shadow texture in the previous section, where objects are projected onto a specific physical plane. Here, the image is made as a view from the light, like a frame of film in a projector.

When rendered, the projected shadow texture modifies the receiver surfaces. It can also be combined with other shadow methods, and sometimes is used primarily for helping aid perception of an object's location. For example, in a platform-hopping video game, the main character might always be given a drop shadow directly below it, even when the character is in full shadow [1343]. More elaborate algorithms can give better results. For example, Eisemann and Décoret [411] assume a rectangular overhead light and create a stack of shadow images of horizontal slices of the object, which are then turned into mipmaps or similar. The corresponding area of each slice is accessed proportional to its distance from the receiver by using its mipmap, meaning that more distant slices will cast softer shadows.

There are some serious drawbacks of texture projection methods. First, the application must identify which objects are occluders and which are their receivers. The receiver must be maintained by the program to be further from the light than the occluder, otherwise the shadow is "cast backward." Also, occluding objects cannot shadow themselves. The next two sections present algorithms that generate correct shadows without the need for such intervention or limitations.

Note that a variety of lighting patterns can be obtained by using prebuilt projective textures. A spotlight is simply a square projected texture with a circle inside of it defining the light. A Venetian blinds effect can be created by a projected texture consisting of horizontal lines. This type of texture is called a *light attenuation mask*, *cookie texture*, or *gobo map*. A prebuilt pattern can be combined with a projected texture created on the fly by simply multiplying the two textures together. Such lights are discussed further in Section 6.9.

7.3 Shadow Volumes

Presented by Heidmann in 1991 [701], a method based on Crow's *shadow volumes* [311] can cast shadows onto arbitrary objects by clever use of the stencil buffer. It can be used on any GPU, as the only requirement is a stencil buffer. It is not image based (unlike the shadow map algorithm described next) and so avoids sampling problems, thus producing correct sharp shadows everywhere. This can sometimes be a disadvantage. For example, a character's clothing may have folds that give thin, hard shadows that alias badly. Shadow volumes are rarely used today, due to their unpredictable cost [1599]. We give the algorithm a brief description here, as it illustrates some important principles and research based on these continues.

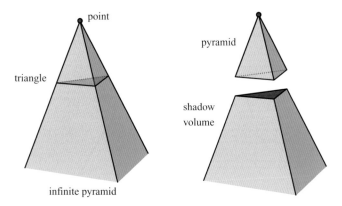

Figure 7.7. Left: the lines from a point light are extended through the vertices of a triangle to form an infinite pyramid. Right: the upper part is a pyramid, and the lower part is an infinite truncated pyramid, also called the shadow volume. All geometry that is inside the shadow volume is in shadow.

To begin, imagine a point and a triangle. Extending the lines from a point through the vertices of a triangle to infinity yields an infinite three-sided pyramid. The part under the triangle, i.e., the part that does not include the point, is a truncated infinite pyramid, and the upper part is simply a pyramid. This is illustrated in Figure 7.7. Now imagine that the point is actually a point light source. Then, any part of an object that is inside the volume of the truncated pyramid (under the triangle) is in shadow. This volume is called a *shadow volume*.

Say we view some scene and follow a ray from the eye through a pixel until the ray hits the object to be displayed on screen. While the ray is on its way to this object, we increment a counter each time it crosses a face of the shadow volume that is frontfacing (i.e., facing toward the viewer). Thus, the counter is incremented each time the ray goes into shadow. In the same manner, we decrement the same counter each time the ray crosses a backfacing face of the truncated pyramid. The ray is then going out of a shadow. We proceed, incrementing and decrementing the counter until the ray hits the object that is to be displayed at that pixel. If the counter is greater than zero, then that pixel is in shadow; otherwise it is not. This principle also works when there is more than one triangle that casts shadows. See Figure 7.8.

Doing this with rays is time consuming. But there is a much smarter solution [701]: A stencil buffer can do the counting for us. First, the stencil buffer is cleared. Second, the whole scene is drawn into the framebuffer with only the color of the unlit material used, to get these shading components in the color buffer and the depth information into the z-buffer. Third, z-buffer updates and writing to the color buffer are turned off (though z-buffer testing is still done), and then the frontfacing triangles of the shadow volumes are drawn. During this process, the stencil operation is set to increment the values in the stencil buffer wherever a triangle is drawn. Fourth, another pass is done with the stencil buffer, this time drawing only the backfacing triangles of the shadow volumes. For this pass, the values in the stencil buffer are decremented when the

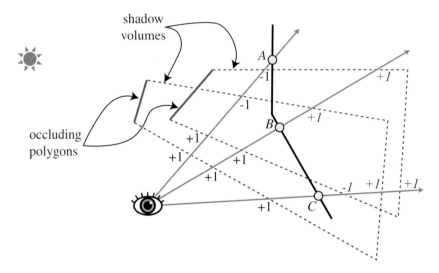

Figure 7.8. A two-dimensional side view of counting shadow-volume crossings using two different counting methods. In z-pass volume counting, the count is incremented as a ray passes through a frontfacing triangle of a shadow volume and decremented on leaving through a backfacing triangle. So, at point A, the ray enters two shadow volumes for $+2$, then leaves two volumes, leaving a net count of zero, so the point is in light. In z-fail volume counting, the counts start beyond the surface (these counts are shown in italics). For the ray at point B, the z-pass method gives a $+2$ count by passing through two frontfacing triangles, and the z-fail gives the same count by passing through two backfacing triangles. Point C shows how z-fail shadow volumes must be capped. The ray starting from point C first hits a frontfacing triangle, giving -1. It then exits two shadow volumes (through their endcaps, necessary for this method to work properly), giving a net count of $+1$. The count is not zero, so the point is in shadow. Both methods always give the same count results for all points on the viewed surfaces.

triangles are drawn. Incrementing and decrementing are done only when the pixels of the rendered shadow-volume face are visible (i.e., not hidden by any real geometry). At this point the stencil buffer holds the state of shadowing for every pixel. Finally, the whole scene is rendered again, this time with only the components of the active materials that are affected by the light, and displayed only where the value in the stencil buffer is 0. A value of 0 indicates that the ray has gone out of shadow as many times as it has gone into a shadow volume—i.e., this location is illuminated by the light.

This counting method is the basic idea behind shadow volumes. An example of shadows generated by the shadow volume algorithm is shown in Figure 7.9. There are efficient ways to implement the algorithm in a single pass [1514]. However, counting problems will occur when an object penetrates the camera's near plane. The solution, called *z-fail*, involves counting the crossings hidden behind visible surfaces instead of in front [450, 775]. A brief summary of this alternative is shown in Figure 7.8.

Creating quadrilaterals for every triangle creates a huge amount of overdraw. That is, each triangle will create three quadrilaterals that must be rendered. A sphere

Figure 7.9. Shadow volumes. On the left, a character casts a shadow. On the right, the extruded triangles of the model are shown. *(Images from Microsoft SDK [1208] sample "ShadowVolume.")*

made of a thousand triangles creates three thousand quadrilaterals, and each of those quadrilaterals may span the screen. One solution is to draw only those quadrilaterals along the silhouette edges of the object, e.g., our sphere may have only fifty silhouette edges, so only fifty quadrilaterals are needed. The geometry shader can be used to automatically generate such silhouette edges [1702]. Culling and clamping techniques can also be used to lower fill costs [1061].

However, the shadow volume algorithm still has a terrible drawback: extreme variability. Imagine a single, small triangle in view. If the camera and the light are in exactly the same position, the shadow-volume cost is minimal. The quadrilaterals formed will not cover any pixels as they are edge-on to the view. Only the triangle itself matters. Say the viewer now orbits around the triangle, keeping it in view. As the camera moves away from the light source, the shadow-volume quadrilaterals will become more visible and cover more of the screen, causing more computation to occur. If the viewer should happen to move into the shadow of the triangle, the shadow volume will entirely fill the screen, costing a considerable amount of time to evaluate compared to our original view. This variability is what makes shadow volumes unusable in interactive applications where a consistent frame rate is important. Viewing toward the light can cause huge, unpredictable jumps in the cost of the algorithm, as can other scenarios.

For these reasons shadow volumes have been for the most part abandoned by applications. However, given the continuing evolution of new and different ways to access data on the GPU, and the clever repurposing of such functionality by researchers, shadow volumes may someday come back into general use. For example, Sintorn et al. [1648] give an overview of shadow-volume algorithms that improve efficiency and propose their own hierarchical acceleration structure.

The next algorithm presented, shadow mapping, has a much more predictable cost and is well suited to the GPU, and so forms the basis for shadow generation in many applications.

7.4 Shadow Maps

In 1978, Williams [1888] proposed that a common z-buffer-based renderer could be used to generate shadows quickly on arbitrary objects. The idea is to render the scene, using the z-buffer, from the position of the light source that is to cast shadows. Whatever the light "sees" is illuminated, the rest is in shadow. When this image is generated, only z-buffering is required. Lighting, texturing, and writing values into the color buffer can be turned off.

Each pixel in the z-buffer now contains the z-depth of the object closest to the light source. We call the entire contents of the z-buffer the *shadow map*, also sometimes known as the *shadow depth map* or *shadow buffer*. To use the shadow map, the scene is rendered a second time, but this time with respect to the viewer. As each drawing primitive is rendered, its location at each pixel is compared to the shadow map. If a rendered point is farther away from the light source than the corresponding value in the shadow map, that point is in shadow, otherwise it is not. This technique is implemented by using texture mapping. See Figure 7.10. Shadow mapping is a popular algorithm because it is relatively predictable. The cost of building the shadow map is roughly linear with the number of rendered primitives, and access time is constant. The shadow map can be generated once and reused each frame for scenes where the light and objects are not moving, such as for computer-aided design.

When a single z-buffer is generated, the light can "look" in only a particular direction, like a camera. For a distant directional light such as the sun, the light's view is set to encompass all objects casting shadows into the viewing volume that the eye sees. The light uses an orthographic projection, and its view needs to be made wide and high enough in x and y to view this set of objects. Local light sources need similar adjustments, as possible. If the local light is far enough away from the shadow-casting objects, a single view frustum may be sufficient to encompass all of these. Alternately, if the local light is a spotlight, it has a natural frustum associated with it, with everything outside its frustum considered not illuminated.

If the local light source is inside a scene and is surrounded by shadow-casters, a typical solution is to use a six-view cube, similar to cubic environment mapping [865]. These are called *omnidirectional shadow maps*. The main challenge for omnidirectional maps is avoiding artifacts along the seams where two separate maps meet. King and Newhall [895] analyze the problems in depth and provide solutions, and Gerasimov [525] provides some implementation details. Forsyth [484, 486] presents a general multi-frustum partitioning scheme for omnidirectional lights that also provides more shadow map resolution where needed. Crytek [1590, 1678, 1679] sets the resolution of each of the six views for a point light based on the screen-space coverage of each view's projected frustum, with all maps stored in a texture atlas.

Not all objects in the scene need to be rendered into the light's view volume. First, only objects that can cast shadows need to be rendered. For example, if it is known that the ground can only receive shadows and not cast one, then it does not have to be rendered into the shadow map.

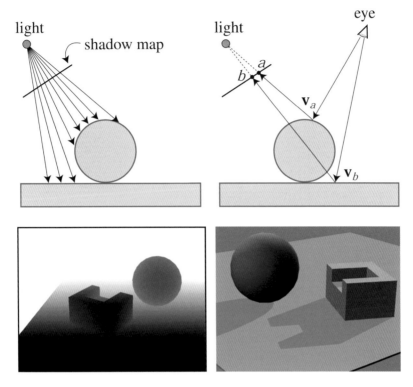

Figure 7.10. Shadow mapping. On the top left, a shadow map is formed by storing the depths to the surfaces in view. On the top right, the eye is shown looking at two locations. The sphere is seen at point $\mathbf{v}_a$, and this point is found to be located at texel a on the shadow map. The depth stored there is not (much) less than point $\mathbf{v}_a$ is from the light, so the point is illuminated. The rectangle hit at point $\mathbf{v}_b$ is (much) farther away from the light than the depth stored at texel b, and so is in shadow. On the bottom left is the view of a scene from the light's perspective, with white being farther away. On the bottom right is the scene rendered with this shadow map.

Shadow casters are by definition those inside the light's view frustum. This frustum can be augmented or tightened in several ways, allowing us to safely disregard some shadow casters [896, 1812]. Think of the set of shadow receivers visible to the eye. This set of objects is within some maximum distance along the light's view direction. Anything beyond this distance cannot cast a shadow on the visible receivers. Similarly, the set of visible receivers may well be smaller than the light's original x and y view bounds. See Figure 7.11. Another example is that if the light source is inside the eye's view frustum, no object outside this additional frustum can cast a shadow on a receiver. Rendering only relevant objects not only can save time rendering, but can also reduce the size required for the light's frustum and so increase the effective resolution of the shadow map, thus improving quality. In addition, it helps if the light frustum's near plane is as far away from the light as possible, and if the far plane is

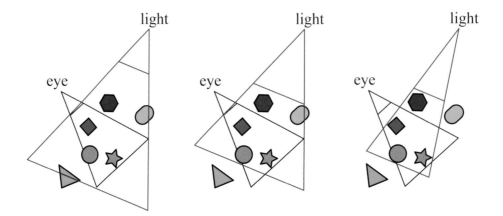

Figure 7.11. On the left, the light's view encompasses the eye's frustum. In the middle, the light's far plane is pulled in to include only visible receivers, so culling the triangle as a caster; the near plane is also adjusted. On the right, the light's frustum sides are made to bound the visible receivers, culling the green capsule.

as close as possible. Doing so increases the effective precision of the z-buffer [1792] (Section 4.7.2).

One disadvantage of shadow mapping is that the quality of the shadows depends on the resolution (in pixels) of the shadow map and on the numerical precision of the z-buffer. Since the shadow map is sampled during the depth comparison, the algorithm is susceptible to aliasing problems, especially close to points of contact between objects. A common problem is *self-shadow aliasing*, often called "surface acne" or "shadow acne," in which a triangle is incorrectly considered to shadow itself. This problem has two sources. One is simply the numerical limits of precision of the processor. The other source is geometric, from the fact that the value of a point sample is being used to represent an area's depth. That is, samples generated for the light are almost never at the same locations as the screen samples (e.g., pixels are often sampled at their centers). When the light's stored depth value is compared to the viewed surface's depth, the light's value may be slightly lower than the surface's, resulting in self-shadowing. The effects of such errors are shown in Figure 7.12.

One common method to help avoid (but not always eliminate) various shadow-map artifacts is to introduce a bias factor. When checking the distance found in the shadow map with the distance of the location being tested, a small bias is subtracted from the receiver's distance. See Figure 7.13. This bias could be a constant value [1022], but doing so can fail when the receiver is not mostly facing the light. A more effective method is to use a bias that is proportional to the angle of the receiver to the light. The more the surface tilts away from the light, the greater the bias grows, to avoid the problem. This type of bias is called the *slope scale bias*. Both biases can be applied by using a command such as OpenGL's `glPolygonOffset`) to shift each polygon away from the light. Note that if a surface directly faces the light, it is not biased backward

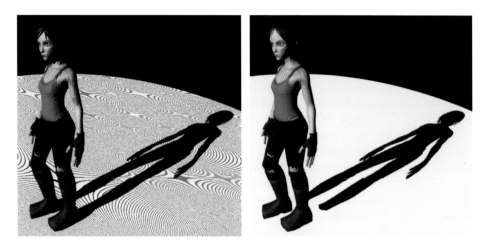

Figure 7.12. Shadow-mapping bias artifacts. On the left, the bias is too low, so self-shadowing occurs. On the right, a high bias causes the shoes to not cast contact shadows. The shadow-map resolution is also too low, giving the shadow a blocky appearance. *(Images generated using a shadow demo by Christoph Peters.)*

at all by slope scale bias. For this reason, a constant bias is used along with slope scale bias to avoid possible precision errors. Slope scale bias is also often clamped at some maximum, since the tangent value can be extremely high when the surface is nearly edge-on when viewed from the light.

Figure 7.13. Shadow bias. The surfaces are rendered into a shadow map for an overhead light, with the vertical lines representing shadow-map pixel centers. Occluder depths are recorded at the × locations. We want to know if the surface is lit at the three samples shown as dots. The closest shadow-map depth value for each is shown with the same color ×. On the left, if no bias is added, the blue and orange samples will be incorrectly determined to be in shadow, since they are farther from the light than their corresponding shadow-map depths. In the middle, a constant depth bias is subtracted from each sample, placing each closer to the light. The blue sample is still considered in shadow because it is not closer to the light than the shadow-map depth it is tested against. On the right, the shadow map is formed by moving each polygon away from the light proportional to its slope. All sample depths are now closer than their shadow-map depths, so all are lit.

Holbert [759, 760] introduced *normal offset bias*, which first shifts the receiver's world-space location a bit along the surface's normal direction, proportional to the sine of the angle between the light's direction and the geometric normal. See Figure 7.24 on page 250. This changes not only the depth but also the x- and y-coordinates where the sample is tested on the shadow map. As the light's angle becomes more shallow to the surface, this offset is increased, in hopes that the sample becomes far enough above the surface to avoid self-shadowing. This method can be visualized as moving the sample to a "virtual surface" above the receiver. This offset is a world-space distance, so Pettineo [1403] recommends scaling it by the depth range of the shadow map. Pesce [1391] suggests the idea of biasing along the camera view direction, which also works by adjusting the shadow-map coordinates. Other bias methods are discussed in Section 7.5, as the shadow method presented there needs to also test several neighboring samples.

Too much bias causes a problem called *light leaks* or *Peter Panning*, in which the object appears to float slightly above the underlying surface. This artifact occurs because the area beneath the object's point of contact, e.g., the ground under a foot, is pushed too far forward and so does not receive a shadow.

One way to avoid self-shadowing problems is to render only the backfaces to the shadow map. Called *second-depth shadow mapping* [1845], this scheme works well for many situations, especially for a rendering system where hand-tweaking a bias is not an option. The problem cases occur when objects are two-sided, thin, or in contact with one another. If an object is a model where both sides of the mesh are visible, e.g., a palm frond or sheet of paper, self-shadowing can occur because the backface and the frontface are in the same location. Similarly, if no biasing is performed, problems can occur near silhouette edges or thin objects, since in these areas backfaces are close to frontfaces. Adding a bias can help avoid surface acne, but the scheme is more susceptible to light leaking, as there is no separation between the receiver and the backfaces of the occluder at the point of contact. See Figure 7.14. Which scheme to choose can be situation dependent. For example, Sousa et al. [1679] found using frontfaces for sun shadows and backfaces for interior lights to work best for their applications.

Note that for shadow mapping, objects must be "watertight" (manifold and closed, i.e., solid; Section 16.3.3), or must have both front- and backfaces rendered to the map, else the object may not fully cast a shadow. Woo [1900] proposes a general method that attempts to, literally, be a happy medium between using just frontfaces or backfaces for shadowing. The idea is to render solid objects to a shadow map and keep track of the two closest surfaces to the light. This process can be performed by depth peeling or other transparency-related techniques. The average depth between the two objects forms an intermediate layer whose depth is used as a shadow map, sometimes called a *dual shadow map* [1865]. If the object is thick enough, self-shadowing and light-leak artifacts are minimized. Bavoil et al. [116] discuss ways to address potential artifacts, along with other implementation details. The main drawbacks are the additional costs

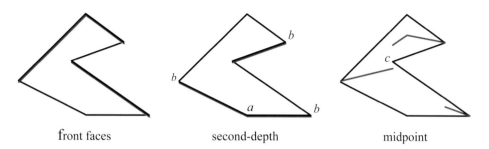

front faces   second-depth   midpoint

Figure 7.14. Shadow-map surfaces for an overhead light source. On the left, surfaces facing the light, marked in red, are sent to the shadow map. Surfaces may be incorrectly determined to shadow themselves ("acne"), so need to be biased away from the light. In the middle, only the backfacing triangles are rendered into the shadow map. A bias pushing these occluders downward could let light leak onto the ground plane near location a; a bias forward can cause illuminated locations near the silhouette boundaries marked b to be considered in shadow. On the right, an intermediate surface is formed at the midpoints between the closest front- and backfacing triangles found at each location on the shadow map. A light leak can occur near point c (which can also happen with second-depth shadow mapping), as the nearest shadow-map sample may be on the intermediate surface to the left of this location, and so the point would be closer to the light.

associated with using two shadow maps. Myers [1253] discusses an artist-controlled depth layer between the occlude and receiver.

As the viewer moves, the light's view volume often changes size as the set of shadow casters changes. Such changes in turn cause the shadows to shift slightly from frame to frame. This occurs because the light's shadow map is sampling a different set of directions from the light, and these directions are not aligned with the previous set. For directional lights, the solution is to force each succeeding shadow map generated to maintain the same relative texel beam locations in world space [927, 1227, 1792, 1810]. That is, you can think of the shadow map as imposing a two-dimensional gridded frame of reference on the whole world, with each grid cell representing a pixel sample on the map. As you move, the shadow map is generated for a different set of these same grid cells. In other words, the light's view projection is forced to this grid to maintain frame to frame coherence.

7.4.1 Resolution Enhancement

Similar to how textures are used, ideally we want one shadow-map texel to cover about one image pixel. If we have a light source located at the same position as the eye, the shadow map perfectly maps one-to-one with the screen-space pixels (and there are no visible shadows, since the light illuminates exactly what the eye sees). As soon as the light's direction changes, this per-pixel ratio changes, which can cause artifacts. An example is shown in Figure 7.15. The shadow is blocky and poorly defined because a large number of pixels in the foreground are associated with each texel of the shadow map. This mismatch is called *perspective aliasing*. Single shadow-map texels can also

Figure 7.15. The image to the left is created using standard shadow mapping; the image to the right using LiSPSM. The projections of each shadow map's texels are shown. The two shadow maps have the same resolution, the difference being that LiSPSM reforms the light's matrices to provide a higher sampling rate nearer the viewer. *(Images courtesy of Daniel Scherzer, Vienna University of Technology.)*

cover many pixels if a surface is nearly edge-on to the light, but faces the viewer. This problem is known as *projective aliasing* [1792]; see Figure 7.16. Blockiness can be decreased by increasing the shadow-map resolution, but at the cost of additional memory and processing.

There is another approach to creating the light's sampling pattern that makes it more closely resemble the camera's pattern. This is done by changing the way the scene projects toward the light. Normally we think of a view as being symmetric, with the view vector in the center of the frustum. However, the view direction merely defines a view plane, but not which pixels are sampled. The window defining the frustum can be shifted, skewed, or rotated on this plane, creating a quadrilateral that gives a different mapping of world to view space. The quadrilateral is still sampled at regular intervals, as this is the nature of a linear transform matrix and its use by the GPU. The sampling rate can be modified by varying the light's view direction and the view window's bounds. See Figure 7.17.

There are 22 degrees of freedom in mapping the light's view to the eye's [896]. Exploration of this solution space led to several different algorithms that attempt

Figure 7.16. On the left the light is nearly overhead. The edge of the shadow is a bit ragged due to a low resolution compared to the eye's view. On the right the light is near the horizon, so each shadow texel covers considerably more screen area horizontally and so gives a more jagged edge. *(Images generated by TheRealMJP's "Shadows" program on Github.)*

to better match the light's sampling rates to the eye's. Methods include *perspective shadow maps* (PSM) [1691], *trapezoidal shadow maps* (TSM) [1132], and *light space perspective shadow maps* (LiSPSM) [1893, 1895]. See Figure 7.15 and Figure 7.26 on page 254 for examples. Techniques in this class are referred to as *perspective warping* methods.

An advantage of these matrix-warping algorithms is that no additional work is needed beyond modifying the light's matrices. Each method has its own strengths and weaknesses [484], as each can help match sampling rates for some geometry and lighting situations, while worsening these rates for others. Lloyd et al. [1062, 1063] analyze the equivalences between PSM, TSM, and LiSPSM, giving an excellent overview of the sampling and aliasing issues with these approaches. These schemes work best when the light's direction is perpendicular to the view's direction (e.g., overhead), as the perspective transform can then be shifted to put more samples closer to the eye.

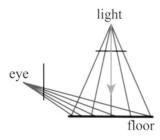
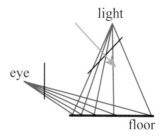

Figure 7.17. For an overhead light, on the left the sampling on the floor does not match the eye's rate. By changing the light's view direction and projection window on the right, the sampling rate is biased toward having a higher density of texels nearer the eye.

One lighting situation where matrix-warping techniques fail to help is when a light is in front of the camera and pointing at it. This situation is known as *dueling frusta*, or more colloquially as "deer in the headlights." More shadow-map samples are needed nearer the eye, but linear warping can only make the situation worse [1555]. This and other problems, such as sudden changes in quality [430] and a "nervous," unstable quality to the shadows produced during camera movement [484, 1227], have made these approaches fall out of favor.

The idea of adding more samples where the viewer is located is a good one, leading to algorithms that generate several shadow maps for a given view. This idea first made a noticeable impact when Carmack described it at his keynote at Quakecon 2004. Blow independently implemented such a system [174]. The idea is simple: Generate a fixed set of shadow maps (possibly at different resolutions), covering different areas of the scene. In Blow's scheme, four shadow maps are nested around the viewer. In this way, a high-resolution map is available for nearby objects, with the resolution dropping for those objects far away. Forsyth [483, 486] presents a related idea, generating different shadow maps for different visible sets of objects. The problem of how to handle the transition for objects spanning the border between two shadow maps is avoided in his setup, since each object has one and only one shadow map associated with it. Flagship Studios developed a system that blended these two ideas. One shadow map is for nearby dynamic objects, another is for a grid section of the static objects near the viewer, and a third is for the static objects in the scene as a whole. The first shadow map is generated each frame. The other two could be generated just once, since the light source and geometry are static. While all these particular systems are now quite old, the ideas of multiple maps for different objects and situations, some precomputed and some dynamic, is a common theme among algorithms that have been developed since.

In 2006 Engel [430], Lloyd et al. [1062, 1063], and Zhang et al. [1962, 1963] independently researched the same basic idea.[1] The idea is to divide the view frustum's volume into a few pieces by slicing it parallel to the view direction. See Figure 7.18. As depth increases, each successive volume has about two to three times the depth range of the previous volume [430, 1962]. For each view volume, the light source can make a frustum that tightly bounds it and then generate a shadow map. By using texture atlases or arrays, the different shadow maps can be treated as one large texture object, thus minimizing cache access delays. A comparison of the quality improvement obtained is shown in Figure 7.19. Engel's name for this algorithm, *cascaded shadow maps* (CSM), is more commonly used than Zhang's term, *parallel-split shadow maps*, but both appear in the literature and are effectively the same [1964].

This type of algorithm is straightforward to implement, can cover huge scene areas with reasonable results, and is robust. The dueling frusta problem can be addressed by sampling at a higher rate closer to the eye, and there are no serious worst-case

---

[1] Tadamura et al. [1735] introduced the idea seven years earlier, but it did not have an impact until other researchers explored its usefulness.

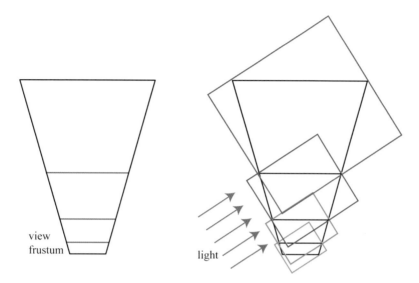

view
frustum

light

Figure 7.18. On the left, the view frustum from the eye is split into four volumes. On the right, bounding boxes are created for the volumes, which determine the volume rendered by each of the four shadow maps for the directional light. *(After Engel [430].)*

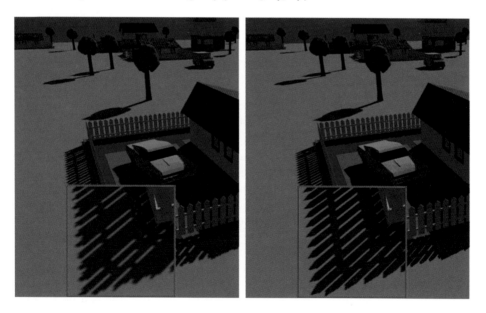

Figure 7.19. On the left, the scene's wide viewable area causes a single shadow map at a 2048×2048 resolution to exhibit perspective aliasing. On the right, four 1024×1024 shadow maps placed along the view axis improve quality considerably [1963]. A zoom of the front corner of the fence is shown in the inset red boxes. *(Images courtesy of Fan Zhang, The Chinese University of Hong Kong.)*

Figure 7.20. Shadow cascade visualization. Purple, green, yellow, and red represent the nearest through farthest cascades. *(Image courtesy of Unity Technologies.)*

problems. Because of these strengths, cascaded shadow mapping is used in many applications.

While it is possible to use perspective warping to pack more samples into subdivided areas of a single shadow map [1783], the norm is to use a separate shadow map for each cascade. As Figure 7.18 implies, and Figure 7.20 shows from the viewer's perspective, the area covered by each map can vary. Smaller view volumes for the closer shadow maps provide more samples where they are needed. Determining how the range of z-depths is split among the maps—a task called *z-partitioning*—can be quite simple or involved [412, 991, 1791]. One method is logarithmic partitioning [1062], where the ratio of far to near plane distances is made the same for each cascade map:

$$r = \sqrt[c]{\frac{f}{n}}, \tag{7.5}$$

where n and f are the near and far planes of the whole scene, c is the number of maps, and r is the resulting ratio. For example, if the scene's closest object is 1 meter away, the maximum distance is 1000 meters, and we have three cascaded maps, then $r = \sqrt[3]{1000/1} = 10$. The near and far plane distances for the closest view would be 1 and 10, the next interval is 10 to 100 to maintain this ratio, and the last is 100 to 1000 meters. The initial near depth has a large effect on this partitioning. If the near depth was only 0.1 meters, then the cube root of 10000 is 21.54, a considerably higher ratio, e.g., 0.1 to 2.154 to 46.42 to 1000. This would mean that each shadow map generated must cover a larger area, lowering its precision. In practice such a partitioning gives considerable resolution to the area close to the near plane, which is wasted if there are no objects in this area. One way to avoid this mismatch is to set the partition distances as a weighted blend of logarithmic and equidistant distributions [1962, 1963], but it would be better still if we could determine tight view bounds for the scene.

The challenge is in setting the near plane. If set too far from the eye, objects may be clipped by this plane, an extremely bad artifact. For a cut scene, an artist can set this value precisely in advance [1590], but for an interactive environment the problem is more challenging. Lauritzen et al. [991, 1403] present *sample distribution shadow maps* (SDSM), which use the z-depth values from the previous frame to determine a better partitioning by one of two methods.

The first method is to look through the z-depths for the minimum and maximum values and use these to set the near and far planes. This is performed using what is called a *reduce* operation on the GPU, in which a series of ever-smaller buffers are analyzed by a compute or other shader, with the output buffer fed back as input, until a 1×1 buffer is left. Normally, the values are pushed out a bit to adjust for the speed of movement of objects in the scene. Unless corrective action is taken, nearby objects entering from the edge of the screen may still cause problems for a frame, though will quickly be corrected in the next.

The second method also analyzes the depth buffer's values, making a graph called a *histogram* that records the distribution of the z-depths along the range. In addition to finding tight near and far planes, the graph may have gaps in it where there are no objects at all. Any partition plane normally added to such an area can be snapped to where objects actually exist, giving more z-depth precision to the set of cascade maps.

In practice, the first method is general, is quick (typically in the 1 ms range per frame), and gives good results, so it has been adopted in several applications [1405, 1811]. See Figure 7.21.

As with a single shadow map, shimmering artifacts due to light samples moving frame to frame are a problem, and can be even worse as objects move between cascades. A variety of methods are used to maintain stable sample points in world space, each with their own advantages [41, 865, 1381, 1403, 1678, 1679, 1810]. A sudden change in a shadow's quality can occur when an object spans the boundary between two shadow maps. One solution is to have the view volumes slightly overlap. Samples taken in these overlap zones gather results from both adjoining shadow maps and are blended [1791]. Alternately, a single sample can be taken in such zone by using dithering [1381].

Due to its popularity, considerable effort has been put into improving efficiency and quality [1791, 1964]. If nothing changes within a shadow map's frustum, that shadow map does not need to be recomputed. For each light, the list of shadow casters can be precomputed by finding which objects are visible to the light, and of these, which can cast shadows on receivers [1405]. Since it is fairly difficult to perceive whether a shadow is correct, some shortcuts can be taken that are applicable to cascades and other algorithms. One technique is to use a low level of detail model as a proxy to actually cast the shadow [652, 1812]. Another is to remove tiny occluders from consideration [1381, 1811]. The more distant shadow maps may be updated less frequently than once a frame, on the theory that such shadows are less important. This idea risks artifacts caused by large moving objects, so needs to be used with care [865, 1389, 1391, 1678, 1679]. Day [329] presents the idea of "scrolling" distant maps from frame to frame, the idea being that most of each static shadow map is

Figure 7.21. Effect of depth bounds. On the left, no special processing is used to adjust the near and far planes. On the right, SDSM is used to find tighter bounds. Note the window frame near the left edge of each image, the area beneath the flower box on the second floor, and the window on the first floor, where undersampling due to loose view bounds causes artifacts. Exponential shadow maps are used to render these particular images, but the idea of improving depth precision is useful for all shadow map techniques. *(Image courtesy of Ready at Dawn Studios, copyright Sony Interactive Entertainment.)*

reusable frame to frame, and only the fringes may change and so need rendering. Games such as *DOOM* (2016) maintain a large atlas of shadow maps, regenerating only those where objects have moved [294]. The farther cascaded maps could be set to ignore dynamic objects entirely, since such shadows may contribute little to the scene. With some environments, a high-resolution static shadow map can be used in place of these farther cascades, which can significantly reduce the workload [415, 1590]. A sparse texture system (Section 19.10.1) can be employed for worlds where a single static shadow map would be enormous [241, 625, 1253]. Cascaded shadow mapping can be combined with baked-in light-map textures or other shadow techniques that are more appropriate for particular situations [652]. Valient's presentation [1811] is noteworthy in that it describes different shadow system customizations and techniques for a wide range of video games. Section 11.5.1 discusses precomputed light and shadow algorithms in detail.

Creating several separate shadow maps means a run through some set of geometry for each. A number of approaches to improve efficiency have been built on the idea of rendering occluders to a set of shadow maps in a single pass. The geometry shader can be used to replicate object data and send it to multiple views [41]. Instanced geometry shaders allow an object to be output into up to 32 depth textures [1456].

Multiple-viewport extensions can perform operations such as rendering an object to a specific texture array slice [41, 154, 530]. Section 21.3.1 discusses these in more detail, in the context of their use for virtual reality. A possible drawback of viewport-sharing techniques is that the occluders for all the shadow maps generated must be sent down the pipeline, versus the set found to be relevant to each shadow map [1791, 1810].

You yourself are currently in the shadows of billions of light sources around the world. Light reaches you from only a few of these. In real-time rendering, large scenes with multiple lights can become swamped with computation if all lights are active at all times. If a volume of space is inside the view frustum but not visible to the eye, objects that occlude this receiver volume do not need to be evaluated [625, 1137]. Bittner et al. [152] use occlusion culling (Section 19.7) from the eye to find all visible shadow receivers, and then render all potential shadow receivers to a stencil buffer mask from the light's point of view. This mask encodes which visible shadow receivers are seen from the light. To generate the shadow map, they render the objects from the light using occlusion culling and use the mask to cull objects where no receivers are located. Various culling strategies can also work for lights. Since irradiance falls off with the square of the distance, a common technique is to cull light sources after a certain threshold distance. For example, the portal culling technique in Section 19.5 can find which lights affect which cells. This is an active area of research, since the performance benefits can be considerable [1330, 1604].

7.5 Percentage-Closer Filtering

A simple extension of the shadow-map technique can provide pseudo-soft shadows. This method can also help ameliorate resolution problems that cause shadows to look blocky when a single light-sample cell covers many screen pixels. The solution is similar to texture magnification (Section 6.2.1). Instead of a single sample being taken off the shadow map, the four nearest samples are retrieved. The technique does not interpolate between the depths themselves, but rather the results of their comparisons with the surface's depth. That is, the surface's depth is compared separately to the four texel depths, and the point is then determined to be in light or shadow for each shadow-map sample. These results, i.e., 0 for shadow and 1 for light, are then bilinearly interpolated to calculate how much the light actually contributes to the surface location. This filtering results in an artificially soft shadow. These penumbrae change, depending on the shadow map's resolution, camera location, and other factors. For example, a higher resolution makes for a narrower softening of the edges. Still, a little penumbra and smoothing is better than none at all.

This idea of retrieving multiple samples from a shadow map and blending the results is called *percentage-closer filtering* (PCF) [1475]. Area lights produce soft shadows. The amount of light reaching a location on a surface is a function of what proportion of the light's area is visible from the location. PCF attempts to approximate a soft shadow for a punctual (or directional) light by reversing the process.

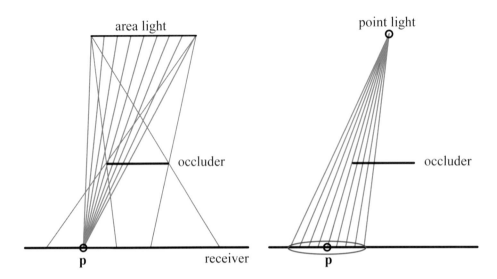

Figure 7.22. On the left, the brown lines from the area light source show where penumbrae are formed. For a single point **p** on the receiver, the amount of illumination received could be computed by testing a set of points on the area light's surface and finding which are not blocked by any occluders. On the right, a point light does not cast a penumbra. PCF approximates the effect of an area light by reversing the process: At a given location, it samples over a comparable area on the shadow map to derive a percentage of how many samples are illuminated. The red ellipse shows the area sampled on the shadow map. Ideally, the width of this disk is proportional to the distance between the receiver and occluder.

Instead of finding the light's visible area from a surface location, it finds the visibility of the punctual light from a set of surface locations near the original location. See Figure 7.22. The name "percentage-closer filtering" refers to the ultimate goal, to find the percentage of the samples taken that are visible to the light. This percentage is how much light then is used to shade the surface.

In PCF, locations are generated nearby to a surface location, at about the same depth, but at different texel locations on the shadow map. Each location's visibility is checked, and these resulting boolean values, lit or unlit, are then blended to get a soft shadow. Note that this process is non-physical: Instead of sampling the light source directly, this process relies on the idea of sampling over the surface itself. The distance to the occluder does not affect the result, so shadows have similar-sized penumbrae. Nonetheless this method provides a reasonable approximation in many situations.

Once the width of the area to be sampled is determined, it is important to sample in a way that avoids aliasing artifacts. There are numerous variations of how to sample and filter nearby shadow-map locations. Variables include how wide of an area to sample, how many samples to use, the sampling pattern, and how to weight the results. With less-capable APIs, the sampling process could be accelerated by a special texture sampling mode similar to bilinear interpolation, which accesses the four neighboring

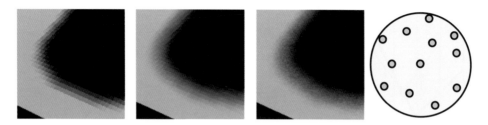

Figure 7.23. The far left shows PCF sampling in a 4×4 grid pattern, using nearest neighbor sampling. The far right shows a 12-tap Poisson sampling pattern on a disk. Using this pattern to sample the shadow map gives the improved result in the middle left, though artifacts are still visible. In the middle right, the sampling pattern is rotated randomly around its center from pixel to pixel. The structured shadow artifacts turn into (much less objectionable) noise. *(Images courtesy of John Isidoro, ATI Research, Inc.)*

locations. Instead of blending the results, each of the four samples is compared to a given value, and the ratio that passes the test is returned [175]. However, performing nearest neighbor sampling in a regular grid pattern can create noticeable artifacts. Using a joint bilateral filter that blurs the result but respects object edges can improve quality while avoiding shadows leaking onto other surfaces [1343]. See Section 12.1.1 for more on this filtering technique.

DirectX 10 introduced single-instruction bilinear filtering support for PCF, giving a smoother result [53, 412, 1709, 1790]. This offers considerable visual improvement over nearest neighbor sampling, but artifacts from regular sampling remain a problem. One solution to minimize grid patterns is to sample an area using a precomputed Poisson distribution pattern, as illustrated in Figure 7.23. This distribution spreads samples out so that they are neither near each other nor in a regular pattern. It is well known that using the same sampling locations for each pixel, regardless of the distribution, can result in patterns [288]. Such artifacts can be avoided by randomly rotating the sample distribution around its center, which turns aliasing into noise. Castaño [235] found that the noise produced by Poisson sampling was particularly noticeable for their smooth, stylized content. He presents an efficient Gaussian-weighted sampling scheme based on bilinear sampling.

Self-shadowing problems and light leaks, i.e., acne and Peter Panning, can become worse with PCF. Slope scale bias pushes the surface away from the light based purely on its angle to the light, with the assumption that a sample is no more than a texel away on the shadow map. By sampling in a wider area from a single location on a surface, some of the test samples may get blocked by the true surface.

A few different additional bias factors have been invented and used with some success to reduce the risk of self-shadowing. Burley [212] describes the *bias cone*, where each sample is moved toward the light proportional to its distance from the original sample. Burley recommends a slope of 2.0, along with a small constant bias. See Figure 7.24.

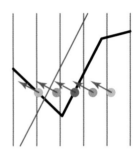

Figure 7.24. Additional shadow bias methods. For PCF, several samples are taken surrounding the original sample location, the center of the five dots. All these samples should be lit. In the left figure, a bias cone is formed and the samples are moved up to it. The cone's steepness could be increased to pull the samples on the right close enough to be lit, at the risk of increasing light leaks from other samples elsewhere (not shown) that truly are shadowed. In the middle figure, all samples are adjusted to lie on the receiver's plane. This works well for convex surfaces but can be counterproductive at concavities, as seen on the left side. In the right figure, normal offset bias moves the samples along the surface's normal direction, proportional to the sine of the angle between the normal and the light. For the center sample, this can be thought of as moving to an imaginary surface above the original surface. This bias not only affects the depth but also changes the texture coordinates used to test the shadow map.

Schüler [1585], Isidoro [804], and Tuft [1790] present techniques based on the observation that the slope of the receiver itself should be used to adjust the depths of the rest of the samples. Of the three, Tuft's formulation [1790] is most easily applied to cascaded shadow maps. Dou et al. [373] further refine and extend this concept, accounting for how the z-depth varies in a nonlinear fashion. These approaches assume that nearby sample locations are on the same plane formed by the triangle. Referred to as *receiver plane depth bias* or other similar terms, this technique can be quite precise in many cases, as locations on this imaginary plane are indeed on the surface, or in front of it if the model is convex. As shown in Figure 7.24, samples near concavities can become hidden. Combinations of constant, slope scale, receiver plane, view bias, and normal offset biasing have been used to combat the problem of self-shadowing, though hand-tweaking for each environment can still be necessary [235, 1391, 1403].

One problem with PCF is that because the sampling area's width remains constant, shadows will appear uniformly soft, all with the same penumbra width. This may be acceptable under some circumstances, but appears incorrect where there is ground contact between the occluder and receiver. See Figure 7.25.

7.6 Percentage-Closer Soft Shadows

In 2005 Fernando [212, 467, 1252] published an influential approach called *percentage-closer soft shadows* (PCSS). It attempts a solution by searching the nearby area on

Figure 7.25. Percentage-closer filtering and percentage-closer soft shadows. On the left, hard shadows with a little PCF filtering. In the middle, constant width soft shadows. On the right, variable-width soft shadows with proper hardness where objects are in contact with the ground. *(Images courtesy of NVIDIA Corporation.)*

the shadow map to find all possible occluders. The average distance of these occluders from the location is used to determine the sample area width:

$$w_{\text{sample}} = w_{\text{light}} \frac{d_r - d_o}{d_r}, \qquad (7.6)$$

where d_r is the distance of the receiver from the light and d_o the average occluder distance. In other words, the width of the surface area to the sample grows as the average occluder gets farther from the receiver and closer to the light. Examine Figure 7.22 and think about the effect of moving the occluder to see how this occurs. Figures 7.2 (page 224), 7.25, and 7.26 show examples.

If there are no occluders found, the location is fully lit and no further processing is necessary. Similarly, if the location is fully occluded, processing can end. Otherwise, then the area of interest is sampled and the light's approximate contribution is computed. To save on processing costs, the width of the sample area can be used to vary the number of samples taken. Other techniques can be implemented, e.g., using lower sampling rates for distant soft shadows that are less likely to be important.

A drawback of this method is that it needs to sample a fair-sized area of the shadow map to find the occluders. Using a rotated Poisson disk pattern can help hide undersampling artifacts [865, 1590]. Jimenez [832] notes that Poisson sampling can be unstable under motion and finds that a spiral pattern formed by using a function halfway between dithering and random gives a better result frame to frame.

Sikachev et al. [1641] discuss in detail a faster implementation of PCSS using features in SM 5.0, introduced by AMD and often called by their name for it, *contact hardening shadows* (CHS). This new version also addresses another problem with basic PCSS: The penumbra's size is affected by the shadow map's resolution. See Figure 7.25. This problem is minimized by first generating mipmaps of the shadow map, then choosing the mip level closest to a user-defined world-space kernel size. An 8×8 area is sampled to find the average blocker depth, needing only 16 `GatherRed()` texture calls. Once a penumbra estimate is found, the higher-resolution mip levels are used for the sharp area of the shadow, while the lower-resolution mip levels are used for softer areas.

CHS has been used in a large number of video games [1351, 1590, 1641, 1678, 1679], and research continues. For example, Buades et al. [206] present *separable soft shadow mapping* (SSSM), where the PCSS process of sampling a grid is split into separable parts and elements are reused as possible from pixel to pixel.

One concept that has proven helpful for accelerating algorithms that need multiple samples per pixel is the hierarchical *min/max shadow map*. While shadow map depths normally cannot be averaged, the minimum and maximum values at each mipmap level can be useful. That is, two mipmaps can be formed, one saving the largest z-depth found in each area (sometimes called *HiZ*), and one the smallest. Given a texel location, depth, and area to be sampled, the mipmaps can be used to rapidly determine fully lit and fully shadowed conditions. For example, if the texel's z-depth is greater than the maximum z-depth stored for the corresponding area of the mipmap, then the texel must be in shadow—no further samples are needed. This type of shadow map makes the task of determining light visibility much more efficient [357, 415, 610, 680, 1064, 1811].

Methods such as PCF work by sampling the nearby receiver locations. PCSS works by finding an average depth of nearby occluders. These algorithms do not directly take into account the area of the light source, but rather sample the nearby surfaces, and are affected by the resolution of the shadow map. A major assumption behind PCSS is that the average blocker is a reasonable estimate of the penumbra size. When two occluders, say a street lamp and a distant mountain, partially occlude the same surface at a pixel, this assumption is broken and can lead to artifacts. Ideally, we want to determine how much of the area light source is visible from a single receiver location. Several researchers have explored *backprojection* using the GPU. The idea is to treat each receiver's location as a viewpoint and the area light source as part of a view plane, and to project occluders onto this plane. Both Schwarz and Stamminger [1593] and Guennebaud et al. [617] summarize previous work and offer their own improvements. Bavoil et al. [116] take a different approach, using depth peeling to create a multi-layer shadow map. Backprojection algorithms can give excellent results, but the high cost per pixel has (so far) meant they have not seen adoption in interactive applications.

7.7 Filtered Shadow Maps

One algorithm that allows filtering of the shadow maps generated is Donnelly and Lauritzen's *variance shadow map* (VSM) [368]. The algorithm stores the depth in one map and the depth squared in another map. MSAA or other antialiasing schemes can be used when generating the maps. These maps can be blurred, mipmapped, put in summed area tables [988], or any other method. The ability to treat these maps as filterable textures is a huge advantage, as the entire array of sampling and filtering techniques can be brought to bear when retrieving data from them.

We will describe VSM in some depth here, to give a sense of how this process works; also, the same type of testing is used for all methods in this class of algorithm. Readers interested in learning more about this area should access the relevant references, and we also recommend the book by Eisemann et al. [412], which gives the topic considerably more space.

To begin, for VSM the depth map is sampled (just once) at the receiver's location to return an average depth of the closest light occluder. When this average depth M_1, called the *first moment*, is greater than the depth on the shadow receiver t, the receiver is considered fully in light. When the average depth is less than the receiver's depth, the following equation is used:

$$p_{\max}(t) = \frac{\sigma^2}{\sigma^2 + (t - M_1)^2}, \tag{7.7}$$

where $p_{\max}$ is the maximum percentage of samples in light, σ^2 is the variance, t is the receiver depth, and M_1 is the average expected depth in the shadow map. The depth-squared shadow map's sample M_2, called the *second moment*, is used to compute the variance:

$$\sigma^2 = M_2 - M_1^2. \tag{7.8}$$

The value $p_{\max}$ is an upper bound on the visibility percentage of the receiver. The actual illumination percentage p cannot be larger than this value. This upper bound is from the one-sided variant of Chebyshev's inequality. The equation attempts to estimate, using probability theory, how much of the distribution of occluders at the surface location is beyond the surface's distance from the light. Donnelly and Lauritzen show that for a planar occluder and planar receiver at fixed depths, $p = p_{\max}$, so Equation 7.7 can be used as a good approximation of many real shadowing situations.

Myers [1251] builds up an intuition as to why this method works. The variance over an area increases at shadow edges. The greater the difference in depths, the greater the variance. The $(t - M_1)^2$ term is then a significant determinant in the visibility percentage. If this value is just slightly above zero, this means the average occluder depth is slightly closer to the light than the receiver, and $p_{\max}$ is then near 1 (fully lit). This would happen along the fully lit edge of the penumbra. Moving into the penumbra, the average occluder depth gets closer to the light, so this term becomes larger and $p_{\max}$ drops. At the same time the variance itself is changing within the penumbra, going from nearly zero along the edges to the largest variance where the occluders differ in depth and equally share the area. These terms balance out to give a linearly varying shadow across the penumbra. See Figure 7.26 for a comparison with other algorithms.

One significant feature of variance shadow mapping is that it can deal with the problem of surface bias problems due to geometry in an elegant fashion. Lauritzen [988] gives a derivation of how the surface's slope is used to modify the value of the second moment. Bias and other problems from numerical stability can be a problem for variance mapping. For example, Equation 7.8 subtracts one large value

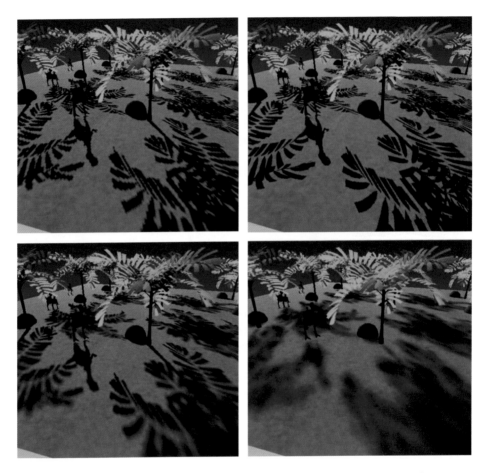

Figure 7.26. In the upper left, standard shadow mapping. Upper right, perspective shadow mapping, increasing the density of shadow-map texel density near the viewer. Lower left, percentage-closer soft shadows, softening the shadows as the occluder's distance from the receiver increases. Lower right, variance shadow mapping with a constant soft shadow width, each pixel shaded with a single variance map sample. *(Images courtesy of Nico Hempe, Yvonne Jung, and Johannes Behr.)*

from another similar value. This type of computation tends to magnify the lack of accuracy of the underlying numerical representation. Using floating point textures helps avoid this problem.

Overall VSM gives a noticeable increase in quality for the amount of time spent processing, since the GPU's optimized texture capabilities are used efficiently. While PCF needs more samples, and hence more time, to avoid noise when generating softer shadows, VSM can work with just a single, high-quality sample to determine the entire area's effect and produce a smooth penumbra. This ability means that shadows can be made arbitrarily soft at no additional cost, within the limitations of the algorithm.

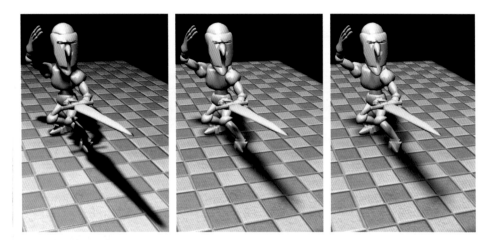

Figure 7.27. Variance shadow mapping, where the distance to the light source increases from left to right. *(Images from the NVIDIA SDK 10 [1300] samples, courtesy of NVIDIA Corporation.)*

As with PCF, the width of the filtering kernel determines the width of the penumbra. By finding the distance between the receiver and the closest occluder, the kernel width can be varied, so giving convincing soft shadows. Mipmapped samples are poor estimators of coverage for a penumbra with a slowly increasing width, creating boxy artifacts. Lauritzen [988] details how to use summed-area tables to give considerably better shadows. An example is shown in Figure 7.27.

One place variance shadow mapping breaks down is along the penumbrae areas when two or more occluders cover a receiver and one occluder is close to the receiver. The Chebyshev inequality from probability theory will produce a maximum light value that is not related to the correct light percentage. The closest occluder, by only partially hiding the light, throws off the equation's approximation. This results in *light bleeding* (a.k.a. light leaks), where areas that are fully occluded still receive light. See Figure 7.28. By taking more samples over smaller areas, this problem can be resolved, turning variance shadow mapping into a form of PCF. As with PCF, speed and performance trade off, but for scenes with low shadow depth complexity, variance mapping works well. Lauritzen [988] gives one artist-controlled method to ameliorate the problem, which is to treat low percentages as fully shadowed and to remap the rest of the percentage range to 0% to 100%. This approach darkens light bleeds, at the cost of narrowing penumbrae overall. While light bleeding is a serious limitation, VSM is good for producing shadows from terrain, since such shadows rarely involve multiple occluders [1227].

The promise of being able to use filtering techniques to rapidly produce smooth shadows generated much interest in filtered shadow mapping; the main challenge is solving the various bleeding problems. Annen et al. [55] introduced the *convolution shadow map*. Extending the idea behind Soler and Sillion's algorithm for planar

Figure 7.28. On the left, variance shadow mapping applied to a teapot. On the right, a triangle (not shown) casts a shadow on the teapot, causing objectionable artifacts in the shadow on the ground. *(Images courtesy of Marco Salvi.)*

receivers [1673], the idea is to encode the shadow depth in a Fourier expansion. As with variance shadow mapping, such maps can be filtered. The method converges to the correct answer, so the light leak problem is lessened.

A drawback of convolution shadow mapping is that several terms need to be computed and accessed, considerably increasing both execution and storage costs [56, 117]. Salvi [1529, 1530] and Annen et al. [56] concurrently and independently came upon the idea of using a single term based on an exponential function. Called an *exponential shadow map* (ESM) or *exponential variance shadow map* (EVSM), this method saves the exponential of the depth along with its second moment into two buffers. An exponential function more closely approximates the step function that a shadow map performs (i.e., in light or not), so this works to significantly reduce bleeding artifacts. It avoids another problem that convolution shadow mapping has, called *ringing*, where minor light leaks can happen at particular depths just past the original occluder's depth.

A limitation with storing exponential values is that the second moment values can become extremely large and so run out of range using floating point numbers. To improve precision, and to allow the exponential function to drop off more steeply, z-depths can be generated so that they are linear [117, 258].

Due to its improved quality over VSM, and its lower storage and better performance compared to convolution maps, the exponential shadow map approach has sparked the most interest of the three filtered approaches. Pettineo [1405] notes several other improvements, such as the ability to use MSAA to improve results and to obtain some limited transparency, and describes how filtering performance can be improved with compute shaders.

More recently, *moment shadow mapping* was introduced by Peters and Klein [1398]. It offers better quality, though at the expense of using four or more moments, increasing storage costs. This cost can be decreased by the use of 16-bit integers to store the moments. Pettineo [1404] implements and compares this new approach with ESM, providing a code base that explores many variants.

Cascaded shadow-map techniques can be applied to filtered maps to improve precision [989]. An advantage of cascaded ESM over standard cascaded maps is that a single bias factor can be set for all cascades [1405]. Chen and Tatarchuk [258] go into detail about various light leak problems and other artifacts encountered with cascaded ESM, and present a few solutions.

Filtered maps can be thought of as an inexpensive form of PCF, one that needs few samples. Like PCF, such shadows have a constant width. These filtered approaches can all be used in conjunction with PCSS to provide variable-width penumbrae [57, 1620, 1943]. An extension of moment shadow mapping also includes the ability to provide light scattering and transparency effects [1399].

7.8 Volumetric Shadow Techniques

Transparent objects will attenuate and change the color of light. For some sets of transparent objects, techniques similar to those discussed in Section 5.5 can be used to simulate such effects. For example, in some situations a second type of shadow map can be generated. The transparent objects are rendered to it, and the closest depth and color or alpha coverage is stored. If the receiver is not blocked by the opaque shadow map, the transparency depth map is then tested and, if occluded, the color or coverage is retrieved as needed [471, 1678, 1679]. This idea is reminiscent of shadow and light projection in Section 7.2, with the stored depths avoiding projection onto receivers between the transparent objects and the light. Such techniques cannot be applied to the transparent objects themselves.

Self-shadowing is critical for realistic rendering of objects such as hair and clouds, where objects are either small or semitransparent. Single-depth shadow maps will not work for these situations. Lokovic and Veach [1066] first presented the concept of *deep shadow maps*, in which each shadow-map texel stores a function of how light drops off with depth. This function is typically approximated by a series of samples at different depths, with each sample having an opacity value. The two samples in the map that bracket a given position's depth are used to find the shadow's effect. The challenge on the GPU is in generating and evaluating such functions efficiently. These algorithms use similar approaches and run into similar challenges found for some order-independent transparency algorithms (Section 5.5), such as compact storage of the data needed to faithfully represent each function.

Kim and Neumann [894] were the first to present a GPU-based method, which they call *opacity shadow maps*. Maps storing just the opacities are generated at a fixed set of depths. Nguyen and Donnelly [1274] give an updated version of this approach, producing images such as Figure 17.2 on page 719. However, the depth slices are all parallel and uniform, so many slices are needed to hide in-between slice opacity artifacts due to linear interpolation. Yuksel and Keyser [1953] improve efficiency and quality by creating opacity maps that more closely follow the shape of the model.

Figure 7.29. Hair and smoke rendering with adaptive volumetric shadow maps [1531]. *(Reprinted by permission of Marco Salvi and Intel Corporation, copyright Intel Corporation, 2010.)*

Doing so allows them to reduce the number of layers needed, as evaluation of each layer is more significant to the final image.

To avoid having to rely on fixed slice setups, more adaptive techniques have been proposed. Salvi et al. [1531] introduce *adaptive volumetric shadow maps*, in which each shadow-map texel stores both the opacities and layer depths. Pixel shaders operations are used to lossily compress the stream of data (surface opacities) as it is rasterized. This avoids needing an unbounded amount of memory to gather all samples and process them in a set. The technique is similar to deep shadow maps [1066], but with the compression step done on the fly in the pixel shader. Limiting the function representation to a small, fixed number of stored opacity/depth pairs makes both compression and retrieval on the GPU more efficient [1531]. The cost is higher than simple blending because the curve needs to be read, updated, and written back, and it depends on the number of points used to represent a curve. In this case, this technique also requires recent hardware that supports UAV and ROV functionality (end of Section 3.8). See Figure 7.29 for an example.

The adaptive volumetric shadow mapping method was used for realistic smoke rendering in the game *GRID2*, with the average cost being below 2 ms/frame [886]. Fürst et al. [509] describe and provide code for their implementation of deep shadow maps for a video game. They use linked lists to store depths and alphas, and use exponential shadow mapping to provide a soft transition between lit and shadowed regions.

Exploration of shadow algorithms continues, with a synthesis of a variety of algorithms and techniques becoming more common. For example, Selgrad et al. [1603] research storing multiple transparent samples with linked lists and using compute shaders with scattered writes to build the map. Their work uses deep shadow-map concepts, along with filtered maps and other elements, which give a more general solution for providing high-quality soft shadows.

7.9 Irregular Z-Buffer Shadows

Shadow-map approaches of various sorts are popular for several reasons. Their costs are predictable and scale well to increasing scene sizes, at worst linear with the number of primitives. They map nicely onto the GPU, as they rely on rasterization to regularly sample the light's view of the world. However, due to this discrete sampling, problems arise because the locations the eye sees do not map one-to-one with those the light sees. Various aliasing problems arise when the light samples a surface less frequently than the eye. Even when sampling rates are comparable, there are biasing problems because the surface is sampled in locations slightly different than those the eye sees.

Shadow volumes provide an exact, analytical solution, as the light's interactions with surfaces result in sets of triangles defining whether any given location is lit or in shadow. The unpredictable cost of the algorithm when implemented on the GPU is a serious drawback. The improvements explored in recent years [1648] are tantalizing, but have not yet had an "existence proof" of being adopted in commercial applications.

Another analytical shadow-testing method may have potential in the longer term: ray tracing. Described in detail in Section 11.2.2, the basic idea is simple enough, especially for shadowing. A ray is shot from the receiver location to the light. If any object is found that blocks the ray, the receiver is in shadow. Much of a fast ray tracer's code is dedicated to generating and using hierarchical data structures to minimize the number of object tests needed per ray. Building and updating these structures each frame for a dynamic scene is a decades-old topic and a continuing area of research.

Another approach is to use the GPU's rasterization hardware to view the scene, but instead of just z-depths, additional information is stored about the edges of the occluders in each grid cell of the light [1003, 1607]. For example, imagine storing at each shadow-map texel a list of triangles that overlap the grid cell. Such a list can be generated by *conservative rasterization*, in which a triangle generates a fragment if any part of the triangle overlaps a pixel, not just the pixel's center (Section 23.1.2). One problem with such schemes is that the amount of data per texel normally needs to be limited, which in turn can lead to inaccuracies in determining the status of every receiver location. Given modern linked-list principles for GPUs [1943], it is certainly possible to store more data per pixel. However, aside from physical memory limits, a problem with storing a variable amount of data in a list per texel is that GPU processing can become extremely inefficient, as a single warp can have a few fragment

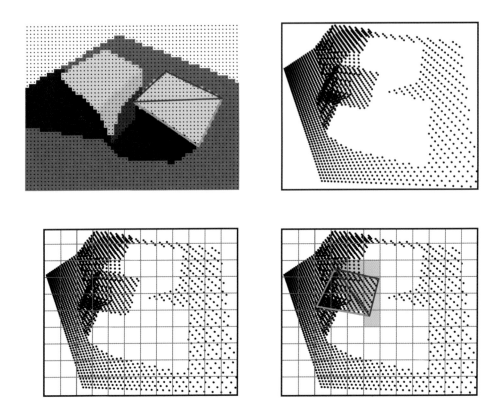

Figure 7.30. Irregular z-buffer. In the upper left, the view from the eye generates a set of dots at the pixel centers. Two triangles forming a cube face are shown. In the upper right, these dots are shown from the light's view. In the lower left, a shadow-map grid is imposed. For each texel a list of all dots inside its grid cell is generated. In the lower right, shadow testing is performed for the red triangle by conservatively rasterizing it. At each texel touched, shown in light red, all dots in its list are tested against the triangle for visibility by the light. *(Underlying raster images courtesy of Timo Aila and Samuli Laine [14].)*

threads that need to retrieve and process many items, while the rest of the threads are idle, having no work to do. Structuring a shader to avoid thread divergence due to dynamic "if" statements and loops is critical for performance.

An alternative to storing triangles or other data in the shadow map and testing receiver locations against them is to flip the problem, storing receiver locations and then testing triangles against each. This concept of saving the receiver locations, first explored by Johnson et al. [839] and Aila and Laine [14], is called the *irregular z-buffer* (IZB). The name is slightly misleading, in that the buffer itself has a normal, regular shape for a shadow map. Rather, the buffer's contents are irregular, as each shadow-map texel will have one or more receiver locations stored in it, or possibly none at all. See Figure 7.30.

Using the method presented by Sintorn et al. [1645] and Wyman et al. [1930, 1932], a multi-pass algorithm creates the IZB and tests its contents for visibility from the light. First, the scene is rendered from the eye, to find the z-depths of the surfaces seen from the eye. These points are transformed to the light's view of the scene, and tight bounds are formed from this set for the light's frustum. The points are then deposited in the light's IZB, each placed into a list at its corresponding texel. Note that some lists may be empty, a volume of space that the light views but that has no surfaces seen by the eye. Occluders are conservatively rasterized to the light's IZB to determine whether any points are hidden, and so in shadow. Conservative rasterization ensures that, even if a triangle does not cover the center of a light texel, it will be tested against points it may overlap nonetheless.

Visibility testing occurs in the pixel shader. The test itself can be visualized as a form of ray tracing. A ray is generated from an image point's location to the light. If a point is inside the triangle and more distant than the triangle's plane, it is hidden. Once all occluders are rasterized, the light-visibility results are used to shade the surface. This testing is also called *frustum tracing*, as the triangle can be thought of as defining a view frustum that checks points for inclusion in its volume.

Careful coding is critical in making this approach work well with the GPU. Wyman et al. [1930, 1932] note that their final version was two orders of magnitude faster than the initial prototypes. Part of this performance increase was straightforward algorithm improvements, such as culling image points where the surface normal was facing away from the light (and so always unlit) and avoiding having fragments generated for empty texels. Other performance gains were from improving data structures for the GPU, and from minimizing thread divergence by working to have short, similar-length lists of points in each texel. Figure 7.30 shows a low-resolution shadow map with long lists for illustrative purposes. The ideal is one image point per list. A higher resolution gives shorter lists, but also increases the number of fragments generated by occluders for evaluation.

As can be seen in the lower left image in Figure 7.30, the density of visible points on the ground plane is considerably higher on the left side than the right, due to the perspective effect. Using cascaded shadow maps helps lower list sizes in these areas by focusing more light-map resolution closer to the eye.

This approach avoids the sampling and bias issues of other approaches and provides perfectly sharp shadows. For aesthetic and perceptual reasons, soft shadows are often desired, but can have bias problems with nearby occluders, such as Peter Panning. Story and Wyman [1711, 1712] explore hybrid shadow techniques. The core idea is to use the occluder distance to blend IZB and PCSS shadows, using the hard shadow result when the occluder is close and soft when more distant. See Figure 7.31. Shadow quality is often most important for nearby objects, so IZB costs can be reduced by using this technique on only a selected subset. This solution has successfully been used in video games. This chapter started with such an image, shown in Figure 7.2 on page 224.

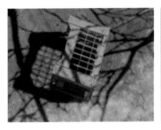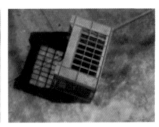

Figure 7.31. On the left, PCF gives uniformly softened shadows for all objects. In the middle, PCSS softens the shadow with distance to the occluder, but the tree branch shadow overlapping the left corner of the crate creates artifacts. On the right, sharp shadows from IZB blended with soft from PCSS give an improved result [1711]. *(Images from "Tom Clancy's The Division," courtesy of Ubisoft.)*

7.10   Other Applications

Treating the shadow map as defining a volume of space, separating light from dark, can also help in determining what parts of objects to shadow. Gollent [555] describes how CD Projekt's terrain shadowing system computes for each area a maximum height that is still occluded, which can then be used to shadow not only terrain but also trees and other elements in the scene. To find each height, a shadow map of the visible area is rendered for the sun. Each terrain heightfield location is then checked for visibility from the sun. If in shadow, the height where the sun is first visible is estimated by increasing the world height by a fixed step size until the sun comes into view and then performing a binary search. In other words, we march along a vertical line and iterate to narrow down the location where it intersects the shadow map's surface that separates light from dark. Neighboring heights are interpolated to find this occlusion height at any location. An example of this technique used for soft shadowing of a terrain heightfield can be seen in Figure 7.32. We will see more use of ray marching through areas of light and dark in Chapter 14.

One last method worth a mention is rendering *screen-space shadows*. Shadow maps often fail to produce accurate occlusions on small features, because of their limited resolution. This is especially problematic when rendering human faces, because we are particularly prone to noticing any visual artifacts on them. For example, rendering glowing nostrils (when not intended) looks jarring. While using higher-resolution shadow maps or a separate shadow map targeting only the area of interest can help, another possibility is to leverage the already-existing data. In most modern rendering engines the depth buffer from the camera perspective, coming from an earlier prepass, is available during rendering. The data stored in it can be treated as a heightfield. By iteratively sampling this depth buffer, we can perform a ray-marching process (Section 6.8.1) and check if the direction toward the light is unoccluded. While costly, as it involves repeatedly sampling the depth buffer, doing so can provide high-quality results for closeups in cut scenes, where spending extra milliseconds is often justified. The method was proposed by Sousa at al. [1678] and is commonly used in many game engines today [384, 1802].

Figure 7.32. Terrain lit with the height where the sun is first seen computed for each heightfield location. Note how trees along the shadow's edge are properly shadowed [555]. *(CD PROJEKT®, The Witcher® are registered trademarks of CD PROJEKT Capital Group. The Witcher game © CD PROJEKT S.A. Developed by CD PROJEKT S.A. All rights reserved. The Witcher game is based on the prose of Andrzej Sapkowski. All other copyrights and trademarks are the property of their respective owners.)*

To summarize this whole chapter, shadow mapping in some form is by far the most common algorithm used for shadows cast onto arbitrary surface shapes. Cascaded shadow maps improve sampling quality when shadows are cast in a large area, such as an outdoor scene. Finding a good maximum distance for the near plane via SDSM can further improve precision. Percentage-closer filtering (PCF) gives some softness to the shadows, percentage-closer soft shadows (PCSS) and its variants give contact hardening, and the irregular z-buffer can provide precise hard shadows. Filtered shadow maps provide rapid soft-shadow computation and work particularly well when the occluder is far from the receiver, as with terrain. Finally, screen-space techniques can be used for additional precision, though at a noticeable cost.

In this chapter, we have focused on key concepts and techniques currently used in applications. Each has its own strengths, and choices depend on world size, composition (static content versus animated), material types (opaque, transparent, hair, or smoke), and number and type of lights (static or dynamic; local or distant; point, spot, or area), as well as factors such as how well the underlying textures can hide any artifacts. GPU capabilities evolve and improve, so we expect to continue seeing new algorithms that map well to the hardware appear in the years ahead. For example, the sparse-texture technique described in Section 19.10.1 has been applied to shadow-map storage to improve resolution [241, 625, 1253]. In an inventive approach, Sintorn,

Figure 7.33. At the top is an image generated with a basic soft-shadows approximation. At the bottom is voxel-based area light shadowing using cone tracing, on a voxelization of the scene. Note the considerably more diffuse shadows for the cars. Lighting also differs due to a change in the time of day. *(Images courtesy of Crytek [865].)*

Kämpe, and others [850, 1647] explore the idea of converting a two-dimensional shadow map for a light into a three-dimensional set of voxels (small boxes; see Section 13.10). An advantage of using a voxel is that it can be categorized as lit or in shadow, thus needing minimal storage. A highly compressed sparse voxel octree representation stores shadows for a huge number of lights and static occluders. Scandolo et al. [1546] combine their compression technique with an interval-based scheme using dual shadow maps, giving still higher compression rates. Kasyan [865] uses voxel cone tracing (Section 13.10) to generate soft shadows from area lights. See Figure 7.33 for an example. More cone-traced shadows are shown in Figure 13.33 on page 585.

Further Reading and Resources

Our focus in this chapter is on basic principles and what qualities a shadow algorithm needs—predictable quality and performance—to be useful for interactive rendering. We have avoiding an exhaustive categorization of the research done in this area of rendering, as two texts tackle the subject. The book *Real-Time Shadows* by Eisemann et al. [412] focuses directly on interactive rendering techniques, discussing a wide range of algorithms along with their strengths and costs. A SIGGRAPH 2012 course provides an excerpt of this book, while also adding references to newer work [413]. Presentations from their SIGGRAPH 2013 course are available at their website, www. realtimeshadows.com. Woo and Poulin's book *Shadow Algorithms Data Miner* [1902] provides an overview of a wide range of shadow algorithms for interactive and batch rendering. Both books supply references to hundreds of research articles in the field.

Tuft's pair of articles [1791, 1792] are an excellent overview of commonly used shadow-mapping techniques and the issues involved. Bjørge [154] presents a range of popular shadow algorithms suitable for mobile devices, along with images comparing various algorithms. Lilley's presentation [1046] gives a solid and extensive overview of practical shadow algorithms, with a focus on terrain rendering for GIS systems. Blog articles by Pettineo [1403, 1404] and Castaño [235] are particularly valuable for their practical tips and solutions, as well as a demo code base. See Scherzer et al. [1558] for a shorter summary of work specifically focused on hard shadows. The survey of algorithms for soft shadows by Hasenfratz et al. [675] is dated, but covers a wide range of early work in some depth.

Chapter 8
Light and Color

"Unweave a rainbow, as it erewhile made
  The tender-person'd Lamia melt into a shade."
    —John Keats

Many of the RGB color values discussed in previous chapters represent intensities and shades of light. In this chapter we will learn about the various physical light quantities measured by these values, laying the groundwork for subsequent chapters, which discuss rendering from a more physically based perspective. We will also learn more about the often-neglected "second half" of the rendering process: the transformation of colors that represent scene linear light quantities into final display colors.

8.1   Light Quantities

The first step in any physically based approach to rendering is to quantify light in a precise manner. Radiometry is presented first, as this is the core field concerned with the physical transmission of light. We follow with a discussion of photometry, which deals with light values that are weighted by the sensitivity of the human eye. Our perception of color is a *psychophysical* phenomenon: the psychological perception of physical stimuli. Color perception is discussed in the section on colorimetry. Finally, we discuss the validity of rendering with RGB color values.

8.1.1   Radiometry

Radiometry deals with the measurement of electromagnetic radiation. As will be discussed in more detail in Section 9.1, this radiation propagates as waves. Electromagnetic waves with different *wavelengths*—the distance between two adjacent points with the same phase, e.g., two adjacent peaks—tend to have different properties. In nature, electromagnetic waves exist across a huge range of wavelengths, from gamma waves less than a hundredth of a nanometer in length to extreme low frequency (ELF) radio waves tens of thousands of kilometers long. The waves that humans can see

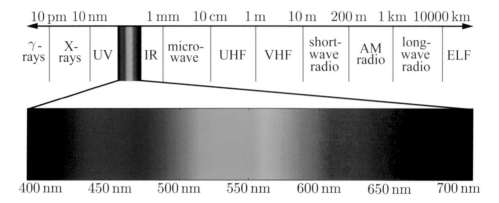

Figure 8.1. The range of wavelengths for visible light, shown in context within the full electromagnetic spectrum.

comprise a tiny subset of that range, extending from about 400 nanometers for violet light to a bit over 700 nanometers for red light. See Figure 8.1.

Radiometric quantities exist for measuring various aspects of electromagnetic radiation: overall energy, power (energy over time), and power density with respect to area, direction, or both. These quantities are summarized in Table 8.1.

In radiometry, the basic unit is *radiant flux*, Φ. Radiant flux is the flow of radiant energy over time—power—measured in *watts* (W).

Irradiance is the density of radiant flux with respect to area, i.e., $d\Phi/dA$. Irradiance is defined with respect to an area, which may be an imaginary area in space, but is most often the surface of an object. It is measured in watts per square meter.

Before we get to the next quantity, we need to first introduce the concept of a *solid angle*, which is a three-dimensional extension of the concept of an angle. An angle can be thought of as a measure of the size of a continuous set of directions in a plane, with a value in radians equal to the length of the arc this set of directions intersects on an enclosing circle with radius 1. Similarly, a solid angle measures the size of a continuous set of directions in three-dimensional space, measured in *steradians* (abbreviated "sr"), which are defined by the area of the intersection patch on an enclosing sphere with radius 1 [544]. Solid angle is represented by the symbol ω.

Name	Symbol	Units
radiant flux	Φ	watt (W)
irradiance	E	W/m^2
radiant intensity	I	W/sr
radiance	L	W/(m^{2}sr)

Table 8.1. Radiometric quantities and units.

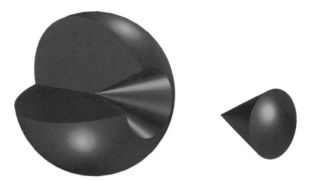

Figure 8.2. A cone with a solid angle of one steradian removed from a cutaway view of a sphere. The shape itself is irrelevant to the measurement. The coverage on the sphere's surface is the key.

In two dimensions, an angle of 2π radians covers the whole unit circle. Extending this to three dimensions, a solid angle of 4π steradians would cover the whole area of the unit sphere. The size of a solid angle of one steradian can be seen in Figure 8.2.

Now we can introduce *radiant intensity*, I, which is flux density with respect to direction—more precisely, solid angle $(d\Phi/d\omega)$. It is measured in watts per steradian.

Finally, *radiance*, L, is a measure of electromagnetic radiation in a single ray. More precisely, it is defined as the density of radiant flux with respect to both area and solid angle $(d^2\Phi/dAd\omega)$. This area is measured in a plane perpendicular to the ray. If radiance is applied to a surface at some other orientation, then a cosine correction factor must be used. You may encounter definitions of radiance using the term "projected area" in reference to this correction factor.

Radiance is what sensors, such as eyes or cameras, measure (see Section 9.2 for more details), so it is of prime importance for rendering. The purpose of evaluating a shading equation is to compute the radiance along a given ray, from the shaded surface point to the camera. The value of L along that ray is the physically based equivalent of the quantity $\mathbf{c}_{\text{shaded}}$ in Chapter 5. The metric units of radiance are watts per square meter per steradian.

The radiance in an environment can be thought of as a function of five variables (or six, including wavelength), called the *radiance distribution* [400]. Three of the variables specify a location, the other two a direction. This function describes all light traveling anywhere in space. One way to think of the rendering process is that the eye and screen define a point and a set of directions (e.g., a ray going through each pixel), and this function is evaluated at the eye for each direction. Image-based rendering, discussed in Section 13.4, uses a related concept, called the *light field*.

In shading equations, radiance often appears in the form $L_o(\mathbf{x}, \mathbf{d})$ or $L_i(\mathbf{x}, \mathbf{d})$, which mean radiance going out from the point $\mathbf{x}$ or entering into it, respectively. The direction vector $\mathbf{d}$ indicates the ray's direction, which by convention always points away from $\mathbf{x}$. While this convention may be somewhat confusing in the case of L_i,

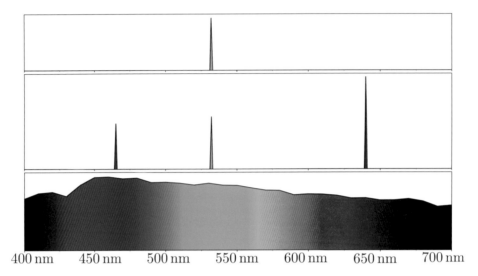

400 nm   450 nm   500 nm   550 nm   600 nm   650 nm   700 nm

Figure 8.3. SPDs (spectral power distributions) for three different light waves. The top SPD is for a green laser, which has an extremely narrow spectral distribution. Its waveform is similar to the simple sine wave in Figure 9.1 on page 294. The middle SPD is for light comprised of the same green laser plus two additional lasers, one red and one blue. The wavelengths and relative intensities of these lasers correspond to an RGB laser projection display showing a neutral white color. The bottom SPD is for the standard D65 illuminant, which is a typical neutral white reference intended to represent outdoor lighting. Such SPDs, with energy continuously spread across the visible spectrum, are typical for natural lighting.

since **d** points in the opposite direction to the light propagation, it is convenient for calculations such as dot products.

An important property of radiance is that it is not affected by distance, ignoring atmospheric effects such as fog. In other words, a surface will have the same radiance regardless of its distance from the viewer. The surface covers fewer pixels when more distant, but the radiance from the surface at each pixel is constant.

Most light waves contain a mixture of many different wavelengths. This is typically visualized as a *spectral power distribution* (SPD), which is a plot showing how the light's energy is distributed across different wavelengths. Figure 8.3 shows three examples. Notably, despite the dramatic differences between the middle and bottom SPDs in Figure 8.3, they are perceived as the same color. Clearly, human eyes make for poor spectrometers. We will discuss color vision in detail in Section 8.1.3.

All radiometric quantities have spectral distributions. Since these distributions are densities over wavelength, their units are those of the original quantity divided by nanometers. For example, the spectral distribution of irradiance has units of watts per square meter per nanometer.

Since full SPDs are unwieldy to use for rendering, especially at interactive rates, in practice radiometric quantities are represented as RGB triples. In Section 8.1.3 we will explain how these triples relate to spectral distributions.

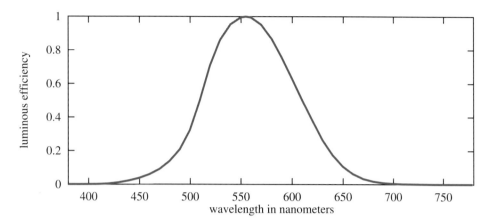

Figure 8.4. The photometric curve.

8.1.2 Photometry

Radiometry deals purely with physical quantities, without taking account of human perception. A related field, *photometry*, is like radiometry, except that it weights everything by the sensitivity of the human eye. The results of radiometric computations are converted to photometric units by multiplying by the *CIE photometric curve*,[1] a bell-shaped curve centered around 555 nm that represents the eye's response to various wavelengths of light [76, 544]. See Figure 8.4.

The conversion curve and the units of measurement are the only difference between the theory of photometry and the theory of radiometry. Each radiometric quantity has an equivalent metric photometric quantity. Table 8.2 shows the names and units of each. The units all have the expected relationships (e.g., lux is lumens per square meter). Although logically the lumen should be the basic unit, historically the candela was defined as a basic unit and the other units were derived from it. In North America, lighting designers measure illuminance using the deprecated Imperial unit of measurement, called the foot-candle (fc), instead of lux. In either case, illuminance is what most light meters measure, and it is important in illumination engineering.

Luminance is often used to describe the brightness of flat surfaces. For example, high dynamic range (HDR) television screens' peak brightness typically ranges from about 500 to 1000 nits. In comparison, clear sky has a luminance of about 8000 nits, a 60-watt bulb about 120,000 nits, and the sun at the horizon 600,000 nits [1413].

---

[1] The full and more accurate name is the "CIE photopic spectral luminous efficiency curve." The word "photopic" refers to lighting conditions brighter than 3.4 candelas per square meter—twilight or brighter. Under these conditions the eye's cone cells are active. There is a corresponding "scotopic" CIE curve, centered around 507 nm, that is for when the eye has become dark-adapted to below 0.034 candelas per square meter—a moonless night or darker. The rod cells are active under these conditions.

Radiometric Quantity: Units	Photometric Quantity: Units
radiant flux: watt (W)	luminous flux: lumen (lm)
irradiance: W/m^2	illuminance: lux (lx)
radiant intensity: W/sr	luminous intensity: candela (cd)
radiance: $W/(m^2 sr)$	luminance: $cd/m^2 = $ nit

Table 8.2. Radiometric and photometric quantities and units.

8.1.3 Colorimetry

In Section 8.1.1 we have seen that our perception of the color of light is strongly connected to the light's SPD (spectral power distribution). We also saw that this is not a simple one-to-one correspondence. The bottom and middle SPDs in Figure 8.3 are completely different yet are perceived as the exact same color. *Colorimetry* deals with the relationship between spectral power distributions and the perception of color.

Humans can distinguish about 10 million different colors. For color perception, the eye works by having three different types of cone receptors in the retina, with each type of receptor responding differently to various wavelengths. Other animals have varying numbers of color receptors, in some cases as many as fifteen [260]. So, for a given SPD, our brain receives only three different signals from these receptors. This is why just three numbers can be used to precisely represent any color stimulus [1707].

But what three numbers? A set of standard conditions for measuring color was proposed by the CIE (*Commission Internationale d'Eclairage*), and color-matching experiments were performed using them. In color matching, three colored lights are projected on a white screen so that their colors add together and form a patch. A test color to match is projected next to this patch. The test color patch is of a single wavelength. The observer can then change the three colored lights using knobs calibrated to a range weighted $[-1, 1]$ until the test color is matched. A negative weight is needed to match some test colors, and such a weight means that the corresponding light is added instead to the wavelength's test color patch. One set of test results for three lights, called r, g, and b, is shown in Figure 8.5. The lights were almost monochromatic, with the energy distribution of each narrowly clustered around one of the following wavelengths: 645 nm for r, 526 nm for g, and 444 nm for b. The functions relating each set of matching weights to the test patch wavelengths are called *color-matching functions*.

What these functions give is a way to convert a spectral power distribution to three values. Given a single wavelength of light, the three colored light settings can be read off the graph, the knobs set, and lighting conditions created that will give an identical sensation from both patches of light on the screen. For an arbitrary spectral distribution, the color-matching functions can be multiplied by the distribution and the area under each resulting curve (i.e., the integral) gives the relative amounts

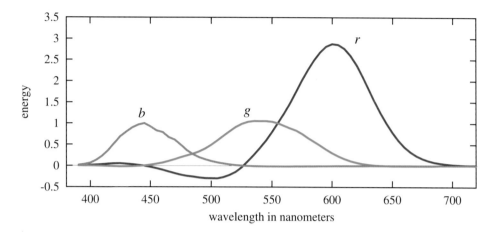

Figure 8.5. The r, g, and b 2-degree color-matching curves, from Stiles and Burch [1703]. These color-matching curves are not to be confused with the spectral distributions of the light sources used in the color-matching experiment, which are pure wavelengths.

to set the colored lights to match the perceived color produced by the spectrum. Considerably different spectral distributions can resolve to the same three weights, i.e., they look the same to an observer. Spectral distributions that give matching weights are called *metamers*.

The three weighted r, g, and b lights cannot directly represent all visible colors, as their color-matching functions have negative weights for various wavelengths. The CIE proposed three different hypothetical light sources with color-matching functions that are positive for all visible wavelengths. These curves are linear combinations of the original r, g, and b color-matching functions. This requires their spectral power distributions of the light sources to be negative at some wavelengths, so these lights are unrealizable mathematical abstractions. Their color-matching functions are denoted $\overline{x}(\lambda)$, $\overline{y}(\lambda)$, and $\overline{z}(\lambda)$, and are shown in Figure 8.6. The color-matching function $\overline{y}(\lambda)$ is the same as the photometric curve (Figure 8.4), as radiance is converted to luminance with this curve.

As with the previous set of color-matching functions, $\overline{x}(\lambda)$, $\overline{y}(\lambda)$, and $\overline{z}(\lambda)$ are used to reduce any SPD $s(\lambda)$ to three numbers via multiplication and integration:

$$X = \int_{380}^{780} s(\lambda)\overline{x}(\lambda)d\lambda, \quad Y = \int_{380}^{780} s(\lambda)\overline{y}(\lambda)d\lambda, \quad Z = \int_{380}^{780} s(\lambda)\overline{z}(\lambda)d\lambda. \tag{8.1}$$

These X, Y, and Z *tristimulus values* are weights that define a color in CIE XYZ space. It is often convenient to separate colors into luminance (brightness) and *chromaticity*. Chromaticity is the character of a color independent of its brightness. For example, two shades of blue, one dark and one light, can have the same chromaticity despite differing in luminance.

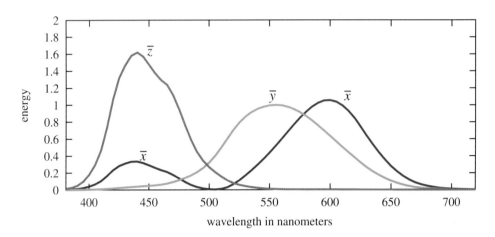

Figure 8.6. The Judd-Vos-modified CIE (1978) 2-degree color-matching functions. Note that the two $\bar{x}$'s are part of the same curve.

For this purpose, the CIE defined a two-dimensional chromaticity space by projecting colors onto the $X + Y + Z = 1$ plane. See Figure 8.7. Coordinates in this space are called x and y, and are computed as follows:

$$x = \frac{X}{X + Y + Z},$$

$$y = \frac{Y}{X + Y + Z},$$

$$z = \frac{Z}{X + Y + Z} = 1 - x - y.$$

(8.2)

The z value gives no additional information, so it is normally omitted. The plot of the *chromaticity coordinates* x and y values is known as the *CIE 1931 chromaticity diagram*. See Figure 8.8. The curved outline in the diagram shows where the colors of the visible spectrum lie, and the straight line connecting the ends of the spectrum is called the *purple line*. The black dot shows the chromaticity of illuminant D65, which is a frequently used *white point*—a chromaticity used to define the white or *achromatic* (colorless) stimulus.

To summarize, we began with an experiment that used three single-wavelength lights and measured how much of each was needed to match the appearance of some other wavelength of light. Sometimes these pure lights had to be added to the sample being viewed in order to match. This gave one set of color-matching functions, which were combined to create a new set without negative values. With this non-negative set of color-matching functions in hand, we can convert any spectral distribution to an XYZ coordinate that defines a color's chromaticity and luminance, which can be reduced to xy to describe just the chromaticity, keeping luminance constant.

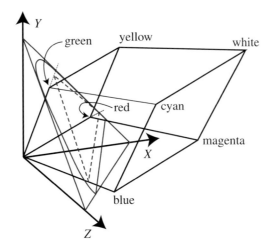

Figure 8.7. The RGB color cube for the CIE RGB primaries is shown in XYZ space, along with its projection (in violet) onto the $X + Y + Z = 1$ plane. The blue outline encloses the space of possible chromaticity values. Each line radiating from the origin has a constant chromaticity value, varying only in luminance.

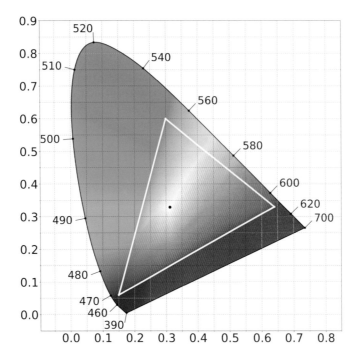

Figure 8.8. The CIE 1931 chromaticity diagram. The curve is labeled with the wavelengths of the corresponding pure colors. The white triangle and black dot show the gamut and white point, respectively, used for the sRGB and Rec. 709 color spaces.

Given a color point (x, y), draw a line from the white point through this point to the boundary (spectral or purple line). The relative distance of the color point compared to the distance to the edge of the region is the *excitation purity* of the color. The point on the region edge defines the *dominant wavelength.* These colorimetric terms are rarely encountered in graphics. Instead, we use *saturation* and *hue*, which correlate loosely with excitation purity and dominant wavelength, respectively. More precise definitions of saturation and hue can be found in books by Stone [1706] and others [456, 789, 1934].

The chromaticity diagram describes a plane. The third dimension needed to fully describe a color is the Y value, luminance. These then define what is called the xyY-coordinate system. The chromaticity diagram is important in understanding how color is used in rendering, and the limits of the rendering system. A television or computer monitor presents colors by using some settings of R, G, and B color values. Each color channel controls a *display primary* that emits light with a particular spectral power distribution. Each of the three primaries is scaled by its respective color value, and these are added together to create a single spectral power distribution that the viewer perceives.

The triangle in the chromaticity diagram represents the *gamut* of a typical television or computer monitor. The three corners of the triangle are the primaries, which are the most saturated red, green, and blue colors the screen can display. An important property of the chromaticity diagram is that these limiting colors can be joined by straight lines to show the limits of the display system as a whole. The straight lines represent the limits of colors that can be displayed by mixing these three primaries. The white point represents the chromaticity that is produced by the display system when the R, G, and B color values are equal to each other. It is important to note that the full gamut of a display system is a three-dimensional volume. The chromaticity diagram shows only the projection of this volume onto a two-dimensional plane. See Stone's book [1706] for more information.

There are several RGB spaces of interest in rendering, each defined by R, G, and B primaries and a white point. To compare them we will use a different type of chromaticity diagram, called the *CIE 1976 UCS* (uniform chromaticity scale) diagram. This diagram is part of the CIELUV color space, which was adopted by the CIE (along with another color space, CIELAB) with the intention of providing more perceptually uniform alternatives to the XYZ space [1707]. Color pairs that are perceptibly different by the same amount can be up to 20 times different in distance in CIE XYZ space. CIELUV improves upon this, bringing the ratio down to a maximum of four times. This increased perceptual uniformity makes the 1976 diagram much better than the 1931 one for the purpose of comparing the gamuts of RGB spaces. Continued research into perceptually uniform color spaces has recently resulted in the IC_TC_P [364] and $J_za_zb_z$ [1527] spaces. These color spaces are more perceptually uniform than CIELUV, especially for the high luminance and saturated colors typical of modern displays. However, chromaticity diagrams based on these color spaces have not yet been widely adopted, so we use the CIE 1976 UCS diagrams in this chapter, for example in the case of Figure 8.9.

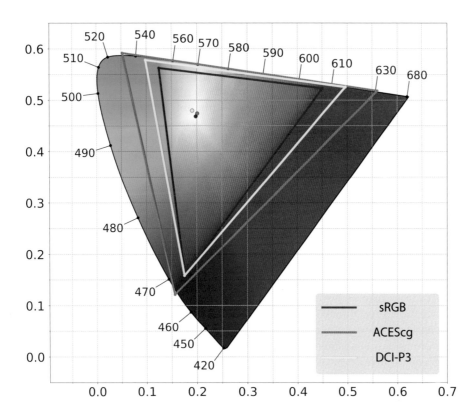

Figure 8.9. A CIE 1976 UCS diagram showing the primaries and white points of three RGB color spaces: sRGB, DCI-P3, and ACEScg. The sRGB plot can be used for Rec. 709 as well, since the two color spaces have the same primaries and white point.

Of the three RGB spaces shown in Figure 8.9, sRGB is by far the most commonly used in real-time rendering. It is important to note that in this section we use "sRGB color space" to refer to a linear color space that has the sRGB primaries and white point, and not to the nonlinear sRGB color encoding that was discussed in Section 5.6. Most computer monitors are designed for the sRGB color space, and the same primaries and white point apply to the Rec. 709 color space as well, which is used for HDTV displays and thus is important for game consoles. However, more displays are being made with wider gamuts. Some computer monitors intended for photo editing use the Adobe 1998 color space (not shown). The DCI-P3 color space—initially developed for feature film production—is seeing broader use. Apple has adopted this color space across their product line from iPhones to Macs, and other manufacturers have been following suit. Although ultra-high definition (UHD) content and displays are specified to use the extremely-wide-gamut Rec. 2020 color space, in many cases DCI-P3 is used as a de facto color space for UHD as well. Rec. 2020 is not shown in

Figure 8.9, but its gamut is quite close to that of the third color space in the figure, ACEScg. The ACEScg color space was developed by the Academy of Motion Picture Arts and Sciences (AMPAS) for feature film computer graphics rendering. It is not intended for use as a display color space, but rather as a *working color space* for rendering, with colors converted to the appropriate display color space after rendering.

While currently the sRGB color space is ubiquitous in real-time rendering, the use of wider color spaces is likely to increase. The most immediate benefit is for applications targeting wide-gamut displays [672], but there are advantages even for applications targeting sRGB or Rec. 709 displays. Routine rendering operations such as multiplication give different results when performed in different color spaces [672, 1117], and there is evidence that performing these operations in the DCI-P3 or ACEScg space produces more accurate results than performing them in linear sRGB space [660, 975, 1118].

Conversion from an RGB space to XYZ space is linear and can be done with a matrix derived from the RGB space's primaries and white point [1048]. Via matrix inversion and concatenation, matrices can be derived to convert from XYZ to any RGB space, or between two different RGB spaces. Note that after such a conversion the RGB values may be negative or greater than one. These are colors that are out of gamut, i.e., not reproducible in the target RGB space. Various methods can be used to map such colors into the target RGB gamut [785, 1241].

One often-used conversion is to transform an RGB color to a grayscale luminance value. Since luminance is the same as the Y coefficient, this operation is just the "Y part" of the RGB-to-XYZ conversion. In other words, it is a dot product between the RGB coefficients and the middle row of the RGB-to-XYZ matrix. In the case of the sRGB and Rec. 709 spaces, the equation is [1704]

$$Y = 0.2126R + 0.7152G + 0.0722B. \tag{8.3}$$

This brings us again to the photometric curve, shown in Figure 8.4 on page 271. This curve, representing how a standard observer's eye responds to light of various wavelengths, is multiplied by the spectral power distributions of the three primaries, and each resulting curve is integrated. The three resulting weights are what form the luminance equation above. The reason that a grayscale intensity value is not equal parts red, green, and blue is because the eye has a different sensitivity to various wavelengths of light.

Colorimetry can tell us whether two color stimuli match, but it cannot predict their appearance. The appearance of a given XYZ color stimulus depends heavily on factors such as the lighting, surrounding colors, and previous conditions. *Color appearance models* (CAM) such as CIECAM02 attempt to deal with these issues and predict the final color appearance [456].

Color appearance modeling is part of the wider field of visual perception, which includes effects such as *masking* [468]. This is where a high-frequency, high-contrast pattern laid on an object tends to hide flaws. In other words, a texture such as a

Persian rug will help disguise color banding and other shading artifacts, meaning that less rendering effort needs to be expended for such surfaces.

8.1.4 Rendering with RGB Colors

Strictly speaking, RGB values represent perceptual rather than physical quantities. Using them for physically based rendering is technically a category error. The correct method would be to perform all rendering computations on spectral quantities, represented either via dense sampling or projection onto a suitable basis, and to convert to RGB colors only at the end.

For example, one of the most common rendering operations is calculating the light reflected from an object. The object's surface typically will reflect light of some wavelengths more than others, as described by its *spectral reflectance* curve. The strictly correct way to compute the color of the reflected light is to multiply the SPD of the incident light by the spectral reflectance at each wavelength, yielding the SPD of the reflected light that would then be converted to an RGB color. Instead, in an RGB renderer the RGB colors of the lights and surface are multiplied together to give the RGB color of the reflected light. In the general case, this does not give the correct result. To illustrate, we will look at a somewhat extreme example, shown in Figure 8.10.

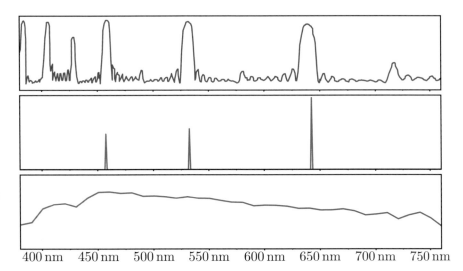

400 nm   450 nm   500 nm   550 nm   600 nm   650 nm   700 nm   750 nm

Figure 8.10. The top plot shows the spectral reflectance of a material designed for use in projection screens. The lower two plots show the spectral power distributions of two illuminants with the same RGB colors: an RGB laser projector in the middle plot and the D65 standard illuminant in the bottom plot. The screen material would reflect about 80% of the light from the laser projector because it has reflectance peaks that line up with the projectors primaries. However, it will reflect less than 20% of the light from the D65 illuminant since most of the illuminant's energy is outside the screen's reflectance peaks. An RGB rendering of this scene would predict that the screen would reflect the same intensity for both lights.

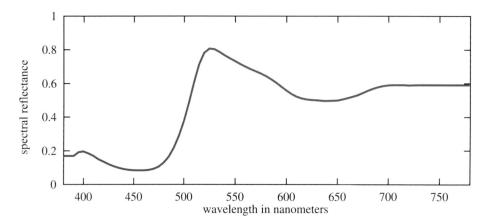

Figure 8.11. The spectral reflectance of a yellow banana [544].

Our example shows a screen material designed for use with laser projectors. It has high reflectance in narrow bands matching laser projector wavelengths and low reflectance for most other wavelengths. This causes it to reflect most of the light from the projector, but absorb most of the light from other light sources. An RGB renderer will produce gross errors in this case.

However, the situation shown in Figure 8.10 is far from typical. The spectral reflectance curves for surfaces encountered in practice are much smoother, such as the one in Figure 8.11. Typical illuminant SPDs resemble the D65 illuminant rather than the laser projector in the example. When both the illuminant SPD and surface spectral reflectance are smooth, the errors introduced by RGB rendering are relatively subtle.

In *predictive rendering* applications, these subtle errors can be important. For example, two spectral reflectance curves may have the same color appearance under one light source, but not another. This problem, called *metameric failure* or *illuminant metamerism*, is of serious concern when painting repaired car body parts, for example. RGB rendering would not be appropriate in an application that attempts to predict this type of effect.

However, for the majority of rendering systems, especially those for interactive applications, that are not aimed at producing predictive simulations, RGB rendering works surprisingly well [169]. Even feature-film offline rendering has only recently started to employ spectral rendering, and it is as yet far from common [660, 1610].

This section has touched on just the basics of color science, primarily to bring an awareness of the relation of spectra to color triplets and to discuss the limitations of devices. A related topic, the transformation of rendered scene colors to display values, will be discussed in the next section.

8.2   Scene to Screen

The next few chapters in this book are focused on the problem of physically based rendering. Given a virtual scene, the goal of physically based rendering is to compute the radiance that would be present in the scene if it were real. However, at that point the work is far from done. The final result—pixel values in the display's framebuffer—still needs to be determined. In this section we will go over some of the considerations involved in this determination.

8.2.1   High Dynamic Range Display Encoding

The material in this section builds upon Section 5.6, which covers display encoding. We decided to defer coverage of high dynamic range (HDR) displays to this section, since it requires background on topics, such as color gamuts, that had not yet been discussed in that part of the book.

Section 5.6 discussed display encoding for standard dynamic range (SDR) monitors, which typically use the sRGB display standard, and SDR televisions, which use the Rec. 709 and Rec. 1886 standards. Both sets of standards have the same RGB gamut and white point (D65), and somewhat similar (but not identical) nonlinear display encoding curves. They also have roughly similar reference white luminance levels (80 cd/m^2 for sRGB, 100 cd/m^2 for Rec. 709/1886). These luminance specifications have not been closely adhered to by monitor and television manufacturers, who in practice tend to manufacture displays with brighter white levels [1081].

HDR displays use the Rec. 2020 and Rec. 2100 standards. Rec. 2020 defines a color space with a significantly wider color gamut, as shown in Figure 8.12, and the same white point (D65) as the Rec. 709 and sRGB color spaces. Rec. 2100 defines two nonlinear display encodings: *perceptual quantizer* (PQ) [1213] and *hybrid log-gamma* (HLG). The HLG encoding is not used much in rendering situations, so we will focus here on PQ, which defines a peak luminance value of $10,000$ cd/m^2.

Although the peak luminance and gamut specifications are important for encoding purposes, they are somewhat aspirational as far as actual displays are concerned. At the time of writing, few consumer-level HDR displays have peak luminance levels that exceed even 1500 cd/m^2. In practice, display gamuts are much closer to that of DCI-P3 (also shown in Figure 8.12) than Rec. 2020. For this reason, HDR displays perform internal tone and gamut mapping from the standard specifications down to the actual display capabilities. This mapping can be affected by metadata passed by the application to indicate the actual dynamic range and gamut of the content [672, 1082].

From the application side, there are three paths for transferring images to an HDR display, though not all three may be available depending on the display and operating system:

1. HDR10—Widely supported on HDR displays as well as PC and console operating systems. The framebuffer format is 32 bits per pixel with 10 unsigned integer bits for each RGB channel and 2 for alpha. It uses PQ nonlinear encoding

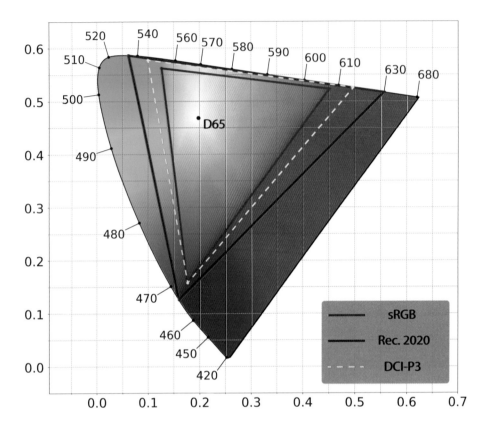

Figure 8.12. A CIE 1976 UCS diagram showing the gamuts and white point (D65) of the Rec. 2020 and sRGB/Rec. 709 color spaces. The gamut of the DCI-P3 color space is also shown for comparison.

and Rec. 2020 color space. Each HDR10 display model performs its own tone mapping, one that is not standardized or documented.

2. scRGB (linear variant)—Only supported on Windows operating systems. Nominally it uses sRGB primaries and white level, though both can be exceeded since the standard supports RGB values less than 0 and greater than 1. The framebuffer format is 16-bit per channel, and stores linear RGB values. It can work with any HDR10 display since the driver converts to HDR10. It is useful primarily for convenience and backward compatibility with sRGB.

3. Dolby Vision—Proprietary format, not yet widely supported in displays or on any consoles (at the time of writing). It uses a custom 12-bit per channel framebuffer format, and uses PQ nonlinear encoding and Rec. 2020 color space. The display internal tone mapping is standardized across models (but not documented).

Lottes [1083] points out that there is actually a fourth option. If the exposure and color are adjusted carefully, then an HDR display can be driven through the regular SDR signal path with good results.

With any option other than scRGB, as part of the display-encoding step the application needs to convert the pixel RGB values from the rendering working space to Rec. 2020—which requires a 3×3 matrix transform—and to apply the PQ encoding, which is somewhat more expensive than the Rec. 709 or sRGB encoding functions [497]. Patry [1360] gives an inexpensive approximation to the PQ curve. Special care is needed when compositing user interface (UI) elements on HDR displays to ensure that the user interface is legible and at a comfortable luminance level [672].

8.2.2   Tone Mapping

In Sections 5.6 and 8.2.1 we discussed display encoding, the process of converting linear radiance values to nonlinear code values for the display hardware. The function applied by display encoding is the inverse of the display's electrical optical transfer function (EOTF), which ensures that the input linear values match the linear radiance emitted by the display. Our earlier discussion glossed over an important step that occurs between rendering and display encoding, one that we are now ready to explore.

Tone mapping or *tone reproduction* is the process of converting scene radiance values to display radiance values. The transform applied during this step is called the *end-to-end transfer function*, or the *scene-to-screen transform*. The concept of *image state* is key to understanding tone mapping [1602]. There are two fundamental image states. *Scene-referred* images are defined in reference to scene radiance values, and *display-referred* images are defined in reference to display radiance values. Image state is unrelated to encoding. Images in either state may be encoded linearly or nonlinearly. Figure 8.13 shows how image state, tone mapping, and display encoding fit together in the *imaging pipeline*, which handles color values from initial rendering to final display.

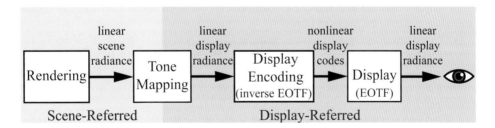

Figure 8.13. The imaging pipeline for synthetic (rendered) images. We render linear scene-referred radiance values, which tone mapping converts to linear display-referred values. Display encoding applies the inverse EOTF to convert the linear display values to nonlinearly encoded values (codes), which are passed to the display. Finally, the display hardware applies the EOTF to convert the nonlinear display values to linear radiance emitted from the screen to the eye.

Figure 8.14. The goal of image reproduction is to ensure that the perceptual impression evoked by the reproduction (right) is as close as possible to that of the original scene (left).

There are several common misconceptions regarding the goal of tone mapping. It is not to ensure that the scene-to-screen transform is an identity transform, perfectly reproducing scene radiance values at the display. It is also not to "squeeze" every bit of information from the high dynamic range of the scene into the lower dynamic range of the display, though accounting for differences between scene and display dynamic range does play an important part.

To understand the goal of tone mapping, it is best to think of it as an instance of image reproduction [757]. The goal of image reproduction is to create a display-referred image that reproduces—as closely as possible, given the display properties and viewing conditions—the perceptual impression that the viewer would have if they were observing the original scene. See Figure 8.14.

There is a type of image reproduction that has a slightly different goal. *Preferred image reproduction* aims at creating a display-referred image that looks better, in some sense, than the original scene. Preferred image reproduction will be discussed later, in Section 8.2.3.

The goal of reproducing a similar perceptual impression as the original scene is a challenging one, considering that the range of luminance in a typical scene exceeds display capabilities by several orders of magnitude. The saturation (purity) of at least some of the colors in the scene are also likely to far outstrip display capabilities. Nevertheless, photography, television, and cinema do manage to produce convincing perceptual likenesses of original scenes, as did Renaissance painters. This achievement is possible by leveraging certain properties of the human visual system.

The visual system compensates for differences in absolute luminance, an ability called *adaptation*. Due to this ability, a reproduction of an outdoor scene shown on a screen in a dim room can produce a similar perception as the original scene, although the luminance of the reproduction is less than 1% of the original. However, the compensation provided by adaptation is imperfect. At lower luminance levels the perceived contrast is decreased (the *Stevens effect*), as is the perceived "colorfulness" (the *Hunt effect*).

Other factors affect actual or perceived contrast of the reproduction. The *surround* of the display (the luminance level outside the display rectangle, e.g., the brightness of the room lighting) may increase or decrease perceived contrast (the *Bartleson-Breneman effect*). *Display flare*, which is unwanted light added to the displayed image via display imperfections or screen reflections, reduces the actual contrast of the image, often to a considerable degree. These effects mean that if we want to preserve a similar perceptual effect as the original scene, we must boost the contrast and saturation of the display-referred image values [1418].

However, this increase in contrast exacerbates an existing problem. Since the dynamic range of the scene is typically much larger than that of the display, we have to choose a narrow window of luminance values to reproduce, with values above and below that window being clipped to black or white. Boosting the contrast further narrows this window. To partially counteract the clipping of dark and bright values, a soft roll-off is used to bring some shadow and highlight detail back.

All this results in a sigmoid (s-shaped) tone-reproduction curve, similar to the one provided by photochemical film [1418]. This is no accident. The properties of photochemical film emulsion were carefully adjusted by researchers at Kodak and other companies to produce effective and pleasing image reproduction. For these reasons, the adjective "filmic" often comes up in discussions of tone mapping.

The concept of *exposure* is critical for tone mapping. In photography, exposure refers to controlling the amount of light that falls on the film or sensor. However, in rendering, exposure is a linear scaling operation performed on the scene-referred image before the tone reproduction transform is applied. The tricky aspect of exposure is to determine what scaling factor to apply. The tone reproduction transform and exposure are closely tied together. Tone transforms are typically designed with the expectation that they will be applied to scene-referred images that have been exposed a certain way.

The process of scaling by exposure and then applying a tone reproduction transform is a type of *global tone mapping*, in which the same mapping is applied to all pixels. In contrast, a *local tone mapping* process uses different mappings pixel to pixel, based on surrounding pixels and other factors. Real-time applications have almost exclusively used global tone mapping (with a few exceptions [1921]), so we will focus on this type, discussing first tone-reproduction transforms and then exposure.

It is important to remember that scene-referred images and display-referred images are fundamentally different. Physical operations are only valid when performed on scene-referred data. Due to display limitations and the various perceptual effects we have discussed, a nonlinear transform is always needed between the two image states.

Tone Reproduction Transform

Tone reproduction transforms are often expressed as one-dimensional curves mapping scene-referred input values to display-referred output values. These curves can be applied either independently to R, G, and B values or to luminance. In the former case, the result will automatically be in the display gamut, since each of the display-referred RGB channel values will be between 0 and 1. However, performing nonlinear operations (especially clipping) on RGB channels may cause shifts in saturation and hue, besides the desired shift in luminance. Giorgianni and Madden [537] point out that the shift in saturation can be perceptually beneficial. The contrast boost that most reproduction transforms use to counteract the Stevens effect (as well as surround and viewing flare effects) will cause a corresponding boost in saturation, which will counteract the Hunt effect as well. However, hue shifts are generally regarded as undesirable, and modern tone transforms attempt to reduce them by applying additional RGB adjustments after the tone curve.

By applying the tone curve to luminance, hue and saturation shifts can be avoided (or at least reduced). However, the resulting display-referred color may be out of the display's RGB gamut, in which case it will need to be mapped back in.

One potential issue with tone mapping is that applying a nonlinear function to scene-referred pixel colors can cause problems with some antialiasing techniques. The issue (and methods to address it) are discussed in Section 5.4.2.

The Reinhard tone reproduction operator [1478] is one of the earlier tone transforms used in real-time rendering. It leaves darker values mostly unchanged, while brighter values asymptotically go to white. A somewhat-similar tone-mapping operator was proposed by Drago et al. [375] with the ability to adjust for output display luminance, which may make it a better fit for HDR displays. Duiker created an approximation to a Kodak film response curve [391, 392] for use in video games. This curve was later modified by Hable [628] to add more user control, and was used in the game *Uncharted 2*. Hable's presentation on this curve was influential, leading to the "Hable filmic curve" being used in several games. Hable [634] later proposed a new curve with a number of advantages over his earlier work.

Day [330] presents a sigmoid tone curve that was used on titles from Insomniac Games, as well as the game *Call of Duty: Advanced Warfare*. Gotanda [571, 572] created tone transforms that simulate the response of film as well as digital camera sensors. These were used on the game *Star Ocean 4* and others. Lottes [1081] points out that the effect of display flare on the effective dynamic range of the display is significant and highly dependent on room lighting conditions. For this reason, it is important to provide user adjustments to the tone mapping. He proposes a tone reproduction transform with support for such adjustments that can be used with SDR as well as HDR displays.

The *Academy Color Encoding System* (ACES) was created by the Science and Technology Council of the Academy of Motion Picture Arts and Sciences as a proposed standard for managing color for the motion picture and television industries. The ACES system splits the scene-to-screen transform into two parts. The first is the *reference rendering transform* (RRT), which transforms scene-referred values into display-referred values in a standard, device-neutral output space called the *output color encoding specification* (OCES). The second part is the *output device transform* (ODT), which converts color values from OCES to the final display encoding. There are many different ODTs, each one designed for a specific display device and viewing condition. The concatenation of the RRT and the appropriate ODT creates the overall transform. This modular structure is convenient for addressing a variety of display types and viewing conditions. Hart [672] recommends the ACES tone mapping transforms for applications that need to support both SDR and HDR displays.

Although ACES was designed for use in film and television, its transforms are seeing growing use in real-time applications. ACES tone mapping is enabled by default in the Unreal Engine [1802], and it is supported by the Unity engine as well [1801]. Narkowicz gives inexpensive curves fitted to the ACES RRT with SDR and HDR ODTs [1260, 1261], as does Patry [1359]. Hart [672] presents a parameterized version of the ACES ODTs to support a range of devices.

Tone mapping with HDR displays requires some care, since the displays will also apply some tone mapping of their own. Fry [497] presents a set of tone mapping transforms used in the Frostbite game engine. They apply a relatively aggressive tone reproduction curve for SDR displays, a less-aggressive one for displays using the HDR10 signal path (with some variation based on the peak luminance of the display), and no tone mapping with displays using the Dolby Vision path (in other words, they rely upon the built-in Dolby Vision tone mapping applied by the display). The Frostbite tone reproduction transforms are designed to be neutral, without significant contrast or hue changes. The intent is for any desired contrast or hue modifications to be applied via color grading (Section 8.2.3). To this end, the tone reproduction transform is applied in the IC_TC_P color space [364], which was designed for perceptual uniformity and orthogonality between the chrominance and luminance axes. The Frostbite transform tone-maps the luminance and increasingly desaturates the chromaticity as the luminance rolls off to display white. This provides a clean transform without hue shifts.

Ironically, following issues with assets (such as fire effects) that were authored to leverage the hue shifts in their previous transform, the Frostbite team ended up modifying the transform, enabling users to re-introduce some degree of hue shifting to the display-referred colors. Figure 8.15 shows the Frostbite transform compared with several others mentioned in this section.

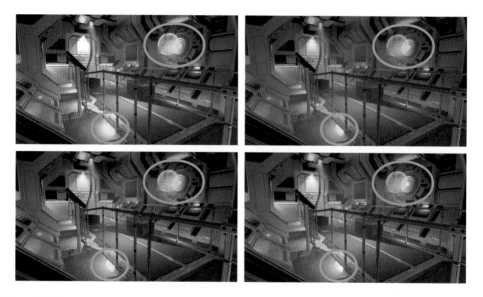

Figure 8.15. A scene with four different tone transforms applied. Differences are primarily seen in the circled areas, where scene pixel values are especially high. Upper left: clipping (plus sRGB OETF); upper right: Reinhard [1478]; lower left: Duiker [392]; lower right: Frostbite (hue-preserving version) [497]. The Reinhard, Duiker, and Frostbite transforms all preserve highlight information lost by clipping. However, the Reinhard curve tends to desaturate the darker parts of the image [628, 629], while the Duiker transform increases saturation in darker regions, which is sometimes regarded as a desirable trait [630]. By design, the Frostbite transform preserves both saturation and hue, avoiding the strong hue shift that can be seen in the lower left circle on the other three images. *(Images courtesy of ©2018 Electronic Arts Inc.)*

Exposure

A commonly used family of techniques for computing exposure relies on analyzing the scene-referred luminance values. To avoid introducing stalls, this analysis is typically done by sampling the previous frame.

Following a recommendation by Reinhard et al. [1478], one metric that was used in earlier implementations is the log-average scene luminance. Typically, the exposure was determined by computing the log-average value for the frame [224, 1674]. This log-average is computed by performing a series of down-sampling post-process passes, until a final, single value for the frame is computed.

Using an average value tends to be too sensitive to outliers, e.g., a small number of bright pixels could affect the exposure for the entire frame. Subsequent implementations ameliorated this problem by instead using a histogram of luminance values. Instead of the average, a histogram allows computing the median, which is more robust. Additional data points in the histogram can be used for improved results. For example, in *The Orange Box* by Valve, heuristics based on the 95th percentile and the median were used to determine exposure [1821]. Mittring describes the use of compute shaders to generate the luminance histogram [1229].

The problem with the techniques discussed so far is that pixel luminance is the wrong metric for driving exposure. If we look at photography practices, such as Ansel Adams' Zone System [10] and how incident light meters are used to set exposure, it becomes clear that it is preferable to use the lighting alone (without the effect of surface albedo) to determine exposure [757]. Doing so works because, to a first approximation, photographic exposure is used to counteract lighting. This results in a print that shows primarily the surface colors of objects, which corresponds to the *color constancy* property of the human visual system. Handling exposure in this way also ensures that correct values are passed to the tone transform. For example, most tone transforms used in the film or television industry are designed to map the exposed scene-referred value 0.18 to the display-referred value 0.1, with the expectation that 0.18 represents an 18% gray card in the dominant scene lighting [1418, 1602].

Although this approach is not yet common in real-time applications, it is starting to see use. For example, the game *Metal Gear Solid V: Ground Zeroes* has an exposure system based on lighting intensity [921]. In many games, static exposure levels are manually set for different parts of the environment based on known scene lighting values. Doing so avoids unexpected dynamic shifts in exposure.

8.2.3 Color Grading

In Section 8.2.2 we mentioned the concept of preferred image reproduction, the idea of producing an image that looks better in some sense than the original scene. Typically this involves creative manipulation of image colors, a process known as *color grading*.

Digital color grading has been used in the movie industry for some time. Early examples include the films *O Brother, Where Art Thou?* (2000) and *Amélie* (2001). Color grading is typically performed by interactively manipulating the colors in an example scene image, until the desired creative "look" is achieved. The same sequence of operations is then re-applied across all the images in a shot or sequence. Color grading spread from movies to games, where it is now widely used [392, 424, 756, 856, 1222].

Selan [1601] shows how to "bake" arbitrary color transformations from a color grading or image editing application into a three-dimensional color lookup table (LUT). Such tables are applied by using the input R, G, and B values as x-, y-, and z-coordinates for looking up a new color in the table, and thus can be used for any mapping from input to output color, up to the limitation of the LUT's resolution. Selan's baking process starts by taking an identity LUT (one that maps every input color to the same color) and "slicing" it to create a two-dimensional image. This sliced LUT image is then loaded into a color grading application, and the operations that define a desired creative look are applied to it. Care is needed to apply only color operations to the LUT, avoiding spatial operations such as blurs. The edited LUT is then saved out, "packed" into a three-dimensional GPU texture, and used in a rendering application to apply the same color transformations on the fly to rendered pixels. Iwanicki [806] presents a clever way to reduce sampling errors when storing a color transform in a LUT, using least-squares minimization.

Figure 8.16. A scene from the game *Uncharted 4*. The screenshot on top has no color grading. The other two screenshots each have a color grading operation applied. An extreme color grading operation (multiplication by a highly saturated cyan color) was chosen for purposes of illustration. In the bottom left screenshot, the color grading was applied to the display-referred (post-tone-mapping) image, and in the bottom right screenshot, it was applied to the scene-referred (pre-tone-mapping) image. (*UNCHARTED 4 A Thief's End* ©/*TM* *2016 SIE. Created and developed by Naughty Dog LLC.*)

In a later publication, Selan [1602] distinguishes between two ways to perform color grading. In one approach, color grading is performed on display-referred image data. In the other, the color grading operations are performed on scene-referred data that is previewed through a display transform. Although the display-referred color grading approach is easier to set up, grading scene-referred data can produce higher-fidelity results.

When real-time applications first adopted color grading, the display-referred approach was predominant [756, 856]. However, the scene-referred approach has since been gaining traction [198, 497, 672] due to its higher visual quality. See Figure 8.16. Applying color grading to scene-referred data also provides the opportunity to save some computation by baking the tone mapping curve into the grading LUT [672], as done in the game *Uncharted 4* [198].

Before LUT lookup, scene-referred data must be remapped to the range [0, 1] [1601]. In the Frostbite engine [497] the perceptual quantizer OETF is used for this purpose, though simpler curves could be used. Duiker [392] uses a log curve, and Hable [635] recommends using a square root operator applied once or twice.

Hable [635] presents a good overview of common color grading operations and implementation considerations.

Further Reading and Resources

For colorimetry and color science, the "bible" is *Color Science* by Wyszecki and Stiles [1934]. Other good colorimetry references include *Measuring Colour* by Hunt [789] and *Color Appearance Models* by Fairchild [456].

Selan's white paper [1602] gives a good overview of image reproduction and the "scene to screen" problem. Readers who want to learn still more about this topic will find *The Reproduction of Colour* by Hunt [788] and *Digital Color Management* by Giorgianni and Madden [537] to be excellent references. The three books in the *Ansel Adams Photography Series* [9, 10, 11], especially *The Negative*, provide an understanding of how the art and science of film photography has influenced the theory and practice of image reproduction to this day. Finally, the book *Color Imaging: Fundamentals and Applications* by Reinhard and others [1480] gives a thorough overview of the whole area of study.

Chapter 9
Physically Based Shading

"Let the form of an object be what it may,—light, shade, and perspective will always make it beautiful."
—John Constable

In this chapter we cover the various aspects of physically based shading. We start with a description of the physics of light-matter interaction in Section 9.1, and in Sections 9.2 to 9.4 we show how these physics connect to the shading process. Sections 9.5 to 9.7 are dedicated to the building blocks used to construct physically based shading models, and the models themselves—covering a broad variety of material types—are discussed in Sections 9.8 to 9.12. Finally, in Section 9.13 we describe how materials are blended together, and we cover filtering methods for avoiding aliasing and preserving surface appearance.

9.1 Physics of Light

The interactions of light and matter form the foundation of physically based shading. To understand these interactions, it helps to have a basic understanding of the nature of light.

In physical optics, light is modeled as an electromagnetic *transverse wave*, a wave that oscillates the electric and magnetic fields perpendicularly to the direction of its propagation. The oscillations of the two fields are coupled. The magnetic and electric field vectors are perpendicular to each other and the ratio of their lengths is fixed. This ratio is equal to the phase velocity, which we will discuss later.

In Figure 9.1 we see a simple light wave. It is, in fact, the simplest possible—a perfect sine function. This wave has a single *wavelength*, denoted with the Greek letter λ (lambda). As we have seen in Section 8.1, the perceived color of light is strongly related to its wavelength. For this reason, light with a single wavelength is called *monochromatic light*, which means "single-colored." However, most light waves encountered in practice are *polychromatic*, containing many different wavelengths.

The light wave in Figure 9.1 is unusually simple in another respect. It is *linearly polarized*. This means that for a fixed point in space, the electric and magnetic fields

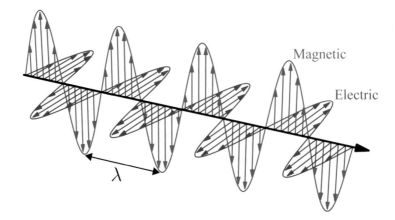

Figure 9.1. Light, an electromagnetic transverse wave. The electric and magnetic field vectors oscillate at 90° to each other and to the direction of propagation. The wave shown in the figure is the simplest possible light wave. It is both monochromatic (has a single wavelength λ) and linearly polarized (the electric and magnetic fields each oscillate along a single line).

each move back and forth along a line. In contrast, in this book we focus on *unpolarized* light, which is much more prevalent. In unpolarized light the field oscillations are spread equally over all directions perpendicular to the propagation axis. Despite their simplicity, it is useful to understand the behavior of monochromatic, linearly polarized waves, since any light wave can be factored into a combination of such waves.

If we track a point on the wave with a given phase (for example, an amplitude peak) over time, we will see it move through space at a constant speed, which is the wave's *phase velocity*. For a light wave traveling through a vacuum, the phase velocity is c, commonly referred to as the speed of light, about 300,000 kilometers per second.

In Section 8.1.1 we discussed the fact that for visible light, the size of a single wavelength is in the range of approximately 400–700 nanometers. To give some intuition for this length, it is about a half to a third of the width of a single thread of spider silk, which is itself less than a fiftieth of the width of a human hair. See Figure 9.2. In optics it is often useful to talk about the size of features relative to light wavelength. In this case we would say that the width of a spider silk thread is about 2λ–3λ (2–3 light wavelengths), and the width of a hair is about 100λ–200λ.

Light waves carry energy. The density of energy flow is equal to the product of the magnitudes of the electric and magnetic fields, which is—since the magnitudes are proportional to each other—proportional to the squared magnitude of the electric field. We focus on the electric field since it affects matter much more strongly than the magnetic field. In rendering, we are concerned with the *average* energy flow over time, which is proportional to the squared wave amplitude. This average energy flow density is the *irradiance*, denoted with the letter E. Irradiance and its relation to other light quantities were discussed in Section 8.1.1.

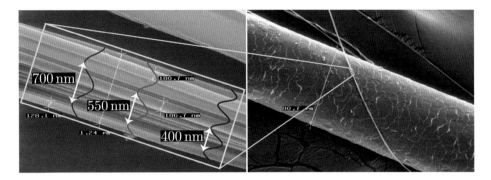

Figure 9.2. On the left visible light wavelengths are shown relative to a single thread of spider silk, which is a bit over 1 micron in width. On the right a similar thread of spider silk is shown next to a human hair, to give some additional context. *(Images courtesy of URnano/University of Rochester.)*

Light waves combine linearly. The total wave is the sum of the component waves. However, since irradiance is proportional to the square of the amplitudes, this would seem to lead to a paradox. For example, would summing two equal waves not lead to a "$1 + 1 = 4$" situation for irradiance? And since irradiance measures energy flow, would this not violate conservation of energy? The answers to these two questions are "sometimes" and "no," respectively.

To illustrate, we will look at a simple case: the addition of n monochromatic waves, identical except for phase. The amplitude of each of the n waves is a. As mentioned earlier, the irradiance E_1 of each wave is proportional to a^2, or in other words $E_1 = ka^2$ for some constant k.

Figure 9.3 shows three example scenarios for this case. On the left, the waves all line up with the same phase and reinforce each other. The combined wave irradiance is

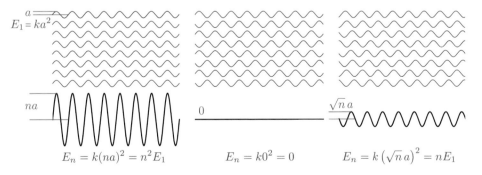

Figure 9.3. Three scenarios where n monochromatic waves with the same frequency, polarization, and amplitude are added together. From left to right: constructive interference, destructive interference, and incoherent addition. In each case the amplitude and irradiance of the combined wave (bottom) is shown relative to the n original waves (top).

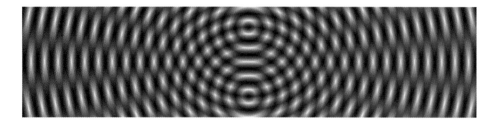

Figure 9.4. Monochromatic waves spreading out from two point sources, with the same frequency. The waves interfere constructively and destructively in different regions of space.

n^2 times that of a single wave, which is n times greater than the sum of the irradiance values of the individual waves. This situation is called *constructive interference*. In the center of the figure, each pair of waves is in opposing phase, canceling each other out. The combined wave has zero amplitude and zero irradiance. This scenario is *destructive interference*.

Constructive and destructive interference are two special cases of *coherent addition*, where the peaks and troughs of the waves line up in some consistent way. Depending on the relative phase relationships, coherent addition of n identical waves can result in a wave with irradiance anywhere between 0 and n^2 times that of an individual wave.

However, most often when waves are added up they are mutually *incoherent*, which means that their phases are relatively random. This is illustrated on the right in Figure 9.3. In this scenario, the amplitude of the combined wave is $\sqrt{n}\,a$, and the irradiance of the individual waves adds up linearly to n times the irradiance of one wave, as one would expect.

It would seem that destructive and constructive interference violate the conservation of energy. But Figure 9.3 does not show the full picture—it shows the wave interaction at only one location. As waves propagate through space, the phase relationship between them changes from one location to another, as shown in Figure 9.4. In some locations the waves interfere constructively, and the irradiance of the combined wave is greater than the sum of the irradiance values of the individual waves. In other locations they interfere destructively, causing the combined irradiance to be less than the sum of the individual wave irradiance values. This does not violate the law of conservation of energy, since the energy gained via constructive interference and the energy lost via destructive interference always cancel out.

Light waves are emitted when the electric charges in an object oscillate. Part of the energy that caused the oscillations—heat, electrical energy, chemical energy—is converted to light energy, which is radiated away from the object. In rendering, such objects are treated as light sources. We first discussed light sources in Section 5.2, and they will be described from a more physically based standpoint in Chapter 10.

After light waves have been emitted, they travel through space until they encounter some bit of matter with which to interact. The core phenomenon underlying the majority of light-matter interactions is simple, and quite similar to the emission case discussed above. The oscillating electrical field pushes and pulls at the electrical charges in the matter, causing them to oscillate in turn. The oscillating charges emit new light waves, which redirect some of the energy of the incoming light wave in new directions. This reaction, called *scattering*, is the basis of a wide variety of optical phenomena.

A scattered light wave has the same frequency as the original wave. When, as is usually the case, the original wave contains multiple frequencies of light, each one interacts with matter separately. Incoming light energy at one frequency does not contribute to emitted light energy at a different frequency, except for specific—and relatively rare—cases such as fluorescence and phosphorescence, which we will not describe in this book.

An isolated molecule scatters light in all directions, with some directional variation in intensity. More light is scattered in directions close to the original axis of propagation, both forward and backward. The molecule's effectiveness as a scatterer—the chance that a light wave in its vicinity will be scattered at all—varies strongly by wavelength. Short-wavelength light is scattered much more effectively than longer-wavelength light.

In rendering we are concerned with collections of many molecules. Light interactions with such aggregates will not necessarily resemble interactions with isolated molecules. Waves scattered from nearby molecules are often mutually coherent, and thus exhibit interference, since they originate from the same incoming wave. The rest of this section is devoted to several important special cases of light scattering from multiple molecules.

9.1.1 Particles

In an *ideal gas*, molecules do not affect each other and thus their relative positions are completely random and uncorrelated. Although this is an abstraction, it is a reasonably good model for air at normal atmospheric pressure. In this case, the phase differences between waves scattered from different molecules are random and constantly changing. As a result, the scattered waves are incoherent and their energy adds linearly, as in the right part of Figure 9.3. In other words, the aggregate light energy scattered from n molecules is n times the light scattered from a single molecule.

In contrast, if the molecules are tightly packed into clusters much smaller than a light wavelength, the scattered light waves in each cluster are in phase and interfere constructively. This causes the scattered wave energy to add up quadratically, as illustrated in the left part of Figure 9.3. Thus the intensity of light scattered from a small cluster of n molecules is n^2 times the light scattered from an individual molecule, which is n times more light than the same number of molecules would scatter in an ideal gas. This relationship means that for a fixed density of molecules per cubic meter, clumping the molecules into clusters will significantly increase the intensity of scattered light. Making the clusters larger, while still keeping the overall molecular density constant, will further increase scattered light intensity, until the cluster diameter becomes close to a light wavelength. Beyond that point, additional increases in cluster size will not further increase the scattered light intensity [469].

This process explains why clouds and fog scatter light so strongly. They are both created by condensation, which is the process of water molecules in the air clumping together into increasingly large clusters. This significantly increases light scattering, even though the overall density of water molecules is unchanged. Cloud rendering is discussed in Section 14.4.2.

When discussing light scattering, the term *particles* is used to refer to both isolated molecules and multi-molecule clusters. Since scattering from multi-molecule particles with diameters smaller than a wavelength is an amplified (via constructive interference) version of scattering from isolated molecules, it exhibits the same directional variation and wavelength dependence. This type of scattering is called *Rayleigh scattering* in the case of atmospheric particles and *Tyndall scattering* in the case of particles embedded in solids.

As particle size increases beyond a wavelength, the fact that the scattered waves are no longer in phase over the entire particle changes the characteristics of the scattering. The scattering increasingly favors the forward direction, and the wavelength dependency decreases until light of all visible wavelengths is scattered equally. This type of scattering is called *Mie scattering*. Rayleigh and Mie scattering are covered in more detail in Section 14.1.

9.1.2 Media

Another important case is light propagating through a *homogeneous medium*, which is a volume filled with uniformly spaced identical molecules. The molecular spacing does not have to be perfectly regular, as in a crystal. Liquids and non-crystalline solids can be optically homogeneous if their composition is pure (all molecules are the same) and they have no gaps or bubbles.

In a homogeneous medium, the scattered waves are lined up so that they interfere destructively in all directions except for the original direction of propagation. After the original wave is combined with all the waves scattered from individual molecules, the final result is the same as the original wave, except for its phase velocity and (in some cases) amplitude. The final wave does not exhibit any scattering—it has effectively been suppressed by destructive interference.

The ratio of the phase velocities of the original and new waves defines an optical property of the medium called the *index of refraction* (IOR) or refractive index, denoted by the letter n. Some media are *absorptive*. They convert part of the light energy to heat, causing the wave amplitude to decrease exponentially with distance. The rate of decrease is defined by the *attenuation index*, denoted by the Greek letter κ (kappa). Both n and κ typically vary by wavelength. Together, these two numbers fully define how the medium affects light of a given wavelength, and they are often combined into a single complex number $n + i\kappa$, called the *complex index of refraction*.

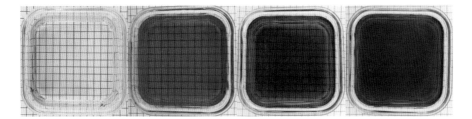

Figure 9.5. Four small containers of liquid with different absorption properties. From left to right: clean water, water with grenadine, tea, and coffee.

The index of refraction abstracts away the molecule-level details of light interaction and enables treating the medium as a continuous volume, which is much simpler.

While the phase velocity of light does not directly affect appearance, *changes* in velocity do, as we will explain later. On the other hand, light absorption has a direct impact on visuals, since it reduces the intensity of light and can (if varying by wavelength) also change its color. Figure 9.5 shows some examples of light absorption.

Nonhomogeneous media can often be modeled as homogeneous media with embedded scattering particles. The destructive interference that suppresses scattering in homogeneous media is caused by the uniform alignment of molecules, and thus of the scattered waves they produce. Any localized change in the distribution of molecules will break this pattern of destructive interference, allowing scattered light waves to propagate. Such a localized change can be a cluster of a different molecule type, an air gap, a bubble, or density variation. In any case, it will scatter light like the particles discussed earlier, with scattering properties similarly dependent on the cluster's size. Even gases can be modeled in this way. For these, the "scattering particles" are transient density fluctuations caused by the constant motion of the molecules. This model enables establishing a meaningful value of n for gases, which is useful for understanding their optical properties. Figure 9.6 shows some examples of light scattering.

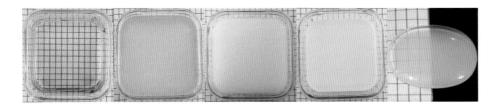

Figure 9.6. From left to right: water, water with a few drops of milk, water with about 10% milk, whole milk, and opalescent glass. Most of milk's scattering particles are larger than visible light wavelengths, so its scattering is primarily colorless, with a faint blue tint apparent in the middle image. The scattering particles in the opalescent glass are all smaller than visible light wavelengths and thus scatter blue light more strongly than red light. Due to the split light and dark background, transmitted light is more visible on the left and scattered light is more visible on the right.

Figure 9.7. The left image shows that, over a distance of multiple meters, water absorbs light, especially red light, quite strongly. The right image shows noticeable light scattering over multiple miles of air, even in the absence of heavy pollution or fog.

Scattering and absorption are both scale-dependent. A medium that does not produce any apparent scattering in a small scene may have quite noticeable scattering at larger scales. For example, light scattering in air and absorption in water are not visible when observing a glass of water in a room. However, in extended environments both effects can be significant, as shown in Figure 9.7.

In the general case, a medium's appearance is caused by some combination of scattering and absorption, as shown in Figure 9.8. The degree of scattering determines cloudiness, with high scattering creating an opaque appearance. With somewhat rare exceptions, such as the opalescent glass in Figure 9.6, particles in solid and liquid media tend to be larger than a light wavelength, and tend to scatter light of all visible wavelengths equally. Thus any color tint is usually caused by the wavelength dependence of the absorption. The lightness of the medium is a result of both phenomena. A white color in particular is the result of a combination of high scattering and low absorption. This is discussed in more detail in Section 14.1.

9.1.3 Surfaces

From an optical perspective, an object surface is a two-dimensional interface separating volumes with different index of refraction values. In typical rendering situations, the outer volume contains air, with a refractive index of about 1.003, often assumed to be 1 for simplicity. The refractive index of the inner volume depends on the substance from which the object is made.

When a light wave strikes a surface, two aspects of that surface have important effects on the result: the substances on either side, and the surface geometry. We will start by focusing on the substance aspect, assuming the simplest-possible surface geometry, a perfectly flat plane. We denote the index of refraction on the "outside" (the side where the incoming, or *incident*, wave originates) as n_1 and the index of refraction on the "inside" (where the wave will be transmitted after passing through the surface) as n_2.

We have seen in the previous section that light waves scatter when they encounter a discontinuity in material composition or density, i.e., in the index of refraction. A

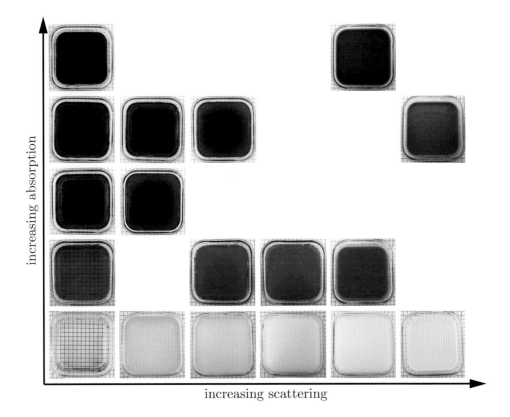

increasing absorption

increasing scattering

Figure 9.8. Containers of liquids that exhibit varying combinations of absorption and scattering.

planar surface separating different indices of refraction is a special type of discontinuity that scatters light in a specific way. The boundary conditions require that the electrical field component parallel to the surface is continuous. In other words, the projection of the electric field vector to the surface plane must match on either side of the surface. This has several implications:

1. At the surface, any scattered waves must be either in phase, or 180° out of phase, with the incident wave. Thus at the surface, the peaks of the scattered waves must line up either with the peaks or the troughs of the incident wave. This restricts the scattered waves to go in only two possible directions, one continuing forward into the surface and one retreating away from it. The first of these is the *transmitted wave*, and the second is the *reflected wave*.

2. The scattered waves must have the same frequency as the incident wave. We assume a monochromatic wave here, but the principles we discuss can be applied to any general wave by first decomposing it into monochromatic components.

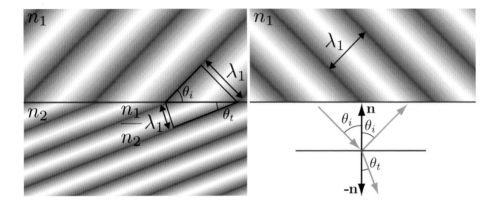

Figure 9.9. A light wave striking a planar surface separating indices of refraction n_1 and n_2. The left side of the figure shows a side view with the incident wave coming in from the upper left. The intensity of the red bands indicate wave phase. The spacing of the waves below the surface is changed proportionally to the ratio (n_1/n_2), which in this case is 0.5. The phases line up along the surface, so the change in spacing bends (refracts) the transmitted wave direction. The triangle construction shows the derivation of Snell's law. For clarity, the upper right of the figure shows the reflected wave separately. It has the same wave spacing as the incident wave, and thus its direction has the same angle with the surface normal. The lower right of the figure shows the wave direction vectors.

3. As a light wave moves from one medium to another, the phase velocity—the speed the wave travels through the medium—changes proportionally to the relative index of refraction (n_1/n_2). Since the frequency is fixed, the wavelength also changes proportionally to (n_1/n_2).

The final result is shown in Figure 9.9. The reflected and incident wave directions have the same angle θ_i with the surface normal. The transmitted wave direction is bent (*refracted*) at an angle θ_t, which has the following relation to θ_i:

$$\sin(\theta_t) = \frac{n_1}{n_2}\sin(\theta_i). \tag{9.1}$$

This equation for refraction is known as *Snell's law*. It is used in global refraction effects, which will be discussed further in Section 14.5.2.

Although refraction is often associated with clear materials such as glass and crystal, it happens at the surface of opaque objects as well. When refraction occurs with opaque objects, the light undergoes scattering and absorption in the object's interior. Light interacts with the object's medium, just as with the various cups of liquid in Figure 9.8. In the case of metals, the interior contains many free electrons (electrons not bound to molecules) that "soak up" the refracted light energy and redirect it into the reflected wave. This is why metals have high absorption as well as high reflectivity.

Figure 9.10. An example of light paths bending due to gradual changes in index of refraction, in this case caused by temperature variations. *("EE Lightnings heat haze," Paul Lucas, used under the CC BY 2.0 license.)*

The surface refraction phenomena we have discussed—reflection and refraction—require an abrupt change in index of refraction, occurring over a distance of less than a single wavelength. A more gradual change in index of refraction does not split the light, but instead causes its path to curve, in a continuous analog of the discontinuous bend that occurs in refraction. This effect commonly can be seen when air density varies due to temperature, such as mirages and heat distortion. See Figure 9.10.

Even an object with a well-defined boundary will have no visible surface if it is immersed in a substance with the same index of refraction. In the absence of an index of refraction change, reflection and refraction cannot occur. An example of this is seen in Figure 9.11.

Until now we have focused on the effect of the substances on either side of a surface. We will now discuss the other important factor affecting surface appearance: geometry. Strictly speaking, a perfectly flat planar surface is impossible. Every surface has irregularities of some kind, even if only the individual atoms comprising the surface. However, surface irregularities much smaller than a wavelength have no effect on light, and surface irregularities much larger than a wavelength effectively tilt the surface without affecting its *local* flatness. Only irregularities with a size in the range of 1–100 wavelengths cause the surface to behave differently than a flat plane, via a phenomenon called *diffraction* that will be discussed further in Section 9.11.

In rendering, we typically use *geometrical optics*, which ignores wave effects such as interference and diffraction. This is equivalent to assuming that all surface irregularities are either smaller than a light wavelength or much larger. In geometrical optics light is modeled as rays instead of waves. At the point a light ray intersects with a surface, the surface is treated locally as a flat plane. The diagram on the bottom right of Figure 9.9 can be seen as a geometrical optics picture of reflection and refraction, in contrast with the wave picture presented in the other parts of that figure. We will

Figure 9.11. The refractive index of these decorative beads is the same as water. Above the water, they have a visible surface due to the difference between their refractive index and that of air. Below the water, the refractive index is the same on both sides of the bead surfaces, so the surfaces are invisible. The beads themselves are visible only due to their colored absorption.

keep to the realm of geometrical optics from this point until Section 9.11, which is dedicated to the topic of shading models based on wave optics.

As we mentioned earlier, surface irregularities much larger than a wavelength change the local orientation of the surface. When these irregularities are too small to be individually rendered—in other words, smaller than a pixel—we refer to them as *microgeometry*. The directions of reflection and refraction depend on the surface normal. The effect of the microgeometry is to change that normal at different points on the surface, thus changing the reflected and refracted light directions.

Even though each specific point on the surface reflects light in only a single direction, each pixel covers many surface points that reflect light in various directions. The appearance is driven by the aggregate result of all the different reflection directions. Figure 9.12 shows an example of two surfaces that have similar shapes on the macroscopic scale but significantly different microgeometry.

For rendering, rather than modeling the microgeometry explicitly, we treat it statistically and view the surface as having a random distribution of microstructure normals. As a result, we model the surface as reflecting (and refracting) light in a continuous spread of directions. The width of this spread, and thus the blurriness of reflected and refracted detail, depends on the statistical variance of the microgeometry normal vectors—in other words, the surface microscale *roughness*. See Figure 9.13.

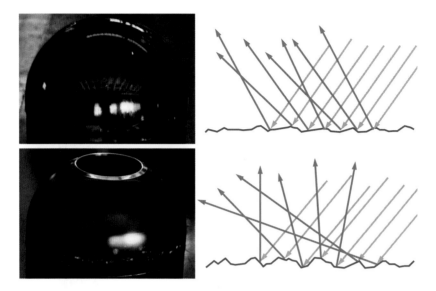

Figure 9.12. On the left we see photographs of two surfaces, with diagrams of their microscopic structures on the right. The top surface has slightly rough microgeometry. Incoming light rays hit surface points that are angled somewhat differently and reflect in a narrow cone of directions. The visible effect is a slight blurring of the reflection. The bottom surface has rougher microgeometry. Surface points hit by incoming light rays are angled in significantly different directions and the reflected light spreads out in a wide cone, causing blurrier reflections.

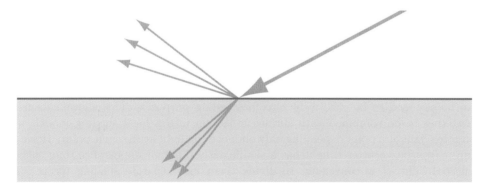

Figure 9.13. When viewed macroscopically, surfaces can be treated as reflecting and refracting light in multiple directions.

9.1.4 Subsurface Scattering

Refracted light continues to interact with the interior volume of the object. As mentioned earlier, metals reflect most incident light and quickly absorb the rest. In contrast, non-metals exhibit a wide variety of scattering and absorption behaviors, which

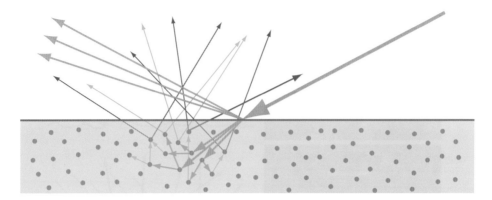

Figure 9.14. The refracted light undergoes absorption as it travels through the material. In this example most of the absorption is at longer wavelengths, leaving primarily short-wavelength blue light. In addition, it scatters from particles inside the material. Eventually some refracted light is scattered back out of the surface, as shown by the blue arrows exiting the surface in various directions.

are similar to those seen in the cups of liquid in Figure 9.8. Materials with low scattering and absorption are transparent, transmitting any refracted light through the entire object. Simple methods for rendering such materials without refraction were discussed in Section 5.5, and refraction will be covered in detail in Section 14.5.2. In this chapter we will focus on opaque objects, in which the transmitted light undergoes multiple scattering and absorption events until finally some of it is re-emitted back from the surface. See Figure 9.14.

This *subsurface-scattered* light exits the surface at varying distances from the entry point. The distribution of entry-exit distances depends on the density and properties of the scattering particles in the material. The relationship between these distances and the shading scale (the size of a pixel, or the distance between shading samples) is important. If the entry-exit distances are small compared to the shading scale, they can be assumed to be effectively zero for shading purposes. This allows subsurface scattering to be combined with surface reflection into a local shading model, with outgoing light at a point depending only on incoming light at the same point. However, since subsurface-scattered light has a significantly different appearance than surface-reflected light, it is convenient to divide them into separate shading terms. The *specular term* models surface reflection, and the *diffuse term* models *local subsurface scattering*.

If the entry-exit distances are large compared to the shading scale, then specialized rendering techniques are needed to capture the visual effect of light entering the surface at one point and leaving it from another. These *global subsurface scattering* techniques are covered in detail in Section 14.6. The difference between local and global subsurface scattering is illustrated in Figure 9.15.

It is important to note that local and global subsurface scattering techniques model exactly the same physical phenomena. The best choice for each situation depends not

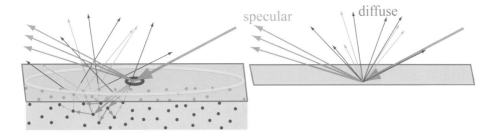

Figure 9.15. On the left, we are rendering a material with subsurface scattering. Two different sampling sizes are shown, in yellow and purple. The large yellow circle represents a single shading sample covering an area larger than the subsurface scattering distances. Thus, those distances can be ignored, enabling subsurface scattering to be treated as the diffuse term in a local shading model, as shown in the separate figure on the right. If we move closer to this surface, the shading sample area becomes smaller, as shown by the small purple circle. The subsurface scattering distances are now large compared to the area covered by a shading sample. Global techniques are needed to produce a realistic image from these samples.

only on the material properties but also on the scale of observation. For example, when rendering a scene of a child playing with a plastic toy, it is likely that global techniques would be needed for an accurate rendering of the child's skin, and that a local diffuse shading model would suffice for the toy. This is because the scattering distances in skin are quite a bit larger than in plastic. However, if the camera is far enough away, the skin scattering distances would be smaller than a pixel and local shading models would be accurate for both the child and the toy. Conversely, in an extreme close-up shot, the plastic would exhibit noticeable non-local subsurface scattering and global techniques would be needed to render the toy accurately.

9.2 The Camera

As mentioned in Section 8.1.1, in rendering we compute the radiance from the shaded surface point to the camera position. This simulates a simplified model of an imaging system such as a film camera, digital camera, or human eye.

Such systems contain a sensor surface composed of many discrete small sensors. Examples include rods and cones in the eye, photodiodes in a digital camera, or dye particles in film. Each of these sensors detects the irradiance value over its surface and produces a color signal. Irradiance sensors themselves cannot produce an image, since they average light rays from all incoming directions. For this reason, a full imaging system includes a light-proof enclosure with a single small *aperture* (opening) that restricts the directions from which light can enter and strike the sensors. A lens placed at the aperture focuses the light so that each sensor receives light from only a small set of incoming directions. The enclosure, aperture, and lens have the combined effect of causing the sensors to be *directionally specific*. They average light over a small area and a small set of incoming directions. Rather than measuring average irradiance—which as we have seen in Section 8.1.1 quantifies the surface density of light flow from all directions—these sensors measure average radiance, which quantifies the brightness and color of a single ray of light.

Historically, rendering has simulated an especially simple imaging sensor called a *pinhole camera*, shown in the top part of Figure 9.16. A pinhole camera has an extremely small aperture—in the ideal case, a zero-size mathematical point—and no lens. The point aperture restricts each point on the sensor surface to collect a single ray of light, with a discrete sensor collecting a narrow cone of light rays with its base covering the sensor surface and its apex at the aperture. Rendering systems model pinhole cameras in a slightly different (but equivalent) way, shown in the middle part of Figure 9.16. The location of the pinhole aperture is represented by the point $\mathbf{c}$, often referred to as the "camera position" or "eye position." This point is also the center of projection for the perspective transform (Section 4.7.2).

When rendering, each shading sample corresponds to a single ray and thus to a sample point on the sensor surface. The process of antialiasing (Section 5.4) can be interpreted as reconstructing the signal collected over each discrete sensor surface. However, since rendering is not bound by the limitations of physical sensors, we can treat the process more generally, as the reconstruction of a continuous image signal from discrete samples.

Although actual pinhole cameras have been constructed, they are poor models for most cameras used in practice, as well as for the human eye. A model of an imaging system using a lens is shown in the bottom part of Figure 9.16. Including a lens allows for the use of a larger aperture, which greatly increases the amount of light collected by the imaging system. However, it also causes the camera to have a limited depth of field (Section 12.4), blurring objects that are too near or too far.

The lens has an additional effect aside from limiting the depth of field. Each sensor location receives a cone of light rays, even for points that are in perfect focus. The idealized model where each shading sample represents a single viewing ray can sometimes introduce mathematical singularities, numerical instabilities, or visual aliasing. Keeping the physical model in mind when we render images can help us identify and resolve such issues.

9.3   The BRDF

Ultimately, physically based rendering comes down to computing the radiance entering the camera along some set of view rays. Using the notation for incoming radiance introduced in Section 8.1.1, for a given view ray the quantity we need to compute is $L_i(\mathbf{c}, -\mathbf{v})$, where $\mathbf{c}$ is the camera position and $-\mathbf{v}$ is the direction along the view ray. We use $-\mathbf{v}$ due to two notation conventions. First, the direction vector in $L_i()$ always points away from the given point, which in this case is the camera location. Second, the view vector $\mathbf{v}$ always points toward the camera.

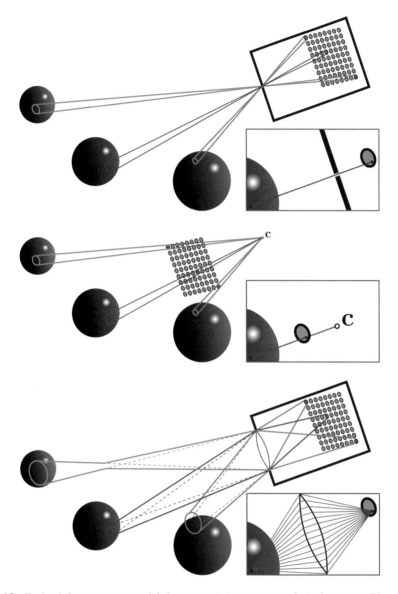

Figure 9.16. Each of these camera model figures contains an array of pixel sensors. The solid lines bound the set of light rays collected from the scene by three of these sensors. The inset images in each figure show the light rays collected by a single point sample on a pixel sensor. The top figure shows a pinhole camera, the middle figure shows a typical rendering system model of the same pinhole camera with the camera point **c**, and the bottom figure shows a more physically correct camera with a lens. The red sphere is in focus, and the other two spheres are out of focus.

In rendering, scenes are typically modeled as collections of objects with media in between them (the word "media" actually comes from the Latin word for "in the middle" or "in between"). Often the medium in question is a moderate amount of relatively clean air, which does not noticeably affect the ray's radiance and can thus be ignored for rendering purposes. Sometimes the ray may travel through a medium that does affect its radiance appreciably via absorption or scattering. Such media are called *participating media* since they participate in the light's transport through the scene. Participating media will be covered in detail in Chapter 14. In this chapter we assume that there are no participating media present, so the radiance entering the camera is equal to the radiance leaving the closest object surface in the direction of the camera:

$$L_i(\mathbf{c}, -\mathbf{v}) = L_o(\mathbf{p}, \mathbf{v}), \tag{9.2}$$

where $\mathbf{p}$ is the intersection of the view ray with the closest object surface.

Following Equation 9.2, our new goal is to calculate $L_o(\mathbf{p}, \mathbf{v})$. This calculation is a physically based version of the shading model evaluation discussed in Section 5.1. Sometimes radiance is directly emitted by the surface. More often, radiance leaving the surface originated from elsewhere and is reflected by the surface into the view ray, via the physical interactions described in Section 9.1. In this chapter we leave aside the cases of transparency (Section 5.5 and Section 14.5.2) and global subsurface scattering (Section 14.6). In other words, we focus on local reflectance phenomena, which redirect light hitting the currently shaded point back outward. These phenomena include surface reflection as well as local subsurface scattering, and depend on only the incoming light direction $\mathbf{l}$ and the outgoing view direction $\mathbf{v}$. Local reflectance is quantified by the *bidirectional reflectance distribution function* (BRDF), denoted as $f(\mathbf{l}, \mathbf{v})$.

In its original derivation [1277] the BRDF was defined for uniform surfaces. That is, the BRDF was assumed to be the same over the surface. However, objects in the real world (and in rendered scenes) rarely have uniform material properties over their surface. Even an object that is composed of a single material, e.g., a statue made of silver, will have scratches, tarnished spots, stains, and other variations that cause its visual properties to change from one surface point to the next. Technically, a function that captures BRDF variation based on spatial location is called a *spatially varying BRDF* (SVBRDF) or *spatial BRDF* (SBRDF). However, this case is so prevalent in practice that the shorter term BRDF is often used and implicitly assumed to depend on surface location.

The incoming and outgoing directions each have two degrees of freedom. A frequently used parameterization involves two angles: elevation θ relative to the surface normal $\mathbf{n}$ and azimuth (horizontal rotation) ϕ about $\mathbf{n}$. In the general case, the BRDF is a function of four scalar variables. *Isotropic* BRDFs are an important special case. Such BRDFs remain the same when the incoming and outgoing directions are rotated around the surface normal, keeping the same relative angles between them. Figure 9.17 shows the variables used in both cases. Isotropic BRDFs are functions of three scalar variables, since only a single angle ϕ between the light's and camera's

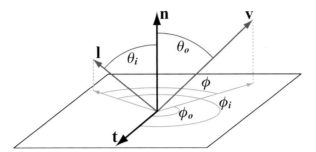

Figure 9.17. The BRDF. Azimuth angles ϕ_i and ϕ_o are given with respect to a given tangent vector **t**. The relative azimuth angle ϕ, used for isotropic BRDFs instead of ϕ_i and ϕ_o, does not require a reference tangent vector.

rotation is needed. What this means is that if a uniform isotropic material is placed on a turntable and rotated, it will appear the same for all rotation angles, given a fixed light and camera.

Since we ignore phenomena such as fluorescence and phosphorescence, we can assume that incoming light of a given wavelength is reflected at the same wavelength. The amount of light reflected can vary based on the wavelength, which can be modeled in one of two ways. Either the wavelength is treated as an additional input variable to the BRDF, or the BRDF is treated as returning a spectrally distributed value. While the first approach is sometimes used in offline rendering [660], in real-time rendering the second approach is always used. Since real-time renderers represent spectral distributions as RGB triples, this simply means that the BRDF returns an RGB value.

To compute $L_o(\mathbf{p}, \mathbf{v})$, we incorporate the BRDF into the *reflectance equation*:

$$L_o(\mathbf{p}, \mathbf{v}) = \int_{\mathbf{l} \in \Omega} f(\mathbf{l}, \mathbf{v}) L_i(\mathbf{p}, \mathbf{l})(\mathbf{n} \cdot \mathbf{l}) d\mathbf{l}. \tag{9.3}$$

The $\mathbf{l} \in \Omega$ subscript on the integral sign means that integration is performed over $\mathbf{l}$ vectors that lie in the unit hemisphere above the surface (centered on the surface normal **n**). Note that **l** is swept continuously over the hemisphere of incoming directions—it is not a specific "light source direction." The idea is that any incoming direction can (and usually will) have some radiance associated with it. We use $d\mathbf{l}$ to denote the differential solid angle around **l** (solid angles are discussed in Section 8.1.1).

In summary, the reflectance equation shows that outgoing radiance equals the integral (over **l** in Ω) of incoming radiance times the BRDF times the dot product between **n** and **l**.

For brevity, for the rest of the chapter we will omit the surface point **p** from $L_i()$, $L_o()$, and the reflectance equation:

$$L_o(\mathbf{v}) = \int_{\mathbf{l} \in \Omega} f(\mathbf{l}, \mathbf{v}) L_i(\mathbf{l})(\mathbf{n} \cdot \mathbf{l}) d\mathbf{l}. \tag{9.4}$$

When computing the reflectance equation, the hemisphere is often parameterized using spherical coordinates ϕ and θ. For this parameterization, the differential solid angle $d\mathbf{l}$ is equal to $\sin\theta_i\,d\theta_i\,d\phi_i$. Using this parameterization, a double-integral form of Equation 9.4 can be derived, which uses spherical coordinates (recall that $(\mathbf{n}\cdot\mathbf{l}) = \cos\theta_i$):

$$L_o(\theta_o,\phi_o) = \int_{\phi_i=0}^{2\pi}\int_{\theta_i=0}^{\pi/2} f(\theta_i,\phi_i,\theta_o,\phi_o)L(\theta_i,\phi_i)\cos\theta_i\sin\theta_i d\theta_i d\phi_i. \qquad (9.5)$$

The angles θ_i, ϕ_i, θ_o, and ϕ_o are shown in Figure 9.17.

In some cases it is convenient to use a slightly different parameterization, with the cosines of the elevation angles $\mu_i = \cos\theta_i$ and $\mu_o = \cos\theta_o$ as variables rather than the angles θ_i and θ_o themselves. For this parameterization, the differential solid angle $d\mathbf{l}$ is equal to $d\mu_i\,d\phi_i$. Using the (μ,ϕ) parameterization yields the following integral form:

$$L_o(\mu_o,\phi_o) = \int_{\phi_i=0}^{2\pi}\int_{\mu_i=0}^{1} f(\mu_i,\phi_i,\mu_o,\phi_o)L(\mu_i,\phi_i)\mu_i d\mu_i d\phi_i. \qquad (9.6)$$

The BRDF is defined only in cases where both the light and view directions are above the surface. The case where the light direction is under the surface can be avoided by either multiplying the BRDF by zero or not evaluating the BRDF for such directions in the first place. But what about view directions under the surface, in other words where the dot product $\mathbf{n}\cdot\mathbf{v}$ is negative? Theoretically this case should never occur. The surface would be facing away from the camera and would thus be invisible. However, interpolated vertex normals and normal mapping, both common in real-time applications, can create such situations in practice. Evaluation of the BRDF for view directions under the surface can be avoided by clamping $\mathbf{n}\cdot\mathbf{v}$ to 0 or using its absolute value, but both approaches can result in artifacts. The Frostbite engine uses the absolute value of $\mathbf{n}\cdot\mathbf{v}$ plus a small number (0.00001) to avoid divides by zero [960]. Another possible approach is a "soft clamp," which gradually goes to zero as the angle between $\mathbf{n}$ and $\mathbf{v}$ increases past 90°.

The laws of physics impose two constraints on any BRDF. The first constraint is *Helmholtz reciprocity*, which means that the input and output angles can be switched and the function value will be the same:

$$f(\mathbf{l},\mathbf{v}) = f(\mathbf{v},\mathbf{l}). \qquad (9.7)$$

In practice, BRDFs used in rendering often violate Helmholtz reciprocity without noticeable artifacts, except for offline rendering algorithms that specifically require reciprocity, such as bidirectional path tracing. However, it is a useful tool to use when determining if a BRDF is physically plausible.

The second constraint is conservation of energy—the outgoing energy cannot be greater than the incoming energy (not counting glowing surfaces that emit light, which are handled as a special case). Offline rendering algorithms such as path tracing require energy conservation to ensure convergence. For real-time rendering, exact energy conservation is not necessary, but approximate energy conservation is important. A surface rendered with a BRDF that significantly violates energy conservation would be too bright, and so may look unrealistic.

The *directional-hemispherical reflectance* $R(\mathbf{l})$ is a function related to the BRDF. It can be used to measure to what degree a BRDF is energy conserving. Despite its somewhat daunting name, the directional-hemispherical reflectance is a simple concept. It measures the amount of light coming from a given direction that is reflected at all, into any outgoing direction in the hemisphere around the surface normal. Essentially, it measures energy loss for a given incoming direction. The input to this function is the incoming direction vector $\mathbf{l}$, and its definition is presented here:

$$R(\mathbf{l}) = \int_{\mathbf{v} \in \Omega} f(\mathbf{l}, \mathbf{v})(\mathbf{n} \cdot \mathbf{v}) d\mathbf{v}. \tag{9.8}$$

Note that here $\mathbf{v}$, like $\mathbf{l}$ in the reflectance equation, is swept over the entire hemisphere and does not represent a singular viewing direction.

A similar but in some sense opposite function, *hemispherical-directional reflectance* $R(\mathbf{v})$ can be similarly defined:

$$R(\mathbf{v}) = \int_{\mathbf{l} \in \Omega} f(\mathbf{l}, \mathbf{v})(\mathbf{n} \cdot \mathbf{l}) d\mathbf{l}. \tag{9.9}$$

If the BRDF is reciprocal, then the hemispherical-directional reflectance and the directional-hemispherical reflectance are equal and the same function can be used to compute either one. *Directional albedo* can be used as a blanket term for both reflectances in cases where they are used interchangeably.

The value of the directional-hemispherical reflectance $R(\mathbf{l})$ must always be in the range $[0, 1]$, as a result of energy conservation. A reflectance value of 0 represents a case where all the incoming light is absorbed or otherwise lost. If all the light is reflected, the reflectance will be 1. In most cases it will be somewhere between these two values. Like the BRDF, the values of $R(\mathbf{l})$ vary with wavelength, so it is represented as an RGB vector for rendering purposes. Since each component (red, green, and blue) is restricted to the range $[0, 1]$, a value of $R(\mathbf{l})$ can be thought of as a simple color. Note that this restriction does not apply to the values of the BRDF. As a distribution function, the BRDF can have arbitrarily high values in certain directions (such as the center of a highlight) if the distribution it describes is highly nonuniform. The requirement for a BRDF to be energy conserving is that $R(\mathbf{l})$ be no greater than one for all possible values of $\mathbf{l}$.

The simplest possible BRDF is Lambertian, which corresponds to the Lambertian shading model briefly discussed in Section 5.2. The Lambertian BRDF has a constant value. The well-known $(\mathbf{n} \cdot \mathbf{l})$ factor that distinguishes Lambertian shading is not part of the BRDF but rather part of Equation 9.4. Despite its simplicity, the Lambertian BRDF is often used in real-time rendering to represent local subsurface scattering (though it is being supplanted by more accurate models, as discussed in Section 9.9). The directional-hemispherical reflectance of a Lambertian surface is also a constant. Evaluating Equation 9.8 for a constant value of $f(\mathbf{l}, \mathbf{v})$ yields the following value for the directional-hemispherical reflectance as a function of the BRDF:

$$R(\mathbf{l}) = \pi f(\mathbf{l}, \mathbf{v}). \tag{9.10}$$

The constant reflectance value of a Lambertian BRDF is typically referred to as the *diffuse color* $\mathbf{c}_{\text{diff}}$ or the *albedo* ρ. In this chapter, to emphasize the connection with subsurface scattering, we will refer to this quantity as the *subsurface albedo* ρ_{ss}. The subsurface albedo is discussed in detail in Section 9.9.1. The BRDF from Equation 9.10 gives the following result:

$$f(\mathbf{l}, \mathbf{v}) = \frac{\rho_{\text{ss}}}{\pi}. \tag{9.11}$$

The $1/\pi$ factor is caused by the fact that integrating a cosine factor over the hemisphere yields a value of π. Such factors are often seen in BRDFs.

One way to understand a BRDF is to visualize it with the input direction held constant. See Figure 9.18. For a given direction of incoming light, the BRDF's values

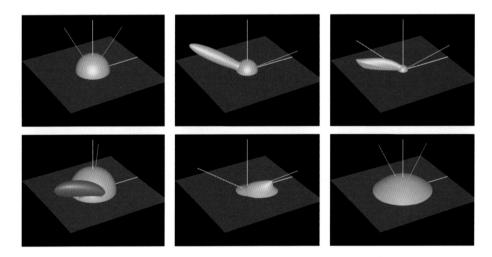

Figure 9.18. Example BRDFs. The solid green line coming from the right of each figure is the incoming light direction, and the dashed green and white line is the ideal reflection direction. In the top row, the left figure shows a Lambertian BRDF (a simple hemisphere). The middle figure shows Blinn-Phong highlighting added to the Lambertian term. The right figure shows the Cook-Torrance BRDF [285, 1779]. Note how the specular highlight is not strongest in the reflection direction. In the bottom row, the left figure shows a close-up of Ward's anisotropic model. In this case, the effect is to tilt the specular lobe. The middle figure shows the Hapke/Lommel-Seeliger "lunar surface" BRDF [664], which has strong retroreflection. The right figure shows Lommel-Seeliger scattering, in which dusty surfaces scatter light toward grazing angles. *(Images courtesy of Szymon Rusinkiewicz, from his "bv" BRDF browser.)*

are displayed for all outgoing directions. The spherical part around the point of intersection is the diffuse component, since outgoing radiance has an equal chance of reflecting in any direction. The ellipsoidal piece is the *specular lobe*. Naturally, such lobes are in the reflection direction from the incoming light, with the thickness of the lobe corresponding to the fuzziness of the reflection. By the principle of reciprocity, these same visualizations can also be thought of as how much each different incoming light direction contributes to a single outgoing direction.

9.4 Illumination

The $L_i(\mathbf{l})$ (incoming radiance) term in the reflectance equation (Equation 9.4) represents light impinging upon the shaded surface point from other parts of the scene. *Global illumination* algorithms calculate $L_i(\mathbf{l})$ by simulating how light propagates and is reflected throughout the scene. These algorithms use the *rendering equation* [846], of which the reflectance equation is a special case. Global illumination is discussed in Chapter 11. In this chapter and the next, we focus on *local illumination*, which uses the reflectance equation to compute shading locally at each surface point. In local illumination algorithms $L_i(\mathbf{l})$ is given and does not need to be computed.

In realistic scenes, $L_i(\mathbf{l})$ includes nonzero radiance from all directions, whether emitted directly from light sources or reflected from other surfaces. Unlike the directional and punctual lights discussed in Section 5.2, real-world light sources are *area lights* that cover a nonzero solid angle. In this chapter, we use a restricted form of $L_i(\mathbf{l})$ comprised of only directional and punctual lights, leaving more general lighting environments to Chapter 10. This restriction allows for a more focused discussion.

Although punctual and directional lights are non-physical abstractions, they can be derived as approximations of physical light sources. Such a derivation is important, because it enables us to incorporate these lights in a physically based rendering framework with confidence that we understand the error involved.

We take a small, distant area light and define $\mathbf{l}_c$ as the vector pointing to its center. We also define the light's color $\mathbf{c}_{\text{light}}$ as the reflected radiance from a white Lambertian surface facing toward the light ($\mathbf{n} = \mathbf{l}_c$). This is an intuitive definition for authoring, since the color of the light corresponds directly to its visual effect.

With these definitions, a directional light can be derived as the limit case of shrinking the size of the area light down to zero while maintaining the value of $\mathbf{c}_{\text{light}}$ [758]. In this case the integral in the reflectance equation (Equation 9.4) simplifies down to a single BRDF evaluation, which is significantly less expensive to compute:

$$L_o(\mathbf{v}) = \pi f(\mathbf{l}_c, \mathbf{v}) \mathbf{c}_{\text{light}} (\mathbf{n} \cdot \mathbf{l}_c). \tag{9.12}$$

The dot product $(\mathbf{n} \cdot \mathbf{l})$ is often clamped to zero, as a convenient method of skipping contributions from lights under the surface:

$$L_o(\mathbf{v}) = \pi f(\mathbf{l}_c, \mathbf{v}) \mathbf{c}_{\text{light}} (\mathbf{n} \cdot \mathbf{l}_c)^+. \tag{9.13}$$

Note the x^+ notation introduced in Section 1.2, which indicates that negative values are clamped to zero.

Punctual lights can be treated similarly. The only differences are that the area light is not required to be distant, and $\mathbf{c}_{\text{light}}$ falls off as the inverse square of the distance to the light, as in Equation 5.11 (page 111). In the case of more than one light source, Equation 9.12 is computed multiple times and the results are summed:

$$L_o(\mathbf{v}) = \pi \sum_{i=1}^{n} f(\mathbf{l}_{c_i}, \mathbf{v}) \mathbf{c}_{\text{light}_i} (\mathbf{n} \cdot \mathbf{l}_{c_i})^+, \tag{9.14}$$

where $\mathbf{l}_{c_i}$ and $\mathbf{c}_{\text{light}_i}$ are the direction and color, respectively, of the ith light. Note the similarities to Equation 5.6 (page 109).

The π factor in Equation 9.14 cancels out the $1/\pi$ factor that often appears in BRDFs (e.g., Equation 9.11). This cancellation moves the divide operation out of the shader and makes the shading equation simpler to read. However, care must be taken when adapting BRDFs from academic papers for use in real-time shading equations. Typically, the BRDF will need to be multiplied by π before use.

9.5 Fresnel Reflectance

In Section 9.1 we discussed light-matter interaction from a high level. In Section 9.3, we covered the basic machinery for expressing these interactions mathematically: the BRDF and the reflectance equation. Now we are ready to start drilling down to specific phenomena, quantifying them so they can be used in shading models. We will start with reflection from a flat surface, first discussed in Section 9.1.3.

An object's surface is an interface between the surrounding medium (typically air) and the object's substance. The interaction of light with a planar interface between two substances follows the *Fresnel equations* developed by Augustin-Jean Fresnel (1788–1827) (pronounced freh-*nel*). The Fresnel equations require a flat interface following the assumptions of geometrical optics. In other words, the surface is assumed to not have any irregularities between 1 light wavelength and 100 wavelengths in size. Irregularities smaller than this range have no effect on the light, and larger irregularities effectively tilt the surface but do not affect its local flatness.

Light incident on a flat surface splits into a reflected part and a refracted part. The direction of the reflected light (indicated by the vector $\mathbf{r}_i$) forms the same angle (θ_i) with the surface normal $\mathbf{n}$ as the incoming direction $\mathbf{l}$. The reflection vector $\mathbf{r}_i$ can be computed from $\mathbf{n}$ and $\mathbf{l}$:

$$\mathbf{r}_i = 2(\mathbf{n} \cdot \mathbf{l})\mathbf{n} - \mathbf{l}. \tag{9.15}$$

See Figure 9.19. The amount of light reflected (as a fraction of incoming light) is described by the *Fresnel reflectance* F, which depends on the incoming angle θ_i.

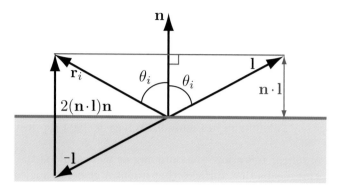

Figure 9.19. Reflection at a planar surface. The light vector **l** is reflected around the normal **n** in order to generate $\mathbf{r}_i$. First, **l** is projected onto **n**, and we get a scaled version of the normal: $(\mathbf{n} \cdot \mathbf{l})\mathbf{n}$. We then negate **l**, and add two times the projected vector to obtain the reflection vector.

As discussed in Section 9.1.3, reflection and refraction are affected by the refractive index of the two substances on either side of the plane. We will continue to use the notation from that discussion. The value n_1 is the refractive index of the substance "above" the interface, where incident and reflected light propagate, and n_2 is the refractive index of the substance "below" the interface, where the refracted light propagates.

The Fresnel equations describe the dependence of F on θ_i, n_1, and n_2. Rather than present the equations themselves, which are somewhat complex, we will describe their important characteristics.

9.5.1   External Reflection

External reflection is the case where $n_1 < n_2$. In other words, the light originates on the side of the surface where the refractive index is lower. Most often, this side contains air, with a refractive index of approximately 1.003. We will assume $n_1 = 1$ for simplicity. The opposite transition, from object to air, is called *internal reflection* and is discussed later in Section 9.5.3.

For a given substance, the Fresnel equations can be interpreted as defining a reflectance function $F(\theta_i)$, dependent only on incoming light angle. In principle, the value of $F(\theta_i)$ varies continuously over the visible spectrum. For rendering purposes its value is treated as an RGB vector. The function $F(\theta_i)$ has the following characteristics:

- When $\theta_i = 0°$, with the light perpendicular to the surface ($\mathbf{l} = \mathbf{n}$), $F(\theta_i)$ has a value that is a property of the substance. This value, F_0, can be thought of as the characteristic specular color of the substance. The case when $\theta_i = 0°$ is called *normal incidence*.

- As θ_i increases and the light strikes the surface at increasingly glancing angles, the value of $F(\theta_i)$ will tend to increase, reaching a value of 1 for all frequencies (white) at $\theta_i = 90°$.

Figure 9.20 shows the $F(\theta_i)$ function, visualized in several different ways, for several substances. The curves are highly nonlinear—they barely change until $\theta_i = 75°$ or so, and then quickly go to 1. The increase from F_0 to 1 is mostly monotonic, though some substances (e.g., aluminum in Figure 9.20) have a slight dip just before going to white.

In the case of mirror reflection, the outgoing or view angle is the same as the incidence angle. This means that surfaces that are at a glancing angle to the incoming

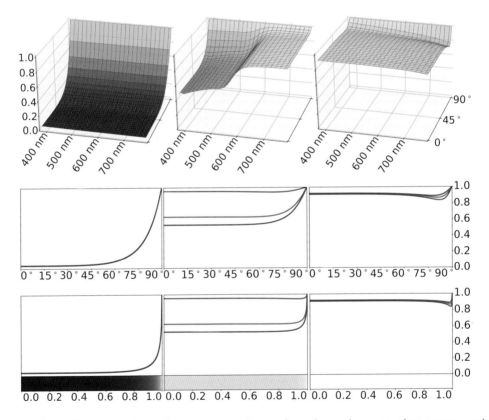

Figure 9.20. Fresnel reflectance F for external reflection from three substances: glass, copper, and aluminum (from left to right). The top row has three-dimensional plots of F as a function of wavelength and incidence angle. The second row shows the spectral value of F for each incidence angle converted to RGB and plotted as separate curves for each color channel. The curves for glass coincide, as its Fresnel reflectance is colorless. In the third row, the R, G, and B curves are plotted against the sine of the incidence angle, to account for the foreshortening shown in Figure 9.21. The same x-axis is used for the strips in the bottom row, which show the RGB values as colors.

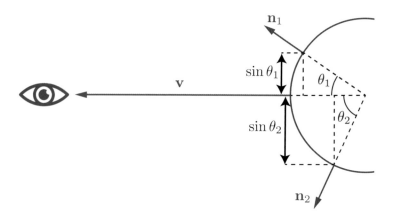

Figure 9.21. Surfaces tilted away from the eye are foreshortened. This foreshortening is consistent with projecting surface points according to the sine of the angle between $\mathbf{v}$ and $\mathbf{n}$ (for mirror reflection this is the same as the incidence angle). For this reason, Fresnel reflectance is plotted against the sine of the incidence angle in Figures 9.20 and 9.22.

light—with values of θ_i close to $90°$—are also at a glancing angle to the eye. For this reason, the increase in reflectance is primarily seen at the edges of objects. Furthermore, the parts of the surface that have the strongest increase in reflectance are foreshortened from the camera's perspective, so they occupy a relatively small number of pixels. To show the different parts of the Fresnel curve proportionally to their visual prominence, the Fresnel reflectance graphs and color bars in Figure 9.22 and the lower half of Figure 9.20 are plotted against $\sin(\theta_i)$ instead of directly against θ_i. Figure 9.21 illustrates why $\sin(\theta_i)$ is an appropriate choice of axis for this purpose.

From this point, we will typically use the notation $F(\mathbf{n},\mathbf{l})$ instead of $F(\theta_i)$ for the Fresnel function, to emphasize the vectors involved. Recall that θ_i is the angle between the vectors $\mathbf{n}$ and $\mathbf{l}$. When the Fresnel function is incorporated as part of a BRDF, a different vector is often substituted for the surface normal $\mathbf{n}$. See Section 9.8 for details.

The increase in reflectance at glancing angles is often called the *Fresnel effect* in rendering publications (in other fields, the term has a different meaning relating to transmission of radio waves). You can see the Fresnel effect for yourself with a short experiment. Take a smartphone and sit in front of a bright area, such as a computer monitor. Without turning it on, first hold the phone close to your chest, look down at it, and angle it slightly so that its screen reflects the monitor. There should be a relatively weak reflection of the monitor on the phone screen. This is because the normal-incidence reflectance of glass is quite low. Now raise the smartphone up so that it is roughly between your eyes and the monitor, and again angle its screen to

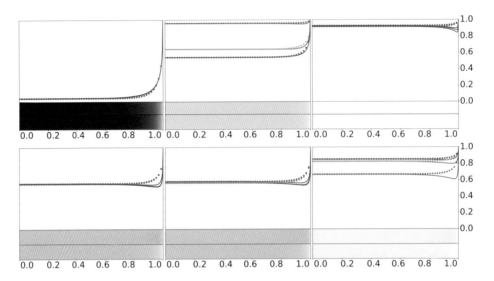

Figure 9.22. Schlick's approximation to Fresnel reflectance compared to the correct values for external reflection from six substances. The top three substances are the same as in Figure 9.20: glass, copper, and aluminum (from left to right). The bottom three substances are chromium, iron, and zinc. Each substance has an RGB curve plot with solid lines showing the full Fresnel equations and dotted lines showing Schlick's approximation. The upper color bar under each curve plot shows the result of the full Fresnel equations, and the lower color bar shows the result of Schlick's approximation.

reflect the monitor. Now the reflection of the monitor on the phone screen should be almost as bright as the monitor itself.

Besides their complexity, the Fresnel equations have other properties that makes their direct use in rendering difficult. They require refractive index values sampled over the visible spectrum, and these values may be complex numbers. The curves in Figure 9.20 suggest a simpler approach based on the characteristic specular color F_0. Schlick [1568] gives an approximation of Fresnel reflectance:

$$F(\mathbf{n}, \mathbf{l}) \approx F_0 + (1 - F_0)(1 - (\mathbf{n} \cdot \mathbf{l})^+)^5. \tag{9.16}$$

This function is an RGB interpolation between white and F_0. Despite this simplicity, the approximation is reasonably accurate.

Figure 9.22 contains several substances that diverge from the Schlick curves, exhibiting noticeable "dips" just before going to white. In fact, the substances in the bottom row were chosen because they diverge from the Schlick approximation to an especially large extent. Even for these substances the resulting errors are quite subtle, as shown by the color bars at the bottom of each plot in the figure. In the rare cases where it is important to precisely capture the behavior of such materials, an alternative approximation given by Gulbrandsen [623] can be used. This approximation can achieve a close match to the full Fresnel equations for metals, though it is more computationally expensive than Schlick's. A simpler option is to modify Schlick's approximation to allow for raising the final term to powers other than 5 (as in Equation 9.18). This would change the "sharpness" of the transition to white at 90°, which could result in a closer match. Lagarde [959] summarizes the Fresnel equations and several approximations to them.

When using the Schlick approximation, F_0 is the only parameter that controls Fresnel reflectance. This is convenient since F_0 has a well-defined range of valid values in $[0, 1]$, is easy to set with standard color-picking interfaces, and can be textured using texture formats designed for colors. In addition, reference values for F_0 are available for many real-world materials. The refractive index can also be used to compute F_0. It is typical to assume that $n_1 = 1$, a close approximation for the refractive index of air, and use n instead of n_2 to represent the refractive index of the object. This simplification gives the following equation:

$$F_0 = \left(\frac{n-1}{n+1} \right)^2 . \tag{9.17}$$

This equation works even with complex-valued refractive indices (such as those of metals) if the magnitude of the (complex) result is used. In cases where the refractive index varies significantly over the visible spectrum, computing an accurate RGB value for F_0 requires first computing F_0 at a dense sampling of wavelengths, and then converting the resulting spectral vector into RGB values using the methods described in Section 8.1.3.

In some applications [732, 947] a more general form of the Schlick approximation is used:

$$F(\mathbf{n}, \mathbf{l}) \approx F_0 + (F_{90} - F_0)(1 - (\mathbf{n} \cdot \mathbf{l})^+)^{\frac{1}{p}} . \tag{9.18}$$

This provides control over the color to which the Fresnel curve transitions at 90°, as well as the "sharpness" of the transition. The use of this more general form is typically motivated by a desire for increased artistic control, but it can also help match physical reality in some cases. As discussed above, modifying the power can lead to closer fits for certain materials. Also, setting F_{90} to a color other than white can help match materials that are not described well by the Fresnel equations, such as surfaces covered in fine dust with grains the size of individual light wavelengths.

9.5.2 Typical Fresnel Reflectance Values

Substances are divided into three main groups with respect to their optical properties. There are *dielectrics*, which are insulators; metals, which are conductors; and semiconductors, which have properties somewhere in between dielectrics and metals.

Fresnel Reflectance Values for Dielectrics
Most materials encountered in daily life are dielectrics—glass, skin, wood, hair, leather, plastic, stone, and concrete, to name a few. Water is also a dielectric. This last may be

Dielectric	Linear	Texture	Color	Notes
Water	0.02	39		
Living tissue	0.02–0.04	39–56		Watery tissues are toward the lower bound, dry ones are higher
Skin	0.028	47		
Eyes	0.025	44		Dry cornea (tears have a similar value to water)
Hair	0.046	61		
Teeth	0.058	68		
Fabric	0.04–0.056	56–67		Polyester highest, most others under 0.05
Stone	0.035–0.056	53–67		Values for the minerals most often found in stone
Plastics, glass	0.04–0.05	56–63		Not including crystal glass
Crystal glass	0.05–0.07	63–75		
Gems	0.05–0.08	63–80		Not including diamonds and diamond simulants
Diamond-like	0.13–0.2	101–124		Diamonds and diamond simulants (e.g., cubic zirconia, moissanite)

Table 9.1. Values of F_0 for external reflection from various dielectrics. Each value is given as a linear number, as a texture value (nonlinearly encoded 8-bit unsigned integer), and as a color swatch. If a range of values is given, then the color swatch is in the middle of the range. Recall that these are specular colors. For example, gems often have vivid colors, but those result from absorption inside the substance and are unrelated to their Fresnel reflectance.

surprising, since in daily life water is known to conduct electricity, but this conductivity is due to various impurities. Dielectrics have fairly low values for F_0—usually 0.06 or lower. This low reflectance at normal incidence makes the Fresnel effect especially visible for dielectrics. The optical properties of dielectrics rarely vary much over the visible spectrum, resulting in colorless reflectance values. The F_0 values for several common dielectrics are shown in Table 9.1. The values are scalar rather than RGB since the RGB channels do not differ significantly for these materials. For convenience, Table 9.1 includes linear values as well as 8-bit values encoded with the sRGB transfer function (the form that would typically be used in a texture-painting application).

The F_0 values for other dielectrics can be inferred by looking at similar substances in the table. For unknown dielectrics, 0.04 is a reasonable default value, not too far off from most common materials.

Metal	Linear	Texture	Color
Titanium	0.542,0.497,0.449	194,187,179	
Chromium	0.549,0.556,0.554	196,197,196	
Iron	0.562,0.565,0.578	198,198,200	
Nickel	0.660,0.609,0.526	212,205,192	
Platinum	0.673,0.637,0.585	214,209,201	
Copper	0.955,0.638,0.538	250,209,194	
Palladium	0.733,0.697,0.652	222,217,211	
Mercury	0.781,0.780,0.778	229,228,228	
Brass (C260)	0.910,0.778,0.423	245,228,174	
Zinc	0.664,0.824,0.850	213,234,237	
Gold	1.000,0.782,0.344	255,229,158	
Aluminum	0.913,0.922,0.924	245,246,246	
Silver	0.972,0.960,0.915	252,250,245	

Table 9.2. Values of F_0 for external reflection from various metals (and one alloy), sorted in order of increasing lightness. The actual red value for gold is slightly outside the sRGB gamut. The value shown is after clamping.

Once the light is transmitted into the dielectric, it may be further scattered or absorbed. Models for this process are discussed in more detail in Section 9.9. If the material is transparent, the light will continue until it hits an object surface "from the inside," which is detailed in Section 9.5.3.

Fresnel Reflectance Values for Metals

Metals have high values of F_0—almost always 0.5 or above. Some metals have optical properties that vary over the visible spectrum, resulting in colored reflectance values. The F_0 values for several metals are shown in Table 9.2.

Similarly to Table 9.1, Table 9.2 has linear values as well as 8-bit sRGB-encoded values for texturing. However, here we give RGB values since many metals have colored Fresnel reflectance. These RGB values are defined using the sRGB (and Rec. 709) primaries and white point. Gold has a somewhat unusual F_0 value. It is the most strongly colored, with a red channel value slightly above 1 (it is just barely outside the sRGB/Rec. 709 gamut) and an especially low blue channel value (the only value in Table 9.2 significantly below 0.5). It is also one of the brightest metals, as can be seen by its position in the table, which is sorted in order of increasing lightness. Gold's bright and strongly colored reflectance probably contributes to its unique cultural and economic significance throughout history.

Recall that metals immediately absorb any transmitted light, so they do not exhibit any subsurface scattering or transparency. All the visible color of a metal comes from F_0.

Substance	Linear	Texture	Color
Diamond	0.171,0.172,0.176	115,115,116	
Silicon	0.345,0.369,0.426	159,164,174	
Titanium	0.542,0.497,0.449	194,187,179	

Table 9.3. The value of F_0 for a representative semiconductor (silicon in crystalline form) compared to a bright dielectric (diamond) and a dark metal (titanium).

Fresnel Reflectance Values for Semiconductors

As one would expect, semiconductors have F_0 values in between the brightest dielectrics and the darkest metals, as shown in Table 9.3. It is rare to need to render such substances in practice, since most rendered scenes are not littered with blocks of crystalline silicon. For practical purposes the range of F_0 values between 0.2 and 0.45 should be avoided unless you are purposely trying to model an exotic or unrealistic material.

Fresnel Reflectance Values in Water

In our discussion of external reflectance, we have assumed that the rendered surface is surrounded by air. If not, the reflectance will change, since it depends on the ratio between the refractive indices on both sides of the interface. If we can no longer assume that $n_1 = 1$, then we need to replace n in Equation 9.17 with the relative index of refraction, n_1/n_2. This yields the following, more general equation:

$$F_0 = \left(\frac{n_1 - n_2}{n_1 + n_2}\right)^2. \tag{9.19}$$

Likely the most frequently encountered case where $n_1 \neq 1$ is when rendering underwater scenes. Since water's refractive index is about 1.33 times higher than that of air, values of F_0 are different underwater. This effect is stronger for dielectrics than for metals, as can be seen in Table 9.4.

Parameterizing Fresnel Values

An often-used parameterization combines the specular color F_0 and the diffuse color ρ_{ss} (the diffuse color will be discussed further in Section 9.9). This parameterization takes advantage of the observation that metals have no diffuse color and that dielectrics have a restricted set of possible values for F_0, and it includes an RGB surface color $\mathbf{c}_{surf}$ and a scalar parameter m, called "metallic" or "metalness." If $m = 1$, then F_0 is set to $\mathbf{c}_{surf}$ and ρ_{ss} is set to black. If $m = 0$, then F_0 is set to a dielectric value (either constant or controlled by an additional parameter) and ρ_{ss} is set to $\mathbf{c}_{surf}$.

The "metalness" parameter first appeared as part of an early shading model used at Brown University [1713], and the parameterization in its current form was first used by Pixar for the film *Wall-E* [1669]. For the *Disney principled* shading model, used in Disney animation films from *Wreck-It Ralph* onward, Burley added an additional

Substance	Linear	Texture	Color
Skin (in air)	0.028	47	
Skin (in water)	0.0007	2	
Schott K7 glass (in air)	0.042	58	
Schott K7 glass (in water)	0.004	13	
Diamond (in air)	0.172	115	
Diamond (in water)	0.084	82	
Iron (in air)	0.562,0.565,0.578	198,198,200	
Iron (in water)	0.470,0.475,0.492	182,183,186	
Gold (in air)	1.000,0.782,0.344	255,229,158	
Gold (in water)	1.000,0.747,0.261	255,224,140	
Silver (in air)	0.972,0.960,0.915	252,250,245	
Silver (in water)	0.964,0.950,0.899	251,249,243	

Table 9.4. A comparison between values of F_0 in air and in water, for various substances. As one would expect from inspecting Equation 9.19, dielectrics with refractive indices close to that of water are affected the most. In contrast, metals are barely affected.

scalar "specular" parameter to control dielectric F_0 within a limited range [214]. This form of the parameterization is used in the Unreal Engine [861], and the Frostbite engine uses a slightly different form with a larger range of possible F_0 values for dielectrics [960]. The game *Call of Duty: Infinite Warfare* uses a variant that packs these metalness and specular parameters into a single value [384], to save memory.

For those rendering applications that use this metalness parameterization instead of using F_0 and ρ_{ss} directly, the motivations include user convenience and saving texture or G-buffer storage. In the game *Call of Duty: Infinite Warfare*, this parameterization is used in an unusual way. Artists paint textures for F_0 and ρ_{ss}, which are automatically converted to the metalness parameterization as a compression method.

Using metalness has some drawbacks. It cannot express some types of materials, such as coated dielectrics with tinted F_0 values. Artifacts can occur on the boundary between a metal and dielectric [960, 1163].

Another parameterization trick used by some real-time applications takes advantage of the fact that no materials have values of F_0 lower than 0.02, outside of special anti-reflective coatings. The trick is used to suppress specular highlights in surface areas that represent cavities or voids. Instead of using a separate specular occlusion texture, values of F_0 below 0.02 are used to "turn off" Fresnel edge brightening. This technique was first proposed by Schüler [1586] and is used in the Unreal [861] and Frostbite [960] engines.

9.5.3 Internal Reflection

Although external reflection is more frequently encountered in rendering, internal reflection is sometimes important as well. Internal reflection happens when $n_1 > n_2$. In

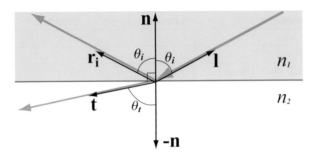

Figure 9.23. Internal reflection at a planar surface, where $n_1 > n_2$.

other words, internal reflection occurs when light is traveling in the interior of a transparent object and encounters the object's surface "from the inside." See Figure 9.23.

Snell's law indicates that, for internal reflection, $\sin\theta_t > \sin\theta_i$. Since these values are both between $0°$ and $90°$, this relationship also implies $\theta_t > \theta_i$, as seen in Figure 9.23. In the case of external reflection the opposite is true—compare this behavior to Figure 9.9 on page 302. This difference is key to understanding how internal and external reflection differ. In external reflection, a valid (smaller) value of $\sin\theta_t$ exists for every possible value of $\sin\theta_i$ between 0 and 1. The same is not true for internal reflection. For values of θ_i greater than a *critical angle* θ_c, Snell's law implies that $\sin\theta_t > 1$, which is impossible. What happens in reality is that there is no θ_t. When $\theta_i > \theta_c$, no transmission occurs, and all the incoming light is reflected. This phenomenon is known as *total internal reflection*.

The Fresnel equations are symmetrical, in the sense that the incoming and transmission vectors can be switched and the reflectance remains the same. In combination with Snell's law, this symmetry implies that the $F(\theta_i)$ curve for internal reflection will resemble a "compressed" version of the curve for external reflection. The value of F_0 is the same for both cases, and the internal reflection curve reaches perfect reflectance at θ_c instead of at $90°$. This is shown in Figure 9.24, which also shows that, on average, reflectance is higher in the case of internal reflection. For example, this is why air bubbles seen underwater have a highly reflective, silvery appearance.

Internal reflection occurs only in dielectrics, as metals and semiconductors quickly absorb any light propagating inside them [285, 286]. Since dielectrics have real-valued refractive indices, computation of the critical angle from the refractive indices or from F_0 is straightforward:

$$\sin\theta_c = \frac{n_2}{n_1} = \frac{1 - \sqrt{F_0}}{1 + \sqrt{F_0}}. \tag{9.20}$$

The Schlick approximation shown in Equation 9.16 is correct for external reflection. It can be used for internal reflection by substituting the transmission angle θ_t for θ_i. If the transmission direction vector $\mathbf{t}$ has been computed (e.g., for rendering refractions—see Section 14.5.2), it can be used for finding θ_t. Otherwise Snell's law could be used

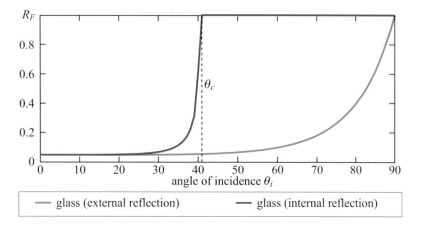

Figure 9.24. Comparison of internal and external reflectance curves at a glass-air interface. The internal reflectance curve goes to 1.0 at the critical angle θ_c.

to compute θ_t from θ_i, but that is expensive and requires the index of refraction, which may not be available.

9.6 Microgeometry

As we discussed earlier in Section 9.1.3, surface irregularities much smaller than a pixel cannot feasibly be modeled explicitly, so the BRDF instead models their aggregate effect statistically. For now we keep to the domain of geometrical optics, which assumes that these irregularities either are smaller than a light wavelength (and so have no effect on the light's behavior) or are much larger. The effects of irregularities that are in the "wave optics domain" (around 1–100 wavelengths in size) will be discussed in Section 9.11.

Each visible surface point contains many microsurface normals that bounce the reflected light in different directions. Since the orientations of individual microfacets are somewhat random, it makes sense to model them as a statistical distribution. For most surfaces, the distribution of microgeometry surface normals is continuous, with a strong peak at the macroscopic surface normal. The "tightness" of this distribution is determined by the surface roughness. The rougher the surface, the more "spread out" the microgeometry normals will be.

The visible effect of increasing microscale roughness is greater blurring of reflected environmental detail. In the case of small, bright light sources, this blurring results in broader and dimmer specular highlights. Those from rougher surfaces are dimmer because the light energy is spread into a wider cone of directions. This phenomenon can be seen in the photographs in Figure 9.12 on page 305.

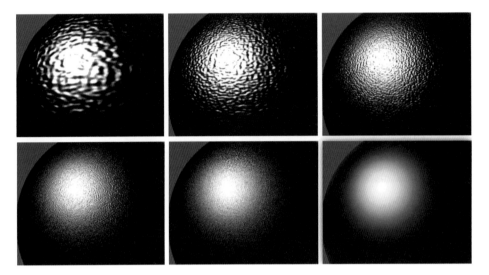

Figure 9.25. Gradual transition from visible detail to microscale. The sequence of images goes top row left to right, then bottom row left to right. The surface shape and lighting are constant. Only the scale of the surface detail changes.

Figure 9.25 shows how visible reflectance results from the aggregate reflections of the individual microscale surface details. The series of images shows a curved surface lit by a single light, with bumps that steadily decrease in scale until in the last image the bumps are much smaller than a single pixel. Statistical patterns in the many small highlights eventually become details in the shape of the resulting aggregate highlight. For example, the relative sparsity of individual bump highlights in the periphery becomes the relative darkness of the aggregate highlight away from its center.

For most surfaces, the distribution of the microscale surface normals is *isotropic*, meaning it is rotationally symmetrical, lacking any inherent directionality. Other surfaces have microscale structure that is *anisotropic*. Such surfaces have anisotropic surface normal distributions, leading to directional blurring of reflections and highlights. See Figure 9.26.

Some surfaces have highly structured microgeometry, resulting in a variety of microscale normal distributions and surface appearances. Fabrics are a commonly encountered example—the unique appearance of velvet and satin is due to the structure of their microgeometry [78]. Fabric models will be discussed in Section 9.10.

Although multiple surface normals are the primary effect of microgeometry on reflectance, other effects can also be important. *Shadowing* refers to occlusion of the light source by microscale surface detail, as shown on the left side of Figure 9.27. *Masking*, where some facets hide others from the camera, is shown in the center of the figure.

Figure 9.26. On the left, an anisotropic surface (brushed metal). Note the directional blurring of reflections. On the right, a photomicrograph showing a similar surface. Note the directionality of the detail. *(Photomicrograph courtesy of the Program of Computer Graphics, Cornell University.)*

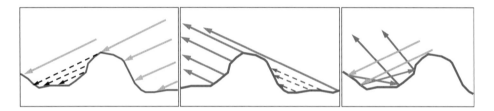

Figure 9.27. Geometrical effects of microscale structure. On the left, the black dashed arrows indicate an area that is shadowed (occluded from the light) by other microgeometry. In the center, the red dashed arrows indicate an area that is masked (occluded from view) by other microgeometry. On the right, interreflection of light between the microscale structures is shown.

If there is a correlation between the microgeometry height and the surface normal, then shadowing and masking can effectively change the normal distribution. For example, imagine a surface where the raised parts have been smoothed by weathering or other processes, and the lower parts remain rough. At glancing angles, the lower parts of the surface will tend to be shadowed or masked, resulting in an effectively smoother surface. See Figure 9.28.

For all surface types, the visible size of the surface irregularities decreases as the incoming angle θ_i to the normal increases. At extremely glancing angles, this effect can decrease the viewed size of the irregularities to be shorter than the light's wavelength, making them "disappear" as far as the light response is concerned. These two effects combine with the Fresnel effect to make surfaces appear highly reflective and mirror-like as the viewing and lighting angles approach 90° [79, 1873, 1874].

Confirm this for yourself. Roll a sheet of non-shiny paper into a long tube. Instead of looking through the hole, move your eye slightly higher, so you are looking down its

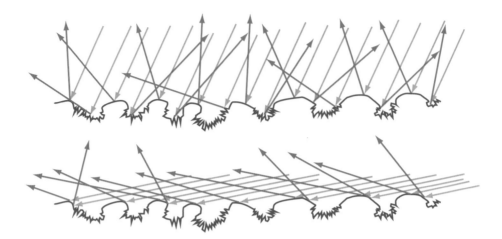

Figure 9.28. The microgeometry shown has a strong correlation between height and surface normal, where the raised areas are smooth and lower areas are rough. In the top image, the surface is illuminated from an angle close to the macroscopic surface normal. At this angle, the rough pits are accessible to many of the incoming light rays, and so many rays are scattered in different directions. In the bottom image, the surface is illuminated from a glancing angle. Shadowing blocks most of the pits, so few light rays hit them, and most rays are reflected from the smooth parts of the surface. In this case, the apparent roughness depends strongly on the angle of illumination.

length. Point your tube toward a brightly lit window or computer screen. With your view angle nearly parallel to the paper you will see a sharp reflection of the window or screen in the paper. The angle has to be extremely close to 90° to see the effect.

Light that was occluded by microscale surface detail does not disappear. It is reflected, possibly onto other microgeometry. Light may undergo multiple bounces in this way before it reaches the eye. Such interreflections are shown on the right side of Figure 9.27. Since the light is being attenuated by the Fresnel reflectance at each bounce, interreflections tend to be subtle in dielectrics. In metals, multiple-bounce reflection is the source of any visible diffuse reflection, since metals lack subsurface scattering. Multiple-bounce reflections from colored metals are more deeply colored than the primary reflection, since they are the result of light interacting with the surface multiple times.

So far we have discussed the effects of microgeometry on specular reflectance, i.e., the surface reflectance. In certain cases, microscale surface detail can affect subsurface reflectance as well. If the microgeometry irregularities are larger than the subsurface scattering distances, then shadowing and masking can cause a *retroreflection* effect, where light is preferentially reflected back toward the incoming direction. This effect occurs because shadowing and masking will occlude lit areas when the viewing and lighting directions differ greatly. See Figure 9.29. Retroreflection tends to give rough surfaces a flat appearance. See Figure 9.30.

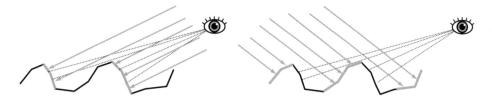

Figure 9.29. Retroreflection due to microscale roughness. Both figures show a rough surface with low Fresnel reflectance and high scattering albedo, so subsurface reflectance is visually important. On the left, the viewing and lighting directions are similar. The parts of the microgeometry that are brightly lit are also the ones that are most visible, leading to a bright appearance. On the right, the viewing and lighting directions differ greatly. In this case, the brightly lit areas are occluded from view and the visible areas are shadowed, leading to a darker appearance.

Figure 9.30. Photographs of two objects exhibiting non-Lambertian, retroreflective behavior due to microscale surface roughness. *(Photograph on the right courtesy of Peter-Pike Sloan.)*

9.7 Microfacet Theory

Many BRDF models are based on a mathematical analysis of the effects of microgeometry on reflectance called *microfacet theory*. This tool was first developed by researchers in the optics community [124]. It was introduced to computer graphics in 1977 by Blinn [159] and again in 1981 by Cook and Torrance [285]. The theory is based on the modeling of microgeometry as a collection of *microfacets*.

Each of these tiny facets is flat, with a single microfacet normal $\mathbf{m}$. The microfacets individually reflect light according to the micro-BRDF $f_\mu(\mathbf{l}, \mathbf{v}, \mathbf{m})$, with the combined reflectance across all the microfacets adding up to the overall surface BRDF. The usual choice is for each microfacet to be a perfect Fresnel mirror, resulting in a specular microfacet BRDF for modeling surface reflection. However, other choices are possible. Diffuse micro-BRDFs have been used to create several local subsurface scattering models [574, 657, 709, 1198, 1337]. A diffraction micro-BRDF was used to create a shading model combining geometrical and wave optics effects [763].

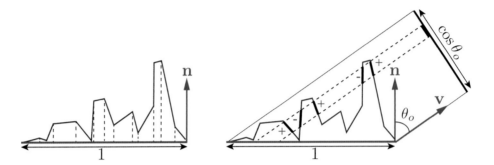

Figure 9.31. Side view of a microsurface. On the left, we see that integrating $D(\mathbf{m})(\mathbf{n} \cdot \mathbf{m})$, the microfacet areas projected onto the macrosurface plane, yields the area (length, in this side view) of the macrosurface, which is 1 by convention. On the right, integrating $D(\mathbf{m})(\mathbf{v} \cdot \mathbf{m})$, the microfacet areas projected onto the plane perpendicular to $\mathbf{v}$, yields the projection of the macrosurface onto that plane, which is $\cos \theta_o$ or $(\mathbf{v} \cdot \mathbf{n})$. When the projections of multiple microfacets overlap, the negative projected areas of the backfacing microfacets cancel out the "extra" frontfacing microfacets. *(After a figure by Matej Drame.)*

An important property of a microfacet model is the statistical distribution of the microfacet normals $\mathbf{m}$. This distribution is defined by the surface's *normal distribution function*, or NDF. Some references use the term *distribution of normals* to avoid confusion with the Gaussian normal distribution. We will use $D(\mathbf{m})$ to refer to the NDF in equations.

The NDF $D(\mathbf{m})$ is the statistical distribution of microfacet surface normals over the microgeometry surface area [708]. Integrating $D(\mathbf{m})$ over the entire sphere of microfacet normals gives the area of the microsurface. More usefully, integrating $D(\mathbf{m})(\mathbf{n} \cdot \mathbf{m})$, the projection of $D(\mathbf{m})$ onto the macrosurface plane, gives the area of the macrosurface patch that is equal to 1 by convention, as shown on the left side of Figure 9.31. In other words, the projection $D(\mathbf{m})(\mathbf{n} \cdot \mathbf{m})$ is normalized:

$$\int_{\mathbf{m} \in \Theta} D(\mathbf{m})(\mathbf{n} \cdot \mathbf{m}) d\mathbf{m} = 1. \tag{9.21}$$

The integral is over the entire sphere, represented here by Θ, unlike previous spherical integrals in this chapter that integrated over only the hemisphere centered on $\mathbf{n}$, represented by Ω. This notation is used in most graphics publications, though some references [708] use Ω to denote the complete sphere. In practice, most microstructure models used in graphics are heightfields, which means that $D(\mathbf{m}) = 0$ for all directions $\mathbf{m}$ outside Ω. However, Equation 9.21 is valid for non-heightfield microstructures as well.

More generally, the projections of the microsurface and macrosurface onto the plane perpendicular to any view direction $\mathbf{v}$ are equal:

$$\int_{\mathbf{m} \in \Theta} D(\mathbf{m})(\mathbf{v} \cdot \mathbf{m}) d\mathbf{m} = \mathbf{v} \cdot \mathbf{n}. \tag{9.22}$$

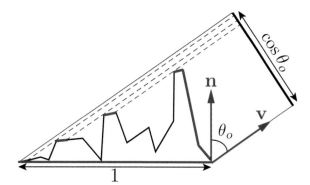

Figure 9.32. Integrating the projected areas of the visible microfacets (in bright red) yields the projected area of the macrosurface onto the plane perpendicular to **v**.

The dot products in Equations 9.21 and 9.22 are not clamped to 0. The right side of Figure 9.31 shows why. Equations 9.21 and 9.22 impose constraints that the function $D(\mathbf{m})$ must obey to be a valid NDF.

Intuitively, the NDF is like a histogram of the microfacet normals. It has high values in directions where the microfacet normals are more likely to be pointing. Most surfaces have NDFs that show a strong peak at the macroscopic surface normal **n**. Section 9.8.1 will cover several NDF models used in rendering.

Take a second look at the right side of Figure 9.31. Although there are many microfacets with overlapping projections, ultimately for rendering we care about only the visible microfacets, i.e., the microfacets that are closest to the camera in each overlapping set. This fact suggests an alternative way of relating the projected microfacet areas to the projected macrogeometry area: The sum of the projected areas of the visible microfacets is equal to the projected area of the macrosurface. We can express this mathematically by defining the *masking function* $G_1(\mathbf{m}, \mathbf{v})$, which gives the fraction of microfacets with normal **m** that are visible along the view vector **v**. The integral of $G_1(\mathbf{m}, \mathbf{v})D(\mathbf{m})(\mathbf{v} \cdot \mathbf{m})^+$ over the sphere then gives the area of the macrosurface projected onto the plane perpendicular to **v**:

$$\int_{\in \Theta} G_1(\mathbf{m}, \mathbf{v})D(\mathbf{m})(\mathbf{v} \cdot \mathbf{m})^+ d\mathbf{m} = \mathbf{v} \cdot \mathbf{n}, \qquad (9.23)$$

as shown in Figure 9.32. Unlike Equation 9.22, the dot product in Equation 9.23 is clamped to zero. This operation is shown with the x^+ notation introduced in Section 1.2. Backfacing microfacets are not visible, so they are not counted in this case. The product $G_1(\mathbf{m}, \mathbf{v})D(\mathbf{m})$ is the *distribution of visible normals* [708].

While Equation 9.23 imposes a constraint on $G_1(\mathbf{m}, \mathbf{v})$, it does not uniquely determine it. There are infinite functions that satisfy the constraint for a given microfacet normal distribution $D(\mathbf{m})$ [708]. This is because $D(\mathbf{m})$ does not fully specify the microsurface. It tells us how many of the microfacets have normals pointing in certain directions, but not how they are arranged.

Although various G_1 functions have been proposed over the years, the dilemma as to which one to use has been solved (at least for now) in an excellent paper by Heitz [708]. Heitz discusses the Smith masking function, which was initially derived for Gaussian normal distributions [1665] and later generalized to arbitrary NDFs [202]. Heitz shows that out of the masking functions proposed in the literature, only two—the Smith function and the Torrance-Sparrow "V-cavity" function [1779]—obey Equation 9.23 and are thus mathematically valid. He further shows that the Smith function is a much closer match to the behavior of random microsurfaces than the Torrance-Sparrow function. Heitz also proves that the Smith masking function is the only possible function that both obeys Equation 9.23 and possesses the convenient property of *normal-masking independence*. This means that the value of $G_1(\mathbf{m}, \mathbf{v})$ does not depend on the direction of $\mathbf{m}$ as long as $\mathbf{m}$ is not backfacing i.e., as long as $\mathbf{m} \cdot \mathbf{v} \geq 0$. The Smith G_1 function has the following form:

$$G_1(\mathbf{m}, \mathbf{v}) = \frac{\chi^+(\mathbf{m} \cdot \mathbf{v})}{1 + \Lambda(\mathbf{v})}, \tag{9.24}$$

where $\chi^+(x)$ is the positive characteristic function

$$\chi^+(x) = \begin{cases} 1, & \text{where } x > 0, \\ 0, & \text{where } x \leq 0. \end{cases} \tag{9.25}$$

The Λ (lambda) function differs for each NDF. The procedure to derive Λ for a given NDF is described in publications by Walter et al. [1833] and Heitz [708].

The Smith masking function does have some drawbacks. From a theoretical standpoint, its requirements are not consistent with the structure of actual surfaces [708], and may even be physically impossible to realize [657]. From a practical standpoint, while it is quite accurate for random surfaces, its accuracy is expected to decrease for surfaces with a stronger dependency between normal direction and masking, such as the surface shown in Figure 9.28, especially if the surface has some repetitive structure (as do most fabrics). Nevertheless, until a better alternative is found, it is the best option for most rendering applications.

Given a microgeometry description including a micro-BRDF $f_\mu(\mathbf{l}, \mathbf{v}, \mathbf{m})$, normal distribution function $D(\mathbf{m})$, and masking function $G_1(\mathbf{m}, \mathbf{v})$, the overall macrosurface BRDF can be derived [708, 1833]:

$$f(\mathbf{l}, \mathbf{v}) = \int_{\mathbf{m} \in \Omega} f_\mu(\mathbf{l}, \mathbf{v}, \mathbf{m}) G_2(\mathbf{l}, \mathbf{v}, \mathbf{m}) D(\mathbf{m}) \frac{(\mathbf{m} \cdot \mathbf{l})^+}{|\mathbf{n} \cdot \mathbf{l}|} \frac{(\mathbf{m} \cdot \mathbf{v})^+}{|\mathbf{n} \cdot \mathbf{v}|} d\mathbf{m}. \tag{9.26}$$

This integral is over the hemisphere Ω centered on $\mathbf{n}$, to avoid collecting light contributions from under the surface. Instead of the masking function $G_1(\mathbf{m}, \mathbf{v})$, Equation 9.26 uses the *joint masking-shadowing function* $G_2(\mathbf{l}, \mathbf{v}, \mathbf{m})$. This function, derived from

G_1, gives the fraction of microfacets with normal $\mathbf{m}$ that are visible from two directions: the view vector $\mathbf{v}$ and the light vector $\mathbf{l}$. By including the G_2 function, Equation 9.26 enables the BRDF to account for masking as well as shadowing, but not for interreflection between microfacets (see Figure 9.27 on page 329). The lack of microfacet interreflection is a limitation shared by all BRDFs derived from Equation 9.26. Such BRDFs are somewhat too dark as a result. In Sections 9.8.2 and 9.9, we will discuss some methods that have been proposed to address this limitation.

Heitz [708] discusses several versions of the G_2 function. The simplest is the separable form, where masking and shadowing are evaluated separately using G_1 and multiplied together:

$$G_2(\mathbf{l}, \mathbf{v}, \mathbf{m}) = G_1(\mathbf{v}, \mathbf{m})G_1(\mathbf{l}, \mathbf{m}). \tag{9.27}$$

This form is equivalent to assuming that masking and shadowing are uncorrelated events. In reality they are not, and the assumption causes over-darkening in BRDFs using this form of G_2.

As an extreme example, consider the case when the view and light directions are the same. In this case G_2 should be equal to G_1, since none of the visible facets are shadowed, but with Equation 9.27 G_2 will be equal to G_1^2 instead.

If the microsurface is a heightfield, which is typically the case for microsurface models used in rendering, then whenever the relative azimuth angle ϕ between $\mathbf{v}$ and $\mathbf{l}$ is equal to $0°$, $G_2(\mathbf{l}, \mathbf{v}, \mathbf{m})$ should be equal to $\min(G_1(\mathbf{v}, \mathbf{m}), G_1(\mathbf{l}, \mathbf{m}))$. See Figure 9.17 on page 311 for an illustration of ϕ. This relationship suggests a general way to account for correlation between masking and shadowing that can be used with any G_1 function:

$$G_2(\mathbf{l}, \mathbf{v}, \mathbf{m}) = \lambda(\phi)G_1(\mathbf{v}, \mathbf{m})G_1(\mathbf{l}, \mathbf{m}) + (1 - \lambda(\phi))\min(G_1(\mathbf{v}, \mathbf{m}), G_1(\mathbf{l}, \mathbf{m})), \tag{9.28}$$

where $\lambda(\phi)$ is some function that increases from 0 to 1 as the angle ϕ increases. Ashikhmin et al. [78] suggested a Gaussian with a standard deviation of $15°$ (~ 0.26 radians):

$$\lambda(\phi) = 1 - e^{-7.3\phi^2}. \tag{9.29}$$

A different λ function was proposed by van Ginneken et al. [534]:

$$\lambda(\phi) = \frac{4.41\phi}{4.41\phi + 1}. \tag{9.30}$$

Regardless of the relative alignment of the light and view directions, there is another reason that masking and shadowing at a given surface point are correlated. Both are related to the point's height relative to the rest of the surface. The probability of masking increases for lower points, and so does the probability of shadowing. If the Smith masking function is used, this correlation can be precisely accounted for by the *Smith height-correlated masking-shadowing function*:

$$G_2(\mathbf{l}, \mathbf{v}, \mathbf{m}) = \frac{\chi^+(\mathbf{m} \cdot \mathbf{v})\chi^+(\mathbf{m} \cdot \mathbf{l})}{1 + \Lambda(\mathbf{v}) + \Lambda(\mathbf{l})}. \tag{9.31}$$

Heitz also describes a form of Smith G_2 that combines direction and height correlation:

$$G_2(\mathbf{l}, \mathbf{v}, \mathbf{m}) = \frac{\chi^+(\mathbf{m} \cdot \mathbf{v})\chi^+(\mathbf{m} \cdot \mathbf{l})}{1 + \max(\Lambda(\mathbf{v}), \Lambda(\mathbf{l})) + \lambda(\mathbf{v}, \mathbf{l}) \min(\Lambda(\mathbf{v}), \Lambda(\mathbf{l}))}, \qquad (9.32)$$

where the function $\lambda(\mathbf{v}, \mathbf{l})$ could be an empirical function such as the ones in Equations 9.29 and 9.30, or one derived specifically for a given NDF [707].

Out of these alternatives, Heitz [708] recommends the height-correlated form of the Smith function (Equation 9.31) since it has a similar cost to the uncorrelated form and better accuracy. This form is the most widely used in practice [861, 947, 960], though some practitioners use the separable form (Equation 9.27) [214, 1937].

The general microfacet BRDF (Equation 9.26) is not used directly for rendering. It is used to derive a closed-form solution (exact or approximate) given a specific choice of micro-BRDF f_μ. The first example of this type of derivation will be shown in the next section.

9.8 BRDF Models for Surface Reflection

With few exceptions, the specular BRDF terms used in physically based rendering are derived from microfacet theory. In the case of specular surface reflection, each microfacet is a perfectly smooth Fresnel mirror. Recall that such mirrors reflect each incoming ray of light in a single reflected direction. This means that the micro-BRDF $f_\mu(\mathbf{l}, \mathbf{v}, \mathbf{m})$ for each facet is equal to zero unless $\mathbf{v}$ is parallel to the reflection of $\mathbf{l}$. For given $\mathbf{l}$ and $\mathbf{v}$ vectors, this configuration is equivalent to the case where the microfacet normal $\mathbf{m}$ is aligned with a vector pointing exactly halfway between $\mathbf{l}$ and $\mathbf{v}$. This vector is the *half vector* $\mathbf{h}$. See Figure 9.33. It is computed by adding $\mathbf{v}$ and $\mathbf{l}$ and normalizing the result:

$$\mathbf{h} = \frac{\mathbf{l} + \mathbf{v}}{\|\mathbf{l} + \mathbf{v}\|}. \qquad (9.33)$$

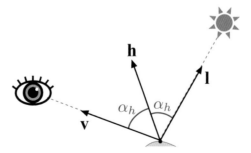

Figure 9.33. The half vector $\mathbf{h}$ forms equal angles (shown in red) with the light and view vectors.

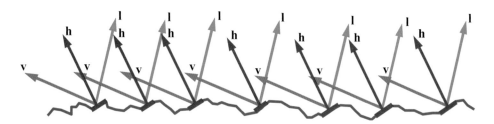

Figure 9.34. Surface composed of microfacets. Only the red microfacets, which have their surface normal aligned with the half vector **h**, participate in the reflection of light from the incoming light vector **l** to the view vector **v**.

When deriving a specular microfacet model from Equation 9.26, the fact that the Fresnel mirror micro-BRDF $f_\mu(\mathbf{l}, \mathbf{v}, \mathbf{m})$ is equal to zero for all $\mathbf{m} \neq \mathbf{h}$ is convenient, since it collapses the integral into an evaluation of the integrated function at $\mathbf{m} = \mathbf{h}$. Doing so yields the specular BRDF term

$$f_{\text{spec}}(\mathbf{l}, \mathbf{v}) = \frac{F(\mathbf{h}, \mathbf{l})G_2(\mathbf{l}, \mathbf{v}, \mathbf{h})D(\mathbf{h})}{4|\mathbf{n} \cdot \mathbf{l}||\mathbf{n} \cdot \mathbf{v}|}. \tag{9.34}$$

Details on the derivation can be found in publications by Walter et al. [1833], Heitz [708], and Hammon [657]. Hammon also shows a method to optimize the BRDF implementation by calculating $\mathbf{n} \cdot \mathbf{h}$ and $\mathbf{l} \cdot \mathbf{h}$ without calculating the vector $\mathbf{h}$ itself.

We use the notation f_{spec} for the BRDF term in Equation 9.34 to denote that it models only surface (specular) reflection. In a full BRDF, it will likely be paired with an additional term that models subsurface (diffuse) shading. To provide some intuition on Equation 9.34, consider that only those microfacets that happen to have their normals aligned with the half vector ($\mathbf{m} = \mathbf{h}$) are correctly oriented to reflect light from $\mathbf{l}$ into $\mathbf{v}$. See Figure 9.34. Thus, the amount of reflected light depends on the concentration of microfacets with normals equal to $\mathbf{h}$. This value is given by $D(\mathbf{h})$, the fraction of those microfacets that are visible from both the light and view directions, which is equal to $G_2(\mathbf{l}, \mathbf{v}, \mathbf{h})$, and the portion of light reflected by each of those microfacets, which is specified by $F(\mathbf{h}, \mathbf{l})$. In the evaluation of the Fresnel function, the vector $\mathbf{h}$ substitutes for the surface normal, e.g., when evaluating the Schlick approximation in Equation 9.16 on page 320.

The use of the half vector in the masking-shadowing function allows for a minor simplification. Since the angles involved can never be greater than $90°$, the χ^+ terms in Equations 9.24, 9.31, and 9.32 can be removed.

9.8.1 Normal Distribution Functions

The normal distribution function has a significant effect on the appearance of the rendered surface. The shape of the NDF, as plotted on the sphere of microfacet normals, determines the width and shape of the cone of reflected rays (the specular

Figure 9.35. The images on the left are rendered with the non-physical Phong reflection model. This model's specular lobe is rotationally symmetrical around the reflection vector. Such BRDFs were often used in the early days of computer graphics. The images in the center are rendered with a physically based microfacet BRDF. The top left and center show a planar surface lit at a glancing angle. The top left shows an incorrect round highlight, while the center displays the characteristic highlight elongation on the microfacet BRDF. This center view matches reality, as shown in the photographs on the right. The difference in highlight shape is far more subtle on the sphere shown in the lower two rendered images, since in this case the surface curvature is the dominating factor for the highlight shape. *(Photographs courtesy of Elan Ruskin.)*

lobe), which in turn determines the size and shape of specular highlights. The NDF affects the overall perception of surface roughness, as well as more subtle visual aspects such as whether highlights have a distinct edge or are surrounded by haze.

However, the specular lobe is not a simple copy of the NDF shape. It, and thus the highlight shape, is distorted to a greater or lesser degree depending on surface curvature and view angle. This distortion is especially strong for flat surfaces viewed at glancing angles, as shown in Figure 9.35. Ngan et al. [1271] present an analysis of the reason behind this distortion.

Isotropic Normal Distribution Functions

Most NDFs used in rendering are *isotropic*—rotationally symmetrical about the macroscopic surface normal $\mathbf{n}$. In this case, the NDF is a function of just one variable, the angle θ_m between $\mathbf{n}$ and the microfacet normal $\mathbf{m}$. Ideally, the NDF can be written as expressions of $\cos\theta_m$ that can be computed efficiently as the dot product of $\mathbf{n}$ and $\mathbf{m}$.

The Beckmann NDF [124] was the normal distribution used in the first microfacet models developed by the optics community. It is still widely used in that community today. It is also the NDF chosen for the Cook-Torrance BRDF [285, 286]. The normalized Beckmann distribution has the following form:

$$D(\mathbf{m}) = \frac{\chi^+(\mathbf{n}\cdot\mathbf{m})}{\pi\alpha_b^2(\mathbf{n}\cdot\mathbf{m})^4}\exp\left(\frac{(\mathbf{n}\cdot\mathbf{m})^2-1}{\alpha_b^2(\mathbf{n}\cdot\mathbf{m})^2}\right).\tag{9.35}$$

The term $\chi^+(\mathbf{n}\cdot\mathbf{m})$ ensures that the value of the NDF is 0 for all microfacet normals that point under the macrosurface. This property tells us that this NDF, like all the other NDFs we will discuss in this section, describes a heightfield microsurface. The α_b parameter controls the surface roughness. It is proportional to the root mean square (RMS) slope of the microgeometry surface, so $\alpha_b = 0$ represents a perfectly smooth surface.

To derive the Smith G_2 function for the Beckmann NDF, we need the corresponding Λ function, to plug into Equation 9.24 (if using the separable form of G_2), 9.31 (for the height correlated form), or 9.32 (for the direction and height correlated form).

The Beckmann NDF is *shape-invariant*, which simplifies the derivation of Λ. As defined by Heitz [708], an isotropic NDF is shape-invariant if the effect of its roughness parameter is equivalent to scaling (stretching) the microsurface. Shape-invariant NDFs can be written in the following form:

$$D(\mathbf{m}) = \frac{\chi^+(\mathbf{n} \cdot \mathbf{m})}{\alpha^2 (\mathbf{n} \cdot \mathbf{m})^4} \, g\left(\frac{\sqrt{1 - (\mathbf{n} \cdot \mathbf{m})^2}}{\alpha(\mathbf{n} \cdot \mathbf{m})} \right), \tag{9.36}$$

where g represents an arbitrary univariate function. For an arbitrary isotropic NDF, the Λ function depends on two variables. The first is the roughness α, and the second is the incidence angle of the vector ($\mathbf{v}$ or $\mathbf{l}$) for which Λ is computed. However, for a shape-invariant NDF, the Λ function depends only on the variable a:

$$a = \frac{\mathbf{n} \cdot \mathbf{s}}{\alpha \sqrt{1 - (\mathbf{n} \cdot \mathbf{s})^2}}, \tag{9.37}$$

where $\mathbf{s}$ is a vector representing either $\mathbf{v}$ or $\mathbf{l}$. The fact that Λ depends on only one variable in this case is convenient for implementation. Univariate functions can be more easily fitted with approximating curves, and can be tabulated in one-dimensional arrays.

The Λ function for the Beckmann NDF is

$$\Lambda(a) = \frac{\mathrm{erf}(a) - 1}{2} + \frac{1}{2a\sqrt{\pi}} \exp(-a^2). \tag{9.38}$$

Equation 9.38 is expensive to evaluate since it includes erf, the error function. For this reason, an approximation [1833] is typically used instead:

$$\Lambda(a) \approx \begin{cases} \frac{1 - 1.259a + 0.396a^2}{3.535a + 2.181a^2}, & \text{where } a < 1.6, \\ 0, & \text{where } a \geq 1.6. \end{cases} \tag{9.39}$$

The next NDF we will discuss is the Blinn-Phong NDF. It was widely used in computer graphics in the past, though in recent times it has been largely superseded by other distributions. The Blinn-Phong NDF is still used in cases where computation is at a premium (e.g., on mobile hardware) because it is less expensive to compute than the other NDFs discussed in this section.

The Blinn-Phong NDF was derived by Blinn [159] as a modification of the (non-physically based) Phong shading model [1414]:

$$D(\mathbf{m}) = \chi^+(\mathbf{n} \cdot \mathbf{m}) \frac{\alpha_p + 2}{2\pi} (\mathbf{n} \cdot \mathbf{m})^{\alpha_p}. \tag{9.40}$$

The power α_p is the roughness parameter of the Phong NDF. High values represent smooth surfaces and low values represent rough ones. The values of α_p can go arbitrarily high for extremely smooth surfaces—a perfect mirror would require $\alpha_p = \infty$. A maximally random surface (uniform NDF) can be achieved by setting α_p to 0. The α_p parameter is not convenient to manipulate directly since its visual impact is highly nonuniform. Small numerical changes have large visual effects for small α_p values, but large values can be changed significantly without much visual impact. For this reason, α_p is typically derived from a user-manipulated parameter via a nonlinear mapping. For example, $\alpha_p = m^s$, where s is a parameter value between 0 and 1 and m is an upper bound for α_p in a given application. This mapping was used by several games, including *Call of Duty: Black Ops*, where m was set to a value of 8192 [998].

Such "interface mappings" are generally useful when the behavior of a BRDF parameter is not perceptually uniform. These mappings are used to interpret parameters set via sliders or painted in textures.

Equivalent values for the Beckmann and Blinn-Phong roughness parameters can be found using the relation $\alpha_p = 2\alpha_b^{-2} - 2$ [1833]. When the parameters are matched in this way, the two distributions are quite close, especially for relatively smooth surfaces, as can be seen in the upper left of Figure 9.36.

The Blinn-Phong NDF is not shape-invariant, and an analytic form does not exist for its Λ function. Walter et al. [1833] suggest using the Beckmann Λ function in conjunction with the $\alpha_p = 2\alpha_b^{-2} - 2$ parameter equivalence.

In the same 1977 paper [159] in which Blinn adapted the Phong shading function into a microfacet NDF, he proposed two other NDFs. Of these three distributions, Blinn recommended one derived by Trowbridge and Reitz [1788]. This recommendation was not widely heeded, but 30 years later the Trowbridge-Reitz distribution was independently rediscovered by Walter et al. [1833], who named it the *GGX distribution*. This time, the seed took root. Within a few years, adoption of the GGX distribution started spreading across the film [214, 1133] and game [861, 960] industries, and today it likely is the most often-used distribution in both. Blinn's recommendation appears to have been 30 years ahead of its time. Although "Trowbridge-Reitz distribution" is technically the correct name, we use the GGX name in this book since it is firmly established.

The GGX distribution is

$$D(\mathbf{m}) = \frac{\chi^+(\mathbf{n} \cdot \mathbf{m})\alpha_g^2}{\pi \left(1 + (\mathbf{n} \cdot \mathbf{m})^2 \left(\alpha_g^2 - 1\right)\right)^2}. \tag{9.41}$$

The roughness control provided by the α_g parameter is similar to that provided by the Beckmann α_b parameter. In the Disney principled shading model, Burley [214] exposes

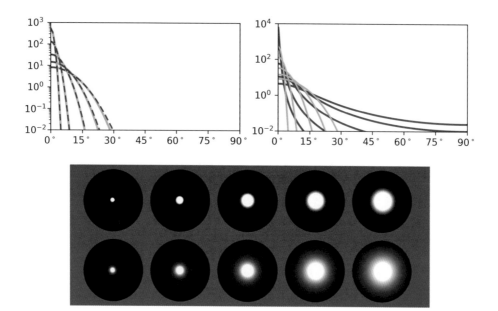

Figure 9.36. On the upper left, a comparison of Blinn-Phong (dashed blue) and Beckmann (green) distributions for values of α_b ranging from 0.025 to 0.2 (using the parameter relation $\alpha_p = 2\alpha_b^{-2} - 2$). On the upper right, a comparison of GGX (red) and Beckmann (green) distributions. The values of α_b are the same as in the left plot. The values of α_g have been adjusted by eye to match highlight size. These same values have been used in the spheres rendered on the bottom image. The top row uses the Beckmann NDF and the bottom row uses GGX.

the roughness control to users as $\alpha_g = r^2$, where r is the user-interface roughness parameter value between 0 and 1. Exposing r as a slider value means that the effect changes in a more linear fashion. This mapping has been adopted by most applications that use the GGX distribution.

The GGX distribution is shape-invariant, and its Λ function is relatively simple:

$$\Lambda(a) = \frac{-1 + \sqrt{1 + \frac{1}{a^2}}}{2}. \tag{9.42}$$

The fact that the variable a appears in Equation 9.42 only as a^2 is convenient, since the square root in Equation 9.37 can be avoided.

Due to the popularity of the GGX distribution and the Smith masking-shadowing function, there has been a focused effort to optimize the combination of the two. Lagarde observes [960] that the height-correlated Smith G_2 for GGX (Equation 9.31) has terms that cancel out when combined with the denominator of the specular microfacet BRDF (Equation 9.34). The combined term can be simplified thusly:

$$\frac{G_2(\mathbf{l}, \mathbf{v})}{4|\mathbf{n} \cdot \mathbf{l}||\mathbf{n} \cdot \mathbf{v}|} \implies \frac{0.5}{\mu_o\sqrt{\alpha^2 + \mu_i(\mu_i - \alpha^2\mu_i)} + \mu_i\sqrt{\alpha^2 + \mu_o(\mu_o - \alpha^2\mu_o)}}. \tag{9.43}$$

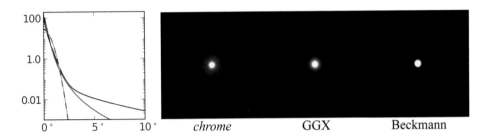

Figure 9.37. NDFs fit to measured chrome from the MERL database. On the left, we have plots of the specular peak against θ_m for chrome (black), GGX (red; $\alpha_g = 0.006$), Beckmann (green; $\alpha_b = 0.013$), and Blinn-Phong (blue dashes; $n = 12000$). Rendered highlights are shown on the right for chrome, GGX, and Beckmann. *(Figure courtesy of Brent Burley [214].)*

The equation uses the variable replacement $\mu_i = (\mathbf{n} \cdot \mathbf{l})^+$ and $\mu_o = (\mathbf{n} \cdot \mathbf{v})^+$ for brevity. Karis [861] proposes an approximated form of the Smith G_1 function for GGX:

$$G_1(\mathbf{s}) \approx \frac{2(\mathbf{n} \cdot \mathbf{s})}{(\mathbf{n} \cdot \mathbf{s})(2 - \alpha) + \alpha}, \tag{9.44}$$

where $\mathbf{s}$ can be replaced with either $\mathbf{l}$ or $\mathbf{v}$. Hammon [657] shows that this approximated form of G_1 leads to an efficient approximation for the combined term composed of the height-correlated Smith G_2 function and the specular microfacet BRDF denominator:

$$\frac{G_2(\mathbf{l}, \mathbf{v})}{4|\mathbf{n} \cdot \mathbf{l}||\mathbf{n} \cdot \mathbf{v}|} \approx \frac{0.5}{\text{lerp}\left(2|\mathbf{n} \cdot \mathbf{l}||\mathbf{n} \cdot \mathbf{v}|, |\mathbf{n} \cdot \mathbf{l}| + |\mathbf{n} \cdot \mathbf{v}|, \alpha\right)}, \tag{9.45}$$

which uses the linear interpolation operator, $\text{lerp}(x, y, s) = x(1 - s) + ys$.

When comparing the GGX and Beckmann distributions in Figure 9.36, it is apparent that the two have fundamentally different shapes. GGX has narrower peaks than Beckmann, as well as longer "tails" surrounding those peaks. In the rendered images at the bottom of the figure, we can see that GGX's longer tails create the appearance of a haze or glow around the core of the highlight.

Many real-world materials show similar hazy highlights, with tails that are typically longer even than those of the GGX distribution [214]. See Figure 9.37. This realization has been a strong contributor to the growing popularity of the GGX distribution, as well as the continuing search for new distributions that would fit measured materials even more accurately.

Burley [214] proposed the *generalized Trowbridge-Reitz* (GTR) NDF with a goal of allowing for more control over the NDF's shape, specifically the tails of the distribution:

$$D(\mathbf{m}) = \frac{k(\alpha, \gamma)}{\pi \left(1 + (\mathbf{n} \cdot \mathbf{m})^2 \left(\alpha_g^2 - 1\right)\right)^\gamma}. \tag{9.46}$$

The γ argument controls the tail shape. When $\gamma = 2$, GTR is the same as GGX. As the value of γ decreases, tails of the distribution become longer, and as it increases, they become shorter. At high values of γ, the GTR distribution resembles Beckmann. The $k(\alpha, \gamma)$ term is the normalization factor, which we give in a separate equation, since it is more complicated than those of other NDFs:

$$k(\alpha, \gamma) = \begin{cases} \frac{(\gamma-1)(\alpha^2-1)}{\left(1-(\alpha^2)^{(1-\gamma)}\right)}, & \text{where } \gamma \neq 1 \text{ and } \alpha \neq 1, \\ \frac{(\alpha^2-1)}{\ln(\alpha^2)}, & \text{where } \gamma = 1 \text{ and } \alpha \neq 1, \\ 1, & \text{where } \alpha = 1. \end{cases} \tag{9.47}$$

The GTR distribution is not shape-invariant, which complicates finding its Smith G_2 masking-shadowing function. It took three years after publication of the NDF for a solution for G_2 to be published [355]. This G_2 solution is quite complex, with a table of analytical solutions for certain values of γ (for intermediate values, interpolation must be used). Another issue with GTR is that the parameters α and γ affect the perceived roughness and "glow" in a non-intuitive manner.

Student's t-distribution (STD) [1491] and *exponential power distribution* (EPD) [763] NDFs include shape control parameters. In contrast to GTR, these functions are shape-invariant with respect to their roughness parameters. At the time of writing, these are newly published, so it is not clear whether they will find use in applications.

Instead of increasing the complexity of the NDF, an alternative solution to better matching measured materials is to use multiple specular lobes. This idea was suggested by Cook and Torrance [285, 286]. It was experimentally tested by Ngan [1271], who found that for many materials adding a second lobe did improve the fit significantly. Pixar's *PxrSurface* material [732] has a "roughspecular" lobe that is intended to be used (in conjunction with the main specular lobe) for this purpose. The additional lobe is a full specular microfacet BRDF with all the associated parameters and terms. Imageworks employs a more surgical approach [947], using a mix of two GGX NDFs that are exposed to the user as an extended NDF, rather than an entire separate specular BRDF term. In this case, the only additional parameters needed are a second roughness value and a blend amount.

Anisotropic Normal Distribution Functions

While most materials have isotropic surface statistics, some have significant anisotropy in their microstructure that noticeably affects their appearance, e.g., Figure 9.26 on page 329. To accurately render such materials, we need BRDFs, especially NDFs that are anisotropic as well.

Unlike isotropic NDFs, anisotropic NDFs cannot be evaluated with just the angle θ_m. Additional orientation information is needed. In the general case, the microfacet normal $\mathbf{m}$ needs to be transformed into the *local frame* or *tangent space* defined by the normal, tangent, and bitangent vectors, respectively, $\mathbf{n}$, $\mathbf{t}$, and $\mathbf{b}$. See Figure 6.32 on page 210. In practice, this transformation is typically expressed as three separate dot products: $\mathbf{m} \cdot \mathbf{n}$, $\mathbf{m} \cdot \mathbf{t}$, and $\mathbf{m} \cdot \mathbf{b}$.

When combining normal mapping with anisotropic BRDFs, it is important to make sure that the normal map perturbs the tangent and bitangent vectors as well as the normal. This procedure is often done by applying the *modified Gram-Schmidt* process to the perturbed normal $\mathbf{n}$ and the interpolated vertex tangent and bitangent vectors $\mathbf{t}_0$ and $\mathbf{b}_0$ (the below assumes that $\mathbf{n}$ is already normalized):

$$\mathbf{t}' = \mathbf{t}_0 - (\mathbf{t}_0 \cdot \mathbf{n})\mathbf{n} \quad \Longrightarrow \mathbf{t} = \frac{\mathbf{t}'}{\|\mathbf{t}'\|},$$

$$\left.\begin{aligned}\mathbf{b}' = \mathbf{b}_0 - (\mathbf{b}_0 \cdot \mathbf{n})\mathbf{n}, \\ \mathbf{b}'' = \mathbf{b}' - (\mathbf{b}' \cdot \mathbf{t})\mathbf{t}\end{aligned}\right\} \Longrightarrow \mathbf{b} = \frac{\mathbf{b}''}{\|\mathbf{b}''\|}. \tag{9.48}$$

Alternatively, after the first line the orthogonal $\mathbf{b}$ vector could be created by taking the cross product of $\mathbf{n}$ and $\mathbf{t}$.

For effects such as brushed metal or curly hair, per-pixel modification of the tangent direction is needed, typically provided by a *tangent map*. This map is a texture that stores the per-pixel tangent, similar to how a normal map stores per-pixel normals. Tangent maps most often store the two-dimensional projection of the tangent vector onto the plane perpendicular to the normal. This representation works well with texture filtering and can be compressed similar to normal maps. Some applications store a scalar rotation amount instead, which is used to rotate the tangent vector around $\mathbf{n}$. Though this representation is more compact, it is prone to texture filtering artifacts where the rotation angle wraps around from $360°$ to $0°$.

A common approach to creating an anisotropic NDF is to generalize an existing isotropic NDF. The general approach used can be applied to any shape-invariant isotropic NDF [708], which is another reason why shape-invariant NDFs are preferable. Recall that isotropic shape-invariant NDFs can be written in the following form:

$$D(\mathbf{m}) = \frac{\chi^+(\mathbf{n} \cdot \mathbf{m})}{\alpha^2(\mathbf{n} \cdot \mathbf{m})^4} \; g\left(\frac{\sqrt{1 - (\mathbf{n} \cdot \mathbf{m})^2}}{\alpha(\mathbf{n} \cdot \mathbf{m})}\right), \tag{9.49}$$

with g representing a one-dimensional function that expresses the shape of the NDF. The anisotropic version is

$$D(\mathbf{m}) = \frac{\chi^+(\mathbf{n} \cdot \mathbf{m})}{\alpha_x \alpha_y (\mathbf{n} \cdot \mathbf{m})^4} \; g\left(\frac{\sqrt{\frac{(\mathbf{t} \cdot \mathbf{m})^2}{\alpha_x^2} + \frac{(\mathbf{b} \cdot \mathbf{m})^2}{\alpha_y^2}}}{(\mathbf{n} \cdot \mathbf{m})}\right). \tag{9.50}$$

The parameters α_x and α_y represent the roughness along the direction of $\mathbf{t}$ and $\mathbf{b}$, respectively. If $\alpha_x = \alpha_y$, Equation 9.50 reduces back to the isotropic form.

The G_2 masking-shadowing function for the anisotropic NDF is the same as the isotropic one, except that the variable a (passed into the Λ function) is calculated differently:

$$a = \frac{\mathbf{n} \cdot \mathbf{s}}{\sqrt{\alpha_x^2(\mathbf{t} \cdot \mathbf{s})^2 + \alpha_y^2(\mathbf{b} \cdot \mathbf{s})^2}}, \tag{9.51}$$

where (as in Equation 9.37) $\mathbf{s}$ represents either $\mathbf{v}$ or $\mathbf{l}$.

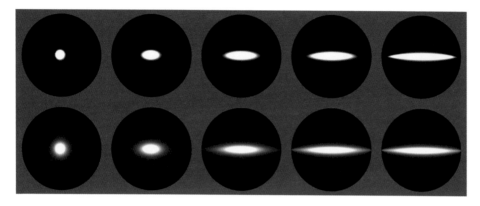

Figure 9.38. Spheres rendered with anisotropic NDFs: Beckmann in the top row and GGX in the bottom row. In both rows α_y is held constant and α_x is increased from left to right.

Using this method, anisotropic versions have been derived for the Beckmann NDF,

$$D(\mathbf{m}) = \frac{\chi^+(\mathbf{n} \cdot \mathbf{m})}{\pi \alpha_x \alpha_y (\mathbf{n} \cdot \mathbf{m})^4} \exp\left(-\frac{\frac{(\mathbf{t} \cdot \mathbf{m})^2}{\alpha_x^2} + \frac{(\mathbf{b} \cdot \mathbf{m})^2}{\alpha_y^2}}{(\mathbf{n} \cdot \mathbf{m})^2}\right), \tag{9.52}$$

and the GGX NDF,

$$D(\mathbf{m}) = \frac{\chi^+(\mathbf{n} \cdot \mathbf{m})}{\pi \alpha_x \alpha_y \left(\frac{(\mathbf{t} \cdot \mathbf{m})^2}{\alpha_x^2} + \frac{(\mathbf{b} \cdot \mathbf{m})^2}{\alpha_y^2} + (\mathbf{n} \cdot \mathbf{m})^2\right)^2}. \tag{9.53}$$

Both are shown in Figure 9.38.

While the most straightforward way to parameterize anisotropic NDFs is to use the isotropic roughness parameterization twice, once for α_x and once for α_y, other parameterizations are sometimes used. In the Disney principled shading model [214], the isotropic roughness parameter r is combined with a second scalar parameter k_{aniso} with a range of $[0, 1]$. The α_x and α_y values are computed from these parameters thusly:

$$k_{\text{aspect}} = \sqrt{1 - 0.9\, k_{\text{aniso}}},$$

$$\alpha_x = \frac{r^2}{k_{\text{aspect}}}, \tag{9.54}$$

$$\alpha_y = r^2\, k_{\text{aspect}}.$$

The 0.9 factor limits the aspect ratio to $10 : 1$.

Imageworks [947] use a different parameterization that allows for an arbitrary degree of anisotropy:

$$
\begin{aligned}
\alpha_x &= r^2 \left(1 + k_{\mathrm{aniso}}\right), \\
\alpha_y &= r^2 \left(1 - k_{\mathrm{aniso}}\right).
\end{aligned}
\tag{9.55}
$$

9.8.2 Multiple-Bounce Surface Reflection

As mentioned earlier in Section 9.7, the microfacet BRDF framework does not account for light that is reflected ("bounced") from the microsurface multiple times. This simplification causes some energy loss and over-darkening, especially for rough metals [712].

A technique used by Imageworks [947] combines elements from previous work [811, 878] to create a term that can be added to the BRDF to simulate multiple-bounce surface reflection:

$$
f_{\mathrm{ms}}(\mathbf{l}, \mathbf{v}) = \frac{\overline{F}\,\overline{R_{\mathrm{sF1}}}}{\pi \left(1 - \overline{R_{\mathrm{sF1}}}\right)\left(1 - \overline{F}(1 - \overline{R_{\mathrm{sF1}}})\right)} \left(1 - R_{\mathrm{sF1}}(\mathbf{l})\right)\left(1 - R_{\mathrm{sF1}}(\mathbf{v})\right), \tag{9.56}
$$

where R_{sF1} is the directional albedo (Section 9.3) of f_{sF1}, which is the specular BRDF term with F_0 set to 1. The function R_{sF1} depends on the roughness α and elevation angle θ. It is relatively smooth, so it can be precomputed numerically (using Equation 9.8 or 9.9) and stored in a small two-dimensional texture. Imageworks found that 32×32 resolution is sufficient.

The function $\overline{R_{\mathrm{sF1}}}$ is the cosine-weighted average value of R_{sF1} over the hemisphere. It depends only on α, so it can be stored in a one-dimensional texture, or an inexpensive curve could be fitted to the data. Since R_{sF1} is rotationally symmetric about $\mathbf{n}$, $\overline{R_{\mathrm{sF1}}}$ can be computed with a one-dimensional integral. We also use the change of variables $\mu = \cos\theta$ (see Equation 9.6 on page 312):

$$
\begin{aligned}
\overline{R_{\mathrm{sF1}}} &= \frac{\int_{\mathbf{s}\in\Omega} R_{\mathrm{sF1}}(\mathbf{s})(\mathbf{n}\cdot\mathbf{s})d\mathbf{s}}{\int_{\mathbf{s}\in\Omega}(\mathbf{n}\cdot\mathbf{s})d\mathbf{s}} = \frac{1}{\pi}\int_{\phi=0}^{2\pi}\int_{\mu=0}^{1} R_{\mathrm{sF1}}(\mu)\,\mu\,d\mu\,d\phi \\
&= 2\int_{\mu=0}^{1} R_{\mathrm{sF1}}(\mu)\,\mu\,d\mu.
\end{aligned}
\tag{9.57}
$$

Finally, $\overline{F}$ is the cosine-weighted average of the Fresnel term, computed in the same way:

$$
\overline{F} = 2\int_{\mu=0}^{1} F(\mu)\,\mu\,d\mu. \tag{9.58}
$$

Imageworks provide a closed-form solution to Equation 9.58 in the case that the generalized Schlick form (Equation 9.18) is used for F:

$$
\overline{F} = \frac{2p^2 F_{90} + (3p+1)F_0}{2p^2 + 3p + 1}. \tag{9.59}
$$

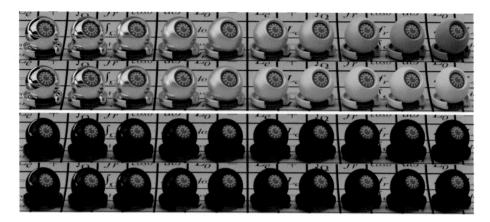

Figure 9.39. In all rows the roughness of the surface increases from left to right. The top two rows show a gold material. The first row is rendered without the Imageworks multiple-bounce term, and the second is rendered with the multiple-bounce term. The difference is most noticeable for the rougher spheres. The next two rows show a black dielectric material. The third row is rendered without the multiple-bounce term, and the fourth row has the multiple-bounce term applied. Here the difference is more subtle, since the specular reflectance is much lower. *(Figure courtesy of Christopher Kulla [947].)*

If the original Schlick approximation is used (Equation 9.16), then the solution simplifies to

$$\overline{F} = \frac{20}{21}F_0 + \frac{1}{21}. \tag{9.60}$$

In the case of anisotropy, Imageworks use an intermediate roughness between α_x and α_y for the purpose of computing f_{ms}. This approximation avoids the need to increase the dimensionality of the R_{sF1} lookup table, and the errors it introduces are small.

The results of the Imageworks multiple-bounce specular term can be seen in Figure 9.39.

9.9 BRDF Models for Subsurface Scattering

In the previous section we discussed surface, or specular, reflection. In this section we will discuss the other side of the issue, namely what happens to light refracted under the surface. As we discussed in Section 9.1.4, this light undergoes some combination of scattering and absorption, and part of it is re-emitted back out of the original surface. We will focus here on BRDF models for local subsurface scattering, or diffuse surface response, in opaque dielectrics. Metals are irrelevant, since they do not have any significant subsurface light interaction. Dielectric materials that are transparent or exhibit global subsurface scattering will be covered in Chapter 14.

We start our discussion of diffuse models with a section on the property of diffuse color and the possible values this color can have in real-world materials. In the following subsection we explain the effect of surface roughness on diffuse shading, and the criteria for choosing whether to use a smooth-surface or rough-surface shading model for a given material. The last two subsections are devoted to the smooth-surface and rough-surface models themselves.

9.9.1   Subsurface Albedo

The subsurface albedo ρ_{ss} of an opaque dielectric is the ratio between the energy of the light that escapes a surface compared to the energy of the light entering into the interior of the material. The value of ρ_{ss} is between 0 (all light is absorbed) and 1 (no light is absorbed) and can depend on wavelength, so ρ_{ss} is modeled as an RGB vector for rendering. For authoring, ρ_{ss} is often referred to as the diffuse color of the surface, just as the normal-incidence Fresnel reflectance F_0 is typically referred to as the specular color. The subsurface albedo is closely related to the scattering albedo discussed in Section 14.1.

Since dielectrics transmit most incoming light rather than reflecting it at the surface, the subsurface albedo ρ_{ss} is usually brighter and thus more visually important than the specular color F_0. Since it results from a different physical process than the specular color—absorption in the interior instead of Fresnel reflectance at the surface—ρ_{ss} typically has a different spectral distribution (and thus RGB color) than F_0. For example, colored plastic is composed of a clear, transparent substrate with pigment particles embedded in its interior. Light reflecting specularly will be uncolored, while light reflecting diffusely will be colored from absorption by the pigment particles; for example, a red plastic ball has a white highlight.

Subsurface albedo can be thought of as the result of a "race" between absorption and scattering—will the light be absorbed before it has had a chance to be scattered back out of the object? This is why foam on a liquid is much brighter than the liquid itself. The process of frothing does not change the absorptivity of the liquid, but the addition of numerous air-liquid interfaces greatly increases the amount of scattering. This causes most of the incoming light to be scattered before it has been absorbed, resulting in a high subsurface albedo and bright appearance. Fresh snow is another example of a substance with a high albedo. There is considerable scattering in the interfaces between snow granules and air, but little absorption, leading to a subsurface albedo of 0.8 or more across the visible spectrum. White paint is slightly less, about 0.7. Many substances encountered in daily life, such as concrete, stone, and soil, average between 0.15 and 0.4. Coal is an example of a material with extremely low subsurface albedo, close to 0.0.

The process by which many materials become darker when wet is the inverse of the liquid froth example. If the material is porous, water penetrates into spaces formerly filled with air. Dielectric materials have an index of refraction that is much closer to water than to air. This decrease in the relative index of refraction decreases the scattering inside the material, and light travels longer distances (on average) before escaping the material. This change causes more light to be absorbed and the subsurface albedo becomes darker [821].

It is a common misconception (even reflected in well-regarded material authoring guidelines [1163]) that values of ρ_{ss} should never go below a lower limit of about 0.015–0.03 (30–50 in 8-bit nonlinear sRGB encoding) for realistic material authoring. However, this lower limit is based on color measurements that include surface (specular) as well as subsurface (diffuse) reflectance, and is thus too high. Actual materials can have lower values. For example, the Federal specification for the "OSHA Black" paint standard [524] has a Y value of 0.35 (out of 100). Given the measurement conditions and surface gloss, this Y corresponds to a ρ_{ss} value of about 0.0035 (11 in 8-bit nonlinear sRGB encoding).

When acquiring spot values or textures for ρ_{ss} from real-world surfaces, it is important to separate out the specular reflectance. This extraction can be done via careful use of controlled lighting and polarization filters [251, 952]. For accurate color, calibration should be performed as well [1153].

Not every RGB triple represents a plausible (or even physically possible) value for ρ_{ss}. Reflectance spectra are more restricted than emissive spectral power distributions: They can never exceed a value of 1 for any wavelength, and they are typically quite smooth. These limitations define a volume in color space that contains all plausible RGB values for ρ_{ss}. Even the relatively small sRGB color gamut contains colors outside this volume, so care must be taken when setting values for ρ_{ss} to avoid specifying unnaturally saturated and bright colors. Besides reducing realism, such colors can cause over-bright secondary reflections when precomputing global illumination (Section 11.5.1). The 2015 paper by Meng et al. [1199] is a good reference for this topic.

9.9.2 Scale of Subsurface Scattering and Roughness

Some BRDF models for local subsurface scattering take account of surface roughness—typically by using microfacet theory with a diffuse micro-BRDF f_μ—and some do not. The deciding factor for which type of model to use is not simply how rough the surface is, though this is a common misconception. The correct deciding factor relates to the relative size of the surface irregularities and the subsurface scattering distances.

See Figure 9.40. If the microgeometry irregularities are larger than the subsurface scattering distances (top left of figure), then the subsurface scattering will exhibit microgeometry-related effects such as retroreflection (Figure 9.29 on page 331). For such surfaces a rough-surface diffuse model should be used. As mentioned above, such models are typically based on microfacet theory, with the subsurface scattering treated as local to each microfacet, thus only affecting the micro-BRDF f_μ.

If the scattering distances are all larger than the irregularities (top right of Figure 9.40), then the surface should be considered flat for the purpose of modeling subsurface scattering, and effects such as retroreflection will not occur. Subsurface

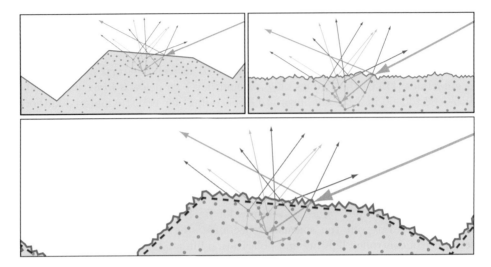

Figure 9.40. Three surfaces with similar NDFs but different relationships between the scale of the microgeometry and the subsurface scattering distances. On the top left, the subsurface scattering distances are smaller than the surface irregularities. On the top right, scattering distances are larger than the surface irregularities. The bottom figure shows a microsurface with roughness at multiple scales. The dashed red line represents the effective surface that only contains microstructure larger than the subsurface scattering distances.

scattering is not local to a microfacet, and cannot be modeled via microfacet theory. In this case, a smooth-surface diffuse model should be used.

In the intermediate case where the surface has roughness at scales both larger and smaller than the scattering distances, then a rough-surface diffuse model should be used, but with an *effective surface* that includes only irregularities larger than the scattering distances. Both diffuse and specular reflectance can be modeled with microfacet theory, but each with a different roughness value. The specular term will use a value based on the roughness of the actual surface, and the diffuse term will use a lower value, based on the roughness of the effective surface.

The scale of observation also ties into this, since it determines the definition of "microgeometry." For example, the moon is often cited as a case where rough-surface diffuse models should be used, since it exhibits significant retroreflection. When we look at the moon from the earth, the scale of observation is such that even a five-foot boulder is "microgeometry." Thus it is not surprising that we observe rough-surface diffuse effects such as retroreflection.

9.9.3 Smooth-Surface Subsurface Models

Here we will discuss smooth-surface subsurface models. These are appropriate for modeling materials where the surface irregularities are smaller than the subsurface scattering distances. Diffuse shading is not directly affected by surface roughness in such materials. If the diffuse and specular terms are coupled, which is the case for some of the models in this section, then surface roughness may affect diffuse shading indirectly.

As mentioned in Section 9.3, real-time rendering applications often model local subsurface scattering with a Lambertian term. In this case the BRDF diffuse term is ρ_{ss} over π:

$$f_{\text{diff}}(\mathbf{l}, \mathbf{v}) = \frac{\rho_{ss}}{\pi}. \tag{9.61}$$

The Lambertian model does not account for the fact that light reflected at the surface is not available for subsurface scattering. To improve this model, there should be an energy trade-off between the surface (specular) and subsurface (diffuse) reflectance terms. The Fresnel effect implies that this surface-subsurface energy trade-off changes with incident light angle θ_i. With increasingly glancing incidence angles, the diffuse reflectance decreases as the specular reflectance increases. A basic way to account for this balance is to multiply the diffuse term by one minus the Fresnel part of the specular term [1626]. If the specular term is that of a flat mirror, the resulting diffuse term is

$$f_{\text{diff}}(\mathbf{l}, \mathbf{v}) = (1 - F(\mathbf{n}, \mathbf{l}))\frac{\rho_{ss}}{\pi}. \tag{9.62}$$

If the specular term is a microfacet BRDF term, then the resulting diffuse term is

$$f_{\text{diff}}(\mathbf{l}, \mathbf{v}) = (1 - F(\mathbf{h}, \mathbf{l}))\frac{\rho_{ss}}{\pi}. \tag{9.63}$$

Equations 9.62 and 9.63 result in a uniform distribution of outgoing light, because the BRDF value does not depend on the outgoing direction $\mathbf{v}$. This behavior makes some sense, since light will typically undergo multiple scattering events before it is re-emitted, so its outgoing direction will be randomized. However, there are two reasons to suspect that the outgoing light is not distributed perfectly uniformly. First, since the diffuse BRDF term in Equation 9.62 varies by incoming direction, Helmholtz reciprocity implies that it must change by outgoing direction as well. Second, the light must undergo refraction on the way out, which will impose some directional preference on the outgoing light.

Shirley et al. proposed a coupled diffuse term for flat surfaces that addresses the Fresnel effect and the surface-subsurface reflectance trade-off, while supporting both energy conservation and Helmholtz reciprocity [1627]. The derivation assumes that the Schlick approximation [1568] (Equation 9.16) is used for Fresnel reflectance:

$$f_{\text{diff}}(\mathbf{l}, \mathbf{v}) = \frac{21}{20\pi}(1 - F_0)\rho_{ss}\left(1 - \left(1 - (\mathbf{n} \cdot \mathbf{l})^+\right)^5\right)\left(1 - \left(1 - (\mathbf{n} \cdot \mathbf{v})^+\right)^5\right). \tag{9.64}$$

Equation 9.64 applies only to surfaces where the specular reflectance is that of a perfect Fresnel mirror. A generalized version that can be used to compute a reciprocal, energy-conserving diffuse term to couple with any specular term was proposed by

Ashikhmin and Shirley [77] and further refined by Kelemen and Szirmay-Kalos [878]:

$$f_{\text{diff}}(\mathbf{l}, \mathbf{v}) = \rho_{\text{ss}} \frac{\left(1 - R_{\text{spec}}(\mathbf{l})\right)\left(1 - R_{\text{spec}}(\mathbf{v})\right)}{\pi \left(1 - \overline{R_{\text{spec}}}\right)}. \tag{9.65}$$

Here, R_{spec} is the directional albedo (Section 9.3) of the specular term, and $\overline{R_{\text{spec}}}$ is its cosine-weighted average over the hemisphere. The value R_{spec} can be precomputed using Equation 9.8 or 9.9 and stored in a lookup table. The average $\overline{R_{\text{spec}}}$ is computed the same way as a similar average we encountered earlier: $\overline{R_{\text{sF1}}}$ (Equation 9.57).

The form in Equation 9.65 has some clear similarities to Equation 9.56, which is not surprising, since the Imageworks multiple-bounce specular term is derived from the Kelemen-Szirmay-Kalos coupled diffuse term. However, there is one important difference. Here, instead of R_{sF1} we use R_{spec}, the directional albedo of the full specular BRDF term including Fresnel, and with the multiple-bounce specular term f_{ms} as well, if one is used. This difference increases the dimensionality of the lookup table for R_{spec} since it depends not only on the roughness α and elevation angle θ, but on the Fresnel reflectance as well.

In Imageworks' implementation of the Kelemen-Szirmay-Kalos coupled diffuse term, they use a three-dimensional lookup table, with the index of refraction as the third axis [947]. They found that the inclusion of the multiple-bounce term in the integral made R_{spec} smoother than R_{sF1}, so a $16 \times 16 \times 16$ table was sufficient. Figure 9.41 shows the result.

If the BRDF uses the Schlick Fresnel approximation and does not include a multiple-bounce specular term, then the value of F_0 can be factored out of the integral. Doing so allows us to use a two-dimensional table for R_{spec}, storing two quantities in each entry, instead of a three-dimensional table, as discussed by Karis [861]. Alternatively, Lazarov [999] presents an analytic function that is fitted to R_{spec}, similarly factoring F_0 out of the integral to simplify the fitted function.

Both Karis and Lazarov use the specular directional albedo R_{spec} for a different purpose, related to image-based lighting. More details on that technique can be found in Section 10.5.2. If both techniques are implemented in the same application, then the same table lookups can be used for both, increasing efficiency.

These models were developed by considering the implications of energy conservation between the surface (specular) and subsurface (diffuse) terms. Other models have been developed from physical principles. Many of these models rely on the work of Subrahmanyan Chandrasekhar (1910–1995), who developed a BRDF model for a semi-infinite, isotropically scattering volume. As demonstrated by Kulla and Conty [947], if the mean free path is sufficiently short, this BRDF model is a perfect match for a scattering volume of arbitrary shape. The Chandrasekhar BRDF can be found in his book [253], though a more accessible form using familiar rendering notation can be found in Equations 30 and 31 of a paper by Dupuy et al. [397].

Since it does not include refraction, the Chandrasekhar BRDF can be used to model only *index-matched surfaces*. These are surfaces where the index of refraction

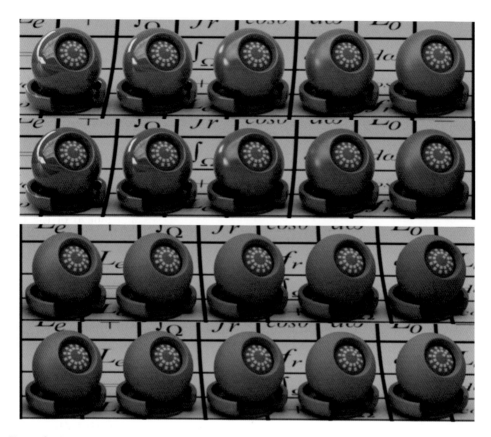

Figure 9.41. The first and third rows show a specular term added to a Lambertian term. The second and fourth rows show the same specular term used with a Kelemen-Szirmay-Kalos coupled diffuse term. The top two rows have lower roughness values than the bottom two. Within each row, roughness increases from left to right. *(Figure courtesy of Christopher Kulla [947].)*

is the same on both sides, as in Figure 9.11 on page 304. To model non-index-matched surfaces, the BRDF must be modified to account for refraction where the light enters and exits the surface. This modification is the focus of work by Hanrahan and Krueger [662] and Wolff [1898].

9.9.4 Rough-Surface Subsurface Models

As part of the Disney principled shading model, Burley [214] included a diffuse BRDF term designed to include roughness effects and match measured materials:

$$f_{\text{diff}}(\mathbf{l}, \mathbf{v}) = \chi^+(\mathbf{n} \cdot \mathbf{l})\chi^+(\mathbf{n} \cdot \mathbf{v})\frac{\rho_{\text{ss}}}{\pi}\big((1 - k_{\text{ss}})f_{\text{d}} + 1.25\,k_{\text{ss}}f_{\text{ss}}\big), \qquad (9.66)$$

where

$$f_{\mathrm{d}} = \left(1 + (F_{\mathrm{D}90} - 1)(1 - \mathbf{n} \cdot \mathbf{l})^5\right)\left(1 + (F_{\mathrm{D}90} - 1)(1 - \mathbf{n} \cdot \mathbf{v})^5\right),$$

$$F_{\mathrm{D}90} = 0.5 + 2\sqrt{\alpha}\,(\mathbf{h} \cdot \mathbf{l})^2,$$

$$f_{\mathrm{ss}} = \left(\frac{1}{(\mathbf{n} \cdot \mathbf{l})(\mathbf{n} \cdot \mathbf{v})} - 0.5\right) F_{\mathrm{SS}} + 0.5, \tag{9.67}$$

$$F_{\mathrm{SS}} = \left(1 + (F_{\mathrm{SS}90} - 1)(1 - \mathbf{n} \cdot \mathbf{l})^5\right)\left(1 + (F_{\mathrm{SS}90} - 1)(1 - \mathbf{n} \cdot \mathbf{v})^5\right),$$

$$F_{\mathrm{SS}90} = \sqrt{\alpha}\,(\mathbf{h} \cdot \mathbf{l})^2,$$

and α is the specular roughness. In the case of anisotropy, an intermediate value between α_x and α_y is used. This equation is often referred to as the *Disney diffuse* model.

The subsurface term f_{ss} is inspired by the Hanrahan-Krueger BRDF [662] and intended as an inexpensive replacement for global subsurface scattering on distant objects. The diffuse model blends between f_{ss} and the f_{d} rough diffuse term based on the user-controlled parameter k_{ss}.

The Disney diffuse model has been used for films [214], as well as games [960] (though without the subsurface term). The full Disney diffuse BRDF also includes a sheen term, which is intended primarily for modeling fabrics, but also helps compensate for the energy lost due to the lack of a multiple-bounce specular term. The Disney sheen term will be discussed in Section 9.10. Several years later, Burley presented [215] an updated model designed to integrate with global subsurface scattering rendering techniques.

Since the Disney diffuse model uses the same roughness as the specular BRDF term, it may have difficulties modeling certain materials. See Figure 9.40. However, it would be a trivial modification to use a separate diffuse roughness value.

Most other rough-surface diffuse BRDFs have been developed using microfacet theory, with various different choices for the NDF D, micro-BRDF f_μ, and masking-shadowing function G_2. The most well-known of these models was proposed by Oren and Nayar [1337]. The Oren-Nayar BRDF uses a Lambertian micro-BRDF, a spherical Gaussian NDF, and the Torrance-Sparrow "V-cavity" masking-shadowing function. The full form of the BRDF models one secondary bounce. Oren and Nayar also included a simplified "qualitative" model in their paper. Several improvements to the Oren-Nayar model have been proposed over the years, including optimizations [573], tweaks to make the "qualitative" model more closely resemble the full model without increasing its cost [504], and changing the micro-BRDF to a more accurate smooth-surface diffuse model [574, 1899].

The Oren-Nayar model assumes a microsurface with quite different normal distribution and masking-shadowing functions than those used in current specular models. Two diffuse microfacet models were derived using the isotropic GGX NDF and height-correlated Smith masking-shadowing function. The first model, by Gotanda [574], is the result of numerically integrating the general microfacet equation (Equation 9.26), using as the micro-BRDF the specular coupled diffuse term in Equation 9.64. An analytic function was then fitted to the numerically integrated data. Gotanda's BRDF does not account for interreflections between facets, and the fitted function is relatively complex.

Using the same NDF, masking-shadowing function, and micro-BRDF as Gotanda, Hammon [657] simulates the BRDF numerically, including interreflections. He shows that interreflections are important for this microfacet configuration, representing as much as half of the total reflectance for rougher surfaces. However, the second bounce contains almost all of the missing energy, so Hammon uses data from a two-bounce simulation. Also, likely because the addition of interreflections smoothed out the data, Hammon was able to fit a fairly simple function to the simulation results:

$$f_{\text{diff}}(\mathbf{l}, \mathbf{v}) = \chi^{+}(\mathbf{n} \cdot \mathbf{l})\chi^{+}(\mathbf{n} \cdot \mathbf{v})\frac{\rho_{\text{ss}}}{\pi}\big((1 - \alpha_g)f_{\text{smooth}} + \alpha_g f_{\text{rough}} + \rho_{\text{ss}}f_{\text{multi}}\big), \quad (9.68)$$

where

$$f_{\text{smooth}} = \frac{21}{20}(1 - F_0)\left(1 - (1 - \mathbf{n} \cdot \mathbf{l})^5\right)\left(1 - (1 - \mathbf{n} \cdot \mathbf{v})^5\right),$$

$$f_{\text{rough}} = k_{\text{facing}}(0.9 - 0.4\,k_{\text{facing}})\left(\frac{0.5 + \mathbf{n} \cdot \mathbf{h}}{\mathbf{n} \cdot \mathbf{h}}\right),$$

$$k_{\text{facing}} = 0.5 + 0.5(\mathbf{l} \cdot \mathbf{v}),$$

$$f_{\text{multi}} = 0.3641\alpha_g,$$

(9.69)

and α_g is the GGX specular roughness. For clarity, the terms here have been factored slightly differently than in Hammon's presentation. Note that f_{smooth} is the coupled diffuse BRDF from Equation 9.64 without the ρ_{ss}/π factor, since this is multiplied in Equation 9.68. Hammon discusses "hybrid" BRDFs that substitute other smooth-surface diffuse BRDFs for f_{smooth}, to increase performance or improve compatibility with assets authored under older models.

Overall, Hammon's diffuse BRDF is inexpensive and is based on sound theoretical principles, although he did not show comparisons with measured data. One caveat is that the assumption that surface irregularities are larger than scattering distances is fundamental to the derivation of the BRDF, which may limit the types of materials it can accurately model. See Figure 9.40.

The simple Lambertian term shown in Equation 9.61 is still implemented by many real-time rendering applications. Besides the Lambertian term's low computational cost, it is easier to use with indirect and baked lighting than other diffuse models, and the visual differences between it and more sophisticated models are often subtle [251, 861]. Nevertheless, the continuing quest for photorealism is driving an increase in the use of more accurate models.

Figure 9.42. A material using the cloth system built for the game *Uncharted 4*. The upper left sphere has a standard BRDF with a GGX microfacet specular and Lambertian diffuse. The upper middle sphere uses the fabric BRDF. Each of the other spheres adds a different type of per-pixel variation, going from left to right and top to bottom: fabric weave details, fabric aging, imperfection details, and small wrinkles. *(UNCHARTED 4 A Thief's End ©/^{TM} 2016 SIE. Created & developed by Naughty Dog LLC.)*

9.10 BRDF Models for Cloth

Cloth tends to have microgeometry that is different from other types of materials. Depending on the fabric type, it may have highly repetitive woven microstructures, cylinders (threads) protruding vertically from the surface, or both. As a result, cloth surfaces have characteristic appearances that typically require specialized shading models, such as anisotropic specular highlights, asperity scattering [919] (bright edge effects caused by light scattering through protruding, translucent fibers), and even color shifts with view direction (caused by threads of different colors running through the fabric).

Aside from the BRDF, most fabrics have high-frequency spatial variation that is also key to creating a convincing cloth appearance [825]. See Figure 9.42.

Cloth BRDF models fall into three main categories: empirical models created from observation, models based on microfacet theory, and micro-cylinder models. We will go over some notable examples from each category.

9.10.1 Empirical Cloth Models

In the game *Uncharted 2* [631], cloth surfaces use the following diffuse BRDF term:

$$f_{\text{diff}}(\mathbf{l}, \mathbf{v}) = \frac{\rho_{ss}}{\pi} \Big(k_{\text{rim}} \big((\mathbf{v} \cdot \mathbf{n})^+ \big)^{\alpha_{\text{rim}}} + k_{\text{inner}} \big(1 - (\mathbf{v} \cdot \mathbf{n})^+ \big)^{\alpha_{\text{inner}}} + k_{\text{diff}} \Big), \qquad (9.70)$$

where k_{rim}, k_{inner}, and k_{diff} are user-controlled scaling factors for a rim lighting term, a term to brighten forward-facing (inner) surfaces, and a Lambertian term, respectively. Also, α_{rim} and α_{inner} control the falloff of the rim and inner terms. This behavior is non-physical, since there are several view-dependent effects but none that depend on the light direction.

In contrast, the cloth in *Uncharted 4* [825] uses either a microfacet or micro-cylinder model, depending on cloth type (as detailed in the following two sections) for the specular term and a "wrap lighting" empirical subsurface scattering approximation for the diffuse term:

$$f_{\text{diff}}(\mathbf{l}, \mathbf{v})(\mathbf{n} \cdot \mathbf{l})^+ \Rightarrow \frac{\rho_{ss}}{\pi} \Big(\mathbf{c}_{\text{scatter}} + (\mathbf{n} \cdot \mathbf{l})^+ \Big)^{\overline{+}} \frac{(\mathbf{n} \cdot \mathbf{l} + w)^{\overline{+}}}{1 + w}. \qquad (9.71)$$

Here we use the $(x)^{\overline{+}}$ notation introduced in Section 1.2, which indicates a clamp between 0 and 1. The odd notation $f_{\text{diff}}(\mathbf{l}, \mathbf{v})(\mathbf{n} \cdot \mathbf{l})^+ \Rightarrow \dots$ indicates that this model affects the lighting as well as the BRDF. The term on the right side of the arrow replaces the term on the left side. The user-specified parameter $\mathbf{c}_{\text{scatter}}$ is a scattering color, and the value w, with range $[0, 1]$, controls the wrap lighting width.

For modeling cloth, Disney use their diffuse BRDF term [214] (Section 9.9.4) with a sheen term added to model asperity scattering:

$$f_{\text{sheen}}(\mathbf{l}, \mathbf{v}) = k_{\text{sheen}} \mathbf{c}_{\text{sheen}} \big(1 - (\mathbf{h} \cdot \mathbf{l})^+ \big)^5, \qquad (9.72)$$

where k_{sheen} is a user parameter that modulates the strength of the sheen term. The sheen color $\mathbf{c}_{\text{sheen}}$ is a blend (controlled by another user parameter) between white and the luminance-normalized value of ρ_{ss}. In other words, ρ_{ss} is divided by its luminance to isolate its hue and saturation.

9.10.2 Microfacet Cloth Models

Ashikhmin et al. [78] proposed using an inverted Gaussian NDF to model velvet. This NDF was slightly modified in subsequent work [81], which also proposed a variant form of the microfacet BRDF for modeling materials in general, with no masking-shadowing term and a modified denominator.

The cloth BRDF used in the game *The Order: 1886* [1266] combines the modified microfacet BRDF and a generalized form of the velvet NDF from Ashikhmin and Premože's later report [81] with the diffuse term from Equation 9.63. The generalized

Figure 9.43. The Imageworks sheen specular term added to a red diffuse term. From left to right, the sheen roughness values are $\alpha = 0.15$, 0.25, 0.40, 0.65, and 1.0. *(Figure courtesy of Alex Conty [442].)*

velvet NDF is

$$D(\mathbf{m}) = \frac{\chi^+(\mathbf{n} \cdot \mathbf{m})}{\pi(1 + k_{\mathrm{amp}}\alpha^2)} \left(1 + \frac{k_{\mathrm{amp}} \exp\left(\frac{(\mathbf{n} \cdot \mathbf{m})^2}{\alpha^2 \left((\mathbf{n} \cdot \mathbf{m})^2 - 1 \right)} \right)}{\left(1 - (\mathbf{n} \cdot \mathbf{m})^2 \right)^2} \right), \qquad (9.73)$$

where α controls the width of the inverted Gaussian and k_{amp} controls its amplitude. The full cloth BRDF is

$$f(\mathbf{l}, \mathbf{v}) = \left(1 - F(\mathbf{h}, \mathbf{l}) \right) \frac{\rho_{\mathrm{ss}}}{\pi} + \frac{F(\mathbf{h}, \mathbf{l}) D(\mathbf{h})}{4 \left(\mathbf{n} \cdot \mathbf{l} + \mathbf{n} \cdot \mathbf{v} - (\mathbf{n} \cdot \mathbf{l})(\mathbf{n} \cdot \mathbf{v}) \right)}. \qquad (9.74)$$

A variation of this BRDF was used in the game *Uncharted 4* [825] for rough fabrics such as wool and cotton.

Imageworks [947] use a different inverted NDF for a sheen term that can be added to any BRDF:

$$D(\mathbf{m}) = \frac{\chi^+(\mathbf{n} \cdot \mathbf{m})(2 + \frac{1}{\alpha})\left(1 - (\mathbf{n} \cdot \mathbf{m})^2 \right)^{\frac{1}{2\alpha}}}{2\pi}. \qquad (9.75)$$

Although there is no closed-form solution to the Smith masking-shadowing function for this NDF, Imageworks were able to approximate the numerical solution with an analytical function. Details on the masking-shadowing function and on energy conservation between the sheen term and the rest of the BRDF are discussed by Estevez and Kulla [442]. See Figure 9.43 for some examples rendered using the Imageworks sheen term.

Each of the cloth models we have seen so far are limited to specific types of fabric. The models discussed in the next section attempt to model cloth in a more general way.

9.10.3 Micro-Cylinder Cloth Models

The micro-cylinder models used for cloth are quite similar to those used for hair, so the discussion of hair models in Section 14.7.2 can provide additional context. The idea behind these models is that the surface is assumed to be covered with one-dimensional lines. Kajiya and Kay developed a simple BRDF model for this case [847], which was given a solid theoretical foundation by Banks [98]. It is alternately known as the *Kajiya-Kay BRDF* or the *Banks BRDF*. The concept is based on the observation that a surface composed of one-dimensional lines has an infinite number of normals at any given location, defined by the *normal plane* perpendicular to the tangent vector **t** at that location. Although many newer micro-cylinder models have been developed from this framework, the original Kajiya-Kay model still sees some use, due to its simplicity. For example, in the game *Uncharted 4* [825], the Kajiya-Kay BRDF was used for the specular term of shiny fabrics such as silk and velvet.

Dreamworks [348, 1937] use a relatively simple and artist-controllable micro-cylinder model for fabric. Textures can be used to vary the roughness, color, and thread direction, which can point out of the surface plane for modeling velvet and similar fabrics. Different parameters can be set for the warp and weft threads to model complex color-changing fabrics, such as shot silk. The model is normalized to be energy-conserving.

Sadeghi et al. [1526] proposed a micro-cylinder model based on measurements from fabric samples as well as individual threads. The model also accounts for inter-thread masking and shadowing between threads.

In some cases actual hair BSDF models (Section 14.7) are used for cloth. Render-Man's *PxrSurface* material [732] has a "fuzz" lobe that uses the R term from the hair model by Marschner et al. [1128] (Section 14.7). One of the models implemented in a real-time cloth rendering system by Wu and Yuksel [1924, 1926] is derived from a hair model used by Disney for animated films [1525].

9.11 Wave Optics BRDF Models

The models we have discussed in the last few sections rely on geometrical optics, which treats light as propagating in rays rather than waves. As discussed on page 303, geometrical optics is based on the assumption that any surface irregularities are either smaller than a wavelength or larger than about 100 wavelengths.

Real-world surfaces are not so obliging. They tend to have irregularities at all scales, including the 1–100 wavelength range. We refer to irregularities with such sizes as *nanogeometry* to distinguish them from the microgeometry irregularities discussed in earlier sections, which are too small to be individually rendered but larger than 100 light wavelengths. The effects of nanogeometry on reflectance cannot be modeled by geometrical optics. These effects depend on the wave nature of light and *wave optics* (also called *physical optics*) is required to model them.

Surface layers, or films, with thicknesses close to a light wavelength also produce optical phenomena related to the wave nature of light.

In this section we touch upon wave optics phenomena such as diffraction and thin-film interference, discussing their (sometimes surprising) importance in realistically rendering what otherwise can seem to be relatively mundane materials.

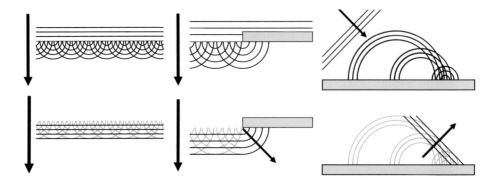

Figure 9.44. To the left, we see a planar wavefront propagating in empty space. If each point on the wavefront is treated as the source of a new spherical wave, the new waves interfere destructively in all directions except forward, resulting in a planar wavefront again. In the center, the waves encounter an obstacle. The spherical waves at the edge of the obstacle have no waves to their right that destructively interfere with them, so some waves diffract or "leak" around the edge. To the right, a planar wavefront is reflected from a flat surface. The planar wavefront encounters surface points on the left earlier than points on the right, so the spherical waves emitting from surface points on the left have had more time to propagate and are therefore larger. The different sizes of spherical wavefronts interfere constructively along the edge of the reflected planar wavefront, and destructively in other directions.

9.11.1 Diffraction Models

Nanogeometry causes a phenomenon called *diffraction*. To explain it we make use of the *Huygens-Fresnel principle*, which states that every point on a wavefront (the set of points that have the same wave phase) can be treated as the source of a new spherical wave. See Figure 9.44. When waves encounter an obstacle, the Huygens-Fresnel principle shows that they will bend slightly around corners, which is an example of diffraction. This phenomenon cannot be predicted by geometrical optics. In the case of light incident on a planar surface, geometrical optics does correctly predict that light will be reflected in a single direction. That said, the Fresnel-Huygens principle provides additional insight. It shows that the spherical waves on the surface line up just right to create the reflected wavefront, with waves in all other directions being eliminated through destructive interference. This insight becomes important when we look at a surface with nanometer irregularities. Due to the different heights of the surface points, the spherical waves on the surface no longer line up so neatly. See Figure 9.45.

As the figure shows, light is scattered in different directions. Some portion of it is specularly reflected, i.e., adds up to a planar wavefront in the reflection direction. The remaining light is diffracted out in a directional pattern that depends on certain properties of the nanogeometry. The division between specularly reflected and diffracted light depends on the height of the nanogeometry bumps, or, more precisely, on the variance of the height distribution. The angular spread of diffracted light around the

Figure 9.45. On the left we see planar wavefronts incident to a surface with rough nanogeometry. In the center we see the spherical waves formed on the surface according to the Fresnel-Huygens principle. On the right we see that after constructive and destructive interference has occurred, some of the resulting waves (in red) form a planar reflected wave. The remainder (in purple) are diffracted, with different amounts of light propagating in each direction, depending on wavelength.

specular reflection direction depends on the width of the nanogeometry bumps relative to the light wavelength. Somewhat counter-intuitively, wider irregularities cause a smaller spread. If the irregularities are larger than 100 light wavelengths, the angle between the diffracted light and the specularly reflected light is so small as to be negligible. Irregularities of decreasing size cause a wider spread of diffracted light, until the irregularities become smaller than a light wavelength, at which point no diffraction occurs.

Diffraction is most clearly visible in surfaces with periodic nanogeometry, since the repeating patterns reinforce the diffracted light via constructive interference, causing a colorful iridescence. This phenomena can be observed in CD and DVD optical disks and certain insects. While diffraction also occurs in non-periodic surfaces, the computer graphics community has assumed for many years that the effect is slight. For this reason, with a handful of exceptions [89, 366, 686, 1688], the computer graphics literature has mostly ignored diffraction for many years.

However, recent analysis of measured materials by Holzschuch and Pacanowski [762] has shown that significant diffraction effects are present in many materials, and may explain the continuing difficulty of fitting these materials with current models. Follow-up work by the same authors [763] introduced a model combining microfacet and diffraction theory, via the use of the general microfacet BRDF (Equation 9.26) with a micro-BRDF that accounts for diffraction. In parallel, Toisoul and Ghosh [1772, 1773] presented methods for capturing the iridescent diffraction effects resulting from periodic nanogeometry, and for rendering them in real time with point light sources as well as image-based lighting.

9.11.2 Models for Thin-Film Interference

Thin-film interference is a wave optics phenomenon that occurs when light paths reflecting from the top and bottom of a thin dielectric layer interfere with each other. See Figure 9.46.

The different wavelengths of light either interfere constructively or destructively, depending on the relationship between the wavelength and the path length difference.

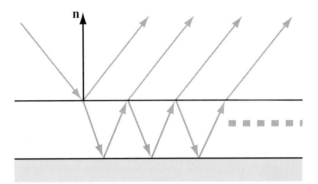

Figure 9.46. Light incident to a thin film on top of a reflective substrate. Besides the primary reflection, there are multiple paths of light refracting, reflecting from the substrate, and either reflecting from the inside of the top thin film surface or refracting through it. These paths are all copies of the same wave, but with short phase delays caused by difference in path length, so they interfere coherently with each other.

Since the path length difference changes with angle, the end result is an iridescent color shift as different wavelengths transition between constructive and destructive interference.

The reason that the film needs to be thin for this effect to occur is related to the concept of *coherence length*. This length is the maximum distance by which a copy of a light wave can be displaced and still interfere coherently with the original wave. This length is inversely proportional to the *bandwidth* of the light, which is the range of wavelengths over which its spectral power distribution (SPD) extends. Laser light, with its extremely narrow bandwidth, has an extremely long coherence length. It can be miles, depending on the type of laser. This relationship makes sense, since a simple sine wave displaced by many wavelengths will still interfere coherently with the original wave. If the laser was truly monochromatic, it would have an infinite coherence length, but in practice lasers have a nonzero bandwidth. Conversely, light with an extremely broad bandwidth will have a chaotic waveform. It makes sense that a copy of such a waveform needs to be displaced only a short distance before it stops interfering coherently with the original.

In theory, ideal white light, which is a mixture of all wavelengths, would have a coherence length of zero. However, for the purposes of visible-light optics, the bandwidth of the human visual system (which senses light only in the 400–700 nm range) determines the coherence length, which is about 1 micrometer. So, in most cases the answer to the question "how thick can a film get before it no longer causes visible interference?" is "about 1 micrometer."

Similarly to diffraction, for many years thin-film interference was thought of as a special case effect that occurs only in surfaces such as soap bubbles and oil stains. However, Akin [27] points out that thin-film interference does lend a subtle coloration

Figure 9.47. A leather material rendered without (on the left) and with (on the right) thin-film interference. The specular coloration caused by thin-film interference increases the realism of the image. *(Image by Atilla Akin, Next Limit Technologies [27].)*

to many everyday surfaces, and shows how modeling this effect can increase realism. See Figure 9.47. His article caused the level of interest in physically based thin-film interference to increase considerably, with various shading models including Render-Man's *PxrSurface* [732] and the Imageworks shading model [947] incorporating support for this effect.

Thin-film interference techniques suitable for real-time rendering have existed for some time. Smits and Meyer [1667] proposed an efficient method to account for thin-film interference between the first- and second-order light paths. They observe that the resulting color is primarily a function of the path length difference, which can be efficiently computed from the film thickness, viewing angle, and index of refraction. Their implementation requires a one-dimensional lookup table with RGB colors. The contents of the table can be computed using dense spectral sampling and converted to RGB colors as a preprocess, which makes the technique quite fast. In the game *Call of Duty: Infinite Warfare*, a different fast thin-film approximation is used as part of a layered material system [386]. These techniques do not model multiple bounces of light in the thin film, as well as other physical phenomena. A more accurate and computationally expensive technique, yet still targeted at real-time implementation, is presented by Belcour and Barla [129].

9.12 Layered Materials

In real life, materials are often layered on top of one another. A surface may be covered with dust, water, ice, or snow; it may be painted with lacquer or some other coating for decorative or protective reasons; or it may have multiple layers as part of its basic construction, such as many biological materials.

One of the simplest and most visually significant cases of layering is a *clear coat*, which is a smooth transparent layer over a substrate of some different material. An example is a smooth coat of varnish over a rough wood surface. The Disney principled shading model [214] includes a clear-coat term, as do the Unreal Engine [1802], RenderMan's *PxrSurface* material [732], and the shading models used by Dreamworks Animation [1937] and Imageworks [947], among others.

The most notable visual result of a clear-coat layer is the double reflection resulting from light reflecting off both the clear-coat and the underlying substrate. This second reflection is most notable when the substrate is a metal, since then the difference between the indices of refraction of the dielectric clear coat and the substrate is largest. When the substrate is a dielectric, its index of refraction is close to that of the clear coat, causing the second reflection to be relatively weak. This effect is similar to underwater materials, shown in Table 9.4 on page 325.

The clear-coat layer can also be tinted. From a physical point of view, this tinting is the result of absorption. The amount of absorbed light depends on the length of the path that light travels through the clear-coat layer, according to the Beer-Lambert law (Section 14.1.2). This path length depends on the angles of the view and light, as well as the index of refraction of the material. The simpler clear-coat implementations, such as those in the Disney principled model and the Unreal Engine, do not model this view-dependence. Others do, such as the implementations in *PxrSurface* and the Imageworks and Dreamworks shading models. The Imageworks model further allows for concatenating an arbitrary number of layers of different types.

In the general case, different layers could have different surface normals. Some examples include rivulets of water running over flat pavement, a smooth sheet of ice on top of bumpy soil, or wrinkled plastic wrap covering a cardboard box. Most layered models used by the movie industry support separate normals per layer. This practice is not common in real-time applications, though the Unreal Engine's clear-coat implementation supports it as an optional feature.

Weidlich and Wilkie [1862, 1863] propose a layered microfacet model, with the assumption that the layer thickness is small compared to the size of the microfacets. Their model supports an arbitrary number of layers, and tracks reflection and refraction events from the top layer down to the bottom and back up again. It is simple enough for real-time implementation [420, 573], but does not account for multiple reflections between layers. Jakob et al. [811, 812] present a comprehensive and accurate framework for simulating layered materials, including multiple reflections. Although not suitable for real-time implementation, the system is useful for ground-truth comparisons, and the ideas used may suggest future real-time techniques.

The game *Call of Duty: Infinite Warfare* uses a layered material system [386] that is especially notable. It allows users to composite an arbitrary number of material layers. It supports refraction, scattering, and path-length-based absorption between

Figure 9.48. Test surface showing various features of the *Call of Duty: Infinite Warfare* multi-layer material system. The material simulates a geometrically complex surface with distortion and scattering, although each side is constructed from only two triangles. *(Image courtesy of Activision Publishing, Inc. 2018.)*

layers, as well as different surface normals per layer. Combined with a highly efficient implementation, this system enables real-time materials of unprecedented complexity, particularly impressive for a game running at 60 Hz. See Figure 9.48.

9.13 Blending and Filtering Materials

Material blending is the process of combining the properties, i.e., the BRDF parameters, of multiple materials. For example, to model a sheet of metal with rust spots, we could paint a mask texture to control the rust spot locations and use it to blend between the material properties (specular color F_0, diffuse color ρ_{ss}, and roughness α) of rust and metal. Each of the materials being blended can also be spatially varying, with parameters stored in textures. Blending can be done as a preprocess to create a new texture, often referred to as "baking," or on the fly in the shader. Although the surface normal **n** is technically not a BRDF parameter, its spatial variation is important for appearance, so material blending typically includes normal map blending as well.

Material blending is critical to many real-time rendering applications. For example, the game *The Order: 1886* has a complex material blending system [1266, 1267, 1410] that allows users to author arbitrarily deep stacks of materials drawn from an extensive library and controlled by various spatial masks. Most of the material blending is done as an offline preprocess, but certain compositing operations can be deferred to runtime as needed. This runtime processing is typically used for environments, to add unique variations to tiled textures. The popular material authoring tools *Substance Painter* and *Substance Designer* use a similar approach for material compositing, as does the *Mari* texture painting tool.

Blending texture elements on the fly provides a diverse set of effects while conserving memory. Games employ material blending for various purposes, such as:

- Displaying dynamic damage on buildings, vehicles, and living (or undead) creatures [201, 603, 1488, 1778, 1822].

- Enabling user customization of in-game equipment and clothing [604, 1748].

- Increasing visual variety in characters [603, 1488] and environments [39, 656, 1038]. See Figure 20.5 on page 891 for an example.

Sometimes one material is blended on top of another with less than 100% opacity, but even fully opaque blends will have pixels (or texels, if baking into textures) on mask boundaries where a partial blend needs to be performed. In either case, the strictly correct approach would be to evaluate the shading model for each material and blend the results. However, blending the BRDF parameters and then evaluating the shading once is much faster. In the case of material properties that have a linear or nearly linear relationship to the final shaded color, such as the diffuse and specular color parameters, little or no error is introduced by such interpolation. In many cases, even for parameters with a highly nonlinear relationship to the final shaded color (such as specular roughness), the errors introduced along mask boundaries are not objectionable.

Blending normal maps requires special consideration. Often good results can be achieved by treating the process as a blend between height maps from which the normal maps are derived [1086, 1087]. In some cases, such as when overlaying a detail normal map on top of a base surface, other forms of blending are preferable [106].

Material filtering is a topic closely related to material blending. Material properties are typically stored in textures, which are filtered via mechanisms such as GPU bilinear filtering and mipmapping. However, these mechanisms are based on the assumption that the quantity being filtered (which is an input to the shading equation) has a linear relationship to the final color (the output of the shading equation). Linearity again holds for some quantities, but not in general. Artifacts can result from using linear mipmapping methods on normal maps, or on textures containing nonlinear BRDF parameters, such as roughness. These artifacts can manifest as specular aliasing (flickering highlights), or as unexpected changes in surface gloss or brightness with a change in the surface's distance from the camera. Of these two, specular aliasing is much more noticeable; techniques for mitigating these artifacts are often referred to as *specular antialiasing* techniques. We will now discuss several of these methods.

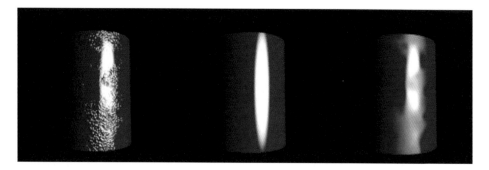

Figure 9.49. On the left, the cylinder is rendered with the original normal map. In the center, a much lower-resolution normal map containing averaged and renormalized normals is used, as shown in the bottom left of Figure 9.50. On the right, the cylinder is rendered with textures at the same low resolution, but containing normal and gloss values fitted to the ideal NDF, as shown in the bottom right of Figure 9.50. The image on the right is a significantly better representation of the original appearance. This surface will also be less prone to aliasing when rendered at low resolution. *(Image courtesy of Patrick Conran, ILM.)*

9.13.1 Filtering Normals and Normal Distributions

The lion's share of material filtering artifacts (primarily from specular aliasing), as well as the most frequently used solutions for them, are related to the filtering of normals and normal distribution functions. Because of its importance, we will discuss this aspect in some depth.

To understand why these artifacts occur and how to solve them, recall that the NDF is a statistical description of subpixel surface structure. When the distance between the camera and surface increases, surface structures that previously covered multiple pixels may be reduced to subpixel size, moving from the realm of bump maps into the realm of the NDF. This transition is intimately tied to the mipmap chain, which encapsulates the reduction of texture details to subpixel size.

Consider how the appearance of an object, such as the cylinder at the left in Figure 9.49, is modeled for rendering. Appearance modeling always assumes a certain scale of observation. *Macroscale* (large-scale) geometry is modeled as triangles, *mesoscale* (middle-scale) geometry is modeled as textures, and *microscale* geometry, smaller than a single pixel, is modeled via the BRDF.

Given the scale shown in the image, it is appropriate to model the cylinder as a smooth mesh (macroscale) and to represent the bumps with a normal map (mesoscale). A Beckmann NDF with a fixed roughness α_b is chosen to model the microscale normal distribution. This combined representation models the cylinder appearance well at this scale. But, what happens when the scale of observation changes?

Study Figure 9.50. The black-framed figure at the top shows a small part of the surface, covered by four normal-map texels. Assume that we are rendering the surface at a scale such that each normal map texel is covered by one pixel on average. For

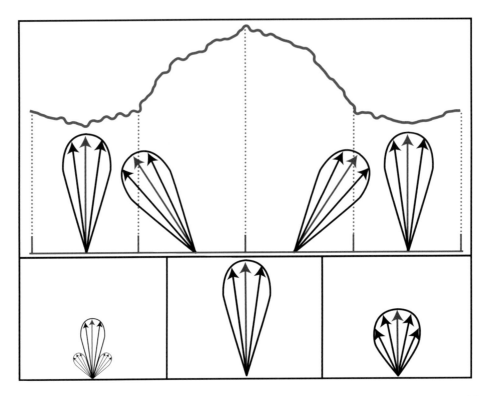

Figure 9.50. Part of the surface from Figure 9.49. The top row shows the normal distributions (the mean normal shown in red) and the implied microgeometry. The bottom row shows three ways to average the four NDFs into one, as done in mipmapping. On the left is the ground truth (averaging the normal distributions), the center shows the result of averaging the mean (normal) and variance (roughness) separately, and the right shows an NDF lobe fitted to the averaged NDF.

each texel, the normal (which is the average, or mean, of the distribution) is shown as a red arrow, surrounded by the Beckmann NDF, shown in black. The normals and NDF implicitly specify an underlying surface structure, shown in cross section. The large hump in the middle is one of the bumps from the normal map, and the small wiggles are the microscale surface structure. Each texel in the normal map, combined with the roughness, can be seen as collecting the distribution of normals across the surface area covered by the texel.

Now assume that the camera has moved further from the object, so that one pixel covers all four of the normal map texels. The ideal representation of the surface at this resolution would exactly represent the distribution of all normals collected across the larger surface area covered by each pixel. This distribution could be found by averaging the NDFs in the four texels of the top-level mipmap. The lower left figure shows this ideal normal distribution. This result, if used for rendering, would most accurately represent the appearance of the surface at this lower resolution.

The bottom center figure shows the result of separately averaging the normals, the mean of each distribution, and the roughness, which corresponds to the width of each. The result has the correct average normal (in red), but the distribution is too narrow. This error will cause the surface to appear too smooth. Worse, since the NDF is so narrow, it will tend to cause aliasing, in the form of flickering highlights.

We cannot represent the ideal normal distribution directly with the Beckmann NDF. However, if we use a roughness map, the Beckmann roughness α_b can be varied from texel to texel. Imagine that, for each ideal NDF, we find the oriented Beckmann lobe that matches it most closely, both in orientation and overall width. We store the center direction of this Beckmann lobe in the normal map, and its roughness value in the roughness map. The results are shown on the bottom right. This NDF is much closer to the ideal. The appearance of the cylinder can be represented much more faithfully with this process than with simple normal averaging, as can be seen in Figure 9.49.

For best results, filtering operations such as mipmapping should be applied to normal distributions, not normals or roughness values. Doing so implies a slightly different way to think about the relationship between the NDFs and the normals. Typically the NDF is defined in the local tangent space determined by the normal map's per-pixel normal. However, when filtering NDFs across different normals, it is more useful to think of the combination of the normal map and roughness map as defining a skewed NDF (one that does not average to a normal pointing straight up) in the tangent space of the underlying geometrical surface.

Early attempts to solve the NDF filtering problem [91, 284, 658] used numerical optimization to fit one or more NDF lobes to the averaged distribution. This approach suffers from robustness and speed issues, and is not used much today. Instead, most techniques currently in use work by computing the variance of the normal distribution. Toksvig [1774] makes a clever observation that if normals are averaged and not renormalized, the length of the averaged normal correlates inversely with the width of the normal distribution. That is, the more the original normals point in different directions, the shorter the normal averaged from them. He presents a method to modify the NDF roughness parameter based on this normal length. Evaluating the BRDF with the modified roughness approximates the spreading effect of the filtered normals.

Toksvig's original equation was intended for use with the Blinn-Phong NDF:

$$\alpha'_p = \frac{\|\overline{\mathbf{n}}\|\alpha_p}{\|\overline{\mathbf{n}}\| + \alpha_p(1 - \|\overline{\mathbf{n}}\|)}, \tag{9.76}$$

where α_p is the original roughness parameter value, α'_p is the modified value, and $\|\overline{\mathbf{n}}\|$ is the length of the averaged normal. The equation can also be used with the Beckmann NDF by applying the equivalence $\alpha_p = 2\alpha_b^{-2} - 2$ (from Walter et al. [1833]), since the shapes of the two NDFs are quite close. Using the method with GGX is less straightforward, since there is no clear equivalence between GGX and Blinn-Phong (or Beckmann). Using the α_b equivalence for α_g gives the same value at the center of the highlight, but the highlight appearance is quite different. More troubling, the variance of the GGX distribution is undefined, which puts this variance-based family of techniques on shaky theoretical ground when used with GGX. Despite these theoretical difficulties, it is fairly common to use Equation 9.76 with the GGX distribution, typically using $\alpha_p = 2\alpha_g^{-2} - 2$. Doing so works reasonably well in practice.

Toksvig's method has the advantage of accounting for normal variance introduced by GPU texture filtering. It also works with the simplest normal mipmapping scheme, linear averaging without normalization. This feature is particularly useful for dynamically generated normal maps such as water ripples, for which mipmap generation must be done on the fly. The method is not as good for static normal maps, since it does not work well with prevailing methods of compressing normal maps. These compression methods rely on the normal being of unit length. Since Toksvig's method relies on the length of the average normal varying, normal maps used with it may have to remain uncompressed. Even then, storing the shortened normals can result in precision issues.

Olano and Baker's LEAN mapping technique [1320] is based on mapping the covariance matrix of the normal distribution. Like Toksvig's technique, it works well with GPU texture filtering and linear mipmapping. It also supports anisotropic normal distributions. Similarly to Toksvig's method, LEAN mapping works well with dynamically generated normals, but to avoid precision issues, it requires a large amount of storage when used with static normals. A similar technique was independently developed by Hery et al. [731, 732] and used in Pixar's animated films to render subpixel details such as metal flakes and small scratches. A simpler variant of LEAN mapping, CLEAN mapping [93], requires less storage at the cost of losing anisotropy support. LEADR mapping [395, 396] extends LEAN mapping to also account for the visibility effects of displacement mapping.

The majority of normal maps used in real-time applications are static, rather than dynamically generated. For such maps, the *variance mapping* family of techniques is commonly used. In these techniques, when the normal map's mipmap chain is generated, the variance that was lost through averaging is computed. Hill [739] notes that the mathematical formulations of Toksvig's technique, LEAN mapping, and CLEAN mapping could each be used to precompute variance in this way, which removes many of the disadvantages of these techniques when used in their original forms. In some cases the precomputed variance values are stored in the mipmap chain of a separate variance texture. More often, these values are used to modify the mipmap chain of an existing roughness map. For example, this method is employed in the variance-mapping technique used in the game *Call of Duty: Black Ops* [998]. The modified roughness values are computed by converting the original roughness values to variance values, adding in the variance from the normal map, and converting the result back to roughness. For the game *The Order: 1886*, Neubelt and Pettineo [1266, 1267] use a technique by Han [658] in a similar way. They convolve the normal map NDF with the NDF of their BRDF's specular term, convert the result to roughness, and store it in a roughness map.

For improved results at the cost of some extra storage, variance can be computed in the texture-space x- and y-directions and stored in an anisotropic roughness map [384, 740, 1823]. By itself this technique is limited to axis-aligned anisotropy, which is typical in man-made surfaces but less so in naturally occurring ones. At the cost of storing one more value, oriented anisotropy can be supported as well [740].

Unlike the original forms of Toksvig, LEAN, and CLEAN mapping, variance mapping techniques do not account for variance introduced by GPU texture filtering. To compensate for this, variance mapping implementations often convolve the top-level mip of the normal map with a small filter [740, 998]. When combining multiple normal maps, e.g., detail normal mapping [106], care needs to be taken to combine the variance of the normal maps correctly [740, 960].

Normal variance can be introduced by high-curvature geometry as well as normal maps. Artifacts resulting from this variance are not mitigated by the previously discussed techniques. A different set of methods exists to address geometry normal variance. If a unique texture mapping exists over the geometry (often the case with characters, less so with environments) then the geometry curvature can be "baked" into the roughness map [740]. The curvature can also be estimated on the fly, using pixel-shader derivative instructions [740, 857, 1229, 1589, 1775, 1823]. This estimation can be done when rendering the geometry, or in a post-process pass, if a normal buffer is available.

The approaches discussed so far focus on specular response, but normal variance can affect diffuse shading as well. Taking account of the effect of normal variance on the $\mathbf{n} \cdot \mathbf{l}$ term can help increase accuracy of both diffuse and specular shading since both are multiplied by this factor in the reflectance integral [740].

Variance mapping techniques approximate the normal distribution as a smooth Gaussian lobe. This is a reasonable approximation if every pixel covers hundreds of thousands of bumps, so that they all average out smoothly. However, in many cases a pixel many cover only a few hundred or a few thousand bumps, which can lead to a "glinty" appearance. An example of this can be seen in Figure 9.25 on page 328, which is a sequence of images showing a sphere with bumps that diminish in size from image to image. The bottom right image shows the result when the bumps are small enough to average into a smooth highlight, but the images on the bottom left and bottom center show bumps that are smaller than a pixel but not small enough to average smoothly. If you were to observe an animated rendering of these spheres, the noisy highlight would appear as glints that sparkle in and out from frame to frame.

If we were to plot the NDF of such a surface, it would look like the left image in Figure 9.51. As the sphere animates, the $\mathbf{h}$ vector moves over the NDF and crosses over bright and dark areas, which causes the "sparkly" appearance. If we were to use variance mapping techniques on this surface, it would effectively approximate this NDF with a smooth NDF similar to the one on the right of Figure 9.51, losing the sparkly details.

In the film industry this is often solved with extensive supersampling, which is not feasible in real-time rendering applications and undesirable even in offline rendering.

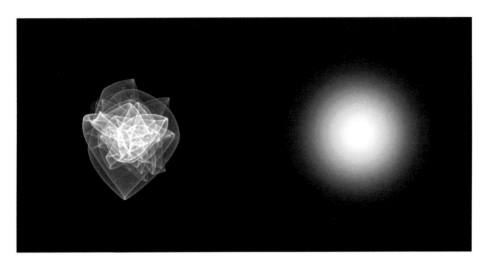

Figure 9.51. On the left is the NDF of a small patch (a few dozen bumps on a side) of a random bumpy surface. On the right is a Beckmann NDF lobe of approximately the same width. *(Image courtesy of Miloš Hašan.)*

Several techniques have been developed to address this issue. Some are unsuitable for real-time use, but may suggest avenues for future research [84, 810, 1941, 1942]. Two techniques have been designed for real-time implementation. Wang and Bowles [187, 1837] present a technique that is used to render sparkling snow in the game *Disney Infinity 3.0*. The technique aims to produce a plausible sparkly appearance rather than simulating a particular NDF. It is intended for use on materials such as snow that have relatively sparse sparkles. Zirr and Kaplanyan's technique [1974] simulates normal distributions on multiple scales, is spatially and temporally stable, and allows for a wider variety of appearances.

We do not have space to cover all of the extensive literature on material filtering, so we will mention a few notable references. Bruneton et al. [204] present a technique for handling variance on ocean surfaces across scales from geometry to BRDF, including environment lighting. Schilling [1565] discusses a variance mapping-like technique that supports anisotropic shading with environment maps. Bruneton and Neyret [205] provide a thorough overview of earlier work in this area.

Further Reading and Resources

McGuire's *Graphics Codex* [1188] and Glassner's *Principles of Digital Image Synthesis* [543, 544] are good references for many of the topics covered in this chapter. Some parts of Dutré's *Global Illumination Compendium* [399] are a bit dated (the BRDF models section in particular), but it is a good reference for rendering mathematics (e.g., spherical and hemispherical integrals). Glassner's and Dutré's references are both freely available online.

For the reader curious to learn more about the interactions of light and matter, we recommend Feynman's incomparable lectures [469] (available online), which were invaluable to our own understanding when writing the physics parts of this chapter. Other useful references include *Introduction to Modern Optics* by Fowles [492], which is a short and accessible introductory text, and *Principles of Optics* by Born and Wolf [177], a heavier (figuratively and literally) book that provides a more in-depth overview. *The Physics and Chemistry of Color* by Nassau [1262] describes the physical phenomena behind the colors of objects in great thoroughness and detail.

Chapter 10
Local Illumination

"Light makes right."
—Andrew Glassner

In Chapter 9 we discussed the theory of physically based materials, and how to evaluate them with punctual light sources. With this content we can perform shading computations by simulating how lights interact with surfaces, in order to measure how much radiance is sent in a given direction to our virtual camera. This spectral radiance is the scene-referred pixel color that will be converted (Section 8.2) to the display-referred color a given pixel will have in the final image.

In reality, the interactions that we need to consider are never punctual. We have seen in Section 9.13.1 how, in order to correctly evaluate shading, we have to solve the integral of the surface BRDF response over the entire *pixel footprint*, which is the projection of the pixel area onto the surface. This process of integration can also be thought as an antialiasing solution. Instead of sampling a shading function that does not have a bound on its frequency components, we pre-integrate.

Up to this point, the effects of only point and directional light sources have been presented, which limits surfaces to receive light from a handful of discrete directions. This description of lighting is incomplete. In reality, surfaces receive light from all incoming directions. Outdoors scenes are not just lit by the sun. If that were true, all surfaces in shadow or facing away from the sun would be black. The sky is an important source of light, caused by sunlight scattering from the atmosphere. The importance of sky light can be seen by looking at a picture of the moon, which lacks sky light because it has no atmosphere. See Figure 10.1.

On overcast days, and at dusk or dawn, outdoor lighting is all sky light. Even on a clear day, the sun subtends a cone when seen from the earth, so is not infinitesimally small. Curiously, the sun and the moon both subtend similar angles, around half a degree, despite their enormous size difference—the sun is two orders of magnitude larger in radius than the moon.

In reality, lighting is never punctual. Infinitesimal entities are useful in some situations as cheap approximations, or as building blocks for more complete models. In order to form a more realistic lighting model, we need to integrate the BRDF

Figure 10.1. Image taken on the moon, which has no sky light due to the lack of an atmosphere to scatter sunlight. This image shows what a scene looks like when it is lit by only a direct light source. Note the pitch-black shadows and lack of any detail on surfaces facing away from the sun. This photograph shows Astronaut James B. Irwin next to the Lunar Roving Vehicle during the Apollo 15 mission. The shadow in the foreground is from the Lunar Module. Photograph taken by Astronaut David R. Scott, Commander. *(Image from NASA's collection.)*

response over the full hemisphere of incident directions on the surface. In real-time rendering we prefer to solve the integrals that the rendering equation (Section 11.1) entails by finding closed-form solutions or approximations of these. We usually avoid averaging multiple samples (rays), as this approach tends to be much slower. See Figure 10.2.

This chapter is dedicated to the exploration of such solutions. In particular, we want to extend our shading model by computing the BRDF with a variety of non-punctual light sources. Often, in order to find inexpensive solutions (or any at all), we will need to approximate the light emitter, the BRDF, or both. It is important to evaluate the final shading results in a perceptual framework, understanding what elements matter most in the final image and so allocate more effort toward these.

We start this chapter with formulae to integrate analytic area light sources. Such emitters are the principal lights in the scene, responsible for most of the direct lighting

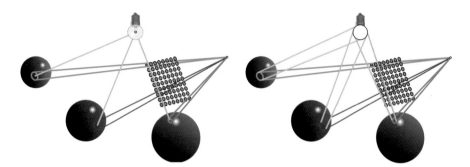

Figure 10.2. On the left, the integrals we have seen in Chapter 9: surface area and punctual light. On the right, the objective of this chapter will be to extend our shading mathematics to account for the integral over the light surface.

intensity, so for these we need to retain all of our chosen material properties. Shadows should be computed for such emitters, as light leaks will result in obvious artifacts. We then investigate ways to represent more general lighting environments, ones that consist of arbitrary distributions over the incoming hemisphere. We typically accept more approximated solutions in these cases. Environment lighting is used for large, complex, but also less intense sources of light. Examples include light scattered from the sky and clouds, *indirect light* bouncing off large objects in the scene, and dimmer direct area light sources. Such emitters are important for the correct balance of the image that would otherwise appear too dark. Even if we consider the effect of indirect light sources, we are still not in the realm of *global illumination* (Chapter 11), which depends on the explicit knowledge of other surfaces in the scene.

10.1 Area Light Sources

In Chapter 9 we described idealized, infinitesimal light sources: punctual and directional. Figure 10.3 shows the incident hemisphere on a surface point, and the difference between an infinitesimal source and an *area light source* with a nonzero size. The light source on the left uses the definitions discussed in Section 9.4. It illuminates the surface from a single direction $\mathbf{l}_c$. Its brightness is represented by its color $\mathbf{c}_{\text{light}}$, defined as the reflected radiance from a white Lambertian surface facing toward the light. The point or directional light's contribution to the outgoing radiance $L_o(\mathbf{v})$ in direction $\mathbf{v}$ is $\pi f(\mathbf{l}_c, \mathbf{v})\mathbf{c}_{\text{light}}(\mathbf{n} \cdot \mathbf{l}_c)^+$ (note the x^+ notation for clamping negative numbers to zero, introduced in Section 1.2). Alternatively, the brightness of the area light source (on the right) is represented by its radiance L_l. The area light *subtends* a solid angle ω_l from the surface location. Its contribution to the outgoing radiance in direction $\mathbf{v}$ is the integral of $f(\mathbf{l}, \mathbf{v})L_l(\mathbf{n} \cdot \mathbf{l})^+$ over ω_l.

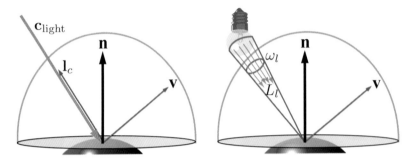

Figure 10.3. A surface illuminated by a light source, considering the hemisphere of possible incoming light directions defined by the surface normal **n**. On the left, the light source is infinitesimal. On the right, it is modeled as an area light source.

The fundamental approximation behind infinitesimal light sources is expressed in the following equation:

$$L_o(\mathbf{v}) = \int_{\mathbf{l} \in \omega_l} f(\mathbf{l}, \mathbf{v}) L_l (\mathbf{n} \cdot \mathbf{l})^+ d\mathbf{l} \approx \pi f(\mathbf{l}_c, \mathbf{v}) \mathbf{c}_{\text{light}} (\mathbf{n} \cdot \mathbf{l}_c)^+. \tag{10.1}$$

The amount that an area light source contributes to the illumination of a surface location is a function of both its radiance (L_l) and its size as seen from that location (ω_l). As we have seen in Section 9.4, point and directional light sources are approximations that cannot be realized in practice since their zero solid angle implies an infinite radiance. Understanding the visual errors that are introduced by the approximation will help to know when to use it, and what approach to take when it cannot be used. These errors will depend on two factors: how large the light source is, measured by the solid angle it covers from the shaded point, and how glossy the surface is.

Figure 10.4 shows how the specular highlight size and shape on a surface depends on both the material roughness and the size of the light source. For a small light source, one that subtends a tiny solid angle compared to the view angle, the error is small. Rough surfaces also tend to show the effect of the light source size less than polished ones. In general, both the area light emission toward a surface point and the specular lobe of the surface BRDF are spherical functions. If we consider the set of directions where the contributions of these two functions are significant, we obtain two solid angles. The determining factor in the error is proportional to the relative size of the emission angle compared to the size of the BRDF specular highlight solid angle.

Finally, note that the highlight from an area light can be approximated by using a punctual light and increasing the surface roughness. This observation is useful for deriving less-costly approximations to the area light integral. It also explains why in practice many real-time rendering system produce plausible results using only punctual sources: Artists compensate for the error. However, doing so is detrimental,

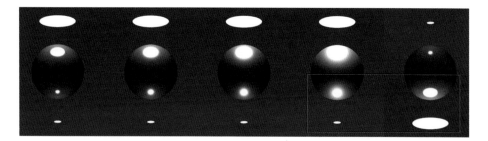

Figure 10.4. From left to right, the material of the sphere increases in surface roughness, using the GGX BRDF. The rightmost image replicates the first in the series, flipped vertically. Notice how the highlight and shading caused by a large disk light on a low-roughness material can look similar to the highlight caused by a smaller light source on a much rougher material.

as it couples material properties with the particular lighting setup. Content created this way will not look right when the lighting scenario is altered.

For the special case of Lambertian surfaces, using a point light for an area light can be exact. For such surfaces, the outgoing radiance is proportional to the irradiance:

$$L_o(\mathbf{v}) = \frac{\rho_{ss}}{\pi} E, \qquad (10.2)$$

where ρ_{ss} is the subsurface albedo, or diffuse color, of the surface (Section 9.9.1). This relationship lets us use the equivalent of Equation 10.1 for computing irradiance, which is much simpler:

$$E = \int_{\mathbf{l} \in \omega_l} L_l (\mathbf{n} \cdot \mathbf{l})^+ d\mathbf{l} \approx \pi \mathbf{c}_{\text{light}} (\mathbf{n} \cdot \mathbf{l}_c)^+. \qquad (10.3)$$

The concept of *vector irradiance* is useful to understand how irradiance behaves in the presence of area light sources. Vector irradiance was introduced by Gershun [526], who called it the *light vector*, and further extended by Arvo [73]. Using vector irradiance, an area light source of arbitrary size and shape can be accurately converted into a point or directional light source.

Imagine a distribution of radiance L_i coming into a point $\mathbf{p}$ in space. See Figure 10.5. We will assume for now that L_i is wavelength-independent and thus can be represented as a scalar. For every infinitesimal solid angle $d\mathbf{l}$ centered on an incoming direction $\mathbf{l}$, a vector is constructed that is aligned with $\mathbf{l}$ and has a length equal to the (scalar) radiance incoming from that direction times $d\mathbf{l}$. Finally, all these vectors are summed to produce the vector irradiance $\mathbf{e}$:

$$\mathbf{e}(\mathbf{p}) = \int_{\mathbf{l} \in \Theta} L_i(\mathbf{p}, \mathbf{l}) \, \mathbf{l} \, d\mathbf{l}, \qquad (10.4)$$

where Θ indicates that the integral is performed over the entire sphere of directions.

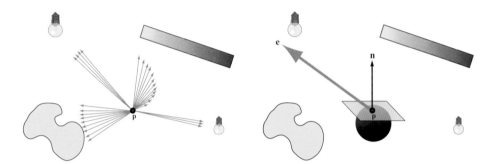

Figure 10.5. Computation of vector irradiance. Left: point **p** is surrounded by light sources of various shapes, sizes, and radiance distributions. The brightness of the yellow color indicates the amount of radiance emitted. The orange arrows are vectors pointing in all directions from which there is any incoming radiance, and each length is equal to the amount of radiance coming from that direction times the infinitesimal solid angle covered by the arrow. In principle there should be an infinite number of arrows. Right: the vector irradiance (large orange arrow) is the sum of all these vectors. The vector irradiance can be used to compute the *net irradiance* of any plane at point **p**.

The vector irradiance **e** can be used to find the net irradiance at **p** through a plane of any orientation by performing a dot product:

$$E(\mathbf{p}, \mathbf{n}) - E(\mathbf{p}, -\mathbf{n}) = \mathbf{n} \cdot \mathbf{e}(\mathbf{p}), \tag{10.5}$$

where **n** is the normal to the plane. The net irradiance through a plane is the difference between the irradiance flowing through the "positive side" of the plane (defined by the plane normal **n**) and that flowing through the "negative side." By itself, the net irradiance is not useful for shading. However, if no radiance is emitted through the "negative side" (in other words, the light distribution being analyzed has no parts for which the angle between **l** and **n** exceeds 90°), then $E(\mathbf{p}, -\mathbf{n}) = 0$ and

$$E(\mathbf{p}, \mathbf{n}) = \mathbf{n} \cdot \mathbf{e}(\mathbf{p}). \tag{10.6}$$

The vector irradiance of a single area light source can be used with Equation 10.6 to light Lambertian surfaces with any normal **n**, as long as **n** does not face more than 90° away from any part of the area light source. See Figure 10.6.

If our assumption that L_i is wavelength-independent does not hold, then in the general case we can no longer define a single vector **e**. However, colored lights often have the same relative spectral distribution at all points, which means that we can factor L_i into a color $\mathbf{c}'$ and a wavelength-independent radiance distribution L_i'. In this case we can compute **e** for L_i' and extend Equation 10.6 by multiplying $\mathbf{n} \cdot \mathbf{e}$ by $\mathbf{c}'$. Doing so results in the same equation used to compute the irradiance from a

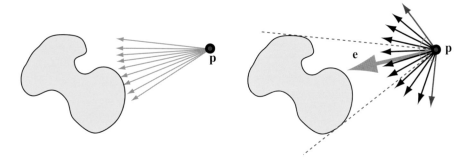

Figure 10.6. Vector irradiance of a single area light source. On the left, the arrows represent the vectors used to compute the vector irradiance. On the right, the large orange arrow is the vector irradiance **e**. The red dashed lines represent the extent of the light source, and the red vectors (each perpendicular to one of the red dashed lines) define the limits of the set of surface normals. Normals outside this set will have an angle greater than 90° with some part of the area light source. Such normals cannot use **e** to compute their irradiance correctly.

directional light source, with the following substitutions:

$$
\mathbf{l}_c = \frac{\mathbf{e}(\mathbf{p})}{\|\mathbf{e}(\mathbf{p})\|},
$$
$$
\mathbf{c}_{\text{light}} = \mathbf{c}' \frac{\|\mathbf{e}(\mathbf{p})\|}{\pi}.
\tag{10.7}
$$

We have effectively converted an area light source of arbitrary shape and size to a directional light source—without introducing any error.

Equation 10.4 for finding the vector irradiance can be solved analytically for simple cases. For example, imagine a spherical light source with a center at $\mathbf{p}_l$ and a radius r_l. The light emits a constant radiance L_l from every point on the sphere, in all directions. For such a light source, Equations 10.4 and 10.7 yield the following:

$$
\mathbf{l}_c = \frac{\mathbf{p}_l - \mathbf{p}}{\|\mathbf{p}_l - \mathbf{p}\|},
$$
$$
\mathbf{c}_{\text{light}} = \frac{r_l^2}{\|\mathbf{p}_l - \mathbf{p}\|^2} L_l.
\tag{10.8}
$$

This equation is the same as an omni light (Section 5.2.2) with $\mathbf{c}_{\text{light}_0} = L_l$, $r_0 = r_l$, and the standard inverse square distance falloff[1] function. This falloff function can be adjusted to account for points inside the sphere, and to bound the light influence to a given maximum distance. More details on such adjustments can be found in Section 5.2.2.

---

[1]Note that while, for spherical lights, the falloff does take the usual inverse square distance formulation (where the distance is taken from the light surface, not its center), this is not in general true for all area light shapes. Notably, disk lights have a falloff proportional to $1/(d^2 + 1)$.

All this is correct only if there is no "negative side" irradiance. Another way to think about it is that no parts of the area light source can be "under the horizon," or occluded by the surface. We can generalize this statement. For Lambertian surfaces, all disparities between area and point light sources result from occlusion differences. The irradiance from a point light source obeys a cosine law for all normals for which the light is not occluded. Snyder derived an analytic expression for a spherical light source, taking occlusion into account [1671]. This expression is quite complex. However, since it depends on only two quantities (r/r_l and θ_i, the angle between $\mathbf{n}$ and $\mathbf{l}_c$), it can be precomputed into a two-dimensional texture. Snyder also gives two functional approximations that are amenable for real-time rendering.

In Figure 10.4 we saw that the effects of area lighting are less noticeable for rough surfaces. This observation allows us also to use a less physically based but still effective method for modeling the effects of area lights on Lambertian surfaces: *wrap lighting*. In this technique, some simple modification is done to the value of $\mathbf{n} \cdot \mathbf{l}$ before it is clamped to 0. One form of wrap lighting is given by Forsyth [487]:

$$E = \pi \mathbf{c}_{\text{light}} \left(\frac{(\mathbf{n} \cdot \mathbf{l}) + k_{\text{wrap}}}{1 + k_{\text{wrap}}} \right)^+, \tag{10.9}$$

where k_{wrap} ranges from 0, for point light sources, to 1, for area light sources covering the entire hemisphere. Another form that mimics the effect of a large area light source is used by Valve [1222]:

$$E = \pi \mathbf{c}_{\text{light}} \left(\frac{(\mathbf{n} \cdot \mathbf{l}) + 1}{2} \right)^2. \tag{10.10}$$

In general, if we compute area lighting, we should also modify our shadowing computations to take into account a non-punctual source. If we do not, some of the visual effect can be canceled out by the harsh shadows [193]. Soft shadows are perhaps the most visible effect of area light sources, as discussed in Chapter 7.

10.1.1 Glossy Materials

The effects of area lights on non-Lambertian surfaces are more involved. Snyder derives a solution for spherical light sources [1671], but it is limited to the original reflection-vector Phong material model and is extremely complex. In practice today approximations are needed.

The primary visual effect of area lights on glossy surfaces is the highlight. See Figure 10.4. Its size and shape are similar to the area light, while the edge of the highlight is blurred according to the roughness of the surface. This observation has led to several empirical approximations of the effect. These can be quite convincing in practice. For example, we could modify the result of our highlight calculation to incorporate a cutoff threshold that creates a large flat highlight area [606]. This can effectively create the illusion of a specular reflection from a spherical light, as in Figure 10.7.

Figure 10.7. Highlights on smooth objects are sharp reflections of the light source shape. On the left, this appearance has been approximated by thresholding the highlight value of a Blinn-Phong shader. On the right, the same object is rendered with an unmodified Blinn-Phong shader for comparison. *(Image courtesy of Larry Gritz.)*

Most of the practical approximations of area lighting effects for real-time rendering are based on the idea of finding, per shaded point, an equivalent punctual lighting setup that would mimic the effects of a non-infinitesimal light source. This methodology is often used in real-time rendering to solve a variety of problems. It is the same principle we saw in Chapter 9 when dealing with BRDF integrals over the pixel footprint of a surface. It yields approximations that are usually inexpensive, as all the work is done by altering the inputs to the shading equation without introducing any extra complexity. Because the mathematics is not otherwise altered, we can often guarantee that, under certain conditions, we revert to evaluating the original shading, thus preserving all its properties. Since most of a typical system's shading code is based on punctual lights, using these for area lights introduces only localized code changes.

One of the first approximations developed is Mittring's *roughness modification* used in the Unreal Engine's "Elemental demo" [1229]. The idea is to first find a cone that contains most of the light source irradiance onto the hemisphere of directions incident to the surface. We then fit a similar cone around the specular lobe, containing "most" of the BRDF. See Figure 10.8. Both cones are then stand-ins for functions on the hemisphere, and they encompass the set of directions where these two functions have values greater than a given, arbitrary cutoff threshold. Having done so, we can approximate the convolution between the light source and the material BRDF by finding a new BRDF lobe, of a different roughness, that has a corresponding cone whose solid angle is equal to the sum of the light lobe angle and the material one.

Karis [861] shows an application of Mittring's principle to the GGX/Trowbridge-Reitz BRDF (Section 9.8.1) and a spherical area light, resulting in a simple modification of the GGX roughness parameter α_g:

$$\alpha_g' = \left(\alpha_g + \frac{r_l}{2\|\mathbf{p}_l - \mathbf{p}\|}\right)^{\overline{\mp}}.$$

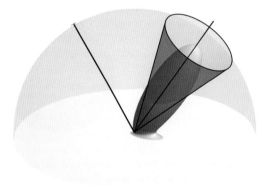

Figure 10.8. The GGX BRDF, and a cone fitted to enclose the set of directions where the specular lobe reflects most of the incoming light radiance.

Note the use of the notation $\overline{x^{\mp}}$, introduced in Section 1.2, for clamping between 0 and 1. This approximation works reasonably well and is extremely inexpensive, but breaks down for shiny, almost mirror-like materials. This failure occurs because the specular lobe is always smooth and cannot mimic the highlight caused by a sharp reflection of an area light source onto a surface. Also, most microfacet BRDF models have a lobe that are not "compact" (localized) but exhibit a wide falloff (specular tail), making roughness remapping less effective. See Figure 10.9.

Instead of varying the material roughness, another idea is to represent the area illumination's source with a light direction that changes based on the point being shaded. This is called a *most representative point* solution, modifying the light vector so it is in the direction of the point on the area light surface that generates the greatest

Figure 10.9. Spherical lighting. From left to right: reference solution computed by numerical integration, roughness modification technique, and representative point technique. *(Image courtesy of Brian Karis, Epic Games Inc.)*

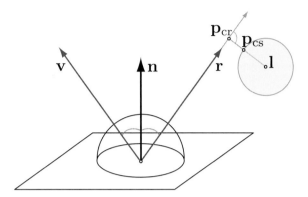

Figure 10.10. Karis representative point approximation for spheres. First, the point on the reflection ray closest to the sphere center $\mathbf{l}$ is computed: $\mathbf{p}_{cr} = (\mathbf{l} \cdot \mathbf{r})\mathbf{r} - \mathbf{l}$. The point on the sphere surface closest to $\mathbf{p}_{cr}$ is then $\mathbf{p}_{cs} = \mathbf{l} + \mathbf{p}_{cr} \cdot \min(1, \frac{\text{radius}}{||\mathbf{p}_{cr}||})$.

energy contribution toward the shaded surface. See Figure 10.9. Picott [1415] uses the point on the light that creates the smallest angle to the reflection ray. Karis [861] improves on Picott's formulation by approximating, for efficiency, the point of smallest angle with the point on the sphere that is at the shortest distance to the reflection ray. He also presents an inexpensive formula to scale the light's intensity to try to preserve the overall emitted energy. See Figure 10.10. Most representative point solutions are convenient and have been developed for a variety of light geometries, so it is important to understand their theoretical background. These approaches resemble the idea of *importance sampling* in Monte Carlo integration, where we numerically compute the value of a definite integral by averaging samples over the integration domain. In order to do so more efficiently, we can try to prioritize samples that have a large contribution to the overall average.

A more stringent justification of their effectiveness lies in the *mean value theorem* of definite integrals, which allows us to replace the integral of a function with a single evaluation of the same function:

$$\int_D f(x)dx = f(c) \int_D 1. \qquad (10.11)$$

If $f(x)$ is continuous in D, then $\int_D 1$ is the area of the domain, with the point $c \in D$ lying on the line between the function minimum and maximum in D. For lighting, the integral we consider is the product of the BRDF and the light irradiance over the area of the hemisphere covered by the light. We usually consider our lights to be irradiating uniformly, so we need to consider only light falloff, and most approximations also assume the domain area D to be fully visible from the shaded point. Even with these assumptions, determining the point c and the normalization factor $\int_D 1$ can still be too expensive, so further approximations are employed.

Representative point solutions can also be framed by the effect they have on the shape of the highlight. On a portion of a surface where the representative point does not change because the reflection vector is outside the cone of directions subtended by the area light, we are effectively lighting with a point light. The shape of the highlight then depends only on the underlying shape of the specular lobe. Alternatively, if we are shading points on the surface where the reflection vector hits the area light, then the representative point will continuously change in order to point toward the direction of maximum contribution. Doing so effectively extends the specular lobe peak, "widening" it, an effect that is similar to the hard thresholding of Figure 10.7.

This wide, constant highlight peak is also one of the remaining sources of error in the approximation. On rougher surfaces the area light reflection looks "sharper" than the ground-truth solution (i.e., obtained via Monte Carlo integration)—an opposite visual defect to the excessive blur of the roughness modification technique. To address this, Iwanicki and Pesce [807] develop approximations obtained by fitting BRDF lobes, soft thresholds, representative point parameters, and scaling factors (for energy conservation) to spherical area lighting results computed via numerical integration. These fitted functions result in a table of parameters that are indexed by material roughness, sphere radius, and the angle between the light source center and the surface normal and view vectors. As it is expensive to directly use such multi-dimensional lookup tables in a shader, closed-form approximations are provided. Recently, de Carpentier [231] derived an improved formulation to better preserve the shape of the highlight from a spherical area source at grazing angles for microfacet-based BRDFs. This method works by finding a representative point that maximizes $\mathbf{n} \cdot \mathbf{h}$, the dot product between the surface normal and the light-view half vector, instead of $\mathbf{n} \cdot \mathbf{r}$ of the original formulation (which was derived for the Phong BRDF).

10.1.2 General Light Shapes

So far we have seen a few ways to compute shading from uniformly emitting spherical area lights and arbitrary glossy BRDFs. Most of these methods employ various approximations in order to arrive at mathematical formulae that are fast to evaluate in real time, and thus display varying degrees of error when compared to a ground-truth solution of the problem. However, even if we had the computational power to derive an exact solution, we would still be committing a large error, one that we embedded in the assumptions of our lighting model. Real-world lights usually are not spheres, and they hardly would be perfect uniform emitters. See Figure 10.11. Spherical area lights are still useful in practice, because they provide the simplest way to break the erroneous correlation between lighting and surface roughness that punctual lights introduce. However, spherical sources are typically a good approximation of most real light fixtures only if these are relatively small.

As the objective of physically based real-time rendering is to generate convincing, plausible images, there is only so far that we can go in this pursuit by limiting ourselves to an idealized scenario. This is a recurring trade-off in computer graphics. We can

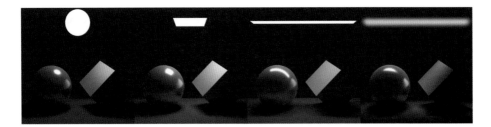

Figure 10.11. Commonly used light shapes. From left to right: sphere, rectangle (card), tube (line), and a tube with focused emission (concentrated along the light surface normal, not evenly spread in the hemisphere). Note the different highlights they create.

usually choose between generating accurate solutions to easier problems that make simplifying assumptions or deriving approximate solutions to more general problems that model reality more closely.

One of the simplest extensions to spherical lights are "tube" lights (also called "capsules"), which can be useful to represent real-world fluorescent tube lights. See Figure 10.12. For Lambertian BRDFs, Picott [1415] shows a closed-form formula of the lighting integral, which is equivalent to evaluating the lighting from two point lights at the extremes of the linear light segment with an appropriate falloff function:

$$\int_{\mathbf{p}_0}^{\mathbf{p}_1} \left(\mathbf{n} \cdot \frac{\mathbf{x}}{\|\mathbf{x}\|} \right) \frac{1}{\|\mathbf{x}\|^2} d\mathbf{x} = \frac{\frac{\mathbf{n} \cdot \mathbf{p}_0}{\|\mathbf{p}_0\|^2} + \frac{\mathbf{n} \cdot \mathbf{p}_1}{\|\mathbf{p}_1\|^2}}{\|\mathbf{p}_0\|\|\mathbf{p}_1\| + (\mathbf{p}_0 \cdot \mathbf{p}_1)}, \tag{10.12}$$

where $\mathbf{p}_0$ and $\mathbf{p}_1$ are the two endpoints of the linear light and $\mathbf{n}$ is the surface normal. Picott also derives a representative point solution for the integral with a Phong specular BRDF, approximating it as the lighting from a point light placed at the position on the light segment that, when joined to the surface point under consideration, forms the

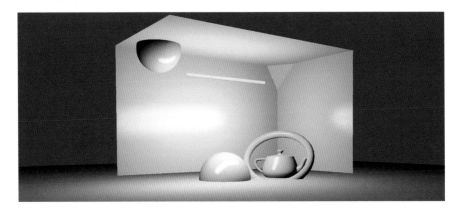

Figure 10.12. A tube light. The image was computed using the representative point solution [807].

smallest angle to the reflection vector. This representative point solution dynamically transforms the linear light into a point one, so we can then use any approximation for spherical light to "thicken" the light fixture into a capsule.

As in the case of spherical lights, Karis [861] presents a more efficient (but somewhat less accurate) variant on Picott's original solution, by using the point on the line with the smallest distance to the reflection vector (instead of the smallest angle), and presents a scaling formula in an attempt to restore energy conservation.

Representative point approximations for many other light shapes could be obtained fairly easily, such as for rings and Bézier segments, but we usually do not want to branch our shaders too much. Good light shapes are ones that can be used to represent many real-world lights in our scenes. One of the most expressive classes of shapes are *planar area lights*, defined as a section of a plane bound by a given geometrical shape, e.g., a rectangle (in which case they are also called *card lights*), a disk, or more generally a polygon. These primitives can be used for emissive panels such as billboards and television screens, to stand in for commonly employed photographic lighting (softboxes, bounce cards), to model the aperture of many more complex lighting fixtures, or to represent lighting reflecting from walls and other large surfaces in a scene.

One of the first practical approximations to card lights (and disks, as well) was derived by Drobot [380]. This again is a representative point solution, but it is particularly notable both because of the complexity of extending this methodology to two-dimensional areas of a plane, and for the overall approach to the solution. Drobot starts from the mean value theorem and, as a first approximation, determines that a good candidate point for light evaluation should lie near the global maximum of the lighting integral.

For a Lambert BRDF, this integral is

$$L_l \int_{\mathbf{l} \in \omega_l} (\mathbf{n} \cdot \mathbf{l})^+ \frac{1}{r_{\mathbf{l}}^2} \, d\mathbf{l}, \tag{10.13}$$

where L_l is the constant radiance emitted by the light, ω_l is the solid angle subtended by the light geometry, $r_{\mathbf{l}}$ is the length of the ray from the surface to the light plane in the direction $\mathbf{l}$, and $(\mathbf{n} \cdot \mathbf{l})^+$ is the usual Lambertian clamped dot product. The maximum of $(\mathbf{n} \cdot \mathbf{l})^+$ is the point $\mathbf{p}_c$ on the boundary of the light region that is closest to the point $\mathbf{p}'$ found by intersecting a ray originating from the surface, in the direction of the normal, with the light plane. Similarly, the maximum of $1/r_{\mathbf{l}}^2$ is the point $\mathbf{p}_r$ on the boundary closest to the point $\mathbf{p}''$ that is the closest on the light plane to the surface point being shaded. See Figure 10.13. The global maximum of the integrand will then lie somewhere on the segment connecting $\mathbf{p}_r$ and $\mathbf{p}_c$: $\mathbf{p}_{\max} = t_m \mathbf{p}_c + (1 - t_m)\mathbf{p}_r$, $t_m \in [0, 1]$. Drobot uses numerical integration to find the best representative point for many different configurations, and then finds a single t_m that works best on average.

Drobot's final solution employs further approximations for both diffuse and specular lighting, all motivated by comparisons with the ground-truth solution found numerically. He also derives an algorithm for the important case of *textured card lights*,

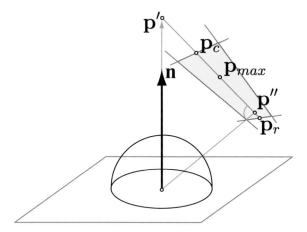

Figure 10.13. Geometric construction of Drobot's rectangular area light representative point approximation.

where the emission is not assumed to be constant but is modulated by a texture, over the rectangular region of the light. This process is executed using a three-dimensional lookup table containing pre-integrated versions of the emission textures over circular footprints of varying radii. Mittring [1228] employs a similar method for glossy reflections, intersecting a reflection ray with a textured, rectangular billboard and indexing precomputed blurred version of the texture depending on the ray intersection distance. This work precedes Drobot's developments, but is a more empirical, less principled approach that does try to match a ground-truth integral solution.

For the more general case of planar *polygonal area lights*, Lambert [967] originally derived an exact closed-form solution for perfectly diffuse surfaces. This method was improved by Arvo [74], allowing for glossy materials modeled as Phong specular lobes. Arvo achieves this by extending the concept of vector irradiance to higher-dimensional *irradiance tensors* and employing *Stoke's theorem* to solve an area integral as a simpler integral along the contour of the integration domain. The only assumptions his method makes are that the light is fully visible from the shaded surface points (a common one to make, which can be circumvented by clipping the light polygon with the plane tangent to the surface) and that the BRDF is a radially symmetric cosine lobe. Unfortunately, in practice Arvo's analytic solution is quite expensive for real-time rendering, as it requires evaluating a formula whose time complexity is linear in the exponent of the Phong lobe used, per each edge of the area light polygon. Recently Lecocq [1004] made this method more practical by finding an $O(1)$ approximation to the contour integral function and extending the solution to general, half-vector-based BRDFs.

All practical real-time area lighting methods described so far employ both certain simplifying assumptions to allow the derivation of analytic constructions and

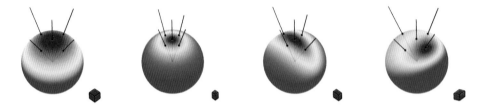

Figure 10.14. The key idea behind the linearly transformed cosine technique is that a simple cosine lobe (on the left) can be easily scaled, stretched, and skewed by using a 3×3 transform matrix. This allows the cosine lobe to take many different shapes on the sphere. *(Image courtesy of Eric Heitz.)*

approximations to deal with the resulting integrals. Heitz et al. [711] take a different approach with *linearly transformed cosines* (LTCs), which yield a practical, accurate, and general technique. Their method starts with devising a category of functions on the sphere that both are highly expressive (i.e., they can take many shapes) and can be integrated easily over arbitrary spherical polygons. See Figure 10.14. LTCs use just a cosine lobe transformed by a 3×3 matrix, so they can be resized, stretched, and rotated over the hemisphere to adapt to a variety of shapes. The integral of a simple cosine lobe (unlike Blinn-Phong, not taken to an exponent) with a spherical polygon is well established, dating back to Lambert [74, 967]. The key observation Heitz et al. make is that extending the integral with a transformation matrix on the lobe does not change its complexity. We can transform the polygonal domain by the inverse of the matrix and cancel the matrix inside the integral, returning to a simple cosine lobe as the integrand. See Figure 10.15. For generic BRDFs and area light shapes, the only remaining work left is to find ways (approximations) to express the BRDF function on the sphere as one or more LTCs, work that can be done offline and tabulated in lookup arrays indexed with the BRDF parameters: roughness, incidence angle, and so

Figure 10.15. Given an LTC and a spherical polygonal domain (on the left), we can transform them both by the inverse of the LTC matrix to obtain a simple cosine lobe and new domain (on the right). The integral of the cosine lobe with the transformed domain is equal to the integral of the LTC over the original domain. *(Image courtesy of Eric Heitz.)*

on. Linearly transformed cosine-based solutions are derived both for general textured polygonal area light sources and for specialized, cheaper-to-compute shapes such as card, disk, and line lights. LTCs can be more expensive than representative point solutions, but are much more accurate.

10.2 Environment Lighting

In principle, reflectance (Equation 9.3) does not distinguish between light arriving directly from a light source and indirect light that has been scattered from the sky or objects in the scene. All incoming directions have radiance, and the reflectance equation integrates over them all. However, in practice direct light is usually distinguished by relatively small solid angles with high radiance values, and indirect light tends to diffusely cover the rest of the hemisphere with moderate to low radiance values. This split provides good practical reasons to handle the two separately.

So far, the area light techniques discussed integrating constant radiance emitted from the light's shape. Doing so creates for each shaded surface point a set of directions that have a constant nonzero incoming radiance. What we examine now are methods to integrate radiance defined by a varying function over all the possible incoming directions. See Figure 10.16.

While we will generally talk about indirect and "environment" lighting here, we are not going to investigate global illumination algorithms. The key distinction is that in this chapter all the shading mathematics does not depend on the knowledge of other surfaces in the scene, but rather on a small set of light primitives. So, while we could, for example, use an area light to model the bounce of the light off a wall, which is a global effect, the shading algorithm does not need to know about the existence of the wall. The only information it has is about a light source, and all the shading is performed locally. Global illumination (Chapter 11) will often be closely related to the concepts of this chapter, as many solutions can be seen as ways to compute the

Figure 10.16. Rendering of a scene under different environment lighting scenarios.

right set of local light primitives to use for every object or surface location in order to simulate the interactions of light bouncing around the scene.

Ambient light is the simplest model of environment lighting, where the radiance does not vary with direction and has a constant value L_A. Even such a basic model of environment lighting improves visual quality significantly. A scene with no consideration of the light indirectly bounced from objects appears highly unrealistic. Objects in shadow or facing away from the light in such a scene would be completely black, which is unlike any scene found in reality. The moonscape in Figure 10.1 on page 376 comes close, but even in such scenes some indirect light reflects off nearby objects.

The exact effects of ambient light will depend on the BRDF. For Lambertian surfaces, the fixed radiance L_A results in a constant contribution to outgoing radiance, regardless of surface normal $\mathbf{n}$ or view direction $\mathbf{v}$:

$$L_o(\mathbf{v}) = \frac{\rho_{ss}}{\pi} L_A \int_{\mathbf{l} \in \Omega} (\mathbf{n} \cdot \mathbf{l}) d\mathbf{l} = \rho_{ss} L_A. \qquad (10.14)$$

When shading, this constant outgoing radiance contribution is added to the contributions from direct light sources. For arbitrary BRDFs, the equivalent equation is

$$L_o(\mathbf{v}) = L_A \int_{\mathbf{l} \in \Omega} f(\mathbf{l}, \mathbf{v})(\mathbf{n} \cdot \mathbf{l}) d\mathbf{l}. \qquad (10.15)$$

The integral in this equation is the same as the directional albedo $R(\mathbf{v})$ (Equation 9.9 in Section 9.3), and so the equation is equivalent to $L_o(\mathbf{v}) = L_A R(\mathbf{v})$. Older real-time rendering applications sometimes assumed a constant value for $R(\mathbf{v})$, referred to as the *ambient color* $\mathbf{c}_{amb}$. This further simplifies the equation to $L_o(\mathbf{v}) = \mathbf{c}_{amb} L_A$.

The reflectance equation ignores occlusion, i.e., that many surface points will be blocked from "seeing" some of the incoming directions by other objects, or other parts of the same object. This simplification reduces realism in general, but it is particularly noticeable for ambient lighting, which appears extremely flat when occlusion is ignored. Methods for addressing this problem will be discussed in Section 11.3, and in Section 11.3.4 in particular.

10.3   Spherical and Hemispherical Functions

To extend environment lighting beyond a constant term, we need a way to represent the incoming radiance from any direction onto an object. To begin, we will consider the radiance to be a function of only the direction being integrated, not the surface position. Doing so works on the assumption that the lighting environment is infinitely far away.

Radiance arriving at a given point can be different for every incoming direction. Lighting can be red from the left and green from the right, or blocked from the top but not from the side. These types of quantities can be represented by *spherical functions*, which are defined over the surface of the unit sphere, or over the space of directions in $\mathbb{R}^3$. We will denote this domain as S. How these functions work is not affected by whether they produce a single value or many values. For example, the same representation used for storing a scalar function can also be used to encode color values, by storing a separate scalar function for every color channel.

Assuming Lambertian surfaces, spherical functions can be used to compute environment lighting by storing a precomputed irradiance function, e.g., radiance convolved with a cosine lobe, for each possible surface normal direction. More sophisticated methods store radiance and compute the integral with a BRDF at runtime, per shaded surface point. Spherical functions are also used extensively in global illumination algorithms (Chapter 11).

Related to spherical functions are those for a *hemisphere*, for cases where values for only half of the directions are defined. For example, these functions are used to describe incoming radiance at a surface where there is no light coming from below.

We will refer to these representations as *spherical bases*, as they are bases for vector spaces of functions defined over a sphere. Even though the ambient/highlight/direction form (Section 10.3.3) is technically not a basis in the mathematical sense, we will also refer to it using this term for simplicity. Converting a function to a given representation is called *projection*, and evaluating the value of a function from a given representation is called *reconstruction*.

Each representation has its own set of trade-offs. Properties we might seek in a given basis are:

- Efficient encoding (projection) and decoding (lookup).

- The ability to represent arbitrary spherical functions with few coefficients and low reconstruction error.

- *Rotational invariance* of projection, which is the result of rotating the projection of a function is the same as rotating the function and then projecting it. This equivalence means that a function approximated with, e.g., spherical harmonics will not change when rotated.

- Ease of computing sums and products of encoded functions.

- Ease of computing spherical integrals and convolutions.

10.3.1 Simple Tabulated Forms

The most straightforward way to represent a spherical (or hemispherical) function is to pick several directions and store a value for each. Evaluating the function involves finding some number of samples around the evaluation direction and reconstructing the value with some form of interpolation.

This representation is simple, yet expressive. Adding or multiplying such spherical functions is as easy as adding or multiplying their corresponding tabulated entries.

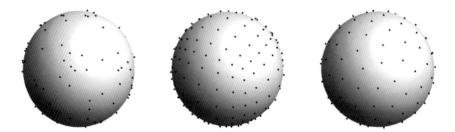

Figure 10.17. A few different ways to distribute points over the surface of a sphere. From left to right: random points, cubical grid points, and spherical t-design.

We can encode many different spherical functions with arbitrarily low error by adding more samples as needed.

It is not trivial to distribute samples over a sphere (see Figure 10.17) in a way that allows efficient retrieval, while representing all directions relatively equally. The most commonly used technique is to first unwrap the sphere into a rectangular domain, then sample this domain with a grid of points. As a two-dimensional texture represents exactly that, a grid of points (texels) on a rectangle, we can use the texels as the underlying storage for the sample values. Doing so lets us leverage GPU-accelerated bilinear texture filtering for fast lookups (reconstruction). Later in this chapter we will discuss environment maps (Section 10.5), which are spherical functions in this form, and discuss different options for unwrapping the sphere.

Tabulated forms have downsides. At low resolutions the quality provided by the hardware filtering is often unacceptable. The computational complexity of calculating convolutions, a common operation when dealing with lighting, is proportional to the number of samples and can be prohibitive. Moreover, projection is not invariant under rotation, which can be problematic for certain applications. For example, imagine encoding the radiance of a light shining from a set of directions as it hits the surface of an object. If the object rotates, the encoded results might reconstruct differently. This can lead to variations in the amount of radiant energy encoded, which can manifest as pulsating artifacts as the scene animates. It is possible to mitigate these issues by employing carefully constructed kernel functions associated with each sample during projection and reconstruction. More commonly, though, just using a dense enough sampling is sufficient to mask these issues.

Typically, tabulated forms are employed when we need to store complex, high-frequency functions that require many data points to be encoded with low error. If we need to encode spherical functions compactly, with only a few parameters, more complex bases can be used.

A popular basis choice, an *ambient cube* (AC) is one of the simplest tabulated forms, constructed out of six squared cosine lobes oriented along the major axes [1193]. It is called an ambient "cube" because it is equivalent to storing data in the faces of a cube and interpolating as we move from one direction to another. For any given direction, only three of the lobes are relevant, so the parameters for the other three do not need to be fetched from memory [766]. Mathematically, the ambient cube can be defined as

$$F_{AC}(\mathbf{d}) = \mathbf{d}d \cdot \text{sel}_+(\mathbf{c}_+, \mathbf{c}_-, \mathbf{d}), \qquad (10.16)$$

where $\mathbf{c}_+$ and $\mathbf{c}_-$ contain the six values for the cube faces and $\text{sel}_+(\mathbf{c}_+, \mathbf{c}_-, \mathbf{d})$ is a vector function that assumes, for each of its components, a value from $\mathbf{c}_+$ or $\mathbf{c}_-$ based on whether the respective component in $\mathbf{d}$ is positive.

An ambient cube is similar to a cube map (Section 10.4) with a single texel on each cube face. In some systems, performing the reconstruction in software for this particular case might be faster than using the GPU's bilinear filtering on cube maps. Sloan [1656] derives a simple formulation to convert between the ambient cube and the spherical harmonic basis (Section 10.3.2).

The quality of reconstruction using the ambient cube is fairly low. Slightly better results can be achieved by storing and interpolating eight values instead of six, corresponding to the cube vertices. More recently, an alternative called *ambient dice* (AD) was presented by Iwanicki and Sloan [808]. The basis is formed from squared and fourth-power cosine lobes oriented along the vertices of an icosahedron. Six out of twelve values stored are needed for reconstruction, and the logic to determine which six are retrieved is slightly more complex than the corresponding logic for ambient cubes, but the quality of the result is much higher.

10.3.2 Spherical Bases

There are an infinite number of ways to project (encode) functions onto representations that use a fixed number of values (coefficients). All we need is a mathematical expression that spans our spherical domain with some parameters we can change. We can then approximate any given function we want by fitting, i.e., finding the values of the parameters that minimize the error between our expression and the given function.

The most minimal possible choice is to use a constant:

$$F_c(\theta, \phi) = c \cdot 1.$$

We can derive the projection of a given function f into this basis by averaging it over the surface area of the unit sphere: $c = \frac{1}{4\pi} \int_\Omega f(\theta, \phi)$. The average c of a periodic function is also known as the *DC component*. This basis has the benefit of simplicity, and even respects some of the properties we are looking for (ease of reconstruction, addition, product, rotational invariance). However, it cannot express most spherical functions well, as it just replaces them with their average. We could construct a slightly more complex approximation using two coefficients, a and b:

$$F_{\text{hemi}}(\theta, \phi) = a + \frac{\cos(\theta) + 1}{2}(b - a),$$

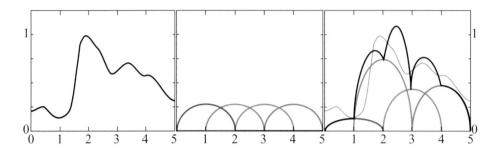

Figure 10.18. A basic example of basis functions. In this case, the space is "functions that have values between 0 and 1 for inputs between 0 and 5." The left plot shows an example of such a function. The middle plot shows a set of basis functions (each color is a different function). The right plot shows an approximation to the target function, formed by multiplying each of the basis functions by a weight and summing them. The basis functions are shown scaled by their respective weights. The black line shows the result of summing, which is an approximation to the original function, shown in gray for comparison.

which creates a representation that can encode exact values at the poles and can interpolate between them across the surface of the sphere. This choice is more expressive, but now projection is more complicated and is not invariant for all rotations. In fact, this basis could be seen as a tabular form with only two samples, placed at the poles.

In general, when we talk about a basis of a function space, we mean that we have a set of functions whose linear combination (weighting and summing) can be used to represent other functions over a given domain. An example of this concept is shown in Figure 10.18. The rest of this section explores some choices of bases that can be used to approximate functions on the sphere.

Spherical Radial Basis Functions

The low quality of reconstruction with tabulated forms using GPU hardware filtering is, at least to some extent, caused by the bilinear shape functions used to interpolate samples. Other functions can be used to weight samples for reconstruction. Such functions may produce higher-quality results than bilinear filtering, and they may have other advantages. One family of functions often used for this purpose are the *spherical radial basis functions* (SRBFs). They are radially symmetric, which makes them functions of only one argument, the angle between the axis along which they are oriented and the evaluation direction. The basis is formed by a set of such functions, called *lobes*, that are spread across the sphere. Representation of a function consists of a set of parameters for each of the lobes. This set can include their directions, but it makes projection much harder (requiring nonlinear, global optimization). For this reason, lobe directions are often assumed to be fixed, spread uniformly across the sphere, and other parameters are used, such as the magnitude of each lobe or its spread, i.e., the angle covered. Reconstruction is performed by evaluating all the lobes for a given direction and summing the results.

Spherical Gaussians

One particularly common choice for an SRBF lobe is a *spherical Gaussian* (SG), also called a *von Mises-Fisher distribution* in directional statistics. We should note that von-Mises-Fisher distributions usually include a normalization constant, one that we avoid in our formulation. A single lobe can be defined as

$$G(\mathbf{v}, \mathbf{d}, \lambda) = e^{\lambda(\mathbf{v} \cdot \mathbf{d} - 1)}, \tag{10.17}$$

where $\mathbf{v}$ is the evaluation direction (a unit vector), $\mathbf{d}$ is the lobe direction axis (mean of the distribution, also normalized), and $\lambda \geq 0$ is the lobe sharpness (which controls its angular width, also called the *concentration parameter* or *spread*) [1838].

To construct the spherical basis, we then use a linear combination of a given number of spherical Gaussians:

$$F_G(\mathbf{v}) = \sum_k w_k G(\mathbf{v}, \mathbf{d}_k, \lambda_k). \tag{10.18}$$

Performing the projection of a spherical function into this representation entails finding the set of parameters $\{w_k, \mathbf{d}_k, \lambda_k\}$ that minimize the reconstruction error. This process is typically done by numerical optimization, often using a nonlinear least-squares optimization algorithm (such as Levenberg-Marquardt). Note that if we allow the complete set parameters to vary in the optimization process, we would not be using a linear combination of functions, so Equation 10.18 does not represent a basis. A proper basis is obtained only when we choose a fixed set of lobes (directions and spreads), so that the entire domain is well covered [1127], and perform projection by fitting only the weights w_k. Doing so also greatly simplifies the optimization problem, as now it can be formulated as ordinary least-squares optimization. This is also a good solution if we need to interpolate between different sets of data (projected functions). For that use case, allowing the lobe directions and sharpness to vary is detrimental, as these parameters are highly nonlinear.

A strength of this representation is that many operations on SGs have simple, analytic forms. The product of two spherical Gaussians is another spherical Gaussian (see [1838]):

$$G_1 G_2 = G\left(\mathbf{v}, \frac{\mathbf{d}'}{||\mathbf{d}'||}, \lambda'\right),$$

where

$$\mathbf{d}' = \frac{\lambda_1 \mathbf{d}_1 + \lambda_2 \mathbf{d}_2}{\lambda_1 + \lambda_2}, \quad \lambda' = (\lambda_1 + \lambda_2)||\mathbf{d}'||.$$

The integral of a spherical Gaussian over the sphere can also be computed analytically:

$$\int_\Omega G(\mathbf{v}) d\mathbf{v} = 2\pi \frac{1 - e^{2\lambda}}{\lambda},$$

which means that the integral of the product of two spherical Gaussians also has a simple formulation.

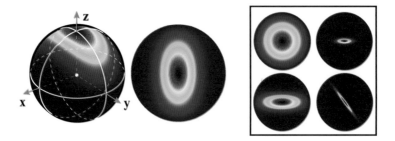

Figure 10.19. Anisotropic spherical Gaussian. Left: an ASG on the sphere and corresponding top-down plot. Right: four other examples of ASG configurations, showing the expressiveness of the formulation. *(Figure courtesy of Xu Kun.)*

If we can express light radiance as spherical Gaussians, then we can integrate its product with a BRDF encoded in the same representation to perform lighting calculations [1408, 1838]. For these reasons, SGs have been used in many research projects [582, 1838] as well as industry applications [1268].

As for Gaussian distributions on the plane, von Mises-Fisher distributions can be generalized to allow anisotropy. Xu et al. [1940] introduced *anisotropic spherical Gaussians* (ASGs; see Figure 10.19), which are defined by augmenting the single direction $\mathbf{d}$ with two supplemental axes $\mathbf{t}$ and $\mathbf{b}$ that together form an orthonormal tangent frame:

$$G(\mathbf{v}, [\mathbf{d}, \mathbf{t}, \mathbf{b}], [\lambda, \mu]) = S(\mathbf{v}, \mathbf{d})e^{-\lambda(\mathbf{v}\cdot\mathbf{t})^2 - \mu(\mathbf{v}\cdot\mathbf{b})^2}, \qquad (10.19)$$

where $\lambda, \mu \geq 0$ control the lobe spread along the two axis of the tangent frame and $S(\mathbf{v}, \mathbf{d}) = (\mathbf{v} \cdot \mathbf{d})^+$ is a smoothing term. This term is the main difference between the Fisher-Bingham distribution used in orientation statistics and the ASGs we employ for computer graphics. Xu et al. also provide analytic approximations for the integral, product, and convolution operators.

While SGs have many desirable properties, one of their drawbacks is that, unlike tabulated forms and in general kernels with a limited extent (bandwidth), they have *global support*. Each lobe is nonzero for the entire sphere, even though its falloff is fairly quick. This global extent means that if we use N lobes to represent a function, we will need all N of them for reconstruction in any direction.

Spherical Harmonics
Spherical harmonics[2] (SH) are an orthogonal set of basis functions over the sphere. An *orthogonal set* of basis functions is a set such that the *inner product* of any two different functions from the set is zero. The inner product is a more general, but similar, concept to the dot product. The inner product of two vectors is their dot product: the sum of the multiplication between pairs of components. We can similarly

---

[2]The basis functions we discuss here are more properly called "real spherical harmonics," since they represent the real part of the complex-valued spherical harmonic functions.

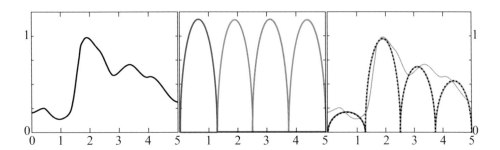

Figure 10.20. Orthonormal basis functions. This example uses the same space and target function as Figure 10.18, but the basis functions have been modified to be orthonormal. The left image shows the target function, the middle shows the orthonormal set of basis functions, and the right shows the scaled basis functions. The resulting approximation to the target function is shown as a dotted black line, and the original function is shown in gray for comparison.

derive a definition of the inner product over two functions by considering the integral of these functions multiplied together:

$$\langle f_i(x), f_j(x) \rangle \equiv \int f_i(x) f_j(x) dx, \tag{10.20}$$

where the integration is performed over the relevant domain. For the functions shown in Figure 10.18, the relevant domain is between 0 and 5 on the x-axis (note that this particular set of functions is not orthogonal). For spherical functions the form is slightly different, but the basic concept is the same:

$$\langle f_i(\mathbf{n}), f_j(\mathbf{n}) \rangle \equiv \int_{\mathbf{n} \in \Theta} f_i(\mathbf{n}) f_j(\mathbf{n}) d\mathbf{n}, \tag{10.21}$$

where $\mathbf{n} \in \Theta$ indicates that the integral is performed over the unit sphere.

An *orthonormal set* is an orthogonal set with the additional condition that the inner product of any function in the set with itself is equal to 1. More formally, the condition for a set of functions $\{f_j()\}$ to be orthonormal is

$$\langle f_i(), f_j() \rangle = \begin{cases} 0, & \text{where } i \neq j, \\ 1, & \text{where } i = j. \end{cases} \tag{10.22}$$

Figure 10.20 shows an example similar to Figure 10.18, where the basis functions are orthonormal. Note that the orthonormal basis functions shown in Figure 10.20 do not overlap. This condition is necessary for an orthonormal set of *non-negative* functions, as any overlap would imply a nonzero inner product. Functions that have negative values over part of their range can overlap and still form an orthonormal set. Such overlap usually leads to better approximations, since it allows the bases to be smooth. Bases with disjoint domains tend to cause discontinuities.

The advantage of an orthonormal basis is that the process to find the closest approximation to the target function is straightforward. To perform projection, the coefficient for each basis function is the inner product of the *target function* $f_{\text{target}}()$ with the appropriate basis function:

$$k_j = \langle f_{\text{target}}(), f_j() \rangle,$$

$$f_{\text{target}}() \approx \sum_{j=1}^{n} k_j f_j(). \tag{10.23}$$

In practice this integral has to be computed numerically, typically by Monte Carlo sampling, averaging n directions distributed evenly over the sphere.

An orthonormal basis is similar in concept to the "standard basis" for three-dimensional vectors introduced in Section 4.2.4. Instead of a function, the target of the standard basis is a point's location. The standard basis is composed of three vectors (one per dimension) instead of a set of functions. The standard basis is orthonormal by the same definition used in Equation 10.22. The method of projecting a point onto the standard basis is also the same, as the coefficients are the result of dot products between the position vector and the basis vectors. One important difference is that the standard basis exactly reproduces every point, while a finite set of basis functions only approximates its target functions. The result can never be exact because the standard basis uses three basis vectors to represent a three-dimensional space. A function space has an infinite number of dimensions, so a finite number of basis functions can never perfectly represent it.

Spherical harmonics are orthogonal and orthonormal, and they have several other advantages. They are rotationally invariant, and SH basis functions are inexpensive to evaluate. They are simple polynomials in the x-, y-, and z-coordinates of unit-length vectors. However, like spherical Gaussians, they have global support, so during reconstruction all of the basis functions need to be evaluated. The expressions for the basis functions can be found in several references, including a presentation by Sloan [1656]. His presentation is noteworthy in that it discusses many practical tips for working with spherical harmonics, including formulae and, in some cases, shader code. More recently Sloan also derived efficient ways to perform SH reconstruction [1657].

The SH basis functions are arranged in *frequency bands*. The first basis function is constant, the next three are linear functions that change slowly over the sphere, and the next five represent quadratic functions that change slightly faster. See Figure 10.21. Functions that are low frequency (i.e., change slowly over the sphere), such as irradiance values, are accurately represented with a relatively small number of SH coefficients (as we will see in Section 10.6.1).

When projecting to spherical harmonics, the resulting coefficients represent the amplitudes of various frequencies of the projected function, i.e., its frequency spectrum. In this spectral domain, a fundamental property holds: The integral of the product of two functions is equal to the dot product of the coefficients of the function projections. This property allows us to compute lighting integrals efficiently.

$l = 0$

$l = 1$

$l = 2$

$l = 3$

$l = 4$

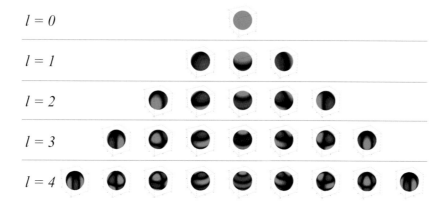

Figure 10.21. The first five frequency bands of spherical harmonics. Each spherical harmonic function has areas of positive values (colored green) and areas of negative values (colored red), fading to black as they approach zero. *(Spherical harmonic visualizations courtesy of Robin Green.)*

Many operations on spherical harmonics are conceptually simple, boiling down to a matrix transform on the vector of coefficients [583]. Among these operations are the important cases of computing the product of two functions projected to spherical harmonics, rotating projected functions, and computing convolutions. A matrix transform in SH in practice means the complexity of these operations is quadratic in the number of coefficients used, which can be a substantial cost. Luckily, these matrices often have peculiar structures that can be exploited to devise faster algorithms. Kautz et al. [869] present a method to optimize the rotation computations by decomposing them into rotations about the x- and z-axes. A popular method for fast rotation of low-order SH projections is given by Hable [633]. Green's survey [583] discusses how to exploit the block structure of the rotation matrix for faster computation. Currently the state of the art is represented by a decomposition into zonal harmonics, as presented by Nowrouzezahrai et al. [1290].

A common problem of spectral transformations such as spherical harmonics and the H-basis, described below, is that they can exhibit a visual artifact called *ringing* (also called the *Gibbs phenomenon*). If the original signal contains rapid changes that cannot be represented by the band-limited approximation, the reconstruction will show oscillation. In extreme cases this reconstructed function can even generate negative values. Various prefiltering methods can be used to combat this problem [1656, 1659].

Other Spherical Representations

Many other representations are possible to encode spherical functions using a finite number of coefficients. Linearly transformed cosines (Section 10.1.2) are an example of a representation that can efficiently approximate BRDF functions, while having the property of being easily integrable over polygonal sections of a sphere.

Spherical wavelets [1270, 1579, 1841] are a basis that balances locality in space (having compact support) and in frequency (smoothness), allowing for compressed representation of high-frequency functions. Spherical piecewise constant basis functions [1939], which partition the sphere into areas of constant value, and biclustering approximations [1723], which rely on matrix factoring, have also been used for environment lighting.

10.3.3 Hemispherical Bases

Even though the above bases can be used to represent hemispherical functions, they are wasteful. Half of the signal is always equal to zero. In these cases the use of representations constructed directly on the hemispherical domain is usually preferred. This is especially relevant for functions defined over surfaces: The BRDF, the incoming radiance, and the irradiance arriving at given point of an object are all common examples. These functions are naturally constrained to the hemisphere centered at the given surface point and aligned with the surface normal; they do not have values for directions that point inside the object.

Ambient/Highlight/Direction

One of the simplest representations along these lines is a combination of a constant function and a single direction where the signal is strongest over the hemisphere. It is usually called the *ambient/highlight/direction* (AHD) basis, and its most common use is to store irradiance. The name AHD denotes what the individual components represent: a constant ambient light, plus a single directional light that approximates the irradiance in the "highlight" direction, and the direction where most of the incoming light is concentrated. The AHD basis usually requires storing eight parameters. Two angles are used for the direction vector and two RGB colors for the ambient and directional light intensities. Its first notable use was in the game *Quake III*, where volumetric lighting for dynamic objects was stored in this way. Since then it has been used in several titles, such as those from the *Call of Duty* franchise.

Projection onto this representation is somewhat tricky. Because it is nonlinear, finding the optimal parameters that approximate the given input is computationally expensive. In practice, heuristics are used instead. The signal is first projected to spherical harmonics, and the optimal linear direction is used to orient the cosine lobe. Given the direction, ambient and highlight values can be computed using least-squares minimization. Iwanicki and Sloan [809] show how to perform this projection while enforcing non-negativity.

Radiosity Normal Mapping/Half-Life 2 Basis

Valve uses a novel representation, which expresses directional irradiance in the context of *radiosity normal mapping*, for the *Half-Life 2* series of games [1193, 1222]. Originally devised to store precomputed diffuse lighting while allowing for normal mapping, it is

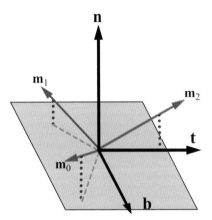

Figure 10.22. *Half-Life 2* lighting basis. The three basis vectors have elevation angles of about 26°
above the tangent plane, and their projections into that plane are spaced equally at 120° intervals
around the normal. They are unit length, and each one is perpendicular to the other two.

often now called the *Half-Life 2 basis*. It represents hemispherical functions on surfaces
by sampling three directions in tangent space. See Figure 10.22. The coordinates of
the three mutually perpendicular basis vectors in tangent space are

$$\mathbf{m}_0 = \left(\frac{-1}{\sqrt{6}}, \frac{1}{\sqrt{2}}, \frac{1}{\sqrt{3}}\right), \quad \mathbf{m}_1 = \left(\frac{-1}{\sqrt{6}}, \frac{-1}{\sqrt{2}}, \frac{1}{\sqrt{3}}\right), \quad \mathbf{m}_2 = \left(\frac{\sqrt{2}}{\sqrt{3}}, 0, \frac{1}{\sqrt{3}}\right). \quad (10.24)$$

For reconstruction, given the tangent-space direction $\mathbf{d}$ we can interpolate the values—
E_0, E_1, and E_2—along the three basis vectors:[3]

$$E(\mathbf{n}) = \frac{\displaystyle\sum_{k=0}^{2} \max(\mathbf{m}_k \cdot \mathbf{n}, 0)^2 E_k}{\displaystyle\sum_{k=0}^{2} \max(\mathbf{m}_k \cdot \mathbf{n}, 0)^2}. \quad (10.25)$$

Green [579] points out that Equation 10.25 can be made significantly less costly if the
following three values are precomputed in the tangent-space direction $\mathbf{d}$ instead:

$$d_k = \frac{\max(\mathbf{m}_k \cdot \mathbf{n}, 0)^2}{\displaystyle\sum_{k=0}^{2} \max(\mathbf{m}_k \cdot \mathbf{n}, 0)^2}, \quad (10.26)$$

---

[3]The formulation given in the GDC 2004 presentation is incorrect. The form in Equation 10.25 is
from a SIGGRAPH 2007 presentation [579].

for $k = 0, 1, 2$. Equation 10.25 then simplifies to

$$E(\mathbf{n}) = \sum_{k=0}^{2} d_k E_k. \qquad (10.27)$$

Green describes several other advantages to this representation, some of which are discussed in Section 11.4.

The *Half-Life 2* basis works well for directional irradiance. Sloan [1654] found that this representation produces results superior to low-order hemispherical harmonics.

Hemispherical Harmonics/H-Basis

Gautron et al. [518] specialize spherical harmonics to the hemispherical domain, which they call *hemispherical harmonics* (HSHs). Various methods are possible to perform this specialization.

For example, Zernike polynomials are orthogonal functions like spherical harmonics, but defined on the unit disk. As with SH, these can be used to transform functions in the frequency domain (spectrum), which yields a number of convenient properties. As we can transform a unit hemisphere into a disk, we can use Zernike polynomials to express hemispherical functions [918]. However, performing reconstruction with these is quite expensive. Gautron et al.'s solution both is more economical and allows for relatively fast rotation by matrix multiplication on the vector of coefficients.

The HSH basis is still more expensive to evaluate than spherical harmonics, however, as it is constructed by shifting the negative pole of the sphere to the outer edge of the hemisphere. This shift operation makes the basis functions non-polynomial, requiring divisions and square roots to be computed, which are typically slow on GPU hardware. Moreover, the basis is always constant at the hemisphere edge as it maps to a single point on the sphere before the shifting. The approximation error can be considerable near the edges, especially if only a few coefficients (spherical harmonic bands) are used.

Habel [627] introduced the *H-basis*, which takes part of the spherical harmonic basis for the longitudinal parameterization and parts of the HSH for the latitudinal one. This basis, one that mixes shifted and non-shifted versions of the SH, is still orthogonal, while allowing for efficient evaluation.

10.4   Environment Mapping

Recording a spherical function in one or more images is called *environment mapping*, as we typically use texture mapping to implement the lookups in the table. This representation is one of the most powerful and popular forms of environment lighting. Compared to other spherical representations, it consumes more memory but is simple and fast to decode in real time. Moreover, it can express spherical signals of arbitrarily high frequency (by increasing the texture's resolution) and accurately capture any range of environment radiance (by increasing each channel's number of bits). Such accuracy comes at a price. Unlike the colors and shader properties stored in other commonly used textures, the radiance values stored in environment maps usually have a high dynamic range. More bits per texel mean environment maps tend to take up more space than other textures and can be slower to access.

We have a basic assumption for any global spherical function, i.e., one used for all objects in the scene, that the incoming radiance L_i is dependent on only the direction. This assumption requires that the objects and lights being reflected are far away, and that the reflector does not reflect itself.

Shading techniques relying on environment mapping are typically not characterized by their ability to represent environment lighting, but by how well we can integrate them with given materials. That is, what kinds of approximations and assumptions do we have to employ on the BRDF in order to perform the integration? *Reflection mapping* is the most basic case of environment mapping, where we assume that the BRDF is a perfect mirror. An optically flat surface or mirror reflects an incoming ray of light to the light's reflection direction $\mathbf{r}_i$ (Section 9.5). Similarly, the outgoing radiance includes incoming radiance from just one direction, the reflected view vector $\mathbf{r}$. This vector is computed in the same way as $\mathbf{r}_i$ (Equation 9.15):

$$\mathbf{r} = 2(\mathbf{n} \cdot \mathbf{v})\mathbf{n} - \mathbf{v}. \tag{10.28}$$

The reflectance equation for mirrors is greatly simplified:

$$L_o(\mathbf{v}) = F(\mathbf{n}, \mathbf{r})L_i(\mathbf{r}), \tag{10.29}$$

where F is the Fresnel term (Section 9.5). Note that unlike the Fresnel terms in half vector-based BRDFs (which use the angle between the half vector $\mathbf{h}$ and $\mathbf{l}$ or $\mathbf{v}$), the Fresnel term in Equation 10.29 uses the angle between the surface normal $\mathbf{n}$ and the reflection vector $\mathbf{r}$ (which is the same as the angle between $\mathbf{n}$ and $\mathbf{v}$).

Since the incoming radiance L_i is dependent on only the direction, it can be stored in a two-dimensional table. This representation enables us to efficiently light a mirror-like surface of any shape with an arbitrary incoming radiance distribution. We do so by computing $\mathbf{r}$ for each point and looking up the radiance in the table. This table is called an *environment map*, as introduced by Blinn and Newell [158]. See Figure 10.23.

The steps of a reflection mapping algorithm are:

- Generate or load a texture representing the environment.

- For each pixel that contains a reflective object, compute the normal at the location on the surface of the object.

- Compute the reflected view vector from the view vector and the normal.

- Use the reflected view vector to compute an index into the environment map that represents the incoming radiance in the reflected view direction.

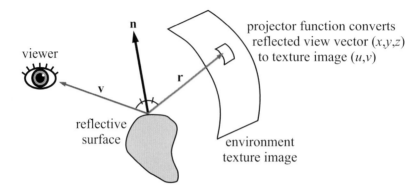

Figure 10.23. Reflection mapping. The viewer sees an object, and the reflected view vector **r** is computed from **v** and **n**. The reflected view vector accesses the environment's representation. The access information is computed by using some projector function to convert the reflected view vector's (x, y, z) to a texture coordinate that is used to retrieve the store radiance of the environment.

- Use the texel data from the environment map as incoming radiance in Equation 10.29.

A potential stumbling block of environment mapping is worth mentioning. Flat surfaces usually do not work well when environment mapping is used. The problem with a flat surface is that the rays that reflect off of it usually do not vary by more than a few degrees. This tight clustering results in a small part of the environment table being mapped onto a relatively large surface. Techniques that also use positional information of where the radiance is emitted from, discussed in Section 11.6.1, can give better results. Also, if we assume completely flat surfaces, such as floors, real-time techniques for planar reflections (Section 11.6.2) may be used.

The idea of illuminating a scene with texture data is also known as *image-based lighting* (IBL), typically when the environment map is obtained from real-world scenes using cameras capturing 360 degree panoramic, high dynamic range images [332, 1479].

Using environment mapping with normal mapping is particularly effective, yielding rich visuals. See Figure 10.24. This combination of features is also historically important. A restricted form of bumped environment mapping was the first use of a dependent texture read (Section 6.2) in consumer-level graphics hardware, giving rise to this ability as a part of the pixel shader.

There are a variety of projector functions that map the reflected view vector into one or more textures. We discuss the more popular mappings here, noting the strengths of each.

10.4.1 Latitude-Longitude Mapping

In 1976, Blinn and Newell [158] developed the first environment mapping algorithm. The mapping they used is the familiar latitude/longitude system used on a globe of

Figure 10.24. A light (at the camera) combined with bump and environment mapping. Left to right: no environment mapping, no bump mapping, no light at the camera, and all three combined. *(Images generated from the three.js example webgl_materials_displacementmap [218], model from AMD GPU MeshMapper.)*

the earth, which is why this technique is commonly referred to as *latitude-longitude mapping* or *lat-long mapping*. Instead of being like a globe viewed from the outside, their scheme is like a map of the constellations in the night sky. Just as the information on a globe can be flattened to a Mercator or other projection map, an environment surrounding a point in space can be mapped to a texture. When a reflected view vector is computed for a particular surface location, the vector is converted to spherical coordinates (ρ, ϕ). Here ϕ, equivalent to the longitude, varies from 0 to 2π radians, and ρ, the latitude, varies from 0 to π radians. The pair (ρ, ϕ) is computed from Equation 10.30, where $\mathbf{r} = (r_x, r_y, r_z)$ is the normalized reflected view vector, with $+z$ being up:

$$\rho = \arccos(r_z) \quad \text{and} \quad \phi = \texttt{atan2}(r_y, r_x). \tag{10.30}$$

See page 8 for a description of `atan2`. These values are then used to access the environment map and retrieve the color seen in the reflected view direction. Note that latitude-longitude mapping is not identical to the Mercator projection. It keeps the distance between latitude lines constant, while Mercator goes to infinity at the poles.

Some distortion is always necessary to unwrap a sphere into a plane, especially if we do not allow multiple cuts, and each projection has its own trade-offs between preserving area, distances, and local angles. One problem with this mapping is that the density of information is nowhere near uniform. As can be seen in the extreme stretching in the top and bottom parts of Figure 10.25, the areas near the poles receive many more texels than those near the equator. This distortion is problematic not only because it does not result in the most efficient encoding, but it can also result in artifacts when employing hardware texture filtering, especially visible at the two pole singularities. The filtering kernel does not follow the stretching of the texture, thus effectively shrinking in areas that have a higher texel density. Note also that while the

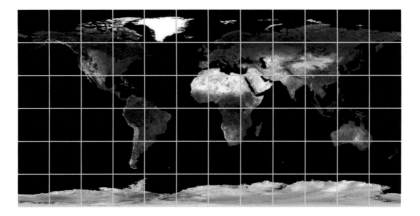

Figure 10.25. The earth with equally spaced latitude and longitude lines, as opposed to the traditional Mercator projection. *(Image from NASA's "Blue Marble" collection.)*

projection mathematics is simple, it might not be efficient, as transcendental functions such as arccosine are costly on GPUs.

10.4.2 Sphere Mapping

Initially mentioned by Williams [1889], and independently developed by Miller and Hoffman [1212], *sphere mapping* was the first environment mapping technique supported in general commercial graphics hardware. The texture image is derived from the appearance of the environment as viewed orthographically in a perfectly reflective sphere, so this texture is called a *sphere map*. One way to make a sphere map of a real environment is to take a photograph of a shiny sphere, such as a Christmas tree ornament. See Figure 10.26.

The resulting circular image is also called a *light probe*, as it captures the lighting situation at the sphere's location. Photographing spherical probes can be an effective

Figure 10.26. A sphere map (left) and the equivalent map in latitude-longitude format (right).

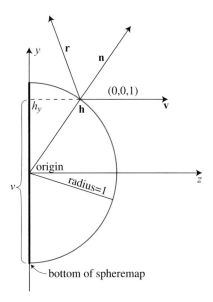

Figure 10.27. Given the constant view direction $\mathbf{v}$ and reflected view vector $\mathbf{r}$ in the sphere map's space, the sphere map's normal $\mathbf{n}$ is halfway between the two. For a unit sphere at the origin, the intersection point $\mathbf{h}$ has the same coordinates as the unit normal $\mathbf{n}$. Also shown is how h_y (measured from the origin) and the sphere map texture coordinate v (not to be confused with the view vector $\mathbf{v}$) are related.

method to capture image-based lighting, even if we use other encodings at runtime. We can always convert between a spherical projection and another form, such as the cube mapping discussed later (Section 10.4.3), if the capture has enough resolution to overcome the differences in distortion between methods.

A reflective sphere shows the entire environment on just the front of the sphere. It maps each reflected view direction to a point on the two-dimensional image of this sphere. Say we wanted to go the other direction, that, given a point on the sphere map, we would want the reflected view direction. To do this, we would take the surface normal on the sphere at that point, and then generate the reflected view direction. So, to reverse the process and get the location on the sphere from the reflected view vector, we need to derive the surface normal on the sphere, which will then yield the (u, v) parameters needed to access the sphere map.

The sphere's normal is the half-angle vector between the reflected view vector $\mathbf{r}$ and the original view vector $\mathbf{v}$, which is $(0, 0, 1)$ in the sphere map's space. See Figure 10.27. This normal vector $\mathbf{n}$ is the sum of the original and reflected view vectors, i.e., $(r_x, r_y, r_z + 1)$. Normalizing this vector gives the unit normal:

$$\mathbf{n} = \left(\frac{r_x}{m}, \frac{r_y}{m}, \frac{r_z + 1}{m} \right), \quad \text{where} \quad m = \sqrt{r_x^2 + r_y^2 + (r_z + 1)^2}. \tag{10.31}$$

If the sphere is at the origin and its radius is 1, then the unit normal's coordinates are also the location $\mathbf{h}$ of the normal on the sphere. We do not need h_z, as (h_x, h_y) describes a point on the image of the sphere, with each value in the range $[-1, 1]$. To map this coordinate to the range $[0, 1)$ to access the sphere map, divide each by two and add a half:

$$m = \sqrt{r_x^2 + r_y^2 + (r_z + 1)^2}, \quad u = \frac{r_x}{2m} + 0.5, \quad \text{and} \quad v = \frac{r_y}{2m} + 0.5. \qquad (10.32)$$

In contrast to latitude-longitude mapping, sphere mapping is much simpler to compute and shows one singularity, located around the edge of the image circle. The drawback is that the sphere map texture captures a view of the environment that is valid for only a single view direction. This texture does capture the entire environment, so it is possible to compute the texture coordinates for a new viewing direction. However, doing so can result in visual artifacts, as small parts of the sphere map become magnified due to the new view, and the singularity around the edge becomes noticeable. In practice, the sphere map is commonly assumed to follow the camera, operating in view space.

Since sphere maps are defined for a fixed view direction, in principle each point on a sphere map defines not just a reflection direction, but also a surface normal. See Figure 10.27. The reflectance equation can be solved for an arbitrary isotropic BRDF, and its result can be stored in a sphere map. This BRDF can include diffuse, specular, retroreflective, and other terms. As long as the illumination and view directions are fixed, the sphere map will be correct. Even a photographic image of a real sphere under actual illumination can be used, as long as the BRDF of the sphere is uniform and isotropic.

It is also possible to index two sphere maps, one with the reflection vector and another with the surface normal, to simulate specular and diffuse environment effects. If we modulate the values stored in the sphere maps to account for the color and roughness of the surface material, we have an inexpensive technique that can generate convincing (albeit view-independent) material effects. This method was popularized by the sculpting software Pixologic ZBrush as "MatCap" shading. See Figure 10.28.

10.4.3 Cube Mapping

In 1986, Greene [590] introduced the *cubic environment map*, usually called a *cube map*. This method is far and away the most popular method today, and its projection is implemented directly in hardware on modern GPUs. The cube map is created by projecting the environment onto the sides of a cube positioned with its center at the camera's location. The images on the cube's faces are then used as the environment map. See Figures 10.29 and 10.30. A cube map is often visualized in a "cross" diagram, i.e., opening the cube and flattening it onto a plane. However, on hardware cube maps are stored as six square textures, not as a single rectangular one, so there is no wasted space.

Figure 10.28. Example of "MatCap" rendering. The objects on the left are shaded using the two sphere maps on the right. The map at the top is indexed using the view-space normal vector, while the bottom one uses the view-space reflection vector, and the values from both are added together. The resulting effect is quite convincing, but moving the viewpoint would reveal that the lighting environment follows the coordinate frame of the camera.

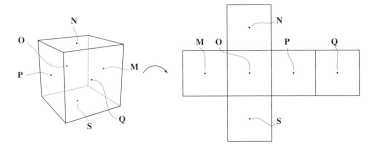

Figure 10.29. Illustration of Greene's environment map, with key points shown. The cube on the left is unfolded into the environment map on the right.

Figure 10.30. The same environment map used in Figure 10.26, transformed to the cube map format.

Figure 10.31. The environment map lighting in *Forza Motorsport 7* updates as the cars change position. *(Image courtesy of Turn 10 Studios, Microsoft.)*

It is possible to create cube maps synthetically by rendering a scene six times with the camera at the center of the cube, looking at each cube face with a 90° view angle. See Figure 10.31. To generate cube maps from real-world environments, usually spherical panoramas acquired by stitching or specialized cameras are projected into the cube map coordinate system.

Cubic environment mapping is *view-independent*, unlike sphere mapping. It also has much more uniform sampling characteristics than latitude-longitude mapping, which oversamples the poles compared to the equator. Wan et al. [1835, 1836] present a mapping called the *isocube* that has an even lower sampling-rate discrepancy than cube mapping, while still leveraging the cube mapping texture hardware for performance.

Accessing the cube map is straightforward. Any vector can be used directly as a three-component texture coordinate to fetch data in the direction it is pointing. So, for reflections we can just pass the reflected view vector **r** to the GPU, without even needing to normalize it. On older GPUs, bilinear filtering could reveal seams along the cube edges, as the texture hardware was unable to properly filter across different cube faces (an operation that is somewhat expensive to perform). Techniques to sidestep this issue were developed, such as making the view projections a bit wider so that a single face would also contain these neighboring texels. All modern GPUs can now correctly perform this filtering across edges, so these methods are no longer necessary.

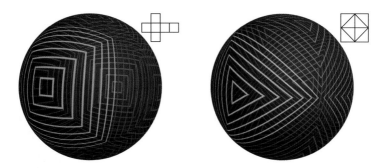

Figure 10.32. Cube map unwrapping of a sphere (left) compared to octahedral unwrapping (right). *(After a Shadertoy by Nimitz.)*

10.4.4 Other Projections

Today the cube map is the most popular tabular representation for environment lighting, due to its versatility, accuracy in reproducing high-frequency details, and execution speed on the GPU. However, a few other projections have been developed that are worth mentioning.

Heidrich and Seidel [702, 704] propose using two textures to perform *dual paraboloid environment mapping*. The idea is like that of sphere mapping, but instead of generating the texture by recording the reflection of the environment off a sphere, two parabolic projections are used. Each paraboloid creates a circular texture similar to a sphere map, with each covering an environment hemisphere.

As with sphere mapping, the reflected view ray is computed in the map's basis, i.e., in its frame of reference. The sign of the z-component of the reflected view vector is used to decide which of the two textures to access. The access function is

$$u = \frac{r_x}{2(1 + r_z)} + 0.5, \quad v = \frac{r_y}{2(1 + r_z)} + 0.5 \tag{10.33}$$

for the front image, and the same, with sign reversals for r_z, for the back image.

The parabolic map has more uniform texel sampling of the environment compared to the sphere map, and even to the cube map. However, care has to be taken for proper sampling and interpolation at the seam between the two projections, which makes accessing a dual paraboloid map more expensive.

Octahedral mapping [434] is another noteworthy projection. Instead of mapping the surrounding sphere to a cube, it is mapped to an octahedron (see Figure 10.32). To flatten this geometry into textures, its eight triangular faces are cut and arranged on a flat plane. Either a square or a rectangular configuration is possible. If we use the square configuration, the mathematics for accessing an octahedral map is quite efficient. Given a reflection direction $\mathbf{r}$, we compute a normalized version using the absolute value L_1 norm:

$$\mathbf{r}' = \frac{\mathbf{r}}{|r_x| + |r_y| + |r_z|}.$$

For the case where r'_y is positive, we can then index the square texture with

$$u = r'_x \cdot 0.5 + 0.5, \quad v = r'_y \cdot 0.5 + 0.5. \tag{10.34}$$

Where r'_y is negative, we need to "fold" the second half of the octahedron outward with the transform

$$u = (1 - |r'_z|) \cdot \text{sign}(r'_x) \cdot 0.5 + 0.5, \quad v = (1 - |r'_x|) \cdot \text{sign}(r'_z) \cdot 0.5 + 0.5. \tag{10.35}$$

The octahedral mapping does not suffer from the filtering issues of the dual paraboloid mapping, as the seams of the parameterization correspond with the edges of the texture used. Texture "wrap-around" sampling modes can automatically access texels from the other side and perform the correct interpolation. Though the mathematics for the projection is slightly more involved, in practice performance is better. The amount of distortion introduced is similar to that for cube maps, so octahedral maps can be a good alternative when cube map texture hardware is not present. Another notable use is as a way of expressing three-dimensional directions (normalized vectors) using only two coordinates, as a mean of compression (Section 16.6).

For the special case of environment maps that are radially symmetric around an axis, Stone [1705] proposes a simple factorization using a single one-dimensional texture storing the radiance values along any meridian line from the symmetry axis. He extends this scheme to two-dimensional textures, storing in each row an environment map pre-convolved with a different Phong lobe. This encoding can simulate a variety of materials, and was employed to encode radiance emitted from a clear sky.

10.5 Specular Image-Based Lighting

While environment mapping was originally developed as a technique for rendering mirror-like surfaces, it can be extended to glossy reflections as well. When used to simulate general specular effects for infinitely distant light sources, environment maps are also known as *specular light probes*. This term is used because they capture the radiance from all directions at a given point in the scene (thus probing), and use that information to evaluate general BRDFs—not only the restricted cases of pure mirrors or Lambertian surfaces. The name *specular cube maps* also is used for the common case of storing the environment lighting in cube maps that have been manipulated to simulate reflections on glossy materials.

To simulate surface roughness, the environment's representation in the texture can be *prefiltered* [590]. By blurring the environment map texture, we can present a specular reflection that looks rougher than perfectly mirror-like reflection. Such blurring should be done in a nonlinear fashion, i.e., different parts of the texture should

Figure 10.33. On the top, the original environment map (left) and shading results applied on a sphere (right). On the bottom, the same environment map blurred with a Gaussian kernel emulates the appearance of a rough material.

be blurred differently. This adjustment is needed because environment map texture representations have a nonlinear mapping to the ideal spherical space of directions. The angular distance between the centers of two adjacent texels is not constant, nor is the solid angle covered by a single texel. Specialized tools to preprocess cube maps, such as AMD's *CubeMapGen* (now open source), take these factors into account when filtering. Neighboring samples from other faces are used to create the mipmap chain, and the angular extent of each texel is factored in. Figure 10.33 shows an example.

Blurring the environment map, while empirically approaching the look of rough surfaces, bears no connection with an actual BRDF. A more principled method is to consider the shape a BRDF function takes on the sphere when a given surface normal and view direction are taken in consideration. We then filter the environment map using this distribution. See Figure 10.34. Filtering an environment map with a specular lobe is not trivial, as a BRDF can assume any shape, depending on its roughness parameters along with the view and normal vectors. There are at least five dimensions of input values (roughness and two polar angles each for the view and normal directions) that control the resulting lobe shape. Storing several environment maps for each choice among these is infeasible.

10.5.1 Prefiltered Environment Mapping

Practical implementations of prefiltering for environment lighting applied to glossy materials require approximations to the BRDF used so that the resulting texture is

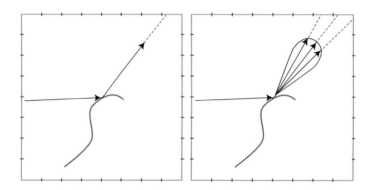

Figure 10.34. The left figure shows an eye ray reflecting off an object to retrieve a perfect mirror reflection from an environment texture (a cube map in this case). The right figure shows a reflected view ray's specular lobe, which is used to sample the environment texture. The green square represents a cross section of the cube map, and the red tick marks denote the boundaries between texels.

independent of the view and normal vectors. If we restrict the shape variation of the BRDF to only the material glossiness, we can compute and store a few environment maps corresponding to different choices of the roughness parameter, and chose the appropriate one to use at runtime. In practice, this means restricting the blur kernels we use, and thus the lobe shapes, to be radially symmetric around the reflection vector.

Imagine some light coming in from near a given reflected view direction. Light directly from the reflected view direction will give the largest contribution, dropping off as the direction to the incoming light increasingly differs from the reflected view direction. The area of the environment map texel multiplied by the texel's BRDF contribution gives the relative effect of this texel. This weighted contribution is multiplied by the color of the environment map texel, and the results are summed to compute **q**. The sum of the weighted contributions, s, is also computed. The final result, **q**/s, is the overall color integrated over the reflected view direction's lobe and is stored in the resulting reflection map.

If we use the Phong material model, the radial symmetry assumption naturally holds, and we can compute environment lighting almost exactly. Phong [1414] derived his model empirically and, in contrast to the BRDFs we have seen in Section 9.8, there is no physical motivation. Both Phong's model and the Blinn-Phong [159] BRDF we discussed in Section 9.8.1 are cosine lobes raised to a power, but in the case of Phong shading, the cosine is formed by the dot product of the reflection (Equation 9.15) and view vectors, instead of the half vector (see Equation 9.33) and the normal. This causes the reflection lobe to be rotationally symmetrical. See Figure 9.35 on page 338.

With a radially symmetric specular lobe, the only effect for which we still cannot accommodate, as it makes the lobe shape dependent on the view direction, is horizon clipping. Think about viewing a shiny (not mirror) sphere. Looking near the center of the sphere's surface gives, say, a symmetric Phong lobe. Viewing the surface near

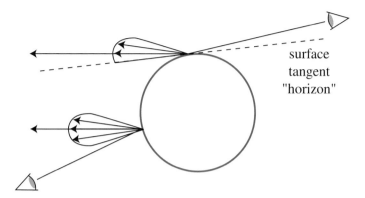

surface
tangent
"horizon"

Figure 10.35. A shiny sphere is seen by two viewers. Separate locations on the sphere give the same reflected view direction for both viewers. The left viewer's surface reflection samples a symmetric lobe. The right viewer's reflection lobe must be chopped off by the horizon of the surface itself, since light cannot reflect off the surface below its horizon.

the sphere's silhouette must in reality have a piece of its lobe cut off, as no light from below the horizon can reach the eye. See Figure 10.35. This is the same issue we saw previously when discussing approximations for area lighting (Section 10.1), and in practice it is often ignored by real-time methods. Doing so can cause excessively bright shading at grazing angles.

Heidrich and Seidel [704] use a single reflection map in this way to simulate the blurriness of a surface. To accommodate for different roughness levels, it is common to employ the mipmaps (Section 6.2.2) of an environment cube map. Each level is used to store blurred versions of the incoming radiance, with higher mip levels storing rougher surfaces, i.e., wider Phong lobes [80, 582, 1150, 1151]. During runtime, we can address the cube map by using the reflection vector and forcing the selection of a given mip level based on the desired Phong exponent (material roughness). See Figure 10.36.

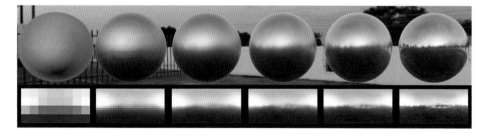

Figure 10.36. Environment map prefiltering. A cube map has been convolved with GGX lobes of varying roughness, and the results are stored in the texture mip chain. With the roughness decreasing from left to right, the resulting texture mips are displayed at the bottom and a sphere is rendered above accessing them in the direction of the reflection vector.

Wider filter areas used by rougher materials remove high frequencies and so require less resolution for adequate results, which maps perfectly to the mipmap structure. Moreover, by employing the GPU hardware's trilinear filtering, it is possible to sample in between prefiltered mip levels, simulating roughness values for which we do not have exact representations. When combined with a Fresnel term, such reflection maps work plausibly well for glossy surfaces.

For performance and aliasing reasons, the selection of the mipmap level to use should take into consideration not only the material roughness at the shaded point, but also the change in normal and roughness over the surface area covered by the screen pixel footprint being shaded. Ashikhmin and Ghosh [80] point out that, for best results, the indices of the two candidate mipmap levels (the minification level computed by the texturing hardware and the level corresponding to the current filter width) should be compared, and the index of the lower-resolution mipmap level should be used. To be more accurate, the widening effect of the surface variance should be taken into account, and a new roughness level, corresponding to a BRDF lobe that best fits the average of lobes in the pixel footprint, should be employed. This problem is exactly the same as BRDF antialiasing (Section 9.13.1), and the same solutions apply.

The filtering scheme presented earlier assumes that all lobes for a given reflected view direction are the same shape and height. This assumption also means that the lobes have to be radially symmetric. Beyond the problem at the horizon, most BRDFs do not have uniform, radially symmetric lobes at all angles. For example, at grazing angles the lobes often become sharper and thinner. Also, the lengths of the lobes normally vary with elevation angle

This effect is not usually perceivable for curved surfaces. However, for flat surfaces such as floors, radially symmetric filters can introduce noticeable errors. (See Figure 9.35 on page 338.)

Convolving the Environment Map

Generating prefiltered environment maps means computing for every texel, corresponding to a direction $\mathbf{v}$, the integral of the environment radiance with the specular lobe D:

$$\int_\Omega D(\mathbf{l}, \mathbf{v}) L_i(\mathbf{l}) d\mathbf{l}.$$

This integral is a *spherical convolution*, and in general cannot be performed analytically, as L_i, for environment maps, is known only in tabular form. A popular numerical solution is to adopt Monte Carlo methods:

$$\int_\Omega D(\mathbf{l}, \mathbf{v}) L_i(\mathbf{l}) d\mathbf{l} \approx \lim_{N \to \infty} \frac{1}{N} \sum_{k=1}^{N} \frac{D(\mathbf{l}_k, \mathbf{v}) L_i(\mathbf{l}_k)}{p(\mathbf{l}_k, \mathbf{v})}, \tag{10.36}$$

where $\mathbf{l}_k$ for $k = 1, 2, \ldots, N$ are discrete samples over the unit sphere (directions), and $p(\mathbf{l}_k, \mathbf{v})$ is the probability function associated with generating a sample in the direction $\mathbf{l}_k$. If we sample the sphere uniformly, then $p(\mathbf{l}_k, \mathbf{v}) = 1$ always. While this summation is correct for each direction $\mathbf{v}$ that we want to integrate, when storing the results in a environment map we also have to take into account the distortion that the projection imposes, by weighting each computed texel by the solid angle it subtends (see Driscoll [376]).

While Monte Carlo methods are simple and correct, they might take a large number of samples to converge to the numerical value of the integral, which can be slow even for an offline process. This situation is especially true for the first levels of the mipmap, where we encode shallow specular lobes (high exponents in the case of Blinn-Phong, low roughness for Cook-Torrance). We not only have more texels to compute (as we need the resolution to store high-frequency details), but also the lobe might be nearly zero for directions that are not close to the one of perfect reflection. Most of the samples are "wasted," as $D(\mathbf{l}_k, \mathbf{v}) \approx 0$ for them.

To avoid this phenomenon, we can use importance sampling, where we generate directions with a probability distribution that tries to match the shape of the specular lobe. Doing so is a common *variance reduction* technique for Monte Carlo integration, and importance-sampling strategies exist for most commonly used lobes [279, 878, 1833]. For even more efficient sampling schemes, it is also possible to consider the distribution of radiance in the environment map jointly with the shape of the specular lobe [270, 819]. However, all techniques relying on point sampling typically are only for offline rendering and ground-truth simulations, as usually hundreds of samples are needed.

To further reduce sampling variance (i.e., noise), we could also estimate the distance between samples and integrate using a sum of cones, instead of single directions. Sampling an environment map using cones can be approximated by point sampling one of its mip levels, choosing the level whose texel size spans a solid angle similar to that of the cone [280]. Doing so introduces bias, but it allows us to greatly reduce the number of samples needed to achieve noise-free results. This type of sampling can be performed at interactive rates with the aid of the GPU.

Also leveraging area samples, McGuire et al. [1175] develop a technique aimed at approximating the results of the convolution with the specular lobe in real time, without any need for precomputation. This process is done by judiciously mixing multiple mipmap levels of a non-prefiltered environment cube map in order to recreate the shape of a Phong lobe. In a similar fashion, Hensley et al. [718, 719, 720] use summed-area tables (Section 6.2.2) to rapidly perform the approximation. Both McGuire et al.'s and Hensley et al.'s techniques are not technically free of any precomputation, because after rendering an environment map they still require us to generate mip levels or prefix sums, respectively. For both cases, efficient algorithms exist so the precomputations required are much faster than performing the full specular lobe convolution. Both techniques are fast enough to even be used in real time for surface shading with environment lighting, but they are not as accurate as other methods relying on ad hoc prefiltering.

Kautz et al. [868] present another variant, a hierarchical technique for rapidly generating filtered parabolic reflection maps. Recently Manson and Sloan [1120] significantly improved the state of the art using an efficient quadratic B-spline filtering scheme to generate the mip levels of an environment map. These specially computed, B-spline filtered mips are then used by combining few samples, in a similar fashion to McGuire et al.'s and Kautz et al.'s techniques, to yield a fast and accurate approximation. Doing so allows generating results in real time that are indistinguishable from the ground truth computed via importance-sampled Monte Carlo techniques.

Fast convolution techniques allow updating prefiltered cube maps in real time, which is necessary when the environment map we want to filter is rendered dynamically. Using environment maps often makes it difficult for an object to move among different lighting situations, e.g., from one room to another. Cubic environment maps can be regenerated on the fly from frame to frame (or once every few frames), so swapping in new specular reflection maps is relatively inexpensive, if efficient filtering schemes are employed.

An alternative to regenerating the full environment map is to add the specular highlights from dynamic light sources onto a static base environment map. The added highlights can be prefiltered "blobs" that are added onto a prefiltered base environment map. Doing so avoids the need to do any filtering at runtime. The limitations are due to the assumptions of environment mapping, that lights and reflected objects are distant and so do not change with the location of the object viewed. These requirements mean that local light sources cannot easily be used.

If the geometry is static, but some light sources (e.g., the sun) move, an inexpensive technique for updating probes that does not require rendering the scene dynamically in a cube map is to store surface attributes (position, normals, materials) in a *G-buffer environment map*. G-buffers are discussed in detail in Section 20.1. We then use these properties to compute the surface's outgoing radiance into an environment map. This technique was used in *Call of Duty: Infinite Warfare* [384], *The Witcher 3* [1778], and *Far Cry 4* [1154], among others.

10.5.2 Split-Integral Approximation for Microfacet BRDFs

The usefulness of environment lighting is so considerable that many techniques have been developed to lessen the BRDF approximation issues inherent in cube map prefiltering.

So far, we have described approximations that work by assuming a Phong lobe and then post-multiplying by a perfect-mirror Fresnel term:

$$\int_{\mathbf{l} \in \Omega} f(\mathbf{l}, \mathbf{v}) L_i(\mathbf{l})(\mathbf{n} \cdot \mathbf{l}) d\mathbf{l} \approx F(\mathbf{n}, \mathbf{v}) \int_{\mathbf{l} \in \Omega} D_{\text{Phong}}(\mathbf{r}) L_i(\mathbf{l})(\mathbf{n} \cdot \mathbf{l}) d\mathbf{l}, \qquad (10.37)$$

where $\int_\Omega D_{\text{Phong}}(\mathbf{r})$ is precomputed for each $\mathbf{r}$ into an environment cube map. If we consider a specular microfacet BRDF f_{smf} using Equation 9.34 on page 337, repeated here for convenience,

$$f_{\mathrm{smf}}(\mathbf{l}, \mathbf{v}) = \frac{F(\mathbf{h}, \mathbf{l}) G_2(\mathbf{l}, \mathbf{v}, \mathbf{h}) D(\mathbf{h})}{4|\mathbf{n} \cdot \mathbf{l}||\mathbf{n} \cdot \mathbf{v}|}, \qquad (10.38)$$

we notice that, even assuming $D(\mathbf{h}) \approx D_{\mathrm{Phong}}(\mathbf{r})$ is valid, we are removing significant parts of the BRDF from the lighting integral. The shadowing term $G_2(\mathbf{l}, \mathbf{v}, \mathbf{h})$ and the half-vector Fresnel term $F(\mathbf{h}, \mathbf{l})$, whose application outside the integral has no theoretical basis, are removed. Lazarov [998] shows that using the perfect-mirror Fresnel that depends on $\mathbf{n} \cdot \mathbf{v}$, instead of $\mathbf{n} \cdot \mathbf{h}$ as in the microfacet BRDF, produces larger errors than not using a Fresnel term at all. Gotanda [573], Lazarov [999], and Karis [861] independently derive a similar *split-integral approximation*:

$$\int_{\mathbf{l} \in \Omega} f_{\mathrm{smf}}(\mathbf{l}, \mathbf{v}) L_i(\mathbf{l}) (\mathbf{n} \cdot \mathbf{l}) d\mathbf{l} \approx \int_{\mathbf{l} \in \Omega} D(\mathbf{r}) L_i(\mathbf{l}) (\mathbf{n} \cdot \mathbf{l}) d\mathbf{l} \int_{\mathbf{l} \in \Omega} f_{\mathrm{smf}}(\mathbf{l}, \mathbf{v}) (\mathbf{n} \cdot \mathbf{l}) d\mathbf{l}. \quad (10.39)$$

Note how even though this solution is commonly called "split integral," we do not factor the integral into two disjoint terms, as that is not a good approximation. Remembering that f_{smf} includes the specular lobe D, we notice that the latter as well as the $\mathbf{n} \cdot \mathbf{l}$ term are instead replicated on both sides. In the split-integral approximation we include in both integrals all the terms that are symmetric around the reflection vector in the environment map. Karis calls his derivation *split-sum* because it is done on the importance-sampled numerical integrator (Equation 10.36) that he uses in the precomputations, but effectively it is the same solution.

The resulting two integrals can both be precomputed efficiently. The first depends only on surface roughness and the reflection vector, with the assumption of a radial-symmetric D lobe. In practice, we can use any lobe, imposing $\mathbf{n} = \mathbf{v} = \mathbf{r}$. This integral can be precomputed and stored in the mip levels of a cube map, as usual. To get a similar highlight between environment lighting and analytic lights when converting half-vector BRDFs to lobes around the reflection vector, the radial-symmetric lobe should use a modified roughness. For example, to convert from a pure Phong-based reflection vector specular term to a Blinn-Phong BRDF using the half-angle, a good fit is obtained by dividing the exponent by four [472, 957].

The second integral is the hemispherical-directional reflectance (Section 9.3) of the specular term, $R_{\mathrm{spec}}(\mathbf{v})$. The R_{spec} function depends on the elevation angle θ, roughness α, and Fresnel term F. Typically F is implemented using Schlick's approximation (Equation 9.16), which is parameterized on only a single value F_0, thus making R_{spec} a function of three parameters. Gotanda precomputes R_{spec} numerically, storing the results in a three-dimensional lookup table. Karis and Lazarov note that the value of F_0 can be factored out of R_{spec}, resulting in two factors each of which depends on two parameters: elevation angle and roughness. Karis uses this insight to reduce the precomputed lookup of R_{spec} to a two-dimensional table that can be stored in a two-channel texture, while Lazarov derives analytical approximations to each of the two factors via function fitting. A more accurate and simpler analytical approximation

Figure 10.37. Karis "split sum" approximation. Left to right: materials with increasing roughness. First row: reference solution. Second row: split-integral approximation. Third row: split-integral with the required radial symmetry added to the specular lobe ($\mathbf{n} = \mathbf{v} = \mathbf{r}$). This last requirement is what introduces the most error. *(Image courtesy of Brian Karis, Epic Games Inc.)*

was later derived by Iwanicki and Pesce [807]. Note that R_{spec} can also be used for improving the accuracy of diffuse BRDF models (see Equation 9.65 on page 352). If both techniques are implemented in the same application, then the implementation of R_{spec} can be used for both, increasing efficiency.

The split-integral solution is exact for a constant environment map. The cube map part provides the lighting intensity that scales the specular reflectance, which is the correct BRDF integral under uniform lighting. Empirically, both Karis and Lazarov observe that the approximation also holds for general environment maps, especially if the frequency content is relatively low, which is not uncommon in outdoor scenes. See Figure 10.37. The greatest source of error in this technique, compared to the ground truth, is the restriction to radial-symmetric, non-clipped specular lobes (Figure 10.35) for the prefiltered environment cube map. Lagarde [960] suggests skewing the vector used to fetch the prefiltered environment map from the reflection direction toward the normal, based on surface roughness, as empirically this reduces the error compared to ground truth. Doing so is justifiable, as it partially compensates for not clipping the lobe with the surface's incoming radiance hemisphere.

10.5.3 Asymmetric and Anisotropic Lobes

The solutions we have seen so far are all restricted to specular lobes that are isotropic, meaning that they do not change when the incoming and outgoing directions are rotated around the surface normal (Section 9.3), and radially symmetric around the

Figure 10.38. Two views of a plot comparing a GGX BRDF (in red) with a GGX NDF lobe adapted to be radially symmetric around the reflection vector (in green). The latter has been scaled to match the peak of the GGX specular lobe, but note how it cannot capture the anisotropic shape of the half-vector-based BRDF. On the right, note the difference in the highlights that the two lobes create on a sphere. *(Images generated using Disney's BRDF Explorer open-source software.)*

reflection vector. Microfacet BRDF lobes are defined around the half vector $\mathbf{h} = (\mathbf{l}+\mathbf{v})/\|\mathbf{l}+\mathbf{v}\|$ (Equation 9.33) and thus never have the symmetry we need, even in the isotropic case. The half vector depends on the light direction $\mathbf{l}$, which for environment lighting is not uniquely defined. So, following Karis [861], for these BRDFs we impose $\mathbf{n} = \mathbf{v} = \mathbf{r}$ and derive a constant roughness correction factor to match the size of the specular highlights to the original half-vector formulation. These assumptions are all considerable sources of error (see Figure 10.38).

Some of the methods that we mentioned in Section 10.5.1 can be used to compute at interactive rates environment lighting with arbitrary BRDFs, such as the ones from Luksch et al. [1093] and Colbert and Křivánek [279, 280]. However, as these methods require tens of samples, they are rarely used in the real-time shading of surfaces. They instead can be seen as fast importance-sampling techniques for Monte Carlo integration.

With prefiltered environment maps created by imposing radial symmetry on specular lobes, and with the simple direct logic of accessing the prefiltered lobe that corresponds to the current surface specular roughness, our results are guaranteed to be correct only when viewing a surface straight on ($\mathbf{n} = \mathbf{v}$). In all other cases there is no such guarantee, and at grazing angles we incur errors regardless of the shape of the BRDF lobe, because we ignore that real lobes cannot dip below the horizon of the shaded surface point. In general, it is likely that the data in the exact direction of specular reflection is not the best match for reality.

Kautz and McCool improve upon naive pre-integration by using a better sampling scheme from radially symmetric lobes stored in a prefiltered environment map [867]. They propose two methods. The first uses a single sample, but tries to find the best lobe to approximate the BRDF in the current view direction instead of relying on a constant correction factor. The second method averages several samples from different lobes. The first method better simulates surfaces at grazing angles. They also derive a correction factor to account for the difference in total energy reflected using the radial-symmetric lobe approximation compared to the original BRDF. The second solution extends the results to include the stretched highlights typical of half-vector models. In both cases, optimization techniques are used to compute tables of parameters that drive the sampling of the prefiltered lobes. Kautz and McCool's technique uses a greedy fitting algorithm and parabolic environment maps.

Recently, Iwanicki and Pesce [807] derived a similar approximation for GGX BRDFs and environment cube maps, using a method called Nelder-Mead minimization. They also analyze the idea of exploiting the hardware anisotropic filtering ability of modern GPUs to accelerate sampling.

The idea of using a single sample from a prefiltered cube map, but adapting its location to the peak of a more complex specular BRDF, is also explored by Revie [1489] for fur rendering combined with deferred shading (Section 20.1). In this context, limitations do not directly stem from environment mapping but rather from the need to encode as few parameters as possible in the G-buffer. McAuley [1154] extends the idea, using this technique for all surfaces in a deferred rendering system.

McAllister et al. [1150, 1151] develop a technique that enables the rendering of a variety of effects, including anisotropy and retroreflection, by exploiting the properties of the Lafortune BRDF. This BRDF [954] is itself an approximation for physically based rendering. It is made of multiple Phong lobes, perturbed around the reflection direction. Lafortune demonstrated the ability of this BRDF to represent complex materials by fitting these lobes to the He-Torrance model [686] and to measurements of real materials from a gonioreflectometer. McAllister's technique relies on noticing that since Lafortune lobes are generalized Phong lobes, a conventional prefiltered environment map can be used, with its mips encoding different Phong exponents. Green et al. [582] propose a similar method, which uses Gaussian lobes instead of Phong lobes. In addition, their approach can be extended to support directional shadowing of the environment map (Section 11.4).

10.6 Irradiance Environment Mapping

The previous section discussed using filtered environment maps for glossy specular reflections. These maps can be used for diffuse reflections as well [590, 1212]. Environment maps for specular reflections have some common properties, whether they are unfiltered and used for mirror reflections, or they are filtered and used for glossy reflections. In both cases, specular environment maps are indexed with the reflected view vector, and they contain radiance values. Unfiltered environment maps contain incoming radiance values, and filtered environment maps contain outgoing radiance values.

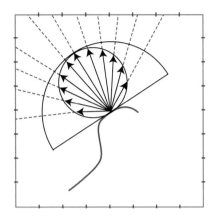

Figure 10.39. Computing an irradiance environment map. The cosine weighted hemisphere around the surface normal is sampled from the environment texture (a cube map in this case) and summed to obtain the irradiance, which is view-independent. The green square represents a cross section of the cube map, and the red tick marks denote the boundaries between texels. Although a cube map representation is shown, any environment representation can be used.

In contrast, environment maps for diffuse reflections are indexed with just the surface normal $\mathbf{n}$, and they contain *irradiance* values. For this reason they are called *irradiance environment maps* [1458]. Figure 10.35 shows that glossy reflections with environment maps have errors under some conditions due to their inherent ambiguity. The same reflected view vector may correspond to different reflection situations. This problem does not happen with irradiance environment maps. The surface normal contains all the relevant information for diffuse reflection. Since irradiance environment maps are extremely blurred compared to the original illumination, they can be stored at significantly lower resolution. Often one of the lowest mip levels of a prefiltered specular environment map is used to store the irradiance data. Moreover, unlike the glossy reflections we have investigated before, we are not integrating against a BRDF lobe that needs to be clipped to the hemisphere around the surface normal. The convolution of the environment lighting with the clamped cosine lobe is exact, not an approximation.

For each texel in the map, we need to sum up the cosine-weighted contributions of all illumination affecting a surface facing in a given normal direction. Irradiance environment maps are created by applying a far-reaching filter, covering the entire visible hemisphere, to the original environment map. The filter includes the cosine factor. See Figure 10.39. The sphere map in Figure 10.26 on page 408 has a corresponding irradiance map shown in Figure 10.40. An example of an irradiance map in use is presented in Figure 10.41.

Irradiance environment maps are stored and accessed separately from the specular environment or reflection map, usually in a view-independent representation such as a cube map. See Figure 10.42. Instead of the reflected view vector, the surface

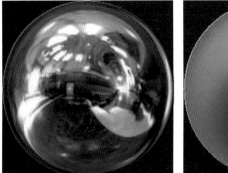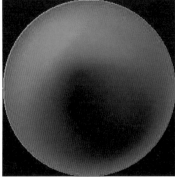

Figure 10.40. Irradiance map formed from the Grace Cathedral sphere map. The left figure is the original sphere map. The right figure is formed by summing the weighted colors in the hemisphere above each pixel. *(Left image courtesy of Paul Debevec, debevec.org; right image courtesy of Ravi Ramamoorthi, Computer Graphics Laboratory, Stanford University.)*

Figure 10.41. Character lighting performed using an irradiance map. *(Image courtesy of the game "Dead or Alive® 3," Tecmo, Ltd. 2001.)*

normal is used to access the cube map to retrieve the irradiance. Values retrieved from the irradiance environment map are multiplied by the diffuse reflectance, and values retrieved from the specular environment map are multiplied by the specular reflectance. The Fresnel effect can also be modeled, increasing specular reflectance (and possibly decreasing diffuse reflectance) at glancing angles [704, 960].

Since the irradiance environment maps use extremely wide filters, it is difficult to create them efficiently on the fly by sampling. King [897] discusses how to perform convolution on the GPU to create irradiance maps. He was able to generate irradiance maps at rates of more than 300 FPS on 2004-era hardware by transforming the environment map to the frequency domain.

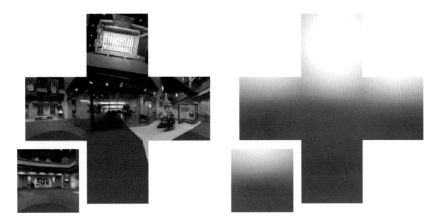

Figure 10.42. A cube map (left) and its corresponding filtered irradiance map (right). *(Reprinted with permission from Microsoft Corporation.)*

Filtered environment maps for diffuse or rough surfaces can be stored at low resolutions, but can also sometimes be generated from relatively small reflection maps of the scene, e.g., a cube map face of 64 × 64 texels. One problem with this approach is that an area light source rendered into such a small texture may "fall between the texels," causing the light to flicker or drop out completely. To avoid this problem, Wiley and Scheuermann [1886] propose representing such light sources by large "cards" (textured rectangles) when rendering the dynamic environment map.

As in the case of glossy reflections, dynamic light sources can also be added into prefiltered irradiance environment maps. An inexpensive method to do this is given by Brennan [195]. Imagine an irradiance map for a single light source. In the direction of the light, the radiance is at a maximum, as the light hits the surface straight on. Radiance for a given surface normal direction (i.e., a given texel) falls off with the cosine of the angle to the light, and is zero where the surface faces away from the light. The GPU can be used to rapidly add this contribution directly to an existing irradiance map by rendering a hemisphere, representing the cosine lobe, centered around the observer, with the pole of the hemisphere along the light's direction.

10.6.1 Spherical Harmonics Irradiance

Although we have discussed representing irradiance environment maps only with textures such as cube maps, other representations are possible, as presented in Section 10.3. Spherical harmonics in particular are quite popular as an irradiance environment map representation, because irradiance from environment lighting is smooth. Convolving radiance with a cosine lobe results in the removal of all the high-frequency components from the environment map.

Ramamoorthi and Hanrahan [1458] show that irradiance environment maps can be represented to an accuracy of about 1% with just the first nine SH coefficients (each coefficient is an RGB vector, so we need to store 27 floating point numbers). Any irradiance environment map can then be interpreted as a spherical function $E(\mathbf{n})$ and projected onto nine RGB coefficients using Equations 10.21 and 10.23. This form is a more compact representation than a cubic or parabolic map, and during rendering the irradiance can be reconstructed by evaluating some simple polynomials, instead of accessing a texture. Often, less precision is needed if the irradiance environment maps represent indirect lighting, a common situation in interactive applications. In this case, four coefficients, for the constant basis function and the three linear basis functions, can often produce good results, since indirect illumination tends to be low frequency, i.e., changes slowly with the angle.

Ramamoorthi and Hanrahan [1458] also show that the SH coefficients for the incoming radiance function $L(\mathbf{l})$ can be converted into coefficients for the irradiance function $E(\mathbf{n})$ by multiplying each coefficient by a constant. Doing so yields a rapid way to filter environment maps into irradiance environment maps, i.e., to project them into the SH basis and then multiply each coefficient by a constant. For example, this is how a fast irradiance filtering implementation by King [897] works. The idea is that the computation of irradiance from radiance is equivalent to performing a spherical convolution between the incoming radiance function $L(\mathbf{l})$ and the clamped cosine function $\cos(\theta_i)^+$. Since the clamped cosine function is rotationally symmetrical about the sphere's z-axis, it assumes a special form in SH: Its projection has only one nonzero coefficient in each frequency band. The nonzero coefficients correspond to the basis functions in the center column of Figure 10.21 (on page 401), which are also known as the *zonal harmonics*.

The result of performing a spherical convolution between a general spherical function and a rotationally symmetrical one (such as the clamped cosine function) is another function over the sphere. This convolution can be performed efficiently on the function's SH coefficients. The SH coefficients of the convolution result is equal to the product (multiplication) of the coefficients of the two functions, scaled by $\sqrt{4\pi/(2l+1)}$, where l is the frequency band index. The SH coefficients of the irradiance function $E(\mathbf{n})$ are then equal to the coefficients of the radiance function $L(\mathbf{l})$ times those of the clamped cosine function $\cos(\theta_i)^+$, scaled by the band constants. The coefficients of $\cos(\theta_i)^+$ beyond the first nine have small values, which explains why nine coefficients suffice for representing the irradiance function $E(\mathbf{n})$. SH irradiance environment maps can be quickly evaluated in this manner. Sloan [1656] describes an efficient GPU implementation.

There is an inherent approximation here, since although the higher-order coefficients of $E(\mathbf{n})$ are small, they are not zero. See Figure 10.43. The approximation is remarkably close, although the "wiggling" of the curve between $\pi/2$ and π, when it should be zero, is called *ringing* in signal processing. It typically occurs when a function with high frequencies is approximated with a small number of basis functions, as seen in Section 10.3.2. The clamp to zero at $\pi/2$ is a sharp change, which means our clamped cosine function has an infinite frequency signal. Ringing is not noticeable in most cases, but it can be seen under extreme lighting conditions as color shifts or

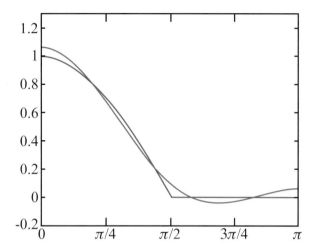

Figure 10.43. The clamped cosine function (in red) versus its nine-coefficient spherical harmonic approximation (in blue). The approximation is quite close. Note the slight dip below and the rise above zero between $\pi/2$ and π.

bright "blobs" on the shadowed sides of objects. If the irradiance environment map is used to store only indirect lighting (as often happens), then ringing is unlikely to be a problem. There are prefiltering methods that minimize the issue [1656, 1659]. See Figure 10.44.

Figure 10.40 shows how an irradiance map derived directly compares to one synthesized by the nine-term function. This SH representation can be evaluated during rendering with the current surface normal **n** [1458], or can be used to rapidly create a cubic or parabolic map for later use. Such lighting is inexpensive and gives good visual results for the diffuse case.

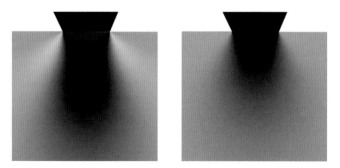

Figure 10.44. Left: example of visual artifacts caused by ringing. Right: a possible solution is to make the original function smoother, so it can be represented without ringing, a process called "windowing." *(Images courtesy of Peter-Pike Sloan.)*

Dynamically rendered cubic environment maps can be projected onto the SH basis [871, 897, 1458]. Since cubic environment maps are a discrete representation of the incoming radiance function, the integral over the sphere in Equation 10.21 becomes a sum over the cube map texels:

$$k_{Lj} = \sum_t f_j(\mathbf{r}[t])L[t]d\omega[t], \tag{10.40}$$

where t is the index of the current cube map texel, $\mathbf{r}[t]$ is the direction vector pointing to the current texel, $f_j(\mathbf{r}[t])$ is the jth SH basis function evaluated at $\mathbf{r}[t]$, $L[t]$ is the radiance stored in the texel, and $d\omega[t]$ is the solid angle subtended by the texel. Kautz [871], King [897], and Sloan [1656] describe how to compute $d\omega[t]$.

To convert the radiance coefficients k_{Lj} into irradiance coefficients, these need to be multiplied by the scaled coefficients of the clamped cosine function $\cos(\theta_i)^+$:

$$k_{Ej} = k'_{\cos^+ j}k_{Lj} = k'_{\cos^+ j} \sum_t f_j(\mathbf{r}[t])L[t]d\omega[t], \tag{10.41}$$

where k_{Ej} is the jth coefficient of the irradiance function $E(\mathbf{n})$, k_{Lj} is the jth coefficient of the incoming radiance function $L(\mathbf{l})$, and $k'_{\cos^+ j}$ is the jth coefficient of the clamped cosine function $\cos(\theta_i)^+$ scaled by $\sqrt{4\pi/(2l+1)}$ (l is the frequency band index).

Given t and the cube map resolution, the factor $k'_{\cos^+ j}f_j(\mathbf{r}[t])d\omega[t]$ is constant for each basis function $f_j()$. These basis factors can be precomputed offline and stored in cube maps, which should be of the same resolution as the dynamic environment maps that will be rendered. The number of textures used can be reduced by packing a separate basis factor in each color channel. To compute an irradiance coefficient for the dynamic cube map, the texels of the appropriate basis factor map are multiplied with those of the dynamic cube map, and the results are summed. Beyond information on dynamic irradiance cube maps, King [897] provides implementation details on GPU SH projection as well.

Dynamic light sources can be added into an existing SH irradiance environment map. This merge is done by computing the SH coefficients of the lights' irradiance contributions and adding them to the existing coefficients. Doing so avoids the need to recompute the entire irradiance environment map. It is a straightforward process, since simple analytical expressions exist for the coefficients of point, disk, and spherical lights [583, 871, 1656, 1690]. Summing the coefficients has the same effect as summing the irradiance. Usually these representations are given in zonal harmonics, for a light aligned with the z-axis, and then rotations can be applied to position the light toward an arbitrary direction. Zonal harmonics rotation is a special case of SH rotation (Section 10.3.2) and is much more efficient, requiring only a dot product instead of a full matrix transform. Coefficients for light sources with more complex shapes can be computed by drawing them into an image that is then numerically projected onto the SH basis [1690]. For the special case of a physical sky model, Habel [626] shows a direct expansion of the Preetham skylight in spherical harmonics.

The ease of projection of common analytical light sources into SH is important, as often environment lighting is used to stand in for distant or less-intense light sources. Fill lights are an important case. In rendering, these light source are placed to simulate the indirect light in the scene, i.e., light bouncing off surfaces. Specular contributions are often not computed for fill lights, especially as these lights can be physically large relative to the shaded object and relatively dim compared to other sources of illumination in the scene. These factors make their specular highlights more spread out and less noticeable. This type of light has a real-world analogy in lighting for film and video, where physical *fill lights* are often used to add lighting in shadows.

In spherical harmonic space it is also simple to do the opposite derivation, that is, to extract analytic light sources from radiance projected in SH. In his survey of SH techniques, Sloan [1656] shows how, given a directional light source with a known axis, it is easy to compute from a SH irradiance representation the intensity that the light should have to minimize the error between itself and the encoded irradiance.

In his previous work [1653] Sloan shows how to select a near-optimal direction by employing only the coefficients in the first (linear) band. The survey also includes a method for extracting multiple directional lights. This work shows that spherical harmonics are a practical basis for light summation. We can project multiple lights into SH and extract a smaller number of directional lights that can closely approximate the projected set. A principled approach to aggregating less important lights is provided by the *lightcuts* [1832] framework.

Although most commonly used for irradiance, SH projections can be employed to simulate glossy, view-dependent BRDF lighting. Ramamoorthi and Hanrahan [1459] describe one such technique. Instead of a single color, they store in a cube map the coefficients of a spherical harmonic projection encoding the view-dependence of the environment map. However, in practice this technique requires much more space than the prefiltered environment map approaches we have seen earlier. Kautz et al. [869] derive a more economical solution using two-dimensional tables of SH coefficients, but this method is limited to fairly low-frequency lighting.

10.6.2 Other Representations

Although cube maps and spherical harmonics are the most popular representations for irradiance environment maps, other representations are possible. See Figure 10.45. Many irradiance environment maps have two dominant colors: a sky color on the top and a ground color on the bottom. Motivated by this observation, Parker et al. [1356] present a *hemisphere lighting* model that uses just two colors. The upper hemisphere is assumed to emit a uniform radiance L_{sky}, and the lower hemisphere is assumed to emit a uniform radiance L_{ground}. The irradiance integral for this case is

$$E = \begin{cases} \pi \left(\left(1 - \dfrac{1}{2} \sin \theta \right) L_{\text{sky}} + \dfrac{1}{2} \sin \theta L_{\text{ground}} \right), & \text{where } \theta < 90°, \\ \pi \left(\dfrac{1}{2} \sin \theta L_{\text{sky}} + \left(1 - \dfrac{1}{2} \sin \theta \right) L_{\text{ground}} \right), & \text{where } \theta \geq 90°, \end{cases} \qquad (10.42)$$

Figure 10.45. Various ways of encoding irradiance. From left to right: the environment map and diffuse lighting computed via Monte Carlo integration for the irradiance; irradiance encoded with an ambient cube; spherical harmonics; spherical Gaussians; and H-basis (which can represent only a hemisphere of directions, so backfacing normals are not shaded). *(Images computed via the* Probulator *open-source software by Yuriy O'Donnell and David Neubelt.)*

where θ is the angle between the surface normal and the sky hemisphere axis. Baker and Boyd propose a faster approximation (described by Taylor [1752]):

$$E = \pi \left(\frac{1 + \cos\theta}{2} L_{\text{sky}} + \frac{1 - \cos\theta}{2} L_{\text{ground}} \right), \qquad (10.43)$$

which is a linear interpolation between sky and ground, using $(\cos\theta + 1)/2$ as the interpolation factor. The term $\cos\theta$ is generally fast to compute as a dot product, and in the common case where the sky hemisphere axis is one of the cardinal axes (e.g., the y- or z-axis), it does not need to be computed at all, since it is equal to one of the world-space coordinates of $\mathbf{n}$. The approximation is reasonably close and significantly faster, so it is preferable to the full expression for most applications.

Forsyth [487] presents an inexpensive and flexible lighting model called the *trilight*, which includes directional, bidirectional, hemispherical, and wrap lighting as special cases.

Valve originally introduced the ambient cube representation (Section 10.3.1) for irradiance. In general, all the spherical function representations we have seen in Section 10.3 can be employed for precomputed irradiance. For the low-frequency signals that irradiance functions represent, we know SH is a good approximation. We tend to create special methods to simplify or use less storage than spherical harmonics.

More complex representations for high frequencies are needed if we want to evaluate occlusions and other global illumination effects, or if we want to incorporate glossy reflections (Section 10.1.1). The general idea of precomputing lighting to account for all interactions is called *precomputed radiance transport* (PRT) and will be discussed in Section 11.5.3. Capturing high frequencies for glossy lighting is also referred to as *all-frequency* lighting. Wavelet representations are often used in this context [1059] as means of compressing environment maps and to devise efficient operators in a similar fashion to the ones we have seen for spherical harmonics. Ng et al. [1269, 1270] demonstrate the use of *Haar wavelets* to generalize irradiance environment mapping to model self-shadowing. They store both the environment map and the shadowing function, which varies over the object surface, in the wavelet basis. This representation is of note because it amounts to a transformation of an environment cube map, performing a two-dimensional wavelet projection of each of the cube faces. Thus, it can be seen as a compression technique for cube maps.

10.7 Sources of Error

To correctly perform shading, we have to evaluate integrals over non-punctual light sources. In practice, this requirement means there are many different techniques we can employ, based on the properties of the lights under consideration. Often real-time engines model a few important lights analytically, approximating integrals over the light area and computing occlusion via shadow maps. All the other light sources—distant lighting, sky, fill lights, and light bouncing over surfaces—are often represented by environment cube maps for the specular component, and spherical bases for diffuse irradiance.

Employing a mix of techniques for lighting means that we are never working directly with a given BRDF model, but with approximations that have varying degrees of error. Sometimes the BRDF approximation is explicit, as we fit intermediate models in order to compute lighting integrals—LTCs are an example. Other times we build approximations that are exact for a given BRDF under certain (often rare) conditions, but are subject to errors in general—prefiltered cube maps fall into this category.

An important aspect to take into consideration when developing real-time shading models is to make sure that the discrepancies between different forms of lighting are not evident. Having coherent light results from different representations might even be more important, visually, than the absolute approximation error committed by each.

Occlusions are also of key importance for realistic rendering, as light "leaking" where there should be none is often more noticeable than not having light where it should be. Most area light representations are not trivial to shadow. Today none of the existing real-time shadowing techniques, even when accounting for "softening" effects (Section 7.6), can accurately consider the light shape. We compute a scalar factor that we multiply to reduce the contribution of a given light when an object casts a shadow, which is not correct; we should take this occlusion into account while performing the integral with the BRDF. The case of environment lighting is particularly hard, as we do not have a defined, dominant light direction, so shadowing techniques for punctual light sources cannot be used.

Even if we have seen some fairly advanced lighting models, it is important to remember that these are not exact representations of real-world sources of illumination. For example, in the case of environment lighting, we assume infinitely distant

Figure 10.46. Production lighting. *(Trailer Park 5. Archival pigment print, 17x22 inches. Production stills from Gregory Crewdson's Beneath the Roses series. ©Gregory Crewdson. Courtesy Gagosian.)*

radiance sources, ones that are never possible. All the analytic lights we have seen work on an even stronger assumption, that the lights emit radiance uniformly over the outgoing hemisphere for each point on their surface. In practice, this assumption can be a source of error, as often real lights are strongly directional. In photographic and cinematic lighting, specially crafted masks and filters called *gobos*, *cuculoris*, or *cookies* are often employed for artistic effect. See for example the sophisticated cinematographic lighting in Figure 10.46, by photographer Gregory Crewdson. To restrict lighting angles while keeping a large area of emission, grids of shielding black material called *honeycombs* can be added in front of large light-emitting panels (so-called *softboxes*). Complex configurations of mirrors and reflectors can also be used in the light's housing, such as in interior lighting, automotive headlights, and flashlights. See Figure 10.47. These optical systems create one or more virtual emitters far from the physical center radiating light, and this offset should be considered when performing falloff computations.

Note that these errors should always be evaluated in a perceptual, result-oriented framework (unless our aim is to do predictive rendering, i.e., to reliably simulate the real-world appearance of surfaces). In the hands of the artists, certain simplifications, even if not realistic, can still result in useful and expressive primitives. Physical models are useful when they make it simpler for artists to create visually plausible images, but they are not a goal in their own.

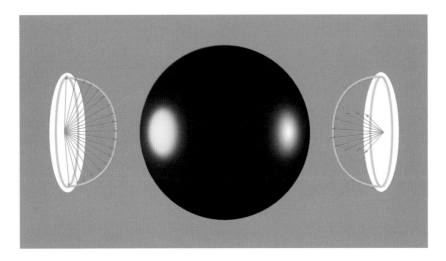

Figure 10.47. The same disk light with two different emission profiles. Left: each point on the disk emits light uniformly over the outgoing hemisphere. Right: emission is focused in a lobe around the disk normal.

Further Reading and Resources

The book *Light Science and Magic: An Introduction to Photographic Lighting* by Hunter [791] is a great reference for understanding real-world photographic lights. For movie lighting *Set Lighting Technician's Handbook: Film Lighting Equipment, Practice, and Electrical Distribution* [188] is a great introduction.

The work pioneered by Debevec in the area of image-based lighting is of great interest to anyone who needs to capture environment maps from real-world scenes. Much of this work is covered in a SIGGRAPH 2003 course [333], as well as in the book *High Dynamic Range Imaging: Acquisition, Display, and Image-Based Lighting* by Reinhard et al. [1479].

One resource that can help simulation are light profiles. The Illuminating Engineering Society (IES) publishes a handbook and file format standard for lighting measurements [960, 961]. Data in this format is commonly available from many manufacturers. The IES standard is limited to describing lights by only their angular emission profile. It does not fully model the effect on the falloff due to optical systems, nor the emission over the light surface area.

Szirmay-Kalos's [1732] state-of-the-art report on specular effects includes many references to environment mapping techniques.

Chapter 11
Global Illumination

> *"If it looks like computer graphics,*
> *it is not good computer graphics."*
> —Jeremy Birn

Radiance is the final quantity computed by the rendering process. So far, we have been using the *reflectance equation* to compute it:

$$L_o(\mathbf{p}, \mathbf{v}) = \int_{\mathbf{l} \in \Omega} f(\mathbf{l}, \mathbf{v}) L_i(\mathbf{p}, \mathbf{l})(\mathbf{n} \cdot \mathbf{l})^+ d\mathbf{l}, \tag{11.1}$$

where $L_o(\mathbf{p}, \mathbf{v})$ is the outgoing radiance from the surface location $\mathbf{p}$ in the view direction $\mathbf{v}$, Ω is the hemisphere of directions above $\mathbf{p}$, $f(\mathbf{l}, \mathbf{v})$ is the BRDF evaluated for $\mathbf{v}$ and the current incoming direction $\mathbf{l}$, $L_i(\mathbf{p}, \mathbf{l})$ is the incoming radiance into $\mathbf{p}$ from $\mathbf{l}$, and $(\mathbf{n} \cdot \mathbf{l})^+$ is the dot product between $\mathbf{l}$ and $\mathbf{n}$, with negative values clamped to zero.

11.1 The Rendering Equation

The reflectance equation is a restricted special case of the full *rendering equation*, presented by Kajiya in 1986 [846]. Different forms have been used for the rendering equation. We will use this version:

$$L_o(\mathbf{p}, \mathbf{v}) = L_e(\mathbf{p}, \mathbf{v}) + \int_{\mathbf{l} \in \Omega} f(\mathbf{l}, \mathbf{v}) L_o(r(\mathbf{p}, \mathbf{l}), -\mathbf{l})(\mathbf{n} \cdot \mathbf{l})^+ d\mathbf{l}, \tag{11.2}$$

where the new elements are $L_e(\mathbf{p}, \mathbf{v})$, which is the emitted radiance from the surface location $\mathbf{p}$ in direction $\mathbf{v}$, and the following replacement:

$$L_i(\mathbf{p}, \mathbf{l}) = L_o(r(\mathbf{p}, \mathbf{l}), -\mathbf{l}). \tag{11.3}$$

This term means that the incoming radiance into location $\mathbf{p}$ from direction $\mathbf{l}$ is equal to the outgoing radiance from some other point in the opposite direction $-\mathbf{l}$. In this case, the "other point" is defined by the *ray casting function* $r(\mathbf{p}, \mathbf{l})$. This function returns the location of the first surface point hit by a ray cast from $\mathbf{p}$ in direction $\mathbf{l}$. See Figure 11.1.

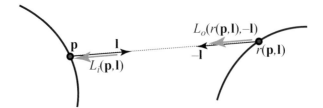

Figure 11.1. The shaded surface location $\mathbf{p}$, lighting direction $\mathbf{l}$, ray casting function $r(\mathbf{p}, \mathbf{l})$, and incoming radiance $L_i(\mathbf{p}, \mathbf{l})$, also represented as $L_o(r(\mathbf{p}, \mathbf{l}), -\mathbf{l})$.

The meaning of the rendering equation is straightforward. To shade a surface location $\mathbf{p}$, we need to know the outgoing radiance L_o leaving $\mathbf{p}$ in the view direction $\mathbf{v}$. This is equal to the emitted radiance L_e plus the reflected radiance. Emission from light sources has been studied in previous chapters, as has reflectance. Even the ray casting operator is not as unfamiliar as it may seem. The z-buffer computes it for rays cast from the eye into the scene, for example.

The only new term is $L_o(r(\mathbf{p}, \mathbf{l}), -\mathbf{l})$, which makes explicit the fact that the incoming radiance into one point must be outgoing from another point. Unfortunately, this is a recursive term. That is, it is computed by yet another summation over outgoing radiance from locations $r(r(\mathbf{p}, \mathbf{l}), \mathbf{l}')$. These in turn need to compute the outgoing radiance from locations $r(r(r(\mathbf{p}, \mathbf{l}), \mathbf{l}'), \mathbf{l}'')$, ad infinitum. It is amazing that the real world can compute all this in real time.

We know this intuitively, that lights illuminate a scene, and the photons bounce around and at each collision are absorbed, reflected, and refracted in a variety of ways. The rendering equation is significant in that it sums up all possible paths in a simple-looking equation.

An important property of the rendering equation is that it is *linear* with respect to the emitted lighting. If we make the lights twice as strong, the result of the shading will be two times brighter. The response of the material for each light is also independent from other sources. That is, one light's presence does not affect the interaction of another light with the material.

In real-time rendering, it is common to use just a local lighting model. Only the surface data at visible points are needed to compute the lighting—and that is exactly what GPUs can most efficiently provide. Primitives are processed and rasterized independently, after which they are discarded. Results of the lighting calculations at point $\mathbf{a}$ cannot be accessed when performing calculations at point $\mathbf{b}$. Transparency, reflections, and shadows are examples of *global illumination* algorithms. They use information from other objects than the one being illuminated. These effects contribute greatly to increasing the realism in a rendered image, and provide cues that help the viewer to understand spatial relationships. At the same time, they are also complex to simulate and might require precomputations or rendering multiple passes that compute some intermediate information.

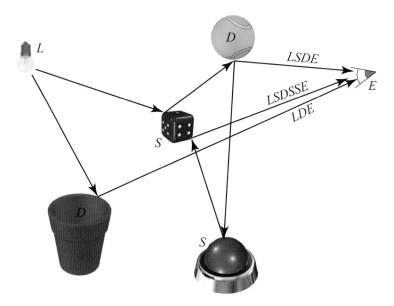

Figure 11.2. Some paths and their equivalent notation as they reach the eye. Note that two paths are shown continuing from the tennis ball.

One way to think of the problem of illumination is by the paths the photons take. In the local lighting model, photons travel from the light to a surface (ignoring intervening objects), then to the eye. Shadowing techniques take into account these intervening objects' direct occlusion effects. An environment map captures illumination traveling from light sources to distant objects, which is then applied to local shiny objects, which mirror-reflect this light to the eye. An irradiance map also captures the effect of light on distant objects, integrated in each direction over a hemisphere. The light reflected from all these objects is weighted and summed to compute the illumination for a surface, which in turn is seen by the eye.

Thinking about the different types and combinations of light transport paths in a more formal manner is helpful in understanding the various algorithms that exist. Heckbert [693] has a notational scheme that is useful for describing the paths simulated by a technique. Each interaction of a photon along its trip from the light (L) to the eye (E) can be labeled as diffuse (D) or specular (S). Categorization can be taken further by adding other surface types, such as "glossy," meaning shiny but not mirror-like. See Figure 11.2. Algorithms can be briefly summarized by regular expressions, showing what types of interactions they simulate. See Table 11.1 for a summary of basic notation.

Photons can take various paths from light to eye. The simplest path is LE, where a light is seen directly by the eye. A basic z-buffer is $L(D|S)E$, or equivalently, $LDE|LSE$. Photons leave the light, reach a diffuse or specular surface, and then

Operator	Description	Example	Explanation
$*$	zero or more	$S*$	zero or more specular bounces
$+$	one or more	$D+$	one or more diffuse bounces
$?$	zero or one	$S?$	zero or one specular bounces
$\|$	either/or	$D\|SS$	either a diffuse or two specular bounces
$()$	group	$(D\|S)*$	zero or more of diffuse or specular

Table 11.1. Regular expression notation.

arrive at the eye. Note that with a basic rendering system, point lights have no physical representation. Giving lights geometry would yield a system $L(D|S)?E$, in which light can also then go directly to the eye.

If environment mapping is added to the renderer, a compact expression is a little less obvious. Though Heckbert's notation reads from light to eye, it is often easier to build up expressions going the other direction. The eye will first see a specular or diffuse surface, $(S|D)E$. If the surface is specular, it could also then, optionally, reflect a (distant) specular or diffuse surface that was rendered into the environment map. So, there is an additional potential path: $((S|D)?S|D)E$. To count in the path where the eye directly sees the light, add in a ? to this central expression to make it optional, and cap with the light itself: $L((S|D)?S|D)?E$.

This expression could be expanded to $LE|LSE|LDE|LSSE|LDSE$, which shows all the possible paths individually, or the shorter $L(D|S)?S?E$. Each has its uses in understanding relationships and limits. Part of the utility of the notation is in expressing algorithm effects and being able to build off of them. For example, $L(S|D)$ is what is encoded when an environment map is generated, and SE is the part that then accesses this map.

The rendering equation itself can be summarized by the simple expression $L(D|S)* E$, i.e., photons from the light can hit zero to nearly infinite numbers of diffuse or specular surfaces before reaching the eye.

Global illumination research focuses on methods for computing light transport along some of these paths. When applying it to real-time rendering, we are often willing to sacrifice some quality or correctness for efficient evaluation. The two most common strategies are to simplify and to precompute. For instance, we could assume that all the light bounces before the one reaching the eye are diffuse, a simplification that can work well for some environments. We could also precalculate some information about inter-object effects offline, such as generating textures that record illumination levels on surfaces, then in real time perform only basic calculations that rely on these stored values. This chapter will show examples of how these strategies can be used to achieve a variety of global illumination effects in real time.

Figure 11.3. Path tracing can generate photorealistic images, but is computationally expensive. The above image uses over two thousand paths per pixel, and each path is up to 64 segments long. It took over two hours to render, and it still exhibits some minor noise. *("Country Kitchen" model by Jay-Artist, Benedikt Bitterli Rendering Resources, licensed under CC BY 3.0 [149]. Rendered using the Mitsuba renderer.)*

11.2 General Global Illumination

Previous chapters have focused on various ways of solving the reflectance equation. We assumed a certain distribution of incoming radiance, L_i, and analyzed how it affected the shading. In this chapter we present algorithms that are designed to solve the full rendering equation. The difference between the two is that the former ignores where the radiance comes from—it is simply given. The latter states this explicitly: Radiance arriving at one point is the radiance that was emitted or reflected from other points.

Algorithms that solve the full rendering equation can generate stunning, photo-realistic images (Figure 11.3). Those methods, however, are too computationally expensive for real-time applications. So, why discuss them? The first reason is that in static or partially static scenes, such algorithms can be run as a preprocess, storing the results for later use during rendering. This is a common approach in games, for example, and we will discuss different aspects of such systems.

The second reason is that global illumination algorithms are built on rigorous theoretical foundations. They are derived directly from the rendering equation, and any approximation they make is meticulously analyzed. A similar type of reasoning can and should be applied when designing real-time solutions. Even when we make certain shortcuts, we should be aware what the consequences are and what is the correct way. As graphics hardware becomes more powerful, we will be able to make fewer compromises and create real-time rendered images that are closer to correct physical results.

Two common ways of solving the rendering equation are finite element methods and Monte Carlo methods. Radiosity is an algorithm based on the first approach; ray tracing in its various forms uses the second. Of the two, ray tracing is far more popular. This is mainly because it can efficiently handle general light transport—including effects such as volumetric scattering—all within the same framework. It also scales and parallelizes more easily.

We will briefly describe both approaches, but interested readers should refer to any of the excellent books that cover the details of solving the rendering equation in a non-real-time setting [400, 1413].

11.2.1 Radiosity

Radiosity [566] was the first computer graphics technique developed to simulate bounced light between diffuse surfaces. It gets its name from the quantity that is computed by the algorithm. In the classic form, radiosity can compute interreflections and soft shadows from area lights. There have been whole books written about this algorithm [76, 275, 1642], but the basic idea is relatively simple. Light bounces around an environment. You turn a light on and the illumination quickly reaches equilibrium. In this stable state, each surface can be considered as a light source in its own right. Basic radiosity algorithms make the simplifying assumption that all indirect light is from diffuse surfaces. This premise fails for places with polished marble floors or large mirrors on the walls, but for many architectural settings this is a reasonable approximation. Radiosity can follow an effectively unlimited number of diffuse bounces. Using the notation introduced at the beginning of this chapter, its light transport set is $LD * E$.

Radiosity assumes that each surface is composed of some number of patches. For each of these smaller areas, it computes a single, average radiosity value, so these patches need to be small enough to capture all the details of the lighting (e.g., shadow edges). However, they do not need to match the underlying surface triangles one to one, or even be uniform in size.

Starting from the rendering equation, we can derive that the radiosity for patch i is equal to

$$B_i = B_i^e + \rho_{\text{ss}} \sum_j F_{ij} B_j, \tag{11.4}$$

where B_i denotes the radiosity of patch i, B_i^e is the radiant *exitance*, i.e., the radiosity emitted by patch i, and ρ_{ss} is the subsurface albedo (Section 9.3). Emission is nonzero only for light sources. F_{ij} is the *form factor* between patches i and j. The form factor is defined as

$$F_{ij} = \frac{1}{A_i} \int_{A_i} \int_{A_j} V(\mathbf{i}, \mathbf{j}) \frac{\cos \theta_i \cos \theta_j}{\pi d_{ij}^2} da_i da_j, \tag{11.5}$$

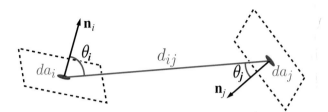

Figure 11.4. The form factor between two surface points.

where A_i is the area of patch i, and $V(\mathbf{i}, \mathbf{j})$ is the visibility function between points $\mathbf{i}$ and $\mathbf{j}$, equal to one if there is nothing blocking light between them and zero otherwise. The values θ_i and θ_j are the angles between the two patch normals and the ray connecting points $\mathbf{i}$ and $\mathbf{j}$. Finally, d_{ij} is the length of the ray. See Figure 11.4.

The form factor is a purely geometric term. It is the fraction of uniform diffuse radiant energy leaving patch i that is incident upon patch j [399]. The area, distance, and orientations of both patches, along with any surfaces that come between them, affect their form factor value. Imagine a patch represented by, say, a computer monitor. Every other patch in the room will directly receive some fraction of any light emitted from the monitor. This fraction could be zero, if the surface is behind or cannot "see" the monitor. These fractions all add up to one. A significant part of the radiosity algorithm is accurately determining the form factors between pairs of patches in the scene.

With the form factors computed, equations for all the patches (Equation 11.4) are combined into a single linear system. The system is then solved, resulting in a radiosity value for every patch. As the number of patches rises, the costs of reducing such a matrix is considerable, due to high computational complexity.

Because the algorithm scales poorly and has other limitations, classical radiosity is rarely used for generating lighting solutions. However, the idea of precomputing the form factors and using them at runtime to perform some form of light propagation is still popular among modern real-time global illumination systems. We will talk about these approaches later in the chapter (Section 11.5.3).

11.2.2 Ray Tracing

Ray casting is the process of firing a ray from a location to determine what objects are in a particular direction. *Ray tracing* uses rays to determine the light transport between various scene elements. In its most basic form, rays are shot from the camera through the pixel grid into the scene. For each ray, the closest object is found. This intersection point is then checked for whether it is in shadow by shooting a ray to each light and finding if any objects are in between. Opaque objects block the light; transparent objects attenuate it. Other rays can be spawned from an intersection point. If a surface is shiny, a ray is generated in the reflection direction. This ray picks up the color of the first object intersected, which in turn has its intersection point tested for shadows. Rays can also be generated in the direction of refraction for transparent solid objects, again recursively evaluated. This basic mechanism is so simple that functional ray tracers have been written that fit on the back of a business card [696].

Classical ray tracing can provide only limited set of effects: sharp reflections and refractions, and hard shadows. However, the same underlying principle can be used to solve the full rendering equation. Kajiya [846] realized that the mechanism of shooting rays and evaluating how much light they carry can be used to compute the integral in Equation 11.2. The equation is recursive, which means that for every ray, we need to evaluate the integral again, at a different position. Fortunately, solid mathematical foundations for handling this problem already existed. *Monte Carlo* methods, developed for physics experiments during the Manhattan Project, were designed specifically to deal with this class of problems. Instead of directly computing the value of the integral in each shading point via quadrature rules, the integrand is evaluated at a number of random points from the domain. These values are then used to compute the estimate for the value of the integral. The more sampling points, the higher the accuracy. The most important property of this method is that only point evaluations of the integrand are needed. Given enough time, we can compute the integral with arbitrary precision. In the context of rendering, this is exactly what ray tracing provides. When we shoot the ray, we point-sample the integrand from Equation 11.2. Even though there is another integral to be evaluated at the intersection point, we do not need its final value, we can just point-sample it again. As the ray bounces across the scene, a *path* is built. The light carried along each path provides one evaluation of the integrand. This procedure is called *path tracing* (Figure 11.5).

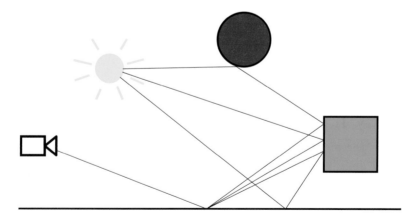

Figure 11.5. Example paths generated by a path tracing algorithm. All three paths pass through the same pixel in the film plane and are used to estimate its brightness. The floor at the bottom of the figure is highly glossy and reflects the rays within a small solid angle. The blue box and red sphere are diffuse and so scatter the rays uniformly around the normal at the point of intersection.

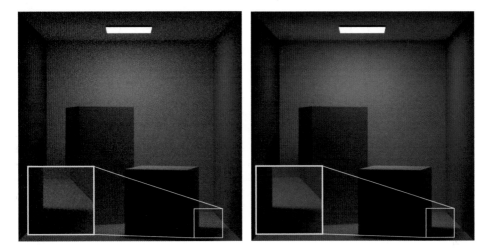

Figure 11.6. Noise resulting from using Monte Carlo path tracing with an insufficient number of samples. The image on the left was rendered with 8 paths per pixel, and the one on the right with 1024 paths per pixel. *("Cornell Box" model from Benedikt Bitterli Rendering Resources, licensed under CC BY 3.0 [149]. Rendered using the Mitsuba renderer.)*

Tracing paths is an extremely powerful concept. Paths can be used for rendering glossy or diffuse materials. Using them, we can generate soft shadows and render transparent objects along with caustic effects. After extending path tracing to sample points in volumes, not just surfaces, it can handle fog and subsurface scattering effects.

The only downside of path tracing is the computational complexity required to achieve high visual fidelity. For cinematic quality images, billions of paths may need to be traced. This is because we never compute the actual value of the integral, only its estimate. If too few paths are used, this approximation will be imprecise, sometimes considerably so. Additionally, results can be vastly different even for points that are next to each other, for which one would expect the lighting to be almost the same. We say that such results have *high variance*. Visually, this manifests itself as noise in the image (Figure 11.6). Many methods have been proposed to combat this effect without tracing additional paths. One popular technique is *importance sampling*. The idea is that variance can be greatly reduced by shooting more rays in the directions from which most of the light comes.

Many papers and books have been published on the subject of path tracing and related methods. Pharr et al. [1413] provide a great introduction to modern offline ray-tracing-based techniques. Veach [1815] lays down the mathematical foundations for modern reasoning about light transport algorithms. We discuss ray and path tracing at interactive rates at the end of this chapter, in Section 11.7.

11.3 Ambient Occlusion

The general global illumination algorithms covered in the previous section are computationally expensive. They can produce a wide range of complex effects, but it can take hours to generate an image. We will begin our exploration of the real-time alternatives with the simplest, yet still visually convincing, solutions and gradually build up to more complex effects throughout the chapter.

One basic global illumination effect is *ambient occlusion* (AO). The technique was developed in the early 2000s by Landis [974], at Industrial Light & Magic, to improve the quality of the environment lighting used on the computer-generated planes in the movie *Pearl Harbor*. Even though the physical basis for the effect includes a fair number of simplifications, the results look surprisingly plausible. This method inexpensively provides cues about shape when lighting lacks directional variation and cannot bring out object details.

11.3.1 Ambient Occlusion Theory

The theoretical background for ambient occlusion can be derived directly from the reflectance equation. For simplicity, we will first focus on Lambertian surfaces. The outgoing radiance L_o from such surfaces is proportional to the surface irradiance E. Irradiance is the cosine-weighted integral of the incoming radiance. In general, it depends on the surface position $\mathbf{p}$ and surface normal $\mathbf{n}$. Again, for simplicity, we will assume that the incoming radiance is constant, $L_i(\mathbf{l}) = L_A$, for all incoming directions $\mathbf{l}$. This results in the following equation for computing irradiance:

$$E(\mathbf{p}, \mathbf{n}) = \int_{\mathbf{l} \in \Omega} L_A (\mathbf{n} \cdot \mathbf{l})^+ d\mathbf{l} = \pi L_A, \tag{11.6}$$

where the integration is performed over the hemisphere Ω of possible incoming directions. With the assumption of constant uniform illumination, the irradiance (and, as a result, the outgoing radiance) does not rely on the surface position or normal, and is constant across the object. This leads to a flat appearance.

Equation 11.6 does not take any visibility into account. Some directions may be blocked by other parts of the object or by other objects in the scene. These directions will have different incoming radiance, not L_A. For simplicity, we will assume that the incoming radiance from the blocked directions is zero. This ignores all the light that might bounce off other objects in the scene and eventually reach point $\mathbf{p}$ from such blocked directions, but it greatly simplifies the reasoning. As a result, we get the following equation, first proposed by Cook and Torrance [285, 286]:

$$E(\mathbf{p}, \mathbf{n}) = L_A \int_{\mathbf{l} \in \Omega} v(\mathbf{p}, \mathbf{l})(\mathbf{n} \cdot \mathbf{l})^+ d\mathbf{l}, \tag{11.7}$$

where $v(\mathbf{p}, \mathbf{l})$ is a visibility function that equals zero if a ray cast from $\mathbf{p}$ in the direction of $\mathbf{l}$ is blocked, and one if it is not.

Figure 11.7. An object rendered with only constant ambient lighting (left) and with ambient occlusion (right). Ambient occlusion brings out object details even when the lighting is constant. (*"Dragon" model by Delatronic, Benedikt Bitterli Rendering Resources, licensed under CC BY 3.0 [149]. Rendered using the Mitsuba renderer.*)

The normalized, cosine-weighted integral of the visibility function is called ambient occlusion:

$$k_A(\mathbf{p}) = \frac{1}{\pi} \int_{\mathbf{l} \in \Omega} v(\mathbf{p}, \mathbf{l})(\mathbf{n} \cdot \mathbf{l})^+ d\mathbf{l}. \tag{11.8}$$

It represents a cosine-weighted percentage of the unoccluded hemisphere. Values range from zero, for fully occluded surface points, to one, for locations with no occlusion. It is worth noting that convex objects, such as spheres or boxes, do not cause occlusion on themselves. If no other objects exist in the scene, a convex object will have an ambient occlusion value of one everywhere. If the object has any concavities, occlusion will be less than one in these areas.

Once k_A is defined, the equation for ambient irradiance in the presence of occlusion is

$$E(\mathbf{p}, \mathbf{n}) = k_A(\mathbf{p})\pi L_A. \tag{11.9}$$

Note that now the irradiance does change with surface location, because k_A does. This leads to much more realistic results, as seen in Figure 11.7 on the right. Surface locations in sharp creases will be dark since their value of k_A is low. Compare surface locations $\mathbf{p}_0$ and $\mathbf{p}_1$ in Figure 11.8. The surface orientation also has an effect, since the visibility function $v(\mathbf{p}, \mathbf{l})$ is weighted by a cosine factor when integrated. Compare $\mathbf{p}_1$ to $\mathbf{p}_2$ in the left side of the figure. Both have an unoccluded solid angle of about the same size, but most of the unoccluded region of $\mathbf{p}_1$ is around its surface normal, so the cosine factor is relatively high, as can be seen by the brightness of the arrows. In contrast, most of the unoccluded region of $\mathbf{p}_2$ is off to one side of the surface normal, with correspondingly lower values for the cosine factor. For this reason, the value of k_A is lower at $\mathbf{p}_2$. From here on, for brevity we will cease to explicitly show dependence on the surface location $\mathbf{p}$.

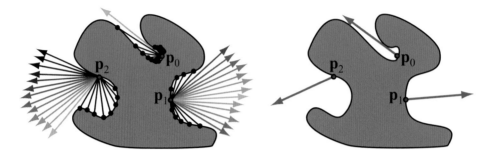

Figure 11.8. An object under ambient illumination. Three points ($\mathbf{p}_0$, $\mathbf{p}_1$, and $\mathbf{p}_2$) are shown. On the left, blocked directions are shown as black rays ending in intersection points (black circles). Unblocked directions are shown as arrows, colored according to the cosine factor, so that those closer to the surface normal are lighter. On the right, each blue arrow shows the average unoccluded direction or bent normal.

In addition to k_A, Landis [974] also computes an average unoccluded direction, known as a *bent normal*. This direction vector is computed as a cosine-weighted average of unoccluded light directions:

$$\mathbf{n}_{\text{bent}} = \frac{\int_{\mathbf{l}\in\Omega} \mathbf{l}\, v(\mathbf{l})(\mathbf{n}\cdot\mathbf{l})^+ d\mathbf{l}}{\|\int_{\mathbf{l}\in\Omega} \mathbf{l}\, v(\mathbf{l})(\mathbf{n}\cdot\mathbf{l})^+ d\mathbf{l}\|}. \tag{11.10}$$

The notation $\|\mathbf{x}\|$ indicates the length of the vector $\mathbf{x}$. The result of the integral is divided by its own length to produce a normalized result. See the right side of Figure 11.8. The resulting vector can be used instead of the geometric normal during shading to provide more accurate results, at no extra performance cost (Section 11.3.7).

11.3.2 Visibility and Obscurance

The visibility function $v(\mathbf{l})$ used to compute the ambient occlusion factor k_A (Equation 11.8) needs to be carefully defined. For an object, such as a character or vehicle, it is straightforward to define $v(\mathbf{l})$ based on whether a ray cast from a surface location in direction $\mathbf{l}$ intersects any other part of the same object. However, this does not account for occlusion by other nearby objects. Often, the object can be assumed to be placed on a flat plane for lighting purposes. By including this plane in the visibility calculation, more realistic occlusion can be achieved. Another benefit is that the occlusion of the ground plane by the object can be used as a contact shadow [974].

Unfortunately, the visibility function approach fails for enclosed geometry. Imagine a scene consisting of a closed room containing various objects. All surfaces will have a k_A value of zero, since all rays from surfaces will hit something. Empirical approaches, which attempt to reproduce the look of ambient occlusion without necessarily simu-

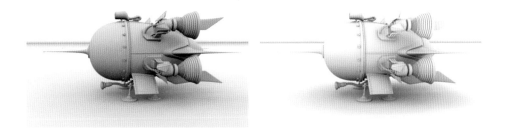

Figure 11.9. Difference between ambient occlusion and obscurance. Occlusion for the spaceship on the left was calculated using rays of infinite length. The image on the right uses finite length rays. *("4060.b Spaceship" model by thecali, Benedikt Bitterli Rendering Resources, licensed under CC BY 3.0 [149]. Rendered using the Mitsuba renderer.)*

lating physical visibility, often work better for such scenes. Some of these approaches were inspired by Miller's concept of *accessibility shading* [1211], which models how nooks and crannies in a surface capture dirt or corrosion.

Zhukov et al. [1970] introduced the idea of *obscurance*, which modifies the ambient occlusion computation by replacing the visibility function $v(\mathbf{l})$ with a distance mapping function $\rho(\mathbf{l})$:

$$k_A = \frac{1}{\pi} \int_{\mathbf{l} \in \Omega} \rho(\mathbf{l})(\mathbf{n} \cdot \mathbf{l})^+ d\mathbf{l}. \qquad (11.11)$$

Unlike $v(\mathbf{l})$, which has only two valid values, 1 for no intersection and 0 for an intersection, $\rho(\mathbf{l})$ is a continuous function based on the distance the ray travels before intersecting a surface. The value of $\rho(\mathbf{l})$ is 0 at an intersection distance of 0 and 1 for any intersection distance greater than a specified distance $d_{\max}$, or when there is no intersection at all. Intersections beyond $d_{\max}$ do not need to be tested, which can considerably speed up the computation of k_A. Figure 11.9 shows the difference between ambient occlusion and ambient obscurance. Notice how the image rendered using ambient occlusion is considerably darker. This is because intersections are detected even at large distances and so affect the value of k_A.

Despite attempts to justify it on physical grounds, obscurance is not physically correct. However, it often gives plausible results that match the viewer's expectations. One drawback is that the value of $d_{\max}$ needs to be set by hand to achieve pleasing results. This type of compromise is often the case in computer graphics, where a technique has no direct physical basis but is "perceptually convincing." The goal is usually a believable image, so such techniques are fine to use. That said, some advantages of methods based on theory are that they can work automatically and can be improved further by reasoning about how the real world works.

Figure 11.10. Difference between ambient occlusion without and with interreflections. The left image uses only information about visibility. The image on the right also uses one bounce of indirect illumination. *("Victorian Style House" model by MrChimp2313, Benedikt Bitterli Rendering Resources, licensed under CC BY 3.0 [149]. Rendered using the Mitsuba renderer.)*

11.3.3 Accounting for Interreflections

Even though the results produced by ambient occlusion are visually convincing, they are darker than those produced by a full global illumination simulation. Compare the images in Figure 11.10.

A significant source of the difference between ambient occlusion and full global illumination are the interreflections. Equation 11.8 assumes that the radiance in the blocked directions is zero, while in reality interreflections will introduce a nonzero radiance from these directions. The effect of this can be seen as darkening in the creases and pits of the model on the left in Figure 11.10, compared to the model on the right. This difference can be addressed by increasing the value of k_A. Using the obscurance distance mapping function instead of the visibility function (Section 11.3.2) can also mitigate this problem, since the obscurance function often has values greater than zero for blocked directions.

Tracking interreflections in a more accurate manner is expensive, since it requires solving a recursive problem. To shade one point, other points must first be shaded, and so on. Computing the value of k_A is significantly less expensive than performing a full global illumination calculation, but it is often desirable to include this missing light in some form, to avoid overdarkening. Stewart and Langer [1699] propose an inexpensive, but surprisingly accurate, method to approximate interreflections. It is based on the observation that for Lambertian scenes under diffuse illumination, the surface locations visible from a given location tend to have similar radiance. By assuming that the radiance L_i from blocked directions is equal to the outgoing radiance L_o from the currently shaded point, the recursion is broken and an analytical expression can be found:

$$E = \frac{\pi k_A}{1 - \rho_{ss}(1 - k_A)} L_i, \tag{11.12}$$

where ρ_{ss} is the subsurface albedo, or diffuse reflectance. This is equivalent to replacing the ambient occlusion factor k_A with a new factor k'_A:

$$k'_A = \frac{k_A}{1 - \rho_{ss}(1 - k_A)}. \tag{11.13}$$

This equation will tend to brighten the ambient occlusion factor, making it visually closer to the result of a full global illumination solution, including interreflections. The effect is highly dependent on the value of ρ_{ss}. The underlying approximation assumes that the surface color is the same in the proximity of the shaded point, to produce an effect somewhat like color bleeding. Hoffman and Mitchell [755] use this method to illuminate terrain with sky light.

A different solution is presented by Jimenez et al. [835]. They perform full, offline path tracing for a number of scenes, each lit by a uniformly white, infinitely distant environment map to obtain occlusion values that properly take interreflections into account. Based on these examples, they fit cubic polynomials to approximate the function f that maps from the ambient occlusion value k_A and subsurface albedo ρ_{ss} to the occlusion value k'_A, which is brightened by the interreflected light. Their method also assumes that the albedo is locally constant, and the color of the incident bounced light can be derived based on the albedo at a given point.

11.3.4 Precomputed Ambient Occlusion

Calculation of the ambient occlusion factors can be time consuming and is often performed offline, prior to rendering. The process of precomputing any lighting-related information, including ambient occlusion, is often called *baking*.

The most common way of precomputing ambient occlusion is via Monte Carlo methods. Rays are cast and checked for intersections with the scene and Equation 11.8 is evaluated numerically. For example, say we pick N random directions $\mathbf{l}$ uniformly distributed over the hemisphere around the normal $\mathbf{n}$, and trace rays in these directions. Based on the intersection results, we evaluate the visibility function v. The ambient occlusion can then be computed as

$$k_A = \frac{1}{N} \sum_i^N v(\mathbf{l}_i)(\mathbf{n} \cdot \mathbf{l}_i)^+. \tag{11.14}$$

When calculating ambient obscurance, the cast rays can be restricted to a maximum distance, and the value of v is based on the intersection distance found.

The computation of ambient occlusion or obscurance factors includes a cosine weighting factor. While it can be included directly, as in Equation 11.14, the more efficient way to incorporate this weighting factor is by means of importance sampling. Instead of casting rays uniformly over the hemisphere and cosine-weighting the results, the distribution of ray directions is cosine weighted. In other words, rays are more likely to be cast closer to the direction of the surface normal, since the results from such directions are likely to matter more. This sampling scheme is called *Malley's method*.

Ambient occlusion precomputations can performed on the CPU or on the GPU. In both cases, libraries that accelerate ray casting against complex geometry are available. The two most popular are Embree [1829], for the CPU, and OptiX [951], for the GPU. In the past, results from the GPU pipeline, such as depth maps [1412] or occlusion queries [493], have also been used for computing ambient occlusion. With the growing popularity of more general ray casting solutions on GPUs, their use is less common today. Most commercially available modeling and rendering software packages provide an option to precompute ambient occlusion.

The occlusion data are unique for every point on the object. They are typically stored in textures, in volumes, or on mesh vertices. The characteristics and problems of the different storage methods are similar, regardless of the type of signal stored. The same methodologies can be used for storing ambient occlusion, directional occlusion, or precomputed lighting, as described in Section 11.5.4.

Precomputed data can also be used to model the ambient occlusion effects of objects on each other. Kontkanen and Laine [924, 925] store the ambient occlusion effect of an object on its surroundings in a cube map, called an *ambient occlusion field*. They model how the ambient occlusion value changes with distance from the object with a reciprocal of a quadratic polynomial. Its coefficients are stored in a cube map, to model directional variation of the occlusion. At runtime, the distance and relative position of the occluding object are used to fetch proper coefficients and reconstruct the occlusion value.

Malmer et al. [1111] show improved results by storing the ambient occlusion factors, and optionally the bent normal, in a three-dimensional grid called an *ambient occlusion volume*. The computation requirements are lower, since the ambient occlusion factor is read directly from the texture, not computed. Fewer scalars are stored compared to Kontkanen and Laine's approach, and the textures in both methods have low resolutions, so the overall storage requirements are similar. Hill [737] and Reed [1469] describe implementations of Malmer et al.'s method in commercial game engines. They discuss various practical aspects of the algorithm as well as useful optimizations. Both methods are meant to work for rigid objects, but they can be extended to articulated objects with small numbers of moving parts, where each part is treated as a separate object.

Whichever method we choose for storing ambient occlusion values, we need to be aware that we are dealing with a continuous signal. When we shoot rays from a particular point in space, we *sample*, and when we interpolate a value from these results before shading, we *reconstruct*. All tools from the signal processing field can be used to improve the quality of the sampling-reconstruction process. Kavan et al. [875] propose a method they call *least-squares baking*. The occlusion signal is sampled uniformly across the mesh. Next, the values for the vertices are derived, so that the total difference between the interpolated and sampled ones is minimized, in the least-squares sense. They discuss the method specifically in the context of storing data at the vertices, but the same reasoning can be used for deriving values to be stored in textures or volumes.

Figure 11.11. *Destiny* uses precomputed ambient occlusion in its indirect lighting calculations. The solution was used on game versions for two different hardware generations, providing high quality and performance. *(Image ©2013 Bungie, Inc. all rights reserved.)*

Destiny is an example of an acclaimed game that uses precomputed ambient occlusion as a basis for its indirect lighting solution (Figure 11.11). The game shipped during the transition period between two generations of console hardware and needed a solution that balanced the high quality expected on new platforms with the limitations, both in performance and memory use, of the older ones. The game features dynamic time of day, so any precomputed solution had to take this correctly into account. The developers chose ambient occlusion for its believable look and low cost. As ambient occlusion decouples the visibility calculations from lighting, the same precomputed data could be used regardless of the time of day. The complete system, including the GPU-based baking pipeline, is described by Sloan et al. [1658].

The *Assassin's Creed* [1692] and *Far Cry* [1154] series from Ubisoft also use a form of precomputed ambient occlusion to augment their indirect illumination solution. They render the world from a top-down view and process the resulting depth map to compute large-scale occlusion. Various heuristics are used to estimate the value based on the distribution of the neighboring depth samples. The resulting world-space AO map is applied to all objects, by projecting their world-space position to texture space. They call this method *World AO*. A similar approach is also described by Swoboda [1728].

11.3.5 Dynamic Computation of Ambient Occlusion

For static scenes, the ambient occlusion factor k_A and bent normal $\mathbf{n}_{\text{bent}}$ can be precomputed. However, for scenes where objects are moving or changing shape, better results can be achieved by computing these factors on the fly. Methods for doing so can be grouped into those that operate in object space, and those that operate in screen space.

Offline methods for computing ambient occlusion usually involve casting a large number of rays, dozens to hundreds, from each surface point into the scene and checking for intersection. This is a costly operation, and real-time methods focus on ways to approximate or avoid much of this computation.

Bunnell [210] computes the ambient occlusion factor k_A and bent normal $\mathbf{n}_{\text{bent}}$ by modeling the surface as a collection of disk-shaped elements placed at the mesh vertices. Disks were chosen since the occlusion of one disk by another can be computed analytically, avoiding the need to cast rays. Simply summing the occlusion factors of a disk by all the other disks leads to overly dark results due to double-shadowing. That is, if one disk is behind another, both will be counted as occluding the surface, even though only the closer of the two should be. Bunnell uses a clever two-pass method to avoid this problem. The first pass computes ambient occlusion including double-shadowing. In the second pass, the contribution of each disk is reduced by its occlusion from the first pass. This is an approximation, but in practice it yields results that are convincing.

Computing occlusion between each pair of elements is an order $O(n^2)$ operation, which is too expensive for all but the simplest scenes. The cost can be reduced by using simplified representations for distant surfaces. Bunnell constructs a hierarchical tree of elements, where each node is a disk that represents the aggregation of the disks below it in the tree. When performing inter-disk occlusion computations, higher-level nodes are used for more distant surfaces. This reduces the computation to order $O(n \log n)$, which is much more reasonable. Bunnell's technique is quite efficient and produces high-quality results. For example, it was used in final renders for the *Pirates of the Caribbean* films [265].

Hoberock [751] proposes several modifications to Bunnell's algorithm that improve quality at a higher computational expense. He also presents a distance attenuation factor, which yields results similar to the obscurance factor proposed by Zhukov et al. [1970].

Evans [444] describes a dynamic ambient occlusion approximation method based on *signed distance fields* (SDF). In this representation, an object is embedded in a three-dimensional grid. Each location in the grid stores the distance to the closest surface of the object. This value is negative for points inside any object and positive for points outside all of them. Evans creates and stores an SDF for a scene in a volume texture. To estimate the occlusion for a location on an object, he uses a heuristic that combines values sampled at some number of points, progressively farther away from the surface, along the normal. The same approach can also be used when the SDF is represented analytically (Section 17.3) instead of stored in a three-dimensional texture, as described by Quílez [1450]. Although the method is non-physical, the results are visually pleasing.

Using signed distance fields for ambient occlusion was further extended by Wright [1910]. Instead of using an ad hoc heuristic to generate occlusion values,

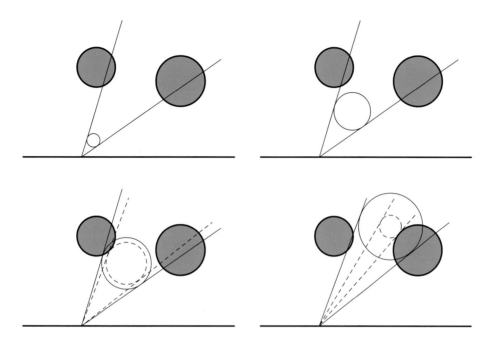

Figure 11.12. Cone tracing is approximated by performing a series of intersections between scene geometry and spheres of increasing radius. The size of the sphere corresponds to the radius of the cone at a given distance from the trace origin. In each step, the cone angle is reduced, to account for occlusion by the scene geometry. The final occlusion factor is estimated as a ratio of the solid angle subtended by the clipped cone to the solid angle of the original cone.

Wright performs *cone tracing*. Cones originate at the location that is being shaded, and are tested for intersections, with the scene representation encoded in the distance field. Cone tracing is approximated by performing a set of steps along the axis and checking for intersections of the SDF with a sphere of increasing radius at each step. If the distance to the nearest occluder (the value sampled from the SDF) is smaller than the sphere's radius, that part of the cone is occluded (Figure 11.12). Tracing a single cone is imprecise and does not allow incorporation of the cosine term. For these reasons, Wright traces a set of cones, covering the entire hemisphere, to estimate the ambient occlusion. To increase visual fidelity, his solution uses not only a global SDF for the scene, but also local SDFs, representing individual objects or logically connected sets of objects.

A similar approach is described by Crassin et al. [305] in the context of a voxel representation of the scene. They use a sparse voxel octree (Section 13.10) to store the voxelization of a scene. Their algorithm for computing ambient occlusion is a special case of a more general method for rendering full global illumination effects (Section 11.5.7).

Figure 11.13. Ambient occlusion effects are blurry and do not reveal details of the occluders. AO calculations can use much simpler representation of the geometry and still achieve plausible effects. The armadillo model (left) is approximated with a set of spheres (right). There is practically no difference in the occlusion cast by the models on the wall behind them. *(Model courtesy of the Stanford Computer Graphics Laboratory.)*

Ren et al. [1482] approximate the occluding geometry as a collection of spheres (Figure 11.13). The visibility function of a surface point occluded by a single sphere is represented using spherical harmonics. The aggregate visibility function for occlusion by a group of spheres is the result of multiplying the individual sphere visibility functions. Unfortunately, computing the product of spherical harmonic functions is an expensive operation. Their key idea is to sum the logarithms of the individual spherical harmonic visibility functions, and exponentiate the result. This produces the same end result as multiplying the visibility functions, but summation of spherical harmonic functions is significantly less expensive than multiplication. The paper shows that, with the right approximations, logarithms and exponentiations can be performed quickly, yielding an overall speedup.

The method computes not just an ambient occlusion factor, but rather a full spherical visibility function, represented with spherical harmonics (Section 10.3.2). The first (order 0) coefficient can be used as the ambient occlusion factor k_A, and the next three (order 1) coefficients can be used to compute the bent normal $\mathbf{n}_{\text{bent}}$. Higher-order coefficients can be used to shadow environment maps or circular light sources. Since geometry is approximated as bounding spheres, occlusion from creases and other small details is not modeled.

Sloan et al. [1655] perform the accumulation of the visibility functions described by Ren in screen space. For each occluder, they consider a set of pixels that are within some prescribed world-space distance from its center. This operation can be achieved by rendering a sphere and either performing the distance test in the shader or using stencil testing. For all the affected screen areas, a proper spherical harmonic value is added to an offscreen buffer. After accumulating visibility for all the occluders, the values in the buffer are exponentiated to get the final, combined visibility functions

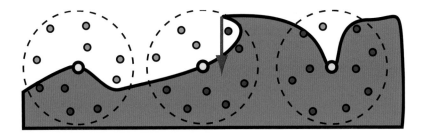

Figure 11.14. Crytek's ambient occlusion method applied to three surface points (the yellow circles). For clarity, the algorithm is shown in two dimensions, with the camera (not shown) above the figure. In this example, ten samples are distributed over a disk around each surface point (in actuality, they are distributed over a sphere). Samples failing the z-test, i.e., those beyond the stored z-buffer values, are shown in red, and samples passing are shown in green. The value of k_A is a function of the ratio of the passing samples to the total samples. We ignore the variable sample weights here for simplicity. The point on the left has 6 passing samples out of 10 total, resulting in a ratio of 0.6, from which k_A is computed. The middle point has three passing samples. One more is outside the object but fails the z-test, as shown by the red arrow. This gives a k_A of 0.3. The point on the right has one passing sample, so k_A is 0.1.

for each screen pixel. Hill [737] uses the same method, but restricts the spherical harmonics visibility functions to only second-order coefficients. With this assumption, the spherical harmonic product is just a handful of scalar multiplies and can be performed by even the GPU's fixed-function blending hardware. This allows us to use the method even on console hardware with limited performance. Because the method uses low-order spherical harmonics, it cannot be used to generate hard shadows with more defined boundaries, rather only mostly directionless occlusion.

11.3.6 Screen-Space Methods

The expense of object-space methods is proportional to scene complexity. However, some information about occlusion can be deduced purely from screen-space data that is already available, such as depth and normals. Such methods have a constant cost, not related to how detailed the scene is, but only to the resolution used for rendering.[1]

Crytek developed a dynamic *screen-space ambient occlusion* (SSAO) approach used in *Crysis* [1227]. They compute ambient occlusion in a full-screen pass, using the z-buffer as the only input. The ambient occlusion factor k_A of each pixel is estimated by testing a set of points, distributed in a sphere around the pixel's location, against the z-buffer. The value of k_A is a function of the number of samples that are in front of the corresponding values in the z-buffer. A smaller number of passing samples results in a lower value for k_A. See Figure 11.14. The samples have weights that decrease with distance from the pixel, similarly to the obscurance factor [1970]. Note that since the samples are not weighted by a $(\mathbf{n} \cdot \mathbf{l})^+$ factor, the resulting ambient occlusion is

---

[1] In practice, the execution time will depend on the distribution of the data in the depth or normal buffers, as this dispersal affects how effectively the occlusion calculation logic uses the GPU caches.

Figure 11.15. The effect of screen-space ambient occlusion is shown in the upper left. The upper right shows the albedo (diffuse color) without ambient occlusion. In the lower left, the two are shown combined. Specular shading and shadows are added for the final image, in the lower right. *(Images from "Crysis" courtesy of Crytek.)*

incorrect. Instead of considering only those samples in the hemisphere above a surface location, all are counted and factored in. This simplification means that samples below the surface are counted when they should not be. Doing so causes a flat surface to be darkened, with edges being brighter than their surroundings. Nonetheless, the results are often visually pleasing. See Figure 11.15.

A similar method was simultaneously developed by Shanmugam and Arikan [1615]. In their paper they describe two approaches. One generates fine ambient occlusion from small, nearby details. The other generates coarse ambient occlusion from larger objects. The results of the two are combined to produce the final ambient occlusion factor. Their fine-scale ambient occlusion method uses a full-screen pass that accesses the z-buffer, along with a second buffer containing the surface normals of the visible pixels. For each shaded pixel, nearby pixels are sampled from the z-buffer. The sampled pixels are represented as spheres, and an occlusion term is computed for the shaded pixel, taking its normal into account. Double-shadowing is not accounted for, so the result is somewhat dark. Their coarse occlusion method is similar to the object-space method of Ren et al. [1482], discussed on page 456, in that the occluding geometry is approximated as a collection of spheres. However, Shanmugam and Arikan accumulate occlusion in screen space, using screen-aligned billboards covering the "area of effect" of each occluding sphere. Double-shadowing is also not accounted for in the coarse occlusion method, unlike the method of Ren et al.

The extreme simplicity of these two methods was quickly noticed by both industry and academia, and spawned numerous follow-up works. Many methods, such as that used in the game *Starcraft II* by Filion et al. [471] and *scalable ambient obscurance* by McGuire et al. [1174], use ad hoc heuristics to generate the occlusion factor. These kinds of methods have good performance characteristics and expose some parameters that can be hand-tweaked to achieve the desired artistic effect.

Other methods aim to provide more principled ways of calculating the occlusion. Loos and Sloan [1072] noticed that Crytek's method could be interpreted as Monte Carlo integration. They call the calculated value *volumetric obscurance* and define it as

$$v_A = \int_{\mathbf{x} \in X} \rho(d(\mathbf{x})) o(\mathbf{x}) d\mathbf{x}, \tag{11.15}$$

where X is a three-dimensional, spherical neighborhood around the point, ρ is the distance-mapping function, analogous to that in Equation 11.11, d is the distance function, and $o(\mathbf{x})$ is the *occupancy function*, equal to zero if $\mathbf{x}$ is not occupied and one otherwise. They note that the $\rho(d)$ function has little impact on the final visual quality and so use a constant function. Given this assumption, volumetric obscurance is an integral of the occupancy function over the neighborhood of a point. Crytek's method samples the three-dimensional neighborhood randomly to evaluate the integral. Loos and Sloan compute the integral numerically in the xy-dimensions, by randomly sampling the screen-space neighborhood of a pixel. The z-dimension is integrated over analytically. If the spherical neighborhood of the point does not contain any geometry, the integral is equal to the length of the intersection between the ray and a sphere representing X. In the presence of geometry, the depth buffer is used as an approximation of the occupancy function, and the integral is computed over only the unoccupied part of each line segment. See the left side of Figure 11.16. The method generates results of quality comparable to Crytek's, but using fewer samples, as integration over one of the dimensions is exact. If the surface normals are available, the method can be extended to take them into account. In that version, the evaluation of the line integral is clamped at the plane defined by the normal at the evaluation point.

Szirmay-Kalos et al. [1733] present another screen-space approach that uses normal information, called *volumetric ambient occlusion*. Equation 11.6 performs the integration over a hemisphere around the normal and includes the cosine term. They propose that this type of integral can be approximated by removing the cosine term from the integrand and clamping the integration range with the cosine distribution. This transforms the integral to be over a sphere instead of a hemisphere, one with half the radius and shifted along the normal, to be fully enclosed within the hemisphere. The volume of its unoccupied portion is calculated just as in the method by Loos and Sloan, by randomly sampling the pixel neighborhood and analytically integrating the occupancy function in the z-dimension. See the right side of Figure 11.16.

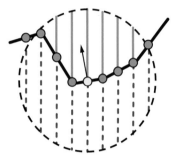 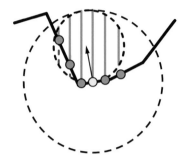

Figure 11.16. Volumetric obscurance (left) estimates the integral of the unoccupied volume around the point using line integrals. Volumetric ambient occlusion (right) also uses line integrals, but to compute the occupancy of the sphere tangent to the shading point, which models the cosine term from the reflectance equation. In both cases, the integral is estimated from the ratio of the unoccupied volume of the sphere (marked with solid green lines) to the total volume of the sphere (the sum of unoccupied and occupied volume, marked with dashed red lines). For both figures the camera is viewing from above. The green dots represent samples read from the depth buffer, and the yellow one is the sample for which the occlusion is being calculated.

A different approach to the problem of estimating local visibility was proposed by Bavoil et al. [119]. They draw inspiration from the *horizon mapping* technique by Max [1145]. Their method, called *horizon-based ambient occlusion* (HBAO), assumes that the data in the z-buffer represents a continuous heightfield. The visibility at a point can be estimated by determining *horizon angles*, the maximum angles above the tangent plane that are occluded by the neighborhood. That is, given a direction from a point, we record the angle of the highest object visible. If we ignore the cosine term, the ambient occlusion factor then can be computed as the integral of the unoccluded portions over the horizon, or, alternatively, as one minus the integral of the occluded parts under the horizon:

$$k_A = 1 - \frac{1}{2\pi} \int_{\phi=-\pi}^{\pi} \int_{\alpha=t(\phi)}^{h(\phi)} W(\omega) \cos(\theta) d\theta d\phi, \tag{11.16}$$

where $h(\phi)$ is the horizon angle above the tangent plane, $t(\phi)$ is the *tangent angle* between the tangent plane and the view vector, and $W(\omega)$ is the attenuation function. See Figure 11.17. The $\frac{1}{2\pi}$ term normalizes the integral so that the result is between zero and one.

By using a linear falloff on the distance to the point that defines the horizon for a given ϕ, we can compute the inner integral analytically:

$$k_A = 1 - \frac{1}{2\pi} \int_{\phi=-\pi}^{\pi} \big(\sin(h(\phi)) - \sin(t(\phi)) \big) W(\phi) d\phi. \tag{11.17}$$

The remaining integral is computed numerically, by sampling a number of directions and finding horizon angles.

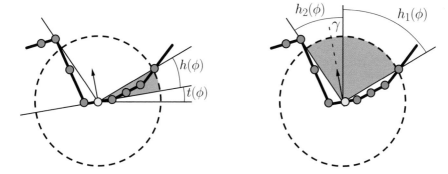

Figure 11.17. Horizon-based ambient occlusion (left) finds the horizon angles h above the tangent plane and integrates the unoccluded angle between them. The angle between the tangent plane and the view vector is denoted as t. Ground-truth ambient occlusion (right) uses the same horizon angles, h_1 and h_2, but also uses the angle between the normal and the view vector, γ, to incorporate the cosine term into the calculations. In both figures the camera is viewing the scene from above. The figures show cross sections, and horizon angles are functions of ϕ, the angle around the view direction. The green dots represent samples read from the depth buffer. The yellow dot is the sample for which the occlusion is being calculated.

The horizon-based approach is also used by Jimenez et al. [835] in a method they call *ground-truth ambient occlusion* (GTAO). Their aim is to achieve ground-truth results, matching those obtained from ray tracing, assuming that the only available information is the heightfield formed by the z-buffer data. Horizon-based ambient occlusion does not include the cosine term in its definition. It also adds the ad hoc attenuation, not present in Equation 11.8, so its results, even though close to those that are ray traced, are not the same. GTAO introduces the missing cosine factor, removes the attenuation function, and formulates the occlusion integral in the reference frame around the view vector. The occlusion factor is defined as

$$k_A = \frac{1}{\pi} \int_0^\pi \int_{h_1(\phi)}^{h_2(\phi)} \cos(\theta - \gamma)^+ |\sin(\theta)| d\theta d\phi, \tag{11.18}$$

where $h_1(\phi)$ and $h_2(\phi)$ are the left and right horizon angles for a given ϕ, and γ is the angle between the normal and the view direction. The normalization term $\frac{1}{\pi}$ is different than for HBAO because the cosine term is included. This makes the open hemisphere integrate to π. Not including the cosine term in the formula makes it integrate to 2π. This formulation matches Equation 11.8 exactly, given the heightfield assumption. See Figure 11.17. The inner integral can still be solved analytically, so only the outer one needs to be computed numerically. This integration is performed the same way as in HBAO, by sampling a number of directions around the given pixel.

The most expensive part of the process in horizon-based methods is sampling the depth buffer along screen-space lines to determine the horizon angles. Timonen [1771] presents a method that aims specifically to improve the performance characteristics of this step. He points out that samples used for estimating the horizon angles for a given direction can be heavily reused between pixels that lay along straight lines in screen space. He splits the occlusion calculations into two steps. First, he performs line traces across the whole z-buffer. At each step of the trace, he updates the horizon angles as he moves along the line, accounting for the prescribed maximum influence distance, and writes this information out to a buffer. One such buffer is created for each screen-space direction used in horizon mapping. The buffers do not need to be the same size as the original depth buffer. Their size depends on the spacing between the lines, and the distance between the steps along the lines, and there is some flexibility in choosing these parameters. Different settings affect the final quality.

The second step is the calculation of the occlusion factors, based on the horizon information stored in the buffers. Timonen uses the occlusion factor defined by HBAO (Equation 11.17), but other occlusion estimators, such as GTAO (Equation 11.18), could be used instead.

A depth buffer is not a perfect representation of the scene, since only the closest object is recorded for a given direction and we do not know what occurs behind it. Many of the methods use various heuristics to try to infer some information about the thickness of the visible objects. These approximations suffice for many situations, and the eye is forgiving of inaccuracies. While there are methods that use multiple layers of depth to mitigate the problem, they never gained wider popularity, due to complex integration with rendering engines and high runtime cost.

The screen-space approaches rely on repeatedly sampling the z-buffer to form some simplified model of the geometry around a given point. Experiments indicate that to achieve a high visual quality, as many as a couple hundred samples are needed. However, to be usable for interactive rendering, no more than 10 to 20 samples can be taken, often even less than that. Jimenez et al. [835] report that, to fit into the performance budget of a 60 FPS game, they could afford to use only one sample per pixel! To bridge the gap between theory and practice, screen-space methods usually employ some form of spatial dithering. In the most common form, every screen pixel uses a slightly different, random set of samples, rotated or shifted radially. After the main phase of AO calculations, a full-screen filtering pass is performed. Joint bilateral filtering (Section 12.1.1) is used to avoid filtering across surface discontinuities and preserve sharp edges. It uses the available information about depth or normals to restrict filtering to use only samples belonging to the same surface. Some of the methods use a randomly changing sampling pattern and experimentally chosen filtering kernel; others use a fixed-size screen-space pattern (for example, 4×4 pixels) of repeating sample sets, and a filter that is restricted to that neighborhood.

Ambient occlusion calculations are also often supersampled over time [835, 1660, 1916]. This process is commonly done by applying a different sampling pattern every frame and performing exponential averaging of the occlusion factors. Data from the previous frame is reprojected to the current view, using the last frame's z-buffer, camera transforms, and information about the motion of dynamic objects. It is then blended with the current frame results. Heuristics based on depth, normal, or velocity are usually used to detect situations when the data from the last frame is not reliable and should be discarded (for instance, because some new object has come into view). Section 5.4.2 explains temporal supersampling and antialiasing techniques in a more general setting. The cost of temporal filtering is small, it is straightforward to implement, and even though it is not always fully reliable, in practice most problems are not noticeable. This is mainly because ambient occlusion is never visualized directly, it only serves as one of the inputs to the lighting calculations. After combining this effect with normal maps, albedo textures, and direct lighting, any minor artifacts are masked out and no longer visible.

11.3.7 Shading with Ambient Occlusion

Even though we have derived the ambient occlusion value in the context of constant, distant illumination, we can also apply it to more complex lighting scenarios. Consider the reflectance equation again:

$$L_o(\mathbf{v}) = \int_{\mathbf{l} \in \Omega} f(\mathbf{l}, \mathbf{v}) L_i(\mathbf{l}) v(\mathbf{l}) (\mathbf{n} \cdot \mathbf{l})^+ d\mathbf{l}. \tag{11.19}$$

The above form contains the visibility function $v(\mathbf{l})$, as introduced in Section 11.3.1.

If we are dealing with a diffuse surface, we can replace $f(\mathbf{l}, \mathbf{v})$ with the Lambertian BRDF, which is equal to the subsurface albedo ρ_{ss} divided by π. We get

$$L_o = \int_{\mathbf{l} \in \Omega} \frac{\rho_{ss}}{\pi} L_i(\mathbf{l}) v(\mathbf{l}) (\mathbf{n} \cdot \mathbf{l})^+ d\mathbf{l} = \frac{\rho_{ss}}{\pi} \int_{\mathbf{l} \in \Omega} L_i(\mathbf{l}) v(\mathbf{l}) (\mathbf{n} \cdot \mathbf{l})^+ d\mathbf{l}. \tag{11.20}$$

We can reformulate the above equation to get

$$
\begin{aligned}
L_o &= \frac{\rho_{ss}}{\pi} \int_{\mathbf{l} \in \Omega} L_i(\mathbf{l}) v(\mathbf{l}) (\mathbf{n} \cdot \mathbf{l})^+ d\mathbf{l} \\
&= \frac{\rho_{ss}}{\pi} \frac{\int_{\mathbf{l} \in \Omega} L_i(\mathbf{l}) v(\mathbf{l}) (\mathbf{n} \cdot \mathbf{l})^+ d\mathbf{l}}{\int_{\mathbf{l} \in \Omega} v(\mathbf{l}) (\mathbf{n} \cdot \mathbf{l})^+ d\mathbf{l}} \int_{\mathbf{l} \in \Omega} v(\mathbf{l}) (\mathbf{n} \cdot \mathbf{l})^+ d\mathbf{l} \\
&= \frac{\rho_{ss}}{\pi} \int_{\mathbf{l} \in \Omega} L_i(\mathbf{l}) \frac{v(\mathbf{l}) (\mathbf{n} \cdot \mathbf{l})^+}{\int_{\mathbf{l} \in \Omega} v(\mathbf{l}) (\mathbf{n} \cdot \mathbf{l})^+ d\mathbf{l}} d\mathbf{l} \int_{\mathbf{l} \in \Omega} v(\mathbf{l}) (\mathbf{n} \cdot \mathbf{l})^+ d\mathbf{l}.
\end{aligned} \tag{11.21}
$$

If we use the definition of the ambient occlusion from Equation 11.8, the above simplifies to

$$L_o = k_A \rho_{ss} \int_{\mathbf{l} \in \Omega} L_i(\mathbf{l}) K(\mathbf{n}, \mathbf{l}) d\mathbf{l}, \tag{11.22}$$

where

$$K(\mathbf{n}, \mathbf{l}) = \frac{v(\mathbf{l}) (\mathbf{n} \cdot \mathbf{l})^+}{\int_{\mathbf{l} \in \Omega} v(\mathbf{l}) (\mathbf{n} \cdot \mathbf{l})^+ d\mathbf{l}}. \tag{11.23}$$

This form gives us a new perspective on the process. The integral in Equation 11.22 can be thought of as applying a directional filtering kernel K to the incoming radiance L_i.

The filter K changes both spatially and directionally in a complicated way, but it has two important properties. First, it covers, at most, the hemisphere around the normal at point $\mathbf{p}$, due to the clamped dot product. Second, its integral over the hemisphere is equal to one, due to the normalization factor in the denominator.

To perform shading, we need to compute an integral of a product of two functions, the incident radiance L_i and the filter function K. In some cases, it is possible to describe the filter in a simplified way and compute this *double product integral* at a fairly low cost, for example, when both L_i and K are represented using spherical harmonics (Section 10.3.2). Another way of dealing with the complexity of this equation is approximating the filter with a simpler one that has similar properties. The most common choice is the normalized cosine kernel H:

$$H(\mathbf{n}, \mathbf{l}) = \frac{(\mathbf{n} \cdot \mathbf{l})^+}{\int_{\mathbf{l} \in \Omega} (\mathbf{n} \cdot \mathbf{l})^+ d\mathbf{l}}. \tag{11.24}$$

This approximation is accurate when there is nothing blocking the incoming lighting. It also covers the same angular extents as the filter we are approximating. It completely ignores visibility, but the ambient occlusion k_A term is still present in Equation 11.22, so there will be some visibility-dependent darkening on the shaded surface.

With this choice of filtering kernel, Equation 11.22 becomes

$$L_o = k_A \rho_{ss} \int_{\mathbf{l} \in \Omega} L_i(\mathbf{l}) \frac{(\mathbf{n} \cdot \mathbf{l})^+}{\int_{\mathbf{l} \in \Omega} (\mathbf{n} \cdot \mathbf{l})^+ d\mathbf{l}} d\mathbf{l} = \frac{k_A}{\pi} \rho_{ss} E. \tag{11.25}$$

This means that, in its simplest form, shading with ambient occlusion can be performed by computing irradiance and multiplying it by the ambient occlusion value. The irradiance can come from any source. For instance, it can be sampled from an irradiance environment map (Section 10.6). The accuracy of the method depends only on how well the approximated filter represents the correct one. For lighting that changes smoothly across the sphere, the approximation gives plausible results. It is also fully accurate if L_i is constant across all possible directions, i.e., as if the scene were lit by an all-white environment map representing the illumination.

This formulation also gives us some insight into why ambient occlusion is a poor approximation of visibility for punctual or small area light sources. They subtend only a small solid angle over the surface—infinitesimally small in case of punctual lights—and the visibility function has an important effect on the value of the lighting integral. It controls the light contribution in an almost binary fashion, i.e., it either enables or disables it entirely. Ignoring visibility, as we did in Equation 11.25, is a significant approximation and, in general, does not yield expected results. Shadows lack definition and do not exhibit any expected directionality, that is, do not appear to be produced by particular lights. Ambient occlusion is not a good choice for modeling visibility of such lights. Other methods, such as shadow maps, should be used instead. It is worth noting, however, that sometimes small, local lights are used to model indirect illumination. In such cases, modulating their contribution with an ambient occlusion value is justified.

Until now we assumed that we are shading a Lambertian surface. When dealing with a more complex, non-constant BRDF, this function cannot be pulled out of the integral, as we did in Equation 11.20. For specular materials, K depends not only on the visibility and normal but also on the viewing direction. A lobe of a typical microfacet BRDF changes significantly across the domain. Approximating it with a single, predetermined shape is too coarse to yield believable results. This is why using ambient occlusion for shading makes most sense for diffuse BRDFs. Other methods, discussed in the upcoming sections, are better for more complex material models.

Using the bent normal (see Equation 11.10 on page 448) can be seen as a way of approximating the filter K more precisely. The visibility term is still not present in the filter, but its maximum matches the average unoccluded direction, which makes it a slightly better approximation to Equation 11.23 overall. In cases where the geometric normal and bent normal do not match, using the latter will give more accurate results. Landis [974] uses it not only for shading with environment maps but also for some of the direct lights, instead of regular shadowing techniques.

For shading with environment maps, Pharr [1412] presents an alternative that uses the GPU's texture filtering hardware to perform the filtering dynamically. The shape of filter K is determined on the fly. Its center is the direction of the bent normal, and its size depends on the value of k_A. This provides an even more precise match to the original filter from Equation 11.23.

11.4 Directional Occlusion

Even though using ambient occlusion alone can increase the visual quality of the image tremendously, it is a greatly simplified model. It gives a poor approximation for visibility when dealing with even large area-light sources, not to mention small or punctual ones. It also cannot correctly deal with glossy BRDFs or more complex lighting setups. Consider a surface lit by a distant dome light, with color changing from red to green across the dome. This might represent ground illuminated by light coming from the sky—given the colors, probably on some distant planet. See Figure 11.18. Even though ambient occlusion will darken the lighting at points **a** and **b**, they will still be illuminated by both red and green portions of the sky. Using bent normals helps mitigate this effect but it is also not perfect. The simple model that we presented before is not flexible enough to deal with such situations. One solution is to describe the visibility in some more expressive way.

We will focus on methods that encode the entire spherical or hemispherical visibility, i.e., ways of describing which directions are blocking the incoming radiance. While this information can be used for shadowing punctual lights, it is not its main purpose. Methods targeting those specific types of lights—discussed extensively in Chapter 7—are able to achieve much better quality, as they need to encode visibility for just a single location or direction for the source. Solutions described here are meant to be used mainly for providing occlusion for large area lights or environment lighting, where

Figure 11.18. Approximated colors of the irradiance in points **a** and **b** under complex lighting conditions. Ambient occlusion does not model any directionality, so the color is the same at both points. Using a bent normal effectively shifts the cosine lobe toward the unoccluded portions of the sky, but because the integration range is not restricted in any way, it is not enough to provide accurate results. Directional methods are able to correctly eliminate lighting coming from the occluded parts of the sky.

the generated shadows are soft, and artifacts caused by approximating visibility are not noticeable. Additionally, these methods can also be used to provide occlusion in cases where regular shadowing techniques are not feasible, such as for self-shadowing of bump map details and for shadowing of extremely large scenes, where shadow maps do not have enough resolution.

11.4.1 Precomputed Directional Occlusion

Max [1145] introduced the concept of *horizon mapping* to describe self-occlusion of a heightfield surface. In horizon mapping, for each point on the surface, the altitude angle of the horizon is determined for some set of azimuth directions, e.g., eight: north, northeast, east, southeast, on around.

Instead of storing horizon angles for some given compass directions, the set of unoccluded three-dimensional directions as a whole can be modeled as an elliptical [705, 866] or circular [1306, 1307] aperture. The latter technique is called *ambient aperture lighting* (Figure 11.19). These techniques have lower storage requirements than horizon maps, but may result in incorrect shadows when the set of unoccluded directions does not resemble an ellipse or circle. For example, a flat plane from which tall spikes protrude at regular intervals should have a star-shaped direction set, which does not map well to the scheme.

There are many variations for occlusion techniques. Wang et al. [1838] use a *spherical signed distance function* (SSDF) to represent visibility. It encodes a signed distance to the boundary of the occluded regions on the sphere. Any of the spherical or hemispherical bases discussed in Section 10.3 can also be used to encode visibility [582, 632, 805, 1267]. Just as with ambient occlusion, directional visibility information can be stored in textures, mesh vertices, or volumes [1969].

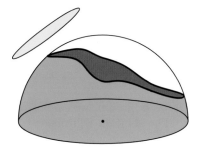 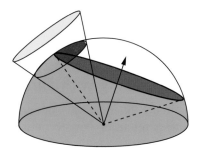

Figure 11.19. Ambient aperture lighting approximates the actual shape of unoccluded regions above the shaded point with a cone. On the left, the area light source is shown in yellow and the visible horizon for the surface location is shown in blue. On the right, the horizon is simplified to a circle, which is the edge of a cone projecting up and to the right from the surface location, shown with dashed lines. Occlusion of the area light is then estimated by intersecting its cone with the occlusion cone, yielding the area shown in red.

11.4.2 Dynamic Computation of Directional Occlusion

Many of the methods used for generating ambient occlusion can also be used to generate directional visibility information. Spherical harmonic exponentiation by Ren et al. [1482], and its screen-space variant by Sloan et al. [1655] generate visibility in a form of spherical harmonic vectors. If more than one SH band is used, these methods natively provide directional information. Using more bands allows encoding visibility with more precision.

Cone tracing methods, such as those from Crassin et al. [305] and Wright [1910], provide one occlusion value for every trace. For quality reasons, even the ambient occlusion estimations are performed using multiple traces, so the available information is already directional. If visibility in a particular direction is needed, we can trace fewer cones.

Iwanicki [806] also uses cone tracing, but he restricts it to just one direction. The results are used to generate soft shadows cast onto static geometry by dynamic characters who are approximated with a set of spheres, similar to Ren et al. [1482] and Sloan et al. [1655]. In this solution, lighting for the static geometry is stored using AHD encoding (Section 10.3.3). Visibility for ambient and directional components can be handled independently. Occlusion of the ambient part is computed analytically. A single cone is traced and intersected with the spheres to calculate the attenuation factor for the directional component.

Many of the screen-space methods can also be extended to provide directional occlusion information. Klehm et al. [904] use the *z*-buffer data to compute *screen-space bent cones*, which are in fact circular apertures, much like those precomputed offline by Oat and Sander [1307]. When sampling the neighborhood of a pixel, they sum the unoccluded directions. The length of the resulting vector can be used to estimate the apex angle of the visibility cone, and its direction defines the axis of this cone. Jimenez et al. [835] estimate the cone axis direction based on the horizon angles, and derive the angle from the ambient occlusion factor.

11.4.3 Shading with Directional Occlusion

With so many different ways of encoding directional occlusion, we cannot provide a single prescription for how to perform shading. The solution will depend on what particular effect we want to achieve.

Let us consider the reflectance equation again, in a version with incoming radiance split into distant lighting L_i and its visibility v:

$$L_o(\mathbf{v}) = \int_{\mathbf{l} \in \Omega} f(\mathbf{l}, \mathbf{v}) L_i(\mathbf{l}) v(\mathbf{l}) (\mathbf{n} \cdot \mathbf{l})^+ d\mathbf{l}. \qquad (11.26)$$

The simplest operation we can do is use the visibility signal to shadow punctual lights. Because of the simplicity of most ways of encoding visibility, the quality of the result will often be unsatisfactory, but it will allow us to follow the reasoning on a basic example. This method can also be used in situations where traditional shadowing methods fail because of insufficient resolution, and the precision of the results is less important than achieving any form of occlusion at all. Examples of such situations include extremely large terrain models, or small surface details represented with bump maps.

Following the discussion in Section 9.4, when dealing with punctual lights, Equation 11.26 becomes

$$L_o(\mathbf{v}) = \pi f(\mathbf{l}_c, \mathbf{v}) \mathbf{c}_{\text{light}} v(\mathbf{l}_c) (\mathbf{n} \cdot \mathbf{l}_c)^+, \qquad (11.27)$$

where $\mathbf{c}_{\text{light}}$ is the radiance reflected from a white, Lambertian surface facing the light, and $\mathbf{l}_c$ is the direction toward the light. We can interpret the above equation as computing a response of the material to the unoccluded light and multiplying the result by the value of the visibility function. If the light direction falls under the horizon (when using horizon mapping), outside the visibility cone (when using ambient aperture lighting), or in the negative area of the SSDF, the visibility function is equal to zero and so any contribution from the light should not be taken into account. It is worth mentioning that even though visibility is defined as binary functions,[2] many representations can return an entire range of values, not only zero or one. Such values convey partial occlusion. Spherical harmonics or the H-basis can even reconstruct negative values, due to ringing. These behaviors might be unwanted, but are just an inherent property of the encoding.

We can perform similar reasoning for lighting with area lights. In this case L_i is equal to zero everywhere, except for within the solid angle subtended by the light,

---

[2]In most situations, at least. There are cases when we want the visibility function to take values other than zero or one, but still in that range. For example, when encoding occlusion caused by a semitransparent material, we might want to use fractional occlusion values.

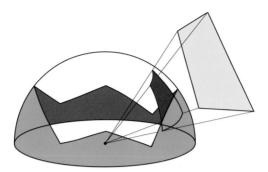

Figure 11.20. A yellow polygonal light source can be projected onto a unit hemisphere over the shaded point to form a spherical polygon. If the visibility is described using horizon mapping, that polygon can be clipped against it. The cosine-weighted integral of the clipped, red polygon can be computed analytically using Lambert's formula.

where it is equal to the radiance emitted by that source. We will refer to it as L_l and assume that it is constant over the light's solid angle. We can replace integration over the entire sphere, Ω, with integration over the solid angle of the light, Ω_l:

$$L_o(\mathbf{v}) = L_l \int_{\mathbf{l} \in \Omega_l} v(\mathbf{l}) f(\mathbf{l}, \mathbf{v}) (\mathbf{n} \cdot \mathbf{l})^+ d\mathbf{l}. \qquad (11.28)$$

If we assume that the BRDF is constant—so we are dealing with a Lambertian surface—it can also be pulled out from under the integral:

$$L_o(\mathbf{v}) = \frac{\rho_{\mathrm{ss}}}{\pi} L_l \int_{\mathbf{l} \in \Omega_l} v(\mathbf{l}) (\mathbf{n} \cdot \mathbf{l})^+ d\mathbf{l}. \qquad (11.29)$$

To determine the occluded lighting, we need to compute the integral of the visibility function multiplied by the cosine term over the solid angle subtended by the light. There are cases when this can be done analytically. Lambert [967] derived a formula to compute the integral of a cosine over a spherical polygon. If our area light is polygonal, and we can clip it against the visibility representation, we then need to use only Lambert's formula to get a precise result (Figure 11.20). This is possible when, for example, we choose horizon angles as our visibility representation. However, if for any reason we settled on another encoding, such as bent cones, the clipping would produce circular segments, for which we can no longer use Lambert's formula. The same applies if we want to use non-polygonal area lights.

Another possibility is to assume that the value of the cosine term is constant across the integration domain. If the size of the area light is small, this approximation is fairly precise. For simplicity, we can use the value of the cosine evaluated in the direction of the center of the area light. This leaves us with the integral of the visibility term over the solid angle of the light. Our options on how to proceed depend, again, on our choice of visibility representation and type of area light. If we use spherical lights and visibility represented with bent cones, the value of the integral is the solid angle of the intersection of the visibility cone and the cone subtended by the light. It can be computed analytically, as shown by Oat and Sander [1307]. While the exact formula is complex, they provide an approximation that works well in practice. If visibility is encoded with spherical harmonics, the integral can also be computed analytically.

For environment lighting we cannot restrict the integration range, because illumination comes from all directions. We need to find a way to calculate the full integral from Equation 11.26. Let us consider the Lambertian BRDF first:

$$L_o(\mathbf{v}) = \frac{\rho_{ss}}{\pi} \int_{\mathbf{l} \in \Omega} L_i(\mathbf{l}) v(\mathbf{l}) (\mathbf{n} \cdot \mathbf{l})^+ d\mathbf{l}. \tag{11.30}$$

The type of integral in this equation is called a *triple product integral*. If the individual functions are represented in certain ways—for instance, as spherical harmonics or wavelets—it can be computed analytically. Unfortunately, this is too expensive for typical real-time applications, though such solutions have been shown to run at interactive frame rates in simple setups [1270].

Our particular case is slightly simpler, though, as one of the functions is the cosine. We can instead write Equation 11.30 as

$$L_o(\mathbf{v}) = \frac{\rho_{ss}}{\pi} \int_{\mathbf{l} \in \Omega} \overline{L_i}(\mathbf{l}) v(\mathbf{l}) d\mathbf{l} \tag{11.31}$$

or

$$L_o(\mathbf{v}) = \frac{\rho_{ss}}{\pi} \int_{\mathbf{l} \in \Omega} L_i(\mathbf{l}) \overline{v}(\mathbf{l}) d\mathbf{l}, \tag{11.32}$$

where

$$\overline{L_i}(\mathbf{l}) = L_i(\mathbf{l})(\mathbf{n} \cdot \mathbf{l})^+,$$
$$\overline{v}(\mathbf{l}) = v(\mathbf{l})(\mathbf{n} \cdot \mathbf{l})^+.$$

Both $\overline{L_i}(\mathbf{l})$ and $\overline{v}(\mathbf{l})$ are spherical functions, like $L_i(\mathbf{l})$ and $v(\mathbf{l})$. Instead of trying to compute a triple product integral, we first multiply the cosine by either L_i (Equation 11.31) or v_i (Equation 11.32). Doing so makes the integrand a product of only two functions. While this might look like just a mathematics trick, it significantly simplifies calculations. If the factors are represented using an orthonormal basis such as spherical harmonics, the double product integral can be trivially computed. It is a dot product of their coefficient vectors (Section 10.3.2).

We still need to compute $\overline{L_i}(\mathbf{l})$ or $\overline{v}(\mathbf{l})$, but because they involve the cosine, this is simpler than for the fully general case. If we represent the functions using spherical harmonics, the cosine projects to zonal harmonics (ZH), a subset of spherical harmonics for which only one coefficient per band is nonzero (Section 10.3.2). The coefficients for this projection have simple, analytic formulae [1656]. The product of an SH and a ZH is much more efficient to compute than a product of an SH and another SH.

If we decide to multiply the cosine by v first (Equation 11.32), we can do it offline and instead store just the visibility. This is a form of *precomputed radiance transfer*, as described by Sloan et al. [1651] (Section 11.5.3). In this form, however, we cannot apply any fine-scale modification of the normal, as the cosine term, which is controlled by the normal, is already fused with the visibility. If we want to model fine-scale normal details, we can multiply the cosine by L_i first (Equation 11.31). Since we do not know the normal direction up front, we can either precompute this product for different normals [805] or perform the multiplication at runtime [809]. Precomputing the products of L_i and cosine offline means that, in turn, any changes to the lighting are restricted, and allowing the lighting to change spatially would require prohibitive amounts of memory. On the other hand, computing the product at runtime is computationally expensive. Iwanicki and Sloan [809] describe how to reduce this cost. Products can be computed at a lower granularity—on vertices, in their case. The result is convolved with the cosine term, projected onto a simpler representation (AHD), then interpolated and reconstructed with the per-pixel normal. This approach allows them to use the method in performance-demanding 60 FPS games.

Klehm et al. [904] present a solution for lighting represented with an environment map and visibility encoded with a cone. They filter the environment map with different-sized kernels that represent the integral of a product of visibility and lighting for different cone openings. They store the results for increasing cone angles in the mip levels of a texture. This is possible because prefiltered results for large cone angles vary smoothly over the sphere and do not need to be stored with high angular resolution. During prefiltering, they assume that the direction of the visibility cone is aligned with the normal, which is an approximation, but in practice gives plausible results. They provide an analysis on how this approximation affects the final quality.

The situation is even more complex if we are dealing with glossy BRDFs and environment lighting. We can no longer pull the BRDF from under the integral, as it is not constant. To handle this, Green et al. [582] suggest approximating the BRDF itself with a set of *spherical Gaussians*. These are radially symmetric functions that can be compactly represented with just three parameters: direction (or mean) $\mathbf{d}$, standard deviation μ, and amplitude w. The approximate BRDF is defined as a sum of spherical Gaussians:

$$f(\mathbf{l}, \mathbf{v}) \approx \sum_k w_k(\mathbf{v}) G(\mathbf{d}_k(\mathbf{v}), \mu_k(\mathbf{v}), \mathbf{l}), \tag{11.33}$$

where $G(\mathbf{d}, \mu, \mathbf{l})$ is the spherical Gaussian lobe, oriented along direction $\mathbf{d}$, with sharpness μ (Section 10.3.2), and w_k in the amplitude of the kth lobe. For an isotropic BRDF, the shape of the lobe depends on only the angle between the normal and the view direction. Approximations can be stored in a one-dimensional lookup table and interpolated.

With this approximation, we can write Equation 11.26 as

$$L_o(\mathbf{v}) \approx \int_{\mathbf{l} \in \Omega} \sum_k w_k(\mathbf{v}) G(\mathbf{d}_k(\mathbf{v}), \mu_k(\mathbf{v}), \mathbf{l}) L_i(\mathbf{l}) v(\mathbf{l}) (\mathbf{n} \cdot \mathbf{l})^+ d\mathbf{l}$$
$$= \sum_k w_k(\mathbf{v}) \int_{\mathbf{l} \in \Omega} G(\mathbf{d}_k(\mathbf{v}), \mu_k(\mathbf{v}), \mathbf{l}) L_i(\mathbf{l}) v(\mathbf{l}) (\mathbf{n} \cdot \mathbf{l})^+ d\mathbf{l}. \quad (11.34)$$

Green et al. also assume that the visibility function is constant across the entire support of each spherical Gaussian, which allows them to pull it out from under the integral. They evaluate the visibility function in the direction of the lobe center:

$$L_o(\mathbf{v}) \approx \sum_k w_k(\mathbf{v}) v_k(\mathbf{d}_k(\mathbf{v})) \int_{\mathbf{l} \in \Omega} G(\mathbf{d}_k(\mathbf{v}), \mu_k(\mathbf{v}), \mathbf{l}) L_i(\mathbf{l}) (\mathbf{n} \cdot \mathbf{l})^+ d\mathbf{l}. \quad (11.35)$$

The remaining integral represents incoming lighting convolved with a spherical Gaussian oriented in a given direction and with a given standard deviation. The results of such convolutions can be precomputed and stored in an environment map, with convolutions for larger μ's stored in lower mip levels. Visibility is encoded with low-order spherical harmonics, but any other representation could also be used, as it is only point-evaluated.

Wang et al. [1838] approximate the BRDF in similar fashion, but handle visibility in a more precise way. Their representation allows them to calculate the integral of a single spherical Gaussian over the support of the visibility function. They use this value to introduce a new spherical Gaussian, one with the same direction and standard deviation, but a different amplitude. They use this new function during lighting calculations.

For certain applications this method may be too expensive. It requires multiple samples from the prefiltered environment maps, and texture sampling is often already a bottleneck during rendering. Jimenez et al. [835] and El Garawany [414] present simpler approximations. To compute the occlusion factor, they represent the entire BRDF lobe with a single cone, ignoring its dependence on viewing angle and considering only parameters such as material roughness (Figure 11.21). They approximate visibility as a cone and compute the solid angle of the intersection of the visibility and BRDF cones, much as done for ambient aperture lighting. The scalar result is used to attenuate lighting. Even though it is a significant simplification, the results are believable.

11.5 Diffuse Global Illumination

The next sections cover various ways of simulating not only occlusion but also full light bounces in real time. They can be roughly divided into algorithms that assume that, right before reaching the eye, light bounces off either a diffuse or specular surface. The

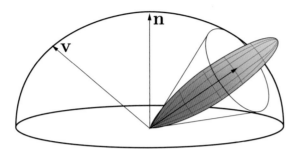

Figure 11.21. For the purpose of computing occlusion, the specular lobe of a glossy material can be represented as a cone. If visibility is approximated as another cone, the occlusion factor can be calculated as a solid angle of the intersection of the two, in a same way as done for ambient aperture lighting (Figure 11.19). The image shows the general principle of representing a BRDF lobe with a cone, but is only meant as an illustration. In practice, to produce plausible occlusion results, the cone would need to be wider.

corresponding light paths can be written as $L(D|S)*DE$ or $L(D|S)*SE$, respectively, with many of the methods placing some constraints on the types of earlier bounces. Solutions in the first group assume that the incoming lighting changes smoothly across the hemisphere above the shading point, or ignore that change entirely. Algorithms in the second group assume a high rate of change across the incident directions. They rely on the fact that the lighting will be accessed within only a relatively small solid angle. Because of these vastly different constraints, it is beneficial to handle these two groups separately. We cover methods for diffuse global illumination in this section, specular in the next, then promising unified approaches in the final section.

11.5.1 Surface Prelighting

Both radiosity and path tracing are designed for offline use. While there have been efforts to use them in real-time settings, the results are still too immature to be used in production. Currently the most common practice is to use them to precompute lighting-related information. The expensive, offline process is run ahead of time, and its results are stored and later used during display to provide high-quality lighting. As mentioned in Section 11.3.4, precomputing in this way for a static scene is referred to as baking.

This practice comes with certain restrictions. If we perform lighting calculations ahead of time, we cannot change the scene setup at runtime. All the scene geometry, lights, and materials need to remain unchanged. We cannot change time of day or blow a hole in a wall. In many cases this limitation is an acceptable trade-off. Architectural visualizations can assume that the user only walks around virtual environments. Games place restrictions on player actions, too. In such applications we can classify geometry into *static* and *dynamic* objects. The static objects are used in the precomputation process and they fully interact with the lighting. Static walls

Figure 11.22. Given a Lambertian surface with a known normal, its irradiance can be precomputed. At runtime this value is multiplied by the actual surface color (for instance, from a texture) to obtain the reflected radiance. Depending on the exact form of the surface color, additional division by π might be needed to ensure energy conservation.

cast shadows and static red carpets bounce red light. Dynamic objects act only as receivers. They do not block light, and they do not generate indirect illumination effects. In such scenarios, dynamic geometry is usually restricted to be relatively small, so its effect on the rest of the lighting can be either ignored or modeled with other techniques, with minimal loss of quality. Dynamic geometry can, for example, use screen-space approaches to generate occlusion. A typical set of dynamic objects includes characters, decorative geometry, and vehicles.

The simplest form of lighting information that can be precomputed is irradiance. For flat, Lambertian surfaces, together with surface color it fully describes the material's response to lighting. Because the effect of a source of illumination is independent of any others, dynamic lights can be added on top of the precomputed irradiance (Figure 11.22).

Quake in 1996 and *Quake II* in 1997 were the first commercial interactive applications to make use of precomputed irradiance values. *Quake* was precomputing the direct contribution from static lights, mainly as a way of improving performance. *Quake II* also included an indirect component, making it the first game that used a global illumination algorithm to generate more realistic lighting. It used a radiosity-based algorithm, since this technique was well suited to computing irradiance in Lambertian environments. Also, memory constraints of the time restricted the lighting to be relatively low resolution, which matched well with the blurry, low-frequency shadows typical of radiosity solutions.

Precomputed irradiance values are usually multiplied with diffuse color or albedo maps stored in a separate set of textures. Although the exitance (irradiance times diffuse color) could in theory be precomputed and stored in a single set of textures, many practical considerations rule out this option in most cases. The color maps are usually quite high frequency, they make use of various kinds of tiling, and their parts are often reused across the model, all to keep the memory usage reasonable. The irradiance values are usually much lower frequency and cannot easily be reused. Keeping lighting and surface color separate consumes much less memory.

Precomputed irradiance is rarely used today, except for the most restrictive hardware platforms. Since, by definition, irradiance is computed for a given normal direction, we cannot use normal mapping to provide high-frequency details. This also means that irradiance can only be precomputed for flat surfaces. If we need to use baked lighting on dynamic geometry, we need other methods to store it. These limitations have motivated a search for ways to store precomputed lighting with a directional component.

11.5.2 Directional Surface Prelighting

To use prelighting together with normal mapping on Lambertian surfaces, we want a way to represent how the irradiance changes with the surface normal. To provide indirect lighting for dynamic geometry, we also need its value for every possible surface orientation. Happily, we already have tools to represent such functions. In Section 10.3 we described various ways of determining lighting dependent on the normal's direction. These include specialized solutions for cases where the function domain is hemispherical and the values on the lower half of the sphere do not matter, as is the case for opaque surfaces.

The most general method is to store full spherical irradiance information, for example by using spherical harmonics. This scheme was first presented by Good and Taylor [564] in the context of accelerating photon mapping, and used in a real-time setting by Shopf et al. [1637]. In both cases directional irradiance was stored in textures. If nine spherical harmonic coefficients are used (third-order SH), the quality is excellent, however the storage and bandwidth costs are high. Using just four coefficients (a second-order SH) is less costly, but many subtleties get lost, the lighting has less contrast, and normal maps are less pronounced.

Chen [257] uses a variation of the method for *Halo 3*, developed to achieve the quality of a third-order SH at a reduced cost. He extracts the most dominant light out of the spherical signal and stores it separately, as a color and a direction. The residue is encoded using a second-order SH. This reduces the number of coefficients from 27 to 18, with little quality loss. Hu [780] describes how these data can be compressed further. Chen and Tatarchuk [258] provide further information on their GPU-based baking pipeline used in production.

The *H-basis* by Habel et al. [627] is another alternative solution. Since it encodes only hemispherical signals, fewer coefficients can provide the same precision as spherical harmonics. Quality comparable to a third-order SH can be obtained with just six coefficients. Because the basis is defined only for a hemisphere, we need some local coordinate system on the surface to properly orient it. Usually, a tangent frame resulting from *uv*-parameterization is used for this purpose. If *H*-basis components are stored in a texture, its resolution should be high enough to adapt to the changes of the underlying tangent space. If multiple triangles with significantly different tangent spaces cover the same texel, the reconstructed signal will not be precise.

Figure 11.23. *Call of Duty: WWII* uses the *AHD* representation to encode the directional variation of the lighting in the light map. The grid is used to visualize the light map density in debug mode. Each square corresponds to a single light map texel. *(Image courtesy of Activision Publishing, Inc. 2018.)*

One problem with both spherical harmonics and the *H*-basis is that they can exhibit ringing (Section 10.6.1). While prefiltering can mitigate this effect, it also smoothes the lighting, which might not always be desirable. Additionally, even the less-expensive variants still have relatively high cost, both in terms of storage and computation. This expense might be prohibitive in more restrictive cases, such as on low-end platforms or when rendering for virtual reality.

Costs are why simple alternatives are still popular. *Half-Life 2* uses a custom, hemispherical basis (Section 10.3.3) that stores three color values, for a total of nine coefficients per sample. The ambient/highlight/direction (AHD) basis (Section 10.3.3) is also a popular choice despite its simplicity. It has been used in games such as the *Call of Duty* [809, 998] series and *The Last of Us* [806]. See Figure 11.23.

A variation was used by Crytek in the game *Far Cry* [1227]. The Crytek representation consists of an average light direction in tangent space, an average light color, and a scalar directionality factor. This last value is used to blend between the ambient and directional components, which both use the same color. This reduces the storage to six coefficients per sample: three values for the color, two for the direction, and one for the directionality factor. The *Unity* engine also uses similar methods in one of its modes [315].

This type of representation is nonlinear, which means that, technically, linearly interpolating individual components, either between texels or vertices, is not mathe-

Figure 11.24. *The Order: 1886* stores incident radiance projected onto a set of spherical Gaussian lobes in its light maps. At runtime, the radiance is convolved with the cosine lobe to compute the diffuse response (left) and with a properly shaped anisotropic spherical Gaussian to generate the specular response (right). *(Image courtesy of Ready at Dawn Studios, copyright Sony Interactive Entertainment.)*

matically correct. If the direction of the dominant light changes rapidly, for instance on shadow boundaries, visual artifacts might appear in shading. Despite these inaccuracies, the results look visually pleasing. Because of the high contrast between the ambient and directionally lit areas, the effects of normal maps are accentuated, which is often desirable. Additionally, the directional component can be used when calculating the specular response of the BRDF to provide a low-cost alternative to environment maps for low-gloss materials.

On the opposite end of the spectrum are methods designed for high visual quality. Neubelt and Pettineo [1268] use texture maps storing coefficients for spherical Gaussians in the game *The Order: 1886* (Figure 11.24). Instead of irradiance, they store incoming radiance, which is projected to a set of Gaussian lobes (Section 10.3.2), defined in a tangent frame. They use between five and nine lobes, depending on the complexity of the lighting in a particular scene. To generate a diffuse response, the spherical Gaussians are convolved with a cosine lobe oriented along the surface normal. The representation is also precise enough to provide low-gloss specular effects, by convolving Gaussians with the specular BRDF lobe. Pettineo describes the full system in detail [1408]. He also provides source code to an application capable of baking and rendering different lighting representations.

If we need information about the lighting in an arbitrary direction, not just within a hemisphere above the surface (for example, to provide indirect lighting for dynamic geometry), we can use methods that encode a full spherical signal. Spherical harmonics are a natural fit here. When memory is less of a concern, third-order SH (nine coefficients per color channel) is the popular choice; otherwise, second-order is used (four coefficients per color channel, which matches the number of components in an RGBA texture, so a single map can store coefficients for one color channel). Spherical Gaussians also work in a fully spherical setting, as the lobes can be distributed across either the entire sphere or only the hemisphere around the normal. However, since the solid angle that needs to be covered by the lobes is twice as large for spherical techniques, we might need to use more lobes to retain the same quality.

If we want to avoid dealing with ringing, but cannot afford to use a high number of lobes, the ambient cube [1193] (Section 10.3.1) is a viable alternative. It consists of six clamped $\cos^2$ lobes, oriented along the major axes. The cosine lobes each cover just one hemisphere, as they have *local support*, meaning they have nonzero values on only a subset of their spherical domain. For this reason, only the three visible lobes out of the six stored values are needed during the reconstruction. This limits the bandwidth cost of lighting calculations. The quality of reconstruction is similar to second-order spherical harmonics.

Ambient dice [808] (also Section 10.3.1) can be used for higher quality than ambient cubes. This scheme uses twelve lobes oriented along the vertices of an icosahedron that are a linear combination of $\cos^2$ and $\cos^4$ lobes. Six values out of the twelve stored are used during a reconstruction. The quality is comparable to third-order spherical harmonics. These and other similar representations (for example, a basis consisting of three $\cos^2$ lobes and a cosine lobe, warped to cover a full sphere) have been used in many commercially successful games, such as *Half-Life 2* [1193], the *Call of Duty* series [766, 808], *Far Cry 3* [533], *Tom Clancy's The Division* [1694], and *Assassin's Creed 4: Black Flag* [1911], to name a few.

11.5.3 Precomputed Transfer

While precomputed lighting can look stunning, it is also inherently static. Any change to geometry or lighting can invalidate the entire solution. Just as in the real world, opening the curtains (local change to the geometry in the scene) may flood the entire room with light (global change to the lighting). Much research effort has been spent on finding solutions that allow for certain types of changes.

If we make the assumption that the scene's geometry does not change, only the lighting, we can precompute how light interacts with the models. Inter-object effects such as interreflections or subsurface scattering can be analyzed up front to a certain degree and the results stored, without operating on actual radiance values. The function that takes the incoming lighting and turns it into a description of the radiance distribution throughout the scene is called a *transfer function*. Solutions that precompute this are called *precomputed transfer* or *precomputed radiance transfer* (PRT) approaches.

As opposed to fully baking the lighting offline, these techniques do have a noticeable runtime cost. When displaying the scene on screen, we need to calculate radiance values for a particular lighting setup. To do this, the actual amount of direct light is "injected" into the system, then the transfer function is applied to propagate it across the scene. Some of the methods assume that this direct lighting comes from an environment map. Other schemes allow the lighting setup to be arbitrary and to change in a flexible fashion.

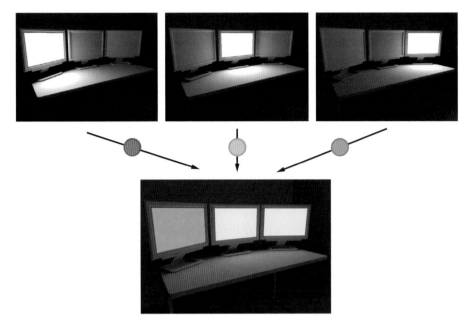

Figure 11.25. Example of rendering using precomputed radiance transfer. Full transport of lighting from each of the three monitors was precomputed separately, obtaining a "unit" response. Because of the linearity of the light transport, these individual solutions can be multiplied by the colors of the screens (pink, yellow, and blue in the example here) to obtain the final lighting.

The concept of precomputed radiance transfer was introduced to graphics by Sloan et al. [1651]. They describe it in terms of spherical harmonics, but the method does not have to use SH. The basic idea is simple. If we describe the direct lighting using some (preferably low) number of "building block" lights, we can precalculate how the scene is lit by each one of them. Imagine a room with three computer monitors inside, and assume that each can display only a single color, but with varying intensity. Consider the maximum brightness of each screen as equal to one, a normalized "unit" lightness. We can independently precompute the effect each monitor has on the room. This process can be done using the methods we covered in Section 11.2. Because light transport is linear, the result of illuminating the scene with all three monitors will be equal to the sum of the light coming from each, directly or indirectly. The illumination from each monitor does not affect the other solutions, so if we set one of the screens to be half as bright, doing so will change only its own contribution to the total lighting.

This allows us to quickly compute the full, bounced lighting within the entire room. We take each precomputed light solution, multiply it by the actual brightness of the screen, and sum the results. We can turn the monitors on and off, make them brighter or darker, even change their colors, and all that is required to get the final lighting are these multiplies and additions (Figure 11.25).

We can write

$$L(\mathbf{p}) = \sum_i L_i(\mathbf{p})\mathbf{w}_i, \tag{11.36}$$

where $L(\mathbf{p})$ is the final radiance at point $\mathbf{p}$, $L_i(\mathbf{p})$ is the precomputed unit contribution from screen i, and $\mathbf{w}_i$ is its current brightness. This equation defines a *vector space* in the mathematical sense, with L_i being the basis vectors for this space. Any possible lighting can be created by a linear combination of the lights' contributions.

The original PRT paper by Sloan et al. [1651] uses the same reasoning, but in the context of an infinitely distant lighting environment represented using spherical harmonics. Instead of storing how the scene responds to a monitor screen, they store how it responds to surrounding light with a distribution defined by spherical harmonic basis functions. By doing so for some number of SH bands, they can render a scene illuminated by an arbitrary lighting environment. They project this lighting onto spherical harmonics, multiply each resulting coefficient by its respective normalized "unit" contribution, and add these all together, just as we did with the monitors.

Note that the choice of the basis used to "inject" light into the scene is independent of the representation used to express the final lighting. For example, we can describe how the scene is illuminated using spherical harmonics, but pick another basis to store how much radiance arrives at any given point. Say we used an ambient cube for storage. We would calculate how much radiance arrives from the top and how much from the sides. The transfer for each of these directions would be stored separately, instead of as a single scalar value representing the total transfer.

The PRT paper by Sloan et al. [1651] analyzes two cases. The first is when the receiver basis is just a scalar irradiance value of the surface. For this, the receiver needs to be a fully diffuse surface, with a predetermined normal, which means that it cannot use normal maps for fine-scale details. The transfer function takes the form of a dot product between the SH projection of the input lighting and the precomputed *transfer vector*, which varies spatially across the scene.

If we need to render non-Lambertian materials, or allow for normal mapping, we can use the second variation presented. In this case, the SH projection of surrounding lighting is transformed to an SH projection of the incident radiance for a given point. Because this operation provides us the full radiance distribution over the sphere (or hemisphere, if we are dealing with a static opaque object), we can properly convolve it with any BRDF. The transfer function maps SH vectors to other SH vectors, and has a form of matrix multiplication. This multiply operation is expensive, both computationally and in terms of memory. If we use third-order SH for both source and receiver, we need to store a 9×9 matrix for every point in the scene, and these data are for just a monochrome transfer. If we want colors, we need three such matrices—an incredible amount of memory per point.

This problem was addressed by Sloan et al. [1652] one year later. Instead of storing the transfer vectors or matrices directly, their whole set is analyzed using a *principal component analysis* (PCA) technique. The transfer coefficients can be considered points in multi-dimensional space (for example, 81-dimensional in the case of 9×9

matrices), but their sets are not uniformly distributed in that space. They form clusters with lower dimensionality. This clustering is just like how three-dimensional points distributed along a line are, effectively, all in a one-dimensional subspace of a three-dimensional space. PCA can efficiently detect such statistical relationships. Once a subspace is discovered, points can be represented using a much lower number of coordinates, as we can store the position in the subspace with a reduced number of dimensions. Using the line analogy, instead of storing the full position of a point using three coordinates, we could just store its distance along the line. Sloan et al. use this method to reduce the dimensionality of the transfer matrices from 625 dimensions (25×25 transfer matrices) to 256 dimensions. While this is still too high for typical real-time applications, many of the later light transport algorithms have adapted PCA as a way of compressing the data.

This type of dimensionality reduction is inherently lossy. In rare cases the data forms a perfect subspace, but most often it is approximate, so projecting data onto it causes some degradation. To increase quality, Sloan et al. divide the set of transfer matrices into clusters and perform PCA on each separately. The process also includes an optimization step that ensures no discontinuities on the cluster boundaries. An extension that allows for limited deformations of the objects is also presented, called *local deformable precomputed radiance transfer* (LDPRT) [1653].

PRT has been used in various forms in several games. It is especially popular in titles in which gameplay focuses on outdoor areas where time of day and weather conditions change dynamically. *Far Cry 3* and *Far Cry 4* use PRT where the source basis is second-order SH and the receiver basis is a custom, four-direction basis [533, 1154]. *Assassin's Creed 4: Black Flag* uses one basis function as a source (sun color), but precomputes the transfer for different times of the day. This representation can be interpreted as having the source basis functions defined over the time dimension instead of directions. The receiver basis is the same as that used in the *Far Cry* titles.

The SIGGRAPH 2005 course [870] on precomputed radiance transfer provides a good overview of research in the area. Lehtinen [1019, 1020] gives a mathematical framework that can be used to analyze the differences between various algorithms and to develop new ones.

The original PRT method assumes infinitely distant surrounding lighting. While this models lighting of an outdoor scene fairly well, it is too restrictive for indoor environments. However, as we noted earlier, the concept is fully agnostic to the initial source of the illumination. Kristensen et al. [941] describe a method where PRT is computed for a set of lights scattered across the entire scene. This corresponds to having a large number of "source" basis functions. The lights are next combined into clusters, and receiving geometry is segmented into zones, with each zone affected by a different subset of lights. This process results in a significant compression of the transfer data. At runtime, the illumination resulting from arbitrarily placed lights is approximated by interpolating data from the closest lights in the precomputed set. Gilabert and Stefanov [533] use the method to generate indirect illumination in the game *Far Cry 3*. This method in its basic form can handle only point lights. While

Figure 11.26. *Enlighten* by Geomerics can generate global illumination effects in real time. The image shows an example of its integration with the *Unity* engine. The user can freely change the time of day as well as turn lights on and off. All the indirect illumination is updated accordingly in real time. *(Courtyard demo © Unity Technologies, 2015.)*

it could be extended to support other types, the cost grows exponentially with the number of degrees of freedom for each light.

The PRT techniques discussed up to this point precompute the transfer from some number of elements, which are then used to model the lights. Another popular class of methods precomputes transfer between surfaces. In this type of system, the actual source of the illumination becomes irrelevant. Any light source can be used, because the input to these methods is the outgoing radiance from some set of surfaces (or some other related quantity, such as irradiance, if the method assumes diffuse-only surfaces). These direct-illumination calculations can use shadowing (Chapter 7), irradiance environment maps (Section 10.6), or the ambient and directional occlusion methods discussed earlier in this chapter. Any surface can also trivially be made emissive by setting its outgoing radiance to a desired value, turning it into an area light source.

The most popular system that works according to these principles is *Enlighten* by Geomerics (Figure 11.26). While the exact details of the algorithm have never been fully publicly revealed, numerous talks and presentations give an accurate picture of this system's principles [315, 1101, 1131, 1435].

The scene is assumed to be Lambertian, but only for the purpose of light transfer. Using Heckbert's notation, the set of paths handled is $LD * (D|S)E$, as the last surface before the eye does not need to be diffuse-only. The system defines a set of "source" elements and another set of "receiver" elements. Source elements exist on surfaces, and share some of their properties, such as diffuse color and normal. The preprocessing step computes how the light is transferred between the source elements and the receivers. The exact form of this information depends on what the source elements are and what basis is used to gather lighting at the receivers. In the simplest form, the source elements can be points, and we are then interested in generating irradiance in the receiving locations. In this case, the transfer coefficient is just the mutual visibility between source and receiver. At runtime, the outgoing radiance for all source elements is provided to the system. From this information we can numerically integrate the reflectance equation (Equation 11.1), using the precomputed visibility and the known information about the position and orientation of the source and receiver. In this way, a single bounce of light is performed. As the majority of the indirect illumination comes from this first bounce, performing one bounce alone is enough to provide plausible illumination. However, we can use this light and run the propagation step again to generate a second bounce of light. This is usually done over the course of several frames, where the output of one frame is used as an input for the next.

Using points as source elements would result in a large number of connections. To improve performance, clusters of points representing areas of similar normal and color can also be used as source sets. In this case the transfer coefficients are the same as the form factors seen in radiosity algorithms (Section 11.2.1). Note that, despite the similarity, the algorithm is different from classical radiosity, as it computes only one bounce of light at a time and does not involve solving a system of linear equations. It draws upon the idea of *progressive radiosity* [275, 1642]. In this system a single patch can determine how much energy it receives from other patches, in an iterative process. The process of transferring the radiance to the receiving location is called *gathering*.

The radiance at the receiving elements can be gathered in different forms. The transfer to the receiving elements may use any of the directional bases that we described before. In this case the single coefficient becomes a vector of values, with the dimensionality equal to the number of functions in the receiving basis. When performing gathering using a directional representation, the result is the same as for the offline solutions described in Section 11.5.2, so it can be used with normal mapping or to provide a low-gloss specular response.

The same general idea is used in many variants. To save memory, Sugden and Iwanicki [1721] use SH transfer coefficients, quantize them, and store them indirectly as an index to an entry in a palette. Jendersie et al. [820] build a hierarchy of source patches, and store references to higher elements in this tree when the solid angle subtended by the children is too small. Stefanov [1694] introduces an intermediate step, where radiance from surface elements is first propagated to a voxelized representation of the scene, one that later acts as a source for the transport.

The (in some sense) ideal split of surfaces into source patches depends on the receiver's position. For distant elements, considering them as separate entities generates unnecessary storage costs, but they should be treated individually when viewed up close. A hierarchy of source patches mitigates this problem to some extent, but does not solve it entirely. Certain patches that could be combined for particular receivers may be far enough apart to prevent such merging. A novel approach to the problem is presented by Silvennoinen and Lehtinen [1644]. Their method does not create the source patches explicitly, but rather generates a different set of them for each receiving position. The objects are rendered to a sparse set of environment maps scattered around the scene. Each map is projected to spherical harmonics, and this low-frequency version is "virtually" projected back onto the environment. Receiving points record how much of this projection they can see, and this process is done for each of the senders' SH basis functions separately. Doing so creates a different set of source elements for every receiver, based on the visibility information from both environment probes and receiver points.

Because the source basis is generated from an environment map projected to an SH, it naturally combines surfaces that are farther away. To pick the probes to use, the receivers use a heuristic that favors nearby ones, which makes the receivers "see" the environment at a similar scale. To limit the amount of data that has to be stored, the transfer information is compressed with clustered PCA.

Another form of precomputed transfer is described by Lehtinen et al. [1021]. In this approach neither the source nor the receiving elements exist on the meshes, but rather are volumetric and can be queried at any location in three-dimensional space. This form is convenient for providing lighting consistency between static and dynamic geometry, but the method is fairly expensive computationally.

Loos et al. [1073] precompute transfer within a modular, unit cell, with different configurations of the side walls. Multiple such cells are then stitched and warped to approximate the geometry of the scene. The radiance is propagated first to the cell borders, which act as interfaces, and then to the neighboring cells using the precomputed models. The method is fast enough to efficiently run even on mobile platforms, but the resulting quality might not be sufficient for more demanding applications.

11.5.4 Storage Methods

Regardless of whether we want to use full precomputed lighting or to precalculate the transfer information and allow for some changes in the lighting, the resulting data has to be stored in some form. GPU-friendly formats are a must.

Light maps are one of the most common way of storing precomputed lighting. These are textures that store the precalculated information. Though sometimes terms such as *irradiance map* are used to denote a specific type of data stored, the term *light maps* is used to collectively describe all of these. At runtime, the GPU's built-in texture mechanisms are used. Values are usually bilinearly filtered, which for some representations might not be entirely correct. For example, when using an AHD representation, the filtered D (direction) component will no longer be a unit length after interpolation and so needs to be renormalized. Using interpolation also means that the A (ambient) and H (highlight) are not exactly what they would be if we computed them directly at the sampling point. That said, the results usually look acceptable, even if the representation is nonlinear.

Figure 11.27. Light baked into a scene, along with the light maps applied to the surfaces. Light mapping uses a unique parameterization. The scene is divided into elements that are flattened and packed into a common texture. For example, the section in the lower left corresponds the ground plane, showing the two shadows of the cubes. *(From the three.js example webgl_materials_lightmap [218].)*

In most cases light maps do not use mipmapping, which is normally not needed because the resolution of the light map is small compared to typical albedo maps or normal maps. Even in high-quality applications, a single light-map texel covers the area of at least roughly 20×20 centimeters, often more. With texels of this size, extra mip levels would almost never be needed.

To store lighting in the texture, objects need to provide an *unique parameterization*. When mapping a diffuse color texture onto a model, it is usually fine for different parts of the mesh to use the same areas of the texture, especially if a model is textured with a general repeating pattern. Reusing light maps is difficult at best. Lighting is unique for every point on the mesh, so every triangle needs to occupy its own, unique area on the light map. The process of creating a parameterization starts with splitting the meshes into smaller chunks. This can be done either automatically, using some heuristics [1036], or by hand, in the authoring tool. Often, the split that is already present for the mapping of other textures is used. Next, each chunk is parameterized independently, ensuring that its parts do not overlap in texture space [1057, 1617]. The resulting elements in texture space are called *charts* or *shells*. Finally, all the charts are packed into a common texture (Figure 11.27). Care must be taken to ensure that not only do charts not overlap, but also their filtering footprints must stay separate. All the texels that can be accessed when rendering a given chart (bilinear filtering accesses four neighboring texels) should be marked as used, so no other chart overlaps them. Otherwise, bleeding between the charts might occur, and lighting from one of them might be visible on the other. Although it is fairly common for light mapping systems to provide a user-controlled "gutter" amount for spacing between the light map charts, this separation is not necessary. The correct filtering footprint of a chart

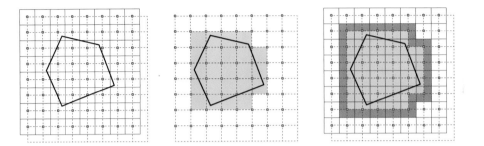

Figure 11.28. To accurately determine the filtering footprint of a chart, we need to find all texels that can be accessed during rendering. If a chart intersects a square spanned between the centers of four neighboring texels, all of them will be used during bilinear filtering. The texel grid is marked with solid lines, texel centers with blue dots, and the chart to be rasterized with thick, solid lines (left). We first conservatively rasterize the chart to a grid shifted by half of a texel size, marked with dashed lined (center). Any texel touching a marked cell is considered occupied (right).

can be determined automatically by rasterizing it in light-map space, using a special set of rules. See Figure 11.28. If shells rasterized this way do not overlap, we are guaranteed that no bleeding will happen.

Avoiding bleeding is another reason why mipmapping is rarely used for light maps. Chart filtering footprints would need to stay separate on all the mip levels, which would lead to excessively large spacing between shells.

Optimally packing charts into textures is an NP-complete problem, which means that there are no known algorithms that can generate an ideal solution with polynomial complexity. As real-time applications may have hundreds of thousands charts in a single texture, all real-world solutions use fine-tuned heuristics and carefully optimized code to generate packing quickly [183, 233, 1036]. If the light map is later block-compressed (Section 6.2.6), to improve the compression quality additional constraints might be added to the packer to ensure that a single block contains only similar values.

A common problem with light maps are *seams* (Figure 11.29). Because the meshes are split into charts and each of these is parameterized independently, it is impossible to ensure that the lighting along split edges is exactly the same on both sides. This manifests as a visual discontinuity. If the meshes are split manually, this problem can be avoided somewhat by splitting them in areas that are not directly visible. Doing so, however, is a laborious process, and cannot be applied when generating the parameterizations automatically. Iwanicki [806] performs a post-process on the final light map that modifies the texels along the split edges to minimize the difference between the interpolated values on both sides. Liu and Ferguson et al. [1058] enforce interpolated values matching along the edge via an equality constraint and solve for texel values that best preserve smoothness. Another approach is to take this constraint into account when creating parameterization and packing charts. Ray et al. [1467] show how *grid-preserving parameterization* can be used to create light maps that do not suffer from seam artifacts.

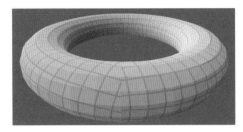
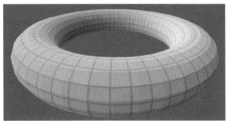

Figure 11.29. To create a unique parameterization for a torus, it needs to be cut and unwrapped. The torus on the left uses a simple mapping, created without considering how the cuts are positioned in texture space. Notice the discontinuities of the grid representing texels on the left. Using more advanced algorithms, we can create a parameterization that ensures that the texel grid lines stay continuous on the three-dimensional mesh, as on the right. Such unwrapping methods are perfect for light mapping, as the resulting lighting does not exhibit any discontinuities.

Precomputed lighting can also be stored at vertices of the meshes. The drawback is that the quality of lighting depends on how finely the mesh is tessellated. Because this decision is usually made at an early stage of authoring, it is hard to ensure that there are enough vertices on the mesh to look good in all expected lighting situations. In addition, tessellation can be expensive. If the mesh is finely tessellated, the lighting signal will be oversampled. If directional methods of storing the lighting are used, the whole representation needs to be interpolated between the vertices by the GPU and passed to the pixel shader stage to perform the lighting calculations. Passing so many parameters between vertex and pixels shaders is fairly uncommon, and generates workloads for which modern GPUs are not optimized, which causes inefficiencies and lower performance. For all these reasons, storing precomputed lighting on vertices is rarely used.

Even though information about the incoming radiance is needed on the surfaces (except when doing volumetric rendering, discussed in Chapter 14), we can precompute and store it volumetrically. Doing so, lighting can be queried at an arbitrary point in space, providing illumination for objects that were not present in the scene during the precomputation phase. Note, however, that these objects will not correctly reflect or occlude lighting.

Greger et al. [594] present the *irradiance volume*, which represents the five-dimensional (three spatial and two directional) irradiance function with a sparse spatial sampling of irradiance environment maps. That is, there is a three-dimensional grid in space, and at each grid point is an irradiance environment map. Dynamic objects interpolate irradiance values from the closest maps. Greger et al. use a two-level adaptive grid for the spatial sampling, but other volume data structures, such as octrees [1304, 1305], can be used.

In the original irradiance volume, Greger et al. stored irradiance at each sample point in a small texture, but this representation cannot be filtered efficiently on the GPU. Today, volumetric lighting data are most often stored in three-dimensional textures, so sampling the volume can use the GPU's accelerated filtering. The most common representations for the irradiance function at the sample points include:

- Spherical harmonics (SH) of second- and third-order, with the former being more common, as the four coefficients needed for a single color channel conveniently pack into four channels of typical texture format.

- Spherical Gaussians.

- Ambient cube or ambient dice.

The AHD encoding, even though technically capable of representing spherical irradiance, generates distracting artifacts. If SH is used, spherical harmonic gradients [54] can further improve quality. All of the above representations have been successfully used in many games [766, 808, 1193, 1268, 1643].

Evans [444] describes a trick used for the irradiance volumes in *LittleBigPlanet*. Instead of a full irradiance map representation, an average irradiance is stored at each point. An approximate directionality factor is computed from the gradient of the irradiance field, i.e., the direction in which the field changes most rapidly. Instead of computing the gradient explicitly, the dot product between the gradient and the surface normal **n** is computed by taking two samples of the irradiance field, one at the surface point **p** and another at a point displaced slightly in the direction of **n**, and subtracting one from the other. This approximate representation is motivated by the fact that the irradiance volumes in *LittleBigPlanet* are computed dynamically.

Irradiance volumes can also be used to provide lighting for static surfaces. Doing so has the advantage of not having to provide a separate parameterization for the light map. The technique also does not generate seams. Both static and dynamic objects can use the same representation, making lighting consistent between the two types of geometry. Volumetric representations are convenient for use in deferred shading (Section 20.1), where all lighting can be performed in a single pass. The main drawback is memory consumption. The amount of memory used by light maps grows with the square of their resolution; for a regular volumetric structure it grows with the cube. For this reason, considerably lower resolutions are used for grid volume representations. Adaptive, hierarchical forms of lighting volumes have better characteristics, but they still store more data than light maps. They are also slower than a grid with regular spacing, as the extra indirections create load dependencies in the shader code, which can result in stalls and slower execution.

Storing surface lighting in volumetric structures is somewhat tricky. Multiple surfaces, sometimes with vastly different lighting characteristics, can occupy the same voxel, making it unclear what data should be stored. When sampling from such voxels, the lighting is frequently incorrect. This happens particularly often near the walls between brightly lit outdoors and dark indoors, and results in either dark patches outside or bright ones inside. The remedy for this is to make the voxel size small enough to never straddle such boundaries, but this is usually impractical because of

Figure 11.30. *Unity* engine uses a tetrahedral mesh to interpolate lighting from a set of probes. *(Book of the Dead © Unity Technologies, 2018.)*

the amount of data needed. The most common ways of dealing with the problem are shifting the sampling position along the normal by some amount, or tweaking the trilinear blending weights used during interpolation. This is often imperfect and manual tweaks to the geometry to mask the problem might be needed. Hooker [766] adds extra clipping planes to the irradiance volumes, which limit their influence to the inside of a convex polytope. Kontkanen and Laine [926] discuss various strategies to minimize bleeding.

The volumetric structure that holds the lighting does not have to be regular. One popular option is to store it in an irregular cloud of points that are then connected to form a Delaunay tetrahedralization (Figure 11.30). This approach was popularized by Cupisz [316]. To look up the lighting, we first find the tetrahedron the sampling position is in. This is an iterative process and can be somewhat expensive. We traverse the mesh, moving between neighboring cells. Barycentric coordinates of the lookup point with respect to the current tetrahedron corners are used to pick the neighbor to visit in the next step (Figure 11.31). Because typical scenes can contain thousands of positions in which the lighting is stored, this process can potentially be time consuming. To accelerate it, we can record a tetrahedron used for lookup in the previous frame (when possible) or use a simple volumetric data structure that provides a good "starting tetrahedron" for an arbitrary point in the scene.

Once the proper tetrahedron is located, the lighting stored on its corners is interpolated, using the already-available barycentric coordinates. This operation is not accelerated by the GPU, but it requires just four values for interpolation, instead of the eight needed for trilinear interpolation on a grid.

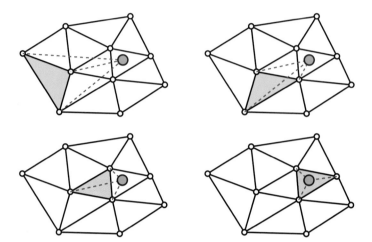

Figure 11.31. Process of a lookup in a tetrahedral mesh illustrated in two dimensions. Steps are shown left to right, top to bottom. Given some starting cell (marked in blue), we evaluate the barycentric coordinates of the lookup point (blue dot) with respect to the cell's corners. In the next step, we move toward the neighbor across the edge opposite to the corner with the most negative coordinate.

The positions for which the lighting gets precomputed and stored can be placed manually [134, 316] or automatically [809, 1812]. They are often referred to as *lighting probes*, or *light probes*, as they probe (or sample) the lighting signal. The term should not be confused with a "light probe" (Section 10.4.2), which is the distant lighting recorded in an environment map.

The quality of the lighting sampled from a tetrahedral mesh is highly dependent upon the structure of that mesh, not just the overall density of the probes. If they are distributed nonuniformly, the resulting mesh can contain thin, elongated tetrahedrons that generate visual artifacts. If probes are placed by hand, problems can be easily corrected, but it is still a manual process. The structure of the tetrahedrons is not related to the structure of the scene geometry, so if not properly handled, lighting will be interpolated across the walls and generate bleeding artifacts, just as with irradiance volumes. In the case of manual probe placement, users can be required to insert additional probes to stop this from happening. When automated placement of probes is used, some form of visibility information can be added to the probes or tetrahedrons to limit their influence to only relevant areas [809, 1184, 1812].

It is a common practice to use different lighting storage methods for static and dynamic geometry. For example, static meshes could use light maps, while dynamic objects could get lighting information from volumetric structures. While popular, this scheme can create inconsistencies between the looks of different types of geometry. Some of these differences can be eliminated by regularization, where lighting information is averaged across the representations.

When baking the lighting, care is needed to compute its values only where they are truly valid. Meshes are often imperfect. Some vertices may be placed inside geometry, or parts of the mesh may self-intersect. The results will be incorrect if we compute incident radiance in such flawed locations. They will cause unwanted darkening or bleeding of incorrectly unshadowed lighting. Kontkanen and Laine [926] and Iwanicki and Sloan [809] discuss different heuristics that can be used to discard invalid samples.

Ambient and directional occlusion signals share many of the spatial characteristics of diffuse lighting. As mentioned in Section 11.3.4, all of the above methods can be used for storing them as well.

11.5.5 Dynamic Diffuse Global Illumination

Even though precomputed lighting can produce impressive-looking results, its main strength is also its main weakness—it requires precomputation. Such offline processes can be lengthy. It is not uncommon for lighting bakes to take many hours for typical game levels. Because lighting computations take so long, artists are usually forced to work on multiple levels at the same time, to avoid downtime while waiting for the bakes to finish. This, in turn, often results in an excessive load on the resources used for rendering, and causes the bakes to take even longer. This cycle can severely impact productivity and cause frustration. In some cases, it is not even possible to precompute the lighting, as the geometry changes at runtime or is created to some extent by the user.

Several methods have been developed to simulate global illumination in dynamic environments. Either they do not require any preprocessing, or the preparation stage is fast enough to be executed every frame.

One of the earliest methods of simulating global illumination in fully dynamic environments was based on "Instant Radiosity" [879]. Despite the name, the method has little in common with the radiosity algorithm. In it, rays are cast outward from the light sources. For each location where a ray hits, a light is placed, representing the indirect illumination from that surface element. These sources are called *virtual point lights* (VPLs). Drawing upon this idea, Tabellion and Lamorlette [1734] developed a method used during production of *Shrek 2* that performs a direct lighting pass of scene surfaces and stores the results in textures. Then, during rendering, the method traces rays and uses the cached lighting to create one-bounce indirect illumination. Tabellion and Lamorlette show that, in many cases, a single bounce is enough to create believable results. This was an offline method, but it inspired a method by Dachsbacher and Stamminger [321] called *reflective shadow maps* (RSM).

Similar to regular shadow maps (Section 7.4), reflective shadow maps are rendered from the point of view of the light. Beyond just depth, they store other information about visible surfaces, such as their albedo, normal, and direct illumination (flux). When performing the final shading, texels of the RSM are treated as point lights to provide a single bounce of indirect lighting. Because a typical RSM contains hundreds of thousands of pixels, only a subset of these are chosen, using an importance-driven

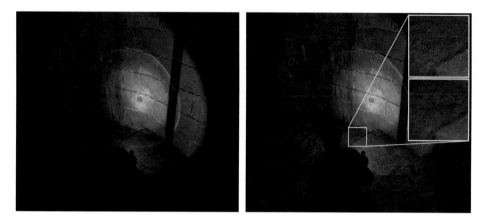

Figure 11.32. The game *Uncharted 4* uses reflective shadow maps to provide indirect illumination from the player's flashlight. The image on the left shows the scene without the indirect contribution. The image on the right has it enabled. The insets show a close-up of the frame rendered without (top) and with (bottom) temporal filtering enabled. It is used to increase the effective number of VPLs that are used for each image pixel. (*UNCHARTED 4 A Thief's End* ©/^{TM} *2016 SIE. Created and developed by Naughty Dog LLC.*)

heuristic. Dachsbacher and Stamminger [322] later show how the method can be optimized by reversing the process. Instead of picking the relevant texels from the RSM for every shaded point, some number of lights are created based on the entire RSM and splatted (Section 13.9) in screen space.

The main drawback of the method is that it does not provide occlusion for the indirect illumination. While this is a significant approximation, results look plausible and are acceptable for many applications.

To achieve high-quality results and maintain temporal stability during light movement, a large number of indirect lights need to be created. If too few are created, they tend to rapidly change their positions when the RSM is regenerated, and cause flickering artifacts. On the other hand, having too many indirect lights is challenging from a performance perspective. Xu [1938] describes how the method was implemented in the game *Uncharted 4*. To stay within the performance constraints, he uses a small number (16) of lights per pixel, but cycles through different sets of them over several frames and filters the results temporally (Figure 11.32).

Different methods have been proposed to address the lack of indirect occlusion. Laine et al. [962] use a dual-paraboloid shadow map for the indirect lights, but add them to the scene incrementally, so in any single frame only a handful of the shadow maps are rendered. Ritschel et al. [1498] use a simplified, point-based representation of the scene to render a large number of *imperfect shadow maps*. Such maps are small and contain many defects when used directly, but after simple filtering provide enough fidelity to deliver proper occlusion effects for indirect illumination.

Some games have used methods that are related to these solutions. *Dust 514* renders a top-down view of the world, with up to four independent layers when required [1110]. These resulting textures are used to perform gathering of indirect illumination, much like the method by Tabellion and Lamorlette. A similar method is used to provide indirect illumination from the terrain in the *Kite* demo, showcasing the Unreal Engine [60].

11.5.6 Light Propagation Volumes

Radiative transfer theory is a general way of modeling how electromagnetic radiation is propagated through a medium. It accounts for scattering, emission, and absorption. Even though real-time graphics strives to show all these effects, except for the simplest cases the methods used for these simulations are orders of magnitude too costly to be directly applied in rendering. However, some of the techniques used in the field have proved useful in real-time graphics.

Light propagation volumes (LPV), introduced by Kaplanyan [854], draw inspiration from the *discrete ordinate methods* in radiative transfer. In his method, the scene is discretized into a regular grid of three-dimensional cells. Each cell will hold a directional distribution of radiance flowing through it. He uses second-order spherical harmonics for these data. In the first step, lighting is injected to the cells that contain directly lit surfaces. Reflective shadow maps are accessed to find these cells, but any other method could be used as well. The injected lighting is the radiance reflected off the lit surfaces. As such, it forms a distribution around the normal, facing away from the surface, and gets its color from the material's color. Next, the lighting is propagated. Each cell analyzes the radiance fields of its neighbors. It then modifies its own distribution to account for the radiance arriving from all the directions. In a single step radiance gets propagated over a distance of only a single cell. Multiple iterations are required to distribute it further (Figure 11.33).

The important advantage of this method is that it generates a full radiance field for each cell. This means that we can use an arbitrary BRDF for the shading, even

Figure 11.33. Three steps of the propagation of the light distribution through a volumetric grid. The left image shows the distribution of the lighting reflected from the geometry illuminated by a directional light source. Notice that only cells directly adjacent to the geometry have a nonzero distribution. In the subsequent steps, light from neighboring cells is gathered and propagated through the grid.

though the quality of the reflections for a glossy BRDF will be fairly low when using second-order spherical harmonics. Kaplanyan shows examples with both diffuse and reflective surfaces.

To allow for the propagation of light over larger distances, as well as to increase the area covered by the volume, while keeping memory usage reasonable, a *cascaded* variant of the method was developed by Kaplanyan and Dachsbacher [855]. Instead of using a single volume with cells of uniform size, they use a set of these with progressively larger cells, nested in one another. Lighting is injected into all the levels and propagated independently. During the lookup, they select the most detailed level available for a given position.

The original implementation did not account for any occlusion of the indirect lighting. The revised approach uses the depth information from the reflective shadow map, as well as the depth buffer from the camera's position, to add information about the light blockers to the volumes. This information is incomplete, but the scene could also be voxelized during the preprocess and so use a more precise representation.

The method shares the problems of other volumetric approaches, the greatest of which is bleeding. Unfortunately, increasing the grid resolution to fix it causes other problems. When using a smaller cell size, more iterations are required to propagate light over the same world-space distance, making the method significantly more costly. Finding a balance between the resolution of the grid and performance is not trivial. The method also suffers from aliasing problems. Limited resolution of the grid, combined with the coarse directional representation of the radiance, causes degradation of the signal as it moves between the neighboring cells. Spatial artifacts, such as diagonal streaks, might appear in the solution after multiple iterations. Some of these problems can be removed by performing spatial filtering after the propagation pass.

11.5.7   Voxel-Based Methods

Introduced by Crassin [304], *voxel cone tracing global illumination* (VXGI) is also based on a voxelized scene representation. The geometry itself is stored in the form of a *sparse voxel octree*, described in Section 13.10. The key concept is that this structure provides a mipmap-like representation of the scene, so that a volume of space can be rapidly tested for occlusion, for example. Voxels also contain information about the amount of light reflected off the geometry they represent. It is stored in a directional form, as the radiance is reflected in six major directions. Using reflective shadow maps, the direct lighting is injected to the lowest levels of the octree first. It is then propagated up the hierarchy.

The octree is used for estimation of the incident radiance. Ideally, we would trace a ray to get an estimate of the radiance coming from a particular direction. However, doing so requires many rays, so whole bundles of these are instead approximated with a cone traced in their average direction, returning just a single value. Exactly testing the cone for intersections with an octree is not trivial, so this operation is approximated with a series of lookups into the tree along the cone's axis. Each lookup reads the

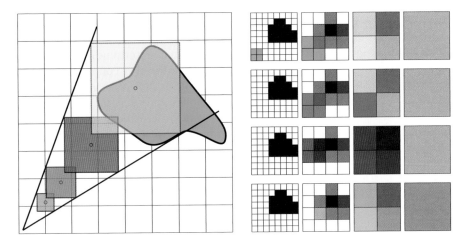

Figure 11.34. Voxel cone tracing approximates an exact cone trace with a series of filtered lookups into a voxel tree. The left side shows a two-dimensional analog of a three-dimensional trace. Hierarchical representation of the voxelized geometry is shown on the right, with each column showing an increasingly coarser level of the tree. Each row shows the nodes of the hierarchy used to provide coverage for a given sample. The levels used are picked so that the size of a node in the coarser level is larger than the lookup size, and in the finer level smaller. A process analogous to trilinear filtering is used to interpolate between these two chosen levels.

level of the tree with a node size corresponding to the cross section of a cone at the given point. The lookup provides the filtered radiance reflected in the direction of the cone origin, as well as the percentage of the lookup footprint that is occupied by geometry. This information is used to attenuate the lighting from subsequent points, in a fashion similar to alpha blending. The occlusion of the entire cone is tracked. In each step it is reduced to account for the percentage of the current sample occupied by geometry. When accumulating the radiance, it is first multiplied by the combined occlusion factor (Figure 11.34). This strategy cannot detect full occlusions that are a result of multiple partial ones, but the results are believable nonetheless.

To compute diffuse lighting, a number of cones are traced. How many are generated and cast is a compromise between performance and precision. Tracing more cones provides higher-quality results, at the cost of more time spent. It is assumed that the cosine term is constant over the entire cone, so that this term can be factored out of the reflectance equation integral. Doing so makes the calculation of the diffuse lighting as simple as computing a weighted sum of the values returned by cone traces.

The method was implemented in a prototype version of the Unreal Engine, as described by Mittring [1229]. He gives several optimizations that the developers needed to make it run as a part of a full rendering pipeline. These improvements include performing the traces at a lower resolution and distributing the cones spatially. This process was done so that each pixel traces only a single cone. The full radiance for the diffuse response is obtained by filtering the results in screen space.

A major problem with using a sparse octree for storing lighting is the high lookup cost. Finding the leaf node containing the given location corresponds to a series of memory lookups, interleaved with a simple logic that determines which subtree to traverse. A typical memory read can take in the order of a couple hundred cycles. GPUs try to hide this latency by executing multiple groups of shader threads (warps or wavefronts) in parallel (Chapter 3). Even though only one group performs ALU operations at any given time, when it needs to wait for a memory read, another group takes its place. The number of warps that can be active at the same time is determined by different factors, but all of them are related to the amount of resources a single group uses (Section 23.3). When traversing hierarchical data structures, most of the time is spent waiting for the next node to be fetched from memory. However, other warps that will be executed during this wait will most likely also perform a memory read. Since there is little ALU work compared to the number of memory accesses, and because the total number of warps in flight is limited, situations where all groups are waiting for memory and no actual work is executed are common.

Having large numbers of stalled warps gives suboptimal performance, and methods that try to mitigate these inefficiencies have been developed. McLaren [1190] replaces the octree with a cascaded set of three-dimensional textures, much like cascaded light propagation volumes [855] (Section 11.5.6). They have the same dimensions, but cover progressively larger areas. In this way, reading the data is accomplished with just a regular texture lookup—no dependent reads are necessary. Data stored in the textures are the same as in the sparse voxel octree. They contain the albedo, occupancy, and bounced lighting information in six directions. Because the position of the cascades changes with the camera movement, objects constantly go in and out of the high-resolution regions. Due to memory constraints, it is not possible to keep these voxelized versions resident all the time, so they are voxelized on demand, when needed. McLaren also describes a number of optimizations that made the technique viable for a 30 FPS game, *The Tomorrow Children* (Figure 11.35).

11.5.8 Screen-Space Methods

Just like screen-space ambient occlusion (Section 11.3.6), some diffuse global illumination effects can be simulated using only surface values stored at screen locations [1499]. These methods are not as popular as SSAO, mainly because the artifacts resulting from the limited amount of data available are more pronounced. Effects such as color bleeding are a result of a strong direct light illuminating large areas of fairly constant color. Surfaces such as this are often impossible to entirely fit in the view. This condition makes the amount of bounced light strongly depend on the current framing, and fluctuate with camera movement. For this reason, screen-space methods are used only to augment some other solution at a fine scale, beyond the resolution achievable by the primary algorithm. This type of system is used in the game *Quantum Break* [1643]. Irradiance volumes are used to model large-scale global illumination effects, and a screen-space solution provides bounced light for limited distances.

Figure 11.35. The game *The Tomorrow Children* uses voxel cone tracing to render indirect illumination effects. *(© 2016 Sony Interactive Entertainment Inc. The Tomorrow Children is a trademark of Sony Interactive Entertainment America LLC.)*

11.5.9 Other Methods

Bunnell's method for calculating ambient occlusion [210] (Section 11.3.5) also allows for dynamically computing global-illumination effects. The point-based representation of the scene (Section 11.3.5) is augmented by storing information about the reflected radiance for each disk. In the gather step, instead of just collecting occlusion, a full incident radiance function can be constructed at each gather location. Just as with ambient occlusion, a subsequent step must be performed to eliminate lighting coming from occluded disks.

11.6 Specular Global Illumination

The methods presented in the previous sections were mainly tailored to simulate diffuse global illumination. We will now look at various methods that can be used to render view-dependent effects. For glossy materials, specular lobes are much tighter than the cosine lobe used for diffuse lighting. If we want to display an extremely shiny material, one with a thin specular lobe, we need a radiance representation that can deliver such high-frequency details. Alternatively, these conditions also mean that evaluation of the reflectance equation needs only the lighting incident from a limited solid angle, unlike a Lambertian BRDF that reflects illumination from the entire hemisphere. This is a completely different requirement than those imposed by diffuse materials. These characteristics explain why different trade-offs need to be made to deliver such effects in real time.

Methods that store the incident radiance can be used to deliver crude view-dependent effects. When using AHD encoding or the HL2 basis, we can compute the specular response as if the illumination was from a directional light arriving from the encoded direction (or three directions, in the case of the HL2 basis). This approach does deliver some specular highlights from indirect lighting, but they are fairly imprecise. Using this idea is especially problematic for AHD encoding, where the directional component can change drastically over small distances. The variance causes the specular highlights to deform in unnatural ways. Artifacts can be reduced by filtering the direction spatially [806]. Similar problems can be observed when using the HL2 basis if the tangent space changes rapidly between neighboring triangles.

Artifacts can also be reduced by representing incoming lighting with higher precision. Neubelt and Pettineo use spherical Gaussian lobes to represent incident radiance in the game *The Order: 1886* [1268]. To render specular effects, they use a method by Xu et al. [1940], who developed an efficient approximation to a specular response of a typical microfacet BRDF (Section 9.8). If the lighting is represented with a set of spherical Gaussians, and the Fresnel term and the masking-shadowing function are assumed constant over their supports, then the reflectance equation can be approximated by

$$L_o(\mathbf{v}) \approx \sum_k \left(M(\mathbf{l}_k, \mathbf{v})(\mathbf{n} \cdot \mathbf{l}_k)^+ \int_{\mathbf{l} \in \Omega} D(\mathbf{l}, \mathbf{v}) L_k(\mathbf{l}) d\mathbf{l} \right), \qquad (11.37)$$

where L_k is the kth spherical Gaussian representing incident radiance, M is the factor combining the Fresnel and masking-shadowing function, and D is the NDF. Xu et al. introduce an *anisotropic spherical Gaussian* (ASG), which they use to model the NDF. They also provide an efficient approximation for computing the integral of a product of SG and ASG, as seen in Equation 11.37.

Neubelt and Pettineo use nine to twelve Gaussian lobes to represent the lighting, which lets them model only moderately glossy materials. They were able to represent most of the game lighting using this method because the game takes place in 19th-century London, and highly polished materials, glass, and reflective surfaces are rare.

11.6.1 Localized Environment Maps

The methods discussed so far are not enough to believably render polished materials. For these techniques the radiance field is too coarse to precisely encode fine details of the incoming radiance, which makes the reflections look dull. The results produced are also inconsistent with the specular highlights from analytical lights, if used on the same material. One solution is to use more spherical Gaussians or a much higher-order SH to get the details we need. This is possible, but we quickly face a performance problem: Both SH and SGs have *global support*. Each basis function is nonzero over the entire sphere, which means that we need all of them to evaluate lighting in a

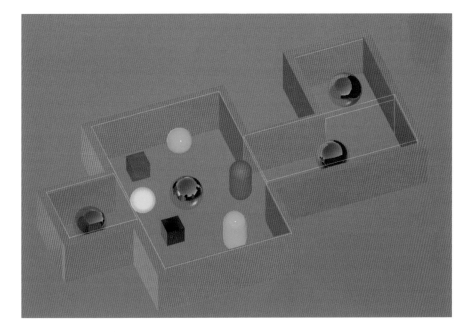

Figure 11.36. A simple scene with localized reflection probes set up. Reflective spheres represent probe locations. Yellow lines depict the box-shaped reflection proxies. Notice how the proxies approximate the overall shape of the scene.

given direction. Doing so becomes prohibitively expensive with fewer basis functions than are needed to render sharp reflections, as we would need thousands. It is also impossible to store that much data at the resolution that is typically used for diffuse lighting.

The most popular solution for delivering specular components for global illumination in real-time settings are *localized environment maps*. They solve both of our earlier problems. The incoming radiance is represented as an environment map, so just a handful of values is required to evaluate the radiance. They are also sparsely distributed throughout the scene, so the spatial precision of the incident radiance is traded for increased angular resolution. Such environment maps, rendered at specific points in the scene, are often called *reflection probes*. See Figure 11.36 for an example.

Environment maps are a natural fit for rendering perfect reflections, which are specular indirect illumination. Numerous methods have been developed that use textures to deliver a wide range of specular effects (Section 10.5). All of these can be used with localized environment maps to render the specular response to indirect illumination.

One of the first titles that tied environment maps to specific points in space was *Half-Life 2* [1193, 1222]. In their system, artists first place sampling locations across the scene. In a preprocessing step a cube map is rendered from each of these positions. Objects then use the nearest location's result as the representation of the incoming radiance during specular lighting calculations. It can happen that the neighboring objects use different environment maps, which causes a visual mismatch, but artists could manually override the automated assignment of cube maps.

If an object is small and the environment map is rendered from its center (after hiding the object so it does not appear in the texture), the results are fairly precise. Unfortunately, this situation is rare. Most often the same reflection probe is used for multiple objects, sometimes with significant spatial extents. The farther the specular surface's location is from the environment map's center, the more the results can vary from reality.

One way of solving this problem was suggested by Brennan [194] and Bjorke [155]. Instead of treating the incident lighting as if it is coming from an infinitely distant surrounding sphere, they assume that it comes from a sphere with a finite size, with the radius being user-defined. When looking up the incoming radiance, the direction is not used directly to index the environment map, but rather is treated as a ray originating from the evaluated surface location and intersected with this sphere. Next, a new direction is computed, one from the environment map's center to the intersection location. This vector serves as the lookup direction. See Figure 11.37. The procedure has the effect of "fixing" the environment map in space. Doing so is often referred to as *parallax correction*. The same method can be used with other primitives, such as boxes [958]. The shapes used for the ray intersection are often called *reflection proxies*. The proxy object used should represent the general shape and size of the geometry rendered into the environment map. Though usually not possible, if they match exactly—for example when a box is used to represent a rectangular room—the method provides perfectly localized reflections.

This technique has gained great popularity in games. It is easy to implement, is fast at runtime, and can be used in both forward and deferred rendering schemes. Artists have direct control over both the look as well as the memory usage. If certain areas need more precise lighting, they can place more reflection probes and fit proxies better. If too much memory is used to store the environment maps, it is easy to remove the probes. When using glossy materials, the distance between the shading point and the intersection with the proxy shape can be used to determine which level of the prefiltered environment map to use (Figure 11.38). Doing so simulates the growing footprint of the BRDF lobe as we move away from the shading point.

When multiple probes cover the same areas, intuitive rules on how to combine them can be established. For example, probes can have a user-set priority parameter that makes those with higher values take precedence over lower ones, or they can smoothly blend into each other.

Unfortunately, the simplistic nature of the method causes a variety of artifacts. Reflection proxies rarely match the underlying geometry exactly. This makes the reflections stretch in unnatural ways in some areas. This is an issue mainly for highly reflective, polished materials. In addition, reflective objects rendered into the envi-

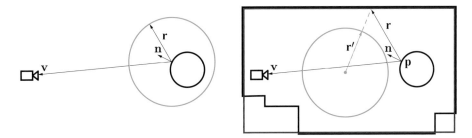

Figure 11.37. The effect of using reflection proxies to spatially localize an environment map (EM). In both cases we want to render a reflection of the environment on the surface of the black circle. On the left is regular environment mapping, represented by the blue circle (but which could be of any representation, e.g., a cube map). Its effect is determined for a point on the black circle by accessing the environment map using the reflected view direction **r**. By using just this direction, the blue circle EM is treated as if it is infinitely large and far away. For any point on the black circle, it is as if the EM is centered there. On the right, we want the EM to represent the surrounding black room as being local, not infinitely far away. The blue circle EM is generated from the center of the room. To access this EM as if it were a room, a reflection ray from position **p** is traced along the reflected view direction and intersected in the shader with a simple proxy object, the red box around the room. This intersection point and the center of the EM are then used to form direction **r′**, which is used to access the EM as usual, by just a direction. By finding **r′**, this process treats the EM as if it has a physical shape, the red box. This proxy box assumption will break down for this room in the two lower corners, since the proxy shape does not match the actual room's geometry.

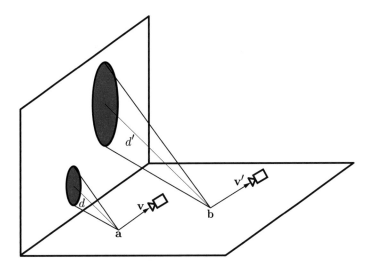

Figure 11.38. The BRDFs at points **a** and **b** are the same, and the view vectors **v** and **v′** are equal. Because the distance d to the reflection proxy from point **a** is shorter than the distance d' from **b**, the footprint of the BRDF lobe on the side of the reflection proxy (marked in red) is smaller. When sampling a prefiltered environment map, this distance can be used along with the roughness at the reflection point to affect the mip level.

ronment map have their BRDFs evaluated from the map's location. Surface locations accessing the environment map will not have the exact same view of these objects, so the texture's stored results are not perfectly correct.

Proxies also cause (sometimes severe) light leaks. Often, the lookup will return values from bright areas of the environment map, because the simplified ray cast misses the local geometry that should cause occlusion. This problem is sometimes mitigated by using directional occlusion methods (Section 11.4). Another popular strategy for mitigating this issue is using the precomputed diffuse lighting, which is usually stored with a higher resolution. The values in the environment map are first divided by the average diffuse lighting at the position from which it was rendered. Doing so effectively removes the smooth, diffuse contribution from the environment map, leaving only higher-frequency components. When the shading is performed, the reflections are multiplied by the diffuse lighting at the shaded location [384, 999]. Doing so can partially alleviate the lack of spatial precision of the reflection probes.

Solutions have been developed that use more sophisticated representation of the geometry captured by the reflection probe. Szirmay-Kalos et al. [1730] store a depth map for each reflection probe and perform a ray trace against it on lookup. This can produce more accurate results, but at an extra cost. McGuire et al. [1184] propose a more efficient way of tracing rays against the probes' depth buffer. Their system stores multiple probes. If the initially chosen probe does not contain enough information to reliably determine the hit location, a fallback probe is selected and the trace continues using the new depth data.

When using a glossy BRDF, the environment map is usually prefiltered, and each mipmap stores the incident radiance convolved with a progressively larger kernel. The prefiltering step assumes that this kernel is radially symmetric (Section 10.5). However, when using parallax correction, the footprint of the BRDF lobe on the shape of the reflection proxy changes depending on the location of the shaded point. Doing so makes the prefiltering slightly incorrect. Pesce and Iwanicki analyze different aspects of this problem and discuss potential solutions [807, 1395].

Reflection proxies do not have to be closed, convex shapes. Simple, planar rectangles can also be used, either instead of or to augment the box or sphere proxies with high-quality details [1228, 1640].

11.6.2 Dynamic Update of Environment Maps

Using localized reflection probes requires that each environment map needs to be rendered and filtered. This work is often done offline, but there are cases where it might be necessary to do it at runtime. In case of an open-world game with a changing time of day, or when the world geometry is generated dynamically, processing all these maps offline might take too long and impact productivity. In extreme cases, when many variants are needed, it might even be impossible to store them all on disk.

In practice, some games render the reflection probes at runtime. This type of system needs to be carefully tuned not to affect the performance in a significant way.

Except for trivial cases, it is not possible to re-render all the visible probes every frame, as a typical frame from a modern game can use tens or even hundreds of them. Fortunately, this is not needed. We rarely require the reflection probes to accurately depict all the geometry around them at all times. Most often we do want them to properly react to changes in the time of day, but we can approximate reflections of dynamic geometry by some other means, such as the screen-space methods described later (Section 11.6.5). These assumptions allow us to render a few probes at load time and the rest progressively, one at a time, as they come into view.

Even when we do want dynamic geometry to be rendered in the reflection probes, we almost certainly can afford to update the probes at a lower frame rate. We can define how much frame time we want to spend rendering reflection probes and update just some fixed number of them every frame. Heuristics based on each probe's distance to the camera, time since the last update, and similar factors can determine the update order. In cases where the time budget is particularly small, we can even split the rendering of a single environment map over multiple frames. For instance, we could render just a single face of a cube map each frame.

High-quality filtering is usually used when performing convolution offline. Such filtering involves sampling the input texture many times, which is impossible to afford at high frame rates. Colbert and Křivánek [279] developed a method to achieve comparable filtering quality with relatively low sample counts (in the order of 64), using importance sampling. To eliminate the majority of the noise, they sample from a cube map with a full mip chain, and use heuristics to determine which mip level should be read by each sample. Their method is a popular choice for fast, runtime prefiltering of environment maps [960, 1154]. Manson and Sloan [1120] construct the desired filtering kernel out of basis functions. The exact coefficients for constructing a particular kernel must be obtained during an optimization process, but it happens only once for a given shape. The convolution is performed in two stages. First, the environment map is downsampled and simultaneously filtered with a simple kernel. Next, samples from the resulting mip chain are combined to construct the final environment map.

To limit the bandwidth used in the lighting passes, as well as the memory usage, it is beneficial to compress the resulting textures. Narkowicz [1259] describes an efficient method for compressing high dynamic range reflection probes to BC6H format (Section 6.2.6), which is capable of storing half-precision floating point values.

Rendering complex scenes, even one cube map face at a time, might be too expensive for the CPU. One solution is to prepare G-buffers for the environment maps offline and calculate only the (much less CPU-demanding) lighting and convolution [384, 1154]. If needed, we can even render dynamic geometry on top of the pregenerated G-buffers.

11.6.3 Voxel-Based Methods

In the most performance-restricted scenarios, localized environment maps are an excellent solution. However, their quality can often be somewhat unsatisfactory. In practice, workarounds have to be used to mask problems resulting from insufficient spatial density of the probes or from proxies being too crude an approximation of the actual geometry. More elaborate methods can be used when more time is available per frame.

Voxel cone tracing—both in the sparse octree [307] as well as the cascaded version [1190] (Section 11.5.7)—can be used for the specular component as well. The method performs cone tracing against a representation of the scene stored in a sparse voxel octree. A single cone trace provides just one value, representing the average radiance coming from the solid angle subtended by the cone. For diffuse lighting, we need to trace multiple cones, as using just a single cone is inaccurate.

It is significantly more efficient to use cone tracing for glossy materials. In the case of specular lighting, the BRDF lobe is narrow, and only radiance coming from a small solid angle needs to be considered. We no longer need to trace multiple cones; in many cases just one is enough. Only specular effects on rougher materials might require tracing multiple cones, but because such reflections are blurry, it is often sufficient to fall back to localized reflection probes for these cases and not trace cones at all.

On the opposite end of the spectrum are highly polished materials. The specular reflection off of these is almost mirror-like. This makes the cone thin, resembling a single ray. With such a precise trace, the voxel nature of the underlying scene representation might be noticeable in the reflection. Instead of polygonal geometry it will show the cubes resulting from the voxelization process. This artifact is rarely a problem in practice, as the reflection is almost never seen directly. Its contribution is modified by textures, which often mask any imperfections. When perfect mirror reflections are needed, other methods can be used that provide them at lower runtime cost.

11.6.4   Planar Reflections

Another alternative is to reuse the regular representation of the scene and re-render it to create a reflected image. If there is a limited number of reflective surfaces, and they are planar, we can use the regular GPU rendering pipeline to create an image of the scene reflected off such surfaces. These images can not only provide accurate mirror reflections, but also render plausible glossy effects with some extra processing of each image.

An ideal reflector follows the *law of reflection*, which states that the angle of incidence is equal to the angle of reflection. That is, the angle between the incident ray and the normal is equal to the angle between the reflected ray and the normal. See Figure 11.39. This figure also shows an "image" of the reflected object. Due to the law of reflection, the reflected image of the object is simply the object itself, physically reflected through the plane. That is, instead of following the reflected ray, we could follow the incident ray through the reflector and hit the same point, but on the reflected object.

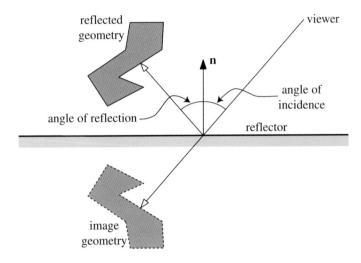

Figure 11.39. Reflection in a plane, showing angle of incidence and reflection, the reflected geometry, and the reflector.

This leads us to the principle that a reflection can be rendered by creating a copy of the object, transforming it into the reflected position, and rendering it from there. To achieve correct lighting, light sources have to be reflected in the plane as well, with respect to both position and direction [1314]. An equivalent method is to instead reflect the viewer's position and orientation through the mirror to the opposite side of the reflector. This reflection can be achieved by simple modification to the projection matrix.

Objects that are on the far side of (i.e., behind) the reflector plane should not be reflected. This problem can be solved by using the reflector's plane equation. The simplest method is to define a clipping plane in the pixel shader. Place the clipping plane so that it coincides with the plane of the reflector [654]. Using this clipping plane when rendering the reflected scene will clip away all reflected geometry that is on the same side as the viewpoint, i.e., all objects that were originally behind the mirror.

11.6.5 Screen-Space Methods

Just as with ambient occlusion and diffuse global illumination, some specular effects can be calculated solely in screen space. Doing so is slightly more precise than in the diffuse case, because of the sharpness of the specular lobe. Information about the radiance is needed from only a limited solid angle around the reflected view vector, not from the full hemisphere, so the screen data are much more likely to contain it. This type of method was first presented by Sousa et al. [1678] and was simultaneously discovered by other developers. The whole family of methods is called *screen-space reflections* (SSR).

Given the position of the point being shaded, the view vector, and the normal, we can trace a ray along the view vector reflected across the normal, testing for intersections with the depth buffer. This testing is done by iteratively moving along the ray, projecting the position to screen space, and retrieving the z-buffer depth from that location. If the point on the ray is further from the camera than the geometry represented by the depth buffer, it means that the ray is inside the geometry and a hit is detected. A corresponding value from the color buffer can then be read to obtain the value of the radiance incident from the traced direction. This method assumes that the surface hit by the ray is Lambertian, but this condition is an approximation common to many methods and is rarely a constraint in practice. The ray can be traced in uniform steps in world space. This method is fairly coarse, so when a hit is detected, a refinement pass can be performed. Over a limited distance, a binary search can be used to accurately locate the intersection position.

McGuire and Mara [1179] note that, because of perspective projection, stepping in uniform world-space intervals creates uneven distributions of sampling points along the ray in screen space. Sections of the rays close to the camera are undersampled, so some hit events might be missed. Those farther away are oversampled, so the same depth buffer pixels are read multiple times, generating unnecessary memory traffic and redundant computations. They suggest performing the ray march in screen space instead, using a *digital differential analyzer* (DDA), a method that can be used for rasterizing lines.

First, both the start and end points of the ray to be traced are projected to screen space. Pixels along this line are each examined in turn, guaranteeing uniform precision. One consequence of this approach is that the intersection test does not require full reconstruction of the view-space depth for every pixel. The reciprocal of the view-space depth, which is the value stored in the z-buffer in the case of a typical perspective projection, changes linearly in screen space. This means that we can compute its derivatives with respect to screen-space x- and y-coordinates before the actual trace, then use simple linear interpolation to get the value anywhere along the screen-space segment. The computed value can be directly compared with the data from the depth buffer.

The basic form of screen-space reflections traces just a single ray, and can provide only mirror reflections. However, perfectly specular surfaces are fairly rare. In modern, physically based rendering pipelines, glossy reflections are needed more often, and SSR can also be used to render these.

In simple, ad hoc approaches [1589, 1812], the reflections are still traced with a single ray, along the reflected direction. The results are stored in an offscreen buffer that is processed in a subsequent step. A series of filtering kernels is applied, often combined with downsampling the buffer to create a set of reflection buffers, each blurred to a different degree. When computing the lighting, the width of the BRDF lobe determines which reflection buffer is sampled. Even though the shape of the filter is often chosen to match the shape of the BRDF lobe, doing so is still only a crude approximation, as screen-space filtering is performed without considering discontinuities, surface orientation, and other factors crucial to the precision of the result. Custom heuristics are added at the end to make the glossy screen-space reflections visually match specular contributions from other sources. Even though it is an approximation, the results are convincing.

Stachowiak [1684] approaches the problem in a more principled way. Computing screen-space reflections is a form of ray tracing, and just like ray tracing it can be used to perform proper Monte Carlo integration. Instead of just using the reflected view direction, he uses importance sampling of the BRDF and shoots rays stochastically. Because of performance constraints, the tracing is done at half resolution and a small number of rays are traced per pixel (between one and four). This is too few rays to produce a noise-free image, so the intersection results are shared between neighboring pixels. It is assumed that the local visibility can be considered the same for pixels within some range. If a ray shot from point $\mathbf{p}_0$ in direction $\mathbf{d}_0$ intersects the scene in point $\mathbf{i}_0$, we can assume that if we shoot a ray from point $\mathbf{p}_1$, in a direction $\mathbf{d}_1$ such that it also passes through $\mathbf{i}_0$, it will also hit the geometry in $\mathbf{i}_0$ and there will not be any intersections before it. This lets us use the ray, without actually tracing it, just by appropriately modifying its contribution to the neighbor's integral. Formally speaking, the direction of a ray shot from a neighboring pixel will have a different probability when computed with respect to the probability distribution function of the BRDF of the current pixel.

To further increase the effective number of rays, the results are filtered temporally. The variance of the final integral is also reduced by performing the scene-independent part of the integration offline and storing it in a lookup table indexed by BRDF parameters. In situations where all the required information for the reflected rays is available in screen space, these strategies allow us to achieve precise, noise-free results, close to path-traced ground-truth images (Figure 11.40).

Tracing rays in screen space is generally expensive. It consists of repeatedly sampling the depth buffer, possibly multiple times, and performing some operations on the lookup results. Because the reads are fairly incoherent, the cache utilization can be poor, leading to long stalls during shader execution from waiting on memory transactions to finish. Much care needs to be put into making the implementation as fast as possible. Screen-space reflections are most often calculated at a reduced resolution [1684, 1812], and temporal filtering is used to make up for the decreased quality.

Uludag [1798] describes an optimization that uses a hierarchical depth buffer (Section 19.7.2) to accelerate tracing. First, a hierarchy is created. The depth buffer is progressively downsampled, by a factor of two in each direction for each step. A pixel on the higher level stores the minimum depth value between the four corresponding pixels at the lower level. Next, the trace is performed through the hierarchy. If in a given step the ray does not hit the geometry stored in the cell it passes through, it is advanced to the cell's boundary, and in the next step a lower-resolution buffer is used. If the ray encounters a hit in the current cell, it is advanced to the hit location, and in the next step a higher-resolution buffer is used. The trace terminates when a hit on the highest-resolution buffer is registered (Figure 11.41).

Figure 11.40. All the specular effects in this image were rendered using a stochastic screen-space reflection algorithm [1684]. Notice the vertical stretching, characteristic of reflections from microfacet models. *(Image courtesy of Tomasz Stachowiak. Scene modeled and textured by Joacim Lunde.)*

The scheme is particularly good for long traces, as it ensures no features will be missed and at the same time allows the ray to advance in large increments. It also accesses the caches well, as the depth buffers are not read in random, distant locations, but rather in a local neighborhood. Many practical tips on implementing this method are presented by Grenier [599].

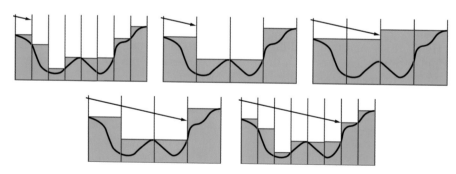

Figure 11.41. Tracing a ray through a hierarchical depth buffer. If the ray does not hit geometry when passing through a pixel, the next step uses a coarser resolution. If a hit is registered, the subsequent step uses finer resolution. This process allows the ray to traverse empty areas in large steps, providing higher performance.

Others avoid tracing the rays entirely. Drobot [384] reuses the location of the intersection with the reflection proxies and looks up the screen-space radiance from there. Cichocki [266] assumes planar reflectors and, instead of tracing the rays, reverses the process and runs a full-screen pass in which every pixel writes its value into the location where it should be reflected.

Just as with other screen-space approaches, reflections can also suffer from artifacts caused by the limited data available. It is common for the reflected rays to leave the screen area before registering a hit, or to hit the backfaces of the geometry, for which no lighting information is available. Such situations need to be handled gracefully, as the validity of the traces is often different even for neighboring pixels. Spatial filters can be used to partially fill the gaps in the traced buffer [1812, 1913].

Another problem with SSR is the lack of information about the thickness of the objects in the depth buffer. Because only a single value is stored, there is no way to tell if the ray hit anything when it goes behind a surface described by depth data. Cupisz [315] discusses various low-cost ways to mitigate the artifacts arising from not knowing the thickness of the objects in the depth buffer. Mara et al. [1123] describe the deep G-buffer, which stores multiple layers of data and so has more information about the surface and environment.

Screen-space reflection is a great tool to provide a specific set of effects, such as local reflections of nearby objects on mostly flat surfaces. They substantially improve the quality of real-time specular lighting, but they do not provide a complete solution. Different methods described in this chapter are often stacked on top of each other, to deliver a complete and robust system. Screen-space reflection serves as a first layer. If it cannot provide accurate results, localized reflection probes are used as a fallback. If none of the probes are applied in a given area, a global, default probe is used [1812]. This type of setup provides a consistent and robust way of obtaining a plausible indirect specular contribution, which is especially important for a believable look.

11.7 Unified Approaches

The methods presented so far can be combined into a coherent system capable of rendering beautiful images. However, they lack the elegance and conceptual simplicity of path tracing. Every aspect of the rendering equation is handled in a different way, each making various compromises. Even though the final image can look realistic, there are many situations when these methods fail and the illusion breaks. For these reasons, real-time path tracing has been the focus of significant research efforts.

The amount of computation needed for rendering images of acceptable quality with path tracing far exceeds the capabilities of even fast CPUs, so GPUs are used instead. Their extreme speed and the flexibility of the compute units make them good candidates for this task. Applications of real-time path tracing include architectural walkthroughs and previsualization for movie rendering. Lower and varying frame rates can be acceptable for these use cases. Techniques such as progressive refinement (Section 13.2) can be used to improve the image quality when the camera is still. High-end systems can expect to have use of multiple GPUs.

In contrast, games need to render frames in final quality, and they need to do it consistently within the time budget. The GPU may also need to perform tasks other than rendering itself. For example, systems such as particle simulations are often offloaded to the GPU to free up some CPU processing power. All these elements combined make path tracing impractical for rendering games today.

There is a saying in the graphics community: "Ray tracing is the technology of the future and it always will be!" This quip implies that the problem is so complex, that even with all the advances in both hardware speed and algorithms, there will always be more efficient ways of handling particular parts of the rendering pipeline. Paying the extra cost and using only ray casting, including for primary visibility, may be hard to justify. There is currently considerable truth to it, because GPUs were never designed to perform efficient ray tracing. Their main goal has always been rasterizing triangles, and they have become extremely good at this task. While ray tracing can be mapped to the GPU, current solutions do not have any direct support from fixed-function hardware. It is difficult at best to always beat hardware rasterization with what is effectively a software solution running on the GPU's compute units.

The more reasonable, less purist approach is to use path-tracing methods for effects that are difficult to handle within the rasterization framework. Rasterize triangles visible from the camera, but instead of relying on approximate reflection proxies, or incomplete screen-space information, trace paths to compute reflections. Instead of trying to simulate area light shadows with ad hoc blurs, trace rays toward the source and compute the correct occlusion. Play to the GPU's strengths and use the more general solution for elements that cannot be handled efficiently in hardware. Such a system would still be a bit of a patchwork, and would lack the simplicity of path tracing, but real-time rendering has always been about compromises. If some elegance has to be given up for a few extra milliseconds, it is the right choice—frame rate is nonnegotiable.

While we perhaps will never be able to call real-time rendering a "solved problem," more use of path tracing would help bring theory and practice closer together. With GPUs getting faster every day, such hybrid solutions should be applicable to even the most demanding applications in the near future. Initial examples of systems built on these principles are already starting to appear [1548].

A ray tracing system relies on an acceleration scheme such as using a *bounding volume hierarchy* (BVH) to accelerate visibility testing. See Section 19.1.1 for more information about this topic. A naive implementation of a BVH does not map well to the GPU. As explained in Chapter 3, GPUs natively execute groups of threads, called warps or wavefronts. A warp is processed in lock-step, with every thread performing the same operation. If some of the threads do not execute particular parts of the

Figure 11.42. Spatiotemporal variance-guided filtering can be used to denoise a one-sample-per-pixel, path-traced image (left) to creates a smooth artifact-free image (center). The quality is comparable to a reference rendered with 2048 samples per pixel (right). *(Image courtesy of NVIDIA Corporation.)*

code, they are temporarily disabled. For this reason, GPU code should be written in a way that minimizes divergent flow control between the threads within the same wavefront. Say each thread processes a single ray. This scheme usually leads to large divergence between threads. Different rays will execute diverging branches of the traversal code, intersecting different bounding volumes along the way. Some rays will finish tree traversal earlier than others. This behavior takes us away from the ideal, where all threads in a warp are using the GPU's compute capabilities. To eliminate these inefficiencies, traversal methods have been developed that minimize divergence and reuse threads that finished early [15, 16, 1947].

Hundreds or thousands of rays may need to be traced per pixel to generate high-quality images. Even with an optimal BVH, efficient tree traversal algorithms, and fast GPUs, doing so is not possible in real time today for any but the simplest scenes. The images that we can generate within the available performance constraints are extremely noisy and are not suitable for display. However, they can be treated with denoising algorithms, to produce mostly noise-free images. See Figure 11.42, as well as Figure 24.2 on page 1044. Impressive advances have been made in the field recently, and algorithms have been developed that can create images visually close to high-quality, path-traced references from input generated by tracing even just a single path per pixel [95, 200, 247, 1124, 1563].

In 2014 PowerVR announced their Wizard GPU [1158]. In addition to typical functionality, it contains units that construct and traverse acceleration structures in hardware (Section 23.11). This system proves that there are both interest and the ability to tailor fixed-function units to accelerate ray casting. It will be exciting to see what the future holds!

Further Reading and Resources

Pharr et al.'s book *Physically Based Rendering* [1413] is an excellent guide to non-interactive global illumination algorithms. What is particularly valuable about their work is that they describe in depth what they found works. Glassner's (now free) *Principles of Digital Image Synthesis* [543, 544] discusses the physical aspects of the interaction of light and matter. *Advanced Global Illumination* by Dutré et al. [400] provides a foundation in radiometry and on (primarily offline) methods of solving Kajiya's rendering equation. McGuire's *Graphics Codex* [1188] is an electronic reference that holds a huge range of equations and algorithms pertaining to computer graphics. Dutré's *Global Illumination Compendium* [399] reference work is quite old, but free. Shirley's series of short books [1628] are an inexpensive and quick way to learn about ray tracing.

Chapter 12
Image-Space Effects

"The world was not wheeling anymore. It was just very clear and bright and inclined to blur at the edges."

—Ernest Hemingway

There is more involved in making an image than simply portraying objects. Part of making an image appear photorealistic is having it look like a photo. Just as a photographer adjusts their final result, we may also wish to modify, say, the color balance. Adding film grain, vignetting, and other subtle changes to the rendered image can make a rendering look more convincing. Alternately, more dramatic effects such as lens flares and bloom can convey a sense of drama. Portraying depth of field and motion blur can increase realism and be used for artistic effect.

The GPU can be used to efficiently sample and manipulate images. In this chapter we first discuss modifying a rendered image with *image processing* techniques. Additional data, such as depths and normals, can be used to enhance these operations, for example, by allowing a noisy area to be smoothed while still retaining sharp edges. Reprojection methods can be used to save on shading computations, or rapidly create missing frames. We conclude by presenting a variety of sample-based techniques to produce lens flares, bloom, depth of field, motion blur, and other effects.

12.1 Image Processing

Graphics accelerators have generally been concerned with creating artificial scenes from geometry and shading descriptions. Image processing is different, where we take an input image and modify it in various ways. The combination of programmable shaders and the ability to use an output image as an input texture opened the way to using the GPU for a wide variety of image processing effects. Such effects can be combined with image synthesis. Typically, an image is generated and then one or more image processing operations is performed on it. Modifying the image after rendering

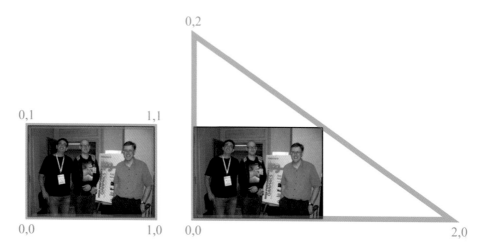

Figure 12.1. On the left, a screen-filling quadrilateral, with (u, v) texture coordinates shown. On the right, a single triangle fills the screen, with its texture coordinates adjusted appropriately to give the same mapping.

is called *post-processing*. A large number of passes, accessing image, depth, and other buffers, can be performed while rendering just a single frame [46, 1918]. For example, the game *Battlefield 4* has over fifty different types of rendering passes [1313], though not all are used in a single frame.

There are a few key techniques for post-processing using the GPU. A scene is rendered in some form to an offscreen buffer, such as a color image, z-depth buffer, or both. This resulting image is then treated as a texture. This texture is applied to a screen-filling quadrilateral. Post-processing is performed by rendering this quadrilateral, as the pixel shader program will be invoked for every pixel. Most image processing effects rely on retrieving each image texel's information at the corresponding pixel. Depending on system limitations and algorithm, this can be done by retrieving the pixel location from the GPU or by assigning texture coordinates in the range $[0, 1]$ to the quadrilateral and scaling by the incoming image size.

In practice a screen-filling triangle can be more efficient than a quadrilateral. For example, image processing proceeds almost 10% faster on the AMD GCN architecture when a single triangle is used instead of a quadrilateral formed from two triangles, due to better cache coherency [381]. The triangle is made large enough to fill the screen [146]. See Figure 12.1. Whatever primitive object is used, the intent is the same: to have the pixel shader be evaluated for every pixel on the screen. This type of rendering is called a *full screen pass*. If available, you can also use compute shaders to perform image processing operations. Doing so has several advantages, described later.

Using the traditional pipeline, the stage is now set for the pixel shader to access the image data. All relevant neighboring samples are retrieved and operations are applied to them. The contribution of the neighbor is weighted by a value depending on its relative location from the pixel being evaluated. Some operations, such as edge detection, have a fixed-size neighborhood (for example, 3×3 pixels) with different weights (sometimes negative) for each neighbor and the pixel's original value itself. Each texel's value is multiplied by its corresponding weight and the results are summed, thus producing the final result.

As discussed in Section 5.4.1, various filter kernels can be used for reconstruction of a signal. In a similar fashion, filter kernels can be used to blur the image. A *rotation-invariant filter kernel* is one that has no dependency on radial angle for the weight assigned to each contributing texel. That is, such filter kernels are described entirely by a texel's distance from the central pixel for the filtering operation. The sinc filter, shown in Equation 5.22 on page 135, is a simple example. The Gaussian filter, the shape of the well-known bell curve, is a commonly used kernel:

$$\text{Gaussian}(x) = \left(\frac{1}{\sigma \sqrt{2\pi}} \right) e^{-\frac{r^2}{2\sigma^2}}, \tag{12.1}$$

where r is the distance from the texel's center and σ is the standard deviation; σ^2 is called the variance. A larger standard deviation makes a wider bell curve. A rough rule of thumb is to make the *support*, the filter size, 3σ pixels wide or greater, as a start [1795]. A wider support gives more blur, at the cost of more memory accesses.

The term in front of the e keeps the area under the continuous curve equal to one. However, this term is irrelevant when forming a discrete filter kernel. The values computed per texel are summed together over the area, and all values are then divided by this sum, so that the final weights sum to one. Because of this normalization process, the constant term serves no purpose, and so often is not shown in filter kernel descriptions. The Gaussian two-dimensional and one-dimensional filters shown in Figure 12.2 are formed this way.

A problem with the sinc and Gaussian filters is that the functions go on forever. One expedient is to clamp such filters to a specific diameter or square area and simply treat anything beyond as having a value of zero. Other filtering kernels are designed for various properties, such as ease of control, smoothness, or simplicity of evaluation. Bjorke [156] and Mitchell et al. [1218], provide some common rotation-invariant filters and other information on image processing on the GPU.

Any full-screen filtering operation will attempt to sample pixels from outside the bounds of the display. For example, if you gather 3×3 samples for, say, the upper left pixel on the screen, you are attempting to retrieve texels that do not exist. One basic solution is to set the texture sampler to clamp to the edge. When an offscreen, nonexistent texel is requested, instead the nearest edge texel is retrieved. This leads to filtering errors at the edges of the image, but these are often not noticeable. Another solution is to generate the image to be filtered at a slightly higher resolution than the display area, so that these offscreen texels exist.

(a)

0.0030	0.0133	0.0219	0.0133	0.0030
0.0133	0.0596	0.0983	0.0596	0.0133
0.0219	0.0983	0.1621	0.0983	0.0219
0.0133	0.0596	0.0983	0.0596	0.0133
0.0030	0.0133	0.0219	0.0133	0.0030

(b)

0.0545	0.2442	0.4026	0.2442	0.0545
0.0545	0.2442	0.4026	0.2442	0.0545
0.0545	0.2442	0.4026	0.2442	0.0545
0.0545	0.2442	0.4026	0.2442	0.0545
0.0545	0.2442	0.4026	0.2442	0.0545

(c)

0.0545	0.0545	0.0545	0.0545	0.0545
0.2442	0.2442	0.2442	0.2442	0.2442
0.4026	0.4026	0.4026	0.4026	0.4026
0.2442	0.2442	0.2442	0.2442	0.2442
0.0545	0.0545	0.0545	0.0545	0.0545

Figure 12.2. One way to perform a Gaussian blur is to sample a 5×5 area, weighting each contribution and summing them. Part (a) of the figure shows these weights for a blur kernel with $\sigma = 1$. A second way is to use separable filters. Two one-dimensional Gaussian blurs, (b) and (c), are performed in series, with the same net result. The first pass, shown in (b) for 5 separate rows, blurs each pixel horizontally using 5 samples in its row. The second pass, (c), applies a 5-sample vertical blur filter to the resulting image from (b) to give the final result. Multiplying the weights in (b) by those in (c) gives the same weights as in (a), showing that this filter is equivalent and therefore separable. Instead of needing 25 samples, as in (a), each of (b) and (c) effectively each use 5 per pixel, for a total of 10 samples.

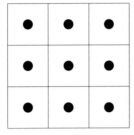 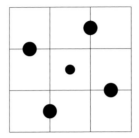 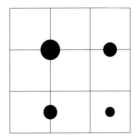

Figure 12.3. On the left, a box filter is applied by performing nine texture samples and averaging the contributions together. In the middle, a symmetric pattern of five samples is used, with the outside samples each representing two texels, and so each is given twice the weight of the center sample. This type of pattern can be useful for other filter kernels, where by moving the outside samples between their two texels, the relative contribution of each texel can be changed. On the right, a more efficient four-sample pattern is used instead. The sample on the upper left interpolates between four texels' values. Those on the upper right and lower left each interpolate the values of two texels. Each sample is given a weight proportional to the number of texels it represents.

One advantage of using the GPU is that built-in interpolation and mipmapping hardware can be used to help minimize the number of texels accessed. For example, say the goal is to use a box filter, i.e., to take the average of the nine texels forming a 3×3 grid around a given texel and display this blurred result. These nine texture samples would then be weighted and summed together by the pixel shader, which would then output the blurred result to the pixel.

Nine explicit sample operations are unnecessary, however. By using bilinear interpolation with a texture, a single texture access can retrieve the weighted sum of up to four neighboring texels [1638]. Using this idea, the 3×3 grid could be sampled with just four texture accesses. See Figure 12.3. For a box filter, where the weights are equal, a single sample could be placed midway among four texels, obtaining the average of the four. For a filter such as the Gaussian, where the weights differ in such a way that bilinear interpolation between four samples can be inaccurate, each sample can still be placed between two texels, but offset closer to one than the other. For instance, imagine one texel's weight was 0.01 and its neighbor was 0.04. The sample could be put so that it was a distance of 0.8 from the first, and so 0.2 from the neighbor, giving each texel its proper proportion. This single sample's weight would be the sum of the two texels' weights, 0.05. Alternatively, the Gaussian could be approximated by using a bilinear interpolated sample for every four texels, finding the offset that gives the closest approximation to the ideal weights.

Some filtering kernels are *separable*. Two examples are the Gaussian and box filters. This means that they can be applied in two separate one-dimensional blurs. Doing so results in considerably less texel access being needed overall. The cost goes from d^2 to $2d$, where d is the kernel diameter or support [815, 1218, 1289]. For example, say the box filter is to be applied in a 5×5 area at each pixel in an image. First the image could be filtered horizontally: The two neighboring texels to the left and two to the right of each pixel, along with the pixel's value itself, are equally weighted by 0.2 and summed together. The resulting image is then blurred vertically, with the two neighboring texels above and below averaged with the central pixel. For example, instead of having to access 25 texels in a single pass, a total of 10 texels are accessed in two passes. See Figure 12.2. Wider filter kernels benefit even more.

Circular disk filters, useful for bokeh effects (Section 12.4), are normally expensive to compute, since they are not separable in the domain of real numbers. However, using complex numbers opens up a wide family of functions that are. Wronski [1923] discusses implementation details for this type of separable filter.

Compute shaders are good for filtering, and the larger the kernel, the better the performance compared to pixel shaders [1102, 1710]. For example, thread group memory can be used to share image accesses among different pixels' filter computations, reducing bandwidth [1971]. A box filter of any radius can be performed for a constant cost by using scattered writes with a compute shader. For the horizontal and vertical passes, the kernel for the first pixel in a row or column is computed. Each successive pixel's result is determined by adding in the next sample at the leading edge of the kernel and subtracting the sample at the far end that was left behind. This "moving average" technique can be used to approximate a Gaussian blur of any size in constant time [531, 588, 817].

Downsampling is another GPU-related technique commonly used when blurring. The idea is to make a smaller version of the image to be manipulated, e.g., halving the resolution along both axes to make a quarter-screen image. Depending on the input data and the algorithm's requirements, the original image may be filtered down in size or simply created at this lower resolution. When this image is accessed to blend into the final, full resolution image, magnification of the texture will use bilinear interpolation to blend between samples. This gives a further blurring effect. Performing manipulations on a smaller version of the original image considerably decreases the overall number of texels accessed. Also, any filters applied to this smaller image have the net effect of increasing the relative size of the filter kernel. For example, applying a kernel with a width of five (i.e., two texels to each side of the central pixel) to the smaller image is similar in effect to applying a kernel with a width of nine to the original image. Quality will be lower, but for blurring large areas of similar color, a common case for many glare effects and other phenomena, most artifacts will be minimal [815]. Reducing the number of bits per pixel is another method that can lower memory access costs. Downsampling can be used for other slowly varying phenomena, e.g., many particle systems can be rendered at half resolution [1391]. This idea of downsampling can be extended to creating a mipmap of an image and sampling from multiple layers to increase the speed of the blurring process [937, 1120].

12.1.1 Bilateral Filtering

Upsampling results and other image processing operations can be improved by using some form of *bilateral filter* [378, 1355]. The idea is to discard or lower the influence

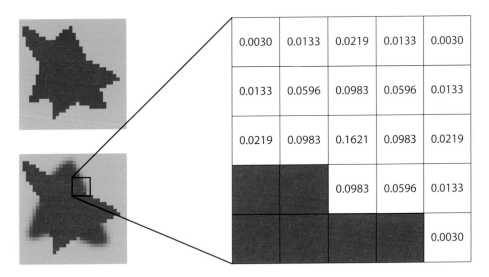

Figure 12.4. Bilateral filter. In the upper left is the original image. In the lower left, we blur and use samples from only those pixels that are not red. On the right, one pixel's filter kernel is shown. The red pixels are ignored when computing the Gaussian blur. The rest of the pixels' colors are multiplied by the corresponding filter weights and summed, and the sum of these weights is also computed. For this case the weights sum to 0.8755, so the color computed is divided by this value.

of samples that appear unrelated to the surface at our center sample. This filter is used to preserve edges. Imagine that you focus a camera on a red object in front of a distant blue object, against a gray background. The blue object should be blurry and the red sharp. A simple bilateral filter would examine the color of the pixel. If red, no blurring would occur—the object stays sharp. Otherwise, the pixel is blurred. All samples that are not red will be used to blur the pixel. See Figure 12.4.

For this example we could determine which pixels to ignore by examining their colors. The *joint*, or *cross*, bilateral filter uses additional information, such as depths, normals, identification values, velocities, or other data to determine whether to use neighboring samples. For example, Ownby et al. [1343] show how patterns can occur when using just a few samples for shadow mapping. Blurring these results looks considerably better. However, a shadow on one object should not affect another unrelated model, and a blur will make shadows bleed outside the edges of the object. They use a bilateral filter, discarding samples on different surfaces by comparing the depth of a given pixel to that of its neighbors. Reducing variability in an area in this way is called *denoising*, and is commonly used in screen-space ambient occlusion algorithms (Section 11.3.6), for example [1971].

Using only the distance from the camera to find edges is often insufficient. For example, a soft shadow crossing the edge formed between two cube faces may fall on only one face, the other facing away from the light. Using just the depth could cause the shadow to bleed from one face to the other when blurred, since this edge would not be detected. We can solve this problem by using only those neighbors where both the depth and surface normal are similar to those of the center sample. Doing so limits samples crossing shared edges, and so such bilateral filters are also called *edge-preserving filters*. Determining whether and how much to weaken or ignore the influence of a neighboring sample is up to the developer, and is dependent on such factors as the models, rendering algorithms, and viewing conditions.

Beyond the additional time spent examining neighbors and summing weights, bilateral filtering has other performance costs. Filtering optimizations such as two-pass separable filtering and bilinear interpolated weighted sampling are more difficult to use. We do not know in advance which samples should be disregarded or weakened in influence, so we cannot use techniques in which the GPU gathers multiple image texels in a single "tap." That said, the speed advantage of a separable two-pass filter has led to approximation methods [1396, 1971].

Paris et al. [1355] discuss many other applications of bilateral filters. Bilateral filters get applied wherever edges must be preserved but samples could be reused to reduce noise. They are also used to decouple shading frequency from the frequency at which geometry is rendered. For example, Yang et al. [1944] perform shading at a lower resolution, then using normals and depths, perform bilateral filtering during upsampling to form the final frame. An alternative is nearest-depth filtering, where the four samples in the low-resolution image are retrieved and the one whose depth is closest to the high-resolution image's depth is used [816]. Hennessy [717] and Pesce [1396] contrast and compare these and other methods for upsampling images. A problem with low-resolution rendering is that fine details can then be lost. Herzog et al. [733] further improve quality by exploiting temporal coherence and reprojection. Note that a bilateral filter is not separable, since the number of samples per pixel can vary. Green [589] notes that the artifacts from treating it as separable can be hidden by other shading effects.

A common way to implement a post-processing pipeline is to use *ping-pong buffers* [1303]. This is simply the idea of applying operations between two offscreen buffers, each used to hold intermediate or final results. For the first pass, the first buffer is the input texture and the second buffer is where output is sent. In the next pass the roles are reversed, with the second now acting as the input texture and the first getting reused for output. In this second pass the first buffer's original contents are overwritten—it is transient, being used as temporary storage for a processing pass. Managing and reusing transient resources is a critical element in designing a modern rendering system [1313]. Making each separate pass perform a particular effect is convenient from an architectural perspective. However, for efficiency, it is best to combine as many effects as possible in a single pass [1918].

In previous chapters, pixel shaders that access their neighbors were used for morphological antialiasing, soft shadows, screen-space ambient occlusion, and other techniques. Post-processing effects are generally run on the final image, and can imitate

Figure 12.5. Image processing using pixel shaders. The original image in the upper left is processed in various ways. The upper right shows a Gaussian difference operation, the lower left edge detection, and lower right a composite of the edge detection blended with the original image. *(Images courtesy of NVIDIA Corporation.)*

thermal imaging [734], reproduce film grain [1273] and chromatic aberration [539], perform edge detection [156, 506, 1218], generate heat shimmer [1273] and ripples [58], posterize an image [58], help render clouds [90], and perform a huge number of other operations [156, 539, 814, 1216, 1217, 1289]. Section 15.2.3 presents a few image processing techniques used for non-photorealistic rendering. See Figure 12.5 for but a few examples. These each use a color image as the only input.

Rather than continue with an exhaustive (and exhausting) litany of all possible algorithms, we end this chapter with some effects achieved using various billboard and image processing techniques.

12.2 Reprojection Techniques

Reprojection is based on the idea of reusing samples computed in previous frames. As its name implies, these samples are reused as possible from a new viewing location and orientation. One goal of reprojection methods is to amortize rendering cost over several frames, i.e., to exploit temporal coherence. Hence, this is also related to temporal antialiasing, covered in Section 5.4.2. Another goal is to form an approximate result if the application fails to finish rendering the current frame in time. This approach is particularly important in virtual reality applications, to avoid simulator sickness (Section 21.4.1).

Reprojection methods are divided into *reverse* reprojection and *forward* reprojection. The basic idea of reverse reprojection [1264, 1556] is shown in Figure 12.6. When a triangle is rendered at time t, the vertex positions are computed for both the current frame (t) and the previous $(t-1)$. Using z and w from vertex shading, the pixel shader can compute an interpolated value z/w for both t and $t-1$, and if they are sufficiently close, a bilinear lookup at $\mathbf{p}_i^{t-1}$ can be done in the previous color buffer and that shaded value can be used instead of computing a new shaded value. For areas that previously were occluded, which then become visible (e.g., the dark green area in Figure 12.6), there are no shaded pixels available. This is called a *cache miss*. On such events, we compute new pixel shading to fill these holes. Since reuse

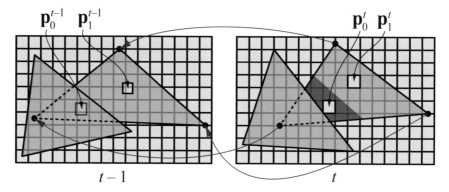

Figure 12.6. A green and a blue triangle at time $t-1$ and the frame after, at time t. The three-dimensional points $\mathbf{p}_i^t$ on the green triangle at the center of two pixels, together with pixel area, are reverse-reprojected to points $\mathbf{p}_i^{t-1}$. As can be seen, $\mathbf{p}_0^{t-1}$ is occluded while $\mathbf{p}_0^t$ is visible, in which case no shaded results can be reused. However, $\mathbf{p}_1$ is visible at both $t-1$ and t, and so shading can potentially be reused for that point. *(Illustration after Nehab et al. [1264].)*

of shaded values assumes that they are independent of any type of motion (objects, camera, light source), it is wise to not reuse shaded values over too many frames. Nehab et al. [1264] suggest that an automatic refresh should always happen after several frames of reuse. One way to do this is to divide the screen into n groups, where each group is a pseudo-random selection of 2×2 pixel regions. Each frame, a single group is updated, which avoids reusing pixel values for too long. Another variant of reverse reprojection is to store a velocity buffer and perform all testing in screen space, which avoids the double transform of vertices.

For better quality, one may also use a *running-average filter* [1264, 1556], which gradually phases out older values. These are particularly recommended for spatial antialiasing, soft shadows, and global illumination. The filter is described by

$$\mathbf{c}_f(\mathbf{p}^t) = \alpha \mathbf{c}(\mathbf{p}^t) + (1 - \alpha)\mathbf{c}(\mathbf{p}^{t-1}), \qquad (12.2)$$

where $\mathbf{c}(\mathbf{p}^t)$ is the newly shaded pixel value at $\mathbf{p}^t$, $\mathbf{c}(\mathbf{p}^{t-1})$ is the reverse-reprojected color from the previous frame, and $\mathbf{c}_f(\mathbf{p}^t)$ is the final color after applying the filter. Nehab et al. use $\alpha = 3/5$ for some use cases, but recommend that different values should be tried depending on what is rendered.

Forward reprojection instead works from the pixels of frame $t - 1$ and projects them into frame t, which thus does not require double vertex shading. This means that the pixels from frame $t - 1$ are *scattered* onto frame t, while reverse reprojection methods *gather* pixel values from frame $t - 1$ to frame t. These methods also need to handle occluded areas that become visible, and this is often done with different heuristic hole-filling approaches, i.e., the values in the missing regions are inferred from the surrounding pixels. Yu et al. [1952] use forward reprojection to compute depth-of-field effects in an inexpensive manner. Instead of classic hole filling, Didyk et al. [350] avoid the holes by adaptively generating a grid over frame $t - 1$ based on motion vectors. This grid is rendered with depth testing, projected into frame t, which means that occlusions and fold-overs are handled as part of rasterizing the adaptive grid triangles with depth testing. Didyk et al. use their method to reproject from the left eye to the right eye in order to generate a stereo pair for virtual reality, where the coherence normally is high between the two images. Later, Didyk et al. [351] present a perceptually motivated method to perform temporal upsampling, e.g., increasing frame rate from 40 Hz to 120 Hz.

Yang and Bowles [185, 1945, 1946] present methods that project from two frames at t and $t + 1$ into a frame at $t + \delta t$ in between these two frames, i.e., $\delta t \in [0, 1]$. These approaches have a greater chance of handling occlusion situations better because they use two frames instead of just one. Such methods are used in games to increase frame rate from 30 FPS to 60 FPS, which is possible since their method runs in less than 1 ms. We recommend their course notes [1946] and the wide-ranging survey on temporal coherence methods by Scherzer et al. [1559]. Valient [1812] also uses reprojection to speed up rendering in *Killzone: Shadow Fall*. See the numerous references near the end of Section 5.4.2 for implementation details in using reprojection for temporal antialiasing.

12.3 Lens Flare and Bloom

Lens flare is a phenomenon caused by light that travels through a lens system or the eye by indirect reflection or other unintended paths. Flare can by classified by several phenomena, most significantly a halo and a ciliary corona. The halo is caused by the radial fibers of the crystalline structure of the lens. It looks like a ring around the light, with its outside edge tinged with red, and its inside with violet. The halo has a constant apparent size, regardless of the distance of the source. The ciliary corona comes from density fluctuations in the lens, and appears as rays radiating from a point, which may extend beyond the halo [1683].

Camera lenses can also create secondary effects when parts of the lens reflect or refract light internally. For example, polygonal patterns can appear due to a camera's aperture blades. Streaks of light can also be seen to smear across a windshield, due to small grooves in the glass [1303]. Bloom is caused by scattering in the lens and other parts of the eye, creating a glow around the light and dimming contrast elsewhere in the scene. A video camera captures an image by converting photons to charge using a *charge-coupled device* (CCD). Bloom occurs in a video camera when a charge site in the CCD gets saturated and overflows into neighboring sites. As a class, halos, coronae, and bloom are called *glare effects*.

In reality, most such artifacts are seen less and less as camera technology improves. Better designs, lens hoods, and anti-reflective coatings can reduce or eliminate these stray ghosting artifacts [598, 786]. However, these effects are now routinely added digitally to real photos. Because there are limits to the light intensity produced by a computer monitor, we can give the impression of increased brightness in a scene or from objects by adding such effects to our images [1951]. The bloom effect and lens flare are almost clichés in photos, films, and interactive computer graphics, due to their common use. Nonetheless, when skillfully employed, such effects can give strong visual cues to the viewer.

To provide a convincing effect, the lens flare should change with the position of the light source. King [899] creates a set of squares with different textures to represent the lens flare. These are then oriented on a line going from the light source position on screen through the screen's center. When the light is far from the center of the screen, these squares are small and more transparent, becoming larger and more opaque as the light moves inward. Maughan [1140] varies the brightness of a lens flare by using the GPU to compute the occlusion of an onscreen area light source. He generates a single-pixel intensity texture that is then used to attenuate the brightness of the effect. Sekulic [1600] renders the light source as a single polygon, using occlusion query hardware to give a pixel count of the area visible (Section 19.7.1). To avoid GPU stalls from waiting for the query to return a value to the CPU, the result is used in the next frame to determine the amount of attenuation. Since the intensity is likely to vary in a fairly continuous and predictable fashion, a single frame of delay causes little perceptual confusion. Gjøl and Svendsen [539] first generate a depth buffer (which they use for other effects as well) and sample it 32 times in a spiral

Figure 12.7. Lens flare, star glare, and bloom effects, along with depth of field and motion blur [1208]. Note the strobing artifacts on some moving balls due to accumulating separate images. *(Image from "Rthdribl," by Masaki Kawase.)*

pattern in the area where the lens flare will appear, using the result to attenuate the flare texture. The visibility sampling is done in the vertex shader while rendering the flare geometry, thus avoiding the delay caused by hardware occlusion queries.

Streaks from bright objects or lights in a scene can be performed in a similar fashion by either drawing semitransparent billboards or performing post-processing filtering on the bright pixels themselves. Games such as *Grand Theft Auto V* use a set of textures applied to billboard for these and other effects [293].

Oat [1303] discusses using a *steerable filter* to produce the streak effect. Instead of filtering symmetrically over an area, this type of filter is given a direction. Texel values along this direction are summed together, which produces a streak effect. Using an image downsampled to one quarter of the width and height, and two passes using ping-pong buffers, gives a convincing streak effect. Figure 12.7 shows an example of this technique.

Figure 12.8. The process of generating sun flare in the game *The Witcher 3*. First, a high-contrast correction curve is applied to the input image to isolate the unoccluded parts of the sun. Next, radial blurs, centered on the sun, are applied to the image. Shown on the left, the blurs are performed in a series, each operating on the output of the previous one. Doing so creates a smooth, high-quality blur, while using a limited number of samples in each pass to improve efficiency. All blurs are performed at half resolution to decrease the runtime cost. The final image of the flare is combined additively with the original scene rendering. *(CD PROJEKT®, The Witcher® are registered trademarks of CD PROJEKT Capital Group. The Witcher game© CD PROJEKT S.A. Developed by CD PROJEKT S.A. All rights reserved. The Witcher game is based on the prose of Andrzej Sapkowski. All other copyrights and trademarks are the property of their respective owners.)*

Many other variations and techniques exist, moving well beyond billboarding. Mittring [1229] uses image processing to isolate bright parts, downsample them, and blur them in several textures. They are then composited again over the final image by duplicating, scaling, mirroring, and tinting. Using this approach, it is not possible for artists to control the look of each flare source independently: The same process is applied to each of the flares. However, any bright parts of the image can generate lens flares, such as specular reflections or emissive parts of a surface, or bright spark particles. Wronski [1919] describes anamorphic lens flares, a byproduct of cinematography equipment used in the 1950s. Hullin et al. [598, 786] provide a physical model for various ghosting artifacts, tracing bundles of rays to compute effects. It gives plausible results that are based on the design of the lens system, along with trade-offs between accuracy and performance. Lee and Eisemann [1012] build on this work, using a linear model that avoids expensive preprocesses. Hennessy [716] gives implementation details. Figure 12.8 shows a typical lens flare system used in production.

The bloom effect, where an extremely bright area spills over onto adjoining pixels, is performed by combining several techniques already presented. The main idea is to create a bloom image consisting only of the bright objects that are to be "overexposed," blur this, then composite it back into the normal image. The blur used is typically a Gaussian [832], though recent matching to reference shots shows that the distribution has more of a spike shape [512]. A common method for making this image is to *bright-pass filter*: Any bright pixels are retained, and all dim pixels are made black, often with some blend or scaling at the transition point [1616, 1674]. For bloom on just a few small objects, a screen bounding box can be computed to limit the extent of the post-processing blur and composite passes [1859].

This bloom image can be rendered at a low resolution, e.g., anywhere from one half to one eighth of the width and height of the original. Doing so saves time and can help increase the effect of filtering. This lower-resolution image is blurred and combined with the original. This reduction in resolution is used in many post-processing effects, as is the technique of compressing or otherwise reducing color resolution [1877]. The bloom image can be downsampled several times and resampled from the set of images produced, giving a wider blur effect while minimizing sampling costs [832, 1391, 1918]. For example, a single bright pixel moving across the screen may cause flicker, as it may not be sampled in some frames.

Because the goal is an image that looks overexposed where it is bright, this image's colors are scaled as desired and added to the original image. Additive blending saturates a color and then goes to white, which is usually just what is desired. An example is shown in Figure 12.9. Alpha blending could be used for more artistic control [1859]. Instead of thresholding, high dynamic range imagery can be filtered for a better result [512, 832]. Low and high dynamic range blooms can be computed separately and composited, to capture different phenomena in a more convincing manner [539]. Other variants are possible, e.g., the previous frame's results can also be added to the current frame, giving animated objects a streaking glow [815].

12.4 Depth of Field

For a camera lens at a given setting, there is a range where objects are in focus, its *depth of field*. Objects outside of this range are blurry—the further outside, the blurrier. In photography, this blurriness is related to aperture size and focal length. Reducing the aperture size increases the depth of field, i.e., a wider range of depths are in focus, but decreases the amount of light forming the image (Section 9.2). A photo taken in an outdoor daytime scene typically has a large depth of field because the amount of light is sufficient to allow a small aperture size, ideally a pinhole camera. Depth of field narrows considerably inside a poorly lit room. So, one way to control a depth-of-field effect is to have it tied to tone mapping, making out-of-focus objects blurrier as the light level decreases. Another is to permit manual artistic control, changing focus and increasing depth of field for dramatic effect as desired. See an example in Figure 12.10.

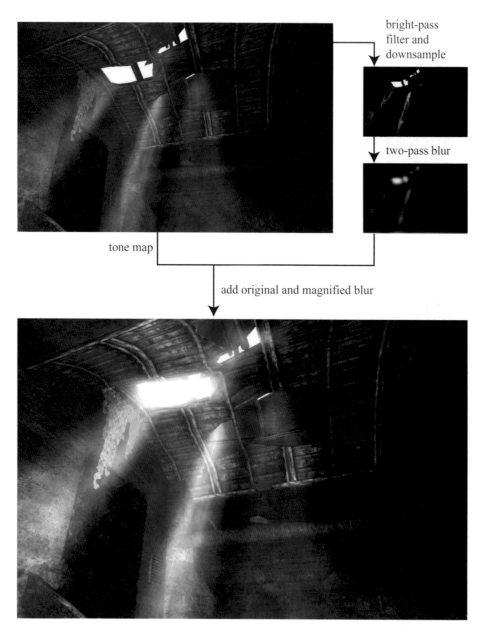

bright-pass filter and downsample

two-pass blur

tone map

add original and magnified blur

Figure 12.9. High dynamic range tone mapping and bloom. The lower image is produced by using tone mapping on, and adding a post-process bloom to, the original image [1869]. *(Image from "Far Cry," courtesy of Ubisoft.)*

Figure 12.10. Depth of field depends on the camera's focus. *(Images rendered in G3D, courtesy of Morgan McGuire [209, 1178].)*

An accumulation buffer can be used to simulate depth of field [637]. See Figure 12.11. By varying the view position on the lens and keeping the point of focus fixed, objects will be rendered blurrier relative to their distance from this focal point. However, as with other accumulation effects, this method comes at a high cost of multiple renderings per image. That said, it does converge to the correct ground-truth

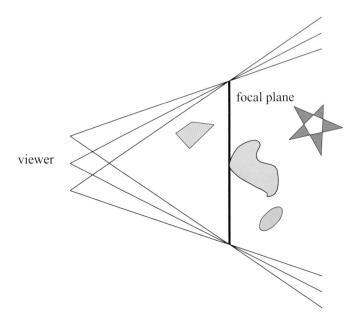

Figure 12.11. Depth of field via accumulation. The viewer's location is moved a small amount, keeping the view direction pointing at the focal point. Each rendered image is summed together and the average of all the images is displayed.

image, which can be useful for testing. Ray tracing can also converge to a physically correct result, by varying the location of the eye ray on the aperture. For efficiency, many methods can use a lower level of detail on objects that are out of focus.

While impractical for interactive applications, the accumulation technique of shifting the view location on the lens provides a reasonable way of thinking about what should be recorded at each pixel. Surfaces can be classified into three zones: those in focus near the focal point's distance (*focus field* or *mid-field*), those beyond (*far field*), and those closer (*near field*). For surfaces at the focal distance, each pixel shows an area in sharp focus, as all the accumulated images have approximately the same result. The focus field is a range of depths where the objects are only slightly out of focus, e.g., less than half a pixel [209, 1178]. This range is what photographers refer to as the depth of field. In interactive computer graphics we use a pinhole camera with perfect focus by default, so depth of field refers to the effect of blurring the near and far field content. Each pixel in the averaged image is a blend of all surface locations seen in the different views, thereby blurring out-of-focus areas, where these locations can vary considerably.

One limited solution to this problem is to create separate image layers. Render one image of just the objects in focus, one of the objects beyond, and one of the objects closer. This can be done by changing the near/far clipping plane locations. The near and far field images are blurred, and then all three images are composited together in back-to-front order [1294]. This *2.5-dimensional* approach, so called because two-dimensional images are given depths and combined, provides a reasonable result under some circumstances. The method breaks down when objects span multiple images, going abruptly from blurry to in focus. Also, all filtered objects have a uniform blurriness, without any variation due to distance [343].

Another way to view the process is to think of how depth of field affects a single location on a surface. Imagine a tiny dot on a surface. When the surface is in focus, the dot is seen through a single pixel. If the surface is out of focus, the dot will appear in nearby pixels, depending on the different views. At the limit, the dot will define a filled circle on the pixel grid. This is termed the *circle of confusion.*

In photography, the aesthetic quality of the areas outside the focus field is called *bokeh*, from the Japanese word meaning "blur." (This word is pronounced "bow-ke," with "bow" as in "bow and arrow" and "ke" as in "kettle.") The light that comes through the aperture is often spread evenly, not in some Gaussian distribution [1681]. The shape of the area of confusion is related to the number and shape of the aperture blades, as well as the size. An inexpensive camera will produce blurs that have a pentagonal shape rather than perfect circles. Currently most new cameras have seven blades, with higher-end models having nine or more. Better cameras have rounded blades, which make the bokeh circular [1915]. For night shots the aperture size is larger and can have a more circular pattern. Similar to how lens flares and bloom are amplified for effect, we sometimes render a hexagonal shape for the circle of confusion to imply that we are filming with a physical camera. The hexagon turns out to be a particularly easy shape to produce in a separable two-pass post-process blur, and so is used in numerous games, as explained by Barré-Brisebois [107].

One way to compute the depth-of-field effect is to take each pixel's location on a surface and scatter its shading value to its neighbors inside this circle or polygon. See the left side of Figure 12.12. The idea of scattering does not map well to pixel shader capabilities. Pixel shaders can efficiently operate in parallel because they do not spread their results to neighbors. One solution is to render a *sprite* (Section 13.5) for every near and far field pixel [1228, 1677, 1915]. Each sprite is rendered to a separate field layer, with the sprite's size determined by the radius of the circle of confusion. Each layer stores the averaged blended sum of all the overlapping sprites, and the layers are then composited one over the next. This method is sometimes referred to as a *forward mapping* technique [343]. Even using image downsampling, such methods can be slow and, worse yet, take a variable amount of time, especially when the field of focus is shallow [1517, 1681]. Variability in performance means that it is difficult to manage the frame budget, i.e., the amount of time allocated to perform all rendering operations. Unpredictability can lead to missed frames and an uneven user experience.

Another way to think about circles of confusion is to make the assumption that the local neighborhood around a pixel has about the same depth. With this idea in place, a gather operation can be done. See the right side of Figure 12.12. Pixel

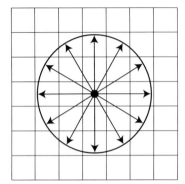 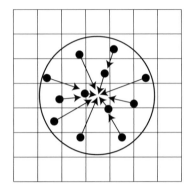

Figure 12.12. A scatter operation takes a pixel's value and spreads it to the neighboring area, for example by rendering a circular sprite. In a gather, the neighboring values are sampled and used to affect a pixel. The GPU's pixel shader is optimized to perform gather operations via texture sampling.

shaders are optimized for gathering results from previous rendering passes. So, one way to perform depth-of-field effects is to blur the surface at each pixel based on its depth [1672]. The depth defines a circle of confusion, which is how wide an area should be sampled. Such gather approaches are called *backward mapping* or *reverse mapping* methods.

Most practical algorithms start with an initial image from one viewpoint. This means that, from the start, some information is missing. The other views of the scene will see parts of surfaces not visible in this single view. As Pesce notes, we should look to do the best we can with what visible samples we have [1390].

Gather techniques have evolved over the years, each improving upon previous work. We present the method by Bukowski et al. [209, 1178] and its solutions to problems encountered. Their scheme generates for each pixel a signed value representing the circle of confusion's radius, based on the depth. This radius could be derived from camera settings and characteristics, but artists often like to control the effect, so the ranges for the near, focus, and far fields optionally can be specified. The radius' sign specifies whether the pixel is in the near or far field, with $-0.5 < r < 0.5$ being in the focus field, where a half-pixel blur is considered in focus.

This buffer containing circle-of-confusion radii is then used to separate the image into two images, near field and the rest, and each is downsampled and blurred in two passes with a separable filter. This separation is performed to address a key problem, that objects in the near field should have blurred edges. If we blurred each pixel based on its radius and output to a single image, the foreground objects could be blurry but with sharp edges. For example, when crossing the silhouette edge from the foreground object to the object in focus, the sample radius will drop to zero, as objects in focus need no blur. This will cause the foreground object's effect on pixels surrounding it to have an abrupt dropoff, resulting in a sharp edge. See Figure 12.13.

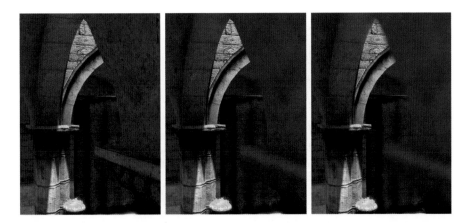

Figure 12.13. Near field blurring. On the left is the original image with no depth-of-field effect. In the middle, pixels in the near field are blurred, but have a sharp edge where adjacent to the focus field. The right shows the effect of using a separate near field image composited atop the more distant content. *(Images generated using G3D [209, 1178].)*

What we want is to have objects in the near field blur smoothly and produce an effect beyond their borders. This is achieved by writing and blurring the near field pixels in a separate image. In addition, each pixel for this near field image is assigned an alpha value, representing its blend factor, which is also blurred. Joint bilateral filtering and other tests are used when creating the two separate images; see the articles [209, 1178] and code provided there for details. These tests serve several functions, such as, for the far field blur, discarding neighboring objects significantly more distant than the sampled pixel.

After performing the separation and blurring based on the circle of confusion radii, compositing is done. The circle-of-confusion radius is used to linearly interpolate between the original, in-focus image and the far field image. The larger this radius, the more the blurry far field result is used. The alpha coverage value in the near field image is then used to blend the near image over this interpolated result. In this way, the near field's blurred content properly spreads atop the scene behind. See Figures 12.10 and 12.14.

This algorithm has several simplifications and tweaks to make it look reasonable. Particles may be handled better in other ways, and transparency can cause problems, since these phenomena involve multiple z-depths per pixel. Nonetheless, with the only inputs being a color and depth buffer and using just three post-processing passes, this method is simple and relatively robust. The ideas of sampling based on the circle of confusion and of separating the near and far fields into separate images (or sets of images) is a common theme among a wide range of algorithms that have been developed to simulate depth of field. We will discuss a few newer approaches used in video games (as the preceding method is), since such methods need to be efficient, be robust, and have a predictable cost.

Figure 12.14. Depth of field in *The Witcher 3*. Near and far field blur convincingly blended with the focus field. *(CD PROJEKT ®, The Witcher ® are registered trademarks of CD PROJEKT Capital Group. The Witcher game © CD PROJEKT S.A. Developed by CD PROJEKT S.A. All rights reserved. The Witcher game is based on the prose of Andrzej Sapkowski. All other copyrights and trademarks are the property of their respective owners.)*

The first method uses an approach we will revisit in the next section: motion blur. To return to the idea of the circle of confusion, imagine turning every pixel in the image into its corresponding circle of confusion, its intensity inversely proportional to the circle's area. Rendering this set of circles in sorted order would give us the best result. This brings us back to the idea of a scatter, and so is generally impractical. It is this mental model that is valuable here. Given a pixel, we want to determine all the circles of confusion that overlap the location and blend these together, in sorted order. See Figure 12.15. Using the maximum circle of confusion radius for the scene, for each pixel we could check each neighbor within this radius and find if its circle of confusion included our current location. All these overlapping-neighbor samples that affect the pixel are then sorted and blended [832, 1390].

This approach is the ideal, but sorting the fragments found would be excessively expensive on the GPU. Instead, an approach called "scatter as you gather" is used, where we gather by finding which neighbors would scatter to the pixel's location. The overlapping neighbor with the lowest z-depth (closest distance) is chosen to represent the nearer image. Any other overlapping neighbors fairly close in z-depth to this have their alpha-blended contributions added in, the average is taken, and the color and alpha are stored in a "foreground" layer. This type of blending requires no sorting. All other overlapping neighbors are similarly summed up and averaged, and the result is put in a separate "background" layer. The foreground and background layers do not correspond to the near and far fields, they are whatever happens to be found for each pixel's region. The foreground image is then composited over the background

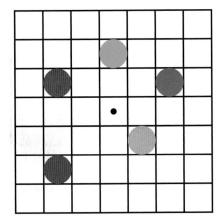 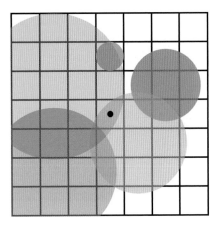

Figure 12.15. Overlapping circles of confusion. On the left is a scene with five dots, all in focus. Imagine that the red dot is closest to the viewer, in the near field, followed by the orange dot; the green dot is in the field of focus; and the blue and violet dots are in the far field, in that order. The right figure shows the circles of confusion that result from applying depth of field, with a larger circle having less effect per pixel. Green is unchanged, since it is in focus. The center pixel is overlapped by only the red and orange circles, so these are blended together, red over orange, to give the pixel color.

image, producing a near field blurring effect. While this approach sounds involved, applying a variety of sampling and filtering techniques makes it efficient. See the presentations by Jimenez [832], Sousa [1681], Sterna [1698], and Courrèges [293, 294] for a few different implementations, and look at the example in Figure 12.16.

One other approach used in a few older video games is based on the idea of computing *heat diffusion*. The image is considered as a heat distribution that diffuses outward, with each circle of confusion representing the thermal conductivity of that pixel. An area in focus is a perfect insulator, with no diffusion. Kass et al. [864] describe how to treat a one-dimensional heat diffusion system as a tridiagonal matrix, which can be solved in constant time per sample. Storing and solving this type of matrix works nicely on a compute shader, so practitioners have developed several implementations in which the image is decomposed along each axis into these one-dimensional systems [612, 615, 1102, 1476]. The problem of visibility for the circles of confusion is still present, and is typically addressed by generating and compositing separate layers based on depths. This technique does not handle discontinuities in the circle of confusion well, if at all, and so is mostly a curiosity today.

A particular depth-of-field effect is caused by bright light sources or reflections in the frame. A light or specular reflection's circle of confusion can be considerably brighter than objects near it in the frame, even with the dimming effect of it being spread over an area. While rendering every blurred pixel as a sprite is expensive, these bright sources of light are higher contrast and so more clearly reveal the aperture shape.

Figure 12.16. Near and far depth of field with pentagonal bokeh on the bright reflective pole in the foreground. *(Image generated using BakingLab demo, courtesy of Matt Pettineo [1408].)*

The rest of the pixels are less differentiated, so the shape is less important. Sometimes the term "bokeh" is (incorrectly) used to describe just these bright areas. Detecting areas of high contrast and rendering just these few bright pixels as sprites, while using a gather technique for the rest of the pixels, gives a result with a defined bokeh while also being efficient [1229, 1400, 1517]. See Figure 12.16. Compute shaders can also be brought to bear, creating high-quality summed-area tables for gather depth of field and efficient splatting for bokeh [764].

We have presented but a few of the many approaches to rendering depth-of-field and bright bokeh effects, describing some techniques used to make the process efficient. Stochastic rasterization, light field processing, and other methods have also been explored. The article by Vaidyanathan et al. [1806] summarizes previous work, and McGuire [1178] gives a summary of some implementations.

12.5 Motion Blur

To render convincing sequences of images, it is important to have a frame rate that is steady and high enough. Smooth and continuous motion is preferable, and too low a frame rate is experienced as jerky motion. Films display at 24 FPS, but theaters are dark and the temporal response of the eye is less sensitive to flicker in dim light. Also, movie projectors change the image at 24 FPS but reduce flickering by redisplaying each image 2–4 times before displaying the next. Perhaps most important, each film frame normally is a motion blurred image; by default, interactive graphics images are not.

In a movie, motion blur comes from the movement of an object across the screen during a frame or from camera motion. The effect comes from the time a camera's

Figure 12.17. On the left, the camera is fixed and the car is blurry. On the right, the camera tracks the car and the background then is blurry. (*Images courtesy of Morgan McGuire et al. [1173].*)

shutter is open for 1/40 to 1/60 of a second during the 1/24 of a second spent on that frame. We are used to seeing this blur in films and consider it normal, so we expect to also see it in video games. Having the shutter be open for 1/500 of a second or less can give a hyperkinetic effect, first seen in films such as *Gladiator* and *Saving Private Ryan*.

Rapidly moving objects appear jerky without motion blur, "jumping" by many pixels between frames. This can be thought of as a type of aliasing, similar to jaggies, but temporal rather than spatial in nature. Motion blur can be thought of as anti-aliasing in the time domain. Just as increasing display resolution can reduce jaggies but not eliminate them, increasing frame rate does not eliminate the need for motion blur. Video games are characterized by rapid motion of the camera and objects, so motion blur can significantly improve their visuals. In fact, 30 FPS with motion blur often looks better than 60 FPS without [51, 437, 584].

Motion blur depends on relative movement. If an object moves from left to right across the screen, it is blurred horizontally on the screen. If the camera is tracking a moving object, the object does not blur—the background does. See Figure 12.17. This is how it works for real-world cameras, and a good director knows to film a shot so that the area of interest is in focus and unblurred.

Similar to depth of field, accumulating a series of images provides a way to create motion blur [637]. A frame has a duration when the shutter is open. The scene is rendered at various times in this span, with the camera and objects repositioned for each. The resulting images are blended together, giving a blurred image where objects are moving relative to the camera's view. For real-time rendering such a process is normally counterproductive, as it can lower the frame rate considerably. Also, if objects move rapidly, artifacts are visible whenever the individual images become discernible. Figure 12.7 on page 525 also shows this problem. Stochastic rasterization can avoid the ghosting artifacts seen when multiple images are blended, producing noise instead [621, 832].

If what is desired is the suggestion of movement instead of pure realism, the accumulation concept can be used in a clever way. Imagine that eight frames of a model in motion have been generated and summed to a high-precision buffer, which is then averaged and displayed. On the ninth frame, the model is rendered again and accumulated, but also at this time the first frame's rendering is performed again and subtracted from the summed result. The buffer now has eight frames of a blurred model, frames 2 through 9. On the next frame, we subtract frame 2 and add in frame 10, again giving the sum of eight frames, 3 through 10. This gives a highly blurred artistic effect, at the cost of rendering the scene twice each frame [1192].

Faster techniques than rendering the frame multiple times are needed for real-time graphics. That depth of field and motion blur can both be rendered by averaging a set of views shows the similarity between the two phenomena. To render these efficiently, both effects need to scatter their samples to neighboring pixels, but we will normally gather. They also need to work with multiple layers of varying blurs, and reconstruct occluded areas given a single starting frame's contents.

There are a few different sources of motion blur, and each has methods that can be applied to it. These can be categorized as camera orientation changes, camera position changes, object position changes, and object orientation changes, in roughly increasing order of complexity. If the camera maintains its position, the entire world can be thought of as a skybox surrounding the viewer (Section 13.3). Changes in just orientation create blurs that have a direction to them, on the image as a whole. Given a direction and a speed, we sample at each pixel along this direction, with the speed determining the filter's width. Such directional blurring is called *line integral convolution* (LIC) [219, 703], and it is also used for visualizing fluid flow. Mitchell [1221] discusses motion-blurring cubic environment maps for a given direction of motion. If the camera is rotating along its view axis, a circular blur is used, with the direction and speed at each pixel changing relative to the center of rotation [1821].

If the camera's position is changing, parallax comes into play, e.g., distant objects move less rapidly and so will blur less. When the camera is moving forward, parallax might be ignored. A radial blur may be sufficient and can be exaggerated for dramatic effect. Figure 12.18 shows an example.

To increase realism, say for a race game, we need a blur that properly computes the motion of each object. If moving sideways while looking forward, called a *pan* in computer graphics,[1] the depth buffer informs us as to how much each object should be blurred. The closer the object, the more blurred. If moving forward, the amount of motion is more complex. Rosado [1509] describes using the previous frame's camera view matrices to compute velocity on the fly. The idea is to transform a pixel's screen location and depth back to a world-space location, then transform this world point using the previous frame's camera to a screen location. The difference between these screen-space locations is the velocity vector, which is used to blur the image for that pixel. Composited objects can be rendered at quarter-screen size, both to save on pixel processing and to filter out sampling noise [1428].

The situation is more complex if objects are moving independently of one another. One straightforward, but limited, method is to model and render the blur itself. This

---

[1]In cinematography a pan means rotating the camera left or right without changing position. Moving sideways is to "truck," and vertically to "pedestal."

Figure 12.18. Radial blurring to enhance the feeling of motion. *(Image from "Assassin's Creed," courtesy of Ubisoft.)*

is the rationale for drawing line segments to represent moving particles. The concept can be extended to other objects. Imagine a sword slicing through the air. Before and behind the blade, two polygons are added along its edge. These could be modeled or generated on the fly. These polygons use an alpha opacity per vertex, so that where a polygon meets the sword, it is fully opaque, and at the outer edge of the polygon, the alpha is fully transparent. The idea is that the model has transparency to it in the direction of movement, simulating the effect that the sword covers these pixels for only part of the time the (imaginary) shutter is open.

This method can work for simple models such as a swinging sword blade, but textures, highlights, and other features should also be blurred. Each surface that is moving can be thought of as individual samples. We would like to scatter these samples, and early approaches to motion blur did so, by expanding the geometry in the direction of movement [584, 1681]. Such geometrical manipulation is expensive, so scatter-as-you-gather approaches have been developed. For depth of field we expanded each sample to the radius of its circle of confusion. For moving samples we instead

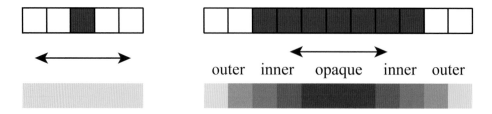

Figure 12.19. On the left, a single sample moving horizontally gives a transparent result. On the right, seven samples give a tapering effect, as fewer samples cover the outer areas. The area in the middle is opaque, as it is always covered by some sample during the whole frame. *(After Jimenez [832].)*

stretch each sample along its path traveled during the frame, similar to LIC. A fast-moving sample covers more area, so has less of an effect at each location. In theory we could take all samples in a scene and draw them as semitransparent line segments, in sorted order. A visualization is shown in Figure 12.19. As more samples are taken, the resulting blur has a smooth transparent gradient on its leading and trailing edges, as with our sword example.

To use this idea, we need to know the velocity of each pixel's surface. A tool that has seen wide adoption is use of a *velocity buffer* [584]. To create this buffer, interpolate the screen-space velocity at each vertex of the model. The velocity can be computed by having two modeling matrices applied to the model, one for the previous frame and one for the current. The vertex shader program computes the difference in positions and transforms this vector to relative screen-space coordinates. A visualization is shown in Figure 12.20. Wronski [1912] discusses deriving velocity buffers and combining motion blur with temporal antialiasing. Courrèges [294] briefly notes how *DOOM* (2016) implements this combination, comparing results.

Once the velocity buffer is formed, the speed of each object at each pixel is known. The unblurred image is also rendered. Note that we encounter a similar problem with motion blur as we did with depth of field, that all data needed to compute the effect is not available from a single image. For depth of field the ideal is to have multiple views averaged together, and some of those views will include objects not seen in others. For interactive motion blur we take a single frame out of a timed sequence and use it as the representative image. We use these data as best we can, but it is important to realize that all the data needed are not always there, which can create artifacts.

Given this frame and the velocity buffer, we can reconstruct what objects affect each pixel, using a scatter-as-you-gather system for motion blur. We begin with the approach described by McGuire et al. [208, 1173], and developed further by Sousa [1681] and Jimenez [832] (Pettineo [1408] provides code). In the first pass, the maximum velocity is computed for each section of the screen, e.g., each 8×8 pixel tile (Section 23.1). The result is a buffer with a maximum velocity per tile, a vector with direction and magnitude. In the second pass, a 3×3 area of this tile-result buffer is examined for each tile, in order to find the highest maximum. This pass ensures that

Figure 12.20. Motion blur due to object and camera movement. Visualizations of the depth and velocity buffers are inset. (*Images courtesy of Morgan McGuire et al. [1173].*)

a rapidly moving object in a tile will be accounted for by neighboring tiles. That is, our initial static view of the scene will be turned into an image where the objects are blurred. These blurs can overlap into neighboring tiles, so such tiles must examine an area wide enough to find these moving objects.

In the final pass the motion blurred image is computed. Similar to depth of field, the neighborhood of each pixel is examined for samples that may be moving rapidly and overlap the pixel. The difference is that each sample has its own velocity, along its own path. Different approaches have been developed to filter and blend the relevant samples. One method uses the magnitude of the largest velocity to determine the direction and width of the kernel. If this velocity is less than half a pixel, no motion blur is needed [1173]. Otherwise, the image is sampled along the direction of maximum velocity. Note that occlusion is important here, as it was with depth of field. A rapidly moving model behind a static object should not have its blur effect bleed over atop this object. If a neighboring sample's distance is found to be near enough to the pixel's z-depth, it is considered visible. These samples are blended together to form the foreground's contribution.

In Figure 12.19 there are three zones for the motion blurred object. The opaque area is fully covered by the foreground object, so needs no further blending. The outer blur areas have, in the original image (the top row of seven blue pixels), a background color available at those pixels over which the foreground can be blended. The inner blur areas, however, do not contain the background, as the original image shows only the foreground. For these pixels, the background is estimated by filtering the neighbor pixels sampled that are not in the foreground, on the grounds that any estimate of the background is better than nothing. An example is shown in Figure 12.20.

There are several sampling and filtering methods that are used to improve the look of this approach. To avoid ghosting, sample locations are randomly jittered half a pixel [1173]. In the outer blur area we have the correct background, but blurring this a bit avoids a jarring discontinuity with the inner blur's estimated background [832]. An object at a pixel may be moving in a different direction than the dominant velocity for its set of 3×3 tiles, so a different filtering method may be used in such situations [621]. Bukowski et al. [208] provide other implementation details and discuss scaling the approach for different platforms.

This approach works reasonably well for motion blur, but other systems are certainly possible, trading off between quality and performance. For example, Andreev [51] uses a velocity buffer and motion blur in order to interpolate between frames rendered at 30 FPS, effectively giving a 60 FPS frame rate. Another concept is to combine motion blur and depth of field into a single system. The key idea is combining the velocity vector and circle of confusion to obtain a unified blurring kernel [1390, 1391, 1679, 1681].

Other approaches have been examined, and research will continue as the capabilities and performance of GPUs improve. As an example, Munkberg et al. [1247] use stochastic and interleaved sampling to render depth of field and motion blur at low sampling rates. In a subsequent pass, they use a fast reconstruction technique [682] to reduce sampling artifacts and recover the smooth properties of motion blur and depth of field.

In a video game the player's experience is usually not like watching a film, but rather is under their direct control, with the view changing in an unpredictable way. Under these circumstances motion blur can sometimes be applied poorly if done in a purely camera-based manner. For example, in first-person shooter games, some users find blur from rotation distracting or a source of motion sickness. In *Call of Duty: Advanced Warfare* onward, there is an option to remove motion blur due to camera rotation, so that the effect is applied only to moving objects. The art team removes rotational blur during gameplay, turning it on for some cinematic sequences. Translational motion blur is still used, as it helps convey speed while running. Alternatively, art direction can be used to modify what is motion blurred, in ways a physical film camera cannot emulate. Say a spaceship moves into the user's view and the camera does not track it, i.e., the player does not turn their head. Using standard motion blur, the ship will be blurry, even though the player's eyes are following it. If we assume the player will track an object, we can adjust our algorithm accordingly, blurring the background as the viewer's eyes follow it and keeping the object unblurred.

Eye tracking devices and higher frame rates may help improve the application of motion blur or eliminate it altogether. However, the effect invokes a cinematic feel, so it may continue to find use in this way or for other reasons, such as connoting illness or dizziness. Motion blur is likely to find continued use, and applying it can be as much art as science.

Further Reading and Resources

Several textbooks are dedicated to traditional image processing, such as Gonzalez and Woods [559]. In particular, we want to note Szeliski's *Computer Vision: Algorithms and Applications* [1729], as it discusses image processing and many other topics and how they relate to synthetic rendering. The electronic version of this book is free for download; see our website realtimerendering.com for the link. The course notes by Paris et al. [1355] provide a formal introduction to bilateral filters, also giving numerous examples of their use.

The articles by McGuire et al. [208, 1173] and Guertin et al. [621] are lucid expositions of their respective work on motion blur; code is available for their implementations. Navarro et al. [1263] provide a thorough report on motion blur for both interactive and batch applications. Jimenez [832] gives a detailed, well-illustrated account of filtering and sampling problems and solutions involved in bokeh, motion blur, bloom, and other cinematic effects. Wronski [1918] discusses restructuring a complex post-processing pipeline for efficiency. For more about simulating a range of optical lens effects, see the lectures presented in a SIGGRAPH course organized by Gotanda [575].

Chapter 13
Beyond Polygons

"Landscape painting is really just a box of air with little marks in it telling you how far back in that air things are."
—Lennart Anderson

Modeling surfaces with triangles is often the most straightforward way to approach the problem of portraying objects in a scene. Triangles are good only up to a point, however. A great advantage of representing an object with an image is that the rendering cost is proportional to the number of pixels rendered, and not to, say, the number of vertices in a geometrical model. So, one use of *image-based rendering* is as a more efficient way to render models. However, image-sampling techniques have a much wider use than this. Many objects, such as clouds and fur, are difficult to represent with triangles. Layered semitransparent images can be used to display such complex surfaces

In this chapter, image-based rendering is first compared and contrasted with traditional triangle rendering, and an overview of algorithms is presented. We then describe commonly used techniques such as sprites, billboards, impostors, particles, point clouds, and voxels, along with more experimental methods.

13.1 The Rendering Spectrum

The goal of rendering is to portray an object on the screen; how we attain that goal is our choice. There is no single correct way to render a scene. Each rendering method is an approximation of reality, at least if photorealism is the goal.

Triangles have the advantage of representing the object in a reasonable fashion from any view. As the camera moves, the representation of the object does not have to change. However, to improve quality, we may wish to substitute a more highly detailed model as the viewer gets closer to the object. Conversely, we may wish to use a simplified form of the model if it is off in the distance. These are called *level*

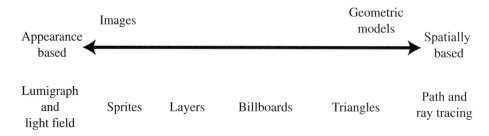

Figure 13.1. The rendering spectrum. *(After Lengyel [1029].)*

of detail techniques (Section 19.9). Their main purpose is to make the scene display faster.

Other rendering and modeling techniques can come into play as an object recedes from the viewer. Speed can be gained by using images instead of triangles to represent the object. It is often less expensive to represent an object with a single image that can be quickly sent to the screen. One way to represent the continuum of rendering techniques comes from Lengyel [1029] and is shown in Figure 13.1. We will first work our way from the left of the spectrum back down to the more familiar territory on the right.

13.2   Fixed-View Effects

For complex geometry and shading models, it can be expensive to re-render an entire scene at interactive rates. Various forms of acceleration can be performed by limiting the viewer's ability to move. The most restrictive situation is one where the camera does not move at all. Under such circumstances, much rendering can be done just once.

For example, imagine a pasture with a fence as the static part of the scene, with a horse moving through it. The pasture and fence are rendered once, then the color and z-buffers are stored away. Each frame, these buffers are used to initialize the color and z-buffer. The horse itself is then all that needs to be rendered to obtain the final image. If the horse is behind the fence, the z-depth values stored and copied will obscure the horse. Note that under this scenario, the horse will not cast a shadow, since the scene is unchanging. Further elaboration can be performed, e.g., the area of effect of the horse's shadow could be determined, and then only this small area of the static scene would need to be evaluated atop the stored buffers. The key point is that there are no limits on when or how the color of each pixel gets set in an image. For a fixed view, much time can be saved by converting a complex geometric model into a simple set of buffers that can be reused for a number of frames.

It is common in computer-aided design (CAD) applications that all modeled objects are static and the view does not change while the user performs various operations. Once the user has moved to a desired view, the color and z-buffers can be stored for immediate reuse, with user interface and highlighted elements then drawn per frame. This allows the user to rapidly annotate, measure, or otherwise interact with a complex static model. By storing additional information in buffers, other operations can be performed. For example, a three-dimensional paint program can be implemented by also storing object IDs, normals, and texture coordinates for a given view and converting the user's interactions into changes to the textures themselves.

A concept related to the static scene is the *golden thread*, also less-poetically called *adaptive refinement* or *progressive refinement*. The idea is that, when the viewer and scene are static, the computer can produce a better and better image over time. Objects in the scene can be made to look more realistic. Such higher-quality renderings can be swapped in abruptly or blended in over a series of frames. This technique is particularly useful in CAD and visualization applications. Many different types of refinement can be done. More samples at different locations within each pixel can be generated over time and the averaged results displayed along the way, so providing antialiasing [1234]. The same applies to depth of field, where samples are randomly stratified over the lens and the pixel [637]. Higher-quality shadow techniques could be used to create a better image. We could also use more involved techniques, such as ray or path tracing, and then fade in the new image.

Some applications take the idea of a fixed view and static geometry a step further in order to allow interactive editing of lighting within a film-quality image. Called *relighting*, the idea is that the user chooses a view in a scene, then uses its data for offline processing, which in turn produces a representation of the scene as a set of buffers or more elaborate structures. For example, Ragan-Kelley et al. [1454] keep shading samples separate from final pixels. This approach allows them to perform motion blur, transparency effects, and antialiasing. They also use adaptive refinement to improve image quality over time. Pellacini et al. [1366] extended basic relighting to include indirect global illumination. These techniques closely resemble those used in deferred shading approaches (described in Section 20.1). The primary difference is that here, the techniques are used to amortize the cost of expensive rendering over multiple frames, and deferred shading uses them to accelerate rendering within a frame.

13.3 Skyboxes

An environment map (Section 10.4) represents the incoming radiance for a local volume of space. While such maps are typically used for simulating reflections, they can also be used directly to represent the surrounding environment. An example is shown in Figure 13.2. Any environment map representation, such as a panorama or cube map, can be used for this purpose. Its mesh is made large enough to encompass the rest of the objects in the scene. This mesh is called a *skybox*.

Pick up this book and look just past the left or right edge toward what is beyond it. Look with just your right eye, then your left. The shift in the book's edge compared

Figure 13.2. A panorama of the Mission Dolores, with three views generated from it at the bottom. Note how the views themselves appear undistorted. *(Images courtesy of Ken Turkowski.)*

to what is behind it is called the *parallax*. This effect is significant for nearby objects, helping us to perceive relative depths as we move. However, for an object or group of objects sufficiently far away from the viewer, and close enough to each other, barely any parallax effect is detectable when the viewer changes position. For example, a distant mountain itself does not normally look appreciably different if you move a meter, or even a thousand meters. It may be blocked from view by nearby objects as you move, but take away those objects and the mountain and its surroundings looks the same.

The skybox's mesh is typically centered around the viewer, moving along with them. The skybox mesh does not have to be large, since by maintaining relative position, it will not appear to change shape. For a scene such as the one shown in Figure 13.2, the viewer may travel only a little distance before they figure out that they are not truly moving relative to the surrounding building. For more large-scale content, such as a star field or distant landscape, the user usually will not move far and fast enough that the lack of change in object size, shape, or parallax breaks the illusion.

Skyboxes are often rendered as cube maps on box meshes, as the texture pixel density on each face is then relatively equal. For a skybox to look good, the cube map texture resolution has to be sufficient, i.e., a texel per screen pixel [1613]. The formula for the necessary resolution is approximately

$$\text{texture resolution} = \frac{\text{screen resolution}}{\tan(\text{fov}/2)}, \tag{13.1}$$

where "fov" is the field of view of the camera. A lower field of view value means that the cube map must have a higher resolution, as a smaller portion of a cube face takes up the same screen size. This formula can be derived from observing that the texture of one face of the cube map must cover a field of view (horizontally and vertically) of 90 degrees.

Other shapes than a box surrounding the world are possible. For example, Gehling [520] describes a system in which a flattened dome is used to represent the sky. This geometric form was found best for simulating clouds moving overhead. The clouds themselves are represented by combining and animating various two-dimensional noise textures.

Because we know that skyboxes are behind all other objects, a few small but worthwhile optimizations are available to us. The skybox never has to write to the z-buffer, because it never blocks anything. If drawn first, the skybox also never has to read from the z-buffer, and the mesh can then be any size desired, since depth is irrelevant. However, drawing the skybox later—after opaque objects, before transparent—has the advantage that objects in the scene will already cover several pixels, lowering the number of pixel shader invocations needed when the skybox is rendered [1433, 1882].

13.4 Light Field Rendering

Radiance can be captured from different locations and directions, at different times and under changing lighting conditions. In the real world, the field of computational photography explores extracting various results from such data [1462]. Purely image-based representations of an object can be used for display. For example, the Lumigraph [567] and light-field rendering [1034] techniques attempt to capture a single object from a set of viewpoints. Given a new viewpoint, these techniques perform an interpolation process between stored views in order to create the new view. This is a complex problem, with high data requirements to store all the views needed. The concept is akin to holography, where a two-dimensional array of views represents the object. A tantalizing aspect of this form of rendering is the ability to capture a real object and be able to redisplay it from any angle. Any object, regardless of surface and lighting complexity, can be displayed at a nearly constant rate. See the book by Szeliski [1729] for more about this subject. In recent years there has been renewed research interest in light field rendering, as it lets the eye properly adjust focus using virtual reality displays [976, 1875]. Such techniques currently have limited use in interactive rendering, but they demarcate what is possible in the field of computer graphics.

Figure 13.3. A still from the animation *Chicken Crossing*, rendered using a Talisman simulator. In this scene, 80 layers of sprites are used, some of which are outlined and shown on the left. Since the chicken wing is partially in front of and behind the tailgate, both were placed in a single sprite. *(Reprinted with permission from Microsoft Corporation.)*

13.5   Sprites and Layers

One of the simplest image-based rendering primitives is the sprite [519]. A sprite is an image that moves around on the screen, e.g., a mouse cursor. The sprite does not have to have a rectangular shape, since some pixels can be rendered as transparent. For simple sprites, each pixel stored will be copied to a pixel on the screen. Animation can be generated by displaying a succession of different sprites.

A more general type of sprite is one rendered as an image texture applied to a polygon that always faces the viewer. This allows the sprite to be resized and warped. The image's alpha channel can provide full or partial transparency to the various pixels of the sprite, thereby also providing an antialiasing effect on edges (Section 5.5). This type of sprite can have a depth, and so a location in the scene itself.

One way to think of a scene is as a series of layers, as is commonly done for two-dimensional cel animation. For example, in Figure 13.3, the tailgate is in front of the chicken, which is in front of the truck's cab, which is in front of the road and trees.

This layering holds true for a large set of viewpoints. Each sprite layer has a depth associated with it. By rendering in a back-to-front order, the *painter's algorithm*, we can build up the scene without need for a z-buffer. Camera zooms just make the object larger, which is simple to handle with the same sprite or an associated mipmap. Moving the camera in or out actually changes the relative coverage of foreground and background, which can be handled by changing each sprite layer's coverage and position. As the viewer moves sideways or vertically, the layers can be moved relative to their depths.

A set of sprites can represent an object, with a separate sprite for a different view. If the object is small enough on the screen, storing a large set of views, even for animated objects, is a viable strategy [361]. Small changes in view angle can also be handled by warping the sprite's shape, though eventually the approximation breaks down and a new sprite needs to be generated. Objects with distinct surfaces can change dramatically from a small rotation, as new polygons become visible and others are occluded.

This layer and image warping process was the basis of the Talisman hardware architecture espoused by Microsoft in the late 1990s [1672, 1776]. While this particular system faded for a number of reasons, the idea of representing a model by one or more image-based representations has been found to be fruitful. Using images in various capacities maps well to GPU strengths, and image-based techniques can be combined with triangle-based rendering. The following sections discuss impostors, depth sprites, and other ways of using images to take the place of polygonal content.

13.6 Billboarding

Orienting a textured rectangle based on the view direction is called *billboarding*, and the rectangle is called a *billboard* [1192]. As the view changes, the orientation of the rectangle is modified in response. Billboarding, combined with alpha texturing and animation, can represent many phenomena that do not have smooth solid surfaces. Grass, smoke, fire, fog, explosions, energy shields, vapor trails, and clouds are just a few of the objects that can be represented by these techniques [1192, 1871]. See Figure 13.4.

A few popular forms of billboards are described in this section. In each, a surface normal and an up direction are found for orienting the rectangle. These two vectors are sufficient to create an orthonormal basis for the surface. In other words, these two vectors describe the rotation matrix needed to rotate the quadrilateral to its final orientation (Section 4.2.4). An *anchor location* on the quadrilateral (e.g., its center) is then used to establish its position in space.

Often, the desired surface normal $\mathbf{n}$ and up vector $\mathbf{u}$ are not perpendicular. In all billboarding techniques, one of these two vectors is established as being a fixed vector that must be maintained in the given direction. The process is always the same to make the other vector perpendicular to this fixed vector. First, create a "right" vector

Figure 13.4. Small billboards representing snow, surfaces, and characters. *(From three.js example programs [218].)*

r, a vector pointing toward the right edge of the quadrilateral. This is done by taking the cross product of **u** and **n**. Normalize this vector **r**, as it will be used as an axis of the orthonormal basis for the rotation matrix. If vector **r** is of zero length, then **u** and **n** must be parallel and the technique [784] described in Section 4.2.4 can be used. If the length of **r** is not quite zero, but nearly so, **u** and **n** are then almost parallel and precision errors can occur.

The process for computing **r** and a new third vector from (non-parallel) **n** and **u** vectors is shown in Figure 13.5. If the normal **n** is to stay the same, as is true for most billboarding techniques, then the new up vector **u**′ is

$$\mathbf{u}' = \mathbf{n} \times \mathbf{r}. \tag{13.2}$$

If, instead, the up direction is fixed (true for axially aligned billboards such as trees on landscape) then the new normal vector **n**′ is

$$\mathbf{n}' = \mathbf{r} \times \mathbf{u}. \tag{13.3}$$

The new vector is then normalized and the three vectors are used to form a rotation matrix. For example, for a fixed normal **n** and adjusted up vector **u**′ the matrix is

$$\mathbf{M} = \left(\ \mathbf{r}, \ \mathbf{u}', \ \mathbf{n} \right). \tag{13.4}$$

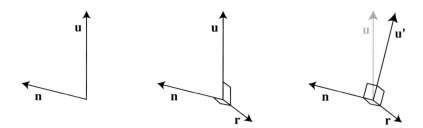

Figure 13.5. For a billboard with a normal direction **n** and an approximate up vector direction **u**, we want to create a set of three mutually perpendicular vectors to orient the billboard. In the middle figure, the "right" vector **r** is found by taking the cross product of **u** and **n**, and so is perpendicular to both of them. In the right figure, the fixed vector **n** is crossed with **r** to give the mutually perpendicular up vector **u**′.

This matrix transforms a quadrilateral in the xy plane with $+y$ pointing toward its top edge, and centered about its anchor position, to the proper orientation. A translation matrix is then applied to move the quadrilateral's anchor point to the desired location.

With these preliminaries in place, the main task that remains is deciding what surface normal and up vector are used to define the billboard's orientation. A few different methods of constructing these vectors are discussed in the following sections.

13.6.1   Screen-Aligned Billboard

The simplest form of billboarding is a *screen-aligned billboard*. This form is the same as a two-dimensional sprite, in that the image is always parallel to the screen and has a constant up vector. A camera renders a scene onto a view plane that is parallel to the near and far planes. We often visualize this imaginary plane at the near plane's location. For this type of billboard, the desired surface normal is the negation of the view plane's normal, where the view plane's normal $\mathbf{v}_n$ points away from the view position. The up vector **u** is from the camera itself. It is a vector in the view plane that defines the camera's up direction. These two vectors are already perpendicular, so all that is needed is the "right" direction vector **r** to form the rotation matrix for the billboard. Since **n** and **u** are constants for the camera, this rotation matrix is the same for all billboards of this type.

In addition to particle effects, screen-aligned billboards are useful for information such as annotation text and map placemarks, as the text will always be aligned with the screen itself, hence the name "billboard." Note that with text annotation the object typically stays a fixed size on the screen. This means that if the user zooms or dollies away from the billboard's location, the billboard will increase in world-space size. The object's size is therefore view-dependent, which can complicate schemes such as frustum culling.

13.6.2   World-Oriented Billboard

We want screen alignment for billboards that display, say, player identities or location names. However, if the camera tilts sideways, such as going into a curve in a flying simulation, we want billboard clouds to tilt in response. If a sprite represents a physical object, it is usually oriented with respect to the world's up direction, not the camera's. Circular sprites are unaffected by a tilt, but other billboard shapes will be. We may want these billboards to remain facing toward the viewer, but also rotate along their view axes in order to stay world oriented.

For such sprites, one way to render these is by using this world up vector to derive the rotation matrix. In this case, the normal is still the negation of the view plane normal, which is the fixed vector, and a new perpendicular up vector is derived from the world's up vector, as explained previously. As with screen-aligned billboards, this matrix can be reused for all sprites, since these vectors do not change within the rendered scene.

Using the same rotation matrix for all sprites carries a risk. Because of the nature of perspective projection, objects that are some distance away from the view axis are warped. See the bottom two spheres in Figure 13.6. The spheres become elliptical, due to projection onto a plane. This phenomenon is not an error and looks fine if a viewer's eyes are the proper distance and location from the screen. That is, if the *geometric field of view* for the virtual camera matches the *display field of view* for the eye, then these spheres look unwarped. Slight mismatches of up to 10%–20% for the field of view are not noticed by viewers [1695]. However, it is common practice to give a wider field of view for the virtual camera, in order to present more of the world to the user. Also, matching the field of view will be effective only if the viewer is centered in front of the display at a given distance. For centuries, artists have realized this problem and compensated as necessary. Objects expected to be round, such as the moon, were painted as circular, regardless of their positions on the canvas [639].

When the field of view or the sprites are small, this warping effect can be ignored and a single orientation aligned to the view plane used. Otherwise, the desired normal needs to equal the vector from the center of the billboard to the viewer's position. This we call a *viewpoint-oriented* billboard. See Figure 13.7. The effect of using different alignments is shown in Figure 13.6. As can be seen, view plane alignment has the effect of making the billboard have no distortion, regardless of where it is on the screen. Viewpoint orientation distorts the sphere image in the same way in which real spheres are distorted by projecting the scene onto the plane.

World-oriented billboarding is useful for rendering many different phenomena. Guymon [624] and Nguyen [1273] both discuss making convincing flames, smoke, and explosions. One technique is to cluster and overlap animated sprites in a random and chaotic fashion. Doing so helps hide the looping pattern of the animated sequences, while also avoiding making each fire or explosion look the same.

Transparent texels in a cutout texture have no effect on the final image but must be processed by the GPU and discarded late in the rasterization pipeline because alpha

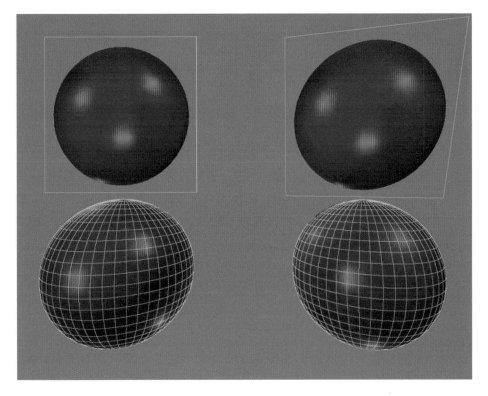

Figure 13.6. A view of four spheres, with a wide field of view. The upper left is a billboard texture of a sphere, using view plane alignment. The upper right billboard is viewpoint oriented. The lower row shows two real spheres.

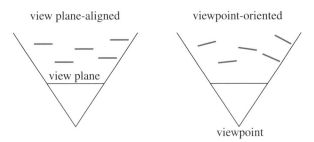

Figure 13.7. A top view of the two billboard alignment techniques. The five billboards face differently, depending on the method.

Figure 13.8. A cloud sprite contains a large transparent fringe. Using the convex hull, shown in green, tighter four- and eight-vertex polygons, in red, are found that enclose fewer transparent texels. Doing so achieves an overall area reduction of 40% and 48%, respectively, compared to the original square particle on the far left. *(Images courtesy of Emil Persson [1382].)*

is zero. An animated set of cutout textures will often have frames with particularly large fringe areas of transparent texels. We typically think of applying a texture to a rectangle primitive. Persson notes a tighter polygon with adjusted texture coordinates can render a sprite more rapidly, since fewer texels are processed [439, 1379, 1382]. See Figure 13.8. He finds that a new polygon with just four vertices can give a substantial performance improvement, and that using more than eight vertices for the new polygon reaches a point of diminishing returns. A "particle cutout" tool to find such polygons is a part of Unreal Engine 4, for example [512].

One common use for billboards is cloud rendering. Dobashi et al. [358] simulate clouds and render them with billboards, and create shafts of light by rendering concentric semitransparent shells. Harris and Lastra [670] also use impostors to simulate clouds. See Figure 13.9.

Wang [1839, 1840] details cloud modeling and rendering techniques used in Microsoft's flight simulator product. Each cloud is formed from 5 to 400 billboards. Only 16 different base sprite textures are needed, as these can be modified using nonuniform scaling and rotation to form a wide variety of cloud types. Modifying transparency based on distance from the cloud center is used to simulate cloud formation and dissipation. To save on processing, distant clouds are all rendered to a set of eight panorama textures surrounding the scene, similar to a skybox.

Flat billboards are not the only cloud rendering technique possible. For example, Elinas and Stuerzlinger [421] generate clouds by rendering sets of nested ellipsoids that become more transparent around the viewing silhouettes. Bahnassi and Bahnassi [90] render ellipsoids they call "mega-particles" and then use blurring and a screen-space turbulence texture to give a convincing cloud-like appearance. Pallister [1347] discusses procedurally generating cloud images and animating these across an overhead sky mesh. Wenzel [1871] uses a series of planes above the viewer for distant clouds. We focus here on the rendering and blending of billboards and other primitives. The shading aspects for cloud billboards are discussed in Section 14.4.2 and true volumetric methods in Section 14.4.2.

Figure 13.9. Clouds created by a set of world-oriented impostors. *(Images courtesy of Mark Harris, UNC-Chapel Hill.)*

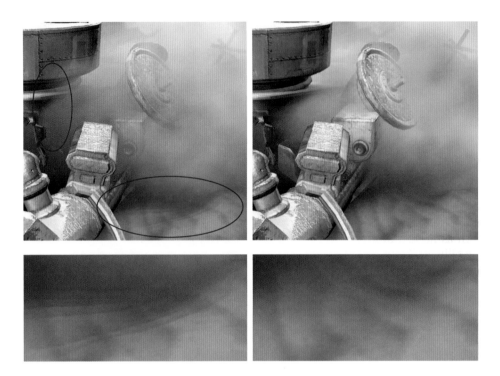

Figure 13.10. On the left, the areas circled show edges and banding due to the dust cloud billboards intersecting with objects. On the right, the billboards fade out where they are near objects, avoiding this problem. At the bottom, the lower circled area is zoomed for comparison. *(Images from NVIDIA SDK 10 [1300] sample "Soft Particles," courtesy of NVIDIA Corporation.)*

As explained in Sections 5.5 and 6.6, to perform compositing correctly, overlapping semitransparent billboards should be rendered in sorted order. Smoke or fog billboards cause artifacts when they intersect solid objects. See Figure 13.10. The illusion is broken, as what should be a volume is seen to be a set of layers. One solution is to have the pixel shader program check the z-depth of the underlying objects while processing each billboard. The billboards test this depth but do not replace it with their own, i.e., do not write a z-depth. If the underlying object is close to the billboard's depth at a pixel, then the billboard fragment is made more transparent. In this way, the billboard is treated more like a volume and the layer artifact disappears. Fading linearly with depth can lead to a discontinuity when the maximum fade distance is reached. An S-curve fadeout function avoids this problem. Persson [1379] notes that the viewer's distance from the particles will change how best to set the fade range. Lorach [1075, 1300] provides more information and implementation details. Billboards that have their transparencies modified in this way are called *soft particles*.

Fadeout using soft particles solves the problem of billboards intersecting solid objects, as shown in Figure 13.10. Other artifacts can occur when explosions move through scenes or the viewer moves through clouds. In the former case, a billboard could move from behind to in front of an object during an animation. This causes a noticeable pop if the billboard moves from entirely invisible to fully visible. Similarly, as the viewer moves through billboards, a billboard can entirely disappear as it moves in front of the near plane, causing a sudden change in what is seen. One quick fix is to make billboards become more transparent as they get closer, fading out to avoid the "pop."

More realistic solutions are possible. Umenhoffer et al. [1799, 1800] introduce the idea of spherical billboards. The billboard object is thought of as actually defining a spherical volume in space. The billboard itself is rendered ignoring z-depth read; the purpose of the billboard is purely to make the pixel shader program execute at locations where the sphere is likely to be. The pixel shader program computes entrance and exit locations on this spherical volume and uses solid objects to change the exit depth as needed and the near clip plane to change the entrance depth. In this way, each billboard's sphere can be properly faded out by increasing the transparency based on the distance that a ray from the camera travels inside the clipped sphere.

A slightly different technique was used in *Crysis* [1227, 1870], using box-shaped volumes instead of spheres to reduce pixel shader cost. Another optimization is to have the billboard represent the front of the volume, rather than its back. This enables the use of z-buffer testing to skip parts of the volume that are behind solid objects. This optimization is viable only when the volume is known to be fully in front of the viewer, so that the billboard is not clipped by the near view plane.

13.6.3 Axial Billboard

The last common type is called *axial billboarding*. In this scheme the textured object does not normally face straight toward the viewer. Instead, it is allowed to rotate around some fixed world-space axis and align itself to face the viewer as much as possible within this range. This billboarding technique can be used for displaying distant trees. Instead of representing a tree with a solid surface, or even with a pair of tree outlines as described in Section 6.6, a single tree billboard is used. The world's up vector is set as an axis along the trunk of the tree. The tree faces the viewer as the viewer moves, as shown in Figure 13.11. This image is a single camera-facing billboard, unlike the "cross-tree" shown in Figure 6.28 on page 203. For this form of billboarding, the world up vector is fixed and the viewpoint direction is used as the second, adjustable vector. Once this rotation matrix is formed, the tree is translated to its position.

This form differs from the world-oriented billboard in what is fixed and what is allowed to rotate. Being world-oriented, the billboard directly faces the viewer and can rotate along this view axis. It is rotated so that the up direction of the billboard aligns as best as possible with the up direction of the world. With an axial billboard, the world's up direction defines the fixed axis, and the billboard is rotated around it so that it faces the viewer as best as possible. For example, if the viewer is nearly

Figure 13.11. As the viewer moves around the scene, the bush billboard rotates to face forward. In this example the bush is lit from the south so that the changing view makes the overall shade change with rotation.

overhead each type of billboard, the world-oriented version will fully face it, while the axial version will be more affixed to the scene.

Because of this behavior, a problem with axial billboarding is that if the viewer flies over the trees and looks down, the illusion is ruined, as the trees will appear nearly edge-on and look like the cutouts they are. One workaround is to add a horizontal cross section texture of the tree (which needs no billboarding) to help ameliorate the problem [908].

Another technique is to use level of detail techniques to change from an image-based model to a mesh-based model [908]. Automated methods of turning tree models from triangle meshes into sets of billboards are discussed in Section 13.6.5. Kharlamov et al. [887] present related tree rendering techniques, and Klint [908] explains data management and representations for large volumes of vegetation. Figure 19.31 on page 857 shows an axial billboard technique used in the commercial SpeedTree package for rendering distant trees.

Just as screen-aligned billboards are good for representing symmetric spherical objects, axial billboards are useful for representing objects with cylindrical symmetry. For example, laser beam effects can be rendered with axial billboards, since their appearance looks the same from any angle around the axis. See Figure 13.12 for an example of this and other billboards. Figure 20.15 on page 913 shows more examples.

These types of techniques illustrate an important idea for these algorithms and ones that follow, that the pixel shader's purpose is to evaluate the true geometry, discarding fragments found outside the represented object's bounds. For billboards such fragments are found when the image texture is fully transparent. As will be seen, more complex pixel shaders can be evaluated to find where the model exists. Geometry's function in any of these methods is to cause the pixel shader to be evaluated, and to give some rough estimate of the z-depth, which may be refined by the pixel shader. We want to avoid wasting time on evaluating pixels outside of the model, but we also do not want to make the geometry so complex that vertex processing and unneeded

Figure 13.12. Billboard examples. The *heads-up display* (HUD) graphics and star-like projectiles are screen-aligned billboards. The large teardrop explosions in the right image are a viewpoint-oriented billboards. The curved beams are axial billboards made of a connected set of quadrilaterals. To create a continuous beam, these quadrilaterals are joined at their corners, and so are no longer fully rectangular. *(Images courtesy of Maxim Garber, Mark Harris, Vincent Scheib, Stephan Sherman, and Andrew Zaferakis, from "BHX: Beamrunner Hypercross.")*

pixel shader invocations outside each triangle (due to 2×2 quads generated along their edges; see Section 18.2.3) become significant costs.

13.6.4 Impostors

An *impostor* is a billboard that is created by rendering a complex object from the current viewpoint into an image texture, which is mapped onto the billboard. The impostor can be used for a few instances of the object or for a few frames, thus amortizing the cost of generating it. In this section different strategies for updating impostors will be presented. Maciel and Shirley [1097] identified several different types of impostors back in 1995, including the one presented in this section. Since that time, the definition of an impostor has narrowed to the one we use here [482].

The impostor image is opaque where the object is present; everywhere else it is fully transparent. It can be use in several ways to replace geometric meshes. For example, imposter images can represent clutter consisting of small static objects [482, 1109]. Impostors are useful for rendering distant objects rapidly, since a complex model is simplified to a single image. A different approach is to instead use a minimal level of detail model (Section 19.9). However, such simplified models often lose shape and color information. Impostors do not have this disadvantage, since the image generated can be made to approximately match the display's resolution [30, 1892]. Another situation in which impostors can be used is for objects located close to the viewer that expose the same side to the viewer as they move [1549].

Before rendering the object to create the impostor image, the viewer is set to view the center of the bounding box of the object, and the impostor rectangle is chosen so that it points directly toward the viewpoint (at the left in Figure 13.13). The size of the

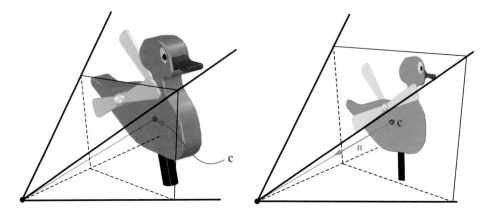

Figure 13.13. At the left, an impostor is created of the object viewed from the side by the viewing frustum. The view direction is toward the center, **c**, of the object, and an image is rendered and used as an impostor texture. This is shown on the right, where the texture is applied to a quadrilateral. The center of the impostor is equal to the center of the object, and the normal (emanating from the center) points directly toward the viewpoint.

impostor's quadrilateral is the smallest rectangle containing the projected bounding box of the object. Alpha is cleared to zero, and wherever the object is rendered, alpha is set to 1.0. The image is then used as a viewpoint-oriented billboard. See the right side of Figure 13.13. When the camera or the impostor object moves, the resolution of the texture may be magnified, which may break the illusion. Schaufler and Stürzlinger [1549] present heuristics that determine when the impostor image needs to be updated.

Forsyth [482] gives many practical techniques for using impostors in games. For example, more frequent updating of the objects closer to the viewer or the mouse cursor can improve perceived quality. When impostors are used for dynamic objects, he describes a preprocessing technique that determines the largest distance, d, any vertex moves during the entire animation. This distance is divided by the number of time steps in the animation, so that $\Delta = d/\text{frames}$. If an impostor has been used for n frames without updating, then $\Delta * n$ is projected onto the image plane. If this distance is larger than a threshold set by the user, the impostor is updated.

Mapping the texture onto a rectangle facing the viewer does not always give a convincing effect. The problem is that an impostor itself does not have a thickness, so can show problems when combined with real geometry. See the upper right image in Figure 13.16. Forsyth suggests instead projecting the texture along the view direction onto the bounding box of the object [482]. This at least gives the impostor a little geometric presence.

Often it is best to just render the geometry when an object moves, and switch to impostors when the object is static [482]. Kavan et al. [874] introduce *polypostors*, in which a model of a person is represented by a set of impostors, one for each limb

Figure 13.14. An impostor technique in which each separate animated element is represented by a set of images. These are rendered in a series of masking and compositing operations that combine to form a convincing model for the given view. *(Image courtesy of Alejandro Beacco, copyright ©2016 John Wiley & Sons, Ltd. [122].)*

and the trunk. This system tries to strike a balance between pure impostors and pure geometry. Beacco et al. [122] describe polypostors and a wide range of other impostor-related techniques for crowd rendering, providing a detailed comparison of the strengths and limitations of each. See Figure 13.14 for one example.

13.6.5 Billboard Representation

A problem with impostors is that the rendered image must continue to face the viewer. If the distant object is changing its orientation, the impostor must be recomputed. To model distant objects that are more like the triangle meshes they represent, Décoret et al. [338] present the idea of a *billboard cloud*. A complex model can often be represented by a small collection of overlapping cutout billboards. Additional information, such as normal or displacement maps and different materials, can be applied to their surfaces to make such models more convincing.

This idea of finding a set of planes is more general than the paper cutout analogy might imply. Billboards can intersect, and cutouts can be arbitrarily complex. For example, several researchers fit billboards to tree models [128, 503, 513, 950]. From

Figure 13.15. On the left, a tree model made of 20,610 triangles. In the middle, the tree modeled with 78 billboards. The overlapping billboards are shown on the right. *(Images courtesy of Dylan Lacewell, University of Utah [950].)*

models with tens of thousands of triangles, they can create convincing billboard clouds consisting of less than a hundred textured quadrilaterals. See Figure 13.15.

Using billboard clouds can cause a considerable amount of overdraw, which can be expensive. Quality can also suffer, as intersecting cutouts can mean that a strict back-to-front draw order cannot be achieved. Alpha to coverage (Section 6.6) can help in rendering complex sets of alpha textures [887]. To avoid overdraw, professional packages such as SpeedTree represent and simplify a model with large meshes of alpha-textured sets of leaves and limbs. While geometry processing then takes more time, this is more than offset by lower overdraw costs. Figure 19.31 on page 857 shows examples. Another approach is to represent such objects with volume textures and render these as a series of layers formed to be perpendicular to the eye's view direction, as described in Section 14.3 [337].

13.7 Displacement Techniques

If the texture of an impostor is augmented with a depth component, this defines a rendering primitive called a *depth sprite* or a *nailboard* [1550]. The texture image is thus an RGB image augmented with a Δ parameter for each pixel, forming an RGBΔ texture. The Δ stores the deviation from the depth sprite rectangle to the correct depth of the geometry that the depth sprite represents. This Δ channel is a heightfield in view space. Because depth sprites contain depth information, they are superior to impostors in that they can merge better with surrounding objects. This is especially evident when the depth sprite rectangle penetrates nearby geometry. Such a case is shown in Figure 13.16. Pixel shaders are able to perform this algorithm by varying the z-depth per pixel.

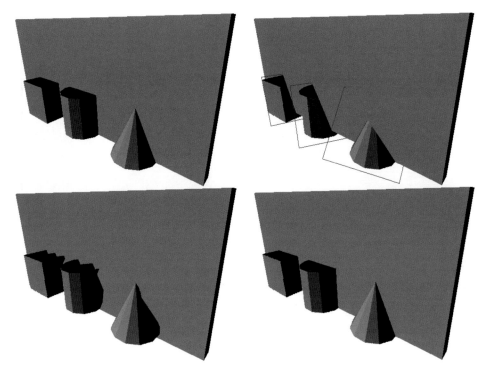

Figure 13.16. The upper left image shows a simple scene rendered with geometry. The upper right image shows what happens if impostors are created and used for the cube, the cylinder, and the cone. The bottom image shows the result when depth sprites are used. The depth sprite in the left image uses 2 bits for depth deviation, while the one on the right uses 8 bits. *(Images courtesy of Gernot Schaufler [1550].)*

Shade et al. [1611] also describe a depth sprite primitive, where they use warping to account for new viewpoints. They introduce a primitive called a *layered depth image*, which has several depths per pixel. The reason for multiple depths is to avoid the gaps that are created due to deocclusion (i.e., where hidden areas become visible) during the warping. Related techniques are also presented by Schaufler [1551] and Meyer and Neyret [1203]. To control the sampling rate, a hierarchical representation called the *LDI tree* was presented by Chang et al. [255].

Related to depth sprites is *relief texture mapping* introduced by Oliveira et al. [1324]. The relief texture is an image with a heightfield that represents the true location of the surface. Unlike a depth sprite, the image is not rendered on a billboard, but rather is oriented on a quadrilateral in world space. An object can be defined by a set of relief textures that match at their seams. Using the GPU, heightfields can be mapped onto surfaces and ray marching can be used to render them, as discussed in Section 6.8.1. Relief texture mapping is also similar to a technique called rasterized bounding volume hierarchies [1288].

Figure 13.17. Woven surface modeled by applying four heightfield textures to a surface and rendered using relief mapping. *(Image courtesy of Fabio Policarpo and Manuel M. Oliveira [1425].)*

Policarpo and Oliveira [1425] use a set of textures on a single quadrilateral to hold the heightfields, and each is rendered in turn. As a simple analogy, any object formed in an injection molding machine can be formed by two heightfields. Each heightfield represents a half of the mold. More elaborate models can be recreated by additional heightfields. Given a particular view of a model, the number of heightfields needed is equal to the maximum number of surfaces found overlapping any pixel. Like spherical billboards, the main purpose of each underlying quadrilateral is to cause evaluation of the heightfield texture by the pixel shader. This method can also be used to create complex geometric details for surfaces; see Figure 13.17.

Beacco et al. [122] use *relief impostors* for crowd scenes. In this representation, the color, normals, and heightfield textures for a model are generated and associated with each face of a box. When a face is rendered, ray marching is performed to find the surface visible at each pixel, if any. A box is associated with each rigid part ("bone") of the model, so that animation can be performed. Skinning is not done, under the assumption that the character is far away. Texturing gives an easy way to reduce the level of detail of the original model. See Figure 13.18.

Gu et al. [616] introduce the *geometry image*. The idea is to transform an irregular mesh into a square image that holds position values. The image itself represents a

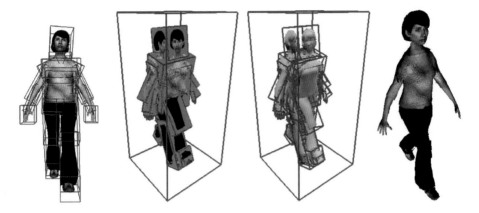

Figure 13.18. Relief impostor. The character's surface model is divided into boxes, and then used to create heightfield, color, and normal textures for each box face. The model is rendered using relief mapping. *(Images courtesy of Alejandro Beacco, copyright © 2016 John Wiley & Sons, Ltd. [122].)*

regular mesh, i.e., the triangles formed are implicit from the grid locations. That is, four neighboring texels in the image form two triangles. The process of forming this image is difficult and rather involved; what is of interest here is the resulting image that encodes the model. The image can clearly be used to generate a mesh. The key feature is that the geometry image can be mipmapped. Different levels of the mipmap pyramid form simpler versions of the model. This blurring of the lines between vertex and texel data, between mesh and image, is a fascinating and tantalizing way to think about modeling. Geometry images have also been used for terrains with feature-preserving maps to model overhangs [852].

At this point in the chapter, we leave behind representing entire polygon objects with images, as the discussion moves to using disconnected, individual samples within particle systems and point clouds.

13.8 Particle Systems

A particle system [1474] is a collection of separate small objects that are set into motion using some algorithm. Applications include simulating fire, smoke, explosions, water flows, whirling galaxies, and other phenomena. As such, a particle system controls animation as well as rendering. Controls for creating, moving, changing, and deleting particles during their lifetimes are part of the system.

Relevant to this chapter is the way that such particles are modeled and rendered. Each particle can be a single pixel or a line segment drawn from the particle's previous location to its current location, but is often represented by a billboard. As mentioned in Section 13.6.2, if the particle is round, then the up vector is irrelevant to its display.

Figure 13.19. Particle systems: a smoke-like simulation (left), fluids (middle), and meteor paths against a galaxy skybox (right). *(WebGL programs "The Spirit" by Edan Kwan, "Fluid Particles" by David Li, and "Southern Delta Aquariids meteor shower" by Ian Webster.)*

In other words, all that is needed is the particle's position to orient it. Figure 13.19 shows some particle system examples. The billboard for each particle can be generated by a geometry shader call, but in practice using the vertex shader to generate sprites may be faster [146]. In addition to an image texture representing a particle, other textures could be included, such as a normal map. Axial billboards can display thicker lines. See Figure 14.18 on page 609 for an example of rain using line segments.

The challenges of rendering transparent objects properly must be addressed if phenomena such as smoke are represented by semitransparent billboard particles. Back-to-front sorting may be needed, but can be expensive. Ericson [439] provides a long set of suggestions for rendering particles efficiently; we list a few here, along with related articles:

- Make smoke from thick cutout textures; avoiding semitransparency means sorting and blending are not needed.

- If semitransparency is needed, consider additive or subtractive blending, which do not need sorting [987, 1971].

- Using a few animated particles can give similar quality and better performance than many static particles.

- To maintain frame rate, use a dynamic cap value on the number of particles rendered.

- Have different particle systems use the same shader to avoid state change costs [987, 1747] (Section 18.4.2).

- A texture atlas or array containing all particle images avoids texture change calls [986].

- Draw smoothly varying particles such as smoke into a lower-resolution buffer and merge [1503], or draw after MSAA is resolved.

This last idea is taken further by Tatarchuk et al. [1747]. They render smoke to a considerably smaller buffer, one-sixteenth size, and use a variance depth map to help compute the cumulative distribution function for the particles' effect. See their presentation for details.

A full sort can be expensive with a large number of particles. Art direction may dictate a rendering order to correctly layer different effects, thus ameliorating the problem. Sorting may not be necessary for small or low-contrast particles. Particles can also sometimes be emitted in a somewhat-sorted order [987]. Weighted blending transparency techniques, which do not need sorting, can be used if the particles are fairly transparent [394, 1180]. More elaborate order-independent transparency systems are also possible. For example, Köhler [920] outlines rendering particles to a nine-layer-deep buffer stored in a texture array, then using a compute shader to perform the sort ordering.

13.8.1 Shading Particles

For shading, it depends on the particle. Emitters such as sparks need no shading and often use additive blending for simplicity. Green [589] describes how fluid systems can be rendered as spherical particles to a depth image, with subsequent steps of blurring the depths, deriving normals from them, and merging the result with the scene. Small particles such as those for dust or smoke can use per-primitive or per-vertex values for shading [44]. However, such lighting can make particles with distinct surfaces look flat. Providing a normal map for the particles can give proper surface normals to illuminate them, but at the cost of additional texture accesses. For round particles using four diverging normals at the four corners of the particle may be sufficient [987, 1650]. Smoke particle systems can have more elaborate models for light scattering [1481]. Radiosity normal mapping (Section 11.5.2) or spherical harmonics [1190, 1503] have also been used to illuminate particles. Tessellation can be used on larger particles, with lighting accumulated at each vertex using the domain shader [225, 816, 1388, 1590].

It is possible to evaluate the lighting per vertex and interpolate over the particle quad [44]. This is fast but produces low quality for large particles, where vertices that are far apart can miss the contribution of small lights. One solution is to shade a particle on a per-pixel basis, but at a lower resolution than used for the final image. To this end, each visible particle allocates a tile in a light-map texture [384, 1682]. The resolution of each tile can be adjusted according to the particle size on screen, e.g., between 1×1 and 32×32 according to the projected area on screen. Once tiles have been allocated, particles are rendered for each tile, writing the world position for the pixel into a secondary texture. A compute shader is then dispatched to evaluate the radiance reaching each of the positions read from the secondary texture. Radiance is gathered by sampling the light sources in the scene, using an acceleration structure in order to evaluate only potentially contributing sources, as described in Chapter 20. The resulting radiance can then be written into the light-map texture as a simple color or as spherical harmonics. When each particle is finally rendered on screen, the lighting is applied by mapping each tile over the particle quad and sampling the radiance per pixel using a texture fetch.

It is also possible to apply the same principle by allocating a tile per emitter [1538]. In this case, having a deep light-map texture will help give volume to the lighting for effects with many particles. It is worth noting that, due to the flat nature of particles that are usually aligned with the viewer, each lighting model presented in this section will produce visible shimmering artifacts if the viewpoint were to rotate around any particle emitter.

In parallel to lighting, the generation of volumetric shadows of particles and self-shadowing requires special care. For receiving shadows from other occluders, small particles can often be tested against the shadow map at just their vertices, instead of every pixel. Because particles are scattered points rendered as simple camera-facing quads, shadow casting onto other objects cannot be achieved using ray marching through a shadow map. However, it is possible to use splatting approaches (Section 13.9). In order to cast shadows on other scene elements from the sun, particles can be splatted into a texture, multiplying their per-pixel transmittance $T_r = 1 - \alpha$ in a buffer first cleared to 1. The texture can consist of a single channel for grayscale or three channels for colored transmittance. These textures, following shadow cascade levels, are applied to the scene by multiplying this transmittance with the visibility resulting from the regular opaque shadow cascade, as presented in Section 7.4. This technique effectively provides a single layer of transparent shadow [44]. The only drawback of this technique is that particles can incorrectly cast shadows back onto opaque elements present between the particles and the sun. This is usually avoided by careful level design.

In order to achieve self-shadowing for particles, more advanced techniques must be used, such as *Fourier opacity mapping* (FOM) [816]. See Figure 13.20. Particles are first rendered from the light's point of view, effectively adding their contribution into the transmittance function represented as Fourier coefficients into the opacity map. When rendering particles from this point of view, it is possible to reconstruct the transmittance signal by sampling the opacity map from the Fourier coefficients. This representation works well for expressing smooth transmittance functions. However, since it uses the Fourier basis with a limited number of coefficients to maintain texture memory requirements, it is subject to ringing for large variations in transmittance. This can result in incorrect bright or dark areas on the rendered particle quad. FOM is a great fit for particles, but other approaches, having different pros and cons, can also be used. These include the adaptive volumetric shadow maps [1531] described in Section 14.3.2 (similar to deep shadow maps [1066]), GPU optimized particle shadow maps [120] (similar to opacity shadow maps [894], but only for camera-facing particles, so it will not work for ribbons or motion-stretched particles), and transmittance function mapping [341] (similar to FOM).

Another approach is to voxelize particles in volumes containing extinction coefficients σ_t [742]. These volumes can be positioned around the camera similar to a clipmap [1739]. This approach is a way to unify the evaluation of volumetric shad-

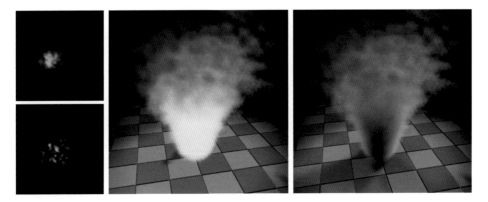

Figure 13.20. Particles casting volumetric shadows using Fourier opacity mapping. On the left, the Fourier opacity map containing the function coefficient from the point of view of one of the spotlights. In the middle, particles are rendered without shadows. On the right, volumetric shadows are cast on particles and other opaque surfaces of the scene. *(Images courtesy of NVIDIA [816].)*

ows from particles and participating media at the same time, since they can both be voxelized in these common volumes. Generating a single deep shadow map [894] that stores T_r per voxel from these "extinction volumes" will automatically lead to volumetric shadows cast from both sources. There are a number of resulting interactions: Particles and participating media can cast shadows on each other, as well as self-shadow; see Figure 14.21 on page 613. The resulting quality is tied to the voxel size, which, to achieve real-time performance, will likely be large. This will result in coarse but visually soft volumetric shadows. See Section 14.3.2 for more details.

13.8.2 Particle Simulation

Efficient and convincing approximation of physical processes using particles is a broad topic beyond the intent of this book, so we will refer you to a few resources. GPUs can generate animation paths for sprites and even perform collision detection. Stream output can control the birth and death of particles. This is done by storing results in a vertex buffer and updating this buffer each frame on the GPU [522, 700]. If unordered access view buffers are available, the particle system can be entirely GPU-based, controlled by the vertex shader [146, 1503, 1911].

Van der Burg's article [211] and Latta's overviews [986, 987] form a quick introduction to the basics of simulation. Bridson's book on fluid simulation for computer graphics [197] discusses theory in depth, including physically based techniques for simulating various forms of water, smoke, and fire. Several practitioners have presented talks on particle systems in interactive renderers. Whitley [1879] goes into details about the particle system developed for *Destiny 2*. See Figure 13.21 for an example image. Evans and Kirczenow [445] discuss their implementation of a fluid-flow algorithm from Bridson's text. Mittring [1229] gives brief details about how particles are

Figure 13.21. Example of particle systems used in the game *Destiny 2*. *(Image ©2017 Bungie, Inc. all rights reserved.)*

controlled in Unreal Engine 4. Vainio [1808] delves into the design and rendering of particle effects for the game *inFAMOUS Second Son*. Wronski [1911] presents a system for generating and rendering rain efficiently. Gjøl and Svendsen [539] discuss smoke and fire effects, along with many other sample-based techniques. Thomas [1767] runs through a compute-shader-based particle simulation system that includes collision detection, transparency sorting, and efficient tile-based rendering. Xiao et al. [1936] present an interactive physical fluid simulator that also computes the isosurface for display. Skillman and Demoreuille [1650] run through their particle system and other image-based effects used to turn the volume up to eleven for the game *Brütal Legend*.

13.9 Point Rendering

In 1985, Levoy and Whitted wrote a pioneering technical report [1033] in which they suggested the use of points as a new primitive to use to render everything. The general idea is to represent a surface using a large set of points and render these. In a subsequent pass, Gaussian filtering is performed to fill in gaps between rendered points. The radius of the Gaussian filter depends on the density of points on the surface, and on the projected density on the screen. Levoy and Whitted implemented this system on a VAX-11/780.

However, it was not until about 15 years later that point-based rendering again became of interest. Two reasons for this resurgence were that computing power reached a level where point-based rendering was possible at interactive rates, and that extremely detailed models obtained from laser range scanners became available [1035]. Since then, a wide range of RGB-D (depth) devices that detect distances have become available, from aerial LIDAR (LIght Detection And Ranging) [779] instruments for terrain mapping, down to Microsoft Kinect sensors, iPhone TrueDepth camera, and Google's Tango devices for short-range data capture. LIDAR systems on self-driving cars can record millions of points per second. Two-dimensional images processed by photogrammetry or other computational photography techniques also are used to provide data sets. The raw output of these various technologies is a set of three-dimensional points with additional data, typically an intensity or color. Additional classification data may also be available, e.g., whether a point is from a building or road surface [37]. These *point clouds* can be manipulated and rendered in a variety of ways.

Such models are initially represented as unconnected three-dimensional points. See Berger et al. [137] for an in-depth overview of point cloud filtering techniques and methods of turning these into meshes. Kotfis and Cozzi [930] present an approach for processing, voxelizing, and rendering these voxelizations at interactive rates. Here we discuss techniques to directly render point cloud data.

QSplat [1519] was an influential point-based renderer first released in 2000. It uses a hierarchy of spheres to represent a model. The nodes in this tree are compressed to allow rendering scenes consisting of several hundred million points. A point is rendered as a shape with a radius, called a *splat*. Different splat shapes that can be used are squares, opaque circles, and fuzzy circles. In other words, splats are particles, though rendered with the intent of representing a continuous surface. See Figure 13.22 for an example. Rendering may stop at any level in the tree. The nodes at that level are rendered as splats with the same radius as the node's sphere. Therefore, the bounding sphere hierarchy is constructed so that no holes are visible at any level. Since traversal of the tree can stop at any level, interactive frame rates can be obtained by stopping the traversal when time runs out. When the user stops moving around, the quality of the rendering can be refined repeatedly until the leaves of the hierarchy are reached.

Around the same time, Pfister et al. [1409] presented the *surfel*—a surface element. It is also a point-based primitive, one that is meant to represent a part of an object's surface and so always includes a normal. An octree (Section 19.1.3) is used to store the sampled surfels: position, normal, and filtered texels. During rendering, the surfels are projected onto the screen and then a visibility splatting algorithm is used to fill in any holes created. The QSplat and surfels papers identify and address some of the key concerns of point cloud systems: managing data set size and rendering convincing surfaces from a given set of points.

QSplat uses a hierarchy, but one that is subdivided down to the level of single points, with inner, parent nodes being bounding spheres, each containing a point that is the average of its children. Gobbetti and Marton [546] introduce layered point clouds, a hierarchical structure that maps better to the GPU and does not create artificial "average" data points. Each inner and child node contains about the same

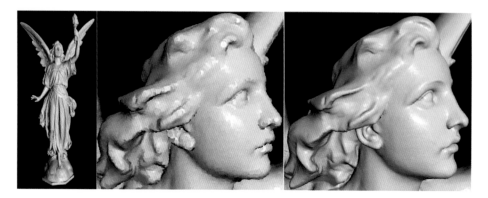

Figure 13.22. These models were rendered with point-based rendering, using circular splats. The left image shows the full model of an angel named Lucy, with 10 million vertices. However, only about 3 million splats were used in the rendering. The middle and right images zoom in on the head. The middle image used about 40,000 splats during rendering. When the viewer stopped moving, the result converged to the image shown to the right, with 600,000 splats. *(Images generated by the QSplat program by Szymon Rusinkiewicz. The model of Lucy was created by the Stanford Graphics Laboratory.)*

number of points, call it n, which are rendered as a set in a single API call. We form the root node by taking n points from the entire set, as a rough representation of the model. Choosing a set in which the distance between points is roughly the same gives a better result than random selection [1583]. Differences in normals or colors can also be used for cluster selection [570]. The remaining points are divided spatially into two child nodes. Repeat the process at each of these nodes, selecting n representative points and dividing the rest into two subsets. This selection and subdivision continues until there are n or fewer points per child. See Figure 13.23. The work by Botsch et al. [180] is a good example of the state of the art, a GPU-accelerated technique that uses deferred shading (Section 20.1) and high-quality filtering. During display, visible

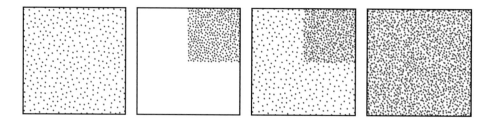

Figure 13.23. Layered point clouds. On the left, the root node contains a sparse subset taken from the children's data. A child node is shown next, then shown combined with the points in the root—note how the child's area is more filled in. Rightmost is the full point cloud, root and all children. *(Images from documentation for Potree [1583], open-source software, potree.org. Figure after Adorjan [12].)*

nodes are loaded and rendered until some limit is met. A node's relative screen size can be used to determine how important the point set is to load, and can provide an estimate of the size of the billboards rendered. By not introducing new points for the parent nodes, memory usage is proportional to the number of points stored. A drawback of this scheme is that, when zoomed in on a single child node, all parent nodes must be sent down the pipeline, even if only a few points are visible in each.

In current point cloud rendering systems, data sets can be huge, consisting of hundreds of billions of points. Because such sets cannot be fully loaded into memory, let alone displayed at interactive rates, a hierarchical structure is used in almost every point cloud rendering system for loading and display. The scheme used can be influenced by the data, e.g., a quadtree is generally a better fit for terrain than an octree. There has been a considerable amount of research on efficient creation and traversal of point cloud data structures. Scheiblauer [1553] provides a summary of research in this area, as well as on surface reconstruction techniques and other algorithms. Adorjan [12] gives an overview of several systems, with a focus on sharing building point clouds generated by photogrammetry.

In theory, splats could be provided individual normals and radii to define a surface. In practice such data takes too much memory and is available only after considerable preprocessing efforts, so billboards of a fixed radius are commonly used. Properly rendering semitransparent splat billboards for the points can be both expensive and artifact-laden, due to sorting and blending costs. Opaque billboards—squares or cutout circles—are often used to maintain interactivity and quality. See Figure 13.24.

If points have no normals, then various techniques to provide shading can be brought to bear. One image-based approach is to compute some form of screen-space ambient occlusion (Section 11.3.6). Typically, all points are first rendered to a depth buffer, with a wide enough radius to form a continuous surface. In the subsequent rendering pass, each point's shade is darkened proportionally to the number of neighboring pixels closer to the viewer. *Eye-dome lighting* (EDL) can further accentuate surface details [1583]. EDL works by examining neighboring pixels' screen depths and finding those closer to the viewer than the current pixel. For each such neighbor, the difference in depth with the current pixel is computed and summed. The average of these differences, negated, is then multiplied by a strength factor and used as an input to the exponential function `exp`. See Figure 13.25.

If each point has a color or intensity along with it, the illumination is already baked in, so can be displayed directly, though glossy or reflective objects will not respond to changes in view. Additional non-graphical attributes, such as object type or elevation, can also be used to display the points. We have touched on only the basics of managing and rendering point clouds. Schuetz [1583] discusses various rendering techniques and provides implementation details, as well as a high-quality open-source system.

Point cloud data can be combined with other data sources. For example, the Cesium program can combine point clouds with high-resolution terrain, images, vector map data, and models generated from photogrammetry. Another scan-related tech-

Figure 13.24. Five million points are selected to render a small town data set of 145 million points. Edges are enhanced by detecting depth differences. Gaps appear where the data are sparse or billboard radius is too small. The row at the bottom shows the selected area when the image budget is 500 thousand, 1 million, and 5 million points, respectively. *(Images generated using Potree [1583], open-source software, potree.org. Model of Retz, Austria, courtesy of RIEGL, riegl.com.)*

Figure 13.25. On the left, points with normals rendered in a single pass. In the middle, a screen-space ambient occlusion rendering of a point cloud without normals; on the right, eye-dome lighting for the same. The last two methods each need to first perform a pass to establish the depths in the image. *(Images generated using CloudCompare, GPL software, cloudcompare.org. Footprint model courtesy of Eugene Liscio.)*

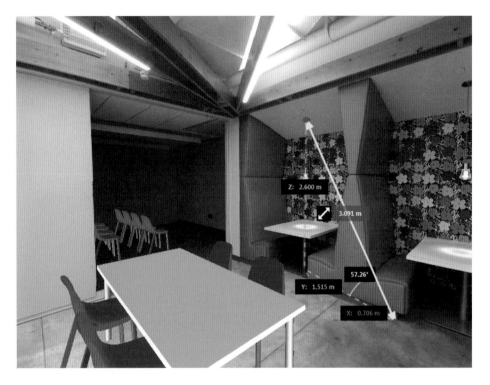

Figure 13.26. An environment with depth available at each pixel. For a fixed view location (but not direction), the user can take measurements between world-space locations and position virtual objects, with occlusion handled properly. *(Images generated using Autodesk ReCap Pro, courtesy of Autodesk, Inc.)*

nique is to capture an environment from a point of view into a skybox, saving both color and depth information, so making the scene capture have a physical presence. For example, the user can add synthetic models into the scene and have them properly merge with this type of skybox, since depths are available for each point in the surrounding image. See Figure 13.26.

The state of the art has progressed considerably, and such techniques are seeing use outside of the field of data capture and display. As an example, we give a brief summary of an experimental point-based rendering system, presented by Evans [446], for the game *Dreams*. Each model is represented by a bounding volume hierarchy (BVH) of clusters, where each cluster is 256 points. The points are generated from signed distance functions (Section 17.3). For level of detail support, a separate BVH, clusters, and points are generated for each level of detail. To transition from high to low detail, the number of points in the higher-density child clusters is reduced stochastically down to 25%, and then the low-detail parent cluster is swapped in. The renderer is based on a compute shader, which splats the points to a framebuffer using atomics to avoid collisions. It implements several techniques, such as stochastic transparency, depth of field (using jittered splats based on the circle of confusion), ambient occlusion, and imperfect shadow maps [1498]. To smooth out artifacts, temporal antialiasing (Section 5.4.2) is performed.

Point clouds represent arbitrary locations in space, and so can be challenging to render, as the gaps between points are often not known or easily available. This problem and other areas of research related to point clouds are surveyed by Kobbelt and Botsch [916]. To conclude this chapter, we turn to a non-polygonal representation where the distance between a sample and its neighbors is always the same.

13.10 Voxels

Just as a pixel is a "picture element" and a texel is a "texture element," a *voxel* is a "volume element." Each voxel represents a volume of space, typically a cube, in a uniform three-dimensional grid. Voxels are the traditional way to store volumetric data, and can represent objects ranging from smoke to 3D-printed models, from bone scans to terrain representations. A single bit can be stored, representing whether the center of the voxel is inside or outside an object. For medical applications, a density or opacity and perhaps a rate of volumetric flow may be available. A color, normal, signed distance, or other values can also be stored to facilitate rendering. No position information is needed per voxel, since the index in the grid determines its location.

13.10.1 Applications

A voxel representation of a model can be used for many different purposes. A regular grid of data lends itself to all sorts of operations having to do with the full object, not just its surface. For example, the volume of an object represented by voxels is simply the sum of the voxels inside of it. The grid's regular structure and a voxel's well-defined local neighborhood mean phenomena such as smoke, erosion, or cloud formation can be simulated by cellular automata or other algorithms. Finite element analysis makes use of voxels to determine an object's tensile strength. Sculpting or carving a model becomes a matter of subtracting voxels. Conversely, building elaborate models can be done by placing a polygonal model into the voxel grid and determining which voxels it overlaps. Such constructive solid geometry modeling operations are efficient, predictable, and guaranteed to work, compared to a more traditional polygonal workflow that must handle singularities and precision problems. Voxel-based systems such as OpenVDB [1249, 1336] and NVIDIA GVDB Voxels [752, 753] are used in film production, scientific and medical visualization, 3D printing, and other applications. See Figure 13.27.

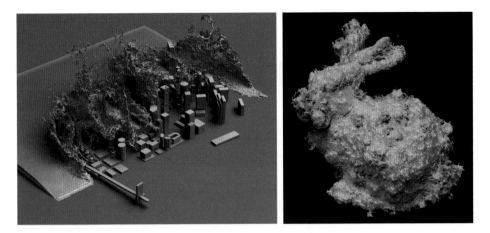

Figure 13.27. Voxel applications. On the left, a fluid simulation is computed directly on a sparse voxel grid and rendered as a volume. On the right, a polygonal bunny model is voxelized into a signed distance field, which is then perturbed with a noise function, and an isosurface is rendered. *(Left image courtesy of NVIDIA® based on research by Wu et al. [1925]. Right image rendered with NVIDIA® GVDB Voxels, courtesy of NVIDIA Corporation.)*

13.10.2 Voxel Storage

Storage of voxels has significant memory requirements, as the data grows according to $O(n^3)$ with the voxel resolution. For example, a voxel grid with a resolution of 1000 in each dimension yields a billion locations. Voxel-based games such as *Minecraft* can have huge worlds. In that game, data are streamed in as chunks of $16 \times 16 \times 256$ voxels each, out to some radius around each player. Each voxel stores an identifier and additional orientation or style data. Every block type then has its own polygonal representation, whether it is a solid chunk of stone displayed using a cube, a semitransparent window using a texture with alpha, or grass represented by a pair of cutout billboards. See Figure 12.10 on page 529 and Figure 19.19 on 842 for examples.

Data stored in voxel grids usually have much coherence, as neighboring locations are likely to have the same or similar values. Depending on the data source, a vast majority of the grid may be empty, which is referred to as a sparse volume. Both coherence and sparseness lead to compact representations. An octree (Section 19.1.3), for example, could be imposed on the grid. At the lowest octree level, each $2 \times 2 \times 2$ set of voxel samples may all be the same, which can be noted in the octree and the voxels discarded. Similarity can be detected on up the tree, and the identical child octree nodes discarded. Only where data differ do they need to be stored. This *sparse voxel octree* (SVO) representation [87, 304, 308, 706] leads to natural level of detail representation, a three-dimensional volumetric equivalent of a mipmap. See Figures 13.28 and 13.29. Laine and Karras [963] provide copious implementation details and various extensions for the SVO data structure.

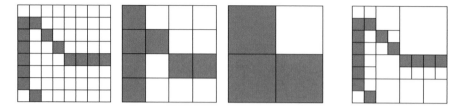

Figure 13.28. Sparse voxel octree, in two-dimensional form. Given a set of voxels on the left, we note which parent nodes have any voxels in them, on up the tree. On the right is a visualization of the final octree, showing the deepest node stored for each grid location. *(Figure after Laine and Karras [963].)*

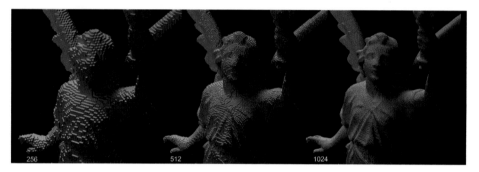

Figure 13.29. Voxel ray tracing at different levels of detail. From left to right, the resolution is 256, 512, and 1024 along each edge of the voxel grid containing the model. *(Images rendered with Optix and NVIDIA® GVDB Voxels, courtesy of NVIDIA Corporation [753].)*

13.10.3 Generation of Voxels

The input to a voxel model can come from a variety of sources. For example, many scanning devices generate data points at arbitrary locations. The GPU can accelerate *voxelization*, the process of turning a point cloud [930], polygonal mesh, or other representation into a set of voxels. For meshes, one quick but rough method from Karabassi et al. [859] is to render the object from six orthographic views: top, bottom, and the four sides. Each view generates a depth buffer, so each pixel holds where the first visible voxel is from that direction. If a voxel's location is beyond the depth stored in each of the six buffers, it is not visible and so is marked as being inside the object. This method will miss any features that cannot be seen in any of the six views, causing some voxels to improperly be marked as inside. Still, for simple models this method can suffice.

Inspired by visual hulls [1139], Loop et al. [1071] use an even simpler system for creating voxelizations of people in the real world. A set of images of a person are captured and the silhouettes extracted. Each silhouette is used to carve away a set of voxels given its camera location—only pixels where you can see the person will have voxels associated with them.

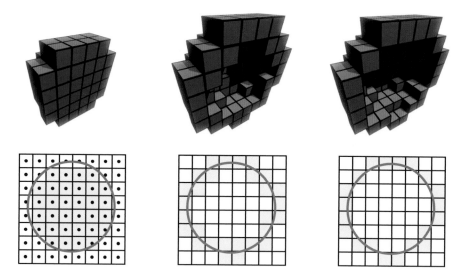

Figure 13.30. A sphere is voxelized three different ways and its cross section is shown. On the left is a solid voxelization, determined by testing the center of each voxel against the sphere. In the middle is a conservative voxelization, where any voxel touched by the sphere's surface is selected. This surface is called a 26-separating voxelization, in which no interior voxel is next to an exterior voxel in its $3 \times 3 \times 3$ neighborhood. In other words, interior and exterior voxels never share a face, edge, or vertex. On the right is a 6-separating voxelization, in which edges and corners can be shared between interior and exterior voxels. *(Figure after Schwarz and Seidel [1594].)*

Voxel grids can also be created from a collection of images, such as with medical image devices that generate slices that are then stacked up. Along the same lines, mesh models can be rendered slice by slice and the voxels found inside the model are duly recorded. The near and far planes are adjusted to bound each slice, which is examined for content. Eisemann and Décoret [409] introduce the idea of a *slicemap*, where the 32-bit target is instead thought of as 32 separate depths, each with a bit flag. The depth of a triangle rendered to this voxel grid is converted to its bit equivalent and stored. The 32 layers can then be rendered in a rendering pass, with more voxel layers available for the pass if wider-channel image formats and multiple render targets are used. Forest et al. [480] give implementation details, noting that on modern GPUs up to 1024 layers can be rendered in a single pass. Note that this slicing algorithm identifies just the surface of the model, its *boundary representation*. The six-views algorithm above also identifies (though sometimes miscategorizes) voxels that are fully inside the model. See Figure 13.30 for three common types of voxelization. Laine [964] provides a thorough treatment of terminology, various voxelization types, and the issues involved in generating and using them.

More efficient voxelization is possible with new functionality available in modern GPUs. Schwarz and Seidel [1594, 1595] and Pantaleoni [1350] present voxelization systems using compute shaders, which offer the ability to directly build an SVO. Crassin and Green [306, 307] describe their open-source system for regular-grid voxelization, which leverages image load/store operations available starting in OpenGL 4.2. These operations allow random read and write access to texture memory. By using conservative rasterization (Section 23.1.2) to determine all triangles overlapping a voxel, their algorithm efficiently computes voxel occupancy, along with an average color and normal. They can also create an SVO with this method, building from the top down and voxelizing only non-empty nodes as they descend, then populating the structure using bottom-up filtering mipmap creation. Schwarz [1595] gives implementation details for both rasterization and compute kernel voxelization systems, explaining the characteristics of each. Rauwendaal and Bailey [1466] include source code for their hybrid system. They provide performance analysis of parallelized voxelization schemes and details for the proper use of conservative rasterization to avoid false positives. Takeshige [1737] discusses how MSAA can be a viable alternative to conservative rasterization, if a small amount of error is acceptable. Baert et al. [87] present an algorithm for creating SVOs that can efficiently run out-of-core, that is, can voxelize a scene to a high precision without needing the whole model to be resident in memory.

Given the large amount of processing needed to voxelize a scene, dynamic objects—those moving or otherwise animated—are a challenge for voxel-based systems. Gaitatzes and Papaioannou [510] tackle this task by progressively updating their voxel representation of the scene. They use the rendering results from the scene camera and any shadow maps generated to clear and set voxels. Voxels are tested against the depth buffers, with those that are found to be closer than the recorded z-depths being cleared. Depth locations in the buffers are then treated as a set of points and transformed to world space. These points' corresponding voxels are determined and set, if not marked before. This clear-and-set process is view-dependent, meaning that parts of the scene that no camera currently sees are effectively unknown and so can be sources of error. However, this fast approximate method makes computing voxel-based global illumination effects practical to perform at interactive rates for dynamic environments (Section 11.5.6).

13.10.4 Rendering

Voxel data are stored in a three-dimensional array, which can also be thought of as, and indeed stored as, a three-dimensional texture. Such data can be displayed in any number of ways. The next chapter discusses ways to visualize voxel data that are semitransparent, such as fog, or where a slicing plane is positioned to examine the data set, such as an ultrasound image. Here we will focus on rendering voxel data representing solid objects.

Imagine the simplest volume representation, where each voxel contains a bit noting whether it is inside or outside an object. There are a few common ways to display such data [1094]. One method is to directly ray-cast the volume [752, 753, 1908] to

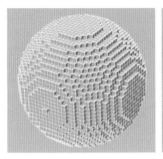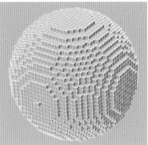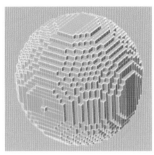

Figure 13.31. Cube culling. On the left, the 17,074 voxel solid sphere is formed of 102,444 quadrilaterals, six per voxel. In the middle, the two quadrilaterals between neighboring solid voxels are removed, reducing the count to 4,770. The look is the same as on left, as the outer shell is untouched. On the right, a fast greedy algorithm merges faces to form larger rectangles, giving 2,100 quadrilaterals. *(Images from Mikola Lysenko's culling program [1094].)*

determine the nearest hit face of each cube. Another technique is to convert the voxel cubes to a set of polygons. Though rendering using a mesh will be fast, this incurs additional cost during voxelization, and is best suited to static volumes. If each voxel's cube is to be displayed as opaque, then we can cull out any faces where two cubes are adjacent, since the shared square between them is not visible. This process leaves us with a hull of squares, hollow on the inside. Simplification techniques (Section 16.5) can reduce the polygon count further. See Figure 13.31.

Shading this set of cube faces is unconvincing for voxels representing curved surfaces. A common alternative to shading the cubes is to create a smoother mesh surface by using an algorithm such as *marching cubes* [558, 1077]. This process is called *surface extraction* or *polygonalization* (a.k.a. *polygonization*). Instead of treating each voxel as a box, we think of it as a point sample. We can then form a cube using the eight neighboring samples in a $2 \times 2 \times 2$ pattern to form the corners. The states of these eight corners can define a surface passing through the cube. For example, if the top four corners of the cube are outside and the bottom four inside, a horizontal square dividing the cube in half is a good guess for the shape of the surface. One corner outside and the rest inside yields a triangle formed by the midpoints of the three cube edges connected to the outside corner. See Figure 13.32. This process of turning a set of cube corners into a corresponding polygonal mesh is efficient, as the eight corner bits can be converted to an index from 0 to 255, which is used to access a table that specifies the number and locations of the triangles for each possible configuration.

Other methods to render voxels, such as level sets [636], are better suited to smooth, curved surfaces. Imagine that each voxel stores the distance to the surface of the object being represented, a positive value for inside and negative for outside. We can use these data to adjust the vertex locations of the mesh formed to more accurately represent the surface, as shown on the right in Figure 13.32. Alternately, we could

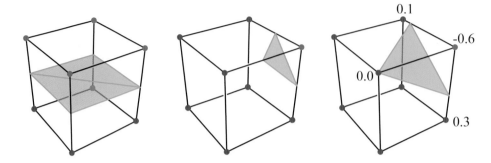

Figure 13.32. Marching cubes. On the left, the four bottom corners are voxel centers inside the object, so a horizontal square of two triangles is formed between the bottom and the top four corners. In the middle, one corner is outside, so a triangle is formed. On the right, if signed distance values are stored at the corners, then we can interpolate the triangle vertices to be at 0.0 along each edge. Note that other cubes sharing a given edge will have a vertex at the same location along that edge, to ensure that the surface has no cracks.

directly ray-trace the level set with an isovalue of zero. This technique is called *level-set rendering* [1249]. It is particularly good at representing the surface and normals of a curved model without any additional voxel attributes.

Voxel data representing differences in density can be visualized in different ways by deciding what forms a surface. For example, some given density may give a good representation of a kidney, another density could show any kidney stones present. Choosing a density value defines an *isosurface*, a set of locations with the same value. Being able to vary this value is particularly useful for scientific visualization. Directly ray tracing any isosurface value is a generalization of level-set ray tracing, where the target value is always zero. Alternatively, one can extract the isosurface and convert it to a polygonal model.

In 2008 Olick [1323] gave an influential talk about how a sparse voxel representation can be rendered directly with ray casting, inspiring further work. Testing rays against regularized voxels is well suited to a GPU implementation, and can be done at interactive frame rates. Many researchers have explored this area of rendering. For an introduction to the subject, start with Crassin's PhD thesis [304] and SIGGRAPH presentation [308], which cover the advantages of voxel-based methods. Crassin exploits the mipmap-like nature of the data by using *cone tracing*. The general idea is to use the regularity and well-defined locality property of voxel representations to define prefiltering schemes for geometry and shading properties, allowing the use of linear filters. A single ray is traced through the scene but is able to gather an approximation of the visibility through a cone emanating from its start point. As the ray moves through space, its radius of interest grows, which means that the voxel hierarchy is sampled higher up the chain, similar to how a mipmap is sampled higher up as more texels fall inside a single pixel. This type of sampling can rapidly compute

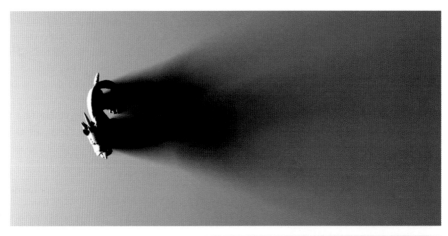

Figure 13.33. Cone-traced shadows. Top: a ray-traced spherical area light rendered in Maya in 20 seconds. Bottom: voxelization and cone tracing for the same scene took ~20 ms. The model is rendered with polygons, with the voxelized version used for shadow computations. *(Images courtesy of Crytek [865].)*

soft shadows and depth of field, for example, as these effects can be decomposed into cone-tracing problems. Area sampling can be valuable for other processes, such as antialiasing and properly filtering varying surface normals. Heitz and Neyret [706] describe previous work and present a new data structure for use with cone tracing that improves visibility calculation results. Kasyan [865] uses voxel cone tracing for area lights, discussing sources of error. A comparison is shown in Figure 13.33. See Figure 7.33 on page 264 for a final result. Cone tracing's use for computing global illumination effects is discussed and illustrated in Section 11.5.7.

Recent trends explore structures beyond octrees on the GPU. A key drawback of octrees is that operations such as ray tracing require a large number of tree traversal hops and so require storage of a significant number of intermediate nodes. Hoetzlein [752] shows that GPU ray tracing of VDB trees, a hierarchy of grids, can achieve significant performance gains over octrees, and are better suited to dynamic changes in volume data. Fogal et al. [477] demonstrate that index tables, rather than octrees, can be used to render large volumes in real-time using a two-pass approach. The first pass identifies visible sub-regions (bricks), and streams in those regions from disk. The second pass renders the regions currently resident in memory. A thorough survey of large-scale volumetric rendering is provided by Beyer et al. [138].

13.10.5   Other Topics

Surface extraction is commonly used to visualize implicit surfaces (Section 17.3), for example. There are different forms of the basic algorithm and some subtleties to how meshes are formed. For example, if every other corner for a cube is found to be inside, should these corners be joined together in the polygonal mesh formed, or kept separate? See the article by de Araújo et al. [67] for a survey of polygonalization techniques for implicit surfaces. Austin [85] runs through the pros and cons of a variety of general polygonalization schemes, finding cubical marching squares to have the most desirable properties.

Other solutions than full polygonalization are possible when using ray casting for rendering. For example, Laine and Karras [963] attach a set of parallel planes to each voxel that approximate the surface, then use a post-process blur to mask discontinuities between voxels. Heitz and Neyret [706] access the signed distance in a linearly filterable representation that permits reconstructing plane equations and determining coverage in a given direction for any spatial location and resolution.

Eisemann and Décoret [409] show how a voxel representation can be used to perform deep shadow mapping (Section 7.8), for situations where semitransparent overlapping surfaces cast shadows. As Kämpe, Sintorn, and others show [850, 1647], another advantage of a voxelized scene is that shadow rays for all lights can be tested using this one representation, versus generating a shadow map for each light source. Compared to directly visible surface rendering, the eye is more forgiving of small errors in secondary effects such as shadows and indirect illumination, and much less voxel data are needed for these tasks. When only occupancy of a voxel is tracked, there can be extremely high self-similarity among many sparse voxel nodes [849, 1817]. For example, a wall will form sets of voxels that are identical over several levels. This means that various nodes and entire sub-trees in a tree are the same, and so we can use a single instance for such nodes and store them in what is called a *directed acyclic graph* (Section 19.1.5). Doing so often leads to vast reductions in the amount of memory needed per voxel-structure.

Further Reading and Resources

Image-based rendering, light fields, computational photography, and many other topics are discussed in Szeliski's *Computer Vision: Algorithms and Applications* [1729]. See our website realtimerendering.com for a link to the free electronic version of this worthwhile volume. A wide range of acceleration techniques taking advantage of limitations in our visual perceptual system is discussed by Weier et al. [1864] in their state-of-the-art report. Dietrich et al. [352] provide an overview of image-based techniques in the sidebars of their report on massive model rendering.

We have touched upon only a few of the ways images, particles, and other non-polygonal methods are used to simulate natural phenomena. See the referenced articles for more examples and details. A few articles discuss a wide range of techniques. The survey of crowd rendering techniques by Beacco et al. [122] discusses many variations on impostors, level of detail methods, and much else. Gjøl and Svendsen's presentation [539] gives image-based sampling and filtering techniques for a wide range of effects, including bloom, len flares, water effects, reflections, fog, fire, and smoke.

Chapter 14

Volumetric and Translucency Rendering

"Those you wish should look farthest away you must make proportionately bluer; thus, if one is to be five times as distant, make it five times bluer."
—Leonardo Da Vinci

Participating media is the term used to describe volumes filled with particles. As we can tell by the name, they are media that participate in light transport, in other words they affect light that passes through them via scattering or absorption. When rendering virtual worlds, we usually focus on the solid surfaces, simple yet complex. These surfaces appear opaque because they are defined by light bouncing off of dense participating media, e.g., a dielectric or metal typically modeled using a BRDF. Less dense well-known media are water, fog, steam, or even air, composed of sparse molecules. Depending on its composition, a medium will interact differently with light traveling through it and bouncing off its particles, an event typically referred to as *light scattering*. The density of particles can be homogeneous (uniform), as in the case of air or water. Or it could be heterogeneous (nonuniform, varying with location in space), as in the case of clouds or steam. Some dense materials often rendered as solid surfaces exhibit high levels of light scattering, such as skin or candle wax. As shown in Section 9.1, diffuse surface shading models are the result of light scattering on a microscopic level. Everything is scattering.

14.1   Light Scattering Theory

In this section, we will describe the simulation and rendering of light in participating media. This is a quantitative treatment of the physical phenomena, scattering and absorption, which were discussed in Sections 9.1.1 and 9.1.2. The radiative transfer equation is described by numerous authors [479, 743, 818, 1413] in the context of path tracing with multiple scattering. Here we will focus on *single scattering* and build a good intuition about how it works. Single scattering considers only one bounce of light

Symbol	Description	Unit
σ_a	Absorption coefficient	m^{-1}
σ_s	Scattering coefficient	m^{-1}
σ_t	Extinction coefficient	m^{-1}
ρ	Albedo	unitless
p	Phase function	sr^{-1}

Table 14.1. Notation used for scattering and participating media. Each of these parameters can depend on the wavelength (i.e., RGB) to achieve colored light absorption or scattering. The units of the phase function are inverse steradians (Section 8.1.1).

on the particles that constitute the participating media. Multiple scattering tracks many bounces per light path and so is much more complex [243, 479]. Results with and without multiple scattering can be seen in Figure 14.51 on page 646. Symbols and units used to represent the participating media properties in scattering equations are presented in Table 14.1. Note that many of the quantities in this chapter, such as σ_a, σ_s, σ_t, p, ρ, v, and T_r are wavelength-dependent, which in practice means that they are RGB quantities.

14.1.1 Participating Media Material

There are four types of events that can affect the amount of radiance propagating along a ray through a medium. These are illustrated in Figure 14.1 and summarized as:

- **Absorption** (function of σ_a)—Photons are absorbed by the medium's matter and transformed into heat or other forms of energy.

- **Out-scattering** (function of σ_s)—Photons are scattered away by bouncing off particles in the medium matter. This will happen according to the phase function p describing the distribution of light bounce directions.

- **Emission**—Light can be emitted when media reaches a high heat, e.g., a fire's black-body radiation. For more details about emission, please refer to the course notes by Fong et al. [479].

- **In-scattering** (function of σ_s)—Photons from any direction can scatter into the current light path after bouncing off particles and contribute to the final radiance. The amount of light in-scattered from a given direction also depends on the phase function p for that light direction.

To sum up, adding photons to a path is a function of in-scattering σ_s and emission. Removing photons is a function of *extinction* $\sigma_t = \sigma_a + \sigma_s$, representing both absorption and out-scattering. As explained by the *radiative transfer equation*, the

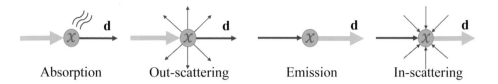

Figure 14.1. Different events change the radiance along a direction **d** in participating media.

set of coefficients represents the derivative of radiance at position **x** and toward direction **v** relative to $L(\mathbf{x}, \mathbf{v})$. That is why these coefficients' values are all in the range $[0, +\infty]$. See the notes by Fong et al. [479] for details. The scattering and absorption coefficients determine the medium's albedo ρ, defined as

$$\rho = \frac{\sigma_s}{\sigma_s + \sigma_a} = \frac{\sigma_s}{\sigma_t}, \tag{14.1}$$

which represents the importance of scattering relative to absorption in a medium for each visible spectrum range considered, i.e., the overall reflectiveness of the medium. The value of ρ is within the range $[0, 1]$. A value close to 0 indicates that most of the light is absorbed, resulting in a murky medium, such as dark exhaust smoke. A value close to 1 indicates that most of the light is scattered instead of being absorbed, resulting in a brighter medium, such as air, clouds, or the earth's atmosphere.

As discussed in Section 9.1.2, the appearance of a medium is a combination of its scattering and absorption properties. Coefficient values for real-world participating media have been measured and published [1258]. For instance, milk has high scattering values, producing a cloudy and opaque appearance. Milk also appears white thanks to a high albedo $\rho > 0.999$. On the other hand, red wine features almost no scattering but instead high absorption, giving it a translucent and colored appearance. See the rendered liquids in Figure 14.2, and compare to the photographed liquids in Figure 9.8 on page 301.

Each of these properties and events are wavelength-dependent. This dependence means that in a given medium, different light frequencies may be absorbed or scattered with differing probabilities. In theory, to account for this we should use spectral values in rendering. For the sake of efficiency, in real-time rendering (and with a few exceptions [660] in offline rendering as well) we use RGB values instead. Where possible, the RGB values of quantities such as σ_a and σ_s should be precomputed from spectral data using color-matching functions (Section 8.1.3).

In earlier chapters, due to the absence of participating media, we could assume that the radiance entering the camera was the same as the radiance leaving the closest surface. More precisely, we assumed (on page 310) that $L_i(\mathbf{c}, -\mathbf{v}) = L_o(\mathbf{p}, \mathbf{v})$, where **c** is the camera position, **p** is the intersection point of the closest surface with the view ray, and **v** is the unit view vector pointing from **p** to **c**.

Once participating media are introduced, this assumption no longer holds and we need to account for the change in radiance along the view ray. As an example, we will

Figure 14.2. Rendered wine and milk, respectively, featuring absorption and scattering at different concentrations. *(Images courtesy of Narasimhan et al. [1258].)*

now describe the computations involved in evaluating scattered light from a punctual light source, i.e., a light source represented by a single infinitesimal point (Section 9.4):

$$L_i(\mathbf{c}, -\mathbf{v}) = T_r(\mathbf{c}, \mathbf{p})L_o(\mathbf{p}, \mathbf{v}) + \int_{t=0}^{\|\mathbf{p}-\mathbf{c}\|} T_r(\mathbf{c}, \mathbf{c} - \mathbf{v}t)L_{\text{scat}}(\mathbf{c} - \mathbf{v}t, \mathbf{v})\sigma_s dt, \quad (14.2)$$

where $T_r(\mathbf{c}, \mathbf{x})$ is the transmittance between a given point $\mathbf{x}$ and the camera position $\mathbf{c}$ (Section 14.1.2) and $L_{\text{scat}}(\mathbf{x}, \mathbf{v})$ is the light scattered along the view ray (Section 14.1.3) at a given point $\mathbf{x}$ on the ray. The different components of the calculation are shown in Figure 14.3 and explained in the following subsections. More details about how Equation 14.2 is derived from the radiative transfer equation can be found in the course notes by Fong et al. [479].

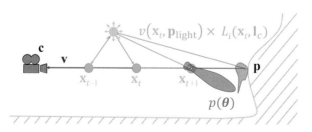

Figure 14.3. Illustration of single scattering integration from a punctual light source. Sample points along the view ray are shown in green, a phase function for one point is shown in red, and the BRDF for an opaque surface S is shown in orange. Here, $\mathbf{l}_c$ is the direction vector to the light center, $\mathbf{p}_{\text{light}}$ is the position of the light, p is the phase function, and the function v is the visibility term.

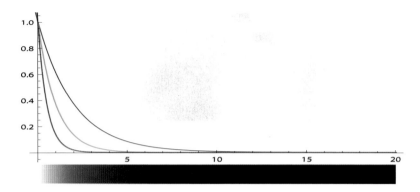

Figure 14.4. Transmittance as a function of depth, with $\sigma_t = (0.5, 1.0, 2.0)$. As expected, a lower extinction coefficient for the red component leads to more red color being transmitted.

14.1.2 Transmittance

The transmittance T_r represents the ratio of light that is able to get through a medium over a certain distance according to

$$T_r(\mathbf{x}_a, \mathbf{x}_b) = e^{-\tau}, \quad \text{where} \quad \tau = \int_{\mathbf{x}=\mathbf{x}_a}^{\mathbf{x}_b} \sigma_t(\mathbf{x}) \, \|d\mathbf{x}\|. \tag{14.3}$$

This relationship is also known as the Beer-Lambert Law. The optical depth τ is unitless and represents the amount of light attenuation. The higher the extinction or distance traversed, the larger the optical depth will be and, in turn, the less light will travel through the medium. An optical depth $\tau = 1$ will remove approximately 60% of the light. For instance, if $\sigma_t = (0.5, 1, 2)$ in RGB, then the light coming through depth $d = 1$ meter will be $T_r = e^{-d\sigma_t} \approx (0.61, 0.37, 0.14)$. This behavior is presented in Figure 14.4. Transmittance needs to be applied on (*i*) the radiance $L_o(\mathbf{p}, \mathbf{v})$ from opaque surfaces, (*ii*) the radiance $L_{\text{scat}}(\mathbf{x}, \mathbf{v})$ resulting from an in-scattering event, and (*iii*) each path from a scattering event to the light source. Visually, (*i*) will result in some fog-like occlusion of surfaces, (*ii*) will result in occlusion of scattered light, giving another visual cue about the media thickness (see Figure 14.6), and (*iii*) will result in volumetric self-shadowing by the participating media (see Figure 14.5). Since $\sigma_t = \sigma_a + \sigma_s$, it is expected that the transmittance is influenced by both the absorption and out-scattering components.

14.1.3 Scattering Events

Integrating in-scattering from punctual light sources in a scene for a given position $\mathbf{x}$ and from direction $\mathbf{v}$ can be done as follows:

$$L_{\text{scat}}(\mathbf{x}, \mathbf{v}) = \pi \sum_{i=1}^{n} p(\mathbf{v}, \mathbf{l}_{c_i}) v(\mathbf{x}, \mathbf{p}_{\text{light}_i}) c_{\text{light}_i}(\|\mathbf{x} - \mathbf{p}_{\text{light}_i}\|), \tag{14.4}$$

Figure 14.5. Example of volumetric shadows from a Stanford bunny made of participating media [744]. Left: without volumetric self-shadowing; middle: with self-shadowing; right: with shadows cast on other scene elements. *(Model courtesy of the Stanford Computer Graphics Laboratory.)*

where n is the number of lights, $p()$ is the phase function, $v()$ is the visibility function, $\mathbf{l}_{c_i}$ is the direction vector to the ith light, and $\mathbf{p}_{\text{light}_i}$ is the position of the ith light. In addition, $c_{\text{light}_i}()$ is the radiance from the ith light as a function of the distance to its position, using the definition from Section 9.4 and the inverse square falloff function from Section 5.2.2. The visibility function $v(\mathbf{x}, \mathbf{p}_{\text{light}_i})$ represents the ratio of light reaching a position $\mathbf{x}$ from a light source at $\mathbf{p}_{\text{light}_i}$ according to

$$v(\mathbf{x}, \mathbf{p}_{\text{light}_i}) = \texttt{shadowMap}(\mathbf{x}, \mathbf{p}_{\text{light}_i}) \cdot \texttt{volShad}(\mathbf{x}, \mathbf{p}_{\text{light}_i}), \qquad (14.5)$$

where $\texttt{volShad}(\mathbf{x}, \mathbf{p}_{\text{light}_i}) = T_r(\mathbf{x}, \mathbf{p}_{\text{light}_i})$. In real-time rendering, shadows result from two kinds of occlusion: opaque and volumetric. Shadows from opaque objects (`shadowMap`) are traditionally computed by using shadow mapping or other techniques from Chapter 7.

The volumetric shadow term $\texttt{volShad}(\mathbf{x}, \mathbf{p}_{\text{light}_i})$ of Equation 14.5 represents the transmittance from light source position $\mathbf{p}_{\text{light}_i}$ to sampled point $\mathbf{x}$, with values in the range $[0, 1]$. Occlusion produced by a volume is a crucial component of volumetric rendering, where the volume element can self-shadow or cast shadows on other scene elements. See Figure 14.5. This result is usually achieved by performing ray marching along the primary ray from the eye through the volume to the first surface, and then along a secondary ray path from each of these samples toward each light source. "Ray marching" refers to the act of sampling the path between two points using n samples, integrating scattered light and transmittance along the way. See Section 6.8.1 for more details on this method of sampling, which in that case was for rendering a heightfield. Ray marching is similar for three-dimensional volumes, with each ray progressing step by step and sampling the volume material or lighting at each point along the way. See Figure 14.3, which shows sample points on a primary ray in green and secondary shadow rays in blue. Many other publications also describe ray marching in detail [479, 1450, 1908].

Being of $O(n^2)$ complexity, where n is the number of samples along each path, ray marching quickly becomes expensive. As a trade-off between quality and performance, specific volumetric shadow representation techniques can be used to store transmit-

Figure 14.6. Stanford dragon with increasing media concentration. From left to right: 0.1, 1.0, and 10.0, with $\sigma_s = (0.5, 1.0, 2.0)$. *(Model courtesy of the Stanford Computer Graphics Laboratory.)*

tance for outgoing directions from a light. These techniques will be explained in the appropriate sections throughout the rest of this chapter.

To gain some intuition about the behavior of light scattering and extinction within a medium, consider $\sigma_s = (0.5, 1, 2)$ and $\sigma_a = (0, 0, 0)$. For a short light path within the medium, in-scattering events will dominate over extinction, e.g., out-scattering in this case, where $T_r \approx 1$ for a small depth. The material will appear blue, since this channel's σ_s value is highest. The deeper that light penetrates into the medium, the fewer photons will get through, due to extinction. In this case, the transmittance color from extinction will start to dominate. This can be explained by the fact that we have $\sigma_t = \sigma_s$, since $\sigma_a = (0, 0, 0)$. As a result, $T_r = e^{-d\sigma_t}$ will decrease much faster than the linear integration of scattered light as a function of the optical depth $d\sigma_s$ using Equation 14.2. For this example, the red light channel will be less subject to extinction through the medium, since this channel's σ_t value is lowest, so it will dominate. This behavior is depicted in Figure 14.6, and is exactly what happens in the atmosphere and sky. When the sun is high (e.g., short light path through the atmosphere, perpendicular to the ground), blue light scatters more, giving the sky its natural blue color. However, when the sun is at the horizon, so that there is a long light path through the atmosphere, the sky will appear redder since more red light is transmitted. This results in the beautiful sunrise and sunset transitions we all know. See Section 14.4.1 for more details about the atmosphere's material composition. For another example of this effect, see the opalescent glass on the right side of Figure 9.6 on page 299.

14.1.4 Phase Functions

A participating medium is composed of particles with varying radii. The distribution of the size of these particles will influence the probability that light will scatter in a given direction, relative to the light's forward travel direction. The physics behind this behavior is explained in Section 9.1.

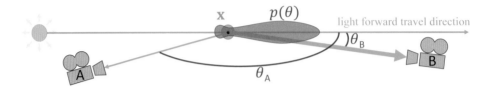

Figure 14.7. Illustration of a phase function (in red) and its influence on scattered light (in green) as a function of θ.

Describing the probability and distribution of scattering directions at a macro level is achieved using a phase function when evaluating in-scattering, as shown in Equation 14.4. This is illustrated in Figure 14.7. The phase function in red is expressed using the parameter θ as the angle between the light's forward travel path in blue and toward direction $\mathbf{v}$ in green. Notice the two main lobes in this phase function example: a small backward-scattering lobe in the opposite direction of the light path, and a large forward-scattering lobe. Camera B is in the direction of the large forward-scattering lobe, so it will receive much more scattered radiance as compared to camera A. To be energy-conserving and -preserving, i.e., no energy gain or loss, the integration of a phase function over the unit sphere must be 1.

A phase function will change the in-scattering at a point according to the directional radiance information reaching that point. The simplest function is isotropic: Light will be scattered uniformly in all directions. This perfect but unrealistic behavior is presented as

$$p(\theta) = \frac{1}{4\pi}, \qquad (14.6)$$

where θ is the angle between the incoming light and out-scattering directions, and 4π is the area of the unit sphere.

Physically based phase functions depend on the relative size s_p of a particle according to

$$s_p = \frac{2\pi r}{\lambda}, \qquad (14.7)$$

where r is the particle radius and λ the considered wavelength [743]:

- When $s_p \ll 1$, there is Rayleigh scattering (e.g., air).

- When $s_p \approx 1$, there is Mie scattering.

- When $s_p \gg 1$, there is geometric scattering.

Rayleigh Scattering

Lord Rayleigh (1842–1919) derived terms for the scattering of light from molecules in the air. These expressions are used, among other applications, to describe light scattering in the earth's atmosphere. This phase function has two lobes, as shown

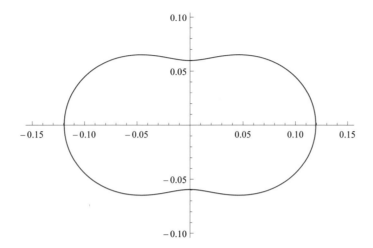

Figure 14.8. Polar plot of the Rayleigh phase as a function of θ. The light is coming horizontally from the left, and the relative intensity is shown for angle θ, measured counterclockwise from the x-axis. The chance of forward and backward scattering is the same.

in Figure 14.8, referred to as *backward and* forward scattering, relative to the light direction. This function is evaluated at θ, the angle between the incoming light and out-scattering directions. The function is

$$p(\theta) = \frac{3}{16\pi}(1 + \cos^2\theta). \qquad (14.8)$$

Rayleigh scattering is highly wavelength-dependent. When viewed as a function of the light wavelength λ, the scattering coefficient σ_s for Rayleigh scattering is proportional to the inverse fourth power of the wavelength:

$$\sigma_s(\lambda) \propto \frac{1}{\lambda^4}. \qquad (14.9)$$

This relationship means that short-wavelength blue or violet light is scattered much more than long-wavelength red light. The spectral distribution from Equation 14.9 can be converted to RGB using spectral color-matching functions (Section 8.1.3): $\sigma_s = (0.490, 1.017, 2.339)$. This value is normalized to a luminance of 1, and should be scaled according to the desired scattering intensity. The visual effects resulting from blue light being scattered more in the atmosphere are explained in Section 14.4.1.

Mie Scattering

Mie scattering [776] is a model that can be used when the size of particles is about the same as the light's wavelength. This type of scattering is not wavelength-dependent. The MiePlot software is useful for simulating this phenomenon [996]. The Mie phase

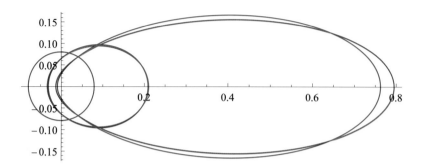

Figure 14.9. Polar plot of the Henyey-Greenstein (in blue) and Schlick approximation (in red) phase as a function of θ. The light is coming horizontally from the left. Parameter g increases from 0 to 0.3 and 0.6, resulting in a strong lobe to the right, meaning that light will be scattered more along its forward path, from the left to the right.

function for a specific particle size is typically a complex distribution with strong and sharp directional lobes, i.e., representing a high probability to scatter photons in specific directions relative to the photon travel direction. Computing such phase functions for volume shading is computationally expensive, but fortunately it is rarely needed. Media typically have a continuous distribution of particle sizes. Averaging the Mie phase functions for all these different sizes results in a smooth average phase function for the overall medium. For this reason, relatively smooth phase functions can be used to represent Mie scattering.

One phase function commonly used for this purpose is the Henyey-Greenstein (HG) phase function, which was originally proposed to simulate light scattering in interstellar dust [721]. This function cannot capture the complexity of every real-world scattering behavior, but it can be a good match to represent one of the phase function lobes [1967], i.e., toward the main scatter direction. It can be used to represent any smoke, fog, or dust-like participating media. Such media can exhibit strong backward or forward scattering, resulting in large visual halos around light sources. Examples include spotlights in fog and the strong silver-lining effect at the edges of clouds in the sun's direction.

The HG phase function can represent more complex behavior than Rayleigh scattering and is evaluated using

$$p_{hg}(\theta, g) = \frac{1 - g^2}{4\pi(1 + g^2 - 2g\cos\theta)^{1.5}}. \tag{14.10}$$

It can result in varied shapes, as shown in Figure 14.9. The g parameter can be used to represent backward ($g < 0$), isotropic ($g = 0$), or forward ($g > 0$) scattering, with g in $[-1, 1]$. Examples of scattering results using the HG phase function are shown in Figure 14.10.

A faster way to obtain similar results to the Henyey-Greenstein phase function is to use an approximation proposed by Blasi et al. [157], which is usually named for the

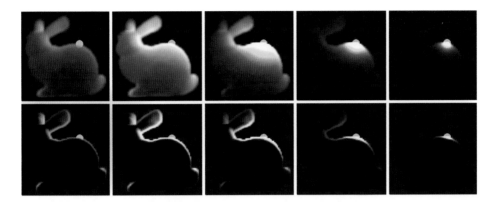

Figure 14.10. Participating-media Stanford bunny showing HG phase function influence, with g ranging from isotropic to strong forward scattering. From left to right: $g = 0.0$, 0.5, 0.9, 0.99, and 0.999. The bottom row uses a ten-times denser participating media. *(Model courtesy of the Stanford Computer Graphics Laboratory.)*

third author as the Schlick phase function:

$$p(\theta, k) = \frac{1 - k^2}{4\pi(1 + k\cos\theta)^2}, \quad \text{where} \quad k \approx 1.55g - 0.55g^3. \tag{14.11}$$

It does not include any complex power function but instead only a square, which is much faster to evaluate. In order to map this function onto the original HG phase function, the k parameter needs to be computed from g. This has to be done only once for participating media having a constant g value. In practical terms, the Schlick phase function is an excellent energy-conserving approximation, as shown in Figure 14.9.

It is also possible to blend multiple HG or Schlick phase functions in order to represent a more complex range of general phase functions [743]. This allows us to represent a phase function having strong forward- and backward-scattering lobes at the same time, similar to how clouds behave, as described and illustrated in Section 14.4.2.

Geometric Scattering

Geometric scattering happens with particles significantly larger than the light's wavelength. In this case, light can refract and reflect within each particle. This behavior can require a complex scattering phase function to simulate it on a macro level. Light polarization can also affect this type of scattering. For instance, a real-life example is the visual rainbow effect. It is caused by internal reflection of light inside water particles in the air, dispersing the sun's light into a visible spectrum over a small visual angle (~ 3 degrees) of the resulting backward scattering. Such complex phase functions can be simulated using the MiePlot software [996]. An example of such a phase function is described in Section 14.4.2.

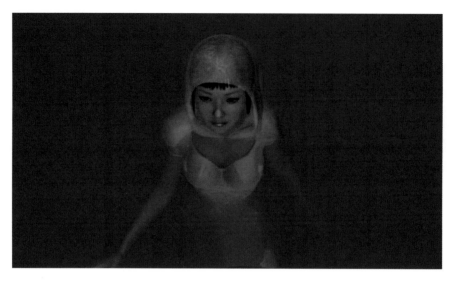

Figure 14.11. Fog used to accentuate a mood. *(Image courtesy of NVIDIA Corporation.)*

14.2   Specialized Volumetric Rendering

This section presents algorithms for rendering volumetric effects in a basic, limited way. Some might even say these are old school tricks, often relying on ad hoc models. The reason they are used is that they still work well.

14.2.1   Large-Scale Fog

Fog can be approximated as a depth-based effect. Its most basic form is the alpha blending of the fog color on top of a scene according to the distance from the camera, usually called *depth fog*. This type of effect is a visual cue to the viewer. First, it can increase the level of realism and drama, as seen in Figure 14.11. Second, it is an important depth cue helping the viewer of a scene determine how far away objects are located. See Figure 14.12. Third, it can be used as a form of occlusion culling. If objects are completely occluded by the fog when too far away, their rendering can safely be skipped, increasing application performance.

One way to represent an amount of fog is to have f in $[0, 1]$ representing a transmittance, i.e., $f = 0.1$ means 10% of the background surface is visible. Assuming that the input color of a surface is c_i and the fog color is c_f, then the final color, c, is determined by

$$\mathbf{c} = f\mathbf{c}_i + (1 - f)\mathbf{c}_f. \tag{14.12}$$

The value f can be evaluated in many different ways. The fog can increase linearly using

$$f = \frac{z_{\text{end}} - z_s}{z_{\text{end}} - z_{\text{start}}}, \tag{14.13}$$

Figure 14.12. Fog is used in this image of a level from *Battlefield 1*, a DICE game, to reveal the complexity of the gameplay area. Depth fog is used to reveal the large-scale nature of the scenery. Height fog, visible on the right at the ground level, reveals the large amount of buildings raising up from the valley. *(Courtesy of DICE, © 2018 Electronic Arts Inc.)*

where z_{start} and z_{end} are user parameters that determine where the fog is to start and end (i.e., become fully foggy), and z_s is the linear depth from the viewer to the surface where fog is to be computed. A physically accurate way to evaluate fog transmittance is to have it increase exponentially with distance, thus following the Beer-Lambert Law for transmittance (Section 14.1.2). This effect can be achieved using

$$f = e^{-d_f z_s}, \tag{14.14}$$

where the scalar d_f is a user parameter that controls the density of the fog. This traditional large-scale fog is a coarse approximation to the general simulation of light scattering and absorption within the atmosphere (Section 14.4.1), but it is still used in games today to great effect. See Figure 14.12.

This is how hardware fog was exposed in legacy OpenGL and DirectX APIs. It is still worthwhile to consider using these models for simpler use cases on hardware such as mobile devices. Many current games rely on more advanced post-processing for atmospheric effects such as fog and light scattering. One problem with fog in a perspective view is that the depth buffer values are computed in a nonlinear fashion (Section 23.7). It is possible to convert the nonlinear depth buffer values back to linear depths z_s using inverse projection matrix mathematics [1377]. Fog can then be applied as a full-screen pass using a pixel shader, enabling more advanced results to be achieved, such as height-dependent fog or underwater shading.

Height fog represents a single slab of participating media with a parameterized height and thickness. For each pixel on screen, the density and scattered light is evaluated as a function of the distance the view ray has traveled through the slab before hitting a surface. Wenzel [1871] proposes a closed-form solution evaluating f for an exponential fall-off of participating media within the slab. Doing so results in a smooth fog transition near the edges of the slab. This is visible in the background fog on the left side of Figure 14.12.

Many variations are possible with depth and height fog. The color $\mathbf{c}_f$ can be a single color, be read from a cube map sampled using the view vector, or even can be the result of complex atmospheric scattering with a per-pixel phase function applied for directional color variations [743]. It is also possible to combine depth f_d and height f_h fog transmittance using $f = f_d f_h$ and have both types of fog interleaved together in a scene.

Depth and height fog are large-scale fog effects. One might want to render more local phenomena such as separated fog areas, for example, in caves or around a few tombs in a cemetery. Shapes such as ellipsoids or boxes can be used to add local fog where needed [1871]. These fog elements are rendered from back to front using their bounding boxes. The front d_f and back d_b intersection along the view vector of each shape is evaluated in the pixel shader. Using volume depth as $d = \max(0, \min(z_s, d_b) - d_f)$, where z_s is the linear depth representing the closest opaque surface, it is possible to evaluate a transmittance T_r (Section 14.1.2), with coverage as $\alpha = 1.0 - T_r$. The amount of scattered light $\mathbf{c}_f$ to add on top can then be evaluated as $\alpha \mathbf{c}_f$. To allow more varied shapes evaluated from meshes, Oat and Scheuermann [1308] give a clever single-pass method of computing both the closest entry point and farthest exit point in a volume. They save the surface distance, d_s, to a surface in one channel, and $1 - d_s$ in another channel. By setting the alpha blending mode to save the minimum value found, after the volume is rendered, the first channel will have the closest value d_f and the second channel will have the farthest value d_b, encoded as $1 - d$, allowing recovery of d.

Water is a participating medium and, as such, exhibits the same type of depth-based color attenuation. Coastal water has a transmittance of about $(0.3, 0.73, 0.63)$ per meter [261], thus using Equation 14.23 we can recover $\sigma_t = (1.2, 0.31, 0.46)$. When rendering dark water using an opaque surface, it is possible to enable the fog logic when the camera is under the water surface, and to turn it off when above. A more advanced solution has been proposed by Wenzel [1871]. If the camera is under water, scattering and transmittance are integrated until a solid or the water surface is hit. If above water, these are integrated from only the distance between the water's top surface to the solid geometry of the seabed.

14.2.2 Simple Volumetric Lighting

Light scattering within participating media can be complex to evaluate. Thankfully, there are many efficient techniques that can be used to approximate such scattering convincingly in many situations.

The simplest way to obtain volumetric effects is to render transparent meshes blended over the framebuffer. We refer to this as a *splatting* approach (Section 13.9). To render light shafts shining through a window, through a dense forest, or from a spotlight, one solution is to use camera-aligned particles with a texture on each. Each textured quad is stretched in the direction of the light shaft while always facing the camera (a cylinder constraint).

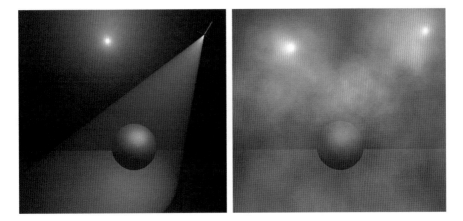

Figure 14.13. Volumetric light scattering from light sources evaluated using the analytical integration from the code snippet on page 603. It can be applied as a post effect assuming homogeneous media (left) or on particles, assuming each of them is a volume with depth (right). *(Image courtesy of Miles Macklin [1098].)*

The drawback with mesh splatting approaches is that accumulating many transparent meshes will increase the required memory bandwidth, likely causing a bottleneck, and the textured quad facing the camera can sometimes be visible. To work around this issue, post-processing techniques using closed-form solutions to light single scattering have been proposed. Assuming a homogeneous and spherical uniform phase function, it is possible to integrate scattered light with correct transmittance along a path assuming a constant medium. The result is visible in Figure 14.13. An example implementation of this technique is shown here in a GLSL shader code snippet [1098]:

```
float inScattering(
vec3 rayStart, vec3 rayDir,
vec3 lightPos, float rayDistance)
{
    // Calculate coefficients.
    vec3  q = rayStart - lightPos;
    float b = dot(rayDir, q);
    float c = dot(q, q);
    float s = 1.0f / sqrt(c - b*b);

    // Factorize some components.
    float x = s * rayDistance;
    float y = s * b;
    return s * atan( (x) / (1.0 + (x + y) * y));
}
```

where **rayStart** is the ray start position, **rayDir** is the ray normalized direction, **rayDistance** the integration distance along the ray, and **lightPos** the light source

Figure 14.14. Light shafts rendered using a screen-space post-process. *(Image courtesy of Kenny Mitchell [1225].)*

position. The solution by Sun et al. [1722] additionally takes into account the scattering coefficient σ_s. It also describes how the diffuse and specular radiance bouncing off Lambertian and Phong surfaces should be affected by the fact that the light would have scattered in non-straight paths before hitting any surface. In order to take into account transmittance and phase functions, a more ALU-heavy solution can be used [1364]. All these models are effective at what they do, but are not able to take into account shadows from depth maps or heterogeneous participating media.

It is possible to approximate light scattering in screen space by relying on a technique known as bloom [539, 1741]. Blurring the framebuffer and adding a small percentage of it back onto itself [44] will make every bright object leak radiance around it. This technique is typically used to approximate imperfections in camera lenses, but in some environments, it is an approximation that works well for short distances and non-occluded scattering. Section 12.3 describes bloom in more detail.

Dobashi et al. [359] present a method of rendering large-scale atmospheric effects using a series of planes sampling the volume. These planes are perpendicular to the view direction and are rendered from back to front. Mitchell [1219] also proposes the same approach to render spotlight shafts, using shadow maps to cast volumetric shadows from opaque objects. Rendering volume by splatting slices is described in detail in Section 14.3.1.

Mitchell [1225] and Rohleder and Jamrozik [1507] present an alternative method working in screen space; see Figure 14.14. It can be used to render light shafts from a distant light such as the sun. First, a fake bright object is rendered around the sun on the far plane in a buffer cleared to black, and a depth buffer test is used to accept non-occluded pixels. Second, a directional blur is applied on the image in order to leak the previously accumulated radiance outward from the sun. It is possible to use a separable filtering technique (Section 12.1) with two passes, each using n samples, to get the same blur result as n^2 samples but rendered faster [1681]. To finish, the final blurred buffer can be added onto the scene buffer. The technique is efficient and, despite the drawback that only the light sources visible on screen can cast light shafts, it provides a significant visual result at a small cost.

14.3   General Volumetric Rendering

In this section, we present volumetric rendering techniques that are more physically based, i.e., that try to represent the medium's material and its interaction with light sources (Section 14.1.1). General volumetric rendering is concerned with spatially varying participating media, often represented using voxels (Section 13.10), with volumetric light interactions resulting in visually complex scattering and shadowing phenomena. A general volumetric rendering solution must also account for the correct composition of volumes with other scene elements, such as opaque or transparent surfaces. The spatially varying media's properties might be the result of a smoke and fire simulation that needs to be rendered in a game environment, together with volumetric light and shadow interactions. Alternately, we may wish to represent solid materials as semitransparent volumes, for applications such as medical visualization.

14.3.1   Volume Data Visualization

Volume data visualization is a tool used for the display and analysis of volume data, usually scalar fields. Computer tomography (CT) and magnetic resonance image (MRI) techniques can be used to create clinical diagnostic images of internal body structures. A data set may be, say, 256^3 voxels, each location holding one or more values. This voxel data can be used to form a three-dimensional image. Voxel rendering can show a solid model, or make various materials (e.g., the skin and skull) appear partially or fully transparent. Cutting planes can be used to show only a sub-volume or parts of the source data. In addition to its use for visualization in such diverse fields as medicine and oil prospecting, volumetric rendering can also produce photorealistic imagery.

There are many voxel rendering techniques [842]. It is possible to use regular path tracing or photon mapping to visualize volumetric data under complex lighting environments. Several less-expensive methods have been proposed to achieve real-time performance.

For solid objects, implicit surface techniques can be used to turn voxels into polygonal surfaces, as described in Section 17.3. For semitransparent phenomena, the volume data set can be sampled by a set of equally spaced slices in layers perpendicular to the view direction. Figure 14.15 shows how this works. It is also possible to render opaque surfaces with this approach [797]. In this case, the solid volume is considered present when the density is greater than a given threshold, and the normal $\mathbf{n}$ can be evaluated as the three-dimensional gradient of the density field.

For semitransparent data, it is possible to store color and opacity per voxel. To reduce the memory footprint and enable users to control the visualization, transfer functions have been proposed. A first solution is to map a voxel density scalar to color and opacity using a one-dimensional transfer texture. However, this does not allow identifying specific material transitions, for instance, human sinuses bone-to-air or bone-to-soft tissue, independently, with separate colors. To solve this issue, Kniss

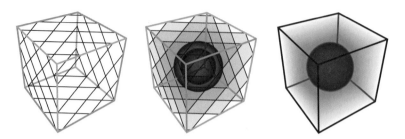

Figure 14.15. A volume is rendered by a series of slices parallel to the view plane. Some slices and their intersection with the volume are shown on the left. The middle shows the result of rendering just these slices. On the right the result is shown when a large series of slices are rendered and blended. *(Figures courtesy of Christof Rezk-Salama, University of Siegen, Germany.)*

et al. [912] suggest using a two-dimensional transfer function that is indexed based on density d and the gradient length of the density field $||\nabla d||$. Regions of change have high gradient magnitudes. This approach results in more meaningful colorization of density transitions. See Figure 14.16.

Figure 14.16. Volume material and opacity evaluated using a one-dimensional (left) and two-dimensional (right) transfer function [912]. In the second case, it is possible to maintain the brown color of the trunk without having it covered with the green color of lighter density representing the leaves. The bottom part of the image represents the transfer functions, with the x-axis being density and the y-axis the gradient length of the density field $||\nabla d||$. *(Image courtesy of Joe Michael Kniss [912].)*

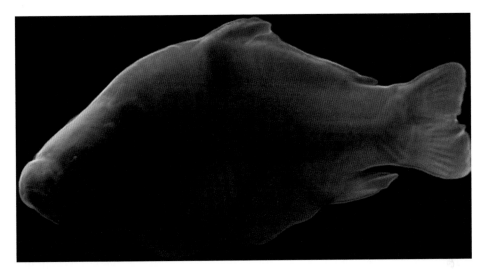

Figure 14.17. Volumetric rendering with forward subsurface scattering using light propagation through half-angle slices. *(Image courtesy of Ikits et al. [797].)*

Ikits et al. [797] discuss this technique and related matters in depth. Kniss et al. [913] extend this approach, instead slicing according to the half-angle. Slices are still rendered back to front but are oriented halfway between the light and view directions. Using this approach, it is possible to render radiance and occlusion from the light's point of view and accumulate each slice in view space. The slice texture can be used as input when rendering the next slice, using occlusion from the light direction to evaluate volumetric shadows, and using radiance to estimate multiple scattering, i.e., light bouncing multiple times within a medium before reaching the eye. Because the previous slice is sampled according to multiple samples in a disk, this technique can synthesize only subsurface phenomena resulting from forward scattering within a cone. The final image is of high quality. See Figure 14.17. This half-angle approach has been extended by Schott et al. [1577, 1578] to evaluate ambient occlusion and depth-of-field blur effects, which improves the depth and volume perception of users viewing the voxel data.

As seen in Figure 14.17, half-angle slicing can render high-quality subsurface scattering. However, the memory bandwidth cost due to rasterization has to be paid for each slice. Tatarchuk and Shopf [1744] perform medical imaging using ray marching in shaders and so pay the rasterization bandwidth cost only once. Lighting and shadowing can be achieved as described in the next section.

14.3.2 Participating Media Rendering

Real-time applications can portray richer scenes by rendering participating media. These effects become more demanding to render when factors such as the time of day, weather, or environment changes such as building destruction are involved. For instance, fog in a forest will look different if it is noon or dusk. Light shafts shining in between trees should adapt to the sun's changing direction and color. Light shafts should also be animated according to the trees' movement. Removing some trees via, say, an explosion would result in a change in the scattered light in that area due to fewer occluders and to the dust produced. Campfires, flashlights, and other sources of light will also generate scattering in the air. In this section, we discuss techniques that can simulate the effects of these dynamic visual phenomena in real time.

A few techniques are focused on rendering shadowed large-scale scattering from a single source. One method is described in depth by Yusov [1958]. It is based on sampling in-scattering along epipolar lines, rays of light that project onto a single line on the camera image plane. A depth map from the light's point of view is used to determine whether a sample is shadowed. The algorithm performs a ray march starting from the camera. A min/max hierarchy along rays is used to skip empty space, while only ray-marching at depth discontinuities, i.e., where it is actually needed to accurately evaluate volumetric shadows. Instead of sampling these discontinuities along epipolar lines, it is possible to do it in view space by rendering a mesh generated from the light-space depth map [765]. In view space, only the volume between front- and backfaces is needed to evaluate the final scattered radiance. To this end, the in-scattering is computed by adding the scattered radiance resulting from frontfaces to the view, and subtracting it for backfaces.

These two methods are effective at reproducing single-scattering events with shadows resulting from opaque surface occlusions [765, 1958]. However, neither can represent heterogeneous participating media, since they both assume that the medium is of a constant material. Furthermore, these techniques cannot take into account volumetric shadows from non-opaque surfaces, e.g., self-shadowing from participating media or transparent shadows from particles (Section 13.8). They are still used in games to great effect, since they can be rendered at high resolution and they are fast, thanks to empty-space skipping [1958].

Splatting approaches have been proposed to handle the more general case of a heterogeneous medium, sampling the volume material along a ray. Without considering any input lighting, Crane et al. [303] use splatting for rendering smoke, fire, and water, all resulting from fluid simulation. In the case of smoke and fire, at each pixel a ray is generated that is ray-marched through the volume, gathering color and occlusion information from the material at regular intervals along its length. In the case of water, the volume sampling is terminated once the ray's first hit point with the water surface is encountered. The surface normal is evaluated as the density field gradient at each sample position. To ensure a smooth water surface, tricubic interpolation is used to filter density values. Examples using these techniques are shown in Figure 14.18.

Taking into account the sun, along with point lights and spotlights, Valient [1812] renders into a half-resolution buffer the set of bounding volumes where scattering from each source should happen. Each of the light volumes is ray-marched with a per-pixel random offset applied to the ray marching start position. Doing so adds a bit of

Figure 14.18. Fog and water rendered using volumetric rendering techniques in conjunction with fluid simulation on the GPU. *(Image on left from "Hellgate: London," courtesy of Flagship Studios, Inc.; image on right courtesy of NVIDIA Corporation [303].)*

noise, which has the advantage of removing banding artifacts resulting from constant stepping. The use of different noise values each frame is a means to hide artifacts. After reprojection of the previous frame and blending with the current frame, the noise will be averaged and thus will vanish. Heterogeneous media are rendered by voxelizing flat particles into a three-dimensional texture mapped onto the camera frustum at one eighth of the screen resolution. This volume is used during ray marching as the material density. The half-resolution scattering result can be composited over the full-resolution main buffer using first a bilateral Gaussian blur and then a bilateral up-sampling filter [816], taking into account the depth difference between pixels. When the depth delta is too high compared to the center pixel, the sample is discarded. This Gaussian blur is not mathematically separable (Section 12.1), but it works well in practice. The complexity of this algorithm depends on the number of light volumes splatted on screen, as a function of their pixel coverage.

This approach has been extended by using blue noise, which is better at producing a uniform distribution of random values over a frame pixel [539]. Doing so results in smoother visuals when up-sampling and blending samples spatially with a bilateral filter. Up-sampling the half-resolution buffer can also be achieved using four stochastic samples blended together. The result is still noisy, but because it gives full-resolution per-pixel noise, it can easily be resolved by a temporal antialiasing post-process (Section 5.4).

The drawback of all these approaches is that depth-ordered splatting of volumetric elements with any other transparent surfaces will never give visually correct ordering of the result, e.g., with large non-convex transparent meshes or large-scale particle effects. All these algorithms need some special handling when it comes to applying volumetric lighting on transparent surfaces, such as a volume containing in-scattering and transmittance in voxels [1812]. So, why not use a voxel-based representation from the start, to represent not only spatially varying participating media properties but also the radiance distribution resulting from light scattering and transmittance? Such techniques have long been used in the film industry [1908].

Wronski [1917] proposes a method where the scattered radiance from the sun and lights in a scene is voxelized into a three-dimensional volume texture V_0 mapped over the view clip space. Scattered radiance is evaluated for each voxel-center world-space position, where the x- and y-axes of the volume correspond to screen coordinates, while the z-coordinate is mapped over camera frustum depth. This volume texture is considerably lower resolution than the final image. A typical implementation of this technique uses a voxel resolution that is one eighth of the screen resolution in the x- and y-axes. Subdivision along the z-coordinate depends on a quality and performance trade-off, with 64 slices being a typical choice. This texture contains the in-scattered radiance $L_{\text{scat}_{\text{in}}}$ in RGB as well as extinction σ_t in alpha. From this input data, the final scattering volume V_f is generated by iterating over each slice from near to far using

$$V_f[x, y, z] = (L'_{\text{scat}} + T'_r L_{\text{scat}_{\text{in}}} d_s, T_{r_{\text{slice}}} T'_r), \tag{14.15}$$

where $L'_{\text{scat}} = V_0[x, y, z-1]_{rgb}$, $T'_r = V_0[x, y, z-1]_a$, and $T_{r_{\text{slice}}} = e^{-\sigma_t d_s}$. This updates slice z from the previous slice $z-1$ data over world-space slice depth d_s. Doing so will result in V_f containing the scattered radiance reaching the viewer and transmittance over the background in each voxel. In Equation 14.15, notice that $L_{\text{scat}_{\text{in}}}$ is affected by only the transmittance from previous slices T'_r. This behavior is incorrect, since $L_{\text{scat}_{\text{in}}}$ should also be affected by the transmittance resulting from σ_t within the current slice.

This problem is discussed by Hillaire [742, 743]. He proposes an analytical solution to the integration of $L_{\text{scat}_{\text{in}}}$ for a constant extinction σ_t over a given depth:

$$V_f[x, y, z] = \left(L'_{\text{scat}} + \frac{L_{\text{scat}_{\text{in}}} - L_{\text{scat}_{\text{in}}} T_{r_{\text{slice}}}}{\sigma_t}, T_{r_{\text{slice}}} T'_r \right). \tag{14.16}$$

The final pixel radiance L_o of an opaque surface with radiance L_s will be modified by L_{scat} and T_r from V_f, sampled with clip-space coordinates as $L_o = T_r L_s + L_{\text{scat}}$. Because V_f is coarse, it is subject to aliasing from camera motion and from high-frequency bright lights or shadows. The previous frame V_f can be reprojected and combined with the new V_f using an exponential moving average [742].

Building over this framework, Hillaire [742] presents a physically based approach for the definition of participating media material as follows: scattering σ_s, absorption σ_a, phase function parameter g, and emitted radiance L_e. This material is mapped to the camera frustum and stored into a participating media material volume texture V_{pm}, being the three-dimensional version of a G-buffer storing an opaque surface material (Section 20.1). Considering single scattering only, and despite voxel discretization, Hillaire shows that using such a physically based material representation results in visuals that are close to path tracing. Analogous to meshes, participating media volumes that are positioned in the world are voxelized into V_{pm} (see Figure 14.19). In each of these volumes, a single material is defined and variation is added, thanks

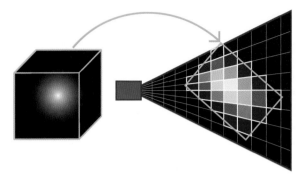

Figure 14.19. An example of a participating media volume placed by an artist in a level and voxelized into camera frustum space [742, 1917]. On the left, a three-dimensional texture, in the shape of a sphere in this case, is mapped onto the volume. The texture defines the volume's appearance, similar to textures on triangles. On the right, this volume is voxelized into the camera frustum by taking into account its world transform. A compute shader accumulates the contribution into each voxel the volume encompass. The resulting material can then be used to evaluate light scattering interactions in each voxel [742]. Note that, when mapped onto camera clip space, voxels take the shape of small frusta and are referred to as *froxels*.

to density sampled from a three-dimensional input texture, resulting in heterogeneous participating media. The result is shown in Figure 14.20. This same approach is also implemented in the Unreal Engine [1802], but instead of using box volumes as sources of participating media, particles are used, assuming a spherical volume instead of a box. It is also possible to represent the material volume texture using a sparse structure [1191], using a topmost volume with each voxel being empty or pointing to a finer-grained volume containing the participating media material data.

The only drawback with camera frustum volume-based approaches [742, 1917] is the low screen-space resolution that is required in order to reach acceptable performance on less powerful platforms (and use a reasonable amount of memory). This is where the previously explained splatting approaches excel, as they produce sharp visual details. As noted earlier, splatting requires more memory bandwidth and provides less of a unified solution, e.g., it is harder to apply on any other transparent surfaces without sorting issues or have participating media cast volume shadows on itself.

Not only direct light, but also illumination that has already bounced, or scattered, can scatter through a medium. Similar to Wronski [1917], the Unreal Engine makes it possible to bake volume light maps, storing irradiance in volumes, and have it scatter back into the media when voxelized in the view volume [1802]. In order to achieve dynamic global illumination in participating media, it is also possible to rely on light propagation volumes [143].

An important feature is the use of volumetric shadows. Without them, the final image in a fog-heavy scene can look too bright and flatter than it should be [742]. Furthermore, shadows are an important visual cue. They help the viewer with perception of depth and volume [1846], produce more realistic images, and can lead to better

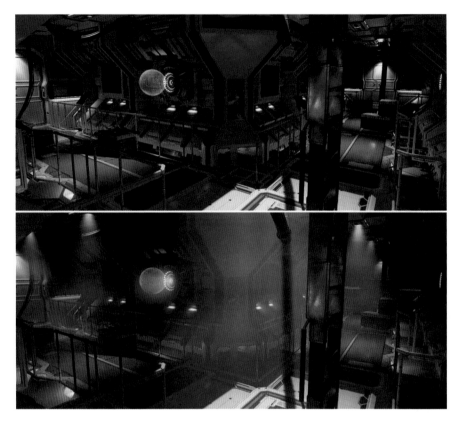

Figure 14.20. A scene rendered without (top) and with (bottom) volumetric lighting and shadowing. Every light in the scene interacts with participating media. Each light's radiance, IES profile, and shadow map are used to accumulate its scattered light contribution [742]. *(Image courtesy of Frostbite, © 2018 Electronic Arts Inc.)*

immersion. Hillaire [742] presents a unified solution to achieve volumetric shadows. Participating media volumes and particles are voxelized into three volumes cascaded around the camera, called *extinction volumes*, according to a clipmap distribution scheme [1777]. These contain extinction σ_t values needed to evaluate T_r and represent a single unified source of data to sample in order to achieve volumetric shadows using an opacity shadow map [742, 894]. See Figure 14.21. Such a solution enables particles and participating media to self-shadow and to cast shadows on each other, as well as any other opaque and transparent elements in a scene.

Volumetric shadows can be represented using opacity shadow maps. However, using a volume texture can quickly become a limitation if high resolutions are needed to catch details. Thus, alternative representations have been proposed to represent T_r more efficiently, for instance using an orthogonal base of functions such as a Fourier [816] or discrete cosine transform [341]. Details are given in Section 7.8.

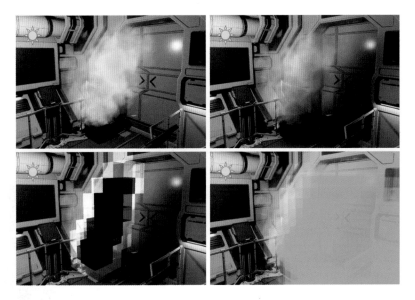

Figure 14.21. At the top, the scene is rendered without (left) and with (right) volumetric shadows. On the bottom, debug views of voxelized particle extinction (left) and volume shadows (right). Greener means less transmittance [742]. *(Image courtesy of Frostbite, © 2018 Electronic Arts Inc.)*

14.4 Sky Rendering

Rendering a world inherently requires a planet sky, atmospheric effects, and clouds. What we call the blue sky on the earth is the result of sunlight scattering in the atmosphere's participating media. The reason why the sky is blue during day and red when the sun is at the horizon is explained in Section 14.1.3. The atmosphere is also a key visual cue since its color is linked to the sun direction, which is related to the time of day. The atmosphere's (sometimes) foggy appearance helps viewers with the perception of relative distance, position, and size of elements in a scene. As such, it is important to accurately render these components required by an increasing number of games and other applications featuring dynamic time of day, evolving weather affecting cloud shapes, and large open worlds to explore, drive around, or even fly over.

14.4.1 Sky and Aerial Perspective

To render atmospheric effects, we need to take into account two main components, as shown in Figure 14.22. First, we simulate the sunlight's interaction with air particles, resulting in wavelength-dependent Rayleigh scattering. This will result in the sky color and a thin fog, also called *aerial perspective*. Second, we need the effect of large particles concentrated near the ground on the sunlight. The concentration of these

Figure 14.22. The two different types of atmospheric light scattering: Rayleigh only at the top and Mie with regular Rayleigh scattering at the bottom. From left to right: density of 0, regular density as described in [203], and exaggerated density. *(Image courtesy of Frostbite, © 2018 Electronic Arts Inc. [743].)*

large particles depends on such factors as weather conditions and pollution. Large particles cause wavelength-independent Mie scattering. This phenomenon will cause a bright halo around the sun, especially with a heavy particle concentration.

The first physically based atmosphere model [1285] rendered the earth and its atmosphere from space, simulating single scattering. Similar results can by achieved using the method proposed by O'Neil [1333]. The earth can be rendered from ground to space using ray marching in a single-pass shader. Expensive ray marching to integrate Mie and Rayleigh scattering is done per vertex when rendering the sky dome. The visually high-frequency phase function is, however, evaluated in the pixel shader. This makes the appearance smooth and avoids revealing the sky geometry due to interpolation. It is also possible to achieve the same result by storing the scattering in a texture and to distribute the evaluation over several frames, accepting update latency for better performance [1871].

Analytical techniques use fitted mathematical models on measured sky radiance [1443] or reference images generated using expensive path tracing of light scattering in the atmosphere [778]. The set of input parameters is generally limited compared to those for a participating media material. For example, *turbidity* represents the contribution of particles resulting in Mie scattering, instead of σ_s and σ_t coefficients. Such a model presented by Preetham et al. [1443] evaluates the sky radiance in any direction using turbidity and sun elevation. It has been improved by adding support for spectral output, better directionality to the scattered radiance around the sun, and a new ground albedo input parameter [778]. Analytical sky models are fast to evaluate. They are, however, limited to ground views, and atmosphere parameters cannot be changed to simulate extra-terrestrial planets or achieve specific art-driven visuals.

Figure 14.23. Real-time rendering of the earth's atmosphere from the ground (left) and from space (right) using a lookup table. *(Image courtesy of Bruneton and Neyret [203].)*

Another approach to rendering skies is to assume that the earth is perfectly spherical, with a layer of atmosphere around it composed of heterogeneous participating media. Extensive descriptions of the atmosphere's composition are given by Bruneton and Neyret [203] as well as Hillaire [743]. Leveraging these facts, precomputed tables can be used to stored transmittance and scattering according to the current view altitude r, the cosine of the view vector angle relative to the zenith μ_v, the cosine of the sun direction angle relative to the zenith μ_s, and the cosine of the view vector angle relative to the sun direction in the azimuthal plane ν. For instance, transmittance from the viewpoint to the atmosphere's boundary can be parameterized by two parameters, r and μ_v. During a precompute step, the transmittance can be integrated in the atmosphere and stored in a two-dimensional lookup table (LUT) texture T_{lut} that can be sampled at runtime using the same parameterization. This texture can be used to apply atmosphere transmittance to sky elements such as the sun, stars, or other celestial bodies.

Considering scattering, Bruneton and Neyret [203] describe a way to store it in a four-dimensional LUT S_{lut} parameterized by all the parameters in the preceding paragraph. They also provide a way to evaluate multiple scattering of order n by iterating n times: (i) Evaluate the single-scattering table S_{lut}, (ii) evaluate S_{lut}^n using S_{lut}^{n-1}, and (iii) add the result to S_{lut}. Do (ii) and (iii) $n-1$ times. More details about the process, as well as source code, are provided by Bruneton and Neyret [203]. See Figure 14.23 for examples of the result. Bruneton and Neyret's parameterization can sometimes exhibit visual artifacts at the horizon. Yusov [1957] has proposed an improved transformation. It is also possible to use an only three-dimensional LUT by ignoring ν [419]. Using this scheme, the earth will not cast shadows in the atmosphere, which can be an acceptable trade-off. The advantage is that this LUT will be much smaller and less expensive to update and sample.

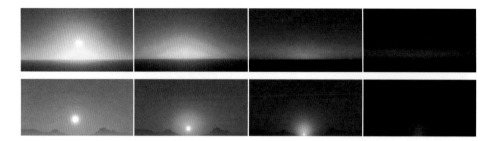

Figure 14.24. Real-time rendering using a fully parameterized model enables the simulation of the earth's atmosphere (top) and the atmosphere of other planets, such as Mars's blue sunset (bottom). *(Top images courtesy of Bruneton and Neyret [203] and bottom images courtesy of Frostbite, © 2018 Electronic Arts Inc. [743].)*

This last three-dimensional LUT approach is used by many Electronic Arts Frostbite real-time games, such as *Need for Speed, Mirror's Edge Catalyst,* and *FIFA* [743]. In this case, artists can drive the physically based atmosphere parameters to reach a target sky visual and even simulate extra-terrestrial atmosphere. See Figure 14.24. The LUT has to be recomputed when atmosphere parameters are changed. To update these LUTs more efficiently, it is also possible to use a function that approximates the integral of the material in the atmosphere instead of ray-marching through it [1587]. The cost of updating the LUTs can be amortized down to 6% of the original by temporally distributing the evaluation of the LUTs and multiple scattering. This is achievable by updating only a sub-part of S_{lut}^n for a given scattering order n, while interpolating the last two solved LUTs, accepting a few frames of latency. As another optimization, to avoid sampling the different LUTs multiple times per pixel, Mie and Rayleigh scattering are baked in voxels of a camera-frustum-mapped low-resolution volume texture. The visually high-frequency phase function is evaluated in the pixel shader in order to produce smooth scattering halos around the sun. Using this type of volume texture also permits applying aerial perspective per vertex on any transparent objects in the scene.

14.4.2 Clouds

Clouds are complex elements in the sky. They can look menacing when representing an incoming storm, or alternately appear discreet, epic, thin, or massive. Clouds change slowly, with both their large-scale shapes and small-scale details evolving over time. Large open-world games with weather and time-of-day changes are more complex cases that require dynamic cloud-rendering solutions. Different techniques can be used depending on the target performance and visual quality.

Clouds are made of water droplets, featuring high-scattering coefficients and complex phase functions that result in a specific look. They are often simulated using participating media, as described in Section 14.1, and their materials have been measured as having a high single-scattering albedo $\rho = 1$ and extinction coefficients σ_t in

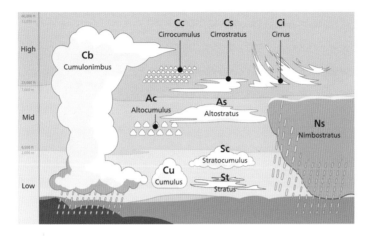

Figure 14.25. Different types of clouds on the earth. *(Image courtesy of Valentin de Bruyn.)*

the range $[0.04, 0.06]$ for stratus (low-level horizontal cloud layers) and $[0.05, 0.12]$ for cumulus [743] (isolated low-level cotton-like fluffy clouds). See Figure 14.25. Given the fact that ρ is close to 1, $\sigma_s = \sigma_t$ can be assumed.

A classic approach to cloud rendering is to use a single panoramic texture composited over the sky using alpha blending. This is convenient when rendering a static sky. Guerrette [620] presents a visual flow technique that gives the illusion of cloud motion in the sky affected by a global wind direction. This is an efficient method that improves over the use of a static set of panoramic cloud textures. However, it will not be able to represent any change to the cloud shapes and lighting.

Clouds as Particles

Harris renders clouds as volumes of particles and impostors [670]. See Section 13.6.2 and Figure 13.9 on page 557.

Another particle-based cloud rendering method is presented by Yusov [1959]. He uses rendering primitives that are called *volume particles*. Each of these is represented by a four-dimensional LUT, allowing retrieval of scattered light and transmittance on the view-facing quad particle as a function of the sun light and view directions. See Figure 14.26. This approach is well suited to render stratocumulus clouds. See Figure 14.25.

When rendering clouds as particles, discretization and popping artifacts can often be seen, especially when rotating around clouds. These problems can be avoided by using *volume-aware* blending. This ability is made possible by using a GPU feature called rasterizer order views (Section 3.8). Volume-aware blending enables the synchronization of pixel shader operations on resources per primitive, allowing deterministic custom blending operations. The closest n particles' depth layers are kept in a buffer at the same resolution as the render target into which we render. This

Figure 14.26. Clouds rendered as volumes of particles. *(Image courtesy of Egor Yusov [1959].)*

buffer is read and used to blend the currently rendered particle by taking into account intersection depth, then finally written out again for the next particle to be rendered. The result is visible in Figure 14.27.

Clouds as Participating Media

Considering clouds as isolated elements, Bouthors et al. [184] represent a cloud with two components: a mesh, showing its overall shape, and a hypertexture [1371], adding high-frequency details under the mesh surface up to a certain depth inside the cloud. Using this representation, a cloud edge can be finely ray-marched in order to gather details, while the inner part can be considered homogeneous. Radiance is integrated while ray marching the cloud structure, and different algorithms are used to gather scattered radiance according to scattering order. Single scattering is integrated using an analytical approach described in Section 14.1. Multiple scattering evaluation is accelerated using offline precomputed transfer tables from disk-shaped light collectors positioned at the cloud's surface. The final result is of high visual quality, as shown in Figure 14.28.

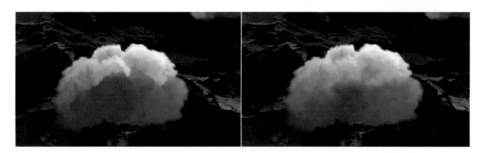

Figure 14.27. On the left, cloud particles rendered the usual way. On the right, particles rendered with volume-aware blending. *(Images courtesy of Egor Yusov [1959].)*

Figure 14.28. Clouds rendered using meshes and hypertextures. *(Image courtesy of Bouthors et al. [184].)*

Instead of rendering clouds as isolated elements, it is possible to model them as a layer of participating media in the atmosphere. Relying on ray marching, Schneider and Vos presented an efficient method to render clouds in this way [1572]. With only a few parameters, it is possible to render complex, animated, and detailed cloud shapes under dynamic time-of-day lighting conditions, as seen in Figure 14.29. The layer is

Figure 14.29. Clouds rendered using a ray-marched cloud layer using Perlin-Worley noise, and featuring dynamic volumetric lighting and shadowing. *(Results by Schneider and Vos [1572], copyright ©2017 Guerrilla Games.)*

built using two levels of procedural noise. The first level gives the cloud its base shape. The second level adds details by eroding this shape. In this case, a mix of Perlin [1373] and Worley [1907] noise is reported to be a good representation of the cauliflower-like shape of cumulus and similar clouds. Source code and tools to generate such textures have been shared publicly [743, 1572]. Lighting is achieved by integrating scattered light from the sun using samples distributed in the cloud layer along the view ray.

Volumetric shadowing can be achieved by evaluating the transmittance for a few samples within the layer, testing toward the sun [743, 1572] as a secondary ray marching. It is possible to sample the lower mipmap levels of the noise textures for these shadow samples in order to achieve better performance and to smooth out artifacts that can become visible when using only a few samples. An alternative approach to avoid secondary ray marching per sample is to encode the transmittance curve from the sun once per frame in textures, using one of the many techniques available (Section 13.8). For instance, the game *Final Fantasy XV* [416] uses transmittance function mapping [341].

Rendering clouds at high resolution with ray marching can become expensive if we want to capture every little detail. To achieve better performance, it is possible to render clouds at a low resolution. One approach is to update only a single pixel within each 4×4 block and reproject the previous frame data to fill up the rest [1572]. Hillaire [743] proposes a variation that always renders at a fixed lower resolution and adds noise on the view ray marching start position. The previous frame result can be reprojected and combined with the new frame using an exponential moving average [862]. This approach renders at lower resolution but can converge faster.

Clouds' phase functions are complex [184]. Here we present two methods that can be used to evaluate them in real time. It is possible to encode the function as a texture and sample it based on θ. If doing so requires too much memory bandwidth, it is possible to approximate the function by combining two Henyey-Greenstein phase functions from Section 14.1.4 [743] as

$$p_{\text{dual}}(\theta, g_0, g_1, w) = p_{\text{dual}_0} + w(p_{\text{dual}_1} - p_{\text{dual}_0}), \qquad (14.17)$$

where the two main scattering eccentricities g_0 and g_1, as well as the blend factor w, can be authored by an artist. This is important in representing both the main forward and backward scattering directions, revealing details in clouds when looking both away from and toward the light source, e.g., the sun or moon. See Figure 14.30.

There are different ways to approximate scattered light from ambient lighting in clouds. A straightforward solution is to use a single radiance input uniformly integrated from a render of the sky into a cube map texture. A bottom-up, dark-to-light gradient can also be used to scale the ambient lighting to approximate occlusion from clouds themselves. It is also possible to separate this input radiance as bottom and top, e.g., ground and sky [416]. Then ambient scattering can analytically be integrated for both contributions, assuming constant media density within the cloud layer [1149].

Figure 14.30. Clouds rendered using a ray-marched cloud layer with dynamic lighting and shadowing using a physically based representation of participating media as described by Hillaire [743]. *(Images courtesy of Sören Hesse (top) and Ben McGrath (bottom) from BioWare, ©2018 Electronic Arts Inc.)*

Multiple Scattering Approximation

Clouds' bright and white look is the result of light scattering multiple times within them. Without multiple scattering, thick clouds would mostly be lit at the edge of their volumes, and they would appear dark everywhere else. Multiple scattering is a key component for clouds to not look smoky or murky. It is excessively expensive to evaluate multiple scattering using path tracing. A way to approximate this phenomenon when ray marching has been proposed by Wrenninge [1909]. It integrates o octaves of scattering and sums them as

$$L_{\mathrm{multiscat}}(\mathbf{x}, \mathbf{v}) = \sum_{n=0}^{o-1} L_{\mathrm{scat}}(\mathbf{x}, \mathbf{v}), \tag{14.18}$$

where the following substitutions are made when evaluating L_{scat} (for instance, using σ_s' instead of σ_s): $\sigma_s' = \sigma_s a^n$, $\sigma_e' = \sigma_e b^n$, and $p'(\theta) = p(\theta c^n)$, where a, b, and c are user-control parameters in $[0, 1]$ that will let the light punch through the participating

Figure 14.31. Clouds rendered using Equation 14.18 as an approximation to multiple scattering. From left to right, n is set to 1, 2, and 3. This enable the sun light to punch through the clouds in a believable fashion. *(Image courtesy of Frostbite, © 2018 Electronic Arts Inc. [743].)*

media. Clouds look softer when these values are closer to 0. In order to make sure this technique is energy-conserving when evaluating $L_{\mathrm{multiscat}}(\mathbf{x}, \mathbf{v})$, we must ensure that $a \leq b$. Otherwise, more light can scatter, because the equation $\sigma_t = \sigma_a + \sigma_s$ would not be respected, as σ_s could end up being larger than σ_t. The advantage of this solution is that it can integrate the scattered light for each of the different octaves on the fly while ray marching. The visual improvement is presented in Figure 14.31. The drawback is that it does a poor job at complex multiple scattering behavior when light could scatter in any direction. However, the look of the clouds is improved, and this method allows lighting artists to easily control the visuals with a few parameters and express their vision, thanks to a wider range of achievable results. With this approach, light can punch through the medium and reveal more internal details.

Clouds and Atmosphere Interactions

When rendering a scene with clouds, it is important to take into account interactions with atmospheric scattering for the sake of visual coherency. See Figure 14.32.

Since clouds are large-scale elements, atmospheric scattering should be applied to them. It is possible to evaluate the atmospheric scattering presented in Section 14.4.1

Figure 14.32. Clouds entirely covering the sky are rendered by taking into account the atmosphere [743]. Left: without atmospheric scattering applied on the clouds, leading to incoherent visuals. Middle: with atmospheric scattering, but the environment appears too bright without shadowing. Right: with clouds occluding the sky, thus affecting the light scattering in the atmosphere and resulting in coherent visuals. *(Image courtesy of Frostbite, © 2018 Electronic Arts Inc. [743].)*

for each sample taken through the cloud layer, but doing so quickly becomes expensive. Instead it is possible to apply the atmospheric scattering on the cloud according to a single depth representing the mean cloud depth and transmittance [743].

If cloud coverage is increased to simulate rainy weather, sunlight scattering in the atmosphere should be reduced under the cloud layer. Only light scattered through the clouds should scatter in the atmosphere under them. The illumination can be modified by reducing the sky's lighting contribution to the aerial perspective and adding scattered light back into the atmosphere [743]. The visual improvement is shown in Figure 14.32.

To conclude, cloud rendering can be achieved with advanced physically based material representation and lighting. Realistic cloud shapes and details can be achieved by using procedural noise. Finally, as presented in this section, it is also important to keep in mind the big picture, such as interactions of clouds with the sky, in order to achieve coherent visual results.

14.5 Translucent Surfaces

Translucent surfaces typically refer to materials having a high absorption together with low scattering coefficients. Such materials include glass, water, or the wine shown in Figure 14.2 on page 592. In addition, this section will also discuss translucent glass with a rough surface. These topics are also covered in detail in many publications [1182, 1185, 1413].

14.5.1 Coverage and Transmittance

As discussed in Section 5.5, a transparent surface can be treated as having a coverage represented by α, e.g., opaque fabric or tissue fibers hiding a percentage of what lies behind. For glass and other materials, we want to compute the translucency, where a solid volume lets a percentage of each light wavelength pass through, acting as a filter over the background as a function of transmittance T_r (Section 14.1.2). With the output color $\mathbf{c}_o$, the surface radiance $\mathbf{c}_s$, and the background color $\mathbf{c}_b$, the blending operation for a transparency-as-coverage surface is

$$\mathbf{c}_o = \alpha \mathbf{c}_s + (1 - \alpha)\mathbf{c}_b. \tag{14.19}$$

In the case of a translucent surface, the blending operation will be

$$\mathbf{c}_o = \mathbf{c}_s + \mathbf{T}_r \mathbf{c}_b, \tag{14.20}$$

where $\mathbf{c}_s$ contains the specular reflection of the solid surface, i.e., glass or a gel. Note that $\mathbf{T}_r$ is a three-valued transmittance color vector. To achieve colored translucency, one can use the dual-source color blending feature of any modern graphics API in order to specify these two output colors to blend with the target buffer color $\mathbf{c}_b$. Drobot [386]

Figure 14.33. Translucency with different absorption factors through multiple layers of a mesh [115]. *(Images courtesy of Louis Bavoil [115].)*

presents the different blending operations that can be used depending on whether, for a given surface, reflection and transmittance are colored or not.

In the general case, it is possible to use a common blending operation for coverage and translucency specified together [1185]. The blend function to use in this case is

$$\mathbf{c}_o = \alpha(\mathbf{c}_s + \mathbf{T}_r\mathbf{c}_b) + (1 - \alpha)\mathbf{c}_b. \tag{14.21}$$

When the thickness varies, the amount of light transmitted can be computed using Equation 14.3, which can be simplified to

$$\mathbf{T}_r = e^{-\boldsymbol{\sigma}_t d}, \tag{14.22}$$

where d is the distance traveled through the material volume. The physical extinction parameter $\boldsymbol{\sigma}_t$ represents the rate at which light drops off as it travels through the medium. For intuitive authoring by artists, Bavoil [115] sets the target color $\mathbf{t}_c$ to be the amount of transmittance at some given distance d. Then extinction $\boldsymbol{\sigma}_t$ can be recovered as

$$\boldsymbol{\sigma}_t = \frac{-\log(\mathbf{t}_c)}{d}. \tag{14.23}$$

For example, with target transmittance color $\mathbf{t}_c = (0.3, 0.7, 0.1)$ and distance $d = 4.0$ meters, we recover

$$\boldsymbol{\sigma}_t = \frac{1}{4}(-\log 0.3, -\log 0.7, -\log 0.1) = (0.3010, 0.0892, 0.5756). \tag{14.24}$$

Note that a transmittance of 0 needs to be handled as a special case. A solution is to subtract a small epsilon, e.g., 0.000001, from each component of $\mathbf{T}_r$. The effect of color filtering is shown in Figure 14.33.

In the case of an empty shell mesh whose surface consists of a single thin layer of translucent material, the background color should be occluded as a function of

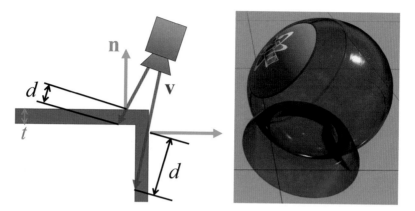

Figure 14.34. Colored transmittance computed from the distance d a view ray $\mathbf{v}$ has traveled within a transparent surface of thickness t. *(Right image courtesy of Activision Publishing, Inc. 2018.)*

the path length d that the light has traveled within the medium. So, viewing such as surface along its normal or tangentially will result in a different amount of background occlusion as a function of its thickness t, because the path length changes with angle. Drobot [386] proposes such an approach where the transmittance $\mathbf{T}_r$ is evaluated as

$$\mathbf{T}_r = e^{-\boldsymbol{\sigma}_t d}, \quad \text{where} \quad d = \frac{t}{\max(0.001, \mathbf{n} \cdot \mathbf{v})}. \tag{14.25}$$

Figure 14.34 shows the result. See Section 9.11.2 for more details about thin-film and multi-layer surfaces.

In the case of solid translucent meshes, computing the actual distance that a ray travels through a transmitting medium can be done in many ways. A common method is to first render the surface where the view ray exits the volume. This surface could be the backface of a crystal ball, or could be the sea floor (i.e., where the water ends). The depth or location of this surface is stored. Then the volume's surface is rendered. The stored exit depth is accessed in the shader, and the distance between it and the current pixel surface is computed. This distance is then used to compute the transmittance to apply over the background.

This method works if it is guaranteed that the volume is closed and convex, i.e., it has one entry and one exit point per pixel, as with a crystal ball. Our seabed example also works because once we exit the water we encounter an opaque surface, so further transmittance will not occur. For more elaborate models, e.g., a glass sculpture or other object with concavities, two or more separate spans may absorb incoming light. Using depth peeling, as discussed in Section 5.5, we can render the volume surfaces in precise back-to-front order. As each frontface is rendered, the distance through the volume is computed and used to compute transmittance. Applying each of these in turn gives the proper final transmittance. Note that if all volumes are made of the

Figure 14.35. Water rendered taking into account the transmittance and reflectance effects. Looking down, we can see into the water with a light blue tint since transmittance is high and blue. Near the horizon the seabed becomes less visible due to a lower transmittance (because light has to travel far into the water volume) and reflection increasing at the expense of transmission, due to the Fresnel effect. *(Image from "Crysis," courtesy of Crytek.)*

same material at the same concentration, the transmittance could be computed once at the end using the summed distances, if the surface has no reflective component. A-buffer or K-buffer methods directly storing object fragments in a single pass can also be used for more efficiency on recent GPUs [115, 230]. Such an example of multi-layer transmittance is shown in Figure 14.33.

In the case of large-scale sea water, the scene depth buffer can be directly used as a representation of the backface seabed. When rendering transparent surfaces, one must consider the Fresnel effect, as described in Section 9.5. Most transmitting media have an index of refraction significantly higher than that of air. At glancing angles, all the light will bounce back from the interface, and none will be transmitted. Figure 14.35 shows this effect, where underwater objects are visible when looking directly into the water, but looking farther out, at a grazing angle, the water surface mostly hides what is beneath the waves. Several articles explain handling reflection, absorption, and refraction for large bodies of water [261, 977].

14.5.2 Refraction

For transmittance we assume that the incoming light comes from directly beyond the mesh volume, in a straight line. This is a reasonable assumption when the front and back surfaces of the mesh are parallel and the thickness is not great, e.g., for a pane

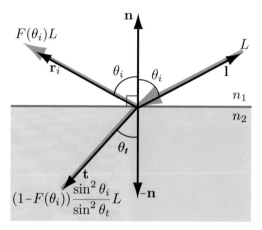

Figure 14.36. Refracted and transmitted radiance as a function of incident angle θ_i and transmission angle θ_t.

of glass. For other transparent media, the index of refraction plays an important role. Snell's law, which describes how light changes direction when a mesh's surface is encountered, is described in Section 9.5.

Due to conservation of energy, any light not reflected is transmitted, so the proportion of transmitted flux to incoming flux is $1 - f$, where f is the amount of reflected light. The proportion of transmitted-to-incident radiance, however, is different. Due to differences in projected area and solid angle between the incident and transmitted rays, the radiance relationship is

$$L_t = (1 - F(\theta_i)) \frac{\sin^2 \theta_i}{\sin^2 \theta_t} L_i. \tag{14.26}$$

This behavior is illustrated in Figure 14.36. Snell's law combined with Equation 14.26 yields a different form for transmitted radiance:

$$L_t = (1 - F(\theta_i)) \frac{n_2^2}{n_1^2} L_i. \tag{14.27}$$

Bec [123] presents an efficient method to compute the refraction vector. For readability (because n is traditionally used for the index of refraction in Snell's equation), we define $\mathbf{N}$ as the surface normal and $\mathbf{l}$ as the direction to the light:

$$\mathbf{t} = (w - k)\mathbf{N} - n\mathbf{l}, \tag{14.28}$$

where $n = n_1/n_2$ is the relative index of refraction, and

$$\begin{aligned} w &= n(\mathbf{l} \cdot \mathbf{N}), \\ k &= \sqrt{1 + (w - n)(w + n)}. \end{aligned} \tag{14.29}$$

Figure 14.37. Left: refraction by glass angels of a cubic environment map, with the map itself used as a skybox background. Right: reflection and refraction by a glass ball with chromatic aberration. *(Left image from the three.js example webgl_materials_cube map_refraction [218], Lucy model from the Stanford 3D scanning repository, texture by Humus. Right image courtesy of Lee Stemkoski [1696].)*

The resulting refraction vector **t** is returned normalized. Water has an index of refraction of approximately 1.33, glass typically around 1.5, and air effectively 1.0.

The index of refraction varies with wavelength. That is, a transparent medium will bend each color of light at a different angle. This phenomenon is called *dispersion*, and explains why prisms spread out white light into a rainbow-colored light cone and why rainbows occur. Dispersion can cause a problem in lenses, termed *chromatic aberration*. In photography, this phenomenon is called *purple fringing*, and can be particularly noticeable along high contrast edges in daylight. In computer graphics we normally ignore this effect, as it is usually an artifact to be avoided. Additional computation is needed to properly simulate the effect, as each light ray entering a transparent surface generates a set of light rays that must then be tracked. As such, normally a single refracted ray is used. It is worthwhile to note that some virtual reality renderers apply an inverse chromatic aberration transform, to compensate for the headset's lenses [1423, 1823].

A general way to give an impression of refraction is to generate a cubic environment map (EM) from the refracting object's position. When this object is then rendered, the EM can be accessed by using the refraction direction computed for the frontfacing surfaces. An example is shown in Figure 14.37. Instead of using an EM, Sousa [1675] proposes a screen-space approach. First, the scene is rendered as usual without any refractive objects into a scene texture **s**. Second, refractive objects are rendered into the alpha channel of **s** that was first cleared to 1. If pixels pass the depth test, a value of 0 is written. Finally, refractive objects are rendered fully, and in the pixel shader **s** is sampled according to pixel position on the screen with a perturbed offset coming from,

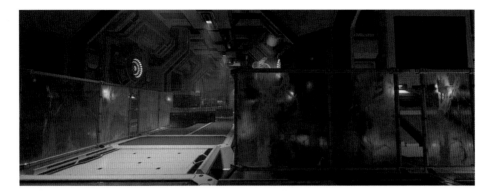

Figure 14.38. Transparent glasses at the bottom of the image features roughness-based background scattering. Elements behind the glass appear more or less blurred, simulating the spreading of refracted rays. *(Image courtesy of Frostbite, © 2018 Electronic Arts Inc.)*

for instance, the scaled surface normal tangent xy-components, simulating refraction. In this context, the color of the perturbed samples is taken into account only if $\alpha = 0$. This test is done to avoid using samples from surfaces that are in front of the refractive object and so having their colors pulled in as if they were behind it. Note that instead of setting $\alpha = 0$, the scene depth map could be used to compare the pixel shader depth against the perturbed scene sample's depth [294]. If the center pixel is farther away, the offset sample is closer; it is then ignored and replaced by the regular scene sample as if there was no refraction.

These techniques give the impression of refraction, but bear little resemblance to physical reality. The ray gets redirected when it enters the transparent solid, but the ray is never bent a second time, when it is supposed to leave the object. This exit interface never comes into play. This flaw sometimes does not matter, because human eyes are forgiving for what the correct appearance should be [1185].

Many games feature refraction through a single layer. For rough refractive surfaces, it is important to blur the background according to material roughness, to simulate the spreading of refracted ray directions caused by the distribution of microgeometry normals. In the game *DOOM* (2016) [1682], the scene is first rendered as usual. It is then downsampled to half resolution and further down to four mipmap levels. Each mipmap level is downsampled according to a Gaussian blur mimicking a GGX BRDF lobe. In the final step, refracting meshes are rendered over the full-resolution scene [294]. The background is composited behind the surfaces by sampling the scene's mipmapped texture and mapping the material roughness to the mipmap level. The rougher the surface, the blurrier the background. Using a general material representation, the same approach is proposed by Drobot [386]. A similar technique is also used within a unified transparency framework from McGuire and Mara [1185]. In this case, a Gaussian point-spread function is used to sample the background in a single pass. See Figure 14.38.

It is also possible to handle the more complex case of refraction through multiple layers. Each layer can be rendered with the depths and normals stored in textures. A procedure in the spirit of relief mapping (Section 6.8.1) can then be used to trace rays through the layers. Stored depths are treated as a heightfield that each ray walks until an intersection is found. Oliveira and Brauwers [1326] present such a framework to handle refraction through backfaces of meshes. Furthermore, nearby opaque objects can be converted into color and depth maps, providing a last opaque layer [1927]. A limitation of all these image-space refraction schemes is that what is outside of the screen's boundaries cannot refract or be refracted.

14.5.3 Caustics and Shadows

Evaluating shadows and caustics resulting from refracted and attenuated light is a complex task. In a non-real-time context, multiple methods, such as bidirectional path tracing or photon mapping [822, 1413], are available to achieve this goal. Luckily, many methods offer approximations of such phenomenon in real time.

Caustics are the visual result of light being diverged from its straight path, for instance by a glass or water surface. The result is that the light will be defocused from some areas, creating shadows, and focused in some others, where ray paths become more dense, resulting in stronger incident lighting. Such paths depend on the curved surface that the light encounters. A classic example for reflection is the cardioid caustic seen inside a coffee mug. Refractive caustics are more noticeable, e.g., light focused through a crystal ornament, a lens, or a glass of water. See Figure 14.39. Caustics can also be created due to light being reflected and refracted by a curved water surface, both above and below. When converging, light will concentrate on opaque surfaces and generate caustics. When under the water surface, converging light paths

Figure 14.39. Real-world caustics from reflection and refraction.

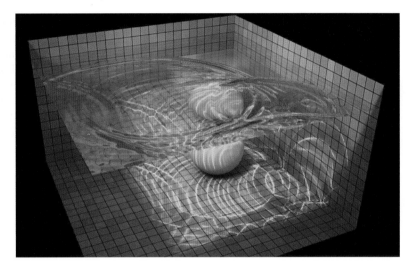

Figure 14.40. Demo of caustic effects in water. *(Image from WebGL Water demo courtesy of Evan Wallace [1831].)*

will become visible within the water volume. This will result in well-known light shafts from photons scattering through water particles. Caustics are a separate factor beyond the light reduction coming from Fresnel interaction at the volume's boundary and the transmittance when traveling through it.

In order to generate caustics from water surfaces, one may apply an animated texture of caustics generated offline as a light map applied on a surface, potentially added on top of the usual light map. Many games have taken advantage of such an approach, such as *Crysis 3* running on CryEngine [1591]. Water areas in a level are authored using *water volumes*. The top surface of the volume can be animated using a bump map texture animation or a physical simulation. The normal resulting from the bump map can be used, when vertically projected above and under the water surface, to generate caustics from their orientation mapped to a radiance contribution. Distance attenuation is controlled using an artist-authored height-based maximum influence distance. The water surface can also be simulated, reacting to object motion in the world and thus generating caustic events matching what is occurring in the environment. An example is shown in Figure 14.40.

When underwater, the same animated water surface can also be used for caustics within the water medium. Lanza [977] propose a two-step method to generate light shafts. First, light positions and refraction directions are rendered from the light's point of view and saved into a texture. Lines can then be rasterized starting from the water surface and extending in the refraction direction in the view. They are accumulated with additive blending, and a final post-process blur can be used to blur out the result in order to mask the low number of lines.

Figure 14.41. On the left, the Buddha refracts both nearby objects and the surrounding skybox [1927]. On the right, caustics are generated via hierarchical maps similar in nature to shadow maps [1929]. *(Images courtesy of Chris Wyman, University of Iowa.)*

Wyman [1928, 1929] presents an image-space technique for caustic rendering. It works by first evaluating photon positions and incident directions after refraction through transparent objects' front- and backfaces. This is achieved by using the background refraction technique [1927] presented in Section 14.5.2. However, instead of storing refracted radiance, textures are used to store the scene intersection position, post-refraction incident direction, and transmittance due to the Fresnel effect. Each texel stores a photon that can then be splatted with the correct intensity back into the view. To achieve this goal there are two possibilities: Splat photons as quads in view space or in light space, with Gaussian attenuation. One result is shown in Figure 14.41. McGuire and Mara [1185] proposed a simpler approach to caustic-like shadows by varying transmittance based on the transparent surface's normal, transmitting more if perpendicular to the incident surface and less otherwise, due to the Fresnel effect. Other volumetric shadow techniques are described in Section 7.8.

14.6   Subsurface Scattering

Subsurface scattering is a complex phenomenon found in solid materials having high scattering coefficients (see Section 9.1.4 for more details). Such materials include wax, human skin, and milk, as seen in Figure 14.2 on page 592.

General light scattering theory has been explained in Section 14.1. In some cases, the scale of scattering is relatively small, as for media with a high optical depth, such as human skin. Scattered light is re-emitted from the surface close to its original point of entry. This shift in location means that subsurface scattering cannot be modeled

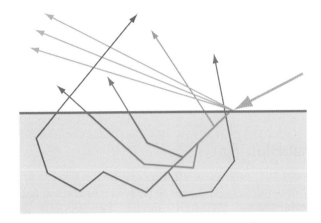

Figure 14.42. Light scattering through an object. Initially the light transmitted into the object travels in the refraction direction, but scattering causes it to change direction repeatedly until it leaves the material. The length of each path through the material determines the percentage of light lost to absorption.

with a BRDF (Section 9.9). That is, when the scattering occurs over a distance larger than a pixel, its more global nature is apparent. Special methods must be used to render such effects.

Figure 14.42 shows light being scattered through an object. Scattering causes incoming light to take many different paths. Since it is impractical to simulate each photon separately (even for offline rendering), the problem must be solved probabilistically, by integrating over possible paths or by approximating such an integral. Besides scattering, light traveling through the material also undergoes absorption.

One important factor that distinguishes the various light paths shown in Figure 14.42 is the number of scattering events. For some paths, the light leaves the material after being scattered once; for others, the light is scattered twice, three times, or more. Scattering paths are commonly grouped as *single scattering* and *multiple scattering*. Different rendering techniques are often used for each group. For some materials, single scattering is a relatively weak part of the total effect, and multiple scattering predominates, e.g., skin. For these reasons, many subsurface scattering rendering techniques focus on simulating multiple scattering. In this section we present several techniques to approximate subsurface scattering.

14.6.1 Wrap Lighting

Perhaps the simplest of the subsurface scattering methods is *wrap lighting* [193]. This technique was discussed on page 382 as an approximation of area light sources. When used to approximate subsurface scattering, we can add a color shift [586]. This accounts for the partial absorption of light traveling through the material. For example, when rendering skin, a red color shift could be applied.

When used in this way, wrap lighting attempts to model the effect of multiple scattering on the shading of curved surfaces. The "leakage" of light from adjacent points into the currently shaded point softens the transition area from light to dark where the surface curves away from the light source. Kolchin [922] points out that this effect depends on surface curvature, and he derives a physically based version. Although the derived expression is somewhat expensive to evaluate, the ideas behind it are useful.

14.6.2 Normal Blurring

Stam [1686] points out that multiple scattering can be modeled as a *diffusion* process. Jensen et al. [823] further develop this idea to derive an analytical *bidirectional surface scattering distribution function* (BSSRDF) model. The BSSRDF is a generalization of the BRDF for the case of global subsurface scattering [1277]. The diffusion process has a spatial blurring effect on the outgoing radiance.

This blurring is applied to only the diffuse reflectance. Specular reflectance occurs at the material surface and is unaffected by subsurface scattering. Since normal maps often encode small-scale variation, a useful trick for subsurface scattering is to apply normal maps to only the specular reflectance [569]. The smooth, unperturbed normal is used for the diffuse reflectance. Since there is no added cost, it is often worthwhile to apply this technique when using other subsurface scattering methods.

For many materials, multiple scattering occurs over a relatively small distance. Skin is an important example, where most scattering takes place over a distance of a few millimeters. For such materials, the technique of not perturbing the diffuse shading normal may be sufficient by itself. Ma et al. [1095] extend this method, based on measured data. They determined the reflected light from scattering objects and found that, while the specular reflectance is based on the geometric surface normals, subsurface scattering makes diffuse reflectance behave as if it uses blurred surface normals. Furthermore, the amount of blurring can vary over the visible spectrum. They propose a real-time shading technique using independently acquired normal maps for the specular reflectance and for the R, G, and B channels of the diffuse reflectance [245]. Using different normal maps for each channel will then result in color bleeding. Since these diffuse normal maps typically resemble blurred versions of the specular map, it is straightforward to modify this technique to use a single normal map, while adjusting the mipmap level, but at the cost of losing the color shift since the normal is the same for each channel.

14.6.3 Pre-Integrated Skin Shading

Combining the idea of wrap lighting and normal blurring, Penner [1369] proposes a pre-integrated skin shading solution.

Scattering and transmittance are integrated and stored in a two-dimensional lookup table. The LUT's first axis is indexed based on $\mathbf{n} \cdot \mathbf{l}$. The second axis is indexed based on $1/r = ||\partial n/\partial p||$, representing the surface curvature. The higher the curvature, the greater the impact on the transmitted and scattered color. Because curvature is constant per triangle, these values must be baked and smoothed offline.

To handle the effect of subsurface scattering on small surface details, Penner modifies the technique by Ma et al. [1095], which was discussed in the previous section. Instead of acquiring separate normal maps for the R, G, and B diffuse reflectance, Penner generates them by blurring the original normal map according to the diffusion profile of the subsurface material for each color channel. Since using four separate normal maps is memory intensive, as an optimization he uses a single smoothed normal map that is blended with the vertex normal for each color channel.

This technique will ignore light diffusion across shadow boundaries, since by default it only relies on curvature. To get the scattering profile to span through shadow boundaries, the shadow penumbra profile can be used to bias the LUT coordinates. Thus, this fast technique is able to approximate the high-quality method presented in the next section [345].

14.6.4 Texture-Space Diffusion

Blurring the diffuse normals accounts for some visual effects of multiple scattering, but not for others, such as softened shadow edges. The concept of *texture-space diffusion* can be used to address these limitations. This idea was introduced by Lensch et al. [1032] as part of a different technique, but the version presented by Borshukov and Lewis [178, 179] has been the most influential. They formalize the idea of multiple scattering as a blurring process. First, the surface irradiance (diffuse lighting) is rendered into a texture. This is done by using texture coordinates as positions for rasterization. The real positions are interpolated separately for use in shading. This texture is blurred and then used for diffuse shading when rendering. The shape and size of the filter depends on the material and on the wavelength. For example, for skin, the R channel is filtered with a wider filter than G or B, causing reddening near shadow edges. The correct filter for simulating subsurface scattering in most materials has a narrow spike in the center and a wide, shallow base. This technique was first presented for use in offline rendering, but real-time GPU implementations were soon proposed by researchers at NVIDIA [345, 586] and ATI [568, 569, 803, 1541].

The presentation by d'Eon and Luebke [345] represents one of the most complete treatments of this technique, including support for complex filters mimicking the effect of multi-layer subsurface structure. Donner and Jensen [369] show that such structures produce the most realistic skin renderings. The full NVIDIA skin rendering system presented by d'Eon and Luebke produces excellent results (see Figure 14.43 for an example), but is quite expensive, requiring a large number of blurring passes. However, it can easily be scaled back to increase performance.

Instead of applying multiple Gaussian passes, Hable [631] presents a single 12-sample kernel. The filter can be applied either in texture space as a preprocess or in the pixel shader when rasterizing the mesh on screen. This makes face rendering much

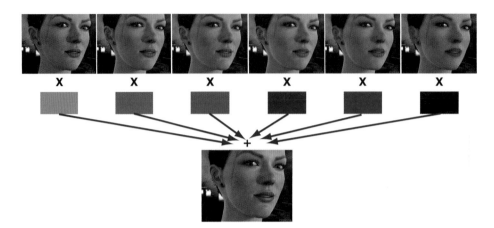

Figure 14.43. Texture-space multi-layer diffusion. Six different blurs are combined using RGB weights. The final image is the result of this linear combination, plus a specular term. *(Images courtesy of NVIDIA Corporation [345].)*

faster at the cost of some realism. When close up, the low amount of sampling can become visible as bands of color. However, from a moderate distance, the difference in quality is not noticeable.

14.6.5 Screen-Space Diffusion

Rendering a light map and blurring it for all the meshes in a scene can quickly become expensive, both computationally and memory-wise. Furthermore, the meshes need to be rendered twice, once in the light map and once in the view, and the light map needs to have a reasonable resolution to be able to represent subsurface scattering from small-scale details.

To counter these issues, Jimenez proposed a screen-space approach [831]. First, the scene is rendered as usual and meshes requiring subsurface scattering, e.g., human faces, will be noted in the stencil buffer. Then a two-pass screen-space process is applied on the stored radiance to simulate subsurface scattering, using the stencil test to apply the expensive algorithm only where it is needed, in pixels containing translucent material. The additional passes apply the two one-dimensional and bilateral blur kernels, horizontally and vertically. The colored blur kernel is separable, but it cannot be applied in a fully separable fashion for two reasons. First, linear view depth must be taken into account to stretch the blur to a correct width, according to surface distance. Second, bilateral filtering avoids light leaking from materials at different depths, i.e., between surfaces that should not interact. In addition, the normal orientation must be taken into account for the blur filter to be applied not only in screen space but tangentially to the surface. In the end, this makes the separability of the blur kernel an approximation, but still a high-quality one. Later, an improved separable filter

Figure 14.44. High-quality render of scanned model faces. Screen-space subsurface scattering makes it possible to render realistic human skin material on many characters with a single post-process. *(Left image: render courtesy of Jorge Jimenez and Diego Gutierrez, Universidad de Zaragoza. Scan courtesy of XYZRGB Inc. Right image: render courtesy of Jorge Jimenez et al., Activision Publishing, Inc., 2013 and Universidad de Zaragoza. Scan courtesy of Lee Perry-Smith, Infinite-Realities [831].)*

was proposed [833]. Being dependent on the material area on screen, this algorithm is expensive for close-ups on faces. However, this cost is justifiable, since high quality in these areas is just what is desired. This algorithm is especially valuable when a scene is composed of many characters, since they will all be processed at the same time. See Figure 14.44.

To further optimize the process, the linear depth can be stored in the alpha channel of the scene texture. The one-dimensional blur relies on a low number of samples, so undersampling can be visible on faces close up. To avoid this issue, the kernel can be rotated per pixel, which will hide ghosting artifacts with noise [833]. The visibility of this noise can be significantly reduced by using temporal antialiasing (Section 5.4.2).

When implementing screen-space diffusion, care must be taken to blur only irradiance and not the diffuse albedo or specular lighting. One way to achieve this goal is to render irradiance and specular lighting into separate screen-space buffers. If deferred shading (Section 20.1) is used, then a buffer with diffuse albedo is already available. To reduce memory bandwidth, Gallagher and Mittring [512] propose storing irradiance and specular lighting in a single buffer, using a checkerboard pattern. After the irradiance has been blurred, the final image is composited by multiplying the diffuse albedo with the blurred irradiance and adding the specular lighting on top.

Within this screen-space framework, it is also possible to render large-scale subsurface scattering phenomena, such as the light traveling through the nose or ears. When rendering the mesh diffuse lighting, the technique presented by Jimenez et al. [827] also adds the subsurface transmission from backface contributions by sampling the incoming light from the opposite side using the negated surface normal $-\mathbf{n}$. The result is modulated by a transmittance value estimated using the depth recovered by sampling a traditional shadow map rendered from the light's point of view, similarly to the method by Dachsbacher and Stamminger [320] described in the next section. To represent forward scattering in a cone, the shadow map can be sampled multiple times. In order to use a low sample count per pixel to reduce the cost of rendering, it is possible to take two shadow samples with a randomized offset or rotation per pixel. Doing so will result in much unwanted visual noise. Thankfully, this noise can automatically be filtered out for free by the screen-space subsurface blur kernel required to achieve the translucent subsurface light diffusion. It is thus possible to render high-quality translucency effects simulating forward light scattering in a cone through the thin parts of a face with only one extra depth-map sample per light source.

14.6.6   Depth-Map Techniques

The techniques discussed so far model light scattering over relatively small distances, e.g., skin. Other techniques are needed for materials exhibiting large-scale scattering, such as light traveling through a hand. Many of these focus on single scattering, which is easier to model than multiple scattering.

The ideal simulation for large-scale single scattering can be seen on the left in Figure 14.45. The light paths change direction on entering and exiting the object, due to refraction. The effects of all the paths need to be summed to shade a single surface point. Absorption also needs to be taken into account—the amount of absorption in a path depends on its length inside the material. Computing all these refracted rays for a single shaded point is expensive even for offline renderers, so the refraction on entering the material is usually ignored, and only the change in direction on exiting the material is taken into account [823]. Since the rays cast are always in the direction of the light, Hery [729, 730] points out that light-space depth maps, typically used for shadowing, can be accessed instead of performing ray casting. See the middle of Figure 14.45. For media that scatter light according to a phase function, the scattering angle also affects the amount of scattered light.

Performing depth-map lookups is faster than ray casting, but the multiple samples required makes Hery's method too slow for most real-time rendering applications. Green [586] proposes a faster approximation, shown on the right in Figure 14.45. Although this method is less physically based, its results can be convincing. One problem is that details on the back side of the object can show through, since every change in object thickness will directly affect the shaded color. Despite this, Green's approximation is effective enough to be used by Pixar for films such as *Ratatouille* [609]. Pixar refers to this technique as *gummi lights*. Another problem with Hery's implementation is that the depth map should not contain multiple objects, or highly non-convex objects. This is because it is assumed that the entire path between the shaded (blue) point and the intersection (red) point lies within the object. Pixar gets around this problem by using a type of deep shadow map [1066].

Modeling large-scale multiple scattering in real time is quite difficult, since each surface point can be influenced by light coming from any other surface point. Dachsbacher and Stamminger [320] propose an extension of shadow mapping, called *translu-*

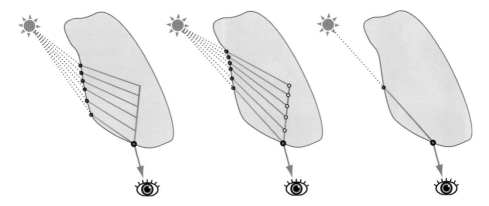

Figure 14.45. On the left, the ideal situation, in which light refracts when entering and exiting the object; all scattering contributions that would properly refract upon leaving the object are correctly gathered via ray marching within the material. The length of each path will be accounted for when evaluating extinction σ_t. This is achievable using path tracing or a few real-time approximations [320]. The middle image shows a computationally simpler situation, in which the rays refract only on exit. This is the usual approximation done in real-time rendering because finding the entry points (in red) from sample points (in yellow) with respect to refraction is not straightforward. The right image shows an approximation, which is therefore faster, where only a single ray is considered instead of multiple samples along the refracted ray [586].

cent shadow mapping, for modeling multiple scattering. Additional information, such as irradiance and the surface normal, is stored in light-space textures. Several samples are taken from these textures, including the depth map, and combined to form an estimation of the scattered radiance. A modification of this technique is used in NVIDIA's skin rendering system [345]. Mertens et al. [1201] propose a similar method, but use a texture in screen space rather than light space.

Leaves in trees also exhibit a strong subsurface scattering effect, appearing as a bright green color when light is coming in from behind. In addition to the albedo and normal textures, a texture representing transmittance T_r through the leaf volume can be mapped onto the surface [1676]. Then, an ad hoc model can be used to approximate the additional subsurface contribution from lights. Since leaves are thin elements, a negated normal can be used as an approximation to the opposite side normal $\mathbf{n}$. The backlit contribution can be evaluated as $(\mathbf{l} \cdot -\mathbf{n})^+ \cdot (-\mathbf{v} \cdot \mathbf{l})^+$, where $\mathbf{l}$ is the light direction and $\mathbf{v}$ is the view direction. It can then be multiplied with the surface albedo and added on top of the direct light contributions.

In a similar fashion, Barré-Brisebois and Bouchard [105] present an inexpensive ad hoc approximation to large-scale subsurface scattering on meshes. First, for each mesh they generate a grayscale texture storing an *averaged local thickness*, which is one minus the ambient occlusion computed from the inward-facing normal $-\mathbf{n}$. This texture, called t_{ss}, is considered an approximation to the transmittance that can be applied to light coming from the opposite side of the surface. The subsurface scattering

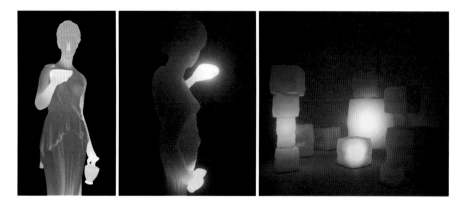

Figure 14.46. On the left, a local thickness texture generated for a statue of Hebe. In the middle, the subsurface light scattering effect that can be achieved with it. On the right, another scene with translucent cubes rendered using the same technique. *(Images courtesy of Colin Barré-Brisebois and Marc Bouchard [105].)*

added to the regular surface lighting is evaluated as

$$t_{\text{ss}}\mathbf{c}_{\text{ss}}\big((\mathbf{v}\cdot-\mathbf{l})^{+}\big)^{p}, \tag{14.30}$$

where $\mathbf{l}$ and $\mathbf{v}$ are the normalized light and view vectors, respectively, p is an exponent approximating a phase function (as shown in Figure 14.10 on page 599), and $\mathbf{c}_{\text{ss}}$ is the subsurface albedo. This expression is then multiplied with the light color, intensity, and distance attenuation. This model is not physically based or energy conserving, but it is able to rapidly render plausible subsurface lighting effects in a single pass. See Figure 14.46.

14.7 Hair and Fur

Hairs are protein filaments that grow out of the dermis layer of mammals. In the case of humans, hair is scattered in different areas of the body, and different types include top-of-head, beard, eyebrows, and eyelashes. Other mammals are often covered with fur (dense, limited-length hair), and fur's properties tend to vary in different locations on an animal's body. Hairs can be straight, wavy, or curly, each with a different strength and roughness. Hair strands can naturally be black, brown, red, blond, gray, or white, and can be dyed (with varying success) all the colors of the rainbow.

Hair and fur structure is fundamentally the same. It consists of three layers [1052, 1128], as shown in Figure 14.47:

- Outside is the cuticle, which represents the surface of the fiber. This surface is not smooth but is composed of overlapping scales tilted by approximately $\alpha = 3°$ compared to the hair's direction, which tilts the normal toward the root.

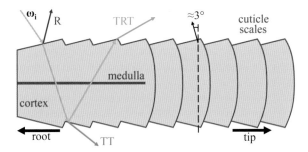

Figure 14.47. Longitudinal cut of a hair strand presenting the different materials composing it, along with lighting components resulting from incoming light along direction ω_i.

- In the middle is the cortex, containing melanin that gives the fiber its color [346]. One such pigment is eumelanin, responsible for brown color with $\sigma_{a,e} = (0.419, 0.697, 1.37)$, and another is pheomelanin, responsible for red hair with $\sigma_{a,p} = (0.187, 0.4, 1.05)$.

- The inner part is the medulla. It is small and often ignored when modeling human hair [1128]. However, it takes up a larger portion of the hair volume for animal fur, where it has greater significance [1052].

It is possible to see hair fibers as analogous to particles, as discretization of a volume, but with curves instead of points. Hair fiber lighting interaction is described using a *bidirectional scattering distribution function* (BSDF). This corresponds to a BRDF but with light integrated over a sphere, instead of just a hemisphere. A BSDF aggregates all the interactions happening within hair fibers through the different layers. It is described in detail in Section 14.7.2. Light scatters within fibers but also bounces off many of them, resulting in complex colored radiance from multiple-scattering phenomena. Furthermore, because fibers absorb light as a function of their material and pigments, it is also important to represent volumetric self-shadows that occur within the hair volume. In this section we describe how recent techniques allow us to render short hairs, such as beard hair, head hair, and, finally, fur.

14.7.1 Geometry and Alpha

Hair strands can be rendered as extruded *hair quads* using vertex shader code around hair guide curves painted by an artist, producing a ribbon of quads following the guides. Each quad ribbon follows its matching hair guide curve according to a specified orientation following the skin and representing a clump of hair [863, 1228, 1560]. This approach is well suited for beard or short and mostly static hairs. It is also efficient, because large quads can result in more visual coverage, and thus less ribbons will be needed to cover a head, which in turn improves performance. If more detail is needed, for instance in the case of thin, long hair animated by a physical simulation, it is possible to use thinner quad ribbons and render thousands of them. In this case, it is better to also orient the generated quads toward the view using a cylinder constraint along the hair curve tangent [36]. Even if a hair simulation is done with just a few hair guides, new strands can be instantiated by interpolating the properties of surrounding hair guides [1954].

All these elements can be rendered as alpha-blended geometry. If used, the rendering order of head hairs will need to be correct to avoid transparency artifacts (Section 5.5). To mitigate this issue, it is possible to use a pre-sorted index buffer, rendering hair strands close to the head first and outer ones last. This work well for short and non-animated hair but not for long interleaved and animated hair strands. Fixing ordering issues by relying on the depth test is possible using alpha testing. However, this can lead to serious aliasing problems for high-frequency geometry and textures. It is possible to use MSAA with alpha testing being done per sample [1228], at the cost of extra samples and memory bandwidth. Alternately, any order-independent transparency method can be used, such as the ones discussed in Section 5.5. For example, TressFX [36] stores the $k = 8$ closest fragments, updated in the pixel shader to keep only the first seven layers ordered, so achieving multi-layer alpha blending [1532].

Another issue is alpha-testing artifacts resulting from mipmapped alpha minification (Section 6.6). Two solutions to this problem are to perform smarter alpha mipmap generation or to use a more advanced hashed alpha test [1933]. When rendering thin long hair strands, it is also possible to modify the hair opacity according to its pixel coverage [36].

Small-scale hairs such as beards, eyelashes, and eyebrows are simpler to render than a head's full volume of hair. Eyelashes and eyebrows can even be geometry skinned to match head and eyelid movements. The hair surface on these small elements can be lit using an opaque BRDF material. It is also possible to shade hair strands by using a BSDF, as presented in the next section.

14.7.2 Hair

Kajiya and Kay [847] developed a BRDF model to render volumes consisting of organized and infinitely small cylinder fibers. This model, discussed in Section 9.10.3, was first developed to render furry elements by ray marching through a volume texture representing density above a surface. The BRDF is used to represent the specular and diffuse light response with the volume, and can also be used on hairs.

The seminal work from Marschner et al. [1128] measures light scattering in human hair fibers and presents a model based on these observations. Different components of scattering in a single hair strand have been observed. These are all depicted in Figure 14.47. First, an R component represents reflection of light at the air/fiber interface on the cuticle, which results in a shifted white specular peak toward the root. Second, the TT component represents light traveling through the hair fiber by being transmitted once from air to hair material, and a second time from hair to air. Finally, a third TRT component represents light traveling in the hair fiber by

Figure 14.48. Path-traced reference of blond (left) and brown (right) hairs rendered with specular glints resulting from fiber eccentricity. *(Image courtesy of d'Eon et al. [346].)*

being transmitted, reflected by the opposite side of the fiber, and then transmitted back outside the hair material. The "R" in the variable name represents one internal reflection. The TRT component is perceived as a secondary specular highlight, shifted compared to R, and is colored since light has been absorbed while traveling through the fiber material.

Visually, the R component is perceived as a colorless specular reflection on the hair. The TT component is perceived as a bright highlight when a volume of hair is lit from behind. The TRT component is crucial to rendering realistic hairs since it will result in glints on strands with eccentricity, i.e., in real-life, a hair's cross section is not a perfect circle but rather an oval. Glints are important for believability, as these keep hairs from looking uniform. See Figure 14.48.

Marschner et al. [1128] propose functions modeling the R, TT, and TRT components as part of the hair BSDF that represents the response of a hair fiber to light. The model properly takes into account the Fresnel effect at transmission and reflection events but ignores the other more-involved light paths such as TRRT, TRRRT, and longer.

This original model is, however, not energy conserving. This has been studied and fixed in the work of d'Eon et al. [346]. The BSDF components have been reformulated and made energy conserving by better taking into account roughness and the contraction of specular cones. The components have also been extended to include longer paths such as TR*T. Transmittance is also controlled using measured melanin extinction coefficients. Similarly to the work by Marschner et al. [1128], their model is able to faithfully render glints on strands with eccentricity. Another energy-conserving model is presented by Chiang et al. [262]. This model gives a parameterization for roughness and multiple scattering color that is more intuitive to author by artists, instead of having them tweak Gaussian variance or melanin concentration coefficients.

Artists may want to author a particular look for the specular term on hair on a character, by changing the roughness parameter, for example. With a physically based energy-conserving and energy-preserving model, the scattered light deep within the

Figure 14.49. Real-time hair rendering with the R, TT, and TRT, as well as a multiple scattering component. *(Image courtesy of Epic Games, Inc. [863, 1802].)*

hair volume will also change. To give more artistic control, it is possible to separate the first few scattering paths (R, TT, TRT) and the multiple scattering parts [1525]. This is achieved by maintaining a second set of BSDF parameters, used only for the multiple scattering paths. In addition, the BSDF R, TT, and TRT components can then be represented with simple mathematical shapes that can be understood and tweaked by artists to further refine the look. The full set is still made energy conserving by normalizing the BSDF according to the in and out directions.

Each BSDF model presented above is complex, expensive to evaluate, and mostly used in movie production path-tracing environments. Thankfully, real-time versions exist. Scheuermann proposes an ad hoc BSDF model that is easy to implement, fast to render, and looks convincing on hair rendered as large quad ribbons [1560]. Going further, it is possible to use the Marschner model [1128] in real time by storing the BSDF in LUT textures indexed by the in and out directions as parameters [1274]. However, this method can make it hard to render a hair with a spatially varying appearance. To avoid this issue, a recent physically based real-time model [863] approximates components from previous work with simplified mathematics to achieve convincing results. See Figure 14.49. However, there is a gap in quality with all these real-time hair rendering models as compared to offline results. The simplified algorithms usually do not feature advanced volumetric shadowing or multiple scattering. Such effects are particularly important for hair with low absorption, e.g., blond hair.

In the case of volumetric shadows, recent solutions [36, 863] rely on a transmittance value computed using d as the distance along the light's direction from the first hair encountered to the current fiber according to a constant absorption σ_a. This approach is practical and straightforward since it relies on the usual shadow map available in any engine. However, it cannot represent local density variations resulting from clumped hair strands, which is especially important for brightly lit hair. See Figure 14.50. To address this, a volumetric shadow representation can be used (Section 7.8).

Multiple scattering is an expensive term to evaluate when rendering hair. There are not many solutions suitable for real-time implementation. Karis [863] proposes a

Figure 14.50. Left: using a depth difference from the first occluder with constant extinction coefficients results in too smooth volumetric shadows. Middle: using deep shadow maps [1953] makes it possible to achieve more transmittance variations matching the way hairs are clumped together within the hair volume. Right: combining deep shadow maps with PCSS achieves smoother volumetric shadows based on the distance to the first occluder (see Section 7.6 for more details). *(Image rendered using a hair model courtesy of USC-HairSalon [781].)*

way to approximate multiple scattering. This ad hoc model uses fake normals (similar to bent normals), wrapped diffuse lighting, and the hairs' base color raised to a depth-dependent power before it is multiplied with lighting, approximating color saturation after light has scattered through many strands.

A more advanced dual-scattering technique has been presented by Zinke et al. [1972]. See Figure 14.51. It is dual because it evaluates the amount of scattered light according to two factors. First, a global transmittance factor Ψ^G is evaluated by combining the BSDF of each hair strand encountered between the shaded pixel and the light's position. Thus, Ψ^G gives the amount of transmittance to apply to the incoming radiance at the shaded position. This value can be evaluated on the GPU by counting the number of hairs and calculating the mean strand orientation on a light path, the latter influencing the BSDF and so also the transmittance. Accumulating these data can be achieved using deep opacity mapping [1953] or occupancy maps [1646]. Second, a local scattering component Ψ^L approximates the fact that the transmitted radiance at the shaded position will scatter in the hair fibers around the current one and contribute to the radiance. Both these terms are added as $\Psi^G + \Psi^G \Psi^L$ and fed through the pixel strand BSDF to accumulate the light source contribution. This technique is more expensive, but it is an accurate real-time approximation to the light multiple scattering phenomenon within hair volumes. It can also be used with any of the BSDFs presented in this chapter.

Environment lighting is another input that is complex to evaluate for animated translucent materials. It is common to simply sample the irradiance from spherical harmonics. The lighting can also be weighted by non-directional pre-integrated ambient occlusion computed from the hair at its rest position [1560]. Using the same fake

Figure 14.51. The first two images present hair rendered using path tracing as a reference for the three hair scattering components (R, TT, TRT) in isolation and then with multiple scattering added. The last two images present results using the dual-scattering approximation: path-traced and then rendered in real time on the GPU. *(Images courtesy of Arno Zinke and Cem Yuksel [1953].)*

normal as for multiple scattering, Karis proposes an ad hoc model for environment lighting [863].

For more information, a comprehensive real-time hair rendering course is available online from Yuksel and Tariq [1954]. Before reading research papers and learning more details, this course will teach you all about the many areas of hair rendering such as simulation, collision, geometry, BSDF, multiple scattering, and volumetric shadows. Hair can look convincing in real-time applications. However, much research is still needed to be able to better approximate physically based environment lighting and multiple scattering in hair.

14.7.3 Fur

As opposed to hair, fur is usually seen as short and semi-organized strands typically found on animals. A concept related to the method of using layers of textures for volumetric rendering is *volumetric textures*, which are volume descriptions that are represented by layers of two-dimensional, semitransparent textures [1203].

For example, Lengyel et al. [1031] use a set of eight textures to represent fur on a surface. Each texture represents a slice through a set of hairs at a given distance from the surface. The model is rendered eight times, with a vertex shader program moving each triangle slightly outward along its vertex normals each time. In this way, each successive model depicts a different height above the surface. Nested models created this way are called *shells*. This rendering technique falls apart along object silhouette edges, as the hairs break up into dots as the layers spread out. To hide this artifact, the fur is also represented by a different hair texture applied on *fins* generated along the silhouette edges. See Figure 14.52 and Figure 19.28 on page 855. The idea of silhouette fin extrusion can be used to create visual complexity for other types of models. For example, Kharlamov et al. [887] use fins and relief mapping to provide tree meshes with complex silhouettes.

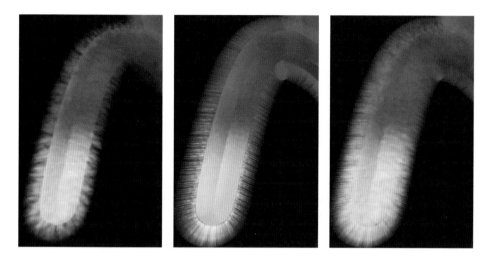

Figure 14.52. Fur using volumetric texturing. The model is rendered eight times, with the surface expanding outward a small amount each pass. On the left is the result of the eight passes. Note the hair breakup along the silhouettes. In the middle, fin rendering is shown. On the right is the final rendering, using both fins and shells. *(Images from NVIDIA SDK 10 [1300] sample "Fur—Shells and Fins," courtesy of NVIDIA Corporation.)*

The introduction of the geometry shader made it possible to actually extrude polyline hairs for surfaces with fur. This technique was used in *Lost Planet* [1428]. A surface is rendered and values are saved at each pixel: fur color, length, and angle. The geometry shader then processes this image, turning each pixel into a semitransparent polyline. By creating one hair per pixel covered, level of detail is automatically maintained. The fur is rendered in two passes. Fur pointing downward in screen space is rendered first, sorted from the bottom to the top of the screen. In this way, blending is performed correctly, back to front. In the second pass, the rest of the fur pointing up is rendered top to bottom, again blending correctly. As the GPU evolves, new techniques become possible and profitable.

It is possible to also use the techniques presented in the previous sections. Strands can be rendered as quads extruded as geometry from a skinned surface such as for Chewbacca in the *Star Wars Battlefront* games or for the TressFX *Rat demo* [36]. When rendering hair strands as thin filaments, Ling-Qi et al. [1052] have proven that it is not enough to simulate hair as a uniform cylinder. For animal fur, the medulla is much darker and larger relative to the hair radius. This reduces the impact of light scattering. As such, a double-cylinder fiber BSDF model is presented that simulates a wider range of hair and fur [1052]. It considers more detailed paths such as TttT, TrRrT, TttRttT, and more, where lowercase letters represent interactions with the medulla. This complex approach results in more realistic visuals, especially for simulation of rougher fur and elaborate scattering effects. Such fur rendering techniques involve the rasterization of many strand instances, and anything that can help to reduce the render time is welcome. Ryu [1523] proposes to decimate the number of strand instances rendered as a level of detail scheme dependent on motion magnitude and distance. This method was used for offline movie rendering and appears to be straightforward to apply in real-time applications.

14.8   Unified Approaches

We have reached a point where volumetric rendering has become affordable in real-time applications. What may be possible to achieve in the future?

At the beginning of this chapter we stated that "everything is scattering." Looking at participating media materials, it is possible to use a high scattering coefficient σ_s in order to achieve a opaque medium. This, together with a complex anisotropic phase function driving diffuse and specular responses, would result in an opaque surface material. In light of that, would there be a way to unify solid and volumetric material representations?

As of today, volumetric and opaque material rendering are separated because the current computational capabilities of GPUs force us to use specific approaches that are efficient for some use cases. We use meshes for opaque surfaces, alpha-blended meshes for transparent materials, particle billboards for smoke volumes, and ray marching for some of the volumetric lighting effects within participating media.

As hinted at by Dupuy et al. [397], it may be possible to represent solid and participating media using a unified representation. One possible representation is to use symmetrical GGX [710] (SGGX), an extension of the GGX normal distribution function presented in Section 9.8.1. In this case, the microflake theory representing oriented flake particles within a volume replaces the microfacet theory used for surface normal distribution representation. In a sense, level of detail would become more practical, as compared to meshes, because it can simply become a volume filtering over the material properties. That could lead to more coherent lighting and representation of large detailed worlds while maintaining lighting, shape, occlusion, or transmittance applied over the background. For example, as shown in Figure 14.53, rendering a forest with a volume filtered tree representation would remove visible tree mesh LOD switching, providing a smooth filtering of thin geometry and avoiding aliasing caused by branches, while also providing the correct occlusion value over the background considering the underlying tree geometry within each voxel.

Further Reading and Resources

These resources have been mentioned throughout the text, but are worth highlighting here as particularly noteworthy. General volumetric rendering is explained in the

Figure 14.53. A forest rendered using SGGX at the top, with decreasing levels of detail from left to right. The bottom part shows the raw unfiltered voxels. *(Images courtesy of Eric Heitz et al. [710].)*

course notes of Fong et al. [479], providing considerable background theory, optimization details, and solutions used in movie production. For sky and cloud rendering, this chapter builds on Hillaire's extensive course notes [743], which have more details than we could include here. The animation of volumetric material is outside the scope of this book. We recommend that the reader reads these articles about real-time simulations [303, 464, 1689] and especially the complete book from Bridson [197]. McGuire's presentation [1182], along with McGuire and Mara's article [1185], gives a wider understanding of transparency-related effects and a range of strategies and algorithms that can be used for various elements. For hair and fur rendering and simulation, we again refer the reader to the extensive course notes by Yuksel and Tariq [1954].

Chapter 15
Non-Photorealistic Rendering

"Using a term like 'nonlinear science' is like referring to the
bulk of zoology as 'the study of nonelephant animals.'"
—Stanislaw Ulam

Photorealistic rendering attempts to make an image indistinguishable from a photograph. *Non-photorealistic rendering* (NPR), also called stylized rendering, has a wide range of goals. One objective of some forms of NPR is to create images similar to technical illustrations. Only those details relevant to the goal of the particular appli-

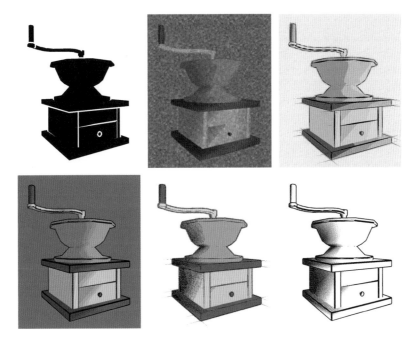

Figure 15.1. A variety of non-photorealistic rendering styles applied to a coffee grinder. *(Generated using LiveArt from Viewpoint DataLabs.)*

cation are the ones that should be displayed. For example, a photograph of a shiny Ferrari engine may be useful in selling the car to a customer, but to repair the engine, a simplified line drawing with the relevant parts highlighted may be more meaningful (as well as less costly to print).

Another area of NPR is in the simulation of painterly styles and natural media, e.g., pen and ink, charcoal, and watercolor. This is a huge field that lends itself to an equally huge variety of algorithms that attempt to capture the feel of various media. Some examples are shown in Figure 15.1. Two older books provide coverage of technical and painterly NPR algorithms [563, 1719]. Given this breadth, we focus here on techniques for rendering strokes and lines. Our goal is to give a flavor of some algorithms used for NPR in real time. This chapter opens with a detailed discussion of ways to implement a cartoon rendering style, then discusses other themes within the field of NPR. The chapter ends with a variety of line rendering techniques.

15.1   Toon Shading

Just as varying the font gives a different feel to the text, different styles of rendering have their own mood, meaning, and vocabulary. There has been a large amount of attention given to one particular form of NPR, *cel* or *toon rendering*. Since this style is identified with cartoons, it has connotations of fantasy and childhood. At its simplest, objects are drawn with solid lines separating areas of different solid colors. One reason this style is popular is what McCloud, in his classic book *Understanding Comics* [1157], calls "amplification through simplification." By simplifying and stripping out clutter, one can amplify the effect of information relevant to the presentation. For cartoon characters, a wider audience will identify with those drawn in a simple style.

The toon rendering style has been used in computer graphics for decades to integrate three-dimensional models with two-dimensional cel animation. It lends itself well to automatic generation by computer because it is easily defined, compared to other NPR styles. Many video games have used it to good effect [250, 1224, 1761]. See Figure 15.2.

The outlines of objects are often rendered in a black color, which amplifies the cartoon look. Finding and rendering these outlines is dealt with in the next section. There are several different approaches to toon surface shading. The two most common methods are to fill the mesh areas with solid (unlit) color or to use a two-tone approach, representing lit and shadowed areas. The two-tone approach, sometimes called *hard shading*, is simple to perform in a pixel shader by using a lighter color when the dot product of the shading normal and light source direction are above some value, and a darker tone if not. When the illumination is more complex, another approach is to quantize the final image itself. Also called *posterization*, this is a process of taking a continuous range of values and converting to a few tones, with a sharp change between each. See Figure 15.3. Quantizing RGB values can cause unpleasant hue shifts, as each separate channel changes in a way not closely related to the others. Working a hue-

Figure 15.2. An example of real-time NPR rendering from the game *Okami*. *(Image courtesy of Capcom Entertainment, Inc.)*

preserving color space such as HSV, HSL, or Y'CbCr is a better choice. Alternately, a one-dimensional function or texture can be defined to remap intensity levels to specific shades or colors. Textures can also be preprocessed using quantization or other filters. Another example, with more color levels, is shown in Figure 15.16 on page 665.

basic   solid   posterization   pencil

Figure 15.3. The basic rendering on the left has solid fill, posterization, and pencil shading techniques applied in turn. *(Jade2 model by Quidam, published by wismo [1449], Creative Commons 2.5 attribution license.)*

Barla et al. [104] add view-dependent effects by using two-dimensional maps in place of one-dimensional shade textures. The second dimension is accessed by the depth or orientation of the surface. This allows objects to smoothly soften in contrast when distant or moving rapidly, for example. This algorithm, combined with a variety of other shading equations and painted textures, is used in the game *Team Fortress 2* to give a blend of cartoon and realistic styles [1224]. Variations on toon shaders can be used for other purposes, such as for exaggerating contrast when visualizing features on surfaces or terrain [1520].

15.2   Outline Rendering

Algorithms used for cel edge rendering reflect some of the major themes and techniques of NPR. Our goal here is to present algorithms that give a flavor of the field. Methods used can be roughly categorized as based on surface shading, procedural geometry, image processing, geometric edge detection, or a hybrid of these.

There are several different types of edges that can be used in toon rendering:

- A *boundary* or *border edge* is one not shared by two triangles, e.g., the edge of a sheet of paper. A solid object typically has no boundary edges.

- A *crease*, *hard*, or *feature edge* is one that is shared by two triangles, and the angle between the two triangles (called the *dihedral angle*) is greater than some predefined value. A good default crease angle is 60 degrees [972]. As an example, a cube has crease edges. Crease edges can be further subcategorized into *ridge* and *valley* edges.

- A *material edge* appears when the two triangles sharing it differ in material or otherwise cause a change in shading. It also can be an edge that the artist wishes to always have displayed, e.g., forehead lines or a line to separate the same colored pants and shirt.

- A *contour edge* is one in which the two neighboring triangles face in different directions compared to some direction vector, typically one from the eye.

- A *silhouette edge* is a contour edge along the outline of the object, i.e., it separates the object from the background in the image plane.

See Figure 15.4. This categorization is based on common usage within the literature, but there are some variations, e.g., what we call crease and material edges are sometimes called boundary edges elsewhere.

We differentiate here between contour and silhouette edges. Both are edges along which one part of the surface faces the viewer, the other part faces away. Silhouette edges are a subset of contour edges, those which separate the object from another object or the background. For example, in a side view of a head, the ears form

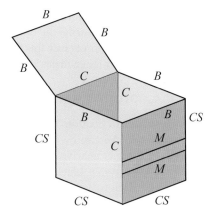

Figure 15.4. A box open on the top, with a stripe on the front. The boundary (B), crease (C), material (M), and silhouette (S) edges are shown. None of the boundary edges are considered silhouette edges by the definitions given, as these edges have only one adjoining polygon.

contour edges, even though they appear within the silhouette outline of the head. Other examples in Figure 15.3 include the nose, two bent fingers, and where the hair parts. In some of the early literature, contour edges are referred to as silhouettes, but the full class of contour edges is usually meant. Also, contour edges should not be confused with contour lines used on topographical maps.

Note that boundary edges are not the same as contour or silhouette edges. Contour and silhouette edges are defined by a view direction, while boundary edges are view-independent. *Suggestive contours* [335] are formed by locations that are almost a contour from the original viewpoint. They provide additional edges that help convey the object's shape. See Figure 15.5. While our focus here is primarily on detect-

Figure 15.5. From left to right: silhouette, contour, and contour together with suggestive contour edges. *(Images courtesy of Doug DeCarlo, Adam Finkelstein, Szymon Rusinkiewicz, and Anthony Santella.)*

ing and rendering contour edges, considerable work has been done for other types of strokes [281, 1014, 1521]. We also focus primarily on finding such edges for polygonal models. Bénard et al. [132] discuss approaches for finding contours of models comprised of subdivision surfaces or other higher-order definitions.

15.2.1 Shading Normal Contour Edges

In a similar fashion to the surface shader in Section 15.1, the dot product between the shading normal and the direction to the eye can be used to give a contour edge [562]. If this value is near zero, then the surface is nearly edge-on to the eye and so is likely to be near a contour edge. Color such areas black, falling off to white as the dot product increases. See Figure 15.6. Before programmable shaders, this algorithm was implemented using a spherical environment map with a black ring, or coloring the topmost levels of a mipmap pyramid texture black [448]. This type of shading today is implemented directly in a pixel shader by going to black as the screen normal becomes perpendicular to the view direction.

This shading is in a sense the opposite of rim lighting, where light illuminates the outline of an object; here the scene is lit from the eye's location and the dropoff is exaggerated, darkening the edges. It can also be thought of as a *thresholding* filter in image processing, where the image is converted to black wherever the surfaces are below a certain intensity, and to white otherwise.

A feature or drawback of this method is that contour lines are drawn with variable width, depending on the curvature of the surface. This method works for curved surface models without crease edges, where areas along the silhouette, for example, will usually have pixels with normals pointing nearly perpendicular to the view direction.

Figure 15.6. Contour edges shaded by darkening the surface as its shading normal becomes perpendicular to the view direction. By widening the falloff angle, a thicker edge is displayed. *(Images courtesy of Kenny Hoff.)*

The algorithm fails on a model such as a cube, since the surface area near a crease edge will not have this property. It can also break up and look bad even on curved surfaces, as when the object is distant and some normals sampled near the contour edges may not be nearly perpendicular. Goodwin et al. [565] note how this basic concept nonetheless has validity as a visual cue, and discuss how lighting, curvature, and distance can be combined to determine stroke thickness.

15.2.2 Procedural Geometry Silhouetting

One of the first techniques for real-time contour edge rendering was presented by Rossignac and van Emmerik [1510], and later refined by Raskar and Cohen [1460]. The general idea is to render the frontfaces normally, then render the backfaces in a way as to make their contour edges visible. There are a variety of methods for rendering these backfaces, each with its own strengths and weaknesses. Each method has as its first step that the frontfaces are drawn. Then frontface culling is turned on and backface culling turned off, so that only backfaces are rendered.

One method to render the contours is to draw only the edges (not the faces) of the backfaces. Using biasing or other techniques (Section 15.4) ensures that some of these lines are drawn just in front of the frontfaces. In this way, only the edges where front- and backfaces meet are visible [969, 1510].

One way to make these lines wider is to render the backfaces themselves in black, again biasing forward. Raskar and Cohen give several biasing methods, such as translating by a fixed amount, or by an amount that compensates for the nonlinear nature of the z-depths, or using a depth-slope bias call such as OpenGL's `glPolygonOffset`. Lengyel [1022] discusses how to provide finer depth control by modifying the perspective matrix. A problem with all these methods is that they do not create lines with a uniform width. To do so, the amount to move forward depends not only on the backface, but also on the neighboring frontface(s). See Figure 15.7. The slope of the backface can be used to bias the polygon forward, but the thickness of the line will also depend on the angle of the frontface.

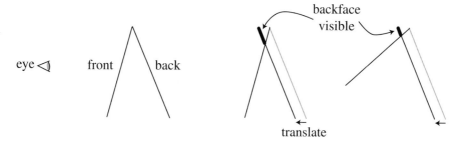

Figure 15.7. The z-bias method of silhouetting, done by translating the backface forward. If the frontface is at a different angle, as shown on the right, a different amount of the backface is visible. *(Illustration after Raskar and Cohen [1460].)*

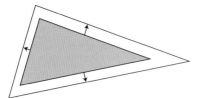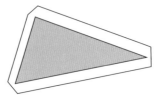

Figure 15.8. Triangle fattening. On the left, a backface triangle is expanded along its plane. Each edge moves a different amount in world space to make the resulting edge the same thickness in screen space. For thin triangles, this technique falls apart, as one corner becomes elongated. On the right, the triangle edges are expanded and joined to form mitered corners to avoid this problem.

Raskar and Cohen [1460, 1461] solve this neighbor dependency problem by instead fattening each backface triangle out along its edges by the amount needed to see a consistently thick line. That is, the slope of the triangle and the distance from the viewer determine how much the triangle is expanded. One method is to expand the three vertices of each triangle outward along its plane. A safer method of rendering the triangle is to move each edge of the triangle outward and connect the edges. Doing so avoids having the vertices stick far away from the original triangle. See Figure 15.8. Note that no biasing is needed with this method, as the backfaces expand beyond the edges of the frontfaces. See Figure 15.9 for results from the three methods. This fattening technique is more controllable and consistent, and has been used successfully for character outlining in video games such as *Prince of Persia* [1138] and *Afro Samurai* [250].

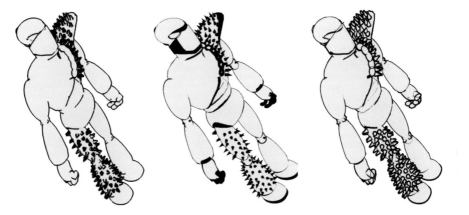

Figure 15.9. Contour edges rendered with backfacing edge drawing with thick lines, z-bias, and fattened triangle algorithms. The backface edge technique gives poor joins between lines and nonuniform lines due to biasing problems on small features. The z-bias technique gives nonuniform edge width because of the dependence on the angles of the frontfaces. *(Images courtesy of Raskar and Cohen [1460].)*

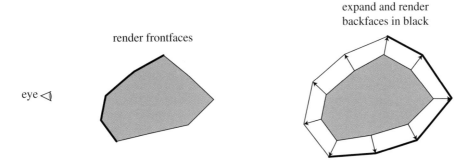

render frontfaces

expand and render
backfaces in black

eye ◁

Figure 15.10. The triangle shell technique creates a second surface by shifting the surface along its vertex normals.

In the method just given, the backface triangles are expanded along their original planes. Another method is to move the backfaces outward by shifting their vertices along the shared vertex normals, by an amount proportional to their z-distance from the eye [671]. This is referred to as the shell or halo method, as the shifted backfaces form a shell around the original object. Imagine a sphere. Render the sphere normally, then expand the sphere by a radius that is 5 pixels wide with respect to the sphere's center. That is, if moving the sphere's center one pixel is equivalent to moving it in world space by 3 millimeters, then increase the radius of the sphere by 15 millimeters. Render only this expanded version's backfaces in black. The contour edge will be 5 pixels wide. See Figure 15.10. Moving vertices outward along their normals is a perfect task for a vertex shader. This type of expansion is sometimes called shell mapping. The method is simple to implement, efficient, robust, and gives steady performance. See Figure 15.11. A forcefield or halo effect can be made by further expanding and shading these backfaces dependent on their angle.

This shell technique has several potential pitfalls. Imagine looking head-on at a cube so that only one face is visible. Each of the four backfaces forming the contour edge will move in the direction of its corresponding cube face, so leaving gaps at the corners. This occurs because while there is a single vertex at each corner, each face has a different vertex normal. The problem is that the expanded cube does not truly form a shell, because each corner vertex is expanding in a different direction. One solution is to force vertices in the same location to share a single, new, average vertex normal. Another technique is to create degenerate geometry at the creases that then gets expanded into triangles with area. Lira et al. [1053] use an additional threshold texture to control how much each vertex is moved.

Shell and fattening techniques waste some fill, since all the backfaces are sent down the pipeline. Other limitations of all these techniques is that there is little control over the edge appearance, and semitransparent surfaces are tricky to render correctly, depending on the transparency algorithm used.

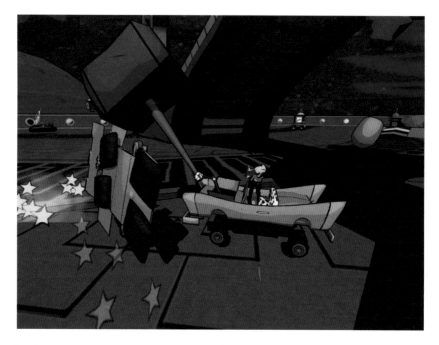

Figure 15.11. An example of real-time toon-style rendering from the game *Cel Damage*, using backface shell expansion to form contour edges, along with explicit crease edge drawing. *(Image courtesy of Pseudo Interactive Inc.)*

One worthwhile feature of this entire class of geometric techniques is that no connectivity information or edge lists are needed during rendering. Each triangle is processed independently from the rest, so such techniques lend themselves to GPU implementation [1461].

This class of algorithms renders only contour edges. Raskar [1461] gives a clever solution for drawing ridge crease edges on deforming models without having to create and access an edge connectivity data structure. The idea is to generate an additional polygon along each edge of the triangle being rendered. These edge polygons are bent away from the triangle's plane by the user-defined critical dihedral angle that determines when a crease should be visible. If at any given moment two adjoining triangles are at greater than this crease angle, the edge polygons will be visible, else they will be hidden by the triangles. See Figure 15.12. Valley edges are possible with a similar technique, but require a stencil buffer and multiple passes.

15.2.3 Edge Detection by Image Processing

The algorithms in the previous section are sometimes classified as image-based, as the screen resolution determines how they are performed. Another type of algorithm is

Figure 15.12. A side view of two triangles joined at an edge, each with a small "fin" attached. As the two triangles bend along the edge, the fins move toward becoming visible. On the right the fins are exposed. Painted black, these appear as a ridge edge.

more directly image-based, in that it operates entirely on data stored in image buffers and does not modify (or even directly know about) the geometry in the scene.

Saito and Takahashi [1528] first introduced this G-buffer concept, which is also used for deferred shading (Section 20.1). Decaudin [336] extended the use of G-buffers to perform toon rendering. The basic idea is simple: NPR can be done by performing image processing algorithms on various buffers of information. Many contour-edge locations can be found by looking for discontinuities in neighboring z-buffer values. Discontinuities in neighboring surface normal values often signal the location of contour and boundary edges. Rendering the scene in ambient colors or with object identification values can be used to detect material, boundary, and true silhouette edges.

Detecting and rendering these edges consists of two parts. First, the scene's geometry is rendered, with the pixel shader saving depth, normal, object IDs, or other data as desired to various render targets. Post-processing passes are then performed, in a similar way as described in Section 12.1. A post-processing pass samples the neighborhood around each pixel and outputs a result based on these samples. For example, imagine we have a unique identification value for each object in the scene. At each pixel we could sample this ID and compare it to the four adjacent pixel ID values at the corners of our test pixel. If any of the IDs differ from the test pixel's ID, output black, else output white. Sampling all eight neighbor pixels is more foolproof, but at a higher sampling cost. This simple kind of test can be used to draw the boundary and outline edges (true silhouettes) of most objects. Material IDs could be used to find material edges.

Contour edges can be found by using various filters on normal and depth buffers. For example, if the difference in depths between neighboring pixels is above some threshold, a contour edge is likely to exist and so the pixel is made black. Rather than a simple decision about whether the neighboring pixels match our sample, other more elaborate edge detection operators are needed. We will not discuss here the pros and cons of various edge detection filters, such as Roberts cross, Sobel, and Scharr, as the image processing literature covers these extensively [559, 1729]. Because the results of such operators are not necessarily boolean, we can adjust their thresholds or fade between black and white when in some zone. Note that the normal buffer can also detect crease edges, as a large difference between normals can signify either a contour or a crease edge. Thibault and Cavanaugh [1761] discuss how they use this technique

Figure 15.13. Modified Sobel edge detection in the game *Borderlands*. The final released version (not shown here) further improved the look by masking out edges for the grass in the foreground [1761]. *(Images courtesy of Gearbox Software, LLC.)*

with the depth buffer for the game *Borderlands*. Among other techniques, they modify the Sobel filter so that it creates single-pixel-wide outlines and the depth computation to improve precision. See Figure 15.13. It is also possible to go the other direction, adding outlines only around shadows by ignoring edges where the neighboring depths differ considerably [1138].

The *dilation operator* is a type of morphological operator that is used for thickening detected edges [226, 1217]. After the edge image is generated, a separate pass is applied. At each pixel, the pixel's value and its surrounding values to within some radius are examined. The darkest pixel value found is returned as output. In this way, a thin black line will be thickened by the diameter of the area searched. Multiple

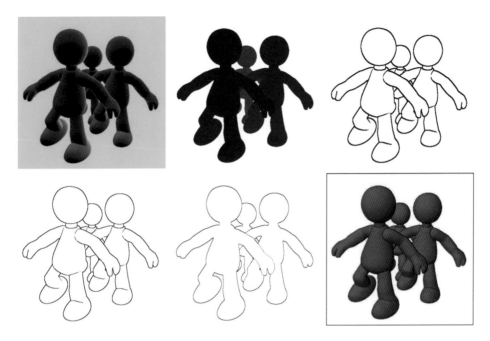

Figure 15.14. The normal map (upper left) and depth map (upper middle) have Sobel edge detection applied to their values, with results shown in the lower left and lower middle, respectively. The image in the upper right is a thickened composite using dilation. The final rendering in the lower right is made by shading the image with Gooch shading and compositing in the edges. *(Images courtesy of Drew Card and Jason L. Mitchell, ATI Technologies Inc.)*

passes can be applied to further thicken lines, the trade-off being that the cost of the additional pass is offset by needing considerably fewer samples for each pass. Different results can have different thicknesses, e.g., the silhouette edges could be made thicker than the other contour edges. The related *erosion operator* can be used for thinning lines or other effects. See Figure 15.14 for some results.

This type of algorithm has several advantages. It handles all types of surfaces, flat or curved, unlike most other techniques. Meshes do not have to be connected or even consistent, since the method is image-based.

There are relatively few flaws with this type of technique. For nearly edge-on surfaces, the z-depth comparison filter can falsely detect a contour-edge pixel across the surface. Another problem with z-depth comparison is that if the differences are minimal, then the contour edge can be missed. For example, a sheet of paper on a desk will usually have its edges missed. Similarly, the normal map filter will miss the edges of this piece of paper, since the normals are identical. This is still not foolproof; for example, a piece of paper folded onto itself will create undetectable edges where the edges overlap [725]. Lines generated show stair-step aliasing, but the various

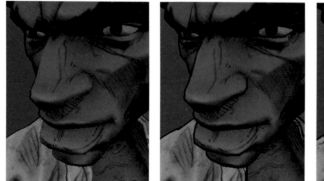

Figure 15.15. Various edge methods. Feature edges such as wrinkles are part of the texture itself, added by the artist in advance. The silhouette of the character is generated with backface extrusion. The contour edges are generated using image processing edge detection, with varying weights. The left image was generated with too little weight, so these edges are faint. The middle shows outlines, on the contour edges of the nose and lips in particular. The right displays artifacts from too great a weight [250]. *(Afro Samurai ® & ©2006 TAKASHI OKAZAKI, GONZO / SAMURAI PROJECT. Program ©2009 BANDAI NAMCO Entertainment America Inc.)*

morphological antialiasing techniques described in Section 5.4.2 work well with this high-contrast output, as well as on techniques such as posterization, to improve edge quality.

Detection can also fail in the opposite way, creating edges where none should exist. Determining what constitutes an edge is not a foolproof operation. For example, imagine the stem of a rose, a thin cylinder. Close up, the stem normals neighboring our sample pixel do not vary all that much, so no edge is detected. As we move away from the rose, the normals will vary more rapidly from pixel to pixel, until at some point a false edge detection may occur near the edges because of these differences. Similar problems can happen with detecting edges from depth maps, with the perspective's effect on depth being an additional factor needing compensation. Decaudin [336] gives an improved method of looking for changes by processing the gradient of the normal and depth maps rather than just the values themselves. Deciding how various pixel differences translate into color changes is a process that often needs to be tuned for the content [250, 1761]. See Figure 15.15.

Once the strokes are generated, further image processing can be performed as desired. Since the strokes can be created in a separate buffer, they can be modified on their own, then composited atop the surfaces. For example, noise functions can be used to fray and wobble the lines and the surfaces separately, creating small gaps between the two and giving a hand-drawn look. The heightfield of the paper can be used to affect the rendering, having solid materials such as charcoal deposited at the tops of bumps or watercolor paint pooled in the valleys. See Figure 15.16 for an example.

Figure 15.16. The fish model on the left is rendered on the right using edge detection, posterization, noise perturbation, blurring, and blending atop the paper. *(Images courtesy of Autodesk, Inc.)*

We have focused here on detecting edges using geometric or other non-graphical data, such as normals, depths, and IDs. Naturally, image processing techniques were developed for images, and such edge detection techniques can be applied to color buffers. One approach is called *difference of Gaussians* (DoG), where the image is processed twice with two different Gaussian filters and one is subtracted from the other. This edge detection method has been found to produce particularly pleasing results for NPR, used to generate images in a variety of artistic styles such as pencil shading and pastels [949, 1896, 1966].

Image post-processing operators feature prominently within many NPR techniques simulating artistic media such as watercolors and acrylic paints. There is considerable research in this area, and for interactive applications much of the challenge is in trying to do the most with the fewest number of texture samples. Bilateral, mean-shift, and Kuwahara filters can be used on the GPU for preserving edges and smoothing areas to appear as if painted [58, 948]. Kyprianidis et al. [949] provide a thorough review and a taxonomy of image processing effects for the field. The work by Montesdeoca et al. [1237] is a fine example of combining a number of straightforward techniques into a watercolor effect that runs at interactive rates. A model rendered with a watercolor style is shown in Figure 15.17.

15.2.4   Geometric Contour Edge Detection

A problem with the approaches given so far is that the stylization of the edges is limited at best. We cannot easily make the lines look dashed, let alone look hand-drawn or like brush strokes. For this sort of operation, we need to find the contour edges and render them directly. Having separate, independent edge entities makes it possible to create other effects, such as having the contours jump in surprise while the mesh is frozen in shock.

Figure 15.17. On the left, a standard realistic render. On the right, the watercolor style softens textures through mean-shift color matching, and increases contrast and saturation, among other techniques. *(Watercolor image courtesy of Autodesk, Inc.)*

A contour edge is one in which one of the two neighboring triangles faces toward the viewer and the other faces away. The test is

$$(\mathbf{n}_0 \cdot \mathbf{v})(\mathbf{n}_1 \cdot \mathbf{v}) < 0, \tag{15.1}$$

where $\mathbf{n}_0$ and $\mathbf{n}_1$ are the two triangle normals and $\mathbf{v}$ is the view direction from the eye to the edge (i.e., to either endpoint). For this test to work correctly, the surface must be consistently oriented (Section 16.3).

The brute-force method for finding the contour edges in a model is to run through the list of edges and perform this test [1130]. Lander [972] notes that a worthwhile optimization is to identify and ignore edges that are inside planar polygons. That is, given a connected triangle mesh, if the two neighboring triangles for an edge lie in the same plane, the edge cannot possibly be a contour edge. Implementing this test on a simple clock model dropped the edge count from 444 edges to 256. Furthermore, if the model defines a solid object, concave edges can never be contour edges. Buchanan and Sousa [207] avoid the need for doing separate dot product tests for each edge by reusing the dot product test for each individual face.

Detecting contour edges each frame from scratch can be costly. If the camera view and the objects move little from frame to frame, it is reasonable to assume that the contour edges from previous frames might still be valid contour edges. Aila and Miettinen [13] associate a valid distance with each edge. This distance is how far the

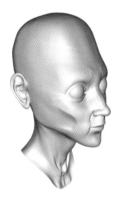 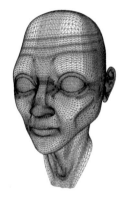 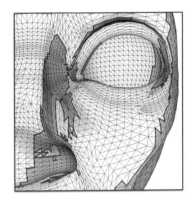

Figure 15.18. Contour loops. On the left is the camera's view of the model. The middle shows the triangles facing away from the camera in blue. A close-up of one area of the face is shown on the right. Note the complexity and how some contour loops are hidden behind the nose. *(Model courtesy of Chris Landreth, images courtesy of Pierre Bénard and Aaron Hertzmann [132].)*

viewer can move and still have the contour edge maintain its state. In any solid model each separate contour always consists of a single closed curve, called a *silhouette loop* or, more properly, a *contour loop*. For contours inside the object's bounds, some part of the loop may be obscured. Even the actual silhouette may consist of a few loops, with parts of loops being inside the outline or hidden by other surfaces. It follows that each vertex must have an even number of contour edges [23]. See Figure 15.18. Note how the loops are often quite jagged in three dimensions when following mesh edges, with the z-depth varying noticeably. If edges forming smoother curves are desired, such as for varying thickness by distance [565], additional processing can be done to interpolate among the triangle's normals to approximate the true contour edge inside a triangle [725, 726].

Tracking loop locations from frame to frame can be faster than recreating loops from scratch. Markosian et al. [1125] start with a set of loops and uses a randomized search algorithm to update this set as the camera moves. Contour loops are also created and destroyed as the model changes orientation. Kalnins et al. [848] note that when two loops merge, corrective measures need to be taken or a noticeable jump from one frame to the next will be visible. They use a pixel search and "vote" algorithm to attempt to maintain contour coherence from frame to frame.

Such techniques can give serious performance increases, but can be inexact. Linear methods are exact but expensive. Hierarchical methods that use the camera to access contour edges combine speed and precision. For orthographic views of non-animated models, Gooch et al. [562] use a hierarchy of Gauss maps for determining contour edges. Sander et al. [1539] use an n-ary tree of normal cones (Section 19.3). Hertzmann and Zorin [726] use a dual-space representation of the model that allows them to impose a hierarchy on the model's edges.

All these explicit edge detection methods are CPU intensive and have poor cache coherency, since edges forming a contour are dispersed throughout the edge list. To avoid these costs, the vertex shader can be used to detect and render contour edges [226]. The idea is to send every edge of the model down the pipeline as two triangles forming a degenerate quadrilateral, with the two adjoining triangle normals attached to each vertex. When an edge is found to be part of the contour, the quadrilateral's points are moved so that it is no longer degenerate (i.e., is made visible). This thin quadrilateral *fin* is then drawn. This technique is based on the same idea as that described for finding contour edges for shadow volume creation (Section 7.3). If the geometry shader is a part of the pipeline, these additional fin quadrilaterals do not need to be stored but can be generated on the fly [282, 299]. A naive implementation will leave chinks and gaps between the fins, which can be corrected by modifying the shape of the fin [723, 1169, 1492].

15.2.5 Hidden Line Removal

Once the contours are found, the lines are rendered. An advantage of explicitly finding the edges is that you can stylize these as pen strokes, paint strokes, or any other medium you desire. Strokes can be basic lines, textured impostors (Section 13.6.4), sets of primitives, or whatever else you wish to try.

A further complication with attempting to use geometric edges is that not all these edges are actually visible. Rendering surfaces to establish the z-buffer can mask hidden geometric edges, which may be sufficient for simple styles such as dotted lines. Cole and Finkelstein [282] extend this for quadrilaterals representing lines by sampling the z-depths along the spine of the line itself. However, with these methods each point along the line is rendered independently, so no well-defined start and end locations are known in advance. For contour loops or other edges where the line segments are meant to define brush strokes or other continuous objects, we need to know when each stroke first appears and when it disappears. Determining visibility for each line segment is known as *hidden line rendering*, where a set of line segments is processed for visibility and a smaller set of (possibly clipped) line segments is returned.

Northrup and Markosian [1287] attack this problem by rendering all the object's triangles and contour edges and assigning each a different identification number. This ID buffer is read back and the visible contour edges are determined from it. These visible segments are then checked for overlaps and linked together to form smooth stroke paths. This approach works if the line segments on the screen are short, but it does not include clipping of the line segments themselves. Stylized strokes are then rendered along these reconstructed paths. The strokes themselves can be stylized in many different ways, including effects of taper, flare, wiggle, overshoot, and fading, as well as depth and distance cues. An example is shown in Figure 15.19.

Cole and Finkelstein [282] present a visibility calculation method for a set of edges. They store each line segment as two world-space coordinate values. A series of passes runs a pixel shader over the whole set of segments, clipping and determining the length

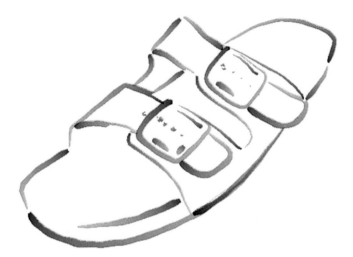

Figure 15.19. An image produced using Northrup and Markosian's hybrid technique. Contour edges are found, built into chains, and rendered as strokes. *(Image courtesy of Lee Markosian.)*

in pixels of each, then creating an atlas for each of these potential pixel locations and determining visibility, and then using this atlas to create visible strokes. While complex, the process is relatively fast on the GPU and provides sets of visible strokes that have known beginning and end locations.

Stylization often consists of applying one or more premade textures to line quadrilaterals. Rougier [1516] discusses a different approach, procedurally rendering dashed patterns. Each line segment accesses a texture that stores all dashed patterns desired. Each pattern is encoded as a set of commands specifying the dashed pattern along with the endcap and join types used. Using the quadrilateral's texture coordinates, each pattern controls a series of tests by the shader for how much of the line covers the pixel at each point in the quadrilateral.

Determining the contour edges, linking them into coherent chains, and then determining visibility for each chain to form a stroke is difficult to fully parallelize. An additional problem when producing high-quality line stylization is that for the next frame each stroke will be drawn again, changing length or possibly appearing for the first time. Bénard et al. [130] present a survey of rendering methods that provide temporal coherence for strokes along edges and patterns on surfaces. This is not a solved problem and can be computationally involved, so research continues [131].

15.3 Stroke Surface Stylization

While toon rendering is a popular style to attempt to simulate, there is an infinite variety of other styles to apply to surfaces. Effects can range from modifying realistic

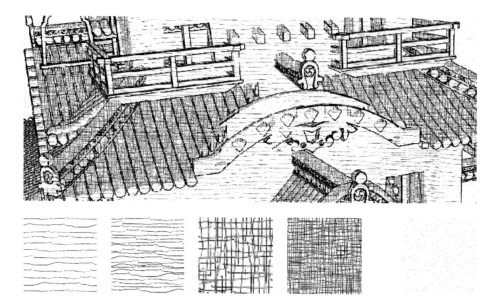

Figure 15.20. An image generated by using a palette of textures, a paper texture, and contour edge rendering. *(Reprinted by permission of Adam Lake and Carl Marshall, Intel Corporation, copyright Intel Corporation 2002.)*

textures [905, 969, 973] to having the algorithm procedurally generate geometric ornamentation from frame to frame [853, 1126]. In this section, we briefly survey techniques relevant to real-time rendering.

Lake et al. [966] discuss using the diffuse shading term to select which texture is used on a surface. As the diffuse term gets darker, a texture with a darker impression is used. The texture is applied with screen-space coordinates to give a hand-drawn look. To further enhance the sketched look, a paper texture is also applied in screen space to all surfaces. See Figure 15.20. A major problem with this type of algorithm is the *shower door effect*, where the objects look like they are viewed through patterned glass during animation. Objects feel as though they are swimming through the texture. Breslav et al. [196] maintain a two-dimensional look for the textures by determining what image transform best matches the movements of some underlying model locations. This can maintain a connection with the screen-based nature of the fill pattern while giving a stronger connection with the object.

One solution is obvious: Apply textures directly to the surface. The challenge is that stroke-based textures need to maintain a relatively uniform stroke thickness and density to look convincing. If the texture is magnified, the strokes appear too thick; if it is minified, the strokes are either blurred away or are thin and noisy (depending on whether mipmapping is used). Praun et al. [1442] present a real-time method of generating stroke-textured mipmaps and applying these to surfaces in a smooth fashion. Doing so maintains the stroke density on the screen as the object's distance

Figure 15.21. *Tonal art maps* (TAMs). Strokes are drawn into the mipmap levels. Each mipmap level contains all the strokes from the textures to the left and above it. In this way, interpolation between mip levels and adjoining textures is smooth. *(Images courtesy of Emil Praun, Princeton University.)*

changes. The first step is to form the textures to be used, called *tonal art maps* (TAMs). This is done by drawing strokes into the mipmap levels. See Figure 15.21. Klein et al. [905] use a related idea in their "art maps" to maintain stroke size for NPR textures. With these textures in place, the model is rendered by interpolating between the tones needed at each vertex. This technique results in images with a hand-drawn feel [1441]. See Figure 15.22.

Webb et al. [1858] present two extensions to TAMs that give better results, one using a volume texture, which allows the use of color, the other using a thresholding scheme, which improves antialiasing. Nuebel [1291] gives a related method of performing charcoal rendering. He uses a noise texture that also goes from dark to light along

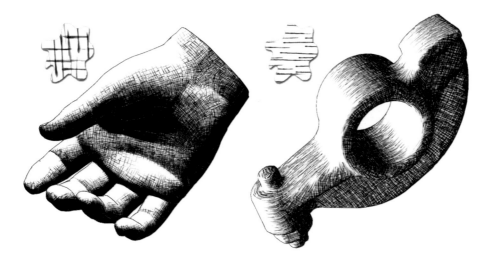

Figure 15.22. Two models rendered using *tonal art maps* (TAMs). The swatches show the lapped texture pattern used to render each. *(Images courtesy of Emil Praun, Princeton University.)*

 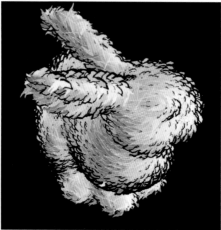

Figure 15.23. Two different graftal styles render the Stanford bunny. *(Images courtesy of Bruce Gooch and Matt Kaplan, University of Utah.)*

one axis. The intensity value accesses the texture along this axis. Lee et al. [1009] use TAMs and other techniques to generate impressive images that appear drawn by pencil.

With regard to strokes, many other operations are possible than those already discussed. To give a sketched effect, edges can be jittered [317, 972, 1009] or can overshoot their original locations, as seen in the upper right and lower middle images in Figure 15.1 on page 651.

Girshick et al. [538] discuss rendering strokes along the principal curve direction lines on a surface. That is, from any given point on a surface, there is a *first principal direction* tangent vector that points in the direction of maximum curvature. The *second principal direction* is the tangent vector perpendicular to this first vector and gives the direction in which the surface is least curved. These direction lines are important in the perception of a curved surface. They also have the advantage of needing to be generated only once for static models, since such strokes are independent of lighting and shading. Hertzmann and Zorin [726] discuss how to clean up and smooth out principal directions. A considerable amount of research and development has explored using these directions and other data in applying textures to arbitrary surfaces, in driving simulation animations, and in other applications. See the report by Vaxman et al. [1814] as a starting point.

The idea of *graftals* [372, 853, 1126] is that geometry or decal textures can be added as needed to a surface to produce a particular effect. They can be controlled by the level of detail needed, by the surface's orientation to the eye, or by other factors. These can also be used to simulate pen or brush strokes. An example is shown in Figure 15.23. Geometric graftals are a form of procedural modeling [407].

This chapter has only barely touched on a few of the directions NPR research has taken. See the "Further Reading and Resources" section at the end for where to go for more information. In this field there is often little or no underlying physically correct answer that we can use as a ground truth. This is both problematic and liberating. Techniques give trade-offs between speed and quality, as well as cost of implementation. Under the tight time constraints of interactive rendering rates, most schemes will bend and break under certain conditions. Determining what works well, or well enough, within your application is what makes the field a fascinating challenge.

Much of our focus has been on a specific topic, contour edge detection and rendering. To conclude, we will turn our attention to lines and text. These two non-photorealistic primitives find frequent use and have some challenges of their own, so deserve separate coverage.

15.4 Lines

Rendering of simple solid "hard" lines is often considered relatively uninteresting. However, they are important in fields such as CAD for seeing underlying model facets and discerning an object's shape. They are also useful in highlighting a selected object and in areas such as technical illustration. In addition, some of the techniques involved are applicable to other problems.

15.4.1 Triangle Edge Rendering

Correctly rendering edges on top of filled triangles is more difficult than it first appears. If a line is at exactly the same location as a triangle, how do we ensure that the line is always rendered in front? One simple solution is to render all lines with a fixed bias [724]. That is, each line is rendered slightly closer than it should truly be, so that it will be above the surface. If the fixed bias is too large, parts of edges that should be hidden appear, spoiling the effect. If the bias is too little, triangle surfaces that are nearly edge-on can hide part or all of the edges. As mentioned in Section 15.2.2, API calls such as OpenGL's `glPolygonOffset` can be used to move backward the surfaces beneath the lines, based on their slopes. This method works reasonably well, but not perfectly.

A scheme by Herrell et al. [724] avoids biasing altogether. It uses a series of steps to mark and clear a stencil buffer, so that edges are drawn atop triangles correctly. This method is impractical for any but the smallest sets of triangles, as each triangle must be drawn separately and the stencil buffer cleared for each, making the process extremely time consuming.

Bærentzen et al. [86, 1295] present a method that maps well to the GPU. They employ a pixel shader that uses the triangle's barycentric coordinates to determine the distance to the closest edge. If the pixel is close to an edge, it is drawn with the edge color. Edge thickness can be any value desired and can be affected by distance or

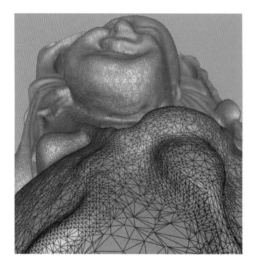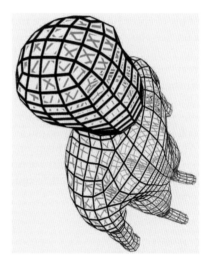

Figure 15.24. Pixel-shader-generated lines. On the left are antialiased single-pixel width edges; on the right are variable thickness lines with haloing. *(Images courtesy of J. Andreas Bærentzen.)*

held constant. See Figure 15.24. The main drawback is that contour edges are drawn half as thick as interior lines, since each triangle draws half of each line's thickness. In practice this mismatch is often not noticeable.

This idea is extended and simplified by Celes and Abraham [242], who also give a thorough summary of previous work. Their idea is to use a one-dimensional set of texture coordinates for each triangle edge, 1.0 for the two vertices defining the edge and 0.0 for the other vertex. They exploit texture mapping and the mip chain to give a constant-width edge. This approach is easy to code and provides some useful controls. For example, a maximum density can be set so that dense meshes do not become entirely filled with edges and so become a solid color.

15.4.2 Rendering Obscured Lines

In normal wireframe drawing, where no surfaces are drawn, all edges of a model are visible. To avoid drawing the lines that are hidden by surfaces, draw all the filled triangles into just the z-buffer, then draw the edges normally [1192]. If you cannot draw all surfaces before drawing all lines, a slightly more costly solution is to draw the surfaces with a solid color that matches the background.

Lines can also be drawn as partially obscured instead of fully hidden. For example, hidden lines could appear in light gray instead of not being drawn at all. This can be done by setting the z-buffer's state appropriately. Draw as before, then reverse the sense of the z-buffer, so that only lines that are *beyond* the current pixel's z-depth are drawn. Also turn off z-buffer modification, so that these drawn lines do not change any depth values. Draw the lines again in the obscured style. Only lines that would

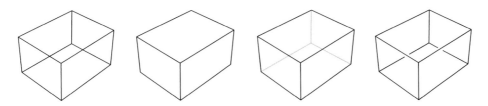

Figure 15.25. Four line rendering styles. From left to right: wireframe, hidden line, obscured line, and haloed line.

be hidden are then drawn. For stylized versions of lines, a full hidden-line-removal process can be used [282].

15.4.3 Haloing

When two lines cross, a common convention is to erase a part of the more distant line, making the ordering obvious. This can be accomplished relatively easily by drawing each line twice, once with a halo [1192]. This method erases the overlap by drawing over it in the background color. First, draw all the lines to the z-buffer, representing each line as a thick quadrilateral that represents the halo. A geometry shader can help with creating such quadrilaterals. Then, draw every line normally in color. The areas masked off by the z-buffer draws will hide lines drawn behind them. A bias or other method has to be used to ensure that each thin black line lies atop the thick z-buffer quadrilateral.

Lines meeting at a vertex can become partially hidden by the competing halos. Shortening the quadrilaterals creating the halos can help, but can lead to other artifacts. The line rendering technique from Bærentzen et al. [86, 1295] can also be used for haloing. See Figure 15.24. The halos are generated per triangle, so there are no interference problems. Another approach is to use image post-processing (Section 15.2.3) to detect and draw the halos.

Figure 15.25 shows results for some of the different line rendering methods discussed here.

15.5 Text Rendering

Given how critical reading text is to civilization, it is unsurprising that considerable attention has been lavished on rendering it well. Unlike many other objects, a single pixel change can make a significant difference, such as turning an "l" into a "1." This section summarizes the major algorithmic approaches used for text rendering.

The eye is more sensitive to differences in intensity than to those in color. This fact has been used since at least the days of the Apple II [527] to improve perceived spatial resolution. One application of this idea is Microsoft's ClearType technology,

technology technology

Figure 15.26. Magnified grayscale antialiased and subpixel antialiased versions of the same word. When a colored pixel is displayed on an LCD screen, the corresponding colored vertical subpixel rectangles making up the pixel are lit. Doing so provides additional horizontal spatial resolution. *(Images generated by Steve Gibson's "Free & Clear" program.)*

which is built upon one of the characteristics of *liquid-crystal display* (LCD) displays. Each pixel on an LCD display consists of three vertical colored rectangles, red, green, and blue—use a magnifying glass on an LCD monitor and see for yourself. Disregarding the colors of these subpixel rectangles, this configuration provides three times as much horizontal resolution as there are pixels. Using different shades fills in different subpixels, and so this technique is sometimes called *subpixel rendering*. The eye blends these colors together, and the reddish and blue fringes become undetectable. See Figure 15.26. This technology was first announced in 1998 and was a great help on large, low-DPI LCD monitors. Microsoft stopped using ClearType in Word 2013, evidently because of problems from blending text with different background colors. Excel uses the technology, as do various web browsers, along with Adobe's CoolType, Apple's Quartz 2D, and libraries such as FreeType and SubLCD. An old yet thorough article by Shemanarev [1618] covers the various subtleties and issues with this approach.

This technique is a sterling example of how much effort is spent on rendering text clearly. Characters in a font, called *glyphs*, typically are described by a series of line segments and quadratic or cubic Bézier curves. See Figure 17.9 on page 726 for an example. All font rendering systems work to determine how a glyph affects the pixels it overlaps. Libraries such as FreeType and Anti-Grain Geometry work by generating a small texture for each glyph and reusing them as needed. Different textures are made for each font size and *emphasis*, i.e., italics or bold.

These systems assume that each texture is pixel-aligned, one texel per pixel, as it normally is for documents. When text is applied to three-dimensional surfaces, these assumptions may no longer hold. Using a texture with a set of glyphs is a simple and popular approach, but there are some potential drawbacks. The application may still align text to face the viewer, but scaling and rotation will break the assumption of a single texel per pixel. Even if screen-aligned, *font hinting* may not be taken into account. Hinting is the process of adjusting the glyph's outline to match up with the pixel cells. For example, the vertical stem of an "I" that is a texel wide is best rendered covering a single column of pixels instead of half-covering two adjacent columns. See Figure 15.27. All these factors mean a raster texture can display blurriness or aliasing problems. Rougier [1515] gives thorough coverage of the issues involved with texture-generation algorithms and shows how FreeType's hinting can be used in an OpenGL-based glyph-rendering system.

The Pathfinder library [1834] is a recent effort that uses the GPU to generate glyphs. It has a low setup time and minimal memory use, and outperforms competing

Figure 15.27. The Verdana font rendered unhinted (top) and hinted (bottom). *(Image courtesy of Nicolas Rougier [1515].)*

CPU-based engines. It uses tessellation and compute shaders to generate and sum up the effects of curves on each pixel, with fallbacks to geometry shaders and OpenCL on less-capable GPUs. Like FreeType, these glyphs are cached and reused. Its high-quality antialiasing, combined with the use of high-density displays, makes hinting nearly obsolete.

Applying text to arbitrary surfaces at different sizes and orientations can be done without elaborate GPU support, while still providing reasonable antialiasing. Green [580] presents such a system, first used by Valve in *Team Fortress 2*. The algorithm uses the *sampled distance field* data structure introduced by Frisken et al. [495]. Each texel holds the signed distance to the nearest edge of a glyph. A distance field attempts to encode the exact bounds of each glyph in a texture description. Bilinear interpolation then gives a good approximation of the alpha coverage of the letter at each sample. See Figure 15.28 for an example. Sharp corners may become smoothed by bilinear interpolation, but can be preserved by encoding more distance values in four separate channels [263]. A limitation of this method is that these signed distance textures are time consuming to create, so they need to be precomputed and stored. Nonetheless, several font rendering libraries are based on this technique [1440], and it adapts well to mobile devices [3]. Reshetov and Luebke [1485] summarize work along these lines and give their own scheme, based on adjusting texture coordinates for samples during magnification.

Even without scaling and rotation concerns, fonts for languages using Chinese characters, for example, may need thousands or more glyphs. A high-quality large character would require a larger texture. Anisotropic filtering of the texture may be needed if the glyph is viewed at an angle. Rendering the glyph directly from its edge and curve description would avoid the need for arbitrarily large textures and avoid the artifacts that come from sampling grids. The Loop-Blinn method [1068, 1069] uses a pixel shader to directly evaluate Bézier curves, and is discussed in Section 17.1.2. This technique requires a tessellation step, which can be expensive when done at load time. Dobbie [360] avoids the issue by drawing a rectangle for the bounding box of each character and evaluating all the glyph outlines in a single pass. Lengyel [1028] presents a robust evaluator for whether a point is inside a glyph, which is critical to avoid artifacts, and discusses evaluation optimizations and effects such as glows, drop shadows, and multiple colors (e.g., for emojis).

Figure 15.28. Vector textures. On the left, the letter "g" shown in its distance field representation [3]. On the right, the "no trespassing" sign is rendered from distance fields. The outline around the text is added by mapping a particular distance range to the outline color [580]. *(Image on left courtesy of ARM Ltd. Image on right from "Team Fortress 2," courtesy of Valve Corp.)*

Further Reading and Resources

For inspiration about non-photorealistic and toon rendering, read Scott McCloud's *Understanding Comics* [1157]. For a view from a researcher's perspective, see Hertzmann's article [728] on using NPR techniques to help build scientific theories about art and illustration.

The book *Advanced Graphics Programming Using OpenGL* [1192], despite being written during the era of fixed-function hardware, has worthwhile chapters on a wide range of technical illustration and scientific visualization techniques. Though also somewhat dated, the books by the Gooches [563] and by Strothotte [1719] are good starting places for NPR algorithms. Surveys of contour edge and stroke rendering techniques are provided by Isenberg et al. [799] and Hertzmann [727]. The lectures from the SIGGRAPH 2008 course by Rusinkiewicz et al. [1521] also examine stroke rendering in detail, including newer work, and Bénard et al. [130] survey frame-to-frame coherence algorithms. For artistic image-processing effects, we refer the interested reader to the overview by Kyprianidis et al. [949]. The proceedings of the *International Symposium on Non-Photorealistic Animation and Rendering* (NPAR) focus on research in the field.

Mitchell et al. [1223] provide a case study about how engineers and artists collaborated to give a distinctive graphic style to the game *Team Fortress 2*. Shodhan and Willmott [1632] discuss the post-processing system in the game *Spore* and include pixel shaders for oil paint, old film, and other effects. The SIGGRAPH 2010 course "Stylized Rendering in Games" is another worthwhile source for practical examples. In particular, Thibault and Cavanaugh [1761] show the evolution of the art style for *Borderlands* and describe the technical challenges along the way. Evans' presentation [446] is a fascinating exploration of a wide range of rendering and modeling techniques to achieve a particular media style.

Pranckevičius [1440] provides a survey of accelerated text rendering techniques filled with links to resources.

Chapter 16
Polygonal Techniques

*"It is indeed wonderful that so simple a figure
as the triangle is so inexhaustible."*
—Leopold Crelle

Up to this point, we have assumed that the model we rendered is available in exactly
the format we need, and with just the right amount of detail. In reality, we are
rarely so lucky. Modelers and data capture devices have their own particular quirks
and limitations, giving rise to ambiguities and errors within the data set, and so
within renderings. Often trade-offs are made among storage size, rendering efficiency,
and quality of the results. In this chapter we discuss a variety of problems that are
encountered within polygonal data sets, along with some of the fixes and workarounds
for these problems. We then cover techniques to efficiently render and store polygonal
models.

The overarching goals for polygonal representation in interactive computer graphics
are visual accuracy and speed. "Accuracy" is a term that depends upon the context.
For example, an engineer wants to examine and modify a machine part at interactive
rates and requires that every bevel and chamfer on the object be visible at every
moment. Compare this to a game, where if the frame rate is high enough, minor
errors or inaccuracies in a given frame are allowable, since they may not occur where
attention is focused, or may disappear in the next frame. In interactive graphics work
it is important to know what the boundaries are to the problem being solved, since
these determine what sorts of techniques can be applied.

The areas covered in this chapter are tessellation, consolidation, optimization, simplification, and compression. Polygons can arrive in many different forms and usually
have to be split into more tractable primitives, such as triangles or quadrilaterals.
This process is called triangulation or, more generally, *tessellation*.[1] *Consolidation*
is our term for the process that encompasses merging separate polygons into a mesh
structure, as well as deriving new data, such as normals, for surface shading. *Optimization* means ordering the polygonal data in a mesh so it will render more rapidly.
Simplification is taking a mesh and removing insignificant features within it. *Com-*

---

[1] "Tessellation," with doubled l's, is probably the most frequently misspelled word in computer
graphics, with "frustum" a close second.

pression is concerned with minimizing the storage space needed for various elements describing the mesh.

Triangulation ensures that a given mesh description is displayed correctly. Consolidation further improves data display and often increases speed, by allowing computations to be shared and reducing the size in memory. Optimization techniques can increase speed still further. Simplification can provide even more speed by removing unneeded triangles. Compression can be used to further reduce the overall memory footprint, which can in turn improve speed by reducing memory and bus bandwidth.

16.1   Sources of Three-Dimensional Data

There are several ways a polygonal model can be created or generated:

- Directly typing in the geometric description.

- Writing programs that create such data. This is called *procedural modeling*.

- Transforming data found in other forms into surfaces or volumes, e.g., taking protein data and converting it into a set of spheres and cylinders.

- Using modeling programs to build up or sculpt an object.

- Reconstructing the surface from one or more photographs of the same object, called *photogrammetry*.

- Sampling a real model at various points, using a three-dimensional scanner, digitizer, or other sensing device.

- Generating an isosurface that represents identical values in some volume of space, such as data from CAT or MRI medical scans, or pressure or temperature samples measured in the atmosphere.

- Using some combination of these techniques.

In the modeling world, there are two main types of modelers: solid-based and surface-based. Solid-based modelers are usually seen in the area of computer aided design (CAD), and often emphasize modeling tools that correspond to actual machining processes, such as cutting, drilling, and planing. Internally, they will have a computational engine that rigorously manipulates the underlying topological boundaries of the objects. For display and analysis, such modelers have *faceters*. A faceter is software that turns the internal model representation into triangles that can then be displayed. For example, a sphere may be represented in a database by a center point and a radius, and the faceter could turn it into any number of triangles or quadrilaterals in order to represent it. Sometimes the best rendering speedup is the simplest: Turning down the visual accuracy required when the faceter is employed can increase speed and save storage space by generating fewer triangles.

An important consideration within CAD work is whether the faceter being used is designed for graphical rendering. For example, there are faceters for the *finite element method* (FEM), which aim to split the surface into nearly equal-area triangles. Such tessellations are strong candidates for simplification, as they contain much graphically useless data. Similarly, some faceters produce sets of triangles that are ideal for creating real-world objects using 3D printing, but that lack vertex normals and are often ill-suited for fast graphical display.

Modelers such as Blender or Maya are not based around a built-in concept of solidity. Instead, objects are defined by their surfaces. Like solid modelers, these *surface-based* systems may use internal representations and faceters to display objects such as spline or subdivision surfaces (Chapter 17). They may also allow direct manipulation of surfaces, such as adding or deleting triangles or vertices. The user can then manually lower the triangle count of a model.

There are other types of modelers, such as implicit surface (including "blobby" metaball) creation systems [67, 558], that work with concepts such as blends, weights, and fields. These modelers can create organic forms by generating surfaces that are defined by the solution to some function $f(x, y, z) = 0$. Polygonalization techniques such as marching cubes are then used to create sets of triangles for display (Section 17.3).

Point clouds are strong candidates for simplification techniques. The data are often sampled at regular intervals, so many samples have a negligible effect on the visual perception of the surfaces formed. Researchers have spent decades of work on techniques for filtering out defective data and reconstructing meshes from point clouds [137]. See Section 13.9 for more about this area.

Any number of cleanup or higher-order operations can be performed on meshes that have been generated from scanned data. For example, *segmentation* techniques analyze a polygonal model and attempt to identify separate parts [1612]. Doing so can aid in creating animations, applying texture maps, matching shapes, and other operations.

There are many other ways in which polygonal data can be generated for surface representation. The key is to understand how the data were created, and for what purpose. Often, the data are not generated specifically for efficient graphical display. Also, there are many different three-dimensional data file formats, and translating between any two is often not a lossless operation. Understanding what sorts of limitations and problems may be encountered with incoming data is a major theme of this chapter.

16.2   Tessellation and Triangulation

Tessellation is the process of splitting a surface into a set of polygons. Here, we focus on tessellating polygonal surfaces; curved surface tessellation is discussed in Section 17.6. Polygonal tessellation can be undertaken for a variety of reasons. The most common is

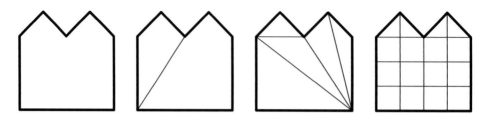

Figure 16.1. Various types of tessellation. The leftmost polygon is not tessellated, the next is partitioned into convex regions, the next is triangulated, and the rightmost is uniformly meshed.

that all graphics APIs and hardware are optimized for triangles. Triangles are almost like atoms, in that any surface can be made from them and rendered. Converting a complex polygon into triangles is called triangulation.

There are several possible goals when tessellating polygons. For example, an algorithm to be used may handle only convex polygons. Such tessellation is called *convex partitioning*. The surface may need to be subdivided (meshed) to store at each vertex the effect of shadows or interreflections using global illumination techniques [400]. Figure 16.1 shows examples of these different types of tessellation. Non-graphical reasons for tessellation include requirements such as having no triangle be larger than some given area, or for triangles to have angles at their vertices all be larger than some minimum angle. *Delaunay triangulation* has a requirement that each circle formed by the vertices of each triangle does not contain any of the remaining vertices, which maximizes the minimum angles. While such restrictions are normally a part of non-graphical applications such as finite element analysis, these can also serve to improve the appearance of a surface. Long, thin triangles are often worth avoiding, as they can cause artifacts when interpolating over distant vertices. They also can be inefficient to rasterize [530].

Most tessellation algorithms work in two dimensions. They assume that all points in the polygon are in the same plane. However, some model creation systems can generate polygon facets that are badly warped and non-planar. A common case of this problem is the warped quadrilateral that is viewed nearly edge-on; this may form what is referred to as an *hourglass* or a *bowtie* quadrilateral. See Figure 16.2. While this particular polygon can be triangulated simply by creating a diagonal edge, more complex warped polygons cannot be so easily managed.

Figure 16.2. Warped quadrilateral viewed edge-on, forming an ill-defined bowtie or hourglass figure, along with the two possible triangulations.

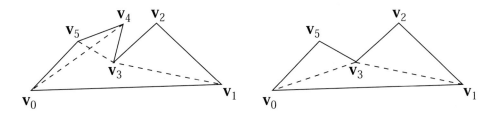

Figure 16.3. Ear clipping. A polygon with potential ears at $\mathbf{v}_2$, $\mathbf{v}_4$, and $\mathbf{v}_5$ shown. On the right, the ear at $\mathbf{v}_4$ is removed. The neighboring vertices $\mathbf{v}_3$ and $\mathbf{v}_5$ are reexamined to see if they now form ears; $\mathbf{v}_5$ does.

When warped polygons are possible, one quick corrective action is to project the vertices onto a plane that is perpendicular to the polygon's approximate normal. The normal for this plane is often found by computing the projected areas on the three orthogonal xy, xz, and yz planes. That is, the polygon's area on the yz plane, found by dropping the x-coordinates, is the value for the x-component, on xz the y, and on xy the z. This method of computing an average normal is called *Newell's formula* [1505, 1738].

The polygon cast onto this plane may still have self-intersection problems, where two or more of its edges cross. More elaborate and computationally expensive methods are then necessary. Zou et al. [1978] discuss previous work based on minimizing surface area or dihedral angles of the resulting tessellation, and present algorithms for optimizing a few non-planar polygons together in a set.

Schneider and Eberly [1574], Held [714], O'Rourke [1339], and de Berg et al. [135] each give an overview of a variety of triangulation methods. The most basic triangulation algorithm is to examine each line segment between any two given points on a polygon and see if it intersects or overlaps any edge of the polygon. If it does, the line segment cannot be used to split the polygon, so we examine the next possible pair of points. Else, split the polygon into two parts using this segment and triangulate these new polygons by the same method. This method is extremely slow, at $O(n^3)$.

A more efficient method is *ear clipping*, which is $O(n^2)$ when done as two processes. First, a pass is made over the polygon to find the ears, that is, to look at all triangles with vertex indices $i, (i+1), (i+2)$ (modulo n) and check if the line segment $i, (i+2)$ does not intersect any polygon edges. If it does not, then triangle $(i+1)$ forms an ear. See Figure 16.3. Each ear available is removed from the polygon in turn, and the triangles at vertices i and $(i+2)$ are reexamined to see if they are now ears or not. Eventually all ears are removed and the polygon is triangulated. Other, more complex methods of triangulation are $O(n \log n)$ and some are effectively $O(n)$ for typical cases. Pseudocode for ear clipping and other, faster triangulation methods is given by Schneider and Eberly [1574].

Rather than triangulating, partitioning a polygon into convex regions can be more efficient, both in storage and further computation costs. Code for a robust convexity

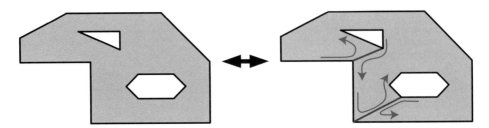

Figure 16.4. A polygon with three outlines converted to a single-outline polygon. Join edges are shown in red. Blue arrows inside the polygon show the order in which vertices are visited to make a single loop.

test is given by Schorn and Fisher [1576]. Convex polygons can easily be represented by fans or strips of triangles, as discussed in Section 16.4. Some concave polygons can be treated as fans (such polygons are called *star-shaped*), but detecting these requires more work [1339, 1444]. Schneider and Eberly [1574] give two convex partitioning methods, a quick and dirty method and an optimal one.

Polygons are not always made of a single outline. Figure 16.4 shows a polygon made of three outlines, also called *loops* or *contours*. Such descriptions can always be converted to a single-outline polygon by carefully generating *join edges* (also called *keyholed* or *bridge edges*) between loops. Eberly [403] discusses how to find the mutually visible vertices that define such edges. This conversion process can also be reversed to retrieve the separate loops.

Writing a robust and general triangulator is a difficult undertaking. Various subtle bugs, pathological cases, and precision problems make foolproof code surprisingly tricky to create. One way to finesse the triangulation problem is to use the graphics accelerator itself to directly render a complex polygon. The polygon is rendered as a triangle fan to the stencil buffer. By doing so, the areas that should be filled are drawn an odd number of times, the concavities and holes drawn an even number. By using the invert mode for the stencil buffer, only the filled areas are marked at the end of this first pass. See Figure 16.5. In the second pass the triangle fan is rendered again, using the stencil buffer to allow only the filled area to be drawn. This method can even be used to render polygons with multiple outlines by drawing the triangles formed by every loop. The major drawbacks are that each polygon has to be rendered using two passes and the stencil buffer clears every frame, and that the depth buffer cannot be used directly. The technique can be useful for display of some user interactions, such as showing the interior of a complex selection area drawn on the fly.

16.2.1 Shading Problems

Sometimes data will arrive as quadrilateral meshes and must be converted into triangles for display. Once in a great while, a quadrilateral will be concave, in which case there is only one way to triangulate it. Otherwise, we may choose either of the two

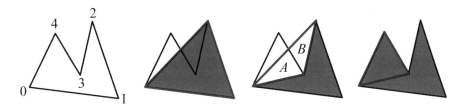

Figure 16.5. Triangulation by rasterization, using odd/even parity for what area is visible. The polygon on the left is drawn into the stencil buffer as a fan of three triangles from vertex 0. The first triangle $[0, 1, 2]$ (middle left) fills in its area, including space outside the polygon. Triangle $[0, 2, 3]$ (middle right) fills its area, changing the parity of areas A and B to an even number of draws, thus making them empty. Triangle $[0, 3, 4]$ (right) fills in the rest of the polygon.

diagonals to split it. Spending a little time picking the better diagonal can sometimes give significantly better visual results.

There are a few different ways to decide how to split a quadrilateral. The key idea is to minimize differences at the vertices of the new edge. For a flat quadrilateral with no additional data at the vertices, it is often best to choose the shortest diagonal. For simple baked global illumination solutions that have a color per vertex, choose the diagonal which has the smaller difference between the colors [17]. See Figure 16.6. This idea of connecting the two least-different corners, as determined by some heuristic, is generally useful in minimizing artifacts.

Sometimes triangles cannot properly capture the intent of the designer. If a texture is applied to a warped quadrilateral, neither diagonal split preserves the intent. That said, simple horizontal interpolation over the non-triangulated quadrilateral, i.e., interpolating values from the left to the right edge, also fails. Figure 16.7 shows the problem. This problem arises because the image being applied to the surface is to be warped when displayed. A triangle has only three texture coordinates, so it can

Figure 16.6. The left figure is rendered as a quadrilateral; the middle is two triangles with upper right and lower left corners connected; the right shows what happens when the other diagonal is used. The middle figure is better visually than the right one.

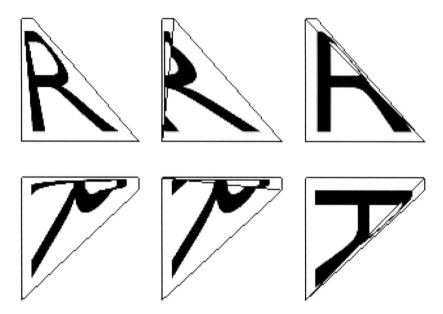

Figure 16.7. The top left shows the intent of the designer, a distorted quadrilateral with a square texture map of an "R." The two images on the right show the two triangulations and how they differ. The bottom row rotates all the polygons; the non-triangulated quadrilateral changes its appearance.

establish an affine transformation, but not a warp. At most, a basic (u, v) texture on a triangle can be sheared, not warped. Woo et al. [1901] discuss this problem further. Several solutions are possible:

- Warp the texture in advance and reapply this new image, with new texture coordinates.

- Tessellate the surface to a finer mesh. This only lessens the problem.

- Use projective texturing to warp the texture on the fly [691, 1470]. This has the undesirable effect of nonuniform spacing of the texture on the surface.

- Use a bilinear mapping scheme [691]. This is achievable with additional data per vertex.

While texture distortion sounds like a pathological case, it happens to some extent any time the texture data applied does not match the proportions of the underlying quadrilateral, i.e., on almost any curved surface. One extreme case occurs with a common primitive: the cone. When a cone is textured and faceted, the triangle vertices at the tip of the cone have different normals. These vertex normals are not shared by the neighboring triangles, so shading discontinuities occur [647].

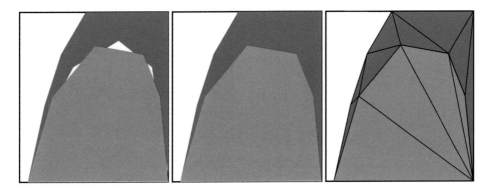

Figure 16.8. The left figure shows cracking where the two surfaces meet. The middle shows the cracking fixed by matching up edge points. The right shows the corrected mesh.

16.2.2 Edge Cracking and T-Vertices

Curved surfaces, discussed in detail in Chapter 17, are usually tessellated into meshes for rendering. This tessellation is done by stepping along the spline curves defining the surface and so computing vertex locations and normals. When we use a simple stepping method, problems can occur where spline surfaces meet. At the shared edge, the points for both surfaces need to coincide. Sometimes this may happen, due to the nature of the model, but often, without sufficient care, the points generated for one spline curve will not match those generated by its neighbor. This effect is called *edge cracking*, and it can lead to disturbing visual artifacts as the viewer peeks through the surface. Even if the viewer cannot see through the cracks, the seam is often visible because of differences in the way the shading is interpolated.

The process of fixing these cracks is called *edge stitching*. The goal is to make sure that all vertices along the (curved) shared edge are shared by both spline surfaces, so that no cracks appear. See Figure 16.8. Section 17.6.2 discusses using adaptive tessellation to avoid cracking for spline surfaces.

A related problem encountered when joining flat surfaces is that of *T-vertices*. This sort of problem can appear whenever two models' edges meet, but do not share all vertices along them. Even though the edges should theoretically meet perfectly, if the renderer does not have enough precision in representing vertex locations on the screen, cracks can appear. Modern graphics hardware uses subpixel addressing [985] to help avoid this problem.

More obvious, and not due to precision, are the shading artifacts that can appear [114]. Figure 16.9 shows the problem, which can be fixed by finding such edges and making sure to share common vertices with bordering faces. An additional problem is the danger of creating degenerate (zero-area) triangles by using a simple fan algorithm. For example, in the figure, say the quadrilateral **abcd** in the upper right is triangulated into the triangles **abc** and **acd**. The triangle **abc** is a degenerate tri-

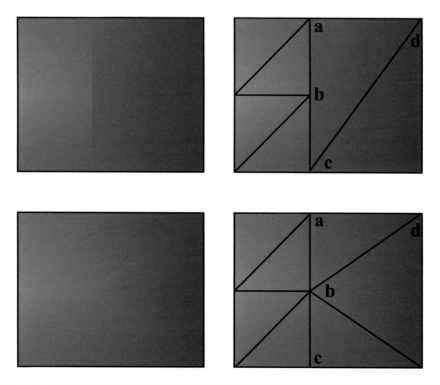

Figure 16.9. In the top row, the underlying mesh of a surface shows a shading discontinuity. Vertex **b** is a T-vertex, as it belongs to the triangles to the left of it, but is not a part of the triangle **acd**. One solution is to add this T-vertex to this triangle and create triangles **abd** and **bcd** (not shown). Long and thin triangles are more likely to cause other shading problems, so retriangulating is often a better solution, shown in the bottom row.

angle, so point **b** is a T-vertex. Lengyel [1023] discusses how to find such vertices and provides code to properly retriangulate convex polygons. Cignoni et al. [267] describe a method to avoid creating degenerate (zero-area) triangles when the T-vertices' locations are known. Their algorithm is $O(n)$ and is guaranteed to produce at most one triangle strip and fan.

16.3 Consolidation

Once a model has passed through any tessellation algorithms needed, we are left with a set of polygons representing the model. There are a few operations that may be useful for displaying these data. The simplest is checking whether the polygon itself is properly formed, that it has at least three unique vertex locations, and that they are not collinear. For example, if two vertices in a triangle match, then it has no area and can be discarded. Note that in this section we are truly referring to polygons, not just triangles. Depending on your goals, it can be more efficient to store each polygon, instead of immediately converting it to triangles for display. Triangulating creates more edges, which in turn creates more work for the operations that follow.

One procedure commonly applied to polygons is *merging*, which finds shared vertices among faces. Another operation is called *orientation*, where all polygons forming a surface are made to face the same direction. Orienting a mesh is important for several different algorithms, such as backface culling, crease edge detection, and correct collision detection and response. Related to orientation is *vertex normal generation*, where surfaces are made to look smooth. We call all these types of techniques *consolidation* algorithms.

16.3.1 Merging

Some data comes in the form of disconnected polygons, often termed a *polygon soup* or *triangle soup*. Storing separate polygons wastes memory, and displaying separate polygons is extremely inefficient. For these reasons and others, individual polygons are usually merged into a *polygon mesh*. At its simplest, a mesh consists of a list of vertices and a set of outlines. Each vertex contains a position and other optional data, such as the shading normal, texture coordinates, tangent vectors, and color. Each polygon outline has a list of integer indices. Each index is a number from 0 to $n - 1$, where n is the number of vertices and so points to a vertex in the list. In this way, each vertex can be stored just once and shared by any number of polygons. A *triangle mesh* is a polygon mesh that contains only triangles. Section 16.4.5 discusses mesh storage schemes in depth.

Given a set of disconnected polygons, merging can be done in several ways. One method is to use hashing [542, 1135]. Initialize a vertex counter to zero. For each polygon, attempt to add each of its vertices in turn to a hash table, hashing based on the vertex values. If a vertex is not already in the table, store it there, along with the vertex counter value, which is then incremented; also store the vertex in the final vertex list. If instead the vertex is found to match, retrieve its stored index. Save the polygon with the indices that point to the vertices. Once all polygons are processed, the vertex and index lists are complete.

Model data sometimes comes in with separate polygons' vertices being extremely close, but not identical. The process of merging such vertices is called *welding*. Efficiently welding vertices can be done by using sorting along with a looser equality function for the position [1135].

16.3.2 Orientation

One quality-related problem with model data is face orientation. Some model data come in oriented properly, with surface normals either explicitly or implicitly pointing in the correct directions. For example, in CAD work, the standard is that the vertices in the polygon outline proceed in a counterclockwise direction when the frontface is viewed. This is called the *winding direction* and the triangles use the *right-hand rule*. Think of the fingers of your right hand wrapping around the polygon's vertices in counterclockwise order. Your thumb then points in the direction of the polygon's normal. This orientation is independent of the left-handed or right-handed view-space or world-coordinate orientation used, as it relies purely on the ordering of the vertices in the world, when looking at the front of the triangle. That said, if a reflection matrix is applied to an oriented mesh, each triangle's normal will be reversed compared to its winding direction.

Given a reasonable model, here is one approach to orient a polygonal mesh:

1. Form edge-face structures for all polygons.

2. Sort or hash the edges to find which edges match.

3. Find groups of polygons that touch each other.

4. For each group, flip faces as needed to obtain consistency.

The first step is to create a set of *half-edge* objects. A half-edge is an edge of a polygon, with a pointer to its associated face (polygon). Since an edge is normally shared by two polygons, this data structure is called a half-edge. Create each half-edge with its first vertex stored before the second vertex, using sorting order. One vertex comes before another in sorting order if its x-coordinate value is smaller. If the x-coordinates are equal, then the y-value is used; if these match, then z is used. For example, vertex $(-3, 5, 2)$ comes before vertex $(-3, 6, -8)$; the -3s match, but $5 < 6$.

The goal is to find which edges are identical. Since each edge is stored so that the first vertex is less than the second, comparing edges is a matter of comparing first to first and second to second vertices. No permutations such as comparing one edge's first vertex to another's second vertex are needed. A hash table can be used to find matching edges [19, 542]. If all vertices have previously been merged, so that half-edges use the same vertex indices, then each half-edge can be matched by putting it on a temporary list associated with its first vertex index. A vertex has an average of 6 edges attached to it, making edge matching extremely rapid once grouped [1487].

Once the edges are matched, connections among neighboring polygons are known, forming an *adjacency graph*. For a triangle mesh, this can be represented as a list for each triangle of its (up to) three neighboring triangle faces. Any edge that does not have two neighboring polygons is a boundary edge. The set of polygons that are connected by edges forms a continuous group. For example, a teapot model has two groups, the pot and the lid.

The next step is to give the mesh orientation consistency, e.g., we usually want all polygons to have counterclockwise outlines. For each continuous group of polygons, choose an arbitrary starting polygon. Check each of its neighboring polygons and determine whether the orientation is consistent. If the direction of traversal for the edge is the same for both polygons, then the neighboring polygon must be flipped. See

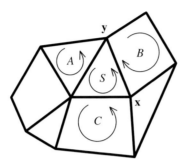

Figure 16.10. A starting polygon S is chosen and its neighbors are checked. Because the vertices in the edge shared by S and B are traversed in the same order (from **x** to **y**), the outline for B needs to be reversed to make it follow the right-hand rule.

Figure 16.10. Recursively check the neighbors of these neighbors, until all polygons in a continuous group are tested once.

Although all the faces are properly oriented at this point, they could all be oriented inward. In most cases we want them facing outward. One quick test for whether all faces should be flipped is to compute the signed volume of the group and check the sign. If it is negative, reverse all the loops and normals. Compute this volume by calculating the signed volume scalar triple product for each triangle and summing these. Look for the volume calculation in our online linear algebra appendix at realtimerendering.com.

This method works well for solid objects but is not foolproof. For example, if the object is a box forming a room, the user wants its normals to face inward toward the camera. If the object is not a solid, but rather a surface description, the problem of orienting each surface can become tricky to perform automatically. If, say, two cubes touch along an edge and are a part of the same mesh, that edge would be shared by four polygons, making orientation more difficult. One-sided objects such as Möbius strips can never be fully oriented, since there is no separation of inside and outside. Even for well-behaved surface meshes it can be difficult to determine which side should face outward. Takayama et al. [1736] discuss previous work and present their own solution, casting random rays from each facet and determining which orientation is more visible from the outside.

16.3.3 Solidity

Informally, a mesh forms a solid if it is oriented and all the polygons visible from the outside have the same orientation. In other words, only one side of the mesh is visible. Such polygonal meshes are called *closed* or *watertight*.

Knowing an object is solid means backface culling can be used to improve display efficiency, as discussed in Section 19.2. Solidity is also a critical property for objects casting shadow volumes (Section 7.3) and for several other algorithms. For example, a 3D printer requires that the mesh it prints be solid.

The simplest test for solidity is to check if every polygon edge in the mesh is shared by exactly two polygons. This test is sufficient for most data sets. Such a surface is loosely referred to as being *manifold*, specifically, *two-manifold*. Technically, a manifold surface is one without any topological inconsistencies, such as having three or more polygons sharing an edge or two or more corners touching each other. A continuous surface forming a solid is a manifold without boundaries.

16.3.4 Normal Smoothing and Crease Edges

Some polygon meshes form curved surfaces, but the polygon vertices do not have normal vectors, so they cannot be rendered with the illusion of curvature. See Figure 16.11.

Many model formats do not provide surface edge information. See Section 15.2 for the various types of edges. These edges are important for several reasons. They can highlight an area of the model made of a set of polygons or can help in nonphotorealistic rendering. Because they provide important visual cues, such edges are often favored to avoid being simplified by progressive mesh algorithms (Section 16.5).

Reasonable crease edges and vertex normals can usually be derived with some success from an oriented mesh. Once the orientation is consistent and the adjacency graph is derived, vertex normals can be generated by *smoothing techniques*. The model's format may provide help by specifying smoothing groups for the polygon

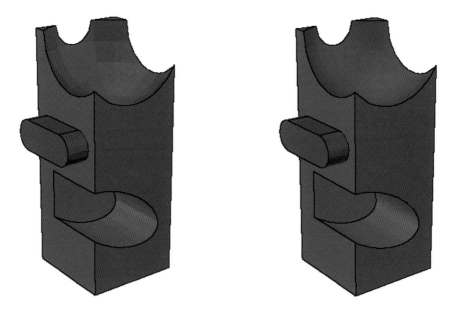

Figure 16.11. The object on the left does not have normals per vertex; the one on the right does.

mesh. Smoothing group values are used to explicitly define which polygons in a group belong together to make up a curved surface. Edges between different smoothing groups are considered sharp.

Another way to smooth a polygon mesh is to specify a crease angle. This value is compared to the *dihedral angle*, which is the angle between the plane normals of two polygons. Values typically range from 20 to 50 degrees. If the dihedral angle between two neighboring polygons is found to be lower than the specified crease angle, then these two polygons are considered to be in the same smoothing group. This technique is sometimes called *edge preservation*.

Using a crease angle can sometimes give an improper amount of smoothing, rounding edges that should be creased, or vice versa. Often experimentation is needed, and no single angle may work perfectly for a mesh. Even smoothing groups have limitations. One example is when you pinch a sheet of paper in the middle. The sheet could be thought of as a single smoothing group, yet it has creases within it, which a smoothing group would smooth away. The modeler then needs multiple overlapping smoothing groups, or direct crease edge definition on the mesh. Another example is a cone made from triangles. Smoothing the cone's whole surface gives the peculiar result that the tip has one normal pointing directly out along the cone's axis. The cone tip is a singularity. For perfect representation of the interpolated normal, each triangle would need to be more like a quadrilateral, with two normals at this tip location [647].

Fortunately, such problematic cases are usually rare. Once a smoothing group is found, vertex normals can be computed for vertices shared within the group. The standard textbook solution for finding the vertex normal is to average the surface normals of the polygons sharing the vertex [541, 542]. However, this method can lead to inconsistent and poorly weighted results. Thürmer and Wüthrich [1770] present an alternate method, in which each polygon normal's contribution is weighted by the angle it forms at the vertex. This method has the desirable property of giving the same result whether a polygon sharing a vertex is triangulated or not. If the tessellated polygon turned into, say, two triangles sharing the vertex, the average normal method would incorrectly exert twice the influence from the two triangles as it would for the original polygon. See Figure 16.12.

Max [1146] gives a different weighting method, based on the assumption that long edges form polygons that should affect the normal less. This type of smoothing may be superior when using simplification techniques, as larger polygons that are formed will be less likely to follow the surface's curvature.

Jin et al. [837] provide a comprehensive survey of these and other methods, concluding that weighting by angle is either the best or among the best under various conditions. Cignoni [268] implements a few methods in *Meshlab* and notes about the same. He also warns against weighting the contribution of each normal by the area of its associated triangle.

For heightfields, Shankel [1614] shows how taking the difference in heights of the neighbors along each axis can be used to rapidly approximate smoothing using the angle-weighted method. For a given point $\mathbf{p}$ and four neighboring points, $\mathbf{p}^{x-1}$ and

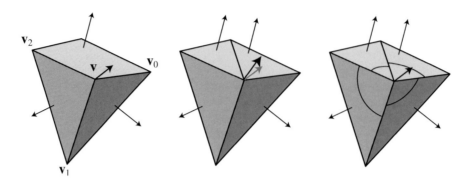

Figure 16.12. On the left, the surface normals of a quadrilateral and two triangles are averaged to give a vertex normal. In the middle, the quadrilateral has been triangulated. This results in the average normal shifting, since each polygon's normal is weighted equally. On the right, Thürmer and Wüthrich's method weights each normal's contribution by its angle between the pair of edges forming it, so triangulation does not shift the normal.

$\mathbf{p}^{x+1}$ on the x-axis of the heightfield and $\mathbf{p}^{y-1}$ and $\mathbf{p}^{y+1}$ on the y-axis, a close approximation of the (unnormalized) normal at $\mathbf{p}$ is

$$\mathbf{n} = \left(p_x^{x+1} - p_x^{x-1}, p_y^{y+1} - p_y^{y-1}, 2 \right). \tag{16.1}$$

16.4 Triangle Fans, Strips, and Meshes

A *triangle list* is the simplest, and usually least efficient, way to store and display a set of triangles. The vertex data for each triangle is put in a list, one after another. Each triangle has its own separate set of three vertices, so there is no sharing of vertex data among triangles. A standard way to increase graphics performance is to send groups of triangles that share vertices through the graphics pipeline. Sharing means fewer calls to the vertex shader, so less points and normals need to be transformed. Here we describe a variety of data structures that share vertex information, starting with triangle fans and strips and progressing to more elaborate, and more efficient, forms for rendering surfaces.

16.4.1 Fans

Figure 16.13 shows a *triangle fan*. This data structure shows how we can form triangles and have the storage cost be less than three vertices per triangle. The vertex shared by all triangles is called the *center vertex* and is vertex 0 in the figure. For the starting triangle 0, send vertices 0, 1, and 2 (in that order). For subsequent triangles, the center vertex is always used together with the previously sent vertex and the vertex currently being sent. Triangle 1 is formed by sending vertex 3, thereby creating a

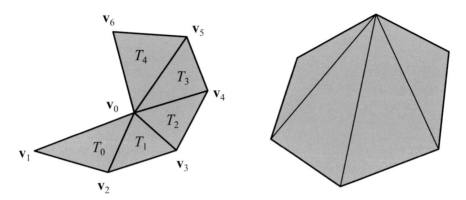

Figure 16.13. The left figure illustrates the concept of a triangle fan. Triangle T_0 sends vertices $\mathbf{v}_0$ (the center vertex), $\mathbf{v}_1$, and $\mathbf{v}_2$. The subsequent triangles, T_i ($i > 0$), send only vertex $\mathbf{v}_{i+2}$. The right figure shows a convex polygon, which can always be turned into one triangle fan.

triangle defined by vertices 0 (always included), 2 (the previously sent vertex), and 3. Triangle 2 is constructed by sending vertex 4, and so on. Note that a general convex polygon is trivial to represent as a triangle fan, since any of its points can be used as the starting, center vertex.

A triangle fan of n vertices is defined as an ordered vertex list

$$\{\mathbf{v}_0, \mathbf{v}_1, \ldots, \mathbf{v}_{n-1}\}, \tag{16.2}$$

where $\mathbf{v}_0$ is the center vertex, with a structure imposed upon the list indicating that triangle i is

$$\triangle \mathbf{v}_0 \mathbf{v}_{i+1} \mathbf{v}_{i+2}, \tag{16.3}$$

where $0 \leq i < n - 2$.

If a triangle fan consists of m triangles, then three vertices are sent for the first, followed by one more for each of the remaining $m - 1$ triangles. This means that the average number of vertices, v_a, sent for a sequential triangle fan of length m, can be expressed as

$$v_a = \frac{3 + (m - 1)}{m} = 1 + \frac{2}{m}. \tag{16.4}$$

As can easily be seen, $v_a \to 1$ as $m \to \infty$. This might not seem to have much relevance for real-world cases, but consider a more reasonable value. If $m = 5$, then $v_a = 1.4$, which means that, on average, only 1.4 vertices are sent per triangle.

16.4.2 Strips

Triangle strips are like triangle fans, in that vertices in previous triangles are reused. Instead of a single center point and the previous vertex getting reused, it is two vertices of the previous triangle that help form the next triangle. Consider Figure 16.14. If

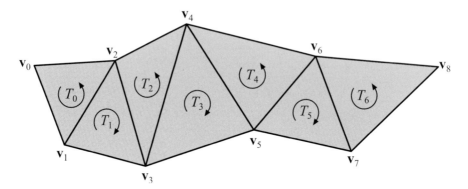

Figure 16.14. A sequence of triangles that can be represented as one triangle strip. Note that the orientation changes from triangle to triangle in the strip, and that the first triangle in the strip sets the orientation of all triangles. Internally, counterclockwise order is kept consistent by traversing vertices [0, 1, 2], [1, 3, 2], [2, 3, 4], [3, 5, 4], and so on.

these triangles are treated as a strip, then a more compact way of sending them to the rendering pipeline is possible. For the first triangle (denoted T_0), all three vertices (denoted $\mathbf{v}_0$, $\mathbf{v}_1$, and $\mathbf{v}_2$) are sent, in that order. For subsequent triangles in this strip, only one vertex has to be sent, since the other two have already been sent with the previous triangle. For example, sending triangle T_1, only vertex $\mathbf{v}_3$ is sent, and the vertices $\mathbf{v}_1$ and $\mathbf{v}_2$ from triangle T_0 are used to form triangle T_1. For triangle T_2, only vertex $\mathbf{v}_4$ is sent, and so on through the rest of the strip.

A sequential triangle strip of n vertices is defined as an ordered vertex list,

$$\{\mathbf{v}_0, \mathbf{v}_1, \ldots, \mathbf{v}_{n-1}\}, \tag{16.5}$$

with a structure imposed upon it indicating that triangle i is

$$\triangle \mathbf{v}_i \mathbf{v}_{i+1} \mathbf{v}_{i+2}, \tag{16.6}$$

where $0 \leq i < n - 2$. This sort of strip is called *sequential* because the vertices are sent in the given sequence. The definition implies that a sequential triangle strip of n vertices has $n - 2$ triangles.

The analysis of the average number of vertices for a triangle strip of length m (i.e., consisting of m triangles), also denoted v_a, is the same as for triangle fans (see Equation 16.4), since they have the same start-up phase and then send only one vertex per new triangle. Similarly, when $m \to \infty$, v_a for triangle strips naturally also tends toward one vertex per triangle. For $m = 20$, $v_a = 1.1$, which is much better than 3 and is close to the limit of 1.0. As with triangle fans, the start-up cost for the first triangle, always costing three vertices, is amortized over the subsequent triangles.

The attractiveness of triangle strips stems from this fact. Depending on where the bottleneck is located in the rendering pipeline, there is a potential for saving up to two thirds of the time spent rendering with simple triangle lists. The speedup is due to avoiding redundant operations such as sending each vertex twice to the graphics hardware, then performing matrix transformations, clipping, and other operations on each. Triangle strips are useful for objects such as blades of grass or other objects where edge vertices are not reused by other strips. Because of its simplicity, strips are used by the geometry shader when multiple triangles are output.

There are several variants on triangles strips, such as not imposing a strict sequence on the triangles, or using doubled vertices or a restart index value so that multiple disconnected strips can be stored in a single buffer. There once was considerable research on how best to decompose an arbitrary mesh of triangles into strips [1076]. Such efforts have died off, as the introduction of indexed triangle meshes allowed better vertex data reuse, leading to both faster display and usually less overall memory needed.

16.4.3 Triangle Meshes

Triangle fans and strips still have their uses, but the norm on all modern GPUs is to use triangle meshes with a single index list (Section 16.3.1) for complex models [1135]. Strips and fans allow some data sharing, but mesh storage allows even more. In a mesh an additional index array keeps track of which vertices form the triangles. In this way, a single vertex can be associated with several triangles.

The Euler-Poincaré formula for *connected planar graphs* [135] helps in determining the average number of vertices that form a closed mesh:

$$v - e + f + 2g = 2. \tag{16.7}$$

Here v is the number of vertices, e is the number of edges, f is the number of faces, and g is the genus. The *genus* is the number of holes in the object. As an example, a sphere has genus 0 and a torus has genus 1. Each face is assumed to have one loop. If faces can have multiple loops, the formula becomes

$$v - e + 2f - l + 2g = 2, \tag{16.8}$$

where l is the number of loops.

For a closed (solid) model, every edge has two faces, and every face has at least three edges, so $2e \geq 3f$. If the mesh is all triangles, as the GPU demands, then $2e = 3f$. Assuming a genus of 0 and substituting $1.5f$ for e in the formula yields $f \leq 2v - 4$. If all faces are triangles, then $f = 2v - 4$.

For large closed triangle meshes, the rule of thumb then is that the number of triangles is about equal to twice the number of vertices. Similarly, we find that each vertex is connected to an average of nearly six triangles (and, therefore, six edges). The number of edges connected to a vertex is called its *valence*. Note that the network of the mesh does not affect the result, only the number of triangles does. Since the average number of vertices per triangle in a strip approaches one, and the number of vertices is twice that of triangles, every vertex has to be sent twice (on average) if a large mesh is represented by triangle strips. At the limit, triangle meshes can send 0.5 vertices per triangle.

Note that this analysis holds for only smooth, closed meshes. As soon as there are *boundary edges* (edges not shared between two polygons), the ratio of vertices to triangles increases. The Euler-Poincaré formula still holds, but the outer boundary of the mesh has to be considered a separate (unused) face bordering all exterior edges. Similarly, each smoothing group in any model is effectively its own mesh, since GPUs need to have separate vertex records with differing normals along sharp edges where two groups meet. For example, the corner of a cube will have three normals at a single location, so three vertex records are stored. Changes in textures or other vertex data can also cause the number of distinct vertex records to increase.

Theory predicts we need to process about 0.5 vertices per triangle. In practice, vertices are transformed by the GPU and put in a *first-in, first-out* (FIFO) cache, or in something approximating a *least recently used* (LRU) system [858]. This cache holds post-transform results for each vertex run through the vertex shader. If an incoming vertex is located in this cache, then the cached post-transform results can be used without calling the vertex shader, providing a significant performance increase. If instead the triangles in a triangle mesh are sent down in random order, the cache is unlikely to be useful. Triangle strip algorithms optimize for a cache size of two, i.e., the last two vertices used. Deering and Nelson [340] first explored the idea of storing vertex data in a larger FIFO cache by using an algorithm to determine in which order to add the vertices to the cache.

FIFO caches are limited in size. For example, the PLAYSTATION 3 system holds about 24 vertices, depending on the number of bytes per vertex. Newer GPUs have not increased this cache significantly, with 32 vertices being a typical maximum.

Hoppe [771] introduces an important measurement of cache reuse, the *average cache miss ratio* (ACMR). This is the average number of vertices that need to be processed per triangle. It can range from 3 (every vertex for every triangle has to be reprocessed each time) to 0.5 (perfect reuse on a large closed mesh; no vertex is reprocessed). If the cache size is as large as the mesh itself, the ACMR is identical to the theoretical vertex to triangle ratio. For a given cache size and mesh ordering, the ACMR can be computed precisely, so describing the efficiency of any given approach for that cache size.

16.4.4   Cache-Oblivious Mesh Layouts

The ideal order for triangles in an mesh is one in which we maximize the use of the vertex cache. Hoppe [771] presents an algorithm that minimizes the ACMR for a mesh, but the cache size has to be known in advance. If the assumed cache size is larger than the actual cache size, the resulting mesh can have significantly less benefit. Solving for different-sized caches may yield different optimal orderings. For when the target cache size is unknown, *cache-oblivious* mesh layout algorithms have been developed that yield orderings that work well, regardless of size. Such an ordering is sometimes called a *universal* index sequence.

Forsyth [485] and Lin and Yu [1047] provide rapid greedy algorithms that use similar principles. Vertices are given scores based on their positions in the cache and by the number of unprocessed triangles attached to them. The triangle with the highest combined vertex score is processed next. By scoring the three most recently used vertices a little lower, the algorithm avoids simply making triangle strips and instead creates patterns similar to a Hilbert curve. By giving higher scores to vertices with fewer triangles still attached, the algorithm tends to avoid leaving isolated triangles behind. The average cache miss ratios achieved are comparable to those of more costly and complex algorithms. Lin and Yu's method is a little more complex but uses related ideas. For a cache size of 12, the average ACMR for a set of 30 unoptimized models was 1.522; after optimization, the average dropped to 0.664 or lower, depending on cache size.

Sander et al. [1544] give an overview of previous work and present their own faster (though not cache-size oblivious) method, called *Tipsify*. One addition is that they also strive to put the outermost triangles early on in the list, to minimize overdraw (Section 18.4.5). For example, imagine a coffee cup. By rendering the triangles forming the outside of the cup first, the later triangles inside are likely to be hidden from view.

Storsjö [1708] contrasts and compares Forsyth's and Sander's methods, and provides implementations of both. He concludes that these methods provide layouts that are near the theoretical limits. A newer study by Kapoulkine [858] compares four cache-aware vertex-ordering algorithms on three hardware vendors' GPUs. Among his conclusions are that Intel uses a 128-entry FIFO, with each vertex using three or more entries, and that AMD's and NVIDIA's systems approximate a 16-entry LRU cache. This architectural difference significantly affects algorithm behavior. He finds that Tipsify [1544] and, to a lesser extent, Forsyth's algorithm [485] perform relatively well across these platforms.

To conclude, offline preprocessing of triangle meshes can noticeably improve vertex cache performance, and the overall frame rate when this vertex stage is the bottleneck. It is fast, effectively $O(n)$ in practice. There are several open-source versions available [485]. Given that such algorithms can be applied automatically to a mesh and that such optimization has no additional storage cost and does not affect other tools in the toolchain, these methods are often a part of a mature development system. Forsyth's algorithm appears to be part of the PLAYSTATION mesh processing toolchain, for example. While the vertex post-transform cache has evolved due to modern GPUs' adoption of a unified shader architecture, avoiding cache misses is still an important concern [530].

16.4.5   Vertex and Index Buffers/Arrays

One way to provide a modern graphics accelerator with model data is by using what DirectX calls *vertex buffers* and OpenGL calls *vertex buffer objects* (VBOs). We will go with the DirectX terminology in this section. The concepts presented have OpenGL equivalents.

The idea of a vertex buffer is to store model data in a contiguous chunk of memory. A vertex buffer is an array of vertex data in a particular format. The format specifies whether a vertex contains a normal, texture coordinates, a color, or other specific information. Each vertex has its data in a group, one vertex after another. The size in bytes of a vertex is called its *stride*. This type of storage is called an *interleaved* buffer. Alternately, a set of *vertex streams* can be used. For example, one stream could hold an array of positions $\{\mathbf{p}_0\mathbf{p}_1\mathbf{p}_2\ldots\}$ and another a separate array of normals $\{\mathbf{n}_0\mathbf{n}_1\mathbf{n}_2\ldots\}$. In practice, a single buffer containing all data for each vertex is generally more efficient on GPUs, but not so much that multiple streams should be avoided [66, 1494]. The main cost of multiple streams is additional API calls, possibly worth avoiding if the application is CPU-bound but otherwise not significant [443].

Wihlidal [1884] discusses different ways multiple streams can help rendering system performance, including API, caching, and CPU processing advantages. For example, SSE and AVX for vector processing on the CPU are easier to apply to a separate stream. Another reason to use multiple streams is for more efficient mesh updating. If, say, just the vertex location stream is changing over time, it is less costly to update this one attribute buffer than to form and send an entire interleaved stream [1609].

How the vertex buffer is accessed is up to the device's `DrawPrimitive` method. The data can be treated as:

1. A list of individual points.

2. A list of unconnected line segments, i.e., pairs of vertices.

3. A single polyline.

4. A triangle list, where each group of three vertices forms a triangle, e.g., vertices $[0, 1, 2]$ form one, $[3, 4, 5]$ form the next, and so on.

5. A triangle fan, where the first vertex forms a triangle with each successive pair of vertices, e.g., $[0, 1, 2]$, $[0, 2, 3]$, $[0, 3, 4]$.

6. A triangle strip, where every group of three contiguous vertices forms a triangle, e.g., $[0, 1, 2]$, $[1, 2, 3]$, $[2, 3, 4]$.

In DirectX 10 on, triangles and triangle strips can also include adjacent triangle vertices, for use by the geometry shader (Section 3.7).

The vertex buffer can be used as is or referenced by an index buffer. The indices in an index buffer hold the locations of vertices in a vertex buffer. Indices are stored as 16-bit unsigned integers, or 32-bit if the mesh is large and the GPU and API support it (Section 16.6). The combination of an index buffer and vertex buffer is used to display the same types of draw primitives as a "raw" vertex buffer. The difference is that each vertex in the index/vertex buffer combination needs to be stored only once in its vertex buffer, versus repetition that can occur in a vertex buffer without indexing.

The triangle mesh structure is represented by an index buffer. The first three indices stored in the index buffer specify the first triangle, the next three the second, and so on. This arrangement is called an *indexed triangle list*, where the indices themselves form a list of triangles. OpenGL binds the index buffer and vertex buffer(s) together with vertex format information in a *vertex array object* (VAO). Indices can also be arranged in triangle strip order, which saves on index buffer space. This format, the *indexed triangle strip*, is rarely used in practice, in that creating such sets of strips for a large mesh takes some effort, and all tools that process geometry also then need to support this format. See Figure 16.15 for examples of vertex and index buffer structures.

Which structure to use is dictated by the primitives and the program. Displaying a simple rectangle is easily done with just a vertex buffer using four vertices as a two-triangle tristrip or fan. One advantage of the index buffer is data sharing, as discussed earlier. Another advantage is simplicity, in that triangles can be in any order and configuration, not having the lock-step requirements of triangle strips. Lastly, the amount of data that needs to be transferred and stored on the GPU is usually smaller when an index buffer is used. The small overhead of including an indexed array is far outweighed by the memory savings achieved by sharing vertices.

An index buffer and one or more vertex buffers provide a way of describing a polygonal mesh. However, the data are typically stored with the goal of GPU rendering efficiency, not necessarily the most compact storage. For example, one way to store a cube is to save its eight corner locations in one array, and its six different normals in another, along with the six four-index loops that define its faces. Each vertex location is then described by two indices, one for the vertex list and one for the normal list. Texture coordinates are represented by yet another array and a third index. This compact representation is used in many model file formats, such as Wavefront OBJ. On the GPU, only one index buffer is available. A single vertex buffer would store 24 different vertices, as each corner location has three separate normals, one for each neighboring face. The index buffer would store indices defining the 12 triangles forming the surface. Masserann [1135] discusses efficiently turning such file descriptions into compact and efficient index/vertex buffers, versus lists of unindexed triangles that do not share vertices. More compact schemes are possible by such methods as storing the mesh in texture maps or buffer textures and using the vertex shader's texture fetch or pulling mechanisms, but they come at the performance penalty of not being able to use the post-transform vertex cache [223, 1457].

For maximum efficiency, the order of the vertices in the vertex buffer should match the order in which they are accessed by the index buffer. That is, the first three vertices referenced by the first triangle in the index buffer should be first three in the vertex buffer. When a new vertex is encountered in the index buffer, it should then be next in the vertex buffer. Giving this order minimizes cache misses in the pre-transform vertex cache, which is separate from the post-transform cache discussed

Three triangles, made of vertex positions
$\mathbf{p}_0$ through $\mathbf{p}_3$, and normals $\mathbf{n}_0$ through $\mathbf{n}_3$

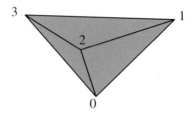

The triangles could be rendered through a series of individual calls: begin, $\mathbf{p}_0$, $\mathbf{n}_0$, $\mathbf{p}_1$, $\mathbf{n}_1$, $\mathbf{p}_2$, $\mathbf{n}_2$, end, begin, $\mathbf{p}_1$, $\mathbf{n}_1$, $\mathbf{p}_3$, $\mathbf{n}_3$, $\mathbf{p}_2$, $\mathbf{n}_2$, end, begin, $\mathbf{p}_2$, $\mathbf{n}_2$, $\mathbf{p}_3$, $\mathbf{n}_3$, $\mathbf{p}_0$, $\mathbf{n}_0$, end.

The positions and normals could be put into two separate lists. These two arrays get treated as a list of triangles, so that each separate trio in the array is a triangle:

| $\mathbf{p}_0$ $\mathbf{p}_1$ $\mathbf{p}_2$ $\mathbf{p}_1$ $\mathbf{p}_3$ $\mathbf{p}_2$ $\mathbf{p}_2$ $\mathbf{p}_3$ $\mathbf{p}_0$ | array of positions |

| $\mathbf{n}_0$ $\mathbf{n}_1$ $\mathbf{n}_2$ $\mathbf{n}_1$ $\mathbf{n}_3$ $\mathbf{n}_2$ $\mathbf{n}_2$ $\mathbf{n}_3$ $\mathbf{n}_0$ | array of normals |

The positions and normals could be put in arrays and every trio define a triangle:

| $\mathbf{p}_0$ $\mathbf{p}_1$ $\mathbf{p}_2$ $\mathbf{p}_3$ $\mathbf{p}_0$ | array of positions |

| $\mathbf{n}_0$ $\mathbf{n}_1$ $\mathbf{n}_2$ $\mathbf{n}_3$ $\mathbf{n}_0$ | array of normals |

Each vertex could be put in a single interleaved array, with each separate trio or every trio (i.e., a tristrip) making a triangle. Here is the array for the tristrip:

| $\mathbf{p}_0$ $\mathbf{n}_0$ $\mathbf{p}_1$ $\mathbf{n}_1$ $\mathbf{p}_2$ $\mathbf{n}_2$ $\mathbf{p}_3$ $\mathbf{n}_3$ $\mathbf{p}_0$ $\mathbf{n}_0$ | array of vertices |

Each vertex could be in a single array, with an index list giving separate triangles:

| $\mathbf{p}_0$ $\mathbf{n}_0$ $\mathbf{p}_1$ $\mathbf{n}_1$ $\mathbf{p}_2$ $\mathbf{n}_2$ $\mathbf{p}_3$ $\mathbf{n}_3$ | array of vertices |

| 0 1 2 1 3 2 2 3 0 | index array |

Each vertex could be in a single array, with an index list defining the triangle strip:

| $\mathbf{p}_0$ $\mathbf{n}_0$ $\mathbf{p}_1$ $\mathbf{n}_1$ $\mathbf{p}_2$ $\mathbf{n}_2$ $\mathbf{p}_3$ $\mathbf{n}_3$ | array of vertices |

| 0 1 2 3 0 | index array |

Figure 16.15. Different ways of defining primitives, in rough order of most to least memory use from top to bottom: separate triangles, as a vertex triangle list, as triangle strips of two or one data streams, and as an index buffer listing separate triangles or in triangle strip order.

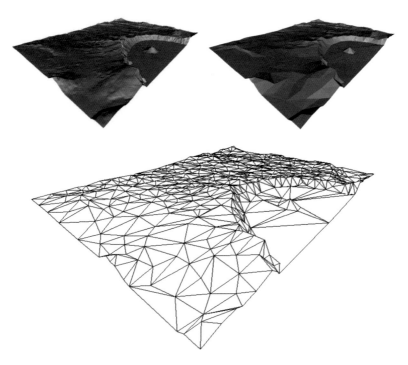

Figure 16.16. In the upper left is a heightfield of Crater Lake rendered with 200,000 triangles. The upper right figure shows this model simplified down to 1000 triangles in a *triangulated irregular network* (TIN). The underlying simplified mesh is shown at the bottom. *(Images courtesy of Michael Garland.)*

in Section 16.4.4. Reordering the data in the vertex buffer is a simple operation, but can be as important to performance as finding an efficient triangle order for the post-transform vertex cache [485].

There are higher-level methods for allocating and using vertex and index buffers to achieve greater efficiency. For example, a buffer that does not change can be stored on the GPU for use each frame, and multiple instances and variations of an object can be generated from the same buffer. Section 18.4.2 discusses such techniques in depth.

The ability to send processed vertices to a new buffer using the pipeline's stream output functionality (Section 3.7.1) allows a way to process vertex buffers on the GPU without rendering them. For example, a vertex buffer describing a triangle mesh could be treated as a simple set of points in an initial pass. The vertex shader could be used to perform per-vertex computations as desired, with the results sent to a new vertex buffer using stream output. On a subsequent pass, this new vertex buffer could be paired with the original index buffer describing the mesh's connectivity, to further process and display the resulting mesh.

16.5 Simplification

Mesh simplification, also known as *data reduction* or *decimation*, is the process of taking a detailed model and reducing its triangle count while attempting to preserve its appearance. For real-time work this process is done to reduce the number of vertices stored and sent down the pipeline. This can be important in making the application scalable, as less powerful machines may need to display lower numbers of triangles. Model data may also be received with more tessellation than is necessary for a reasonable representation. Figure 16.16 gives a sense of how the number of stored triangles can be reduced by data reduction techniques.

Luebke [1091, 1092] identifies three types of mesh simplification: static, dynamic, and view-dependent. Static simplification is the idea of creating separate level of detail (LOD) models before rendering begins, and the renderer chooses among these. This form is covered in Section 19.9. Offline simplification can also be useful for other tasks, such as providing coarse meshes for subdivision surfaces to refine [1006, 1007]. Dynamic simplification gives a continuous spectrum of LOD models instead of a few discrete models, and so such methods are referred to as *continuous level of detail* (CLOD) algorithms. View-dependent techniques are meant for where the level of detail varies within the model. Specifically, terrain rendering is a case in which the nearby areas in view need detailed representation while those in the distance are at a lower level of detail. These two types of simplification are discussed in this section.

16.5.1 Dynamic Simplification

One method of reducing the triangle count is to use an *edge collapse* operation, where an edge is removed by moving its two vertices to coincide. See Figure 16.17 for an example of this operation in action. For a solid model, an edge collapse removes a total of two triangles, three edges, and one vertex. So, a closed model with 3000 triangles would have 1500 edge collapses applied to it to reduce it to zero faces. The rule of thumb is that a closed triangle mesh with v vertices has about $2v$ faces and $3v$ edges. This rule can be derived using the Euler-Poincaré formula that $f - e + v = 2$ for a solid's surface (Section 16.4.3).

The edge collapse process is reversible. By storing the edge collapses in order, we can start with the simplified model and reconstruct the complex model from it. This characteristic can be useful for network transmission of models, in that the edge-collapsed version of the database can be sent in an efficiently compressed form and progressively built up and displayed as the model is received [768, 1751]. Because of this feature, this simplification process is often referred to as *view-independent progressive meshing* (VIPM).

In Figure 16.17, **u** was collapsed into the location of **v**, but **v** could have been collapsed into **u**. A simplification system limited to just these two possibilities is using a *subset placement* strategy. An advantage of this strategy is that, if we limit the possibilities, we may implicitly encode the choice made [516, 768]. This strategy

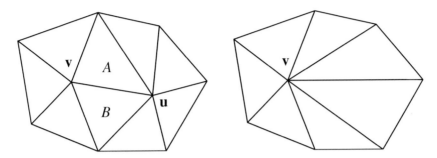

Figure 16.17. On the left is the figure before the **uv** edge collapse occurs; the right figure shows point **u** collapsed into point **v**, thereby removing triangles A and B and edge **uv**.

is faster because fewer possibilities need to be evaluated, but it also can yield lower-quality approximations because a smaller solution space is examined.

When using an *optimal placement* strategy, we examine a wider range of possibilities. Instead of collapsing one vertex into another, both vertices for an edge are contracted to a new location. Hoppe [768] examines the case in which **u** and **v** both move to some location on the edge joining them. He notes that to improve compression of the final data representation, the search can be limited to checking the midpoint. Garland and Heckbert [516] go further, solving a quadratic equation to find an optimal position, one that may be located off of the edge. The advantage of optimal placement strategies is that they tend to give higher-quality meshes. The disadvantages are extra processing, code, and memory for recording this wider range of possible placements.

To determine the best point placement, we perform an analysis on the local neighborhood. This locality is an important and useful feature for several reasons. If the cost of an edge collapse depends on just a few local variables (e.g., edge length and face normals near the edge), the cost function is easy to compute, and each collapse affects only a few of its neighbors. For example, say a model has 3000 possible edge collapses that are computed at the start. The edge collapse with the lowest cost-function value is performed. Because it influences only a few nearby triangles and their edges, only those edge collapse possibilities whose cost functions are affected by these changes need to be recomputed (say, 10 instead of 3000), and the list requires only a minor bit of resorting. Because an edge-collapse affects only a few other edge-collapse cost values, a good choice for maintaining this list of cost values is a heap or other priority queue [1649].

Some contractions must be avoided regardless of cost. See an example in Figure 16.18. These can be detected by checking whether a neighboring triangle flips its normal direction due to a collapse.

The collapse operation itself is an edit of the model's database. Data structures for storing these collapses are well documented [481, 770, 1196, 1726]. Each edge collapse is analyzed with a cost function, and the one with the smallest cost value is performed

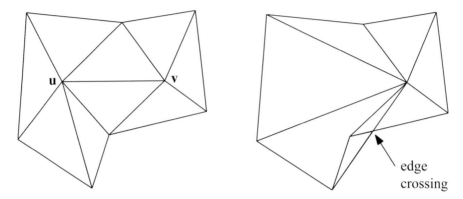

Figure 16.18. Example of a bad collapse. On the left is a mesh before collapsing vertex **u** into **v**. On the right is the mesh after the collapse, showing how edges now cross.

next. The best cost function can and will vary with the type of model and other factors [1092]. Depending on the problem being solved, the cost function may make trade-offs among speed, quality, robustness, and simplicity. It may also be tailored to maintain surface boundaries, material locations, lighting effect, symmetry along an axis, texture placement, volume, or other constraints.

We will present Garland and Heckbert's *quadric error metric* (QEM) cost function [515, 516] in order to give a sense of how such functions work. This function is of general use in a large number of situations. In contrast, in earlier research Garland and Heckbert [514] found using the Hausdorff distance best for terrain simplification, and others have borne this out [1496]. This function is simply the longest distance a vertex in the simplified mesh is from the original mesh. Figure 16.16 shows a result from using this metric.

For a given vertex there is a set of triangles that share it, and each triangle has a plane equation associated with it. The QEM cost function for moving a vertex is the sum of the squared distances between each of these planes and the new location. More formally,

$$c(\mathbf{v}) = \sum_{i=1}^{m}(\mathbf{n}_i \cdot \mathbf{v} + d_i)^2$$

is the cost function for new location **v** and m planes, where $\mathbf{n}_i$ is the plane i's normal and d_i its offset from the origin.

An example of two possible contractions for the same edge is shown in Figure 16.19. Say the cube is two units wide. The cost function for collapsing **e** into **c** ($\mathbf{e} \rightarrow \mathbf{c}$) will be 0, because the point **e** does not move off of the planes it shares when it goes to **c**. The cost function for $\mathbf{c} \rightarrow \mathbf{e}$ will be 1, because **c** moves away from the plane of the right face of the cube by a squared distance of 1. Because it has a lower cost, the $\mathbf{e} \rightarrow \mathbf{c}$ collapse would be preferred over $\mathbf{c} \rightarrow \mathbf{e}$.

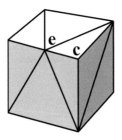 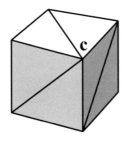 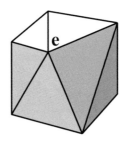

Figure 16.19. The left figure shows a cube with an extra point along one edge. The middle figure shows what happens if this point **e** is collapsed to corner **c**. The right figure shows **c** collapsed to **e**.

This cost function can be modified in various ways. Imagine two triangles that share an edge that form a sharp edge, e.g., they are part of a fish's fin or turbine blade. The cost function for collapsing a vertex on this edge is low, because a point sliding along one triangle does not move far from the other triangle's plane. The basic function's cost value is related to the volume change of removing the feature, but is not a good indicator of its visual importance. One way to maintain an edge with a sharp crease is to add an extra plane that includes the edge and has a normal that is the average of the two triangle normals. Now vertices that move far from this edge will have a higher cost function [517]. A variation is to weight the cost function by the change in the areas of the triangles.

Another type of extension is to use a cost function based on maintaining other surface features. For example, the crease and boundary edges of a model are important in portraying it, so these should be made less likely to be modified. See Figure 16.20. Other surface features worth preserving are locations where there are material changes, texture map edges, and color-per-vertex changes [772]. See Figure 16.21.

One serious problem that occurs with most simplification algorithms is that textures often deviate in a noticeable way from their original appearance [1092]. As edges are collapsed, the underlying mapping of the texture to the surface can become distorted. Also, texture coordinate values can match at boundaries but belong to different regions where the texture is applied, e.g., along a central edge where a model is mirrored. Caillaud et al. [220] survey a variety of previous approaches and present their own algorithm that handles texture seams.

Speed can be another concern. In systems where users create their own content, such as in a CAD system, level of detail models need to be created on the fly. Performing simplification using the GPU has met with some success [1008]. Another approach is to use a simpler simplification algorithm, such as *vertex clustering* [1088, 1511]. The core idea of this approach is to overlay the model with a three-dimensional voxel grid or similar structure. Any vertices in a voxel are moved to a "best" vertex location for that cell. Doing so may eliminate some triangles, when two or more of each triangle's vertices land in the same location, making it degenerate. This algorithm is robust, the connectivity of the mesh is not needed, and separate meshes can easily be aggregated

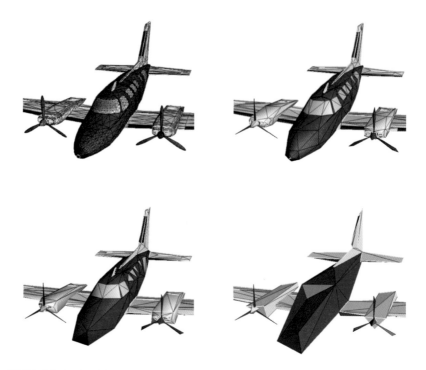

Figure 16.20. Mesh simplification. Upper left shows the original mesh of 13,546 faces, upper right is simplified to 1,000 faces, lower left to 500 faces, lower right to 150 faces [770]. *(Images © 1996 Microsoft. All rights reserved.)*

into one. However, the basic vertex clustering algorithm rarely gives as good a result as a full QEM approach. Willmott [1890] discusses how his team made this clustering approach work in a robust and efficient manner for the user-created content in the game *Spore*.

Turning a surface's original geometry into a normal map for bump mapping is an idea related to simplification. Small features such as buttons or wrinkles can be represented by a texture with little loss in fidelity. Sander et al. [1540] discuss previous work in this area and provide a solution. Such algorithms are commonly used in developing models for interactive applications, with a high-quality model baked into a textured representation [59].

Simplification techniques can produce a large number of *level of detail* (LOD) models from a single complex model. A problem found in using LOD models is that the transition can sometimes be seen if one model instantly replaces another between one frame and the next [508]. This problem is called "popping." One solution is to use *geomorphs* [768] to increase or decrease the level of detail. Since we know how the vertices in the more complex model map to the simple model, it is possible to create a smooth transition. See Section 19.9.1 for more details.

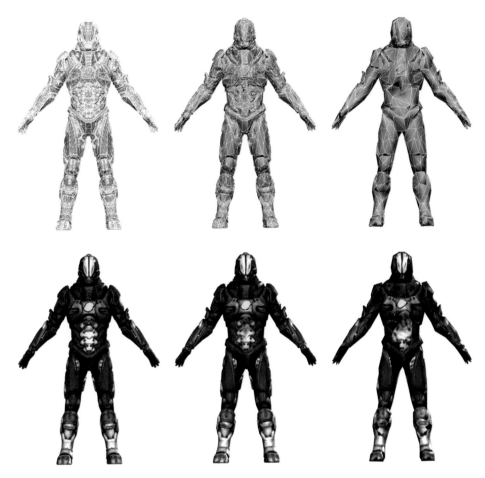

Figure 16.21. Mesh simplification. Top row: with mesh and simple gray material. Bottom row: with textures. From left to right: the models contain 51,123, 6,389, and 1,596 triangles. The texture on the model is maintained as possible, though some distortion creeps in as the triangle count falls. *(Images ©2016 Microsoft. All rights reserved.)*

One advantage of using view-independent progressive meshing is that a single vertex buffer can be created once and shared among copies of the same model at different levels of detail [1726]. However, under the basic scheme, a separate index buffer needs to be made for each copy. Another problem is efficiency. Because the order of collapses determines the triangle display order, vertex cache coherency is poor. Forsyth [481] discusses several practical solutions to improve efficiency when forming and sharing index buffers.

Mesh reduction techniques can be useful, but fully automated systems are not a panacea. The problem of maintaining symmetry is shown in Figure 16.22. A talented model maker can create low-triangle-count objects that are better in quality than

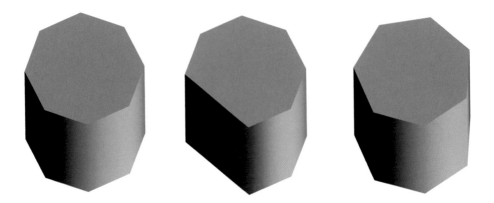

Figure 16.22. Symmetry problem. The cylinder on the left has 10 flat faces (including top and bottom). The middle cylinder has 9 flat faces after 1 face is eliminated by automatic reduction. The right cylinder has 9 flat faces after being regenerated by the modeler's faceter.

those generated by automated procedures. For example, the eyes and mouth are the most important part of the face. A naive algorithm will smooth these away as inconsequential. *Retopology* is a process where edges are added to a model to keep various features separate when modeling, smoothing, or simplification techniques are applied. Simplification-related algorithms continue to be developed and automated as possible.

16.6   Compression and Precision

Triangle mesh data can have its data compressed in various ways, and can accrue similar benefits. Just as PNG and JPEG image file formats use lossless and lossy compression for textures, a variety of algorithms and formats have been developed for the compression of triangle mesh data.

Compression minimizes the room spent for data storage, at the cost of time spent encoding and decoding. The time saved by transferring a smaller representation must outweigh the extra time spent decompressing the data. When transmitted on the Internet, a slow download speed implies that more elaborate algorithms can be used. Mesh connectivity can be compressed and efficiently decoded using TFAN [1116], adopted in MPEG-4. Encoders such as Open3DGC, OpenCTM, and Draco can create model files that can be one fourth of the size or smaller compared to using only gzip compression [1335]. Decompression using these schemes is meant to be a one-time operation, something that is relatively slow—a few million triangles per second—but that can more than pay for itself by saving on time spent transmitting data. Maglo et al. [1099] provide a thorough review of algorithms. Here we focus on compression techniques directly involving the GPU itself.

Much of this chapter has been devoted to various ways in which a triangle mesh's storage is minimized. The major motivation for doing so is rendering efficiency. Reusing, versus repeating, vertex data among several triangles will lead to fewer cache misses. Removing triangles that have little visual impact saves both vertex processing and memory. A smaller memory size leads to lower bandwidth costs and better cache use. There are also limits to what the GPU can store in memory, so data reduction techniques can lead to more triangles that can be displayed.

Vertex data can be compressed using fixed-rate compression, for similar reasons as when textures are compressed (Section 6.2.6). By *fixed-rate compression* we mean methods in which the final compressed storage size is known. Having a self-contained form of compression for each vertex means that decoding can happen on the GPU. Calver [221] presents a variety of schemes that use the vertex shader for decompression. Zarge [1961] notes that data compression can also help align vertex formats to cache lines. Purnomo et al. [1448] combine simplification and vertex quantization techniques, and optimize the mesh for a given target mesh size, using an image-space metric.

One simple form of compression is found within the index buffer's format. An index buffer consists of an array of unsigned integers that give the array positions for vertices in the vertex buffer. If there are less than or equal to 2^{16} vertices in the vertex buffer, then the index buffer can use unsigned shorts instead of unsigned longs. Some APIs support unsigned bytes for meshes with less than 2^8 vertices, but using these can cause costly alignment issues, so are generally avoided. It is worth noting that OpenGL ES 2.0, unextended WebGL 1.0, and some older desktop and laptop GPUs have a limitation that unsigned long index buffers are not supported, so unsigned shorts must be used.

The other compression opportunity is with triangle mesh data itself. As a basic example, some triangle meshes store one or more colors per vertex to represent baked-in lighting, simulation results, or other information. On a typical monitor a color is represented by 8 bits of red, green, and blue, so the data could be stored in the vertex record as three unsigned bytes instead of three floats. The GPU's vertex shader can turn this field into separate values that are then interpolated during triangle traversal. However, care should be taken on many architectures. For example, Apple recommends on iOS padding 3-byte data fields to 4 bytes to avoid extra processing [66]. See the middle illustration in Figure 16.23.

Another compression method is to not store any color at all. If the color data are, say, showing temperature results, the temperature itself can be stored as a single number that is then converted to an index in a one-dimensional texture for a color. Better yet, if the temperature value is not needed, then a single unsigned byte could be used to reference this color texture.

Even if the temperature itself is stored, it may be needed to only a few decimal places. A floating point number has a total precision of 24 bits, a little more than 7 decimal digits. Note that 16 bits give almost 5 decimal digits of precision. The range of temperature values is likely to be small enough that the exponent part of the floating point format is unnecessary. By using the lowest value as an offset and the

Single-precision
float data

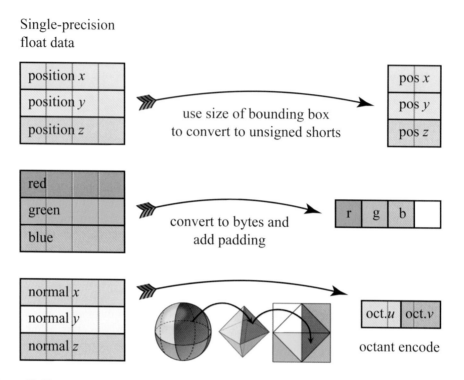

Figure 16.23. Typical fixed-rate compression methods for vertex data. *(Octant conversion figure from Cigolle et al. [269], courtesy of Morgan McGuire.)*

highest minus the lowest as a scale, the values can be evenly spread over a limited range. For example, if values range from 28.51 to 197.12, an unsigned short value would be converted to a temperature by first dividing it by $2^{16} - 1$, then multiplying the result by a scale factor of $(197.12 - 28.51)$, and finally adding the offset 28.51. By storing the scale and offset factors for the data set and passing these to the vertex shader program, the data set itself can be stored in half the space. This type of transformation is called *scalar quantization* [1099].

Vertex position data are usually a good candidate for such a reduction. Single meshes span a small area in space, so having a scale and offset vector (or a 4×4 matrix) for the whole scene can save considerable space without a significant loss in fidelity. For some scenes it may be possible to generate a scale and offset for each object, so increasing precision per model. However, doing so may cause cracks to appear where separate meshes touch [1381]. Vertices originally in the same world location but in separate models may be scaled and offset to slightly different locations. When all models are relatively small compared to the scene as a whole, one solution is to use the same scale for all models and align the offsets, which can give a few more bits of precision [1010].

Sometimes even floating point storage for vertex data is not sufficient to avoid precision problems. A classic example is the space shuttle rendered over the earth. The shuttle model itself may be specified down to a millimeter scale, but the earth's surface is over 100,000 meters away, giving an 8 decimal-place difference in scale. When the shuttle's world-space position is computed relative to the earth, the vertex locations generated need higher precision. When no corrective action is taken, the shuttle will jitter around the screen when the viewer moves near it. While the shuttle example is an extreme version of this problem, massive multiplayer worlds can suffer the same effects if a single coordinate system is used throughout. Objects on the fringes will lose enough precision that the problem becomes visible—animated objects will jerk around, individual vertices snap at different times, and shadow map texels will jump with the slightest camera move. One solution is to redo the transform pipeline so that, for each origin-centered object, the world and camera translations are first concatenated together and so mostly cancel out [1379, 1381]. Another approach is to segment the world and redefine the origin to be in the center of each segment, with the challenge then being travel from one segment to another. Ohlarik [1316] and Cozzi and Ring [299] discuss these problems and solutions in depth.

Other vertex data can have particular compression techniques associated with them. Texture coordinates are often limited to the range of $[0.0, 1.0]$ and so can normally be safely reduced to unsigned shorts, with an implicit offset of 0 and scale divisor of $2^{16} - 1$. There are usually pairs of values, which nicely fit into two unsigned shorts [1381], or even just 3 bytes [88], depending on precision requirements.

Unlike other coordinate sets, normals are usually normalized, so the set of all normalized normals forms a sphere. For this reason researchers have studied transforms of a sphere onto a plane for the purpose of efficiently compressing normals. Cigolle et al. [269] analyze the advantages and trade-offs of various algorithms, along with code samples. They conclude that octant and spherical projections are the most practical, minimizing error while being efficient to decode and encode. Pranckevičius [1432] and Pesce [1394] discuss normal compression when generating G-buffers for deferred shading (Section 20.1).

Other data may have properties that can be leveraged to reduce storage. For example, the normal, tangent, and bitangent vectors are commonly used for normal mapping. When these three vectors are mutually perpendicular (not skew), and if the handedness is consistent, then only two of the vectors could be stored and the third derived by a cross product. More compact yet, a single 4-byte quaternion with a handedness bit saved along with a 7-bit w can represent the rotation matrix that the basis forms [494, 1114, 1154, 1381, 1639]. For more precision, the largest of the four quaternion values can be left out and the other three stored at 10 bits each. The remaining 2 bits identify which of the four values is not stored. Since the squares of the quaternion sum to 1, we can then derive the fourth value from the other three [498]. Doghramachi et al. [363] use a tangent/bitangent/normal scheme storing the axis and angle. It is also 4 bytes and, compared to quaternion storage, takes about half the shader instructions to decode.

See Figure 16.23 for a summary of some fixed-rate compression methods.

Further Reading and Resources

Meshlab is an open-source mesh visualization and manipulation system that implements a huge number of algorithms, including mesh cleanup, normal derivation, and simplification. *Assimp* is an open-source library that reads and writes a wide variety of three-dimensional file formats. For more software recommendations, see this book's website, realtimerendering.com.

Schneider and Eberly [1574] present a wide variety of algorithms concerning polygons and triangles, along with pseudocode.

Luebke's practical survey [1091] is old but still a good introduction to simplification algorithms. The book *Level of Detail for 3D Graphics* [1092] covers simplification and related topics in depth.

Chapter 17

Curves and Curved Surfaces

"Where there is matter, there is geometry."
—Johannes Kepler

The triangle is a basic atomic rendering primitive. It is what graphics hardware is tuned to rapidly turn into shaded fragments and put into the framebuffer. However, objects and animation paths that are created in modeling systems can have many different underlying geometric descriptions. Curves and curved surfaces can be described precisely by equations. These equations are evaluated and sets of triangles are then created and sent down the pipeline to be rendered.

The beauty of using curves and curved surfaces is at least fourfold: (1) They have a more compact representation than a set of triangles, (2) they provide scalable geometric primitives, (3) they provide smoother and more continuous primitives than straight lines and planar triangles, and (4) animation and collision detection may become simpler and faster.

Compact curve representation offers several advantages for real-time rendering. First, there is savings in memory for model storage (and so some gain in memory cache efficiency). This is especially useful for game consoles, which typically do not have as much memory as a PC. Transforming curved surfaces generally involves fewer matrix multiplications than transforming a mesh representing the surface. If the graphics hardware can accept such curved surface descriptions directly, the amount of data the host CPU has to send to the graphics hardware is usually much less than sending a triangle mesh.

Curved model descriptions such as PN triangles and subdivision surfaces have the worthwhile property that a model with few polygons can be made more convincing and realistic. The individual polygons are treated as curved surfaces, so creating more vertices on the surface. The result of a higher vertex density is better lighting of the surface and silhouette edges with higher quality. See Figure 17.1 for an example.

Another major advantage of curved surfaces is that they are scalable. A curved surface description could be turned into 2 triangles or 2000. Curved surfaces are a natural form of on the fly level of detail modeling: When the curved object is close, sample the analytical representation more densely and generate more triangles. For

Figure 17.1. A scene from *Call of Duty: Advanced Warfare*, where the character Ilona's face was rendered using Catmull-Clark subdivision surfaces with the adaptive quadtree algorithm from Section 17.6.3. *(Image from "Call of Duty," courtesy of Activision Publishing, Inc. 2018.)*

animation, curved surfaces have the advantage that a much smaller number of points needs to be animated. These points can be used to form a curved surface, and a smooth tessellation can then be generated. Also, collision detection can potentially be more efficient and accurate [939, 940].

The topic of curves and curved surfaces has been the subject of entire books [458, 777, 1242, 1504, 1847]. Our goal here is to cover curves and surfaces that find common use in real-time rendering.

17.1 Parametric Curves

In this section we will introduce parametric curves. These are used in many different contexts and are implemented using a great many different methods. For real-time graphics, parametric curves are often used to move the viewer or some object along a predefined path. This may involve changing both the position and the orientation. However, in this chapter, we consider only positional paths. See Section 4.3.2 for information on orientation interpolation. Another use is to render hair, as seen in Figure 17.2.

Say you want to move the camera from one point to another in a certain amount of time, independent of the performance of the underlying hardware. As an example, assume that the camera should move between these points in one second, and that the rendering of one frame takes 50 ms. This means that we will be able to render 20 frames along the way during that second. On a faster computer, one frame might take only 25 ms, which would be equal to 40 frames per second, and so we would want to

Figure 17.2. Hair rendering using tessellated cubic curves [1274]. *(Image from "Nalu" demo, courtesy of NVIDIA Corporation.)*

move the camera to 40 different locations. Finding either set of points is possible to do with parametric curves.

A parametric curve describes points using some formula as a function of a parameter t. Mathematically, we write this as $\mathbf{p}(t)$, which means that this function delivers a point for each value of t. The parameter t may belong to some interval, called the *domain*, e.g., $t \in [a, b]$. The generated points are continuous, that is, as $\epsilon \to 0$ then $\mathbf{p}(t + \epsilon) \to \mathbf{p}(t)$. Loosely speaking, this means that if ϵ is a minuscule number, then $\mathbf{p}(t)$ and $\mathbf{p}(t + \epsilon)$ are two points that are extremely close to each other.

In the next section, we will start with an intuitive and geometrical description of Bézier curves, a common form of parametric curves, and then put this into a mathematical setting. Then we discuss how to use piecewise Bézier curves and explain the concept of continuity for curves. In Section 17.1.4 and 17.1.5, we will present two other useful curves, namely cubic Hermites and Kochanek-Bartels splines. Finally, we cover rendering of Bézier curves using the GPU in Section 17.1.2.

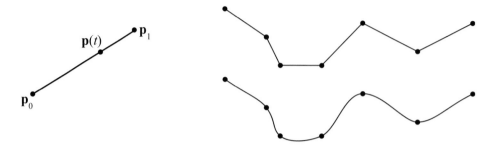

Figure 17.3. Linear interpolation between two points is the path on a straight line (left). For seven points, linear interpolation is shown at the upper right, and some sort of smoother interpolation is shown at the lower right. What is most objectionable about using linear interpolation are the discontinuous changes (sudden jerks) at the joints between the linear segments.

17.1.1 Bézier Curves

Linear interpolation traces out a path, which is a straight line, between two points, $\mathbf{p}_0$ and $\mathbf{p}_1$. This is as simple as it gets. See the left illustration in Figure 17.3. Given these points, the following function describes a linearly interpolated point $\mathbf{p}(t)$, where t is the curve parameter, and $t \in [0, 1]$:

$$\mathbf{p}(t) = \mathbf{p}_0 + t(\mathbf{p}_1 - \mathbf{p}_0) = (1 - t)\mathbf{p}_0 + t\mathbf{p}_1. \tag{17.1}$$

The parameter t controls where on the line the point $\mathbf{p}(t)$ will land; $\mathbf{p}(0) = \mathbf{p}_0$, $\mathbf{p}(1) = \mathbf{p}_1$, and $0 < t < 1$ gives us a point on the straight line between $\mathbf{p}_0$ and $\mathbf{p}_1$. So, if we would like to move the camera from $\mathbf{p}_0$ to $\mathbf{p}_1$ linearly in 20 steps during one second, then we would use $t_i = i/(20 - 1)$, where i is the frame number (starting from 0 and ending at 19).

When you are interpolating between only two points, linear interpolation may suffice, but for more points on a path, it often does not. For example, when several points are interpolated, the sudden changes at the points (also called joints) that connect two segments become unacceptable. This is shown at the right of Figure 17.3.

To solve this, we take the approach of linear interpolation one step further, and linearly interpolate repeatedly. By doing this, we arrive at the geometrical construction of the Bézier (pronounced *beh*-zee-eh) curve. As a historical note, the Bézier curves were developed independently by Paul de Casteljau and Pierre Bézier for use in the French car industry. They are called *Bézier* curves because Bézier was able to make his research publicly available before de Casteljau, even though de Casteljau wrote his technical report before Bézier [458].

First, to be able to repeat the interpolation, we have to add more points. For example, three points, $\mathbf{a}$, $\mathbf{b}$, and $\mathbf{c}$, called the *control points*, could be used. Say we want to find $\mathbf{p}(1/3)$, that is, the point on the curve for $t = 1/3$. We compute two new points $\mathbf{d}$ and $\mathbf{e}$ by linear interpolation from $\mathbf{a}$ & $\mathbf{b}$ and $\mathbf{b}$ & $\mathbf{c}$ using $t = 1/3$. See Figure 17.4. Finally, we compute $\mathbf{f}$ by linear interpolation from $\mathbf{d}$ and $\mathbf{e}$ again using

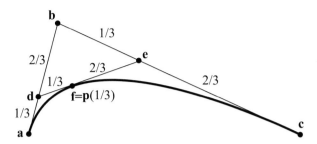

Figure 17.4. Repeated linear interpolation gives a Bézier curve. This curve is defined by three control points, **a**, **b**, and **c**. Assuming we want to find the point on the curve for the parameter $t = 1/3$, we first linearly interpolate between **a** and **b** to get **d**. Next, **e** is interpolated from **b** and **c**. The final point, $\mathbf{p}(1/3) = \mathbf{f}$ is found by interpolating between **d** and **e**.

$t = 1/3$. We define $\mathbf{p}(t) = \mathbf{f}$. Using this technique, we get the following relationship:

$$
\begin{aligned}
\mathbf{p}(t) &= (1-t)\mathbf{d} + t\mathbf{e} \\
&= (1-t)[(1-t)\mathbf{a} + t\mathbf{b}] + t[(1-t)\mathbf{b} + t\mathbf{c}] \\
&= (1-t)^2\mathbf{a} + 2(1-t)t\mathbf{b} + t^2\mathbf{c},
\end{aligned}
\tag{17.2}
$$

which is a parabola since the maximum degree of t is two. In fact, given $n+1$ control points, it turns out that the degree of the curve is n. This means that more control points gives more degrees of freedom for the curve. A first degree curve is a straight line (called *linear*), a second degree curve is called a *quadratic*, a third degree curve is called a *cubic*, a fourth degree curve is called a *quartic*, and so on.

This kind of repeated or recursive linear interpolation is often referred to as the *de Casteljau algorithm* [458, 777]. An example of what this looks like when using five control points is shown in Figure 17.5. To generalize, instead of using points **a**–**f**, as in this example, the following notation is used. The control points are denoted $\mathbf{p}_i$, so in the example, $\mathbf{p}_0 = \mathbf{a}$, $\mathbf{p}_1 = \mathbf{b}$, and $\mathbf{p}_2 = \mathbf{c}$. Then, after linear interpolation has been applied k times, intermediate control points $\mathbf{p}_i^k$ are obtained. In our example,

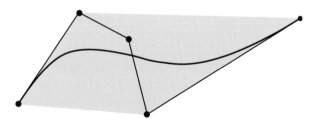

Figure 17.5. Repeated linear interpolation from five points gives a fourth degree (quartic) Bézier curve. The curve is inside the convex hull (green region) of the control points, marked by black dots. Also, at the first point, the curve is tangent to the line between the first and second point. The same also holds for the other end of the curve.

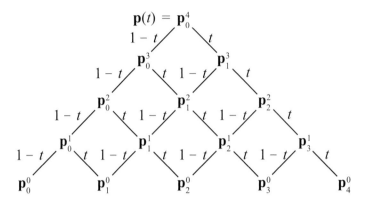

Figure 17.6. An illustration of how repeated linear interpolation works for Bézier curves. In this example, the interpolation of a quartic curve is shown. This means there are five control points, $\mathbf{p}_i^0$, $i = 0, 1, 2, 3, 4$, shown at the bottom. The diagram should be read from the bottom up, that is, $\mathbf{p}_0^1$ is formed from weighting $\mathbf{p}_0^0$ with weight $1 - t$ and adding that with $\mathbf{p}_1^0$ weighted by t. This goes on until the point of the curve $\mathbf{p}(t)$ is obtained at the top. *(Illustration after Goldman [551].)*

we have $\mathbf{p}_0^1 = \mathbf{d}$, $\mathbf{p}_1^1 = \mathbf{e}$, and $\mathbf{p}_0^2 = \mathbf{f}$. The Bézier curve for $n + 1$ control points can be described with the recursion formula shown below, where $\mathbf{p}_i^0 = \mathbf{p}_i$ are the initial control points:

$$\mathbf{p}_i^k(t) = (1 - t)\mathbf{p}_i^{k-1}(t) + t\mathbf{p}_{i+1}^{k-1}(t), \qquad \begin{cases} k = 1 \ldots n, \\ i = 0 \ldots n - k. \end{cases} \qquad (17.3)$$

Note that a point on the curve is described by $\mathbf{p}(t) = \mathbf{p}_0^n(t)$. This is not as complicated as it looks. Consider again what happens when we construct a Bézier curve from three points, $\mathbf{p}_0$, $\mathbf{p}_1$, and $\mathbf{p}_2$, which are equivalent to $\mathbf{p}_0^0$, $\mathbf{p}_1^0$, and $\mathbf{p}_2^0$. Three controls points means that $n = 2$. To shorten the formulae, sometimes "(t)" is dropped from the $\mathbf{p}$'s. In the first step $k = 1$, which gives $\mathbf{p}_0^1 = (1 - t)\mathbf{p}_0 + t\mathbf{p}_1$, and $\mathbf{p}_1^1 = (1 - t)\mathbf{p}_1 + t\mathbf{p}_2$. Finally, for $k = 2$, we get $\mathbf{p}_0^2 = (1 - t)\mathbf{p}_0^1 + t\mathbf{p}_1^1$, which is the same as sought for $\mathbf{p}(t)$. An illustration of how this works in general is shown in Figure 17.6.

Now that we have the basics in place on how Bézier curves work, we can take a look at a more mathematical description of the same curves.

Bézier Curves Using Bernstein Polynomials

As seen in Equation 17.2, the quadratic Bézier curve could be described using an algebraic formula. It turns out that every Bézier curve can be described with such an algebraic formula, which means that you do not need to do the repeated interpolation. This is shown below in Equation 17.4, which yields the same curve as described by Equation 17.3. This description of the Bézier curve is called the *Bernstein form*:

$$\mathbf{p}(t) = \sum_{i=0}^{n} B_i^n(t)\mathbf{p}_i. \qquad (17.4)$$

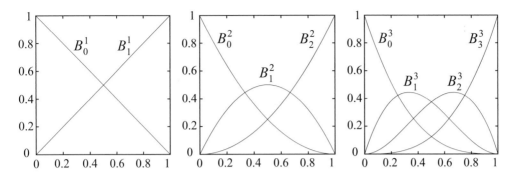

Figure 17.7. Bernstein polynomials for $n = 1$, $n = 2$, and $n = 3$ (left to right). The left figure shows linear interpolation, the middle quadratic interpolation, and the right cubic interpolation. These are the blending functions used in the Bernstein form of Bézier curves. So, to evaluate a quadratic curve (middle diagram) at a certain t-value, just find the t-value on the x-axis, and then go vertically until the three curves are encountered, which gives the weights for the three control points. Note that $B_i^n(t) \geq 0$, when $t \in [0, 1]$, and the symmetry of these blending functions: $B_i^n(t) = B_{n-i}^n(1 - t)$.

This function contains the Bernstein polynomials, also sometimes called Bézier basis functions,

$$B_i^n(t) = \binom{n}{i} t^i (1 - t)^{n-i} = \frac{n!}{i!(n - i)!} t^i (1 - t)^{n-i}. \qquad (17.5)$$

The first term, the binomial coefficient, in this equation is defined in Equation 1.6 in Chapter 1. Two basic properties of the Bernstein polynomial are the following:

$$B_i^n(t) \in [0, 1], \text{ when } t \in [0, 1], \quad \text{and} \quad \sum_{i=0}^{n} B_i^n(t) = 1. \qquad (17.6)$$

The first formula means that the Bernstein polynomials are in the interval between 0 to 1 when t also is from 0 to 1. The second formula means that all the Bernstein polynomial terms in Equation 17.4 sum to one for all different degrees of the curve (this can be seen in Figure 17.7). Loosely speaking, this means that the curve will stay "close" to the control points, $\mathbf{p}_i$. In fact, the entire Bézier curve will be located in the convex hull (see our online linear algebra appendix) of the control points, which follows from Equations 17.4 and 17.6. This is a useful property when computing a bounding area or volume for the curve. See Figure 17.5 for an example.

In Figure 17.7 the Bernstein polynomials for $n = 1$, $n = 2$, and $n = 3$ are shown. These are also called *blending functions*. The case when $n = 1$ (linear interpolation) is illustrative, in the sense that it shows the curves $y = 1 - t$ and $y = t$. This implies that when $t = 0$, then $\mathbf{p}(0) = \mathbf{p}_0$, and when t increases, the blending weight for $\mathbf{p}_0$ decreases, while the blending weight for $\mathbf{p}_1$ increases by the same amount, keeping the sum of the weights equal to 1. Finally, when $t = 1$, $\mathbf{p}(1) = \mathbf{p}_1$. In general, it holds for all Bézier curves that $\mathbf{p}(0) = \mathbf{p}_0$ and $\mathbf{p}(1) = \mathbf{p}_n$, that is, the endpoints are interpolated (i.e., are on the curve). It is also true that the curve is tangent to the vector $\mathbf{p}_1 - \mathbf{p}_0$ at $t = 0$, and to $\mathbf{p}_n - \mathbf{p}_{n-1}$ at $t = 1$. Another useful property is that instead of computing points on a Bézier curve, and then rotating the curve, the control points can first be rotated, and then the points on the curve can be computed. There are usually fewer control points than generated points on the curve, so it is more efficient to transform the control points first.

As an example on how the Bernstein version of the Bézier curve works, assume that $n = 2$, i.e., a quadratic curve. Equation 17.4 is then

$$\mathbf{p}(t) = B_0^2 \mathbf{p}_0 + B_1^2 \mathbf{p}_1 + B_2^2 \mathbf{p}_2$$

$$= \binom{2}{0} t^0 (1-t)^2 \mathbf{p}_0 + \binom{2}{1} t^1 (1-t)^1 \mathbf{p}_1 + \binom{2}{2} t^2 (1-t)^0 \mathbf{p}_2 \qquad (17.7)$$

$$= (1-t)^2 \mathbf{p}_0 + 2t(1-t)\mathbf{p}_1 + t^2 \mathbf{p}_2,$$

which is the same as Equation 17.2. Note that the blending functions above, $(1-t)^2$, $2t(1-t)$, and t^2, are the functions displayed in the middle of Figure 17.7. In the same manner, a cubic curve is simplified into

$$\mathbf{p}(t) = (1-t)^3 \mathbf{p}_0 + 3t(1-t)^2 \mathbf{p}_1 + 3t^2 (1-t)\mathbf{p}_2 + t^3 \mathbf{p}_3. \qquad (17.8)$$

This equation can be rewritten in matrix form as

$$\mathbf{p}(t) = \begin{pmatrix} 1 & t & t^2 & t^3 \end{pmatrix} \begin{pmatrix} 1 & 0 & 0 & 0 \\ -3 & 3 & 0 & 0 \\ 3 & -6 & 3 & 0 \\ -1 & 3 & -3 & 1 \end{pmatrix} \begin{pmatrix} \mathbf{p}_0 \\ \mathbf{p}_1 \\ \mathbf{p}_2 \\ \mathbf{p}_3 \end{pmatrix}, \qquad (17.9)$$

which is sometimes useful when doing mathematical simplifications.

By collecting terms of the form t^k in Equation 17.4, it can be seen that every Bézier curve can be written in the following form, called the *power form*, where the $\mathbf{c}_i$ are points that fall out by collecting terms:

$$\mathbf{p}(t) = \sum_{i=0}^{n} t^i \mathbf{c}_i. \qquad (17.10)$$

It is straightforward to differentiate Equation 17.4, in order to get the derivative of the Bézier curve. The result, after reorganizing and collecting terms, is shown below [458]:

$$\frac{d}{dt}\mathbf{p}(t) = n \sum_{i=0}^{n-1} B_i^{n-1}(t)(\mathbf{p}_{i+1} - \mathbf{p}_i). \qquad (17.11)$$

The derivative is, in fact, also a Bézier curve, but with one degree lower than $\mathbf{p}(t)$.

A potential downside of Bézier curves is that they do not pass through all the control points (except the endpoints). Another problem is that the degree increases with the number of control points, making evaluation more and more expensive. A solution to this is to use a simple, low degree curve between each pair of subsequent control points, and see to it that this kind of piecewise interpolation has a high enough degree of continuity. This is the topic of Sections 17.1.3–17.1.5.

Rational Bézier Curves

While Bézier curves can be used for many things, they do not have that many degrees of freedom—only the position of the control points can be chosen freely. Also, not every curve can be described by Bézier curves. For example, the circle is normally considered a simple shape, but it cannot be defined by one or a collection of Bézier curves. One alternative is the *rational Bézier curve*. This type of curve is described by the formula shown in Equation 17.12:

$$\mathbf{p}(t) = \frac{\sum_{i=0}^{n} w_i B_i^n(t) \mathbf{p}_i}{\sum_{i=0}^{n} w_i B_i^n(t)}. \tag{17.12}$$

The denominator is a weighted sum of the Bernstein polynomials, while the numerator is a weighted version of the standard Bézier curve (Equation 17.4). For this type of curve, the user has the weights, w_i, as additional degrees of freedom. More about these curves can be found in Hoschek and Lasser's [777] and in Farin's book [458]. Farin also describes how a circle can be described by three rational Bézier curves.

17.1.2 Bounded Bézier Curves on the GPU

A method for rendering Bézier curves on the GPU will be presented [1068, 1069]. Specifically, the target is "bounded Bézier curves," where the region between the curve and the straight line between the first and last control points is filled. There is a surprisingly simple way to do this by rendering a triangle with a specialized pixel shader.

We use a quadratic, i.e., degree two, Bézier curve, with control points $\mathbf{p}_0$, $\mathbf{p}_1$, and $\mathbf{p}_2$. If we set the texture coordinates at these vertices to $\mathbf{t}_0 = (0,0)$, $\mathbf{t}_1 = (0.5, 0)$, and $\mathbf{t}_2 = (1,1)$, the texture coordinates will be interpolated as usual during rendering of the triangle $\Delta \mathbf{p}_0 \mathbf{p}_1 \mathbf{p}_2$. We also evaluate the following scalar function inside the triangle for each pixel, where u and v are interpolated texture coordinates:

$$f(u, v) = u^2 - v. \tag{17.13}$$

The pixel shader then determines whether the pixel is inside ($f(u, v) < 0$), or otherwise outside. This is illustrated in Figure 17.8. When rendering a perspective-projected triangle with this pixel shader, we will get the corresponding projected Bézier curve. A proof of this is given by Loop and Blinn [1068, 1069].

This type of technique can be used to render TrueType fonts, for example. This is illustrated in Figure 17.9. Loop and Blinn also show how to render rational quadratic

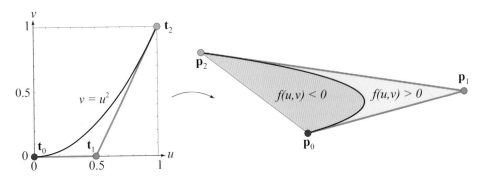

Figure 17.8. Bounded Bézier curve rendering. Left: the curve is shown in canonical texture space. Right: the curve is rendered in screen space. If the condition $f(u,v) \geq 0$ is used to kill pixels, then the light blue region will result from the rendering.

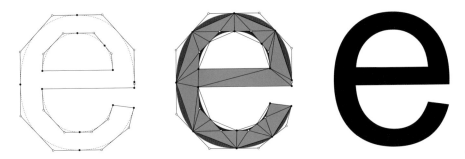

Figure 17.9. An e is represented by several straight lines and quadratic Bézier curves (left). In the middle, this representation has been "tessellated" into several bounded Bézier curves (red and blue), and triangles (green). The final letter is shown to the right. *(Reprinted with permission from Microsoft Corporation.)*

curves and cubic curves, and how do to antialiasing using this representation. Because of the importance of text rendering, research in this area has continued. See Section 15.5 for related algorithms.

17.1.3 Continuity and Piecewise Bézier Curves

Assume that we have two Bézier curves that are cubic, that is, defined by four control points each. The first curve is defined by $\mathbf{q}_i$, and the second by $\mathbf{r}_i$, $i = 0, 1, 2, 3$. To join the curves, we could set $\mathbf{q}_3 = \mathbf{r}_0$. This point is called a *joint*. However, as shown in Figure 17.10, the joint will not be smooth using this simple technique. The composite curve formed from several curve pieces (in this case two) is called a *piecewise Bézier curve*, and is denoted $\mathbf{p}(t)$ here. Further, assume we want $\mathbf{p}(0) = \mathbf{q}_0$, $\mathbf{p}(1) = \mathbf{q}_3 = \mathbf{r}_0$, and $\mathbf{p}(3) = \mathbf{r}_3$. Thus, the times for when we reach $\mathbf{q}_0$, $\mathbf{q}_3 = \mathbf{r}_0$, and $\mathbf{r}_3$, are $t_0 = 0.0$,

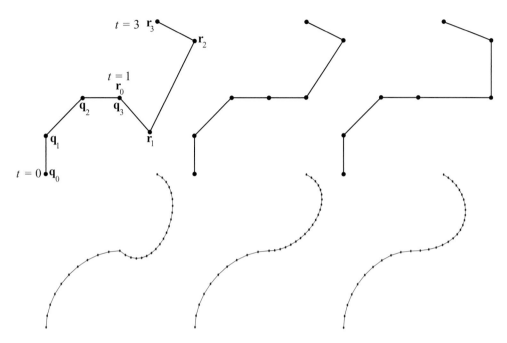

Figure 17.10. This figure shows from left to right C^0, G^1, and C^1 continuity between two cubic Bézier curves (four control points each). The top row shows the control points, and the bottom row the curves, with 10 sample points for the left curve, and 20 for the right. The following time-point pairs are used for this example: $(0.0, \mathbf{q}_0)$, $(1.0, \mathbf{q}_3)$, and $(3.0, \mathbf{r}_3)$. With C^0 continuity, there is a sudden jerk at the join (where $\mathbf{q}^3 = \mathbf{r}^0$). This is improved with G^1 by making the tangents at the join parallel (and equal in length). Though, since $3.0 - 1.0 \neq 1.0 - 0.0$, this does not give C^1 continuity. This can be seen at the join where there is a sudden acceleration of the sample points. To achieve C^1, the right tangent at the join has to be twice as long as the left tangent.

$t_1 = 1.0$, and $t_2 = 3.0$. See Figure 17.10 for notation. From the previous section we know that a Bézier curve is defined for $t \in [0, 1]$, so this works out fine for the first curve segment defined by the $\mathbf{q}_i$'s, since the time at $\mathbf{q}_0$ is 0.0, and the time at $\mathbf{q}_3$ is 1.0. But what happens when $1.0 < t \leq 3.0$? The answer is simple: We must use the second curve segment, and then translate and scale the parameter interval from $[t_1, t_2]$ to $[0, 1]$. This is done using the formula below:

$$t' = \frac{t - t_1}{t_2 - t_1}. \tag{17.14}$$

Hence, it is the t' that is fed into the Bézier curve segment defined by the $\mathbf{r}_i$'s. This is simple to generalize to stitching several Bézier curves together.

A better way to join the curves is to use the fact that at the first control point of a Bézier curve the tangent is parallel to $\mathbf{q}_1 - \mathbf{q}_0$ (Section 17.1.1). Similarly, at the last control point the cubic curve is tangent to $\mathbf{q}_3 - \mathbf{q}_2$. This behavior can be seen in Figure 17.5. So, to make the two curves join tangentially at the joint, the tangent for the first and the second curve should be parallel there. Put more formally, the following should hold:

$$(\mathbf{r}_1 - \mathbf{r}_0) = c(\mathbf{q}_3 - \mathbf{q}_2) \quad \text{for } c > 0. \tag{17.15}$$

This simply means that the incoming tangent, $\mathbf{q}_3 - \mathbf{q}_2$, at the joint should have the same direction as the outgoing tangent, $\mathbf{r}_1 - \mathbf{r}_0$.

It is possible to achieve even better continuity than that, using in Equation 17.15 the c defined by Equation 17.16 [458]:

$$c = \frac{t_2 - t_1}{t_1 - t_0}. \tag{17.16}$$

This is also shown in Figure 17.10. If we instead set $t_2 = 2.0$, then $c = 1.0$, so when the time intervals on each curve segment are equal, then the incoming and outgoing tangent vectors should be identical. However, this does not work when $t_2 = 3.0$. The curves will look identical, but the speed at which $\mathbf{p}(t)$ moves on the composite curve will not be smooth. The constant c in Equation 17.16 takes care of this.

Some advantages of using piecewise curves are that lower-degree curves can be used, and that the resulting curves will go through a set of points. In the example above, a degree of three, i.e., a cubic, was used for each of the two curve segments. Cubic curves are often used for this, as those are the lowest-degree curves that can describe an *S-shaped* curve, called an *inflection*. The resulting curve $\mathbf{p}(t)$ interpolates, i.e., goes through, the points $\mathbf{q}_0$, $\mathbf{q}_3 = \mathbf{r}_0$, and $\mathbf{r}_3$.

At this point, two important continuity measures have been introduced by example. A slightly more mathematical presentation of the continuity concept for curves follows. For curves in general, we use the C^n notation to differentiate between different kinds of continuity at the joints. This means that all the nth first derivatives should be continuous and nonzero all over the curve. Continuity of C^0 means that the segment should join at the same point, so linear interpolation fulfills this condition. This was the case for the first example in this section. Continuity of C^1 means that if we derive once at any point on the curve (including joints), the result should also be continuous. This was the case for the third example in this section, where Equation 17.16 was used.

There is also a measure that is denoted G^n. Let us look at G^1 (geometrical) continuity as an example. For this, the tangent vectors from the curve segments that meet at a joint should be parallel and have the same direction, but nothing about the lengths is assumed. In other words, G^1 is a weaker continuity than C^1, and a curve that is C^1 is always G^1 except when the velocities of two curves go to zero at the point where the curves join and they have different tangents just before the join. The concept of geometrical continuity can be extended to higher dimensions. The middle illustration in Figure 17.10 shows G^1-continuity.

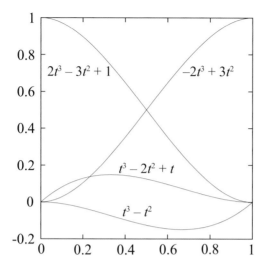

Figure 17.11. Blending functions for Hermite cubic interpolation. Note the asymmetry of the blending functions for the tangents. Negating the blending function $t^3 - t^2$ and $\mathbf{m}_1$ in Equation 17.17 would give a symmetrical look.

17.1.4 Cubic Hermite Interpolation

Bézier curves are good for describing the theory behind the construction of smooth curves, but are sometimes not predictable to work with. In this section, we will present cubic Hermite interpolation, and these curves tend to be simpler to control. The reason is that instead of giving four control points to describe a cubic Bézier curve, the cubic Hermite curve is defined by starting and ending points, $\mathbf{p}_0$ and $\mathbf{p}_1$, and starting and ending tangents, $\mathbf{m}_0$ and $\mathbf{m}_1$. The Hermite interpolant, $\mathbf{p}(t)$, where $t \in [0, 1]$, is

$$\mathbf{p}(t) = (2t^3 - 3t^2 + 1)\mathbf{p}_0 + (t^3 - 2t^2 + t)\mathbf{m}_0 + (t^3 - t^2)\mathbf{m}_1 + (-2t^3 + 3t^2)\mathbf{p}_1. \quad (17.17)$$

We also call $\mathbf{p}(t)$ a Hermite curve segment or a cubic spline segment. This is a cubic interpolant, since t^3 is the highest exponent in the blending functions in the above formula. The following holds for this curve:

$$\mathbf{p}(0) = \mathbf{p}_0, \quad \mathbf{p}(1) = \mathbf{p}_1, \quad \frac{\partial \mathbf{p}}{\partial t}(0) = \mathbf{m}_0, \quad \frac{\partial \mathbf{p}}{\partial t}(1) = \mathbf{m}_1. \quad (17.18)$$

This means that the Hermite curve interpolates $\mathbf{p}_0$ and $\mathbf{p}_1$, and the tangents at these points are $\mathbf{m}_0$ and $\mathbf{m}_1$. The blending functions in Equation 17.17 are shown in Figure 17.11, and they can be derived from Equations 17.4 and 17.18. Some examples of cubic Hermite interpolation can be seen in Figure 17.12. All these examples interpolate the same points, but have different tangents. Note also that different lengths

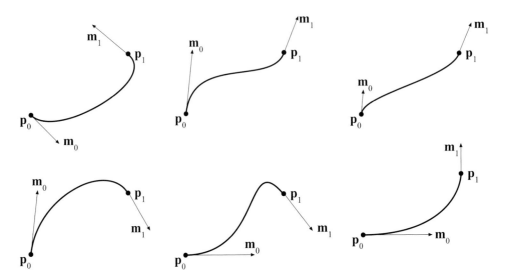

Figure 17.12. Hermite interpolation. A curve is defined by two points, $\mathbf{p}_0$ and $\mathbf{p}_1$, and a tangent, $\mathbf{m}_0$ and $\mathbf{m}_1$, at each point.

of the tangents give different results; longer tangents have a greater impact on the overall shape.

Cubic Hermite interpolation is used to render the hair in the Nalu demo [1274]. See Figure 17.2. A coarse control hair is used for animation and collision detection, tangents are computed, and cubic curves are tessellated and rendered.

17.1.5 Kochanek-Bartels Curves

When interpolating between more than two points, you can connect several Hermite curves. However, when doing this, there are degrees of freedom in selecting the shared tangents that provide different characteristics. Here, we will present one way to compute such tangents, called Kochanek-Bartels curves. Assume that we have n points, $\mathbf{p}_0, \ldots, \mathbf{p}_{n-1}$, which should be interpolated with $n-1$ Hermite curve segments. We assume that there is only one tangent at each point, and we start to look at the "inner" tangents, $\mathbf{m}_1, \ldots, \mathbf{m}_{n-2}$. A tangent at $\mathbf{p}_i$ can be computed as a combination of the two chords [917]: $\mathbf{p}_i - \mathbf{p}_{i-1}$, and $\mathbf{p}_{i+1} - \mathbf{p}_i$, as shown at the left in Figure 17.13.

First, a tension parameter, a, is introduced that modifies the length of the tangent vector. This controls how sharp the curve is going to be at the joint. The tangent is computed as

$$\mathbf{m}_i = \frac{1-a}{2}\big((\mathbf{p}_i - \mathbf{p}_{i-1}) + (\mathbf{p}_{i+1} - \mathbf{p}_i)\big). \tag{17.19}$$

The top row at the right in Figure 17.13 shows different tension parameters. The default value is $a = 0$; higher values give sharper bends (if $a > 1$, there will be a

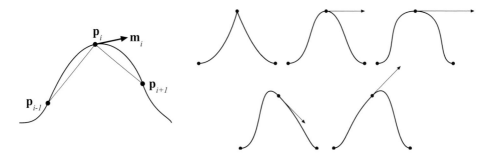

Figure 17.13. One method of computing the tangents is to use a combination of the chords (left). The upper row at the right shows three curves with different tension parameters (a). The left curve has $a \approx 1$, which means high tension; the middle curve has $a \approx 0$, which is default tension; and the right curve has $a \approx -1$, which is low tension. The bottom row of two curves at the right shows different bias parameters. The curve on the left has a negative bias, and the right curve has a positive bias.

loop at the joint), and negative values give less taut curves near the joints. Second, a bias parameter, b, is introduced that influences the direction of the tangent (and, indirectly, the length of the tangent). Using both tension and bias gives us

$$\mathbf{m}_i = \frac{(1-a)(1+b)}{2}(\mathbf{p}_i - \mathbf{p}_{i-1}) + \frac{(1-a)(1-b)}{2}(\mathbf{p}_{i+1} - \mathbf{p}_i), \qquad (17.20)$$

where the default value is $b = 0$. A positive bias gives a bend that is more directed toward the chord $\mathbf{p}_i - \mathbf{p}_{i-1}$, and a negative bias gives a bend that is more directed toward the other chord: $\mathbf{p}_{i+1} - \mathbf{p}_i$. This is shown in the bottom row on the right in Figure 17.13. The user can either set the tension and bias parameters or let them have their default values, which produces what is often called a Catmull-Rom spline [236]. The tangents at the first and the last points can also be computed with these formulae, where one of the chords is simply set to a length of zero.

Yet another parameter that controls the behavior at the joints can be incorporated into the tangent equation [917]. However, this requires the introduction of two tangents at each joint, one incoming, denoted $\mathbf{s}_i$ (for source) and one outgoing, denoted $\mathbf{d}_i$ (for destination). See Figure 17.14. Note that the curve segment between $\mathbf{p}_i$ and $\mathbf{p}_{i+1}$ uses the tangents $\mathbf{d}_i$ and $\mathbf{s}_{i+1}$. The tangents are computed as below, where c is the *continuity* parameter:

$$\begin{aligned}
\mathbf{s}_i &= \frac{1-c}{2}(\mathbf{p}_i - \mathbf{p}_{i-1}) + \frac{1+c}{2}(\mathbf{p}_{i+1} - \mathbf{p}_i), \\
\mathbf{d}_i &= \frac{1+c}{2}(\mathbf{p}_i - \mathbf{p}_{i-1}) + \frac{1-c}{2}(\mathbf{p}_{i+1} - \mathbf{p}_i).
\end{aligned} \qquad (17.21)$$

Again, $c = 0$ is the default value, which makes $\mathbf{s}_i = \mathbf{d}_i$. Setting $c = -1$ gives $\mathbf{s}_i = \mathbf{p}_i - \mathbf{p}_{i-1}$, and $\mathbf{d}_i = \mathbf{p}_{i+1} - \mathbf{p}_i$, producing a sharp corner at the joint, which is only C^0. Increasing the value of c makes $\mathbf{s}_i$ and $\mathbf{d}_i$ more and more alike. For $c = 0$,

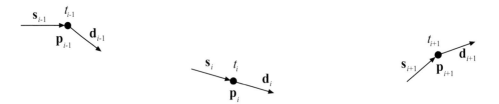

Figure 17.14. Incoming and outgoing tangents for Kochanek-Bartels curves. At each control point $\mathbf{p}_i$, its time t_i is also shown, where $t_i > t_{i-1}$, for all i.

then $\mathbf{s}_i = \mathbf{d}_i$. When $c = 1$ is reached, we get $\mathbf{s}_i = \mathbf{p}_{i+1} - \mathbf{p}_i$, and $\mathbf{d}_i = \mathbf{p}_i - \mathbf{p}_{i-1}$. Thus, the continuity parameter c is another way to give even more control to the user, and it makes it possible to get sharp corners at the joints, if desired.

The combination of tension, bias, and continuity, where the default parameter values are $a = b = c = 0$, is

$$
\begin{aligned}
\mathbf{s}_i &= \frac{(1-a)(1+b)(1-c)}{2}(\mathbf{p}_i - \mathbf{p}_{i-1}) + \frac{(1-a)(1-b)(1+c)}{2}(\mathbf{p}_{i+1} - \mathbf{p}_i), \\
\mathbf{d}_i &= \frac{(1-a)(1+b)(1+c)}{2}(\mathbf{p}_i - \mathbf{p}_{i-1}) + \frac{(1-a)(1-b)(1-c)}{2}(\mathbf{p}_{i+1} - \mathbf{p}_i).
\end{aligned}
\tag{17.22}
$$

Both Equations 17.20 and 17.22 work only when all curve segments are using the same time interval length. To account for different time length of the curve segments, the tangents have to be adjusted, similar to what was done in Section 17.1.3. The adjusted tangents, denoted $\mathbf{s}_i'$ and $\mathbf{d}_i'$, are

$$
\mathbf{s}_i' = \mathbf{s}_i \frac{2\Delta_i}{\Delta_{i-1} + \Delta_i} \quad \text{and} \quad \mathbf{d}_i' = \mathbf{d}_i \frac{2\Delta_{i-1}}{\Delta_{i-1} + \Delta_i},
\tag{17.23}
$$

where $\Delta_i = t_{i+1} - t_i$.

17.1.6 B-Splines

Here, we will provide a brief introduction to the topic of B-splines, and we will focus in particular on cubic uniform B-splines. In general, a *B-spline* is quite similar to a Bézier curve, and can be expressed as a function of t (using shifted basis functions), β_n (weighted by control points), and c_k: e.g.,

$$
s_n(t) = \sum_k c_k \beta_n(t - k).
\tag{17.24}
$$

In this case, this is a curve where t is the x-axis and $s_n(t)$ is the y-axis, and the control points are simply evenly spaced y-values. For much more extensive coverage, see the texts by the Killer B's [111], Farin [458], and Hoschek and Lasser [777].

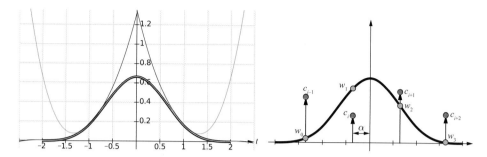

Figure 17.15. Left: the $\beta_3(t)$ basis function is shown as a fat black curve, which is constructed from two piecewise cubic functions (red and green). The green curve is used when $|t| < 1$, the red curve when $1 \leq |t| < 2$, and the curve is zero elsewhere. Right: to create a curve segment using four control points, c_k, $k \in \{i - 1, i, i + 1, i + 2\}$, we will only obtain a curve between the t-coordinate of c_i and of $c_i + 1$. The α is fed into the w functions to evaluate the basis function, and these values are then multiplied by the corresponding control point. Finally, all values are added together, which gives us a point on the curve. See Figure 17.16. *(Illustration on the right after Ruijters et al. [1518].)*

Here, we will follow the presentation by Ruijters et al. [1518] and present the special case of a uniform cubic B-spline. The basis function, $\beta_3(t)$, is stitched together by three pieces:

$$\beta_3(t) = \begin{cases} 0, & |t| \geq 2, \\ \frac{1}{6}(2 - |t|)^3, & 1 \leq |t| < 2, \\ \frac{2}{3} - \frac{1}{2}|t|^2(2 - |t|), & |t| < 1. \end{cases} \qquad (17.25)$$

The construction of this basis function is shown on the left in Figure 17.15. This function has C^2 continuity everywhere, which means that if several B-spline curve segments are stitched together, the composite curve will also be C^2. A cubic curve has C^2 continuity, and in general, a curve of degree n has C^{n-1} continuity. In general, the basis functions are created as follows. The $\beta_0(t)$ is a "square" function, i.e., it is 1 if $|t| < 0.5$, it is 0.5 if $|t| = 0.5$, and it is 0 elsewhere. The next basis function, $\beta_1(t)$ is created by integrating $\beta_0(t)$, which gives us a tent function. The basis function after that is created by integrating $\beta_1(t)$, which gives a smoother function, which is C^1. This process is repeated to get C^2, and so on.

How to evaluate a curve segment is illustrated on the right in Figure 17.15, and its formula is

$$s_3(i + \alpha) = w_0(\alpha)c_{i-1} + w_1(\alpha)c_i + w_2(\alpha)c_{i+1} + w_3(\alpha)c_{i+2}. \qquad (17.26)$$

Note that only four control points will be used at any time, and this means that the curve has local support, i.e., a limited number of control points is needed. The functions $w_k(\alpha)$ are defined using $\beta_3()$ as

$$\begin{aligned} w_0(\alpha) &= \beta_3(-\alpha - 1), & w_1(\alpha) &= \beta_3(-\alpha), \\ w_2(\alpha) &= \beta_3(1 - \alpha), & w_3(\alpha) &= \beta_3(2 - \alpha). \end{aligned} \qquad (17.27)$$

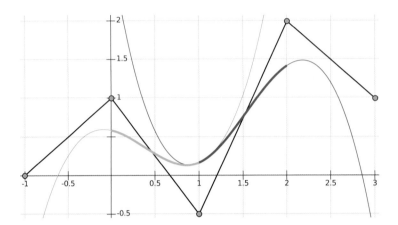

Figure 17.16. The control points c_k (green circles) define a uniform cubic spline in this example. Only the two fat curves are part of the piecewise B-spline curve. The left (green) curve is defined by the four leftmost control points, and the right (red) curve is defined by the four rightmost control points. The curves meet at $t = 1$ with C^2 continuity.

Ruijters et al. [1518] show that these can be rewritten as

$$w_0(\alpha) = \frac{1}{6}(1-\alpha)^3, \qquad\qquad w_1(\alpha) = \frac{2}{3} - \frac{1}{2}\alpha^2(2-\alpha),$$

$$w_2(\alpha) = \frac{2}{3} - \frac{1}{2}(1-\alpha)^2(1+\alpha), \quad w_3(\alpha) = \frac{1}{6}\alpha^3. \tag{17.28}$$

In Figure 17.16, we show the results of stitching two uniform cubic B-spline curves together as one. A major advantage is that the curves are continuous with the same continuity as the basis functions, $\beta(t)$, which are C^2 in the case of a cubic B-spline. As can be seen in the figure, there is no guarantee that the curve will go through any of the control points. Note that we can also create a B-spline for the x-coordinates, which would give a general curve in the plane (and not just a function). The resulting two-dimensional points would then be $(s_3^x(i+\alpha), s_3^y(i+\alpha))$, i.e., simply two different evaluations of Equation 17.26, one for x and one for y.

We have shown how to use only B-splines that are uniform. If the spacing between the control points is nonuniform, the equations become a bit more elaborate but more flexible [111, 458, 777].

17.2   Parametric Curved Surfaces

A natural extension of parametric curves is parametric surfaces. An analogy is that a triangle or polygon is an extension of a line segment, in which we go from one to two dimensions. Parametric surfaces can be used to model objects with curved surfaces. A parametric surface is defined by a small number of control points. Tessellation of a parametric surface is the process of evaluating the surface representation at several positions, and connecting these to form triangles that approximate the true surface. This is done because graphics hardware can efficiently render triangles. At runtime, the surface can then be tessellated into as many triangles as desired. Thus, parametric surfaces are perfect for making a trade-off between quality and speed, since more triangles take more time to render, but give better shading and silhouettes. Another advantage of parametric surfaces is that the control points can be animated and then the surface can be tessellated. This is in contrast to animating a large triangle mesh directly, which can be more expensive.

This section starts by introducing *Bézier patches*, which are curved surfaces with rectangular domains. These are also called *tensor-product Bézier surfaces*. Then *Bézier triangles* are presented, which have triangular domains, followed by a discussion about continuity in Section 17.2.3. In Sections 17.2.4 and 17.2.5, two methods are presented that replace each input triangle with a Bézier triangle. These techniques are called PN triangles and Phong tessellation, respectively. Finally, B-spline patches are presented in Section 17.2.6.

17.2.1 Bézier Patches

The concept of Bézier curves, introduced in Section 17.1.1, can be extended from using one parameter to using two parameters, thus forming surfaces instead of curves. Let us start with extending linear interpolation to *bilinear interpolation*. Now, instead of just using two points, we use four points, called $\mathbf{a}$, $\mathbf{b}$, $\mathbf{c}$, and $\mathbf{d}$, as shown in Figure 17.17. Instead of using one parameter called t, we now use two parameters (u, v). Using u to linearly interpolate $\mathbf{a}$ & $\mathbf{b}$ and $\mathbf{c}$ & $\mathbf{d}$ gives $\mathbf{e}$ and $\mathbf{f}$:

$$\mathbf{e} = (1 - u)\mathbf{a} + u\mathbf{b}, \quad \mathbf{f} = (1 - u)\mathbf{c} + u\mathbf{d}. \tag{17.29}$$

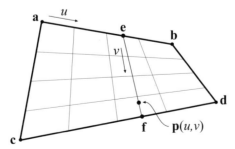

Figure 17.17. Bilinear interpolation using four points.

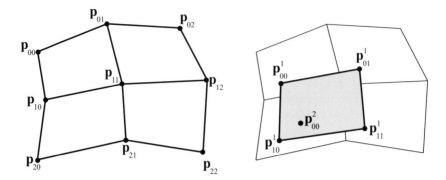

Figure 17.18. Left: a biquadratic Bézier surface, defined by nine control points, $\mathbf{p}_{ij}$. Right: to generate a point on the Bézier surface, four points $\mathbf{p}_{ij}^1$ are first created using bilinear interpolation from the nearest control points. Finally, the point surface $\mathbf{p}(u,v) = \mathbf{p}_{00}^2$ is bilinearly interpolated from these created points.

Next, the linearly interpolated points, $\mathbf{e}$ and $\mathbf{f}$, are linearly interpolated in the other direction, using v. This yields bilinear interpolation:

$$
\begin{aligned}
\mathbf{p}(u,v) &= (1-v)\mathbf{e} + v\mathbf{f} \\
&= (1-u)(1-v)\mathbf{a} + u(1-v)\mathbf{b} + (1-u)v\mathbf{c} + uv\mathbf{d}.
\end{aligned}
\tag{17.30}
$$

Note that this is the same type of equation used for bilinear interpolation for texture mapping (Equation 6.1 on page 179). Equation 17.30 describes the simplest nonplanar parametric surface, where different points on the surface are generated using different values of (u,v). The domain, i.e., the set of valid values, is $(u,v) \in [0,1] \times [0,1]$, which means that both u and v should belong to $[0,1]$. When the domain is rectangular, the resulting surface is often called a *patch*.

To extend a Bézier curve from linear interpolation, more points were added and the interpolation repeated. The same strategy can be used for patches. Assume nine points, arranged in a 3×3 grid, are used. This is shown in Figure 17.18, where the notation is shown as well. To form a biquadratic Bézier patch from these points, we first need to bilinearly interpolate four times to create four intermediate points, also shown in Figure 17.18. Next, the final point on the surface is bilinearly interpolated from the previously created points.

The repeated bilinear interpolation described above is the extension of de Casteljau's algorithm to patches. At this point we need to define some notation. The degree of the surface is n. The control points are $\mathbf{p}_{i,j}$, where i and j belong to $[0\ldots n]$. Thus, $(n+1)^2$ control points are used for a patch of degree n. Note that the control points should be superscripted with a zero, i.e., $\mathbf{p}_{i,j}^0$, but this is often omitted, and sometimes we use the subscript $_{ij}$ instead of $_{i,j}$ when there can be no confusion. The Bézier patch using de Casteljau's algorithm is described in the equation that follows:

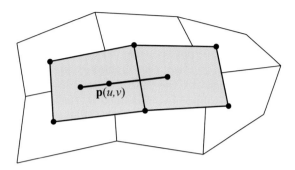

Figure 17.19. Different degrees in different directions.

de Casteljau [patches]:

$$\mathbf{p}_{i,j}^k(u,v) = (1-u)(1-v)\mathbf{p}_{i,j}^{k-1} + u(1-v)\mathbf{p}_{i,j+1}^{k-1} + (1-u)v\mathbf{p}_{i+1,j}^{k-1} + uv\mathbf{p}_{i+1,j+1}^{k-1}$$
$$k = 1 \ldots n, \quad i = 0 \ldots n-k, \quad j = 0 \ldots n-k. \tag{17.31}$$

Similar to the Bézier curve, the point at (u,v) on the Bézier patch is $\mathbf{p}_{0,0}^n(u,v)$. The Bézier patch can also be described in Bernstein form using Bernstein polynomials, as shown in Equation 17.32:

Bernstein [patches]:

$$\mathbf{p}(u,v) = \sum_{i=0}^{m} B_i^m(u) \sum_{j=0}^{n} B_j^n(v)\mathbf{p}_{i,j} = \sum_{i=0}^{m}\sum_{j=0}^{n} B_i^m(u)B_j^n(v)\mathbf{p}_{i,j},$$
$$= \sum_{i=0}^{m}\sum_{j=0}^{n} \binom{m}{i}\binom{n}{j} u^i(1-u)^{m-i}v^j(1-v)^{n-j}\mathbf{p}_{i,j}. \tag{17.32}$$

Note that in Equation 17.32, there are two parameters, m and n, for the degree of the surface. The "compound" degree is sometimes denoted $m \times n$. Most often $m = n$, which simplifies the implementation a bit. The consequence of, say, $m > n$ is to first bilinearly interpolate n times, and then linearly interpolate $m-n$ times. This is shown in Figure 17.19. A different interpretation of Equation 17.32 is found by rewriting it as

$$\mathbf{p}(u,v) = \sum_{i=0}^{m} B_i^m(u) \sum_{j=0}^{n} B_j^n(v)\mathbf{p}_{i,j} = \sum_{i=0}^{m} B_i^m(u)\mathbf{q}_i(v). \tag{17.33}$$

Here, $\mathbf{q}_i(v) = \sum_{j=0}^{n} B_j^n(v)\mathbf{p}_{i,j}$ for $i = 0 \ldots m$. As can be seen in the bottom row in Equation 17.33, this is just a Bézier curve when we fix a v-value. Assuming $v = 0.35$, the points $\mathbf{q}_i(0.35)$ can be computed from a Bézier curve, and then Equation 17.33 describes a Bézier curve on the Bézier surface, for $v = 0.35$.

Next, some useful properties of Bézier patches will be presented. By setting $(u, v) = (0, 0)$, $(u, v) = (0, 1)$, $(u, v) = (1, 0)$, and $(u, v) = (1, 1)$ in Equation 17.32, it is simple to prove that a Bézier patch interpolates, that is, goes through, the corner control points, $\mathbf{p}_{0,0}$, $\mathbf{p}_{0,n}$, $\mathbf{p}_{n,0}$, and $\mathbf{p}_{n,n}$. Also, each boundary of the patch is described by a Bézier curve of degree n formed by the control points on the boundary. Therefore, the tangents at the corner control points are defined by these boundary Bézier curves. Each corner control point has two tangents, one in each of the u- and v-directions. As was the case for Bézier curves, the patch also lies within the convex hull of its control points, and

$$\sum_{i=0}^{m} \sum_{j=0}^{n} B_i^m(u) B_j^n(v) = 1 \tag{17.34}$$

for $(u, v) \in [0, 1] \times [0, 1]$. Finally, rotating the control points and then generating points on the patch is the same mathematically as (though usually faster than) generating points on the patch and then rotating these.

Partially differentiating Equation 17.32 gives [458] the equations below:

Derivatives [patches]:

$$\frac{\partial \mathbf{p}(u, v)}{\partial u} = m \sum_{j=0}^{n} \sum_{i=0}^{m-1} B_i^{m-1}(u) B_j^n(v) [\mathbf{p}_{i+1,j} - \mathbf{p}_{i,j}],$$

$$\frac{\partial \mathbf{p}(u, v)}{\partial v} = n \sum_{i=0}^{m} \sum_{j=0}^{n-1} B_i^m(u) B_j^{n-1}(v) [\mathbf{p}_{i,j+1} - \mathbf{p}_{i,j}]. \tag{17.35}$$

As can be seen, the degree of the patch is reduced by one in the direction that is differentiated. The unnormalized normal vector is then formed as

$$\mathbf{n}(u, v) = \frac{\partial \mathbf{p}(u, v)}{\partial u} \times \frac{\partial \mathbf{p}(u, v)}{\partial v}. \tag{17.36}$$

In Figure 17.20, the control mesh together with the actual Bézier patch is shown. The effect of moving a control point is shown in Figure 17.21.

Rational Bézier Patches

Just as the Bézier curve could be extended into a rational Bézier curve (Section 17.1.1), and thus introduce more degrees of freedom, so can the Bézier patch be extended into a rational Bézier patch:

$$\mathbf{p}(u, v) = \frac{\sum_{i=0}^{m} \sum_{j=0}^{n} w_{i,j} B_i^m(u) B_j^n(v) \mathbf{p}_{i,j}}{\sum_{i=0}^{m} \sum_{j=0}^{n} w_{i,j} B_i^m(u) B_j^n(v)}. \tag{17.37}$$

Consult Farin's book [458] and Hochek and Lasser's book [777] for information about this type of patch. Similarly, the rational Bézier triangle is an extension of the Bézier triangle, treated next.

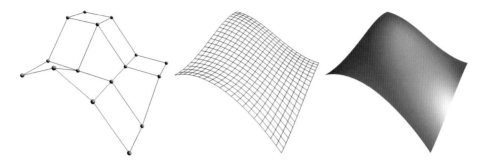

Figure 17.20. Left: control mesh of a 4 × 4 Bézier patch of degree 3 × 3. Middle: the actual quadrilaterals that were generated on the surface. Right: shaded Bézier patch.

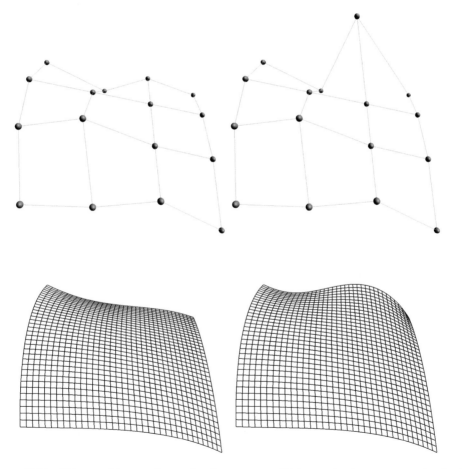

Figure 17.21. This set of images shows what happens to a Bézier patch when one control point is moved. Most of the change is near the moved control point.

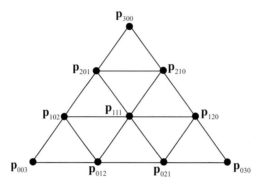

Figure 17.22. The control points of a Bézier triangle with degree three (cubic).

17.2.2 Bézier Triangles

Even though the triangle often is considered a simpler geometric primitive than the rectangle, this is not the case when it comes to Bézier surfaces: Bézier triangles are not as straightforward as Bézier patches. This type of patch is worth presenting as it is used in forming PN triangles and for Phong tessellation, which are fast and simple. Note that some game engines, such as the Unreal Engine, Unity, and Lumberyard, support Phong tessellation and PN triangles.

The control points are located in a triangular grid, as shown in Figure 17.22. The degree of the Bézier triangle is n, and this implies that there are $n + 1$ control points per side. These control points are denoted $\mathbf{p}_{i,j,k}^0$ and sometimes abbreviated to $\mathbf{p}_{ijk}$. Note that $i + j + k = n$, and $i, j, k \geq 0$ for all control points. Thus, the total number of control points is

$$\sum_{x=1}^{n+1} x = \frac{(n+1)(n+2)}{2}. \tag{17.38}$$

It should come as no surprise that Bézier triangles also are based on repeated interpolation. However, due to the triangular shape of the domain, barycentric coordinates (Section 22.8) must be used for the interpolation. Recall that a point within a triangle $\Delta \mathbf{p}_0 \mathbf{p}_1 \mathbf{p}_2$, can be described as $\mathbf{p}(u,v) = \mathbf{p}_0 + u(\mathbf{p}_1 - \mathbf{p}_0) + v(\mathbf{p}_2 - \mathbf{p}_0) = (1-u-v)\mathbf{p}_0 + u\mathbf{p}_1 + v\mathbf{p}_2$, where (u,v) are the barycentric coordinates. For points inside the triangle the following must hold: $u \geq 0$, $v \geq 0$, and $1 - (u+v) \geq 0 \Leftrightarrow u + v \leq 1$. Based on this, the de Casteljau algorithm for Bézier triangles is

de Casteljau [triangles]:

$$\mathbf{p}_{i,j,k}^l(u,v) = u\mathbf{p}_{i+1,j,k}^{l-1} + v\mathbf{p}_{i,j+1,k}^{l-1} + (1-u-v)\mathbf{p}_{i,j,k+1}^{l-1},$$
$$l = 1 \ldots n, \quad i + j + k = n - l. \tag{17.39}$$

The final point on the Bézier triangle at (u,v) is $\mathbf{p}_{000}^n(u,v)$. The Bézier triangle in Bernstein form is

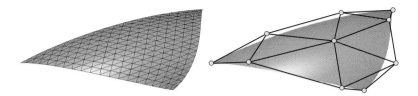

Figure 17.23. Left: wireframe of a tessellated Bézier triangle. Right: shaded surface together with control points.

Bernstein [triangles]: $\quad \mathbf{p}(u,v) = \sum_{i+j+k=n} B_{ijk}^{n}(u,v)\mathbf{p}_{ijk}.$ $\quad\quad$ (17.40)

The Bernstein polynomials now depend on both u and v, and are therefore computed differently, as shown below:

$$B_{ijk}^{n}(u,v) = \frac{n!}{i!j!k!}u^i v^j (1-u-v)^k, \quad i+j+k=n. \quad\quad (17.41)$$

The partial derivatives are [475]

Derivatives [triangles]:

$$
\begin{aligned}
\frac{\partial \mathbf{p}(u,v)}{\partial u} &= \sum_{i+j+k=n-1} nB_{ijk}^{n-1}(u,v)\big(\mathbf{p}_{i+1,j,k} - \mathbf{p}_{i,j,k+1}\big), \\
\frac{\partial \mathbf{p}(u,v)}{\partial v} &= \sum_{i+j+k=n-1} nB_{ijk}^{n-1}(u,v)\big(\mathbf{p}_{i,j+1,k} - \mathbf{p}_{i,j,k+1}\big).
\end{aligned}
$$
$\quad\quad$ (17.42)

Some unsurprising properties of Bézier triangles are that they interpolate (pass through) the three corner control points, and that each boundary is a Bézier curve described by the control points on that boundary. Also, the surfaces lies in the convex hull of the control points. A Bézier triangle is shown in Figure 17.23.

17.2.3 Continuity

When constructing a complex object from Bézier surfaces, one often wants to stitch together several different Bézier surfaces to form one composite surface. To get a good-looking result, care must be taken to ensure that reasonable continuity is obtained across the surfaces. This is in the same spirit as for curves, in Section 17.1.3.

Assume two bicubic Bézier patches should be pieced together. These have 4×4 control points each. This is illustrated in Figure 17.24, where the left patch has control points, $\mathbf{a}_{ij}$, and the right has control points, $\mathbf{b}_{ij}$, for $0 \le i,j \le 3$. To ensure C^0 continuity, the patches must share the same control points at the border, that is, $\mathbf{a}_{3j} = \mathbf{b}_{0j}$.

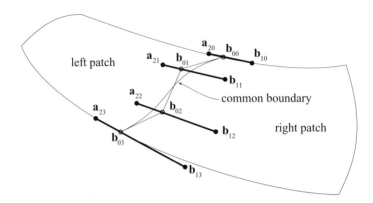

Figure 17.24. How to stitch together two Bézier patches with C^1 continuity. All control points on bold lines must be collinear, and they must have the same ratio between the two segment lengths. Note that $\mathbf{a}_{3j} = \mathbf{b}_{0j}$ to get a shared boundary between patches. This can also be seen to the right in Figure 17.25.

However, this is not sufficient to get a nice looking composite surface. Instead, a simple technique will be presented that gives C^1 continuity [458]. To achieve this we must constrain the position of the two rows of control points closest to the shared control points. These rows are $\mathbf{a}_{2j}$ and $\mathbf{b}_{1j}$. For each j, the points $\mathbf{a}_{2j}$, $\mathbf{b}_{0j}$, and $\mathbf{b}_{1j}$ must be collinear, that is, they must lie on a line. Moreover, they must have the same ratio, which means that $||\mathbf{a}_{2j} - \mathbf{b}_{0j}|| = k||\mathbf{b}_{0j} - \mathbf{b}_{1j}||$. Here, k is a constant, and it must be the same for all j. Examples are shown in Figure 17.24 and 17.25.

This sort of construction uses up many degrees of freedom of setting the control points. This can be seen even more clearly when stitching together four patches, sharing one common corner. The construction is visualized in Figure 17.26. The result is shown to the right in this figure, where the locations of the eight control points around the shared control point are shown. These nine points must all lie in the same plane, and they must form a bilinear patch, as shown in Figure 17.17. If one is satisfied with G^1 continuity at the corners (and only there), it suffices to make the nine points coplanar. This uses fewer degrees of freedom.

Continuity for Bézier triangles is generally more complex, as well as the G^1 conditions for both Bézier patches and triangles [458, 777]. When constructing a complex object of many Bézier surfaces, it is often hard to see to it that reasonable continuity is obtained across all borders. One solution to this is to turn to subdivision surfaces, treated in Section 17.5.

Note that C^1 continuity is required for good-looking texturing across borders. For reflections and shading, a reasonable result is obtained with G^1 continuity. C^1 or higher gives even better results. An example is shown in Figure 17.25.

In the following two subsections, we will present two methods that exploit the normals at triangle vertices to derive a Bézier triangle per input (flat) triangle.

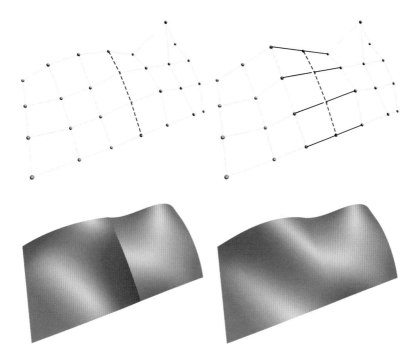

Figure 17.25. The left column shows two Bézier patches joined with only C^0 continuity. Clearly, there is a shading discontinuity between the patches. The right column shows similar patches joined with C^1 continuity, which looks better. In the top row, the dashed lines indicate the border between the two joined patches. To the upper right, the black lines show the collinearity of the control points of the joining patches.

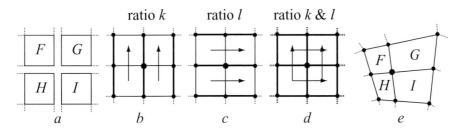

Figure 17.26. (*a*) Four patches, F, G, H, and I, are to be stitched together, where all patches share one corner. (*b*) In the vertical direction, the three sets of three points (on each bold line) must use the same ratio, k. This relationship is not shown here; see the rightmost figure. A similar process is done for (*c*), where, in the horizontal direction, both patches must use the same ratio, l. (*d*) When stitched together, all four patches must use ratio k vertically, and l horizontally. (*e*) The result is shown, in which the ratios are correctly computed for the nine control points closest to (and including) the shared control point.

17.2.4   PN Triangles

Given an input triangle mesh with normals at each vertex, the goal of the *PN triangle* scheme by Vlachos et al. [1819] is to construct a better-looking surface compared to using just triangles. The letters "PN" are short for "point and normal," since that is all the data you need to generate the surfaces. They are also called *N-patches*. This scheme attempts to improve the triangle mesh's shading and silhouettes by creating a curved surface to replace each triangle. Tessellation hardware is able to make each surface on the fly because the tessellation is generated from each triangle's points and normals, with no neighbor information needed. See Figure 17.27 for an example. The algorithm presented here builds upon work by van Overveld and Wyvill [1341].

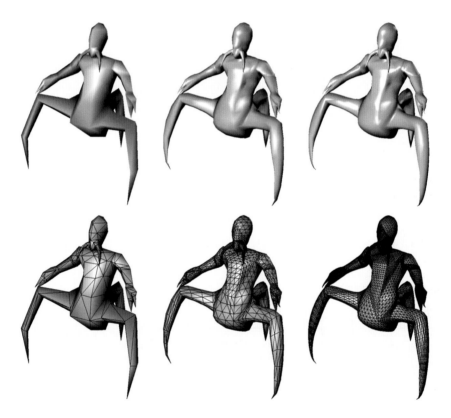

Figure 17.27. The columns show different levels of detail of the same model. The original triangle data, consisting of 414 triangles, is shown on the left. The middle model has 3,726 triangles, while the right has 20,286 triangles, all generated with the presented algorithm. Note how the silhouette and the shading improve. The bottom row shows the models in wireframe, which reveals that each original triangle generates the same amount of subtriangles. *(Model courtesy of id Software. Images from ATI Technologies Inc. demo.)*

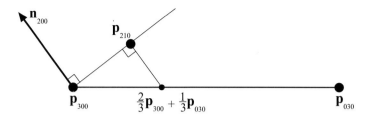

Figure 17.28. How the Bézier point $\mathbf{p}_{210}$ is computed using the normal $\mathbf{n}_{200}$ at $\mathbf{p}_{300}$, and the two corner points $\mathbf{p}_{300}$ and $\mathbf{p}_{030}$.

Assume that we have a triangle with vertices $\mathbf{p}_{300}$, $\mathbf{p}_{030}$, and $\mathbf{p}_{003}$ with normals $\mathbf{n}_{200}$, $\mathbf{n}_{020}$, and $\mathbf{n}_{002}$. The basic idea is to use this information to create a cubic Bézier triangle for each original triangle, and to generate as many triangles as we wish from the Bézier triangle.

To shorten notation, $w = 1 - u - v$ will be used. A cubic Bézier triangle is given by

$$
\begin{aligned}
\mathbf{p}(u, v) &= \sum_{i+j+k=3} B_{ijk}^3(u, v)\mathbf{p}_{ijk} \\
&= u^3\mathbf{p}_{300} + v^3\mathbf{p}_{030} + w^3\mathbf{p}_{003} + 3u^2v\mathbf{p}_{210} + 3u^2w\mathbf{p}_{201} \\
&\quad + 3uv^2\mathbf{p}_{120} + 3v^2w\mathbf{p}_{021} + 3vw^2\mathbf{p}_{012} + 3uw^2\mathbf{p}_{102} + 6uvw\mathbf{p}_{111}.
\end{aligned}
\tag{17.43}
$$

See Figure 17.22. To ensure C^0 continuity at the borders between two PN triangles, the control points on the edge can be determined from the corner control points and the normals at those corners. (assuming that normals are shared between adjacent triangles).

Say that we want to compute $\mathbf{p}_{210}$ using the control points $\mathbf{p}_{300}$, $\mathbf{p}_{030}$ and the normal $\mathbf{n}_{200}$ at $\mathbf{p}_{300}$, as illustrated in Figure 17.28. Simply take the point $\frac{2}{3}\mathbf{p}_{300} + \frac{1}{3}\mathbf{p}_{030}$ and project it in the direction of the normal, $\mathbf{n}_{200}$, onto the tangent plane defined by $\mathbf{p}_{300}$ and $\mathbf{n}_{200}$ [457, 458, 1819]. Assuming normalized normals, the point $\mathbf{p}_{210}$ is computed as

$$
\mathbf{p}_{210} = \frac{1}{3}\left(2\mathbf{p}_{300} + \mathbf{p}_{030} - (\mathbf{n}_{200} \cdot (\mathbf{p}_{030} - \mathbf{p}_{300}))\mathbf{n}_{200}\right).
\tag{17.44}
$$

The other border control points can be computed similarly, so it only remains to compute the interior control point, $\mathbf{p}_{111}$. This is done as shown in the next equation, and this choice follows a quadratic polynomial [457, 458]:

$$
\mathbf{p}_{111} = \frac{1}{4}(\mathbf{p}_{210} + \mathbf{p}_{120} + \mathbf{p}_{102} + \mathbf{p}_{201} + \mathbf{p}_{021} + \mathbf{p}_{012}) - \frac{1}{6}(\mathbf{p}_{300} + \mathbf{p}_{030} + \mathbf{p}_{003}).
\tag{17.45}
$$

Instead of using Equation 17.42 to compute the two tangents on the surface, and subsequently the normal, Vlachos et al. [1819] choose to interpolate the normal using

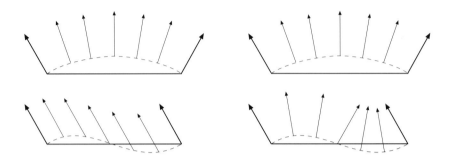

Figure 17.29. This figure illustrates why quadratic interpolation of normals is needed, and why linear interpolation is not sufficient. The left column shows what happens when linear interpolation of normals is used. This works fine when the normals describe a convex surface (top), but breaks down when the surface has an inflection (bottom). The right column illustrates quadratic interpolation. *(Illustration after van Overveld and Wyvill [1342].)*

a quadratic scheme, as shown here:

$$\mathbf{n}(u,v) = \sum_{i+j+k=2} B_{ijk}^2(u,v)\mathbf{n}_{ijk}$$
$$= u^2\mathbf{n}_{200} + v^2\mathbf{n}_{020} + w^2\mathbf{n}_{002} + 2(uv\mathbf{n}_{110} + uw\mathbf{n}_{101} + vw\mathbf{n}_{011}).$$

(17.46)

This can be thought of as a Bézier triangle of degree two, where the control points are six different normals. In Equation 17.46, the choice of the degree, i.e., quadratic, is quite natural, since the derivatives are of one degree lower than the actual Bézier triangle, and because linear interpolation of the normals cannot describe an inflection. See Figure 17.29.

To be able to use Equation 17.46, the normal control points $\mathbf{n}_{110}$, $\mathbf{n}_{101}$, and $\mathbf{n}_{011}$ need to be computed. One intuitive, but flawed, solution is to use the average of $\mathbf{n}_{200}$ and $\mathbf{n}_{020}$ (normals at the vertices of the original triangle) to compute $\mathbf{n}_{110}$. However, when $\mathbf{n}_{200} = \mathbf{n}_{020}$, then the problem shown at the lower left in Figure 17.29 will once again be encountered. Instead, $\mathbf{n}_{110}$ is constructed by first taking the average of $\mathbf{n}_{200}$ and $\mathbf{n}_{020}$, and then reflecting this normal in the plane π, which is shown in Figure 17.30. This plane has a normal parallel to the difference between the endpoints $\mathbf{p}_{300}$ and $\mathbf{p}_{030}$. Since only normal vectors will be reflected in π, we can assume that π passes through the origin because normals are independent of the position on the plane. Also, note that each normal should be normalized. Mathematically, the unnormalized version of $\mathbf{n}_{110}$ is expressed as [1819]

$$\mathbf{n}_{110}' = \mathbf{n}_{200} + \mathbf{n}_{020} - 2\frac{(\mathbf{p}_{030} - \mathbf{p}_{300}) \cdot (\mathbf{n}_{200} + \mathbf{n}_{020})}{(\mathbf{p}_{030} - \mathbf{p}_{300}) \cdot (\mathbf{p}_{030} - \mathbf{p}_{300})}(\mathbf{p}_{030} - \mathbf{p}_{300}).$$

(17.47)

Originally, van Overveld and Wyvill used a factor of 3/2 instead of the 2 in this equation. Which value is best is hard to judge from looking at images, but using 2 gives the nice interpretation of a true reflection in the plane.

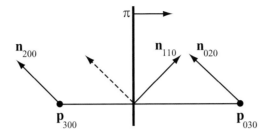

Figure 17.30. Construction of $\mathbf{n}_{110}$ for PN triangles. The dashed normal is the average of $\mathbf{n}_{200}$ and $\mathbf{n}_{020}$, and $\mathbf{n}_{110}$ is this normal reflected in the plane π. The plane π has a normal that is parallel to $\mathbf{p}_{030} - \mathbf{p}_{300}$.

At this point, all Bézier points of the cubic Bézier triangle and all the normal vectors for quadratic interpolation have been computed. It only remains to create triangles on the Bézier triangle so that they can be rendered. Advantages of this approach are that the surface gets a better silhouette and shape for relatively lower cost.

One way to specify levels of detail is the following. The original triangle data are considered LOD 0. The LOD number then increases with the number of newly introduced vertices on a triangle edge. So, LOD 1 introduces one new vertex per edge, and so creates four subtriangles on the Bézier triangle, and LOD 2 introduces two new vertices per edge, generating nine subtriangles. In general, LOD n generates $(n+1)^2$ subtriangles. To prevent cracking between Bézier triangles, each triangle in the mesh must be tessellated with the same LOD. This is a serious disadvantage, since a tiny triangle will be tessellated as much as a large triangle. Techniques such as adaptive tessellation (Section 17.6.2) and fractional tessellation (Section 17.6.1) can be used to avoid these problems.

One problem with PN triangles is that creases are hard to control, and often one needs to insert extra triangles near a desired crease. The continuity between Bézier triangles is only C^0, but they still look acceptable in many cases. This is mainly because the normals are continuous across triangles, so that a set of PN triangles mimics a G^1 surface. A better solution is suggested by Boubekeur et al. [181], where a vertex can have two normals, and two such connected vertices generate a crease. Note that to get good-looking texturing, C^1 continuity is required across borders between triangles (or patches). Also worth knowing is that cracks will appear if two adjacent triangles do not share the same normals. A technique to further improve the quality of the continuity across PN triangles is described by Grün [614]. Dyken et al. [401] present a technique inspired by PN triangles, where only the silhouettes as seen from the viewer are adaptively tessellated and, hence, become more curved. These silhouette curves are derived in similar ways as the PN triangle curves. To get smooth transitions, they blend between coarse silhouettes and tessellated silhouettes. For improved continuity, Fünfzig et al. [505] present PNG1 triangles, which is a modification of PN triangles that have G^1 continuity everywhere. McDonald and Kilgard [1164] present another extension of PN triangles, which can handle different normals on adjacent triangles.

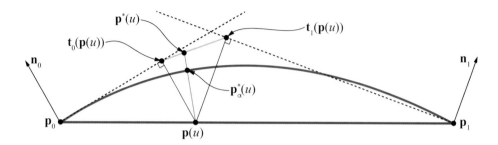

Figure 17.31. Phong tessellation construction illustrated using curves instead of surfaces, which means that $\mathbf{p}(u)$ is only a function of u instead of (u, v), and similarly for $\mathbf{t}_i$. Note that $\mathbf{p}(u)$ is first projected onto the tangent planes, which generates $\mathbf{t}_0$ and $\mathbf{t}_1$. After that, $\mathbf{p}^*(u)$ is created by a linear interpolation from $\mathbf{t}_0$ and $\mathbf{t}_1$. As a final step, a shape factor α is used to blend between the base triangle and $\mathbf{p}^*(u)$. In this example, we used $\alpha = 0.75$.

17.2.5 Phong Tessellation

Boubekeur and Alexa [182] presented a surface construction called *Phong tessellation*, which has many similarities with PN triangles, but is faster to evaluate and simpler to implement. Call the vertices of a base triangle $\mathbf{p}_0$, $\mathbf{p}_1$, and $\mathbf{p}_2$, and let the corresponding normalized normals be $\mathbf{n}_0$, $\mathbf{n}_1$, and $\mathbf{n}_2$. First, recall that a point on the base triangle at the barycentric coordinates (u, v) is computed as

$$\mathbf{p}(u, v) = (u, v, 1 - u - v) \cdot (\mathbf{p}_0, \mathbf{p}_1, \mathbf{p}_2). \tag{17.48}$$

In Phong shading, the normals are interpolated over the flat triangle, also using the equation above, but with the points replaced by normals. Phong tessellation attempts to create a geometric version of Phong shading normal interpolation using repeated interpolation, which results in a Bézier triangle. For this discussion, we will refer to Figure 17.31. The first step is to create a function that projects a point $\mathbf{q}$ on the base triangle up to the tangent plane defined by a point and a normal. This is done as

$$\mathbf{t}_i(\mathbf{q}) = \mathbf{q} - ((\mathbf{q} - \mathbf{p}_i) \cdot \mathbf{n}_i)\mathbf{n}_i. \tag{17.49}$$

Instead of using the triangle vertices to perform linear interpolation (Equation 17.48), linear interpolation is done using the function $\mathbf{t}_i$, which results in

$$\mathbf{p}^*(u, v) = (u, v, 1 - u - v) \cdot (\mathbf{t}_0(u, v), \mathbf{t}_1(u, v), \mathbf{t}_2(u, v)). \tag{17.50}$$

To add some flexibility, a shape factor α is added that interpolates between the base triangle and Equation 17.50, which results in the final formula for Phong tessellation:

$$\mathbf{p}^*_\alpha(u, v) = (1 - \alpha)\mathbf{p}(u, v) + \alpha\mathbf{p}^*(u, v), \tag{17.51}$$

where $\alpha = 0.75$ is a recommended setting [182]. The only information needed to generate this surface is the vertices and normals of the base triangle and a user-

Figure 17.32. Phong tessellation applied to the monster frog. From left to right: base mesh with flat shading, base mesh with Phong shading, and finally, Phong tessellation applied to the base mesh. Note the improved silhouettes. In this example, we used $\alpha = 0.6$. *(Images generated using Tamy Boubekeur's demo program.)*

supplied α, which makes evaluation of this surface fast. The resulting triangular path is quadratic, i.e., of lower degree than PN triangles. The normals are simply linearly interpolated, just as in standard Phong shading. See Figure 17.32 for an example illustrating the effect of Phong tessellation applied to a mesh.

17.2.6 B-Spline Surfaces

Section 17.1.6 briefly introduced B-spline curves, and here we will do the same for introducing B-spline surfaces. Equation 17.24 on page 732 can be generalized to B-spline patches as

$$\mathbf{s}_n(u, v) = \sum_k \sum_l \mathbf{c}_{k,l} \beta_n(u - k) \beta_n(v - l), \tag{17.52}$$

which is fairly similar to the Bézier patch formula (Equation 17.32). Note that $\mathbf{s}_n(u, v)$ is a three-dimensional point on the surface. If this function were to be used for texture filtering, Equation 17.52 would be a height field and $c_{k,l}$ would be one-dimensional, i.e., heights.

For a bicubic B-spline patch, the $\beta_3(t)$ function from Equation 17.25 would be used in Equation 17.52. A total of 4×4 control points, $\mathbf{c}_{k,l}$, would be needed, and the actual surface patch described by Equation 17.52 would be inside the innermost 2×2 control points. This is illustrated in Figure 17.33. Note that bi-cubic B-spline patches are essential to Catmull-Clark subdivision surfaces (Section 17.5.2), as well. There are many good books with more information about B-spline surfaces [111, 458, 777].

17.3 Implicit Surfaces

To this point, only parametric curves and surfaces have been discussed. *Implicit surfaces* form another useful class for representing models. Instead of using some

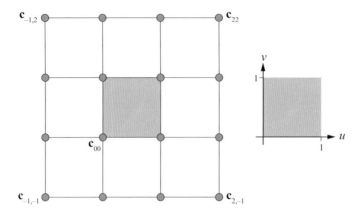

Figure 17.33. The setting for a bicubic B-spline patch, which has 4×4 control points, $\mathbf{c}_{k,l}$. The domain for (u, v) is the unit square as shown to the right.

parameters, say u and v, to explicitly describe a point on the surface, the following form, called the implicit function, is used:

$$f(x, y, z) = f(\mathbf{p}) = 0. \tag{17.53}$$

This is interpreted as follows: A point $\mathbf{p}$ is on the implicit surface if the result is zero when the point is inserted into the implicit function f. Implicit surfaces are often used in intersection testing with rays (Sections 22.6–22.9), as they can be simpler to intersect than the corresponding (if any) parametric surface. Another advantage of implicit surfaces is that *constructive solid geometry* algorithms can be applied easily to them, that is, objects can be subtracted from each other, logically AND:ed or OR:ed with each other. Also, objects can be easily blended and deformed.

Some examples of implicit surfaces, located at the origin, are

$$
\begin{aligned}
f_s(\mathbf{p}, r) &= ||\mathbf{p}|| - r, & \text{sphere;} \\
f_{xz}(\mathbf{p}) &= p_y, & \text{plane in } xz; \\
f_{rb}(\mathbf{p}, \mathbf{d}, r) &= ||\max(|\mathbf{p}| - \mathbf{d}, 0)|| - r, & \text{rounded box.}
\end{aligned} \tag{17.54}
$$

These deserve some explanation. The sphere is simply the distance from $\mathbf{p}$ to the origin subtracted by the radius, so $f_s(\mathbf{p}, r)$ is equal to 0 if $\mathbf{p}$ is on the sphere with radius r. Otherwise, a signed distance will be returned where negative means that $\mathbf{p}$ is inside the sphere, and positive outside. Therefore, these functions are sometimes also called *signed distance functions* (SDFs). The plane $f_{xz}(\mathbf{p})$ is just the y-coordinate of $\mathbf{p}$, i.e., the side where the y-axis is positive. For the expression for the rounded box, we assume that the absolute value ($|\mathbf{p}|$) and the maximum of a vector are calculated per component. Also, $\mathbf{d}$ is a vector of the half sides of the box. See the rounded box illustrated in Figure 17.34; the formula is explained in the caption. To get a non-rounded box, simply set $r = 0$.

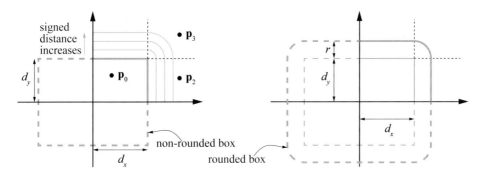

Figure 17.34. Left: a non-rounded box, whose signed distance function is $\|\max(|\mathbf{p}|-\mathbf{d},0)\|$, where $\mathbf{p}$ is the point to be tested and $\mathbf{d}$'s components are the half sides as shown. Note that $|\mathbf{p}|$ makes the rest of the computations occur in the top right quadrant (in 2D). Subtracting $\mathbf{d}$ means that $|p_x|-d_x$ will be negative if $\mathbf{p}$ is inside the box along x, and likewise for the other axes. Only positive values are retained, while negative ones are clamped to zero by $\max()$. Hence, $\|\max(|\mathbf{p}|-\mathbf{d},0)\|$ computes the closest distance to the box sides, and this means that the signed distance field outside the box gets rounded if more than one value is positive after evaluating $\max()$. Right: the rounded box is obtained by subtracting r from the non-rounded box, which expands the box by r is all directions.

The normal of an implicit surface is described by the partial derivatives, called the gradient and denoted ∇f:

$$\nabla f(x,y,z) = \left(\frac{\partial f}{\partial x}, \frac{\partial f}{\partial y}, \frac{\partial f}{\partial z}\right). \tag{17.55}$$

To be able to evaluate it exactly, f in Equation 17.55 must be differentiable, and thus also continuous. In practice, one often use a numerical technique called central differences, which samples using the scene function f [495]:

$$\nabla f_x \approx f(\mathbf{p}+\epsilon\mathbf{e}_x) - f(\mathbf{p}-\epsilon\mathbf{e}_x), \tag{17.56}$$

and similarly for ∇f_y and ∇f_z. Recall that $\mathbf{e}_x = (1,0,0)$, $\mathbf{e}_y = (0,1,0)$, and $\mathbf{e}_z = (0,0,1)$ and that ϵ is a small number.

To build a scene with the primitives in Equation 17.54, the union operator, $\cup$, is used. For example, $f(\mathbf{p}) = f_s(\mathbf{p},1) \cup f_{xz}(\mathbf{p})$ is a scene consisting of a sphere and a plane. The union operator is implemented by taking the smallest of its two operands, since we want to find the surface closest to $\mathbf{p}$. Translation is done by translating $\mathbf{p}$ before calling the signed distance function, i.e., $f_s(\mathbf{p}-\mathbf{t},1)$ is a sphere translated by $\mathbf{t}$. Rotations and other transforms can be done in the same spirit, i.e., with the inverse transform applied to $\mathbf{p}$. It is also straightforward to repeat an object over the entire space by using $\mathbf{r} = \mathrm{mod}(\mathbf{p},\mathbf{c}) - 0.5\mathbf{c}$ instead of $\mathbf{p}$ as the argument to the signed distance function.

Blending of implicit surfaces is a nice feature that can be used in what is often referred to as blobby modeling [161], soft objects, or metaballs [67, 558]. See Figure 17.35 for some examples. The basic idea is to use several simple primitives, such

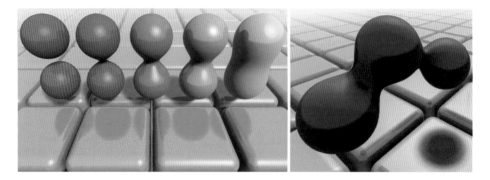

Figure 17.35. Left: pairs of spheres blended with different increasing (from left to right) blend radii and with a ground floor composed of repeated rounded boxes. Right: three spheres blended together.

as spheres, ellipsoids, or whatever is available, and blend these smoothly. Each object can be seen as an atom, and after blending the molecule of the atoms is obtained. Blending can be done in many different ways. An often-used method [1189, 1450] to blend two distances, d_1 and d_2, with a blend radius, r_b, is

$$h = \min\left(\max(0.5 + 0.5(d_2 - d_1)/r_b, 0.0), 1.0\right),$$
$$d = (1 - h)d_2 + hd_1 + r_b h(1 - h), \tag{17.57}$$

where d is the blended distance. While this function only blends the shortest distances to two objects, the function can be use repeatedly to blend more objects (see the right part of Figure 17.35).

To visualize a set of implicit functions, the usual method used is ray marching [673]. Once you can ray-march through a scene, it is also possible to generate shadows, reflections, ambient occlusion, and other effects. Ray marching within a signed distance field is illustrated in Figure 17.36. At the first point, $\mathbf{p}$, on the ray, we evaluate the

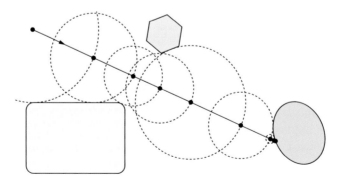

Figure 17.36. Ray marching with signed distance fields. The dashed circles indicate the distance to the closest surface from their centers. A position can advance along the ray to the border of the previous position's circle.

Figure 17.37. Rain forest (left) and a snail (right) created procedurally using signed distance functions and ray marching. The trees were generated using ellipsoids displaced with procedural noise. *(Images generated with Shadertoy using programs from Iñigo Quilez.)*

shortest distance, d, to the scene. Since this indicates that there is a sphere around $\mathbf{p}$ of radius d with no other object being any closer, we can move the ray d units along the ray direction and so on until we reach the surface within some epsilon, or when a predefined ray-march steps have been met, in which case we can assume that the background is hit. Two excellent examples are shown in Figure 17.37.

Every implicit surface can also be turned into a surface consisting of triangles. There are several algorithms available for performing this operation [67, 558]. One well-known example is the marching cubes algorithm, described in Section 13.10. Code for performing polygonalization using algorithms by Wyvill and Bloomenthal is available on the web [171], and de Araújo et al. [67] present a survey on recent techniques for polygonalization of implicit surfaces. Tatarchuk and Shopf [1744] describe a technique they call *marching tetrahedra*, in which the GPU can be used to find isosurfaces in a three-dimensional data set. Figure 3.13 on page 48 shows an example of isosurface extraction using the geometry shader. Xiao et al. [1936] present a fluid simulation system in which the GPU computes the locations of 100k particles and uses them to display the isosurface, all at interactive rates.

17.4 Subdivision Curves

Subdivision techniques are used to create smooth curves and surfaces. One reason why they are used in modeling is that they bridge the gap between discrete surfaces (triangle meshes) and continuous surfaces (e.g., a collection of Bézier patches), and can therefore be used for level of detail techniques (Section 19.9). Here, we will first describe how subdivision curves work, and then discuss the more popular subdivision surface schemes.

Subdivision curves are best explained by an example that uses *corner cutting*. See Figure 17.38. The corners of the leftmost polygon are cut off, creating a new polygon

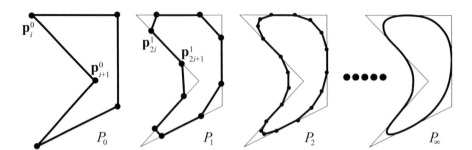

Figure 17.38. Chaikin's subdivision scheme in action. The initial control polygon P_0 is subdivided once into P_1, and then again into P_2. As can be seen, the corners of each polygon, P_i, are cut off during subdivision. After infinitely many subdivisions, the limit curve P_∞ is obtained. This is an approximating scheme as the curve does not go through the initial points.

with twice as many vertices. Then the corners of this new polygon are cut off, and so on to infinity (or, more practically, until we cannot see any difference). The resulting curve, called the *limit curve*, is smooth since all corners are cut off. This process can also be thought of as a low-pass filter since all sharp corners (high frequency) are removed. This process is often written as $P_0 \to P_1 \to P_2 \cdots \to P_\infty$, where P_0 is the starting polygon, also called the *control polygon*, and P_∞ is the limit curve.

This subdivision process can be done in many different ways, and each is characterized by a subdivision scheme. The one shown in Figure 17.38 is called Chaikin's scheme [246] and works as follows. Assume the n vertices of a polygon are $P_0 = \{\mathbf{p}_0^0, \ldots, \mathbf{p}_{n-1}^0\}$, where the superscript denotes the level of subdivision. Chaikin's scheme creates two new vertices between each subsequent pair of vertices, say $\mathbf{p}_i^k$ and $\mathbf{p}_{i+1}^k$, of the original polygon as

$$\mathbf{p}_{2i}^{k+1} = \frac{3}{4}\mathbf{p}_i^k + \frac{1}{4}\mathbf{p}_{i+1}^k \quad \text{and} \quad \mathbf{p}_{2i+1}^{k+1} = \frac{1}{4}\mathbf{p}_i^k + \frac{3}{4}\mathbf{p}_{i+1}^k. \tag{17.58}$$

As can be seen, the superscript changes from k to $k+1$, which means that we go from one subdivision level to the next, i.e., $P_k \to P_{k+1}$. After such a subdivision step is performed, the original vertices are discarded and the new points are reconnected. This kind of behavior can be seen in Figure 17.38, where new points are created $1/4$ away from the original vertices toward neighboring vertices. The beauty of subdivision schemes comes from the simplicity of rapidly generating smooth curves. However, you do not immediately have a parametric form of the curve as in Section 17.1, though it can be shown that Chaikin's algorithm generates a quadratic B-spline [111, 458, 777, 1847]. So far, the presented scheme works for (closed) polygons, but most schemes can be extended to work for open polylines as well. In the case of Chaikin, the only difference is that the two endpoints of the polyline are kept in each subdivision step (instead of being discarded). This makes the curve go through the endpoints.

There are two different classes of subdivision schemes, namely *approximating* and *interpolating*. Chaikin's scheme is approximating, as the limit curve, in general, does

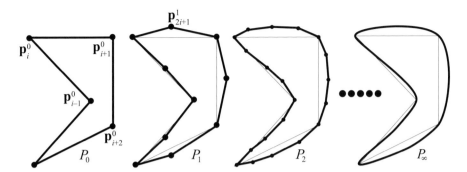

Figure 17.39. The 4-point subdivision scheme in action. This is an interpolating scheme as the curve goes through the initial points, and in general curve P_{i+1} goes through the points of P_i. Note that the same control polygon is used in Figure 17.38.

not lie on the vertices of the initial polygon. This is because the vertices are discarded (or updated, for some schemes). In contrast, an interpolating scheme keeps all the points from the previous subdivision step, and so the limit curve P_∞ goes through all the points of P_0, P_1, P_2, and so on. This means that the scheme interpolates the initial polygon. An example, using the same polygon as in Figure 17.38, is shown in Figure 17.39. This scheme uses the four nearest points to create a new point [402]:

$$\mathbf{p}_{2i}^{k+1} = \mathbf{p}_i^k,$$
$$\mathbf{p}_{2i+1}^{k+1} = \left(\frac{1}{2} + w\right)(\mathbf{p}_i^k + \mathbf{p}_{i+1}^k) - w(\mathbf{p}_{i-1}^k + \mathbf{p}_{i+2}^k). \tag{17.59}$$

The first line in Equation 17.59 simply means that we keep the points from the previous step without changing them (i.e., interpolating), and the second line is for creating a new point in between $\mathbf{p}_i^k$ and $\mathbf{p}_{i+1}^k$. The weight w is called a *tension parameter.* When $w = 0$, linear interpolation is the result, but when $w = 1/16$, we get the kind of behavior shown in Figure 17.39. It can be shown [402] that the resulting curve is C^1 when $0 < w < 1/8$. For open polylines we run into problems at the endpoints because we need two points on both sides of the new point, and we only have one. This can be solved if the point next to the endpoint is reflected across the endpoint. So, for the start of the polyline, $\mathbf{p}_1$ is reflected across $\mathbf{p}_0$ to obtain $\mathbf{p}_{-1}$. This point is then used in the subdivision process. The creation of $\mathbf{p}_{-1}$ is shown in Figure 17.40.

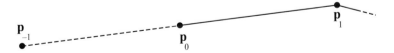

Figure 17.40. The creation of a reflection point, $\mathbf{p}_{-1}$, for open polylines. The reflection point is computed as: $\mathbf{p}_{-1} = \mathbf{p}_0 - (\mathbf{p}_1 - \mathbf{p}_0) = 2\mathbf{p}_0 - \mathbf{p}_1$.

Another approximating scheme uses the following subdivision rules:

$$\mathbf{p}_{2i}^{k+1} = \frac{3}{4}\mathbf{p}_i^k + \frac{1}{8}(\mathbf{p}_{i-1}^k + \mathbf{p}_{i+1}^k),$$

$$\mathbf{p}_{2i+1}^{k+1} = \frac{1}{2}(\mathbf{p}_i^k + \mathbf{p}_{i+1}^k). \tag{17.60}$$

The first line updates the existing points, and the second computes the midpoint on the line segment between two neighboring points. This scheme generates a cubic B-spline curve (Section 17.1.6). Consult the SIGGRAPH course on subdivision [1977], the Killer B's book [111], Warren and Weimer's subdivision book [1847], or Farin's CAGD book [458] for more about these curves.

Given a point $\mathbf{p}$ and its neighboring points, it is possible to directly "push" that point to the limit curve, i.e., determine what the coordinates of $\mathbf{p}$ would be on P_∞. This is also possible for tangents. See, for example, Joy's online introduction to this topic [843].

Many of the concepts for subdivision curves also apply to subdivision surfaces, which are presented next.

17.5 Subdivision Surfaces

Subdivision surfaces are a powerful paradigm for defining smooth, continuous, crackless surfaces from meshes with arbitrary topology. As with all other surfaces in this chapter, subdivision surfaces also provide infinite level of detail. That is, you can generate as many triangles or polygons as you wish, and the original surface representation is compact. An example of a surface being subdivided is shown in Figure 17.41. Another advantage is that subdivision rules are simple and easily implemented. A disadvantage is that the analysis of surface continuity often is mathematically involved. However, this sort of analysis is often of interest only to those who wish to create new subdivision schemes, and is out of the scope of this book. For such details, consult Warren and Weimer's book [1847] and the SIGGRAPH course on subdivision [1977].

In general, the subdivision of surfaces (and curves) can be thought of as a two-phase process [915]. Starting with a polygonal mesh, called the *control mesh* or the *control cage*, the first phase, called the *refinement phase*, creates new vertices and reconnects to create new, smaller triangles. The second, called the *smoothing phase*, typically computes new positions for some or all vertices in the mesh. This is illustrated in Figure 17.42. It is the details of these two phases that characterize a subdivision scheme. In the first phase, a polygon can be split in different ways, and in the second phase, the choice of subdivision rules give different characteristics such as the level of continuity, and whether the surface is approximating or interpolating, which are properties described in Section 17.4.

A subdivision scheme can be characterized by being *stationary* or *non-stationary*, by being *uniform* or *nonuniform*, and whether it is *triangle-based* or *polygon-based*. A stationary scheme uses the same subdivision rules at every subdivision step, while

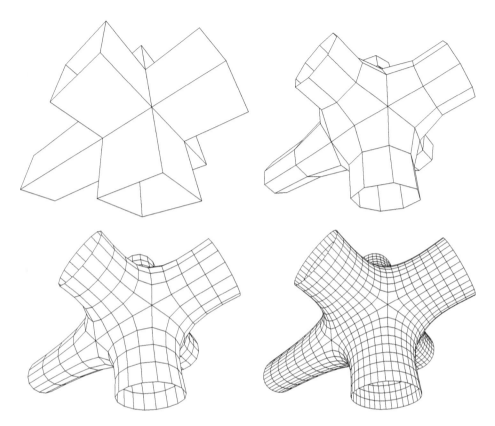

Figure 17.41. The top left image shows the control mesh, i.e., that original mesh, which is the only geometrical data that describes the resulting subdivision surface. The following images are subdivided one, two, and three times. As can be seen, more and more polygons are generated and the surface gets smoother and smoother. The scheme used here is the Catmull-Clark scheme, described in Section 17.5.2.

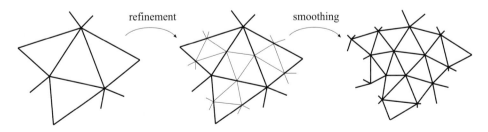

Figure 17.42. Subdivision as refinement and smoothing. The refinement phase creates new vertices and reconnects to create new triangles, and the smoothing phase computes new positions for the vertices.

Figure 17.43. The connectivity of two subdivision steps for schemes such as Loop's method. Each triangle generates four new triangles.

a nonstationary may change the rules depending on which step currently is being processed. The schemes treated below are all stationary. A uniform scheme uses the same rules for every vertex or edge, while a nonuniform scheme may use different rules for different vertices or edges. As an example, a different set of rules is often used for edges that are on the boundaries of a surface. A triangle-based scheme only operates on triangles, and thus only generates triangles, while a polygon-based scheme operates on arbitrary polygons.

Several different subdivision schemes are presented next. Following these, two techniques are presented that extend the use of subdivision surfaces, along with methods for subdividing normals, texture coordinates, and colors. Finally, some practical algorithms for subdivision and rendering are presented.

17.5.1 Loop Subdivision

Loop's method [767, 1067] was the first subdivision scheme for triangles. It is like the last scheme in Section 17.4 in that it is approximating, and that it updates each existing vertex and creates a new vertex for each edge. The connectivity for this scheme is shown in Figure 17.43. As can be seen, each triangle is subdivided into four new triangles, so after n subdivision steps, a triangle has been subdivided into 4^n triangles.

First, let us focus on an existing vertex $\mathbf{p}^k$, where k is the number of subdivision steps. This means that $\mathbf{p}^0$ is the vertex of the control mesh.

After one subdivision step, $\mathbf{p}^0$ turns into $\mathbf{p}^1$. In general, $\mathbf{p}^0 \rightarrow \mathbf{p}^1 \rightarrow \mathbf{p}^2 \rightarrow \cdots \rightarrow \mathbf{p}^\infty$, where $\mathbf{p}^\infty$ is the limit point. If $\mathbf{p}^k$ has n neighboring vertices, $\mathbf{p}_i^k$, $i \in \{0, 1, \ldots, n-1\}$, then we say that the *valence* of $\mathbf{p}^k$ is n. See Figure 17.44 for the notation described above. Also, a vertex that has valence 6 is called *regular* or *ordinary*. Otherwise it is called *irregular* or *extraordinary*.

Below, the subdivision rules for Loop's scheme are given, where the first formula is the rule for updating an existing vertex $\mathbf{p}^k$ into $\mathbf{p}^{k+1}$, and the second formula is for creating a new vertex, $\mathbf{p}_i^{k+1}$, between $\mathbf{p}^k$ and each of the $\mathbf{p}_i^k$. Again, n is the valence of $\mathbf{p}^k$:

$$\mathbf{p}^{k+1} = (1 - n\beta)\mathbf{p}^k + \beta(\mathbf{p}_0^k + \cdots + \mathbf{p}_{n-1}^k),$$

$$\mathbf{p}_i^{k+1} = \frac{3\mathbf{p}^k + 3\mathbf{p}_i^k + \mathbf{p}_{i-1}^k + \mathbf{p}_{i+1}^k}{8}, \quad i = 0 \ldots n-1. \tag{17.61}$$

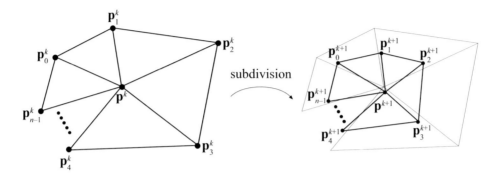

Figure 17.44. The notation used for Loop's subdivision scheme. The left neighborhood is subdivided into the neighborhood to the right. The center point $\mathbf{p}^k$ is updated and replaced by $\mathbf{p}^{k+1}$, and for each edge between $\mathbf{p}^k$ and $\mathbf{p}_i^k$, a new point is created ($\mathbf{p}_i^{k+1}$, $i \in 1, \ldots, n$).

Note that we assume that the indices are computed modulo n, so that if $i = n - 1$, then for $i + 1$, we use index 0, and likewise when $i = 0$, then for $i - 1$, we use index $n - 1$. These subdivision rules can easily be visualized as masks, also called stencils. See Figure 17.45. The major use of these is that they communicate almost an entire subdivision scheme using only a simple illustration. Note that the weights sum to one for both masks. This is a characteristic that is true for all subdivision schemes, and the rationale for this is that a new point should lie in the neighborhood of the weighted points. In Equation 17.61, the constant β is actually a function of n, and is given by

$$\beta(n) = \frac{1}{n}\left(\frac{5}{8} - \frac{(3 + 2\cos(2\pi/n))^2}{64}\right). \tag{17.62}$$

Loop's suggestion [1067] for the β function gives a surface of C^2 continuity at every regular vertex, and C^1 elsewhere [1976], that is, at all irregular vertices. As only regular vertices are created during subdivision, the surface is only C^1 at the

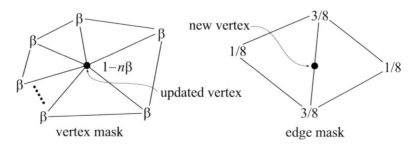

Figure 17.45. The masks for Loop's subdivision scheme (black circles indicate which vertex is updated/generated). A mask shows the weights for each involved vertex. For example, when updating an existing vertex, the weight $1 - n\beta$ is used for the existing vertex, and the weight β is used for all the neighboring vertices, called the 1-ring.

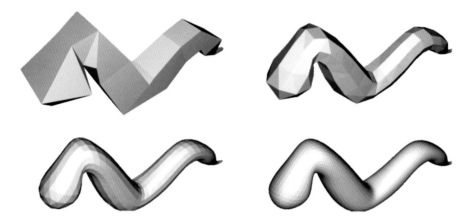

Figure 17.46. A worm subdivided three times with Loop's subdivision scheme.

places where we had irregular vertices in the control mesh. See Figure 17.46 for an example of a mesh subdivided with Loop's scheme. A variant of Equation 17.62, which avoids trigonometric functions, is given by Warren and Weimer [1847]:

$$\beta(n) = \frac{3}{n(n+2)}. \tag{17.63}$$

For regular valences, this gives a C^2 surface, and C^1 elsewhere. The resulting surface is hard to distinguish from a regular Loop surface. For a mesh that is not closed, we cannot use the presented subdivision rules. Instead, special rules have to be used for such boundaries. For Loop's scheme, the reflection rules of Equation 17.60 can be used. This is also treated in Section 17.5.3.

The surface after infinitely many subdivision steps is called the limit surface. Limit surface points and limit tangents can be computed using closed form expressions. The limit position of a vertex is computed [767, 1977] using the formula on the first row in Equation 17.61, by replacing $\beta(n)$ with

$$\gamma(n) = \frac{1}{n + \frac{3}{8\beta(n)}}. \tag{17.64}$$

Two limit tangents for a vertex $\mathbf{p}^k$ can be computed by weighting the immediate neighboring vertices, called the *1-ring* or *1-neighborhood*, as shown below [767, 1067]:

$$\mathbf{t}_u = \sum_{i=0}^{n-1} \cos(2\pi i/n)\mathbf{p}_i^k, \quad \mathbf{t}_v = \sum_{i=0}^{n-1} \sin(2\pi i/n)\mathbf{p}_i^k. \tag{17.65}$$

The normal is then $\mathbf{n} = \mathbf{t}_u \times \mathbf{t}_v$. Note that this often is less expensive [1977] than the methods described in Section 16.3, which need to compute the normals of the neighboring triangles. More importantly, this gives the exact normal at the point.

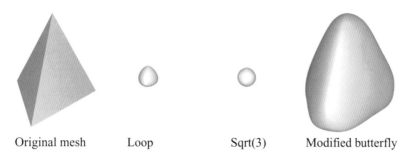

| Original mesh | Loop | Sqrt(3) | Modified butterfly |

Figure 17.47. A tetrahedron is subdivided five times with Loop's, the $\sqrt{3}$, and the *modified butterfly* (MB) scheme [1975]. Loop's and the $\sqrt{3}$-scheme [915] are both approximating, while MB is interpolating, where the latter means that the initial vertices are located on the final surface. We cover only approximating schemes in this book due to their popularity in games and offline rendering.

A major advantage of approximating subdivision schemes is that the resulting surface tends to get fair. *Fairness* is, loosely speaking, related to how smoothly a curve or surface bends [1239]. A higher degree of fairness implies a smoother curve or surface. Another advantage is that approximating schemes converge faster than interpolating schemes. However, this means that the shapes often shrink. This is most notable for small, convex meshes, such as the tetrahedron shown in Figure 17.47. One way to decrease this effect is to use more vertices in the control mesh, i.e., care must be taken while modeling it. Maillot and Stam present a framework for combining subdivision schemes so that the shrinking can be controlled [1106]. A characteristic that can be used to great advantage at times is that a Loop surface is contained inside the convex hull of the original control points [1976].

The Loop subdivision scheme generates a generalized three-directional quartic box spline.[1] So, for a mesh consisting only of regular vertices, we could actually describe the surface as a type of spline surface. However, this description is not possible for irregular settings. Being able to generate smooth surfaces from any mesh of vertices is one of the great strengths of subdivision schemes. See also Sections 17.5.3 and 17.5.4 for different extensions to subdivision surfaces that use Loop's scheme.

17.5.2 Catmull-Clark Subdivision

The two most famous subdivision schemes that can handle polygonal meshes (rather than just triangles) are Catmull-Clark [239] and Doo-Sabin [370].[2] Here, we will only briefly present the former. Catmull-Clark surfaces have been used in Pixar's short film *Geri's Game* [347], *Toy Story 2*, and in all subsequent feature films from Pixar. This subdivision scheme is also commonly used for making models for games, and is probably the most popular one. As pointed out by DeRose et al. [347], Catmull-

---

[1]These spline surfaces are out of the scope of this book. Consult Warren's book [1847], the SIGGRAPH course [1977], or Loop's thesis [1067].

[2]Incidentally, both were presented in the same issue of the same journal.

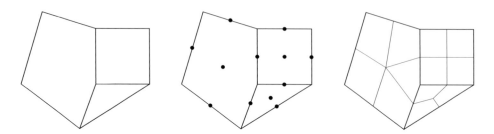

Figure 17.48. The basic idea of Catmull-Clark subdivision. Each polygon generates a new point, and each edge generates a new point. These are then connected as shown to the right. Weighting of the original points is not shown here.

Clark surfaces tend to generate more symmetrical surfaces. For example, an oblong box results in a symmetrical ellipsoid-like surface, which agrees with intuition. In contrast, a triangular-based subdivision scheme would treat each cube face as two triangles, and would hence generate different results depending on how the square is split.

The basic idea for Catmull-Clark surfaces is shown in Figure 17.48, and an actual example of Catmull-Clark subdivision is shown in Figure 17.41 on page 757. As can be seen, this scheme only generates faces with four vertices. In fact, after the first subdivision step, only vertices of valence 4 are generated, thus such vertices are called ordinary or regular (compared to valence 6 for triangular schemes).

Following the notation from Halstead et al. [655], let us focus on a vertex $\mathbf{v}^k$ with n surrounding edge points $\mathbf{e}_i^k$, where $i = 0 \ldots n - 1$. See Figure 17.49. Now, for each face, a new face point $\mathbf{f}^{k+1}$ is computed as the face centroid, i.e., the mean of the points of the face. Given this, the subdivision rules are [239, 655, 1977]

$$
\begin{aligned}
\mathbf{v}^{k+1} &= \frac{n-2}{n}\mathbf{v}^k + \frac{1}{n^2}\sum_{j=0}^{n-1}\mathbf{e}_j^k + \frac{1}{n^2}\sum_{j=0}^{n-1}\mathbf{f}_j^{k+1}, \\
\mathbf{e}_j^{k+1} &= \frac{\mathbf{v}^k + \mathbf{e}_j^k + \mathbf{f}_{j-1}^{k+1} + \mathbf{f}_j^{k+1}}{4}.
\end{aligned}
\tag{17.66}
$$

As can be seen, the vertex $\mathbf{v}^{k+1}$ is computed as weighting of the considered vertex, the average of the edge points, and the average of the newly created face points. On the other hand, new edge points are computed by the average of the considered vertex, the edge point, and the two newly created face points that have the edge as a neighbor.

The Catmull-Clark surface describes a generalized bicubic B-spline surface. So, for a mesh consisting only of regular vertices we could actually describe the surface as a bicubic B-spline surface (Section 17.2.6) [1977]. However, this is not possible for irregular mesh settings, and being able to handle these using subdivision surfaces is one of the scheme's strengths. Limit positions and tangents are also possible to

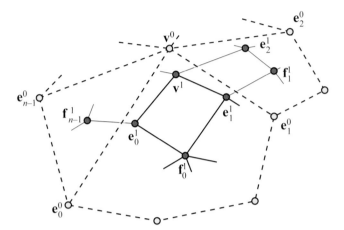

Figure 17.49. Before subdivision, we have the blue vertices and corresponding edges and faces. After one step of Catmull-Clark subdivision, we obtain the red vertices, and all new faces are quadrilaterals. *(Illustration after Halstead et al. [655].)*

compute, even at arbitrary parameter values using explicit formulae [1687]. Halstead et al. [655] describe a different approach to computing limit points and normals.

See Section 17.6.3 for a set of efficient techniques that can render Catmull-Clark subdivision surfaces using the GPU.

17.5.3 Piecewise Smooth Subdivision

In a sense, curved surfaces may be considered boring because they lack detail. Two ways to improve such surfaces are to use bump or displacement maps (Section 17.5.4). A third approach, *piecewise smooth subdivision*, is described here. The basic idea is to change the subdivision rules so that *darts*, *corners*, and *creases* can be used. This increases the range of different surfaces that can be modeled and represented. Hoppe et al. [767] first described this for Loop's subdivision surfaces. See Figure 17.50 for a comparison of a standard Loop subdivision surface, and one with piecewise smooth subdivision.

To actually be able to use such features on the surface the edges that we want to be sharp are first tagged, so we know where to subdivide differently. The number of sharp edges coming in at a vertex is denoted s. Then the vertices are classified into: smooth $(s = 0)$, dart $(s = 1)$, crease $(s = 2)$, and corner $(s > 2)$. Therefore, a crease is a curve on the surface, where the continuity across the curve is C^0. A dart is a non-boundary vertex where a crease ends and smoothly blends into the surface. Finally, a corner is a vertex where three or more creases come together. Boundaries can be defined by marking each boundary edge as sharp.

After classifying the various vertex types, Hoppe et al. use a table to determine which mask to use for the various combinations. They also show how to compute

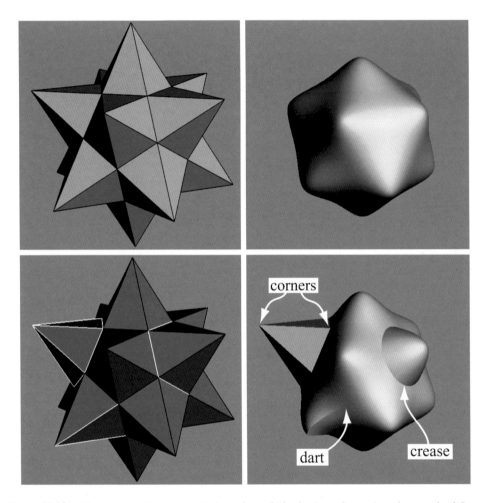

Figure 17.50. The top row shows a control mesh, and the limit surface using the standard Loop subdivision scheme. The bottom row shows piecewise smooth subdivision with Loop's scheme. The lower left image shows the control mesh with tagged edges (sharp) shown in a light gray. The resulting surface is shown to the lower right, with corners, darts, and creases marked. *(Image courtesy of Hugues Hoppe.)*

limit surface points and limit tangents. Biermann et al. [142] present several improved subdivision rules. For example, when extraordinary vertices are located on a boundary, the previous rules could result in gaps. This is avoided with the new rules. Also, their rules make it possible to specify a normal at a vertex, and the resulting surface will adapt to get that normal at that point. DeRose et al. [347] present a technique for creating soft creases. They allow an edge to first be subdivided as sharp a number of times (including fractions), and after that, standard subdivision is used.

17.5.4 Displaced Subdivision

Bump mapping (Section 6.7) is one way to add detail to otherwise smooth surfaces. However, this is just an illusionary trick that changes the normal or local occlusion at each pixel. The silhouette of an object looks the same with or without bump mapping. The natural extension of bump mapping is *displacement mapping* [287], where the surface is displaced. This is usually done along the direction of the normal. So, if the point of the surface is $\mathbf{p}$, and its normalized normal is $\mathbf{n}$, then the point on the displaced surface is

$$\mathbf{s}(u,v) = \mathbf{p}(u,v) + d(u,v)\mathbf{n}(u,v). \tag{17.67}$$

The scalar d is the displacement at the point $\mathbf{p}$. The displacement could also be vector-valued [938].

In this section, the *displaced subdivision surface* [1006] will be presented. The general idea is to describe a displaced surface as a coarse control mesh that is subdivided into a smooth surface that is then displaced along its normals using a scalar field. In the context of displaced subdivision surfaces, $\mathbf{p}$ in Equation 17.67 is the limit point on the subdivision surface (of the coarse control mesh), and $\mathbf{n}$ is the normalized normal at $\mathbf{p}$, computed as

$$\mathbf{n} = \frac{\mathbf{n}'}{||\mathbf{n}'||}, \quad \text{where} \quad \mathbf{n}' = \mathbf{p}_u \times \mathbf{p}_v, \tag{17.68}$$

In Equation 17.68, $\mathbf{p}_u$ and $\mathbf{p}_v$ are the first-order derivative of the subdivision surface. Thus, they describe two tangents at $\mathbf{p}$. Lee et al. [1006] use a Loop subdivision surface for the coarse control mesh, and its tangents can be computed using Equation 17.65. Note that the notation is slightly different here; we use $\mathbf{p}_u$ and $\mathbf{p}_v$ instead of $\mathbf{t}_u$ and $\mathbf{t}_v$. Equation 17.67 describes the displaced position of the resulting surface, but we also need a normal, $\mathbf{n}_s$, on the displaced subdivision surface in order to render it correctly. It is computed analytically as shown below [1006]:

$$\mathbf{n}_s = \mathbf{s}_u \times \mathbf{s}_v, \quad \text{where}$$
$$\mathbf{s}_u = \frac{\partial \mathbf{s}}{\partial u} = \mathbf{p}_u + d_u\mathbf{n} + d\mathbf{n}_u \quad \text{and} \quad \mathbf{s}_v = \frac{\partial \mathbf{s}}{\partial v} = \mathbf{p}_v + d_v\mathbf{n} + d\mathbf{n}_v. \tag{17.69}$$

To simplify computations, Blinn [160] suggests that the third term can be ignored if the displacements are small. Otherwise, the following expressions can be used to compute $\mathbf{n}_u$ (and similarly $\mathbf{n}_v$) [1006]:

$$\bar{\mathbf{n}}_u = \mathbf{p}_{uu} \times \mathbf{p}_v + \mathbf{p}_u \times \mathbf{p}_{uv},$$
$$\mathbf{n}_u = \frac{\bar{\mathbf{n}}_u - (\bar{\mathbf{n}}_u \cdot \mathbf{n})\mathbf{n}}{||\mathbf{n}'||}. \tag{17.70}$$

Note that $\bar{\mathbf{n}}_u$ is not any new notation, it is merely a "temporary" variable in the computations. For an ordinary vertex (valence $n = 6$), the first and second

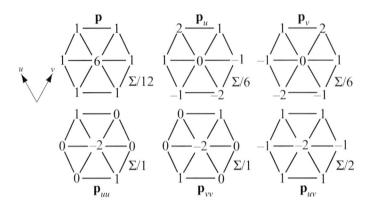

Figure 17.51. The masks for an ordinary vertex in Loop's subdivision scheme. Note that after using these masks, the resulting sum should be divided as shown. *(Illustration after Lee et al. [1006].)*

order derivatives are particularly simple. Their masks are shown in Figure 17.51. For an extraordinary vertex (valence $n \neq 6$), the third term in rows one and two in Equation 17.69 is omitted. An example using displacement mapping with Loop subdivision is shown in Figure 17.52.

When a displaced surface is far away from the viewer, standard bump mapping could be used to give the illusion of this displacement. Doing so saves on geometry processing. Some bump mapping schemes need a tangent-space coordinate system at the vertex, and the following can be used for that: $(\mathbf{b}, \mathbf{t}, \mathbf{n})$, where $\mathbf{t} = \mathbf{p}_u / \|\mathbf{p}_u\|$ and $\mathbf{b} = \mathbf{n} \times \mathbf{t}$.

Nießner and Loop [1281] present a similar method as the one presented above by Lee et al., but they use Catmull-Clark surfaces and use direct evaluation of the derivatives on the displacement function, which is faster. They also use the hardware tessellation pipeline (Section 3.6) for rapid tessellation.

Figure 17.52. To the left is a coarse mesh. In the middle, it is subdivided using Loop's subdivision scheme. The right image shows the displaced subdivision surface. *(Image courtesy of Aaron Lee, Henry Moreton, and Hugues Hoppe.)*

17.5.5   Normal, Texture, and Color Interpolation

In this section, we will present different strategies for dealing with normals, texture coordinates and color per vertex.

As shown for Loop's scheme in Section 17.5.1, limit tangents, and thus, limit normals can be computed explicitly. This involves trigonometric functions that may be expensive to evaluate. Loop and Schaefer [1070] present an approximative technique where Catmull-Clark surfaces always are approximated by bicubic Bézier surfaces (Section 17.2.1). For normals, two tangent patches are derived, that is, one in the u-direction and one the v-direction. The normal is then found as the cross product between those vectors. In general, the derivatives of a Bézier patch are computed using Equation 17.35. However, since the derived Bézier patches approximate the Catmull-Clark surface, the tangent patches will not form a continuous normal field. Consult Loop and Schaefer's paper [1070] on how to overcome these problems. Alexa and Boubekeur [29] argue that it can be more efficient in terms of quality per computation to also subdivide the normals, which gives nicer continuity in the shading. We refer to their paper for the details on how to subdivide the normals. More types of approximations can also be found in Ni et al.'s SIGGRAPH course [1275].

Assume that each vertex in a mesh has a texture coordinate and a color. To be able to use these for subdivision surfaces, we also have to create colors and texture coordinates for each newly generated vertex, too. The most obvious way to do this is to use the same subdivision scheme as we used for subdividing the polygon mesh. For example, you can treat the colors as four-dimensional vectors (RGBA), and subdivide these to create new colors for the new vertices. This is a reasonable way to do it, since the color will have a continuous derivative (assuming the subdivision scheme is at least C^1), and thus abrupt changes in colors are avoided over the surface The same can certainly be done for texture coordinates [347]. However, care must be taken when there are boundaries in texture space. For example, assume we have two patches sharing an edge but with different texture coordinates along this edge. The geometry should be subdivided with the surface rules as usual, but the texture coordinates should be subdivided using boundary rules in this case.

A sophisticated scheme for texturing subdivision surfaces is given by Piponi and Borshukov [1419].

17.6   Efficient Tessellation

To display a curved surface in a real-time rendering context, we usually need to create a triangle mesh representation of the surface. This process is known as *tessellation*. The simplest form of tessellation is called *uniform tessellation*. Assume that we have a parametric Bézier patch, $\mathbf{p}(u, v)$, as described in Equation 17.32. We want to tessellate this patch by computing 11 points per patch side, resulting in $10 \times 10 \times 2 = 200$ triangles. The simplest way to do this is to sample the uv-space uniformly. Thus, we evaluate $\mathbf{p}(u, v)$ for all $(u_k, v_l) = (0.1k, 0.1l)$, where both k and l can be any

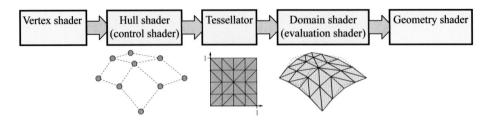

Figure 17.53. Pipeline with hardware tessellation, where the new stages are shown in the middle three (blue) boxes. We use the naming conventions from DirectX here, with the OpenGL counterparts in parenthesis. The hull shader computes new locations of control points and computes tessellation factors as well, which dictates how many triangles the subsequent step should generate. The tessellator generates points in the uv-space, in this case a unit square, and connects them into triangles. Finally, the domain shader computes the positions at each uv-coordinate using the control points.

integer from 0 to 10. This can be done with two nested `for`-loops. Two triangles can be created for the four surface points $\mathbf{p}(u_k, v_l)$, $\mathbf{p}(u_{k+1}, v_l)$, $\mathbf{p}(u_{k+1}, v_{l+1})$, and $\mathbf{p}(u_k, v_{l+1})$.

While this certainly is straightforward, there are faster ways to do it. Instead of sending tessellated surfaces, consisting of many triangles, over the bus from the CPU to the GPU, it makes more sense to send the curved surface representation to the GPU and let it handle the data expansion. Recall that the tessellation stage is described in Section 3.6. For a quick refresher, see Figure 17.53.

The tessellator may use a fractional tessellation technique, which is described in the following section. Then follows a section on adaptive tessellation, and finally, we describe how to render Catmull-Clark surfaces and displacement mapped surfaces with tessellation hardware.

17.6.1 Fractional Tessellation

To obtain smoother level of detail for parametric surfaces, Moreton introduced *fractional tessellation factors* [1240]. These factors enable a limited form of adaptive tessellation, since different tessellation factors can be used on different sides of the parametric surface. Here, an overview of how these techniques work will be presented.

In Figure 17.54, constant tessellation factors for rows and columns are shown on the left, and independent tessellation factors for all four edges on the right. Note that the tessellation factor of an edge is the number of points generated on that edge, minus one. In the patch on the right, the greater of the top and bottom factors is used in the interior for both of these edges, and similarly the greater of the left and right factors is used in the interior. Thus, the basic tessellation rate is 4×8. For the sides with smaller factors, triangles are filled in along the edges. Moreton [1240] describes this process in more detail.

The concept of fractional tessellation factors is shown for an edge in Figure 17.55. For an integer tessellation factor of n, $n + 1$ points are generated at k/n, where $k = 0, \ldots, n$. For a fractional tessellation factor, r, $\lceil r \rceil$ points are generated at k/r,

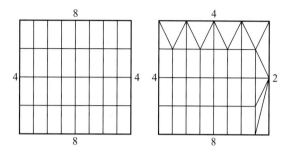

Figure 17.54. Left: normal tessellation—one factor is used for the rows, and another for the columns. Right: independent tessellation factors on all four edges. *(Illustration after Moreton [1240].)*

Figure 17.55. Top: integer tessellation. Middle: fractional tessellation, with the fraction to the right. Bottom: fractional tessellation with the fraction in the middle. This configuration avoids cracks between adjacent patches.

where $k = 0, \ldots, \lfloor r \rfloor$. Here, $\lceil r \rceil$ computes the *ceiling* of r, which is the closest integer toward $+\infty$, and $\lfloor r \rfloor$ computes the *floor*, which is the closest integer toward $-\infty$. Then, the rightmost point is just "snapped" to the rightmost endpoint. As can be seen in the middle illustration in Figure 17.55, this pattern in not symmetric. This leads to problems, since an adjacent patch may generate the points in the other direction, and so give cracks between the surfaces. Moreton solves this by creating a symmetric pattern of points, as shown at the bottom of Figure 17.55. See also Figure 17.56 for an example.

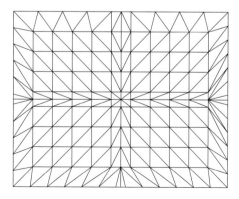

Figure 17.56. A patch with the rectangular domain fractionally tessellated. *(Illustration after Moreton [1240].)*

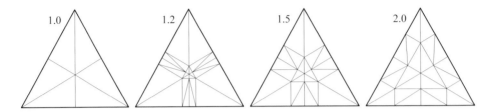

Figure 17.57. Fractional tessellation of a triangle, with tessellation factors shown. Note that the tessellation factors may not correspond exactly to those produced by actual tessellation hardware. (*Illustration after Tatarchuk [1745].*)

So far, we have seen methods for tessellating surfaces with a rectangular domain, e.g., Bézier patches. However, triangles can also be tessellated using fractions [1745], as shown in Figure 17.57. Like the quadrilaterals, it is also possible to specify an independent fractional tessellation rate per triangle edge. As mentioned, this enables adaptive tessellation (Section 17.6.2), as illustrated in Figure 17.58, where displacement mapped terrain is rendered. Once triangles or quadrilaterals have been created, they can be forwarded to the next step in the pipeline, which is treated in the next subsection.

17.6.2 Adaptive Tessellation

Uniform tessellation gives good results if the sampling rate is high enough. However, in some regions on a surface there may not be as great a need for high tessellation as in other regions. This may be because the surface bends more rapidly in some area and therefore may need higher tessellation there, while other parts of the surface are almost flat or far away, and only a few triangles are needed to approximate them. A solution to the problem of generating unnecessary triangles is *adaptive tessellation*, which refers to algorithms that adapt the tessellation rate depending on some measure (for example

Figure 17.58. Displaced terrain rendering using adaptive fractional tessellation. As can be seen in the zoomed-in mesh to the right, independent fractional tessellation rates are used for the edges of the red triangles, which gives us adaptive tessellation. (*Images courtesy of Game Computing Applications Group, Advanced Micro Devices, Inc.*)

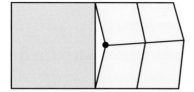 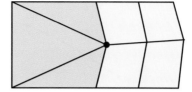

Figure 17.59. To the left, a crack is visible between the two regions. This is because the right has a higher tessellation rate than the left. The problem lies in that the right region has evaluated the surface where there is a black circle, and the left region has not. The standard solution is shown to the right.

curvature, triangle edge length, or some screen size measure). Figure 17.58 shows an example of adaptive tessellation for terrain.

Care must be taken to avoid cracks that can appear between different tessellated regions. See Figure 17.59. When using fractional tessellation, it is common to base the edge tessellation factors on information that comes from only the edge itself, since the edge data are all that is shared between the two connected patches. This is a good start, but due to floating point inaccuracies, there can still be cracks. Nießner et al. [1279] discuss how to make the computations fully watertight, e.g., by making sure that, for an edge, the exact same point is returned regardless of whether tessellation is done from $\mathbf{p}_0$ to $\mathbf{p}_1$, or vice versa.

In this section, we will present some general techniques that can be used to compute fractional tessellation rates, or to decide when to terminate further tessellation and when to split larger patches into a set of smaller ones.

Terminating Adaptive Tessellation

To provide adaptive tessellation, we need to determine when to stop the tessellation, or equivalently how to compute fractional tessellation factors. Either you can use only the information of an edge to determine if tessellation should be terminated, or use information from an entire triangle, or a combination.

It should also be noted that with adaptive tessellation, one can get swimming or popping artifacts from frame to frame if the tessellation factors for a certain edge change too much from one frame to the next. This may be a factor to take into consideration when computing tessellation factors as well. Given an edge, $(\mathbf{a}, \mathbf{b})$, with an associated curve, i.e., a patch edge curve, we can try to estimate how flat the curve is between $\mathbf{a}$ and $\mathbf{b}$. See Figure 17.60. The midpoint in parametric space between $\mathbf{a}$ and $\mathbf{b}$ is found, and its three-dimensional counterpart, $\mathbf{c}$, is computed. Finally, the length, l, between $\mathbf{c}$ and its projection, $\mathbf{d}$, onto the line between $\mathbf{a}$ and $\mathbf{b}$, is computed. This length, l, is used to determine whether the curve segment on that edge if flat enough. If l is small enough, it is considered flat. Note that this method may falsely consider an S-shaped curve segment to be flat. A solution to this is to randomly perturb the parametric sample point [470]. An alternative to using just l is to use

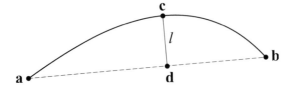

Figure 17.60. The points **a** and **b** have already been generated on this surface. The question is: Should a new point, that is **c**, be generated on the surface?

the ratio $l/\|\mathbf{a} - \mathbf{b}\|$, giving a relative measure [404]. Note that this technique can be extended to consider a triangle as well, where you simply compute the surface point in the middle of the triangle and use the distance from that point to the triangle's plane. To be certain that this type of algorithm terminates, it is common to set some upper limit on how many subdivisions can be made. When that limit is reached, the subdivision ends. For fractional tessellation, the vector from **c** to **d** can be projected onto the screen, and its (scaled) length used as a tessellation rate.

So far we have discussed how to determine the tessellation rate from only the shape of the surface. Other factors that typically are used for on-the-fly tessellation include whether the local neighborhood of a vertex is [769, 1935]:

1. Inside the view frustum.

2. Frontfacing.

3. Occupying a large area in screen space.

4. Close to the silhouette of the object.

These factors will be discussed in turn here. For view frustum culling, one can place a sphere to enclose the edge. This sphere is then tested against the view frustum. If it is outside, we do not subdivide that edge further.

For face culling, the normals at **a**, **b**, and possibly **c** can be computed from the surface description. These normals, together with **a**, **b**, and **c**, define three planes. If all are backfacing, it is likely that no further subdivision is needed for that edge.

There are many different ways to implement screen-space coverage (see also Section 19.9.2). All methods project some simple object onto the screen and estimate the length or area in screen space. A large area or length implies that tessellation should proceed. A fast estimation of the screen-space projection of a line segment from **a** to **b** is shown in Figure 17.61. First, the line segment is translated so that its midpoint is on the view ray. Then, the line segment is assumed to be parallel to the near plane, n, and the screen-space projection, s, is computed from this line segment. Using the points of the line segment $\mathbf{a}'$ and $\mathbf{b}'$ to the right in the illustration, the screen-space projection is then

$$s = \frac{\sqrt{(\mathbf{a}' - \mathbf{b}') \cdot (\mathbf{a}' - \mathbf{b}')}}{\mathbf{v} \cdot (\mathbf{a}' - \mathbf{e})}. \tag{17.71}$$

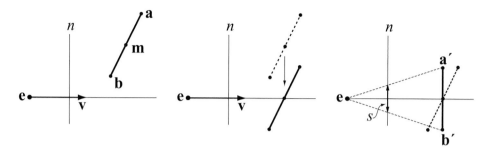

Figure 17.61. Estimation of the screen-space projection, s, of the line segment.

The numerator is simply the length of the line segment. This is divided by the distance from the eye, $\mathbf{e}$, to the line segment's midpoint. The computed screen-space projection, s, is then compared to a threshold, t, representing the maximum edge length in screen space. Rewriting the previous equation to avoid computing the square root, if the following condition is true, the tessellation should continue:

$$s > t \quad \Longleftrightarrow \quad (\mathbf{a}' - \mathbf{b}') \cdot (\mathbf{a}' - \mathbf{b}') > t^2 (\mathbf{v} \cdot (\mathbf{a}' - \mathbf{e}))^2. \tag{17.72}$$

Note that t^2 is a constant and so can be precomputed. For fractional tessellation, s from Equation 17.71 can be used as the tessellation rate, possibly with a scaling factor applied. Another way to measure projected edge length is to place a sphere at the center of the edge, make the radius half the edge length, and then use the projection of the sphere as the edge tessellation factor [1283]. This test is proportional to the area, while the test above is proportional to edge length.

Increasing the tessellation rate for the silhouettes is important, since they play a prime role for the perceived quality of the object. Finding if a triangle is near a silhouette edge can be done by testing whether the dot product between the normal at $\mathbf{a}$ and the vector from the eye to $\mathbf{a}$ is close to zero. If this is true for any of $\mathbf{a}$, $\mathbf{b}$, or $\mathbf{c}$, further tessellation should be done.

For displaced subdivision, Nießner and Loop [1281] use one of the following factors for each base mesh vertex $\mathbf{v}$, which is connected to n edge vectors $\mathbf{e}_i$, $i \in \{0, 1, \ldots, n - 1\}$:

$$
\begin{aligned}
f_1 &= k_1 \cdot \|\mathbf{c} - \mathbf{v}\|, \\
f_2 &= k_2 \sqrt{\sum \mathbf{e}_i \times \mathbf{e}_{i+1}}, \\
f_3 &= k_3 \max \left(\|\mathbf{e}_0\|, \|\mathbf{e}_1\|, \ldots, \|\mathbf{e}_{n-1}\| \right),
\end{aligned}
\tag{17.73}
$$

where the loop index, i, goes over all n edges $\mathbf{e}_i$ connected to $\mathbf{v}$, $\mathbf{c}$ is the position of the camera, and k_i are user-supplied constants. Here, f_1 is simply based on the distance to the vertex from the camera, f_2 computes the area of the quads connected to $\mathbf{v}$, and f_3 uses the largest edge length. The tessellation factor for a vertex is then computed as the maximum of the edge's two base vertices' tessellation factors. The inner tessellation factors are computed as the maximum of the opposite edge's tessellation factor (in u and v). This method can be used with any of the edge tessellation factor methods presented in this section.

Notably, Nießner et al. [1279] recommend using a single global tessellation factor for characters, which depends on the distance to the character. The number of subdivisions is then $\lceil \log_2 f \rceil$, where f is the per-character tessellation factor, which can be computed using any of the methods above.

It is hard to say what methods will work in all applications. The best advice is to test several of the presented heuristics, and combinations of them.

Split and Dice Methods

Cook et al. [289] introduced a method called *split and dice*, with the goal being to tessellate surfaces so that each triangle becomes pixel-sized, to avoid geometrical aliasing. For real-time purposes, this tessellation threshold should be increased to what the GPU can handle. Each patch is first split recursively into a set of subpatches until it is estimated that if uniform tessellation is used for a certain subpatch, the triangles will have the desired size. Hence, this is also a type of adaptive tessellation.

Imagine a single large patch being used for a landscape. In general, there is no way that fractional tessellation can adapt so that the tessellation rate is higher closer to the camera and lower farther away, for example. The core of split and dice may therefore be useful for real-time rendering, even if the target tessellation rate is to have larger triangles than pixel-sized in our case.

Next, we describe the general method for split and dice in a real-time graphics scenario. Assume that a rectangular patch is used. Then start a recursive routine with the entire parametric domain, i.e., the square from $(0,0)$ to $(1,1)$. Using the adaptive termination criteria just described, test whether the surface is tessellated enough. If it is, then terminate tessellation. Otherwise, split this domain into four different equally large squares and call the routine recursively for each of the four subsquares. Continue recursively until the surface is tessellated enough or a predefined recursion level is reached. The nature of this algorithm implies that a quadtree is recursively created during tessellation. However, this will give cracks if adjacent subsquares are tessellated to different levels. The standard solution is to ensure that two adjacent subsquares only differ in one level at most. This is called a *restricted quadtree*. Then the technique shown to the right in Figure 17.59 is used to fill in the cracks. A disadvantage with this method is that the bookkeeping is more involved.

Liktor et al. [1044] present a variant of split and dice for the GPU. The problem is to avoiding swimming artifacts and popping effects when suddenly deciding to split one more time due to, e.g., the camera having moved closer to a surface. To solve that, they use a fractional split method, inspired by fractional tessellation. This is illustrated in Figure 17.62. Since the split is smoothly introduced from one side toward the center of the curve, or toward the center of the patch side, swimming and popping artifacts are avoided. When the termination criteria for the adaptive tessellation have

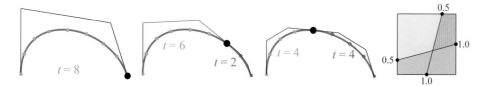

Figure 17.62. Fractional splitting is applied to a cubic Bézier curve. The tessellation rate t is shown for each curve. The split point is the large black circle, which is moved in from the right side of the curve toward the center of the curve. To fractionally split the cubic curve, the black point is smoothly moved toward the curve's center and the original curve is replaced with two cubic Bézier segments that together generate the original curve. To the right, the same concept is illustrated for a patch, which has been split into four smaller subpatches, where 1.0 indicates that the split point is on the center point of the edge, and 0.0 means that it is at the patch corner. (*Illustration after Liktor et al. [1044].*)

been reached, each remaining subpatch is tessellated by the GPU using fractional tessellation as well.

17.6.3 Fast Catmull-Clark Tessellation

Catmull-Clark surfaces (Section 17.5.2) are frequently used in modeling software and in feature film rendering, and hence it is attractive to be able to render these efficiently using graphics hardware as well. Fast tessellation methods for Catmull-Clark surfaces have been an active research field over recent years. Here, we will present a handful of these methods.

Approximating Approaches

Loop and Schaefer [1070] present a technique to convert Catmull-Clark surfaces into a representation that can be evaluated quickly in the domain shader, without the need to know the polygons' neighbors.

As mentioned in Section 17.5.2, the Catmull-Clark surface can be described as many small B-spline surfaces when all vertices are ordinary. Loop and Schaefer convert a quadrilateral (quad) polygon in the original Catmull-Clark subdivision mesh to a bi-cubic Bézier surface (Section 17.2.1). This is not possible for non-quadrilaterals, and so we assume that there are no such polygons (recall that after the first step of subdivision there are only quadrilateral polygons). When a vertex has a valence different from four, it is not possible to create a bicubic Bézier patch that is identical to the Catmull-Clark surface. Hence, an approximative representation is proposed, which is exact for quads with valence-four vertices, and close to the Catmull-Clark surface elsewhere. To this end, both *geometry patches* and *tangent patches* are used, which will be described next.

The geometry patch is simply a bicubic Bézier patch with 4×4 control points. We will describe how these control points are computed. Once this is done, the patch can be tessellated and the domain shader can evaluate the Bézier patch quickly at

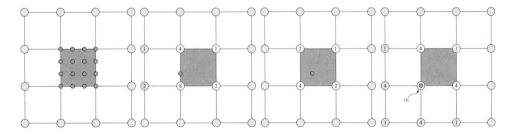

Figure 17.63. Left: part of a quad mesh, where we want to compute a Bézier patch for the gray quad. Note that the gray quad has vertices with only valence four. The blue vertices are neighboring quads' vertices, and the green circles are the control points of the Bézier patch. The following three illustrations show the different masks used to compute the green control points. For example, to compute one of the inner control points, the middle right mask is used, and the vertices of the quad are weighted with the weight shown in the mask.

any parametric coordinate (u, v). So, assuming we have a mesh consisting of only quads with vertices of valence four, we want to compute the control points of the corresponding Bézier patch for a certain quad in the mesh. To that end, the neighborhood around the quad is needed. The standard way of doing this is illustrated in Figure 17.63, where three different masks are shown. These can be rotated and reflected in order to create all the 16 control points. Note that in an implementation the weights for the masks should sum to one, a process that is omitted here for clarity.

The above technique computes a Bézier patch for the ordinary case. When there is at least one extraordinary vertex, we compute an extraordinary patch [1070]. The masks for this are shown in Figure 17.64, where the lower left vertex in the gray quad is an extraordinary vertex.

Note that this results in a patch that approximates the Catmull-Clark subdivision surface, and, it is only C^0 along edges with an extraordinary vertex. This often looks distracting when shading is added, and hence a similar trick as used for N-patches (Section 17.2.4) is suggested. However, to reduce the computational complexity, two

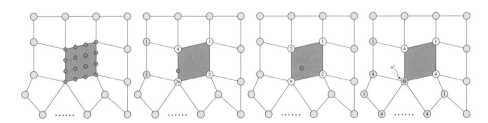

Figure 17.64. Left: a Bézier patch for the gray quad of the mesh is to be generated. The lower left vertex in the gray quad is extraordinary, since its valence is $n \neq 4$. The blue vertices are neighboring quads' vertices, and the green circles are the control points of the Bézier patch. The following three illustrations show the different masks used to compute the green control points.

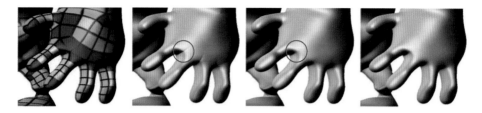

Figure 17.65. Left: quad structure of a mesh. White quads are ordinary, green have one extraordinary vertex, and blue have more than one. Middle left: geometry patch approximation. Middle right: geometry patches with tangent patches. Note that the obvious (red circle) shading artifacts disappeared. Right: true Catmull-Clark surface. *(Image courtesy of Charles Loop and Scott Schaefer, reprinted with permission from Microsoft Corporation.)*

tangent patches are derived: one in the u-direction, and one the v-direction. The normal is then found as the cross product between those vectors. In general, the derivatives of a Bézier patch are computed using Equation 17.35. However, since the derived Bézier patches approximate the Catmull-Clark surface, the tangent patches will not form a continuous normal field. Consult Loop and Schaefer's paper [1070] on how to overcome these problems. Figure 17.65 shows an example of the types of artifacts that can occur.

Kovacs et al. [931] describe how the method above can be extended to also handle creases and corners (Section 17.5.3), and implement these extensions in Valve's Source engine.

Feature Adaptive Subdivision and OpenSubdiv

Pixar presented an open-source system called OpenSubdiv that implements a set of techniques called *feature adaptive subdivision* (FAS) [1279, 1280, 1282]. The basic approach is rather different from the previous technique just discussed. The foundation of this work lies in that subdivision is equivalent to bicubic B-spline patches (Section 17.2.6) for regular faces, i.e., quads where each vertex is regular, which means that the vertex has valence four. So, subdivision continues recursively only for non-regular faces, up until some maximum subdivision level is reached. This is illustrated on the left in Figure 17.66. FAS can also handle creases and semi-smooth creases [347], and the FAS algorithm also needs to subdivide around such creases, which is illustrated on the right in Figure 17.66. The bicubic B-spline patches can be rendered directly using the tessellation pipeline.

The method starts by creating a table using the CPU. This table encodes indices to vertices that need to be accessed during subdivision up to a specified level. As such, the base mesh can be animated since the indices are independent of the vertex positions. As soon as a bicubic B-spline patch is generated, recursion needs not to be continued, which means that the table usually becomes relatively small. The base mesh and the table with indices and additional valence and crease data are uploaded to the GPU once.

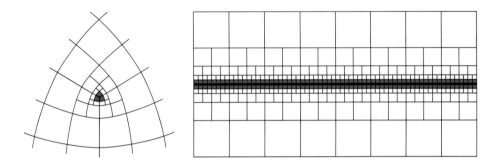

Figure 17.66. Left: recursive subdivision around an extraordinary vertex, i.e., the middle vertex has three edges. As recursion continues, it leaves a band of regular patches (with four vertices, each with four incoming edges) behind. Right: subdivision around a smooth crease indicated by the bold line in the middle. (*Illustration after Nießner et al. [1279].*)

To subdivide the mesh one step, new face points are computed first, followed by new edge points, and finally the vertices are updated, and one compute shader is used for each of these types. For rendering, a distinction between full patches and transition patches is made. A full patch (FP) only shares edges with patches of the same subdivision level, and a regular FP is directly rendered as a bicubic B-spline patch using the GPU tessellation pipeline. Subdivision continues otherwise. The adaptive subdivision process ensures that there is at most a difference of one subdivision level between neighboring patches. A transition patch (TP) has a difference in subdivision level against at least one neighbor. To get crack-free renderings, each TP is split into several subpatches as shown in Figure 17.67. In this way, tessellated vertices match along both sides of each edge. Each type of subpatch is rendered using different hull and domain shaders that implement interpolation variants. For example, the leftmost case in Figure 17.67 is rendered as three triangular B-spline patches. Around extraordinary vertices, another domain shader is used where limit positions and limit normals are computed using the method of Halstead et al. [655]. An example of Catmull-Clark surface rendering using OpenSubdiv is shown in Figure 17.68.

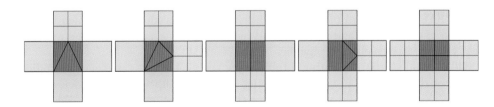

Figure 17.67. Red squares are transition patches, and each has four immediate neighbors, which are either blue (current subdivision level) or green (next subdivision level). This illustration shows the five configurations that can occur, and how they are stitched together. (*Illustration after Nießner et al. [1279].*)

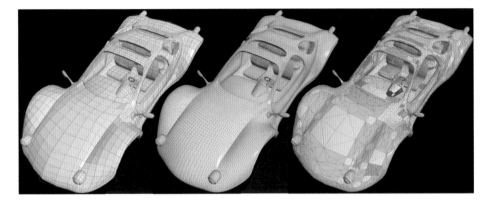

Figure 17.68. Left: the control mesh in green and red lines with the gray surface (8k vertices) generated using one subdivision step. Middle: the mesh subdivided an additional two steps (102k vertices). Right: the surface generated using adaptive tessellation (28k vertices). (*Images generated using OpenSubdiv's dxViewer.*)

The FAS algorithm handles creases, semi-smooth creases, hierarchical details, and adaptive level of detail. We refer to the FAS paper [1279] and Nießner's PhD thesis [1282] for more details. Schäfer et al. [1547] presents a variant of FAS, called DFAS, which is even faster.

Adaptive Quadtrees

Brainerd et al. [190] present a method called *adaptive quadtrees*. It is similar to the approximating scheme by Loop and Schaefer [1070] in that a single tessellated primitive is submitted per quad of the original base mesh. In addition, it precomputes a subdivision plan, which is a quadtree that encodes the hierarchical subdivision (similar to feature adaptive subdivision) from an input face, down to some maximum subdivision level. The subdivision plan also contains a list of stencil masks of the control points needed by the subdivided faces.

During rendering, the quadtree is traversed, making it possible to map (u, v)-coordinates to a patch in the subdivision hierarchy, which can be directly evaluated. A quadtree leaf is a subregion of the domain of the original face, and the surface in this subregion can be directly evaluated using the control points in the stencil. An iterative loop is used to traverse the quadtree in the domain shader, whose input is a parametric (u, v)-coordinate. Traversal needs to continue until a leaf node is reached in which the (u, v)-coordinates are located. Depending on the type of node reached in the quadtree, different actions are taken. For example, when reaching a subregion that can be evaluated directly, the 16 control points for its corresponding bicubic B-spline patch are retrieved, and the shader continues with evaluating that patch.

See Figure 17.1 on page 718 for an example rendered using this technique. This method is the fastest to date that renders Catmull-Clark subdivision surfaces exactly,

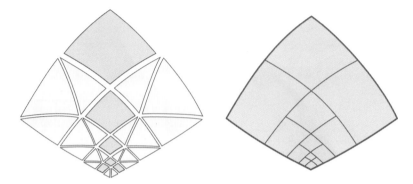

Figure 17.69. Left: hierarchical subdivision according to feature adaptive subdivision (FAS), where each triangle and quad is rendered as a separate tessellated primitive. Right: hierarchical subdivision using adaptive quadtrees, where the entire quad is rendered as a single tessellated primitive. (*Illustration after Brainerd et al. [190].*)

and handles creases and other topological features. An additional advantage of using adaptive quadtrees over FAS is illustrated in Figure 17.69 and further shown in Figure 17.70. Adaptive quadtrees also provide more uniform tessellations since there is a one-to-one mapping between each submitted quad and tessellated primitive.

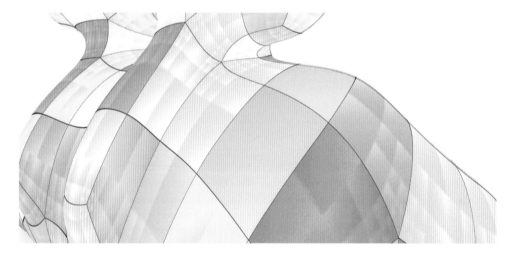

Figure 17.70. Subdivision patches using adaptive quadtrees. Each patch, corresponding to a base mesh face, is surrounded by black curves on the surface and the subdivision steps are illustrated hierarchically inside each patch. As can be seen, there is one patch with uniform color in the center. This implies that it was rendered as a bicubic B-spline patch, while others (with extraordinary vertices) clearly show their underlying adaptive quadtrees. (*Image courtesy of Wade Brainerd.*)

Further Reading and Resources

The topic of curves and surfaces is huge, and for more information, it is best to consult the books that focus solely on this topic. Mortenson's book [1242] serves as a good general introduction to geometric modeling. Books by Farin [458, 460], and by Hoschek and Lasser [777] are general and treat many aspects of *Computer Aided Geometric Design* (CAGD). For implicit surfaces, consult the book by Gomes et al. [558] and the more recent article by de Araújo et al. [67]. For much more information on subdivision surfaces, consult Warren and Heimer's book [1847] and the SIGGRAPH course notes on "Subdivision for Modeling and Animation" by Zorin et al. [1977]. The course on substitutes for subdivision surfaces by Ni et al. [1275] is a useful resource here as well. The survey by Nießner et al. [1283] and Nießner's PhD thesis [1282] are great for information on real-time rendering of subdivision surfaces using the GPU.

For spline interpolation, we refer the interested reader to the Killer B's book [111] in addition to the books above by Farin [458] and Hoschek and Lasser [777]. Many properties of Bernstein polynomials, both for curves and surfaces, are given by Goldman [554]. Almost everything you need to know about triangular Bézier surfaces can be found in Farin's article [457]. Another class of rational curves and surfaces is the nonuniform rational B-spline (NURBS) [459, 1416, 1506], often used in CAD.

Chapter 18
Pipeline Optimization

"We should forget about small efficiencies, say about 97% of the time: Premature optimization is the root of all evil."
—Donald Knuth

Throughout this volume, algorithms have been presented within a context of quality, memory, and performance trade-offs. In this chapter we will discuss performance problems and opportunities that are not associated with particular algorithms. Bottleneck detection and optimization are the focus, starting with making small, localized changes, and ending with techniques for structuring an application as a whole to take advantage of multiprocessing capabilities.

As we saw in Chapter 2, the process of rendering an image is based on a pipelined architecture with four conceptual stages: *application*, *geometry processing*, *rasterization*, and *pixel processing*. There is always one stage that is the bottleneck—the slowest process in the pipeline. This implies that this bottleneck stage sets the limit for the throughput, i.e., the total rendering performance, and so is a prime candidate for *optimization*.

Optimizing the performance of the rendering pipeline resembles the procedure of optimizing a pipelined processor (CPU) [715] in that it consists mainly of two steps. First, the bottleneck of the pipeline is located. Second, that stage is optimized in some way; and after that, step one is repeated if the performance goals have not been met. Note that the bottleneck may or may not be located at the same place after the optimization step. It is a good idea to put only enough effort into optimizing the bottleneck stage so that the bottleneck moves to another stage. Several other stages may have to be optimized before this stage becomes the bottleneck again. For this reason, effort should not be wasted on over-optimizing a stage.

The location of the bottleneck may change within a frame, or even within a draw call. At one moment the geometry stage may be the bottleneck because many tiny triangles are rendered. Later in the frame pixel processing could be the bottleneck because a heavyweight procedural shader is evaluated at each pixel. In a pixel shader execution may stall because the texture queue is full, or take more time as a particular loop or branch is reached. So, when we talk about, say, the application stage being the bottleneck, we mean it is the bottleneck most of the time during that frame. There is rarely only one bottleneck.

Another way to capitalize on the pipelined construction is to recognize that when the slowest stage cannot be optimized further, the other stages can be made to work just as much as the slowest stage. This will not change performance, since the speed of the slowest stage will not be altered, but the extra processing can be used to improve image quality [1824]. For example, say that the bottleneck is in the application stage, which takes 50 milliseconds (ms) to produce a frame, while the others each take 25 ms. This means that without changing the speed of the rendering pipeline (50 ms equals 20 frames per second), the geometry and the rasterizer stages could also do their work in 50 ms. For example, we could use a more sophisticated lighting model or increase the level of realism with shadows and reflections, assuming that this does not increase the workload on the application stage.

Compute shaders also change the way we think about bottlenecks and unused resources. For example, if a shadow map is being rendered, vertex and pixel shaders are simple and the GPU computational resources might be underutilized if fixed-function stages such as the rasterizer or the pixel merger become the bottleneck. Overlapping such draws with asynchronous compute shaders can keep the shader units busy when these conditions arise [1884]. Task-based multiprocessing is discussed in the final section of this chapter.

Pipeline optimization is a process in which we first maximize the rendering speed, then allow the stages that are not bottlenecks to consume as much time as the bottleneck. That said, it is not always a straightforward process, as GPUs and drivers can have their own peculiarities and fast paths. When reading this chapter, the dictum

KNOW YOUR ARCHITECTURE

should always be in the back of your mind, since optimization techniques vary greatly for different architectures. That said, be wary of optimizing based on a specific GPU's implementation of a feature, as hardware can and will change over time [530]. A related dictum is, simply,

MEASURE, MEASURE, MEASURE.

18.1 Profiling and Debugging Tools

Profiling and debugging tools can be invaluable in finding performance problems in your code. Capabilities vary and can include:

- Frame capture and visualization. Usually step-by-step frame replay is available, with the state and resources in use displayed.

- Profiling of time spent across the CPU and GPU, including time spent calling the graphics API.

- Shader debugging, and possibly hot editing to see the effects of changing code.

- Use of debug markers set in the application, to help identify areas of code.

Profiling and debugging tools vary with the operating system, the graphics API, and often the GPU vendor. There are tools for most combinations, and that's why the gods created Google. That said, we will mention a few package names specifically for interactive graphics to get you started on your quest:

- *RenderDoc* is a high-quality Windows debugger for DirectX, OpenGL, and Vulkan, originally developed by Crytek and now open source.

- *GPU PerfStudio* is AMD's suite of tools for their graphics hardware offerings, working on Windows and Linux. One notable tool provided is a static shader analyzer that gives performance estimates without needing to run the application. AMD's Radeon GPU Profiler is a separate, related tool.

- *NVIDIA Nsight* is a performance and debugging system with a wide range of features. It integrates with Visual Studio on Windows and Eclipse on Mac OS and Linux.

- Microsoft's *PIX* has long been used by Xbox developers and has been brought back for DirectX 12 on Windows. Visual Studio's *Graphics Diagnostics* can be used with earlier versions of DirectX.

- *GPUView* from Microsoft uses Event Tracing for Windows (ETW), an efficient event logging system. GPUView is one of several programs that are consumers of ETW sessions. It focuses on the interaction between CPU and GPU, showing which is the bottleneck [783].

- *Graphics Performance Analyzers* (GPA) is a suite from Intel, not specific to their graphics chips, that focuses on performance and frame analysis.

- Xcode on OSX provides *Instruments*, which has several tools for timing, performance, networking, memory leaks, and more. Worth mentioning are *OpenGL ES Analysis*, which detects performance and correctness problems and proposes solutions, and *Metal System Trace*, which provides tracing information from the application, driver, and GPU.

These are the major tools that have existed for a few years. That said, sometimes no tool will do the job. *Timer query* calls are built into most APIs to help profile a GPU's performance. Some vendors provide libraries to access GPU counters and thread traces as well.

18.2 Locating the Bottleneck

The first step in optimizing a pipeline is to locate the largest bottleneck [1679]. One way of finding bottlenecks is to set up several tests, where each test decreases the amount of work a particular stage performs. If one of these tests causes the frames per second to increase, the bottleneck stage has been found. A related way of testing a stage is to reduce the workload on the other stages without reducing the workload on the stage being tested. If performance does not change, the bottleneck is the stage where the workload was not altered. Performance tools can provide detailed information on which API calls are expensive, but do not necessarily pinpoint exactly what stage in the pipeline is slowing down the rest. Even when they do, it is useful to understand the idea behind each test.

What follows is a brief discussion of some of the ideas used to test the various stages, to give a flavor of how such testing is done. A perfect example of the importance of understanding the underlying hardware comes with the advent of the *unified shader architecture*. It forms the basis of many GPUs from the end of 2006 on. The idea is that vertex, pixel, and other shaders all use the same functional units. The GPU takes care of load balancing, changing the proportion of units assigned to vertex versus pixel shading. As an example, if a large quadrilateral is rendered, only a few shader units could be assigned to vertex transformation, while the bulk are given the task of fragment processing. Pinpointing whether the bottleneck is in the vertex or pixel shader stage is less obvious [1961]. Either shader processing as a whole or another stage will still be the bottleneck, however, so we discuss each possibility in turn.

18.2.1 Testing the Application Stage

If the platform being used is supplied with a utility for measuring the workload on the processor(s), that utility can be used to see if your program uses 100% (or near that) of the CPU processing power. If the CPU is in constant use, your program is likely to be *CPU-limited*. This is not always foolproof, since the application may at times be waiting for the GPU to complete a frame. We talk about a program being CPU- or GPU-limited, but the bottleneck can change over the lifetime of a frame.

A smarter way to test for CPU limits is to send down data that causes the GPU to do little or no work. For some systems this can be accomplished by simply using a null driver (a driver that accepts calls but does nothing) instead of a real driver. This effectively sets an upper limit on how fast you can get the entire program to run, because you do not use the graphics hardware nor call the driver, and thus, the application on the CPU is always the bottleneck. By doing this test, you get an idea on how much room for improvement there is for the GPU-based stages not run in the application stage. That said, be aware that using a null driver can also hide any bottleneck due to driver processing itself and communication between CPU and GPU. The driver can often be the cause of a CPU-side bottleneck, a topic we discuss in depth later on.

Another more direct method is to underclock the CPU, if possible [240]. If performance drops in direct proportion to the CPU rate, the application is CPU-bound to at least some extent. This same underclocking approach can be done for GPUs. If the GPU is slowed down and performance decreases, then at least some of the time the application is GPU-bound. These underclocking methods can help identify a bottleneck, but can sometimes cause a stage that was not a bottleneck before to become one. The other option is to overclock, but you did not read that here.

18.2.2 Testing the Geometry Processing Stage

The geometry stage is the most difficult stage to test. This is because if the workload on this stage is changed, then the workload on one or both of the other stages is often changed as well. To avoid this problem, Cebenoyan [240] gives a series of tests working from the rasterizer stages back up the pipeline.

There are two main areas where a bottleneck can occur in the geometry stage: vertex fetching and processing. To see if the bottleneck is due to object data transfer, increase the size of the vertex format. This can be done by sending several extra texture coordinates per vertex, for example. If performance falls, this area is the bottleneck.

Vertex processing is done by the vertex shader. For the vertex shader bottleneck, testing consists of making the shader program longer. Some care has to be taken to make sure the compiler is not optimizing away these additional instructions.

If your pipeline also uses geometry shaders, their performance is a function of output size and program length. If you are using tessellation shaders, again program length affects performance, as well as the tessellation factor. Varying any of these elements, while avoiding changes in the work other stages perform, can help determine whether any are the bottleneck.

18.2.3 Testing the Rasterization Stage

This stage consists of triangle setup and triangle traversal. Shadow map generation, which uses extremely simple pixel shaders, can bottleneck in the rasterizer or merging stages. Though normally rare [1961], it is possible for triangle setup and rasterization to be the bottleneck for small triangles from tessellation or objects such as grass or foliage. However, small triangles can also increase the use of both vertex and pixel shaders. More vertices in a given area clearly increases vertex shader load. Pixel shader load also increases because each triangle is rasterized by a set of 2×2 quads, so the number of pixels outside of each triangle increases [59]. This is sometimes called *quad overshading* (Section 23.1). To find if rasterization is truly the bottleneck, increase the execution time of both the vertex and pixel shaders by increasing their program sizes. If the render time per frame does not increase, then the bottleneck is in the rasterization stage.

18.2.4 Testing the Pixel Processing Stage

The pixel shader program's effect can be tested by changing the screen resolution. If a lower screen resolution causes the frame rate to rise appreciably, the pixel shader is likely to be the bottleneck, at least some of the time. Care has to be taken if a level of detail system is in place. A smaller screen is likely to also simplify the models displayed, lessening the load on the geometry stage.

Lowering the display resolution can also affect costs from triangle traversal, depth testing and blending, and texture access, among other factors. To avoid these factors and isolate the bottleneck, one approach is the same as that taken with vertex shader programs, to add more instructions to see the effect on execution speed. Again, it is important to determine that these additional instructions are not optimized away by the compiler. If frame rendering time increases, the pixel shader is the bottleneck (or at least has become the bottleneck at some point as its execution cost increased). Alternately, the pixel shader could be simplified to a minimum number of instructions, something often difficult to do in a vertex shader. If overall rendering time decreases, a bottleneck has been found. Texture cache misses can also be costly. If replacing a texture with a 1×1 resolution version gives considerably faster performance, then texture memory access is a bottleneck.

Shaders are separate programs that have their own optimization techniques. Persson [1383, 1385] presents several low-level shader optimizations, as well as specifics about how graphics hardware has evolved and how best practices have changed.

18.2.5 Testing the Merging Stage

In this stage depth and stencil tests are made, blending is done, and surviving results are written to buffers. Changing the output bit depth for these buffers is one way to vary the bandwidth costs for this stage and see if it could be the bottleneck. Turning alpha blending on for opaque objects or using other blending modes also affects the amount of memory access and processing performed by raster operations.

This stage can be the bottleneck with post-processing passes, shadows, particle system rendering, and, to a lesser extent, rendering hair and grass, where the vertex and pixel shaders are simple and so do little work.

18.3 Performance Measurements

To optimize we need to measure. Here we discuss different measures of GPU speed. Graphics hardware manufacturers used to present peak rates such as *vertices per second* and *pixels per second*, which were at best hard to reach. Also, since we are dealing with a pipelined system, true performance is not as simple as listing these kinds of numbers. This is because the location of the bottleneck may move from one time to another, and the different pipeline stages interact in different ways during execution.

Because of this complexity, GPUs are marketed in part on their physical properties, such as the number and clock rate of cores, memory size, speed, and bandwidth.

All that said, GPU counters and thread traces, if available, are important diagnostic tools when used well. If the peak performance of some given part is known and the count is lower, then this area is unlikely to be the bottleneck. Some vendors present counter data as a utilization percentage for each stage. These values are over a given time period during which the bottleneck can move, and so are not perfect, but help considerably in finding the bottleneck.

More is better, but even seemingly simple physical measurements can be difficult to compare precisely. For example, the clock rate for the same GPU can vary among IHV partners, as each has its own cooling solution and so overclocks its GPUs to what it considers safe. Even FPS benchmark comparisons on a single system are not always as simple as they sound. NVIDIA's *GPU Boost* [1666] and AMD's *PowerTune* [31] technology are good examples of our dictum "know your architecture." NVIDIA's GPU Boost arose in part because some synthetic benchmarks worked many parts of the GPU's pipeline simultaneously and so pushed power usage to the limit, meaning that NVIDIA had to lower its base clock rate to keep the chip from overheating. Many applications do not exercise all parts of the pipeline to such an extent, so can safely be run at a higher clock rate. The GPU Boost technology tracks GPU power and temperature characteristics and adjusts the clock rate accordingly. AMD and Intel have similar power/performance optimizations with their GPUs. This variability can cause the same benchmark to run at different speeds, depending on the initial temperature of the GPU. To avoid this problem, Microsoft provides a method in DirectX 12 to lock the GPU core clock frequency in order to get stable timings [121]. Examining power states is possible for other APIs, but is more complex [354].

When it comes to measuring performance for CPUs, the trend has been to avoid IPS (*instructions per second*), FLOPS (*floating point operations per second*), gigahertz, and simple short benchmarks. Instead, the preferred method is to measure wall clock times for a range of different, real programs [715], and then compare the running times for these. Following this trend, most independent graphics benchmarks measure the actual frame rate in FPS for several given scenes, and for a variety of different screen resolutions, along with antialiasing and quality settings. Many graphics-heavy games include a benchmarking mode or have one created by a third party, and these benchmarks are commonly used in comparing GPUs.

While FPS is useful shorthand for comparing GPUs running benchmarks, it should be avoided when analyzing a series of frame rates. The problem with FPS is that it is a reciprocal measure, not linear, and so can lead to analysis errors. For example, imagine you find the frame rate of your application at different times is 50, 50, and 20 FPS. If you average these values you get 40 FPS. That value is misleading at best. These frame rates translate to 20, 20, and 50 milliseconds, so the average frame time is 30 ms, which is 33.3 FPS. Similarly, milliseconds are pretty much required when measuring the performance of individual algorithms. For a specific benchmarking situation with a given test and a given machine, it is possible to say that some particular shadow algorithm or post-process effect "costs" 7 FPS, and that the benchmark ran this much slower. However, it is meaningless to generalize this statement, since this value also depends on how much time it takes to process everything else in the frame and because you cannot add together the FPS of different techniques (but you can add times) [1378].

To be able to see the potential effects of pipeline optimization, it is important to measure the total rendering time per frame with double buffering disabled, i.e., in single-buffer mode by turning vertical synchronization off. This is because with double buffering turned on, swapping of the buffers occurs only in synchronization with the frequency of the monitor, as explained in the example in Section 2.1. De Smedt [331] discusses analyzing frame times to find and fix frame stutter problems from spikes in the CPU workload, as well as other useful tips for optimizing performance. Using statistical analysis is usually necessary. It is also possible to use GPU timestamps to learn what is happening within a frame [1167, 1422].

Raw speed is important, but for mobile devices another goal is optimizing power consumption. Purposely lowering the frame rate but keeping the application interactive can significantly extend battery life and have little effect on the user's experience [1200]. Akenine-Möller and Johnsson [25, 840] note that performance per watt is like frames per second, with the same drawbacks as FPS. They argue a more useful measure is joules per task, e.g., joules per pixel.

18.4 Optimization

Once a bottleneck has been located, we want to optimize that stage to boost the performance. In this section we present optimization techniques for the application, geometry, rasterization, and pixel processing stages.

18.4.1 Application Stage

The application stage is optimized by making the code faster and the memory accesses of the program faster or fewer. Here we touch upon some of the key elements of code optimization that apply to CPUs in general.

For code optimization, it is crucial to locate the place in the code where most of the time is spent. A good code profiler is critical in finding these code hot spots, where most time is spent. Optimization efforts are then made in these places. Such locations in the program are often *inner loops*, pieces of the code that are executed many times each frame.

The basic rule of optimization is to try a variety of tactics: Reexamine algorithms, assumptions, and code syntax, trying variants as possible. CPU architecture and compiler performance often limit the user's ability to form an intuition about how to write the fastest code, so question your assumptions and keep an open mind.

One of the first steps is to experiment with the optimization flags for the compiler. There are usually a number of different flags to try. Make few, if any, assumptions about what optimization options to use. For example, setting the compiler to use more aggressive loop optimizations could result in slower code. Also, if possible, try different compilers, as these are optimized in different ways, and some are markedly superior. Your profiler can tell you what effect any change has.

Memory Issues

Years ago the number of arithmetic instructions was the key measure of an algorithm's efficiency; now the key is memory access patterns. Processor speed has increased much more rapidly than the data transfer rate for DRAM, which is limited by the pin count. Between 1980 and 2005, CPU performance doubled about every two years, and DRAM performance doubled about every six [1060]. This problem is known as the *Von Neumann bottleneck* or the *memory wall. Data-oriented design* focuses on cache coherency as a means of optimization.[1]

On modern GPUs, what matters is the distance traveled by data. Speed and power costs are proportional to this distance. Cache access patterns can make up to an orders-of-magnitude performance difference [1206]. A cache is a small fast-memory area that exists because there is usually much coherence in a program, which the cache can exploit. That is, nearby locations in memory tend to be accessed one after another (spatial locality), and code is often accessed sequentially. Also, memory locations tend to be accessed repeatedly (temporal locality), which the cache also exploits [389]. Processor caches are fast to access, second only to registers for speed. Many fast algorithms work to access data as locally (and as little) as possible.

Registers and local caches form one end of the *memory hierarchy*, which extends next to dynamic random access memory (DRAM), then to storage on SSDs and hard disks. At the top are small amounts of fast, expensive memory, at the bottom are large amounts of slow and inexpensive storage. Between each level of the hierarchy the speed drops by some noticeable factor. See Figure 18.1. For example, processor registers are usually accessed in one clock cycle, while L1 cache memory is accessed in a few cycles. Each change in level has an increase in latency in this way. As discussed in Section 3.10, sometimes latency can be hidden by the architecture, but it is always a factor that must be kept in mind.

Bad memory access patterns are difficult to directly detect in a profiler. Good patterns need to be built into the design from the start [1060]. Below is a list of pointers that should be kept in consideration when programming.

- Data that is accessed sequentially in the code should also be stored sequentially in memory. For example, when rendering a triangle mesh, store texture coordinate #0, normal #0, color #0, vertex #0, texture coordinate #1, and normal #1, sequentially in memory if they are accessed in that order. This can also be

---

[1]This area of study should not be confused with *data-driven design*, which can mean any number of things, from the AWK programming language to A/B testing.

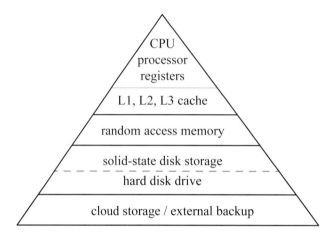

Figure 18.1. The memory hierarchy. Speed and cost decrease as we descend the pyramid.

important on the GPU, as with the post-transform vertex cache (Section 16.4.4). Also see Section 16.4.5 for why storing separate streams of data can be beneficial.

- Avoid pointer indirection, jumps, and function calls (in critical parts of the code), as these may significantly decrease CPU performance. You get pointer indirection when you follow a pointer to another pointer and so on. Modern CPUs try to speculatively execute instructions (branch prediction) and fetch memory (cache prefetching) to keep all their functional units busy running code. These techniques are highly effective when the code flow is consistent in a loop, but fail with branching data structures such as binary trees, linked lists, and graphs; use arrays instead, as possible. McVoy and Staelin [1194] show a code example that follows a linked list through pointers. This causes cache misses for data both before and after, and their example stalls the CPU more than 100 times longer than it takes to follow the pointer (if the cache could provide the address of the pointer). Smits [1668] notes how flattening a pointer-based tree into a list with skip pointers considerably improves hierarchy traversal. Using a van Emde Boas layout is another way to help avoid cache misses—see Section 19.1.4. High-branching trees are often preferable to binary trees because they reduce the tree depth and so reduce the amount of indirection.

- Aligning frequently used data structures to multiples of the cache line size can significantly improve overall performance. For example, 64 byte cache lines are common on Intel and AMD processors [1206]. Compiler options can help, but it is wise to design your data structures with alignment, called *padding*, in mind. Tools such as *VTune* and *CodeAnalyst* for Windows and Linux, *Instruments* for the Mac, and the open-source *Valgrind* for Linux can help identify caching bottlenecks. Alignment can also affect GPU shader performance [331].

- Try different organizations of data structures. For example, Hecker [698] shows how a surprisingly large amount of time was saved by testing a variety of matrix structures for a simple matrix multiplier. An array of structures,

```
struct Vertex {float x,y,z;};
Vertex myvertices[1000];
```

or a structure of arrays,

```
struct VertexChunk {float x[1000],y[1000],z[1000];};
VertexChunk myvertices;
```

may work better for a given architecture. This second structure is better for using SIMD commands, but as the number of vertices goes up, the chance of a cache miss increases. As the array size increases, a hybrid scheme,

```
struct Vertex4 {float x[4],y[4],z[4];};
Vertex4 myvertices[250];
```

may be the best choice.

- It is often better to allocate a large pool of memory at start-up for objects of the same size, and then use your own allocation and free routines for handling the memory of that pool [113, 736]. Libraries such as *Boost* provide pool allocation. A set of contiguous records is more likely to be cache coherent than those created by separate allocations. That said, for languages with garbage collection, such as C# and Java, pools can actually reduce performance.

While not directly related to memory access patterns, it is worthwhile to avoid allocating or freeing memory within the rendering loop. Use pools and allocate scratch space once, and have stacks, arrays, and other structures only grow (using a variable or flags to note which elements should be treated as deleted).

18.4.2 API Calls

Throughout this book we have given advice based on general trends in hardware. For example, indexed vertex buffers objects are usually the fastest way to provide the accelerator with geometric data (Section 16.4.5). This section is about how to best call the graphics API itself. Most graphics APIs have similar architectures, and there are well-established ways of using them efficiently.

Understanding object buffer allocation and storage is basic to efficient rendering [1679]. For a desktop system with a CPU and a separate, discrete GPU, each normally has its own memory. The graphics driver is usually in control of where objects reside, but it can be given hints of where best to store them. A common classification is static versus dynamic buffers. If the buffer's data are changing each frame, using a dynamic buffer, which requires no permanent storage space on the GPU, is preferable. Consoles, laptops with low-power integrated GPUs, and mobile devices usually have unified memory, where the GPU and CPU share the same physical memory. Even in these setups, allocating a resource in the right pool matters. Correctly tagging a resource as CPU-only or GPU-only can still yield benefits. In general, if a memory area has to be accessed by both chips, when one writes to it the other has to invalidate its caches—an expensive operation—to be sure not to get stale data.

If an object is not deforming, or the deformations can be carried out entirely by shader programs (e.g., skinning), then it is profitable to store the data for the object in GPU memory. The unchanging nature of this object can be signaled by storing it as a static buffer. In this way, it does not have to be sent across the bus for every frame rendered, thus avoiding any bottleneck at this stage of the pipeline. The internal memory bandwidth on a GPU is normally much higher than the bus between CPU and GPU.

State Changes

Calling the API has several costs associated with it. On the application side, more calls mean more application time spent, regardless of what the calls actually do. This cost can be minimal or noticeable, and a null driver can help identify it. Query functions that depend on values from the GPU can potentially halve the frame rate due to stalls from synchronization with the CPU [1167]. Here we will delve into optimizing a common graphics operation, preparing the pipeline to draw a mesh. This operation may involve changing the state, e.g., setting the shaders and their uniforms, attaching textures, changing the blend state or the color buffer used, and so on.

A major way for the application to improve performance is to minimize state changes by grouping objects with a similar rendering state. Because the GPU is an extremely complex state machine, perhaps the most complex in computer science, changing the state can be expensive. While a little of the cost can involve the GPU, most of the expense is from the driver's execution on the CPU. If the GPU maps well to the API, the state change cost tends to be predictable, though still significant. If the GPU has a tight power constraint or limited silicon footprint, such as with some mobile devices, or has a hardware bug to work around, the driver may have to perform heroics that cause unexpectedly high costs. State change costs are mostly on the CPU side, in the driver.

One concrete example is how the PowerVR architecture supports blending. In older APIs blending is specified using a fixed-function type of interface. PowerVR's blending is programmable, which means that their driver has to patch the current blend state into the pixel shader [699]. In this case a more advanced design does not map well to the API and so incurs a significant setup cost in the driver. While throughout this chapter we note that hardware architecture and the software running it can affect the importance of various optimizations, this is particularly true for state change costs. Even the specific GPU type and driver release may have an effect. While reading, please imagine the phrase "your mileage may vary" stamped in large red letters over every page of this section.

Everitt and McDonald [451] note that different types of state changes vary considerably in cost, and give some rough idea as to how many times a second a few could be performed on an NVIDIA OpenGL driver. Here is their order, from most expensive to least, as of 2014:

- Render target (framebuffer object), ~60k/sec.

- Shader program, ~300k/sec.

- Blend mode (ROP), such as for transparency.

- Texture bindings, ~1.5M/sec.

- Vertex format.

- Uniform buffer object (UBO) bindings.

- Vertex bindings.

- Uniform updates, ~10M/sec.

This approximate cost order is borne out by others [488, 511, 741]. One even more expensive change is switching between the GPU's rendering mode and its compute shader mode [1971]. Avoiding state changes can be achieved by sorting the objects to be displayed by grouping them by shader, then by textures used, and so on down the cost order. Sorting by state is sometimes called *batching*.

Another strategy is to restructure the objects' data so that more sharing occurs. A common way to minimize texture binding changes is to put several texture images into one large texture or, better yet, a texture array. If the API supports it, bindless textures are another option to avoid state changes (Section 6.2.5). Changing the shader program is usually relatively expensive compared to updating uniforms, so variations within a class of materials may be better represented by a single shader that uses "if" statements. You might also be able to make larger batches by sharing a shader [1609]. Making shaders more complex can also lower performance on the GPU, however. Measuring to see what is effective is the only foolproof way to know.

Making fewer, more effective calls to the graphics API can yield some additional savings. For example, often several uniforms can be defined and set as a group, so binding a single uniform buffer object is considerably more efficient [944]. In DirectX these are called *constant buffers*. Using these properly saves both time per function and time spent error-checking inside each individual API call [331, 613].

Modern drivers often defer setting state until the first draw call encountered. If redundant API calls are made before then, the driver will filter these out, thus avoiding the need to perform a state change. Often a dirty flag is used to note that a state change is needed, so going back to a base state after each draw call may become costly. For example, you may want to assume state X is off by default when you are about to draw an object. One way to achieve this is "Enable(X); Draw(M_1); Disable(X);" then "Enable(X); Draw(M_2); Disable(X);" thus restoring the state after each draw. However, it is also likely to waste significant time setting the state again between the two draw calls, even though no actual state change occurs between them.

Usually the application has higher-level knowledge of when a state change is needed. For example, changing from a "replace" blending mode for opaque surfaces to an "over" mode for transparent ones normally needs to be done once during the frame. Issuing the blend mode before rendering each object can easily be avoided. Galeano [511] shows how ignoring such filtering and issuing unneeded state calls would have cost their WebGL application up to nearly 2 ms/frame. However, if the driver already does such redundancy filtering efficiently, performing this same testing per call in the application can be a waste. How much effort to spend filtering out API calls primarily depends on the underlying driver [443, 488, 741].

Consolidating and Instancing

Using the API efficiently avoids having the CPU be the bottleneck. One other concern with the API is the small batch problem. If ignored, this can be a significant factor affecting performance in modern APIs. Simply put, a few triangle-filled meshes are much more efficient to render than many small, simple ones. This is because there is a fixed-cost overhead associated with each draw call, a cost paid for processing a primitive, regardless of size.

Back in 2003, Wloka [1897] showed that drawing two (relatively small) triangles per batch was a factor of 375 away from the maximum throughput for the GPU tested.[2] Instead of 150 million triangles per second, the rate was 0.4 million, for a 2.7 GHz CPU. For a scene rendered consisting of many small and simple objects, each with only a few triangles, performance is entirely CPU-bound by the API; the GPU has no ability to increase it. That is, the processing time on the CPU for the draw call is greater than the amount of time the GPU takes to actually draw the mesh, so the GPU is starved.

Wloka's rule of thumb is that "You get X batches per frame." This is a maximum number of draw calls you can make per frame, purely due to the CPU being the limiting factor. In 2003, the breakpoint where the API was the bottleneck was about 130 triangles per object. Figure 18.2 shows how the breakpoint rose in 2006 to 510 triangles per mesh. Times have changed. Much work was done to ameliorate this draw call problem, and CPUs became faster. The recommendation back in 2003 was 300 draw calls per frame; in 2012, 16,000 draw calls per frame was one team's ceiling [1381]. That said, even this number is not enough for some complicated scenes. With modern APIs such as DirectX 12, Vulkan, and Metal, the driver cost may itself be minimized—this is one of their major advantages [946]. However, the GPU can have its own fixed costs per mesh.

---

[2]Wloka used *batch* to mean a single mesh rendered with a draw call. This term has widened out over the years, now sometimes meaning a group of separate objects to be rendered that have the same state, as the API overhead can then be reduced.

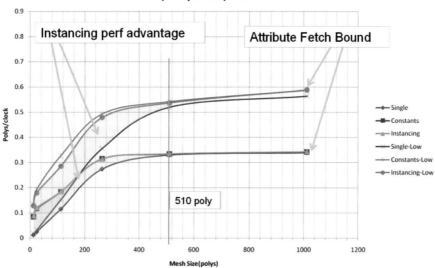

Figure 18.2. Batch performance benchmarks for an Intel Core 2 Duo 2.66 GHz CPU using an NVIDIA G80 GPU, running DirectX 10. Batches of varying size were run and timed under different conditions. The "Low" conditions are for triangles with just the position and a constant-color pixel shader; the other set of tests is for reasonable meshes and shading. "Single" is rendering a single batch many times. "Instancing" reuses the mesh data and puts the per-instance data in a separate stream. "Constants" is a DirectX 10 method where instance data are put in constant memory. As can be seen, small batches hurt all methods, but instancing gives proportionally much faster performance. At a few hundred triangles, performance levels out, as the bottleneck becomes how fast vertices are retrieved from the vertex buffer and caches. *(Graph courtesy of NVIDIA Corporation.)*

One way to reduce the number of draw calls is to consolidate several objects into a single mesh, which needs only one draw call to render the set. For sets of objects that use the same state and are static, at least with respect to one another, consolidation can be done once and the batch can be reused each frame [741, 1322]. Being able to consolidate meshes is another reason to consider avoiding state changes by using a common shader and texture-sharing techniques. The cost savings from consolidation are not just from avoiding API draw calls. There are also savings from the application itself handling fewer objects. However, having batches that are considerably larger than needed can make other algorithms, such as frustum culling, be less effective [1381]. One practice is to use a bounding volume hierarchy to help find and group static objects that are near each other. Another concern with consolidation is selection, since all the static objects are undifferentiated, in one mesh. A typical solution is to store an object identifier at each vertex in the mesh.

The other approach to minimize application processing and API costs is to use some form of *instancing* [232, 741, 1382]. Most APIs support the idea of having an object and drawing it several times in a single call. This is typically done by specifying a base model and providing a separate data structure that holds information about each specific instance desired. Beyond position and orientation, other attributes could be specified per instance, such as leaf colors or curvature due to the wind, or anything else that could be used by shader programs to affect the model. Lush jungle scenes can be created by liberal use of instancing. See Figure 18.3. Crowd scenes are a good fit for instancing, with each character appearing unique by selecting different body parts from a set of choices. Further variation can be added by random coloring and decals. Instancing can also be combined with level of detail techniques [122, 1107, 1108]. See Figure 18.4 for an example.

A concept that combines consolidation and instancing is called *merge-instancing*, where a consolidated mesh contains objects that may in turn be instanced [146, 1382].

In theory, the geometry shader can be used for instancing, as it can create duplicate data of an incoming mesh. In practice, if many instances are needed, this method can be slower than using instancing API commands. The intent of the geometry shader is to perform local, small-scale amplification of data [1827]. In addition, for some architectures, such as Mali's tile-based renderer, the geometry shader is implemented in software. To quote Mali's best practices guide [69], "Find a better solution to your problem. Geometry shaders are not your solution."

18.4.3 Geometry Stage

The geometry stage is responsible for transforms, per-vertex lighting, clipping, projection, and screen mapping. Other chapters discuss ways to reduce the amount of data flowing through the pipeline. Efficient triangle mesh storage, model simplification, and vertex data compression (Chapter 16) all save both processing time and memory. Techniques such as frustum and occlusion culling (Chapter 19) avoid sending the full primitive itself down the pipeline. Adding such large-scale techniques on the CPU can entirely change performance characteristics of the application and so are worth trying early on in development. On the GPU such techniques are less common. One notable example is how the compute shader can be used to perform various types of culling [1883, 1884].

The effect of elements of lighting can be computed per vertex, per pixel (in the pixel processing stage), or both. Lighting computations can be optimized in several ways. First, the types of light sources being used should be considered. Is lighting needed for all triangles? Sometimes a model only requires texturing, texturing with colors at the vertices, or simply colors at the vertices.

If light sources are static with respect to geometry, then the diffuse and ambient lighting can be precomputed and stored as colors at the vertices. Doing so is often referred to as "baking" on the lighting. A more elaborate form of prelighting is to precompute the diffuse global illumination in a scene (Section 11.5.1). Such illumination can be stored as colors or intensities at the vertices or as light maps.

Figure 18.3. Vegetation instancing. All objects the same color in the lower image are rendered in a single draw call [1869]. *(Image from CryEngine1, courtesy of Crytek.)*

Figure 18.4. Crowd scene. Using instancing minimizes the number of draw calls needed. Level of detail techniques are also used, such as rendering impostors for distant models [1107, 1108]. *(Image courtesy of Jonathan Maïm, Barbara Yersin, Mireille Clavien, and Daniel Thalmann.)*

For forward rendering systems the number of light sources influences the performance of the geometry stage. More light sources means more computation. A common way to lessen work is to disable or trim down local lighting and instead use an environment map (Section 10.5).

18.4.4 Rasterization Stage

Rasterization can be optimized in a few ways. For closed (solid) objects and for objects that will never show their backfaces (for example, the back side of a wall in a room), backface culling should be turned on (Section 19.3). This reduces the number of triangles to be rasterized by about half and so reduces the load on triangle traversal. In addition, this can be particularly beneficial when the pixel shading computation is expensive, as backfaces are then never shaded.

18.4.5 Pixel Processing Stage

Optimizing pixel processing is often profitable, since usually there are many more pixels to shade than vertices. There are notable exceptions. Vertices always have to be processed, even if a draw ends up not generating any visible pixels. Ineffective culling in the rendering engine might make the vertex shading cost exceed pixel shading. Too small a triangle not only causes more vertex shading evaluation than may be needed, but also can create more partial-covered quads that cause additional work. More important, textured meshes that cover only a few pixels often have low thread occupancy rates. As discussed in Section 3.10, there is a large time cost in sampling a texture, which the GPU hides by switching to execute shader programs on other fragments, returning later when the texture data has been fetched. Low occupancy can result in poor latency hiding. Complex shaders that use a high number of registers can also lead to low occupancy by allowing fewer threads to be available at one time (Section 23.3). This condition is referred to as high *register pressure*. There are other subtleties, e.g., frequent switching to other warps may cause more cache misses. Wronski [1911, 1914] discusses various occupancy problems and solutions.

To begin, use native texture and pixel formats, i.e., use the formats that the graphics accelerator uses internally, to avoid a possible expensive transform from one format to another [278]. Two other texture-related techniques are loading only the mipmap levels needed (Section 19.10.1) and using texture compression (Section 6.2.6). As usual, smaller and fewer textures mean less memory used, which in turn means lower transfer and access times. Texture compression also can improve cache performance, since the same amount of cache memory is occupied by more pixels.

One level of detail technique is to use different pixel shader programs, depending on the distance of the object from the viewer. For example, with three flying saucer models in a scene, the closest might have an elaborate bump map for surface details that the two farther away do not need. In addition, the farthest saucer might have specular highlighting simplified or removed altogether, both to simplify computations and to reduce "fireflies," i.e., sparkle artifacts from undersampling. Using a color per vertex on simplified models can give the additional benefit that no state change is needed due to the texture changing.

The pixel shader is invoked only if the fragment is visible at the time the triangle is rasterized. The GPU's early-z test (Section 23.7) checks the z-depth of the fragment against the z-buffer. If not visible, the fragment is discarded without any pixel shader evaluation, saving considerable time. While the z-depth can be modified by the pixel shader, doing so means that early-z testing cannot be performed.

To understand the behavior of a program, and especially the load on the pixel processing stage, it is useful to visualize the depth complexity, which is the number of surfaces that cover a pixel. Figure 18.5 shows an example. One simple method of generating a depth complexity image is to use a call like OpenGL's glBlendFunc(GL_ONE,GL_ONE), with z-buffering disabled. First, the image is cleared to black. All objects in the scene are then rendered with the color $(1/255, 1/255, 1/255)$. The effect of the blend function setting is that for each primitive rendered, the values of the written pixels will increase by one intensity level. A pixel with a depth complexity of 0 is then black and a pixel of depth complexity 255 is full white, $(255, 255, 255)$.

The amount of *pixel overdraw* is related to how many surfaces actually were rendered. The number of times the pixel shader is evaluated can be found by rendering the scene again, but with the z-buffer enabled. Overdraw is the amount of effort

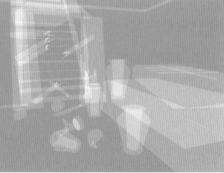

Figure 18.5. The depth complexity of the scene on the left is shown on the right. *(Images created using NVPerfHUD from NVIDIA Corporation.)*

wasted computing a shade for a surface that is then hidden by a later pixel shader invocation. An advantage of deferred rendering (Section 20.1), and ray tracing for that matter, is that shading is performed after all visibility computations are performed.

Say two triangles cover a pixel, so the depth complexity is two. If the farther triangle is drawn first, the nearer triangle overdraws it, and the amount of overdraw is one. If the nearer is drawn first, the farther triangle fails the depth test and is not drawn, so there is no overdraw. For a random set of opaque triangles covering a pixel, the average number of draws is the *harmonic series* [296]:

$$H(n) = 1 + \frac{1}{2} + \frac{1}{3} + \ldots + \frac{1}{n}. \tag{18.1}$$

The logic behind this is that the first triangle rendered is one draw. The second triangle is either in front or behind the first, a 50/50 chance. The third triangle can have one of three positions compared to the first two, giving one chance in three of it being frontmost. As n goes to infinity,

$$\lim_{n \to \infty} H(n) = \ln(n) + \gamma, \tag{18.2}$$

where $\gamma = 0.57721\ldots$ is the Euler-Mascheroni constant. Overdraw rises rapidly when depth complexity is low, but quickly tapers off. For example, a depth complexity of 4 gives an average of 2.08 draws, 11 gives 3.02 draws, but it takes a depth complexity of 12,367 to reach an average of 10.00 draws.

So, overdraw is not necessarily as bad as it seems, but we would still like to minimize it, without costing too much CPU time. Roughly sorting and then drawing the opaque objects in a scene in an approximate front-to-back order (near to far) is a common way to reduce overdraw [240, 443, 488, 511]. Occluded objects that are drawn later will not write to the color or z-buffers (i.e., overdraw is reduced). Also, the pixel fragment can be rejected by occlusion culling hardware before even reaching

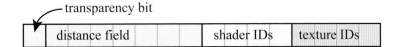

Figure 18.6. Example sort key for draw order. Keys are sorted from low to high. Setting the transparency bit means that the object is transparent, as transparent objects are to be rendered after all opaque objects. The object's distance from the camera is stored as an integer with low precision. For transparent objects the distance is reversed or negated, since we want objects in a back-to-front order. Shaders are each given a unique identification number, as are textures.

the pixel shader program (Section 23.5). Sorting can be accomplished by any number of methods. An explicit sort based on the distance along the view direction of the centroids of all opaque objects is one simple technique. If a bounding volume hierarchy or other spatial structure is already in use for frustum culling, we can choose the closer child to be traversed first, on down the hierarchy.

Another technique can be useful for surfaces with complex pixel shader programs. Performing a z-prepass renders the geometry to just the z-buffer first, then the whole scene is rendered normally [643]. This eliminates all overdraw shader evaluations, but at the cost of an entire separate run through all the geometry. Pettineo [1405] writes that the primary reason his team used a depth prepass in their video game was to avoid overdraw. However, drawing in a rough front-to-back order may provide much of the same benefit without the need for this extra work. A hybrid approach is to identify and first draw just a few large, simple occluders likely to give the most benefit [1768]. As McGuire [1177] notes, a full-draw prepass did not help performance for his particular system. Measuring is the only way to know which technique, if any, is most effective for your application.

Earlier we recommended grouping by shader and texture to minimize state changes; here we talk about rendering objects sorted by distance. These two goals usually give different object draw orders and so conflict with each other. There is always some ideal draw order for a given scene and viewpoint, but this is difficult to find in advance. Hybrid schemes are possible, e.g., sorting nearby objects by depth and sorting everything else by material [1433]. A common, flexible solution [438, 488, 511, 1434, 1882] is to create a sorting key for each object that encapsulates all the relevant criteria by assigning each a set of bits. See Figure 18.6.

We can choose to favor sorting by distance, but by limiting the number of bits storing the depth, we can allow grouping by shader to become relevant for objects in a given range of distances. It is not uncommon to sort draws into even as few as two or three depth partitions. If some objects have the same depth and use the same shader, then the texture identifier is used to sort the objects, which then groups objects with the same texture together.

This is a simple example and is situational, e.g., the rendering engine may itself keep opaque and transparent objects separate so that the transparency bit is not necessary. The number of bits for the other fields certainly varies with the maximum

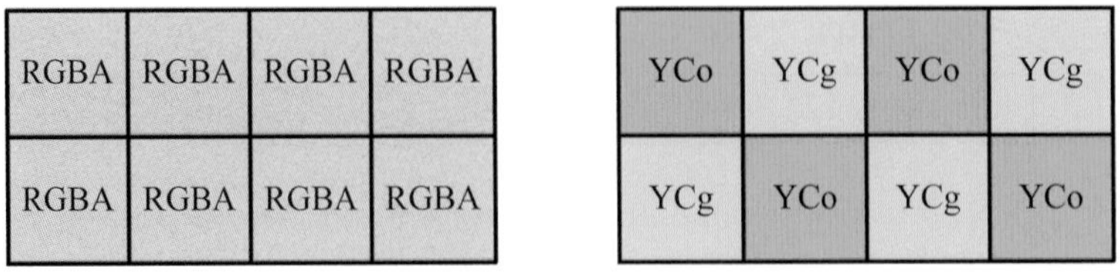

Figure 18.7. Left: 4×2 pixels, each storing four color components (RGBA). Right: an alternative representation where each pixel stores the luminance, Y, and either the first (C_o) or the second (C_g) chrominance component, in a checkerboard pattern.

number of shaders and textures expected. Other fields may be added or substituted in, such as one for blend state and another for z-buffer read and write. Most important of all is the architecture. For example, some tile-based GPU renderers on mobile devices do not gain anything from sorting front to back, so state sorting is the only important element to optimize [1609]. The main idea here is that putting all attributes into a single integer key lets you perform an efficient sort, thus minimizing overdraw and state changes as possible.

18.4.6 Framebuffer Techniques

Rendering a scene often incurs a vast amount of accesses to the framebuffer and many pixel shader executions. To reduce the pressure on the cache hierarchy, a common piece of advice is to reduce the storage size of each pixel of the framebuffer. While a 16-bit floating point value per color channel provides more accuracy, an 8-bit value is half the size, which means faster accesses assuming that the accuracy is sufficient. The chrominance is often subsampled in many image and video compression schemes, such as JPEG and MPEG. This can often be done with negligible visual effect due to fact that the human visual system is more sensitive to luminance than to chrominance. For example, the Frostbite game engine [1877] uses this idea of *chroma subsampling* to reduce bandwidth costs for post-processing their 16-bits-per-channel images.

Mavridis and Papaioannou [1144] propose that the lossy YCoCg transform, described on page 197, is used to achieve a similar effect for the color buffer during rasterization. Their pixel layout is shown in Figure 18.7. Compared to RGBA, this halves the color buffer storage requirements (assuming A is not needed) and often increases performance, depending on architecture. Since each pixel has only one of the chrominance components, a reconstruction filter is needed to infer a full YCoCg per pixel before converting back to RGB before display. For a pixel missing the C_o-value, for example, the average of the four closest C_o-values can be used. However, this does not reconstruct edges as well as desired. Therefore, a simple edge-aware filter is used instead, which is implemented as

$$C_o = \sum_{i=0}^{3} w_i C_{o,i}, \quad \text{where } w_i = 1.0 - \text{step}(t - |L_i - L|), \tag{18.3}$$

for a pixel that does not have C_o, where $C_{o,i}$ and L_i are the values to the left, right, top, and bottom of the current pixel, L is the luminance of the current pixel, and t is a threshold value for edge detection. Mavridis and Papaioannou used $t = 30/255$. The step(x) function is 0 if $x < 0$, and 1 otherwise. Hence, the filter weights w_i are either 0 or 1, where they are zero if the luminance gradient, $|L_i - L|$, is greater than t. A WebGL demo with source code is available online [1144].

Because of the continuing increase in display resolutions and the shader execution cost savings, using a checkerboard pattern for rendering has been used in several systems [231, 415, 836, 1885]. For virtual reality applications, Vlachos [1824] uses a checkerboard pattern for pixels around the periphery of the view, and Answer [59] reduces each 2×2 quad by one to three samples.

18.4.7 Merging Stage

Make sure to enable blend modes only when useful. In theory "over" compositing could be set for every triangle, opaque or transparent, since opaque surfaces using "over" will fully overwrite the value in the pixel. However, this is more costly than a simple "replace" raster operation, so tracking objects with cutout texturing and materials with transparency is worthwhile. Alternately, there are some raster operations that cost nothing extra. For example, when the z-buffer is being used, on some systems it costs no additional time to also access the stencil buffer. This is because the 8-bit stencil buffer value is stored in the same word as the 24-bit z-depth value [890].

Thinking through when various buffers need to be used or cleared is worthwhile. Since GPUs have fast clear mechanisms (Section 23.5), the recommendation is to always clear both color and depth buffers since that increases the efficiency of memory transfers for these buffers.

You should normally avoid reading back render targets from the GPU to the CPU if you can help it. Any framebuffer access by the CPU causes the entire GPU pipeline to be flushed before the rendering is returned, losing all parallelism there [1167, 1609].

If you do find that the merging stage is your bottleneck, you may need to rethink your approach. Can you use lower-precision output targets, perhaps through compression? Is there any way to reorder your algorithm to mitigate the stress on this stage? For shadows, are there ways to cache and reuse parts where nothing has moved?

In this section we have discussed ways of using each stage well by searching for bottlenecks and tuning performance. That said, be aware of the dangers of repeatedly optimizing an algorithm when you may be better served by using an entirely different technique.

18.5 Multiprocessing

Traditional APIs have evolved toward issuing fewer calls that each do more [443, 451]. The new generation of APIs—DirectX 12, Vulkan, Metal—take a different strategy.

For these APIs the drivers are streamlined and minimal, with much of the complexity and responsibility for validating the state shifted to the calling application, as well as memory allocation and other functions [249, 1438, 1826]. This redesign in good part was done to minimize draw call and state change overhead, which comes from having to map older APIs to modern GPUs. The other element these new APIs encourage is using multiple CPU processors to call the API.

Around 2003 the trend of ever-rising clock speeds for CPUs flattened out at around 3.4 GHz, due to several physical issues such as heat dissipation and power consumption [1725]. These limits gave rise to multiprocessing CPUs, where instead of higher clock rates, more CPUs were put in a single chip. In fact, many small cores provide the best performance per unit area [75], which is the major reason why GPUs themselves are so effective. Creating efficient and reliable programs that exploit concurrency has been the challenge ever since. In this section we will cover the basic concepts of efficient multiprocessing on CPU cores, at the end discussing how graphics APIs have evolved to enable more concurrency within the driver itself.

Multiprocessor computers can be broadly classified into *message-passing* architectures and *shared memory multiprocessors*. In message-passing designs, each processor has its own memory area, and messages are sent between the processors to communicate results. These are not common in real-time rendering. Shared memory multiprocessors are just as they sound; all processors share a logical address space of memory among themselves. Most popular multiprocessor systems use shared memory, and most of these have a *symmetric multiprocessing* (SMP) design. SMP means that all the processors are identical. A multicore PC system is an example of a symmetric multiprocessing architecture.

Here, we will present two general methods for using multiple processors for real-time graphics. The first method—*multiprocessor pipelining*, also called temporal parallelism—will be covered in more detail than the second—*parallel processing*, also called spatial parallelism. These two methods are illustrated in Figure 18.8. These two types of parallelism are then brought together with *task-based multiprocessing*, where the application creates jobs that can each be picked up and processed by an individual core.

18.5.1 Multiprocessor Pipelining

As we have seen, pipelining is a method for speeding up execution by dividing a job into certain pipeline stages that are executed in parallel. The result from one pipeline stage is passed on to the next. The ideal speedup is n times for n pipeline stages, and the slowest stage (the bottleneck) determines the actual speedup. Up to this point, we have seen pipelining used with a single CPU core and a GPU to run the application, geometry processing, rasterization, and pixel processing in parallel. Pipelining can also be used when multiple processors are available on the host, and in these cases, it is called *multiprocess pipelining* or *software pipelining*.

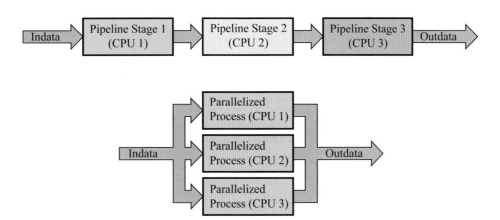

Figure 18.8. Two different ways of using multiple processors. At the top we show how three processors (CPUs) are used in a *multiprocessor pipeline*, and at the bottom we show *parallel* execution on three CPUs. One of the differences between these two implementations is that lower latency can be achieved if the configuration at the bottom is used. On the other hand, it may be easier to use a multiprocessor pipeline. The ideal speedup for both of these configurations is linear, i.e., using n CPUs would give a speedup of n times.

Here we describe one type of software pipelining. Endless variations are possible and the method should be adapted to the particular application. In this example, the application stage is divided into three stages [1508]: APP, CULL, and DRAW. This is coarse-grained pipelining, which means that each stage is relatively long. The APP stage is the first stage in the pipeline and therefore controls the others. It is in this stage that the application programmer can put in additional code that does, for example, collision detection. This stage also updates the viewpoint. The CULL stage can perform:

- Traversal and hierarchical view frustum culling on a scene graph (Section 19.4).

- Level of detail selection (Section 19.9).

- State sorting, as discussed in Section 18.4.5.

- Finally (and always performed), generation of a simple list of all objects that should be rendered.

The DRAW stage takes the list from the CULL stage and issues all graphics calls in this list. This means that it simply walks through the list and feeds the GPU. Figure 18.9 shows some examples of how this pipeline can be used.

If one processor core is available, then all three stages are run on that core. If two CPU cores are available, then APP and CULL can be executed on one core and DRAW on the other. Another configuration would be to execute APP on one core and CULL

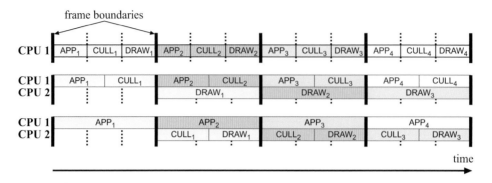

Figure 18.9. Different configurations for a multiprocessor pipeline. The thick lines represent synchronization between the stages, and the subscripts represent the frame number. At the top, a single CPU pipeline is shown. In the middle and at the bottom are shown two different pipeline subdivisions using two CPUs. The middle has one pipeline stage for **APP** and **CULL** and one pipeline stage for **DRAW**. This is a suitable subdivision if **DRAW** has much more work to do than the others. At the bottom, **APP** has one pipeline stage and the other two have another. This is suitable if **APP** has much more work than the others. Note that the bottom two configurations have more time for the **APP**, **CULL**, and **DRAW** stages.

and **DRAW** on the other. Which is the best depends on the workloads for the different stages. Finally, if the host has three cores available, then each stage can be executed on a separate core. This possibility is shown in Figure 18.10.

The advantage of this technique is that the throughput, i.e., the rendering speed, increases. The downside is that, compared to parallel processing, the latency is greater. Latency, or temporal delay, is the time it takes from the polling of the user's actions to the final image [1849]. This should not be confused with frame rate, which is the number of frames displayed per second. For example, say the user is using an unteth-

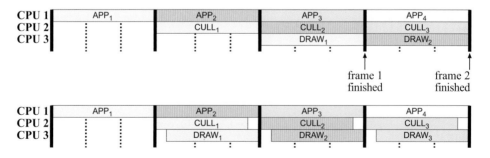

Figure 18.10. At the top, a three-stage pipeline is shown. In comparison to the configurations in Figure 18.9, this configuration has more time for each pipeline stage. The bottom illustration shows a way to reduce the latency: The **CULL** and the **DRAW** are overlapped with FIFO buffering in between.

ered head-mounted display. The determination of the head's position may take 10 milliseconds to reach the CPU, then it takes 15 milliseconds to render the frame. The latency is then 25 milliseconds from initial input to display. Even though the frame rate is 66.7 Hz (1/0.015 seconds), if no location prediction or other compensation is performed, interactivity can feel sluggish because of the delay in sending the position changes to the CPU. Ignoring any delay due to user interaction (which is a constant under both systems), multiprocessing has more latency than parallel processing because it uses a pipeline. As is discussed in detail in the next section, parallel processing breaks up the frame's work into pieces that are run concurrently.

In comparison to using a single CPU on the host, multiprocessor pipelining gives a higher frame rate and the latency is about the same or a little greater due to the cost of synchronization. The latency increases with the number of stages in the pipeline. For a well-balanced application the speedup is n times for n CPUs.

One technique for reducing the latency is to update the viewpoint and other latency-critical parameters at the end of the APP stage [1508]. This reduces the latency by (approximately) one frame. Another way to reduce latency is to execute CULL and DRAW overlapped. This means that the result from CULL is sent over to DRAW as soon as anything is ready for rendering. For this to work, there has to be some buffering, typically a FIFO, between those stages. The stages are stalled on empty and full conditions; i.e., when the buffer is full, then CULL has to stall, and when the buffer is empty, DRAW has to starve. The disadvantage is that techniques such as state sorting cannot be used to the same extent, since primitives have to be rendered as soon as they have been processed by CULL. This latency reduction technique is visualized in Figure 18.10.

The pipeline in this figure uses a maximum of three CPUs, and the stages have certain tasks. However, this technique is in no way limited to this configuration—rather, you can use any number of CPUs and divide the work in any way you want. The key is to make a smart division of the entire job to be done so that the pipeline tends to be balanced. The multiprocessor pipelining technique requires a minimum of synchronization in that it needs to synchronize only when switching frames. Additional processors can also be used for parallel processing, which needs more frequent synchronization.

18.5.2 Parallel Processing

A major disadvantage of using a multiprocessor pipeline technique is that the latency tends to increase. For some applications, such as flight simulators, first person shooters, and virtual reality rendering, this is not acceptable. When moving the viewpoint, you usually want instant (next-frame) response but when the latency is long this will not happen. That said, it all depends. If multiprocessing raised the frame rate from 30 FPS with 1 frame latency to 60 FPS with 2 frames latency, the extra frame delay would have no perceptible difference.

If multiple processors are available, one can also try to run sections of the code concurrently, which may result in shorter latency. To do this, the program's tasks must possess the characteristics of *parallelism*. There are several different methods for parallelizing an algorithm. Assume that n processors are available. Using static assignment [313], the total work package, such as the traversal of an acceleration structure, is divided into n work packages. Each processor then takes care of a work package, and all processors execute their work packages in parallel. When all processors have completed their work packages, it may be necessary to merge the results from the processors. For this to work, the workload must be highly predictable.

When this is not the case, dynamic assignment algorithms that adapt to different workloads may be used [313]. These use one or more work pools. When jobs are generated, they are put into the work pools. CPUs can then fetch one or more jobs from the queue when they have finished their current job. Care must be taken so that only one CPU can fetch a particular job, and so that the overhead in maintaining the queue does not damage performance. Larger jobs mean that the overhead for maintaining the queue becomes less of a problem, but, on the other hand, if the jobs are too large, then performance may degrade due to imbalance in the system—i.e., one or more CPUs may starve.

As for the multiprocessor pipeline, the ideal speedup for a parallel program running on n processors would be n times. This is called *linear speedup*. Even though linear speedup rarely happens, actual results can sometimes be close to it.

In Figure 18.8 on page 807, both a multiprocessor pipeline and a parallel processing system with three CPUs are shown. Temporarily assume that these should do the same amount of work for each frame and that both configurations achieve linear speedup. This means that the execution will run three times faster in comparison to serial execution (i.e., on a single CPU). Furthermore, we assume that the total amount of work per frame takes 30 ms, which would mean that the maximum frame rate on a single CPU would be $1/0.03 \approx 33$ frames per second.

The multiprocessor pipeline would (ideally) divide the work into three equal-sized work packages and let each of the CPUs be responsible for one work package. Each work package should then take 10 ms to complete. If we follow the work flow through the pipeline, we will see that the first CPU in the pipeline does work for 10 ms (i.e., one third of the job) and then sends it on to the next CPU. The first CPU then starts working on the first part of the next frame. When a frame is finally finished, it has taken 30 ms for it to complete, but since the work has been done in parallel in the pipeline, one frame will be finished every 10 ms. So, the latency is 30 ms, and the speedup is a factor of three (30/10), resulting in 100 frames per second.

A parallel version of the same program would also divide the jobs into three work packages, but these three packages will execute at the same time on the three CPUs. This means that the latency will be 10 ms, and the work for one frame will also take 10 ms. The conclusion is that the latency is much shorter when using parallel processing than when using a multiprocessor pipeline.

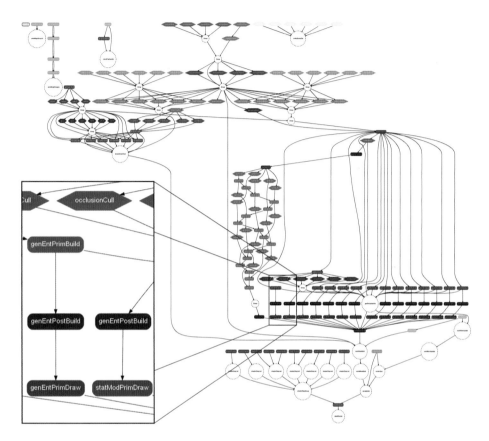

Figure 18.11. Frostbite CPU job graph, with one small zoomed-in part inset [45]. *(Figure courtesy of Johan Andersson—Electronic Arts.)*

18.5.3 Task-Based Multiprocessing

Knowing about pipelining and parallel processing techniques, it is natural to combine both in a single system. If there are only a few processors available, it might make sense to have a simple system of explicitly assigning systems to a particular core. However, given the large number of cores on many CPUs, the trend has been to use task-based multiprocessing. Just as one can create several tasks (also called *jobs*) for a process that can be parallelized, this idea can be broadened to include pipelining. Any task generated by any core is put into the work pool as it is generated. Any free processor gets a task to work on.

One way to convert to multiprocessing is to take an application's workflow and determine which systems are dependent on others. See Figure 18.11.

Having a processor stall while waiting for synchronization means a task-based version of the application could even become slower due to this cost and the overhead for task management [1854]. However, many programs and algorithms do have a large number of tasks that can be performed at the same time and can therefore benefit.

The next step is to determine what parts of each system can be decomposed into tasks. Characteristics of a piece of code that is a good candidate to become a task include [45, 1060, 1854]:

• The task has a well-defined input and output.

• The task is independent and stateless when run, and always completes.

• It is not so large a task that it often becomes the only process running.

Languages such as C++11 have facilities built into them for multithreading [1445]. On Intel-compatible systems, Intel's open-source *Threading Building Blocks* (TBB) is an efficient library that simplifies task generation, pooling, and synchronization [92].

Having the application create its own sets of tasks that are multiprocessed, such as simulation, collision detection, occlusion testing, and path planning, is a given when performance is critical [45, 92, 1445, 1477, 1854]. We note here again that there are also times when the GPU cores tend to be idle. For example, these are usually underused during shadow map generation or a depth prepass. During such idle times, compute shaders can be applied to other tasks [1313, 1884]. Depending on the architecture, API, and content, it is sometimes the case that the rendering pipeline cannot keep all the shaders busy, meaning that there is always some pool available for compute shading. We will not tackle the topic of optimizing these, as Lauritzen makes a convincing argument that writing fast and portable compute shaders is not possible, due to hardware differences and language limitations [993]. How to optimize the core rendering pipeline itself is the subject of the next section.

18.5.4 Graphics API Multiprocessing Support

Parallel processing often does not map to hardware constraints. For example, DirectX 10 and earlier allow only one thread to access the graphics driver at a time, so parallel processing for the actual draw stage is more difficult [1477].

There are two operations in a graphics driver that can potentially use multiple processors: resource creation and render-related calls. Creating resources such as textures and buffers can be purely CPU-side operations and so are naturally parallelizable. That said, creation and deletion can also be blocking tasks, as they might trigger operations on the GPU or need a particular device context. In any case, older APIs were created before consumer-level multiprocessing CPUs existed, so needed to be rewritten to support such concurrency.

A key construct used is the *command buffer* or *command list*, which harks back to an old OpenGL concept called the *display list*. A command buffer (CB) is a list of API state change and draw calls. Such lists can be created, stored, and replayed as

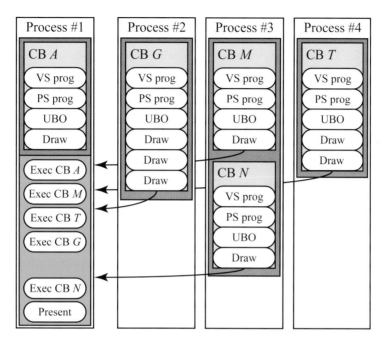

Figure 18.12. Command buffers. Each processor uses its deferred context, shown in orange, to create and populate one or more command buffers, shown in blue. Each command buffer is sent to Process #1, which executes these as desired, using its immediate context, shown in green. Process #1 can do other operations while waiting for command buffer N from Process #3. *(After Zink et al. [1971].)*

desired. They may also be combined to form longer command buffers. Only a single CPU processor communicates with the GPU via the driver and so can send it a CB for execution. However, every processor (including this single processor) can create or concatenate stored command buffers in parallel.

In DirectX 11, for example, the processor that communicates with the driver sends its render calls to what is called the *immediate context*. The other processors each use a *deferred context* to generate command buffers. As the name implies, these are not directly sent to the driver. Instead, these are sent to the immediate context for rendering. See Figure 18.12. Alternately, a command buffer can be sent to another deferred context, which inserts it into its own CB. Beyond sending a command buffer to the driver for execution, the main operations that the immediate context can perform that the deferred cannot are GPU queries and readbacks. Otherwise, command buffer management looks the same from either type of context.

An advantage of command buffers, and their predecessor, display lists, is that they can be stored and replayed. Command buffers are not fully bound when created, which aids in their reuse. For example, say a CB contains a view matrix. The camera moves, so the view matrix changes. However, the view matrix is stored in a constant buffer. The constant buffer's contents are not stored in the CB, only the reference to them. The contents of the constant buffer can be changed without having to rebuild the CB. Determining how best to maximize parallelism involves choosing a suitable granularity—per view, per object, per material—to create, store, and combine command buffers [1971].

Such multithreading draw systems existed for years before command buffers were made a part of modern APIs [1152, 1349, 1552, 1554]. API support makes the process simpler and lets more tools work with the system created. However, command lists do have creation and memory costs associated with them. Also, the expense of mapping an API's state settings to the underlying GPU is still a costly operation with DirectX 11 and OpenGL, as discussed in Section 18.4.2. Within these systems command buffers can help when the application is the bottleneck, but can be detrimental when the driver is.

Certain semantics in these earlier APIs did not allow the driver to parallelize various operations, which helped motivate the development of Vulkan, DirectX 12, and Metal. A thin draw submission interface that maps well to modern GPUs minimizes the driver costs of these newer APIs. Command buffer management, memory allocation, and synchronization decisions become the responsibility of the application instead of the driver. In addition, command buffers with these newer APIs are validated once when formed, so repeated playback has less overhead than those used with earlier APIs such as DirectX 11. All these elements combine to improve API efficiency, allow multiprocessing, and lessen the chances that the driver is the bottleneck.

Further Reading and Resources

Mobile devices can have a different balance of where time is spent, especially if they use a tile-based architecture. Merry [1200] discusses these costs and how to use this type of GPU effectively. Pranckevičius and Zioma [1433] provide an in-depth presentation on many aspects of optimizing for mobile devices. McCaffrey [1156] compares mobile versus desktop architectures and performance characteristics. Pixel shading is often the largest cost on mobile GPUs. Sathe [1545] and Etuaho [443] discuss shader precision issues and optimization on mobile devices.

For the desktop, Wiesendanger [1882] gives a thorough walkthrough of a modern game engine's architecture. O'Donnell [1313] presents the benefits of a graph-based rendering system. Zink et al. [1971] discuss DirectX 11 in depth. De Smedt [331] provides guidance as to the common hotspots found in video games, including optimizations for DirectX 11 and 12, for multiple-GPU configurations, and for virtual reality. Coombes [291] gives a rundown of DirectX 12 best practices, and Kubisch [946] provides a guide for when to use Vulkan. There are numerous presentations about porting from older APIs to DirectX 12 and Vulkan [249, 536, 699, 1438]. By the time you read this, there will undoubtedly be more. Check IHV developer sites, such as NVIDIA, AMD, and Intel; the Khronos Group; and the web at large, as well as this book's website.

Though a little dated, Cebenoyan's article [240] is still relevant. It gives an overview of how to find the bottleneck and techniques to improve efficiency. Some popular optimization guides for C++ are Fog's [476] and Isensee's [801], free on the web. Hughes et al. [783] provide a modern, in-depth discussion of how to use trace tools and GPUView to analyze where bottlenecks occur. Though focused on virtual reality systems, the techniques discussed are applicable to any Windows-based machine.

Sutter [1725] discusses how CPU clock rates leveled out and multiprocessor chipsets arose. For more on why this change occurred and for information on how chips are designed, see the in-depth report by Asanovic et al. [75]. Foley [478] discusses various forms of parallelism in the context of graphics application development. *Game Engine Gems 2* [1024] has several articles on programming multithreaded elements for game engines. Preshing [1445] explains how Ubisoft uses multithreading and gives specifics on using C++11's threading support. Tatarchuk [1749, 1750] gives two detailed presentations on the multithreaded architecture and shading pipeline used for the game *Destiny*.

Chapter 19
Acceleration Algorithms

"*Now here, you see, it takes all the running you can do to keep in the same place. If you want to get somewhere else, you must run at least twice as fast as that!*"

—Lewis Carroll

One of the great myths concerning computers is that one day we will have enough processing power. Even in a relatively simple application such as word processing, we find that additional power can be applied to all sorts of features, such as on-the-fly spell and grammar checking, antialiased text display, and dictation.

In real-time rendering, we have at least four performance goals: more frames per second, higher resolution and sampling rates, more realistic materials and lighting, and increased geometrical complexity. A speed of 60–90 frames per second is generally considered fast enough. Even with motion blurring, which can lower the frame rate needed for image quality, a fast rate is still needed to minimize latency when interacting with a scene [1849].

Today, we have 4k displays with 3840×2160 resolution; 8k displays with 7680×4320 resolution exist, but are not common yet. A 4k display typically has around 140–150 dots per inch (DPI), sometimes called pixels per inch (PPI). Mobile phone displays have values ranging on up to around 400 DPI. A resolution of 1200 DPI, 64 times the number of pixels of a 4k display, is offered by many printer companies today. Even with a limit on screen resolution, antialiasing increases the number of samples needed for generating high-quality images. As discussed in Section 23.6, the number of bits per color channel can also be increased, which drives the need for higher-precision (and therefore more costly) computations.

As previous chapters have shown, describing and evaluating an object's material can be computationally complex. Modeling the interplay of light and surface can soak up an arbitrarily high amount of computing power. This is true because an image should ultimately be formed by the contributions of light traveling down a limitless number of paths from an illumination source to the eye.

Frame rate, resolution, and shading can always be made more complex, but there is some sense of diminishing returns to increasing any of these. However, there is no

Figure 19.1. A "reduced" Boeing model with a mere 350 million triangles rendered with ray tracing. Sectioning is performed by using a user-defined clipping plane. *(Image courtesy of Computer Graphics Group, Saarland University. Source 3D data provided by and used with permission of the Boeing Company.)*

real upper limit on scene complexity. The rendering of a Boeing 777 includes 132,500 unique parts and over 3,000,000 fasteners, which yields a polygonal model with over 500,000,000 polygons [310]. See Figure 19.1. Even if most of those objects are not seen due to their small size or position, some work must be done to determine that this is the case. Neither z-buffering nor ray tracing can handle such models without the use of techniques to reduce the sheer number of computations needed. Our conclusion: Acceleration algorithms will always be needed.

In this chapter we offer a smörgåsbord of algorithms for accelerating computer graphics rendering, in particular the rendering of large amounts of geometry. The core of many such algorithms is based on *spatial data structures*, which are described in the next section. Based on that knowledge, we then continue with *culling techniques*. These are algorithms that try to rapidly determine which objects are visible and need to be treated further. *Level of detail* techniques reduce the complexity of rendering the remaining objects. To close the chapter, we discuss systems for rendering huge models, including virtual texturing, streaming, transcoding, and terrain rendering.

19.1 Spatial Data Structures

A spatial data structure is one that organizes geometry in some n-dimensional space. Only two- and three-dimensional structures are used in this book, but the concepts can often easily be extended to higher dimensions. These data structures can be used to accelerate queries about whether geometric entities overlap. Such queries are used in a wide variety of operations, such as culling algorithms, during intersection testing and ray tracing, and for collision detection.

The organization of spatial data structures is usually hierarchical. This means, loosely speaking, that the topmost level contains some children, each defining its own volume of space and which in turn contains its own children. Thus, the structure is nested and of a recursive nature. Geometry is referenced by some of the elements in this hierarchy. The main reason for using a hierarchy is that different types of queries get significantly faster, typically an improvement from $O(n)$ to $O(\log n)$. That is, instead of searching through all n objects, we visit a small subset when performing operations such as finding the closest object in a given direction. Construction time of a spatial data structure can be expensive, and depends on both the amount of geometry inside it and the desired quality of the data structure. However, major advances in this field have reduced construction times considerably, and in some situations it can be done in real time. With lazy evaluation and incremental updates, the construction time can be reduced further still.

Some common types of spatial data structures are *bounding volume hierarchies*, variants of *binary space partitioning* (BSP) trees, quadtrees, and octrees. BSP trees and octrees are data structures based on *space subdivision*. This means that the entire space of the scene is subdivided and encoded in the data structure. For example, the union of the space of all the leaf nodes is equal to the entire space of the scene. Normally the leaf nodes' volumes do not overlap, with the exception of less common structures such as loose octrees. Most variants of BSP trees are *irregular*, which means that the space can be subdivided more arbitrarily. The octree is *regular*, meaning that space is split in a uniform fashion. Though more restrictive, this uniformity can often be a source of efficiency. A bounding volume hierarchy, on the other hand, is not a space subdivision structure. Rather, it encloses the regions of the space surrounding geometrical objects, and thus the BVH need not enclose all space at each level.

BVHs, BSP trees, and octrees are all described in the following sections, along with the *scene graph*, which is a data structure more concerned with model relationships than with efficient rendering.

19.1.1 Bounding Volume Hierarchies

A *bounding volume* (BV) is a volume that encloses a set of objects. The idea of a BV is that it should be a much simpler geometrical shape than the contained objects, so that tests using a BV can be done much faster than using the objects themselves. Examples of BVs are spheres, *axis-aligned bounding boxes* (AABBs), *oriented bounding boxes* (OBBs), and k-DOPs. See Section 22.2 for definitions. A BV does not contribute visually to the rendered image. Instead, it is used as a *proxy* in place of the bounded objects, to speed up rendering, selection, queries, and other computations.

For real-time rendering of three-dimensional scenes, the bounding volume hierarchy is often used for hierarchical view frustum culling (Section 19.4). The scene is organized in a hierarchical tree structure, consisting of a set of connected nodes. The topmost node is the *root*, which has no parents. An *internal node* has pointers to its children, which are other nodes. The root is thus an internal node, unless it is the only node in the tree. A *leaf node* holds the actual geometry to be rendered, and it

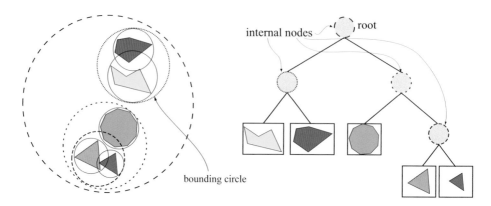

Figure 19.2. The left part shows a simple scene with five objects, with bounding circles that are used in the bounding volume hierarchy to the right. A single circle encloses all objects, and then smaller circles are inside the large circle, in a recursive manner. The right part shows the bounding volume hierarchy (tree) that is used to represent the object hierarchy on the left.

does not have any children nodes. Each node, including leaf nodes, in the tree has a bounding volume that encloses the geometry in its entire subtree. One may also decide to exclude BVs from the leaf nodes, and instead include them in an internal node just above each leaf node. This setup is where the name *bounding volume hierarchy* stems from. Each node's BV encloses the geometry of all the leaf nodes in its subtree. This means that the root has a BV that contains the entire scene. An example of a BVH is shown in Figure 19.2. Note that some of the larger bounding circles could be made tighter, as each node needs to contain only the geometry in its subtree, not the BVs of the descendant nodes. For bounding circles (or spheres), forming such tighter nodes can be expensive, as all geometry in its subtree would have to be examined by each node. In practice, a node's BV is often formed "bottom up" through the tree, by making a BV that contains the BVs of its children.

The underlying structure of a BVH is a tree, and in the field of computer science the literature on tree data structures is vast. Here, only a few important results will be mentioned. For more information, see, for example, the book *Introduction to Algorithms* by Cormen et al. [292].

Consider a k-ary tree, that is, a tree where each internal node has k children. A tree with only one node (the root) is said to be of height 0. A leaf node of the root is at height 1, and so on. A balanced tree is a tree in which all leaf nodes either are at height h or $h - 1$. In general, the height, h, of a balanced tree is $\lfloor \log_k n \rfloor$, where n is the total number of nodes (internal and leaves) in the tree. Note that a higher k gives a tree with a lower height, which means that it takes fewer steps to traverse the tree, but it also requires more work at each node. The binary tree is often the simplest choice, and one that gives reasonable performance. However, there is evidence that a higher k (e.g., $k = 4$ or $k = 8$) gives better performance for some applications [980, 1829]. Using $k = 2$, $k = 4$, or $k = 8$ makes it simple to construct trees; just subdivide along the longest axis for $k = 2$, and for the two longest axes for $k = 4$, and for all axes for $k = 8$. It is more difficult to form good trees for other values of k. Trees with a higher number, e.g., $k = 8$, of children per node are often preferred from a performance perspective, since they reduce average tree depth and the number of indirections (pointers from parent to child) to follow.

BVHs are excellent for performing various queries. For example, assume that a ray should be intersected with a scene, and the first intersection found should be returned, as would be the case for a shadow ray. To use a BVH for this, testing starts at the root. If the ray misses its BV, then the ray misses all geometry contained in the BVH. Otherwise, testing continues recursively, that is, the BVs of the children of the root are tested. As soon as a BV is missed by the ray, testing can terminate on that subtree of the BVH. If the ray hits a leaf node's BV, the ray is tested against the geometry at this node. The performance gains come partly from the fact that testing the ray with the BV is fast. This is why simple objects such as spheres and boxes are used as BVs. The other reason is the nesting of BVs, which allows us to avoid testing large regions of space due to early termination in the tree.

Often the closest intersection, not the first found, is what is desired. The only additional data needed are the distance and identity of the closest object found while traversing the tree. The current closest distance is also used to cull the tree during traversal. If a BV is intersected, but its distance is beyond the closest distance found so far, then the BV can be discarded. When examining a parent box, we intersect all children BVs and find the closest. If an intersection is found in this BV's descendants, this new closest distance is used to cull out whether the other children need to be traversed. As will be seen, a BSP tree has an advantage over normal BVHs in that it can guarantee front-to-back ordering, versus this rough sort that BVHs provide.

BVHs can be used for dynamic scenes as well [1465]. When an object contained in a BV has moved, simply check whether it is still contained in its parent's BV. If it is, then the BVH is still valid. Otherwise, the object node is removed and the parent's BV recomputed. The node is then recursively inserted back into the tree from the root. Another method is to grow the parent's BV to hold the child recursively up the tree as needed. With either method, the tree can become unbalanced and inefficient as more and more edits are performed. Another approach is to put a BV around the limits of movement of the object over some period of time. This is called a *temporal bounding volume* [13]. For example, a pendulum could have a bounding box that enclosed the entire volume swept out by its motion. One can also perform a bottom-up refit [136] or select parts of the tree to refit or rebuild [928, 981, 1950].

To create a BVH, one must first be able to compute a tight BV around a set of objects. This topic is treated in Section 22.3. Then, the actual hierarchy of BVs must be created. See the collision detection chapter at realtimerendering.com for more on BV building strategies.

19.1.2   BSP Trees

Binary space partitioning trees, or BSP trees for short, exist as two noticeably different variants in computer graphics, which we call *axis-aligned* and *polygon-aligned*. The trees are created by using a plane to divide the space in two, and then sorting the geometry into these two spaces. This division is done recursively. One worthwhile property is that if a BSP tree is traversed in a certain way, the geometrical contents of the tree can be sorted front to back from any point of view. This sorting is approximate for axis-aligned and exact for polygon-aligned BSPs. Note that the axis-aligned BSP tree is also called a *k*-d tree

Axis-Aligned BSP Trees (k-D Trees)

An axis-aligned BSP tree is created as follows. First, the whole scene is enclosed in an *axis-aligned bounding box* (AABB). The idea is then to recursively subdivide this box into smaller boxes. Now, consider a box at any recursion level. One axis of the box is chosen, and a perpendicular plane is generated that divides the space into two boxes. Some schemes fix this partitioning plane so that it divides the box exactly in half; others allow the plane to vary in position. With varying plane position, called nonuniform subdivision, the resulting tree can become more balanced. With a fixed plane position, called uniform subdivision, the location in memory of a node is implicitly given by its position in the tree.

An object intersecting the plane can be treated in any number of ways. For example, it could be stored at this level of the tree, or made a member of both child boxes, or truly split by the plane into two separate objects. Storing at the tree level has the advantage that there is only one copy of the object in the tree, making object deletion straightforward. However, small objects intersected by the splitting plane become lodged in the upper levels of the tree, which tends to be inefficient. Placing intersected objects into both children can give tighter bounds to larger objects, as all objects percolate down to one or more leaf nodes, but only those they overlap. Each child box contains some number of objects, and this plane-splitting procedure is repeated, subdividing each AABB recursively until some criterion is fulfilled to halt the process. See Figure 19.3 for an example of an axis-aligned BSP tree.

Rough front-to-back sorting is an example of how axis-aligned BSP trees can be used. This is useful for occlusion culling algorithms (Sections 19.7 and 23.7), as well as for generally reducing pixel shader costs by minimizing pixel overdraw. Assume that a node called N is currently traversed. Here, N is the root at the start of traversal. The splitting plane of N is examined, and tree traversal continues recursively on the side of the plane where the viewer is located. Thus, it is only when the entire half of the tree has been traversed that we start to traverse the other side. This traversal does not give exact front-to-back sorting, since the contents of the leaf nodes are not sorted, and because objects may be in many nodes of the tree. However, it gives a rough sorting, which often is useful. By starting traversal on the other side of a node's plane when compared to the viewer's position, rough back-to-front sorting can

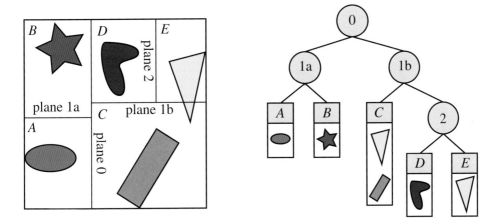

Figure 19.3. Axis-aligned BSP tree. In this example, the space partitions are allowed to be anywhere along the axis, not just at its midpoint. The spatial volumes formed are labeled A through E. The tree on the right shows the underlying BSP data structure. Each leaf node represents an area, with that area's contents shown beneath it. Note that the triangle is in the object list for two areas, C and E, because it overlaps both.

be obtained. This is useful for transparency sorting. BSP traversal can also be used to test a ray against the scene geometry. The ray's origin is simply exchanged for the viewer's location.

Polygon-Aligned BSP Trees

The other type of BSP tree is the polygon-aligned form [4, 500, 501]. This data structure is particularly useful for rendering static or rigid geometry in an exact sorted order. This algorithm was popular for games like *DOOM* (2016), back when there was no hardware z-buffer. It still has occasional use, such as for collision detection and intersection testing.

In this scheme, a polygon is chosen as the divider, splitting space into two halves. That is, at the root, a polygon is selected. The plane in which the polygon lies is used to divide the rest of the polygons in the scene into two sets. Any polygon that is intersected by the dividing plane is broken into two separate pieces along the intersection line. Now in each half-space of the dividing plane, another polygon is chosen as a divider, which divides only the polygons in its half-space. This is done recursively until all polygons are in the BSP tree. Creating an efficient polygon-aligned BSP tree is a time-consuming process, and such trees are normally computed once and stored for reuse. This type of BSP tree is shown in Figure 19.4. It is generally best to form a balanced tree, i.e., one where the depth of each leaf node is the same, or at most off by one.

The polygon-aligned BSP tree has some useful properties. One is that, for a given view, the structure can be traversed strictly from back to front (or front to back).

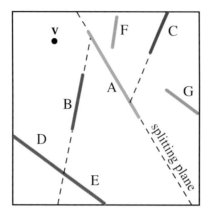 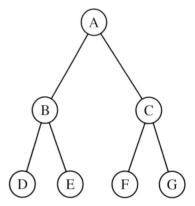

Figure 19.4. Polygon-aligned BSP tree. Polygons A through G are shown from above. Space is first split by polygon A, then each half-space is split separately by B and C. The splitting plane formed by polygon B intersects the polygon in the lower left corner, splitting it into separate polygons D and E. The BSP tree formed is shown on the right.

This is in comparison to the axis-aligned BSP tree, which normally gives only a rough sorted order. Determine on which side of the root plane the camera is located. The set of polygons on the far side of this plane is then beyond the near side's set. Now with the far side's set, take the next level's dividing plane and determine which side the camera is on. The subset on the far side is again the subset farthest away from the camera. By continuing recursively, this process establishes a strict back-to-front order, and a *painter's algorithm* can be used to render the scene. The painter's algorithm does not need a z-buffer. If all objects are drawn in a back-to-front order, each closer object is drawn in front of whatever is behind it, and so no z-depth comparisons are required.

For example, consider what is seen by a viewer **v** in Figure 19.4. Regardless of the viewing direction and frustum, **v** is to the left of the splitting plane formed by A, so C, F, and G are behind B, D, and E. Comparing **v** to the splitting plane of C, we find G to be on the opposite side of this plane, so it is displayed first. A test of B's plane determines that E should be displayed before D. The back-to-front order is then G, C, F, A, E, B, D. Note that this order does not guarantee that one object is closer to the viewer than another. Rather, it provides a strict occlusion order, a subtle difference. For example, polygon F is closer to **v** than polygon E, even though it is farther back in occlusion order.

19.1.3 Octrees

The octree is similar to the axis-aligned BSP tree. A box is split simultaneously along all three axes, and the split point must be the center of the box. This creates eight new boxes—hence the name *octree*. This makes the structure regular, which can make some queries more efficient.

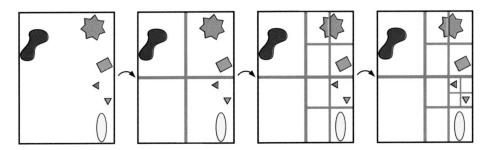

Figure 19.5. The construction of a quadtree. The construction starts from the left by enclosing all objects in a bounding box. Then the boxes are recursively divided into four equal-sized boxes until each box (in this case) is empty or contains one object.

An octree is constructed by enclosing the entire scene in a minimal axis-aligned box. The rest of the procedure is recursive in nature and ends when a stopping criterion is fulfilled. As with axis-aligned BSP trees, these criteria can include reaching a maximum recursion depth, or obtaining a certain number of primitives in a box [1535, 1536]. If a criterion is met, the algorithm binds the primitives to the box and terminates the recursion. Otherwise, it subdivides the box along its main axes using three planes, thereby forming eight equal-sized boxes. Each new box is tested and possibly subdivided again into $2 \times 2 \times 2$ smaller boxes. This is illustrated in two dimensions, where the data structure is called a *quadtree*, in Figure 19.5. Quadtrees are the two-dimensional equivalent of octrees, with a third axis being ignored. They can be useful in situations where there is little advantage to categorizing the data along all three axes.

Octrees can be used in the same manner as axis-aligned BSP trees, and thus, can handle the same types of queries. A BSP tree can, in fact, give the same partitioning of space as an octree. If a cell is first split along the middle of, say, the x-axis, then the two children are split along the middle of, say, y, and finally those children are split in the middle along z, eight equal-sized cells are formed that are the same as those created by one application of an octree division. One source of efficiency for the octree is that it does not need to store information needed by more flexible BSP tree structures. For example, the splitting plane locations are known and so do not have to be described explicitly. This more compact storage scheme also saves time by accessing fewer memory locations during traversal. Axis-aligned BSP trees can still be more efficient, as the additional memory cost and traversal time due to the need for retrieving the splitting plane's location can be outweighed by the savings from better plane placement. There is no overall best efficiency scheme; it depends on the nature of the underlying geometry, the usage pattern of how the structure is accessed, and the architecture of the hardware running the code, to name a few factors. Often the locality and level of cache-friendliness of the memory layout is the most important factor. This is the focus of the next section.

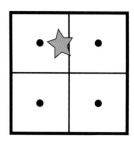 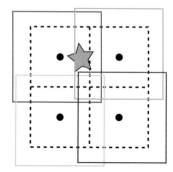

Figure 19.6. An ordinary octree compared to a loose octree. The dots indicate the center points of the boxes (in the first subdivision). To the left, the star pierces through one splitting plane of the ordinary octree. Thus, one choice is to put the star in the largest box (that of the root). To the right, a loose octree with $k = 1.5$ (that is, boxes are 50% larger) is shown. The boxes are slightly displaced, so that they can be discerned. The star can now be placed fully in the red box to the upper left.

In the above description, objects are always stored in leaf nodes. Therefore, certain objects have to be stored in more than one leaf node. Another option is to place the object in the box that is the smallest that contains the entire object. For example, the star-shaped object in the figure should be placed in the upper right box in the second illustration from the left. This has a significant disadvantage in that, for example, a (small) object that is located at the center of the octree will be placed in the topmost (largest) node. This is not efficient, since a tiny object is then bounded by the box that encloses the entire scene. One solution is to split the objects, but that introduces more primitives. Another is to put a pointer to the object in each leaf box it is in, losing efficiency and making octree editing more difficult.

Ulrich presents a third solution, *loose octrees* [1796]. The basic idea of loose octrees is the same as for ordinary octrees, but the choice of the size of each box is relaxed. If the side length of an ordinary box is l, then kl is used instead, where $k > 1$. This is illustrated for $k = 1.5$, and compared to an ordinary octree, in Figure 19.6. Note that the boxes' center points are the same. By using larger boxes, the number of objects that cross a splitting plane is reduced, so that the object can be placed deeper down in the octree. An object is always inserted into only one octree node, so deletion from the octree is trivial. Some advantages accrue by using $k = 2$. First, insertion and deletion of objects is $O(1)$. Knowing the object's size means immediately knowing the level of the octree it can successfully be inserted in, fully fitting into one loose box. In practice, it is sometimes possible to push the object to a deeper box in the octree. Also, if $k < 2$, the object may have to be pushed up the tree if it does not fit.

The object's centroid determines into which loose octree box it is put. Because of these properties, this structure lends itself well to bounding dynamic objects, at the expense of some BV efficiency, and the loss of a strong sort order when traversing the structure. Also, often an object moves only slightly from frame to frame, so that the previous box still is valid in the next frame. Therefore, only a fraction of animated objects in the loose octree need updating each frame. Cozzi [302] notes that after each object/primitive has been assigned to the loose octree, one may compute a minimal AABB around the objects in each node, which essentially becomes a BVH at that point. This approach avoids splitting objects across nodes.

19.1.4 Cache-Oblivious and Cache-Aware Representations

Since the gap between the bandwidth of the memory system and the computing power of CPUs increases every year, it is critical to design algorithms and spatial data structure representations with caching in mind. In this section, we will give an introduction to cache-aware (or cache-conscious) and cache-oblivious spatial data structures. A cache-aware representation assumes that the size of cache blocks is known, and hence we optimize for a particular architecture. In contrast, a cache-oblivious algorithm is designed to work well for all types of cache sizes, and are hence platform-independent.

To create a cache-aware data structure, you must first find out what the size of a cache block is for your architecture. This may be 64 bytes, for example. Then try to minimize the size of your data structure. For example, Ericson [435] shows how it is sufficient to use only 32 bits for a k-d tree node. This is done in part by appropriating the two least significant bits of the node's 32-bit value. These 2 bits can represent four types: a leaf node, or the internal node split on one of the three axes. For leaf nodes, the upper 30 bits hold a pointer to a list of objects; for internal nodes, these represent a (slightly lower-precision) floating point split value. Hence, it is possible to store a four-level deep binary tree of 15 nodes in a single cache block of 64 bytes. The sixteenth node indicates which children exist and where they are located. See his book for details. The key concept is that data access is considerably improved by ensuring that structures pack cleanly to cache boundaries.

One popular and simple cache-oblivious ordering for trees is the van Emde Boas layout [68, 422, 435]. Assume we have a tree, $\mathcal{T}$, with height h. The goal is to compute a cache-oblivious layout, or ordering, of the nodes in the tree. The key idea is that, by recursively breaking a hierarchy into smaller and smaller chunks, at some level a set of chunks will fit in the cache. These chunks are near each other in the tree, so the cached data will be valid for a longer time than if, for example, we simply listed all nodes from the top level on down. A naive listing such as that would lead to large jumps between memory locations.

Let us denote the van Emde Boas layout of $\mathcal{T}$ as $v(\mathcal{T})$. This structure is defined recursively, and the layout of a single node in a tree is just the node itself. If there are more than one node in $\mathcal{T}$, the tree is split at half the height, $\lfloor h/2 \rfloor$. The topmost $\lfloor h/2 \rfloor$ levels are put in a tree denoted $\mathcal{T}_0$, and the children subtree starting at the leaf nodes of $\mathcal{T}_0$ are denoted $\mathcal{T}_1, \ldots, \mathcal{T}_n$. The recursive nature of the tree is described as follows:

$$v(\mathcal{T}) = \begin{cases} \{\mathcal{T}\}, & \text{if there is single node in } \mathcal{T}, \\ \{\mathcal{T}_0, \mathcal{T}_1, \ldots, \mathcal{T}_n\}, & \text{else.} \end{cases} \tag{19.1}$$

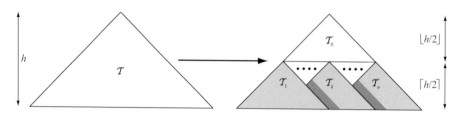

Figure 19.7. The van Emde Boas layout of a tree, $\mathcal{T}$, is created by splitting the height, h, of the tree in two. This creates the subtrees, $\mathcal{T}_0, \mathcal{T}_1, \ldots, \mathcal{T}_n$, and each subtree is split recursively in the same manner until only one node per subtree remains.

Note that all the subtrees $\mathcal{T}_i$, $0 \leq i \leq n$, are also defined by the recursion above. This means, for example, that $\mathcal{T}_1$ has to be split at half its height, and so on. See Figure 19.7 for an example.

In general, creating a cache-oblivious layout consists of two steps: clustering and ordering of the clusters. For the van Emde Boas layout, the clustering is given by the subtrees, and the ordering is implicit in the creation order. Yoon et al. [1948, 1949] develop techniques that are specifically designed for efficient bounding volume hierarchies and BSP trees. They develop a probabilistic model that takes into account both the locality between a parent and its children, and the spatial locality. The idea is to minimize cache misses when a parent has been accessed, by making sure that the children are inexpensive to access. Furthermore, nodes that are close to each other are grouped closer together in the ordering. A greedy algorithm is developed that clusters nodes with the highest probabilities. Generous increases in performance are obtained without altering the underlying algorithm—it is only the ordering of the nodes in the BVH that is different.

19.1.5 Scene Graphs

BVHs, BSP trees, and octrees all use some sort of tree as their basic data structure. It is in how they partition the space and store the geometry that they differ. They also store geometrical objects, and nothing else, in a hierarchical fashion. However, rendering a three-dimensional scene is about so much more than just geometry. Control of animation, visibility, and other elements are usually performed using a scene graph, which is called a *node hierarchy* in glTF. This is a user-oriented tree structure that is augmented with textures, transforms, levels of detail, render states (material properties, for example), light sources, and whatever else is found suitable. It is represented by a tree, and this tree is traversed in some order to render the scene. For example, a light source can be put at an internal node, which affects only the contents of its subtree. Another example is when a material is encountered in the tree. The material can be applied to all the geometry in that node's subtree, or possibly be overridden by a child's settings. See also Figure 19.34 on page 861 on how different levels of detail can be supported in a scene graph. In a sense, every graphics application uses some

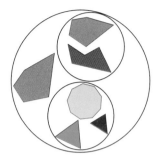
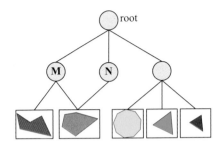

Figure 19.8. A scene graph with different transforms **M** and **N** applied to internal nodes, and their respective subtrees. Note that these two internal nodes also point to the same object, but since they have different transforms, two different objects appear (one is rotated and scaled).

form of scene graph, even if the graph is just a root node with a list of children to display.

One way of animating objects is to vary transforms of internal nodes in the tree. Scene graph implementations then transform the entire contents of that node's subtree. Since a transform can be put in any internal node, hierarchical animation can be done. For example, the wheels of a car can spin, and the car as a whole can move forward.

When several nodes may point to the same child node, the tree structure is called a *directed acyclic graph* (DAG) [292]. The term *acyclic* means that it must not contain any loops or cycles. By *directed*, we mean that as two nodes are connected by an edge, they are also connected in a certain order, e.g., from parent to child. Scene graphs are often DAGs because they allow for instantiation, i.e., when we want to make several copies (instances) of an object without replicating its geometry. An example is shown in Figure 19.8, where two internal nodes have different transforms applied to their subtrees. Using instances saves memory, and GPUs can render multiple copies of an instance rapidly via API calls (Section 18.4.2).

When objects are to move in the scene, the scene graph has to be updated. This can be done with a recursive call on the tree structure. Transforms are updated on the way from the root toward the leaves. The matrices are multiplied in this traversal and stored in relevant nodes. However, when transforms have been updated, any BVs attached are obsolete. Therefore, the BVs are updated on the way back from the leaves toward the root. A too relaxed tree structure complicates these tasks enormously, so DAGs are often avoided, or a limited form of DAGs is used, where only the leaf nodes are shared. See Eberly's book [404] for more information on this topic. Note also that when JavaScript-based APIs, such as WebGL, are used, then it is of extreme importance to move over as much work as possible to the GPU with as little feedback to the CPU as possible [876].

Scene graphs themselves can be used to provide some computational efficiency. A node in the scene graph often has a bounding volume, and is thus quite similar to a BVH. A leaf in the scene graph stores geometry. It is important to realize that entirely unrelated efficiency schemes can be used alongside a scene graph. This is the idea of *spatialization*, in which the user's scene graph is augmented with a separate data structure (e.g., BSP tree or BVH) created for a different task, such as faster culling or picking. The leaf nodes, where most models are located, are shared, so the expense of an additional spatial efficiency structure is relatively low.

19.2 Culling Techniques

To *cull* means to "remove from a flock," and in the context of computer graphics, this is exactly what culling techniques do. The flock is the whole scene that we want to render, and the removal is limited to those portions of the scene that are not considered to contribute to the final image. The rest of the scene is sent through the rendering pipeline. Thus, the term *visibility culling* is also often used in the context of rendering. However, culling can also be done for other parts of a program. Examples include collision detection (by doing less accurate computations for offscreen or hidden objects), physics computations, and AI. Here, only culling techniques related to rendering will be presented. Examples of such techniques are *backface culling*, *view frustum culling*, and *occlusion culling*. These are illustrated in Figure 19.9. Backface culling eliminates triangles facing away from the viewer. View frustum culling eliminates groups of triangles outside the view frustum. Occlusion culling eliminates objects hidden by groups of other objects. It is the most complex culling technique, as it requires computing how objects affect each other.

The actual culling can theoretically take place at any stage of the rendering pipeline, and for some occlusion culling algorithms, it can even be precomputed. For culling algorithms that are implemented on the GPU, we can sometimes only enable/disable, or set some parameters for, the culling function. The fastest triangle

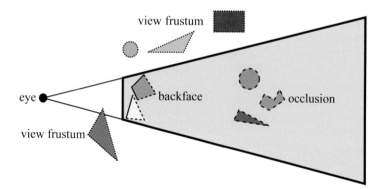

Figure 19.9. Different culling techniques. Culled geometry is dashed. *(Illustration after Cohen-Or et al. [277].)*

to render is the one never sent to the GPU. Next to that, the earlier in the pipeline culling can occur, the better. Culling is often achieved by using geometric calculations, but is in no way limited to these. For example, an algorithm may also use the contents of the frame buffer.

The ideal culling algorithm would send only the *exact visible set* (EVS) of primitives through the pipeline. In this book, the EVS is defined as all primitives that are partially or fully visible. One such data structure that allows for ideal culling is the *aspect graph*, from which the EVS can be extracted, given any point of view [532]. Creating such data structures is possible in theory, but not in practice, since worst-time complexity can be as bad as $O(n^9)$ [277]. Instead, practical algorithms attempt to find a set, called the *potentially visible set* (PVS), that is a prediction of the EVS. If the PVS fully includes the EVS, so that only invisible geometry is discarded, the PVS is said to be *conservative*. A PVS may also be *approximate*, in which the EVS is not fully included. This type of PVS may therefore generate incorrect images. The goal is to make these errors as small as possible. Since a conservative PVS always generates correct images, it is often considered more useful. By overestimating or approximating the EVS, the idea is that the PVS can be computed much faster. The difficulty lies in how these estimations should be done to gain overall performance. For example, an algorithm may treat geometry at different granularities, i.e., triangles, whole objects, or groups of objects. When a PVS has been found, it is rendered using the z-buffer, which resolves the final per-pixel visibility.

Note that there are algorithms that reorder the triangles in a mesh in order to provide better occlusion culling, i.e., reduced overdraw, and improved vertex cache locality at the same time. While these are somewhat related to culling, we refer the interested reader to the references [256, 659].

In Sections 19.3–19.8, we treat backface culling, view frustum culling, portal culling, detail culling, occlusion culling, and culling systems.

19.3 Backface Culling

Imagine that you are looking at an opaque sphere in a scene. Approximately half of the sphere will not be visible. The conclusion from this observation is that what is invisible need not be rendered since it does not contribute to the image. Therefore, the back side of the sphere need not be processed, and that is the idea behind backface culling. This type of culling can also be done for whole groups at a time, and so is called clustered backface culling.

All backfacing triangles that are part of a solid opaque object can be culled away from further processing, assuming the camera is outside of, and does not penetrate (i.e., near clip into), the object. A consistently oriented triangle (Section 16.3) is backfacing if the projected triangle is known to be oriented in, say, a clockwise fashion in screen space. This test can be implemented by computing the signed area of the triangle in two-dimensional screen space. A negative signed area means that the

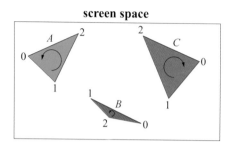
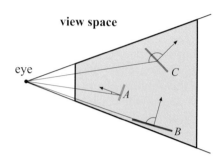

Figure 19.10. Two different tests for determining whether a triangle is backfacing. The left figure shows how the test is done in screen space. The two triangles to the left are frontfacing, while the right triangle is backfacing and can be omitted from further processing. The right figure shows how the backface test is done in view space. Triangles A and B are frontfacing, while C is backfacing.

triangle should be culled. This can be implemented immediately after the screen-mapping procedure has taken place.

Another way to determine whether a triangle is backfacing is to create a vector from an arbitrary point on the plane in which the triangle lies (one of the vertices is the simplest choice) to the viewer's position. For orthographic projections, the vector to the eye position is replaced with the negative view direction, which is constant for the scene. Compute the dot product of this vector and the triangle's normal. A negative dot product means that the angle between the two vectors is greater than $\pi/2$ radians, so the triangle is not facing the viewer. This test is equivalent to computing the signed distance from the viewer's position to the plane of the triangle. If the sign is positive, the triangle is frontfacing. Note that the distance is obtained only if the normal is normalized, but this is unimportant here, as only the sign is of interest. Alternatively, after the projection matrix has been applied, form vertices $\bar{\mathbf{v}} = (v_x, v_y, v_w)$ in clip space and compute the determinant $d = |\bar{\mathbf{v}}_0, \bar{\mathbf{v}}_1, \bar{\mathbf{v}}_2|$ [1317]. If $d \leq 0$, the triangle can be culled. These culling techniques are illustrated in Figure 19.10.

Blinn points out that these two tests are geometrically the same [165]. In theory, what differentiates these tests is the space where the tests are computed—nothing else. In practice, the screen-space test is often safer, because edge-on triangles that appear to face slightly backward in view space can become slightly forward in screen space. This happens because the view-space coordinates get rounded off to screen-space subpixel coordinates.

Using an API such as OpenGL or DirectX, backface culling is normally controlled with a few functions that either enable backface or frontface culling or disable all culling. Be aware that a mirroring transform (i.e., a negative scaling operation) turns backfacing triangles into frontfacing ones and vice versa [165] (Section 4.1.3). Finally, it is possible to find out in the pixel shader whether a triangle is frontfacing. In OpenGL, this is done by testing `gl_FrontFacing` and in DirectX it is called `SV_IsFrontFace`. Prior to this addition the main way to display two-sided objects

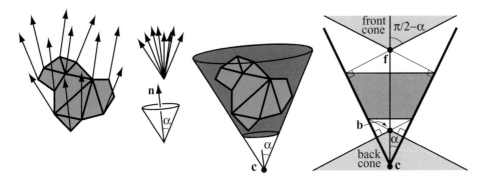

Figure 19.11. Left: a set of triangles and their normals. Middle left: the normals are collected (top), and a minimal cone (bottom), defined by one normal **n**, and a half-angle, α, is constructed. Middle right: the cone is anchored at a point **c**, and truncated so that it also contains all points on the triangles. Right: a cross section of a truncated cone. The light gray region on the top is the frontfacing cone, and the light gray region at the bottom is the backfacing cone. The points **f** and **b** are respectively the apexes of the front- and backfacing cones.

properly was to render them twice, first culling backfaces then culling frontfaces and reversing the normals.

A common misconception about standard backface culling is that it cuts the number of triangles rendered by about half. While backface culling will remove about half of the triangles in many objects, it will provide little gain for some types of models. For example, the walls, floor, and ceiling of interior scenes are usually facing the viewer, so there are relatively few backfaces of these types to cull in such scenes. Similarly, with terrain rendering often most of the triangles are visible, and only those on the back sides of hills or ravines benefit from this technique.

While backface culling is a simple technique for avoiding rasterizing individual triangles, it would be even faster if one could decide with a single test if a whole set of triangles could be culled. Such techniques are called *clustered backface culling* algorithms, and some of these will be reviewed here. The basic concept that many such algorithms use is the *normal cone* [1630]. For some section of a surface, a truncated cone is created that contains all the normal directions and all the points. Note that two distances along the normal are needed to truncate the cone. See Figure 19.11 for an example. As can be seen, a cone is defined by a normal, **n**, and half-angle, α, and an anchor point, **c**, and some offset distances along the normal that truncates the cone. In the right part of Figure 19.11, a cross section of a normal cone is shown. Shirman and Abi-Ezzi [1630] prove that if the viewer is located in the frontfacing cone, then all faces in the cone are frontfacing, and similarly for the backfacing cone. Engel [433] uses a similar concept called the exclusion volume for GPU culling.

For static meshes, Haar and Aaltonen [625] suggest that a minimal cube is computed around n triangles, and each cube face is split into $r \times r$ "pixels," each encoding an n-bit mask that indicates whether the corresponding triangle is visible over that

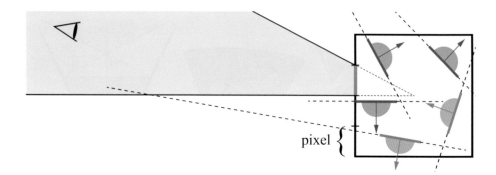

Figure 19.12. A set of five static triangles, viewed edge on, surrounded by a square in two dimensions. The square face to the left has been split into 4 "pixels," and we focus on the one second from the top, whose frustum outside the box has been colored blue. The positive half-space formed by the triangle's plane is indicated with a half-circle (red and green). All triangles that do not have any part of the blue frustum in its positive half-space are conservatively backfacing (marked red) from all points in the frustum. Green indicates those that are frontfacing.

"pixel." This is illustrated in Figure 19.12. If the camera is outside the cube, one finds the corresponding frustum in which the camera is located and can immediately look up its bitmask and know which triangles are backfacing (conservatively). If the camera is inside the cube, all triangles are considered visible (unless one wants to perform further computations). Haar and Aaltonen use only one bitmask per cube face and encode $n = 64$ triangles at a time. By counting the number of bits that are set in the bitmask, one can allocate memory for the non-culled triangles in an efficient manner. This work has been used in *Assassin's Creed Unity*.

Next, we will use a non-truncated normal cone, in contrast to the one in Figure 19.11, and so it is defined by only a center point $\mathbf{c}$, normal $\mathbf{n}$, and an angle α. To compute such a normal cone of a number of triangles, take all the normals of the triangle planes, put them in the same position, and compute a minimal circle on the unit sphere surface that includes all the normals [101]. As a first step, assume that from a point $\mathbf{e}$ we want to backface-test all normals, sharing the same origin $\mathbf{c}$, in the cone. A normal cone is backfacing from $\mathbf{e}$ if the following is true [1883, 1884]:

$$\mathbf{n} \cdot (\mathbf{e} - \mathbf{c}) < \underbrace{\cos\left(\alpha + \frac{\pi}{2}\right)}_{-\sin\alpha} \iff \mathbf{n} \cdot (\mathbf{c} - \mathbf{e}) < \sin\alpha. \qquad (19.2)$$

However, this test only works if all the geometry is located at $\mathbf{c}$. Next, we assume that all geometry is inside a sphere with center point $\mathbf{c}$ and radius r. The test then becomes

$$\mathbf{n} \cdot (\mathbf{e} - \mathbf{c}) < \underbrace{\cos\left(\alpha + \beta + \frac{\pi}{2}\right)}_{-\sin(\alpha+\beta)} \iff \mathbf{n} \cdot (\mathbf{c} - \mathbf{e}) < \sin(\alpha + \beta), \qquad (19.3)$$

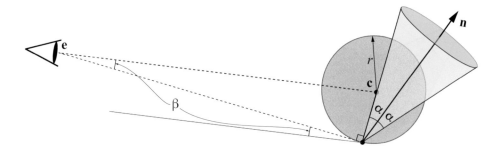

Figure 19.13. This situation shows the limit when the normal cone, defined by $\mathbf{c}$, $\mathbf{n}$, and α, is just about to become visible to $\mathbf{e}$ from the most critical point inside the circle with radius r and center point $\mathbf{c}$. This happens when the angle between the vector from $\mathbf{e}$ to a point on the circle such that the vector is tangent to the circle, and the side of the normal cone is $\pi/2$ radians. Note that the normal cone has been translated down from $\mathbf{c}$ so its origin coincides with the sphere border.

where $\sin \beta = r/||\mathbf{c} - \mathbf{e}||$. The geometry involved in deriving this test is shown in Figure 19.13. Quantized normals can be stored in 8×4 bits, which may be sufficient for some applications.

To conclude this section, we note that backface culling for motion blurred triangles, where each vertex has a linear motion over a frame, is not as simple as one may think. A triangle with linearly moving vertices over time can be backfacing at the start of a frame, turn frontfacing, and then turn backfacing again, all within the same frame. Hence, incorrect results will be generated if a triangle is culled due to the motion blurred triangle being backfacing at the start and end of a frame. Munkberg and Akenine-Möller [1246] present a method where the vertices in the standard backface test are replaced with linearly moving triangles vertices. The test is rewritten in Bernstein form, and the convex property of Bézier curves is used as a conservative test. For depth of field, if the entire lens is in the negative half-space of the triangle (in other words, behind it), the triangle can be culled safely.

19.4 View Frustum Culling

As seen in Section 2.3.3, only primitives that are entirely or partially inside the view frustum need to be rendered. One way to speed up the rendering process is to compare the bounding volume of each object to the view frustum. If the BV is outside the frustum, then the geometry it encloses can be omitted from rendering. If instead the BV is inside or intersecting the frustum, then the contents of that BV may be visible and must be sent through the rendering pipeline. See Section 22.14 for methods of testing for intersection between various bounding volumes and the view frustum.

By using a spatial data structure, this kind of culling can be applied hierarchically [272]. For a bounding volume hierarchy, a preorder traversal [292] from the root

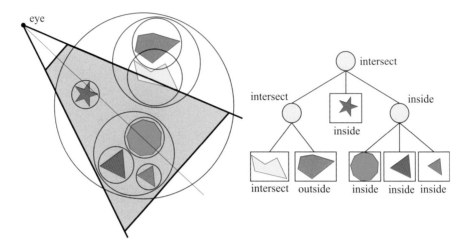

Figure 19.14. A set of geometry and its bounding volumes (spheres) are shown on the left. This scene is rendered with view frustum culling from the point of the eye. The BVH is shown on the right. The BV of the root intersects the frustum, and the traversal continues with testing its children's BVs. The BV of the left subtree intersects, and one of that subtree's children intersects (and thus is rendered), and the BV of the other child is outside and therefore is not sent through the pipeline. The BV of the middle subtree of the root is entirely inside and is rendered immediately. The BV of the right subtree of the root is also fully inside, and the entire subtree can therefore be rendered without further tests.

does the job. Each node with a bounding volume is tested against the frustum. If the BV of the node is outside the frustum, then that node is not processed further. The tree is pruned, since the BV's contents and children are outside the view. If the BV is fully inside the frustum, its contents must all be inside the frustum. Traversal continues, but no further frustum testing is needed for the rest of such a subtree. If the BV intersects the frustum, then the traversal continues and its children are tested. When a leaf node is found to intersect, its contents (i.e., its geometry) is sent through the pipeline. The primitives of the leaf are not guaranteed to be inside the view frustum. An example of view frustum culling is shown in Figure 19.14. It is also possible to use multiple BV tests for an object or cell. For example, if a sphere BV around a cell is found to overlap the frustum, it may be worthwhile to also perform the more accurate (though more expensive) OBB-versus-frustum test if this box is known to be much smaller than the sphere [1600].

A useful optimization for the "intersects frustum" case is to keep track of which frustum planes the BV is fully inside [148]. This information, usually stored as a bitmask, can then be passed with the intersector for testing children of this BV. This technique is sometimes called *plane masking*, as only those planes that intersected the BV need to be tested against the children. The root BV will initially be tested against all 6 frustum planes, but with successive tests the number of plane/BV tests done at each child will go down. Assarsson and Möller [83] note that temporal coherence can also be used. The frustum plane that rejects a BV could be stored with the BV and then be the first plane tested for rejection in the next frame. Wihlidal [1883, 1884] notes that if view frustum culling is done on a per-object level on the CPU, then it suffices to perform view frustum culling against the left, right, bottom, and top planes when finer-grained culling is done on the GPU. Also, to improve performance, a construction called the apex point map can be used to provide tighter bounding volumes. This is described in more detail in Section 22.13.4. Sometimes fog is used in the distance to avoid the effect of objects suddenly disappearing at the far plane.

For large scenes or certain camera views, only a fraction of the scene might be visible, and it is only this fraction that needs to be sent through the rendering pipeline. In such cases a large gain in speed can be expected. View frustum culling techniques exploit the spatial coherence in a scene, since objects that are located near each other can be enclosed in a BV, and nearby BVs may be clustered hierarchically.

It should be noted that some game engines do not use hierarchical BVHs, but rather just a linear list of BVs, one for each object in the scene [283]. The main motivation is that it is simpler to implement algorithms using SIMD and multiple threads, so giving better performance. However, for some applications, such as CAD, most or all of the geometry is inside the frustum, in which case one should avoid using these types of algorithms. Hierarchical view frustum culling may still be applied, since if a node is inside the frustum, its geometry can immediately be drawn.

19.5 Portal Culling

For architectural models, there is a set of algorithms that goes under the name of *portal culling*. The first of these were introduced by Airey et al. [17, 18]. Later, Teller and Séquin [1755, 1756] and Teller and Hanrahan [1757] constructed more efficient and more complex algorithms for portal culling. The rationale for all portal-culling algorithms is that walls often act as large occluders in indoor scenes. Portal culling is thus a type of occlusion culling, discussed in the next section. This occlusion algorithm uses a view frustum culling mechanism through each portal (e.g., door or window). When traversing a portal, the frustum is diminished to fit closely around the portal. Therefore, this algorithm can be seen as an extension of view frustum culling as well. Portals that are outside the view frustum are discarded.

Portal-culling methods preprocess the scene in some way. The scene is divided into *cells* that usually correspond to rooms and hallways in a building. The doors and windows that connect adjacent rooms are called *portals*. Every object in a cell and the walls of the cell are stored in a data structure that is associated with the cell. We also store information on adjacent cells and the portals that connect them in an adjacency graph. Teller presents algorithms for computing this graph [1756]. While this technique worked back in 1992 when it was introduced, for modern complex scenes automating the process is extremely difficult. For that reason defining cells and creating the graph is currently done by hand.

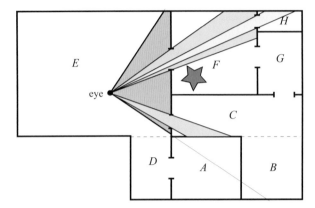

Figure 19.15. Portal culling: Cells are enumerated from A to H, and portals are openings that connect the cells. Only geometry seen through the portals is rendered. For example, the star in cell F is culled.

Luebke and Georges [1090] use a simple method that requires just a small amount of preprocessing. The only information that is needed is the data structure associated with each cell, as described above. The key idea is that each portal defines the view into its room and beyond. Imagine that you are looking through a doorway to a room with three windows. The doorway defines a frustum, which you use to cull out the objects not visible in the room, and you render those that can be seen. You cannot see two of the windows through the doorway, so the cells visible through those windows can be ignored. The third window is visible but partially blocked by the doorframe. Only the contents in the cell visible through both the doorway and this window needs to be sent down the pipeline. The cell rendering process depends on tracking this visibility, in a recursive manner.

The portal culling algorithm is illustrated in Figure 19.15 with an example. The viewer or eye is located in cell E and therefore rendered together with its contents. The neighboring cells are C, D, and F. The original frustum cannot see the portal to cell D and is therefore omitted from further processing. Cell F is visible, and the view frustum is therefore diminished so that it goes through the portal that connects to F. The contents of F are then rendered with that diminished frustum. Then, the neighboring cells of F are examined—G is not visible from the diminished frustum and so is omitted, while H is visible. Again, the frustum is diminished with the portal of H, and thereafter the contents of H are rendered. H does not have any neighbors that have not been visited, so traversal ends there. Now, recursion falls back to the portal into cell C. The frustum is diminished to fit the portal of C, and then rendering of the objects in C follows, with frustum culling. No more portals are visible, so rendering is complete.

Each object may be tagged when it has been rendered, to avoid rendering objects more than once. For example, if there were two windows into a room, the contents

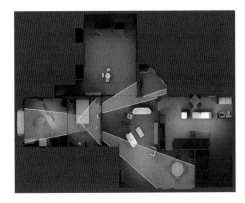 

Figure 19.16. Portal culling. The left image is an overhead view of the Brooks House. The right image is a view from the master bedroom. Cull boxes for portals are in white and for mirrors are in red. *(Images courtesy of David Luebke and Chris Georges, UNC-Chapel Hill.)*

of the room are culled against each frustum separately. Without tagging, an object visible through both windows would be rendered twice. This is both inefficient and can lead to rendering errors, such as when an object is transparent. To avoid having to clear this list of tags each frame, each object is tagged with the frame number when visited. Only objects that store the current frame number have already been visited.

An optimization that can well be worth implementing is to use the stencil buffer for more accurate culling. In practice, portals are overestimated with an AABB; the real portal will most likely be smaller. The stencil buffer can be used to mask away rendering outside that real portal. Similarly, a scissor rectangle around the portal can be set for the GPU to increase performance [13]. Using stencil and scissor functionality also obviates the need to perform tagging, as transparent objects may be rendered twice but will affect visible pixels in each portal only once.

See Figure 19.16 for another view of the use of portals. This form of portal culling can also be used to trim content for planar reflections (Section 11.6.2). The left image shows a building viewed from the top; the white lines indicate the way in which the frustum is diminished with each portal. The red lines are created by reflecting the frustum at a mirror. The actual view is shown in the image on the right side, where the white rectangles are the portals and the mirror is red. Note that it is only the objects inside any of the frusta that are rendered. Other transformations can be used to create other effects, such as simple refractions.

19.6 Detail and Small Triangle Culling

Detail culling is a technique that sacrifices quality for speed. The rationale for detail culling is that small details in the scene contribute little or nothing to the rendered

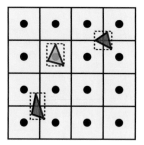 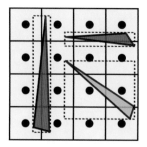

Figure 19.17. Small triangle culling using `any(round(min) == round(max))`. Red triangles are culled, while green triangles need to be rendered. Left: the green triangle overlaps with a sample, so cannot be culled. The red triangles both round all AABB coordinates to the same pixel corners. Right: the red triangles can be culled because one of AABB coordinates is rounded to the same integer. The green triangle does not overlap any samples, but cannot be culled by this test.

images when the viewer is in motion. When the viewer stops, detail culling is usually disabled. Consider an object with a bounding volume, and project this BV onto the projection plane. The area of the projection is then estimated in pixels, and if the number of pixels is below a user-defined threshold, the object is omitted from further processing. For this reason, detail culling is sometimes called *screen-size culling*. Detail culling can also be done hierarchically on a scene graph. These types of techniques are often used in game engines [283].

With one sample at the center of each pixel, small triangles are rather likely to fall between the samples. In addition, small triangles are rather inefficient to rasterize. Some graphics hardware actually cull triangles falling between samples, but when culling is done using code on the GPU (Section 19.8), it may be beneficial to add some code to cull small triangles. Wihlidal [1883, 1884] presents a simple method, where the AABB of the triangle is first computed. The triangle can be culled in a shader if the following is true:

$$\texttt{any(round(min) == round(max))}, \tag{19.4}$$

where `min` and `max` represent the two-dimensional AABB around the triangle. The function `any` returns true if any of the vector components are true. Recall also that pixel centers are located at $(x+0.5, y+0.5)$, which means that Equation 19.4 is true if either the x- or y-coordinates, or both, round to the same coordinates. Some examples are shown in Figure 19.17.

19.7 Occlusion Culling

As we have seen, visibility may be solved via the z-buffer. Even though it solves visibility correctly, the z-buffer is relatively simple and brute-force, and so not always

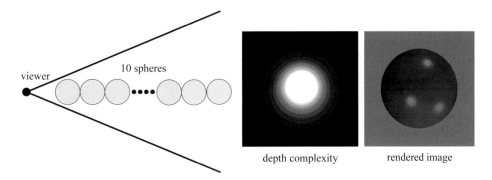

Figure 19.18. An illustration of how occlusion culling can be useful. Ten spheres are placed in a line, and the viewer is looking along this line (left) with perspective. The depth complexity image in the middle shows that some pixels are written to several times, even though the final image (on the right) only shows one sphere.

the most efficient solution. For example, imagine that the viewer is looking along a line where 10 spheres are placed. This is illustrated in Figure 19.18. An image rendered from this viewpoint will show but one sphere, even though all 10 spheres will be rasterized and compared to the z-buffer, and then potentially written to the color buffer and z-buffer. The middle part of Figure 19.18 shows the depth complexity for this scene from the given viewpoint. Depth complexity is the number of surfaces covered by a pixel. In the case of the 10 spheres, the depth complexity is 10 for the pixel in the middle as all 10 spheres are located there, assuming backface culling is on. If the scene is rendered back to front, the pixel in the middle will be pixel shaded 10 times, i.e., there are 9 unnecessary pixel shader executions. Even if the scene is rendered front to back, the triangles for all 10 spheres will still be rasterized, and depth will be computed and compared to the depth in the z-buffer, even though an image of a single sphere is generated. This uninteresting scene is not likely to be found in reality, but it describes (from the given viewpoint) a densely populated model. These sorts of configurations are found in real scenes such as those of a rain forest, an engine, a city, and the inside of a skyscraper. See Figure 19.19 for an example.

Given the examples in the previous paragraph, it seems plausible that an algorithmic approach to avoid this kind of inefficiency may pay off in performance. Such approaches go under the name of *occlusion culling algorithms*, since they try to cull away objects that are occluded, that is, hidden by other objects in the scene. The optimal occlusion culling algorithm would select only the objects that are visible. In a sense, the z-buffer selects and renders only those objects that are visible, but not without having to send all objects inside the view frustum through most of the pipeline. The idea behind efficient occlusion culling algorithms is to perform some simple tests early on to cull sets of hidden objects. In a sense, backface culling is a simple form of occlusion culling. If we know in advance that an object is solid and is opaque, then the backfaces are occluded by the frontfaces and so do not need to be rendered.

Figure 19.19. A *Minecraft* scene, called Neu Rungholt, with occlusion culling visualized where the viewer is located in the lower right corner. Lightly shaded geometry is culled, while darker is rendered. The final image is shown to the lower left. *(Reprinted by permission of Jon Hasselgren, Magnus Andersson, and Tomas Akenine-Möller and Intel Corporation, copyright Intel Corporation, 2016. Neu Rungholt map is courtesy of kescha.)*

There are two major forms of occlusion culling algorithms, namely point-based and cell-based. These are illustrated in Figure 19.20. Point-based visibility is just what is normally used in rendering, that is, what is seen from a single viewing location. Cell-based visibility, on the other hand, is done for a cell, which is a region of the space containing a set of viewing locations, normally a box or a sphere. An invisible object in cell-based visibility must be invisible from all points within the cell. The advantage

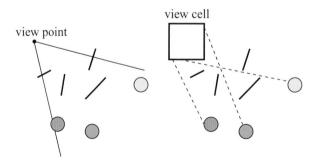

Figure 19.20. The left figure shows point-based visibility, while the right shows cell-based visibility, where the cell is a box. As can be seen, the circles are occluded to the left from the viewpoint. To the right, however, the circles are visible, since rays can be drawn from somewhere within the cell to the circles without intersecting any occluder.

```
        OcclusionCullingAlgorithm(G)
1:      O_R =empty
2:      P =empty
3:      for each object g ∈ G
4:          if(isOccluded(g,O_R))
5:              Skip(g)
6:          else
7:              Render(g)
8:              Add(g, P)
9:              if(LargeEnough(P))
10:                 Update(O_R, P)
11:                 P =empty
12:             end
13:         end
14:     end
```

Figure 19.21. Pseudocode for a general occlusion culling algorithm. G contains all the objects in the scene, and O_R is the occlusion representation. P is a set of potential occluders, that are merged into O_R when it contains sufficiently many objects. *(After Zhang [1965].)*

of cell-based visibility is that once it is computed for a cell, it can usually be used for a few frames, as long as the viewer is inside the cell. However, it is usually more time consuming to compute than point-based visibility. Therefore, it is often done as a preprocessing step. Point-based and cell-based visibility are similar in nature to point and area light sources, where the light can be thought of as viewing the scene. For an object to be invisible, this is equivalent to it being in the umbra region, i.e., fully in shadow.

One can also categorize occlusion culling algorithms into those that operate in *image space*, *object space*, or *ray space*. Image-space algorithms do visibility testing in two dimensions after some projection, while object-space algorithms use the original three-dimensional objects. Ray-space methods [150, 151, 923] perform their tests in a dual space. Each point of interest, often two-dimensional, is converted to a ray in this dual space. For real-time graphics, of the three, image-space occlusion culling algorithms are the most widely used.

Pseudocode for one type of occlusion culling algorithm is shown in Figure 19.21, where the function isOccluded, often called the *visibility test*, checks whether an object is occluded. G is the set of geometrical objects to be rendered, O_R is the occlusion representation, and P is a set of potential occluders that can be merged with O_R. Depending on the particular algorithm, O_R represents some kind of occlusion information. O_R is set to be empty at the beginning. After that, all objects (that pass the view frustum culling test) are processed.

Consider a particular object. First, we test whether the object is occluded with respect to the occlusion representation O_R. If it is occluded, then it is not processed further, since we then know that it will not contribute to the image. If the object cannot be determined to be occluded, then that object has to be rendered, since it probably contributes to the image (at that point in the rendering). Then the object is added to P, and if the number of objects in P is large enough, then we can afford to merge the *occluding power* of these objects into O_R. Each object in P can thus be used as an *occluder*.

Note that for most occlusion culling algorithms, the performance is dependent on the order in which objects are drawn. As an example, consider a car with a motor inside it. If the hood of the car is drawn first, then the motor will (probably) be culled away. On the other hand, if the motor is drawn first, then nothing will be culled. Sorting and rendering in rough front-to-back order can give a considerable performance gain. Also, it is worth noting that small objects potentially can be excellent occluders, since the distance to the occluder determines how much it can occlude. As an example, a matchbox can occlude the Golden Gate Bridge if the viewer is sufficiently close to the matchbox.

19.7.1 Occlusion Queries

GPUs support occlusion culling by using a special rendering mode. The user can query the GPU to find out whether a set of triangles is visible when compared to the current contents of the z-buffer. The triangles most often form the bounding volume (for example, a box or k-DOP) of a more complex object. If none of these triangles are visible, then the object can be culled. The GPU rasterizes the triangles of the query and compares their depths to the z-buffer, i.e., it operates in image space. A count of the number of pixels n in which these triangles are visible is generated, though no pixels nor any depths are actually modified. If n is zero, all triangles are occluded or clipped.

However, a count of zero is not quite enough to determine if a bounding volume is not visible. More precisely, no part of the camera frustum's visible near plane should be inside the bounding volume. Assuming this condition is met, then the entire bounding volume is completely occluded, and the contained objects can safely be discarded. If $n > 0$, then a fraction of the pixels failed the test. If n is smaller than a threshold number of pixels, the object could be discarded as being unlikely to contribute much to the final image [1894]. In this way, speed can be traded for possible loss of quality. Another use is to let n help determine the LOD (Section 19.9) of an object. If n is small, then a smaller fraction of the object is (potentially) visible, and so a less-detailed LOD can be used.

When the bounding volume is found to be obscured, we gain performance by avoiding sending a potentially complex object through the rendering pipeline. However, if the test fails, we actually lose a bit of performance, as we spent additional time testing this bounding volume to no benefit.

There are variants of this test. For culling purposes, the exact number of visible fragments is not needed—it suffices with a boolean indicating whether at least one fragment passes the depth test. OpenGL 3.3 and DirectX 11 and later support this type of occlusion query, enumerated as `ANY_SAMPLES_PASSED` in OpenGL [1598]. These tests can be faster since they can terminate the query as soon as one fragment is visible. OpenGL 4.3 and later also allows a faster variant of this query, called `ANY_SAMPLES_PASSED_CONSERVATIVE`. The implementation may choose to provide a less-precise test as long as it is conservative and errs on the correct side. A hardware vendor could implement this by performing the depth test against only the coarse depth buffer (Section 23.7) instead of the per-pixel depths, for example.

The latency of a query is often a relatively long time. Usually, hundreds or thousands of triangles can be rendered within this time—see Section 23.3 for more about latency. Hence, this GPU-based occlusion culling method is worthwhile when the bounding boxes contain a large number of objects and a relatively large amount of occlusion is occurring. GPUs use an occlusion query model in which the CPU can send off any number of queries to the GPU, then it periodically checks to see if any results are available, that is, the query model is asynchronous. For its part, the GPU performs each query and puts the result in a queue. The queue check by the CPU is extremely fast, and the CPU can continue to send down queries or actual renderable objects without having to stall. Both DirectX and OpenGL support predicated/conditional occlusion queries, where both the query and an ID to the corresponding draw call are submitted at the same time. The corresponding draw call is automatically processed by the GPU only if it is indicated that the geometry of the occlusion query is visible. This makes the model substantially more useful.

In general, queries should be performed on objects most likely to be occluded. Kovalèík and Sochor [932] collect running statistics on queries over several frames for each object while the application is running. The number of frames in which an object was found to be hidden affects how often it is tested for occlusion in the future. That is, objects that are visible are likely to stay visible, and so can be tested less frequently. Hidden objects get tested every frame, if possible, since these objects are most likely to benefit from occlusion queries. Mattausch et al. [1136] present several optimizations for occlusion queries (OCs) without predicated/conditional rendering. They use batching of OCs, combining a few OCs into a single OC, use several bounding boxes instead of a single larger one, and use temporally jittered sampling for scheduling of previously visible objects.

The schemes discussed here give a flavor of the potential and problems with occlusion culling methods. When to use occlusion queries, or use most occlusion schemes in general, is not often clear. If everything is visible, an occlusion algorithm can only cost additional time, never save it. One challenge is rapidly determining that the algorithm is not helping, and so cutting back on its fruitless attempts to save time. Another problem is deciding what set of objects to use as occluders. The first objects that are inside the frustum must be visible, so spending queries on these is wasteful. Deciding in what order to render and when to test for occlusion is a struggle in implementing most occlusion-culling algorithms.

19.7.2 Hierarchical Z-Buffering

Hierarchical z-buffering (HZB) [591, 593] has had significant influence on occlusion culling research. Though the original CPU-side form is rarely used, the algorithm is the basis for the GPU hardware method of z-culling (Section 23.7) and for custom occlusion culling using software running on the GPU or on the CPU. We first describe the basic algorithm, followed by how the technique has been adopted in various rendering engines.

The algorithm maintains the scene model in an octree, and a frame's z-buffer as an image pyramid, which we call a z-pyramid. The algorithm thus operates in image space. The octree enables hierarchical culling of occluded regions of the scene, and the z-pyramid enables hierarchical z-buffering of primitives. The z-pyramid is thus the occlusion representation of this algorithm. Examples of these data structures are shown in Figure 19.22.

The finest (highest-resolution) level of the z-pyramid is simply a standard z-buffer. At all other levels, each z-value is the farthest z in the corresponding 2×2 window of the adjacent finer level. Therefore, each z-value represents the farthest z for a square region of the screen. Whenever a z-value is overwritten in the z-buffer, it is propagated through the coarser levels of the z-pyramid. This is done recursively until the top of the image pyramid is reached, where only one z-value remains. Pyramid formation is illustrated in Figure 19.23.

Hierarchical culling of octree nodes is done as follows. Traverse the octree nodes in a rough front-to-back order. A bounding box of the octree is tested against the z-pyramid using an extended occlusion query (Section 19.7.1). We begin testing at the coarsest z-pyramid cell that encloses the box's screen projection. The box's nearest depth within the cell (z_{near}) is then compared to the z-pyramid value, and if z_{near} is farther, the box is known to be occluded. This testing continues recursively down the z-pyramid until the box is found to be occluded, or until the bottom level of the z-pyramid is reached, at which point the box is known to be visible. For visible octree boxes, testing continues recursively down in the octree, and finally potentially visible geometry is rendered into the hierarchical z-buffer. This is done so that subsequent tests can use the occluding power of previously rendered objects.

The full HZB algorithm is not used these days, but it has been simplified and adapted to work well with compute passes using custom culling on the GPU or using software rasterization on the CPU. In general, most occlusion culling algorithms based on HZB work like this:

1. Generate a full hierarchical z-pyramid using some occluder representation.

2. To test if an object is occluded, project its bounding volume to screen space and estimate the mip level in the z-pyramid.

3. Test occlusion against the selected mip level. Optionally continue testing using a finer mip level if results are ambiguous.

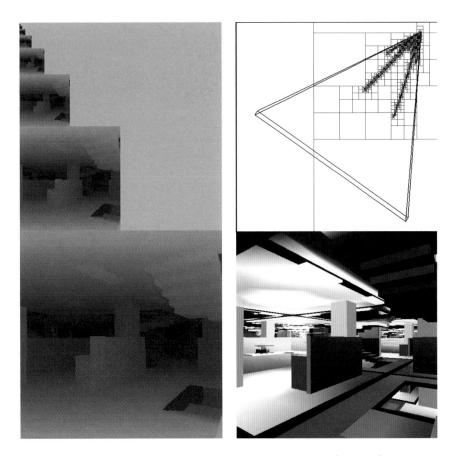

Figure 19.22. Example of occlusion culling with the HZB algorithm [591, 593], showing a scene with high depth complexity (lower right) with the corresponding z-pyramid (on the left), and octree subdivision (upper right). By traversing the octree from front to back and culling occluded octree nodes as they are encountered, this algorithm visits only visible octree nodes and their children (the nodes portrayed at the upper right) and renders only the triangles in visible boxes. In this example, culling of occluded octree nodes reduces the depth complexity from 84 to 2.5. *(Images courtesy of Ned Greene/Apple Computer.)*

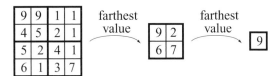

Figure 19.23. On the left, a 4×4 piece of the z-buffer is shown. The numerical values are the actual z-values. This is downsampled to a 2×2 region where each value is the farthest (largest) of the four 2×2 regions on the left. Finally, the farthest value of the remaining four z-values is computed. These three maps compose an image pyramid that is called the hierarchical z-buffer.

Most implementations do not use an octree or any BVH, nor do they update the z-pyramid after an object has been rendered since this is considered too expensive to perform.

Step 1 can be done using the "best" occluders [1637], which could be selected as the closest set of n objects [625], using simplified artist-generated occluder primitives, or using statistics concerning the set of objects that were visible the previous frame. Alternatively, one may use the z-buffer from the previous frame [856], however this is not conservative in that objects may sometimes just pop up due to incorrect culling, especially under quick camera or object movement. Haar and Aaltonen [625] both render the best occluders and combine them with a reprojection of 1/16 low resolution of the previous frame's depth. The z-pyramid is then constructed, as shown in Figure 19.23, using the GPU. Some use the HTILE of the AMD GCN architecture (Section 23.10.3) to speed up z-pyramid generation [625].

In step 2, the bounding volume of an object is projected to screen space. Common choices for BVs are spheres, AABBs, and OBBs. The longest side, l (in pixels), of the projected BV is used to compute the mip level, λ, as [738, 1637, 1883, 1884]

$$\lambda = \min\left(\left\lceil \log_2\left(\max(l,1)\right)\right\rceil, n-1\right), \tag{19.5}$$

where n is the maximum number of mip levels in the z-pyramid. The max operator is there to avoid getting negative mip levels, and the min avoids accessing mip levels that do not exist. Equation 19.5 selects the lowest integer mip level such that the projected BV covers at most 2×2 depth values. The reason for this choice is that it makes the cost predictable—at most four depth values need to be read and tested. Also, Hill and Collin [738] argue that this test can be seen as "probabilistic" in the sense that large objects are more likely to be visible than small ones, so there is no reason to read more depth values in those cases.

When reaching step 3, we know that the projected BV is bounded by a certain set of, at most, 2×2 depth values at that mip level. For a given-sized BV, it may fall entirely inside one depth texel on the mip level. However, depending on how it falls on the grid, it may cover up to all four texels. The minimum depth of the BV is computed, either exactly or conservatively. With an AABB in view space, this depth is simply the minimum depth of the box, and for an OBB, one may project all vertices onto the view vector and select the smallest distance. For spheres, Shopf et al. [1637] compute the closest point on the sphere as $\mathbf{c} - r\mathbf{c}/\|\mathbf{c}\|$, where $\mathbf{c}$ is the sphere center in view space and r is the sphere radius. Note that if the camera is inside a BV, then the BV covers the entire screen and the object is then rendered. The minimum depth, $z_{\min}$, of the BV is compared to the (at most) 2×2 depths in the hierarchical z-buffer, and if $z_{\min}$ is always larger, then the BV is occluded. It is possible to stop testing here and just render the object if it was not detected as occluded.

One may also continue testing against the next deeper (higher-resolution) level in the pyramid. We can see if such testing is warranted by using another z-pyramid that stores the minimum depths. We test the maximum distance, $z_{\max}$, to the BV against the corresponding depths in this new buffer. If z_{max} is smaller than all these depths, then the BV is definitely visible and can be rendered immediately. Otherwise, the z_{min} and z_{max} of the BV overlap the depth of the two hierarchical z-buffers, in which case Kaplanyan [856] suggests testing be continued on a higher-resolution mip level. Note that testing 2×2 texels in the hierarchical z-buffer against a single depth is quite similar to percentage-closer filtering (Section 7.5). In fact, the test can be done using bilinear filtering with percentage-closer filtering, and if the test returns a positive value, then at least one texel is visible.

Haar and Altonen [625] also present a two-pass method that always renders at least all visible objects. First, occlusion culling for all objects is done against the previous frame's z-pyramid, and the "visible" objects are rendered. Alternatively, one can use the last frame's visibility list to directly render the z-pyramid. While this is an approximation, all the objects that were rendered serve as an excellent guess for the "best" occluders for the current frame, especially in scenarios with high frame-to-frame coherency. The second pass takes the depth buffer of these rendered objects and creates a new z-pyramid. Then, the objects that were occlusion culled in the first pass are tested for occlusion, and rendered if not culled. This method generates a fully correct image even if the camera moves quickly or objects move rapidly over the screen. Kubisch and Tavenrath [944] use a similar method.

Doghramachi and Bucci [363] rasterize oriented bounding boxes of the occludees against the previous frame's depth buffer, which has been downsampled and reprojected. They force the shader to use early-z (Section 23.7), and for each box the visible fragments mark the object as visible in a buffer location, which is uniquely determined from the object ID [944]. This provides higher culling rates since oriented boxes are used and since per-pixel testing is done, instead of using a custom test against a mip level using Equation 19.5.

Collin [283] uses a 256×144 float z-buffer (not hierarchical) and rasterizes artist-generated occluders with low complexity. This is done in software either using the CPU or using the SPUs (on PLAYSTATION 3) with highly optimized SIMD code. To perform occlusion testing, the screen-space AABB of an object is computed and its z_{min} is compared against all relevant depths in the small z-buffer. Only objects that survive culling are sent to the GPU. This approach works but is not conservatively correct, since a lower resolution than the final framebuffer's resolution is used. Wihlidal [1883] suggests that the low-resolution z-buffer also be used to load z_{max}-values into the HiZ (Section 23.7) of the GPU, e.g., priming the HTILE structure on AMD GCN. Alternatively, if HZB is used for compute-pass culling, then the software z-buffer can be used to generate the z-pyramid. In this way, the algorithms exploit all information generated in software.

Hasselgren et al. [683] present a different approach, where each 8×4 tile has one bit per pixel and two z_{max}-values [50], resulting in an overall cost of 3 bits per pixel. By using z_{max}-values, it is possible to handle depth discontinuities better, since a background object can use one of the z_{max}-values and a foreground object uses the other. This representation, called a *masked hierarchical depth buffer* (MHDB), is conservative and can also be used for z_{max}-culling. Only coverage masks and a single maximum depth value are generated per tile during software triangle rasterization, which makes rasterization to the MHDB quick and efficient. During rasterization of triangles to the MDHB, occlusion testing of the triangles can be done to the MDHB as well, which optimizes the rasterizer. The MDHB is updated for each triangle, which is a strength that few of the other methods have. Two usage modes are evaluated. The first is to use special occlusion meshes and render these using the software rasterizer to the MDHB. After that, an AABB tree over the occludees is traversed and hierarchically tested against the MDHB. This can be highly effective, especially if there are many small objects in a scene. For the second approach, the entire scene is stored in an AABB tree and traversal of the scene is done in roughly front-to-back order using a heap. At each step, frustum culling and occlusion queries are done against the MDHB. The MDHB is also updated whenever an object is rendered. The scene in Figure 19.19 was rendered using this method. The open-source code is heavily optimized for AVX2 [683].

There are also middleware packages specifically for culling and for occlusion culling in particular. Umbra is one such framework, which has been integrated extensively with various game engines [13, 1789].

19.8 Culling Systems

Culling systems have evolved considerably over the years, and continue to do so. In this section, we describe some overarching ideas and point to the literature for details. Some systems execute effectively all culling in the GPU's compute shader, while others combine coarse culling on the CPU with a later finer culling on the GPU.

A typical culling system works on many granularities, as shown in Figure 19.24. A cluster or chunk of an object is simply a subset of the triangles of the object. One may use triangle strips with 64 vertices [625], or groups of 256 triangles [1884], for example. At each step, a combination of culling techniques can be used. El Mansouri [415] uses small triangle culling, detail culling, view frustum culling, and occlusion culling on objects. Since a cluster is geometrically smaller than an object, it makes sense to use the same culling techniques even for clusters since they are more likely to be culled. One may use, for example, detail, frustum, clustered backface, and occlusion culling on clusters.

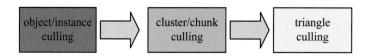

Figure 19.24. An example culling system that works on three different granularities. First, culling is done on a per-object level. Surviving objects are then culled on a per-cluster level. Finally, triangle culling is done, which is further described in Figure 19.25.

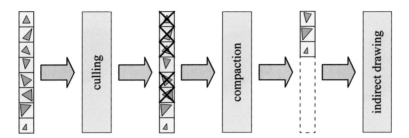

Figure 19.25. Triangle culling system, where a battery of culling algorithms first is applied to all individual triangles. To be able to use indirect drawing, i.e., without a GPU/CPU round trip, the surviving triangles are then compacted into a shorter list. This list is rendered by the GPU using indirect drawing.

After culling has been done on a per-cluster level, one can perform an additional step where culling is done on a per-triangle level. To make this occur entirely on the GPU, the approach illustrated in Figure 19.25 can be used. Culling techniques for triangles include frustum culling after division by w, i.e., comparing the extents of the triangle against ± 1, backface testing, degenerate triangle culling, small triangle culling, and possibly occlusion culling as well. The triangles that remain after all the culling tests are then compacted into a minimal list, which is done in order to process only surviving triangles in the next step [1884]. The idea is to instruct the culling compute shader to send a draw command from the GPU to itself in this step. This is done using an *indirect draw command*. These calls are called "multi-draw indirect" in OpenGL and "execute indirect" in DirectX [433]. The number of triangles is written to a location in a GPU buffer, which together with the compacted list can be used by the GPU to render the list of triangles.

There are many ways to combine culling algorithms together with where they are executed, i.e., either on the CPU or on the GPU, and there are many flavors of each culling algorithm as well. The ultimate combination has yet to be found, but it is safe to say that the best approach depends on the target architecture and the content to be rendered. Next, we point to some important work in the field of CPU/GPU culling systems that has influenced the field substantially. Shopf et al. [1637] did all AI simulations for characters on the GPU, and as a consequence, the position of each character was only available in GPU memory. This led them to explore culling and LOD management using the compute shader, and most of the systems that followed have been heavily influenced by their work. Haar and Aaltonen [625] describe the system they developed for *Assassin's Creed Unity*. Wihlidal [1883, 1884] explains the culling system used in the Frostbite engine. Engel [433] presents a system for culling that helps improve a pipeline using a visibility buffer (Section 20.5). Kubisch and Tavenrath [944] describe methods for rendering massive models with a large number of parts and optimize using different culling methods and API calls. One noteworthy method they use to occlusion-cull boxes is to create the visible sides of a bounding box using the geometry shader and then let early-z quickly cull occluded geometry.

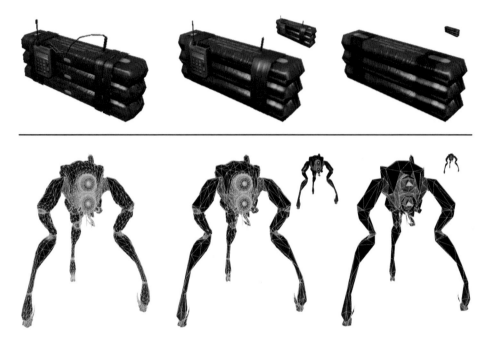

Figure 19.26. Here, we show three different levels of detail for models of C4 explosives (top) and a Hunter (bottom). Elements are simplified or removed altogether at lower levels of detail. The small inset images show the simplified models at the relative sizes at which they might be used. *(Top row of images courtesy of Crytek; bottom row courtesy of Valve Corp.)*

19.9 Level of Detail

The basic idea of *levels of detail* (LODs) is to use simpler versions of an object as it makes less and less of a contribution to the rendered image. For example, consider a detailed car that may consist of a million triangles. This representation can be used when the viewer is close to the car. When the object is farther away, say covering only 200 pixels, we do not need all one million triangles. Instead, we can use a simplified model that has only, say, 1000 triangles. Due to the distance, the simplified version looks approximately the same as the more detailed version. See Figure 19.26. In this way, a significant performance increase can be expected. In order to reduce the total work involved in applying LOD techniques, they are best applied after culling techniques. For example, LOD selection is computed only for objects inside the view frustum.

LOD techniques can also be used in order to make an application work at the desired frame rates on a range of devices with different performance. On systems with lower speeds, less-detailed LODs can be used to increase performance. Note that while LOD techniques help first and foremost with a reduction in vertex processing, they also reduce pixel-shading costs. This occurs because the sum of all triangle edge lengths for a model will be lower, which means that quad overshading is reduced (Sections 18.2 and 23.1).

Fog and other participating media, described in Chapter 14, can be used together with LODs. This allows us to completely skip the rendering of an object as it enters fully opaque fog, for example. Also, the fogging mechanism can be used to implement time-critical rendering (Section 19.9.3). By moving the far plane closer to the viewer, more objects can be culled early on, increasing the frame rate. In addition, a lower LOD can often be used in the fog.

Some objects, such as spheres, Bézier surfaces, and subdivision surfaces, have levels of detail as part of their geometrical description. The underlying geometry is curved, and a separate LOD control determines how it is tessellated into displayable triangles. See Section 17.6.2 for algorithms that adapt the quality of tessellations for parametric surfaces and subdivision surfaces.

In general, LOD algorithms consist of three major parts, namely, *generation, selection*, and *switching*. LOD generation is the part where different representations of a model are generated with varying amounts of detail. The simplification methods discussed in Section 16.5 can be used to generate the desired number of LODs. Another approach is to make models with different numbers of triangles by hand. The selection mechanism chooses a level of detail model based on some criteria, such as estimated area on the screen. Finally, we need to change from one level of detail to another, and this process is termed *LOD switching*. Different LOD switching and selection mechanisms are presented in this section.

While the focus in this section is on choosing among different geometric representations, the ideas behind LODs can also be applied to other aspects of the model, or even to the rendering method used. Lower level of detail models can also use lower-resolution textures, thereby further saving memory as well as possibly improving cache access [240]. Shaders themselves can be simplified depending on distance, importance, or other factors [688, 1318, 1365, 1842]. Kajiya [845] presents a hierarchy of scale showing how surface lighting models overlap texture mapping methods, which in turn overlap geometric details. Another technique is that fewer bones can be used for skinning operations for distant objects.

When static objects are relatively far away, billboards and impostors (Section 13.6.4) are a natural way to represent them at little cost [1097]. Other surface rendering methods, such as bump or relief mapping, can be used to simplify the representation of a model. Figure 19.27 gives an example. Teixeira [1754] discusses how to bake normal maps onto surfaces using the GPU. The most noticeable flaw with this simplification technique is that the silhouettes lose their curvature. Loviscach [1085] presents a method of extruding fins along silhouette edges to create curved silhouettes.

An example of the range of techniques that can be used to represent an object comes from Lengyel et al. [1030, 1031]. In this research, fur is represented by geometry when extremely close up, by alpha-blended polylines when farther away, then by a

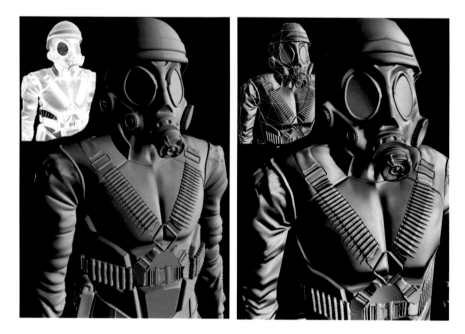

Figure 19.27. On the left, the original model consists of 1.5 million triangles. On the right, the model has 1100 triangles, with surface details stored as heightfield textures and rendered using relief mapping. *(Image courtesy of Natalya Tatarchuk, ATI Research, Inc.)*

blend with volume texture "shells," and finally by a texture map when far away. See Figure 19.28. Knowing when and how best to switch from one set of modeling and rendering techniques to another and so maximize frame rate and quality is still an art and an open area for exploration.

19.9.1 LOD Switching

When switching from one LOD to another, an abrupt model substitution is often noticeable and distracting. This difference is called *popping*. Several different ways to perform this switching will be described here, and they each have different popping traits.

Discrete Geometry LODs

In the simplest type of LOD algorithm, the various representations are models of the same object containing different numbers of primitives. This algorithm is well suited for modern graphics hardware [1092], because these separate static meshes can be stored in GPU memory and reused (Section 16.4.5). A more detailed LOD has a higher number of primitives. Three LODs of objects are shown in Figures 19.26 and 19.29. The first figure also shows the LODs at different distances from the viewer.

Figure 19.28. From a distance, the bunny's fur is rendered with volumetric textures. When the bunny comes closer, the hair is rendered with alpha-blended polylines. When close up, the fur along the silhouette is rendered with graftal fins. *(Image courtesy of Jed Lengyel and Michael Cohen, Microsoft Research.)*

Figure 19.29. A part of a cliff at three different levels of detail, with 72,200, 13,719, and 7,713 triangles from left to right. *(Images courtesy of Quixel Megascans.)*

The switching from one LOD to another is sudden. That is, on the current frame a certain LOD is used, then on the next frame, the selection mechanism selects another LOD and immediately uses that for rendering. Popping is typically the worst for this type of LOD method, but it can work well if switching occurs at distances when the difference in the rendered LODs is barely visible. Better alternatives are described next.

Blend LODs

Conceptually, a simple way to switch is to do a linear blend between the two LODs over a short period of time. Doing so will certainly make for a smoother switch. Rendering two LODs for one object is naturally more expensive than just rendering one LOD, so this somewhat defeats the purpose of LODs. However, LOD switching usually takes place during only a short amount of time, and often not for all objects in a scene at the same time, so the quality improvement may well be worth the cost.

Assume a transition between two LODs—say LOD1 and LOD2—is desired, and that LOD1 is the current LOD being rendered. The problem is in how to render and blend both LODs in a reasonable fashion. Making both LODs semitransparent will result in a semitransparent (though somewhat more opaque) object being rendered to the screen, which looks strange.

Giegl and Wimmer [528] propose a blending method that works well in practice and is simple to implement. First draw LOD1 opaquely to the framebuffer (both color and z). Then fade in LOD2 by increasing its alpha value from 0 to 1 and using the "over" blend mode. When LOD2 has faded in so it is completely opaque, it is turned into the current LOD, and LOD1 is then faded out. The LOD that is being faded (in or out) should be rendered with the z-test enabled and z-writes disabled. To avoid distant objects that are drawn later drawing over the results of rendering the faded LOD, simply draw all faded LODs in sorted order after all opaque content, as is normally done for transparent objects. Note that in the middle of the transition, both LODs are rendered opaquely, one on top of the other. This technique works best if the transition intervals are kept short, which also helps keep the rendering overhead small. Mittring [1227] discusses a similar method, except that screen-door transparency (potentially at the subpixel level) is used to dissolve between versions.

Scherzer and Wimmer [1557] avoid rendering both LODs by only updating one of the LODs on each frame and reuse the other LOD from the previous frame. Back-projection of the previous frame is performed together with a combination pass using visibility textures. Faster rendering and better-behaved transitions are the main results.

Some objects lend themselves to other switching techniques. For example, the SpeedTree package [887] smoothly shifts or scales parts of their tree LOD models to avoid pops. See Figure 19.30 for one example. A set of LODs are shown in Figure 19.31, along with a billboard LOD technique used for distant trees.

Figure 19.30. Tree branches (and their leaves, not shown) are shrunk and then removed as the viewer moves away from the tree model. *(Images courtesy of SpeedTree.)*

Alpha LODs

A simple method that avoids popping altogether is to use what we call alpha LODs. This technique can be used by itself or combined with other LOD switching techniques. It is used on the simplest visible LOD, which can be the original model if only one LOD is available. As the metric used for LOD selection (e.g., distance to this object) increases, the overall transparency of the object is increased (α is decreased), and the object finally disappears when it reaches full transparency ($\alpha = 0.0$). This happens

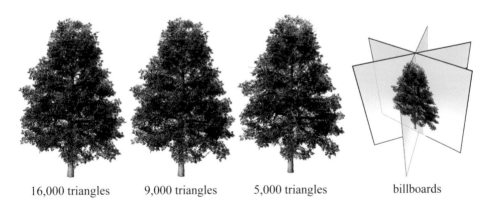

16,000 triangles   9,000 triangles   5,000 triangles   billboards

Figure 19.31. Tree LOD models, near to far. When the tree is in the distance, it is represented by one of a set of billboards, shown on the right. Each billboard is a rendering of the tree from a different view, and consists of a color and normal map. The billboard most facing the viewer is selected. In practice 8 to 12 billboards are formed (6 are shown here), and the transparent sections are trimmed away to avoid spending time discarding fully transparent pixels (Section 13.6.2). *(Images courtesy of SpeedTree.)*

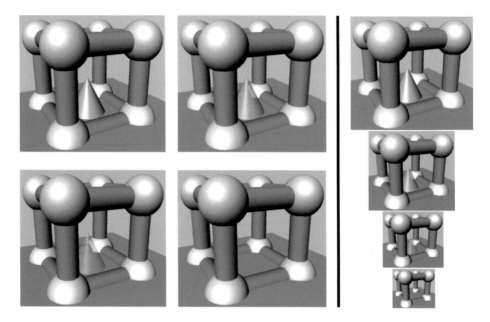

Figure 19.32. The cone in the middle is rendered using an alpha LOD. The transparency of the cone is increased when the distance to it increases, and it finally disappears. The images on the left are shown from the same distance for viewing purposes, while the images to the right of the line are shown at different sizes.

when the metric value is larger than a user-defined invisibility threshold. When the invisibility threshold has been reached, the object need not be sent through the rendering pipeline at all as long as the metric value remains above the threshold. When an object has been invisible and its metric falls below the invisibility threshold, then it decreases its transparency and starts to be visible again. An alternative is to use the hysteresis method described in Section 19.9.2.

The advantage of using this technique standalone is that it is experienced as much more continuous than the discrete geometry LOD method, and so avoids popping. Also, since the object finally disappears altogether and need not be rendered, a significant speedup can be expected. The disadvantage is that the object entirely disappears, and it is only at this point that a performance increase is obtained. Figure 19.32 shows an example of alpha LODs.

One problem with using alpha transparency is that sorting by depth needs to be done to ensure transparent objects blend correctly. To fade out distant vegetation, Whatley [1876] discusses how a noise texture can be used for screen-door transparency. This has the effect of a dissolve, with more texels on the object disappearing as the distance increases. While the quality is not as good as a true alpha fade, screen-door transparency means that no sorting or blending is necessary.

CLODs and Geomorph LODs

The process of mesh simplification can be used to create various LOD models from a single complex object. Algorithms for performing this simplification are discussed in Section 16.5.1. One approach is to create a set of discrete LODs and use these as discussed previously. However, edge collapse methods have a property that allows other ways of making a transition between LODs. Here, we present two methods that exploit such information. These are useful as background, but are currently rarely used in practice.

A model has two fewer triangles after each edge collapse operation is performed. What happens in an edge collapse is that an edge is shrunk until its two endpoints meet and it disappears. If this process is animated, a smooth transition occurs between the original model and its slightly simplified version. For each edge collapse, a single vertex is joined with another. Over a series of edge collapses, a set of vertices move to join other vertices. By storing the series of edge collapses, this process can be reversed, so that a simplified model can be made more complex over time. The reversal of an edge collapse is called a *vertex split*. So, one way to change the level of detail of an object is to precisely base the number of triangles visible on the LOD selection value. At 100 meters away, the model might consist of 1000 triangles, and moving to 101 meters, it might drop to 998 triangles. Such a scheme is called a *continuous level of detail* (CLOD) technique. There is not, then, a discrete set of models, but rather a huge set of models available for display, each one with two less triangles than its more complex neighbor.

While appealing, using such a scheme in practice has some drawbacks. Not all models in the CLOD stream look good. Triangle meshes, which can be rendered much more rapidly than single triangles, are more difficult to use with CLOD techniques than with static models. If there are several instances of the same object in the scene, then each CLOD object needs to specify its own specific set of triangles, since it does not match any others. Forsyth [481] discuss solutions to these and other problems. While most CLOD techniques are rather serial in nature, they are not automatically a good fit for implementation on GPUs. Therefore, Hu et al. [780] present a modification of CLOD that better fits the parallel nature of the GPU. Their technique is also view-dependent in that if an object intersects, say, the left side of the view frustum, fewer triangles can be used outside the frustum, connecting to a higher-density mesh inside.

In a vertex split, one vertex becomes two. What this means is that every vertex on a complex model comes from some vertex on a simpler version. *Geomorph LODs* [768] are a set of discrete models created by simplification, with the connectivity between vertices maintained. When switching from a complex model to a simple one, the complex model's vertices are interpolated between their original positions and those of the simpler version. When the transition is complete, the simpler level of detail model is used to represent the object. See Figure 19.33 for an example of a transition. There are several advantages to geomorphs. The individual static models can be selected in advance to be of high quality, and easily can be turned into triangle meshes. Like CLOD, popping is also avoided by smooth transitions. The main drawback is that

Figure 19.33. The left and right images show a low-detail model and a higher-detail model. The image in the middle shows a geomorph model interpolated approximately halfway between the left and right models. Note that the cow in the middle has equally many vertices and triangles as the model to the right. *(Images generated using Melax's "Polychop" simplification demo [1196].)*

each vertex needs to be interpolated; CLOD techniques usually do not use interpolation, so the set of vertex positions themselves never changes. Another drawback is that the objects always appear to be changing, which may be distracting. This is especially true for textured objects. Sander and Mitchell [1543] describe a system in which geomorphing is used in conjunction with static, GPU-resident vertex and index buffers. It is also possible to combine the screen-door transparency of Mittring [1227] (described above) with geomorphs for an even smoother transition.

A related idea called fractional tessellation is supported by GPUs. In such schemes, the tessellation factor for a curved surface can be set to any floating point number, and so popping can be avoided. Fractional tessellation can be used for Bézier patches and displacement mapping primitives, for example. See Section 17.6.1 for more on these techniques.

19.9.2 LOD Selection

Given that different levels of detail of an object exist, a choice must be made for which one of them to render, or which ones to blend. This is the task of LOD selection, and a few different techniques for this will be presented here. These techniques can also be used to select good occluders for occlusion culling algorithms.

In general, a metric, also called the *benefit function*, is evaluated for the current viewpoint and the location of the object, and the value of this metric picks an appropriate LOD. This metric may be based on, for example, the projected area of the bounding volume of the object or the distance from the viewpoint to the object. The value of the benefit function is denoted r here. See also Section 17.6.2 on how to rapidly estimate the projection of a line onto the screen.

Range-Based

A common way of selecting a LOD is to associate the different LODs of an object with different distance ranges. The most detailed LOD has a range from zero to some

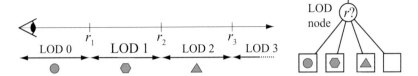

Figure 19.34. The left part of this illustration shows how range-based LODs work. Note that the fourth LOD is an empty object, so when the object is farther away than r_3, nothing is drawn, because the object is not contributing enough to the image to be worth the effort. The right part shows a LOD node in a scene graph. Only one of the children of a LOD node is descended based on r.

user-defined value r_1, which means that this LOD is visible when the distance to the object is less than r_1. The next LOD has a range from r_1 to r_2 where $r_2 > r_1$. If the distance to the object is greater than or equal to r_1 and less than r_2, then this LOD is used, and so on. Examples of four different LODs with their ranges, and their corresponding LOD node used in a scene graph, are illustrated in Figure 19.34.

Unnecessary popping can occur if the metric used to determine which LOD to use varies from frame to frame around some value, r_i. A rapid cycling back and forth between levels can occur. This can be solved by introducing some hysteresis around the r_i value [898, 1508]. This is illustrated in Figure 19.35 for a range-based LOD, but applies to any type. Here, the upper row of LOD ranges are used only when r is increasing. When r is decreasing, the bottom row of ranges is used.

Blending two LODs in the transition ranges is illustrated in Figure 19.36. However, this is not ideal, since the distance to an object may reside in the transition range for a long time, which increases the rendering burden due to blending two LODs. Instead, Mittring [1227] performs LOD switching during a finite amount of time, when the object reaches a certain transition range. For best results, this should be combined with the hysteresis approach above.

Projected Area-Based

Another common metric for LOD selection is the projected area of the bounding volume, or an estimation of it. Here, we will show how the number of pixels of that

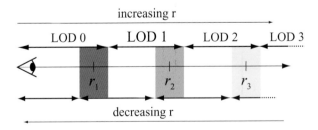

Figure 19.35. The colored areas illustrate the hysteresis regions for the LOD technique.

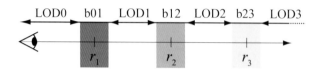

Figure 19.36. The colored areas illustrate ranges where blending is done between the two closest LODs, where b01 means blend between LOD0 and LOD1, for example, and LODk means that only LODk is rendered in the corresponding range.

area, called the *screen-space coverage*, can be estimated for spheres and boxes with perspective viewing.

Starting with spheres, the estimation is based on the fact that the size of the projection of an object diminishes with the distance from the viewer along the view direction. This is shown in Figure 19.37, which illustrates how the size of the projection is halved if the distance from the viewer is doubled, which holds for planar objects facing the viewer. We define a sphere by its center point $\mathbf{c}$ and a radius r. The viewer is located at $\mathbf{v}$ looking along the normalized direction vector $\mathbf{d}$. The distance from $\mathbf{c}$ to $\mathbf{v}$ along the view direction is simply the projection of the sphere's center onto the view vector: $\mathbf{d} \cdot (\mathbf{v} - \mathbf{c})$. We also assume that the distance from the viewer to the near plane of the view frustum is n. The near plane is used in the estimation so that an object that is located on the near plane returns its original size. The estimation of the radius of the projected sphere is then

$$p = \frac{nr}{\mathbf{d} \cdot (\mathbf{v} - \mathbf{c})}. \tag{19.6}$$

The area of the projection in pixels is thus $\pi p^2 wh$, where $w \times h$ is the screen resolution. A higher value selects a more detailed LOD. This is an approximation. In fact,

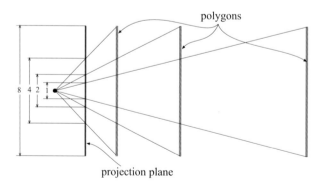

Figure 19.37. This illustration shows how the size of the projection of objects, without any thickness, is halved when the distance is doubled.

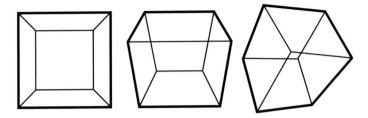

Figure 19.38. Three cases of projection of a cube, showing (from left to right) one, two, and three frontfaces. The outlines consist of four, six, and six vertices, respectively, and the area of each outline is computed for each polygon formed. *(Illustration after Schmalstieg and Tobler [1569].)*

the projection of a three-dimensional sphere is an ellipse, as shown by Mara and McGuire [1122]. They also derive a method for computing conservative bounding polygons even in the case when the sphere intersects the near plane.

It is common practice to simply use a bounding sphere around an object's bounding box. Another estimate is to use the screen bounds of the bounding box. However, thin or flat objects can vary considerably in the amount of projected area actually covered. For example, imagine a strand of spaghetti that has one end at the upper left corner of the screen, the other at the lower right. Its bounding sphere will cover the screen, as do the minimum and maximum two-dimensional screen bounds of its bounding box.

Schmalstieg and Tobler [1569] present a rapid routine for calculating the projected area of a box. The idea is to classify the viewpoint of the camera with respect to the box, and to use this classification to determine which projected vertices are included in the silhouette of the projected box. This process is done via a lookup table. Using these vertices, the area in view can be computed. The classification is categorized into three major cases, shown in Figure 19.38. Practically, this classification is done by determining on which side of the planes of the bounding box the viewpoint is located. For efficiency, the viewpoint is transformed into the coordinate system of the box, so that only comparisons are needed for classification. The result of the comparisons are put into a bitmask, which is used as an index into the LUT. This LUT determines how many vertices there are in the silhouette as seen from the viewpoint. Then, another lookup is used to actually find the silhouette vertices. After they have been projected to the screen, the area of the outline is computed. To avoid (sometimes drastic) estimation errors, it is worthwhile to clip the polygon formed to the view frustum's sides. Source code is available on the web. Lengyel [1026] presents an optimization to this scheme, where a more compact LUT can be used.

It is not always a good idea to base the LOD selection on range or projection alone. For example, if an object has a certain AABB with some large and some small triangles in it, then the small triangles may alias badly and decrease performance due to quad overshading. If another object has the exact same AABB but with medium and large triangles in it, then both range-based and projection-based selection methods will select the same LOD. To avoid this, Schulz and Mader [1590] use the geometric mean, g, to help select the LOD:

$$g = \sqrt[n]{t_0 t_1 \cdots t_{n-1}}, \tag{19.7}$$

where t_i are the sizes of the triangles of the object. The reason to use a geometric mean instead of an arithmetic mean (average) is that many small triangles will make g smaller even if there are a few large triangles. This value is computed offline for the highest-resolution model, and is used to precompute a distance where the first switch should occur. The subsequent switch distances are simple functions of the first distance. This allows their system to use lower LODs more often, which increases performance.

Another approach is to compute the geometric error of each discrete LOD, i.e., an estimation of how many meters that simplified model deviates at most from the original model. This distance can then be projected to determine what the effect is in screen space to use that LOD. The lowest LOD, that also meets a user-defined screen-space error, is then selected.

Other Selection Methods

Range-based and projected area-based LOD selection are typically the most common metrics used. However, many others are possible, and we will mention a few here. Besides projected area, Funkhouser and Séquin [508] also suggest using the importance of an object (e.g., walls are more important than a clock on the wall), motion, hysteresis (when switching LODs, the benefit is lowered), and focus. This last, the viewer's focus of attention, can be an important factor. For example, in a sports game, the figure controlling the ball is where the user will be paying the most attention, so the other characters can have relatively lower levels of detail [898]. Similarly, when eye tracking is used in a virtual reality application, higher LODs should be used where the viewer looks.

Depending on the application, other strategies may be fruitful. Overall visibility can be used, e.g., a nearby object seen through dense foliage can be rendered with a lower LOD. More global metrics are possible, such as limiting the overall number of highly detailed LODs used in order to stay within a given triangle budget [898]. See the next section for more on this topic. Other factors are visibility, colors, and textures. Perceptual metrics can also be used to choose a LOD [1468].

McAuley [1154] presents a vegetation system, where trunk and leaf clusters have three LODs before they become impostors. He preprocesses visibility, from different viewpoints and from different distances, between clusters for each object. Since a cluster in the back of the tree may be quite hidden by closer clusters, it is possible to select lower LODs for such clusters even if the tree is up close. For grass rendering, it is common to use geometry close to the viewer, billboards a bit farther away, and a simple ground texture at significant distances [1352].

19.9.3 Time-Critical LOD Rendering

It is often a desirable feature of a rendering system to have a constant frame rate. In fact, this is what often is referred to as "hard real-time" or time-critical rendering.. Such a system is given a specific amount of time, say 16 ms, and must complete its task (e.g., render the image) within that time. When time is up, the system has to stop processing. A hard real-time rendering system will be able to show the user more or all of the scene each frame if the objects in a scene are represented by LODs, versus drawing only a few highly detailed models in the time allotted.

Funkhouser and Séquin [508] have presented a heuristic algorithm that adapts the selection of the level of detail for all visible objects in a scene to meet the requirement of constant frame rate. This algorithm is *predictive* in the sense that it selects the LOD of the visible objects based on desired frame rate and on which objects are visible. Such an algorithm contrasts with a *reactive* algorithm, which bases its selection on the time it took to render the previous frame.

An object is called O and is rendered at a level of detail called L, which gives (O, L) for each LOD of an object. Two heuristics are then defined. One heuristic estimates the cost of rendering an object at a certain level of detail: $\text{Cost}(O, L)$. Another estimates the benefit of an object rendered at a certain level of detail: $\text{Benefit}(O, L)$. The benefit function estimates the contribution to the image of an object at a certain LOD.

Assume the objects inside or intersecting the view frustum are called S. The main idea behind the algorithm is then to optimize the selection of the LODs for the objects S using the heuristically chosen functions. Specifically, we want to maximize

$$\sum_S \text{Benefit}(O, L) \tag{19.8}$$

under the constraint

$$\sum_S \text{Cost}(O, L) \leq T, \tag{19.9}$$

where T is the target frame time.

In other words, we want to select the level of detail for the objects that gives us "the best image" within the desired frame rate. Next we describe how the cost and benefit functions can be estimated, and then we present an optimization algorithm for the above equations.

Both the cost function and the benefit function are hard to define so that they work under all circumstances. The cost function can be estimated by timing the rendering of a LOD several times with different viewing parameters. See Section 19.9.2 for different benefit functions. In practice, the projected area of the BV of the object may suffice as a benefit function.

Finally, we will discuss how to choose the level of detail for the objects in a scene. First, we note the following: For some viewpoints, a scene may be too complex to be able to keep up with the desired frame rate. To solve this, we can define a LOD for each object at its lowest detail level, which is simply an object with no primitives—i.e., we avoid rendering the object [508]. Using this trick, we render only the most important objects and skip the unimportant ones.

To select the "best" LODs for a scene, Equation 19.8 has to be optimized under the constraint shown in Equation 19.9. This is an NP-complete problem, which means that to solve it correctly, the only thing to do is to test all different combinations and select the best. This is clearly infeasible for any kind of algorithm. A simpler, more feasible approach is to use a greedy algorithm that tries to maximize the Value = Benefit(O, L)/Cost(O, L) for each object. This algorithm treats all the objects inside the view frustum and chooses to render the objects in descending order, i.e., the one with the highest value first. If an object has the same value for more than one LOD, then the LOD with the highest benefit is selected and rendered. This approach gives the most "bang for the buck." For n objects inside the view frustum, the algorithm runs in $O(n \log n)$ time, and it produces a solution that is at least half as good as the best [507, 508]. It is also possible to exploit frame-to-frame coherence to speed up the sorting of the values.

More information about LOD management and the combination of LOD management and portal culling can be found in Funkhouser's PhD thesis [507]. Maciel and Shirley [1097] combine LODs with impostors and present an approximately constant-time algorithm for rendering outdoor scenes. The general idea is that a hierarchy of different representations (e.g., a set of LODs and hierarchical impostors) of an object is used. Then the tree is traversed in some fashion to give the best image given a certain amount of time. Mason and Blake [1134] present an incremental hierarchical LOD selection algorithm. Again, the different representations of an object can be arbitrary. Eriksson et al. [441] present hierarchical levels of detail (HLODs). Using these, a scene can be rendered with constant frame rate as well, or rendered such that the rendering error is bounded. Related to this is rendering on a power budget. Wang et al. [1843] present an optimization framework that selects good parameters for reducing power usage, which is important for mobile phones and tablets.

Related to time-critical rendering is another set of techniques that apply to static models. When the camera is not moving, the full model is rendered and accumulation buffering can be used for antialiasing, depth of field, and soft shadows, with a progressive update. However, when the camera moves, the levels of detail of all objects can be lowered and detail culling can be used to completely cull small objects in order to meet a certain frame rate.

19.10 Rendering Large Scenes

So far it has been implied that the scene to be rendered fits into the main memory of the computer. This may not always be the case. Some consoles only have 8 GB of internal memory, for example, while some game worlds can consist of hundreds of gigabytes of data. Therefore, we present methods for streaming and transcoding of textures, some general streaming techniques, and finally terrain rendering algorithms. Note that these methods are almost always combined with culling techniques and level of detail methods, described earlier in this chapter.

19.10.1 Virtual Texturing and Streaming

Imagine that you want to use a texture with an incredibly large resolution in order to be able to render a huge terrain data set, and that this texture is so large that it does not fit into GPU memory. As an example, some virtual textures in the game *RAGE* have a resolution of 128k × 128k, which would consume 64 GB of GPU memory [1309]. When memory is limited on the CPU, operating systems use virtual memory for memory management, swapping in data from the drive to CPU memory as needed [715]. This functionality is what *sparse textures* [109, 248] provide, making it possible to allocate a huge virtual texture, also known as a *megatexture*. These sets of techniques are sometimes called *virtual texturing* or *partially resident texturing*. The application determines which regions (tiles) of each mipmap level should be resident in GPU memory. A tile is typically 64 kB and its texture resolution depends on the texture format. Here, we present virtual texturing and streaming techniques.

The key observation about an efficient texturing system using mipmapping is that the number of texels needed should ideally be proportional to the resolution of the final image being rendered, independent of the resolutions of the textures themselves. As a consequence, we only require the texels that are visible to be located in physical GPU memory, which is a rather limited set compared to all texels in an entire game world. The main concept is illustrated in Figure 19.39, where the entire mipmap chain is divided into tiles in both virtual and physical memory. These structures are sometimes called *virtual mipmaps* or *clipmaps* [1739], where the latter term refers to a smaller part of the larger mipmap being clipped out for use. Since the size of physical memory is much smaller than virtual memory, only a small set of the virtual texture tiles can fit into the physical memory. The geometry uses a global uv-parameterization into the virtual texture, and before such uv-coordinates are used in a pixel shader, they need to be translated into texture coordinates that point into physical texture memory. This is done using either a GPU-supported page table (shown in Figure 19.39) or an indirection texture, if done in software on the GPU. The GPU in the Nintendo GameCube has virtual texture support. More recently, the PLAYSTATION 4, Xbox One, and many other GPUs have support for hardware virtual texturing. The indirection texture needs to be updated with correct offsets as tiles are mapped and unmapped to physical memory. Using a huge virtual texture and a small physical texture works well because distant geometry only needs to load a few higher-level mipmap tiles into physical memory, while geometry close to the camera can load a few lower-level mipmap tiles. Note that virtual texturing can be used for streaming huge textures from disk but also for sparse shadow mapping [241], for example.

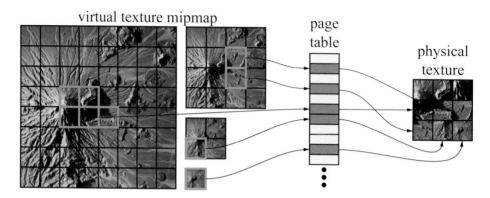

Figure 19.39. In virtual texturing, a large virtual texture with its mipmap hierarchy is divided into tiles (left) of, say, 128×128 pixels each. Only a small set (3×3 tiles in this case) can fit into physical memory (right). To find the location of a virtual texture tile, a translation from a virtual address to physical address is required, which here is done via a page table. Note that, in order to reduce clutter, not all tiles in physical memory have arrows from the virtual texture. *(Image texture of the Bazman volcano, Iran. From NASA's "Visible Earth" project.)*

Since physical memory is limited, all engines using virtual texturing need a way to determine which tiles should be resident, i.e., located in physical memory, and which should not. There are several such methods. Sugden and Iwanicki [1721] use a feedback rendering approach, where a first render pass writes out all the information required to know which texture tile a fragment will access. When that pass is done, the texture is read back to the CPU and analyzed to find which tiles are needed. The tiles that are not resident are read and mapped to physical memory, and tiles in physical memory that are not needed are unmapped. Their approach does not work for shadows, reflections, and transparency. However, screen-door techniques (Section 5.5) can be used for transparent effects, which work reasonably well. Feedback rendering is also used by van Waveren and Hart [1855]. Note that such a pass could either be a separate rendering pass or be combined with a z-prepass. When a separate pass is used, a resolution of only 80×60 pixels can be used, as an approximation, to reduce processing time. Hollemeersch et al. [761] use a compute pass instead of reading back the feedback buffer to the CPU. The result is a compact list of tile identifiers created on the GPU, and sent back to the CPU for mapping.

With GPU-supported virtual texturing, it is the responsibility of the driver to create and destroy resources, to map and unmap tiles, and to make sure that physical allocations are backed by virtual allocations [1605]. With GPU-hardware virtual texturing, a `sparseTexture` lookup returns a code indicating whether the corresponding tile is resident, in addition to the filtered value (for resident tiles) [1605]. With software-supported virtual texturing, all these tasks fall back on the developer. We refer to van Waveren's report for more information on this topic [1856].

Figure 19.40. High-resolution texture mapping accessing a huge image database using texture streaming in *DOOM* (2016). *(Image from the game "DOOM," courtesy of id Software.)*

To make sure everything fits into physical memory, van Waveren adjusts a global texture LOD bias until the working set fits [1854]. In addition, when only a higher-level mipmap tile is available than what is desired, that higher-level mipmap tile needs to be used until the lower-level mipmap tile becomes available. In such cases, the higher-level mipmap tile can be upscaled immediately and used, and then the new tile can be blended in over time to make for a smooth transition when it becomes available.

Barb [99] instead always loads all textures that are smaller than or equal to 64 kB, and hence, some texturing can always be done, albeit at lower quality if the higher-resolution mipmap levels have not yet been loaded. He uses offline feedback rendering to precompute, for various locations, how much solid angle around the player each mipmap level covers for each material at a nominal texture and screen resolution. At runtime this information is streamed in and adjusted for both the resolution of each texture with that material and the final screen resolution. This yields an importance value per texture, per mipmap. Each importance value is then divided by the number of texels in the corresponding mipmap level, which generates a reasonable final metric since it is invariant even if a texture is subdivided into smaller, identically mapped textures. See Barb's presentation for more information [99]. An example rendering is shown in Figure 19.40.

Widmark [1881] describes how streaming can be combined with procedural texture generation for a more varied and detailed texture. Chen extends Widmark's scheme to handle textures an order of magnitude larger [259].

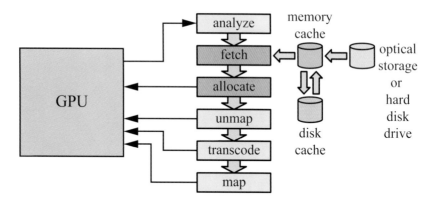

Figure 19.41. A texture streaming system using virtual texturing with transcoding. *(Illustration after van Waveren and Hart [1855].)*

19.10.2 Texture Transcoding

To make a virtual texturing system work even better, it can be combined with *transcoding*. This is the process of reading an image compressed with, typically, a variable-rate compression scheme, such as JPEG, from disk, decoding it, and then encoding it using one of the GPU-supported texture compression schemes (Section 6.2.6). One such system is illustrated in Figure 19.41. The purpose of the feedback rendering pass is to determine which tiles are needed for the current frame, and either of the methods described in Section 19.10.1 can be used here. The fetch step acquires the data through a hierarchy of storage, from optical storage or hard disk drive (HDD), through an optional disk cache, and then via a memory cache managed by software. Unmapping refers to deallocating a resident tile. When new data has been read, it is transcoded and finally mapped to a new resident tile.

The advantages of using transcoding are that a higher compression ratio can be used when the texture data are stored on disk, and that a GPU-supported texture compression format is used when accessing the texture data through the texture sampler. This requires both fast decompression of the variable-rate compression format and fast compression to the GPU-supported format [1851]. It is also possible to compress an already-compressed texture to reduce file size further [1717]. The advantage with such an approach is that when the texture is read from disk and decompressed, it is already in the texture compression format that can be consumed by the GPU. The *crunch* library [523], with free source code, uses a similar approach and reaches results of 1–2 bits per texel. See Figure 19.42 for an example. The successor, called *basis*, is a proprietary format with variable-bit compression for blocks, which transcodes quickly to texture compression formats [792]. Rapid methods for compression on the GPU are available for BC1/BC4 [1376], BC6H/BC7 [933, 935, 1259], and PVRTC [934]. Sugden and Iwanicki [1721] use a variant of Malvar's compression scheme [1113] for a variable rate compression scheme on disk. For normals they achieve a 40 : 1 compres-

Figure 19.42. Illustration of transcoding quality. Left to right: original partial parrot image, zoom-in on the eye for the original (24 bits per pixel), ETC compressed image (4 bits per pixel), and crunched ETC image (1.21 bits per pixel). *(Images compressed by Unity.)*

sion ratio, and for albedo textures 60 : 1 using the YCoCg transform (described in Equation 6.6 on page 197). Khronos is working on a standard universal compressed file format for textures.

When high texture quality is desired and texture loading times need to be small, Olano et al. [1321] use a variable-rate compression algorithm to store compressed textures on disk. The textures are also compressed in GPU memory until they are needed, at which time the GPU decompresses them using its own algorithm, and after that, they are used in uncompressed form.

19.10.3 General Streaming

In a game or other real-time rendering application with models larger than physical memory, a streaming system is also needed for actual geometry, scripts, particles, and AIs, for example. A plane can be tiled by regular convex polygons using either triangles, squares, or hexagons. Hence, these are also common building blocks for streaming systems, where each polygon is associated with all the assets in that polygon. This is illustrated in Figure 19.43. It should be noted that squares and hexagons are most commonly used [134, 1522], likely because these have fewer immediate neighbors than triangles. The viewer is located in the dark blue polygons in Figure 19.43, and the streaming system ensures that the immediate neighbors (light blue and green) are loaded into memory. This is to make sure that the surrounding geometry is available for rendering and to guarantee that the data are there when the viewer moves into a neighboring polygon. Note that triangles and squares have two types of neighbors: one that shares an edge and one that shares only a vertex.

Ruskin [1522] uses hexagons, each having a low- and a high-resolution geometrical LOD. Due to the small memory footprint of the low-resolution LODs, the entire world's low-resolution LODs are loaded at all times. Hence, only high-resolution LODs and textures are streamed in and out of memory. Bentley [134] uses squares, where each square covers 100×100 m^2. High-resolution mipmaps are streamed separately from the rest of the assets. This system uses 1–3 LODs for near- to mid-range viewing, and then baked impostors for far viewing. For a car-racing game, Tector [1753] instead

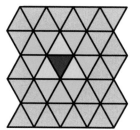 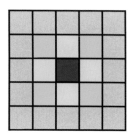 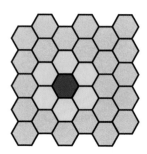

Figure 19.43. Tilings of the two-dimensional plane by regular polygons using triangles (left), squares (middle), and hexagons (right). The tiling is typically overlaid on a game world seen from above, and all assets inside a polygon are associated with that polygon. Assuming that the viewer is located in the dark blue polygons, the neighboring polygons' assets are loaded as well.

loads data along the race track as the car advances. He stores data compressed using the zip format on disk and loads blocks into a compressed software cache. The blocks are then decompressed as needed and used by the memory hierarchies of the CPU and GPU.

In some applications, it may be necessary to tile the three-dimensional space, instead of just using a two-dimensional tiling as described above. Note that the cube is the only regular polyhedron that also tiles three-dimensional space, so it is the natural choice for such applications.

19.10.4   Terrain Rendering

Terrain rendering is an important part of many games and applications, e.g., Google Earth and the Cesium open-source engine for large world rendering [299, 300]. An example is shown in Figure 19.44. We describe several popular methods that perform well on current GPUs. It should be noted that any of these can add on fractal noise in order to provide high levels of detail when zooming in on the terrain. Also, many systems procedurally generate the terrain on the fly when the game or a level is loaded.

One such method is the geometry clipmap [1078]. It is similar to texture clipmaps [1739] in that it uses a hierarchical structure related to mipmapping, i.e., the geometry is filtered into a pyramid of coarser and coarser levels toward the top. This is illustrated in Figure 19.45. When rendering huge terrain data sets, only $n \times n$ samples, i.e., heights, are cached in memory for each level around the viewer. When the viewer moves, the windows in Figure 19.45 move accordingly, and new data are loaded and old possibly evicted. To avoid cracks between levels, a transition region between every two successive levels is used. In such a transition level, both geometry and textures are smoothly interpolated into the next coarser level. This is implemented in vertex and pixel shaders. Asirvatham and Hoppe [82] present an efficient GPU implementation where the terrain data are stored as vertex textures. The vertex shader accesses these in order to obtain the height of the terrain. Normal maps can

Figure 19.44. A 50 cm terrain and 25 cm imagery of Mount Chamberlin captured by airborne photogrammetry. *(Image courtesy of Cesium and Fairbanks Fodar.)*

be used to augment the visual detail on the terrain, and when zooming in closely, Losasso and Hoppe [1078] also add fractal noise displacement for further details. See Figure 19.46 for an example. Gollent uses a variant of geometry clipmaps in *The Witcher 3* [555]. Pangerl [1348] and Torchelsen et al. [1777] give related methods for geometry clipmaps that also fit well with the GPU's capabilities.

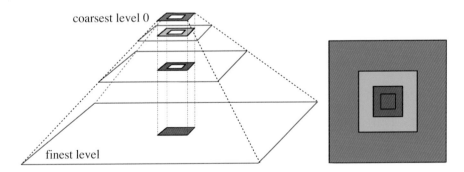

Figure 19.45. Left: the geometry clipmap structure, where an equal-size square window is cached in each resolution level. Right: a top view of the geometry, where the viewer is in the middle purple region. Note that the finest level renders its entire square, while the others are hollow inside. *(Illustration after Asirvatham and Hoppe [82].)*

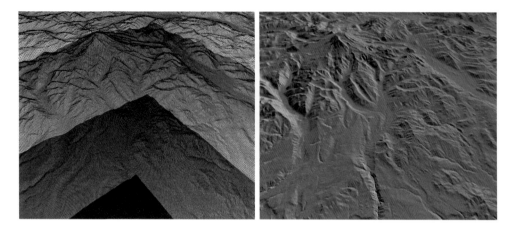

Figure 19.46. Geometry clipmapping. Left: wireframe rendering where the different mipmap levels clearly are visible. Right: the blue transition regions indicate where interpolation between levels occurs. *(Images generated using Microsoft's "Rendering of Terrains Using Geometry Clipmaps" program.)*

Several schemes focus on creating tiles and rendering them. One approach is that the heightfield array is broken up into tiles of, say, 17×17 vertices each. For a highly detailed view, a single tile can be rendered instead of sending individual triangles or small fans to the GPU. A tile can have multiple levels of detail. For example, by using only every other vertex in each direction, a 9×9 tile can be formed. Using every fourth vertex gives a 5×5 tile, every eighth a 2×2, and finally the four corners a 1×1 tile of two triangles. Note that the original 17×17 vertex buffer can be stored on the GPU and reused; only a different index buffer needs to be provided to change the number of triangles rendered. A method using this data layout is presented next.

Another method for rendering large terrain rapidly on the GPU is called *chunked LOD* [1797]. The idea is to represent the terrain using n discrete levels of detail, where each finer LOD is split $4\times$ compared to its parent, as illustrated in Figure 19.47. This structure is then encoded in a quadtree and traversed from the root for rendering. When a node is visited, it will be rendered if its screen-space error (which is described next) is below a certain pixel-error threshold, τ. Otherwise, each of the four children are visited recursively. This results in better resolution where needed, for example, close to the viewer. In a more advanced variant, terrain quads are loaded from disk as needed [1605, 1797]. The traversal is similar to the method described above, except that the children are only visited recursively if they are already loaded into memory (from disk). If they are not loaded, they are queued for loading, and the current node is rendered.

Ulrich [1797] computes the screen-space error as

$$s = \frac{\epsilon w}{2d \tan \frac{\theta}{2}}, \tag{19.10}$$

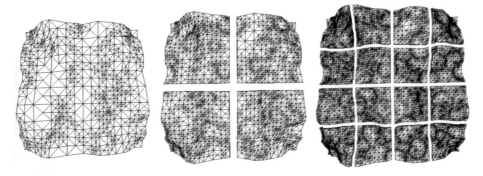

Figure 19.47. Chunked LOD representation of terrain. *(Images courtesy of Thatcher Ulrich.)*

where w is the width of the screen, d is the distance from the camera to the terrain tile, θ is the horizontal field of view in radians, and ϵ is a geometric error in the same units as d. For the geometric error term, the Hausdorff distance between two meshes is often used [906, 1605]. For each point on the original mesh, find its closest point on the simplified mesh, and call the smallest of these distances d_1. Now perform the same procedure for each point on the simplified mesh, finding the closest point on the original, and call the smallest of the distances d_2. The Hausdorff distance is $\epsilon = \max(d_1, d_2)$. This is illustrated in Figure 19.48. Note that the closest point to the simplified mesh from $\mathbf{o}$ is $\mathbf{s}$, while the closest point to the original mesh from $\mathbf{s}$ is $\mathbf{a}$, which is the reason why the measurement must be done in both combinations, from the original to the simplified mesh and vice versa. Intuitively, the Hausdorff distance is the error when using a simplified mesh instead of the original. If an application cannot afford to compute the Hausdorff distance, one may use constants that are manually adjusted for each simplification, or find the errors during simplification [1605].

To avoid popping effects when switching from one LOD to another, Ulrich [1797] proposes a simple morphing technique, where a vertex (x, y, z) from a high-resolution tile is linearly interpolated with a vertex (x, y', z), which is approximated from the parent tile (e.g., using bilinear interpolation). The linear interpolation factor is computed as $2s\tau - 1$, which is clamped to $[0, 1]$. Note that only the higher-resolution tile is needed during morphing, since the next-lower-resolution tile's vertices are also in the higher-resolution tile.

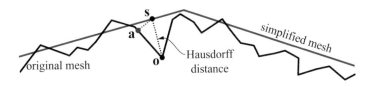

Figure 19.48. The Hausdorff distance between an original mesh and a simplified mesh. *(Illustration after Sellers et al. [1605].)*

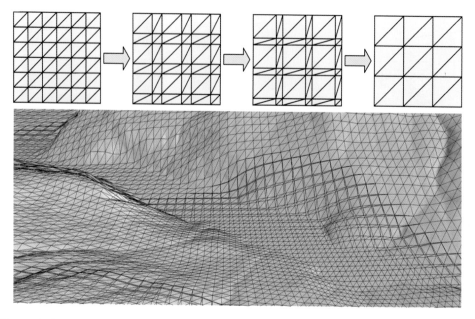

Figure 19.49. Crack avoidance using the chunked LOD system by Strugar [1720]. The top left shows a higher-resolution tile that is morphed into a lower-resolution terrain tile at the top right. In between, we show two interpolated and morphed variants. In reality, this occurs in a smooth way as the LOD is changed, which is shown in the screen shot at the bottom. *(Bottom image generated by a program by Filip Strugar [1720].)*

Heuristics, such as the one in Equation 19.10, can be used to determine the level of detail used for each tile. The main challenge for a tiling scheme is crack repair. For example, if one tile is at 33×33 resolution and its neighbor is at 9×9, there will be cracking along the edge where they meet. One corrective measure is to remove the highly detailed triangles along the edge and then form sets of triangles that properly bridge the gap between the two tiles [324, 1670]. Cracks will appear when two neighboring areas have different levels of detail. Ulrich describes a method using extra ribbon geometry, which is a reasonable solution if τ is set to less than 5 pixels. Cozzi and Bagnell [300] instead fill the cracks using a screen-space post-process pass, where the fragments around the crack, but not in the crack, are weighted using a Gaussian kernel. Strugar [1720] has an elegant way of avoiding cracks without screen-space methods or extra geometry. This is shown in Figure 19.49 and can be implemented with a simple vertex shader.

For improved performance, Sellers et al. [1605] combine chunked LOD with view frustum culling and horizon culling. Kang et al. [852] present a scheme similar to chunked LOD, with the largest difference being that they use GPU-based tessellation to tessellate a node and make sure that the edge tessellation factors match up to avoid cracks. They also show how geometry images with feature-preserving maps can be

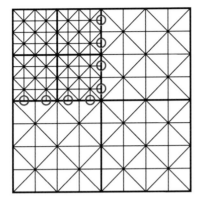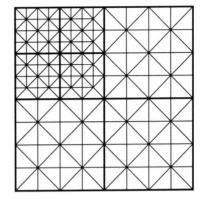

Figure 19.50. A restricted quadtree of terrain tiles, in which each tile can neighbor tiles at most one level higher or lower in level of detail. Each tile has 5×5 vertices, except in the upper left corner, where there are 2×2 higher-resolution tiles. The rest of the terrain is filled by three lower-resolution tiles. On the left, there are vertices on the edges of the upper left tile that do not match ones on the adjacent lower-resolution tiles, which would result in cracking. On the right, the more-detailed tile's edges are modified to avoid the problem. Each tile is rendered in a single draw call. *(Illustration after Andersson [40].)*

used to render terrain with overhangs, which heightfield-based terrain cannot handle. Strugar [1720] presents an extension of the chunked LOD scheme, with better and more flexible distribution of the triangles. In contrast to Ulrich's method, which uses a per-node LOD, Strugar uses morphing per vertex with individual levels of detail. While he uses only distance as a measure for determining LOD, other factors can be used as well, e.g., how much depth variation there is in the vicinity, which can generate better silhouettes.

The source terrain data are typically represented by uniform heightfield grids. View-independent methods of simplification can be used on these data, as seen in Figure 16.16 on page 705. The model is simplified until some limiting criterion is met [514]. Small surface details can be captured by color or bump map textures. The resulting static mesh, often called a *triangulated irregular network* (TIN), is a useful representation when the terrain area is small and relatively flat in various areas [1818].

Andersson [40] uses a restricted quadtree to bridge the gaps and lower the total number of draw calls needed for large terrains. Instead of a uniform grid of tiles rendered at different resolutions, he uses a quadtree of tiles. Each tile has the same base resolution of 33×33, but each can cover a different amount of area. The idea of a restricted quadtree is that each tile's neighbors can be no more than one level of detail different. See Figure 19.50. This restriction means that there are a limited number of situations in which the resolutions of the neighboring tiles differ. Instead of creating gaps and having additional index buffers rendered to fill these gaps, the idea is to store all the possible permutations of index buffers that create a tile that also include the gap transition triangles. Each index buffer is formed by full-resolution

Figure 19.51. Terrain rendering at many levels of detail in action. *(Courtesy of DICE, © 2016 Electronic Arts Inc.)*

edges (33 vertices on an edge) and lower level of detail edges (17 vertices only, since the quadtree is restricted). An example of this modern terrain rendering is shown in Figure 19.51. Widmark [1881] describes a complete terrain rendering system, which is used in the Frostbite 2 engine. It has useful features, such as decals, water, terrain decoration, composition of different material shaders using artist-generated or procedurally generated masks [40], and procedural terrain displacement.

A simple technique that can be used for ocean rendering is to employ a uniform grid, transformed to camera space each frame [749]. This is shown in Figure 19.52. Bowles [186] provides many tricks on how to overcome certain quality problems.

In addition to the terrain techniques above, which tend to reduce the size of the data set that needs to be kept in memory at any time, one can also use compression

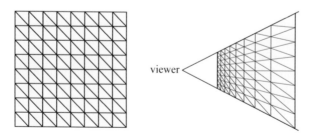

Figure 19.52. Left: a uniform grid. Right: the grid transformed to camera space. Note how the transformed grid allows higher detail closer to the viewer.

techniques. Yusov [1956] compresses the vertices using the quadtree data structure, with a simple prediction scheme, where only the differences are encoded (using few bits). Schneider and Westermann [1573] use a compressed format that is decoded by the vertex shader and explore geomorphing between levels of detail, while maximizing cache coherency. Lindstrom and Cohen [1051] use a streaming codec with linear prediction and residual encoding for lossless compression. In addition, they use quantization to provide further improved compression rates, though the results are then lossy. Decompression can be done using the GPU, with compression rates from $3:1$ up to $12:1$.

There are many other approaches to terrain rendering. Kloetzli [909] uses a custom compute shader in *Civilization V* to create an adaptive tessellation for terrain, which is then fed to the GPU for rendering. Another technique is to use the GPU's tessellator to handle the tessellation [466] per patch. Note that many of the techniques used for terrain rendering can also be used for water rendering. For example, Gonzalez-Ochoa and Holder [560] used a variant of geometry clipmaps in *Uncharted 3*, adapted for water. They avoid T-junctions by dynamically adding triangles between levels. Research on this topic will continue as the GPU evolves.

Further Reading and Resources

Though the focus is collision detection, Ericson's book [435] has relevant material about forming and using various space subdivision schemes.

There is a wealth of literature about occlusion culling. Two good starting places for early work on algorithms are the visibility surveys by Cohen-Or et al. [277] and Durand [398]. Aila and Miettinen [13] describe the architecture of a commercial culling system for dynamic scenes. Nießner et al. [1283] present a survey of existing methods for backfacing-patch, view frustum, and occlusion culling of displaced subdivision surfaces. A worthwhile resource for information on the use of LODs is the book *Level of Detail for 3D Graphics* by Luebke et al. [1092].

Dietrich et al. [352] present an overview of research in the area of rendering massive models. Another nice overview of massive model rendering is provided by Gobbetti et al. [547]. The SIGGRAPH course by Sellers et al. [1605] is a more recent resource with excellent material. Cozzi and Ring's book [299] presents techniques for terrain rendering and large-scale data set management, along with methods dealing with precision issues. The Cesium blog [244] provides many implementation details and further acceleration techniques for large world and terrain rendering.

Chapter 20
Efficient Shading

"*Never put off till to-morrow what you can*
do the day after to-morrow just as well."
—Mark Twain

For simple scenes—relatively little geometry, basic materials, a few lights—we can use the standard GPU pipeline to render images without concerns about maintaining frame rate. Only when one or more elements become expensive do we need to use more involved techniques to rein in costs. In the previous chapter we focused on culling triangles and meshes from processing further downstream. Here we concentrate on techniques for reducing costs when evaluating materials and lights. For many of these methods, there is an additional processing cost, with the hope being that this expense is made up by the savings obtained. Others trade off between bandwidth and computation, often shifting the bottleneck. As with all such schemes, which is best depends on your hardware, scene structure, and many other factors.

Evaluating a pixel shader for a material can be expensive. This cost can be reduced by various shader level of detail simplification techniques, as noted in Section 19.9. When there are several light sources affecting a surface, two different strategies can be used. One is to build a shader that supports multiple light sources, so that only a single pass is needed. Another is *multi-pass shading*, where we create a simple one-light pixel shader for a light and evaluate it, adding each result to the framebuffer. So, for three lights, we would draw the primitive three times, changing the light for each evaluation. This second method might be more efficient overall than a single-pass system, because each shader used is simpler and faster. If a renderer has many different types of lights, a one-pass pixel shader must include them all and test for whether each is used, making for a complex shader.

In Section 18.4.5 we discussed avoiding unnecessary pixel shader evaluations by minimizing or eliminating overdraw. If we can efficiently determine that a surface does not contribute to the final image, then we can save the time spent shading it. One technique performs a *z*-prepass, where the opaque geometry is rendered and only *z*-depths are written. The geometry is then rendered again fully shaded, and the *z*-buffer from the first pass culls away all fragments that are not visible. This type of pass is an attempt to decouple the process of finding what geometry is visible from the operation of subsequently shading that geometry. This idea of separating these two processes is an important concept used throughout this chapter, and is employed by several alternative rendering schemes.

For example, a problem with using a z-prepass is that you have to render the geometry twice. This is an additional expense compared to standard rendering, and could cost more time than it saves. If the meshes are formed via tessellation, skinning, or some other involved process, the cost of this added pass can be considerable [992, 1177]. Objects with cutout alpha values need to have their texture's alpha retrieved each pass, adding to the expense, or must be ignored altogether and rendered only in the second pass, risking wasted pixel shader evaluations. For these reasons, sometimes only large occluders (in screen or world space) are drawn in this initial pass. Performing a full prepass may also be needed by other screen-space effects, such as ambient occlusion or reflection [1393]. Some of the acceleration techniques presented in this chapter require an accurate z-prepass that is then used to help cull lists of lights.

Even with no overdraw, a significant expense can arise from a large number of dynamic lights evaluated for a visible surface. Say you have 50 light sources in a scene. A multi-pass system can render the scene successfully, but at the cost of 50 vertex and shader passes per object. One technique to reduce costs is to limit the effect of each local light to a sphere of some radius, cone of some height, or other limited shape [668, 669, 1762, 1809]. The assumption is that each light's contribution becomes insignificant past a certain distance. For the rest of this chapter, we will refer to lights' volumes as spheres, with the understanding that other shapes can be used. Often the light's intensity is used as the sole factor determining its radius. Karis [860] discusses how the presence of glossy specular materials will increase this radius, since such surfaces are more noticeably affected by lights. For extremely smooth surfaces this distance may go to infinity, such that environment maps or other techniques may need to be used instead.

A simple preprocess is to create for each mesh a list of lights that affects it. We can think of this process as performing collision detection between a mesh and the lights, finding those that may overlap [992]. When shading the mesh, we use this list of lights, thus reducing the number of lights applied. There are problems with this type of approach. If objects or lights move, these changes affect the composition of the lists. For performance, geometry sharing the same material is often consolidated into larger meshes (Section 18.4.2), which could cause a single mesh to have some or all of the lights in a scene in its list [1327, 1330]. That said, meshes can be consolidated and then split spatially to provide shorter lists [1393].

Another approach is to bake static lights into world-space data structures. For example, in the lighting system for *Just Cause 2*, a world-space top-down grid stores light information for a scene. A grid cell represents a 4 meter × 4 meter area. Each cell is stored as a texel in an RGBα texture, thus holding a list of up to four lights. When a pixel is rendered, the list in its area is retrieved and the relevant lights are applied [1379]. A drawback is that there is a fixed storage limit to the number of

Figure 20.1. A complicated lighting situation. Note that the small light on the shoulder and every bright dot on the building structure are light sources. The lights in the far distance in the upper right are light sources, which are rendered as point sprites at that distance. *(Image from "Just Cause 3," courtesy of Avalanche Studios [1387].)*

lights affecting a given area. While potentially useful for carefully designed outdoor scenes, buildings with a number of stories can quickly overwhelm this storage scheme.

Our goal is to handle dynamic meshes and lights in an efficient way. Also important is predictable performance, where a small change in the view or scene does not cause a large change in the cost of rendering it. Some levels in *DOOM* (2016) have 300 visible lights [1682]; some scenes in *Ashes of the Singularity* have 10,000. See Figure 20.1 and Figure 20.15 on page 913. In some renderers a large number of particles can each be treated as small light sources. Other techniques use light probes (Section 11.5.4) to illuminate nearby surfaces, which can be thought of as short-range light sources.

20.1 Deferred Shading

So far throughout this book we have described *forward shading*, where each triangle is sent down the pipeline and, at the end of its travels, the image on the screen is updated with its shaded values. The idea behind *deferred shading* is to perform all visibility testing and surface property evaluations before performing any material lighting computations. The concept was first introduced in a hardware architecture in 1988 [339], later included as a part of the experimental PixelFlow system [1235], and used as an offline software solution to help produce non-photoreal styles via image processing [1528]. Calver's extensive article [222] in mid-2003 lays out the basic ideas of using deferred shading on the GPU. Hargreaves and Harris [668, 669] and Thibieroz [1762] promoted its use the following year, at a time when the ability to write to multiple render targets was becoming more widely available.

In forward shading we perform a single pass using a shader and a mesh representing the object to compute the final image. The pass fetches material properties—constants, interpolated parameters, or values in textures—then applies a set of lights to these values. The z-prepass method for forward rendering can be seen as a mild decoupling of geometry rendering and shading, in that a first geometry pass aims at only determining visibility, while all shading work, including material parameter retrieval, is deferred to a second geometry pass performed to shade all visible pixels. For interactive rendering, deferred shading specifically means that all material parameters associated with the visible objects are generated and stored by an initial geometry pass, then lights are applied to these stored surface values using a post-process. Values saved in this first pass include the position (stored as z-depth), normal, texture coordinates, and various material parameters. This pass establishes all geometry and material information for the pixel, so the objects are no longer needed, i.e., the contribution of the models' geometry has been fully decoupled from lighting computations. Note that overdraw can happen in this initial pass, the difference being that the shader's execution is considerably less—transferring values to buffers—than that of evaluating the effect of a set of lights on the material. There is also less of the additional cost found in forward shading, where sometimes not all the pixels in a 2×2 quad are inside a triangle's boundaries but all must be fully shaded [1393] (Section 23.8). This sounds like a minor effect, but imagine a mesh where each triangle covers a single pixel. Four fully shaded samples will be generated and three of these discarded with forward shading. Using deferred shading, each shader invocation is less expensive, so discarded samples have a considerably lower impact.

The buffers used to store surface properties are commonly called *G-buffers* [1528], short for "geometric buffers." Such buffers are also occasionally called *deep buffers*, though this term can also mean a buffer storing multiple surfaces (fragments) per pixel, so we avoid it here. Figure 20.2 shows the typical contents of some G-buffers. A G-buffer can store anything a programmer wants it to contain, i.e., whatever is needed to complete the required subsequent lighting computations. Each G-buffer is a separate render target. Typically three to five render targets are used as G-buffers, but systems have gone as high as eight [134]. Having more targets uses more bandwidth, which increases the chance that this buffer is the bottleneck.

After the pass creating the G-buffers, a separate process is used to compute the effect of illumination. One method is to apply each light one by one, using the G-buffers to compute its effect. For each light we draw a screen-filling quadrilateral (Section 12.1) and access the G-buffers as textures [222, 1762]. At each pixel we can determine the location of the closest surface and whether it is in range of the light. If it is, we compute the effect of the light and place the result in an output buffer. We do this for each light in turn, adding its contribution via blending. At the end, we have all lights' contributions applied.

Figure 20.2. Geometric buffers for deferred shading, in some cases converted to colors for visualization. Left column, top to bottom: depth map, normal buffer, roughness buffer, and sunlight occlusion. Right column: texture color (a.k.a. albedo texture), light intensity, specular intensity, and near-final image (without motion blur). *(Images from "Killzone 2," courtesy of Guerrilla BV [1809].)*

This process is about the most inefficient way to use G-buffers, since every stored pixel is accessed for every light, similar to how basic forward rendering applies all lights to all surface fragments. Such an approach can end up being slower than forward shading, due to the extra cost of writing and reading the G-buffers [471]. As a start on improving performance, we could determine the screen bounds of a light volume (a sphere) and use them to draw a screen-space quadrilateral that covers a smaller part of the image [222, 1420, 1766]. In this way, pixel processing is reduced, often significantly. Drawing an ellipse representing the sphere can further trim pixel processing that is outside the light's volume [1122]. We can also use the third screen dimension, z-depth. By drawing a rough sphere mesh encompassing the volume, we can trim the sphere's area of effect further still [222]. For example, if the sphere is hidden by the depth buffer, the light's volume is behind the closest surface and so has no effect. To generalize, if a sphere's minimum and maximum depths at a pixel do not overlap the closest surface, the light cannot affect this pixel. Hargreaves [668] and Valient [1809] discuss various options and caveats for efficiently and correctly determining this overlap, along with other optimizations. We will see this idea of testing for depth overlap between the surface and the light used in several of the algorithms ahead. Which is most efficient depends on the circumstances.

For traditional forward rendering, the vertex and pixel shader programs retrieve each light's and material's parameters and compute the effect of one on the other. Forward shading needs either one complex vertex and pixel shader that covers all possible combinations of materials and lights, or shorter, specialized shaders that handle specific combinations. Long shaders with dynamic branches often run considerably more slowly [414], so a large number of smaller shaders can be more efficient, but also require more work to generate and manage. Since all shading functions are done in a single pass with forward shading, it is more likely that the shader will need to change when the next object is rendered, leading to inefficiency from swapping shaders (Section 18.4.2).

The deferred shading method of rendering allows a strong separation between lighting and material definition. Each shader is focused on parameter extraction or lighting, but not both. Shorter shaders run faster, both due to length and the ability to optimize them. The number of registers used in a shader determines occupancy (Section 23.3), a key factor in how many shader instances can be run in parallel. This decoupling of lighting and material also simplifies shader system management. For example, this split makes experimentation easy, as only one new shader needs to be added to the system for a new light or material type, instead of one for each combination [222, 927]. This is possible since material evaluations are done in the first pass, and lighting is then applied to this stored set of surface parameters in the second pass.

For single-pass forward rendering, all shadow maps usually must be available at the same time, since all lights are evaluated at once. With each light handled fully in a single pass, deferred shading permits having only one shadow map in memory at a time [1809]. However, this advantage disappears with the more complex light assignment schemes we cover later, as lights are evaluated in groups [1332, 1387].

Basic deferred shading supports just a single material shader with a fixed set of parameters, which constrains what material models can be portrayed. One way to support different material descriptions is to store a material ID or mask per pixel in

	R8	G8	B8	A8	
RT0	world normal (RGB10)				GI
RT1	base color (sRGB8)			config (A8)	
RT2	metalness (R8)	glossiness (G8)	cavity (B8)	aliased value (A8)	
RT3	velocity.xy (RGB8)			velocity.z (A8)	

Figure 20.3. An example of a possible G-buffer layout, used in *Rainbow Six Siege*. In addition to depth and stencil buffers, four render targets (RTs) are used as well. As can be seen, anything can be put into these buffers. The "GI" field in RT0 is "GI normal bias (A2)." *(Illustration after El Mansouri [415].)*

some given field. The shader can then perform different computations based on the G-buffer contents. This approach could also modify what is stored in the G-buffers, based on this ID or mask value [414, 667, 992, 1064]. For example, one material might use 32 bits to store a second layer color and blend factor in a G-buffer, while another may use these same bits to store two tangent vectors that it requires. These schemes entail using more complex shaders, which can have performance implications.

Basic deferred shading has some other drawbacks. G-buffer video memory requirements can be significant, as can the related bandwidth costs in repeatedly accessing these buffers [856, 927, 1766]. We can mitigate these costs by storing lower-precision values or compressing the data [1680, 1809]. An example is shown in Figure 20.3. In Section 16.6 we discussed compression of world-space data for meshes. G-buffers can contain values that are in world-space or screen-space coordinates, depending on the needs of the rendering engine. Pesce [1394] discusses the trade-offs in compressing screen-space versus world-space normals for G-buffers and provides pointers to related resources. A world-space octahedral mapping for normals is a common solution, due to its high precision and quick encoding and decoding times.

Two important technical limitations of deferred shading involve transparency and antialiasing. Transparency is not supported in a basic deferred shading system, since we can store only one surface per pixel. One solution is to use forward rendering for transparent objects after the opaque surfaces are rendered with deferred shading. For early deferred systems this meant that all lights in a scene had to be applied to each transparent object, a costly process, or other simplifications had to be performed. As we will explore in the sections ahead, improved GPU capabilities have led to the development of methods that cull lights for both deferred and forward shading. While it is possible to now store lists of transparent surfaces for pixels [1575] and use a pure deferred approach, the norm is to mix deferred and forward shading as desired for transparency and other effects [1680].

An advantage of forward methods is that antialiasing schemes such as MSAA are easily supported. Forward techniques need to store only N depth and color samples per pixel for $N\times$ MSAA. Deferred shading could store all N samples per element in the G-buffers to perform antialiasing, but the increases in memory cost, fill rate, and computation make this approach expensive [1420]. To overcome this limitation,

Shishkovtsov [1631] uses an edge detection method for approximating edge coverage computations. Other morphological post-processing methods for antialiasing (Section 5.4.2) can also be used [1387], as well as temporal antialiasing. Several deferred MSAA methods avoid computing the shade for every sample by detecting which pixels or tiles have edges in them [43, 990, 1064, 1299, 1764]. Only those with edges need to have multiple samples evaluated. Sousa [1681] builds on this type of approach, using stenciling to identify pixels with multiple samples that need more complex processing. Pettineo [1407] describes a newer way to track such pixels, using a compute shader to move edge pixels to a list in thread group memory for efficient stream processing.

Antialiasing research by Crassin et al. [309] focuses on high-quality results and summarizes other research in this area. Their technique performs a depth and normal geometry prepass and groups similar subsamples together. They then generate G-buffers and perform a statistical analysis of the best value to use for each group of subsamples. These depth-bounds values are then used to shade each group and the results are blended together. While as of this writing such processing at interactive rates is impractical for most applications, this approach gives a sense of the amount of computational power that can and will be brought to bear on improving image quality.

Even with these limitations, deferred shading is a practical rendering method used in commercial programs. It naturally separates geometry from shading, and lighting from materials, meaning that each element can be optimized on its own. One area of particular interest is decal rendering, which has implications for any rendering pipeline.

20.2 Decal Rendering

A decal is some design element, such as a picture or other texture, applied on top of a surface. Decals are often seen in video games in such forms as tire marks, bullet holes, or player tags sprayed onto surfaces. Decals are used in other applications for applying logos, annotations, or other content. For terrain systems or cities, for example, decals can allow artists to avoid obvious repetition by layering on detailed textures, or by recombining various patterns in different ways.

A decal can blend with the underlying material in a variety of ways. It might modify the underlying color but not the bump map, like a tattoo. Alternately, it might replace just the bump mapping, such as an embossed logo does. It could define a different material entirely, for example, placing a sticker on a car window. Multiple decals might be applied to the same geometry, such as footprints on a path. A single decal might span multiple models, such as graffiti on a subway car's surfaces. These variations have implications for how forward and deferred shading systems store and process decals.

To begin, the decal must be mapped to the surface, like any other texture. Since multiple texture coordinates can be stored at each vertex, it is possible to bind a few decals to a single surface. This approach is limited, since the number of values that can be saved per vertex is relatively low. Each decal needs its own set of texture coordinates. A large number of small decals applied to a surface would mean saving these texture coordinates at every vertex, even though each decal affects only a few triangles in the mesh.

To render decals attached to a mesh, one approach is to have the pixel shader sample every decal and blend one atop the next. This complicates the shader, and if the number of decals varies over time, frequent recompilation or other measures may be required. Another approach that keeps the shader independent from the decal system is to render the mesh again for each decal, layering and blending each pass over the previous one. If a decal spans just a few triangles, a separate, shorter index buffer can be created to render just this decal's sub-mesh. One other decal method is to modify the material's texture. If used on just one mesh, as in a terrain system, modifying this texture provides a simple "set it and forget it" solution [447]. If the material texture is used on a few objects, we need to create a new texture with the material and decal composited together. This baked solution avoids shader complexity and wasted overdraw, but at the cost of texture management and memory use [893, 1393]. Rendering the decals separately is the norm, as different resolutions can then be applied to the same surface, and the base texture can be reused and repeated without needing additional modified copies in memory.

These solutions can be reasonable for a computer-aided design package, where the user may add a single logo and little else. They are also used for decals applied to animated models, where the decal needs to be projected before the deformation so it stretches as the object does. However, such techniques become inefficient and cumbersome for more than a few decals.

A popular solution for static or rigid objects is to treat the decal as a texture orthographically projected through a limited volume [447, 893, 936, 1391, 1920]. An oriented box is placed in the scene, with the decal projected from one of the box faces to its opposite face, like a film projector. See Figure 20.4. The faces of the box are rasterized, as a way to drive the pixel shader's execution. Any geometry found inside this volume has the decal applied over its material. This is done by converting the surface's depth and screen position into a location in the volume, which then gives a (u, v) texture coordinate for the decal. Alternately, the decal could be a true volume texture [888, 1380]. Decals can affect only certain objects in the volume by assigning IDs [900], assigning a stencil bit [1778], or relying on the rendering order. They are also often faded or clamped to the angle of the surface and the projection direction, to avoid having a decal stretch or distort wherever the surface becomes more edge-on [893].

Deferred shading excels at rendering such decals. Instead of needing to illuminate and shade each decal, as with standard forward shading, the decal's effect can be applied to the G-buffers. For example, if a decal of a tire's tread mark replaces the shading normals on a surface, these changes are made directly to the appropriate G-buffer. Each pixel is later shaded by lights with only the data found in the G-buffers, so avoiding the shading overdraw that occurs with forward shading [1680]. Since

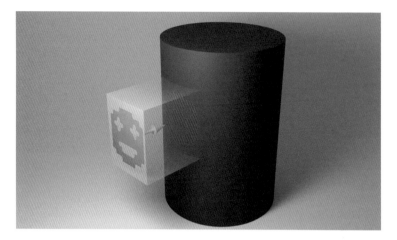

Figure 20.4. A box defines a decal projection, and a surface inside that box has the decal applied to it. The box is shown with exaggerated thickness to display the projector and its effect. In practice the box is made as thin and tight to the surface as possible, to minimize the number of pixels that are tested during decal application.

the decal's effect can be captured entirely by G-buffer storage, the decal is then not needed during shading. This integration also avoids a problem with multi-pass forward shading, that the surface parameters of one pass may need to affect the lighting or shading of another pass [1380]. This simplicity was a major factor in the decision to switch from forward to deferred shading for the Frostbite 2 engine, for example [43]. Decals can be thought of as the same as lights, in that both are applied by rendering a volume of space to determine its effect on the surfaces enclosed. As we will see in Section 20.4, by using this fact, a modified form of forward shading can capitalize on similar efficiencies, along with other advantages.

Lagarde and de Rousiers [960] describe several problems with decals in a deferred setting. Blending is limited to what operations are available during the merge stage in the pipeline [1680]. If the material and decal both have normal maps, achieving a properly blended result can be difficult, and harder still if some bump texture filtering technique is in use [106, 888]. Black or white fringing artifacts can occur, as described in Section 6.5. Techniques such as signed distance fields can be used to sharply divide such materials [263, 580], though doing so can cause aliasing problems. Another concern is fringing along silhouette edges of decals, caused by gradient errors due to using screen-space information projected back into world space. One solution is to restrict or ignore mipmapping for such decals; more elaborate solutions are discussed by Wronski [1920].

Decals can be used for dynamic elements, such as skid marks or bullet holes, but are also useful for giving different locations some variation. Figure 20.5 shows a scene with decals applied to building walls and elsewhere. The wall textures can be reused, while the decals provide customized details that give each building a unique character.

Figure 20.5. In the top image the areas where color and bump decals are overlaid are shown with checkerboards. The middle shows the building with no decals applied. The bottom image shows the scene with about 200 decals applied. *(Images courtesy of IO Interactive.)*

20.3 Tiled Shading

In basic deferred shading, each light is evaluated separately and the result is added to the output buffer. This was a feature for early GPUs, where evaluating more than a few lights could be impossible, due to limitations on shader complexity. Deferred shading could handle any number of lights, at the cost of accessing the G-buffers each time. With hundreds or thousands of lights, basic deferred shading becomes expensive, since all lights need to be processed for each overlapped pixel, and each light evaluated at a pixel involves a separate shader invocation. Evaluating several lights in a single shader invocation is more efficient. In the sections that follow, we discuss several algorithms for rapidly processing large numbers of lights at interactive rates, for both deferred and forward shading.

Various hybrid G-buffer systems have been developed over the years, balancing between material and light storage. For example, imagine a simple shading model with diffuse and specular terms, where the material's texture affects only the diffuse term. Instead of retrieving the texture's color from a G-buffer for each light, we could first compute each light's diffuse and specular terms separately and store these results. These accumulated terms are added together in light-based G-buffers, sometimes called L-buffers. At the end, we retrieve the texture's color once, multiply it by the diffuse term, and then add in the specular. The texture's effect is factored out of the equation, as it is used only a single time for all lights. In this way, fewer G-buffer data points are accessed per light, saving on bandwidth. A typical storage scheme is to accumulate the diffuse color and the specular intensity, meaning four values can be output via additive blending to a single buffer. Engel [431, 432] discusses several of these early *deferred lighting* techniques, also known as *pre-lighting* or *light prepass* methods. Kaplanyan [856] compares different approaches, aiming to minimize G-buffer storage and access. Thibieroz [1766] also stresses shallower G-buffers, contrasting several algorithms' pros and cons. Kircher [900] describes using lower-resolution G-buffers and L-buffers for lighting, which are upsampled and bilateral-filtered during a final forward shading pass. This approach works well for some materials, but can cause artifacts if the lighting's effect changes rapidly, e.g., a roughness or normal map is applied to a reflective surface. Sousa et al. [1681] use the idea of subsampling alongside Y'CbCr color encoding of the albedo texture to help reduce storage costs. Albedo affects the diffuse component, which is less prone to high-frequency changes.

There are many more such schemes [892, 1011, 1351, 1747], each varying such elements as which components are stored and factored, what passes are performed, and how shadows, transparency, antialiasing, and other phenomena are rendered. A major goal of all these is the same—the efficient rendering of light sources—and such techniques are still in use today [539]. One limitation of some schemes is that they can require even more restricted material and lighting models [1332]. For example, Shulz [1589] notes that moving to a physically based material model meant that the specular reflectance then needed to be stored to compute the Fresnel term from the lighting. This increase in the light prepass requirements helped push his group to move from a light prepass to a fully deferred shading system.

Accessing even a small number of G-buffers per light can have significant bandwidth costs. Faster still would be to evaluate only the lights that affect each pixel, in a single pass. Zioma [1973] was one of the first to explore creating lists of lights for forward shading. In his scheme, light volumes are rendered and the light's relative location, color, and attenuation factor are stored for each pixel overlapped. Depth peeling is used to handle storing the information for light sources that overlap the same pixels. The scene's geometry is then rendered, using the stored light representation. While viable, this scheme is limited by how many lights can overlap any pixel. Trebilco [1785] takes the idea of creating light lists per pixel further. He performs a z-prepass to avoid overdraw and to cull hidden light sources. The light volumes are rendered and stored as ID values per pixel, which are then accessed during the forward rendering pass. He gives several methods for storing multiple lights in a single buffer, including a bit-shifting and blending technique that allows four lights to be stored without the need for multiple depth-peeling passes.

Tiled shading was first presented by Balestra and Engstad [97] in 2008 for the game *Uncharted: Drake's Fortune*, soon followed by presentations about its use in the Frostbite engine [42] and PhyreEngine [1727], among others. The core idea of tiled shading is to assign light sources to tiles of pixels, so limiting both the number of lights that need to be evaluated at each surface, and the amount of work and storage required. These per-tile light lists are then accessed in a single shader invocation, instead of deferred shading's method of calling a shader for each light [990].

A tile for light classification is a square set of pixels on the screen, for example, 32×32 pixels in size. Note that there are other ways tiling the screen is used for interactive rendering; for instance, mobile processors render an image by processing tiles [145], and GPU architectures use screen tiles for a variety of tasks (Chapter 23). Here the tiles are a construct chosen by the developer and often have relatively little to do with the underlying hardware. A tiled rendering of the light volumes is something like a low-resolution rendering of the scene, a task that can be performed on the CPU or in, say, a compute shader on the GPU [42, 43, 139, 140, 1589].

Lights that potentially affect a tile are recorded in a list. When rendering is performed, a pixel shader in a given tile uses the tile's corresponding list of lights to shade the surface. This is illustrated on the left side of Figure 20.6. As can be seen, not all lights overlap with every tile. The screen-space bounds of the tile form an asymmetrical frustum, which is used to determine overlap. Each light's spherical volume of effect can quickly be tested on the CPU or in a compute shader for overlap with each tile's frustum. Only if there is an overlap do we need to process that light further for the pixels in the tile. By storing light lists per tile instead of per pixel, we err on the side of being conservative—a light's volume may not overlap the whole tile—in exchange for much reduced processing, storage, and bandwidth costs [1332].

To determine whether a light overlaps with a tile, we can use frustum testing against a sphere, which is described in Section 22.14. The test there assumes a large, wide frustum and relatively small spheres. However, since the frustum here originates from a screen-space tile, it is often long, thin, and asymmetrical. This decreases the

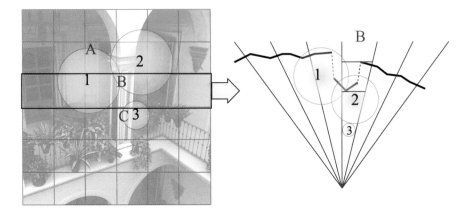

Figure 20.6. Illustration of tiling. Left: the screen has been divided into 6×6 tiles, and three lights sources, 1–3, are lighting this scene. Looking at tiles A–C, we see that tile A is potentially affected by lights 1 and 2, tile B by lights 1–3, and tile C by light 3. Right: the black outlined row of tiles on the left is visualized as seen from above. For tile B, the depth bounds are indicated by red lines. On the screen, tile B appears to be overlapped by all lights, but only lights 1 and 2 overlap with the depth bounds as well.

efficiency of the cull, since the number of reported intersections can increase (i.e., false positives). See the left part of Figure 20.7. Instead one can add a sphere/box test (Section 22.13.2) after testing against the planes of the frustum [1701, 1768], which is illustrated on the right in Figure 20.7. Mara and McGuire [1122] run through alternative tests for a projected sphere, including their own GPU-efficient version. Zhdan [1968] notes that this approach does not work well for spotlights, and discusses optimization techniques using hierarchical culling, rasterization, and proxy geometry.

This light classification process can be used with deferred shading or forward rendering, and is described in detail by Olsson and Assarsson [1327]. For *tiled deferred shading*, the G-buffers are established as usual, the volume of each light is recorded in the tiles it overlaps, and then these lists are applied to the G-buffers to compute the final result. In basic deferred shading each light is applied by rendering a proxy object such as a quadrilateral to force the pixel shader to be evaluated for that light. With tiled shading, a compute shader or a quad rendered for the screen or per tile is used to drive shader evaluation for each pixel. When a fragment is then evaluated, all lights in the list for that tile are applied. Applying lists of lights has several advantages, including:

- For each pixel the G-buffers are read at most one time total, instead of one time per overlapping light.

- The output image buffer is written to only one time, instead of accumulating the results of each light.

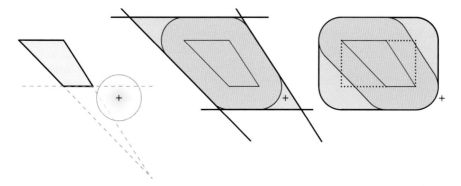

Figure 20.7. Left: with a naive sphere/frustum test, this circle would be reported as intersecting since it overlaps with the bottom and right planes of the frustum. Middle: an illustration of the test to the left, where the frustum has grown and the origin (plus sign) of the circle is tested against just the thick black planes. False intersections are reported in the green regions. Right: a box, shown with dotted lines, is placed around the frustum, and a sphere/box test is added after the plane test in the middle, forming the thick-outlined shape shown. Note how this test would produce other false intersections in its green areas, but with both tests applied these areas are reduced. Since the origin of the sphere is outside the shape, the sphere is correctly reported as not overlapping the frustum.

- Shader code can factor out any common terms in the rendering equation and compute these once, instead of per light [990].

- Each fragment in a tile evaluates the same list of lights, ensuring coherent execution of the GPU warps.

- After all opaque objects are rendered, transparent objects can be handled using forward shading, using the same light lists.

- Since the effects of all lights are computed in a single pass, framebuffer precision can be low, if desired.

This last item, framebuffer precision, can be important in a traditional deferred shading engine [1680]. Each light is applied in a separate pass, so the final result can suffer from banding and other artifacts if the results are accumulated in a framebuffer with only 8 bits per color channel. That said, being able to use a lower precision is not relevant for many modern rendering systems, since these need higher-precision output for performing tone mapping and other operations.

Tiled light classification can also be used with forward rendering. This type of system is called *tiled forward shading* [144, 1327] or *forward+* [665, 667]. First a *z*-prepass of the geometry is performed, both to avoid overdraw in the final pass and to permit further light culling. A compute shader classifies the lights by tiles. A second geometry pass then performs forward shading, with each shader accessing the light lists based on the fragment's screen-space location.

Tiled forward shading has been used in such games as *The Order: 1886* [1267, 1405]. Pettineo [1401] provides an open-source test suite to compare implementations of deferred [990] and forward classification of tiled shading. For antialiasing each sample was stored when using deferred shading. Results were mixed, with each scheme outperforming the other under various test conditions. With no antialiasing, deferred tended to win out on many GPUs as the number of lights increased up to 1024, and forward did better as the antialiasing level was increased. Stewart and Thomas [1700] analyze one GPU model with a wider range of tests, finding similar results.

The z-prepass can also be used for another purpose, culling lights by depth. The idea is shown on the right in Figure 20.6. The first step is finding the minimum and maximum z-depths of objects in a tile, $z_{\min}$ and $z_{\max}$. Each of these is determined by performing a *reduce* operation, in which a shader is applied to the tile's data and the $z_{\min}$ and $z_{\max}$ values are computed by sampling in one or more passes [43, 1701, 1768]. As an example, Harada et al. [667] use a compute shader and unordered access views to efficiently perform frustum culling and reduction of the tiles. These values can then be used to quickly cull any lights that do not overlap this range in the tile. Empty tiles, e.g., where only the sky is visible, can also be ignored [1877]. The type of scene and the application affect whether it is worthwhile to compute and use the minimums, maximums, or both [144]. Culling in this way can also be applied to tiled deferred shading, since the depths are present in the G-buffers.

Since the depth bounds are found from opaque surfaces, transparency must be considered separately. To handle transparent surfaces, Neubelt and Pettineo [1267] render an additional set of passes to create per-tile lights, used to light and shade only transparent surfaces. First, the transparent surfaces are rendered on top of the opaque geometry's z-prepass buffer. The $z_{\min}$ of the transparent surfaces are kept, while the $z_{\max}$ of the opaque surfaces are used to cap the far end of the frustum. The second pass performs a separate light classification pass, where new per-tile light lists are generated. The third pass sends only the transparent surfaces through the renderer, in a similar fashion as tiled forward shading. All such surfaces are shaded and lit with the new light lists.

For scenes with a large number of lights, a range of valid z-values is critical in culling most of these out from further processing. However, this optimization provides little benefit for a common case, depth discontinuities. Say a tile contains a nearby character framed against a distant mountain. The z range between the two is enormous, so is mostly useless for culling lights. This depth range problem can affect a large percentage of a scene, as illustrated in Figure 20.8. This example is not an extreme case. A scene in a forest or with tall grass or other vegetation can contain discontinuities in a higher percentage of tiles [1387].

One solution is to make a single split, halfway between $z_{\min}$ and $z_{\max}$. Called *bimodal clusters* [992] or *HalfZ* [1701, 1768], this test categorizes an intersected light as overlapping the closer, farther, or full range, compared to the midpoint. Doing so directly attacks the case of two objects in a tile, one near and one far. It does not address all concerns, e.g., the case of a light volume overlapping neither object, or

Figure 20.8. A visualization of tiles where large depth discontinuities exist. *(Image from "Just Cause 3," courtesy of Avalanche Studios [1387].)*

more than two objects overlapping at different depths. Nonetheless, it can provide a noticeable reduction in lighting calculations overall.

Harada et al. [666, 667] present a more elaborate algorithm called *2.5D culling*, where each tile's depth range, z_{min} and z_{max}, is split into n cells along the depth direction. This process is illustrated in Figure 20.9. A geometry bitmask of n bits is created, and each bit is set to 1 where there is geometry. For efficiency, they use $n = 32$. Iteration over all lights follows, and a light bitmask is created for every light that overlaps the tile frustum. The light bitmask indicates in which cells the light is located. The geometry bitmask is AND:ed with the light mask. If the result is zero, then that light does not affect any geometry in that tile. This is shown on the right in Figure 20.9. Otherwise, the light is appended to the tile's light list. For one GPU architecture, Stewart and Thomas [1700] found that when the number of lights rose to be over 512, HalfZ began outperforming basic tiled deferred, and when the number rose beyond 2300, 2.5D culling began to dominate, though not significantly so.

Mikkelsen [1210] prunes the light lists further by using the pixel locations of the opaque objects. A list for each 16×16 pixel tile is generated with a screen-space bounding rectangle for each light, along with the z_{min} and z_{max} geometry bounds for culling. This list is then culled further by having each of 64 compute-shader threads compare four pixels in the tile against each light. If none of the pixels' world-space locations in a tile are found to be inside a light's volume, the light is culled from the list. The resulting set of lights can be quite accurate, since only those lights guaranteed to affect at least one pixel are saved. Mikkelsen found that, for his scenes, further culling procedures using the z-axis decreased overall performance.

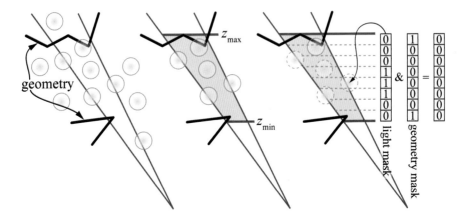

Figure 20.9. Left: a frustum for a tile in blue, some geometry in black, and set of circular yellow light sources. Middle: with tiled culling the z_{min} and z_{max} values in red are used to cull light sources that do not overlap with the gray area. Right: with clustered culling, the region between z_{min} and z_{max} is split into n cells, where $n = 8$ in this example. A geometry bitmask (10000001) is computed using the depths of the pixels, and a light bitmask is computed for each light. If the bitwise AND between these is 0, then that light is not considered further for that tile. The topmost light has 11000000 and so is the only light that will be processed for lighting computations, since 11000000 AND 10000001 gives 10000000, which is nonzero.

With lights placed into lists and evaluated as a set, shader complexity for a deferred system can become quite complex. A single shader must be able to handle all materials and all light types. Tiles can help reduce this complexity. The idea is to store a bitmask in every pixel, with each bit associated with a shader feature the material uses in that pixel. For each tile, these bitmasks are OR:ed together to determine the smallest number of features used in that tile. The bitmasks can also be AND:ed together to find features that are used by all pixels, meaning that the shader does not need an "if" test to check whether to execute this code. A shader fulfilling these requirements is then used for all pixels in the tile [273, 414, 1877]. This shader specialization is important not only because less instructions need to be executed, but also because the resulting shaders might achieve higher occupancy (Section 23.3), as otherwise the shader has to allocate registers for the worst-case code path. Attributes other than materials and lights can be tracked and used to affect the shader. For example, for the game *Split/Second*, Knight et al. [911] classify 4×4 tiles by whether they are fully or partially in shadow, if they contain polygon edges that need antialiasing, and other tests.

20.4 Clustered Shading

Tiled light classification uses the two-dimensional spatial extents of a tile and, optionally, the depth bounds of the geometry. *Clustered shading* divides the view frustum

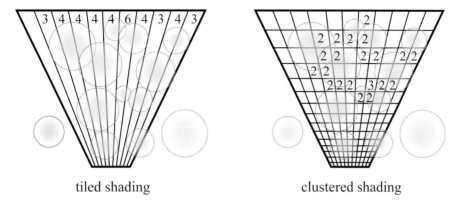

tiled shading   clustered shading

Figure 20.10. Tiled and clustered shading, shown in two dimensions. The view frustum is subdivided and a scene's light volumes are categorized by which regions they overlap. Tiled shading subdivides in screen space, while clustered also divides by z-depth slices. Each volume contains a list of lights; values are shown for lists of length two or more. If z_{min} and z_{max} are not computed for tiled shading from the scene's geometry (not shown), light lists could contain large numbers of unneeded lights. Clustered shading does not need rendered geometry to cull its lists, though such a pass can help. *(Figure after Persson [1387].)*

into a set of three-dimensional cells, called clusters. Unlike the z-depth approaches for tiled shading, this subdivision is performed on the whole view frustum, independent of the geometry in the scene. The resulting algorithms have less performance variability with camera position [1328], and behave better when a tile contains depth discontinuities [1387]. Clustered shading can be applied to both forward and deferred shading systems.

Due to perspective, a tile's cross-section area increases with distance from the camera. Uniform subdivision schemes will create squashed or long and thin voxels for the tile's frustum, which are not optimal. To compensate, Olsson et al. [1328, 1329] cluster geometry exponentially in view space, without any dependency on geometry's z_{min} and z_{max}, to make clusters be more cubical. As an example, the developers for *Just Cause 3* use 64×64 pixel tiles with 16 depth slices, and have experimented with larger resolutions along each axis, as well as using a fixed number of screen tiles regardless of resolution [1387]. The Unreal Engine uses the same size tiles and typically 32 depth slices [38]. See Figure 20.10.

Lights are categorized by the clusters they overlap, and lists are formed. By not depending on the scene geometry's z-depths, the clusters can be computed from just the view and the set of lights [1387]. Each surface, opaque or transparent, then uses its location to retrieve the relevant light list. Clustering provides an efficient, unified lighting solution that works for all objects in the scene, including transparent and volumetric ones.

Like tiled approaches, algorithms using clustering can be combined with forward or deferred shading. For example, *Forza Horizon 2* computes its clusters on the GPU, and then uses forward shading because this provides MSAA support without any additional work [344, 1002, 1387]. While overdraw is possible when forward shading in a single pass, other methods, such as rough front-to-back sorting [892, 1766] or performing a prepass for only a subset of objects [145, 1768], can avoid much overdraw without a second full geometry pass. That said, Pettineo [1407] finds that, even using such optimizations, using a separate z-prepass is faster. Alternately, deferred shading can be performed for opaque surfaces, with the same light list structure then used for forward shading on transparent surfaces. This approach is used in *Just Cause 3*, which creates the light lists on the CPU [1387]. Dufresne [390] also generates cluster light lists in parallel on the CPU, since this process has no dependence on the geometry in the scene.

Clustered light assignment gives fewer lights per list, and has less view dependence than tiled methods [1328, 1332]. The long, thin frusta defined by tiles can have considerable changes in their contents from just small movements of the camera. A straight line of streetlights, for example, can align to fill one tile [1387]. Even with z-depth subdivision methods, the near and far distances found from surfaces in each tile can radically shift due to a single pixel change. Clustering is less susceptible to such problems.

Several optimizations for clustered shading are explored by Olsson et al. [1328, 1329] and others, as noted. One technique is to form a BVH for the lights, which is then used to rapidly determine which light volumes overlap a given cluster. This BVH needs to be rebuilt as soon as at least one light moves. One option, usable with deferred shading, is to cull using quantized normal directions for the surfaces in a cluster. Olsson et al. categorize surface normals by direction into a structure holding 3×3 direction sets per face on a cube, 54 locations in total, in order to form a normal cone (Section 19.3). This structure can then be used to further cull out light sources when creating the cluster's list, i.e., those behind all surfaces in the cluster. Sorting can become expensive for a large number of lights, and van Oosten [1334] explores various strategies and optimizations.

When the visible geometry locations are available, as with deferred shading or from a z-prepass, other optimizations are possible. Clusters containing no geometry can be eliminated from processing, giving a sparse grid that requires less processing and storage. Doing so means that the scene must first be processed to find which clusters are occupied. Because this requires access to the depth buffer data, cluster formation must then be performed on the GPU. The geometry overlapping a cluster may have a small extent compared to the cluster's volume. More lights may be culled by using these samples to form a tight AABB to test against [1332]. An optimized system can handle upward of a million light sources and scales well as this number increases, while also being efficient for just a few lights.

There is no requirement to subdivide the screen z-axis using an exponential function, and such a subdivision may have a negative effect for scenes with many distant lights. With an exponential distribution, cluster volume increases with depth, which can result in a distant cluster's light list being excessively long. Limiting the cluster set's maximum distance, the "far plane" for light clustering, is one solution, with more distant lights faded out, represented as particles or glares, or baked in [293, 432, 1768]. Simpler shaders, lightcuts [1832], or other level of detail techniques can also be used. Conversely, the volume closest to the viewer may be relatively unpopulated but heavily subdivided. One approach is to force the classifying frustum's "near plane" to some reasonable distance and categorize lights closer than this depth to fall into the first depth slice [1387].

In *DOOM* (2016), the developers [294, 1682] implemented their forward shading system using a combination of clustering methods from Olsson et al. [1328] and Persson [1387]. They first perform a z-prepass, which takes about 0.5 ms. Their list-building scheme can be thought of as clip-space voxelization. Light sources, environment light probes, and decals are inserted by testing each for intersection with an AABB representing each cell. The addition of decals is a significant improvement, as the clustered forward system gains the advantages that deferred shading has for these entities. During forward shading the engine loops through all decals found in a cell. If a decal overlaps the surface location, its texture values are retrieved and blended in. Decals can be blended with the underlying surface in any way desired, instead of being limited to only the operations available in the blending stage, as done with deferred shading. With clustered forward shading decals can also be rendered on transparent surfaces. All relevant lights in the cell are then applied.

The CPU can be used to build light lists because the scene's geometry is not necessary, and because analytically testing light volume spheres and cluster boxes for overlap is inexpensive. However, if a spotlight or other light volume shape is involved, using a spherical bounding volume around it can result in adding such a light to many clusters where it has no effect, and the precise analytic intersection test can be expensive. Along these lines, Persson [1387] provides a rapid method for voxelizing a sphere into a set of clusters.

The GPU's rasterization pipeline can be used to categorize light volumes to avoid these problems. Örtegren and Persson [1340] describe a two-pass process to build the light lists. In the shell pass, each light is represented by a low-resolution mesh that encompasses it. Conservative rasterization (Section 23.1.2) is used to render each of these shells into the cluster grid, recording the minimum and maximum cluster each overlaps. In the fill pass, a compute shader adds the light to a linked list for each cluster between these bounds. Using meshes instead of bounding spheres gives tighter bounds for spotlights, and geometry can directly occlude light visibility, culling the lists further still. When conservative rasterization is not available, Pettineo [1407] describes a method that employs surface gradients to conservatively estimate the z bounds of a triangle at each pixel. For example, if the farthest distance is needed at a pixel, the x- and y-depth gradients are used to select which corner of the pixel is farthest away and to compute the depth at that point. Because such points may be off the triangle, he also clamps to the z-depth range of the light as a whole, to avoid having a triangle that is nearly edge-on throw the estimated z-depth far off. Wronski [1922] explores a variety of solutions, landing on the idea of putting a bounding sphere around

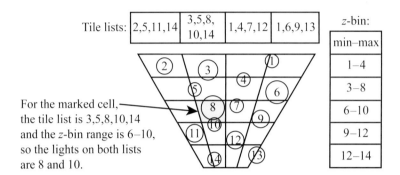

Figure 20.11. Using z-binning, each light is given an ID based on its z-depth. A list for each tile is generated. Each z-bin stores a minimum and maximum ID, a conservative range of lights that may overlap the slice. For any pixels in the marked cell, we retrieve both lists and find the overlap.

a grid cell and performing an intersection test against the cone. This test is quick to evaluate and works well when the cells are nearly cubic, less so when elongated.

Drobot [385] describes how meshes were used for inserting lights in *Call of Duty: Infinite Warfare.* Think of a static spotlight. It forms a volume in space, such as a cone. Without further processing, that cone could extend some considerable distance, either to the extents of the scene or to some maximum distance defined for the light. Now imagine a shadow map for this spotlight, generated using static geometry in the scene. This map defines a maximum distance for each direction in which the light shines. In a baking process, this shadow map is turned into a low-resolution mesh that then serves as the light's effective volume. The mesh is conservative, formed using the maximum depths in each shadow map area, so that it fully encompasses the volume of space that is illuminated by the light. This representation of the spotlight will likely overlap fewer clusters than the original cone's volume.

Independent of this process, the light list storage and access method, called *z-binning*, takes considerably less memory than clustered shading. In it, the lights are sorted by screen z-depth and given IDs based on these depths. A set of z-slices, each of the same depth thickness instead of exponential, is then used to classify these lights. Each z-slice stores just the minimum and maximum ID of the lights overlapping it. See Figure 20.11. Tiled shading lists are also generated, with geometry culling being optional. Each surface location then accesses this two-dimensional tiling structure and the one-dimensional z-bin ID range per slice. The tiling list gives all lights in a tile that may affect the pixel. The pixel's depth retrieves the range of IDs that may overlap that z-slice. The overlap of these two is computed on the fly and gives the valid light list for the cluster.

Instead of creating and storing a list for every cluster in a three-dimensional grid, this algorithm needs only a list per two-dimensional tile and a small fixed-sized array for the set of z-slices. Less storage, bandwidth use, and precomputing are needed, at the cost of a bit more work to determine the relevant lights at each pixel. Using

z-binning may lead to some lights being miscategorized, but Drobot found that for man-made environments there was often little overlap between lights in both the xy screen coordinates and the z-depths. Using pixel and compute shaders, this scheme is able to give near-perfect culling in tiles with depth discontinuities.

Three-dimensional data structures for accessing objects often can be categorized as volume-related, where a grid or octree is imposed on the space; object-related, where a bounding volume hierarchy is formed; or hybrid, such as using a bounding volume around the contents in a grid cell. Bezrati [139, 140] performs tiled shading in a compute shader to form an enhanced light list, where each light includes its minimum and maximum z-depth. In this way, a fragment can quickly reject any lights that do not overlap it. O'Donnell and Chajdas [1312] present *tiled light trees*, which they form on the CPU side. They use tiled light lists with depth bounds for each light and form a bounding interval hierarchy. That is, instead of forming a separate three-dimensional hierarchy of all lights, as done by Olsson et al. [1328], they create a simpler one-dimensional hierarchy from the z extents of each light in a tile. This structure maps well to the GPU's architecture, and is better able to handle cases where a large number of lights fall into a single tile. They also provide a hybrid algorithm that chooses between dividing the tile into cells—the normal clustered shading approach— or using light trees. Light trees work best in situations where the average overlap between a cell and its lights is low.

The idea of local light lists can be used on mobile devices, but there are different limitations and opportunities. For example, rendering one light at a time in a traditional deferred fashion can be the most efficient method on mobile, because of the unique property that mobile keeps the G-buffer in local memory. Tiled forward shading can be implemented on devices that support OpenGL ES 2.0, which is almost a given on mobile GPUs. With OpenGL ES 3.0 and an extension called *pixel local storage*, the tile-based rendering system available in ARM GPUs can be used to efficiently generate and apply light lists. See Billeter's presentation [145] for more information. Nummelin [1292] discusses conversion of the Frostbite engine from the desktop to mobile, including trade-offs with light classification schemes because compute shaders have less support on mobile hardware. Due to mobile devices using tile-based rendering, G-buffer data generated for deferred shading can be maintained in local memory. Smith and Einig [1664] describe using *framebuffer fetch* and pixel local storage to do so, finding that these mechanisms reduce overall bandwidth costs by more than half.

In summary, tiled, clustered, or other light-list culling techniques can be used with deferred or forward shading, and each can also be applied to decals. Algorithms for light-volume culling focus on minimizing the number of lights that are evaluated for each fragment, while the idea of decoupling geometry and shading can be used to balance processing and bandwidth costs to maximize efficiency. Just as frustum culling will cost additional time with no benefit if all objects are always in view, so will some techniques provide little benefit under various conditions. If the sun is the only light source, a light culling preprocess is not necessary. If there is little surface

	Trad. forward	Trad. deferred	Tiled/clust. defer.	Tiled/clust. fwd.
Geometry passes	1	1	1	1–2
Light passes	0	1 per light	1	1
Light culling	per mesh	per pixel	per volume	per volume
Transparency	easy	no	w/fwd→	easy
MSAA	built-in	hard	hard	built-in
Bandwidth	low	high	medium	low
Vary shading models	simple	hard	involved	simple
Small triangles	slow	fast	fast	slow
Register pressure	poss. high	low	poss. low	poss. high
Shadow map reuse	no	yes	no	no
Decals	expensive	cheap	cheap	expensive

Table 20.1. For a typical desktop GPU, comparison of traditional single-pass forward, deferred, and tiled/clustered light classification using deferred and forward shading. *(After Olsson [1332].)*

overdraw and few lights, deferred shading may cost more time overall. For scenes with many limited-effect sources of illumination, spending time to create localized light lists is worth the effort, whether using forward or deferred shading. When geometry is complex to process or surfaces are expensive to render, deferred shading provides a way to avoid overdraw, minimize driver costs such as program and state switches, and use fewer calls to render larger consolidated meshes. Keep in mind that several of these methods can be used in rendering a single frame. What makes for the best mix of techniques is not only dependent on the scene, but can also vary on a per-object or per-light basis [1589].

To conclude this section, we summarize the main differences among approaches in Table 20.1. The right arrow in the "Transparency" row means that deferred shading is applied to opaque surfaces, with forward shading needed for transparent ones. "Small triangles" notes an advantage of deferred shading, that quad shading (Section 23.1) can be inefficient when forward rendering, due to all four samples being fully evaluated. "Register pressure" refers to the overall complexity of the shaders involved. Using many registers in a shader can mean fewer threads formed, leading to the GPU's warps being underused [134]. It can become low for tiled and clustered deferred techniques if shader streamlining methods are employed [273, 414, 1877]. Shadow map reuse is often not as critical as it once was, when GPU memory was more limited [1589].

Shadows are a challenge when a large number of light sources are present. One response is to ignore shadow computations for all but the closest and brightest lights, and the sun, at the risk of light leaks from the lesser sources. Harada et al. [667] discuss how they use ray casting in a tiled forward system, spawning a ray for each visible surface pixel to each nearby light source. Olsson et al. [1330, 1331] discuss generating shadow maps using occupied grid cells as proxies for geometry, with samples created as needed. They also present a hybrid system, combining these limited shadow maps with ray casting.

Using world space instead of screen space for generating light lists is another way to structure space for clustered shading. This approach can be reasonable in some situations, though might be worth avoiding for large scenes because of memory constraints [385] and because distant clusters will be pixel-sized, hurting performance. Persson [1386] provides code for a basic clustered forward system where static lights are stored in a three-dimensional world-space grid.

20.5 Deferred Texturing

Deferred shading avoids overdraw and its costs of computing a fragment's shade and then having these results discarded. However, when forming G-buffers, overdraw still occurs. One object is rasterized and all its parameters are retrieved, performing several texture accesses along the way. If another object is drawn later that occludes these stored samples, all the bandwidth spent for rendering the first object was wasted. Some deferred shading systems perform a partial or full z-prepass to avoid texture access for a surface that is later drawn over by another object [38, 892, 1401]. However, an additional geometry pass is something many systems avoid if possible. Bandwidth is used by texture fetches, but also by vertex data access and other data. For detailed geometry, an extra pass can use more bandwidth than it might save in texture access costs.

The higher the number of G-buffers formed and accessed, the higher the memory and bandwidth costs. In some systems bandwidth may not be a concern, as the bottleneck could be predominantly within the GPU's processor. As discussed at length in Chapter 18, there is always a bottleneck, and it can and will change from moment to moment. A major reason why there are so many efficiency schemes is that each is developed for a given platform and type of scene. Other factors, such as how hard it is to implement and optimize a system, the ease of authoring content, and a wide variety of other human factors, can also determine what is built.

While both computational and bandwidth capabilities of GPUs have risen over time, they have increased at different rates, with compute rising faster. This trend, combined with new functionality on the GPU, has meant that a way to future-proof your system is by aiming for the bottleneck to be GPU computation instead of buffer access [217, 1332].

A few different schemes have been developed that use a single geometry pass and avoid retrieving textures until needed. Haar and Aaltonen [625] describe how virtual *deferred texturing* is used in *Assassin's Creed Unity*. Their system manages a local 8192×8192 texture atlas of visible textures, each with 128×128 resolution, selected from a much larger set. This atlas size permits storing (u, v) texture coordinates that can be used to access any texel in the atlas. There are 16 bits used to store a coordinate; with 13 bits needed for 8192 locations, this leaves 3 bits, i.e., 8 levels, for sub-texel precision. A 32-bit tangent basis is also stored, encoded as a quaternion [498] (Section 16.6). Doing so means only a single 64-bit G-buffer is needed. With no texture accesses performed in the geometry pass, overdraw can be extremely inexpensive. After this G-buffer is established, the virtual texture is then accessed during shading. Gradients are needed for mipmapping, but are not stored. Rather, each pixel's neighbors are examined and those with the closest (u, v) values are used

Figure 20.12. In the first pass of the visibility buffer [217], just triangle and instance IDs are rendered and stored in a single G-buffer, here visualized with a different color per triangle. *(Image courtesy of Graham Wihlidal—Electronic Arts [1885].)*

to compute the gradients on the fly. The material ID is also derived from determining which texture atlas tile is accessed, done by dividing the texture coordinate values by 128, i.e., the texture resolution.

Another technique used in this game to reduce shading costs is to render at a quarter resolution and use a special form of MSAA. On consoles using AMD GCN, or systems using OpenGL 4.5, OpenGL ES 3.2, or other extensions [2, 1406], the MSAA sampling pattern can be set as desired. Haar and Aaltonen set a grid pattern for 4× MSAA, so that each grid sample corresponds directly to the center of a full-screen pixel. By rendering at a quarter resolution, they can take advantage of the multisampling nature of MSAA. The (u, v) and tangent bases can be interpolated across the surface with no loss, and 8× MSAA (equivalent to 2× MSAA per pixel) is also possible. When rendering scenes with considerable overdraw, such as foliage and trees, their technique significantly reduces the number of shader invocations and bandwidth costs for the G-buffers.

Storing just the texture coordinates and basis is pretty minimal, but other schemes are possible. Burns and Hunt [217] describe what they call the *visibility buffer*, in which they store two pieces of data, a triangle ID and an instance ID. See Figure 20.12. The geometry pass shader is extremely quick, having no texture accesses and needing to store just these two ID values. All triangle and vertex data—positions, normals, color, material, and so on—are stored in global buffers. During the deferred shading pass, the triangle and instance IDs stored for each pixel are used to retrieve these data. The view ray for the pixel is intersected against the triangle to find the barycentric coordinates, which are used to interpolate among the triangle's vertex data. Other computations that are normally done less frequently must also be performed per pixel, such as vertex shader calculations. Texture gradient values are also computed from scratch for each pixel, instead of being interpolated. All these data are then used to shade the pixel, applying lights using any classification scheme desired.

While this all sounds expensive, remember that computational power is growing faster than bandwidth capabilities. This research favors a compute-heavy pipeline that minimizes bandwidth losses due to overdraw. If there are less than 64k meshes in the scene, and each mesh has less than 64k triangles, each ID is then 16 bits in length and the G-buffer can be as small as 32 bits per pixel. Larger scenes push this to 48 or 64 bits.

Stachowiak [1685] describes a variant of the visibility buffer that uses some capabilities available on the GCN architecture. During the initial pass, the barycentric coordinates for the location on the triangle are also computed and stored per pixel. A GCN fragment (i.e., pixel) shader can compute the barycentric coordinates inexpensively, compared to later performing an individual ray/triangle intersection per pixel. While costing additional storage, this approach has an important advantage. With animated meshes the original visibility buffer scheme needs to have any modified mesh data streamed out to a buffer, so that the modified vertex locations can be retrieved during deferred shading. Saving the transformed mesh coordinates consumes additional bandwidth. By storing the barycentric coordinates in the first pass, we are done with the vertex positions, which do not have to be fetched again, a disadvantage of the original visibility buffer. However, if the distance from the camera is needed, this value must also be stored in the first pass, since it cannot later be reconstructed.

This pipeline lends itself to decoupling geometry and shading frequency, similar to previous schemes. Aaltonen [2] notes that the MSAA grid sampling method can be applied to each, leading to further reductions in the average amount of memory required. He also discusses variations in storage layout and differences in compute costs and capabilities for these three schemes. Schied and Dachsbacher [1561, 1562] go the other direction, building on the visibility buffer and using MSAA functionality to reduce memory consumption and shading computations for high-quality antialiasing.

Pettineo [1407] notes that the availability of bindless texture functionality (Section 6.2.5) makes implementing deferred texturing simpler still. His deferred texturing system creates a larger G-buffer, storing the depth, a separate material ID, and depth gradients. Rendering the Sponza model, this system's performance was compared against a clustered forward approach, with and without z-prepass. Deferred texturing was always faster than forward shading when MSAA was off, slowing when MSAA was applied. As noted in Section 5.4.2, most video games have moved away from MSAA as screen resolutions have increased, instead relying on temporal antialiasing, so in practical terms such support is not all that important.

Engel [433] notes that the visibility buffer concept has become more attractive due to API features exposed in DirectX 12 and Vulkan. Culling sets of triangles (Section 19.8) and other removal techniques performed using compute shaders reduce the number of triangles rasterized. DirectX 12's `ExecuteIndirect` command can be used to create the equivalent of an optimized index buffer that displays only those triangles that were not culled. When used with an advanced culling system [1883, 1884], his analysis determined that the visibility buffer outperformed deferred shading at all resolutions and antialiasing settings on the San Miguel scene. As the screen resolution rose, the performance gap increased. Future changes to the GPU's API and capabilities are likely to further improve performance. Lauritzen [993] discusses the visibility buffer and how there is a need to evolve the GPU to improve the way material shaders are accessed and processed in a deferred setting.

Doghramachi and Bucci [363] discuss their deferred texturing system in detail, which they call *deferred+*. Their system integrates aggressive culling techniques early on. For example, the previous frame's depth buffer is downsampled and reprojected in a way that provides a conservative culling depth for each pixel in the current scene. These depths help test occlusion for rendering bounding volumes of all meshes visible in the frustum, as briefly discussed in Section 19.7.2. They note that the alpha cutout texture, if present, must be accessed in any initial pass (or any z-prepass, for that matter), so that objects behind cutouts are not hidden. The result of their culling and rasterization process is a set of G-buffers that include the depth, texture coordinates, tangent space, gradients, and material ID, which are used to shade the pixels. While its number of G-buffers is higher than in other deferred texturing schemes, it does avoid unneeded texture accesses. For two simplified scene models from *Deus Ex: Mankind Divided*, they found that deferred+ ran faster than clustered forward shading, and believe that more complex materials and lighting would further widen the gap. They also noted that warp usage was significantly better, meaning that tiny triangles caused fewer problems, so GPU tessellation performed better. Their implementation of deferred texturing has several other advantages over deferred shading, such as being able to handle a wider range of materials more efficiently. The main drawbacks are those common to most deferred schemes, relating to transparency and antialiasing.

20.6 Object- and Texture-Space Shading

The idea of decoupling the rate at which the geometry is sampled from the rate at which shading values are computed is a recurring theme in this chapter. Here we cover several alternate approaches that do not easily fit in the categories covered so far. In particular, we discuss hybrids that draw upon concepts first seen in the *Reyes*[1] batch renderer [289], used for many years by Pixar and others to make their films. Now studios primarily use some form of ray or path tracing for rendering, but for its day, Reyes solved several rendering problems in an innovative and efficient way.

The key concept of Reyes is the idea of *micropolygons*. Every surface is diced into an extremely fine mesh of quadrilaterals. In the original system, dicing is done

---

[1]The name "Reyes" was inspired by Point Reyes peninsula, and is sometimes capitalized as "REYES," an acronym meaning "Renders Everything You Ever Saw."

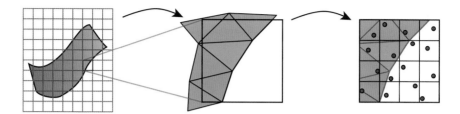

Figure 20.13. Reyes rendering pipeline. Each object is tessellated into micropolygons, which are then individually shaded. A set of jittered samples for each pixel (in red) are compared to the micropolygons and the results are used to render the image.

with respect to the eye, with the goal of having each micropolygon be about half the width and height of a pixel, so that the Nyquist limit (Section 5.4.1) is maintained. Quadrilaterals outside the frustum or facing away from the eye are culled. In this system, the micropolygon was shaded and assigned a single color. This technique evolved to shading the vertices in the micropolygon grid [63]. Our discussion here focuses on the original system, for the ideas it explored.

Each micropolygon is inserted into a jittered 4×4 sample grid in a pixel—a supersampled z-buffer. Jittering is done to avoid aliasing by producing noise instead. Because shading happens with respect to a micropolygon's coverage, before rasterization, this type of technique is called *object-based shading*. Compare this to forward shading, where shading takes place in screen space during rasterization, and deferred shading, where it takes place after. See Figure 20.13.

One advantage of shading in object space is that material textures are often directly related to their micropolygons. That is, the geometric object can be subdivided such that there is a power-of-two number of texels in each micropolygon. During shading the exact filtered mipmap sample can then be retrieved for the micropolygon, since it directly correlates to the surface area shaded. The original Reyes system also meant that cache coherent access of a texture occurs, since micropolygons are accessed in order. This advantage does not hold for all textures, e.g., environment textures used as reflection maps must be sampled and filtered in traditional ways.

Motion blur and depth-of-field effects can also work well with this type of arrangement. For motion blur each micropolygon is assigned a position along its path at a jittered time during the frame interval. So, each micropolygon will have a different location along the direction of movement, giving a blur. Depth of field is achieved in a similar fashion, distributing the micropolygons based on the circle of confusion.

There are some disadvantages to the Reyes algorithm. All objects must be able to be tessellated, and must be diced to a fine degree. Shading occurs before occlusion testing in the z-buffer, so can be wasted due to overdraw. Sampling at the Nyquist limit does not mean that high-frequency phenomena such as sharp specular highlights are captured, but rather that sampling is sufficient to reconstruct lower frequencies.

Generally, every object must be "chartable," in other words, must have (u, v) texture values for the vertices that give a unique texel for each different area on the model. See Figure 2.9 on page 23 and Figure 6.6 on page 173 for examples. Object-based shading can be thought of as first baking in the shading, with the camera used to determine view-dependent effects and possibly limit the amount of effort expended for each surface area. One simple method of performing object-based shading on the GPU is to tessellate the object to a fine subpixel level, then shade each vertex on the mesh. Doing so can be costly because the setup costs for each triangle are not amortized over a number of pixels. The expense is made worse still because a single-pixel triangle generates four pixel shader invocations, due to quad rendering (Section 23.1). GPUs are optimized to render triangles that cover a fair number of pixels, e.g., 16 or more (Section 23.10.3).

Burns et al. [216] explore object-space shading by performing it after establishing which object locations are visible. They determine these with a "polygon grid" for an object that is diced, culled as possible, and then rasterized. An independent object-space "shading grid" is then used to shade the visible areas, with each texel corresponding to an area of the surface. The shading grid can be a different resolution than the polygon grid. They found that a finely tessellated geometric surface provided little benefit, so decoupling the two led to more efficient use of the resources. They implemented their work only in a simulator, but their techniques have influenced newer research and development.

Considerable research that draws inspiration from Reyes has examined faster shading methods on the GPU for various phenomena. Ragan-Kelley et al. [1455] propose a hardware extension based on decoupled sampling, applying their idea to motion blur and depth of field. Samples have five dimensions: two for the subpixel location, two for the lens location, and one for time. Visibility and shading are sampled separately. A "decoupling mapping" determines the shading sample needed for a given visibility sample. Liktor and Dachsbacher [1042, 1043] present a deferred shading system in a similar vein, where shading samples are cached when computed and used during stochastic rasterization. Effects such as motion blur and depth of field do not require high sampling rates, so shading computations can be reused. Clarberg et al. [271] present hardware extensions for computing shading in texture space. These eliminate the quad overshading problem and hence allow for smaller triangles. Since shading is computed in texture space, the pixel shader can use a bilinear filter or a more complex one, when looking up the shading from the texture. This allows reducing shading costs by turning down the texture resolution. For low-frequency terms, this technique usually works well, since filtering can be used.

Andersson et al. [48] take a different approach, called *texture-space shading*. Each triangle is tested for frustum and backface culling, then its charted surface is applied to a corresponding area of an output target, shading this triangle based on its (u, v) parameterization. At the same time, using a geometry shader, each visible triangle's size in the camera's view is computed. This size value is used to determine in which mipmap-like level the triangle is inserted. In this way, the amount of shading performed for an object is related to its screen coverage. See Figure 20.14. They use stochastic rasterization to render the final image. Each fragment generated looks up

Figure 20.14. Object-space texture shading. On the left is the final rendering, including motion blur. In the middle the visible triangles in the chart are shown. On the right each triangle is inserted at its proper mipmap level based on screen coverage of the triangle, for use during the final camera-based rasterization pass. *(Reprinted by permission of M. Andersson [48] and Intel Corporation, copyright Intel Corporation, 2014.)*

its shaded color from the texture. Again, computed shading values can be reused for motion blur and depth-of-field effects.

Hillesland and Yang [747, 748] build upon the texture-space shading concept, along with caching concepts similar to Liktor and Dachsbacher's. They draw geometry to the final view, use a compute shader to populate a mipmap-like structure of object-based shading results, and render the geometry again to access this texture and display the final shade. A triangle ID visibility buffer is also saved in the first pass, so that their compute shader can later access vertex attributes for interpolation. Their system includes coherence over time. Since the shading is in object space, the same area is associated with the same output texture location for each frame. If a surface area's shade at a given mipmap level was computed previously and is not too old, it is reused instead of being recomputed. Results will vary with the material, lighting, and other factors, but they found that reusing a shading sample every other frame at 60 FPS led to negligible errors. They also determined that the mipmap level could be selected not only by screen size, but also by variation in other factors, such as the change in normal direction over an area. A higher mipmap level means that less shading is computed per screen fragment, which they found could lead to considerable savings.

Baker [94] describes Oxide Games' renderer for the game *Ashes of the Singularity*. It is inspired by Reyes, though the implementation details are considerably different, and uses texture-space shading for each model as a whole. Objects may have any number of materials covering their surfaces, which are differentiated by using masks. Their process is:

- Several large—4k × 4k, 16 bits per channel—"master" textures are allocated for shading.

- All objects are evaluated. If in view, an object's estimated area on the screen is computed.

- This area is used to assign a proportion of a master texture to each object. If the total requested area is larger than the texture space, proportions are scaled down to make the requests fit.

- Texture-based shading is performed in a compute shader, with each material attached to the model applied in turn. Results from each material are accumulated in the assigned master texture.

- Mipmap levels are computed for the master textures as needed.

- Objects are then rasterized, with the master textures used to shade them.

Using multiple materials per object allows such effects as having a single terrain model include dirt, roads, ground cover, water, snow, and ice, each with its own material BRDF. Antialiasing works on both a pixel level and a shader level, if desired, as the full information about an object's surface area and its relationship to the master texture is accessible during shading. This ability allows the system to stably handle models with extremely high specular powers, for example. Because shaded results are attached to objects as a whole, regardless of visibility, shading can also be computed at a different frame rate than rasterization. Shading at 30 FPS was found to be adequate, with rasterization occurring at 60 FPS, or 90 FPS for virtual reality systems. Having asynchronous shading means that the frame rate for the geometry can be maintained even if the shader load becomes too high.

There are several challenges in implementing such a system. About twice as many batches are sent overall, compared to a typical game engine, since each object's "material quadrilateral" is processed with a compute shader during the object-shading step, then the object is drawn during rasterization. Most batches are simple, however, and APIs such as DirectX 12 and Vulkan help remove overhead. How the master textures are allocated to objects based on their size makes a significant difference in image quality. Objects that are large on the screen, or otherwise vary in texel density, such as terrain, can have issues. Performing an additional stitching process is used to maintain a smooth transition among terrain tiles of different resolutions in the master texture. Screen-space techniques, such as ambient occlusion, are a challenge to implement. Like the original visibility buffer, animation affecting object shape must be done twice, for shading and for rasterization. Objects are shaded, then occluded, which is a source of waste. For an application with low depth complexity, such as a real-time strategy game, this cost can be relatively low. Each material is simple to evaluate, unlike complex deferred shaders, and shading is done on a chart for the whole object. Objects with simple shaders, such as particles and trees, receive little benefit from this technique. For performance, these effects can instead be rendered with forward shading. As can be seen in Figure 20.15, being able to handle many lights gives a richness to the rendered scene.

We end our discussion of efficient shading here. We have only touched upon a panoply of specialized techniques to improve speed and quality of results used in

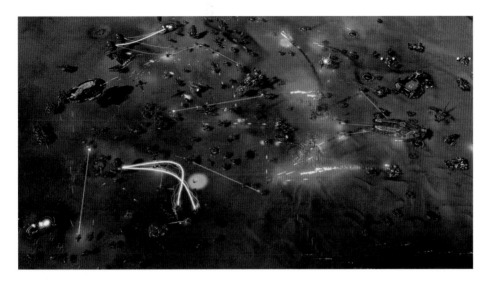

Figure 20.15. A scene from *Ashes of the Singularity* lit by approximately a thousand lights. These include at least one light source for each vehicle and each bullet. *(Image courtesy of Oxide Games and Stardock Entertainment.)*

different applications. Our goal here is to present popular algorithms used to accelerate shading and explain how and why they arose. As graphics hardware capabilities and APIs evolve, and as screen resolutions, art workflows, and other elements change over time, efficient shading techniques will continue to be researched and developed in new and, likely, unanticipated ways.

If you have read the book through to this point, you now have working knowledge of the major algorithms that go into a modern interactive rendering engine. One of our goals is to get you up to speed so that you can comprehend current articles and presentations in the field. If you wish to see how these elements work together, we highly recommend you read the excellent articles on different commercial renderers by Courrèges [293, 294] and Anagnostou [38]. After this point, the chapters that follow delve deeper into several fields, such as rendering for virtual and augmented reality, algorithms for intersection and collision detection, and architectural features of graphics hardware.

Further Reading and Resources

So, of the various mixes of these approaches—deferred, forward, tiled, clustered, visibility—which is better? Each has its own strengths, and the answer is "it depends." Factors such as platform, scene characteristics, illumination model, and design goals can all play a part. As a starting spot, we recommend Pesce's extensive discussions [1393, 1397] about the effectiveness and trade-offs of various schemes.

The SIGGRAPH course "Real-Time Many-Light Management and Shadows with Clustered Shading" [145, 1331, 1332, 1387] presents a thorough run-through of tiled and clustered shading techniques and their use with deferred and forward shading, along with related topics such as shadow mapping and implementing light classification on mobile devices. An earlier presentation by Stewart and Thomas [1700] explains tiled shading and presents copious timing results showing how various factors affect performance. Pettineo's open-source framework [1401] compares tiled forward and deferred systems, and includes results for a wide range of GPUs.

For implementation details, the book on DirectX 11 by Zink et al. [1971] has about 50 pages on the subject of deferred shading and includes numerous code samples. The NVIDIA GameWorks code samples [1299] include an implementation of MSAA for deferred shading. The articles by Mikkelsen [1210] and Örtegren and Persson [1340] in the book *GPU Pro 7* describe modern GPU-based systems for tiled and clustered shading. Billeter et al. [144] give coding details on implementing tiled forward shading, and Stewart [1701] walks through code for performing tiled culling in a compute shader. Lauritzen [990] provides a full implementation for tiled deferred shading, and Pettineo [1401] builds a framework to compare it to tiled forward. Dufresne [390] has demo code for clustered forward shading. Persson [1386] provides code for a basic world-space clustered forward rendering solution. Finally, van Oosten [1334] discusses various optimizations and gives a demo system with code that implements different forms of clustered, tiled, and vanilla forward rendering, showing the performance differences.

Chapter 21
Virtual and Augmented Reality

"Reality is that which, when you stop believing in it, doesn't go away."
—Philip K. Dick

Virtual reality (VR) and augmented reality (AR) are technologies that attempt to stimulate your senses in the same way the real world does. Within the field of computer graphics, augmented reality integrates synthetic objects with the world around us; virtual reality replaces the world completely. See Figure 21.1. This chapter focuses on rendering techniques specific to these two technologies, which are sometimes grouped together using the umbrella term "XR," where the X can stand for any letter. Much of the focus here will be on virtual reality techniques, since this technology is more widespread as of this writing.

Rendering is but a small part of these fields. From a hardware standpoint, some type of GPU is used, which is a well-understood piece of the system. Creating accurate and comfortable head-tracking sensors [994, 995], effective input devices (possibly with haptic feedback or eye-tracking control), and comfortable headgear and optics, along with convincing audio, are among the challenges system creators face. Balancing performance, comfort, freedom of movement, price, and other factors make this a demanding design space.

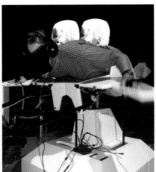

Figure 21.1. The first three authors using various VR systems. Tomas using an HTC Vive; Eric in the Birdly fly-like-a-bird simulator; Naty using an Oculus Rift.

We concentrate on interactive rendering and the ways these technologies influence how images are generated, starting with a brief survey of various virtual and augmented reality systems currently available. The capabilities and goals of some systems' SDKs and APIs are then discussed. We end with specific computer graphics techniques that should be avoided or modified to give the best user experience.

21.1   Equipment and Systems Overview

Aside from CPUs and GPUs, virtual and augmented reality equipment for graphics can be categorized as either sensors or displays. Sensors include trackers that detect the rotation and position of the user, along with a myriad of input methods and devices. For display, some systems rely on using a mobile phone's screen, which is logically split into two halves. Dedicated systems often have two separate displays. The display is all the user sees in a virtual reality system. For augmented reality, the virtual is combined with a view of the real world by use of specially designed optics.

Virtual and augmented reality are old fields that have undergone a recent explosion in new, lower-cost systems, in good part directly or indirectly due to the availability of various mobile and console technologies [995]. Phones can be used for immersive experiences, sometimes surprisingly well. A mobile phone can be placed inside a *head-mounted display* (HMD), ranging from a simple viewer, such as Google Cardboard, to those that are hands-free and provide additional input devices, such as GearVR. The phone's orientation sensors for gravity, magnetic north, and other mechanisms allow the orientation of the display to be determined. The orientation, also called *attitude*, has three degrees of freedom, e.g., yaw, pitch, and roll, as discussed in Section 4.2.1.[1] APIs can return the orientation as a set of Euler angles, a rotation matrix, or a quaternion. Real-world content such as fixed-view panoramas and videos can work well with these devices, as the costs of presenting the correct two-dimensional view for the user's orientation are reasonably low.

Mobile devices' relatively modest computational capabilities, as well as the power requirements for extended use of GPU and CPU hardware, limit what can be done with them. Tethered virtual reality devices, in which the user's headset is connected by a set of wires to a stationary computer, limit mobility, but allow more powerful processors to be used.

We will briefly describe the sensors for just two systems, the Oculus Rift and the HTC Vive. Both provide six degrees of freedom (6-DOF) tracking: orientation and position. The Rift tracks the location of the HMD and controllers by up to three separate infrared cameras. When the headset's position is determined by stationary external sensors, this is called *outside-in tracking*. An array of infrared LEDs on the outside of the headset allow it to be tracked. The Vive uses a pair of "lighthouses" that shine non-visible light into a room at rapid intervals, which sensors in the headset and

---

[1] Many phones' inertial measurement units have six degrees of freedom, but positional tracking errors can accumulate rapidly.

controllers detect in order to triangulate their positions. This is a form of *inside-out tracking*, where the sensors are part of the HMD.

Hand controllers are a standard piece of equipment, being trackable and able to move with the user, unlike mice and keyboards. Many other types of input devices have been developed for VR, based on a wide range of technologies. Devices include gloves or other limb or body tracking devices, eye tracking, and those simulating in-place movement, such as pressure pads, single- or omni-directional treadmills, stationary bicycles, and human-sized hamster balls, to name but a few. Aside from optical systems, tracking methods based on magnetic, inertia, mechanical, depth detection, and acoustic phenomena have been explored.

Augmented reality is defined as computer-generated content combined with a user's real-world view. Any application providing a heads-up display (HUD) with text data overlaid on an image is a basic form of augmented reality. Yelp Monocle, introduced in 2009, overlays business user ratings and distances on the camera's view. The mobile version of Google Translate can replace signs with translated equivalents. Games such as *Pokémon GO* overlay imaginary creatures in real environments. Snapchat can detect facial features and add costume elements or animations.

Of more interest for synthetic rendering, *mixed reality* (MR) is a subset of augmented reality in which real-world and three-dimensional virtual content blend and interact in real time [1570]. A classic use case for mixed reality is in surgery, where scanned data for a patient's organs are merged with the camera view of the external body. This scenario assumes a tethered system with considerable computing power and precision. Another example is playing "tag" with a virtual kangaroo, where the real-world walls of the house can hide your opponent. In this case, mobility is more important, with registration or other factors affecting quality being less critical.

One technology used in this field is to mount a video camera on the front of an HMD. For example, every HTC Vive has a front-mounted camera that the developer can access. This view of the world is sent to the eyes, and synthetic imagery can be composited with it. This is sometimes called *pass-through* AR or VR, or *mediated reality* [489], in which the user is not directly viewing the environment. One advantage of using such a video stream is that it allows more control of merging the virtual objects with the real. The downside is that the real world is perceived with some lag. Vrvana's Totem and Occipital's Bridge are examples of AR systems using a head-mounted display with this type of arrangement.

Microsoft's HoloLens is the most well-known mixed-reality system as of this book's writing. It is an untethered system, with CPU, GPU, and what Microsoft terms an HPU (holographic processing unit) all built into the headset. The HPU is a custom chip consisting of 24 digital signal processing cores that draws less than 10 watts. These cores are used to process world data from a Kinect-like camera that views the environment. This view, along with other sensors such as accelerometers, perform inside-out tracking, with the additional advantage that no lighthouses, QR codes (a.k.a. fiducials), or other external elements are needed. The HPU is used to identify a limited set of hand gestures, meaning that no additional input device is necessary for basic interactions. While scanning the environment, the HPU also extracts depths and derives geometry data, such as planes and polygons representing surfaces in the world. This geometry can then be used for collision detection, e.g., having virtual objects sit on a real-world tabletop.

Tracking using the HPU allows a wider range of motion, effectively anywhere in the world, by creating real-world waypoints, called *spatial anchors*. A virtual object's position is then set relative to a particular spatial anchor [1207]. The device's estimates of these anchor positions can also improve over time. Such data can be shared, meaning that a few users can see the same content in the same location. Anchors can also be defined so that users at different locations can collaborate on the same model.

A pair of transparent screens allow the user to see the world along with whatever is projected onto these screens. Note that this is unlike a phone's use of augmented reality, where the view of the world is captured by camera. One advantage of using transparent screens is that the world itself never has latency or display problems, and consumes no processing power. A disadvantage of this type of display system is that virtual content can only add luminance to the user's view of the world. For example, a dark virtual object will not occlude brighter real world objects behind it, since light can only be increased. This can give virtual objects a translucent feel. The HoloLens also has an LCD dimmer that can help avoid this effect. With proper adjustment, the system can be effective in showing three-dimensional virtual objects merged with reality.

Apple's ARKit and Google's ARCore help developers create augmented reality apps for phones and tablets. The norm is to display a single (not stereoscopic) view, with the device held some distance from the eyes. Objects can be fully opaque, since they are overlaid on the video camera's view of the world. See Figure 21.2. For ARKit, inside-out tracking is performed by using the device's motion-sensing hardware along with a set of notable features visible to the camera. Tracking these feature points from frame to frame helps precisely determine the device's current position and orientation. Like the HoloLens, horizontal and vertical surfaces are discovered and the extents determined, with this information then made available to the developer [65].

Intel's Project Alloy is an untethered head-mounted display that, like the HoloLens, has a sensor array to detect large objects and walls in the room. Unlike the HoloLens, the HMD does not let the user directly view the world. However, its ability to sense its surroundings gives what Intel calls "merged reality," where real-world objects can have a convincing presence in a virtual world. For example, the user could reach out to a control console in the virtual world and touch a table in the real world.

Virtual and augmented reality sensors and controllers are undergoing rapid evolution, with fascinating technologies arising at a breakneck pace. These offer the promise of less-intrusive headsets, more mobility, and better experiences. For example, Google's Daydream VR and Qualcomm's Snapdragon VR headsets are untethered and use inside-out positional tracking that does not need external sensors or devices. Systems from HP, Zotac, and MSI, where the computer is mounted on your back, make for untethered systems that provide more compute power. Intel's WiGig wire-

Figure 21.2. An image from ARKit. The ground plane is detected and displayed as a blue grid. The closest beanbag chair is a virtual object added on the ground plane. It is missing shadows, though these could be added for the object and blended over the scene. *(Image courtesy of Autodesk, Inc.)*

less networking technology uses a short-range 90 GHz radio to send images from a PC to a headset. Another approach is to compute expensive lighting computations on the cloud, then send this compressed information to be rendered by a lighter, less powerful GPU in a headset [1187]. Software methods such as acquiring point clouds, voxelizing these, and rendering the voxelized representations at interactive rates [930] open up new ways for the virtual and real to merge.

Our focus for most of this chapter is on the display and its use in VR and AR. We first run through some of the physical mechanics of how images are displayed on the screen and some of the issues involved. The chapter continues with what the SDKs and hardware systems provide to simplify programming and enhance the user's perception of the scene. This section is followed by information about how these various factors affect image generation, with a discussion of how some graphical techniques need to be modified or possibly avoided altogether. We end with a discussion of rendering methods and hardware enhancements that improve efficiency and the participant's experience.

21.2 Physical Elements

This section is about the various components and characteristics of modern VR and AR systems, in particular those related to image display. This information gives a framework for understanding the logic behind the tools provided by vendors.

21.2.1   Latency

Mitigating the effects of latency is particularly important in VR and AR systems, often the most critical concern [5, 228]. We discussed how the GPU hides memory latency in Chapter 3. That type of latency, caused by operations such as texture fetches, is specific to a small portion of the entire system. What we mean here is the "motion-to-photon" latency of the system as a whole. That is, say you begin to turn your head to the left. How much time elapses between your head coming to face in a particular direction and the view generated from that direction being displayed? Processing and communication costs for each piece of hardware in the chain, from the detection of a user input (e.g., your head orientation) to the response (the new image being displayed), all add up to tens of milliseconds of latency.

Latency in a system with a regular display monitor (i.e., one not attached to your face) is annoying at worst, breaking the sense of interactivity and connection. For augmented and mixed reality applications, lower latency will help increase "pixel stick," or how well the virtual objects in the scene stay affixed to the real world. The more latency in the system, the more the virtual objects will appear to swim or float relative to their real-world counterparts. With immersive virtual reality, where the display is the only visual input, latency can create a much more drastic set of effects. Though not a true illness or disease, it is called *simulation sickness* and can cause sweating, dizziness, nausea, and worse. If you begin to feel unwell, immediately take off the HMD—you are not able to "power through" this discomfort, and will just become more ill [1183]. To quote Carmack [650], "Don't push it. We don't need to be cleaning up sick in the demo room." In reality, actual vomiting is rare, but the effects can nonetheless be severe and debilitating, and can be felt for up to a day.

Simulation sickness in VR arises when the display images do not match the user's expectations or perceptions through other senses, such as the inner ears' vestibular system for balance and motion. The lower the lag between head motion and the proper matching displayed image, the better. Some research points to 15 ms being imperceptible. A lag of more than 20 ms can definitely be perceived and has a deleterious effect [5, 994, 1311]. As a comparison, from mouse move to display, video games generally have a latency of 50 ms or more, 30 ms with vsync off (Section 23.6.2). A display rate of 90 FPS is common among VR systems, which gives a frame time of 11.1 ms. On a typical desktop system it takes about 11 ms to scan the frame over a cable to the display, so even if you could render in 1 ms, you would still have 12 ms of latency.

There are a wide variety of application-based techniques that can prevent or ameliorate discomfort [1089, 1183, 1311, 1802]. These can range from minimizing visual flow, such as not tempting the user to look sideways while traveling forward and avoiding going up staircases, to more psychological approaches, such as playing ambient music or rendering a virtual object representing the user's nose [1880]. More muted colors and dimmer lighting can also help avoid simulator sickness. Making the system's response match the user's actions and expectations is the key to providing an enjoyable VR experience. Have all objects respond to head movements, do not zoom the camera or otherwise change the field of view, properly scale the virtual world, and do not take control of the camera away from the user, to name a few guidelines. Having a fixed visual reference around the user, such as a car or airplane cockpit, can also diminish simulator sickness. Visual accelerations applied to a user can cause discomfort, so using a constant velocity is preferable. Hardware solutions may also prove useful. For example, Samsung's Entrim 4D headphones emit tiny electrical impulses that affect the vestibular system, making it possible to match what the user sees to what their sense of balance tells them. Time will tell as to the efficacy of this technique, but it is a sign of how much research and development is being done to mitigate the effects of simulator sickness.

The *tracking pose*, or simply the *pose*, is the orientation and, if available, position of the viewer's head in the real world. The pose is used to form the camera matrices needed for rendering. A rough prediction of the pose may be used at the start of a frame to perform simulation, such as collision detection of a character and elements in the environment. When rendering is about to start, a newer pose prediction can be retrieved at that moment and used to update the camera's view. This prediction will be more accurate, since it is retrieved later and is for a shorter duration. When the image is about to be displayed, another pose prediction that is more accurate still can be retrieved and used to warp this image to better match the user's position. Each later prediction cannot fully compensate for computations based on an earlier, inaccurate prediction, but using them as possible can considerably improve the overall experience. Hardware enhancements in various rigs provide the ability to rapidly query and obtain updated head poses at the moment they are needed.

There are elements other than visuals that make interaction with a virtual environment convincing, but getting the graphics wrong dooms the user to an unpleasant experience at best. Minimizing latency and improving realism in an application can help achieve *immersion* or *presence*, where the interface falls away and the participant feels physically a part of the virtual world.

21.2.2 Optics

Designing precise physical optics that map a head-mounted display's contents to the corresponding locations on the retina is an expensive proposition. What makes virtual reality display systems affordable is that the images produced by the GPU are then distorted in a separate post-process so that they properly reach our eyes.

A VR system's lenses present the user with a wide field-of-view image that has pincushion distortion, where the edges of the image appear to curve inward. This effect is canceled out by warping each generated image using barrel distortion, as seen on the right in Figure 21.3. Optical systems usually also suffer from *chromatic aberration*, where the lenses cause the colors to separate, like a prism does. This problem can also be compensated for by the vendor's software, by generating images that have an inverted chromatic separation. It is chromatic aberration "in the other

Figure 21.3. The original rendered targets (left) and their distorted versions (right) for display on an HTC Vive [1823]. *(Images courtesy of Valve.)*

direction." These separate colors combine properly when displayed through the VR system's optics. This correction can be seen in the orange fringing around the edges of the images in the distorted pair.

There are two types of displays, rolling and global [6]. For both types of display, the image is sent in a serial stream. In a *rolling display*, this stream is immediately displayed as received, scanline by scanline. In a *global display*, once the whole image is received, it is then displayed in a single, short burst. Each type of display is used in virtual reality systems, and each has its own advantages. In comparison to a global display, which must wait for the entire image to be present before display, a rolling display can minimize latency, in that the results are shown as soon as available. For example, if images are generated in strips, each strip could be sent as rendered, just before display, "racing the beam" [1104]. A drawback is that different pixels are illuminated at different times, so images can be perceived as wobbly, depending on the relative movement between the retinas and the display. Such mismatches can be particularly disconcerting for augmented reality systems. The good news is that the compositor usually compensates by interpolating the predicted head poses across a block of scan lines. This mostly addresses wobble or shearing that would otherwise happen with fast head rotation, though cannot correct for objects moving in the scene.

Global displays do not have this type of timing problem, as the image must be fully formed before it is shown. Instead, the challenge is technological, as a single short timed burst rules out several display options. Organic light-emitting diode (OLED) displays are currently the best option for global displays, as they are fast enough to keep up with the 90 FPS display rates popular for VR use.

21.2.3 Stereopsis

As can be seen in Figure 21.3, two images are offset, with a different view for each eye. Doing so stimulates *stereopsis*, the perception of depth from having two eyes.While an important effect, stereopsis weakens with distance, and is not our only way of perceiving depth.We do not use it at all, for example, when looking at an image on a standard monitor. Object size, texture pattern changes, shadows, relative movement (parallax), and other visual depth cues work with just one eye.

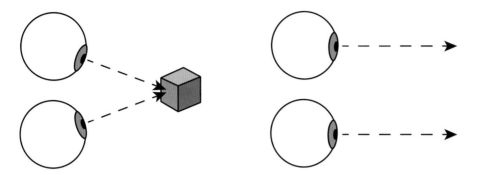

Figure 21.4. How much two eyes rotate to see an object is the vergence. Convergence is the motion of the eyes inward to focus on an object, as on the left. Divergence is the outward motion when they change to look at objects in the distance, off the right edge of the page. The lines of sight for viewing distant objects are effectively parallel.

How much the eyes must adjust shape to bring something into focus is known as *accommodative demand*. For example, the Oculus Rift's optics are equivalent to looking at a screen located about 1.3 meters from the user. How much the eyes need to turn inward to focus on an object is called *vergence demand*. See Figure 21.4. In the real world the eyes change lens shape and turn inward in unison, a phenomenon known as the *accommodation-convergence reflex*. With a display, the accommodative demand is a constant, but the vergence demand changes as the eyes focus on objects at different perceived depths. This mismatch can cause eye strain, so Oculus recommends that any objects the user is going to see for an extended period of time be placed about 0.75 to 3.5 meters away [1311, 1802]. This mismatch can also have perceptual effects in some AR systems, for example, where the user may focus on a distant object in the real world, but then must refocus on an associated virtual billboard that is at a fixed depth near the eye. Hardware that can adjust the perceived focal distance based on the user's eye movements, sometimes called an *adaptive focus* or *varifocal* display, is under research and development by a number of groups [976, 1186, 1875].

The rules for generating stereo pairs for VR and AR are different than those for single-display systems where some technology (polarized lens, shutter glasses, multi-view display optics) presents separate images to each eye from the same screen. In VR each eye has a separate display, meaning that each must be positioned in a way that the images projected onto the retinas will closely match reality. The distance from eye to eye is called the *interpupillary distance* (IPD). In one study of 4000 U.S. Army soldiers, the IPD was found to range from 52 mm to 78 mm, with an average of 63.5 mm [1311]. VR and AR systems have calibration methods to determine and adjust to the user's IPD, thus improving image quality and comfort. The system's API controls a camera model that includes this IPD. It is best to avoid modifying a user's perceived IPD to achieve an effect. For example, increasing the eye-separation distance could enhance the perception of depth, but can also lead to eye strain.

Stereo rendering for head-mounted displays is challenging to perform properly from scratch. The good news is that much of the process of setting up and using the proper camera transform for each eye is handled by the API, the subject of the next section.

21.3   APIs and Hardware

Let us say this from the start: Always use the VR software development kit (SDK) and application programming interface (API) provided by the system provider, unless you have an excellent reason to do otherwise. For example, you might believe your own distortion shader is faster and looks about right. In practice, however, it may well cause serious user discomfort—you will not necessarily know whether this is true without extensive testing. For this and other reasons, application-controlled distortion has been removed from all major APIs; getting VR display right is a system-level task. There is much careful engineering done on your behalf to optimize performance and maintain quality. This section discusses what support various vendors' SDKs and APIs provide.

The process for sending rendered images of a three-dimensional scene to a headset is straightforward. Here we will talk about it using elements common to most virtual and augmented reality APIs, noting vendor-specific functionality along the way. First, the time when the frame about to be rendered will be displayed is determined. There is usually support for helping you estimate this time delay. This value is needed so that the SDK can compute an estimate of where and in which direction the eyes will be located at the moment the frame is seen. Given this estimated latency, the API is queried for the pose, which contains information about the camera settings for each eye. At a minimum this consists of the head's orientation, along with the position, if sensors also track this information. The OpenVR API also needs to know if the user is standing or seated, which can affect what location is used as the origin, e.g., the center of the tracked area or the position of the user's head. If the prediction is perfect, then the rendered image will be displayed at the moment the head reaches the predicted location and orientation. In this way, the effect of latency can be minimized.

Given the predicted pose for each eye, you generally render the scene to two separate targets.[2] These targets are sent as textures to the SDK's *compositor*. The compositor takes care of converting these images into a form best viewed on the headset. The compositor can also composite various layers together. For example, if a monoscopic heads-up display is needed, one where the view is the same for both eyes, a single texture containing this element can be provided as a separate layer that is composited atop each eye's view. Textures can be different resolutions and formats, with the compositor taking care of conversion to the final eye buffers. Doing so can allow optimizations such as dynamically lowering the resolution of the three-dimensional scene's layer to save time on rendering [619, 1357, 1805], while maintaining high resolution and quality for the other layers [1311]. Once images are composed for each

---

[2]Some APIs instead accept a single target split into two views.

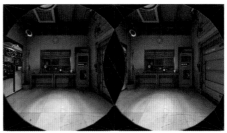

Figure 21.5. On the left, the red areas in the display image show pixels that are rendered and then warped, but that are not visible to the HMD user. Note that the black areas are outside the bounds of the transformed rendered image. On the right, these red areas are instead masked out in advance with the red-edged mesh at the start of rendering, resulting in this rendered (pre-warped) image needing fewer pixels to be shaded [1823]. Compare the right image with the original, on the left in Figure 21.3. *(Images courtesy of Valve.)*

eye, distortion, chromatic aberration, and any other processes needed are performed by the SDK and the results are then displayed.

If you rely on the API, you do not need to fully understand the algorithms behind some of these steps, since the vendor does much of the work for you. However, knowing a bit about this area is still worthwhile, if only to realize that the most obvious solution is not always the best one. To start, consider compositing. The most efficient way is to first composite all the layers together, and then to apply the various corrective measures on this single image. Instead, Oculus first performs these corrections separately to each layer, then composites these distorted layers to form the final, displayed image. One advantage is that each layer's image is warped at its own resolution, which can improve text quality, for example, because treating the text separately means that resampling and filtering during the distortion process is focused on just the text's content [1311].

The field of view a user perceives is approximately circular. What this means is that we do not need to render some of the pixels on the periphery of each image, near the corners. While these pixels will appear on the display, they are nearly undetectable by the viewer. To avoid wasting time generating these, we can first render a mesh to hide these pixels in the original images we generate. This mesh is rendered into the stencil buffer as a mask, or into the z-buffer at the front. Subsequent rendered fragments in these areas are then discarded before being evaluated. Vlachos [1823] reports that this reduces the fill rate by about 17% on the HTC Vive. See Figure 21.5. Valve's OpenVR API calls this pre-render mask the "hidden area mesh."

Once we have our rendered image, it needs to be warped to compensate for the distortion from the system's optics. The concept is to define a remapping of the original image to the desired shape for the display, as shown in Figure 21.3. In other words, given a pixel sample on the incoming rendered image, to where does this sample move in the displayed image? A ray casting approach can give the precise answer and adjust by wavelength [1423], but is impractical for most hardware. One method is

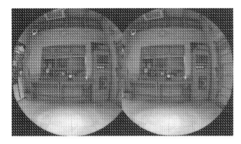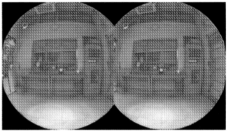

Figure 21.6. On the left, the mesh for the final, displayed image is shown. In practice, this mesh can be trimmed back to the culled version on the right, since drawing black triangles adds nothing to the final image [1823]. *(Images courtesy of Valve.)*

to treat the rendered image as a texture and draw a screen-filling quadrilateral to run a post-process. The pixel shader computes the exact location on this texture that corresponds to the output display pixel [1430]. However, this method can be expensive, as this shader has to evaluate distortion equations at every pixel.

Applying the texture to a mesh of triangles is more efficient. This mesh's shape can be modified by the distortion equation and rendered. Warping the mesh just once will not correct for chromatic aberration. Three separate sets of (u, v)-coordinates are used to distort the image, one for each color channel [1423, 1823]. That is, each triangle in the mesh is rendered once, but for each pixel the rendered image is sampled three times in slightly different locations. These red, green, and blue channel values then form the output pixel's color.

We can apply a regularly spaced mesh to the rendered image and warp to the displayed image, or vice versa. An advantage of applying the gridded mesh to the displayed image and warping back to the rendered image is that fewer 2×2 quads are likely to be generated, as no thin triangles will be displayed. In this case the mesh locations are not warped but rendered as a grid, and only the vertices' texture coordinates are adjusted in order to distort the image applied to the mesh. A typical mesh is 48×48 quadrilaterals per eye. See Figure 21.6. The texture coordinates are computed once for this mesh by using per-channel display-to-render image transforms. By storing these values in the mesh, no complex transforms are needed during shader execution. GPU support for anisotropic sampling and filtering of a texture can be used to produce a sharp displayable image.

The rendered stereo pair on the right in Figure 21.5 gets distorted by the display mesh. The slice removed in the center of this image corresponds to how the warping transform generates the displayable images—note how this slice is missing from where the images meet in the displayed version on the left in Figure 21.5. By trimming back the displayed warping mesh to only visible areas, as shown on the right in Figure 21.6, we can reduce the cost for the final distortion pass by about 15%.

To sum up the optimizations described, we first draw a hidden area mesh to avoid evaluating fragments in areas we know will be undetectable or unused (such as the middle slice). We render the scene for both eyes. We then apply this rendered image to a gridded mesh that has been trimmed to encompass only the relevant rendered areas. Rendering this mesh to a new target gives us the image to display. Some or all of these optimizations are built in to virtual and augmented reality systems' API support.

21.3.1 Stereo Rendering

Rendering two separate views seems like it would be twice the work of rendering a single view. However, as Wilson notes [1891], this is not true for even a naive implementation. Shadow map generation, simulation and animation, and other elements are view-independent. The number of pixel shader invocations does not double, because the display itself is split in half between the two views. Similarly, post-processing effects are resolution-dependent, so those costs do not change either. View-dependent vertex processing is doubled, however, and so many have explored ways to reduce this cost.

Frustum culling is often performed before any meshes are sent down the GPU's pipeline. A single frustum can be used to encompass both eye frusta [453, 684, 1453]. Since culling happens before rendering, the exact rendered views to use may be retrieved after culling occurs. However, this means that a safety margin is needed during culling, since this retrieved pair of views could otherwise view models removed by the frustum. Vlachos [1823] recommends adding about 5 degrees to the field of view for predictive culling. Johansson [838] discusses how frustum culling and other strategies, such as instancing and occlusion cull queries, can be combined for VR display of large building models.

One method of rendering the two stereo views is to do so in a series, rendering one view completely and then the other. Trivial to implement, this has the decided disadvantage that state changes are also then doubled, something to avoid (Section 18.4.2). For tile-based renderers, changing your view and render target (or scissor rectangle) frequently will result in terrible performance. A better alternative is to render each object twice as you go, switching the camera transform in between. However, the number of API draw calls is still doubled, causing additional work. One approach that comes to mind is using the geometry shader to duplicate the geometry, creating triangles for each view. DirectX 11, for example, has support for the geometry shader sending its generated triangles to separate targets. Unfortunately, this technique has been found to lower geometry throughput by a factor of three or more, and so is not used in practice. A better solution is to use instancing, where each object's geometry is drawn twice by a single draw call [838, 1453]. User-defined clip planes are set to keep each eye's view separate. Using instancing is much faster than using geometry shaders, and is a good solution barring any additional GPU support [1823, 1891]. Another approach is to form a command list (Section 18.5.4) when rendering one eye's image, shift referenced constant buffers to the other eye's transform, and then replay this list to render the second eye's image [453, 1473].

There are several extensions that avoid sending geometry twice (or more) down the pipeline. On some mobile phones, an OpenGL ES 3.0 extension called *multi-view* adds support for sending the geometry only once and rendering it to two or more views, making adjustments to screen vertex positions and any view-dependent variables [453, 1311]. The extension gives more much freedom in implementing a stereo renderer. For example, the simplest extension is likely to use instancing in the driver, issuing the geometry twice, while an implementation requiring GPU support could send each triangle to each of the views. Different implementations have various advantages, but since API costs always are reduced, any of these methods can help CPU-bound applications. The more complex implementations can increase texture cache efficiency [678] and perform vertex shading of view-independent attributes only once, for example. Ideally, the entire matrix can be set for each view and any per-vertex attributes can also be shaded for each view. To make a hardware implementation use less transistors, a GPU can implement a subset of these features.

Multi-GPU solutions tuned for VR stereo rendering are available from AMD and NVIDIA. For two GPUs, each renders a separate eye's view. Using an *affinity mask*, the CPU sets a bit for all GPUs that are to receive particular API calls. In this way, calls can be sent to one or more GPUs [1104, 1453, 1473, 1495]. With affinity masks the API still needs to be called twice if a call differs between the right and left eye's view.

Another style of rendering provided by vendors is what NVIDIA calls *broadcasting*, where rendering to both eyes is provided using a single draw call, i.e., it is broadcast to all GPUs. Constant buffers are used to send different data, e.g., eye positions, to the different GPUs. Broadcasting creates both eyes' images with hardly any more CPU overhead than a single view, as the only cost is setting a second constant buffer.

Separate GPUs mean separate targets, but the compositor often needs a single rendered image. There is a special sub-rectangle transfer command that shifts render target data from one GPU to the other in a millisecond or less [1471]. It is asynchronous, meaning that the transfer can happen while the GPU does other work. With two GPUs running in parallel, both may also separately create the shadow buffer needed for rendering. This is duplicated effort, but is simpler and usually faster than attempting to parallelize the process and transfer between GPUs. This entire two-GPU setup results in about a 30 to 35% rendering speedup [1824]. For applications that are already tuned for single GPUs, multiple GPUs can instead apply their extra compute on additional samples for a better antialiased result.

Parallax from stereo viewing is important for nearby models, but is negligible for distant objects. Palandri and Green [1346] take advantage of this fact on the mobile GearVR platform by using a separating plane perpendicular to the view direction. They found a plane distance of about 10 meters was a good default. Opaque objects closer than this are rendered in stereo, and those beyond with a monoscopic camera placed between the two stereo cameras. To minimize overdraw, the stereo views are drawn first, then the intersection of their depth buffers is used to initialize the z-buffer for the single monoscopic render. This image of distant objects is then composited

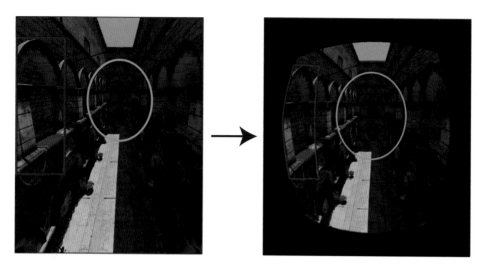

Figure 21.7. On the left is the rendered image for one eye. On the right is the warped image for display. Note how the green oval in the center maintains about the same area. On the periphery, a larger area (red outline) in the rendered image is associated with a smaller displayed area [1473]. *(Images courtesy of NVIDIA Corporation.)*

with each stereo view. Transparent content is rendered last for each view. While more involved, and with objects spanning the separating plane needing an additional pass, this method produced consistent overall savings of about 25%, with no loss in quality or depth perception.

As can be seen in Figure 21.7, a higher density of pixels is generated in the periphery of each eye's image, due to distortion needed by the optics. In addition, the periphery is usually less important, as the user looks toward the center of the screen a considerable amount of the time. For these reasons, various techniques have been developed for applying less effort to pixels on the periphery of each eye's view.

One method to lower the resolution along the periphery is called *multi-resolution shading* by NVIDIA and *variable rate shading* by AMD. The idea is to divide the screen into, e.g., 3×3 sections and render areas around the periphery at lower resolutions [1473], as shown in Figure 21.8. NVIDIA has had support for this partitioning scheme since their Maxwell architecture, but with Pascal on, a more general type of projection is supported. This is called *simultaneous multi-projection* (SMP). Geometry can be processed by up to 16 individual projections times 2 separate eye locations, allowing a mesh to be replicated up to 32 times without additional cost on the application side. The second eye location must be equal to the first eye location offset along the x-axis. Each projection can be independently tilted or rotated around an axis [1297].

Using SMP, one can implement *lens matched shading*, where the goal is to better match the rendered resolution to what is displayed. See Figure 21.7. Four frusta

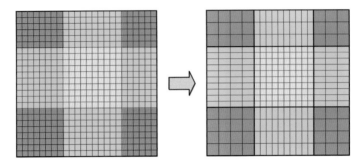

Figure 21.8. Assume that we want to render the view on the left with lower resolution at the periphery. We can reduce the resolution of any area as desired, but it is usually better to keep the same resolution along shared edges. On the right, we show how the blue regions are reduced in number of pixels by 50% and the red regions by 75%. The field of view remains the same, but the resolution used for the peripheral areas is reduced.

with tilted planes are rendered, as shown on the left in Figure 21.9. These modified projections provide more pixel density at the center of the image and less around the periphery. This gives a smoother transition between sections than multi-resolution shading. There are a few drawbacks, e.g., effects such as blooms need to be reworked to display properly. Unity and Unreal Engine 4 have integrated this technique into their systems [1055]. Toth et al. [1782] formally compare and contrast these and other multi-view projection algorithms, and use up to 3×3 views per eye to reduce pixel shading further. Note that SMP can be applied to both eyes simultaneously, as illustrated on the right in Figure 21.9.

To save on fragment processing, an application-level method, called *radial density masking*, renders the periphery pixels in a checkerboard pattern of quads. In other words, every other 2×2 quad of fragments is not rendered. A post-process pass is then used to reconstruct the missing pixels from their neighbors [1824]. This technique can

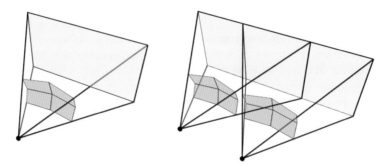

Figure 21.9. Left: simultaneous multi-projection (SMP) using four projection planes for one eye. Right: SMP using four projection planes for each of the two eyes.

be particularly valuable for a system with a single, low-end GPU. Rendering using this method will cut down on pixel shader invocations, though may not gain you anything if the costs of skipping and then performing a reconstruction filter are too high. Sony's London studio goes a step further with this process, dropping one, two, or three quads out of the set of 2×2, with the number dropped increasing near the edge of the image. Missing quads are filled in a similar way, and the dither pattern is changed each frame. Applying temporal antialiasing also helps hide stair-stepping artifacts. Sony's system saves about 25% GPU time [59].

Another method is to render two separate images per eye, one of a central circular area and the other of the ring forming the periphery. These two images can then be composited and warped to form the displayed image for that eye. The periphery's image can be generated at a lower resolution to save on pixel shader invocations, at the expense of sending the geometry to form four different images. This technique dovetails well with GPU support for sending geometry to multiple views, as well as providing a natural division of work for systems with two or four GPUs. Though meant to reduce the excessive pixel shading on the periphery due to the optics involved in the HMD, Vlachos calls this technique *fixed foveated rendering* [1824]. This term is a reference to a more advanced concept, *foveated rendering*.

21.3.2   Foveated Rendering

To understand this rendering technique, we must know a bit more about our eyes. The fovea is a small depression on each of our eyes' retinas that is packed with a high density of cones, the photoreceptors associated with color vision. Our visual acuity is highest in this area, and we rotate our eyes to take advantage of this capability, such as tracking a bird in flight, or reading text on a page. Visual acuity drops off rapidly, about 50% for every 2.5 degrees from the fovea's center for the first 30 degrees, and more steeply farther out. Our eyes have a field of view for binocular vision (where both eyes can see the same object) of 114 horizontal degrees. First-generation consumer headsets have a somewhat smaller field of view, around 80 to 100 horizontal degrees for both eyes, with this likely to rise. The area in the central 20 degrees of view cover about 3.6% of the display for HMDs from 2016, dropping to 2% for those expected around 2020 [1357]. Display resolutions are likely to rise by an order of magnitude during this time [8].

With the vast preponderance of the display's pixels being seen by the eye in areas of low visual acuity, this provides an opportunity to perform less work by using foveated rendering [619, 1358]. The idea is to render the area at which the eyes are pointed with high resolution and quality, with less effort expended on everything else. The problem is that the eyes move, so knowing which area to render will change. For example, when studying an object, the eyes perform a series of rapid shifts called *saccades*, moving as rapidly as a speed of 900 degrees a second, i.e., possibly 10 degrees per frame in a 90 FPS system. Precise eye-tracking hardware could potentially provide a large performance boost by performing less rendering work outside the foveal area, but such sensors are a technical challenge [8]. In addition, rendering "larger" pixels in the periphery tends to increase the problem of aliasing. The rendering of peripheral areas with a lower resolution can potentially be improved by attempting to maintain contrast and avoiding large changes over time, making such areas more perceptually acceptable [1357]. Stengel et al. [1697] discuss previous methods of foveated rendering to reduce the number of shader invocations and present their own.

21.4 Rendering Techniques

What works for a single view of the world does not necessarily work for two. Even within stereo, there is a considerable difference between what techniques work on a single, fixed screen compared to a screen that moves with the viewer. Here we discuss specific algorithms that may work fine on a single screen, but are problematic for VR and AR. We have drawn on the expertise of Oculus, Valve, Epic Games, Microsoft, and others. Research by these companies continues to be folded into user manuals and discussed in blogs, so we recommend visiting their sites for current best practices [1207, 1311, 1802].

As the previous section emphasizes, vendors expect you to understand their SDKs and APIs and use them appropriately. The view is critical, so follow the head model provided by the vendor and get the camera projection matrix exactly right. Effects such as strobe lights should be avoided, as flicker can lead to headaches and eye strain. Flickering near the edge of the field of view can cause simulator sickness. Both flicker effects and high-frequency textures, such as thin stripes, can also trigger seizures in some people.

Monitor-based video games often use a heads-up display with overlaid data about health, ammo, or fuel remaining. However, for VR and AR, binocular vision means that objects closer to the viewer have a larger shift between the two eyes—vergence (Section 21.2.3). If the HUD is placed on the same portion of the screen for both eyes, the perceptual cue is that the HUD must be far away, as shown in Figure 21.4 on page 923. However, the HUD is drawn in front of everything. This perceptual mismatch makes it hard for users to fuse the two images and understand what they are seeing, and it can cause discomfort [684, 1089, 1311]. Shifting the HUD content to be rendered with a nearby depth to the eyes solves this, but still at the cost of screen real estate. See Figure 21.10. There is also still a risk of a depth conflict if, say, a nearby wall is closer than a cross-hair, since the cross-hair icon is still rendered on top at a given depth. Casting a ray and finding the nearest surface's depth for a given direction can be used in various ways to adjust this depth, either using it directly or smoothly moving it closer if need be [1089, 1679].

Bump mapping works poorly with any stereo viewing system in some circumstances, as it is seen for what it is, shading painted onto a flat surface. It can work for fine surface details and distant objects, but the illusion rapidly breaks down for normal maps that represent larger geometric shapes and that the user can approach.

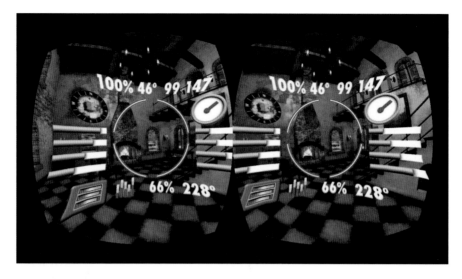

Figure 21.10. A busy heads-up display that dominates the view. Note how HUD elements must be shifted for each eye in order to avoid confusing depth cues. A better solution is to consider putting such information into devices or displays that are part of the virtual world itself or on the player's avatar, since the user can tilt or turn their head [1311]. To see the stereo effect here, get close and place a small, stiff piece of paper perpendicular to the page between the images so that one eye looks at each. *(Image courtesy of Oculus VR, LLC.)*

See Figure 21.11. Basic parallax mapping's swimming problem is more noticeable in stereo, but can be improved by a simple correction factor [1171]. In some circumstances more costly techniques, such as steep parallax mapping, parallax occlusion mapping (Section 6.8.1), or displacement mapping [1731], may be needed to produce a convincing effect.

Figure 21.11. Normal maps for smaller surface features, such as the two textures on the left and in the middle, can work reasonably well in VR. Bump textures representing sizable geometric features, such as the image on the right, will be unconvincing up close when viewed in stereo [1823]. *(Image courtesy of Valve.)*

Billboards and impostors can sometimes be unconvincing when viewed in stereo, since these lack surface z-depths. Volumetric techniques or meshes may be more appropriate [1191, 1802]. Skyboxes need to be sized such that they are rendered "at infinity" or thereabouts, i.e., the difference in eye positions should not affect their rendering. If tone mapping is used, it should be applied to both rendered images equally, to avoid eye strain [684]. Screen-space ambient occlusion and reflection techniques can create incorrect stereo disparities [344]. In a similar vein, post-processing effects such as blooms or flares need to be generated in a way that respects the z-depth for each eye's view so that the images fuse properly. Underwater or heat-haze distortion effects can also need rework. Screen-space reflection techniques produce reflections that could have problems matching up, so reflection probes may be more effective [1802]. Even specular highlighting may need modification, as stereo vision can affect how glossy materials are perceived. There can be large differences in highlight locations between the two eye images. Researchers have found that modifying this disparity can make the images easier to fuse and be more convincing. In other words, the eye locations may be moved a bit closer to each other when computing the glossy component. Conversely, differences in highlights from objects in the distance may be imperceptible between the images, possibly leading to sharing shading computations [1781]. Sharing shading between the eye's images can be done if the computations are completed and stored in texture space [1248].

The demands on display technology for VR are extremely high. Instead of, say, using a monitor with a 50 degree horizontal field of view, resulting in perhaps around 50 pixels per degree, the 110 degree field of view on a VR display results in about 15 pixels per degree [1823] for the Vive's 1080×1200 pixel display for each eye. The transform from a rendered image to a displayed image also complicates the process of resampling and filtering properly. The user's head is constantly moving, even if just a small bit, resulting in increased temporal aliasing. For these reasons, high-quality antialiasing is practically a requirement to improve quality and fusion of images. Temporal antialiasing is often recommended against [344], due to potential blurring, though at least one team at Sony has used it successfully [59]. They found there are trade-offs, but that it was more important to remove flickering pixels than to provide a sharper image. However, for most VR applications the sharper visuals provided by MSAA are preferred [344]. Note that $4\times$ MSAA is good, $8\times$ is better, and jittered supersampling better still, if you can afford it. This preference for MSAA works against using various deferred rendering approaches, which are costly for multiple samples per pixel.

Banding from a color slowly changing over a shaded surface (Section 23.6) can be particularly noticeable on VR displays. This artifact can be masked by adding in a little dithered noise [1823].

Motion blur effects should not be used, as they muddy the image, beyond whatever artifacts occur due to eye movement. Such effects are at odds with the low-persistence nature of VR displays that run at 90 FPS. Because our eyes do move to take in the wide field of view, often rapidly (saccades), depth-of-field techniques should be avoided. Such methods make the content in the periphery of the scene look blurry for no real reason, and can cause simulator sickness [1802, 1878].

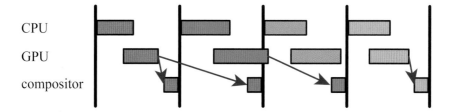

Figure 21.12. Judder. Four frames are shown in a row, with the CPU and GPU attempting to compute an image for each. The image for the first frame, shown in pink, is computed in time to send it to the compositor for this frame. The next image, in blue, is not finished in time for display in the second frame, so the first image must be displayed again. The green third image is again not ready in time, so the (now-completed) second image is sent to the compositor for the third frame. The orange fourth image is completed in time, so is displayed. Note the results of the third frame's rendering computations never get displayed. *(Illustration after Oculus [1311].)*

Mixed reality systems pose additional challenges, such as applying similar illumination to virtual objects as what is present in the real-world environment. In some situations the real-world lighting can be controlled and converted to virtual lighting in advance. When this is not possible, you can use various *light estimation* techniques to capture and approximate the environment's lighting conditions on the fly. Kronander et al. [942] provide an in-depth survey of various lighting capture and representation methods.

21.4.1 Judder

Even with perfect tracking and properly maintained correspondence between the virtual and real worlds, latency is still a problem. A finite amount of time is needed to generate an image at 45 to 120 FPS, the update rates for a range of VR equipment [125].

A *dropped frame* occurs when an image is not generated in time to be sent to the compositor and displayed. An examination of early launch titles for the Oculus Rift showed they dropping about 5% of their frames [125]. Dropped frames can increase the perception of *judder*, a smearing and strobing artifact in VR headsets that is most visible when the eye is moving relative to the display. See Figure 21.12. If pixels are illuminated for the duration of the frame, smears are received on the eyes' retinas. Lowering the *persistence*, the length of time the pixels are lit by the display during a frame, gives less smearing. However, it can instead lead to strobing, where if there is a large change between frames, multiple separate images are perceived. Abrash [7] discusses judder in depth and how it relates to display technologies.

Vendors provide methods that can help minimize latency and judder effects. One set of techniques, which Oculus calls *timewarp* and *spacewarp*, take the generated image and warp or modify it to better match the user's orientation and position. To start, imagine that we are not dropping frames and we detect the user is rotating their head. We use the detected rotation to predict the location and direction of view for each eye. With perfect prediction, the images we generate are exactly as needed.

Say instead that the user is rotating their head and is slowing down. For this scenario our prediction will overshoot, with the images generated being a bit ahead of where they should be at display time. Estimating the rotational acceleration in addition to the velocity can help improve prediction [994, 995].

A more serious case occurs when a frame is dropped. Here, we must use the previous frame's image, as something needs to be put on the screen. Given our best prediction of the user's view, we can modify this image to approximate the missing frame's image. One operation we can perform is a two-dimensional image warp, what Oculus calls a timewarp. It compensates for only the rotation of the head pose. This warp operation is a quick corrective measure that is much better than doing nothing. Van Waveren [1857] discusses the trade-offs for various timewarp implementations, including those run on CPUs and digital signal processors (DSPs), concluding that GPUs are by far the fastest for this task. Most GPUs can perform this image warp process in less than half a millisecond [1471]. Rotating the previously displayed image can cause the black border of the displayed image to become visible in the user's peripheral vision. Rendering a larger image than is needed for the current frame is one way to avoid this problem. In practice, however, this fringe area is almost unnoticeable [228, 1824, 1857].

Beyond speed, an advantage of purely rotational warping is that the other elements in the scene are all consistent. The user is effectively at the center of an environmental skybox (Section 13.3), changing only view direction and orientation. The technique is fast and works well for what it does. Missing frames is bad enough, but variable and unpredictable lag due to intermittent dropped frames appears to bring on simulator sickness more rapidly [59, 1311]. To provide a smoother frame rate, Valve has its *interleaved reprojection* system kick in when frame drops are detected, dropping the rendering rate to 45 FPS and warping every other frame. Similarly, one version of VR on the PLAYSTATION has a 120-Hz refresh rate, in which rendering is performed at 60 Hz and reprojection is done to fill in the alternating frames [59].

Correcting just for rotation is not always sufficient. Even if the user does not move or shift their position, when the head rotates or tilts, the eyes do change locations. For example, the distance between eyes will appear to narrow when using just image warping, since the new image is generated using eye separation for eyes pointing in a different direction [1824]. This is a minor effect, but not compensating properly for positional changes can lead to user disorientation and sickness if there are objects near the viewer, or if the viewer is looking down at a textured ground plane. To adjust for positional changes, you can perform a full three-dimensional reprojection (Section 12.2). All pixels in the image have a depth associated with them, so the process can be thought of as projecting these pixels into their locations in the world, moving the eye location, and then reprojecting these points back to the screen. Oculus calls this process *positional timewarp* [62]. Such a process has several drawbacks, beyond its sheer expense. One problem is that when the eye moves, some surfaces can come into or go out of view. This can happen in different ways, e.g., the face of a cube could become visible, or parallax can cause an object in the foreground to shift relative to the background and so hide or reveal details there. Reprojection algorithms attempt to identify objects at different depths and use local image warping to fill in any gaps found [1679]. Such techniques can cause *disocclusion trails*, where the warping makes distant details appear to shift and animate as an object passes in front of them. Transparency cannot be handled by basic reprojection, since only one surface's depth is known. For example, this limitation can affect the appearance of particle systems [652, 1824].

A problem with both image warp and reprojection techniques is that the fragments' colors are computed with respect to the old locations. We can shift the positions and visibility of these fragments, but any specular highlights or reflections will not change. Dropped frames can show judder from these surface highlights, even if the surfaces themselves are shifted perfectly. Even without any head movement, the basic versions of these methods cannot compensate for object movement or animation within a scene [62]. Only the positions of the surfaces are known, not their velocities. As such, objects will not appear to move on their own from frame to frame for an extrapolated image. Objects' movements can be captured in a velocity buffer, as discussed in Section 12.5. Doing so allows reprojection techniques to also adjust for such changes.

Both rotational and positional compensation techniques are often run in a separate, asynchronous process, as a form of insurance against frame drops. Valve calls this *asynchronous reprojection*, and Oculus *asynchronous timewarp* and *asynchronous spacewarp*. Spacewarp extrapolates the missed frame by analyzing previous frames, taking into account camera and head translation as well as animation and controller movement. The depth buffer is not used in spacewarp. Along with normal rendering, an extrapolated image is computed independently at the same time. Being image-based, this process takes a fairly predictable amount of time, meaning that a reprojected image is usually available if rendering cannot be completed in time. So, instead of deciding whether to keep trying to finish the frame or instead use timewarp or spacewarp reprojection, both are done. The spacewarp result is then available if the frame is not completed in time. Hardware requirements are modest, and these warping techniques are meant primarily as an aid for less-capable systems. Reed and Beeler [1471] discuss different ways GPU sharing can be accomplished and how to use asynchronous warps effectively, as do Hughes et al. [783].

Rotational and positional techniques are complementary, each providing its own improvement. Rotational warping can be perfect for accommodating head rotation when viewing distant static scenes or images. Positional reprojection is good for nearby animated objects [126]. Changes in orientation generally cause much more significant registration problems than positional shifts, so even just rotational correction alone offers a considerable improvement [1857].

Our discussion here touches on the basic ideas behind these compensating processes. There is certainly much more written about the technical challenges and limitations of these methods, and we refer the interested reader to relevant references [62, 125, 126, 228, 1311, 1824].

21.4.2 Timing

While asynchronous timewarp and spacewarp techniques can help avoid judder, the best advice for maintaining quality is for the application itself to avoid dropping frames as best it can [59, 1824]. Even without judder, we noted that the user's actual pose at the time of display may differ from the predicted pose. As such, a technique called *late orientation warping* may be useful to better match what the user should see. The idea is to get the pose and generate the frame as usual, then later on in the frame to retrieve an updated prediction for the pose. If this new pose differs from the original pose used to render the scene, then rotational warping (timewarp) is performed on this frame. Since warping usually takes less than half a millisecond, this investment is often worthwhile. In practice, this technique is often the responsibility of the compositor itself.

The time spent getting this later orientation data can be minimized by making this process run on a separate CPU thread, using a technique called *late latching* [147, 1471]. This CPU thread periodically sends the predicted pose to a private buffer for the GPU, which grabs the latest setting at the last possible moment before warping the image. Late latching can be used to provide all head pose data directly to the GPU. Doing so has the limitation that the view matrix for each eye is not available to the application at that moment, since only the GPU is provided this information. AMD has an improved version called *latest data latch*, which allows the GPU to grab the latest pose at the moment it needs these data [1104].

You may have noticed in Figure 21.12 that there is considerable downtime for the CPU and GPU, as the CPU does not start processing until the compositor is done. This is a simplified view for a single CPU system, where all work happens in a single frame. As discussed in Section 18.5, most systems have multiple CPUs that can be kept working in a variety of ways. In practice, the CPUs often work on collision detection, path planning, or other tasks, and prepare data for the GPU to render in the next frame. Pipelining is done, where the GPU works on whatever the CPUs have set up in the previous frame [783]. To be effective, the CPU and GPU work per frame should each take less than a single frame. See Figure 21.13. The compositor often uses a method to know when the GPU is done. Called a *fence*, it is issued as a command by the application, and becomes signaled when all the GPU calls made before it have been fully executed. Fences are useful for knowing when the GPU is finished with various resources.

The GPU durations shown in the figure represent the time spent rendering the images. Once the compositor is done creating and displaying the final frame, the GPU is ready to start rendering the next frame. The CPU needs to wait until compositing is done before it can issue commands to the GPU for the next frame. However, if we wait until the image is displayed, there is then time spent while the application generates new commands on the CPU, which are interpreted by the driver, and commands are finally issued to the GPU. During this time, which can be as high as 2 ms, the GPU is idle. Valve and Oculus avoid this downtime by providing support called

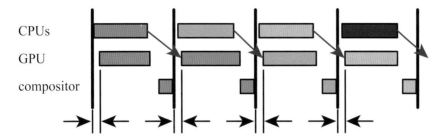

Figure 21.13. Pipelining. To maximize use of resources, the CPUs perform tasks during one frame, and the GPU is used for rendering in the next. By using running start/adaptive queue ahead, the gaps shown at the bottom could instead be added to the GPU's execution time for each frame.

running start and *adaptive queue ahead*, respectively. This type of technique can be implemented on any system. The intent is to have the GPU immediately start working after it is done with the previous frame, by timing when the previous frame is expected to complete and issuing commands just before then. Most VR APIs provide some implicit or explicit mechanism for releasing the application to work on the next frame at a regular cadence, and with enough time to maximize throughput. We provide a simplified view in this section of pipelining and this gap, to give a sense of the benefit of this optimization. See Vlachos' [1823] and Mah's [1104] presentations for in-depth discussions of pipelining and timing strategies.

We end our discussion of virtual and augmented reality systems here. Given the lag between writing and publication, we expect any number of new technologies to arise and supersede those presented here. Our primary goal has been to provide a sense of the rendering issues and solutions involved in this rapidly evolving field. One fascinating direction that recent research has explored is using ray casting for rendering. For example, Hunt [790] discusses the possibilities and provides an open-source CPU/GPU hybrid ray caster that evaluates over ten billion rays per second. Ray casting directly addresses many of the issues facing rasterizer-based systems, such as wide field of view and lens distortion, while also working well with foveated rendering. McGuire [1186] notes how rays can be cast at pixels just before a rolling display shows them, reducing the latency of that part of the system to next to nothing. This, along with many other research initiatives, leads him to conclude that we will use VR in the future but not call it VR, as it will simply be everyone's interface for computing.

Further Reading and Resources

Abrash's blog [5] has worthwhile articles about the basics of virtual reality displays, latency, judder, and other relevant topics. For effective application design and rendering techniques, the Oculus best practices site [1311] and blog [994] have much useful information, as does Epic Games' Unreal VR page [1802]. You may wish to study

OpenXR as a representative API and architecture for cross-platform virtual reality development. Ludwig's case study of converting *Team Fortress 2* to VR [1089] covers a range of user-experience issues and solutions.

McGuire [1186, 1187] gives an overview of NVIDIA's research efforts into a number of areas for VR and AR. Weier et al. [1864] provide a comprehensive state-of-the-art report that discusses human visual perception and how its limitations can be exploited in computer graphics. The SIGGRAPH 2017 course organized by Patney [1358] includes presentations on virtual and augmented reality research related to visual perception. Vlachos' GDC presentations [1823, 1824] discuss specific strategies for efficient rendering, and give more details for several techniques that we covered only briefly. NVIDIA's GameWorks blog [1055] includes worthwhile articles about GPU improvements for VR and how best to use them. Hughes et al. [783] provide an in-depth tutorial on using the tools XPerf, ETW, and GPUView to tune your VR rendering system to perform well. Schmalstieg and Hollerer's recent book *Augmented Reality* [1570] covers a wide range of concepts, methods, and technologies relate to this field.

Chapter 22
Intersection Test Methods

"I'll sit and see if that small sailing cloud
Will hit or miss the moon."
—Robert Frost

Intersection testing is often used in computer graphics. We may wish to determine whether two objects collide, or to find the distance to the ground so we can keep the camera at a constant height. Another important use is finding whether an object should be sent down the pipeline at all. All these operations can be performed with intersection tests. In this chapter, we cover the most common ray/object and object/object intersection tests.

In collision detection algorithms, which are also built upon hierarchies, the system must decide whether or not two primitive objects collide. These objects include triangles, spheres, axis-aligned bounding boxes (AABBs), oriented bounding boxes (OBBs), and discrete oriented polytopes (k-DOPs).

As we have seen in Section 19.4, view frustum culling is a means for efficiently discarding geometry that is outside the view frustum. Tests that decide whether a bounding volume (BV) is fully outside, fully inside, or partially inside a frustum are needed to use this method.

In all these cases we have encountered a certain class of problems that require *intersection tests*. An intersection test determines whether two objects, A and B, intersect, which may mean that A is fully inside B (or vice versa), that the boundaries of A and B intersect, or that they are disjoint. However, sometimes more information may be needed, such as the closest intersection point to some location, or the amount and direction of penetration.

In this chapter we focus on fast intersection test methods. We not only present the basic algorithms, but also give advice on how to construct new and efficient intersection test methods. Naturally, the methods presented in this chapter are also of use in offline computer graphics applications. For example, the ray intersection algorithms presented in Sections 22.6 through 22.9 are used in ray tracing programs.

After briefly covering hardware-accelerated picking methods, this chapter continues with some useful definitions, followed by algorithms for forming bounding volumes around primitives. Rules of thumb for constructing efficient intersection test methods are presented next. Finally, the bulk of the chapter consists of a cookbook of intersection test methods.

22.1 GPU-Accelerated Picking

It is often desirable to let the user select a certain object by *picking* (clicking) on it with the mouse or any other input device. Naturally, the performance of such an operation needs to be high.

If you need *all* the objects at a point or larger area on the screen, regardless of visibility, a CPU-side picking solution may be warranted. This type of picking is sometimes seen in modeling or CAD software packages. It can be solved efficiently on the CPU by using a bounding volume hierarchy (Section 19.1.1). A ray is formed at the pixel's location, passing from the near to the far plane of the view frustum. This ray is then tested for intersection with the bounding volume hierarchy as needed, similar to what is done to accelerate tracing rays in global illumination algorithms. For a rectangular area formed by the user defining a rectangle on the screen, we would create a frustum instead of a ray and test it against the hierarchy.

Intersection testing on the CPU has several drawbacks, depending on the requirements. Meshes with thousands of triangles can become expensive to test triangle by triangle unless some acceleration structure such as a hierarchy or grid is imposed on the mesh itself. If accuracy is important, geometry generated by displacement mapping or GPU tessellation needs to be matched by the CPU. For alpha-mapped objects such as tree foliage, the user should not be able to select fully transparent texels. A considerable amount of work on the CPU is needed to emulate texture access, along with any other shaders that discard texels for any reason.

Often we need only what is visible at a pixel or in an area of the screen. For this type of selection, use the GPU pipeline itself. One method was first presented by Hanrahan and Haeberli [661]. To support picking, the scene is rendered with each triangle, polygon, or mesh object having a unique identifier value, which can be thought of as a color. This idea is similar in intent to the visibility buffer, forming an image similar to that in Figure 20.12 on page 906. The image formed is stored offscreen and is then used for extremely rapid picking. When the user clicks on a pixel, the color identifier is looked up in this image and the object is immediately identified. These identifier values can be rendered to a separate render target while performing standard rendering using simple shaders, so the cost is relatively low. The main expense may be that from reading pixels back from the GPU to CPU.

Any other type of information that the pixel shader receives or computes can also be stored in an offscreen target. For example, the normal or texture coordinates are obvious candidates. It is also possible to find the relative location of a point inside a triangle using such a system [971] by taking advantage of interpolation. In a separate render target each triangle is rendered with the colors of the triangle vertices as red

$(255, 0, 0)$, green $(0, 255, 0)$, and blue $(0, 0, 255)$. Say that the interpolated color of the selected pixel is $(23, 192, 40)$, This means that the red vertex contributes with a factor $23/255$, the green with $192/255$, and the red with $40/255$. The values are barycentric coordinates, which are discussed further in Section 22.8.1.

Picking using the GPU was originally presented as part of a three-dimensional paint system. Such picking is particularly well adapted for such systems, where the camera and the objects are not moving, as the entire picking buffer can be generated once and reused. For picking when the camera is moving, another approach is to render the scene again to a tiny target, e.g., 3×3, using an off-axis camera focusing on a minute part of the screen. CPU-side frustum culling should eliminate almost all geometry and only a few pixels are shaded, making this pass relatively quick. For picking all objects (not just visible ones), this tiny window method could be performed several times, using depth peeling or simply not rendering previously selected objects [298].

22.2 Definitions and Tools

This section introduces notation and definitions useful for this entire chapter.

A ray, $\mathbf{r}(t)$, is defined by an origin point, $\mathbf{o}$, and a direction vector, $\mathbf{d}$ (which, for convenience, is usually normalized, so $\|\mathbf{d}\| = 1$). Its mathematical formula is shown in Equation 22.1, and an illustration of a ray is shown in Figure 22.1:

$$\mathbf{r}(t) = \mathbf{o} + t\mathbf{d}. \qquad (22.1)$$

The scalar t is a variable that is used to generate different points on the ray, where t-values of less than zero are said to lie behind the ray origin (and so are not part of the ray), and the positive t-values lie in front of it. Also, since the ray direction is normalized, a t-value generates a point on the ray that is situated t distance units from the ray origin.

In practice, we often also store a current distance l, which is the maximum distance we want to search along the ray. For example, while picking, we usually want the closest intersection along the ray; objects beyond this intersection can safely be ignored.

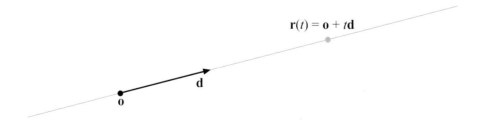

Figure 22.1. A simple ray and its parameters: $\mathbf{o}$ (the ray origin), $\mathbf{d}$ (the ray direction), and t, which generates different points on the ray, $\mathbf{r}(t) = \mathbf{o} + t\mathbf{d}$.

The distance l starts at ∞. As objects are successfully intersected, l is updated with the intersection distance. Once l is set, the ray becomes a line segment for testing. In the ray/object intersection tests we will be discussing, we will normally not include l in the discussion. If you wish to use l, all you have to do is perform the ordinary ray/object test, then check l against the intersection distance computed and take the appropriate action.

When talking about surfaces, we distinguish *implicit* surfaces from *explicit* surfaces. An implicit surface is defined by Equation 22.2:

$$f(\mathbf{p}) = f(p_x, p_y, p_z) = 0. \tag{22.2}$$

Here, $\mathbf{p}$ is any point on the surface. This means that if you have a point that lies on the surface and you plug this point into f, then the result will be 0. Otherwise, the result from f will be nonzero. An example of an implicit surface is $p_x^2 + p_y^2 + p_z^2 = r^2$, which describes a sphere located at the origin with radius r. It is easy to see that this can be rewritten as $f(\mathbf{p}) = p_x^2 + p_y^2 + p_z^2 - r^2 = 0$, which means that it is indeed implicit. Implicit surfaces are briefly covered in Section 17.3, while modeling and rendering with a wide variety of implicit surface types is well covered in Gomes et al. [558] and de Araújo et al. [67].

An explicit surface, on the other hand, is defined by a vector function $\mathbf{f}$ and some parameters (ρ, ϕ), rather than a point on the surface. These parameters yield points, $\mathbf{p}$, on the surface. Equation 22.3 below shows the general idea:

$$\mathbf{p} = \begin{pmatrix} p_x \\ p_y \\ p_z \end{pmatrix} = \mathbf{f}(\rho, \phi) = \begin{pmatrix} f_x(\rho, \phi) \\ f_y(\rho, \phi) \\ f_z(\rho, \phi) \end{pmatrix}. \tag{22.3}$$

An example of an explicit surface is again the sphere, this time expressed in spherical coordinates, where ρ is the latitude and ϕ longitude, as shown in Equation 22.4:

$$\mathbf{f}(\rho, \phi) = \begin{pmatrix} r\sin\rho\cos\phi \\ r\sin\rho\sin\phi \\ r\cos\rho \end{pmatrix}. \tag{22.4}$$

As another example, a triangle, $\triangle\mathbf{v}_0\mathbf{v}_1\mathbf{v}_2$, can be described in explicit form like this: $\mathbf{t}(u, v) = (1 - u - v)\mathbf{v}_0 + u\mathbf{v}_1 + v\mathbf{v}_2$, where $u \geq 0$, $v \geq 0$ and $u + v \leq 1$ must hold.

Finally, we shall give definitions of some common bounding volumes other than the sphere.

Definition. An *axis-aligned bounding box* (also called a *rectangular box*), AABB for short, is a box whose faces have normals that coincide with the standard basis axes. For example, an AABB A is described by two diagonally opposite points, $\mathbf{a}^{\min}$ and $\mathbf{a}^{\max}$, where $\mathbf{a}_i^{\min} \leq \mathbf{a}_i^{\max}$, $\forall i \in \{x, y, z\}$.

Figure 22.2 contains an illustration of a three-dimensional AABB together with notation.

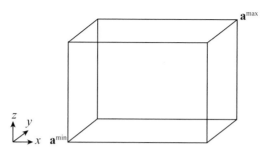

Figure 22.2. A three-dimensional AABB, A, with its extreme points, $\mathbf{a}^{\min}$ and $\mathbf{a}^{\max}$, and the axes of the standard basis.

Definition. An *oriented bounding box*, OBB for short, is a box whose faces have normals that are all pairwise orthogonal—i.e., it is an AABB that is arbitrarily rotated. An OBB, B, can be described by the center point of the box, $\mathbf{b}^c$, and three normalized vectors, $\mathbf{b}^u$, $\mathbf{b}^v$, and $\mathbf{b}^w$, that describe the side directions of the box. Their respective positive half-lengths are denoted h_u^B, h_v^B, and h_w^B, which is the distance from $\mathbf{b}^c$ to the center of the respective face.

A three-dimensional OBB and its notation are depicted in Figure 22.3.

Definition. A k-DOP (*discrete oriented polytope*) is defined by $k/2$ (where k is even) normalized normals (orientations), $\mathbf{n}_i$, $1 \leq i \leq k/2$, and with each $\mathbf{n}_i$ two associated scalar values $d_i^{\min}$ and $d_i^{\max}$, where $d_i^{\min} < d_i^{\max}$. Each triple $(\mathbf{n}_i, d_i^{\min}, d_i^{\max})$ describes a *slab*, S_i, which is the volume between the two planes, $\pi_i^{\min} : \mathbf{n}_i \cdot \mathbf{x} + d_i^{\min} = 0$ and $\pi_i^{\max} : \mathbf{n}_i \cdot \mathbf{x} + d_i^{\max} = 0$, and where the intersection of all slabs, $\bigcap_{1 \leq l \leq k/2} S_l$, is the actual k-DOP volume. The k-DOP is defined as the tightest set of slabs that bound

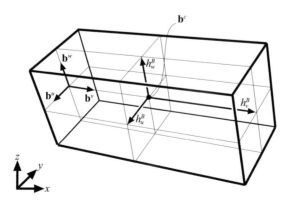

Figure 22.3. A three-dimensional OBB, B, with its center point, $\mathbf{b}^c$, and its normalized, positively oriented side vectors, $\mathbf{b}^u$, $\mathbf{b}^v$, and $\mathbf{b}^w$. The half-lengths of the sides, h_u^B, h_v^B, and h_w^B, are the distances from the center of the box to the center of the faces, as shown.

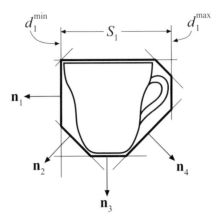

Figure 22.4. An example of a two-dimensional 8-DOP for a tea cup, with all normals, $\mathbf{n}_i$, shown along with the first slab, S_1, and the "size" of the slab: $d_1^{\min}$ and $d_1^{\max}$.

the object [435]. AABBs and OBBs can be represented as 6-DOPs, as each has six planes defined by three slabs. Figure 22.4 depicts an 8-DOP in two dimensions.

For the definition of a convex polyhedron, it is useful to use the concept of *half-spaces* of a plane. The positive half-space includes all points $\mathbf{x}$ where $\mathbf{n} \cdot \mathbf{x} + d \geq 0$, and the negative half-space is $\mathbf{n} \cdot \mathbf{x} + d \leq 0$.

Definition. A *convex polyhedron* is a finite volume defined by the intersection of the negative half-spaces of p planes, where the normal of each plane points away from the polyhedron.

AABBs, OBBs, and k-DOPs, as well as any view frustum, are all particular forms of convex polyhedra. More complex k-DOPs and convex polyhedra are used primarily for collision detection algorithms, where computing precise intersection of the underlying meshes can be costly. The extra planes used to form these bounding volumes can trim additional volume from the object and so justify the additional cost involved.

Two other bounding volumes of interest are line swept spheres and rectangle swept spheres. These are also more commonly called capsules and lozenges, respectively, and examples are shown in Figure 22.5.

A *separating axis* specifies a line in which two objects that do not overlap (are disjoint) have projections onto that line that also do not overlap. Similarly, where a plane can be inserted between two three-dimensional objects, that plane's normal defines a separating axis. An important tool for intersection testing [576, 592] follows, one that works for convex polyhedra such as AABBs, OBBs, and k-DOPs. It is an aspect of the *separating hyperplane theorem* [189].[1]

---

[1]This test is sometimes known as the "separating axis theorem" in computer graphics, a misnomer we helped promulgate in previous editions. It is not a theorem itself, but is rather a special case of the separating hyperplane theorem.

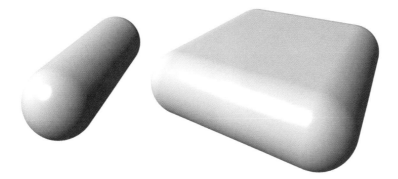

Figure 22.5. A line swept sphere and rectangle swept sphere, a.k.a. capsule and lozenge.

Separating Axis Test (SAT). For any two arbitrary, convex, disjoint polyhedra, A and B, there exists at least one separating axis where the projections of the polyhedra, which form intervals on the axis, are also disjoint. This does not hold if one object is concave. For example, the walls of a well and a bucket inside may not touch, but no plane can divide them. Furthermore, if A and B are disjoint, then they can be separated by an axis that is orthogonal (i.e., by a plane that is parallel) to one of the following [577]:

1. A face of A.

2. A face of B.

3. An edge from each polyhedron (e.g., a cross product).

The first two tests say that if one object is entirely on the far side of any face of the other object, they cannot overlap. With the faces handled by the first two tests, the last test is based on the edges of the objects. To separate the objects with the third test, we want to squeeze in a plane (whose normal is the separating axis) as close to both objects as possible, and such a plane cannot lie any closer to an object than on one of its edges. So, the separating axes to test are each formed by the cross product of an edge from each of the two objects. This test is illustrated for two boxes in Figure 22.6.

Note that the definition of a convex polyhedron is liberal here. A line segment and a convex polygon such as a triangle are also convex polyhedra (though degenerate, since they enclose no volume). A line segment A does not have a face, so the first test disappears. This test is used in deriving the triangle/box overlap test in Section 22.12 and the OBB/OBB overlap test in Section 22.13.5. Gregorius [597] notes an important optimization for any intersection test using the separating axis: temporal coherence. If a separating axis was found in this frame, store this axis as the first to test for the pair of objects in the next frame.

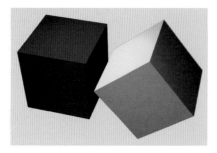

Figure 22.6. Separating axis. Call the blue box A and the yellow box B. The first image shows B fully to the right of the right face of A, the second shows A fully below the lower left face of B. In the third no face forms a plane that excludes the other box, so an axis formed from the cross product of the upper right edge of A and lower left of B defines the normal of a plane separating the two objects.

To return to the discussion of methods that can be brought to bear, a common technique for optimizing intersection tests is to make some simple calculations early on that can determine whether the ray or object misses the other object. Such a test is called a *rejection test*, and if the test succeeds, the intersection is said to be *rejected*.

Another approach often used in this chapter is to project the three-dimensional objects onto the "best" orthogonal plane (xy, xz, or yz), and solve the problem in two dimensions instead.

Finally, due to numerical imprecision, we often use a minuscule number in the intersection tests. This number is denoted ϵ (epsilon), and its value will vary from test to test. However, often an epsilon is chosen that works for the programmer's problem cases (what Press et al. [1446] call a "convenient fiction"), as opposed to doing careful roundoff error analysis and epsilon adjustment. Such code used in another setting may well break because of differing conditions. Ericson's book [435] discusses the area of numerical robustness in depth in the context of geometric computation. This caveat firmly in place, we sometimes do attempt to provide epsilons that are at least reasonable starting values for "normal" data, small scale (say less than 100, more than 0.1) and near the origin.

22.3 Bounding Volume Creation

Given a collection of objects, finding a tight fitting bounding volume is important to minimizing intersection costs. The chance that an arbitrary ray will hit any convex object is proportional to that object's surface area (Section 22.4). Minimizing this area increases the efficiency of any intersection algorithm, as a rejection is never slower to compute than an intersection. In contrast, it is often better to minimize the volume of each BV for collision detection algorithms. This section briefly covers methods of finding optimal or near-optimal bounding volumes given a collection of polygons.

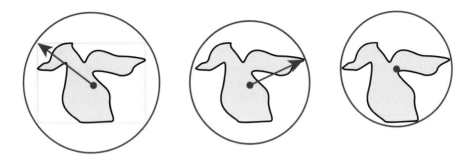

Figure 22.7. Bounding spheres. At its simplest, on the left, an object can have a bounding sphere around its bounding box. If the object does not extend to any corner of the bounding box, the sphere can be improved by using the box's center and running through all the vertices to find the most distant for setting the sphere's radius, as in the middle image. A smaller radius is possible by moving the sphere's center, as shown on the right.

22.3.1 AABB and *k*-DOP Creation

The simplest bounding volume to create is an AABB. Take the minimum and maximum extents of the set of polygon vertices along each axis and the AABB is formed. The k-DOP is an extension of the AABB: Project the vertices onto each normal, $\mathbf{n}_i$, of the k-DOP, and the extreme values (min,max) of these projections are stored in $d^i_{\min}$ and $d^i_{\max}$. These two values define the tightest slab for that direction. Together, all such values define a minimal k-DOP.

22.3.2 Sphere Creation

Bounding sphere formation is not as straightforward as determining slab extents. There are a number of algorithms that perform this task, and these have speed versus quality trade-offs. A fast, constant-time single pass algorithm is to form an AABB for the polygon set and then use the center and the diagonal of this box to form the sphere. This sometimes gives a poor fit, which can possibly be improved by another pass: Starting with the center of the AABB as the center of the sphere BV, go through all vertices once again and find the one that is farthest from this center (comparing against the square of the distance, to avoid taking the square root). This is then the new radius. See Figure 22.7.

These two techniques need only slight modification if you are nesting child spheres inside a parent sphere. If all the child spheres have the same radius, the centers can be treated as vertices and this child radius is added to the parent sphere's radius at the end of either process. If the radii vary, the AABB bounds can be found by including these radii in the bounds calculations to find a reasonable center. If the second pass is performed, add each radius to the distance of the point from the parent's center.

Ritter [1500] presents a simple algorithm that creates a near-optimal bounding sphere. The idea is to find the vertex that is at the minimum and the vertex at the maximum along each of the x-, y-, and z-axes. For these three pairs of vertices, find the pair with the largest distance between them. Use this pair to form a sphere with its center at the midpoint between them and a radius equal to the distance to them. Go through all the other vertices and check their distance d to the center of the sphere. If the vertex is outside the sphere's radius r, move the sphere's center toward the vertex by $(d - r)/2$, set the radius to $(d + r)/2$, and continue. This step has the effect of enclosing the vertex and the existing sphere in a new sphere. After this second time through the list, the bounding sphere is guaranteed to enclose all vertices.

Welzl [1867] presents a more complex algorithm, which is implemented by Eberly [404, 1574] and Ericson [435] among others, with code on the web. The idea is to find a supporting set of points defining a sphere. A sphere can be defined by a set of two, three, or four points on its surface. When a vertex is found to be outside the current sphere, its location is added to the supporting set (and possibly old support vertices removed from the set), the new sphere is computed, and the entire list is run through again. This process repeats until the sphere contains all vertices. While more complex than the previous methods, this algorithm guarantees that an optimal bounding sphere is found.

Ohlarik [1315] compares the speed of variants of both Ritter's and Welzl's algorithms. A simplified form of Ritter's can cost only 20% more than the basic version, however it can sometimes give worse results, so running both is worthwhile. Eberly's implementation of Welzl's algorithm is expected to be linear for a randomized list of points, but runs slower by an order of magnitude or so.

22.3.3   Convex Polyhedron Creation

One general form of bounding volume is the convex polyhedron. Convex objects can be used with the separating axis test. AABBs, k-DOPs, and OBBs are all convex polyhedra, but tighter bounds can be found. Just as k-DOPs can be thought of as trimming off more volume from an object by adding additional pairs of planes, a convex polyhedron can be defined by an arbitrary set of planes. By trimming off additional volume, more expensive tests involving the whole mesh of the enclosed polygonal object can be avoided. We want to "shrink-wrap" our polygonal object and find this set of planes, which form the *convex hull*. Figure 22.8 shows an example. The convex hull can be found with, for example, the *Quickhull* algorithm [100, 596]. Despite the name, the process is slower than linear time, and so generally is performed as an offline preprocess for complex models.

As can be seen, this process may result in a large number of planes, each defined by a polygon on the convex hull. In practice we may not need this level of precision. First creating a simplified version of the original mesh, possibly expanded outward to fully encompass the original, will yield a less accurate but simpler convex hull. Also note that for k-DOPs, as k increases, the BV increasingly resembles the convex hull.

Figure 22.8. The convex hull of a teapot computed using Quickhull [596]. *(Image courtesy of Dirk Gregorius, Valve Corporation.)*

22.3.4 OBB Creation

An object may have a natural OBB, in that it starts with an AABB and then undergoes a rotation that thus makes the AABB into an OBB. However, the OBB then used may not be optimal. Imagine a flagpole modeled to extend from a building at an angle. An AABB around it is not as tight as an OBB extending along its length. For models without obvious best axes, OBB formation, with its arbitrary basis orientation, is even more involved than finding a reasonable bounding sphere.

A noticeable amount of work has been done on creating algorithms for this problem. An exact solution by O'Rourke [1338] from 1985 runs in $O(n^3)$ time. Gottschalk [577] presents a faster, simpler method that gives an approximation for the best OBB. It first computes the convex hull of the polygonal mesh, to avoid model vertices inside this volume that could bias the results. Principle component analysis (PCA), which runs in linear time, is then used to find reasonable OBB axes. A drawback of this method is that the boxes are sometimes loose-fitting [984]. Eberly describes a method for computing a minimum-volume OBB using a minimization technique. He samples a set of possible directions for the box, and uses the axes whose OBB is smallest as a starting point for the numeric minimizer. Powell's direction set method [1446] is then used to find the minimum volume box. Eberly has code for this operation on the web [404]. There are yet other algorithms; Chang et al. [254] give a reasonable overview of previous work and present their own minimization technique that uses a genetic algorithm to help search the solution space.

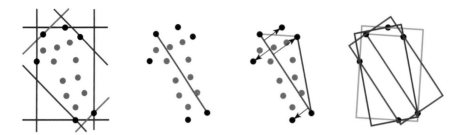

Figure 22.9. Near-optimal OBB formation; keep in mind that all the points are in three dimensions. For each k-DOP's slab (marked by a pair of colored lines), there is a pair of points at its limits, marked in black; the two vertices at the bottom are each at the extreme for two slab planes. The other vertices, marked in gray, are not used in the following steps. Of the four pairs, the two vertices farthest apart are used to form an edge. The extremal point farthest from this edge's line is used to form a triangle with the edge. Three boxes are formed, each using a triangle edge to define its axes and the remaining extremal points to define its boundaries. Of these three, the best box is saved.

Here we present an algorithm from Larsson and Källberg [984], a near-optimal method that does not need the convex hull and executes in linear time. It usually provides better quality than Gottschalk's PCA-based method, is considerably faster to execute, lends itself to SIMD parallelization, and has code provided by the authors. First a k-DOP is formed for the object, and a pair (any pair) of vertices touching the opposite sides of each k-DOP slab is saved. All these pairs of vertices together are called the *extremal points* of the object. So, for example, a 26-DOP generates 13 pairs of points, and some of these points may specify the same vertex, possibly giving a smaller overall set. The "best OBB" is initialized to the AABB surrounding the object. The algorithm then proceeds by finding OBB orientations that are likely to provide a better fit. A large base triangle is constructed, and two tetrahedra are extended from its face. These create a set of seven triangles that yield potentially near-optimal OBBs.

The pair of points that are farthest away from each other form one edge of the base triangle. The vertex from the remaining extremal points that is farthest from this edge's line forms the third point of the triangle. Each triangle edge and the normal to the edge in the triangle's plane are used to form two axes for a potential new OBB. The remaining extremal points are projected onto these axes to find the two-dimensional bounds in the plane for each of the three OBBs. See Figure 22.9. The smallest surrounding two-dimensional rectangle is used to choose the best OBB from the three. Since the height, the distance along the triangle's normal, of any of these three OBBs will be the same, the two-dimensional bounding box around each is sufficient to decide which is the best.

The remaining extremal points are then used to find the extents of this OBB in three dimensions by projection against the triangle's normal. This fully formed OBB is checked against the initial AABB to see which is better. The two extremal points found during this process, one at the maximum and one at the minimum height, are then used to form two tetrahedra, with the original large triangle as the base of each. Each tetrahedron in turn forms three additional triangles, and the process of evaluating the triangle's three candidate OBBs is performed for each as done for the original triangle. The best two-dimensional OBB for each triangle is similarly extended along its height, as before, but only to get the final size of the candidate OBB, not to form yet more triangles. A total of seven triangles is formed, and one full OBB is generated and compared from each.

Once the best OBB is found, all points in the original object are projected onto its axes to increase its size as needed. A final check is made against the original AABB to see if this OBB actually gives a better fit. This whole process is faster than previous techniques and benefits from using a small set of extremal points for most steps. Notably, the authors prefer optimizing the bounding box based on surface area, not volume, for reasons we cover in the next section.

22.4 Geometric Probability

Common geometric operations include whether a plane or ray intersects an object, and whether a point is inside it. A related question is what is the relative probability that a point, ray, or plane intersects an object. The relative probability of a random point in space being inside an object is fairly obvious: It is directly proportional to the volume of the object. So, a $1 \times 2 \times 3$ box is 6 times as likely to contain a randomly chosen point as is a $1 \times 1 \times 1$ box.

For an arbitrary ray in space, what is the relative chance of a ray intersecting one object versus another? This question is related to another question: What is the average number of pixels covered by an arbitrarily oriented object when using an orthographic projection? An orthographic projection can be thought of as a set of parallel rays in the view volume, with a ray traveling through each pixel. Given a randomly oriented object, the number of pixels covered is equal to the number of rays intersecting the object.

The answer is surprisingly simple: The average projected area of any convex solid object is one fourth of its surface area. This is clearly true for a sphere on the screen, where its orthographic projection is always a circle with area πr^2 and its surface area is $4\pi r^2$. This same ratio holds as the average projected for any other arbitrarily oriented convex object, such as a box or k-DOP. See Nienhuys' article [1278] for an informal proof.

A sphere, box, or other convex object always has a front and a back at each pixel, so the depth complexity is two. The probability measure can be extended to any polygon, as a (two-sided) polygon always has a depth complexity of one. As such, the average projected area of any polygon is one half its surface area.

This metric is referred to as the *surface area heuristic* (SAH) [71, 1096, 1828] in the ray tracing literature, and it is important in forming efficient visibility structures for data sets. One use is in comparing bounding volume efficiency. For example, a sphere has a relative probability of 1.57 ($\pi/2$) of being hit by a ray, compared to an inscribed cube (i.e., a cube with its corners touching the sphere). Similarly, a cube has a relative probability of 1.91 ($6/\pi$) of being hit, versus a sphere inscribed inside it.

This type of probability measurement can be useful in areas such as level of detail computation. For example, imagine a long and thin object that covers many fewer pixels than a rounder object, yet both have the same bounding sphere size. Knowing the hit ratio in advance from the area of its bounding box, the long and thin object may be considered relatively less important in visual impact.

We now have a point's probability of enclosure as being related to volume, and a ray's probability of intersection as being related to surface area. The chance of a plane intersecting a box is directly proportional to the sum of the extents of the box in three dimensions [1580]. This sum is called the object's *mean width*. For example, a cube with an edge length of 1 has a mean width of $1 + 1 + 1 = 3$. A box's mean width is proportional to its chance of being hit by a plane. So, a $1 \times 1 \times 1$ box has a measure of 3, and a $1 \times 2 \times 3$ box a measure of 6, meaning that the second box is twice as likely to be intersected by an arbitrary plane.

However, this sum is larger than the true geometric mean width, which is the average projected length of an object along a fixed axis over the set of all possible orientations. There is no easy relationship (such as surface area) among different convex object types for mean width computation. A sphere of diameter d has a geometric mean width of d, since the sphere spans this same length for any orientation. We will leave this topic by simply stating that multiplying the sum of a box's dimensions (i.e., its mean width) by 0.5 gives its geometric mean width, which can be compared directly to a sphere's diameter. So, the $1 \times 1 \times 1$ box with measure 3 has a geometric mean width of $3 \times 0.5 = 1.5$. A sphere bounding this box has a diameter of $\sqrt{3} = 1.732$. Therefore a sphere surrounding a cube is $1.732/1.5 = 1.155$ times as likely to be intersected by an arbitrary plane.

These relationships are useful for determining the benefits of various algorithms. Frustum culling is a prime candidate, as it involves intersecting planes with bounding volumes. Another use is for determining whether and where to best split a BSP node containing objects, so that frustum culling performance becomes better (Section 19.1.2).

22.5　Rules of Thumb

Before we begin studying the specific intersection methods, here are some rules of thumb that can lead to faster, more robust, and more exact intersection tests. These should be kept in mind when designing, inventing, and implementing an intersection routine:

- Perform computations and comparisons early on that might trivially *reject* or *accept* various types of intersections to obtain an early escape from further computations.

- If possible, exploit the results from previous tests.

- If more than one rejection or acceptance test is used, then try changing their internal order (if possible), since a more efficient test may result. Do not assume that what appears to be a minor change will have no effect.

- Postpone expensive calculations (especially trigonometric functions, square roots, and divisions) until they are truly needed (Section 22.8 for an example of delaying an expensive division).

- The intersection problem can often be simplified considerably by *reducing the dimension* of the problem (for example, from three dimensions to two dimensions or even to one dimension). See Section 22.9 for an example.

- If a single ray or object is being compared to many other objects at a time, look for precalculations that can be done just once before the testing begins.

- Whenever an intersection test is expensive, it is often good to start with a sphere or other simple BV around the object to give a first level of quick rejection.

- Make it a habit always to perform timing comparisons on your computer, and use real data and testing situations for the timings.

- Exploit results from the previous frame, e.g., if a certain axis was found to be separating two objects the previous frame, it might be a good idea to try that axis first on the next frame.

- Finally, try to make your code *robust*. This means it should work for all special cases and that it will be insensitive to as many floating point precision errors as possible. Be aware of any limitations it may have. For more information about numerical and geometrical robustness, we refer to Ericson's book [435].

Finally, we emphasize on the fact that it is hard to determine whether there is a "best" algorithm for a particular test. For evaluation, random data with a set of different, predetermined hit rates are often used, but this shows only part of the truth. The algorithm will get used in real scenarios, e.g., in a game, and it is best evaluated in that context. The more test scenes used, the better understanding of performance issues you get. Some architectures, such as GPUs and wide-SIMD implementations, may lose performance due to multiple rejection branches needing execution. It is best to avoid making assumptions and instead create a solid test plan.

22.6 Ray/Sphere Intersection

Let us start with a mathematically simple intersection test—namely, that between a ray and a sphere. As we will see later, the straightforward mathematical solution can be made faster if we begin thinking of the geometry involved [640].

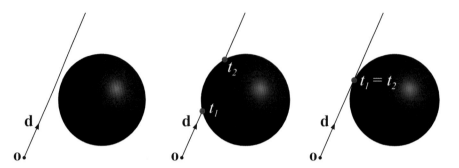

Figure 22.10. The left image shows a ray that misses a sphere and consequently $b^2 - c < 0$. The middle image shows a ray that intersects a sphere at two points ($b^2 - c > 0$) determined by the scalars t_1 and t_2. The right image illustrates the case where $b^2 - c = 0$, which means that the two intersection points coincide.

22.6.1 Mathematical Solution

A sphere can be defined by a center point, $\mathbf{c}$, and a radius, r. A more compact implicit formula (compared to the one previously introduced) for the sphere is then

$$f(\mathbf{p}) = ||\mathbf{p} - \mathbf{c}|| - r = 0, \tag{22.5}$$

where $\mathbf{p}$ is any point on the sphere's surface. To solve for the intersections between a ray and a sphere, the ray $\mathbf{r}(t)$ simply replaces $\mathbf{p}$ in Equation 22.5 to yield

$$f(\mathbf{r}(t)) = ||\mathbf{r}(t) - \mathbf{c}|| - r = 0. \tag{22.6}$$

Using Equation 22.1, that $\mathbf{r}(t) = \mathbf{o} + t\mathbf{d}$, Equation 22.6 is simplified as follows:

$$||\mathbf{r}(t) - \mathbf{c}|| - r = 0$$
$$\Longleftrightarrow$$
$$||\mathbf{o} + t\mathbf{d} - \mathbf{c}|| = r$$
$$\Longleftrightarrow$$
$$(\mathbf{o} + t\mathbf{d} - \mathbf{c}) \cdot (\mathbf{o} + t\mathbf{d} - \mathbf{c}) = r^2 \tag{22.7}$$
$$\Longleftrightarrow$$
$$t^2(\mathbf{d} \cdot \mathbf{d}) + 2t(\mathbf{d} \cdot (\mathbf{o} - \mathbf{c})) + (\mathbf{o} - \mathbf{c}) \cdot (\mathbf{o} - \mathbf{c}) - r^2 = 0$$
$$\Longleftrightarrow$$
$$t^2 + 2t(\mathbf{d} \cdot (\mathbf{o} - \mathbf{c})) + (\mathbf{o} - \mathbf{c}) \cdot (\mathbf{o} - \mathbf{c}) - r^2 = 0.$$

The last step comes from the fact that $\mathbf{d}$ is assumed to be normalized, i.e., $\mathbf{d} \cdot \mathbf{d} = ||\mathbf{d}||^2 = 1$. Not surprisingly, the resulting equation is a polynomial of the second order, which means that if the ray intersects the sphere, it does so at up to two points. See Figure 22.10. If the solutions to the equation are imaginary, then the ray misses the sphere. If not, the two solutions t_1 and t_2 can be inserted into the ray equation to compute the intersection points on the sphere.

The resulting Equation 22.7 can be written as a quadratic equation:

$$t^2 + 2bt + c = 0, \qquad (22.8)$$

where $b = \mathbf{d} \cdot (\mathbf{o} - \mathbf{c})$ and $c = (\mathbf{o} - \mathbf{c}) \cdot (\mathbf{o} - \mathbf{c}) - r^2$. The solutions of the second-order equation are shown below:

$$t = -b \pm \sqrt{b^2 - c}. \qquad (22.9)$$

Note that if $b^2 - c < 0$, then the ray misses the sphere and the intersection can be rejected and calculations avoided (e.g., the square root and some additions). If this test is passed, both $t_0 = -b - \sqrt{b^2 - c}$ and $t_1 = -b + \sqrt{b^2 - c}$ can be computed. An additional comparison needs to be done to find the smallest positive value of t_0 and t_1. See the collision detection chapter at realtimerendering.com for an alternate way of solving this quadratic equation that is more numerically stable [1446].

If these computations are instead viewed from a geometric point of view, then better rejection tests can be discovered. The next subsection describes such a routine.

22.6.2 Optimized Solution

For the ray/sphere intersection problem, we begin by observing that intersections behind the ray origin are not needed. For example, this is normally the case in picking. To check for this condition early on, we first compute a vector $\mathbf{l} = \mathbf{c} - \mathbf{o}$, which is the vector from the ray origin to the center of the sphere. All notation that is used is depicted in Figure 22.11. Also, the squared length of this vector is computed, $l^2 = \mathbf{l} \cdot \mathbf{l}$. Now if $l^2 < r^2$, this implies that the ray origin is inside the sphere, which, in turn, means that the ray is guaranteed to hit the sphere and we can exit if we want to detect only whether or not the ray hits the sphere; otherwise, we proceed. Next, the projection of $\mathbf{l}$ onto the ray direction, $\mathbf{d}$, is computed: $s = \mathbf{l} \cdot \mathbf{d}$.

Now, here comes the first rejection test: If $s < 0$ and the ray origin is outside the sphere, then the sphere is behind the ray origin and we can reject the intersection. Otherwise, the squared distance from the sphere center to the projection is computed using the Pythagorean theorem: $m^2 = l^2 - s^2$. The second rejection test is even simpler than the first: If $m^2 > r^2$ the ray will definitely miss the sphere and the rest of the calculations can safely be omitted. If the sphere and ray pass this last test, then the ray is guaranteed to hit the sphere and we can exit if that was all we were interested in finding out.

To find the real intersection points, a little more work has to be done. First, the squared distance $q^2 = r^2 - m^2$ is calculated.[2] See Figure 22.11. Since $m^2 \leq r^2$, q^2 is greater than or equal to zero, and this means that $q = \sqrt{q^2}$ can be computed. Finally, the distances to the intersections are $t = s \pm q$, whose solution is quite similar to that of the second-order equation obtained in the previous mathematical solution section.

---

[2]The scalar r^2 could be computed once and stored within the data structure of the sphere in an attempt to gain further efficiency. In practice such an "optimization" may be slower, as more memory is then accessed, a major factor for algorithm performance.

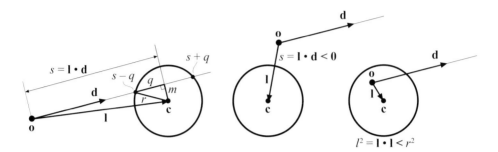

Figure 22.11. The notation for the geometry of the optimized ray/sphere intersection. In the left figure, the ray intersects the sphere in two points, where the distances are $t = s \pm q$ along the ray. The middle case demonstrates a rejection made when the sphere is behind the ray origin. Finally, at the right, the ray origin is inside the sphere, in which case the ray always hits the sphere.

If we are interested in only the first, positive intersection point, then we should use $t_1 = s - q$ for the case where the ray origin is outside the sphere and $t_2 = s + q$ when the ray origin is inside. The true intersection point(s) are found by inserting the t-value(s) into the ray equation (Equation 22.1).

Pseudocode for the optimized version is shown in the box below. The routine returns a boolean value that is REJECT if the ray misses the sphere and INTERSECT otherwise. If the ray intersects the sphere, then the distance, t, from the ray origin to the intersection point, along with the intersection point, **p**, are also returned.

RaySphereIntersect(o, d, c, r)
returns ({REJECT, INTERSECT}, t, **p**)
1 : $\mathbf{l} = \mathbf{c} - \mathbf{o}$
2 : $s = \mathbf{l} \cdot \mathbf{d}$
3 : $l^2 = \mathbf{l} \cdot \mathbf{l}$
4 :   if$(s < 0$ and $l^2 > r^2)$ return (REJECT, 0, **0**);
5 : $m^2 = l^2 - s^2$
6 :   if$(m^2 > r^2)$ return (REJECT, 0, **0**);
7 : $q = \sqrt{r^2 - m^2}$
8 :   if$(l^2 > r^2)$ $t = s - q$
9 :   else $t = s + q$
10 :   return (INTERSECT, t, $\mathbf{o} + t\mathbf{d}$);

Note that after line 3, we can test whether **p** is inside the sphere and, if all we want to know is whether the ray and sphere intersect, the routine can terminate if they do so. Also, after line 6, the ray is guaranteed to hit the sphere. If we do an operation count (counting adds, multiplies, compares, and similar), we find that the geometric solution, when followed to completion, is approximately equivalent to the algebraic solution presented earlier. The important difference is that the rejection tests are done much earlier in the process, making the overall cost of this algorithm lower on average.

Optimized geometric algorithms exist for computing the intersection between a ray and some other quadrics and hybrid objects. For example, there are methods for the cylinder [318, 713, 1621], cone [713, 1622], ellipsoid, capsule, and lozenge [404].

22.7 Ray/Box Intersection

Three methods for determining whether a ray intersects a solid box are given below. The first handles both AABBs and OBBs. The second is a variant that is often faster, but deal with only the simpler AABB. The third is based on the separating axis test on page 947, and handles only line segments versus AABBs. Here, we use the definitions and notation of the BVs from Section 22.2.

22.7.1 Slabs Method

One scheme for ray/AABB intersection is based on Kay and Kajiya's slab method [640, 877], which in turn is inspired by the Cyrus-Beck line clipping algorithm [319].

We extend this scheme to handle the more general OBB volume. It returns the closest positive t-value (i.e., the distance from the ray origin $\mathbf{o}$ to the point of intersection, if any exists). Optimizations for the AABB will be treated after we present the general case. The problem is approached by computing all t-values for the ray and all planes belonging to the faces of the OBB. The box is considered as a set of three slabs, as illustrated in two dimensions in the left part of Figure 22.12. For each slab, there is a minimum and a maximum t-value, and these are called $t_i^{\min}$ and $t_i^{\max}$,

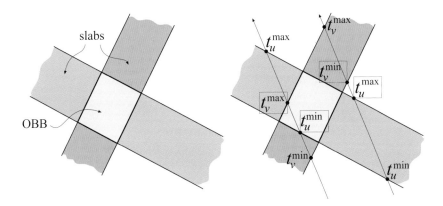

Figure 22.12. The left figure shows a two-dimensional OBB formed by two slabs, while the right shows two rays that are tested for intersection with the OBB. All t-values are shown, and they are subscripted with u for the green slab and with v for the orange. The extreme t-values are marked with boxes. The left ray hits the OBB since $t^{\min} < t^{\max}$, and the right ray misses since $t^{\max} < t^{\min}$.

$\forall i \in \{u, v, w\}$. The next step is to compute the variables in Equation 22.10:

$$t^{\min} = \max(t_u^{\min}, t_v^{\min}, t_w^{\min}),$$
$$t^{\max} = \min(t_u^{\max}, t_v^{\max}, t_w^{\max}). \tag{22.10}$$

Now, the clever test: If $t^{\min} \leq t^{\max}$, then the line defined by the ray intersects the box; otherwise it misses. In other words, we find the near and far intersection distances for each slab. If the farthest "near" distance found is less than or equal to the nearest "far" distance, then the line defined by the ray hits the box. You should convince yourself of this by inspecting the illustration on the right side of Figure 22.12. These two distances define intersection points for the line, so if the nearest "far" distance is not negative, the ray itself hits the box, i.e., the box is not behind the ray.

Pseudocode for the ray/OBB intersection test, between an OBB (A) and a ray (described by Equation 22.1) follows. The code returns a boolean indicating whether or not the ray intersects the OBB (INTERSECT or REJECT), and the distance to the intersection point (if it exists). Recall that for an OBB A, the center is denoted $\mathbf{a}^c$, and $\mathbf{a}^u$, $\mathbf{a}^v$, and $\mathbf{a}^w$ are the normalized side directions of the box; h_u, h_v, and h_w are the positive half-lengths (from the center to a box face).

RayOBBIntersect($\mathbf{o}, \mathbf{d}, A$)
returns ($\{\text{REJECT}, \text{INTERSECT}\}, t$);

```
 1 :  tmin = −∞
 2 :  tmax = ∞
 3 :  p = a^c − o
 4 :  for each i ∈ {u, v, w}
 5 :      e = a^i · p
 6 :      f = a^i · d
 7 :      if(|f| > ε)
 8 :          t₁ = (e + h_i)/f
 9 :          t₂ = (e − h_i)/f
10 :          if(t₁ > t₂) swap(t₁, t₂);
11 :          if(t₁ > tmin) tmin = t₁
12 :          if(t₂ < tmax) tmax = t₂
13 :          if(tmin > tmax) return (REJECT, 0);
14 :          if(tmax < 0) return (REJECT, 0);
15 :      else if(− e − h_i > 0 or − e + h_i < 0) return (REJECT, 0);
16 :  if(tmin > 0) return (INTERSECT, tmin);
17 :  else return (INTERSECT, tmax);
```

Line 7 checks whether the ray direction is not perpendicular to the normal direction of the slab currently being tested. In other words, it tests whether the ray is not parallel to the slab planes and so can intersect them. Note that ϵ is a minuscule number here, on the order of 10^{-20}, simply to avoid overflow when the division occurs. Lines 8 and 9 show a division by f; in practice, it is usually faster to compute $1/f$ once and multiply by this value, since division is often expensive. Line 10 ensures that the minimum of t_1 and t_2 is stored in t_1, and consequently, the maximum of these is stored in t_2. In practice, the swap does not have to be made; instead lines 11 and 12 can be repeated for the branch, and t_1 and t_2 can change positions there. Should line 13 return, then the ray misses the box, and similarly, if line 14 returns, then the box is behind the ray origin. Line 15 is executed if the ray is parallel to the slab (and so cannot intersect it); it tests if the ray is outside the slab. If so, then the ray misses the box and the test terminates. For even faster code, Haines discusses a way of unwinding the loop and thereby avoiding some code [640].

There is an additional test not shown in the pseudocode that is worth adding in actual code. As mentioned when we defined the ray, we usually want to find the closest object. So, after line 15, we could also test whether $t^{\min} \geq l$, where l is the current ray length. This effectively treats the ray as a line segment. If the new intersection is not closer, the intersection is rejected. This test could be deferred until after the entire ray/OBB test has been completed, but it is usually more efficient to try for an early rejection inside the loop.

There are other optimizations for the special case of an OBB that is an AABB. Lines 5 and 6 change to $e = p_i$ and $f = d_i$, which makes the test faster. Normally the $\mathbf{a}^{\min}$ and $\mathbf{a}^{\max}$ corners of the AABB are used on lines 8 and 9, so the addition and subtraction is avoided. Kay and Kajiya [877] and Smits [1668] note that line 7 can be avoided by allowing division by 0 and interpreting the processor's results correctly. Kensler [1629] gives code for a minimal version of this test. Williams et al. [1887] provide implementation details to handle division by 0 correctly, along with other optimizations. Aila et al. [16] show how the maximum of minimums test, or vice versa, can be performed in a single GPU operation on some NVIDIA architectures. It is also possible to derive a test using SAT for the ray and box, but then the intersection distance is not part of the result, which is often useful.

A generalization of the slabs method can be used to compute the intersection of a ray with a k-DOP, frustum, or any convex polyhedron; code is available on the web [641].

22.7.2 Ray Slope Method

In 2007 Eisemann et al. [410] presented a method of intersecting boxes that appears to be faster than previous methods. Instead of a three-dimensional test, the ray is tested against three projections of the box in two dimensions. The key idea is that for each two-dimensional test, there are two box corners that define the extreme extents of what the ray "sees," akin to the silhouette edges of a model. To intersect this projection of the box, the slope of the ray must be between the two slopes defined by the ray's origin and these two points. If this test passes for all three projections, the ray must hit the box. The method is extremely fast because some of the comparison terms rely entirely on the ray's values. By computing these terms once, the ray can then efficiently be compared against a large number of boxes. This method can return just whether the box was hit, or can also return the intersection distance, at a little additional cost.

22.8   Ray/Triangle Intersection

In real-time graphics libraries and APIs, triangle geometry is usually stored as a set of vertices with associated shading normals, and each triangle is defined by three such vertices. The normal of the plane in which the triangle lies is often not stored, in which case it must be computed if needed. There exist many different ray/triangle intersection tests, and many of them first compute the intersection point between the ray and the triangle's plane. Thereafter, the intersection point and the triangle vertices are projected on the axis-aligned plane (xy, yz, or xz) where the area of the triangle is maximized. By doing this, we reduce the problem to two dimensions, and we need only decide whether the (two-dimensional) point is inside the (two-dimensional) triangle. Several such methods exist, and they have been reviewed and compared by Haines [642], with code available on the web. See Section 22.9 for one popular algorithm using this technique. A wealth of algorithms have been evaluated for different CPU architectures, compilers, and hit ratios [1065], and it could not be concluded that there is a single best test in all cases.

Here, the focus will be on an algorithm that does not presume that normals are precomputed. For triangle meshes, this can amount to significant memory savings. For dynamic geometry we do not need to recompute the plane equation of the triangle every frame. Instead of testing a ray against the triangle's plane and then checking the intersection point for inclusion inside a two-dimensional version of the triangle, the check is performed against just the triangle's vertices. This algorithm, along with optimizations, was discussed by Möller and Trumbore [1231], and their presentation is used here. Kensler and Shirley [882] noted that most ray/triangle tests operating directly in three dimensions are computationally equivalent. They develop new tests using SSE to test four rays against a triangle, and use a genetic algorithm to find the best order of the operations in this equivalent test. Code for the best-performing test is in their paper. Note that there is a wealth of different methods for this. For example, Baldwin and Weber [96] provide a method with a different space-speed trade-off. One potential problem with this class of tests is that a ray exactly intersecting a triangle's edge or vertex may be judged to miss the triangle. This means that a ray could potentially pass through a mesh by hitting an edge shared by two triangles. Woop et al. [1906] present a ray/triangle intersection test that is watertight on both edges and vertices. Performance is a bit lower depending on which type of traversal is used.

The ray from Equation 22.1 is used to test for intersection with a triangle defined by three vertices, $\mathbf{p}_1$, $\mathbf{p}_2$, and $\mathbf{p}_3$—i.e., $\triangle\mathbf{p}_1\mathbf{p}_2\mathbf{p}_3$.

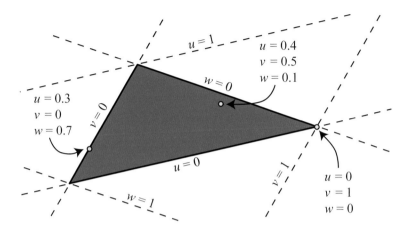

Figure 22.13. Barycentric coordinates for a triangle, along with example point values. The values u, v, and w all vary from 0 to 1 inside the triangle, and the sum of these three is always 1 over the entire plane. These values can be used as weights for how data at each of the three vertices influence any point on the triangle. Note how at each vertex, one value is 1 and the others 0, and along edges, one value is always 0.

22.8.1 Intersection Algorithm

A point, $\mathbf{f}(u, v)$, on a triangle is given by the explicit formula

$$\mathbf{f}(u, v) = (1 - u - v)\mathbf{p}_0 + u\mathbf{p}_1 + v\mathbf{p}_2, \tag{22.11}$$

where (u, v) are two of the *barycentric coordinates*, which must fulfill $u \geq 0$, $v \geq 0$, and $u + v \leq 1$. Note that (u, v) can be used for operations such as texture mapping and normal or color interpolation. That is, u and v are the amounts by which to weight each vertex's contribution to a particular location, with $w = (1 - u - v)$ being the third weight. These coordinates are often denoted in other works as α, β, and γ. We use u, v, and w here for readability and consistency of notation. See Figure 22.13.

Computing the intersection between the ray, $\mathbf{r}(t)$, and the triangle, $\mathbf{f}(u, v)$, is equivalent to $\mathbf{r}(t) = \mathbf{f}(u, v)$, which yields

$$\mathbf{o} + t\mathbf{d} = (1 - u - v)\mathbf{p}_0 + u\mathbf{p}_1 + v\mathbf{p}_2. \tag{22.12}$$

Rearranging the terms gives

$$\begin{pmatrix} -\mathbf{d} & \mathbf{p}_1 - \mathbf{p}_0 & \mathbf{p}_2 - \mathbf{p}_0 \end{pmatrix} \begin{pmatrix} t \\ u \\ v \end{pmatrix} = \mathbf{o} - \mathbf{p}_0. \tag{22.13}$$

This means the barycentric coordinates (u, v) and the distance t from the ray origin to the intersection point can be found by solving this linear system of equations.

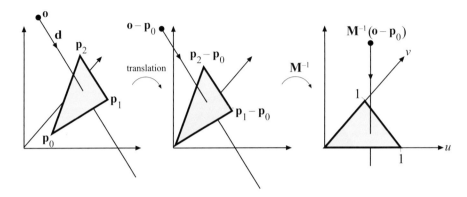

Figure 22.14. Translation and change of base of the ray origin.

This manipulation can be thought of geometrically as translating the triangle to the origin and transforming it to a unit triangle in y and z with the ray direction aligned with x. This is illustrated in Figure 22.14. If $\mathbf{M} = (-\mathbf{d} \;\; \mathbf{p}_1 - \mathbf{p}_0 \;\; \mathbf{p}_2 - \mathbf{p}_0)$ is the matrix in Equation 22.13, then the solution is found by multiplying Equation 22.13 with $\mathbf{M}^{-1}$.

Denoting $\mathbf{e}_1 = \mathbf{p}_1 - \mathbf{p}_0$, $\mathbf{e}_2 = \mathbf{p}_2 - \mathbf{p}_0$, and $\mathbf{s} = \mathbf{o} - \mathbf{p}_0$, the solution to Equation 22.13 is obtained by using Cramer's rule:

$$\begin{pmatrix} t \\ u \\ v \end{pmatrix} = \frac{1}{\det(-\mathbf{d}, \mathbf{e}_1, \mathbf{e}_2)} \begin{pmatrix} \det(\mathbf{s}, \mathbf{e}_1, \mathbf{e}_2) \\ \det(-\mathbf{d}, \mathbf{s}, \mathbf{e}_2) \\ \det(-\mathbf{d}, \mathbf{e}_1, \mathbf{s}) \end{pmatrix}. \tag{22.14}$$

From linear algebra, we know that $\det(\mathbf{a}, \mathbf{b}, \mathbf{c}) = |\mathbf{a} \; \mathbf{b} \; \mathbf{c}| = -(\mathbf{a} \times \mathbf{c}) \cdot \mathbf{b} = -(\mathbf{c} \times \mathbf{b}) \cdot \mathbf{a}$. Equation 22.14 can therefore be rewritten as

$$\begin{pmatrix} t \\ u \\ v \end{pmatrix} = \frac{1}{(\mathbf{d} \times \mathbf{e}_2) \cdot \mathbf{e}_1} \begin{pmatrix} (\mathbf{s} \times \mathbf{e}_1) \cdot \mathbf{e}_2 \\ (\mathbf{d} \times \mathbf{e}_2) \cdot \mathbf{s} \\ (\mathbf{s} \times \mathbf{e}_1) \cdot \mathbf{d} \end{pmatrix} = \frac{1}{\mathbf{q} \cdot \mathbf{e}_1} \begin{pmatrix} \mathbf{r} \cdot \mathbf{e}_2 \\ \mathbf{q} \cdot \mathbf{s} \\ \mathbf{r} \cdot \mathbf{d} \end{pmatrix}, \tag{22.15}$$

where $\mathbf{q} = \mathbf{d} \times \mathbf{e}_2$ and $\mathbf{r} = \mathbf{s} \times \mathbf{e}_1$. These factors can be used to speed up the computations.

If you can afford some extra storage, this test can be reformulated in order to reduce the number of computations. Equation 22.15 can be rewritten as

$$\begin{pmatrix} t \\ u \\ v \end{pmatrix} = \frac{1}{(\mathbf{d} \times \mathbf{e}_2) \cdot \mathbf{e}_1} \begin{pmatrix} (\mathbf{s} \times \mathbf{e}_1) \cdot \mathbf{e}_2 \\ (\mathbf{d} \times \mathbf{e}_2) \cdot \mathbf{s} \\ (\mathbf{s} \times \mathbf{e}_1) \cdot \mathbf{d} \end{pmatrix}$$

$$= \frac{1}{-(\mathbf{e}_1 \times \mathbf{e}_2) \cdot \mathbf{d}} \begin{pmatrix} (\mathbf{e}_1 \times \mathbf{e}_2) \cdot \mathbf{s} \\ (\mathbf{s} \times \mathbf{d}) \cdot \mathbf{e}_2 \\ -(\mathbf{s} \times \mathbf{d}) \cdot \mathbf{e}_1 \end{pmatrix} = \frac{1}{-\mathbf{n} \cdot \mathbf{d}} \begin{pmatrix} \mathbf{n} \cdot \mathbf{s} \\ \mathbf{m} \cdot \mathbf{e}_2 \\ -\mathbf{m} \cdot \mathbf{e}_1 \end{pmatrix}, \tag{22.16}$$

where $\mathbf{n} = \mathbf{e}_1 \times \mathbf{e}_2$ is the unnormalized normal of the triangle, and hence constant (for static geometry), and $\mathbf{m} = \mathbf{s} \times \mathbf{d}$. If we store $\mathbf{p}_0$, $\mathbf{e}_1$, $\mathbf{e}_2$, and $\mathbf{n}$ for each triangle, we can avoid many ray triangle intersection computations. Most of the gain comes from avoiding a cross product. It should be noted that this defies the original idea of the algorithm, namely to store minimal information with the triangle. However, if speed is of utmost concern, this may a reasonable alternative. The trade-off is whether the savings in computation is outweighed by the additional memory accesses. Only careful testing can ultimately show what is fastest.

22.8.2 Implementation

The algorithm is summarized in the pseudocode below. Besides returning whether or not the ray intersects the triangle, the algorithm also returns the previously described triple (u, v, t). The code does not cull backfacing triangles, and it returns intersections for negative t-values, but these can be culled too, if desired.

$$
\begin{array}{ll}
& \mathbf{RayTriIntersect}(\mathbf{o}, \mathbf{d}, \mathbf{p}_0, \mathbf{p}_1, \mathbf{p}_2) \\
& \text{returns} \ (\{\text{REJECT}, \text{INTERSECT}\}, u, v, t); \\
1: & \mathbf{e}_1 = \mathbf{p}_1 - \mathbf{p}_0 \\
2: & \mathbf{e}_2 = \mathbf{p}_2 - \mathbf{p}_0 \\
3: & \mathbf{q} = \mathbf{d} \times \mathbf{e}_2 \\
4: & a = \mathbf{e}_1 \cdot \mathbf{q} \\
5: & \text{if}(a > -\epsilon \ \text{and} \ a < \epsilon) \ \text{return} \ (\text{REJECT}, 0, 0, 0); \\
6: & f = 1/a \\
7: & \mathbf{s} = \mathbf{o} - \mathbf{p}_0 \\
8: & u = f(\mathbf{s} \cdot \mathbf{q}) \\
9: & \text{if}(u < 0.0) \ \text{return} \ (\text{REJECT}, 0, 0, 0); \\
10: & \mathbf{r} = \mathbf{s} \times \mathbf{e}_1 \\
11: & v = f(\mathbf{d} \cdot \mathbf{r}) \\
12: & \text{if}(v < 0.0 \ \text{or} \ u + v > 1.0) \ \text{return} \ (\text{REJECT}, 0, 0, 0); \\
13: & t = f(\mathbf{e}_2 \cdot \mathbf{r}) \\
14: & \text{return} \ (\text{INTERSECT}, u, v, t);
\end{array}
$$

A few lines may require some explanation. Line 4 computes a, which is the determinant of the matrix $\mathbf{M}$. This is followed by a test that avoids determinants close to zero. With a properly adjusted value of ϵ, this algorithm is extremely robust. For floating point precision and "normal" conditions, $\epsilon = 10^{-5}$ works fine. In line 9, the value of u is compared to an edge of the triangle ($u = 0$).

C-code for this algorithm, including both culling and nonculling versions, is available on the web [1231]. The C-code has two branches: one that efficiently culls all backfacing triangles, and one that performs intersection tests on two-sided triangles. All computations are delayed until they are required. For example, the value of v is not computed until the value of u is found to be within the allowable range (this can be seen in the pseudocode as well).

The one-sided intersection routine eliminates all triangles where the value of the determinant is negative. This procedure allows the routine's only division operation to be delayed until an intersection has been confirmed.

22.9 Ray/Polygon Intersection

Even though triangles are the most common rendering primitive, a routine that computes the intersection between a ray and a polygon is useful to have. A polygon of n vertices is defined by an ordered vertex list $\{\mathbf{v}_0, \mathbf{v}_1, \ldots, \mathbf{v}_{n-1}\}$, where vertex $\mathbf{v}_i$ forms an edge with $\mathbf{v}_{i+1}$ for $0 \leq i < n-1$ and the polygon is closed by the edge from $\mathbf{v}_{n-1}$ to $\mathbf{v}_0$. The plane of the polygon is denoted $\pi_p : \mathbf{n}_p \cdot \mathbf{x} + d_p = 0$.

We first compute the intersection between the ray (Equation 22.1) and π_p, which is easily done by replacing $\mathbf{x}$ by the ray. The solution is presented below:

$$\mathbf{n}_p \cdot (\mathbf{o} + t\mathbf{d}) + d_p = 0 \quad \Longleftrightarrow \quad t = \frac{-d_p - \mathbf{n}_p \cdot \mathbf{o}}{\mathbf{n}_p \cdot \mathbf{d}}. \tag{22.17}$$

If the denominator $|\mathbf{n}_p \cdot \mathbf{d}| < \epsilon$, where ϵ is a minuscule number, then the ray is considered parallel to the polygon plane and no intersection occurs. In this computation an epsilon of 10^{-20} or smaller can work, as the goal is to avoid overflowing when dividing. We ignore the case where the ray is in the polygon's plane.

Otherwise, the intersection point, $\mathbf{p}$, of the ray and the polygon plane is computed: $\mathbf{p} = \mathbf{o} + t\mathbf{d}$, where the t-value is that from Equation 22.17. Thereafter, the problem of deciding whether $\mathbf{p}$ is inside the polygon is reduced from three to two dimensions. This is done by projecting all vertices and $\mathbf{p}$ to one of the xy-, xz-, or yz-planes where the area of the projected polygon is maximized. In other words, the coordinate component that corresponds to $\max(|n_{p,x}|, |n_{p,y}|, |n_{p,z}|)$ can be skipped and the others kept as two-dimensional coordinates. For example, given a normal $(0.6, -0.692, 0.4)$, the y-component has the largest magnitude, so all y-coordinates are ignored. The largest magnitude is chosen to avoid projecting onto a plane that might create a degenerate, zero-area triangle. Note that this component information could be precomputed once and stored within the polygon for efficiency. The topology of the polygon and the intersection point is conserved during this projection (assuming the polygon is indeed flat; see Section 16.2 for more on this topic). The projection procedure is shown in Figure 22.15.

The question left is whether the two-dimensional ray/plane intersection point $\mathbf{p}$ is contained in the two-dimensional polygon. Here, we will review just one of the more useful algorithms—the "crossings" test. Haines [642] and Schneider and Eberly [1574] provide extensive surveys of two-dimensional, point-in-polygon strategies. A more formal treatment can be found in the computational geometry literature [135, 1339,

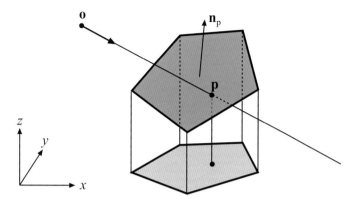

Figure 22.15. Orthographic projection of polygon vertices and intersection point **p** onto the xy-plane, where the area of the projected polygon is maximized. This is an example of using dimension reduction to obtain simpler calculations.

1444]. Lagae and Dutré [955] provide a fast method for ray/quadrilateral intersection based on the Möller and Trumbore ray/triangle test. Walker [1830] provides a method for rapid testing of polygons with more than 10 vertices. Nishita et al. [1284] discuss point inclusion testing for shapes with curved edges.

22.9.1   The Crossings Test

The crossings test is based on the *Jordan Curve Theorem*, a result from topology. From it, a point is inside a polygon if a ray from this point in an arbitrary direction in the plane crosses an odd number of polygon edges. The Jordan Curve Theorem actually limits itself to non-self-intersecting loops. For self-intersecting loops, this ray test causes some areas visibly inside the polygon to be considered outside. This is shown in Figure 22.16. This test is also known as the parity or the even-odd test.

The crossings algorithm works by shooting a ray from the projection of the point **p** in the positive x-direction (or in any direction; the x-direction is simply efficient to code). Then the number of crossings between the polygon edges and this ray is computed. As the Jordan Curve Theorem proves, an odd number of crossings indicates that the point is inside the polygon.

The test point **p** can also be thought of as being at the origin, and the (translated) edges are tested against the positive x-axis instead. This option is depicted in Figure 22.17. If the y-coordinates of a polygon edge have the same sign, then that edge cannot cross the x-axis. Otherwise, it can, and then the x-coordinates are checked. If both are positive, then the number of crossings is incremented, since the test ray must hit this edge. If they differ in sign, the x-coordinate of the intersection between the edge and the x-axis must be computed, and if it is positive, the number of crossings is incremented.

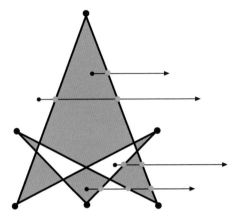

Figure 22.16. A general polygon that is self-intersecting and concave, yet all its enclosed areas are not considered inside (only brown areas are inside). Vertices are marked with large, black dots. Three points being tested are shown, along with their test rays. According to the Jordan Curve Theorem, a point is inside if the number of crossings with the edges of the polygon is odd. Therefore, the uppermost and the bottommost points are inside (one and three crossings, respectively). The two middle points each cross two edges and are thus considered outside the polygon.

In Figure 22.17 all enclosed areas could be categorized as inside as well. This variant test finds the *winding number*, the number of times the polygon loop goes around the test point. See Haines' article [642] for treatment.

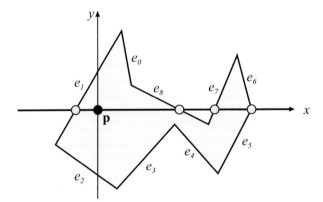

Figure 22.17. The polygon has been translated by $-\mathbf{p}$ ($\mathbf{p}$ is the point to be tested for containment in the polygon), and so the number of crossings with the positive x-axis determines whether $\mathbf{p}$ is inside the polygon. Edges e_0, e_2, e_3, and e_4 do not cross the x-axis. The intersection between edge e_1 and the x-axis must be computed, but will not yield a crossing, since the intersection has a negative x-component. Edges e_7 and e_8 will each increase the number of crossings, since the two vertices of each edge have positive x-components and one negative and one positive y-component. Finally, the edges e_5 and e_6 share a vertex where $y = 0$ and $x > 0$, and they will together increase the number of crossings by one. By considering vertices on the x-axis as above the ray, e_5 is classified as crossing the ray, e_6 as above the ray.

Problems might occur when the test ray intersects a vertex, since two crossings might be detected. These problems are solved by considering the vertex infinitesimally above the ray, which, in practice, is done by interpreting the vertices with $y \geq 0$ as also lying above the x-axis (the ray). The code becomes simpler and speedier, as then no vertices are intersected [640].

The pseudocode for an efficient form of the crossings test follows. It was inspired by the work of Joseph Samosky [1537] and Mark Haigh-Hutchinson, and the code is available on the web [642]. A two-dimensional test point $\mathbf{t}$ and polygon P with vertices $\mathbf{v}_0$ through $\mathbf{v}_{n-1}$ are compared.

```
       bool PointInPolygon(t, P)
       returns ({TRUE, FALSE});
1 :    bool inside = FALSE
2 :    e₀ = vₙ₋₁
3 :    bool y₀ = (e₀ᵧ ≥ tᵧ)
4 :    for i = 0 to n − 1
5 :        e₁ = vᵢ
6 :        bool y₁ = (e₁ᵧ ≥ tᵧ)
7 :        if(y₀ ≠ y₁)
8 :            if(((e₁ᵧ − tᵧ)(e₀ₓ − e₁ₓ) ≥ (e₁ₓ − tₓ)(e₀ᵧ − e₁ᵧ)) == y₁)
9 :                inside = ¬inside
10 :       y₀ = y₁
11 :       e₀ = e₁
12 :   return inside;
```

Line 3 checks whether the y-value of the last vertex in the polygon is greater than or equal to the y-value of the test point $\mathbf{t}$, and stores the result in the boolean y_0. In other words, it tests whether the first endpoint of the first edge we will test is above or below the x-axis. Line 7 tests whether the endpoints e_0 and e_1 are on different sides of the x-axis formed by the test point. If so, then line 8 tests whether the x-intercept is positive. Actually, it is a bit faster than that: To avoid the divide normally needed for computing the intercept, we perform a sign-canceling operation here. By inverting *inside*, line 9 records that a crossing took place. Lines 10 through 12 move on to the next vertex.

In the pseudocode we do not perform a test after line 7 to see whether both endpoints have larger or smaller x-coordinates compared to the test point. Although we presented the algorithm with using a quick accept or reject of these types of edges, code based on the pseudocode presented often runs faster without this test. A major factor is the number of vertices in the polygons tested—with more vertices, checking the x-coordinate differences first can be more efficient.

The advantages of the crossings test is that it is relatively fast and robust, and requires no additional information or preprocessing for the polygon. A disadvantage of this method is that it does not yield anything beyond the indication of whether a point is inside or outside the polygon. Other methods, such as the ray/triangle test in Section 22.8.1, can also compute barycentric coordinates that can be used to interpolate additional information about the test point [642]. Note that barycentric coordinates can be extended to handle convex and concave polygons with more than three vertices [474, 773]. Jiménez et al. [826] provide an optimized algorithm based on barycentric coordinates that aims to include all points along the edges of the polygon and is competitive with the crossings test.

The more general problem of determining whether a point is inside a closed outline formed of line segments and Bézier curvescurves!Bézier can be performed in a similar fashion, counting ray crossings. Lengyel [1028] gives a robust algorithm for this process, using it in a pixel shader for rendering text.

22.10 Plane/Box Intersection

We can know the distance of a point to a plane by inserting the point into the plane's equation, $\pi : \mathbf{n} \cdot \mathbf{x} + d = 0$. The absolute value of the result is the distance to the plane. Plane/sphere testing is then simple: Insert the sphere's center into the plane equation and see if the absolute value is less than or equal to the sphere's radius.

One way to determine whether a box intersects a plane is to insert all the vertices of the box into the plane equation. If both a positive and a negative result (or a zero) is obtained, then vertices are located on both sides of (or on) the plane, and therefore, an intersection has been detected. There are smarter, faster ways to do this test, which are presented in the next two sections, one for the AABB, and one for the OBB.

The idea behind both methods is that only two of the eight corners need to be inserted into the plane equation. For an arbitrarily oriented box, intersecting a plane or not, there are two diagonally opposite corners on the box that are the maximum distance apart, when measured along the plane's normal. Every box has four diagonals, formed by its corners. Taking the dot product of each diagonal's direction with the plane's normal, the largest value identifies the diagonal with these two furthest points. By testing just these two corners, the box as a whole is tested against a plane.

22.10.1 AABB

Assume we have an AABB, B, defined by a center point, $\mathbf{c}$, and a positive half diagonal vector, $\mathbf{h}$. Note that $\mathbf{c}$ and $\mathbf{h}$ can easily be derived from the minimum and maximum corners, $\mathbf{b}^{\min}$ and $\mathbf{b}^{\max}$ of B, that is, $\mathbf{c} = (\mathbf{b}^{\max} + \mathbf{b}^{\min})/2$, and $\mathbf{h} = (\mathbf{b}^{\max} - \mathbf{b}^{\min})/2$.

Now, we want to test B against a plane $\mathbf{n} \cdot \mathbf{x} + d = 0$. There is a surprisingly fast way of performing this test. The idea is to compute the "extent," here denoted e, of the box when projected onto the plane normal, $\mathbf{n}$. In theory, this can be done by projecting all the eight different half diagonals of the box onto the normal, and picking the longest one. In practice, however, this can be implemented rapidly as

$$e = h_x|n_x| + h_y|n_y| + h_z|n_z|. \tag{22.18}$$

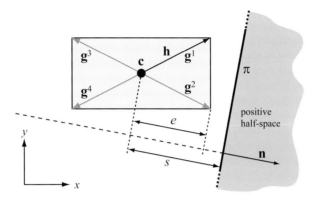

Figure 22.18. An axis-aligned box with center, **c**, and positive half diagonal, **h**, is tested against a plane, π. The idea is to compute the signed distance, s, from the center of the box to the plane, and compare that to the "extent," e, of the box. The vectors $\mathbf{g}^i$ are the different possible diagonals of the two-dimensional box, where **h** is equal to $\mathbf{g}^1$ in this example. Note also that the signed distance s is negative, and its magnitude is larger than e, indicating that the box is inside the plane ($s + e < 0$).

Why is this equivalent to finding the maximum of the eight different half diagonals projections? These eight half diagonals are the combinations: $\mathbf{g}^i = (\pm h_x, \pm h_y, \pm h_z)$, and we want to compute $\mathbf{g}^i \cdot \mathbf{n}$ for all eight i. The dot product $\mathbf{g}^i \cdot \mathbf{n}$ will reach its maximum when each term in the dot product is positive. For the x-term, this will happen when n_x has the same sign as h_x^i, but since we know that h_x is positive already, we can compute the max term as $h_x|n_x|$. Doing this for y and z as well gives us Equation 22.18.

Next, we compute the signed distance, s, from the center point, **c**, to the plane. This is done with: $s = \mathbf{c} \cdot \mathbf{n} + d$. Both s and e are illustrated in Figure 22.18. Assuming that the "outside" of the plane is the positive half-space, we can simply test if $s - e > 0$, which then indicates that the box is fully outside the plane. Similarly, $s + e < 0$ indicates that the box is fully inside. Otherwise, the box intersects the plane. This technique is based on ideas by Ville Miettinen and his clever implementation. Pseudocode is below:

PlaneAABBIntersect(B, π)
returns({OUTSIDE, INSIDE, INTERSECTING});
1 : $\quad \mathbf{c} = (\mathbf{b}^{\mathrm{max}} + \mathbf{b}^{\mathrm{min}})/2$
2 : $\quad \mathbf{h} = (\mathbf{b}^{\mathrm{max}} - \mathbf{b}^{\mathrm{min}})/2$
3 : $\quad e = h_x|n_x| + h_y|n_y| + h_z|n_z|$
4 : $\quad s = \mathbf{c} \cdot \mathbf{n} + d$
5 : $\quad \text{if}(s - e > 0) \text{ return (OUTSIDE)};$
9 : $\quad \text{if}(s + e < 0) \text{ return (INSIDE)};$
10 : $\text{return (INTERSECTING)};$

22.10.2 OBB

Testing an OBB against a plane differs only slightly from the AABB/plane test from the previous section. It is only the computation of the "extent" of the box that needs to be changed, which is done as

$$e = h_u^B |\mathbf{n} \cdot \mathbf{b}^u| + h_v^B |\mathbf{n} \cdot \mathbf{b}^v| + h_w^B |\mathbf{n} \cdot \mathbf{b}^w|. \tag{22.19}$$

Recall that $(\mathbf{b}^u, \mathbf{b}^v, \mathbf{b}^w)$ are the coordinate system axes (see the definition of the OBB in Section 22.2) of the OBB, and (h_u^B, h_v^B, h_w^B) are the lengths of the box along these axes.

22.11 Triangle/Triangle Intersection

Since graphics hardware uses the triangle as its most important (and optimized) drawing primitive, it is only natural to perform collision detection tests on this kind of data as well. So, the deepest levels of a collision detection algorithm typically have a routine that determines whether or not two triangles intersect. Given two triangles, $T_1 = \triangle \mathbf{p}_1 \mathbf{p}_2 \mathbf{p}_3$ and $T_2 = \triangle \mathbf{q}_1 \mathbf{q}_2 \mathbf{q}_3$ (which lie in the planes π_1 and π_2, respectively), we want to determine whether or not they intersect.

From a high level, it is common to start by checking whether T_1 intersects with π_2, and whether T_2 intersects with π_1 [1232]. If either of these tests fails, there can be no intersection. Assuming the triangles are not coplanar, we know that the intersection of the planes, π_1 and π_2, will be a line, L. This is illustrated in Figure 22.19. From the figure, it can be concluded that if the triangles intersect, their intersections on L will also have to overlap. Otherwise, there will be no intersection. There are different ways to implement this, and we present the method by Guigue and Devillers [622] next.

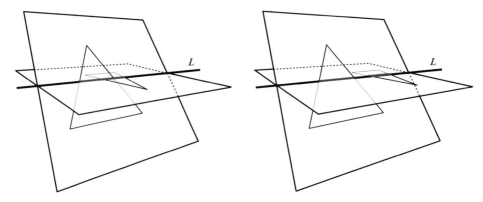

Figure 22.19. Triangles and the planes in which they lie. Intersection intervals are marked in red in both figures. Left: the intervals along the line L overlap, as well as the triangles. Right: there is no intersection; the two intervals do not overlap.

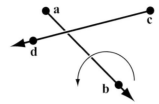

Figure 22.20. Illustration of the screw vector $\mathbf{b} - \mathbf{a}$ in the direction of $\mathbf{d} - \mathbf{c}$.

In this implementation, there is heavy use of 4×4 determinants from four three-dimensional vectors, $\mathbf{a}$, $\mathbf{b}$, $\mathbf{c}$, and $\mathbf{d}$:

$$[\mathbf{a}, \mathbf{b}, \mathbf{c}, \mathbf{d}] = - \begin{vmatrix} a_x & b_x & c_x & d_x \\ a_y & b_y & c_y & d_y \\ a_z & b_z & c_z & d_z \\ 1 & 1 & 1 & 1 \end{vmatrix} = (\mathbf{d} - \mathbf{a}) \cdot ((\mathbf{b} - \mathbf{a}) \times (\mathbf{c} - \mathbf{a})). \quad (22.20)$$

Geometrically, Equation 22.20 has an intuitive interpretation. The cross product, $(\mathbf{b} - \mathbf{a}) \times (\mathbf{c} - \mathbf{a})$, can be seen as computing the normal of a triangle, $\triangle \mathbf{abc}$. By taking the dot product between this normal and the vector from $\mathbf{a}$ to $\mathbf{d}$, we get a value that is positive if $\mathbf{d}$ is in the positive half-space of the triangle's plane, $\triangle \mathbf{abc}$. An alternative interpretation is that the sign of the determinant tells us whether a screw in the direction of $\mathbf{b} - \mathbf{a}$ turns in the same direction as indicated by $\mathbf{d} - \mathbf{c}$. This is illustrated in Figure 22.20.

We first test whether T_1 intersects with π_2, and vice versa. This can be done using the specialized determinants from Equation 22.20 by evaluating $[\mathbf{q}_1, \mathbf{q}_2, \mathbf{q}_3, \mathbf{p}_1]$, $[\mathbf{q}_1, \mathbf{q}_2, \mathbf{q}_3, \mathbf{p}_2]$, and $[\mathbf{q}_1, \mathbf{q}_2, \mathbf{q}_3, \mathbf{p}_3]$. The first test is equivalent to computing the normal of T_2, and then testing which half-space the point $\mathbf{p}_1$ is in. If the signs of these determinants are the same and nonzero, there can be no intersection, and the test ends. If all are zero, the triangles are coplanar, and a separate test is performed to handle this case. Otherwise, we continue testing whether T_2 intersects with π_1, using the same type of test.

At this point, two intervals, $I_1 = [i, j]$ and $I_2 = [k, l]$, on L are to be computed, where I_1 is computed from T_1 and I_2 from T_2. To do this, the vertices for each triangle are reordered so the first vertex is alone on one side of the other triangle's plane. If I_1 overlaps with I_2, then the two triangles intersect, and this occurs only if $k \leq j$ and $i \leq l$. To implement $k \leq j$, we can use the sign test of the determinant (Equation 22.20), and note that j is derived from $\mathbf{p}_1 \mathbf{p}_2$, and k from $\mathbf{q}_1 \mathbf{q}_2$. Using the interpretation of the "screw test" of the determinant computation, we can conclude that $k \leq j$ if $[\mathbf{p}_1, \mathbf{p}_2, \mathbf{q}_1, \mathbf{q}_2] \leq 0$. The final test then becomes

$$[\mathbf{p}_1, \mathbf{p}_2, \mathbf{q}_1, \mathbf{q}_2] \leq 0 \quad \text{and} \quad [\mathbf{p}_1, \mathbf{p}_3, \mathbf{q}_3, \mathbf{q}_1] \leq 0. \quad (22.21)$$

The entire test starts with six determinant tests, and the first three share the first arguments, so many computations can be shared. In principle, the determinant can be computed using many smaller 2×2 subdeterminants, and when these occur in more than one 4×4 determinant, the computations can be shared. There is code on the web for this test [622], and it is also possible to augment the code to compute the actual line segment of intersection.

If the triangles are coplanar, they are projected onto the axis-aligned plane where the areas of the triangles are maximized (Section 22.9). Then, a simple two-dimensional triangle-triangle overlap test is performed. First, test all closed edges (i.e., including endpoints) of T_1 for intersection with the closed edges of T_2. If any intersection is found, the triangles intersect. Otherwise, we must test whether T_1 is entirely contained in T_2 or vice versa. This can be done by performing a point-in-triangle test (Section 22.8) for one vertex of T_1 against T_2, and vice versa.

Note that the separating axis test (see page 947) can be used to derive a triangle/triangle overlap test. We instead presented a test by Guigue and Devillers [622], which is faster than using SAT. Other algorithms exist for performing triangle/triangle intersection [713, 1619, 1787] as well. Architectural and compiler differences, as well as variation in expected hit ratios, mean that we cannot recommend a single algorithm that always performs best. Note that precision problems can occur as with any geometrical tests. Robbins and Whitesides [1501] use the exact arithmetic by Shewchuk [1624] to avoid this.

22.12 Triangle/Box Intersection

This section presents an algorithm for determining whether a triangle intersects an axis-aligned box. Such a test is useful for voxelization and for collision detection.

Green and Hatch [581] present an algorithm that can determine whether an arbitrary polygon overlaps a box. Akenine-Möller [21] developed a faster method that is based on the separating axis test (page 947), and which we present here. Triangle/sphere testing can also be performed using this test, see Ericson's article [440] for details.

We focus on testing an axis-aligned bounding box (AABB), defined by a center $\mathbf{c}$, and a vector of half lengths, $\mathbf{h}$, against a triangle $\Delta \mathbf{u}_0 \mathbf{u}_1 \mathbf{u}_2$. To simplify the tests, we first move the box and the triangle so that the box is centered around the origin, i.e., $\mathbf{v}_i = \mathbf{u}_i - \mathbf{c}$, $i \in \{0, 1, 2\}$. This translation and the notation used is shown in Figure 22.21. To test against an oriented box, we would first rotate the triangle vertices by the inverse box transform, then use the test here. Based on the separating axis test (SAT), we test the following 13 axes:

1. [3 tests] $\mathbf{e}_0 = (1, 0, 0)$, $\mathbf{e}_1 = (0, 1, 0)$, $\mathbf{e}_2 = (0, 0, 1)$ (the normals of the AABB). In other words, test the AABB against the minimal AABB around the triangle.

2. [1 test] $\mathbf{n}$, the normal of $\Delta \mathbf{u}_0 \mathbf{u}_1 \mathbf{u}_2$. We use a fast plane/AABB overlap test (Section 22.10.1), which tests only the two vertices of the box diagonal whose direction is most closely aligned to the normal of the triangle.

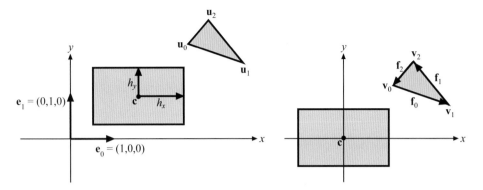

Figure 22.21. Notation used for the triangle/box overlap test. To the left, the initial position of the box and the triangle is shown, while to the right, the box and the triangle have been translated so that the box center coincides with the origin.

3. [9 tests] $\mathbf{a}_{ij} = \mathbf{e}_i \times \mathbf{f}_j$, $i, j \in \{0, 1, 2\}$, where $\mathbf{f}_0 = \mathbf{v}_1 - \mathbf{v}_0$, $\mathbf{f}_1 = \mathbf{v}_2 - \mathbf{v}_1$, and $\mathbf{f}_2 = \mathbf{v}_0 - \mathbf{v}_2$, i.e., edge vectors. These tests are similar in form and we will only show the derivation of the case where $i = 0$ and $j = 0$ (see below).

As soon as a separating axis is found the algorithm terminates and returns "no overlap." If all tests pass, i.e., there is no separating axis, then the triangle overlaps the box.

Here we derive one of the nine tests, where $i = 0$ and $j = 0$, in Step 3. This means that $\mathbf{a}_{00} = \mathbf{e}_0 \times \mathbf{f}_0 = (0, -f_{0z}, f_{0y})$. So, now we need to project the triangle vertices onto $\mathbf{a}_{00}$ (hereafter called $\mathbf{a}$):

$$
\begin{aligned}
p_0 &= \mathbf{a} \cdot \mathbf{v}_0 = (0, -f_{0z}, f_{0y}) \cdot \mathbf{v}_0 = v_{0z}v_{1y} - v_{0y}v_{1z}, \\
p_1 &= \mathbf{a} \cdot \mathbf{v}_1 = (0, -f_{0z}, f_{0y}) \cdot \mathbf{v}_1 = v_{0z}v_{1y} - v_{0y}v_{1z} = p_0, \\
p_2 &= \mathbf{a} \cdot \mathbf{v}_2 = (0, -f_{0z}, f_{0y}) \cdot \mathbf{v}_2 = (v_{1y} - v_{0y})v_{2z} - (v_{1z} - v_{0z})v_{2y}.
\end{aligned}
\tag{22.22}
$$

Normally, we would have had to find $\min(p_0, p_1, p_2)$ and $\max(p_0, p_1, p_2)$, but fortunately $p_0 = p_1$, which simplifies the computations. Now we only need to find $\min(p_0, p_2)$ and $\max(p_0, p_2)$, which is significantly faster because conditional statements are expensive on modern CPUs.

After the projection of the triangle onto $\mathbf{a}$, we need to project the box onto $\mathbf{a}$ as well. We compute a "radius," r, of the box projected on $\mathbf{a}$ as

$$
r = h_x|a_x| + h_y|a_y| + h_z|a_z| = h_y|a_y| + h_z|a_z|,
\tag{22.23}
$$

where the last step comes from that $a_x = 0$ for this particular axis. Then, this axis test becomes

$$\mathtt{if(\ min}(p_0, p_2) > r \ \mathtt{or}\ \ \max(p_0, p_2) < -r)\ \mathtt{return\ false;}
\tag{22.24}$$

Code is available on the web [21].

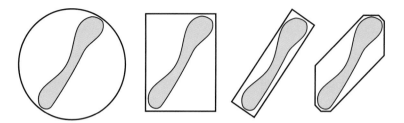

Figure 22.22. A sphere (left), an AABB (middle left), an OBB (middle right), and a k-DOP (right) are shown for an object, where the OBB and the k-DOP clearly have less empty space than the others.

22.13   Bounding-Volume/Bounding-Volume Intersection

The purpose of a bounding volume is to provide simpler intersection tests and make more efficient rejections. For example, to test whether or not two cars collide, first find their BVs and test if these overlap. If they do not, then the cars are guaranteed not to collide (which we assume is the most common case). We then have avoided testing each primitive of one car against each primitive of the other, thereby saving computation.

A fundamental operation is to test whether or not two bounding volumes overlap. Methods of testing overlap for the AABB, the k-DOP, and the OBB are presented in the following sections. See Section 22.3 for algorithms that form BVs around primitives.

The reason for using more complex BVs than the sphere and the AABB is that more complex BVs often have a tighter fit. This is illustrated in Figure 22.22. Other bounding volumes are possible, of course. For example, cylinders and ellipsoids are sometimes used as bounding volumes for objects. Also, several spheres can be placed to enclose a single object [782, 1582].

For capsule and lozenge BVs it is a relatively quick operation to compute the minimum distance. Therefore, they are often used in tolerance verification applications, where one wants to verify that two (or more) objects are at least a certain distance apart. Eberly [404] and Larsen et al. [979] derive formulae and efficient algorithms for these types of bounding volumes.

22.13.1   Sphere/Sphere Intersection

For spheres, the intersection test is simple and quick: Compute the distance between the two spheres' centers and then reject if this distance is greater than the sum of the two spheres' radii. Otherwise, they intersect. In implementing this algorithm, it is best to use the squared distances of these two quantities, since all that is desired is the result of the comparison. In this way, computing the square root (an expensive operation) is avoided. Ericson [435] gives SSE code for testing four separate pairs of spheres simultaneously.

22.13.2 Sphere/Box Intersection

An algorithm for testing whether a sphere and an AABB intersect was first presented by Arvo [70] and is surprisingly simple. The idea is to find the point on the AABB that is closest to the sphere's center, $\mathbf{c}$. One-dimensional tests are used, one for each of the three axes of the AABB. The sphere's center coordinate for an axis is tested against the bounds of the AABB. If it is outside the bounds, the distance between the sphere center and the box along this axis (a subtraction) is computed and squared. After we have done this along the three axes, the sum of these squared distances is compared to the squared radius, r^2, of the sphere. If the sum is less than the squared radius, the closest point is inside the sphere, and the box overlaps. As Arvo shows, this algorithm can be modified to handle hollow boxes and spheres, as well as axis-aligned ellipsoids.

Larsson et al. [982] present some variants of this algorithm, including a considerably faster SSE vectorized version. Their insight is to use simple rejection tests early on, either per axis or all at the start. The rejection test is to see if the center-to-box distance along an axis is greater than the radius. If so, testing can end early, since the sphere then cannot possibly overlap with the box. When the chance of overlap is low, this early rejection method is noticeably faster. What follows is the QRI (quick rejections intertwined) version of their test. The early out tests are at lines 4 and 7, and can be removed if desired.

$$
\begin{array}{l}
\text{bool } \mathbf{SphereAABB\_intersect}(\mathbf{c}, r, A) \\
\text{returns}(\{\texttt{OVERLAP}, \texttt{DISJOINT}\}); \\
1: \quad d = 0 \\
2: \quad \text{for each } i \in \{x, y, z\} \\
3: \quad\quad \text{if } ((e = c_i - a_i^{\min}) < 0) \\
4: \quad\quad\quad \text{if } (e < -r)\text{return (DISJOINT)}; \\
5: \quad\quad\quad d = d + e^2; \\
6: \quad\quad \text{else if } ((e = c_i - a_i^{\max}) > 0) \\
7: \quad\quad\quad \text{if } (e > r)\text{return (DISJOINT)}; \\
8: \quad\quad\quad d = d + e^2; \\
9: \quad\quad \text{if } (d > r^2) \text{ return (DISJOINT)}; \\
10: \quad \text{return (OVERLAP)};
\end{array}
$$

For a fast vectorized (using SSE) implementation, Larsson et al. propose to eliminate most of the branches. The idea is to evaluate lines 3 and 6 simultaneously using the following expression:

$$e = \max(a_i^{\min} - c_i, 0) + \max(c_i - a_i^{\max}, 0). \tag{22.25}$$

Normally, we would then update d as $d = d + e^2$. However, using SSE, we can evaluate Equation 22.25 for x, y, and z in parallel. Pseudocode for the full test is given below.

---

bool **SphereAABB_intersect**$(\mathbf{c}, r, A)$
returns($\{$OVERLAP, DISJOINT$\}$);
1 : $\mathbf{e} = (\max(a_x^{\min} - c_x, 0), \max(a_y^{\min} - c_y, 0), \max(a_z^{\min} - c_z, 0))$
2 : $\mathbf{e} = \mathbf{e} + (\max(c_x - a_x^{\max}, 0), \max(c_y - a_y^{\max}, 0), \max(c_z - a_z^{\max}, 0))$
3 : $d = \mathbf{e} \cdot \mathbf{e}$
4 : if $(d > r^2)$ return (DISJOINT);
5 : return (OVERLAP);

Note that lines 1 and 2 can be implemented using a parallel SSE max function. Even though there are no early outs in this test, it is still faster than the other techniques. This is because branches have been eliminated and parallel computations used. Another approach to SSE is to vectorize the object pairs. Ericson [435] presents SIMD code to compare four spheres with four AABBs at the same time.

For sphere/OBB intersection, first transform the sphere's center into the OBB's space. That is, use the OBB's normalized axes as the basis for transforming the sphere's center. Now this center point is expressed relative to the OBB's axes, so the OBB can be treated as an AABB. The sphere/AABB algorithm is then used to test for intersection.

Larsson [983] gives an efficient method for ellipsoid/OBB intersection testing. First, both objects are scaled so that the ellipsoid becomes a sphere and the OBB a parallelepiped. Sphere/slab intersection testing can be performed for quick acceptance and rejection. Finally, the sphere is tested for intersection with only those parallelograms facing it.

22.13.3 AABB/AABB Intersection

An AABB is, as its name implies, a box whose faces are aligned with the main axis directions. Therefore, two points are sufficient to describe such a volume. Here we use the definition of the AABB presented in Section 22.2.

Due to their simplicity, AABBs are commonly employed both in collision detection algorithms and as bounding volumes for the nodes in a scene graph. The test for intersection between two AABBs, A and B, is trivial and is summarized below:

---

bool **AABB_intersect**(A, B)
returns($\{$OVERLAP, DISJOINT$\}$);
1 : for each $i \in \{x, y, z\}$
2 :   if$(a_i^{\min} > b_i^{\max}$ or $b_i^{\min} > a_i^{\max})$
3 :   return (DISJOINT);
4 : return (OVERLAP);

Lines 1 and 2 loop over all three standard axis directions x, y, and z. Ericson [435] provides SSE code for testing four separate pairs of AABBs simultaneously.

22.13.4 k-DOP/k-DOP Intersection

The intersection test for a k-DOP with another k-DOP consists of only $k/2$ interval overlap tests. Klosowski et al. [910] have shown that, for moderate values of k, the overlap test for two k-DOPs is an order of magnitude faster than the test for two OBBs. In Figure 22.4 on page 946, a simple two-dimensional k-DOP is depicted. Note that the AABB is a special case of a 6-DOP where the normals are the positive and negative main axis directions. OBBs are also a form of 6-DOP, but this fast test can be used only when the two OBBs share the same axes.

The intersection test that follows is simple and extremely fast, inexact but conservative. If two k-DOPs, A and B (superscripted with indices A and B), are to be tested for intersection, then test all parallel pairs of slabs (S_i^A, S_i^B) for overlap; $s_i = S_i^A \cap S_i^B$ is a one-dimensional interval overlap test, which is solved with ease. This is an example of dimension reduction, as the rules of thumb in Section 22.5 recommend. Here, a three-dimensional slab test is simplified into a one-dimensional interval overlap test.

If at any time $s_i = \emptyset$ (i.e., the empty set), then the BVs are disjoint and the test is terminated. Otherwise, the slab overlap tests continues. If and only if all $s_i \neq \emptyset$, $1 \leq i \leq k/2$, then the BVs are considered overlapping. According to the separating axis test (Section 22.2), one also needs to test an axis parallel to the cross product of one edge from each k-DOP. However, these tests are often omitted because they cost more than they give back in performance. Therefore, if the test below returns that the k-DOPs overlap, then they might actually be disjoint. Here is the pseudocode for the k-DOP/k-DOP overlap test:

$$
\begin{aligned}
&\textbf{kDOP\_intersect}(d_1^{A,\min}, \ldots, d_{k/2}^{A,\min}, d_1^{A,\max}, \ldots, d_{k/2}^{A,\max}, \\
&\qquad\qquad d_1^{B,\min}, \ldots, d_{k/2}^{B,\min}, d_1^{B,\max}, \ldots, d_{k/2}^{B,\max})
\end{aligned}
$$

```
      returns({OVERLAP, DISJOINT});
1 :   for each i ∈ {1, ..., k/2}
2 :       if(d_i^{B,min} > d_i^{A,max} or d_i^{A,min} > d_i^{B,max})
3 :          return (DISJOINT);
4 :   return (OVERLAP);
```

Note that only k scalar values need to be stored with each instance of the k-DOP (the normals, $\mathbf{n}_i$, are stored once for all k-DOPs since they are static). If the k-DOPs are translated by $\mathbf{t}^A$ and $\mathbf{t}^B$, respectively, the test gets a tiny bit more complicated. Project $\mathbf{t}^A$ onto the normals, $\mathbf{n}_i$, e.g., $p_i^A = \mathbf{t}^A \cdot \mathbf{n}_i$ (note that this is independent of any k-DOP and therefore needs to be computed only once for each $\mathbf{t}^A$ or $\mathbf{t}^B$) and add p_i^A to $d_i^{A,\min}$ and $d_i^{A,\max}$ in the `if`-statement. The same is done for $\mathbf{t}^B$. In other words, a translation changes the distance of the k-DOP along each normal's direction.

Laine and Karras [965] present an extension to k-DOPs called the *apex point map*. The idea is to map a set of plane normals to various points on the k-DOP, such that each point stored represents the most distant location along that direction. This point and the direction form a plane that fully contains the model in one half-space, i.e., the point is at the apex of the model's k-DOP. During testing, the apex point retrieved for a given direction can be used for a more accurate intersection test between k-DOPs, for improved frustum culling, and for finding tighter AABBs after rotation, as some examples.

22.13.5 OBB/OBB Intersection

In this section we briefly outline a fast method for testing intersection between two OBBs, A and B [436, 576, 577]. The algorithm uses the separating axis test, and is about an order of magnitude faster than previous methods, which use closest features or linear programming. The definition of the OBB may be found in Section 22.2.

The test is done in the coordinate system formed by A's center and axes. This means that the origin is $\mathbf{a}^c = (0, 0, 0)$ and that the main axes in this coordinate system are $\mathbf{a}^u = (1, 0, 0)$, $\mathbf{a}^v = (0, 1, 0)$, and $\mathbf{a}^w = (0, 0, 1)$. Moreover, B is assumed to be located relative to A, with a translation $\mathbf{t}$ and a rotation (matrix) $\mathbf{R}$.

According to the separating axis test, it is sufficient to find one axis that separates A and B to be sure that they are disjoint (do not overlap). Fifteen axes have to be tested: three from the faces of A, three from the faces of B, and $3 \cdot 3 = 9$ from combinations of edges from A and B. This is shown in two dimensions in Figure 22.23.

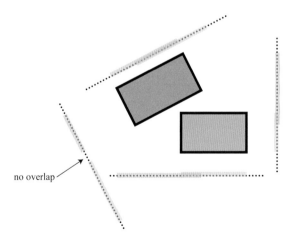

Figure 22.23. To determine whether two OBBs overlap, the separating axis test can be used. Here, it is shown in two dimensions. The four separating axes are orthogonal to the faces of the two OBBs, two axes for each box. The OBBs are then projected onto the axes. If both projections overlap on all axes, then the OBBs overlap; otherwise, they do not. So, it is sufficient to find one axis that separates the projections to know that the OBBs do not overlap. In this example, the lower left axis is the only axis that separates the projections. *(Figure after Ericson [436].)*

As a consequence of the orthonormality of the matrix $\mathbf{A} = (\mathbf{a}^u \ \mathbf{a}^v \ \mathbf{a}^w)$, the potential separating axes that should be orthogonal to the faces of A are simply the axes $\mathbf{a}^u$, $\mathbf{a}^v$, and $\mathbf{a}^w$. The same holds for B. The remaining nine potential axes, formed by one edge each from both A and B, are then $\mathbf{c}^{ij} = \mathbf{a}^i \times \mathbf{b}^j$, $\forall i \in \{u, v, w\}$ and $\forall j \in \{u, v, w\}$. Luckily, there is optimized code online for this [1574].

22.14 View Frustum Intersection

As has been seen in Section 19.4, hierarchical view frustum culling is essential for rapid rendering of a complex scene. One of the few operations called during bounding-volume-hierarchy cull traversal is the intersection test between the view frustum and a bounding volume. These operations are thus critical to fast execution. Ideally, they should determine whether the BV is fully inside (inclusion), it is entirely outside (exclusion), or it intersects the frustum.

To review, a view frustum is a pyramid that is truncated by a near and a far plane (which are parallel), making the volume finite. In fact, it becomes a polyhedron. This is shown in Figure 22.24, where the names of the six planes, *near*, *far*, *left*, *right*, *top*, and *bottom* also are marked. The view frustum volume defines the parts of the scene that should be visible and thus rendered (in perspective for a pyramidal frustum).

The most common bounding volumes used for internal nodes in a hierarchy (e.g., a scene graph) and for enclosing geometry are spheres, AABBs, and OBBs. Therefore frustum/sphere and frustum/AABB/OBB tests will be discussed and derived here.

To see why we need the three return results outside/inside/intersect, we will examine what happens when traversing the bounding volume hierarchy. If a BV is found to be entirely outside the view frustum, then that BV's subtree will not be traversed further and none of its geometry will be rendered. On the other hand, if the BV is fully inside, then no more frustum/BV tests need to be computed for that subtree and every renderable leaf will be drawn. For a partially visible BV, i.e., one that intersects the frustum, the BV's subtree is tested recursively against the frustum. If the BV is for a leaf, then that leaf must be rendered.

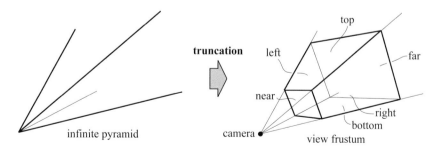

Figure 22.24. The illustration on the left is an infinite pyramid, which then is cropped by the parallel near and far planes to construct a view frustum. The names of the other planes are also shown, and the position of the camera is at the apex of the pyramid.

The complete test is called an *exclusion/inclusion/intersection test.* Sometimes the third state, intersection, may be considered too costly to compute. In this case, the BV is classified as "probably inside." We call such a simplified algorithm an *exclusion/inclusion test.* If a BV cannot be excluded successfully, there are two choices. One is to treat the "probably inside" state as an inclusion, meaning that everything inside the BV is rendered. This is often inefficient, as no further culling is performed. The other choice is to test each node in the subtree in turn for exclusion. Such testing is often without benefit, as much of the subtree may indeed be inside the frustum. Because neither choice is particularly good, some attempt at quickly differentiating between intersection and inclusion is often worthwhile, even if the test is imperfect.

It is important to realize that the quick classification tests do not have to be exact for scene-graph culling, just conservative. For differentiating exclusion from inclusion, all that is required is that the test err on the side of inclusion. That is, objects that should actually be excluded can erroneously be included. Such mistakes simply cost extra time. On the other hand, objects that should be included should never be quickly classified as excluded by the tests, otherwise rendering errors will occur. With inclusion versus intersection, either type of incorrect classification is usually legal. If a fully included BV is classified as intersecting, time is wasted testing its subtree for intersection. If an intersected BV is considered fully inside, time is wasted by rendering all objects, some of which could have been culled.

Before we introduce the tests between a frustum and a sphere, AABB, or OBB, we shall describe an intersection test method between a frustum and a general object. This test is illustrated in Figure 22.25. The idea is to transform the test from a BV/frustum test to a point/volume test. First, a point relative to the BV is selected. Then the BV is moved along the outside of the frustum, as closely as possible to it without overlapping. During this movement, the point relative to the BV is traced, and its trace forms a new volume (a polygon with thick edges in Figure 22.25). The fact that the BV was moved as close as possible to the frustum means that if the point relative to the BV (in its original position) lies inside the traced-out volume, then the BV intersects or is inside the frustum. So, instead of testing the BV for intersection against a frustum, the point relative to the BV is tested against another new volume, which is traced out by the point. In the same way, the BV can be moved along the inside of the frustum and as close as possible to the frustum. This will trace out a new, smaller frustum with planes parallel to the original frustum [83]. If the point relative to the object is inside this new volume, then the BV is fully inside the frustum. This technique is used to derive tests in the subsequent sections. Note that the creation of the new volumes is independent of the position of the actual BV—it is dependent solely on the position of the point relative to the BV and the shape of the BV. This means that a BV with an arbitrary position can be tested against the same volumes.

Saving just a parent BV's intersection state with each child is a useful optimization. If the parent is known to be fully inside the frustum, none of the descendants need any further frustum testing. The plane masking and temporal coherence techniques dis-

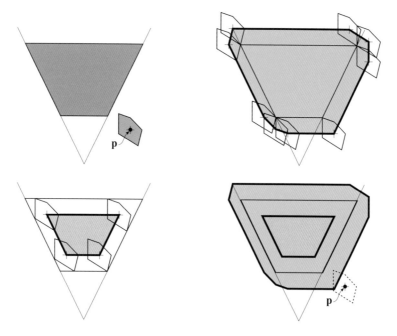

Figure 22.25. The upper left image shows a frustum (blue) and a general bounding volume (green), where a point **p** relative to the object has been selected. By tracing the point **p** where the object moves on the outside (upper right) and on the inside (lower left) of the frustum, as close as possible to the frustum, the frustum/BV can be reformulated into testing the point **p** against an outer and an inner volume. This is shown on the lower right. If the point **p** is outside the orange volume, then the BV is outside the frustum. The BV intersects the frustum if **p** is inside the orange area, and the BV is fully inside the frustum if **p** is inside the violet area.

cussed in Section 19.4 can also noticeably improve testing against a bounding volume hierarchy, though are less useful with a SIMD implementation [529].

First, we derive the plane equations of the frustum, since these are needed for these sorts of tests. Frustum/sphere intersection is presented next, followed by an explanation of frustum/box intersection.

22.14.1 Frustum Plane Extraction

To do view frustum culling, the plane equations for the six different sides of the frustum are needed. We present here a clever and fast way of deriving these. Assume that the view matrix is $\mathbf{V}$ and that the projection matrix is $\mathbf{P}$. The composite transform is then $\mathbf{M} = \mathbf{PV}$. A point $\mathbf{s}$ (where $s_w = 1$) is transformed into $\mathbf{t}$ as $\mathbf{t} = \mathbf{Ms}$. At this point, $\mathbf{t}$ may have $t_w \neq 1$ due to, for example, perspective projection. Therefore, all components in $\mathbf{t}$ are divided by t_w to obtain a point $\mathbf{u}$ with $u_w = 1$. For points inside the view frustum, it holds that $-1 \leq u_i \leq 1$, for $i \in x, y, z$, i.e., the point $\mathbf{u}$ is inside a unit cube. This is for the OpenGL type of projection matrices (Section 4.7). For DirectX, the same holds, except that $0 \le u_z \le 1$. The planes of the frustum can be derived directly from the rows of the composite transform matrix.

Focus for a moment on the volume on the right side of the left plane of the unit cube, for which $-1 \le u_x$. This is expanded below:

$$-1 \le u_x \iff -1 \le \frac{t_x}{t_w} \iff t_x + t_w \ge 0 \iff \tag{22.26}$$
$$\iff (\mathbf{m}_{0,} \cdot \mathbf{s}) + (\mathbf{m}_{3,} \cdot \mathbf{s}) \ge 0 \iff (\mathbf{m}_{0,} + \mathbf{m}_{3,}) \cdot \mathbf{s} \ge 0.$$

In the derivation, $\mathbf{m}_{i,}$ denotes the ith row in $\mathbf{M}$. The last step $(\mathbf{m}_0, +\mathbf{m}_{3,}) \cdot \mathbf{s} \ge 0$ is, in fact, denoting a (half) plane equation of the left plane of the view frustum. This is so because the left plane in the unit cube has been transformed back to world coordinates. Also note that $s_w = 1$, which makes the equation a plane. To make the normal of the plane point outward from the frustum, the equation must be negated (as the original equation described the inside of the unit cube). This gives $-(\mathbf{m}_{3,} +\mathbf{m}_{0,}) \cdot (x, y, z, 1) = 0$ for the left plane of the frustum (where we use $(x, y, z, 1)$ instead to use a plane equation of the form: $ax + by + cz + d = 0$). To summarize, all the planes are

$$\begin{aligned}
-(\mathbf{m}_{3,} + \mathbf{m}_{0,}) \cdot (x, y, z, 1) &= 0 & [\textbf{left}], \\
-(\mathbf{m}_{3,} - \mathbf{m}_{0,}) \cdot (x, y, z, 1) &= 0 & [\textbf{right}], \\
-(\mathbf{m}_{3,} + \mathbf{m}_{1,}) \cdot (x, y, z, 1) &= 0 & [\textbf{bottom}], \\
-(\mathbf{m}_{3,} - \mathbf{m}_{1,}) \cdot (x, y, z, 1) &= 0 & [\textbf{top}], \\
-(\mathbf{m}_{3,} + \mathbf{m}_{2,}) \cdot (x, y, z, 1) &= 0 & [\textbf{near}], \\
-(\mathbf{m}_{3,} - \mathbf{m}_{2,}) \cdot (x, y, z, 1) &= 0 & [\textbf{far}].
\end{aligned} \tag{22.27}$$

Code for doing this in OpenGL and DirectX is available on the web [600].

22.14.2 Frustum/Sphere Intersection

A frustum for an orthographic view is a box, so the overlap test in this case becomes a sphere/OBB intersection and can be solved using the algorithm presented in Section 22.13.2. To further test whether the sphere is entirely inside the box, we first check if the sphere's center is between the box's boundaries along each axis by a distance greater than its radius. If it is between these in all three dimensions, it is fully contained. For an efficient implementation of this modified algorithm, along with code, see Arvo's article [70].

Following the method for deriving a frustum/BV test, for an arbitrary frustum we select the center of the sphere as the point $\mathbf{p}$ to trace. This is shown in Figure 22.26. If the sphere, with radius r, is moved along the inside and along the outside of the frustum and as close to the frustum as possible, then the trace of $\mathbf{p}$ gives us the volumes that are needed to reformulate the frustum/sphere test. The actual volumes are shown in the middle segment of Figure 22.26. As before, if $\mathbf{p}$ is outside the orange

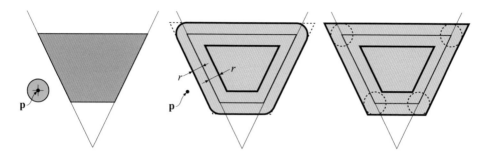

Figure 22.26. At the left, a frustum and a sphere are shown. The exact frustum/sphere test can be formulated as testing **p** against the orange and violet volumes in the middle figure. At the right is a reasonable approximation of the volumes in the middle. If the center of the sphere is located outside a rounded corner, but inside all outer planes, it will be incorrectly classified as intersecting, even though it is outside the frustum.

volume, then the sphere is outside the frustum. If **p** is inside the violet area, then the sphere is completely inside the frustum. If the point is inside the orange area, the sphere intersects the frustum sides planes. In this way, the exact test can be done. However, for the sake of efficiency we use the approximation that appears on the right side of Figure 22.26. Here, the orange volume has been extended in order to avoid the more complicated computations that the rounded corners would require. Note that the outer volume consists of the planes of the frustum moved r distance units outward in the direction of the frustum plane normal, and that the inner volume can be created by moving the planes of the frustum r distance units inward in the direction of the frustum plane normals.

Assume that the plane equations of the frustum are such that the positive half-space is located outside of the frustum. Then, an actual implementation would loop over the six planes of the frustum, and for each frustum plane, compute the signed distance from the sphere's center to the plane. This is done by inserting the sphere center into the plane equation. If the distance is greater than the radius r, then the sphere is outside the frustum. If the distances to all six planes are less than $-r$, then the sphere is inside the frustum; otherwise the sphere intersects it. More correctly, we *say* that the sphere intersects the frustum, but the sphere center may be located in one of the sharp corner areas outside the rounded corners shown in Figure 22.26. This would mean that the sphere is outside the frustum, but we report it to be intersecting, to be conservatively correct.

To make the test more accurate, it is possible to add extra planes for testing if the sphere is outside. However, for the purposes of quickly culling out scene-graph nodes, occasional false hits simply cause unnecessary testing, not algorithm failure, and this additional testing will cost more time overall. Another more accurate, though still imprecise, method is described in Section 20.3, useful for when these sharp corner areas are significant.

For efficient shading techniques, the frusta are often highly asymmetrical and a special method for that is described in Figure 20.7 on page 895. Assarsson and Möller [83] provide a method that eliminates three planes from each test by dividing the frustum into octants and finding in which octant the center of the object is located.

22.14.3 Frustum/Box Intersection

If the view's projection is orthographic (i.e., the frustum has a box shape), precise testing can be done using OBB/OBB intersection testing (Section 22.13.5). For general frustum/box intersection testing, there are two methods commonly used. One simple method is to transform all eight box corners to the frustum's coordinate system by using the view and projection matrices for the frustum. Perform clip testing for the canonical view volume that extends $[-1, 1]$ along each axis (Section 4.7.1). If all points are outside one boundary, the box is rejected; if all are in, the box is fully contained [529]. As this method emulates clipping, it can be used for any object delimited by a set of points, such as a line segment, triangle, or k-DOP. An advantage of this method is that no frustum plane extraction is needed. Its self-contained simplicity lends it to efficient use in a compute shader [1883, 1884].

A method that is considerably more efficient on the CPU is to use the plane/box intersection test described in Section 22.10. Like the frustum/sphere test, the OBB or AABB is checked against the six view frustum planes. Instead of computing the signed distance of all eight corners from a plane, in the plane/box test we check at most two corners, determined by the plane's normal. If the nearest corner is outside the plane, the box is fully outside and testing can end early. If the farthest corner for every plane is inside, then the box is contained inside the frustum. Note that the dot product distance computations for the near and far planes can be shared, since these planes are parallel. The only additional cost for this second method is that the frustum's planes must first be derived, a trivial expense if a few boxes are to be tested.

Like the frustum/sphere algorithm, the test suffers from classifying boxes as intersecting that are actually fully outside. Those kinds of errors are shown in Figure 22.27. Quílez [1452] notes that this can happen more frequently with fixed-size terrain meshes or other large objects. When an intersection is reported, his solution is to then also test the corners of the frustum against each of the planes forming the bounding box. If all points are outside a box's plane, the frustum and box do not intersect. This additional test is equivalent to the second part of the separating axis test, where the axis tested is orthogonal to the second object's faces. That said, such additional testing can be more costly than the benefits accrued. For his GIS renderer, Eng [425] found that this optimization cost 2 ms per frame of CPU time to save only a few draw calls.

Wihlidal [1884] goes the other direction with frustum culling, using only the four frustum side planes and not performing the near and far plane cull tests. He notes that these two planes do not help much in video games. The near plane is mostly

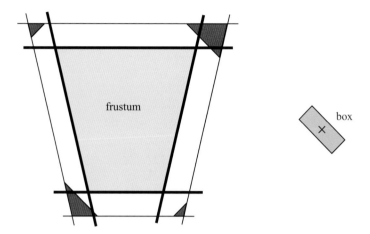

Figure 22.27. The bold black lines are the planes of the frustum. When testing the box (left) against the frustum using the presented algorithm, the box can be incorrectly classified as intersecting when it is outside. For the situation in the figure, this happens when the box's center is located in the red areas.

redundant, since the side planes trim out almost all the space it does, and the far plane is normally set to view all objects in the scene.

Another approach is to use the separating axis test (found in Section 22.13) to derive an intersection routine. Several authors use the separating axis test for a general solution for two convex polyhedra [595, 1574]. A single optimized test can then be used for any combination of line segments, triangles, AABBs, OBBs, k-DOPs, frusta, and convex polyhedra.

22.15   Line/Line Intersection

In this section, both two- and three-dimensional line/line intersection tests are derived and examined. Lines, rays, and line segments are intersected with one another, and methods that are both fast and elegant are described.

22.15.1   Two Dimensions

First Method
From a theoretical viewpoint, this first method of computing the intersection between a pair of two-dimensional lines is truly beautiful. Consider two lines, $\mathbf{r}_1(s) = \mathbf{o}_1 + s\mathbf{d}_1$ and $\mathbf{r}_2(t) = \mathbf{o}_2 + t\mathbf{d}_2$. Since $\mathbf{a} \cdot \mathbf{a}^{\perp} = 0$ (the perp dot product [735] from Section 1.2.1), the intersection calculations between $\mathbf{r}_1(s)$ and $\mathbf{r}_2(t)$ become elegant and simple. Note

that all vectors are two-dimensional in this section:

$$1: \qquad \mathbf{r}_1(s) = \mathbf{r}_2(t)$$
$$\Longleftrightarrow$$
$$2: \qquad \mathbf{o}_1 + s\mathbf{d}_1 = \mathbf{o}_2 + t\mathbf{d}_2$$
$$\Longleftrightarrow$$
$$3: \quad \begin{cases} s\mathbf{d}_1 \cdot \mathbf{d}_2^{\perp} = (\mathbf{o}_2 - \mathbf{o}_1) \cdot \mathbf{d}_2^{\perp} \\ t\mathbf{d}_2 \cdot \mathbf{d}_1^{\perp} = (\mathbf{o}_1 - \mathbf{o}_2) \cdot \mathbf{d}_1^{\perp} \end{cases} \qquad (22.28)$$
$$\Longleftrightarrow$$
$$4: \quad \begin{cases} s = \dfrac{(\mathbf{o}_2 - \mathbf{o}_1) \cdot \mathbf{d}_2^{\perp}}{\mathbf{d}_1 \cdot \mathbf{d}_2^{\perp}} \\[2ex] t = \dfrac{(\mathbf{o}_1 - \mathbf{o}_2) \cdot \mathbf{d}_1^{\perp}}{\mathbf{d}_2 \cdot \mathbf{d}_1^{\perp}} \end{cases}$$

If $\mathbf{d}_1 \cdot \mathbf{d}_2^{\perp} = 0$, then the lines are parallel and no intersection occurs. For lines of infinite length, all values of s and t are valid, but for line segments (with normalized directions), say of length l_1 and l_2 (starting at $s = 0$ and $t = 0$ and ending at $s = l_1$ and $t = l_2$), we have a valid intersection if and only if $0 \le s \le l_1$ and $0 \le t \le l_2$. Or, if you set $\mathbf{o}_1 = \mathbf{p}_1$ and $\mathbf{d}_1 = \mathbf{p}_2 - \mathbf{p}_1$ (meaning that the line segment starts at $\mathbf{p}_1$ and ends at $\mathbf{p}_2$) and do likewise for $\mathbf{r}_2$ with start and end points $\mathbf{q}_1$ and $\mathbf{q}_2$, then a valid intersection occurs if and only if $0 \le s \le 1$ and $0 \le t \le 1$. For rays with origins, the valid range is $s \ge 0$ and $t \ge 0$. The point of intersection is obtained either by plugging s into $\mathbf{r}_1$ or by plugging t into $\mathbf{r}_2$.

Second Method

Antonio [61] describes another way of deciding whether two line segments (i.e., of finite length) intersect by doing more compares and early rejections and by avoiding the expensive calculations (divisions) in the previous formulae. This method is therefore faster. The previous notation is used again, i.e., the first line segment goes from $\mathbf{p}_1$ to $\mathbf{p}_2$ and the second from $\mathbf{q}_1$ to $\mathbf{q}_2$. This means $\mathbf{r}_1(s) = \mathbf{p}_1 + s(\mathbf{p}_2 - \mathbf{p}_1)$ and $\mathbf{r}_2(t) = \mathbf{q}_1 + t(\mathbf{q}_2 - \mathbf{q}_1)$. The result from Equation 22.28 is used to obtain a solution to $\mathbf{r}_1(s) = \mathbf{r}_2(t)$:

$$\begin{cases} s = \dfrac{-\mathbf{c} \cdot \mathbf{a}^{\perp}}{\mathbf{b} \cdot \mathbf{a}^{\perp}} = \dfrac{\mathbf{c} \cdot \mathbf{a}^{\perp}}{\mathbf{a} \cdot \mathbf{b}^{\perp}} = \dfrac{d}{f}, \\[2ex] t = \dfrac{\mathbf{c} \cdot \mathbf{b}^{\perp}}{\mathbf{a} \cdot \mathbf{b}^{\perp}} = \dfrac{e}{f}. \end{cases} \qquad (22.29)$$

In Equation 22.29, $\mathbf{a} = \mathbf{q}_2 - \mathbf{q}_1$, $\mathbf{b} = \mathbf{p}_2 - \mathbf{p}_1$, $\mathbf{c} = \mathbf{p}_1 - \mathbf{q}_1$, $d = \mathbf{c} \cdot \mathbf{a}^{\perp}$, $e = \mathbf{c} \cdot \mathbf{b}^{\perp}$, and $f = \mathbf{a} \cdot \mathbf{b}^{\perp}$. The simplification step for the factor s comes from the fact that $\mathbf{a}^{\perp} \cdot \mathbf{b} = -\mathbf{b}^{\perp} \cdot \mathbf{a}$ and $\mathbf{a} \cdot \mathbf{b}^{\perp} = \mathbf{b}^{\perp} \cdot \mathbf{a}$. If $\mathbf{a} \cdot \mathbf{b}^{\perp} = 0$, then the lines are collinear. Antonio [61] observes that the denominators for both s and t are the same, and that, since s and t are not needed explicitly, the division operation can be omitted. Define $s = d/f$ and $t = e/f$. To test if $0 \le s \le 1$ the following code is used:

```
1 : if (f > 0)
2 :    if (d < 0 or d > f) return NO_INTERSECTION;
3 : else
4 :    if (d > 0 or d < f) return NO_INTERSECTION;
```

After this test, it is guaranteed that $0 \leq s \leq 1$. The same is then done for $t = e/f$ (by replacing d by e in the code). If the routine has not returned after this test, the line segments do intersect, since the t-value is then also valid.

Source code for an integer version of this routine is available on the web [61], and is easily converted for use with floating point numbers.

22.15.2 Three Dimensions

Say we want to compute in three dimensions the intersection between two lines (defined by rays, Equation 22.1). The lines are again called $\mathbf{r}_1(s) = \mathbf{o}_1 + s\mathbf{d}_1$ and $\mathbf{r}_2(t) = \mathbf{o}_2 + t\mathbf{d}_2$, with no limitation on the value of t. The three-dimensional counterpart of the perp dot product is, in this case, the cross product, since $\mathbf{a} \times \mathbf{a} = 0$, and therefore the derivation of the three-dimensional version is much like that of the two-dimensional version. The intersection between two lines is derived below:

$$1: \qquad \mathbf{r}_1(s) = \mathbf{r}_2(t)$$

$$\Longleftrightarrow$$

$$2: \qquad \mathbf{o}_1 + s\mathbf{d}_1 = \mathbf{o}_2 + t\mathbf{d}_2$$

$$\Longleftrightarrow$$

$$3: \qquad \begin{cases} s\mathbf{d}_1 \times \mathbf{d}_2 = (\mathbf{o}_2 - \mathbf{o}_1) \times \mathbf{d}_2 \\ t\mathbf{d}_2 \times \mathbf{d}_1 = (\mathbf{o}_1 - \mathbf{o}_2) \times \mathbf{d}_1 \end{cases}$$

$$\Longleftrightarrow$$

$$4: \qquad \begin{cases} s(\mathbf{d}_1 \times \mathbf{d}_2) \cdot (\mathbf{d}_1 \times \mathbf{d}_2) = \big((\mathbf{o}_2 - \mathbf{o}_1) \times \mathbf{d}_2\big) \cdot (\mathbf{d}_1 \times \mathbf{d}_2) \\ t(\mathbf{d}_2 \times \mathbf{d}_1) \cdot (\mathbf{d}_2 \times \mathbf{d}_1) = \big((\mathbf{o}_1 - \mathbf{o}_2) \times \mathbf{d}_1\big) \cdot (\mathbf{d}_2 \times \mathbf{d}_1) \end{cases} \qquad (22.30)$$

$$\Longleftrightarrow$$

$$5: \qquad \begin{cases} s = \dfrac{\det(\mathbf{o}_2 - \mathbf{o}_1, \mathbf{d}_2, \mathbf{d}_1 \times \mathbf{d}_2)}{||\mathbf{d}_1 \times \mathbf{d}_2||^2} \\[4mm] t = \dfrac{\det(\mathbf{o}_2 - \mathbf{o}_1, \mathbf{d}_1, \mathbf{d}_1 \times \mathbf{d}_2)}{||\mathbf{d}_1 \times \mathbf{d}_2||^2} \end{cases}$$

Step 3 comes from subtracting $\mathbf{o}_1$ ($\mathbf{o}_2$) from both sides and then crossing with $\mathbf{d}_2$ ($\mathbf{d}_1$), and Step 4 is obtained by dotting with $\mathbf{d}_1 \times \mathbf{d}_2$ ($\mathbf{d}_2 \times \mathbf{d}_1$). Finally, Step 5, the solution, is found by rewriting the right sides as determinants (and changing some signs in the bottom equation) and then by dividing by the term located to the right of s (t).

Goldman [548] notes that if the denominator $||\mathbf{d}_1 \times \mathbf{d}_2||^2$ equals 0, then the lines are parallel. He also observes that if the lines are skew (i.e., they do not share a common plane), then the s and t parameters represent the points of closest approach.

If the lines are to be treated like line segments, with lengths l_1 and l_2 (assuming the direction vectors $\mathbf{d}_1$ and $\mathbf{d}_2$ are normalized), then check whether $0 \leq s \leq l_1$ and $0 \leq t \leq l_2$ both hold. If not, then the intersection is rejected.

Rhodes [1490] gives an in-depth solution to the problem of intersecting two lines or line segments. He gives robust solutions that deal with special cases, and he discusses optimizations and provides source code.

22.16 Intersection between Three Planes

Given three planes, each described by a normalized normal vector, $\mathbf{n}_i$, and an arbitrary point on the plane, $\mathbf{p}_i$, $i = 1$, 2, and 3, the unique point, $\mathbf{p}$, of intersection between those planes is given by Equation 22.31 [549]. Note that the denominator, the determinant of the three plane normals, is zero if two or more planes are parallel:

$$\mathbf{p} = \frac{(\mathbf{p}_1 \cdot \mathbf{n}_1)(\mathbf{n}_2 \times \mathbf{n}_3) + (\mathbf{p}_2 \cdot \mathbf{n}_2)(\mathbf{n}_3 \times \mathbf{n}_1) + (\mathbf{p}_3 \cdot \mathbf{n}_3)(\mathbf{n}_1 \times \mathbf{n}_2)}{|\mathbf{n}_1 \ \mathbf{n}_2 \ \mathbf{n}_3|}. \tag{22.31}$$

This formula can be used to compute the corners of a BV consisting of a set of planes. An example is a k-DOP, which consists of k plane equations. Equation 22.31 can calculate the corners of the convex polyhedron if it is fed with the proper planes.

If, as is usual, the planes are given in implicit form, i.e., $\pi_i : \mathbf{n}_i \cdot \mathbf{x} + d_i = 0$, then we need to find the points $\mathbf{p}_i$ in order to be able to use the equation. Any arbitrary point on the plane can be chosen. We compute the point closest to the origin, since those calculations are inexpensive. Given a ray from the origin pointing along the plane's normal, intersect this with the plane to get the point closest to the origin:

$$\left. \begin{array}{c} \mathbf{r}_i(t) = t\mathbf{n}_i \\ \mathbf{n}_i \cdot \mathbf{x} + d_i = 0 \end{array} \right\} \Rightarrow$$

$$\mathbf{n}_i \cdot \mathbf{r}_i(t) + d_i = 0 \iff t\mathbf{n}_i \cdot \mathbf{n}_i + d_i = 0 \iff t = -d_i \tag{22.32}$$
$$\Rightarrow$$
$$\mathbf{p}_i = \mathbf{r}_i(-d_i) = -d_i\mathbf{n}_i.$$

This result should not come as a surprise, since d_i in the plane equation simply holds the perpendicular, negative distance from the origin to the plane (the normal must be of unit length if this is to be true).

Further Reading and Resources

Ericson's *Real-Time Collision Detection* [435] and Eberly's *3D Game Engine Design* [404] cover a wide variety of object/object intersection tests and hierarchy traversal methods, along with much else, and include source code. Schneider and Eberly's

Geometric Tools for Computer Graphics [1574] provides many practical algorithms for two- and three-dimensional geometric intersection testing. The open-access *Journal of Computer Graphics Techniques* publishes improved algorithms and code for intersection testing. The older *Practical Linear Algebra* [461] is a good source for two-dimensional intersection routines and many other geometric manipulations useful in computer graphics. The *Graphics Gems* series [72, 540, 695, 902, 1344] includes many different kinds of intersection routines, and code is available on the web. The free *Maxima* [1148] software is good for manipulating equations and deriving formulae. This book's website includes a page, realtimerendering.com/intersections.html, summarizing resources available for many object/object intersection tests.

Chapter 23
Graphics Hardware

"When we get the final hardware, the performance is just going to skyrocket."
—J. Allard

Although graphics hardware is evolving at a rapid pace, there are some general concepts and architectures that are commonly used in its design. Our goal in this chapter is to give an understanding of the various hardware elements of a graphics system and how they relate to one another. Other parts of the book discuss their use with particular algorithms. Here, we present hardware on its own terms. We begin by describing how to rasterize lines and triangles, which is followed by a presentation of how the massive compute capabilities of a GPU work and how tasks are scheduled, including dealing with latency and occupancy. We then discuss memory systems, caching, compression, color buffering, and everything related to the depth system in a GPU. Details about the texture system are then presented, followed by a section about architecture types for GPUs. Case studies of three different architectures are presented in Section 23.10, and finally, ray tracing architectures are briefly discussed.

23.1 Rasterization

An important feature of any GPU is its speed at drawing triangles and lines. As described in Section 2.4, rasterization consists of triangle setup and triangle traversal. In addition, we will describe how to interpolate attributes over a triangle, which is closely tied to triangle traversal. We end with conservative rasterization, which is an extension of standard rasterization.

Recall that the center of a pixel is given by $(x+0.5, y+0.5)$, where $x \in [0, W-1]$ and $y \in [0, H-1]$ are integers, and $W \times H$ is the screen resolution, e.g., 3840×2160. Let the non-transformed vertices be called $\mathbf{v}_i$, $i \in \{0, 1, 2\}$ and the transformed vertices, including projection but excluding division by w, be $\mathbf{q}_i = \mathbf{M}\mathbf{v}_i$. The two-dimensional screen-space coordinates are then $\mathbf{p}_i = \big((q_{ix}/q_{iw} + 1)W/2, (q_{iy}/q_{iw} + 1)H/2\big)$, i.e., the perspective divide by the w-component is performed and the value is scaled and translated to match screen resolution. This setup is illustrated in Figure 23.1. As can

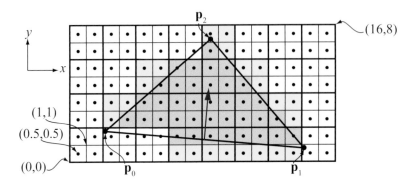

Figure 23.1. A triangle, with three two-dimensional vertices $\mathbf{p}_0$, $\mathbf{p}_1$, and $\mathbf{p}_2$ in screen space. The size of the screen is 16×8 pixels. Notice that the center of a pixel (x, y) is $(x + 0.5, y + 0.5)$. The normal vector (scaled in length by 0.25) for the bottom edge is shown in red. Only the green pixels are inside the triangle. Helper pixels, in yellow, belong to quads (2×2 pixels) where at least one pixel is considered inside, and where the helper pixel's sample point (center) is outside the triangle. Helper pixels are needed to compute derivatives using finite differences.

be seen, the pixel grid is divided into groups of 2×2 pixels, called quads. To be able to compute derivatives, which are needed for texture level of detail (Section 23.8), pixel shading is computed for all quads where at least one pixel is inside the triangle (also discussed in Section 3.8). This is a central design of most, if not all, GPUs and influences many of the following stages. The smaller the triangle, the greater the ratio of helper pixels to pixels inside the triangle. This relationship means that small triangles are expensive (in proportion to triangle area) when performing pixel shading. The worst scenario is a triangle covering a single pixel, which means that it needs three helper pixels. The number of helper pixels is sometimes referred to as *quad overshading*.

To determine whether a pixel center, or any other sample position, is inside a triangle, the hardware uses an *edge function* for each triangle edge [1417]. These are based on line equations, i.e.,

$$\mathbf{n} \cdot \big((x, y) - \mathbf{p}\big) = 0, \tag{23.1}$$

where $\mathbf{n}$ is a vector, sometimes called the normal of the edge, which is orthogonal to the edge, and $\mathbf{p}$ is a point on the line. Such equations can be rewritten as $ax + by + c = 0$. Next, we will derive the edge function $e_2(x, y)$ through $\mathbf{p}_0$ and $\mathbf{p}_1$. The edge vector is $\mathbf{p}_1 - \mathbf{p}_0$, and so the normal is that edge rotated 90 degrees counterclockwise, i.e., $\mathbf{n}_2 = (-(p_{1y} - p_{0y}), p_{1x} - p_{0x})$, which points to the inside of the triangle, as shown in Figure 23.1. By inserting $\mathbf{n}_2$ and $\mathbf{p}_0$ into Equation 23.1, $e_2(x, y)$ becomes

$$\begin{aligned}
e_2(x, y) &= -(p_{1y} - p_{0y})(x - p_{0x}) + (p_{1x} - p_{0x})(y - p_{0y}) \\
&= -(p_{1y} - p_{0y})x + (p_{1x} - p_{0x})y + (p_{1y} - p_{0y})p_{0x} - (p_{1x} - p_{0x})p_{0y} \\
&= a_2 x + b_2 y + c_2. \tag{23.2}
\end{aligned}$$

For points (x, y) exactly on an edge, we have $e(x, y) = 0$. Having the normal point to the inside of the triangle means that $e(x, y) > 0$ for points that are on the same side of the edge as the normal points. The edge divides the space into two parts and $e(x, y) > 0$ is sometimes called the positive half-space and $e(x, y) < 0$ is called the negative half-space. These properties can be exploited to determine whether a point is inside a triangle or not. Call the edges of the triangle e_i, $i \in \{0, 1, 2\}$. If a sample point (x, y) is inside the triangle or on the edges, then it must hold that $e_i(x, y) \geq 0$ for all i.

It is often required by the graphics API specification that the floating point vertex coordinates in screen space are converted to fixed-point coordinates. This is enforced in order to define tie-breaker rules (described later) in a consistent manner. It can also make the inside test for a sample more efficient. Both p_{ix} and p_{iy} can be stored in, for example, 1.14.8 bits, i.e., 1 sign bit, 14 bits for the integer coordinates, and 8 bits for the fractional position inside a pixel. In this case, this means that there can be 2^8 possible positions in both x and y inside a pixel, and the integer coordinates must be in the range of $[-(2^{14} - 1), 2^{14} - 1]$. In practice, this snapping is done before the edge equations are computed.

Another important feature of edge functions is their incremental property. Assume we have evaluated an edge function at a certain pixel center $(x, y) = (x_i + 0.5, y_i + 0.5)$, where (x_i, y_i) are integer pixel coordinates, i.e., we have evaluated $e(x, y) = ax + by + c$. To evaluate the pixel to the right, for example, we want to compute $e(x + 1, y)$, which can be rewritten as

$$e(x + 1, y) = a(x + 1) + by + c = a + ax + by + c = a + e(x, y), \qquad (23.3)$$

i.e., this is just the edge function evaluated at the current pixel, $e(x, y)$, plus a. Similar reasoning can be applied in the y-direction, and these properties are often exploited to quickly evaluate the three edge equations in a small *tile* of pixels, e.g., 8×8 pixels, to "stamp" out a coverage mask with one bit per pixel indicating whether the pixel is inside or not. This type of hierarchical traversal is explained a little later in this section.

It is important to consider what happens when an edge or vertex goes exactly through a pixel center. For example, assume that two triangles share an edge and this edge goes through a pixel center. Should it belong to the first triangle, the second, or even both? From an efficiency perspective, both is the wrong answer since the pixel would first be written to by one of the triangles and then overwritten by the other triangle. For this purpose, it is common to use a tie-breaker rule, and here we present the *top-left rule* used in DirectX. Pixels where $e_i(x, y) > 0$, for all $i \in \{0, 1, 2\}$, are always considered to be inside. The top-left rule comes into play when an edge goes through a pixel. The pixel is considered inside if its center lies on an edge that is either a top edge or a left edge. An edge is a top edge if it is horizontal and the other edges are below it. An edge is a left edge if it is non-horizontal and is on the left side of the triangle, which means that a triangle can have at most two left edges. It

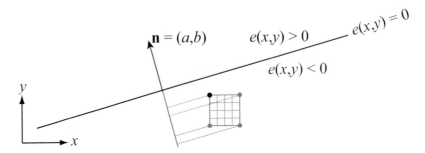

Figure 23.2. The negative half-space, $e(x,y) < 0$, of an edge function is always considered to be outside the triangle. Here, the corners of a 4×4 pixel tile are projected onto the edge's normal. Only the corner with the black circle needs to be tested against this edge, since its projection onto **n** is greatest. It then can be concluded that this tile is outside the triangle.

is simple to detect whether an edge is top or left. A top edge has $a = 0$ (horizontal) and $b < 0$, while a left edge has $a > 0$. The entire test to determine if a sample point (x, y) is inside a triangle is sometimes referred to as an *inside test*.

We have not yet explained how lines can be traversed. In general, a line can be rendered as an oblong, pixel-wide rectangle, which either can be composed of two triangles or an additional edge equation can be used for the rectangle. The advantage of such designs is that the same hardware for edge equations is used also for lines. Points are drawn as quadrilaterals.

To improve efficiency, it is common to perform triangle traversal in a hierarchical manner [1162]. Typically, the hardware computes the bounding box of the screen-space vertices, and then determines which tiles are inside the bounding box and also overlap with the triangle. Determining whether a tile is outside an edge can be done with a technique that is a two-dimensional version of the AABB/plane test from Section 22.10.1. The general principle is shown in Figure 23.2. To adapt this to tiled triangle traversal, one can first determine which tile corner should be tested against an edge before traversal starts [24]. The tile corner to use is the same for all tiles for a particular edge, since the closest tile corner only depends on the edge normal. The edge equations are evaluated for these predetermined corners, and if this selected corner is outside its edge, then the entire tile is outside and the hardware does not need to perform any per-pixel inside tests in that tile. To move to a neighboring tile, the incremental property described above can be used per tile. For example, to move horizontally by 8 pixels to the right, one needs to add $8a$.

With a tile/edge intersection test in place, it is possible to hierarchically traverse a triangle. This is shown in Figure 23.3. The tiles need to be traversed in some order as well, and this can be done in zigzag order or using some space-filling curve [1159], both of which tend to increase coherency. Additional levels in the hierarchical traversal can be added if needed. For example, one can first visit 16×16 tiles, and for each such tile that is overlapping the triangle, 4×4 subtiles are then tested [1599].

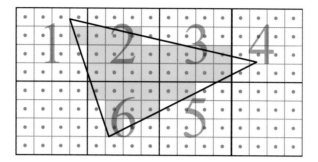

Figure 23.3. A possible traversal order when using tiled traversal with 4 × 4 pixel tiles. Traversal starts at the top left in this example, and continues to the right. Each of the top tiles overlap with the triangle, though the top right tile has no pixels it. Traversal continues to the tile directly below, which is completely outside, and so no per-pixel inside tests are needed there. Traversal then continues to the left, and the following two tiles are found to overlap the triangle, while the bottom left tile does not.

The main advantage of tiled traversal over, say, traversing the triangle in scanline order, is that pixels are processed in a more coherent manner, and as a consequence, texels also are visited more coherently. It also has the benefit of exploiting locality better when accessing color and depth buffers. Consider, for example, a large triangle being traversed in scanline order. Texels are cached, so that the most recently accessed texels remain in the cache for reuse. Assume that mipmapping is used for texturing, which increases the level of reuse from the texels in the cache. If we access pixels in scanline order, the texels used at the beginning of the scanline are likely already evicted from the cache when the end of the scanline is reached. Since it is more efficient to reuse texels in the cache, versus fetching them from memory repeatedly, triangles are often traversed in tiles [651, 1162]. This gives a great benefit for texturing [651], depth buffering [679], and color buffering [1463]. In fact, textures and depth and color buffers are also stored in tiles much for the same reasons. This will be discussed further in Section 23.4.

Before triangle traversal starts, GPUs typically have a triangle setup stage. The purpose of this stage is to compute factors that are constant over the triangle so that traversal can proceed efficiently. For example, the edge equations' (Equation 23.2) constants a_i, b_i, c_i, $i \in \{0, 1, 2\}$, of a triangle are computed here once and then used in the entire traversal step for the current triangle. Triangle setup is also responsible for computing constants related to attribute interpolation (Section 23.1.1). As the discussion continues, we will also discover other constants than can be computed once in the triangle setup.

By necessity, clipping is done before triangle setup since clipping may generate more triangles. Clipping a triangle against the view volume in clip space is an expensive process, and so GPUs avoid doing this if not absolutely necessary. Clipping against the near plane is always needed, and this can generate either one or two trian-

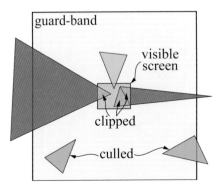

Figure 23.4. Guard-bands to attempt to avoid full clipping. Assume that the guard-band region is $\pm 16K$ pixels in both x and y. The screen in the middle is then approximately 6500×4900 pixels, which indicates that these triangles are huge. The two green triangles at the bottom are culled either as part of triangle setup or in previous steps. The common case is the blue triangle in the middle, which intersects the screen area and is fully inside the guard-band. No full clipping operation is needed, since just the visible tiles are processed. The red triangles are outside the guard band and intersect the screen area, and so these need clipping. Note that the red triangle to the right is clipped into two triangles.

gles. For the edges of the screen, most GPUs then use *guard-band clipping*, a simpler scheme that avoids the more complex full clip process. The algorithm is visualized in Figure 23.4.

23.1.1   Interpolation

In Section 22.8.1, barycentric coordinates were generated as a byproduct of computing the intersection of a ray and a triangle. Any per-vertex attribute, a_i, $i \in \{0, 1, 2\}$, can be interpolated using the barycentric coordinates (u, v) as

$$a(u, v) = (1 - u - v)a_0 + ua_1 + va_2, \qquad (23.4)$$

where $a(u, v)$ is the interpolated attribute at (u, v) over the triangle. The definitions of the barycentric coordinates are

$$u = \frac{A_1}{A_0 + A_1 + A_2}, \quad v = \frac{A_2}{A_0 + A_1 + A_2}, \qquad (23.5)$$

where A_i are the areas of the subtriangles shown on the left in Figure 23.5. The third coordinate $w = A_0/(A_0 + A_1 + A_2)$ is part of the definition as well, which shows that $u + v + w = 1$, i.e., $w = 1 - u - v$. We use the term $1 - u - v$ here instead of w.

The edge equation in Equation 23.2 can be expressed using the normal of the edge, $\mathbf{n}_2 = (a_2, b_2)$, as

$$e_2(x, y) = e_2(\mathbf{p}) = \mathbf{n}_2 \cdot \big((x, y) - \mathbf{p}_0\big) = \mathbf{n}_2 \cdot (\mathbf{p} - \mathbf{p}_0), \qquad (23.6)$$

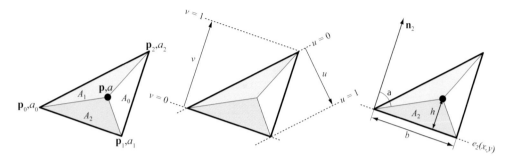

Figure 23.5. Left: a triangle with scalar attributes (a_0, a_1, a_2) at the vertices. The barycentric coordinates at the point $\mathbf{p}$ are proportional to the signed areas (A_1, A_2, A_0). Middle: illustration of how the barycentric coordinates (u, v) change over the triangle. Right: the length of the normal $\mathbf{n}_2$ is the edge $\mathbf{p}_0\mathbf{p}_1$ rotated 90 degrees counterclockwise. The area A_2 is then $bh/2$.

where $\mathbf{p} = (x, y)$. From the definition of the dot product, this can be rewritten as

$$e_2(\mathbf{p}) = ||\mathbf{n}_2|| \, ||\mathbf{p} - \mathbf{p}_0|| \cos \alpha, \qquad (23.7)$$

where α is the angle between $\mathbf{n}_2$ and $\mathbf{p} - \mathbf{p}_0$. Note that $b = ||\mathbf{n}_2||$ is equal to the length of the edge $\mathbf{p}^0\mathbf{p}^1$, since $\mathbf{n}_2$ is the edge rotated 90 degrees. The geometric interpretation of the second term, $||\mathbf{p} - \mathbf{p}_0|| \cos \alpha$, is the length of the vector obtained when projecting $\mathbf{p} - \mathbf{p}_0$ onto $\mathbf{n}_2$, and that length is exactly the height, h, of the subtriangle whose area is A_2. This is shown on the right in Figure 23.5. Noteworthy, then, we have $e_2(\mathbf{p}) = ||\mathbf{n}_2|| \, ||\mathbf{p} - \mathbf{p}_0|| \cos \alpha = bh = 2A_2$, which is excellent since we need the areas of the subtriangles in order to compute the barycentric coordinates. This means that

$$\bigl(u(x, y), v(x, y)\bigr) = \frac{(A_1, A_2)}{A_0 + A_1 + A_2} = \frac{\bigl(e_1(x, y), e_2(x, y)\bigr)}{e_0(x, y) + e_1(x, y) + e_2(x, y)}. \qquad (23.8)$$

The triangle setup often computes $1/(A_0 + A_1 + A_2)$ since the area of the triangle does not change, which also avoids the division for each pixel. So, when we traverse a triangle using the edge equations, we get all terms of Equation 23.8 as a byproduct of the inside tests. These are useful when interpolating depth, as we will see, or for orthogonal projections, but for perspective projection, barycentric coordinates do not generate the expected results, as illustrated in Figure 23.6.

Perspective-correct barycentric coordinates require a division per pixel [163, 694]. The derivation [26, 1317] is omitted here, and instead we summarize the most important results. Since linear interpolation is inexpensive, and we know how to compute (u, v), we would like to use linear interpolation in screen space as much as possible, even for perspective correction. Somewhat surprisingly, it turns out that it is possible to linearly interpolate both a/w and $1/w$ over the triangle, where w is the fourth component of a vertex after all transforms. Recovering the interpolated attribute, a,

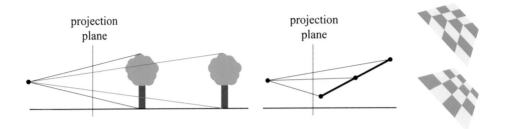

Figure 23.6. Left: in perspective, the projected image of geometry shrinks with distance. Middle: an edge-on triangle projection. Note how the upper half of the triangle covers a smaller portion on the projection plane than the lower half. Right: a quadrilateral with a checkerboard texture. The top image was rendered using barycentric coordinates for texturing, while the bottom image used perspective-correct barycentric coordinates.

is a matter of using these two interpolated values,

$$\frac{\overbrace{a/w}^{\text{linearly interpolated}}}{\underbrace{1/w}_{\text{linearly interpolated}}} = \frac{aw}{w} = a. \tag{23.9}$$

This is the per-pixel division that was mentioned earlier.

A concrete example shows the effect. Say we interpolate along a horizontal triangle edge, with $a_0 = 4$ at the left end and $a_1 = 6$ at the right. What is the value for the midpoint between these two endpoints? For orthographic projection (or when the w values at the endpoints match), the answer is simply $a = 5$, the value halfway between a_0 and a_1.

Say instead that the w values for the endpoints are $w_0 = 1$ and $w_1 = 3$. In this case we need to interpolate twice, to get a/w and $1/w$. For a/w, the left endpoint is $4/1 = 4$ and the right is $6/3 = 2$, so the midpoint value is 3. For $1/w$ we have $1/1$ and $1/3$, so the midpoint is $2/3$. Dividing 3 by $2/3$ gives us $a = 4.5$ for the perspective midpoint value.

In practice, we often need to interpolate several attributes using perspective correction over a triangle. Therefore, it is common to compute perspective-correct barycentric coordinates, which we denote $(\tilde{u}, \tilde{v})$, and then use these for all attribute interpolation. To this end, we introduce the following helper functions [26]:

$$f_0(x, y) = \frac{e_0(x, y)}{w_0}, \quad f_1(x, y) = \frac{e_1(x, y)}{w_1}, \quad f_2(x, y) = \frac{e_2(x, y)}{w_2}. \tag{23.10}$$

Note that since $e_0(x, y) = a_0 x + b_0 y + c_0$, the triangle setup can compute and store a_0/w_0 and other similar terms to make evaluation per pixel faster. Alternatively, all

f_i-functions can be multiplied by $w_0 w_1 w_2$; e.g., we store $w_1 w_2 f_0(x,y)$, $w_0 w_2 f_1(x,y)$, and $w_0 w_1 f_2(x,y)$ [1159]. The perspective-correct barycentric coordinates are

$$\big(\tilde{u}(x,y), \tilde{v}(x,y)\big) = \frac{\big(f_1(x,y), f_2(x,y)\big)}{f_0(x,y) + f_1(x,y) + f_2(x,y)}, \tag{23.11}$$

which need to be computed once per pixel and can then be used to interpolate any attribute with correct perspective foreshortening. Note that these coordinates are not proportional to the areas of the subtriangles as is the case for (u,v). In addition, the denominator is not constant, as is the case for barycentric coordinates, which is the reason why this division must be performed per pixel.

Finally, note that since depth is z/w, we can see in Equation 23.10 that we should not use those equations since they already are divided by w. Hence, z_i/w_i should be computed per vertex, and then linearly interpolated using (u,v). This has several advantages, e.g., for compression of depth buffers (Section 23.7).

23.1.2 Conservative Rasterization

From DirectX 11 and through using extensions in OpenGL, a new type of triangle traversal called *conservative rasterization* (CR) is available. CR comes in two types called overestimated CR (OCR) and underestimated CR (UCR). Sometimes they are also called outer-conservative rasterization and inner-conservative rasterization. These are illustrated in Figure 23.7.

Loosely speaking, all pixels that overlap or are inside a triangle are visited with OCR and only pixels that are fully inside the triangle are visited with UCR. Both OCR and UCR can be implemented using tiled traversal by shrinking the tile size to one pixel [24]. When no support is available in hardware, one can implement OCR using the geometry shader or using triangle expansion [676]. For more information about CR, we refer to the specifications of the respective API. CR can be useful for collision detection in image space, occlusion culling, shadow computations [1930], and antialiasing, among other algorithms.

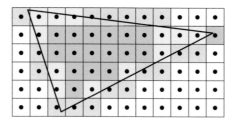

Figure 23.7. Conservative rasterization of a triangle. All colored pixels belong to the triangle when using outer-conservative rasterization. The yellow and green pixels are inside the triangle using standard rasterization, and only the green pixels are generated using inner-conservative rasterization.

Finally, we note that all types of rasterization act as a bridge between geometry and pixel processing. To compute the final locations of the triangle vertices and to compute the final color of the pixels, a massive amount of flexible compute power is needed in the GPU. This is explained next.

23.2   Massive Compute and Scheduling

To provide an enormous amount of compute power that can be used for arbitrary computations, most, if not all, GPU architectures employ unified shader architectures using SIMD-processing with multiple threads, sometimes called SIMT-processing or hyperthreading. See Section 3.10 for a refresher on the terms thread, SIMD-processing, warps, and thread groups. Note that we use the term warp, which is NVIDIA terminology, but on AMD hardware these are instead called waves or wavefronts. In this section, we will first look at a typical unified *arithmetic logic unit* (ALU) used in GPUs.

An ALU is a piece of hardware optimized for executing a program for one entity, e.g., a vertex or fragment, in this context. Sometimes we use the term *SIMD lane* instead of ALU. A typical ALU for a GPU is visualized on the left in Figure 23.8. The main compute units are a floating point (FP) unit and an integer unit. FP units typically adhere to the IEEE 754 FP standard and support a fused-multiply and add (FMA) instruction as one of its most complex instructions. An ALU typically also contains move/compare and load/store capabilities and a branch unit, in addition to transcendental operations, such as cosine, sine, and exponential. It should be noted, however, that some of these may be located in separate hardware units on some architectures, e.g., a small set of, say, transcendental hardware units may operate to

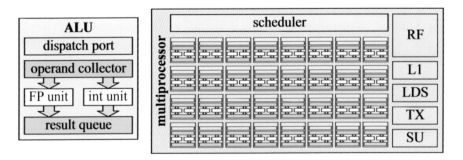

Figure 23.8. Left: an example of an arithmetic logic unit built for execution of one item at a time. The dispatch port receives information about the current instruction to be executed and the operand collector reads the registers required by the instruction. Right: here, 8 × 4 ALUs have been assembled together with several other hardware units into a block called a multiprocessor. The 32 ALUs, sometimes called SIMD lanes, would execute the same program in lock-step, i.e., they constitute a SIMD engine. There is also a register file, an L1 cache, local data storage, texture units, and special units for various instructions not handled in the ALUs.

serve a larger number of ALUs. This could be the case for operations that are not executed as often as others. These are grouped together in the special unit (SU) block, shown on the right in Figure 23.8. The ALU architecture is usually built using a few hardware pipeline stages, i.e., there are several actual blocks built in silicon that are executed in parallel. For example, while the current instruction performs a multiplication, the next instruction can fetch registers. With n pipeline stages, the throughput can be increased by factor of n, ideally. This is often called *pipeline parallelism*. Another important reason to pipeline is that the slowest hardware block in a pipelined processor dictates the maximum clock frequency in which the block can be executed. Increasing the number of pipeline stages makes the number of hardware blocks per pipeline stage smaller, which usually makes it possible to increase the clock frequency. However, to simplify the design, an ALU usually has few pipeline stages, e.g., 4–10.

The unified ALU is different from a CPU core in that it does not have many of the bells and whistles, such as branch prediction, register renaming, and deep instruction pipelining. Instead, much of the chip area is spent on duplicating the ALUs to provide massive compute power and on increased register file size, so that warps can be switched in and out. For example, the NVIDIA GTX 1080 Ti has 3584 ALUs. For efficient scheduling of the work that is issued to the GPU, most GPUs group ALUs in numbers of, say, 32. They are executed in lock-step, which means that the entire set of 32 ALUs is a SIMD engine. Different vendors use different names for such a group together with additional hardware units, and we use the general term *multiprocessor* (MP). For example, NVIDIA uses the term streaming multiprocessor, Intel uses execution unit, and AMD uses compute unit. An example of an MP is shown on the right in Figure 23.8. An MP typically has a scheduler that dispatches work to the SIMD engine(s), and there is also an L1 cache, local data storage (LDS), texture units (TX), and a special unit for handling instructions not executed in the ALUs. An MP dispatches instructions onto the ALUs, where the instructions are executed in lock-step, i.e., SIMD-processing (Section 3.10). Note that the exact content of an MP varies from vendor to vendor and from one architecture generation to the next.

SIMD-processing makes sense for graphics workloads since there are many of the same, e.g., vertices and fragments, that execute the same program. Here, the architecture exploits *thread-level parallelism*, i.e., the fact that vertices and fragments, say, can execute their shaders independent of other vertices and fragments. Furthermore, with any type of SIMD/SIMT-processing, *data-level parallelism* is exploited since an instruction is executed for all the lanes in the SIMD machine. There is also *instruction-level parallelism*, which means that if the processor can find instructions that are independent of each other, they can be executed at the same time, given that there are resources that can execute in parallel.

Close to an MP is a (warp) scheduler that receives large chunks of work that are to be executed on that MP. The task of the warp scheduler is to assign the work in warps to the MP, allocate registers in the register file (RF) to the threads in the warp, and then prioritize the work in the best possible way. Usually, downstream work has higher priority than upstream work. For example, pixel shading is at the end of the programmable stages and has higher priority than vertex shading, which is earlier in the pipeline. This avoids stalling, since stages toward the end are less likely to block earlier stages. See Figure 3.2 on page 34 for a refresher on the graphics pipeline diagram. An MP can handle hundreds or even thousands of threads in order to hide latency of, for example, memory accesses. The scheduler can switch out the warp currently executing (or waiting) on the MP for a warp that is ready for execution. Since the scheduler is implemented in dedicated hardware, this can often be done with zero overhead [1050]. For instance, if the current warp executes a texture load instruction, which is expected to have long latency, the scheduler can immediately switch out the current warp, replace it with another, and continue execution for that warp instead. In this way, the compute units are better utilized.

Note that for pixel shading work, the warp scheduler dispatches several full quads, since pixels are shaded at quad granularity in order to compute derivatives. This was mentioned in Section 23.1 and will be discussed further in Section 23.8. So, if the size of a warp is 32, then $32/4 = 8$ quads can be scheduled for execution. There is an architectural design choice here, where one can choose to lock an entire warp to a single triangle, or to have the possibility of letting each quad in a warp belong to a different triangle. The former is simpler to implement, but for smaller triangles, efficiency suffers. The latter is more complex, but is more efficient for smaller triangles.

In general, MPs are also duplicated to obtain higher compute density on the chip, and as a result, a GPU usually has a higher-level scheduler as well. Its task is then to assign work to the different warp schedulers based on work that is submitted to the GPU. Having many threads in a warp generally also means that the work for a thread needs to be independent of the work of other threads. This is, of course, often the case in graphics processing. For example, shading a vertex does not generally depend on other vertices, and the color of a fragment is generally not dependent on other fragments.

Note that there are many differences between architectures. Some of these will be highlighted in Section 23.10, where a few different case studies are presented. At this point, we know how rasterization is done and how shading can be computed using many duplicated unified ALUs. A large remaining piece is the memory system, all the related buffers, and texturing. These are the topics of the following sections starting at Section 23.4, but first we present some more information about latency and occupancy.

23.3 Latency and Occupancy

In general, the latency is the time between making a query and receiving its result. As an example, one may ask for the value at a certain address in memory, and the time it takes from the query to getting the result is the latency. Another example is to request a filtered color from a texture unit, which may take hundreds or possibly even thousands of clock cycles from the time of the request until the value is available. This latency needs to be hidden for efficient usage of the compute resources in a GPU. If these latencies are not hidden, memory accesses can easily dominate execution times.

One hiding mechanism for this is the multithreading part of SIMD-processing, which is illustrated in Figure 3.1 on page 33. In general, there is a maximum number of warps that an MP can handle. The number of *active* warps depends on register usage and may also depend on usage of texture samplers, L1 caching, interpolants, and other factors. Here, we define the *occupancy*, *o*, as

$$o = \frac{w_{\text{active}}}{w_{\text{max}}}, \tag{23.12}$$

where w_{max} is the maximum number of warps allowed on an MP and w_{active} is the number of currently active warps. That is, o is a measure of how well the compute resources are kept in use. As an example, assume that $w_{\text{max}} = 32$, that a shader processor has 256 kB registers, and that one shader program for a single thread uses 27 32-bit floating point registers and another uses 150. Furthermore, we assume that register usage is what dictates the number of active warps. Assuming that SIMD width is 32, we can compute the active number of warps for these two cases respectively as

$$w_{\text{active}} = \frac{256 \cdot 1024}{27 \cdot 4 \cdot 32} \approx 75.85, \quad w_{\text{active}} = \frac{256 \cdot 1024}{150 \cdot 4 \cdot 32} \approx 13.65. \tag{23.13}$$

In the first case, i.e., for the short program using 27 registers, $w_{\text{active}} > 32$, so the occupancy is $o = 1$, which is ideal and therefore bodes well for hiding latency. However, in the second case, $w_{\text{active}} \approx 13.65$, so $o \approx 13.65/32 \approx 0.43$. Since there are fewer active warps, the occupancy is lower, which may hinder latency hiding. Hence, it is important to design an architecture with a well-balanced number of maximum warps, maximum registers, and other shared resources.

Sometimes a too high occupancy can be counter-productive in that it may thrash the caches if your shaders use many memory accesses [1914]. Another hiding mechanism is to continue executing the same warp after a memory request, which is possible if there are instructions that are independent of the result from the memory access. While this uses more registers, it can sometimes be more efficient to have low occupancy [1914]. An example is loop unrolling, which opens up for more possibilities for instruction-level parallelism, because longer independent instruction chains are often generated, which makes it possible to execute longer before switching warps. However, this would also use more temporary registers. A general rule is to strive after higher occupancy. Low occupancy means that it is less likely to be possible to switch to another warp when a shader requests texture access, for example.

A different type of latency is that from reading back data from the GPU to CPU. A good mental model is to think of the GPU and CPU as separate computers working asynchronously, with communication between the two taking some effort. Latency from changing the direction of the flow of information can seriously hurt performance. When data are read back from the GPU, the pipeline may have to be flushed before the read. During this time, the CPU is waiting for the GPU to finish its work. For architectures, such as Intel's GEN architecture [844], where the GPU and CPU are on the same chip and use a shared memory model, this type of latency is greatly reduced. The lower-level caches are shared between the CPU and the GPU, while the higher-level caches are not. The reduced latency of the shared caches allows different types of optimization and other kinds of algorithms. For example, this feature has been used to speed up ray tracing, where rays are communicated back and forth between the graphics processor and the CPU cores at no cost [110].

An example of a read-back mechanism that does not produce a CPU stall is the occlusion query. See Section 19.7.1. For occlusion testing, the mechanism is to perform the query and then occasionally check the GPU to see if the results of the query are available. While waiting for the results, other work can then be done on both the CPU and GPU.

23.4 Memory Architecture and Buses

Here, we will introduce some terminology, discuss a few different types of memory architectures, and then present compression and caching.

A *port* is a channel for sending data between two devices, and a *bus* is a shared channel for sending data among more than two devices. *Bandwidth* is the term used to describe throughput of data over the port or bus, and is measured in bytes per second, B/s. Ports and buses are important in computer graphics architecture because, simply put, they glue together different building blocks. Also important is that bandwidth is a scarce resource, and so a careful design and analysis must be done before building a graphics system. Since ports and buses both provide data transfer capabilities, ports are often referred to as buses, a convention we will follow here.

For many GPUs, it is common to have exclusive GPU memory on the graphics accelerator, and this memory is often called *video memory*. Access to this memory is usually much faster than letting the GPU access system memory over a bus, such as, for example, PCI Express (PCIe), used in PCs. Sixteen-lane PCIe v3 can provide 15.75 GB/s in both directions and PCIe v4 can provide 31.51 GB/s. However, the video memory of the Pascal architecture for graphics (GTX 1080) provides 320 GB/s.

Traditionally, textures and render targets are stored in video memory, but it can serve to store other data as well. Many objects in a scene do not appreciably change shape from frame to frame. Even a human character is typically rendered with a set of unchanging meshes that use GPU-side vertex blending at the joints. For this type of data, animated purely by modeling matrices and vertex shader programs, it is common to use *static* vertex and index buffers, which are placed in video memory. Doing so makes for fast access by the GPU. For vertices that are updated by the CPU each frame, *dynamic* vertex and index buffers are used, and these are placed in system memory that can be accessed over a bus, such as PCI Express. One nice property of PCIe is that queries can be pipelined, so that several queries can be requested before results return.

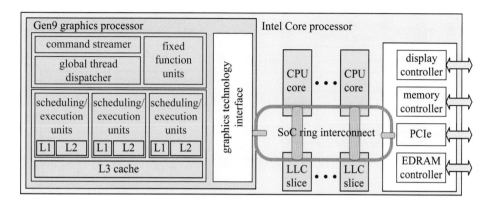

Figure 23.9. A simplified view of the memory architecture of Intel's system-on-a-chip (SoC) Gen9 graphics architecture connected with CPU cores and a shared memory model. Note that the last-level caches (LLCs) are shared between both the graphics processor and the CPU cores. (*Illustration after Junkins [844].*)

Most game consoles, e.g., all Xboxes and the PLAYSTATION 4, use a *unified memory architecture* (UMA), which means that the graphics accelerator can use any part of the host memory for textures and different kinds of buffers [889]. Both the CPU and the graphics accelerator use the same memory, and thus also the same bus. This is clearly different from using dedicated video memory. Intel also uses UMA so that memory is shared between the CPU cores and the GEN9 graphics architecture [844], which is illustrated in Figure 23.9. However, not all caches are shared. The graphics processor has its own set of L1 caches, L2 caches, and an L3 cache. The last-level cache is the first shared resource in the memory hierarchy. For any computer or graphics architecture, it is important to have a cache hierarchy. Doing so decreases the average access time to memory, if there is some kind of locality in the accesses. In the following section we discuss caching and compression for GPUs.

23.5 Caching and Compression

Caches are located in several different parts of each GPU, but they differ from architecture to architecture, as we will see in Section 23.10. In general, the goal of adding a cache hierarchy to an architecture is to reduce memory latency and bandwidth usage by exploiting locality of memory access patterns. That is, if the GPU accesses one item, it is likely that it will access this same or a nearby item soon thereafter [715]. Most buffers and texture formats are stored in tiled formats, which also helps increase locality [651]. Say that a cache line consists of 512 bits, i.e., 64 bytes, and that the currently used color format uses 4 B per pixel. One design choice would then be to store all the pixels inside a 4×4 region, also called a tile, in 64 B. That is, the entire color buffer would be split into 4×4 tiles. A tile may also span several cache lines.

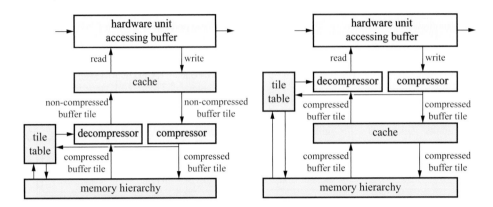

Figure 23.10. Block diagrams of hardware techniques for compression and caching of render targets in a GPU. Left: post-cache compression, where the compressor/decompressor hardware units are located after (below) the cache. Right: pre-cache compression, where the compressor/decompressor hardware units are located before (above) the cache.

To obtain an efficient GPU architecture, one needs to work on all fronts to reduce bandwidth usage. Most GPUs contain hardware units that compress and decompress render targets on the fly, e.g., as images are being rendered. It is important to realize that these types of compression algorithms are lossless; that is, it is always possible to reproduce the original data exactly. Central to these algorithms is what we call the *tile table*, which has additional information stored for each tile. This can be stored on chip or accessed through a cache via the memory hierarchy. Block diagrams for these two types of systems are shown in Figure 23.10. In general, the same setup can be used for depth, color, and stencil compression, sometimes with some modifications. Each element in the tile table stores the state of a tile of pixels in the framebuffer. The state of each tile can be either compressed, uncompressed, or cleared (discussed next). In general there could also be different types of compressed blocks. For example, one compressed mode might compress down to 25% and another to 50%. It is important to realize that the levels of compression depend on the size of the memory transfers that the GPU can handle. Say the smallest memory transfer is 32 B in a particular architecture. If the tile size is chosen to be 64 B, then it would only be possible to compress to 50%. However, with a tile size of 128 B, one can compress to 75% (96 B), 50% (64 B), and 25% (32 B).

The tile table is often also used to implement fast clearing of the render target. When the system issues a clear of the render target, the state of each tile in the table is set to *cleared*, and the framebuffer proper is not touched. When the hardware unit accessing the render target needs to read the cleared render target, the *decompressor* unit first checks the state in the table to see if the tile is cleared. If so, the render target tile is placed in the cache with all values set to the clear value, without any need to read and decompress the actual render target data. In this way, access to the render target itself is minimized during clears, which saves bandwidth. If the state is not cleared, then the render target for that tile has to be read. The tile's stored data are read and, if compressed, passed through the decompressor before being sent on.

When the hardware unit accessing the render target has finished writing new values, and the tile is eventually evicted from the cache, it is sent to the *compressor*, where an attempt is made at compressing it. If there are two compression modes, both could be tried, and the one that can compress that tile with fewest bits is used. Since the APIs require lossless render target compression, a fallback to using uncompressed data is needed if all compression techniques fail. This also implies that lossless render target compression never can reduce memory usage in the actual render target—such techniques only reduce memory bandwidth usage. If compression succeeds, the tile's state is set to *compressed* and the information is sent in a compressed form. Otherwise, it is sent uncompressed and the state is set to *uncompressed*.

Note that the compressor and decompressor units can be either after (called *post-cache*) or before (*pre-cache*) the cache, as shown in Figure 23.10. Pre-cache compression can increase the effective cache size substantially, but it usually also increases the complexity of the system [681] There are specific algorithms for compressing depth [679, 1238, 1427] and color [1427, 1463, 1464, 1716]. The latter include research on lossy compression, which, however, is not available in any hardware we know of [1463]. Most of the algorithms encode an anchor value, which represents all the pixels in a tile, and then the differences are encoded in different ways with respect to that anchor value. For depth, it is common to store a set of plane equations [679] or use a difference-of-differences technique [1238], which both give good results since depth is linear in screen space.

23.6 Color Buffering

Rendering using the GPU involves accessing several different buffers, for example, color, depth, and stencil buffers. Note that, though it is called a "color" buffer, any sort of data can be rendered and stored in it.

The color buffer usually has a few color modes, based on the number of bytes representing the color. These modes include:

- High color—2 bytes per pixel, of which 15 or 16 bits are used for the color, giving 32,768 or 65,536 colors, respectively.

- True color or RGB color—3 or 4 bytes per pixel, of which 24 bits are used for the color, giving $16,777,216 \approx 16.8$ million different colors.

- Deep color—30, 36, or 48 bits per pixel, giving at least a billion different colors.

The high color mode has 16 bits of color resolution to use. Typically, this amount is split into at least 5 bits each for red, green, and blue, giving 32 levels per color channel.

Figure 23.11. As the rectangle is shaded from white to black, banding appears. Although each of the 32 grayscale bars has a solid intensity level, each can appear to be darker on the left and lighter on the right due to the Mach band illusion.

This leaves one bit, which is usually given to the green channel, resulting in a 5-6-5 division. The green channel is chosen because it has the largest luminance effect on the eye, and so requires greater precision. High color has a speed advantage over true and deep color. This is because 2 bytes of memory per pixel may usually be accessed more quickly than three or more bytes per pixel. That said, the use of high color mode is quite rare to non-existent at this point. Differences in adjacent color levels are easily discernible with only 32 or 64 levels of color in each channel. This problem is sometimes called *banding* or *posterization*. The human visual system further magnifies these differences due to a perceptual phenomenon called *Mach banding* [543, 653]. See Figure 23.11. Dithering [102, 539, 1081], where adjacent levels are intermingled, can lessen the effect by trading spatial resolution for increased effective color resolution. Banding on gradients can be noticeable even on 24-bit monitors. Adding noise to the framebuffer image can be used to mask this problem [1823].

True color uses 24 bits of RGB color, 1 byte per color channel. On PC systems, the ordering is sometimes reversed to BGR. Internally, these colors are often stored using 32 bits per pixel, because most memory systems are optimized for accessing 4-byte elements. On some systems the extra 8 bits can also be used to store an alpha channel, giving the pixel an RGBA value. The 24-bit color (no alpha) representation is also called the *packed pixel format*, which can save framebuffer memory in comparison to its 32-bit, unpacked counterpart. Using 24 bits of color is almost always acceptable for real-time rendering. It is still possible to see banding of colors, but much less likely than with only 16 bits.

Deep color uses 30, 36, or 48 bits per color for RGB, i.e., 10, 12, or 16 bits per channel. If alpha is added, these numbers increase to 40/48/64. HDMI 1.3 on supports all 30/36/48 modes, and the DisplayPort standard also has support for up to 16 bits per channel.

Color buffers are often compressed and cached as described in Section 23.5. In addition, blending incoming fragment data with the color buffers is further described in each of the case studies in Section 23.10. Blending is handled by raster operation (ROP) units, and each ROP is usually connected to a memory partition, using, for example, a generalized checkerboard pattern [1160]. We next will discuss the video display controller, which takes a color buffer and makes it appear on the display. Single, double, and triple buffering are then examined.

23.6.1 Video Display Controller

In each GPU, there is a *video display controller* (VDC), also called a *display engine* or *display interface*, which is responsible for making a color buffer appear on the display. This is a hardware unit in the GPU, which may support a variety of interfaces, such as high-definition multimedia interface (HDMI), DisplayPort, digital visual interface (DVI), and video graphics array (VGA). The color buffer to be displayed may be located in the same memory as the CPU uses for its tasks, in dedicated frame-buffer memory, or in video memory, where the latter can contain any GPU data but is not directly accessible to the CPU. Each of the interfaces uses its standard's protocol to transfer parts of the color buffer, timing information, and sometimes even audio. The VDC may also perform image scaling, noise reduction, composition of several image sources, and other functions.

The rate at which a display, e.g., an LCD, updates the image is typically between 60 and 144 times per second (Hertz). This is also called the *vertical refresh rate*. Most viewers notice flicker at rates less than 72 Hz. See Section 12.5 for more information on this topic.

Monitor technology has advanced on several fronts, including refresh rate, bits per component, gamut, and sync. The refresh rate used to be 60 Hz, but 120 Hz is becoming more common, and up to 600 Hz is possible. For high refresh rates, the image is typically shown multiple times, and sometimes black frames are inserted, to minimize smearing artifacts due to the eyes moving during frame display [7, 646]. Monitors can also have more than 8 bits per channel, and HDR monitors could be the next big thing in display technology. These can use 10 bits per channel or more. Dolby has HDR display technology that uses a lower-resolution array of LED backlights to enhance their LCD monitors. Doing so gives their display about 10 times the brightness and 100 times the contrast of a typical monitor [1596]. Monitors with wider color gamuts are also becoming more common. These can display a wider range of colors by having pure spectral hues become representable, e.g., more vivid greens. See Section 8.1.3 for more information about color gamuts.

To reduce tearing effects, companies have developed adaptive synchronization technologies, such as AMD's FreeSync and NVIDIA's G-sync. The idea here is to adapt the update rate of the display to what the GPU can produce instead of using a fixed predetermined rate. For example, if one frame takes 10 ms and the next takes 30 ms to render, the image update to the display will start immediately after each image has finished rendering. Rendering appears much smoother with such technologies. In addition, if the image is not updated, then the color buffer needs not to be sent to the display, which saves power.

23.6.2 Single, Double, and Triple Buffering

In Section 2.4, we mentioned that double buffering ensures that the image is not shown on the display until rendering has finished. Here, we will describe single, double, and even triple buffering.

Assume that we have only a single buffer. This buffer has to be the one that is currently shown on the display. As triangles for a frame are drawn, more and more of them will appear as the monitor refreshes—an unconvincing effect. Even if our frame rate is equal to the monitor's update rate, single buffering has problems. If we decide to clear the buffer or draw a large triangle, then we will briefly be able to see the actual partial changes to the color buffer as the video display controller transfers those areas of the color buffer that are being drawn. Sometimes called *tearing*, because the image displayed looks as if it were briefly ripped in two, this is not a desirable feature for real-time graphics. On some ancient systems, such as the Amiga, you could test where the beam was and so avoid drawing there, thus allowing single buffering to work. These days, single buffering is rarely used, with the possible exception of virtual reality systems, where "racing the beam" can be a way to reduce latency [6].

To avoid the tearing problem, double buffering is commonly used. A finished image is shown in the *front buffer*, while an offscreen *back buffer* contains the image that is currently being drawn. The back buffer and the front buffer are then swapped by the graphics driver, typically just after an entire image has been transferred to the display to avoid tearing. Swapping is often done by just swapping two color buffer pointers. For CRT displays, this event is called the *vertical retrace*, and the video signal during this time is called the *vertical synchronization* pulse, or *vsync* for short. For LCD displays, there is no physical retrace of a beam, but we use the same term to indicate that the entire image has just been transferred to the display. Instantly swapping back and front buffers after rendering completes is useful for benchmarking a rendering system, and is also used in many applications because it maximizes frame rate. Not updating on the vsync also leads to tearing, but because there are two fully formed images, the artifact is not as bad as with single buffering. Immediately after the swap, the (new) back buffer is then the recipient of graphics commands, and the new front buffer is shown to the user. This process is shown in Figure 23.12.

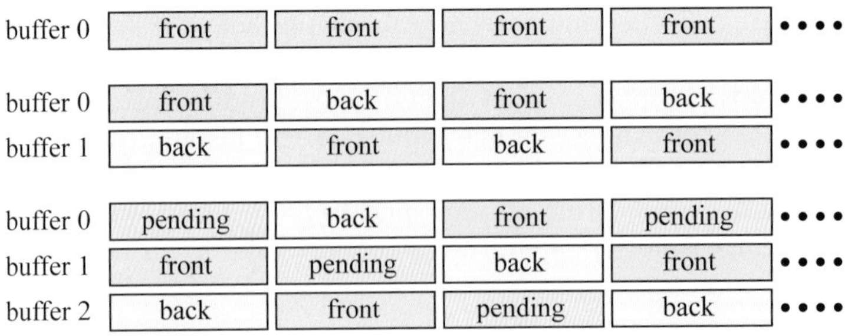

buffer 0	front	front	front	front	• • • •

buffer 0	front	back	front	back	• • • •
buffer 1	back	front	back	front	• • • •

buffer 0	pending	back	front	pending	• • • •
buffer 1	front	pending	back	front	• • • •
buffer 2	back	front	pending	back	• • • •

Figure 23.12. For single buffering (top), the front buffer is always shown. For double buffering (middle), first buffer 0 is in front and buffer 1 is in the back. Then they swap from front to back and vice versa for each frame. Triple buffering (bottom) works by having a pending buffer as well. Here, first a buffer is cleared and rendering to it is begun (pending). Second, the system continues to use the buffer for rendering until the image has been completed (back). Finally, the buffer is shown (front).

Double buffering can be augmented with a second back buffer, which we call the *pending buffer*. This is called *triple buffering* [1155]. The pending buffer is like the back buffer in that it is also offscreen, and that it can be modified while the front buffer is being displayed. The pending buffer becomes part of a three-buffer cycle. During one frame, the pending buffer can be accessed. At the next swap, it becomes the back buffer, where the rendering is completed. Then it becomes the front buffer and is shown to the viewer. At the next swap, the buffer again turns into a pending buffer. This course of events is visualized at the bottom of Figure 23.12.

Triple buffering has one major advantage over double buffering. Using it, the system can access the pending buffer while waiting for the vertical retrace. With double buffering, while waiting for the vertical retrace so that a swap can take place, the construction must simply keep waiting. This is so because the front buffer must be shown to the viewer, and the back buffer must remain unchanged because it has a finished image in it, waiting to be shown. The drawback of triple buffering is that the latency increases up to one entire frame. This increase delays the reaction to user inputs, such as keystrokes and mouse or joystick moves. Controls can feel sluggish because these user events are deferred after the rendering begins in the pending buffer.

In theory, more than three buffers could be used. If the amount of time to compute a frame varies considerably, more buffers give more balance and an overall higher display rate, at the cost of more potential latency. To generalize, multibuffering can be thought of as a circular structure. There is a rendering pointer and a display pointer, each pointing at a different buffer. The rendering pointer leads the display pointer, moving to the next buffer when the current rendering buffer is done being computed. The only rule is that the display pointer should never be the same as the rendering pointer.

A related method of achieving additional acceleration for PC graphics accelerators is to use *SLI* mode. Back in 1998 3dfx used SLI as an acronym for *scanline interleave*, where two graphics chipsets run in parallel, one handling the odd scanlines and the other the even. NVIDIA (who bought 3dfx's assets) uses this abbreviation for an entirely different way of connecting two (or more) graphics cards, called *scalable link interface*. AMD calls it CrossFire X. This form of parallelism divides the work by either splitting the screen into two (or more) horizontal sections, one per card, or by having each card fully render its own frame, alternating output. There is also a mode that allows the cards to accelerate antialiasing of the same frame. The most common use is having each GPU render a separate frame, called *alternate frame rendering* (AFR). While this scheme sounds as if it should increase latency, it can often have little or no effect. Say a single GPU system renders at 10 FPS. If the GPU is the bottleneck, two GPUs using AFR could render at 20 FPS, or even four at 40 FPS. Each GPU takes the same amount of time to render its frame, so latency does not necessarily change.

Screen resolutions continue to increase, posing a serious challenge to renderers based on per-pixel sampling. One way to maintain frame rate is to adaptively change the pixel shading rate over the screen [687, 1805] and surfaces [271].

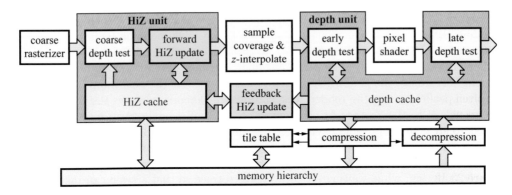

Figure 23.13. A possible implementation of the depth pipeline, where z-interpolate simply computes the depth value using interpolation. *(Illustration after Andersson et al. [46].)*

23.7 Depth Culling, Testing, and Buffering

In this section, we will cover everything that has to do with depth, including resolution, testing, culling, compression, caching, buffering, and early-z.

Depth resolution is important because it helps avoid rendering errors. For example, say you modeled a sheet of paper and placed it on a desk, ever so slightly above the desk's surface. With precision limits of the z-depths computed for the desk and paper, the desk can poke through the paper at various spots. This problem is sometimes called *z-fighting*. Note that if the paper were placed exactly at the same height as the desk, i.e., the paper and desk were made coplanar, then there would be no right answer without additional information about their relationship. This problem is due to poor modeling and cannot be resolved by better z precision.

As we saw in Section 2.5.2, the z-buffer (also called the depth buffer) can be used to resolve visibility. This kind of buffer typically has 24 bits or 32 bits per pixel (or sample), and may use floating point or fixed-point representations [1472]. For orthographic viewing, the distance values are proportional to the z-values, and so a uniform distribution is obtained. However, for perspective viewing, the distribution is nonuniform, as we have seen on seen on pages 99–102. After applying the perspective transform (Equations 4.74 or 4.76), a division by the w-component is required (Equation 4.72). The depth component then becomes $p_z = q_z/q_w$, where $\mathbf{q}$ is the point after multiplication by the projection matrix. For fixed-point representations, the value $p_z = q_z/q_w$ is mapped from its valid range (e.g., $[0, 1]$ for DirectX) to the integer range $[0, 2^b - 1]$ and is stored in the z-buffer, where b is the number of bits. See pages 99–102 for more information about depth precision.

The hardware depth pipeline is shown in Figure 23.13. The main goal of this pipeline is to test each incoming depth, generated when rasterizing a primitive, against the depth buffer, and possibly to write the incoming depth to the depth buffer if the fragment passes the depth test. At the same time, this pipeline needs to be efficient. The left part of the figure starts with coarse rasterization, i.e., rasterization on a tile level (Section 23.1). At this point, only tiles that overlap a primitive are passed through to the next stage, called the HiZ unit, where z-culling techniques are executed.

The HiZ unit starts with a block called the *coarse depth test*, and two types of tests are often performed here. We start by describing z_{max}-culling, which is a simplification of Greene's hierarchical z-buffering algorithm [591], presented in Section 19.7.2. The idea is to store the maximum, called z_{max}, of all the depths within each tile. The tile size is architecture-dependent, but 8×8 pixels is commonly used [1238]. These z_{max}-values can be stored in a fixed on-chip memory or be accessed through a cache. In Figure 23.13, we refer to this as the *HiZ cache*. Briefly, we want to test if the triangle is fully occluded in a tile. To do this we need to compute the minimum z-value, $z_{\mathrm{min}}^{\mathrm{tri}}$, on the triangle inside the tile. If $z_{\mathrm{min}}^{\mathrm{tri}} > z_{\mathrm{max}}$, it is guaranteed that the triangle is occluded by previously rendered geometry in that tile. Processing of the triangle in that tile can be terminated, which saves per-pixel depth testing. Note that it does not save any pixel shader executions, since the per-sample depth test would eliminate fragments that are hidden later in the pipeline anyway. In practice, we cannot afford to compute the exact value of $z_{\mathrm{min}}^{\mathrm{tri}}$, so instead, a conservative estimate is computed. Several different ways to compute $z_{\mathrm{min}}^{\mathrm{tri}}$ are possible, each with its own advantages and disadvantages:

1. The minimum z-value of the three vertices of a triangle can be used. This is not always accurate, but has little overhead.

2. Evaluate the z-value at the four corners of a tile using the plane equation of the triangle, and use the minimum of those.

The best culling performance is obtained if these two strategies are combined. This is done by taking the larger of the two z_{min} values.

The other type of coarse depth test is z_{min}-culling, and the idea is to store z_{min} of all the pixels in a tile [22]. There are two uses for this. First, it can be used to avoid z-buffer reads. If a triangle being rendered is definitely in front of all previously rendered geometry, per-pixel depth testing is unnecessary. In some cases, z-buffer reads can be completely avoided, which further boosts performance. Second, it can be used to support different types of depth tests. For the z_{max}-culling method, we assumed the standard "less than" depth test. However, it would be beneficial if culling could be used with other depth tests as well, and if z_{min} and z_{max} are both available, all depth tests can be supported using this culling process. A more detailed hardware description of the depth pipeline is found in Andersson's PhD thesis [49].

The green boxes in Figure 23.13 are concerned with different ways to update a tile's z_{max} and z_{min} values. If a triangle is covering an entire tile, the update can be done directly in the HiZ unit. Otherwise, the per-sample depths of an entire tile need to be read and reduced to minimum and maximum values and sent back to the HiZ unit, which introduces some latency. Andersson et al. [50] present a way to perform this without the more expensive feedback from the depth cache and are still able to retain most of the culling efficiency.

For tiles that survive the coarse depth test, pixel or sample coverage is determined (using edge equations as described in Section 23.1) and per-sample depths are computed (called z-interpolate in Figure 23.13). These values are forwarded to the depth unit, shown on the right in the figure. Per the API descriptions, pixel shader evaluation should follow. However, under some circumstances, which will be covered below, an additional test, called *early-z* [1220, 1542] or *early depth*, can be performed without altering the expected behavior. Early-z is actually just the per-sample depth test performed before the pixel shader, and occluded fragments are discarded. This process thus avoids unnecessary execution of the pixel shader. The early-z test is often confused with z-culling, but it is performed by entirely separate hardware. Either technique can be used without the other.

All of z_{max}-culling, z_{min}-culling, and early-z are automatically used by the GPU under many circumstances. However, these have to be disabled if, for example, the pixel shader writes a custom depth, uses a `discard` operation, or writes a value to an unordered access view [50]. If early-z cannot be used, then the depth test is done after the pixel shader (called a *late depth test*).

On newer hardware, it may be possible to perform atomic read-modify-write operations, loads, and stores to an image from shaders. In these cases, you can explicitly enable early-z and override these constraints, if you know it is safe to do so. Another feature, which can be used when the pixel shader outputs custom depth, is conservative depth. In this case, early-z can be enabled if the programmer guarantees that the custom depth is greater than the triangle depth. For this example, z_{max}-culling could also be enabled, but not early-z and z_{min}-culling.

As always, occlusion culling benefits from rendering front to back. Another technique with a similar name, and similar intent, is the z-prepass. The idea is that the programmer first renders the scene while writing only depth, disabling pixel shading, and writing to the color buffer. When rendering subsequent passes, an "equal" test is used, meaning that only the frontmost surfaces will be shaded since the z-buffer already has been initialized. See Section 18.4.5.

To conclude this section, we will briefly describe caching and compression for the depth pipeline, which is shown on the lower right of Figure 23.13. The general compression system is similar to the system described in Section 23.5. Each tile can be compressed to a few select sizes, and there is always a fallback to uncompressed data, which is used when compression fails to reach any of the selected sizes. Fast clear is used to save bandwidth usage when clearing the depth buffer. Since depth is linear in screen space, typical compression algorithms either store plane equations with high precision, use a difference-of-differences technique with delta encoding, or use some anchor method [679, 1238, 1427]. The tile table and the HiZ cache may be stored entirely in on-chip buffers, or they may communicate though the rest of the memory hierarchy, as does the depth cache. Storing on chip is expensive, since these buffers need to be large enough to handle the largest supported resolution.

23.8 Texturing

While texture operations, including fetching, filtering, and decompression, certainly can be implemented in pure software running on the GPU multiprocessors, it has been shown that fixed-function hardware for texturing can be up to 40 times faster [1599]. The texture unit performs addressing, filtering, clamping, and decompression of texture formats (Chapter 6). It is used in conjunction with a texture cache to reduce bandwidth usage. We start by discussing filtering and what consequence that has on the texture unit.

To be able to use minification filters, such as mipmapping and anisotropic filtering, the derivatives of the texture coordinates in screen space are needed. That is, to compute the texture level of detail λ, we need $\partial u/\partial x$, $\partial v/\partial x$, $\partial u/\partial y$, and $\partial v/\partial y$. These tell us what extent of the texture's area or function is represented by the fragment. If the texture coordinates, which are passed from the vertex shader, are used to directly access the texture, then the derivatives can be computed analytically. If the texture coordinates are transformed using some function, e.g., $(u', v') = (\cos v, \sin u)$, then it becomes more complicated to compute derivatives analytically. It is, however, still possible, using the chain rule or symbolic differentiation [618]. Notwithstanding, none of these methods are used by graphics hardware, since the situation can be arbitrarily complex. Imagine computing the reflections on a surface, with normals being bump mapped, using an environment map. It is difficult to compute analytically, for example, the derivatives of a reflection vector bouncing off a normal map that are then used to access an environment map. As a result, the derivatives are usually computed numerically using finite differences in x and y on a quad basis, i.e, over 2×2 pixels. This is also the reason why GPU architectures are focused around scheduling quads.

In general, derivative computations happen under the hood, i.e., they are hidden from the user. The actual implementation is often done using cross-lane instructions (shuffle/swizzle) over a quad, and such instructions may be inserted by the compiler. Some GPUs instead use fixed-function hardware to compute these derivatives. There is no exact specification of how derivatives should be computed. Some common methods are shown in Figure 23.14. OpenGL 4.5 and DirectX 11 support functions for both coarse and fine derivatives [1368].

Texture caching [362, 651, 794, 795] is used by all GPUs to reduce bandwidth usage for textures. Some architectures use a dedicated cache for texturing, or even two dedicated levels of texture caching, while others share a cache between all types of accesses, including texturing. Typically a small on-chip memory (usually SRAM) is used to implement a texture cache. This cache stores the results of recent texture reads, and access is quick. The replacement policies and sizes are architecture-dependent. If neighboring pixels need to access the same or closely located texels, they are likely to find these in the cache. As mentioned in Section 23.4, memory accesses are often done in a tiled fashion, so instead of texels being stored in a scanline order, they are stored in small tiles, e.g., 4×4 texels, which increases efficiency [651] since a tile of

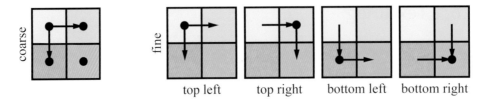

Figure 23.14. Illustration of how derivatives may be computed. Arrows indicate that the difference is computed between the pixel where the arrow ends and the pixel where it starts. For example, the top left horizontal difference is computed as the top right pixel minus the top left pixel. For coarse derivatives (left), a single horizontal difference and a single vertical difference are used for all four pixels within the quad. For fine derivatives (right), one uses the differences closest to the pixel. *(Illustration after Penner [1368].)*

texels is fetched together. The tile size in bytes is typically the same as the cache line size, e.g., 64 bytes. Another way to store the texture is to use a *swizzled* pattern. Assume that the texture coordinates have been transformed to fixed-point numbers: (u, v), where each of u and v have n bits. The bit with number i of u is denoted u_i. Then the remapping of (u, v) to a swizzled texture address, A, is

$$A(u, v) = B + (v_{n-1} u_{n-1} v_{n-2} u_{n-2} \ldots v_1 u_1 v_0 u_0) \cdot T, \qquad (23.14)$$

where B is the base address of the texture and T is the number of bytes occupied by one texel. The advantage of this remapping is that it gives rise to the texel order shown in Figure 23.15. As can be seen, this is a space-filling curve, called a *Morton sequence* [1243], and it is known to improve coherency [1825]. In this case, the curve is two-dimensional, since textures normally are, too.

The texture units also contain custom silicon to decompress several different texture formats (Section 6.2.6). These are usually many times more efficient when implemented in fixed-function hardware, compared to software implementations. Note that when using a texture both as a render target and for texture mapping, other compression opportunities occur. If compression of the color buffer is enabled (Section 23.5), then there are two design options when accessing such a render target as a texture. When the render target has finished its rendering, one option is to decompress the entire render target from its color buffer compression format and to store it uncompressed for subsequent texture accesses. The second option is to add hardware support in the texture unit to decompress the color buffer compression formats [1716]. The latter is the more efficient option, since the render target can stay compressed even during access as a texture. More information about caches and compression can be found in Section 23.4.

Mipmapping is important for texture cache locality, since it enforces a maximum texel-pixel ratio. When traversing a triangle, each new pixel represents a step in texture space of approximately one texel. Mipmapping is one of the few cases in rendering where a technique improves both visuals and performance.

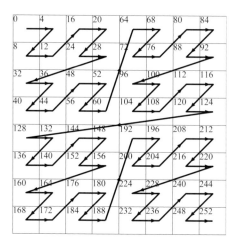

Figure 23.15. Texture swizzling increases coherency of texel memory accesses. Note that texel size here is 4 bytes, and that the texel address is shown in each texel's upper left corner.

23.9 Architecture

The best way of achieving faster graphics is to exploit parallelism, and this can be done in practically all stages in a GPU. The idea is to compute multiple results simultaneously and then merge these at a later stage. In general, a parallel graphics architecture has the appearance shown in Figure 23.16. The application sends tasks to the GPU, and after some scheduling, geometry processing starts in parallel in several *geometry units*. The results from geometry processing are forwarded to a set of *rasterizer units*, which perform rasterization. Pixel shading and blending are then performed, also in parallel, by a set of *pixel processing units*. Finally, the resulting image is sent to the display for viewing.

For both software and hardware, it is important to realize that if there is a serial part of your code or hardware, it will limit the amount of total possible performance

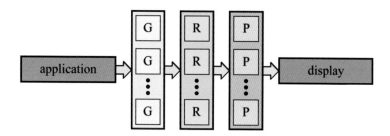

Figure 23.16. The general architecture for a high-performance, parallel computer graphics architecture, consisting of several geometry units (G's), rasterizer units (R's), and pixel processing units (P's).

improvement. This is expressed by Amdahl's law, i.e.,

$$a(s,p) = \frac{1}{s + \frac{1-s}{p}}, \tag{23.15}$$

where s is the serial percentage of a program/hardware, and hence $1-s$ is the percentage that is amenable for parallelization. Furthermore, p is the maximum performance improvement factor that can be achieved through parallelizing the program or hardware. For example, if we originally had one multiprocessor and added three more, then $p = 4$. Here, $a(s,p)$ is the acceleration factor that you get from your improvement. If we have an architecture where, say, 10% is serialized, i.e., $s = 0.1$, and we improve our architecture so that the remaining (non-serial) part can be improved by a factor of 20, i.e., $p = 20$, then we get $a = 1/(0.1 + 0.9/20) \approx 6.9$. As can be seen, we do not get a speedup of 20, and the reason is that the serial part of the code/hardware seriously limits performance. In fact, as $p \to \infty$, we get $a = 10$. Whether it is better to spend effort on improving the parallel part or on the serial part is not always clear, but after the parallel part has been improved substantially, the serial part will limit performance more.

For graphics architectures, multiple results are computed in parallel, but primitives in draw calls are expected to be processed in the order they were submitted by the CPU. Therefore, some kind of sorting must be done, so that the parallel units together render the image that the user intended. Specifically, the sorting needed is from model space to screen space (Section 2.3.1 and 2.4). It should be noted that the geometry units and pixel processing units may be mapped to identical units, i.e., unified ALUs. All the architectures in our case study section use unified shader architectures (Section 23.10). Even if this is the case, it is important to understand where this sorting takes place. We present a taxonomy [417, 1236] for parallel architectures. The sort can occur anywhere in the pipeline, which gives rise to four different classes of work distribution in parallel architectures, as shown in Figure 23.17. These are called *sort-first*, *sort-middle*, *sort-last fragment*, and *sort-last image*. Note that these architectures give rise to different ways to distribute work among the parallel units in the GPU.

A sort-first-based architecture sorts primitives before the geometry stage. The strategy is to divide the screen into a set of regions, and the primitives inside a region are sent to a complete pipeline that "owns" that region. See Figure 23.18. A primitive is initially processed enough to know which region(s) it needs to be sent— this is the sorting step. Sort-first is the least explored architecture for a single machine [418, 1236]. It is a scheme that does see use when driving a system with multiple screens or projectors forming a large display, as a single computer is dedicated to each screen [1513]. A system called Chromium [787] has been developed, which can implement any type of parallel rendering algorithm using a cluster of workstations. For example, sort-first and sort-last can be implemented with high rendering performance.

The Mali architecture (Section 23.10.1) is of the type sort-middle. The geometry processing units are given approximately the same amount of geometry to process.

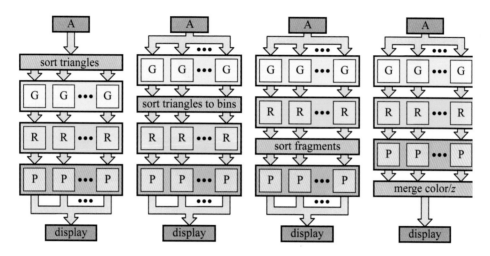

Figure 23.17. Taxonomy of parallel graphics architectures. A is the application, G's are geometry units, R's are rasterizer units, and P's are pixel processing units. From left to right, the architectures are sort-first, sort-middle, sort-last fragment, and sort-last image. *(Illustration after Eldridge et al. [417].)*

Then transformed geometry is sorted into non-overlapping rectangles, called *tiles*, that together cover the entire screen. Note that a transformed triangle may overlap with several tiles and so may be processed by several rasterizer and pixel processing units. Key to efficiency here is that each pair of rasterizer and pixel processing units have a tile-sized framebuffer on chip, which means that all framebuffer accesses are fast. When all geometry has been sorted to tiles, rasterization and pixel processing of each tile can commence independently of each other. Some sort-middle architectures perform a z-prepass per tile for opaque geometry, which means that each pixel is only shaded once. However, not all sort-middle architectures do this.

The sort-last fragment architecture sorts the fragments after rasterization (sometimes called fragment generation) and before pixel processing. An example is the GCN architecture, described in Section 23.10.3. Just as with sort-middle, primitives are spread as evenly as possible across the geometry units. One advantage with sort-last fragment is that there will not be any overlap, meaning that a generated fragment is sent to only one pixel processing unit, which is optimal. Imbalance can occur if one rasterizer unit deals with large triangles, while another one deals with only small triangles.

Finally, the sort-last image architecture sorts after pixel processing. A visualization is shown in Figure 23.19. This architecture can be seen as a set of independent pipelines. The primitives are spread across the pipelines, and each pipeline renders an image with depth. In a final composition stage, all the images are merged with respect to their z-buffers. It should be noted that sort-last image systems cannot fully implement an API such as OpenGL and DirectX, because they require that primitives

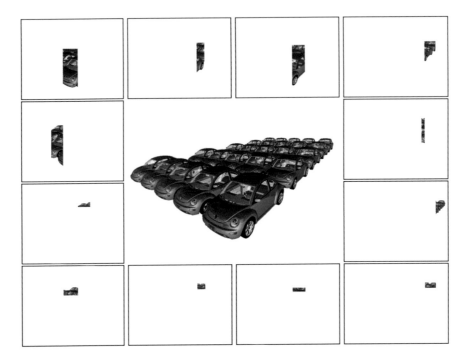

Figure 23.18. Sort-first splits the screen into separate tiles and assigns a processor to each tile, as shown here. A primitive is then sent to the processors whose tiles they overlap. This is in contrast to sort-middle architecture, which needs to sort *all* triangles after geometry processing has occurred. Only after all triangles have been sorted can per-pixel rasterization start. *(Images courtesy of Marcus Roth and Dirk Reiners.)*

be rendered in the order they are sent. PixelFlow [455, 1235] is an example of the sort-last image architecture. The PixelFlow architecture is also noteworthy because it uses deferred shading, meaning that it shades only visible fragments. It should be noted, however, that no current architectures use sort-last image due to the substantial bandwidth usage toward the end of the pipelines.

One problem with a pure sort-last image scheme for large tiled display systems is the sheer amount of image and depth data that needs to be transferred between rendering nodes. Roth and Reiners [1513] optimize data transfer and composition costs by using the screen and depth bounds of each processor's results.

Eldridge et al. [417, 418] present Pomegranate, a sort-everywhere architecture. Briefly, it inserts sort stages between the geometry stage and the rasterizer units (R's), between R's and pixel processing units (P's), and between P's and the display. The work is therefore kept more balanced as the system scales (i.e., as more pipelines are added). The sorting stages are implemented as a high-speed network with point-to-point links. Simulations show a nearly linear performance increase as more pipelines are added.

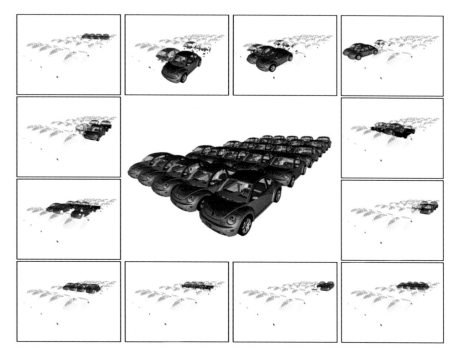

Figure 23.19. In sort-last image, different objects in the scene are sent to different processors. Transparency is difficult to deal with when compositing separate rendered images, so transparent objects are usually sent to all nodes. *(Images courtesy of Marcus Roth and Dirk Reiners.)*

All the components in a graphics system (host, geometry processing, rasterization, and pixel processing) connected together give us a multiprocessing system. For such systems there are two problems that are well known, and almost always associated with multiprocessing: *load balancing* and *communication* [297]. FIFO (first-in, first-out) queues are often inserted into many different places in the pipeline, so that jobs can be queued to avoid stalling parts of the pipeline. For example, it is possible to put a FIFO between the geometry and rasterizer units, so that geometry-processed triangles can be buffered if the rasterizer units cannot keep up with the pace of the geometry units, due to huge triangle size, for example.

The different sort architectures described have distinct load balancing advantages and disadvantages. Consult Eldridge's PhD thesis [418] or the paper by Molnar et al. [1236] for more information on these. The programmer can also affect load balancing; techniques for doing so are discussed in Chapter 18. Communication can be a problem if the bandwidth of the buses is too low, or is used unwisely. Therefore, it is of extreme importance to design an application's rendering system so that the bottleneck does not occur in any of the buses, e.g., the bus from the host to the graphics hardware. Section 18.2 deals with different methods to detect bottlenecks.

23.10   Case Studies

In this section, three different graphics hardware architectures will be presented. The ARM Mali G71 Bifrost architecture, targeting mobile devices and televisions, is presented first. NVIDIA's Pascal architecture follows next. We end with a description of the AMD GCN architecture called Vega.

Note that graphics hardware companies often base their design decisions on extensive software simulations of GPUs that have not yet been built. That is, several applications, e.g., games, are run through their parameterized simulator with several different configurations. Possible parameters are number of MPs, clock frequency, number of caches, number of raster engines/tessellator engines, and number of ROPs, for example. Simulations are used to gather information about such factors as performance, power usage, and memory bandwidth usage. At the end of the day, the best possible configuration, which works best in most use cases, is chosen and a chip is built from that configuration. In addition, simulations may help find typical bottlenecks in the architecture, which then can be addressed, e.g., increasing the size of a cache. For a particular GPU, the reason for various speeds and numbers of units is, simply, "it works best this way."

23.10.1   Case Study: ARM Mali G71 Bifrost

The Mali product line encompasses all GPU architectures from ARM, and Bifrost is their architecture from 2016. The target for this architecture is mobile and embedded systems, e.g., mobile phones, tablets, and televisions. In 2015, 750 million Mali-based GPUs were shipped. Since many of these are powered by batteries, it is important to design an energy-efficient architecture, rather than just focusing on performance. Therefore, it makes sense to use a sort-middle architecture, where all framebuffer accesses are kept on chip, which lowers power consumption. All Mali architectures are of the sort-middle type, sometimes called a *tiling architecture.* A high-level overview of the GPU is shown in Figure 23.20. As can be seen, the G71 can support up to 32 unified shader engines. ARM uses the term shader core instead of shader engine, but we use the term shader engine to avoid confusion with the rest of the chapter. A shader engine is capable of executing instructions for 12 threads at a time, i.e., it has 12 ALUs. The choice of 32 shader engines was specifically for the G71, but the architecture scales beyond 32 engines.

The driver software feeds the GPU with work. The job manager, i.e., a scheduler, then divides this work among the shader engines. These engines are connected through a GPU fabric, which is a bus on which the engines can communicate with the other units in the GPU. All memory accesses are sent through the memory management unit (MMU), which translates from a virtual memory address to a physical address.

An overview of a shader engine is shown in Figure 23.21. As can be seen, it contains three execution engines, centered around executing shading for quads. Therefore, they have been designed as a small general-purpose processor with SIMD width 4. Each

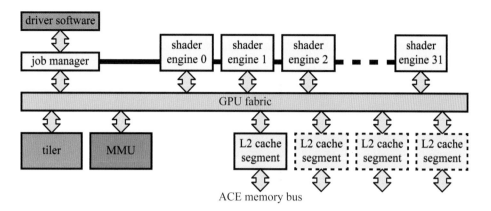

Figure 23.20. The Bifrost G71 GPU architecture, which is scalable up to 32 shader engines, where each shader engine is the one shown in Figure 23.21. *(Illustration after Davies [326].)*

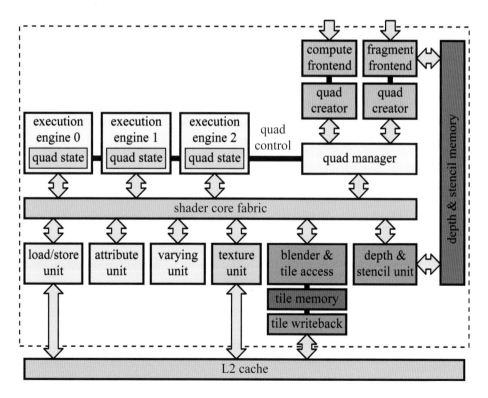

Figure 23.21. The Bifrost shader engine architecture, where the tile memory is on chip, which makes for fast local framebuffer accesses. *(Illustration after Davies [326].)*

execution engine contains four fused-multiply-and-add (FMA) units for 32-bit floating point and four 32-bit adders, among other things. This means that there are 3×4 ALUs, i.e., 12 SIMD lanes, per shader engine. The quad is equivalent to a warp, in the terminology we use here. To hide latency for texture accesses, for example, the architecture can keep at least 256 threads in flight per shader engine.

Note that the shader engines are unified and can perform compute, vertex, and pixel shading, to name a few. The execution engine also contains support for many of the transcendental functions, such as sine and cosine. In addition, performance is up to 2× when using 16-bit floating point precision. These units also have support for bypassing register content in cases when a register result is used only as input to an instruction that follows. This saves power since the register file does not need to be accessed. In addition, when performing a texture or other memory access, for example, a single quad can be switched in by the quad manager, similar to how other architectures hide the latency of such operations. Note that this happens at a small-grain level, swapping 4 threads instead of all 12. The load/store unit takes care of general memory accesses, memory address translation, and coherent caching [264]. The attribute unit handles attribute indexing and addressing. It sends its accesses to the load/store unit. The varying unit performs interpolation of varying attributes.

The core idea of tiling architectures (sort-middle) is to first perform all geometry processing, so that the screen-space position of each primitive to render is found. At the same time, a *polygon list*, containing pointers to all the primitives overlapping a tile, is built for each tile in the framebuffer. After this step, the set of primitives overlapping a tile is known. Hence, the primitives in a tile can be rasterized and shaded, and the results are stored in the on-chip tile memory. When the tile has finished rendering all its primitives, the data from the tile memory is written back to external memory through the L2 cache. This reduces memory bandwidth usage. Then the next tile is rasterized, and so on, until the entire frame has been rendered. The first tiling architecture was Pixel-Planes 5 [502], and that system has some high-level similarities to the Mali architectures.

Geometry processing and pixel processing are visualized in Figure 23.22. As can be seen, the vertex shader is split into one part that only performs position shading and another part called varying shading, which is done after tiling. This saves memory bandwidth compared to ARM's previous architectures. The only information needed to perform *binning*, i.e, determining which tiles a primitive overlaps, is the position of the vertices. The tiler unit, which performs binning, works in a hierarchical fashion as illustrated in Figure 23.23. This helps make the memory footprint for binning smaller and more predictable, since it is no longer proportional to primitive size.

When the tiler has finished binning all primitives in the scene, it is known exactly which primitives overlap a certain tile. As such, the remaining rasterization, pixel processing, and blending can be performed in parallel for any number of tiles, as long as there are available shader engines that can work in parallel. In general, a tile is submitted to a shader engine that handles all the primitives in that tile. While this work is done for all the tiles, it is also possible to start with geometry processing

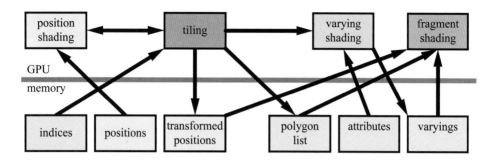

Figure 23.22. Illustration of how the geometry flows through the Bifrost architecture. The vertex shader consists of position shading, which is used by the tiler, and varying shading which is executed only when needed, after tiling. *(Illustration after Choi [264].)*

and tiling for the next frame. This processing model implies that there may be more latency in a tiling architecture.

At this point, rasterization, pixel shader execution, blending, and other per-pixel operations follow. The single most important feature of a tiling architecture is that the framebuffer (including color, depth, and stencil, for example) for a single tile can be stored in quick on-chip memory, here called the *tile memory*. This is affordable because the tiles are small (16×16 pixels). When all rendering in a tile has finished, the desired output (usually color, and possibly depth) of the tile is copied to an off-chip framebuffer (in external memory) of the same size as the screen. This means that all accesses to the framebuffer during per-pixel processing are effectively for free. Avoiding using the external buses is highly desirable, because this use comes with a high energy cost [22]. Framebuffer compression can still be used when evicting the content of the on-chip tile memory to the off-chip framebuffer.

Bifrost supports *pixel local storage* (PLS), which is a set of extensions that generally are supported on sort-middle architectures. Using PLS, one can let the pixel shader access the color of the framebuffer and hence implement custom blending techniques. In contrast, blending is usually configured using the API and is not programmable in

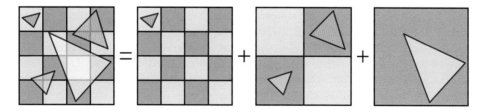

Figure 23.23. The hierarchical tiler of the Bifrost architecture. In this example, binning is done on three different levels, where each triangle has been assigned to the level at which it overlaps a single square. *(Illustration after Bratt [191].)*

the way that a pixel shader is. One can also store arbitrary fixed-size data structures per pixel using the tile memory. This allows the programmer to implement, for example, deferred shading techniques efficiently. The G-buffer (e.g., normal, position, and diffuse texture) is stored in PLS in a first pass. The second pass performs the lighting calculations and accumulates the results in PLS. The third pass uses the information in the PLS to compute the final pixel color. Note that, for a single tile, all these computations occur while the entire tile memory is kept on the chip, which makes it fast.

All Mali architectures have been designed from the ground up with multisampling antialiasing (MSAA) in mind, and they implement the rotated grid supersampling (RGSS) scheme described on page 143, using four samples per pixel. Sort-middle architectures are well suited for antialiasing. This is because filtering is done just before the tile leaves the GPU and is sent out to external memory. Hence, the framebuffer in external memory needs to store only a single color per pixel. A standard architecture would need a framebuffer to be four times as large. For a tiling architecture, you need to increase only the on-chip tile buffer by four times, or effectively use smaller tiles (half the width and height).

The Mali Bifrost architecture can also selectively choose to use either multisampling or supersampling on a batch of rendering primitives. This means that the more expensive supersampling approach, where you execute the pixel shader for each sample, can be used when it is needed. An example would be rendering a textured tree with alpha mapping, where you need high-quality sampling to avoid visual artifacts. For these primitives, supersampling could be enabled. When this complex situation ends and simpler objects are to be rendered, one can switch back to using the less expensive multisampling approach. The architecture also supports 8× and 16× MSAA.

Bifrost (and the previous architecture called Midgard) also supports a technique called *transaction elimination*. The idea is to avoid memory transfers from the tile memory to off-chip memory for parts of a scene that do not change from frame to frame. For the current frame, a unique signature is computed for each tile when the tile is evicted to the off-chip framebuffer. This signature is a type of checksum. For the next frame, the signature is computed for tiles that are about to be evicted. If the signature from the previous frame is the same as the signature for the current frame for a certain tile, then the architecture avoids writing out the color buffer to off-chip memory since the correct content is already there. This is particularly useful for casual mobile games (e.g., *Angry Birds*), where a smaller percentage of the scene is updated each frame. Note also that this type of technique is difficult to implement on sort-last architectures, since they do not operate on a per-tile basis. The G71 also supports *smart composition*, which is transaction elimination applied to user interface composition. It can avoid reading, compositing, and writing a block of pixels if all sources are the same as the previous frame's and the operations are the same.

Low-level power-saving techniques, such as clock gating and power gating, are also heavily used in this architecture. This means that unused or inactive parts of the pipeline are shut down or kept idle at lower energy consumption to reduce power usage.

To reduce texture bandwidth, there is a texture cache with dedicated decompression units for ASTC and ETC. In addition, compressed textures are stored in compressed form in the cache, as opposed to decompressing them and then putting the texels in the cache. This means that when a request for a texel is made, the hardware reads the block from the cache and then decompresses the texels of the block on the fly. This configuration increases the effective size of the cache, which boosts efficiency.

An advantage of the tiling architecture, in general, is that it is inherently designed parallel processing of tiles. For example, more shader engines could be added, where each shader engine is responsible for independently rendering to a single tile at a time. A disadvantage of tiling architectures is that the entire scene data needs to be sent to the GPU for tiling and processed geometry streamed out to memory. In general, sort-middle architectures are not ideal for handling geometry amplification such as applying geometry shaders and tessellation, since more geometry adds to the amount of memory transfers for shuffling geometry back and forth. For the Mali architecture, both geometry shading (Section 18.4.2) and tessellation are handled in software on the GPU, and the Mali best practices guide [69] recommends never using the geometry shader. For most content, sort-middle architectures work well for mobile and embedded systems.

23.10.2 Case Study: NVIDIA Pascal

Pascal is a GPU architecture built by NVIDIA. It exists both as a graphics part [1297] and as a compute part [1298], where the latter targets high-performance computing and deep learning applications. In this presentation, we will focus mostly on the graphics part, and in particular on a certain configuration called the GeForce GTX 1080. We will present the architecture in a bottom-up fashion, starting with the smallest unified ALU and then building up toward the entire GPU. We will mention some of the other chip configurations briefly at the end of this section.

The unified ALU —*CUDA core* in NVIDIA terminology—used in the Pascal graphics architecture has the same high-level diagram as the ALU on the left in Figure 23.8 on page 1002. The focus of the ALUs is on floating point and integer arithmetic, but they also support other operations. To increase computational power, several such ALUs are combined into a streaming multiprocessor (SM). In the graphics part of Pascal, the SM consists of four processing blocks, where each block has 32 ALUs. This means that the SM can execute 4 warps of 32 threads at the same time. This is illustrated in Figure 23.24.

Each processing block, i.e., a SIMT engine with width 32, also has 8 load/store (LD/ST) units and 8 special function units (SFUs). The load/store units handle reading and writing values to registers in the register file, which is $16,384 \times 4$ bytes, i.e., 64 kB, per processing block, which sums to 256 kB per SM. The SFUs handle transcendental function instructions, such as sine, cosine, exponential (base 2), logarithm (base 2), reciprocal, and reciprocal square root. They also have support for attribute interpolation [1050].

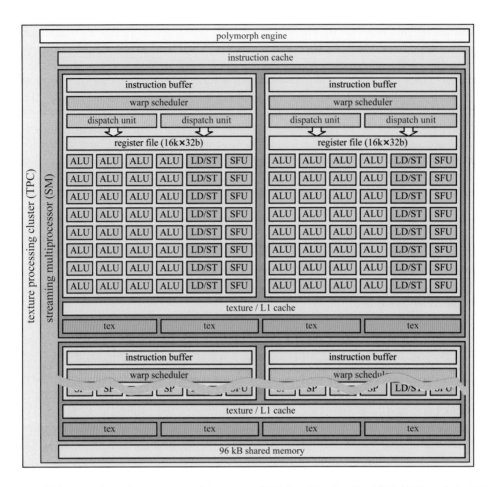

Figure 23.24. The Pascal streaming multiprocessor (SM) has $32 \times 2 \times 2$ unified ALUs and the SM is encapsulated with a polymorph engine, which together form a texture processing cluster (TPC). Note that the top dark gray box has been duplicated just below it, but parts of that duplication have been left out. *(Illustration after NVIDIA white paper [1297].)*

All ALUs in the SM share a single instruction cache, while each SIMT engine has its own instruction buffer with a local set of recently loaded instructions to further increase the instruction cache hit ratio. The warp scheduler is capable of dispatching two warp instructions per clock cycle [1298], e.g., work can be scheduled to both the ALUs and the LD/ST units in the same clock cycle. Note that there are also two L1 caches per SM, each having 24 kB of storage, i.e., 48 kB per SM. The reason to have two L1 caches is likely that a larger L1 cache would need more read and write ports, which increases the complexity of the cache and makes the implementation larger on chip. In addition, there are 8 texture units per SM.

Because shading must be done in 2×2 pixel quads, the warp scheduler finds work of 8 different pixel quads and groups them together for execution in the 32 SIMT lanes [1050]. Since this is a unified ALU design, the warp scheduler can group one of vertices, pixels, primitives, or compute shader work into warps. Note that an SM can handle different types of warps (such as vertices, pixels, and primitives) at the same time. The architecture also has zero overhead for switching out a currently executing warp for a warp that is ready for execution. The details of what warp is next selected for execution on Pascal are not public, but a previous NVIDIA architecture gives us some hints. In the NVIDIA Tesla architecture from 2008 [1050], a *scoreboard* was used to qualify each warp for issue each clock cycle. A scoreboard is a general mechanism that allows for out-of-order execution without conflicts. The warp scheduler chooses among the warps that are ready for execution, e.g., not waiting for a texture load to return, and chooses the one with the highest priority. Warp type, instruction type, and "fairness" are the parameters that are used to select the highest-priority warp.

The SM works in conjunction with the *polymorph engine* (PM). This unit was introduced in its first incarnation in the Fermi chip [1296]. The PM performs several geometry-related tasks, including vertex fetch, tessellation, simultaneous multiprojection, attribute setup, and stream output. The first stage fetches vertices from a global vertex buffer and dispatches warps to SMs for vertex and hull shading. Then follows an optional tessellation stage (Section 17.6), where newly generated (u, v) patch coordinates are dispatched to the SMs for domain shading and, optionally, geometry shading. The third stage handles viewport transform and perspective correction. In addition, an optional simultaneous multi-projection step is executed here, which can be used for efficient VR rendering, for example (Section 21.3.1). Next comes an optional fourth stage, where vertices are streamed out to memory. Finally, the results are forwarded to the relevant raster engines.

A raster engine has three tasks, namely, triangle setup, triangle traversal, and z-culling. Triangle setup fetches vertices, computes edge equations, and performs backface culling. Triangle traversal uses a hierarchical tiled traversal technique to visit the tiles overlapping a triangle. It uses the edge equations to perform tile tests and to perform the inside tests. On Fermi, each rasterizer can process up to 8 pixels per clock cycle [1296]. There are no public numbers for this on Pascal. The z-culling unit handles culling on a per-tile basis using the techniques described in Section 23.7. If a tile is culled, then processing is immediately terminated for that tile. For surviving triangles, per-vertex attributes are converted into plane equations for efficient evaluation in the pixel shader.

A streaming processor coupled with a polymorph engine is called a *texture processing cluster* (TPC). On a higher level, five TPCs are grouped into a *graphics processing cluster* (GPC) that has a single raster engine serving these five TPCs. A GPC can be thought of as a small GPU, and its goal is to provide a balanced set of hardware units for graphics, e.g., vertex, geometry, raster, texture, pixel, and ROP units. As we will see at the end of this section, creating separate functional units allows designers to more easily create a family of GPU chips with a range of capabilities.

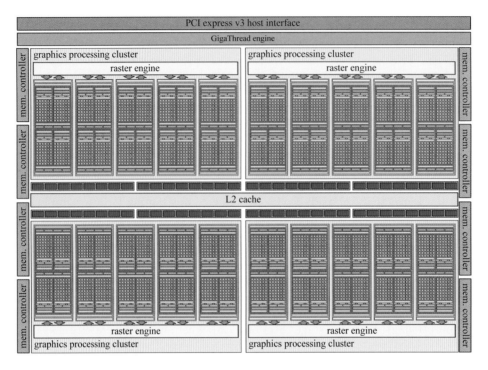

Figure 23.25. The Pascal GPU in its GTX 1080 configuration with 20 SMs, 20 polymorph engines, 4 raster engines, $8 \times 20 = 160$ texture units (with a peak rate of 277.3 Gtexels/s), $256 \times 20 = 5120$ kB worth of register file, and a total of $20 \times 128 = 2560$ unified ALUs. *(Illustration after NVIDIA white paper [1297].)*

At this point, we have most of the building blocks for the GeForce GTX 1080. It consists of four GPCs, and this general setup is shown in Figure 23.25. Notice that there is another level of scheduling here, powered by the GigaThread engine, along with an interface to PCIe v3. The GigaThread engine is a global work distribution engine that schedules blocks of threads to all the GPCs.

The raster operation units are also displayed in Figure 23.25, albeit somewhat hidden. They are located immediately above and below the L2 cache in the middle of the figure. Each blue block is one ROP unit, and there are 8 groups, each with 8 ROPs for a total of 64. The major tasks of the ROP units are to write output to pixels and other buffers, and to perform various operations such as blending. As can be seen on the left and right in the figure, there are a total of eight 32-bit memory controllers, which sums to 256 bits in total. Eight ROP units are tied to a single memory controller and 256 kB of the L2 cache. This gives a total of 2 MB of the L2 cache for the entire chip. Each ROP is tied to a certain memory partition, which means that a ROP handles a certain subset of the pixels in a buffer. The ROP units also handle lossless compression. There are three different compression modes

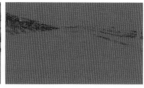

Figure 23.26. The rendered image is shown on the left, while the compression results are visualized for Maxwell (middle), the architecture before Pascal, and for Pascal (right). The more purple the image is, the higher the success rate of buffer compression. *(Images from NVIDIA white paper [1297].)*

in addition to supporting uncompressed and fast clears [1297]. For 2 : 1 compression (e.g., from 256 B to 128 B), a reference color value is stored per tile and the differences are encoded between pixels, where each difference is encoded with fewer bits than its uncompressed form. Then 4 : 1 compression is an extension of the 2 : 1 mode, but this mode can only be enabled if the differences can be encoded using even fewer bits, and it works for only those tiles with smoothly varying content. There is also an 8 : 1 mode, which is a combination of 4 : 1 constant color compression of 2×2 pixel blocks with the 2 : 1 mode above. The 8 : 1 mode has priority over 4 : 1, which has priority over 2 : 1, i.e., the mode with the highest compression rate that also succeeds at compressing the tile is always used. If all these compression attempts fail, the tile has to be transferred and stored in memory as uncompressed. The efficiency of the Pascal compression system is illustrated in Figure 23.26.

The video memory used is GDDRX5 with a clock rate of 10 GHz. Above we saw that the eight memory controllers provide 256 bits = 32 B in total. This gives a total of 320 GB/s of total peak memory bandwidth, but the many levels of caching combined with the compression techniques give an impression of a higher effective rate.

The base clock frequency of the chip is 1607 MHz, and it can operate in boost mode (1733 MHz) for when there is sufficient power budget. The peak compute capability is

$$\underbrace{2}_{\text{FMA}} \cdot \underbrace{2560}_{\text{num. SPs}} \cdot \underbrace{1733}_{\text{clock freq.}} = 8,872,960 \text{ MFLOPS} \approx 8.9 \text{ TFLOPS}, \qquad (23.16)$$

where the 2 comes from the fact that a fused-multiply-and-add often is counted as two floating point operations and we have divided by 10^6 to convert from MFLOPS to TFLOPS. The GTX 1080 Ti has 3584 ALUs, which results in 12.3 TFLOPS.

NVIDIA has developed sort-last fragment architectures for a long time. However, since Maxwell, they also support a new type of rendering called *tiled caching*, which is somewhat between sort-middle and sort-last fragment. This architecture is illustrated in Figure 23.27. The idea is to exploit locality and the L2 cache. Geometry is processed in small enough chunks so that the output can stay in this cache. In addition, the framebuffer stays in L2 as well, as long as the geometry overlapping that tile has not finished pixel shading.

There are four raster engines in Figure 23.25, but as we know the graphics APIs must (in most cases) respect primitive submission order [1598]. The framebuffer is

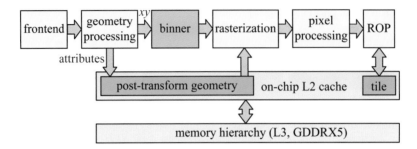

Figure 23.27. Tiled caching introduces a binner that sorts geometry into tiles and lets the transformed geometry stay in the L2 cache. The currently processed tile also stays in L2 until the geometry in that tile for the current chunk is done.

often split into tiles using a generalized checkerboard pattern [1160], and each raster engine "owns" a set of the tiles. The current triangle is sent to each raster engine that has at least one of its tiles overlapping with the triangle, which solves the ordering problem independently for each tile. This makes for better load balancing. There are usually also several FIFO queues in a GPU architecture, which are there to reduce starvation of hardware units. These queues are not shown in our diagrams.

The display controller has 12 bits per color component and has BT.2020 wide color gamut support. It also supports HDMI 2.0b and HDCP 2.2. For video processing, it supports SMPTE 2084, which is a transfer function for high dynamic range video. Venkataraman [1816] describes how NVIDIA architectures from Fermi and after have one or more *copy engines*. These are memory controllers that can perform *direct memory access* (DMA) transfers. A DMA transfer occur between the CPU and the GPU, and such a transfer is typically started on either of these. The starting processing unit can continue doing other computations during the transfer. The copy engines can initiate DMA transfers of data between the CPU and the GPU memory, and they can execute independently of the rest of the GPU. Hence, the GPU can render triangles and perform other functions while information is transferred from the CPU to the GPU or vice versa.

The Pascal architecture can also be configured for non-graphical applications, such as for training neural networks or large-scale data analysis. The Tesla P100 is one such configuration [1298]. Some of the differences from the GTX 1080 include that it uses high-bandwidth memory 2 (HBM2) with 4096 bits for the memory bus, providing a total memory bandwidth of 720 GB/s. In addition, they have native 16-bit floating point support, with up to 2× the performance of 32-bit floating point, and substantially faster double precision processing. The SM configuration is also different, as well as the register file setup [1298].

The GTX 1080 Ti (titanium) is a higher-end configuration. It has 3584 ALUs, a 352-bit memory bus, 484 GB/s in total memory bandwidth, 88 ROPs, and 224 texture units, compared to 2560, 256-bit, 320 GB/s, 64, and 160 for the GTX 1080.

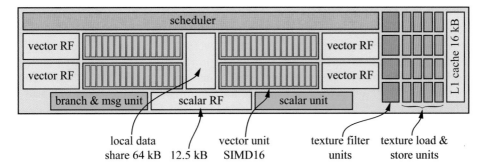

Figure 23.28. The GCN compute unit of the Vega architecture. Each of the vector register files has a 64 kB capacity, while the scalar RF has 12.5 kB, and local data share has 64 kB. Note that there are four units of 16 SIMD lanes (light green), with 32-bit floating point, for compute in each CU. *(Illustration after Mah [1103] and AMD white paper [35].)*

It is configured using six GPCs, i.e., it has six raster engines, compared to four in the GTX 1080. Four of the GPCs are exactly the same as in the GTX 1080, while the remaining two are somewhat smaller with only four TPCs instead of five. The 1080 Ti is built from 12 billion transistors for the chip, while the 1080 uses 7.2 billion. The Pascal architecture is flexible in that it can also scale down. For example, the GTX 1070 is a GTX 1080 minus one GPC, and the GTX 1050 consists of two GPCs, each with three SMs.

23.10.3   Case Study: AMD GCN Vega

The AMD Graphics Core Next (GCN) architecture is used in several AMD graphics card products as well as in the Xbox One and PLAYSTATION 4. Here, we describe general elements of the GCN Vega architecture [35], which is an evolution of the architectures used in these consoles.

A core building block of the GCN architecture is the compute unit (CU), which is illustrated in Figure 23.28. The CU has four SIMD units, each having 16 SIMD lanes, i.e., 16 unified ALUs (using the terminology from Section 23.2). Each SIMD unit executes instructions for 64 threads, which is called a *wavefront*. One single-precision floating point instruction per clock cycle can be issued per SIMD unit. Because the architecture processes a wavefront of 64 threads per SIMD unit, it takes 4 clock cycles before a wavefront has been fully issued [1103]. Note also that a CU can run code from different kernels at the same time. Since each SIMD unit has 16 lanes and one instruction can be issued per clock cycle, the maximum throughput for the entire CU is 4 SIMD units per CU × 16 SIMD lanes per unit = 64 single-precision FP operations per clock cycle. The CU can also execute twice as many half-precision (16-bit floating point) instructions compared to single-precision FP, which can be useful for cases where less accuracy is needed. This can include machine learning and shader computations, for example. Note that two 16-bit FP values are packed into a single

32-bit FP register. Each SIMD unit has a 64 kB register file, which amounts to $65,536/(4 \cdot 64) = 256$ registers per thread, since a single-precision FP uses 4 bytes and there are 64 threads per wavefront. The ALUs have four hardware pipeline stages [35].

Each CU has an instruction cache (not shown in the figure) that is shared between up to four SIMD units. The relevant instructions are forwarded to a SIMD unit's instruction buffer (IB). Each IB has storage for handling 10 wavefronts, which can be switched in and out of the SIMD unit as needed in order to hide latency. This means that the CU can handle 40 wavefronts. This, in turn, is equivalent to $40 \cdot 64 = 2560$ threads. The CU scheduler in Figure 23.28 can thus handle 2560 threads at a time, and its task is to distribute work to the different units of the CU. Each clock cycle, all wavefronts on the current CU are considered for instruction issues, and up to one instruction can be issued to each execution port. The execution ports of the CU include branches, scalar/vector ALU, scalar/vector memory, local data share, global data share or export, and special instructions [32], that is, each execution port maps roughly to one unit of the CU.

The scalar unit is a 64-bit ALU that is shared between the SIMD units as well. It has its own scalar register file and a scalar data cache (not shown). The scalar RF has 800 32-bit registers per SIMD unit, i.e., $800 \cdot 4 \cdot 4 = 12.5$ kB. Execution is tightly coupled to the wavefronts. Since it takes four clock cycles to fully issue an instruction into a SIMD unit, the scalar unit can serve a particular SIMD unit only every fourth clock cycle. The scalar unit handles control flow, pointer arithmetic, and other computations that can be shared among the threads in a warp. Conditional and unconditional branch instructions are sent from the scalar unit for execution in the branch and message unit. Each SIMD unit has a single 48-bit program counter (PC) that is shared between lanes. This is sufficient, since all of them execute the same instructions. For taken branches, the program counter is updated. Messages that can be sent by this unit include debug messages, special graphics synchronization messages, and CPU interrupts [1121].

The Vega 10 architecture [35] is illustrated in Figure 23.29. The top part includes a graphics command processor, two hardware schedulers (HWSs) and eight asynchronous compute engines (ACEs) [33]. The task of the GPC is to dispatch graphics tasks onto the graphics pipelines and compute engines of the GPU. The HWSs' buffers work in queues that they assign to the ACEs as soon as it is possible. The task of an ACE is to schedule compute tasks onto the compute engines. There are also two DMA engines that can handle copy tasks (not shown in the figure). The GPC, ACEs, and DMA engines can work in parallel and submit work to the GPU, which improves utilization, since tasks can be interleaved from different queues. Work can be dispatched from any queue without waiting for other work to finish, which means that independent tasks can execute on the compute engines simultaneously. The ACEs can synchronize via cache or memory. They can support task graphs together, so that one ACE's task can depend on another ACE's task, or on the graphics pipeline's tasks. It is recommended that smaller compute and copy tasks are interleaved with heavier graphics tasks [33].

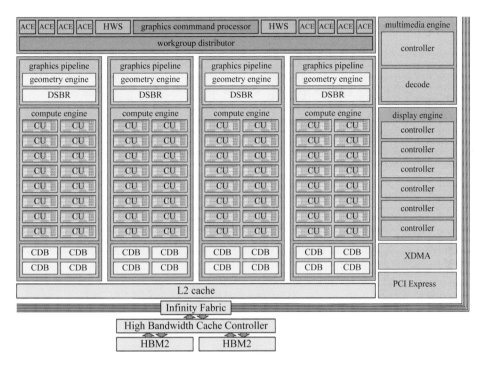

Figure 23.29. A Vega 10 GPU built with 64 CUs. Note that each CU contains the hardware shown in Figure 23.28. *(Illustration after AMD white paper [35].)*

As can be seen in Figure 23.29, there are four graphics pipelines and four compute engines. Each compute engine has 16 CUs, which sums to 64 CUs in total. The graphics pipeline has two blocks, namely a geometry engine and draw-stream binning rasterizer (DSBR). The geometry engine includes a geometry assembler, tessellation unit, and vertex assembler. In addition, a new *primitive shader* is supported. The idea of the primitive shader is to enable more flexible geometry processing and faster culling of primitives [35]. The DSBR combines the advantages of sort-middle and sort-last architectures, which also is the goal of tiled caching (Section 23.10.2). The image is divided into tiles in screen space, and after geometry processing, each primitive is assigned to the tiles they overlap. During rasterization of a tile, all data (e.g., tile buffers) required are kept in the L2 cache, which improves performance. Pixel shading can be deferred automatically until all the geometry in a tile has been processed. Hence, a z-prepass is done under the hood and pixels shaded only once. Deferred shading can be turned on and off; e.g., for transparent geometry it needs to be off.

To handle depth, stencil, and color buffers, the GCN architecture has a building block called the color and depth block (CDB). They handle color, depth, and stencil

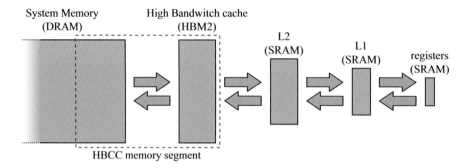

Figure 23.30. The cache hierarchy of the Vega architecture.

read and writes, in addition to color blending. A CDB can compress the color buffer using the general approach described in Section 23.5. A delta compression technique is used where one pixel's color is stored uncompressed per tile, and the rest of the color values are encoded relative to that pixel color [34, 1238]. In order to increase efficiency, the tile size can be dynamically chosen based on access patterns. For a tile originally stored using 256 bytes, the maximum rate is 8 : 1, i.e., compression down to 32 bytes. A compressed color buffer can be used as a texture in a subsequent pass, in which case the texture unit will decompress the compressed tile, which provides further bandwidth savings [1716].

The rasterizers can rasterize up to four primitives per clock cycle. The CDBs connected to the graphics pipeline and compute engine can write 16 pixels per clock cycle. That is, triangles smaller than 16 pixels reduce efficiency. The rasterizer also handles coarse depth testing (HiZ) and hierarchical stencil testing. The buffer for HiZ is called *HTILE* and can be programmed by the developer, e.g., for feeding occlusion information to the GPU.

The cache hierarchy of Vega is shown in Figure 23.30. At the top of the hierarchy (rightmost in the figure), we have registers, followed by the L1 and L2 caches. Then, there is high-bandwidth memory 2 (HBM2), which is located on the graphics card as well, and finally system memory located on the CPU side. A new feature of Vega is the High-Bandwidth Cache Controller (HBCC), shown at the bottom of Figure 23.29. It allows the video memory to behave like a last-level cache. This means that if a memory access is made and the corresponding content is not in the video memory, i.e., HBM2, then the HBCC will automatically fetch the relevant system memory page(s) over the PCIe bus and put it in video memory. Less recently used pages in the video memory may be swapped out as a consequence. The memory pool shared between the HBM2 and system memory is called the HBCC memory segment (HMS). All graphics blocks also access memory through the L2 cache, which differs from previous architectures. The architecture also supports virtual memory (Section 19.10.1).

Note that all the on-chip blocks, e.g., HBCC, XDMA (CrossFire DMA), PCI express, display engines, and multimedia engines, communicate over an interconnect called the *Infinity Fabric* (IF). AMD CPUs can also be connected to the IF. The Infinity Fabric can connect blocks on different chip dies. The IF is also coherent, meaning that all blocks get to see the same view of the content in memory.

The base clock frequency of the chip is 1677 MHz, i.e., the peak compute capability is

$$\underbrace{2}_{\text{FMA}} \cdot \underbrace{4096}_{\text{num SPs}} \cdot \underbrace{1677}_{\text{clock freq.}} = 13,737,984 \text{ MFLOPS} \approx 13.7 \text{ TFLOPS}, \qquad (23.17)$$

where the FMA and TFLOPS calculations match those in Equation 23.16. The architecture is flexible and extendable, so many more configurations are expected.

23.11 Ray Tracing Architectures

This section will give a brief introduction to ray tracing hardware. We will not list all recent references on this topic, but rather provide a set of pointers that the reader is encouraged to follow. Research in this field was started by Schmittler et al. [1571] in 2002, where focus was on traversal and intersection, and shading was computed using a fixed-function unit. This work was later followed up by Woop et al. [1905], who presented an architecture with programmable shaders.

The commercial interest in this topic has increased considerably over the past few years. This can be seen in the fact that companies, such as Imagination Technologies [1158], LG Electronics [1256], and Samsung [1013], have presented their own hardware architectures for real-time ray tracing. However, only Imagination Technologies has released a commercial product at the time of writing.

There are several common traits in these architectures. First, they often use a bounding volume hierarchy based on axis-aligned bounding boxes. Second, they tend to reduce hardware complexity by reducing precision in the ray/box intersection tests (Section 22.7). Finally, they use programmable cores to support programmable shading, which is more or less a requirement today. For example, Imagination Technologies extend their traditional chip design by adding a ray tracing unit, which can exploit the shader cores for shading, for example. The ray tracing unit consists of a ray intersection processor and a coherency engine [1158], where the latter gathers rays with similar properties and processes them together to exploit locality for faster ray tracing. The architecture from Imagination Technologies also includes a dedicated unit for building BVHs.

Research in this field continues to explore several areas, including reduced precision for efficient implementation of traversal [1807], compressed representations for BVHs [1045], and energy efficiency [929]. There is undoubtedly more research to be done.

Further Reading and Resources

A great set of resources are the course notes on computer graphics architectures by Akeley and Hanrahan [20] and Hwu and Kirk [793]. The book by Kirk and Hwu [903] is also an excellent resource for information about programming with CUDA on GPUs. The annual *High-Performance Graphics* and *SIGGRAPH* conference proceedings are good sources for presentations on new architectural features. Giesen's trip down the graphics pipeline is a wonderful online resource for anyone wanting to learn more about the details of GPUs [530]. We also refer the interested reader to Hennessy and Patterson's book [715] for detailed information about memory systems. Information on mobile rendering is scattered among many sources. Of note, the book *GPU Pro 5* has seven articles on mobile rendering techniques.

Chapter 24
The Future

"Pretty soon, computers will be fast."
—Billy Zelsnack

"Prediction is difficult, especially of the future."
—Niels Bohr or Yogi Berra

"The best way to predict the future is to create it."
—Alan Kay

There are two parts to the future: you and everything else. This chapter is about both. First, we will make some predictions, a few of which may even come true. More important is the second part, about where you could go next. It is something of an extended *Further Reading and Resources* section, but it also discusses ways to proceed from here—general sources of information, conferences, code, and more. But first, an image: See Figure 24.1.

Figure 24.1. A glimpse of one future, through the game *Destiny 2. (Image ©2017 Bungie, Inc. all rights reserved.)*

24.1 Everything Else

Graphics helps sell games, and games help sell chips. One of the best features of real-time rendering from a chip-maker's marketing perspective is that graphics eats huge amounts of processing power and other resources. Hardware-related features such as frame rate, resolution, and color depth can also grow to some extent, further increasing the load. A minimum solid frame rate of 90 FPS is the norm for virtual reality applications, and 4k pixel displays are already testing the abilities of graphics systems to keep up [1885].

The complex task of simulating the effect of light in a scene is plenty on its own for absorbing compute power. Adding more objects or lights to a scene is one way in which rendering can clearly become more expensive. The types of objects (both solid and volumetric, such as fog), the way these objects' surfaces are portrayed, and the types of lights used are just some factors where complexity can increase. Many algorithms improve in quality if we can take more samples, evaluate more accurate equations, or simply use more memory. Increasing complexity makes graphics a nearly bottomless pit for processing power to attempt to fill.

To solve performance concerns in the long run, rosy-eyed optimists like to turn to Moore's Law. This observation gives an acceleration rate of $2\times$ every 1.5 years or, more usefully, about $10\times$ speedup every 5 years [1663]. However, processor speed is usually not the bottleneck, and probably will be less so as time goes on. Bandwidth is, as it increases by a factor of 10 every 10 years, not 5 [1332].

Algorithms from the film industry often find their way into real-time rendering, since the fields share the same goal of generating realistic images. Looking at their practices, we see statistics such as that a single frame of the 2016 movie *The Jungle Book* includes millions of hairs in some scenes, with render times of 30 to 40 hours a frame [1960]. While GPUs are purpose-built for real-time rendering and so have a noticeable advantage over CPUs, going from $1/(40 \times 60 \times 60) = 0.00000694$ FPS to 60 FPS is about seven orders of magnitude.

We promised some predictions. "Faster and more flexible" is a simple one to make. As far as GPU architecture goes, one possibility is that the z-buffer triangle rasterization pipeline will continue to rule the roost. All but the simplest games use the GPU for rendering. Even if tomorrow some incredible technique supplanted the current pipeline, one that was a hundred times faster and that consisted of downloading a system patch, it could still take years for the industry to move to this new technology. One catch would be whether the new method could use exactly the same APIs as existing ones. If not, adoption would take a while. A complex game costs tens of millions of dollars or more to develop and takes years to make. The target platforms are chosen early in the process, which informs decisions about everything from the algorithms and shaders used, to the size and complexity of artwork produced. Beyond those factors, the tools needed to work with or produce these elements need to be made and users need to become proficient in their use. The momentum that the current rasterizer pipeline has behind it gives it several years of life, even with a miracle occurring.

Change still happens. In reality, the simple "one rasterizer to rule them all" idea has already begun to fade. Throughout this book we have discussed how the compute shader is able to take on various tasks, proof that rasterization is hardly the only service a GPU can offer. If new techniques are compelling, retooling the workflow will happen, percolating out from game companies to commercial engines and content creation tools.

So, what of the long-term? Dedicated fixed-function GPU hardware for rendering triangles, accessing textures, and blending resulting samples still gives critical boosts to performance. The needs of mobile devices change this equation, as power consumption becomes as much of a factor as raw performance. However, the "fire-and-forget" concept of the basic pipeline, where we send a triangle down the pipeline once and are entirely done with it for that frame, is not the model used in modern rendering engines. The basic pipeline model of transform, scan, shade, and blend has evolved almost beyond recognition. The GPU has become a large cluster of stream-based processors to use as you wish.

APIs and GPUs have coevolved to adapt to this reality. The mantra is "flexibility." Methods are explored by researchers, then implemented on existing hardware by developers, who identify functionality they wish was available. Independent hardware vendors can use these findings and their own research to develop general capabilities, in a virtuous cycle. Optimizing for any single algorithm is a fool's errand. Creating new, flexible ways to access and process data on the GPU is not.

With that in mind, we see ray/object intersection as a general tool with numerous uses. We know that perfectly unbiased sampling using path tracing eventually yields the correct, ground-truth image, to the limits of the scene description. It is the word "eventually" that is the catch. As discussed in Section 11.7, there are currently serious challenges for path tracing as a viable algorithm. The main problem is the sheer number of samples needed to get a result that is not noisy, and that does not twinkle when animated. That said, the purity and simplicity of path tracing make it extremely appealing. Instead of the current state of interactive rendering, where a multitude of specialized techniques are tailored for particular situations, just one algorithm does it all. Film studios have certainly come to realize this, as the past decade has seen them move entirely to ray and path tracing methods. Doing so lets them optimize on just one set of geometric operations for light transport.

Real-time rendering—all rendering for that matter—is ultimately about sampling and filtering. Aside from increasing the efficiency of ray shooting, path tracing can benefit from smarter sampling and filtering. As it is, almost every offline path tracer is biased, regardless of marketing literature [1276]. Reasonable assumptions are made about where to send sample rays, vastly improving performance. The other area where path tracing can benefit is intelligent filtering—literally. Deep learning is currently a white-hot area of research and development, with the initial resurgence of interest due to impressive gains in 2012 when it considerably outpaced hand-tweaked algorithms for image recognition [349]. The use of neural nets for denoising [95, 200, 247] and antialiasing [1534] are fascinating developments. See Figure 24.2. We are already

Figure 24.2. Image reconstruction with a neural net. On the left, a noisy image generated with path tracing. On the right, the image cleaned up using a GPU-accelerated denoiser at interactive rates. *(Image courtesy of NVIDIA Corporation [200], using the Amazon Lumberyard Bistro scene.)*

seeing a large uptick in the number of research papers using neural nets for rendering-related tasks, not to mention modeling and animation.

Dating back to AT&T's *Pixel Machine* in 1987, interactive ray tracing has long been possible for small scenes, low resolutions, few lights, and compositions with only sharp reflections, refractions, and shadows. Microsoft's addition of ray tracing functionality to the DirectX API, called *DXR*, simplifies the process of shooting rays and is likely to inspire hardware vendors to add support for ray intersection. Ray shooting, enhanced with denoising or other filtering, will at first be just another technique for improving rendering quality of various elements, such as shadows or reflections. It will compete with many other algorithms, with each rendering engine making choices based on such factors as speed, quality, and ease of use. See Figure 24.3.

Hierarchical ray shooting as a fundamental operation is not an explicit part of any mainstream commercial GPU as of this writing. We take PowerVR's Wizard GPU [1158] as a good sign, in that a mobile device company is considering hardware support for testing rays against a hierarchical scene description. Newer GPUs with direct support for shooting rays will change the equations of efficiency and could create a virtuous cycle, one where various rendering effects are less customized and specialized. Rasterization for the eye rays and ray tracing or compute shaders for almost everything else is one approach, already being used in various DXR demos [1, 47, 745]. With improved denoising algorithms, faster GPUs for tracing rays, and previous research reapplied as well as new investigations, we expect to soon see the equivalent of a $10\times$ performance improvement.

We expect DXR to be a boon to developers and researchers in other ways. For games, baking systems that cast rays can now be run on the GPU and use similar

Figure 24.3. These images were rendered at interactive rates with two reflection ray bounces per pixel, a shadow ray for the screen location and both bounces, and two ambient occlusion rays, for a total of seven rays per pixel. Denoising filters were used for shadows and reflections. *(Images courtesy of NVIDIA Corporation.)*

or the same shaders as found in the interactive renderer, with improved performance as a result. Ground-truth images can be more easily generated, making it simpler to test and even auto-tune algorithms. The idea of architectural changes that allow more flexible generation of GPU tasks, e.g., shaders creating shader work, seems a powerful one that will likely have other applications.

There are certainly other fascinating possibilities of how GPUs might evolve. Another idealized view of the world is one in which all matter is voxelized. Such a representation has any number of advantages for light transport and simulation, as discussed in Section 13.10. The large amount of data storage needed, and difficulties with dynamic objects in the scene, make the likelihood of a complete switchover extremely unlikely. Nonetheless, we believe voxels are likely to get more attention, for their use in a wide range of areas, including high-quality volumetric effects, 3D printing, and unconstrained object modification (e.g., *Minecraft*). Certainly a related representation, point clouds, will be part of much more research in the years to come, given the massive amounts of such data generated by self-driving car systems, LIDAR, and other sensors. Signed distance fields (SDFs) are another intriguing scene description method. Similarly to voxels, SDFs enable unconstrained modification of the scene and can accelerate ray tracing as well.

Sometimes, the unique constraints of a given application allow its developers to "break the mold" and use techniques previously considered exotic or infeasible. Games such as Media Molecule's *Dreams* and *Claybook* by Second Order, pictured in Figure 24.4, can give us intriguing glimpses into possible rendering futures where unorthodox algorithms hold sway.

Figure 24.4. *Claybook* is a physics-based puzzle game with a world of clay that can be freely sculpted by users. The clay world is modeled using signed distance fields and rendered with ray tracing, including primary rays as well as ray-traced shadows and AO. Solid and liquid physics are simulated on the GPU. *(Claybook.* © *2017 Second Order, Ltd.)*

Virtual and mixed reality deserve a mention. When VR works well, it is breathtaking. Mixed reality has enchanting demos of synthetic content merging with the real world. Everyone wants the lightweight glasses that do both, which is likely to be in the "personal jetpacks, underwater cities" category in the short term. But who knows? Given the huge amount of research and development behind these efforts [1187], there are likely to be some breakthroughs, possibly world-changing ones.

24.2 You

So, while you and your children's children are waiting for The Singularity, what do you do in the meantime? Program, of course: Discover new algorithms, create applications, or do whatever else you enjoy. Decades ago graphics hardware for one machine cost more than a luxury car; now it is built into just about every device with a CPU, and these devices often fit in the palm of your hand. Graphics hacking is inexpensive and mainstream. In this section, we cover various resources we have found to be useful in learning more about the field of real-time rendering.

This book does not exist in a vacuum; it draws upon a huge number of sources of information. If you are interested in a particular algorithm, track down the original publications. Our website has a page of all articles we reference, so you can look there for the link to the resource, if available. Most research articles can be found using

Google Scholar, the author's website, or, if all else fails, ask the author for a copy—almost everyone likes to have their work read and appreciated. If not found for free, services such as the *ACM Digital Library* have a huge number of articles available. If you are a member of SIGGRAPH, you automatically have free access to many of their graphics articles and talks. There are several journals that publish technical articles, such as the *ACM Transactions on Graphics* (which now includes the SIGGRAPH proceedings as an issue), *The Journal of Computer Graphics Techniques* (which is open access), *IEEE Transactions on Visualization and Computer Graphics, Computer Graphics Forum*, and *IEEE Computer Graphics and Applications*, to mention a few. Finally, some professional blogs have excellent information, and graphics developers and researchers on Twitter often point out wonderful new resources.

One of the fastest ways to learn and meet others is to attend a conference. Odds are high that another person is doing something you are, or might get, interested in. If money is tight, contact the organizers and ask about volunteer opportunities or scholarships. The SIGGRAPH and SIGGRAPH Asia annual conferences are premier venues for new ideas, but hardly the only ones. Other technical gatherings, such as the Eurographics conference and the Eurographics Symposium on Rendering (EGSR), the Symposium on Interactive 3D Graphics and Games (I3D), and the High Performance Graphics (HPG) forum present and publish a significant amount of material relevant to real-time rendering. There are also developer-specific conferences, such as the well-established Game Developers Conference (GDC). Say hello to strangers when you are waiting in line or at an event. At SIGGRAPH in particular keep an eye out for *birds of a feather* (BOF) gatherings in your areas of interest. Meeting people and exchanging ideas face to face is both rewarding and energizing.

There are a few electronic resources relevant to interactive rendering. Of particular note, the *Graphics Codex* [1188] is a high-quality, purely electronic reference that has the advantage of being continually updated. The site *immersive linear algebra* [1718], created in part by a coauthor of this book, includes interactive demos to aid in learning this topic. Shirley [1628] has an excellent series of short Kindle books on ray tracing. We look forward to more inexpensive and quick-access resources of this sort.

Printed books still have their place. Beyond general texts and field-specific volumes, edited collections of articles include a significant amount of research and development information, many of which we reference in this book. Recent examples are the *GPU Pro* and *GPU Zen* books. Older books such as *Game Programming Gems, GPU Gems* (free online), and the *ShaderX* series still have relevant articles—algorithms do not rot. All these books allow game developers to present their methods without having to write a formal conference paper. Such collections also allow academics to discuss technical details about their work that do not fit into a research paper. For a professional developer, an hour saved by reading about some implementation detail found in an article more than pays back the cost of the entire book. If you cannot wait for a book to be delivered, using the "Look Inside" feature on Amazon or searching for the text on Google Books may yield an excerpt to get you started.

When all is said and done, code needs to be written. With the rise of GitHub, Bitbucket, and similar repositories, there is a rich storehouse to draw upon. The hard part is knowing what does not fall under Sturgeon's Law. Products such as the Unreal Engine have made their source open access, and thus an incredible resource. The ACM is now encouraging code to be released for any technical article published. Authors you respect sometimes have their code available. Search around.

One site of particular note is Shadertoy, which often uses ray marching in a pixel shader to show off various techniques. While many programs are first and foremost eye candy, the site has numerous educational demos, all with code visible, and all runnable within your browser. Another source for browser-based demos is the three.js repository and related sites. "Three" is a wrapper around WebGL that encourages experimentation, as just a few lines of code produces a rendering. The ability to publish demos on the web for anyone to run and dissect, just a hyperlink click away, is wonderful for educational uses and for sharing ideas. One of the authors of this book created an introductory graphics course for Udacity based on three.js [645].

We refer you one more time to our website at realtimerendering.com. There you will find many other resources, such as lists of recommended and new books (including a few that are free and of high quality [301, 1729]), as well as pointers to worthwhile blogs, research sites, course presentations, and many other sources of information. Happy hunting!

Our last words of advice are to go and learn and do. The field of real-time computer graphics is continually evolving, and new ideas and features are constantly being invented and integrated. You can be involved. The wide array of techniques employed can seem daunting, but you do not need to implement a laundry list of buzzwords-du-jour to get good results. Cleverly combining a small number of techniques, based on the constraints and visual style of your application, can result in distinctive visuals. Share your results on GitHub, which can also be used to host a blog. Get involved!

One of the best parts of this field is that it reinvents itself every few years. Computer architectures change and improve. What did not work a few years ago may now be worth pursuing. With each new GPU offering comes a different mix of functionality, speed, and memory. What is efficient and what is a bottleneck changes and evolves. Even areas that seem old and well-established are worth revisiting. Creation is said to be a matter of bending, breaking, and blending other ideas, not making something from nothing.

This edition comes 44 years after one of the milestone papers in the field of computer graphics, "A Characterization of Ten Hidden-Surface Algorithms" by Sutherland, Sproull, and Schumacker, published in 1974 [1724]. Their 55-page paper is an incredibly thorough comparison. The algorithm described as "ridiculously expensive," the brute-force technique not even dignified with a researcher's name, and mentioned only in the appendices, is what is now called the z-buffer. In fairness, Sutherland was the adviser of the inventor of the z-buffer, Ed Catmull, whose thesis discussing this concept would be published a few months later [237].

This eleventh hidden-surface technique won out because it was easy to implement in hardware and because memory densities went up and costs went down. The "Ten Algorithms" survey done by Sutherland et al. was perfectly valid for its time. As conditions change, so do the algorithms used. It will be exciting to see what happens in the years to come. How will it feel when we look back on this current era of rendering technology? No one knows, and each person can have a significant effect on the way the future turns out. There is no one future, no course that must occur. You create it.

What do you want to do next? *(CD PROJEKT®, The Witcher® are registered trademarks of CD PROJEKT Capital Group. The Witcher game © CD PROJEKT S.A. Developed by CD PROJEKT S.A. All rights reserved. The Witcher game is based on the prose of Andrzej Sapkowski. All other copyrights and trademarks are the property of their respective owners.)*

Bibliography

[1] Aalto, Tatu, "Experiments with DirectX Raytracing in Remedy's Northlight Engine," *Game Developers Conference*, Mar. 19, 2018. Cited on p. 1044

[2] Aaltonen, Sebastian, "Modern Textureless Deferred Rendering Techniques," *Beyond3D Forum*, Feb. 28, 2016. Cited on p. 906, 907

[3] Abbas, Wasim, "Practical Analytic 2D Signed Distance Field Generation," in *ACM SIGGRAPH 2016 Talks*, article no. 68, July 2016. Cited on p. 677, 678

[4] Abrash, Michael, *Michael Abrash's Graphics Programming Black Book*, Special Edition, The Coriolis Group, Inc., 1997. Cited on p. 823

[5] Abrash, Michael, "Latency—The *sine qua non* of AR and VR," *Ramblings in Valve Time* blog, Dec. 29, 2012. Cited on p. 920, 939

[6] Abrash, Michael, "Raster-Scan Displays: More Than Meets The Eye," *Ramblings in Valve Time* blog, Jan. 28, 2013. Cited on p. 922, 1012

[7] Abrash, Michael, "Down the VR Rabbit Hole: Fixing Judder," *Ramblings in Valve Time* blog, July 26, 2013. Cited on p. 935, 1011

[8] Abrash, Michael, "Oculus Chief Scientist Predicts the Next 5 Years of VR Technology," *Road to VR* website, Nov. 4, 2016. Cited on p. 931, 932

[9] Adams, Ansel, *The Camera*, Little, Brown and Company, 1980. Cited on p. 291

[10] Adams, Ansel, *The Negative*, Little, Brown and Company, 1981. Cited on p. 289, 291

[11] Adams, Ansel, *The Print*, Little, Brown and Company, 1983. Cited on p. 291

[12] Adorjan, Matthias, *OpenSfM: A Collaborative Structure-from-Motion System*, Diploma thesis in Visual Computing, Vienna University of Technology, 2016. Cited on p. 574, 575

[13] Aila, Timo, and Ville Miettinen, "dPVS: An Occlusion Culling System for Massive Dynamic Environments," *IEEE Computer Graphics and Applications*, vol. 24, no. 2, pp. 86–97, Mar. 2004. Cited on p. 666, 821, 839, 850, 879

[14] Aila, Timo, and Samuli Laine, "Alias-Free Shadow Maps," in *Eurographics Symposium on Rendering*, Eurographics Association, pp. 161–166, June 2004. Cited on p. 260

[15] Aila, Timo, and Samuli Laine, "Understanding the Efficiency of Ray Traversal on GPUs," *High Performance Graphics*, June 2009. Cited on p. 511

[16] Aila, Timo, Samuli Laine, and Tero Karras, "Understanding the Efficiency of Ray Traversal on GPUs—Kepler and Fermi Addendum," Technical Report NVR-2012-02, NVIDIA, 2012. Cited on p. 511, 961

[17] Airey, John M., John H. Rohlf, and Frederick P. Brooks Jr., "Towards Image Realism with Interactive Update Rates in Complex Virtual Building Environments," *ACM SIGGRAPH Computer Graphics (Symposium on Interactive 3D Graphics)*, vol. 24, no. 2, pp. 41–50, Mar. 1990. Cited on p. 687, 837

[18] Airey, John M., *Increasing Update Rates in the Building Walkthrough System with Automatic Model-Space Subdivision and Potentially Visible Set Calculations*, PhD thesis, Technical Report TR90-027, Department of Computer Science, University of North Carolina at Chapel Hill, July 1990. Cited on p. 837

[19] Akeley, K., P. Haeberli, and D. Burns, `tomesh.c`, a C-program on the *SGI Developer's Toolbox CD*, 1990. Cited on p. 692

[20] Akeley, Kurt, and Pat Hanrahan, "Real-Time Graphics Architectures," Course CS448A Notes, Stanford University, Fall 2001. Cited on p. 1040

[21] Akenine-Möller, Tomas, "Fast 3D Triangle-Box Overlap Testing," *journal of graphics tools*, vol. 6, no. 1, pp. 29–33, 2001. Cited on p. 974, 975

[22] Akenine-Möller, Tomas, and Jacob Ström, "Graphics for the Masses: A Hardware Rasterization Architecture for Mobile Phones," *ACM Transactions on Graphics*, vol. 22, no. 3, pp. 801–808, 2003. Cited on p. 146, 1015, 1027

[23] Akenine-Möller, Tomas, and Ulf Assarsson, "On the Degree of Vertices in a Shadow Volume Silhouette," *journal of graphics tools*, vol. 8, no. 4, pp. 21–24, 2003. Cited on p. 667

[24] Akenine-Möller, T., and T. Aila, "Conservative and Tiled Rasterization Using a Modified Triangle Setup," *journal of graphics tools*, vol. 10, no. 3, pp. 1–8, 2005. Cited on p. 996, 1001

[25] Akenine-Möller, Tomas, and Björn Johnsson, "Performance per What?" *Journal of Computer Graphics Techniques*, vol. 1, no. 18, pp. 37–41, 2012. Cited on p. 790

[26] Akenine-Möller, Tomas, "Some Notes on Graphics Hardware," *Tomas Akenine-Möller* webpage, Nov. 27, 2012. Cited on p. 999, 1000

[27] Akin, Atilla, "Pushing the Limits of Realism of Materials," *Maxwell Render* blog, Nov. 26, 2014. Cited on p. 362, 363

[28] Alexa, Marc, "Recent Advances in Mesh Morphing," *Computer Graphics Forum*, vol. 21, no. 2, pp. 173–197, 2002. Cited on p. 87, 88, 102

[29] Alexa, M., and T. Boubekeur, "Subdivision Shading," *ACM Transactions on Graphics*, vol. 27, no. 5, pp. 142:1–142:3, 2008. Cited on p. 767

[30] Aliaga, Daniel G., and Anselmo Lastra, "Automatic Image Placement to Provide a Guaranteed Frame Rate," in *SIGGRAPH '99: Proceedings of the 26th Annual Conference on Computer Graphics and Interactive Techniques*, ACM Press/Addison-Wesley Publishing Co., pp. 307–316, Aug. 1999. Cited on p. 561

[31] AMD, "AMD PowerTune Technology," AMD website, 2011. Cited on p. 789

[32] AMD, "AMD Graphics Cores Next (GCN) Architecture," AMD website, 2012. Cited on p. 1036

[33] AMD, "Asynchronous Shaders: Unlocking the Full Potential of the GPU," AMD website, 2015. Cited on p. 1036

[34] AMD, "Radeon: Dissecting the Polaris Architecture," AMD website, 2016. Cited on p. 1038

[35] AMD, "Radeon's Next-Generation Vega Architecture," AMD website, 2017. Cited on p. 1035, 1036, 1037

[36] AMD, GPUOpen, "TressFX," *GitHub* repository, 2017. Cited on p. 642, 644, 647

[37] American Society for Photogrammetry & Remote Sensing, "LAS Specification, Version 1.4—R13," *asprs.org*, July 15, 2013. Cited on p. 573

[38] Anagnostou, Kostas, "How Unreal Renders a Frame," *Interplay of Light* blog, Oct. 24, 2017. Cited on p. 899, 905, 913

[39] Anderson, Eric A., "Building Obduction: Cyan's Custom UE4 Art Tools," *Game Developers Conference*, Mar. 2016. Cited on p. 366

[40] Andersson, Johan, "Terrain Rendering in Frostbite Using Procedural Shader Splatting," *SIG-GRAPH Advanced Real-Time Rendering in 3D Graphics and Games course*, Aug. 2007. Cited on p. 43, 175, 218, 877, 878

[41] Andersson, Johan, and Daniel Johansson, "Shadows & Decals: D3D10 Techniques from Frostbite," *Game Developers Conference*, Mar. 2009. Cited on p. 245, 246, 247

[42] Andersson, Johan, "Parallel Graphics in Frostbite—Current & Future," *SIGGRAPH Beyond Programmable Shading course*, Aug. 2009. Cited on p. 893

[43] Andersson, Johan, "DirectX 11 Rendering in *Battlefield 3*," *Game Developers Conference*, Mar. 2011. Cited on p. 147, 888, 890, 893, 896

[44] Andersson, Johan, "Shiny PC Graphics in *Battlefield 3*," *GeForce LAN*, Oct. 2011. Cited on p. 569, 570, 604

[45] Andersson, Johan, "Parallel Futures of a Game Engine," *Intel Dynamic Execution Environment Symposium*, May 2012. Cited on p. 811, 812

[46] Andersson, Johan, "The Rendering Pipeline—Challenges & Next Steps," *SIGGRAPH Open Problems in Real-Time Rendering course*, Aug. 2015. Cited on p. 156, 514, 1014

[47] Andersson, Johan, and Colin Barré-Brisebois, "Shiny Pixels and Beyond: Real-Time Raytracing at SEED," *Game Developers Conference*, Mar. 2018. Cited on p. 1044

[48] Andersson, M., J. Hasselgren, R. Toth, and T. Akenine-Möller, "Adaptive Texture Space Shading for Stochastic Rendering," *Computer Graphics Forum*, vol. 33, no. 2, pp. 341–350, 2014. Cited on p. 910, 911

[49] Andersson, Magnus, *Algorithmic Improvements for Stochastic Rasterization & Depth Buffering*, PhD thesis, Lund University, Oct. 2015. Cited on p. 1015

[50] Andersson, M., J. Hasselgren, and T. Akenine-Möller, "Masked Depth Culling for Graphics Hardware," *ACM Transactions on Graphics*, vol. 34, no. 6, pp. 188:1–188:9, 2015. Cited on p. 849, 1015, 1016

[51] Andreev, Dmitry, "Real-Time Frame Rate Up-Conversion for Video Games," in *ACM SIGGRAPH 2010 Talks*, ACM, article no. 16, July 2010. Cited on p. 537, 542

[52] Andreev, Dmitry, "Anti-Aliasing from a Different Perspective," *Game Developers Conference*, Mar. 2011. Cited on p. 147

[53] Anguelov, Bobby, "DirectX10 Tutorial 10: Shadow Mapping Part 2," *Taking Initiative* blog, May 25, 2011. Cited on p. 249

[54] Annen, Thomas, Jan Kautz, Frédo Durand, and Hans-Peter Seidel, "Spherical Harmonic Gradients for Mid-Range Illumination," in *Proceedings of the Fifteenth Eurographics Conference on Rendering Techniques*, Eurographics Association, pp. 331–336, June 2004. Cited on p. 488

[55] Annen, Thomas, Tom Mertens, Philippe Bekaert, Hans-Peter Seidel, and Jan Kautz, "Convolution Shadow Maps," in *Proceedings of the 18th Eurographics Conference on Rendering Techniques*, Eurographics Association, pp. 51–60, June 2007. Cited on p. 255

[56] Annen, Thomas, Tom Mertens, Hans-Peter Seidel, Eddy Flerackers, and Jan Kautz, "Exponential Shadow Maps," in *Graphics Interface 2008*, Canadian Human-Computer Communications Society, pp. 155–161, May 2008. Cited on p. 256

[57] Annen, Thomas, Zhao Dong, Tom Mertens, Philippe Bekaert, Hans-Peter Seidel, and Jan Kautz, "Real-Time, All-Frequency Shadows in Dynamic Scenes," *ACM Transactions on Graphics*, vol. 27, no. 3, article no. 34, Aug. 2008. Cited on p. 257

[58] Ansari, Marwan Y., "Image Effects with DirectX 9 Pixel Shaders," in Wolfgang Engel, ed., *ShaderX²: Shader Programming Tips and Tricks with DirectX 9*, pp. 481–518, Wordware, 2004. Cited on p. 521, 665

[59] Answer, James, "Fast and Flexible: Technical Art and Rendering for The Unknown," *Game Developers Conference*, Mar. 2016. Cited on p. 710, 787, 805, 931, 934, 936, 938

[60] Antoine, François, Ryan Brucks, Brian Karis, and Gavin Moran, "The Boy, the Kite and the 100 Square Mile Real-Time Digital Backlot," in *ACM SIGGRAPH 2015 Talks*, ACM, article no. 20, Aug. 2015. Cited on p. 493

[61] Antonio, Franklin, "Faster Line Segment Intersection," in David Kirk, ed., *Graphics Gems III*, pp. 199–202, Academic Press, 1992. Cited on p. 988, 989

[62] Antonov, Michael, "Asynchronous Timewarp Examined," *Oculus Developer Blog*, Mar. 3, 2015. Cited on p. 936, 937

[63] Apodaca, Anthony A., and Larry Gritz, *Advanced RenderMan: Creating CGI for Motion Pictures*, Morgan Kaufmann, 1999. Cited on p. 37, 909

[64] Apodaca, Anthony A., "How PhotoRealistic RenderMan Works," in *Advanced RenderMan: Creating CGI for Motion Pictures*, Morgan Kaufmann, Chapter 6, 1999. Also in *SIGGRAPH Advanced RenderMan 2: To RI_INFINITY and Beyond course*, July 2000. Cited on p. 51

[65] Apple, "ARKit," Apple developer website. Cited on p. 918

[66] Apple, "OpenGL ES Programming Guide for iOS," Apple developer website. Cited on p. 177, 702, 713

[67] de Araújo, B. R., D. S. Lopes, P. Jepp, J. A. Jorge, and B. Wyvill, "A Survey on Implicit Surface Polygonization," *ACM Computing Surveys*, vol. 47, no. 4, pp. 60:1–60:39, 2015. Cited on p. 586, 683, 751, 753, 781, 944

[68] Arge, L., G. S. Brodal, and R. Fagerberg, "Cache-Oblivious Data Structures," in *Handbook of Data Structures*, CRC Press, Chapter 34, 2005. Cited on p. 827

[69] ARM Limited, "ARM®Mali^{TM}Application Developer Best Practices, Version 1.0," ARM documentation, Feb. 27, 2017. Cited on p. 48, 798, 1029

[70] Arvo, James, "A Simple Method for Box-Sphere Intersection Testing," in Andrew S. Glassner, ed., *Graphics Gems*, Academic Press, pp. 335–339, 1990. Cited on p. 977, 984

[71] Arvo, James, "Ray Tracing with Meta-Hierarchies," *SIGGRAPH Advanced Topics in Ray Tracing course*, Aug. 1990. Cited on p. 953

[72] Arvo, James, ed., *Graphics Gems II*, Academic Press, 1991. Cited on p. 102, 991

[73] Arvo, James, "The Irradiance Jacobian for Partially Occluded Polyhedral Sources," in *SIGGRAPH '94: Proceedings of the 21st Annual Conference on Computer Graphics and Interactive Techniques*, ACM, pp. 343–350, July 1994. Cited on p. 379

[74] Arvo, James, "Applications of Irradiance Tensors to the Simulation of non-Lambertian Phenomena," in *SIGGRAPH '95: Proceedings of the 22nd Annual Conference on Computer Graphics and Interactive Techniques*, ACM, pp. 335–342, Aug. 1995. Cited on p. 389, 390

[75] Asanovic, Krste, et al., "The Landscape of Parallel Computing Research: A View from Berkeley," Technical Report No. UCB/EECS-2006-183, EECS Department, University of California, Berkeley, 2006. Cited on p. 806, 815

[76] Ashdown, Ian, *Radiosity: A Programmer's Perspective*, John Wiley & Sons, Inc., 1994. Cited on p. 271, 442

[77] Ashikhmin, Michael, and Peter Shirley, "An Anisotropic Phong Light Reflection Model," Technical Report UUCS-00-014, Computer Science Department, University of Utah, June 2000. Cited on p. 352

[78] Ashikhmin, Michael, Simon Premože, and Peter Shirley, "A Microfacet-Based BRDF Generator," in *SIGGRAPH '00: Proceedings of the 27th Annual Conference on Computer Graphics and Interactive Techniques*, ACM Press/Addison-Wesley Publishing Co., pp. 67–74, July 2000. Cited on p. 328, 335, 357

[79] Ashikhmin, Michael, "Microfacet-Based BRDFs," *SIGGRAPH State of the Art in Modeling and Measuring of Surface Reflection course*, Aug. 2001. Cited on p. 329

[80] Ashikhmin, Michael, Abhijeet Ghosh, "Simple Blurry Reflections with Environment Maps," *journal of graphics tools*, vol. 7, no. 4, pp. 3–8, 2002. Cited on p. 417, 418

[81] Ashikhmin, Michael, and Simon Premože, "Distribution-Based BRDFs," Technical Report, 2007. Cited on p. 357

[82] Asirvatham, Arul, and Hugues Hoppe, "Terrain Rendering Using GPU-Based Geometry Clipmaps," in Matt Pharr, ed., *GPU Gems 2*, Addison-Wesley, pp. 27–45, 2005. Cited on p. 872, 873

[83] Assarsson, Ulf, and Tomas Möller, "Optimized View Frustum Culling Algorithms for Bounding Boxes," *journal of graphics tools*, vol. 5, no. 1, pp. 9–22, 2000. Cited on p. 836, 982, 986

[84] Atanasov, Asen, and Vladimir Koylazov, "A Practical Stochastic Algorithm for Rendering Mirror-Like Flakes," in *ACM SIGGRAPH 2016 Talks*, article no. 67, July 2016. Cited on p. 372

[85] Austin, Michael, "Voxel Surfing," *Game Developers Conference*, Mar. 2016. Cited on p. 586

[86] Bærentzen, J. Andreas, Steen Lund Nielsen, Mikkel Gjøl, and Bent D. Larsen, "Two Methods for Antialiased Wireframe Drawing with Hidden Line Removal," in *SCCG '08 Proceedings of the 24th Spring Conference on Computer Graphics*, ACM, pp. 171–177, Apr. 2008. Cited on p. 673, 675

[87] Baert, J., A. Lagae, and Ph. Dutré, "Out-of-Core Construction of Sparse Voxel Octrees," *Computer Graphics Forum*, vol. 33, no. 6, pp. 220–227, 2014. Cited on p. 579, 582

[88] Bagnell, Dan, "Graphics Tech in Cesium—Vertex Compression," *Cesium* blog, May 18, 2015. Cited on p. 715

[89] Bahar, E., and S. Chakrabarti, "Full-Wave Theory Applied to Computer-Aided Graphics for 3D Objects," *IEEE Computer Graphics and Applications*, vol. 7, no. 7, pp. 46–60, July 1987. Cited on p. 361

[90] Bahnassi, Homam, and Wessam Bahnassi, "Volumetric Clouds and Mega-Particles," in Wolfgang Engel, ed., *ShaderX^5*, Charles River Media, pp. 295–302, 2006. Cited on p. 521, 556

[91] Baker, Dan, "Advanced Lighting Techniques," *Meltdown 2005*, July 2005. Cited on p. 369

[92] Baker, Dan, and Yannis Minadakis, "Firaxis' Civilization V: A Case Study in Scalable Game Performance," *Game Developers Conference*, Mar. 2010. Cited on p. 812

[93] Baker, Dan, "Spectacular Specular—LEAN and CLEAN Specular Highlights," *Game Developers Conference*, Mar. 2011. Cited on p. 370

[94] Baker, Dan, "Object Space Lighting," *Game Developers Conference*, Mar. 2016. Cited on p. 911

[95] Bako, Steve, Thijs Vogels, Brian McWilliams, Mark Meyer, Jan Novák, Alex Harvill, Pradeep Sen, Tony DeRose, and Fabrice Rousselle, "Kernel-Predicting Convolutional Networks for Denoising Monte Carlo Renderings," *ACM Transactions on Graphics*, vol. 36, no. 4, article no. 97, 2017. Cited on p. 511, 1043

[96] Baldwin, Doug, and Michael Weber, "Fast Ray-Triangle Intersections by Coordinate Transformation," *Journal of Computer Graphics Techniques*, vol. 5, no. 3, pp. 39–49, 2016. Cited on p. 962

[97] Balestra, C., and P.-K. Engstad, "The Technology of Uncharted: Drake's Fortune," *Game Developers Conference*, Mar. 2008. Cited on p. 893

[98] Banks, David, "Illumination in Diverse Codimensions," in *SIGGRAPH '94: Proceedings of the 21st Annual Conference on Computer Graphics and Interactive Techniques*, ACM, pp. 327–334, July 1994. Cited on p. 359

[99]   Barb, C., "Texture Streaming in *Titanfall 2*," *Game Developers Conference*, Feb.–Mar. 2017. Cited on p. 869

[100] Barber, C. B., D. P. Dobkin, and H. Huhdanpaa, "The Quickhull Algorithm for Convex Hull," Technical Report GCG53, Geometry Center, July 1993. Cited on p. 950

[101] Barequet, G., and G. Elber, "Optimal Bounding Cones of Vectors in Three Dimensions," *Information Processing Letters*, vol. 93, no. 2, pp. 83–89, 2005. Cited on p. 834

[102] Barkans, Anthony C., "Color Recovery: True-Color 8-Bit Interactive Graphics," *IEEE Computer Graphics and Applications*, vol. 17, no. 1, pp. 67–77, Jan./Feb. 1997. Cited on p. 1010

[103] Barkans, Anthony C., "High-Quality Rendering Using the Talisman Architecture," in *Proceedings of the ACM SIGGRAPH/EUROGRAPHICS Workshop on Graphics Hardware*, ACM, pp. 79–88, Aug. 1997. Cited on p. 189

[104] Barla, Pascal, Joëlle Thollot, and Lee Markosian, "X-Toon: An Extended Toon Shader," in *Proceedings of the 4th International Symposium on Non-Photorealistic Animation and Rendering*, ACM, pp. 127–132, 2006. Cited on p. 654

[105] Barré-Brisebois, Colin, and Marc Bouchard, "Approximating Translucency for a Fast, Cheap and Convincing Subsurface Scattering Look," *Game Developers Conference*, Feb.–Mar. 2011. Cited on p. 639, 640

[106] Barré-Brisebois, Colin, and Stephen Hill, "Blending in Detail," *Self-Shadow* blog, July 10, 2012. Cited on p. 366, 371, 890

[107] Barré-Brisebois, Colin, "Hexagonal Bokeh Blur Revisited," *ZigguratVertigo's Hideout* blog, Apr. 17, 2017. Cited on p. 531

[108] Barrett, Sean, "Blend Does Not Distribute Over Lerp," *Game Developer*, vol. 11, no. 10, pp. 39–41, Nov. 2004. Cited on p. 160

[109] Barrett, Sean, "Sparse Virtual Textures," *Game Developers Conference*, Mar. 2008. Cited on p. 867

[110] Barringer, R., M. Andersson, and T. Akenine-Möller, "Ray Accelerator: Efficient and Flexible Ray Tracing on a Heterogeneous Architecture," *Computer Graphics Forum*, vol. 36, no. 8, pp. 166–177, 2017. Cited on p. 1006

[111] Bartels, Richard H., John C. Beatty, and Brian A. Barsky, *An Introduction to Splines for use in Computer Graphics and Geometric Modeling*, Morgan Kaufmann, 1987. Cited on p. 732, 734, 749, 754, 756, 781

[112] Barzel, Ronen, ed., *Graphics Tools—The jgt Editors' Choice*, A K Peters, Ltd., 2005. Cited on p. 1058, 1064, 1065, 1084, 1091, 1111, 1115, 1133, 1138, 1143

[113] Batov, Vladimir, "A Quick and Simple Memory Allocator," *Dr. Dobbs's Portal*, Jan. 1, 1998. Cited on p. 793

[114] Baum, Daniel R., Stephen Mann, Kevin P. Smith, and James M. Winget, "Making Radiosity Usable: Automatic Preprocessing and Meshing Techniques for the Generation of Accurate Radiosity Solutions," *Computer Graphics (SIGGRAPH '91 Proceedings)*, vol. 25, no. 4, pp. 51–60, July 1991. Cited on p. 689

[115] Bavoil, Louis, Steven P. Callahan, Aaron Lefohn, João L. D. Comba, and Cláudio T. Silva, "Multi-Fragment Effects on the GPU Using the k-Buffer," in *Proceedings of the 2007 Symposium on Interactive 3D Graphics and Games*, ACM, pp. 97–104, Apr.–May 2007. Cited on p. 156, 624, 626

[116] Bavoil, Louis, Steven P. Callahan, and Cláudio T. Silva, "Robust Soft Shadow Mapping with Backprojection and Depth Peeling," *journal of graphics tools*, vol. 13, no. 1, pp. 16–30, 2008. Cited on p. 238, 252

[117] Bavoil, Louis, "Advanced Soft Shadow Mapping Techniques," *Game Developers Conference*, Feb. 2008. Cited on p. 256

[118] Bavoil, Louis, and Kevin Myers, "Order Independent Transparency with Dual Depth Peeling," NVIDIA White Paper, Feb. 2008. Cited on p. 155, 157

[119] Bavoil, Louis, and Miguel Sainz, and Rouslan Dimitrov, "Image-Space Horizon-Based Aambient Occlusion," in *ACM SIGGRAPH 2008 Talks*, ACM, article no. 22, Aug. 2008. Cited on p. 460

[120] Bavoil, Louis, and Jon Jansen, "Particle Shadows and Cache-Efficient Post-Processing," *Game Developers Conference*, Mar. 2013. Cited on p. 570

[121] Bavoil, Louis, and Iain Cantlay, "SetStablePowerState.exe: Disabling GPU Boost on Windows 10 for more deterministic timestamp queries on NVIDIA GPUs," *NVIDIA GameWorks* blog, Sept. 14, 2016. Cited on p. 789

[122] Beacco, A., N. Pelechano, and C. Andújar, "A Survey of Real-Time Crowd Rendering," *Computer Graphics Forum*, vol. 35, no. 8, pp. 32–50, 2016. Cited on p. 563, 566, 567, 587, 798

[123] Bec, Xavier, "Faster Refraction Formula, and Transmission Color Filtering," *Ray Tracing News*, vol. 10, no. 1, Jan. 1997. Cited on p. 627

[124] Beckmann, Petr, and André Spizzichino, *The Scattering of Electromagnetic Waves from Rough Surfaces*, Pergamon Press, 1963. Cited on p. 331, 338

[125] Beeler, Dean, and Anuj Gosalia, "Asynchronous Timewarp on Oculus Rift," *Oculus Developer Blog*, Mar. 25, 2016. Cited on p. 935, 937

[126] Beeler, Dean, Ed Hutchins, and Paul Pedriana, "Asynchronous Spacewarp," *Oculus Developer Blog*, Nov. 10, 2016. Cited on p. 937

[127] Beers, Andrew C., Maneesh Agrawala, and Navin Chaddha, "Rendering from Compressed Textures," in *SIGGRAPH '96: Proceedings of the 23rd Annual Conference on Computer Graphics and Interactive Techniques*, ACM, pp. 373–378, Aug. 1996. Cited on p. 192

[128] Behrendt, S., C. Colditz, O. Franzke, J. Kopf, and O. Deussen, "Realistic Real-Time Rendering of Landscapes Using Billboard Clouds," *Computer Graphics Forum*, vol. 24, no. 3, pp. 507–516, 2005. Cited on p. 563

[129] Belcour, Laurent, and Pascal Barla, "A Practical Extension to Microfacet Theory for the Modeling of Varying Iridescence," *ACM Transactions on Graphics (SIGGRAPH 2017)*, vol. 36, no. 4, pp. 65:1–65:14, July 2017. Cited on p. 363

[130] Bénard, Pierre, Adrien Bousseau, and Jöelle Thollot, "State-of-the-Art Report on Temporal Coherence for Stylized Animations," *Computer Graphics Forum*, vol. 30, no. 8, pp. 2367–2386, 2011. Cited on p. 669, 678

[131] Bénard, Pierre, Lu Jingwan, Forrester Cole, Adam Finkelstein, and Jöelle Thollot, "Active Strokes: Coherent Line Stylization for Animated 3D Models," in *Proceedings of the International Symposium on Non-Photorealistic Animation and Rendering*, Eurographics Association, pp. 37–46, 2012. Cited on p. 669

[132] Bénard, Pierre, Aaron Hertzmann, and Michael Kass, "Computing Smooth Surface Contours with Accurate Topology," *ACM Transactions on Graphics*, vol. 33, no. 2, pp. 19:1–19:21, 2014. Cited on p. 656, 667

[133] Benson, David, and Joel Davis, "Octree Textures," *ACM Transactions on Graphics (SIGGRAPH 2002)*, vol. 21, no. 3, pp. 785–790, July 2002. Cited on p. 190

[134] Bentley, Adrian, "*inFAMOUS Second Son* Engine Postmortem," *Game Developers Conference*, Mar. 2014. Cited on p. 54, 490, 871, 884, 904

[135] de Berg, M., M. van Kreveld, M. Overmars, and O. Schwarzkopf, *Computational Geometry—Algorithms and Applications*, Third Edition, Springer-Verlag, 2008. Cited on p. 685, 699, 967

[136] van den Bergen, G., "Efficient Collision Detection of Complex Deformable Models Using AABB Trees," *journal of graphics tools*, vol. 2, no. 4, pp. 1–13, 1997. Also collected in [112]. Cited on p. 821

[137] Berger, Matthew, Andrea Tagliasacchi, Lee M. Seversky, Pierre Alliez, Gaël Guennebaud, Joshua A. Levine, Andrei Sharf, and Claudio T. Silva, "A Survey of Surface Reconstruction from Point Clouds," *Computer Graphics Forum*, vol. 36, no. 1, pp. 301–329, 2017. Cited on p. 573, 683

[138] Beyer, Johanna, Markus Hadwiger, and Hanspeter Pfister, "State-of-the-Art in GPU-Based Large-Scale Volume Visualization," *Computer Graphics Forum*, vol. 34, no. 8, pp. 13–37, 2015. Cited on p. 586

[139] Bezrati, Abdul, "Real-Time Lighting via Light Linked List," *SIGGRAPH Advances in Real-Time Rendering in Games course*, Aug. 2014. Cited on p. 893, 903

[140] Bezrati, Abdul, "Real-Time Lighting via Light Linked List," in Wolfgang Engel, ed., *GPU Pro⁶*, CRC Press, pp. 183–193, 2015. Cited on p. 893, 903

[141] Bier, Eric A., and Kenneth R. Sloan, Jr., "Two-Part Texture Mapping," *IEEE Computer Graphics and Applications*, vol. 6, no. 9, pp. 40–53, Sept. 1986. Cited on p. 170

[142] Biermann, Henning, Adi Levin, and Denis Zorin, "Piecewise Smooth Subdivision Surface with Normal Control," in *SIGGRAPH '00: Proceedings of the 27th Annual Conference on Computer Graphics and Interactive Techniques*, ACM Press/Addison-Wesley Publishing Co., pp. 113–120, July 2000. Cited on p. 764

[143] Billeter, Markus, Erik Sintorn, and Ulf Assarsson, "Real-Time Multiple Scattering Using Light Propagation Volumes," in *Proceedings of the ACM SIGGRAPH Symposium on Interactive 3D Graphics and Games*, ACM, pp. 119–126, 2012. Cited on p. 611

[144] Billeter, Markus, Ola Olsson, and Ulf Assarsson, "Tiled Forward Shading," in Wolfgang Engel, ed., *GPU Pro⁴*, CRC Press, pp. 99–114, 2013. Cited on p. 895, 896, 914

[145] Billeter, Markus, "Many-Light Rendering on Mobile Hardware," *SIGGRAPH Real-Time Many-Light Management and Shadows with Clustered Shading course*, Aug. 2015. Cited on p. 893, 900, 903, 914

[146] Bilodeau, Bill, "Vertex Shader Tricks: New Ways to Use the Vertex Shader to Improve Performance," *Game Developers Conference*, Mar. 2014. Cited on p. 51, 87, 514, 568, 571, 798

[147] Binstock, Atman, "Optimizing VR Graphics with Late Latching," *Oculus Developer Blog*, Mar. 2, 2015. Cited on p. 938

[148] Bishop, L., D. Eberly, T. Whitted, M. Finch, and M. Shantz, "Designing a PC Game Engine," *IEEE Computer Graphics and Applications*, vol. 18, no. 1, pp. 46–53, Jan./Feb. 1998. Cited on p. 836

[149] Bitterli, Benedikt, *Benedikt Bitterli Rendering Resources*, https://benedikt-bitterli.me/resources, licensed under CC BY 3.0, https://creativecommons.org/licenses/by/3.0. Cited on p. 441, 445, 447, 449, 450

[150] Bittner, Jiří, and Jan Přikryl, "Exact Regional Visibility Using Line Space Partitioning," Technical Report TR-186-2-01-06, Institute of Computer Graphics and Algorithms, Vienna University of Technology, Mar. 2001. Cited on p. 843

[151] Bittner, Jiří, Peter Wonka, and Michael Wimmer, "Visibility Preprocessing for Urban Scenes Using Line Space Subdivision," in *Pacific Graphics 2001*, IEEE Computer Society, pp. 276–284, Oct. 2001. Cited on p. 843

[152] Bittner, Jiří, Oliver Mattausch, Ari Silvennoinen, and Michael Wimmer, "Shadow Caster Culling for Efficient Shadow Mapping," in *Symposium on Interactive 3D Graphics and Games*, ACM, pp. 81–88, 2011. Cited on p. 247

[153] Bjørge, Marius, Sam Martin, Sandeep Kakarlapudi, and Jan-Harald Fredriksen, "Efficient Rendering with Tile Local Storage," in *ACM SIGGRAPH 2014 Talks*, ACM, article no. 51, July 2014. Cited on p. 156

[154] Bjørge, Marius, "Moving Mobile Graphics," *SIGGRAPH Advanced Real-Time Shading course*, July 2016. Cited on p. 247, 265

[155] Bjorke, Kevin, "Image-Based Lighting," in Randima Fernando, ed., *GPU Gems*, Addison-Wesley, pp. 308–321, 2004. Cited on p. 500

[156] Bjorke, Kevin, "High-Quality Filtering," in Randima Fernando, ed., *GPU Gems*, Addison-Wesley, pp. 391–424, 2004. Cited on p. 515, 521

[157] Blasi, Philippe, Bertrand Le Saec, and Christophe Schlick, "A Rendering Algorithm for Discrete Volume Density Objects," *Computer Graphics Forum*, vol. 12, no. 3, pp. 201–210, 1993. Cited on p. 598

[158] Blinn, J. F., and M. E. Newell, "Texture and Reflection in Computer Generated Images," *Communications of the ACM*, vol. 19, no. 10, pp. 542–547, Oct. 1976. Cited on p. 405, 406

[159] Blinn, James F., "Models of Light Reflection for Computer Synthesized Pictures," *ACM Computer Graphics (SIGGRAPH '77 Proceedings)*, vol. 11, no. 2, pp. 192–198, July 1977. Cited on p. 331, 340, 416

[160] Blinn, James, "Simulation of Wrinkled Surfaces," *Computer Graphics (SIGGRAPH '78 Proceedings)*, vol. 12, no. 3, pp. 286–292, Aug. 1978. Cited on p. 209, 765

[161] Blinn, James F., "A Generalization of Algebraic Surface Drawing," *ACM Transactions on Graphics*, vol. 1, no. 3, pp. 235–256, 1982. Cited on p. 751

[162] Blinn, Jim, "Me and My (Fake) Shadow," *IEEE Computer Graphics and Applications*, vol. 8, no. 1, pp. 82–86, Jan. 1988. Also collected in [165]. Cited on p. 225, 227

[163] Blinn, Jim, "Hyperbolic Interpolation," *IEEE Computer Graphics and Applications*, vol. 12, no. 4, pp. 89–94, July 1992. Also collected in [165]. Cited on p. 999

[164] Blinn, Jim, "Image Compositing—Theory," *IEEE Computer Graphics and Applications*, vol. 14, no. 5, pp. 83–87, Sept. 1994. Also collected in [166]. Cited on p. 160

[165] Blinn, Jim, *Jim Blinn's Corner: A Trip Down the Graphics Pipeline*, Morgan Kaufmann, 1996. Cited on p. 27, 832, 1059

[166] Blinn, Jim, *Jim Blinn's Corner: Dirty Pixels*, Morgan Kaufmann, 1998. Cited on p. 165, 1059

[167] Blinn, Jim, "A Ghost in a Snowstorm," *IEEE Computer Graphics and Applications*, vol. 18, no. 1, pp. 79–84, Jan./Feb. 1998. Also collected in [168], Chapter 9. Cited on p. 165

[168] Blinn, Jim, *Jim Blinn's Corner: Notation, Notation, Notation*, Morgan Kaufmann, 2002. Cited on p. 165, 1059

[169] Blinn, Jim, "What Is a Pixel?" *IEEE Computer Graphics and Applications*, vol. 25, no. 5, pp. 82–87, Sept./Oct. 2005. Cited on p. 165, 280

[170] Bloomenthal, Jules, "Edge Inference with Applications to Antialiasing," *Computer Graphics (SIGGRAPH '83 Proceedings)*, vol. 17, no. 3, pp. 157–162, July 1983. Cited on p. 146

[171] Bloomenthal, Jules, "An Implicit Surface Polygonizer," in Paul S. Heckbert, ed., *Graphics Gems IV*, Academic Press, pp. 324–349, 1994. Cited on p. 753

[172] Blow, Jonathan, "Mipmapping, Part 1," *Game Developer*, vol. 8, no. 12, pp. 13–17, Dec. 2001. Cited on p. 184

[173] Blow, Jonathan, "Mipmapping, Part 2," *Game Developer*, vol. 9, no. 1, pp. 16–19, Jan. 2002. Cited on p. 184

[174] Blow, Jonathan, "Happycake Development Notes: Shadows," *Happycake Development Notes* website, Aug. 25, 2004. Cited on p. 242

[175] Blythe, David, "The Direct3D 10 System," *ACM Transactions on Graphics*, vol. 25, no. 3, pp. 724–734, July 2006. Cited on p. 29, 39, 42, 47, 48, 50, 249

[176] Bookout, David, "Programmable Blend with Pixel Shader Ordering," *Intel Developer Zone* blog, Oct. 13, 2015. Cited on p. 52

[177] Born, Max, and Emil Wolf, *Principles of Optics: Electromagnetic Theory of Propagation, Interference and Diffraction of Light*, Seventh Edition, Cambridge University Press, 1999. Cited on p. 373

[178] Borshukov, George, and J. P. Lewis, "Realistic Human Face Rendering for *The Matrix Reloaded*," in *ACM SIGGRAPH 2003 Sketches and Applications*, ACM, July 2003. Cited on p. 635

[179] Borshukov, George, and J. P. Lewis, "Fast Subsurface Scattering," *SIGGRAPH Digital Face Cloning course*, Aug. 2005. Cited on p. 635

[180] Botsch, Mario, Alexander Hornung, Matthias Zwicker, and Leif Kobbelt, "High-Quality Surface Splatting on Today's GPUs," in *Proceedings of the Second Eurographics / IEEE VGTC Symposium on Point-Based Graphics*, Eurographics Association, pp. 17–24, June 2005. Cited on p. 574

[181] Boubekeur, Tamy, Patrick Reuter, and Christophe Schlick, "Scalar Tagged PN Triangles," in *Eurographics 2005 Short Presentations*, Eurographics Association, pp. 17–20, Sept. 2005. Cited on p. 747

[182] Boubekeur, T., and Marc Alexa, "Phong Tessellation," *ACM Transactions on Graphics*, vol. 27, no. 5, pp. 141:1–141:5, 2008. Cited on p. 748

[183] Boulton, Mike, "Static Lighting Tricks in *Halo 4*," *Game Developers Conference*, Mar. 2013. Cited on p. 486

[184] Bouthors, Antoine, Fabrice Neyret, Nelson Max, Eric Bruneton, and Cyril Crassin, "Interactive Multiple Anisotropic Scattering in Clouds," in *Proceedings of the 2008 Symposium on Interactive 3D Graphics and Games*, ACM, pp. 173–182, 2008. Cited on p. 618, 619, 620

[185] Bowles, H., K. Mitchell, B. Sumner, J. Moore, and M. Gross, "Iterative Image Warping," *Computer Graphics Forum*, vol. 31, no. 2, pp. 237–246, 2012. Cited on p. 523

[186] Bowles, H., "Oceans on a Shoestring: Shape Representation, Meshing and Shading," *SIGGRAPH Advances in Real-Time Rendering in Games course*, July 2013. Cited on p. 878

[187] Bowles, Huw, and Beibei Wang, "Sparkly but not too Sparkly! A Stable and Robust Procedural Sparkle Effect," *SIGGRAPH Advances in Real-Time Rendering in Games course*, Aug. 2015. Cited on p. 372

[188] Box, Harry, *Set Lighting Technician's Handbook: Film Lighting Equipment, Practice, and Electrical Distribution*, Fourth Edition, Focal Press, 2010. Cited on p. 435

[189] Boyd, Stephen, and Lieven Vandenberghe, *Convex Optimization*, Cambridge University Press, 2004. Freely downloadable. Cited on p. 946

[190] Brainerd, W., T. Foley, M. Kraemer, H. Moreton, and M. Nießner, "Efficient GPU Rendering of Subdivision Surfaces Using Adaptive Quadtrees," *ACM Transactions on Graphics*, vol. 35, no. 4, pp. 113:1–113:12, 2016. Cited on p. 779, 780

[191] Bratt, I., "The ARM Mali T880 Mobile GPU," *Hot Chips* website, 2015. Cited on p. 1027

[192] Brawley, Zoe, and Natalya Tatarchuk, "Parallax Occlusion Mapping: Self-Shadowing, Perspective-Correct Bump Mapping Using Reverse Height Map Tracing," in Wolfgang Engel, ed., *ShaderX³*, Charles River Media, pp. 135–154, Nov. 2004. Cited on p. 217

[193] Bredow, Rob, "Fur in *Stuart Little*," *SIGGRAPH Advanced RenderMan 2: To RI_INFINITY and Beyond course*, July 2000. Cited on p. 382, 633

[194] Brennan, Chris, "Accurate Environment Mapped Reflections and Refractions by Adjusting for Object Distance," in Wolfgang Engel, ed., *Direct3D ShaderX: Vertex & Pixel Shader Tips and Techniques*, Wordware, pp. 290–294, May 2002. Cited on p. 500

[195] Brennan, Chris, "Diffuse Cube Mapping," in Wolfgang Engel, ed., *Direct3D ShaderX: Vertex & Pixel Shader Tips and Techniques*, Wordware, pp. 287–289, May 2002. Cited on p. 427

[196] Breslav, Simon, Karol Szerszen, Lee Markosian, Pascal Barla, and Joëlle Thollot, "Dynamic 2D Patterns for Shading 3D Scenes," *ACM Transactions on Graphics*, vol. 27, no. 3, pp. 20:1–20:5, 2007. Cited on p. 670

[197] Bridson, Robert, *Fluid Simulation for Computer Graphics*, Second Edition, CRC Press, 2015. Cited on p. 571, 649

[198] Brinck, Waylon, and Andrew Maximov, "The Technical Art of *Uncharted 4*," *SIGGRAPH production session*, July 2016. Cited on p. 290

[199] Brinkmann, Ron, *The Art and Science of Digital Compositing*, Morgan Kaufmann, 1999. Cited on p. 149, 151, 159, 160

[200] Brisebois, Vincent, and Ankit Patel, "Profiling the AI Performance Boost in OptiX 5," *NVIDIA News Center*, July 31, 2017. Cited on p. 511, 1043, 1044

[201] Brown, Alistair, "Visual Effects in *Star Citizen*," *Game Developers Conference*, Mar. 2015. Cited on p. 366

[202] Brown, Gary S., "Shadowing by Non-gaussian Random Surfaces," *IEEE Transactions on Antennas and Propagation*, vol. 28, no. 6, pp. 788–790, 1980. Cited on p. 334

[203] Bruneton, Eric, and Fabrice Neyret, "Precomputed Atmospheric Scattering," *Computer Graphics Forum*, vol. 27, no. 4, pp. 1079–1086, 2008. Cited on p. 614, 615, 616

[204] Bruneton, Eric, Fabrice Neyret, and Nicolas Holzschuch, "Real-Time Realistic Ocean Lighting Using Seamless Transitions from Geometry to BRDF," *Computer Graphics Forum*, vol. 29, no. 2, pp. 487–496, 2010. Cited on p. 372

[205] Bruneton, Eric, and Fabrice Neyret, "A Survey of Non-linear Pre-filtering Methods for Efficient and Accurate Surface Shading," *IEEE Transactions on Visualization and Computer Graphics*, vol. 18, no. 2, pp. 242–260, 2012. Cited on p. 372

[206] Buades, Jose María, Jesús Gumbau, and Miguel Chover, "Separable Soft Shadow Mapping," *The Visual Computer*, vol. 32, no. 2, pp. 167–178, Feb. 2016. Cited on p. 252

[207] Buchanan, J. W., and M. C. Sousa, "The Edge Buffer: A Data Structure for Easy Silhouette Rendering," in *Proceedings of the 1st International Symposium on Non-photorealistic Animation and Rendering*, ACM, pp. 39–42, June 2000. Cited on p. 666

[208] Bukowski, Mike, Padraic Hennessy, Brian Osman, and Morgan McGuire, "Scalable High Quality Motion Blur and Ambient Occlusion," *SIGGRAPH Advances in Real-Time Rendering in 3D Graphics and Games course*, Aug. 2012. Cited on p. 540, 542, 543

[209] Bukowski, Mike, Padraic Hennessy, Brian Osman, and Morgan McGuire, "The *Skylanders* SWAP Force Depth-of-Field Shader," in Wolfgang Engel, ed., *GPU Pro⁴*, CRC Press, pp. 175–184, 2013. Cited on p. 529, 530, 532, 533

[210] Bunnell, Michael, "Dynamic Ambient Occlusion and Indirect Lighting," in Matt Pharr, ed., *GPU Gems 2*, Addison-Wesley, pp. 223–233, 2005. Cited on p. 454, 497

[211] van der Burg, John, "Building an Advanced Particle System," *Gamasutra*, June 2000. Cited on p. 571

[212] Burley, Brent, "Shadow Map Bias Cone and Improved Soft Shadows: Disney Bonus Section," *SIGGRAPH RenderMan for Everyone course*, Aug. 2006. Cited on p. 249, 250

[213] Burley, Brent, and Dylan Lacewell, "Ptex: Per-Face Texture Mapping for Production Rendering," in *Proceedings of the Nineteenth Eurographics Conference on Rendering*, Eurographics Association, pp. 1155–1164, 2008. Cited on p. 191

[214] Burley, Brent, "Physically Based Shading at Disney," *SIGGRAPH Practical Physically Based Shading in Film and Game Production course*, Aug. 2012. Cited on p. 325, 336, 340, 342, 345, 353, 354, 357, 364

[215] Burley, Brent, "Extending the Disney BRDF to a BSDF with Integrated Subsurface Scattering," *SIGGRAPH Physically Based Shading in Theory and Practice course*, Aug. 2015. Cited on p. 354

[216] Burns, Christopher A., Kayvon Fatahalian, and William R. Mark, "A Lazy Object-Space Shading Architecture with Decoupled Sampling," in *Proceedings of the Conference on High-Performance Graphics*, Eurographics Association, pp. 19–28, June 2010. Cited on p. 910

[217] Burns, C. A., and W. A. Hunt, "The Visibility Buffer: A Cache-Friendly Approach to Deferred Shading," *Journal of Computer Graphics Techniques*, vol. 2, no. 2, pp. 55–69, 2013. Cited on p. 905, 906

[218] Cabello, Ricardo, et al., *Three.js source code*, Release r89, Dec. 2017. Cited on p. 41, 50, 115, 189, 201, 407, 485, 552, 628

[219] Cabral, Brian, and Leith (Casey) Leedom, "Imaging Vector Fields Using Line Integral Convolution," in *SIGGRAPH '93: Proceedings of the 20th Annual Conference on Computer Graphics and Interactive Techniques*, ACM, pp. 263–270, Aug. 1993. Cited on p. 538

[220] Caillaud, Florian, Vincent Vidal, Florent Dupont, and Guillaume Lavoué, "Progressive Compression of Arbitrary Textured Meshes," *Computer Graphics Forum*, vol. 35, no. 7, pp. 475–484, 2016. Cited on p. 709

[221] Calver, Dean, "Vertex Decompression in a Shader," in Wolfgang Engel, ed., *Direct3D ShaderX: Vertex & Pixel Shader Tips and Techniques*, Wordware, pp. 172–187, May 2002. Cited on p. 713

[222] Calver, Dean, "Photo-Realistic Deferred Lighting," *Beyond3D.com* website, July 30, 2003. Cited on p. 883, 884, 886

[223] Calver, Dean, "Accessing and Modifying Topology on the GPU," in Wolfgang Engel, ed., *ShaderX³*, Charles River Media, pp. 5–19, 2004. Cited on p. 703

[224] Calver, Dean, "Deferred Lighting on PS 3.0 with High Dynamic Range," in Wolfgang Engel, ed., *ShaderX³*, Charles River Media, pp. 97–105, 2004. Cited on p. 288

[225] Cantlay, Iain, and Andrei Tatarinov, "From Terrain to Godrays: Better Use of DX11," *Game Developers Conference*, Mar. 2014. Cited on p. 44, 569

[226] Card, Drew, and Jason L. Mitchell, "Non-Photorealistic Rendering with Pixel and Vertex Shaders," in Wolfgang Engel, ed., *Direct3D ShaderX: Vertex & Pixel Shader Tips and Techniques*, Wordware, pp. 319–333, May 2002. Cited on p. 662, 668

[227] Carling, Richard, "Matrix Inversion," in Andrew S. Glassner, ed., *Graphics Gems*, Academic Press, pp. 470–471, 1990. Cited on p. 68

[228] Carmack, John, "Latency Mitigation Strategies," *AltDevBlog*, Feb. 22, 2013. Cited on p. 920, 936, 937

[229] do Carmo, Manfred P., *Differential Geometry of Curves and Surfaces*, Prentice-Hall, Inc., 1976. Cited on p. 81

[230] Carpenter, Loren, "The A-Buffer, an Antialiased Hidden Surface Method," *Computer Graphics (SIGGRAPH '84 Proceedings)*, vol. 18, no. 3, pp. 103–108, July 1984. Cited on p. 155, 626

[231] Carpentier, Giliam, and Kohei Ishiyama, "*Decima*, Advances in Lighting and AA," *SIGGRAPH Advances in Real-Time Rendering in Games course*, Aug. 2017. Cited on p. 146, 148, 386, 805

[232] Carucci, Francesco, "Inside Geometry Instancing," in Matt Pharr, ed., *GPU Gems 2*, Addison-Wesley, pp. 47–67, 2005. Cited on p. 797

[233] Castaño, Ignacio, "Lightmap Parameterization,' *The Witness Blog*, Mar. 30, 2010. Cited on p. 486

[234] Castaño, Ignacio, "Computing Alpha Mipmaps," *The Witness Blog*, Sept. 9, 2010. Cited on p. 204, 206

[235] Castaño, Ignacio, "Shadow Mapping Summary—Part 1,' *The Witness Blog*, Sept. 23, 2013. Cited on p. 249, 250, 265

[236] Catmull, E., and R. Rom, "A Class of Local Interpolating Splines," in R. Barnhill & R. Riesenfeld, eds., *Computer Aided Geometric Design*, Academic Press, pp. 317–326, 1974. Cited on p. 731

[237] Catmull, E., *A Subdivision Algorithm for Computer Display of Curved Surfaces*, PhD thesis, University of Utah, Dec. 1974. Cited on p. 1048

[238] Catmull, Edwin, "Computer Display of Curved Surfaces," in *Proceedings of the IEEE Conference on Computer Graphics, Pattern Recognition and Data Structures*, IEEE Press, pp. 11–17, May 1975. Cited on p. 24

[239] Catmull, E., and J. Clark, "Recursively Generated B-Spline Surfaces on Arbitrary Topological Meshes," *Computer-Aided Design*, vol. 10, no. 6, pp. 350–355, Sept. 1978. Cited on p. 761, 762

[240] Cebenoyan, Cem, "Graphics Pipeline Performance," in Randima Fernando, ed., *GPU Gems*, Addison-Wesley, pp. 473–486, 2004. Cited on p. 787, 802, 815, 853

[241] Cebenoyan, Cem, "Real Virtual Texturing—Taking Advantage of DirectX11.2 Tiled Resources," *Game Developers Conference*, Mar. 2014. Cited on p. 246, 263, 867

[242] Celes, Waldemar, and Frederico Abraham, "Fast and Versatile Texture-Based Wireframe Rendering," *The Visual Computer*, vol. 27, no. 10, pp. 939–948, 2011. Cited on p. 674

[243] Cerezo, Eva, Frederic Pérez, Xavier Pueyo, Francisco J. Seron, and François X. Sillion, "A Survey on Participating Media Rendering Techniques," *The Visual Computer*, vol. 21, no. 5, pp. 303–328, June 2005. Cited on p. 590

[244] *The Cesium Blog*, http://cesiumjs.org/blog/, 2017. Cited on p. 879

[245] Chabert, Charles-Félix, Wan-Chun Ma, Tim Hawkins, Pieter Peers, and Paul Debevec, "Fast Rendering of Realistic Faces with Wavelength Dependent Normal Maps," in *ACM SIGGRAPH 2007 Posters*, ACM, article no. 183, Aug. 2007. Cited on p. 634

[246] Chaikin, G., "An Algorithm for High Speed Curve Generation," *Computer Graphics and Image Processing*, vol. 4, no. 3, pp. 346–349, 1974. Cited on p. 754

[247] Chaitanya, Chakravarty R. Alla, Anton S. Kaplanyan, Christoph Schied, Marco Salvi, Aaron Lefohn, Derek Nowrouzezahrai, and Timo Aila, "Interactive Reconstruction of Monte Carlo Image Sequences Using a Recurrent Denoising Autoencoder," *ACM Transactions on Graphics*, vol. 36, no. 4, article no. 98, pp. 2017. Cited on p. 511, 1043

[248] Chajdas, Matthäus G., Christian Eisenacher, Marc Stamminger, and Sylvain Lefebvre, "Virtual Texture Mapping 101," in Wolfgang Engel, ed., *GPU Pro*, A K Peters, Ltd., pp. 185–195, 2010. Cited on p. 867

[249] Chajdas, Matthäus G., "D3D12 and Vulkan: Lessons Learned," *Game Developers Conference*, Mar. 2016. Cited on p. 40, 806, 814

[250] Chan, Danny, and Bryan Johnston, "Style in Rendering: The History and Technique Behind *Afro Samurai*'s Look," *Game Developers Conference*, Mar. 2009. Cited on p. 652, 658, 664

[251] Chan, Danny, "Real-World Measurements for *Call of Duty: Advanced Warfare*," in *SIGGRAPH Physically Based Shading in Theory and Practice course*, Aug. 2015. Cited on p. 349, 355

[252] Chan, Eric, and Frédo Durand, "Fast Prefiltered Lines," in Matt Pharr, ed., *GPU Gems 2*, Addison-Wesley, pp. 345–359, 2005. Cited on p. 133

[253] Chandrasekhar, Subrahmanyan, *Radiative Transfer*, Oxford University Press, 1950. Cited on p. 352

[254] Chang, Chia-Tche, Bastien Gorissen, and Samuel Melchior, "Fast Oriented Bounding Box Optimization on the Rotation Group $SO(3, \mathbb{R})$," *ACM Transactions on Graphics*, vol. 30, no. 5, pp. 122:1–122:16, Oct. 2011. Cited on p. 951

[255] Chang, Chun-Fa, Gary Bishop, and Anselmo Lastra, "LDI Tree: A Hierarchical Representation for Image-Based Rendering," in *SIGGRAPH '99: Proceedings of the 26th Annual Conference on Computer Graphics and Interactive Techniques*, ACM Press/Addison-Wesley Publishing Co., pp. 291–298, Aug. 1999. Cited on p. 565

[256] Chen, G. P. Sander, D. Nehab, L. Yang, and L. Hu, "Depth-Presorted Triangle Lists," *ACM Transactions on Graphics*, vol. 31, no. 6, pp. 160:1–160:9, 2016. Cited on p. 831

[257] Chen, Hao, "Lighting and Material of *Halo 3*," *Game Developers Conference*, Mar. 2008. Cited on p. 475

[258] Chen, Hao, and Natalya Tatarchuk, "Lighting Research at Bungie," *SIGGRAPH Advances in Real-Time Rendering in 3D Graphics and Games course*, Aug. 2009. Cited on p. 256, 257, 475

[259] Chen, K., "Adaptive Virtual Texture Rendering in *Far Cry 4*," *Game Developers Conference*, Mar. 2015. Cited on p. 869

[260] Chen, Pei-Ju, Hiroko Awata, Atsuko Matsushita, En-Cheng Yang, and Kentaro Arikawa, "Extreme Spectral Richness in the Eye of the Common Bluebottle Butterfly, Graphium sarpedon," *Frontiers in Ecology and Evolution*, vol. 4, pp.18, Mar. 8, 2016. Cited on p. 272

[261] Chi, Yung-feng, "True-to-Life Real-Time Animation of Shallow Water on Todays GPUs," in Wolfgang Engel, ed., *ShaderX⁴*, Charles River Media, pp. 467–480, 2005. Cited on p. 602, 626

[262] Chiang, Matt Jen-Yuan, Benedikt Bitterli, Chuck Tappan, and Brent Burley, "A Practical and Controllable Hair and Fur Model for Production Path Tracing," *Computer Graphics Forum (Eurographics 2016)*, vol. 35, no. 2, pp. 275–283, 2016. Cited on p. 643

[263] Chlumský, Viktor, *Shape Decomposition for Multi-channel Distance Fields*, MSc thesis, Department of Theoretical Computer Science, Czech Technical University in Prague, May 2015. Cited on p. 677, 890

[264] Choi, H., "Bifrost—The GPU Architecture for Next Five Billion," *ARM Tech Forum*, June 2016. Cited on p. 1026, 1027

[265] Christensen, Per H., "Point-Based Approximate Color Bleeding," Technical memo, Pixar Animation Studios, 2008. Cited on p. 454

[266] Cichocki, Adam, "Optimized Pixel-Projected Reflections for Planar Reflectors," *SIGGRAPH Advances in Real-Time Rendering in Games course*, Aug. 2017. Cited on p. 509

[267] Cignoni, P., C. Montani, and R. Scopigno, "Triangulating Convex Polygons Having T-Vertices," *journal of graphics tools*, vol. 1, no. 2, pp. 1–4, 1996. Also collected in [112]. Cited on p. 690

[268] Cignoni, Paolo, "On the Computation of Vertex Normals," *Meshlab Stuff* blog, Apr. 10, 2009. Also collected in [112]. Cited on p. 695

[269] Cigolle, Zina H., Sam Donow, Daniel Evangelakos, Michael Mara, Morgan McGuire, and Quirin Meyer, "A Survey of Efficient Representations for Independent Unit Vectors," *Journal of Computer Graphics Techniques*, vol. 3, no. 1, pp. 1–30, 2014. Cited on p. 222, 714, 715

[270] Clarberg, Petrik, and Tomas Akenine-Möller, "Practical Product Importance Sampling for Direct Illumination," *Computer Graphics Forum*, vol. 27, no. 2, pp. 681–690, 2008. Cited on p. 419

[271] Clarberg, P., R. Toth, J. Hasselgren, J. Nilsson, and T. Akenine-Möller, "AMFS: Adaptive Multi-frequency Shading for Future Graphics Processors," *ACM Transactions on Graphics*, vol. 33, no. 4, pp. 141:1–141:12, 2014. Cited on p. 910, 1013

[272] Clark, James H., "Hierarchical Geometric Models for Visible Surface Algorithms," *Communications of the ACM*, vol. 19, no. 10, pp. 547–554, Oct. 1976. Cited on p. 835

[273] Coffin, Christina, "SPU Based Deferred Shading in *Battlefield 3* for Playstation 3," *Game Developers Conference*, Mar. 2011. Cited on p. 898, 904

[274] Cohen, Jonathan D., Marc Olano, and Dinesh Manocha, "Appearance-Preserving Simplification," in *SIGGRAPH '98: Proceedings of the 25th Annual Conference on Computer Graphics and Interactive Techniques*, ACM, pp. 115–122, July 1998. Cited on p. 212

[275] Cohen, Michael F., and John R. Wallace, *Radiosity and Realistic Image Synthesis*, Academic Press Professional, 1993. Cited on p. 442, 483

[276] Cohen-Or, Daniel, Yiorgos Chrysanthou, Frédo Durand, Ned Greene, Vladlen Kulton, and Cláudio T. Silva, *SIGGRAPH Visibility, Problems, Techniques and Applications course*, Aug. 2001. Cited on p.

[277] Cohen-Or, Daniel, Yiorgos Chrysanthou, Cláudio T. Silva, and Frédo Durand, "A Survey of Visibility for Walkthrough Applications," *IEEE Transactions on Visualization and Computer Graphics*, vol. 9, no. 3, pp. 412–431, July–Sept. 2003. Cited on p. 830, 831, 879

[278] Cok, Keith, Roger Corron, Bob Kuehne, and Thomas True, *SIGGRAPH Developing Efficient Graphics Software: The Yin and Yang of Graphics course*, July 2000. Cited on p. 801

[279] Colbert, Mark, and Jaroslav Křivánek, "GPU-Based Importance Sampling," in Hubert Nguyen, ed., *GPU Gems 3*, Addison-Wesley, pp. 459–475, 2007. Cited on p. 419, 423, 503

[280] Colbert, Mark, and Jaroslav Křivánek, "Real-Time Shading with Filtered Importance Sampling," in *ACM SIGGRAPH 2007 Technical Sketches*, ACM, article no. 71, Aug. 2007. Cited on p. 419, 423

[281] Cole, Forrester, Aleksey Golovinskiy, Alex Limpaecher, Heather Stoddart Barros, Adam Finkelstein, Thomas Funkhouser, and Szymon Rusinkiewicz, "Where Do People Draw Lines?" *ACM Transactions on Graphics (SIGGRAPH 2008)*, vol. 27, no. 3, pp. 88:1–88:11, 2008. Cited on p. 656

[282] Cole, Forrester, and Adam Finkelstein, "Two Fast Methods for High-Quality Line Visibility," *IEEE Transactions on Visualization and Computer Graphics*, vol. 16, no. 5, pp. 707–717, Sept./Oct. 2010. Cited on p. 668, 675

[283] Collin, D., "Culling the Battlefield," *Game Developers Conference*, Mar. 2011. Cited on p. 837, 840, 849

[284] Conran, Patrick, "SpecVar Maps: Baking Bump Maps into Specular Response," in *ACM SIGGRAPH 2005 Sketches*, ACM, article no. 22, Aug. 2005. Cited on p. 369

[285] Cook, Robert L., and Kenneth E. Torrance, "A Reflectance Model for Computer Graphics," *Computer Graphics (SIGGRAPH '81 Proceedings)*, vol. 15, no. 3, pp. 307–316, July 1981. Cited on p. 314, 326, 331, 338, 343, 446

[286] Cook, Robert L., and Kenneth E. Torrance, "A Reflectance Model for Computer Graphics," *ACM Transactions on Graphics*, vol. 1, no. 1, pp. 7–24, Jan. 1982. Cited on p. 326, 338, 343, 446

[287] Cook, Robert L., "Shade Trees," *Computer Graphics (SIGGRAPH '84 Proceedings)*, vol. 18, no. 3, pp. 223–231, July 1984. Cited on p. 37, 765

[288] Cook, Robert L., "Stochastic Sampling in Computer Graphics," *ACM Transactions on Graphics*, vol. 5, no. 1, pp. 51–72, Jan. 1986. Cited on p. 249

[289] Cook, Robert L., Loren Carpenter, and Edwin Catmull, "The Reyes Image Rendering Architecture," *Computer Graphics (SIGGRAPH '87 Proceedings)*, vol. 21, no. 4, pp. 95–102, July 1987. Cited on p. 26, 774, 908

[290] Cook, Robert L., and Tony DeRose, "Wavelet Noise," *ACM Transactions on Graphics (SIGGRAPH 2005)*, vol. 24, no. 3, pp. 803–811, 2005. Cited on p. 199

[291] Coombes, David, "DX12 Do's and Don'ts, Updated!" *NVIDIA GameWorks* blog, Nov. 12, 2015. Cited on p. 814

[292] Cormen, T. H., C. E. Leiserson, R. Rivest, and C. Stein, *Introduction to Algorithms*, MIT Press, 2009. Cited on p. 820, 829, 835

[293] Courrèges, Adrian, "*GTA V*—Graphics Study," *Adrian Courrèges* blog, Nov. 2, 2015. Cited on p. 525, 535, 901, 913

[294] Courrèges, Adrian, "*DOOM* (2016)—Graphics Study," *Adrian Courrèges* blog, Sept. 9, 2016. Cited on p. 246, 535, 540, 629, 901, 913

[295] Courrèges, Adrian, "Beware of Transparent Pixels," *Adrian Courrèges* blog, May 9, 2017. Cited on p. 160, 208

[296] Cox, Michael, and Pat Hanrahan, "Pixel Merging for Object-Parallel Rendering: A Distributed Snooping Algorithm," in *Proceedings of the 1993 Symposium on Parallel Rendering*, ACM, pp. 49–56, Nov. 1993. Cited on p. 802

[297] Cox, Michael, David Sprague, John Danskin, Rich Ehlers, Brian Hook, Bill Lorensen, and Gary Tarolli, *SIGGRAPH Developing High-Performance Graphics Applications for the PC Platform course*, July 1998. Cited on p. 1023

[298] Cozzi, Patrick, "Picking Using the Depth Buffer," *AGI Blog*, Mar. 5, 2008. Cited on p. 943

[299] Cozzi, Patrick, and Kevin Ring, *3D Engine Design for Virtual Globes*, A K Peters/CRC Press, 2011. Cited on p. 668, 715, 872, 879

[300] Cozzi, P., and D. Bagnell, "A WebGL Globe Rendering Pipeline," in Wolfgang Engel, ed., *GPU Pro⁴*, CRC Press, pp. 39–48, 2013. Cited on p. 872, 876

[301] Cozzi, Patrick, ed., *WebGL Insights*, CRC Press, 2015. Cited on p. 129, 1048

[302] Cozzi, Patrick, "Cesium 3D Tiles," *GitHub* repository, 2017. Cited on p. 827

[303] Crane, Keenan, Ignacio Llamas, and Sarah Tariq, "Real-Time Simulation and Rendering of 3D Fluids," in Hubert Nguyen, ed., *GPU Gems 3*, Addison-Wesley, pp. 633–675, 2007. Cited on p. 608, 609, 649

[304] Crassin, Cyril, *GigaVoxels: A Voxel-Based Rendering Pipeline For Efficient Exploration Of Large And Detailed Scenes*, PhD thesis, University of Grenoble, July 2011. Cited on p. 494, 579, 584

[305] Crassin, Cyril, Fabrice Neyret, Miguel Sainz, Simon Green, and Elmar Eisemann, "Interactive Indirect Illumination Using Voxel Cone Tracing," *Computer Graphics Forum*, vol. 30, no. 7, pp. 1921–1930, 2011. Cited on p. 455, 467

[306] Crassin, Cyril, and Simon Green, "Octree-Based Sparse Voxelization Using the GPU Hardware Rasterizer," in Patrick Cozzi & Christophe Riccio, eds., *OpenGL Insights*, CRC Press, pp. 303–319, 2012. Cited on p. 582

[307] Crassin, Cyril, "Octree-Based Sparse Voxelization for Real-Time Global Illumination," *NVIDIA GPU Technology Conference*, Feb. 2012. Cited on p. 504, 582

[308] Crassin, Cyril, "Dynamic Sparse Voxel Octrees for Next-Gen Real-Time Rendering," *SIGGRAPH Beyond Programmable Shading course*, Aug. 2012. Cited on p. 579, 584

[309] Crassin, Cyril, Morgan McGuire, Kayvon Fatahalian, and Aaron Lefohn, "Aggregate G-Buffer Anti-Aliasing," *IEEE Transactions on Visualization and Computer Graphics*, vol. 22, no. 10, pp. 2215–2228, Oct. 2016. Cited on p. 888

[310] Cripe, Brian, and Thomas Gaskins, "The DirectModel Toolkit: Meeting the 3D Graphics Needs of Technical Applications," *Hewlett-Packard Journal*, pp. 19–27, May 1998. Cited on p. 818

[311] Crow, Franklin C., "Shadow Algorithms for Computer Graphics," *Computer Graphics (SIGGRAPH '77 Proceedings)*, vol. 11, no. 2, pp. 242–248, July 1977. Cited on p. 230

[312] Crow, Franklin C., "Summed-Area Tables for Texture Mapping," *Computer Graphics (SIGGRAPH '84 Proceedings)*, vol. 18, no. 3, pp. 207–212, July 1984. Cited on p. 186

[313] Culler, David E., and Jaswinder Pal Singh, with Anoop Gupta, *Parallel Computer Architecture: A Hardware/Software Approach*, Morgan Kaufmann, 1998. Cited on p. 810

[314] Cunningham, Steve, "3D Viewing and Rotation Using Orthonormal Bases," in Andrew S. Glassner, ed., *Graphics Gems*, Academic Press, pp. 516–521, 1990. Cited on p. 74

[315] Cupisz, Kuba, and Kasper Engelstoft, "Lighting in Unity," *Game Developers Conference*, Mar. 2015. Cited on p. 476, 482, 509

[316] Cupisz, Robert, "Light Probe Interpolation Using Tetrahedral Tessellations," *Game Developers Conference*, Mar. 2012. Cited on p. 489, 490

[317] Curtis, Cassidy, "Loose and Sketchy Animation," in *ACM SIGGRAPH '98 Electronic Art and Animation Catalog*, ACM, p. 145, July 1998. Cited on p. 672

[318] Cychosz, J. M., and W. N. Waggenspack, Jr., "Intersecting a Ray with a Cylinder," in Paul S. Heckbert, ed., *Graphics Gems IV*, Academic Press, pp. 356–365, 1994. Cited on p. 959

[319] Cyrus, M., and J. Beck, "Generalized Two- and Three-Dimensional Clipping," *Computers and Graphics*, vol. 3, pp. 23–28, 1978. Cited on p. 959

[320] Dachsbacher, Carsten, and Marc Stamminger, "Translucent Shadow Maps," in *Proceedings of the 14th Eurographics Workshop on Rendering*, Eurographics Association, pp. 197–201, June 2003. Cited on p. 638, 639

[321] Dachsbacher, Carsten, and Marc Stamminger, "Reflective Shadow Maps," in *Proceedings of the 2005 Symposium on Interactive 3D Graphics and Games*, ACM, pp. 203–231, 2005. Cited on p. 491

[322] Dachsbacher, Carsten, and Marc Stamminger, "Splatting of Indirect Illumination," in *Proceedings of the 2006 Symposium on Interactive 3D Graphics and Games*, ACM, pp. 93–100, 2006. Cited on p. 492

[323] Dachsbacher, C., and N. Tatarchuk, "Prism Parallax Occlusion Mapping with Accurate Silhouette Generation," *Symposium on Interactive 3D Graphics and Games poster*, Apr.–May 2007. Cited on p. 220

[324] Dallaire, Chris, "Binary Triangle Trees for Terrain Tile Index Buffer Generation," *Gamasutra*, Dec. 21, 2006. Cited on p. 876

[325] Dam, Erik B., Martin Koch, and Martin Lillholm, "Quaternions, Interpolation and Animation," Technical Report DIKU-TR-98/5, Department of Computer Science, University of Copenhagen, July 1998. Cited on p. 81

[326] Davies, Jem, "The Bifrost GPU Architecture and the ARM Mali-G71 GPU," *Hot Chips*, Aug. 2016. Cited on p. 1025

[327] Davies, Leigh, "OIT to Volumetric Shadow Mapping, 101 Uses for Raster-Ordered Views Using DirectX 12," *Intel Developer Zone* blog, Mar. 5, 2015. Cited on p. 52, 139, 156

[328] Davies, Leigh, "Rasterizer Order Views 101: A Primer," *Intel Developer Zone* blog, Aug. 5, 2015. Cited on p. 52, 156

[329] Day, Mike, "CSM Scrolling: An Acceleration Technique for the Rendering of Cascaded Shadow Maps," presented by Mike Acton, *SIGGRAPH Advances in Real-Time Rendering in Games course*, Aug. 2012. Cited on p. 245

[330] Day, Mike, "An Efficient and User-Friendly Tone Mapping Operator," *Insomniac R&D Blog*, Sept. 18, 2012. Cited on p. 286

[331] De Smedt, Matthijs, "PC GPU Performance Hot Spots," *NVIDIA GameWorks* blog, Aug. 10, 2016. Cited on p. 790, 792, 795, 814

[332] Debevec, Paul E., "Rendering Synthetic Objects into Real Scenes: Bridging Traditional and Image-Based Graphics with Global Illumination and High Dynamic Range Photography," in *SIGGRAPH '98: Proceedings of the 25th Annual Conference on Computer Graphics and Interactive Techniques*, ACM, pp. 189–198, July 1998. Cited on p. 406

[333] Debevec, Paul, Rod Bogart, Frank Vitz, and Greg Ward, *SIGGRAPH HDRI and Image-Based Lighting course*, July 2003. Cited on p. 435

[334] DeBry, David (grue), Jonathan Gibbs, Devorah DeLeon Petty, and Nate Robins, "Painting and Rendering Textures on Unparameterized Models," *ACM Transactions on Graphics (SIGGRAPH 2002)*, vol. 21, no. 3, pp. 763–768, July 2002. Cited on p. 190

[335] DeCarlo, Doug, Adam Finkelstein, and Szymon Rusinkiewicz, "Interactive Rendering of Suggestive Contours with Temporal Coherence," in *Proceedings of the 3rd International Symposium on Non-Photorealistic Animation and Rendering*, ACM, pp. 15–24, June 2004. Cited on p. 655

[336] Decaudin, Philippe, "Cartoon-Looking Rendering of 3D-Scenes," Technical Report INRIA 2919, Université de Technologie de Compiègne, France, June 1996. Cited on p. 661, 664

[337] Decaudin, Philippe, and Fabrice Neyret, "Volumetric Billboards," *Computer Graphics Forum*, vol. 28, no. 8, pp. 2079–2089, 2009. Cited on p. 564

[338] Décoret, Xavier, Frédo Durand, François Sillion, and Julie Dorsey, "Billboard Clouds for Extreme Model Simplification," *ACM Transactions on Graphics (SIGGRAPH 2003)*, vol. 22, no. 3, pp. 689–696, 2003. Cited on p. 563

[339] Deering, M., S. Winnder, B. Schediwy, C. Duff, and N. Hunt, "The Triangle Processor and Normal Vector Shader: A VLSI System for High Performance Graphics," *Computer Graphics (SIGGRAPH '88 Proceedings)*, vol. 22, no. 4, pp. 21–30, Aug. 1988. Cited on p. 883

[340] Deering, Michael, "Geometry Compression," in *SIGGRAPH '95: Proceedings of the 22nd Annual Conference on Computer Graphics and Interactive Techniques*, ACM, pp. 13–20, Aug. 1995. Cited on p. 700

[341] Delalandre, Cyril, Pascal Gautron, Jean-Eudes Marvie, and Guillaume François, "Transmittance Function Mapping," *Symposium on Interactive 3D Graphics and Games*, 2011. Cited on p. 570, 612, 620

[342] Delva, Michael, Julien Hamaide, and Ramses Ladlani, "Semantic Based Shader Generation Using Shader Shaker," in Wolfgang Engel, ed., *GPU Pro^6*, CRC Press, pp. 505–520, 2015. Cited on p. 128

[343] Demers, Joe, "Depth of Field: A Survey of Techniques," in Randima Fernando, ed., *GPU Gems*, Addison-Wesley, pp. 375–390, 2004. Cited on p. 531

[344] Demoreuille, Pete, "Optimizing the Unreal Engine 4 Renderer for VR," *Oculus Developer Blog*, May 25, 2016. Cited on p. 900, 934

[345] d'Eon, Eugene, and David Luebke, "Advanced Techniques for Realistic Real-Time Skin Rendering," in Hubert Nguyen, ed., *GPU Gems 3*, Addison-Wesley, pp. 293–347, 2007. Cited on p. 635, 636, 639

[346] d'Eon, Eugene, Guillaume François, Martin Hill, Joe Letteri, and Jean-Mary Aubry, "An Energy-Conserving Hair Reflectance Model," *Computer Graphics Forum*, vol. 30, no. 4, pp. 1467–8659, 2011. Cited on p. 641, 643

[347] DeRose, T., M. Kass, and T. Truong, "Subdivision Surfaces in Character Animation," in *SIGGRAPH '98: Proceedings of the 25th Annual Conference on Computer Graphics and Interactive Techniques*, ACM, pp. 85–94, July 1998. Cited on p. 761, 764, 767, 777

[348] Deshmukh, Priyamvad, Feng Xie, and Eric Tabellion, "DreamWorks Fabric Shading Model: From Artist Friendly to Physically Plausible," in *ACM SIGGRAPH 2017 Talks*, article no. 38, July 2017. Cited on p. 359

[349] Deshpande, Adit, "The 9 Deep Learning Papers You Need To Know About," *Adit Deshpande* blog, Aug. 24, 2016. Cited on p. 1043

[350] Didyk, P., T. Ritschel, E. Eisemann, K. Myszkowski, and H.-P. Seidel, "Adaptive Image-Space Stereo View Synthesis," in *Proceedings of the Vision, Modeling, and Visualization Workshop 2010*, Eurographics Association, pp. 299–306, 2010. Cited on p. 523

[351] Didyk, P., E. Eisemann, T. Ritschel, K. Myszkowski, and H.-P. Seidel, "Perceptually-Motivated Real-Time Temporal Upsampling of 3D Content for High-Refresh-Rate Displays," *Computer Graphics Forum*, vol. 29, no. 2, pp. 713–722, 2011. Cited on p. 523

[352] Dietrich, Andreas, Enrico Gobbetti, and Sung-Eui Yoon, "Massive-Model Rendering Techniques," *IEEE Computer Graphics and Applications*, vol. 27, no. 6, pp. 20–34, Nov./Dec. 2007. Cited on p. 587, 879

[353] Dietrich, Sim, "Attenuation Maps," in Mark DeLoura, ed., *Game Programming Gems*, Charles River Media, pp. 543–548, 2000. Cited on p. 221

[354] Dimitrijević, Aleksandar, "Performance State Tracking," in Patrick Cozzi & Christophe Riccio, eds., *OpenGL Insights*, CRC Press, pp. 527–534, 2012. Cited on p. 789

[355] Dimov, Rossen, "Deriving the Smith Shadowing Function for the GTR BRDF," Chaos Group White Paper, June 2015. Cited on p. 343

[356] Ding, Vivian, "In-Game and Cinematic Lighting of *The Last of Us*," *Game Developers Conference*, Mar. 2014. Cited on p. 229

[357] Dmitriev, Kirill, and Yury Uralsky, "Soft Shadows Using Hierarchical Min-Max Shadow Maps," *Game Developers Conference*, Mar. 2007. Cited on p. 252

[358] Dobashi, Yoshinori, Kazufumi Kaneda, Hideo Yamashita, Tsuyoshi Okita, and Tomoyuki Nishita, "A Simple, Efficient Method for Realistic Animation of Clouds," in *SIGGRAPH '00: Proceedings of the 27th Annual Conference on Computer Graphics and Interactive Techniques*, ACM Press/Addison-Wesley Publishing Co., pp. 19–28, July 2000. Cited on p. 556

[359] Dobashi, Yoshinori, Tsuyoshi Yamamoto, and Tomoyuki Nishita, "Interactive Rendering of Atmospheric Scattering Effects Using Graphics Hardware," in *Graphics Hardware 2002*, Eurographics Association, pp. 99–107, Sept. 2002. Cited on p. 604

[360] Dobbie, Will, "GPU Text Rendering with Vector Textures," *Will Dobbie* blog, Jan. 21, 2016. Cited on p. 677

[361] Dobbyn, Simon, John Hamill, Keith O'Conor, and Carol O'Sullivan, "Geopostors: A Real-Time Geometry/Impostor Crowd Rendering System," in *Proceedings of the 2005 Symposium on Interactive 3D Graphics and Games*, ACM, pp. 95–102, Apr. 2005. Cited on p. 551

[362] Doggett, M., "Texture Caches," *IEEE Micro*, vol. 32, no. 3, pp. 136–141, 2005. Cited on p. 1017

[363] Doghramachi, Hawar, and Jean-Normand Bucci, "Deferred+: Next-Gen Culling and Rendering for the Dawn Engine," in Wolfgang Engel, ed., *GPU Zen*, Black Cat Publishing, pp. 77–103, 2017. Cited on p. 715, 849, 908

[364] Dolby Laboratories Inc., "ICtCp Dolby White Paper," Dolby website. Cited on p. 276, 287

[365] Dominé, Sébastien, "OpenGL Multisample," *Game Developers Conference*, Mar. 2002. Cited on p. 145

[366] Dong, Zhao, Bruce Walter, Steve Marschner, and Donald P. Greenberg, "Predicting Appearance from Measured Microgeometry of Metal Surfaces," *ACM Transactions on Graphics*, vol. 35, no. 1, article no. 9, 2015. Cited on p. 361

[367] Donnelly, William, "Per-Pixel Displacement Mapping with Distance Functions," in Matt Pharr, ed., *GPU Gems 2*, Addison-Wesley, pp. 123–136, 2005. Cited on p. 218

[368] Donnelly, William, and Andrew Lauritzen, "Variance Shadow Maps," in *Proceedings of the 2006 Symposium on Interactive 3D Graphics*, ACM, pp. 161–165, 2006. Cited on p. 252

[369] Donner, Craig, and Henrik Wann Jensen, "Light Diffusion in Multi-Layered Translucent Materials," *ACM Transactions on Graphics (SIGGRAPH 2005)*, vol. 24, no. 3, pp. 1032–1039, 2005. Cited on p. 635

[370] Doo, D., and M. Sabin, "Behaviour of Recursive Division Surfaces Near Extraordinary Points," *Computer-Aided Design*, vol. 10, no. 6, pp. 356–360, Sept. 1978. Cited on p. 761

[371] Dorn, Jonathan, Connelly Barnes, Jason Lawrence, and Westley Weimer, "Towards Automatic Band-Limited Procedural Shaders," *Computer Graphics Forum (Pacific Graphics 2015)*, vol. 34, no. 7, pp. 77–87, 2015. Cited on p. 200

[372] Doss, Joshua A., "Art-Based Rendering with Graftal Imposters," in Mark DeLoura, ed., *Game Programming Gems 7*, Charles River Media, pp. 447–454, 2008. Cited on p. 672

[373] Dou, Hang, Yajie Yan, Ethan Kerzner, Zeng Dai, and Chris Wyman, "Adaptive Depth Bias for Shadow Maps," *Journal of Computer Graphics Techniques*, vol. 3, no. 4, pp. 146–162, 2014. Cited on p. 250

[374] Dougan, Carl, "The Parallel Transport Frame," in Mark DeLoura, ed., *Game Programming Gems 2*, Charles River Media, pp. 215–219, 2001. Cited on p. 102

[375] Drago, F., K. Myszkowski, T. Annen, and N. Chiba, "Adaptive Logarithmic Mapping for Displaying High Contrast Scenes,' *Computer Graphics Forum*, vol. 22, no. 3, pp. 419–426, 2003. Cited on p. 286

[376] Driscoll, Rory, "Cubemap Texel Solid Angle," *CODEITNOW* blog, Jan. 15, 2012. Cited on p. 419

[377] Drobot, Michal, "Quadtree Displacement Mapping with Height Blending," in Wolfgang Engel, ed., *GPU Pro*, A K Peters, Ltd., pp. 117–148, 2010. Cited on p. 220

[378] Drobot, Michał, "A Spatial and Temporal Coherence Framework for Real-Time Graphics," in Eric Lengyel, ed., *Game Engine Gems 2*, A K Peters, Ltd., pp. 97–118, 2011. Cited on p. 518

[379] Drobot, Michal, "Lighting of *Killzone: Shadow Fall*," *Digital Dragons* conference, Apr. 2013. Cited on p. 116

[380] Drobot, Michal, "Physically Based Area Lights," in Wolfgang Engel, ed., *GPU Pro^5*, CRC Press, pp. 67–100, 2014. Cited on p. 116, 388

[381] Drobot, Michal, "GCN Execution Patterns in Full Screen Passes," *Michal Drobot* blog, Apr. 1, 2014. Cited on p. 514

[382] Drobot, Michał, "Hybrid Reconstruction Anti Aliasing," *SIGGRAPH Advances in Real-Time Rendering in Games course*, Aug. 2014. Cited on p. 141, 142, 146, 165

[383] Drobot, Michał, "Hybrid Reconstruction Antialiasing," in Wolfgang Engel, ed., *GPU Pro^6*, CRC Press, pp. 101–139, 2015. Cited on p. 141, 146, 165

[384] Drobot, Michal, "Rendering of *Call of Duty Infinite Warfare*," *Digital Dragons* conference, May 2017. Cited on p. 262, 325, 371, 420, 502, 503, 509, 569

[385] Drobot, Michal, "Improved Culling for Tiled and Clustered Rendering," *SIGGRAPH Advances in Real-Time Rendering in Games course*, Aug. 2017. Cited on p. 902, 905

[386] Drobot, Michał, "Practical Multilayered Materials in *Call of Duty Infinite Warfare*," *SIGGRAPH Physically Based Shading in Theory and Practice course*, Aug. 2017. Cited on p. 151, 363, 364, 623, 625, 629

[387] Duff, Tom, "Compositing 3-D Rendered Images," *Computer Graphics (SIGGRAPH '85 Proceedings)*, vol. 19, no. 3, pp. 41–44, July 1985. Cited on p. 149

[388] Duff, Tom, James Burgess, Per Christensen, Christophe Hery, Andrew Kensler, Max Liani, and Ryusuke Villemin, "Building an Orthonormal Basis, Revisited," *Journal of Computer Graphics Techniques*, vol. 6, no. 1, pp. 1–8, 2017. Cited on p. 75

[389] Duffy, Joe, "CLR Inside Out," *MSDN Magazine*, vol. 21, no. 10, Sept. 2006. Cited on p. 791

[390] Dufresne, Marc Fauconneau, "Forward Clustered Shading," *Intel Software Developer Zone*, Aug. 5, 2014. Cited on p. 900, 914

[391] Duiker, Haarm-Pieter, and George Borshukov, "Filmic Tone Mapping," Presentation at Electronic Arts, Oct. 27, 2006. Cited on p. 286

[392] Duiker, Haarm-Pieter, "Filmic Tonemapping for Real-Time Rendering," *SIGGRAPH Color Enhancement and Rendering in Film and Game Production course*, July 2010. Cited on p. 286, 288, 289, 290

[393] Dummer, Jonathan, "Cone Step Mapping: An Iterative Ray-Heightfield Intersection Algorithm," *lonesock* website, 2006. Cited on p. 219

[394] Dunn, Alex, "Transparency (or Translucency) Rendering," *NVIDIA GameWorks* blog, Oct. 20, 2014. Cited on p. 155, 157, 159, 204, 569

[395] Dupuy, Jonathan, Eric Heitz, Jean-Claude Iehl, Pierre Poulin, Fabrice Neyret, and Victor Ostromoukhov, "Linear Efficient Antialiased Displacement and Reflectance Mapping," *ACM Transactions on Graphics*, vol. 32, no. 6, pp. 211:1–211:11, Nov. 2013. Cited on p. 370

[396] Dupuy, Jonathan, "Antialiasing Physically Based Shading with LEADR Mapping," *SIGGRAPH Physically Based Shading in Theory and Practice course*, Aug. 2014. Cited on p. 370

[397] Dupuy, Jonathan, Eric Heitz, and Eugene d'Eon, "Additional Progress Towards the Unification of Microfacet and Microflake Theories," in *Proceedings of the Eurographics Symposium on Rendering: Experimental Ideas & Implementations*, Eurographics Association, pp. 55–63, 2016. Cited on p. 352, 648

[398] Durand, Frédo, *3D Visibility: Analytical Study and Applications*, PhD thesis, Université Joseph Fourier, Grenoble, July 1999. Cited on p. 879

[399] Dutré, Philip, *Global Illumination Compendium*, webpage, Sept. 29, 2003. Cited on p. 372, 443, 512

[400] Dutré, Philip, Kavita Bala, and Philippe Bekaert, *Advanced Global Illumination*, Second Edition, A K Peters, Ltd., 2006. Cited on p. 269, 442, 512, 684

[401] Dyken, C., M. Reimers, and J. Seland, "Real-Time GPU Silhouette Refinement Using Adaptively Blended Bézier Patches," *Computer Graphics Forum*, vol. 27, no. 1, pp. 1–12, 2008. Cited on p. 747

[402] Dyn, Nira, David Levin, and John A. Gregory, "A 4-Point Interpolatory Subdivision Scheme for Curve Design," *Computer Aided Geometric Design*, vol. 4, no. 4, pp. 257–268, 1987. Cited on p. 755

[403] Eberly, David, "Triangulation by Ear Clipping," *Geometric Tools* website, 2003. Cited on p. 686

[404] Eberly, David, *3D Game Engine Design: A Practical Approach to Real-Time Computer Graphics*, Second Edition, Morgan Kaufmann, 2006. Cited on p. 82, 772, 829, 950, 951, 959, 976, 990

[405] Eberly, David, "Reconstructing a Height Field from a Normal Map," *Geometric Tools* blog, May 3, 2006. Cited on p. 214

[406] Eberly, David, "A Fast and Accurate Algorithm for Computing SLERP," *Journal of Graphics, GPU, and Game Tools*, vol. 15, no. 3, pp. 161–176, 2011. Cited on p. 82

[407] Ebert, David S., John Hart, Bill Mark, F. Kenton Musgrave, Darwyn Peachey, Ken Perlin, and Steven Worley, *Texturing and Modeling: A Procedural Approach*, Third Edition, Morgan Kaufmann, 2002. Cited on p. 198, 200, 222, 672

[408] Eccles, Allen, "The Diamond Monster 3Dfx Voodoo 1," *GameSpy Hall of Fame*, 2000. Cited on p. 1

[409] Eisemann, Martin, and Xavier Décoret, "Fast Scene Voxelization and Applications," in *ACM SIGGRAPH 2006 Sketches*, ACM, article no. 8, 2006. Cited on p. 581, 586

[410] Eisemann, Martin, Marcus Magnor, Thorsten Grosch, and Stefan Müller, "Fast Ray/Axis-Aligned Bounding Box Overlap Tests Using Ray Slopes," *journal of graphics tools*, vol. 12, no. 4, pp. 35–46, 2007. Cited on p. 961

[411] Eisemann, Martin, and Xavier Décoret, "Occlusion Textures for Plausible Soft Shadows," *Computer Graphics Forum*, vol. 27, no. 1, pp. 13–23, 2008. Cited on p. 230

[412] Eisemann, Martin, Michael Schwarz, Ulf Assarsson, and Michael Wimmer, *Real-Time Shadows*, A K Peters/CRC Press, 2011. Cited on p. 223, 244, 249, 253, 265

[413] Eisemann, Martin, Michael Schwarz, Ulf Assarsson, and Michael Wimmer, *SIGGRAPH Efficient Real-Time Shadows course*, Aug. 2012. Cited on p. 265

[414] El Garawany, Ramy, "Deferred Lighting in *Uncharted 4*," *SIGGRAPH Advances in Real-Time Rendering in Games course*, July 2016. Cited on p. 472, 886, 887, 898, 904

[415] El Mansouri, Jalal, "Rendering Tom Clancy's Rainbow Six Siege," *Game Developers Conference*, Mar. 2016. Cited on p. 146, 246, 252, 805, 850, 887

[416] Elcott, Sharif, Kay Chang, Masayoshi Miyamoto, and Napaporn Metaaphanon, "Rendering Techniques of *Final Fantasy XV*," in *ACM SIGGRAPH 2016 Talks*, ACM, article no. 48, July 2016. Cited on p. 620

[417] Eldridge, Matthew, Homan Igehy, and Pat Hanrahan, "Pomegranate: A Fully Scalable Graphics Architecture," in *SIGGRAPH '00: Proceedings of the 27th Annual Conference on Computer Graphics and Interactive Techniques*, ACM Press/Addison-Wesley Publishing Co., pp. 443–454, July 2000. Cited on p. 1020, 1021, 1022

[418] Eldridge, Matthew, *Designing Graphics Architectures around Scalability and Communication*, PhD thesis, Stanford University, June 2001. Cited on p. 1020, 1022, 1023

[419] Elek, Oskar, "Rendering Parametrizable Planetary Atmospheres with Multiple Scattering in Real Time," *Central European Seminar on Computer Graphics*, 2009. Cited on p. 615

[420] Elek, Oskar, "Layered Materials in Real-Time Rendering," in *Proceedings of the 14th Central European Seminar on Computer Graphics*, Vienna University of Technology, pp. 27–34, May 2010. Cited on p. 364

[421] Elinas, Pantelis, and Wolfgang Stuerzlinger, "Real-Time Rendering of 3D Clouds," *journal of graphics tools*, vol. 5, no. 4, pp. 33–45, 2000. Cited on p. 556

[422] van Emde Boas, P., R. Kaas, and E. Zijlstra, "Design and Implementation of an Efficient Priority Queue," *Mathematical Systems Theory*, vol. 10, no. 1, pp. 99–127, 1977. Cited on p. 827

[423] Enderton, Eric, Erik Sintorn, Peter Shirley, and David Luebke, "Stochastic Transparency," *IEEE Transactions on Visualization and Computer Graphics*, vol. 17, no. 8, pp. 1036–1047, 2011. Cited on p. 149, 206

[424] Endres, Michael, and Frank Kitson, "Perfecting The Pixel: Refining the Art of Visual Styling," *Game Developers Conference*, Mar. 2010. Cited on p. 289

[425] Eng, Austin, "Tighter Frustum Culling and Why You May Want to Disregard It," *Cesium* blog, Feb. 2, 2017. Cited on p. 986

[426] Engel, Wolfgang, ed., *Direct3D ShaderX: Vertex & Pixel Shader Tips and Techniques*, Wordware, 2002. Cited on p. xvii

[427] Engel, Wolfgang, ed., *ShaderX²: Introduction & Tutorials with DirectX 9*, Wordware, 2004. Cited on p. xvi

[428] Engel, Wolfgang, ed., *ShaderX²: Shader Programming Tips & Tricks with DirectX 9*, Wordware, 2004. Cited on p. xvi

[429] Engel, Wolfgang, ed., *ShaderX³*, Charles River Media, 2004. Cited on p. 1148

[430] Engel, Wolfgang, "Cascaded Shadow Maps," in Wolfgang Engel, ed., *ShaderX⁵*, Charles River Media, pp. 197–206, 2006. Cited on p. 242, 243

[431] Engel, Wolfgang, "Designing a Renderer for Multiple Lights: The Light Pre-Pass Renderer," in Wolfgang Engel, ed., *ShaderX⁷*, Charles River Media, pp. 655–666, 2009. Cited on p. 892

[432] Engel, Wolfgang, "Light Pre-Pass; Deferred Lighting: Latest Development," *SIGGRAPH Advances in Real-Time Rendering in Games course*, Aug. 2009. Cited on p. 892, 901

[433] Engel, Wolfgang, "The Filtered and Culled Visibility Buffer," *Game Developers Conference Europe*, Aug. 2016. Cited on p. 833, 851, 907

[434] Engelhardt, Thomas, and Carsten Dachsbacher, "Octahedron Environment Maps," in *Proceedings of the Vision, Modeling, and Visualization Conference 2008*, Aka GmbH, pp. 383–388 Oct. 2008. Cited on p. 413

[435] Ericson, Christer, *Real-Time Collision Detection*, Morgan Kaufmann, 2005. Cited on p. 827, 879, 946, 948, 950, 955, 977, 978, 979, 990

[436] Ericson, Christer, "Collisions Using Separating-Axis Tests," *Game Developers Conference*, Mar. 2007. Cited on p. 980

[437] Ericson, Christer, "More Capcom/CEDEC Bean-Spilling," *realtimecollisiondetection.net—the blog*, Oct. 1, 2007. Cited on p. 537

[438] Ericson, Christer, "Order Your Graphics Draw Calls Around!" *realtimecollisiondetection .net—the blog*, Oct. 3, 2008. Cited on p. 803

[439] Ericson, Christer, "Optimizing the Rendering of a Particle System," *realtimecollision detection.net—the blog*, Jan. 2, 2009. Cited on p. 556, 568

[440] Ericson, Christer, "Optimizing a Sphere-Triangle Intersection Test," *realtimecollision detection.net—the blog*, Dec. 30, 2010. Cited on p. 974

[441] Eriksson, Carl, Dinesh Manocha, and William V. Baxter III, "HLODs for Faster Display of Large Static and Dynamic Environments," in *Proceedings of the 2001 Symposium on Interactive 3D Graphics*, ACM, pp. 111–120, 2001. Cited on p. 866

[442] Estevez, Alejandro Conty, and Christopher Kulla, "Production Friendly Microfacet Sheen BRDF," Technical Report, Sony Imageworks, 2017. Cited on p. 358

[443] Etuaho, Olli, "Bug-Free and Fast Mobile WebGL," in Patrick Cozzi, ed., *WebGL Insights*, CRC Press, pp. 123–137, 2015. Cited on p. 702, 796, 802, 805, 814

[444] Evans, Alex, "Fast Approximations for Global Illumination on Dynamic Scenes," *SIGGRAPH Advanced Real-Time Rendering in 3D Graphics and Games course*, Aug. 2006. Cited on p. 454, 488

[445] Evans, Alex, and Anton Kirczenow, "Voxels in *LittleBigPlanet 2*," *SIGGRAPH Advances in Real-Time Rendering in Games course*, Aug. 2011. Cited on p. 571

[446] Evans, Alex, "Learning from Failure: A Survey of Promising, Unconventional and Mostly Abandoned Renderers for 'Dreams PS4', a Geometrically Dense, Painterly UGC Game," *SIGGRAPH Advances in Real-Time Rendering in Games course*, Aug. 2015. Cited on p. 577, 679

[447] Evans, Martin, "Drawing Stuff on Other Stuff with Deferred Screenspace Decals," *Blog 3.0*, Feb. 27, 2015. Cited on p. 889

[448] Everitt, Cass, "One-Pass Silhouette Rendering with GeForce and GeForce2," NVIDIA White Paper, June 2000. Cited on p. 656

[449] Everitt, Cass, "Interactive Order-Independent Transparency," NVIDIA White Paper, May 2001. Cited on p. 154

[450] Everitt, Cass, and Mark Kilgard, "Practical and Robust Stenciled Shadow Volumes for Hardware-Accelerated Rendering," NVIDIA White Paper, Mar. 2002. Cited on p. 232

[451] Everitt, Cass, and John McDonald, "Beyond Porting," *Steam Dev Days*, Feb. 2014. Cited on p. 795, 805

[452] Everitt, Cass, Graham Sellers, John McDonald, and Tim Foley, "Approaching Zero Driver Overhead," *Game Developers Conference*, Mar. 2014. Cited on p. 191, 192

[453] Everitt, Cass, "Multiview Rendering," *SIGGRAPH Moving Mobile Graphics course*, July 2016. Cited on p. 927, 928

[454] Ewins, Jon P., Marcus D. Waller, Martin White, and Paul F. Lister, "MIP-Map Level Selection for Texture Mapping," *IEEE Transactions on Visualization and Computer Graphics*, vol. 4, no. 4, pp. 317–329, Oct.–Dec. 1998. Cited on p. 185

[455] Eyles, J., S. Molnar, J. Poulton, T. Greer, A. Lastra, N. England, and L. Westover, "PixelFlow: The Realization," in *Proceedings of the ACM SIGGRAPH/EUROGRAPHICS Workshop on Graphics Hardware*, ACM, pp. 57–68, Aug. 1997. Cited on p. 1022

[456] Fairchild, Mark D., *Color Appearance Models*, Third Edition, John Wiley & Sons, Inc., 2013. Cited on p. 276, 278, 291

[457] Farin, Gerald, "Triangular Bernstein-Bézier Patches," *Computer Aided Geometric Design*, vol. 3, no. 2, pp. 83–127, 1986. Cited on p. 745, 781

[458] Farin, Gerald, *Curves and Surfaces for Computer Aided Geometric Design—A Practical Guide*, Fourth Edition, Academic Press Inc., 1996. Cited on p. 718, 720, 721, 724, 725, 728, 732, 734, 738, 742, 745, 749, 754, 756, 781

[459] Farin, Gerald E., *NURBS: From Projective Geometry to Practical Use*, Second Edition, A K Peters, Ltd., 1999. Cited on p. 781

[460] Farin, Gerald, and Dianne Hansford, *The Essentials of CAGD*, A K Peters, Ltd., 2000. Cited on p. 781

[461] Farin, Gerald E., and Dianne Hansford, *Practical Linear Algebra: A Geometry Toolbox*, A K Peters, Ltd., 2004. Cited on p. 102, 991

[462] Fatahalian, Kayvon, and Randy Bryant, *Parallel Computer Architecture and Programming course*, Carnegie Mellon University, Spring 2017. Cited on p. 30, 55

[463] Fauconneau, M., "High-Quality, Fast DX11 Texture Compression with ISPC," *Game Developers Conference*, Mar. 2015. Cited on p. 198

[464] Fedkiw, Ronald, Jos Stam, and Henrik Wann Jensen, "Visual Simulation of Smoke," in *SIGGRAPH '01: Proceedings of the 27th Annual Conference on Computer Graphics and Interactive Techniques*, ACM, pp. 15–22, Aug. 2001. Cited on p. 649

[465] Fenney, Simon, "Texture Compression Using Low-Frequency Signal Modulation," in *Graphics Hardware 2003*, Eurographics Association, pp. 84–91, July 2003. Cited on p. 196

[466] Fernandes, António Ramires, and Bruno Oliveira, "GPU Tessellation: We Still Have a LOD of Terrain to Cover," in Patrick Cozzi & Christophe Riccio, eds., *OpenGL Insights*, CRC Press, pp. 145–161, 2012. Cited on p. 46, 879

[467] Fernando, Randima, "Percentage-Closer Soft Shadows," in *ACM SIGGRAPH 2005 Sketches*, ACM, article no. 35, Aug. 2005. Cited on p. 250

[468] Ferwerda, James, "Elements of Early Vision for Computer Graphics," *IEEE Computer Graphics and Applications*, vol. 21, no. 5, pp. 22–33, Sept./Oct. 2001. Cited on p. 278

[469] Feynman, Richard, Robert B. Leighton, and Matthew Sands, *The Feynman Lectures on Physics*, 1963. Available at *Feynman Lectures* website, 2006. Cited on p. 298, 373

[470] de Figueiredo, L. H., "Adaptive Sampling of Parametric Curves," in Alan Paeth, ed., *Graphics Gems V*, Academic Press, pp. 173–178, 1995. Cited on p. 771

[471] Filion, Dominic, and Rob McNaughton, "Starcraft II: Effects and Techniques," *SIGGRAPH Advances in Real-Time Rendering in 3D Graphics and Games course*, Aug. 2008. Cited on p. 257, 459, 885

[472] Fisher, F., and A. Woo, "R.E versus N.H Specular Highlights," in Paul S. Heckbert, ed., *Graphics Gems IV*, Academic Press, pp. 388–400, 1994. Cited on p. 421

[473] Flavell, Andrew, "Run Time Mip-Map Filtering," *Game Developer*, vol. 5, no. 11, pp. 34–43, Nov. 1998. Cited on p. 185, 186

[474] Floater, Michael, Kai Hormann, and Géza Kós, "A General Construction of Barycentric Coordinates over Convex Polygons," *Advances in Computational Mathematics*, vol. 24, no. 1–4, pp. 311–331, Jan. 2006. Cited on p. 970

[475] Floater, M., "Triangular Bézier Surfaces," Technical Report, University of Oslo, Aug. 2011. Cited on p. 741

[476] Fog, Agner, "Optimizing Software in C++," *Software Optimization Resources*, 2007. Cited on p. 815

[477] Fogal, Thomas, Alexander Schiewe, and Jens Krüger, "An Analysis of Scalable GPU-Based Ray-Guided Volume Rendering," in *Proceedings of the IEEE Symposium on Large Data Analysis and Visualization (LDAV 13)*, IEEE Computer Society, pp. 43–51, 2013. Cited on p. 586

[478] Foley, Tim, "Introduction to Parallel Programming Models," *SIGGRAPH Beyond Programmable Shading course*, Aug. 2009. Cited on p. 815

[479] Fong, Julian, Magnus Wrenninge, Christopher Kulla, and Ralf Habel, *SIGGRAPH Production Volume Rendering course*, Aug. 2017. Cited on p. 589, 590, 591, 592, 594, 649

[480] Forest, Vincent, Loic Barthe, and Mathias Paulin, "Real-Time Hierarchical Binary-Scene Voxelization," *journal of graphics, GPU, and game tools*, vol. 14, no. 3, pp. 21–34, 2011. Cited on p. 581

[481] Forsyth, Tom, "Comparison of VIPM Methods," in Mark DeLoura, ed., *Game Programming Gems 2*, Charles River Media, pp. 363–376, 2001. Cited on p. 707, 711, 859

[482] Forsyth, Tom, "Impostors: Adding Clutter," in Mark DeLoura, ed., *Game Programming Gems 2*, Charles River Media, pp. 488–496, 2001. Cited on p. 561, 562

[483] Forsyth, Tom, "Making Shadow Buffers Robust Using Multiple Dynamic Frustums," in Wolfgang Engel, ed., *ShaderX⁴*, Charles River Media, pp. 331–346, 2005. Cited on p. 242

[484] Forsyth, Tom, "Extremely Practical Shadows," *Game Developers Conference*, Mar. 2006. Cited on p. 234, 241, 242

[485] Forsyth, Tom, "Linear-Speed Vertex Cache Optimisation," *TomF's Tech Blog*, Sept. 28, 2006. Cited on p. 701, 705

[486] Forsyth, Tom, "Shadowbuffers," *Game Developers Conference*, Mar. 2007. Cited on p. 234, 242

[487] Forsyth, Tom, "The Trilight: A Simple General-Purpose Lighting Model for Games," *TomF's Tech Blog*, Mar. 22, 2007. Cited on p. 382, 432

[488] Forsyth, Tom, "Renderstate Change Costs," *TomF's Tech Blog*, Jan. 27, 2008. Cited on p. 795, 796, 802, 803

[489] Forsyth, Tom, "VR, AR and Other Realities," *TomF's Tech Blog*, Sept. 16, 2012. Cited on p. 917

[490] Forsyth, Tom, "Premultiplied Alpha Part 2," *TomF's Tech Blog*, Mar. 18, 2015. Cited on p. 208

[491] Forsyth, Tom, "The sRGB Learning Curve," *TomF's Tech Blog*, Nov. 30, 2015. Cited on p. 161, 162, 163

[492] Fowles, Grant R., *Introduction to Modern Optics*, Second Edition, Holt, Reinhart, and Winston, 1975. Cited on p. 373

[493] Franklin, Dustin, "Hardware-Based Ambient Occlusion," in Wolfgang Engel, ed., *ShaderX⁴*, Charles River Media, pp. 91–100, 2005. Cited on p. 452

[494] Frey, Ivo Zoltan, "Spherical Skinning with Dual-Quaternions and QTangents," in *ACM SIGGRAPH 2011 Talks*, article no. 11, Aug. 2011. Cited on p. 209, 210, 715

[495] Frisken, Sarah, Ronald N. Perry, Alyn P. Rockwood, and Thouis R. Jones, "Adaptively Sampled Distance Fields: A General Representation of Shape for Computer Graphics," in *SIGGRAPH '00: Proceedings of the 27th Annual Conference on Computer Graphics and Interactive Techniques*, ACM Press/Addison-Wesley Publishing Co., pp. 249–254, July 2000. Cited on p. 677, 751

[496] Frisvad, Jeppe Revall, "Building an Orthonormal Basis from a 3D Unit Vector Without Normalization," *journal of graphics tools*, vol. 16, no. 3, pp. 151–159, 2012. Cited on p. 75

[497] Fry, Alex, "High Dynamic Range Color Grading and Display in Frostbite," *Game Developers Conference*, Feb.–Mar. 2017. Cited on p. 283, 287, 288, 290

[498] Frykholm, Niklas, "The BitSquid Low Level Animation System," *Autodesk Stingray* blog, Nov. 20, 2009. Cited on p. 715, 905

[499] Frykholm, Niklas, "What Is Gimbal Lock and Why Do We Still Have to Worry about It?" *Autodesk Stingray* blog, Mar. 15, 2013. Cited on p. 73

[500] Fuchs, H., Z. M. Kedem, and B. F. Naylor, "On Visible Surface Generation by A Priori Tree Structures," *Computer Graphics (SIGGRAPH '80 Proceedings)*, vol. 14, no. 3, pp. 124–133, July 1980. Cited on p. 823

[501] Fuchs, H., G. D. Abram, and E. D. Grant, "Near Real-Time Shaded Display of Rigid Objects," *Computer Graphics (SIGGRAPH '83 Proceedings)*, vol. 17, no. 3, pp. 65–72, July 1983. Cited on p. 823

[502] Fuchs, H., J. Poulton, J. Eyles, T. Greer, J. Goldfeather, D. Ellsworth, S. Molnar, G. Turk, B. Tebbs, and L. Israel, "Pixel-Planes 5: A Heterogeneous Multiprocessor Graphics System Using Processor-Enhanced Memories," *Computer Graphics (SIGGRAPH '89 Proceedings)*, vol. 23, no. 3, pp. 79–88, July 1989. Cited on p. 8, 1026

[503] Fuhrmann, Anton L., Eike Umlauf, and Stephan Mantler, "Extreme Model Simplification for Forest Rendering," in *Proceedings of the First Eurographics Conference on Natural Phenomena*, Eurographics Association, pp. 57–66, 2005. Cited on p. 563

[504] Fujii, Yasuhiro, "A Tiny Improvement of Oren-Nayar Reflectance Model," http://mimosa-pudica.net, Oct. 9, 2013. Cited on p. 354

[505] Fünfzig, C., K. Müller, D. Hansford, and G. Farin, "PNG1 Triangles for Tangent Plane Continuous Surfaces on the GPU," in *Graphics Interface 2008*, Canadian Information Processing Society, pp. 219–226, 2008. Cited on p. 747

[506] Fung, James, "Computer Vision on the GPU," in Matt Pharr, ed., *GPU Gems 2*, Addison-Wesley, pp. 649–666, 2005. Cited on p. 521

[507] Funkhouser, Thomas A., *Database and Display Algorithms for Interactive Visualization of Architectural Models*, PhD thesis, University of California, Berkeley, 1993. Cited on p. 866

[508] Funkhouser, Thomas A., and Carlo H. Séquin, "Adaptive Display Algorithm for Interactive Frame Rates During Visualization of Complex Virtual Environments," in *SIGGRAPH '93: Proceedings of the 20th Annual Conference on Computer Graphics and Interactive Techniques*, ACM, pp. 247–254, Aug. 1993. Cited on p. 710, 864, 865, 866

[509] Fürst, René, Oliver Mattausch, and Daniel Scherzer, "Real-Time Deep Shadow Maps," in Wolfgang Engel, ed., *GPU Pro⁴*, CRC Press, pp. 253–264, 2013. Cited on p. 258

[510] Gaitatzes, Athanasios, and Georgios Papaioannou, "Progressive Screen-Space Multichannel Surface Voxelization," in Wolfgang Engel, ed., *GPU Pro⁴*, CRC Press, pp. 137–154, 2013. Cited on p. 582

[511] Galeano, David, "Rendering Optimizations in the Turbulenz Engine," in Patrick Cozzi, ed., *WebGL Insights*, CRC Press, pp. 157–171, 2015. Cited on p. 795, 796, 802, 803

[512] Gallagher, Benn, and Martin Mittring, "Building Paragon in UE4," *Game Developers Conference*, Mar. 2016. Cited on p. 527, 556, 637

[513] Garcia, Ismael, Mateu Sbert, and Lázló Szirmay-Kalos, "Tree Rendering with Billboard Clouds," *Third Hungarian Conference on Computer Graphics and Geometry*, Jan. 2005. Cited on p. 563

[514] Garland, Michael, and Paul S. Heckbert, "Fast Polygonal Approximation of Terrains and Height Fields," Technical Report CMU-CS-95-181, Carnegie Mellon University, 1995. Cited on p. 708, 877

[515] Garland, Michael, and Paul S. Heckbert, "Surface Simplification Using Quadric Error Metrics," in *SIGGRAPH '97: Proceedings of the 24th Annual Conference on Computer Graphics and Interactive Techniques*, ACM Press/Addison-Wesley Publishing Co., pp. 209–216, Aug. 1997. Cited on p. 708

[516] Garland, Michael, and Paul S. Heckbert, "Simplifying Surfaces with Color and Texture Using Quadric Error Metrics," in *Proceedings of IEEE Visualization 98*, IEEE Computer Society, pp. 263–269, July 1998. Cited on p. 706, 707, 708

[517] Garland, Michael, *Quadric-Based Polygonal Surface Simplification*, PhD thesis, Technical Report CMU-CS-99-105, Carnegie Mellon University, 1999. Cited on p. 709

[518] Gautron, Pascal, Jaroslav Křivánek, Sumanta Pattanaik, and Kadi Bouatouch, "A Novel Hemispherical Basis for Accurate and Efficient Rendering," on *Proceedings of the Fifteenth Eurographics Conference on Rendering Techniques*, Eurographics Association, pp. 321–330, June 2004. Cited on p. 404

[519] Geczy, George, "2D Programming in a 3D World: Developing a 2D Game Engine Using DirectX 8 Direct3D," *Gamasutra*, June 2001. Cited on p. 550

[520] Gehling, Michael, "Dynamic Skyscapes," *Game Developer*, vol. 13, no. 3, pp. 23–33, Mar. 2006. Cited on p. 549

[521] Geiss, Ryan, "Generating Complex Procedural Terrains Using the GPU," in Hubert Nguyen, ed., *GPU Gems 3*, Addison-Wesley, pp. 7–37, 2007. Cited on p. 171

[522] Geiss, Ryan, and Michael Thompson, "NVIDIA Demo Team Secrets—Cascades," *Game Developers Conference*, Mar. 2007. Cited on p. 171, 571

[523] Geldreich, Rich, "crunch/crnlib v1.04," *GitHub* repository, 2012. Cited on p. 870

[524] General Services Administration, "Colors Used in Government Procurement," Document ID FED-STD-595C, Jan. 16, 2008. Cited on p. 349

[525] Gerasimov, Philipp, "Omnidirectional Shadow Mapping," in Randima Fernando, ed., *GPU Gems*, Addison-Wesley, pp. 193–203, 2004. Cited on p. 234

[526] Gershun, Arun, "The Light Field," Moscow, 1936, translated by P. Moon and G. Timoshenko, *Journal of Mathematics and Physics*, vol. 18, no. 2, pp. 51–151, 1939. Cited on p. 379

[527] Gibson, Steve, "The Distant Origins of Sub-Pixel Font Rendering," *Sub-pixel Font Rendering Technology*, Aug, 4, 2006. Cited on p. 675

[528] Giegl, Markus, and Michael Wimmer, "Unpopping: Solving the Image-Space Blend Problem for Smooth Discrete LOD Transition," *Computer Graphics Forum*, vol. 26, no. 1, pp. 46–49, 2007. Cited on p. 856

[529] Giesen, Fabian, "View Frustum Culling," *The ryg blog*, Oct. 17, 2010. Cited on p. 983, 986

[530] Giesen, Fabian, "A Trip through the Graphics Pipeline 2011," *The ryg blog*, July 9, 2011. Cited on p. 32, 42, 46, 47, 48, 49, 52, 53, 54, 55, 141, 247, 684, 701, 784, 1040

[531] Giesen, Fabian, "Fast Blurs 1," *The ryg blog*, July 30, 2012. Cited on p. 518

[532] Gigus, Z., J. Canny, and R. Seidel, "Efficiently Computing and Representing Aspect Graphs of Polyhedral Objects," *IEEE Transactions on Pattern Analysis and Machine Intelligence*, vol. 13, no. 6, pp. 542–551, 1991. Cited on p. 831

[533] Gilabert, Mickael, and Nikolay Stefanov, "Deferred Radiance Transfer Volumes," *Game Developers Conference*, Mar. 2012. Cited on p. 478, 481

[534] van Ginneken, B., M. Stavridi, and J. J. Koenderink, "Diffuse and Specular Reflectance from Rough Surfaces," *Applied Optics*, vol. 37, no. 1, Jan. 1998. Cited on p. 335

[535] Ginsburg, Dan, and Dave Gosselin, "Dynamic Per-Pixel Lighting Techniques," in Mark DeLoura, ed., *Game Programming Gems 2*, Charles River Media, pp. 452–462, 2001. Cited on p. 211, 221

[536] Ginsburg, Dan, "Porting Source 2 to Vulkan," *SIGGRAPH An Overview of Next Generation APIs course*, Aug. 2015. Cited on p. 814

[537] Giorgianni, Edward J., and Thomas E. Madden, *Digital Color Management: Encoding Solutions*, Second Edition, John Wiley & Sons, Inc., 2008. Cited on p. 286, 291

[538] Girshick, Ahna, Victoria Interrante, Steve Haker, and Todd Lemoine, "Line Direction Matters: An Argument for the Use of Principal Directions in 3D Line Drawings," in *Proceedings of the 1st International Symposium on Non-photorealistic Animation and Rendering*, ACM, pp. 43–52, June 2000. Cited on p. 672

[539] Gjøl, Mikkel, and Mikkel Svendsen, "The Rendering of *Inside*," *Game Developers Conference*, Mar. 2016. Cited on p. 521, 524, 527, 572, 587, 604, 609, 892, 1010

[540] Glassner, Andrew S., ed., *Graphics Gems*, Academic Press, 1990. Cited on p. 102, 991

[541] Glassner, Andrew S., "Computing Surface Normals for 3D Models," in Andrew S. Glassner, ed., *Graphics Gems*, Academic Press, pp. 562–566, 1990. Cited on p. 695

[542] Glassner, Andrew, "Building Vertex Normals from an Unstructured Polygon List," in Paul S. Heckbert, ed., *Graphics Gems IV*, Academic Press, pp. 60–73, 1994. Cited on p. 691, 692, 695

[543] Glassner, Andrew S., *Principles of Digital Image Synthesis*, vol. 1, Morgan Kaufmann, 1995. Cited on p. 372, 512, 1010

[544] Glassner, Andrew S., *Principles of Digital Image Synthesis*, vol. 2, Morgan Kaufmann, 1995. Cited on p. 268, 271, 280, 372, 512

[545] Gneiting, A., "Real-Time Geometry Caches," in *ACM SIGGRAPH 2014 Talks*, ACM, article no. 49, Aug. 2014. Cited on p. 92

[546] Gobbetti, Enrico, and Fabio Marton, "Layered Point Clouds," *Symposium on Point-Based Graphics*, Jun. 2004. Cited on p. 573

[547] Gobbetti, E., D. Kasik, and S.-E. Yoon, "Technical Strategies for Massive Model Visualization," *ACM Symposium on Solid and Physical Modeling*, June 2008. Cited on p. 879

[548] Goldman, Ronald, "Intersection of Two Lines in Three-Space," in Andrew S. Glassner, ed., *Graphics Gems*, Academic Press, p. 304, 1990. Cited on p. 990

[549] Goldman, Ronald, "Intersection of Three Planes," in Andrew S. Glassner, ed., *Graphics Gems*, Academic Press, p. 305, 1990. Cited on p. 990

[550] Goldman, Ronald, "Matrices and Transformations," in Andrew S. Glassner, ed., *Graphics Gems*, Academic Press, pp. 472–475, 1990. Cited on p. 75

[551] Goldman, Ronald, "Some Properties of Bézier Curves," in Andrew S. Glassner, ed., *Graphics Gems*, Academic Press, pp. 587–593, 1990. Cited on p. 722

[552] Goldman, Ronald, "Recovering the Data from the Transformation Matrix," in James Arvo, ed., *Graphics Gems II*, Academic Press, pp. 324–331, 1991. Cited on p. 74

[553] Goldman, Ronald, "Decomposing Linear and Affine Transformations," in David Kirk, ed., *Graphics Gems III*, Academic Press, pp. 108–116, 1992. Cited on p. 74

[554] Goldman, Ronald, "Identities for the Univariate and Bivariate Bernstein Basis Functions," in Alan Paeth, ed., *Graphics Gems V*, Academic Press, pp. 149–162, 1995. Cited on p. 781

[555] Gollent, M., "Landscape Creation and Rendering in REDengine 3," *Game Developers Conference*, Mar. 2014. Cited on p. 262, 263, 873

[556] Golub, Gene, and Charles Van Loan, *Matrix Computations*, Fourth Edition, Johns Hopkins University Press, 2012. Cited on p. 102

[557] Golus, Ben, "Anti-aliased Alpha Test: The Esoteric Alpha to Coverage," *Medium.com* website, Aug. 12, 2017. Cited on p. 204, 205, 206, 207

[558] Gomes, Abel, Irina Voiculescu, Joaquim Jorge, Brian Wyvill, and Callum Galbraith, *Implicit Curves and Surfaces: Mathematics, Data Structures and Algorithms*, Springer, 2009. Cited on p. 583, 683, 751, 753, 781, 944

[559] Gonzalez, Rafael C., and Richard E. Woods, *Digital Image Processing*, Third Edition, Addison-Wesley, 2007. Cited on p. 130, 543, 661

[560] Gonzalez-Ochoa, C., and D. Holder, "Water Technology in *Uncharted*," *Game Developers Conference*, Mar. 2012. Cited on p. 879

[561] Gooch, Amy, Bruce Gooch, Peter Shirley, and Elaine Cohen, "A Non-Photorealistic Lighting Model for Automatic Technical Illustration," in *SIGGRAPH '98: Proceedings of the 25th Annual Conference on Computer Graphics and Interactive Techniques*, ACM, pp. 447–452, July 1998. Cited on p. 103

[562] Gooch, Bruce, Peter-Pike J. Sloan, Amy Gooch, Peter Shirley, and Richard Riesenfeld, "Interactive Technical Illustration," in *Proceedings of the 1999 Symposium on Interactive 3D Graphics*, ACM, pp. 31–38, 1999. Cited on p. 656, 667

[563] Gooch, Bruce or Amy, and Amy or Bruce Gooch, *Non-Photorealistic Rendering*, A K Peters, Ltd., 2001. Cited on p. 652, 678

[564] Good, Otavio, and Zachary Taylor, "Optimized Photon Tracing Using Spherical Harmonic Light Maps," in *ACM SIGGRAPH 2005 Sketches*, article no. 53, Aug. 2005. Cited on p. 475

[565] Goodwin, Todd, Ian Vollick, and Aaron Hertzmann, "Isophote Distance: A Shading Approach to Artistic Stroke Thickness," *Proceedings of the 5th International Symposium on Non-Photorealistic Animation and Rendering*, ACM, pp. 53–62, Aug. 2007. Cited on p. 657, 667

[566] Goral, Cindy M., Kenneth E. Torrance, Donald P. Greenberg, and Bennett Battaile, "Modelling the Interaction of Light Between Diffuse Surfaces," *Computer Graphics (SIGGRAPH '84 Proceedings)*, vol. 18, no. 3, pp. 212–222, July 1984. Cited on p. 442

[567] Gortler, Steven J., Radek Grzeszczuk, Richard Szeliski, and Michael F. Cohen, "The Lumigraph," in *SIGGRAPH '96: Proceedings of the 23rd Annual Conference on Computer Graphics and Interactive Techniques*, ACM, pp. 43–54, Aug. 1996. Cited on p. 549

[568] Gosselin, David R., Pedro V. Sander, and Jason L. Mitchell, "Real-Time Texture-Space Skin Rendering," in Wolfgang Engel, ed., *ShaderX³*, Charles River Media, pp. 171–183, 2004. Cited on p. 635

[569] Gosselin, David R., "Real Time Skin Rendering," *Game Developers Conference*, Mar. 2004. Cited on p. 634, 635

[570] Goswami, Prashant, Yanci Zhang, Renato Pajarola, and Enrico Gobbetti, "High Quality Interactive Rendering of Massive Point Models Using Multi-way kd-Trees," *Pacific Graphics 2010*, Sept. 2010. Cited on p. 574

[571] Gotanda, Yoshiharu, "*Star Ocean 4*: Flexible Shader Management and Post-Processing," *Game Developers Conference*, Mar. 2009. Cited on p. 286

[572] Gotanda, Yoshiharu, "Film Simulation for Videogames," *SIGGRAPH Color Enhancement and Rendering in Film and Game Production course*, July 2010. Cited on p. 286

[573] Gotanda, Yoshiharu, "Beyond a Simple Physically Based Blinn-Phong Model in Real-Time," *SIGGRAPH Physically Based Shading in Theory and Practice course*, Aug. 2012. Cited on p. 354, 364, 421

[574] Gotanda, Yoshiharu, "Designing Reflectance Models for New Consoles," *SIGGRAPH Physically Based Shading in Theory and Practice course*, Aug. 2014. Cited on p. 331, 354, 355

[575] Gotanda, Yoshiharu, Masaki Kawase, and Masanori Kakimoto, *SIGGRAPH Real-Time Rendering of Physically Based Optical Effect in Theory and Practice course*, Aug. 2015. Cited on p. 543

[576] Gottschalk, S., M. C. Lin, and D. Manocha, "OBBTree: A Hierarchical Structure for Rapid Interference Detection," in *SIGGRAPH '96: Proceedings of the 23rd Annual Conference on Computer Graphics and Interactive Techniques*, ACM, pp. 171–180, Aug. 1996. Cited on p. 946, 980

[577] Gottschalk, Stefan, *Collision Queries Using Oriented Bounding Boxes*, PhD thesis, Department of Computer Science, University of North Carolina at Chapel Hill, 2000. Cited on p. 947, 951, 980

[578] Gouraud, H., "Continuous Shading of Curved Surfaces," *IEEE Transactions on Computers*, vol. C-20, pp. 623–629, June 1971. Cited on p. 118

[579] Green, Chris, "Efficient Self-Shadowed Radiosity Normal Mapping," *SIGGRAPH Advanced Real-Time Rendering in 3D Graphics and Games course*, Aug. 2007. Cited on p. 403

[580] Green, Chris, "Improved Alpha-Tested Magnification for Vector Textures and Special Effects," *SIGGRAPH Advanced Real-Time Rendering in 3D Graphics and Games course*, Aug. 2007. Cited on p. 206, 677, 678, 890

[581] Green, D., and D. Hatch, "Fast Polygon-Cube Intersection Testing," in Alan Paeth, ed., *Graphics Gems V*, Academic Press, pp. 375–379, 1995. Cited on p. 974

[582] Green, Paul, Jan Kautz, and Frédo Durand, "Efficient Reflectance and Visibility Approximations for Environment Map Rendering," *Computer Graphics Forum*, vol. 26, no. 3, pp. 495–502, 2007. Cited on p. 398, 417, 424, 466, 471

[583] Green, Robin, "Spherical Harmonic Lighting: The Gritty Details," *Game Developers Conference*, Mar. 2003. Cited on p. 401, 430

[584] Green, Simon, "Stupid OpenGL Shader Tricks," *Game Developers Conference*, Mar. 2003. Cited on p. 537, 539, 540

[585] Green, Simon, "Summed Area Tables Using Graphics Hardware," *Game Developers Conference*, Mar. 2003. Cited on p. 188

[586] Green, Simon, "Real-Time Approximations to Subsurface Scattering," in Randima Fernando, ed., *GPU Gems*, Addison-Wesley, pp. 263–278, 2004. Cited on p. 633, 635, 638, 639

[587] Green, Simon, "Implementing Improved Perlin Noise," in Matt Pharr, ed., *GPU Gems 2*, Addison-Wesley, pp. 409–416, 2005. Cited on p. 199

[588] Green, Simon, "DirectX 10/11 Visual Effects," *Game Developers Conference*, Mar. 2009. Cited on p. 518

[589] Green, Simon, "Screen Space Fluid Rendering for Games," *Game Developers Conference*, Mar. 2010. Cited on p. 520, 569

[590] Greene, Ned, "Environment Mapping and Other Applications of World Projections," *IEEE Computer Graphics and Applications*, vol. 6, no. 11, pp. 21–29, Nov. 1986. Cited on p. 410, 414, 424

[591] Greene, Ned, Michael Kass, and Gavin Miller, "Hierarchical Z-Buffer Visibility," in *SIGGRAPH '93: Proceedings of the 20th Annual Conference on Computer Graphics and Interactive Techniques*, ACM, pp. 231–238, Aug. 1993. Cited on p. 846, 847, 1015

[592] Greene, Ned, "Detecting Intersection of a Rectangular Solid and a Convex Polyhedron," in Paul S. Heckbert, ed., *Graphics Gems IV*, Academic Press, pp. 74–82, 1994. Cited on p. 946

[593] Greene, Ned, *Hierarchical Rendering of Complex Environments*, PhD thesis, Technical Report UCSC-CRL-95-27, University of California at Santa Cruz, June 1995. Cited on p. 846, 847

[594] Greger, Gene, Peter Shirley, Philip M. Hubbard, and Donald P. Greenberg, "The Irradiance Volume," *IEEE Computer Graphics and Applications*, vol. 18, no. 2, pp. 32–43, Mar./Apr. 1998. Cited on p. 487

[595] Gregorius, Dirk, "The Separating Axis Test between Convex Polyhedra," *Game Developers Conference*, Mar. 2013. Cited on p. 987

[596] Gregorius, Dirk, "Implementing QuickHull," *Game Developers Conference*, Mar. 2014. Cited on p. 950, 951

[597] Gregorius, Dirk, "Robust Contact Creation for Physics Simulations," *Game Developers Conference*, Mar. 2015. Cited on p. 947

[598] Grenier, Jean-Philippe, "Physically Based Lens Flare," *Autodesk Stingray* blog, July 3, 2017. Cited on p. 524, 526

[599] Grenier, Jean-Philippe, "Notes on Screen Space HIZ Tracing," *Autodesk Stingray* blog, Aug. 14, 2017. Cited on p. 508

[600] Gribb, Gil, and Klaus Hartmann, "Fast Extraction of Viewing Frustum Planes from the World-View-Projection Matrix," *gamedevs.org*, June 2001. Cited on p. 984

[601] Griffin, Wesley, and Marc Olano, "Objective Image Quality Assessment of Texture Compression," in *Proceedings of the 18th Meeting of the ACM SIGGRAPH Symposium on Interactive 3D Graphics and Games*, ACM, pp. 119–126, Mar. 1999. Cited on p. 198

[602] Griffiths, Andrew, "Real-Time Cellular Texturing," in Wolfgang Engel, ed., *ShaderX^5*, Charles River Media, pp. 519–532, 2006. Cited on p. 199

[603] Grimes, Bronwen, "Shading a Bigger, Better Sequel: Techniques in *Left 4 Dead 2*," *Game Developers Conference*, Mar. 2010. Cited on p. 366

[604] Grimes, Bronwen, "Building the Content that Drives the *Counter-Strike: Global Offensive* Economy," *Game Developers Conference*, Mar. 2014. Cited on p. 366

[605] Gritz, Larry, "Shader Antialiasing," in *Advanced RenderMan: Creating CGI for Motion Pictures*, Morgan Kaufmann, Chapter 11, 1999. Also (as "Basic Antialiasing in Shading Language") in *SIGGRAPH Advanced RenderMan: Beyond the Companion course*, Aug. 1999. Cited on p. 200

[606] Gritz, Larry, "The Secret Life of Lights and Surfaces," *SIGGRAPH Advanced RenderMan 2: To RI_INFINITY and Beyond course*, July 2000. Also in "Illumination Models and Light," in *Advanced RenderMan: Creating CGI for Motion Pictures*, Morgan Kaufmann, 1999. Cited on p. 382

[607] Gritz, Larry, and Eugene d'Eon, "The Importance of Being Linear," in Hubert Nguyen, ed., *GPU Gems 3*, Addison-Wesley, pp. 529–542, 2007. Cited on p. 161, 166, 184

[608] Gritz, Larry, ed., "Open Shading Language 1.9: Language Specification," Sony Pictures Imageworks Inc., 2017. Cited on p. 37

[609] Gronsky, Stefan, "Lighting Food," *SIGGRAPH Anyone Can Cook—Inside Ratatouille's Kitchen course*, Aug. 2007. Cited on p. 638

[610] Gruen, Holger, "Hybrid Min/Max Plane-Based Shadow Maps," in Wolfgang Engel, ed., *GPU Pro*, A K Peters, Ltd., pp. 447–454, 2010. Cited on p. 252

[611] Gruen, Holger, and Nicolas Thibieroz, "OIT and Indirect Illumination Using Dx11 Linked Lists," *Game Developers Conference*, Mar. 2010. Cited on p. 155

[612] Gruen, Holger, "An Optimized Diffusion Depth Of Field Solver (DDOF)," *Game Developers Conference*, Mar. 2011. Cited on p. 535

[613] Gruen, Holger, "Constant Buffers without Constant Pain," *NVIDIA GameWorks* blog, Jan. 14, 2015. Cited on p. 795

[614] Grün, Holger, "Smoothed N-Patches," in Wolfgang Engel, ed., *ShaderX^5*, Charles River Media, pp. 5–22, 2006. Cited on p. 747

[615] Grün, Holger, "Implementing a Fast DDOF Solver," Eric Lengyel, ed., *Game Engine Gems 2*, A K Peters, Ltd., pp. 119–133, 2011. Cited on p. 535

[616] Gu, Xianfeng, Steven J. Gortler, and Hugues Hoppe, "Geometry Images," *ACM Transactions on Graphics (SIGGRAPH 2002)*, vol. 21, no. 3, pp. 355–361, 2002. Cited on p. 566

[617] Guennebaud, Gaël, Loïc Barthe, and Mathias Paulin, "High-Quality Adaptive Soft Shadow Mapping," *Computer Graphics Forum*, vol. 26, no. 3, pp. 525–533, 2007. Cited on p. 252

[618] Guenter, B., J. Rapp, and M. Finch, "Symbolic Differentiation in GPU Shaders," Technical Report MSR-TR-2011-31, Microsoft, Mar. 2011. Cited on p. 1017

[619] Guenter, Brian, Mark Finch, Steven Drucker, Desney Tan, and John Snyder, "Foveated 3D Graphics," *ACM Transactions on Graphics*, vol. 31, no. 6, article no. 164, 2012. Cited on p. 924, 931

[620] Guerrette, Keith, "Moving The Heavens," *Game Developers Conference*, Mar. 2014. Cited on p. 617

[621] Guertin, Jean-Philippe, Morgan McGuire, and Derek Nowrouzezahrai, "A Fast and Stable Feature-Aware Motion Blur Filter," Technical Report, NVIDIA, Nov. 2013. Cited on p. 537, 542, 543

[622] Guigue, Philippe, and Olivier Devillers, "Fast and Robust Triangle-Triangle Overlap Test Using Orientation Predicates," *journals of graphics tools*, vol. 8, no. 1, pp. 25–42, 2003. Cited on p. 972, 974

[623] Gulbrandsen, Ole, "Artist Friendly Metallic Fresnel," *Journal of Computer Graphics Techniques*, vol. 3, no. 4, pp. 64–72, 2014. Cited on p. 320

[624] Guymon, Mel, "Pyro-Techniques: Playing with Fire," *Game Developer*, vol. 7, no. 2, pp. 23–27, Feb. 2000. Cited on p. 554

[625] Haar, Ulrich, and Sebastian Aaltonen, "GPU-Driven Rendering Pipelines," *SIGGRAPH Advances in Real-Time Rendering in Games course*, Aug. 2015. Cited on p. 246, 247, 263, 833, 848, 849, 850, 851, 905

[626] Habel, Ralf, Bogdan Mustata, and Michael Wimmer, "Efficient Spherical Harmonics Lighting with the Preetham Skylight Model," in *Eurographics 2008—Short Papers*, Eurographics Association, pp. 119–122, 2008. Cited on p. 430

[627] Habel, Ralf, and Michael Wimmer, "Efficient Irradiance Normal Mapping," in *Proceedings of the 2010 ACM SIGGRAPH Symposium on Interactive 3D Graphics and Games*, ACM, pp. 189–195, Feb. 2010. Cited on p. 404, 475

[628] Hable, John, "*Uncharted 2*: HDR Lighting," *Game Developers Conference*, Mar. 2010. Cited on p. 286, 288

[629] Hable, John, "Why Reinhard Desaturates Your Blacks," *Filmic Worlds Blog*, May 17, 2010. Cited on p. 288

[630] Hable, John, "Why a Filmic Curve Saturates Your Blacks," *Filmic Worlds Blog*, May 24, 2010. Cited on p. 288

[631] Hable, John, "*Uncharted 2*: Character Lighting and Shading," *SIGGRAPH Advances in Real-Time Rendering in Games course*, July 2010. Cited on p. 357, 635

[632] Hable, John, "Next-Gen Characters: From Facial Scans to Facial Animation," *Game Developers Conference*, Mar. 2014. Cited on p. 466

[633] Hable, John, "Simple and Fast Spherical Harmonic Rotation," *Filmic Worlds Blog*, July 2, 2014. Cited on p. 401

[634] Hable, John, "Filmic Tonemapping with Piecewise Power Curves," *Filmic Worlds Blog*, Mar. 26, 2017. Cited on p. 286

[635] Hable, John, "Minimal Color Grading Tools," *Filmic Worlds Blog*, Mar. 28, 2017. Cited on p. 290

[636] Hadwiger, Markus, Christian Sigg, Henning Scharsach, Khatja Bühler, and Markus Gross, "Real-Time Ray-Casting and Advanced Shading of Discrete Isosurfaces," *Computer Graphics Forum*, vol. 20, no. 3, pp. 303–312, 2005. Cited on p. 583

[637] Haeberli, P., and K. Akeley, "The Accumulation Buffer: Hardware Support for High-Quality Rendering," *Computer Graphics (SIGGRAPH '90 Proceedings)*, vol. 24, no. 4, pp. 309–318, Aug. 1990. Cited on p. 139, 529, 537, 547

[638] Haeberli, Paul, and Mark Segal, "Texture Mapping as a Fundamental Drawing Primitive," in *4th Eurographics Workshop on Rendering*, Eurographics Association, pp. 259–266, June 1993. Cited on p. 200

[639] Hagen, Margaret A., "How to Make a Visually Realistic 3D Display," *Computer Graphics*, vol. 25, no. 2, pp. 76–81, Apr. 1991. Cited on p. 554

[640] Haines, Eric, "Essential Ray Tracing Algorithms," in Andrew Glassner, ed., *An Introduction to Ray Tracing*, Academic Press Inc., Chapter 2, 1989. Cited on p. 955, 959, 961, 969

[641] Haines, Eric, "Fast Ray-Convex Polyhedron Intersection," in James Arvo, ed., *Graphics Gems II*, Academic Press, pp. 247–250, 1991. Cited on p. 961

[642] Haines, Eric, "Point in Polygon Strategies," in Paul S. Heckbert, ed., *Graphics Gems IV*, Academic Press, pp. 24–46, 1994. Cited on p. 962, 966, 968, 969, 970

[643] Haines, Eric, and Steven Worley, "Fast, Low-Memory Z-Buffering when Performing Medium-Quality Rendering," *journal of graphics tools*, vol. 1, no. 3, pp. 1–6, 1996. Cited on p. 803

[644] Haines, Eric, "Soft Planar Shadows Using Plateaus," *journal of graphics tools*, vol. 6, no. 1, pp. 19–27, 2001. Also collected in [112]. Cited on p. 229

[645] Haines, Eric, "Interactive 3D Graphics," *Udacity Course 291*, launched May 2013. Cited on p. 1048

[646] Haines, Eric, "60 Hz, 120 Hz, 240 Hz...," *Real-Time Rendering Blog*, Nov. 5, 2014. Cited on p. 1011

[647] Haines, Eric, "Limits of Triangles," *Real-Time Rendering Blog*, Nov. 10, 2014. Cited on p. 688, 695

[648] Haines, Eric, "GPUs Prefer Premultiplication," *Real-Time Rendering Blog*, Jan. 10, 2016. Cited on p. 160, 208

[649] Haines, Eric, "A PNG Puzzle," *Real-Time Rendering Blog*, Feb. 19, 2016. Cited on p. 160

[650] Haines, Eric, "Minecon 2016 Report," *Real-Time Rendering Blog*, Sept. 30, 2016. Cited on p. 920

[651] Hakura, Ziyad S., and Anoop Gupta, "The Design and Analysis of a Cache Architecture for Texture Mapping," in *Proceedings of the 24th Annual International Symposium on Computer Architecture*, ACM, pp. 108–120, June 1997. Cited on p. 997, 1007, 1017

[652] Hall, Chris, Rob Hall, and Dave Edwards, "Rendering in *Cars 2*," *SIGGRAPH Advances in Real-Time Rendering in 3D Graphics and Games course*, Aug. 2011. Cited on p. 245, 246, 937

[653] Hall, Roy, *Illumination and Color in Computer Generated Imagery*, Springer-Verlag, 1989. Cited on p. 1010

[654] Hall, Tim, "A How To for Using OpenGL to Render Mirrors," *comp.graphics.api.opengl* newsgroup, Aug. 1996. Cited on p. 505

[655] Halstead, Mark, Michal Kass, and Tony DeRose, "Efficient, Fair Interpolation Using Catmull-Clark Surfaces," in *SIGGRAPH '93: Proceedings of the 20th Annual Conference on Computer Graphics and Interactive Techniques*, ACM, pp. 35–44, Aug. 1993. Cited on p. 762, 763, 778

[656] Hamilton, Andrew, and Kenneth Brown, "Photogrammetry and *Star Wars Battlefront*," *Game Developers Conference*, Mar. 2016. Cited on p. 366

[657] Hammon, Earl, Jr., "PBR Diffuse Lighting for GGX+Smith Microsurfaces," *Game Developers Conference*, Feb.–Mar. 2017. Cited on p. 331, 334, 337, 342, 355

[658] Han, Charles, Bo Sun, Ravi Ramamoorthi, and Eitan Grinspun, "Frequency Domain Normal Map Filtering," *ACM Transactions on Graphics (SIGGRAPH 2007)*, vol. 26, no. 3, pp. 28:1–28::11, July 2007. Cited on p. 369, 370

[659] Han, S., and P. Sander, "Triangle Reordering for Reduced Overdraw in Animated Scenes," in *Proceedings of the 20th ACM SIGGRAPH Symposium on Interactive 3D Graphics and Games*, ACM, pp. 23–27, 2016. Cited on p. 831

[660] Hanika, Johannes, "Manuka: Weta Digital's Spectral Renderer," *SIGGRAPH Path Tracing in Production course*, Aug. 2017. Cited on p. 278, 280, 311, 591

[661] Hanrahan, P., and P. Haeberli, "Direct WYSIWYG Painting and Texturing on 3D Shapes," *Computer Graphics (SIGGRAPH '90 Proceedings)*, vol. 24, no. 4, pp. 215–223, Aug. 1990. Cited on p. 942

[662] Hanrahan, Pat, and Wolfgang Krueger, "Reflection from Layered Surfaces due to Subsurface Scattering," in *SIGGRAPH '93: Proceedings of the 20th Annual Conference on Computer Graphics and Interactive Techniques*, ACM, pp. 165–174, Aug. 1993. Cited on p. 353, 354

[663] Hanson, Andrew J., *Visualizing Quaternions*, Morgan Kaufmann, 2006. Cited on p. 102

[664] Hapke, B., "A Theoretical Photometric Function for the Lunar Surface," *Journal of Geophysical Research*, vol. 68, no. 15, pp. 4571–4586, Aug. 1, 1963. Cited on p. 314

[665] Harada, T., J. McKee, and J. Yang, "Forward+: Bringing Deferred Lighting to the Next Level," in *Eurographics 2012—Short Papers*, Eurographics Association, pp. 5–8, May 2012. Cited on p. 895

[666] Harada, T., "A 2.5D culling for Forward+," in *SIGGRAPH Asia 2012 Technical Briefs*, ACM, pp. 18:1–18:4, Dec. 2012. Cited on p. 897

[667] Harada, Takahiro, Jay McKee, and Jason C. Yang, "Forward+: A Step Toward Film-Style Shading in Real Time," in Wolfgang Engel, ed., *GPU Pro⁴*, CRC Press, pp. 115–135, 2013. Cited on p. 887, 895, 896, 897, 904

[668] Hargreaves, Shawn, "Deferred Shading," *Game Developers Conference*, Mar. 2004. Cited on p. 882, 884, 886

[669] Hargreaves, Shawn, and Mark Harris, "Deferred Shading," *NVIDIA Developers Conference*, June 29, 2004. Cited on p. 882, 884

[670] Harris, Mark J., and Anselmo Lastra, "Real-Time Cloud Rendering," *Computer Graphics Forum*, vol. 20, no. 3, pp. 76–84, 2001. Cited on p. 556, 617

[671] Hart, Evan, Dave Gosselin, and John Isidoro, "Vertex Shading with Direct3D and OpenGL," *Game Developers Conference*, Mar. 2001. Cited on p. 659

[672] Hart, Evan, "UHD Color for Games," NVIDIA White Paper, June 2016. Cited on p. 161, 165, 278, 281, 283, 287, 290

[673] Hart, J. C., D. J. Sandin, and L. H. Kauffman, "Ray Tracing Deterministic 3-D Fractals," *Computer Graphics (SIGGRAPH '89 Proceedings)*, vol. 23, no. 3, pp. 289–296, 1989. Cited on p. 752

[674] Hart, John C., George K. Francis, and Louis H. Kauffman, "Visualizing Quaternion Rotation," *ACM Transactions on Graphics*, vol. 13, no. 3, pp. 256–276, 1994. Cited on p. 102

[675] Hasenfratz, Jean-Marc, Marc Lapierre, Nicolas Holzschuch, and François Sillion, "A Survey of Real-Time Soft Shadows Algorithms," *Computer Graphics Forum*, vol. 22, no. 4, pp. 753–774, 2003. Cited on p. 265

[676] Hasselgren, J., T. Akenine-Möller, and L. Ohlsson, "Conservative Rasterization," in Matt Pharr, ed., *GPU Gems 2*, Addison-Wesley, pp. 677–690, 2005. Cited on p. 1001

[677] Hasselgren, J., T. Akenine-Möller, and S. Laine, "A Family of Inexpensive Sampling Schemes," *Computer Graphics Forum*, vol. 24, no. 4, pp. 843–848, 2005. Cited on p. 146

[678] Hasselgren, J., and T. Akenine-Möller, "An Efficient Multi-View Rasterization Architecture," in *Proceedings of the 17th Eurographics Conference on Rendering Techniques*, Eurographics Association, pp. 61–72, June 2006. Cited on p. 928

[679] Hasselgren, J., and T. Akenine-Möller, "Efficient Depth Buffer Compression," in *Graphics Hardware 2006*, Eurographics Association, pp. 103–110, Sept. 2006. Cited on p. 997, 1009, 1016

[680] Hasselgren, J., and T. Akenine-Möller, "PCU: The Programmable Culling Unit," *ACM Transactions on Graphics*, vol. 26, no. 3, pp. 92.1–91.20, 2007. Cited on p. 252

[681] Hasselgren, J., M. Andersson, J. Nilsson, and T. Akenine-Möller, "A Compressed Depth Cache," *Journal of Computer Graphics Techniques*, vol. 1, no. 1, pp. 101–118, 2012. Cited on p. 1009

[682] Hasselgren, Jon, Jacob Munkberg, and Karthik Vaidyanathan, "Practical Layered Reconstruction for Defocus and Motion Blur," *Journal of Computer Graphics Techniques*, vol. 4, no. 2, pp. 45–58, 2012. Cited on p. 542

[683] Hasselgren, J., M. Andersson, and T. Akenine-Möller, "Masked Software Occlusion Culling," *High-Performance Graphics*, June 2016. Cited on p. 849, 850

[684] Hast, Anders, "3D Stereoscopic Rendering: An Overview of Implementation Issues," in Eric Lengyel, ed., *Game Engine Gems*, Jones & Bartlett, pp. 123–138, 2010. Cited on p. 927, 932, 934

[685] Hathaway, Benjamin, "Alpha Blending as a Post-Process," in Wolfgang Engel, ed., *GPU Pro*, A K Peters, Ltd., pp. 167–184, 2010. Cited on p. 208

[686] He, Xiao D., Kenneth E. Torrance, François X. Sillion, and Donald P. Greenberg, "A Comprehensive Physical Model for Light Reflection," *Computer Graphics (SIGGRAPH '91 Proceedings)*, vol. 25, no. 4, pp. 175–186, July 1991. Cited on p. 361, 424

[687] He, Y., Y. Gu, and K. Fatahalian, "Extending the Graphics Pipeline with Adaptive, Multirate Shading," *ACM Transactions on Graphics*, vol. 33, no. 4, pp. 142:1–142:12, 2014. Cited on p. 1013

[688] He, Y., T. Foley, N. Tatarchuk, and K. Fatahalian, "A System for Rapid, Automatic Shader Level-of-Detail," *ACM Transactions on Graphics*, vol. 34, no. 6, pp. 187:1–187:12, 2015. Cited on p. 853

[689] Hearn, Donald, and M. Pauline Baker, *Computer Graphics with OpenGL*, Fourth Edition, Prentice-Hall, Inc., 2010. Cited on p. 102

[690] Heckbert, Paul, "Survey of Texture Mapping," *IEEE Computer Graphics and Applications*, vol. 6, no. 11, pp. 56–67, Nov. 1986. Cited on p. 222

[691] Heckbert, Paul S., "Fundamentals of Texture Mapping and Image Warping," Technical Report 516, Computer Science Division, University of California, Berkeley, June 1989. Cited on p. 187, 189, 222, 688

[692] Heckbert, Paul S., "What Are the Coordinates of a Pixel?" in Andrew S. Glassner, ed., *Graphics Gems*, Academic Press, pp. 246–248, 1990. Cited on p. 176

[693] Heckbert, Paul S., "Adaptive Radiosity Textures for Bidirectional Ray Tracing," *Computer Graphics (SIGGRAPH '90 Proceedings)*, vol. 24, no. 4, pp. 145–154, Aug. 1990. Cited on p. 439

[694] Heckbert, Paul S., and Henry P. Moreton, "Interpolation for Polygon Texture Mapping and Shading," *State of the Art in Computer Graphics: Visualization and Modeling*, Springer-Verlag, pp. 101–111, 1991. Cited on p. 22, 999

[695] Heckbert, Paul S., ed., *Graphics Gems IV*, Academic Press, 1994. Cited on p. 102, 991

[696] Heckbert, Paul S., "A Minimal Ray Tracer," in Paul S. Heckbert, ed., *Graphics Gems IV*, Academic Press, pp. 375–381, 1994. Cited on p. 444

[697] Heckbert, Paul S., and Michael Herf, "Simulating Soft Shadows with Graphics Hardware," Technical Report CMU-CS-97-104, Carnegie Mellon University, Jan. 1997. Cited on p. 228

[698] Hecker, Chris, "More Compiler Results, and What To Do About It," *Game Developer*, pp. 14–21, Aug./Sept. 1996. Cited on p. 793

[699] Hector, Tobias, "Vulkan: High Efficiency on Mobile," *Imagination Blog*, Nov. 5, 2015. Cited on p. 40, 794, 814

[700] Hegeman, Kyle, Nathan A. Carr, and Gavin S. P. Miller, "Particle-Based Fluid Simulation on the GPU," in *Computational Science—ICCS 2006*, Springer, pp. 228–235, 2006. Cited on p. 571

[701] Heidmann, Tim, "Real Shadows, Real Time," *Iris Universe*, no. 18, pp. 23–31, Nov. 1991. Cited on p. 230, 231

[702] Heidrich, Wolfgang, and Hans-Peter Seidel, "View-Independent Environment Maps," in *Proceedings of the ACM SIGGRAPH/EUROGRAPHICS Workshop on Graphics Hardware*, ACM, pp. 39–45, Aug. 1998. Cited on p. 413

[703] Heidrich, Wolfgang, Rüdifer Westermann, Hans-Peter Seidel, and Thomas Ertl, "Applications of Pixel Textures in Visualization and Realistic Image Synthesis," in *Proceedings of the 1999 Symposium on Interactive 3D Graphics*, ACM, pp. 127–134, Apr. 1999. Cited on p. 538

[704] Heidrich, Wolfgang, and Hans-Peter Seidel, "Realistic, Hardware-Accelerated Shading and Lighting," in *SIGGRAPH '99: Proceedings of the 26th Annual Conference on Computer Graphics and Interactive Techniques*, ACM Press/Addison-Wesley Publishing Co., pp. 171–178, Aug. 1999. Cited on p. 413, 417, 426

[705] Heidrich, Wolfgang, Katja Daubert, Jan Kautz, and Hans-Peter Seidel, "Illuminating Micro Geometry Based on Precomputed Visibility," in *SIGGRAPH '00: Proceedings of the 27th Annual Conference on Computer Graphics and Interactive Techniques*, ACM Press/Addison-Wesley Publishing Co., pp. 455–464, July 2000. Cited on p. 466

[706] Heitz, Eric, and Fabrice Neyret, "Representing Appearance and Pre-filtering Subpixel Data in Sparse Voxel Octrees," in *Proceedings of the Fourth ACM SIGGRAPH / Eurographics Conference on High-Performance Graphics*, Eurographics Association, pp. 125–134, June 2012. Cited on p. 579, 585, 586

[707] Heitz, Eric, Christophe Bourlier, and Nicolas Pinel, "Correlation Effect between Transmitter and Receiver Azimuthal Directions on the Illumination Function from a Random Rough Surface," *Waves in Random and Complex Media*, vol. 23, no. 3, pp. 318–335, 2013. Cited on p. 336

[708] Heitz, Eric, "Understanding the Masking-Shadowing Function in Microfacet-Based BRDFs," *Journal of Computer Graphics Techniques*, vol. 3, no. 4, pp. 48–107, 2014. Cited on p. 332, 333, 334, 335, 336, 337, 339, 344

[709] Heitz, Eric, and Jonathan Dupuy, "Implementing a Simple Anisotropic Rough Diffuse Material with Stochastic Evaluation," Technical Report, 2015. Cited on p. 331

[710] Heitz, Eric, Jonathan Dupuy, Cyril Crassin, and Carsten Dachsbacher, "The SGGX Microflake Distribution," *ACM Transactions on Graphics (SIGGRAPH 2015)*, vol. 34, no. 4, pp. 48:1–48:11, Aug. 2015. Cited on p. 648, 649

[711] Heitz, Eric, Jonathan Dupuy, Stephen Hill, and David Neubelt, "Real-Time Polygonal-Light Shading with Linearly Transformed Cosines," *ACM Transactions on Graphics (SIGGRAPH 2016)*, vol. 35, no. 4, pp. 41:1–41:8, July 2016. Cited on p. 390

[712] Heitz, Eric, Johannes Hanika, Eugene d'Eon, and Carsten Dachsbacher, "Multiple-Scattering Microfacet BSDFs with the Smith Model," *ACM Transactions on Graphics (SIGGRAPH 2016)*, vol. 35, no. 4, pp. 58:1–58:8, July 2016. Cited on p. 346

[713] Held, Martin, "ERIT—A Collection of Efficient and Reliable Intersection Tests," *journal of graphics tools*, vol. 2, no. 4, pp. 25–44, 1997. Cited on p. 959, 974

[714] Held, Martin, "FIST: Fast Industrial-Strength Triangulation of Polygons," *Algorithmica*, vol. 30, no. 4, pp. 563–596, 2001. Cited on p. 685

[715] Hennessy, John L., and David A. Patterson, *Computer Architecture: A Quantitative Approach*, Fifth Edition, Morgan Kaufmann, 2011. Cited on p. 12, 30, 783, 789, 867, 1007, 1040

[716] Hennessy, Padraic, "Implementation Notes: Physically Based Lens Flares," *Placeholder Art* blog, Jan. 19, 2015. Cited on p. 526

[717] Hennessy, Padraic, "Mixed Resolution Rendering in *Skylanders: SuperChargers*," *Game Developers Conference*, Mar. 2016. Cited on p. 520

[718] Hensley, Justin, and Thorsten Scheuermann, "Dynamic Glossy Environment Reflections Using Summed-Area Tables," in Wolfgang Engel, ed., *ShaderX⁴*, Charles River Media, pp. 187–200, 2005. Cited on p. 188, 419

[719] Hensley, Justin, Thorsten Scheuermann, Greg Coombe, Montek Singh, and Anselmo Lastra, "Fast Summed-Area Table Generation and Its Applications," *Computer Graphics Forum*, vol. 24, no. 3, pp. 547–555, 2005. Cited on p. 188, 419

[720] Hensley, Justin, "Shiny, Blurry Things," *SIGGRAPH Beyond Programmable Shading course*, Aug. 2009. Cited on p. 419

[721] Henyey, L. G., and J. L. Greenstein, "Diffuse Radiation in the Galaxy," in *Astrophysical Journal*, vol. 93, pp. 70–83, 1941. Cited on p. 598

[722] Herf, M., and P. S. Heckbert, "Fast Soft Shadows," in *ACM SIGGRAPH '96 Visual Proceedings*, ACM, p. 145, Aug. 1996. Cited on p. 228

[723] Hermosilla, Pedro, and Pere-Pau Vázquez, "NPR Effects Using the Geometry Shader," in Wolfgang Engel, ed., *GPU Pro*, A K Peters, Ltd., pp. 149–165, 2010. Cited on p. 668

[724] Herrell, Russ, Joe Baldwin, and Chris Wilcox, "High-Quality Polygon Edging," *IEEE Computer Graphics and Applications*, vol. 15, no. 4, pp. 68–74, July 1995. Cited on p. 673

[725] Hertzmann, Aaron, "Introduction to 3D Non-Photorealistic Rendering: Silhouettes and Outlines," *SIGGRAPH Non-Photorealistic Rendering course*, Aug. 1999. Cited on p. 663, 667

[726] Hertzmann, Aaron, and Denis Zorin, "Illustrating Smooth Surfaces," in *SIGGRAPH '00: Proceedings of the 27th Annual Conference on Computer Graphics and Interactive Techniques*, ACM Press/Addison-Wesley Publishing Co., pp. 517–526, July 2000. Cited on p. 667, 672

[727] Hertzmann, Aaron, "A Survey of Stroke-Based Rendering," *IEEE Computer Graphics and Applications*, vol. 23, no. 4, pp. 70–81, July/Aug. 2003. Cited on p. 678

[728] Hertzmann, Aaron, "Non-Photorealistic Rendering and the Science of Art," in *Proceedings of the 8th International Symposium on Non-Photorealistic Animation and Rendering*, ACM, pp. 147–157, 2010. Cited on p. 678

[729] Hery, Christophe, "On Shadow Buffers," *Stupid RenderMan/RAT Tricks*, SIGGRAPH 2002 RenderMan Users Group meeting, July 2002. Cited on p. 638

[730] Hery, Christophe, "Implementing a Skin BSSRDF (or Several)," *SIGGRAPH RenderMan, Theory and Practice course*, July 2003. Cited on p. 638

[731] Hery, Christophe, Michael Kass, and Junyi Ling, "Geometry into Shading," Technical memo, Pixar Animation Studios, 2014. Cited on p. 370

[732] Hery, Christophe, and Junyi Ling, "Pixar's Foundation for Materials: PxrSurface and PxrMarschnerHair," *SIGGRAPH Physically Based Shading in Theory and Practice course*, Aug. 2017. Cited on p. 321, 343, 359, 363, 364, 370

[733] Herzog, Robert, Elmar Eisemann, Karol Myszkowski, and H.-P. Seidel, "Spatio-Temporal Upsampling on the GPU," in *Proceedings of the 2010 ACM SIGGRAPH Symposium on Interactive 3D Graphics and Games*, ACM, pp. 91–98, 2010. Cited on p. 520

[734] Hicks, Odell, "A Simulation of Thermal Imaging," in Wolfgang Engel, ed., *ShaderX³*, Charles River Media, pp. 169–170, 2004. Cited on p. 521

[735] Hill, F. S., Jr., "The Pleasures of 'Perp Dot' Products," in Paul S. Heckbert, ed., *Graphics Gems IV*, Academic Press, pp. 138–148, 1994. Cited on p. 6, 987

[736] Hill, Steve, "A Simple Fast Memory Allocator," in David Kirk, ed., *Graphics Gems III*, Academic Press, pp. 49–50, 1992. Cited on p. 793

[737] Hill, Stephen, "Rendering with Conviction," *Game Developers Conference*, Mar. 2010. Cited on p. 452, 457

[738] Hill, Stephen, and Daniel Collin, "Practical, Dynamic Visibility for Games," in Wolfgang Engel, ed., *GPU Pro²*, A K Peters/CRC Press, pp. 329–348, 2011. Cited on p. 848

[739] Hill, Stephen, "Specular Showdown in the Wild West," *Self-Shadow* blog, July 22, 2011. Cited on p. 370

[740] Hill, Stephen, and Dan Baker, "Rock-Solid Shading: Image Stability Without Sacrificing Detail," *SIGGRAPH Advances in Real-Time Rendering in Games course*, Aug. 2012. Cited on p. 371

[741] Hillaire, Sébastien, "Improving Performance by Reducing Calls to the Driver," in Patrick Cozzi & Christophe Riccio, eds., *OpenGL Insights*, CRC Press, pp. 353–363, 2012. Cited on p. 795, 796, 797

[742] Hillaire, Sébastien, "Physically-Based and Unified Volumetric Rendering in Frostbite," *SIGGRAPH Advances in Real-Time Rendering course*, Aug. 2015. Cited on p. 570, 610, 611, 612, 613

[743] Hillaire, Sébastien, "Physically Based Sky, Atmosphere and Cloud Rendering in Frostbite," *SIGGRAPH Physically Based Shading in Theory and Practice course*, July 2016. Cited on p. 589, 596, 599, 602, 610, 614, 615, 616, 617, 620, 621, 622, 623, 649

[744] Hillaire, Sébastien, "Volumetric Stanford Bunny," *Shadertoy*, Mar. 25, 2017. Cited on p. 594

[745] Hillaire, Sébastien, "Real-Time Raytracing for Interactive Global Illumination Workflows in Frostbite," *Game Developers Conference*, Mar. 2018. Cited on p. 1044

[746] Hillesland, Karl, "Real-Time Ptex and Vector Displacement," in Wolfgang Engel, ed., *GPU Pro⁴*, CRC Press, pp. 69–80, 2013. Cited on p. 191

[747] Hillesland, K. E., and J. C. Yang, "Texel Shading," in *Eurographics 2016—Short Papers*, Eurographics Association, pp. 73–76, May 2016. Cited on p. 911

[748] Hillesland, Karl, "Texel Shading," *GPUOpen* website, July 21, 2016. Cited on p. 911

[749] Hinsinger, D., F. Neyret, and M.-P. Cani, "Interactive Animation of Ocean Waves," in *Proceedings of the 2002 ACM SIGGRAPH/Eurographics Symposium on Computer Animation*, ACM, pp. 161–166, 2002. Cited on p. 878

[750] Hirche, Johannes, Alexander Ehlert, Stefan Guthe, and Michael Doggett, "Hardware Accelerated Per-Pixel Displacement Mapping," in *Graphics Interface 2004*, Canadian Human-Computer Communications Society, pp. 153–158, 2004. Cited on p. 220

[751] Hoberock, Jared, and Yuntao Jia, "High-Quality Ambient Occlusion," in Hubert Nguyen, ed., *GPU Gems 3*, Addison-Wesley, pp. 257–274, 2007. Cited on p. 454

[752] Hoetzlein, Rama, "GVDB: Raytracing Sparse Voxel Database Structures on the GPU," *High Performance Graphics*, June 2016. Cited on p. 578, 582, 586

[753] Hoetzlein, Rama, "NVIDIA®GVDB Voxels: Programming Guide," NVIDIA website, May 2017. Cited on p. 578, 580, 582

[754] Hoffman, Donald D., *Visual Intelligence*, W. W. Norton & Company, 2000. Cited on p. 150

[755] Hoffman, Naty, and Kenny Mitchell, "Photorealistic Terrain Lighting in Real Time," *Game Developer*, vol. 8, no. 7, pp. 32–41, July 2001. More detailed version in "Real-Time Photorealistic Terrain Lighting," *Game Developers Conference*, Mar. 2001. Also collected in [1786]. Cited on p. 451

[756] Hoffman, Naty, "Color Enhancement for Videogames," *SIGGRAPH Color Enhancement and Rendering in Film and Game Production course*, July 2010. Cited on p. 289, 290

[757] Hoffman, Naty, "Outside the Echo Chamber: Learning from Other Disciplines, Industries, and Art Forms," Opening keynote of *Symposium on Interactive 3D Graphics and Games*, Mar. 2013. Cited on p. 284, 289

[758] Hoffman, Naty, "Background: Physics and Math of Shading," *SIGGRAPH Physically Based Shading in Theory and Practice course*, July 2013. Cited on p. 315

[759] Holbert, Daniel, "Normal Offset Shadows," *Dissident Logic* blog, Aug. 27, 2010. Cited on p. 238

[760] Holbert, Daniel, "Saying 'Goodbye' to Shadow Acne," *Game Developers Conference poster*, Mar. 2011. Cited on p. 238

[761] Hollemeersch, C.-F., B. Pieters, P. Lambert, and R. Van de Walle, "Accelerating Virtual Texturing Using CUDA," in Wolfgang Engel, ed., *GPU Pro*, A K Peters, Ltd., pp. 623–642, 2010. Cited on p. 868

[762] Holzschuch, Nicolas, and Romain Pacanowski, "Identifying Diffraction Effects in Measured Reflectances," *Eurographics Workshop on Material Appearance Modeling*, June 2015. Cited on p. 361

[763] Holzschuch, Nicolas, and Romain Pacanowski, "A Two-Scale Microfacet Reflectance Model Combining Reflection and Diffraction," *ACM Transactions on Graphics (SIGGRAPH 2017)*, vol. 36, no. 4, pp. 66:1–66:12, July 2017. Cited on p. 331, 343, 361

[764] Hoobler, Nathan, "High Performance Post-Processing," *Game Developers Conference*, Mar. 2011. Cited on p. 54, 536

[765] Hoobler, Nathan, "Fast, Flexible, Physically-Based Volumetric Light Scattering," *Game Developers Conference*, Mar. 2016. Cited on p. 608

[766] Hooker, JT, "Volumetric Global Illumination at Treyarch," *SIGGRAPH Advances in Real-Time Rendering in Games course*, July 2016. Cited on p. 395, 478, 488, 489

[767] Hoppe, H., T. DeRose, T. Duchamp, M. Halstead, H. Jin, J. McDonald, J. Schweitzer, and W. Stuetzle, "Piecewise Smooth Surface Reconstruction," in *SIGGRAPH '94: Proceedings of the 21st Annual Conference on Computer Graphics and Interactive Techniques*, ACM, pp. 295–302, July 1994. Cited on p. 758, 760, 763

[768] Hoppe, Hugues, "Progressive Meshes," in *SIGGRAPH '96: Proceedings of the 23rd Annual Conference on Computer Graphics and Interactive Techniques*, ACM, pp. 99–108, Aug. 1996. Cited on p. 706, 707, 710, 859

[769] Hoppe, Hugues, "View-Dependent Refinement of Progressive Meshes," in *SIGGRAPH '97: Proceedings of the 24th Annual Conference on Computer Graphics and Interactive Techniques*, ACM Press/Addison-Wesley Publishing Co., pp. 189–198, Aug. 1997. Cited on p. 772

[770] Hoppe, Hugues, "Efficient Implementation of Progressive Meshes," *Computers and Graphics*, vol. 22, no. 1, pp. 27–36, 1998. Cited on p. 707, 710

[771] Hoppe, Hugues, "Optimization of Mesh Locality for Transparent Vertex Caching," in *SIGGRAPH '99: Proceedings of the 26th Annual Conference on Computer Graphics and Interactive Techniques*, ACM Press/Addison-Wesley Publishing Co., pp. 269–276, Aug. 1999. Cited on p. 700

[772] Hoppe, Hugues, "New Quadric Metric for Simplifying Meshes with Appearance Attributes," in *Proceedings of Visualization '99*, IEEE Computer Society, pp. 59–66, Oct. 1999. Cited on p. 709

[773] Hormann, K., and M. Floater, 'Mean Value Coordinates for Arbitrary Planar Polygons," *ACM Transactions on Graphics*, vol. 25, no. 4, pp. 1424–1441, Oct. 2006. Cited on p. 970

[774] Hormann, Kai, Bruno Lévy, and Alla Sheffer, *SIGGRAPH Mesh Parameterization: Theory and Practice course*, Aug. 2007. Cited on p. 173

[775] Hornus, Samuel, Jared Hoberock, Sylvain Lefebvre, and John Hart, "*ZP+*: Correct *Z-Pass* Stencil Shadows," in *Proceedings of the 2005 Symposium on Interactive 3D Graphics and Games*, ACM, pp. 195–202, Apr. 2005. Cited on p. 232

[776] Horvath, Helmuth, "Gustav Mie and the Scattering and Absorption of Light by Particles: Historic Developments and Basics," *Journal of Quantitative Spectroscopy and Radiative Transfer*, vol. 110, no. 11, pp. 787–799, 2009. Cited on p. 597

[777] Hoschek, Josef, and Dieter Lasser, *Fundamentals of Computer Aided Geometric Design*, A K Peters, Ltd., 1993. Cited on p. 718, 721, 725, 732, 734, 738, 742, 749, 754, 781

[778] Hosek, Lukas, and Alexander Wilkie, "An Analytic Model for Full Spectral Sky-Dome Radiance," *ACM Transaction on Graphics*, vol. 31, no. 4, pp. 1–9, July 2012. Cited on p. 614

[779] Hu, Jinhui, Suya You, and Ulrich Neumann, "Approaches to Large-Scale Urban Modeling," *IEEE Computer Graphics and Applications*, vol. 23, no. 6, pp. 62–69, Nov./Dec. 2003. Cited on p. 573

[780] Hu, L., P. Sander, and H. Hoppe, "Parallel View-Dependent Level-of-Detail Control," *IEEE Transactions on Visualization and Computer Graphics*, vol. 16, no. 5, pp. 718–728, 2010. Cited on p. 475, 859

[781] Hu, Liwen, Chongyang Ma, Linjie Luo, and Hao Li, "Single-View Hair Modeling Using a Hairstyle Database," *ACM Transaction on Graphics*, vol. 34, no. 4, pp. 1–9, July 2015. Cited on p. 645

[782] Hubbard, Philip M., "Approximating Polyhedra with Spheres for Time-Critical Collision Detection," *ACM Transactions on Graphics*, vol. 15, no. 3, pp. 179–210, 1996. Cited on p. 976

[783] Hughes, James, Reza Nourai, and Ed Hutchins, "Understanding, Measuring, and Analyzing VR Graphics Performance," in Wolfgang Engel, ed., *GPU Zen*, Black Cat Publishing, pp. 253–274, 2017. Cited on p. 785, 815, 937, 938, 940

[784] Hughes, John F., and Tomas Möller, "Building an Orthonormal Basis from a Unit Vector," *journal of graphics tools*, vol. 4, no. 4, pp. 33–35, 1999. Also collected in [112]. Cited on p. 75, 552

[785] Hughes, John F., Andries van Dam, Morgan McGuire, David F. Sklar, James D. Foley, Steven K. Feiner, and Kurt Akeley, *Computer Graphics: Principles and Practice*, Third Edition, Addison-Wesley, 2013. Cited on p. 102, 278

[786] Hullin, Matthias, Elmar Eisemann, Hans-Peter Seidel, and Sungkil Lee, "Physically-Based Real-Time Lens Flare Rendering," *ACM Transactions on Graphics (SIGGRAPH 2011)*, vol. 30, no. 4, pp. 108:1–108:10, July 2011. Cited on p. 524, 526

[787] Humphreys, Greg, Mike Houston, Ren Ng, Randall Frank, Sean Ahern, Peter D. Kirchner, and James t. Klosowski, "Chromium: A Stream-Processing Framework for Interactive Rendering on Clusters," *ACM Transactions on Graphics*, vol. 21, no. 3, pp. 693–702, July 2002. Cited on p. 1020

[788] Hunt, R. W. G., *The Reproduction of Colour*, Sixth Edition, John Wiley & Sons, Inc., 2004. Cited on p. 291

[789] Hunt, R. W. G., and M. R. Pointer, *Measuring Colour*, Fourth Edition, John Wiley & Sons, Inc., 2011. Cited on p. 276, 291

[790] Hunt, Warren, "Real-Time Ray-Casting for Virtual Reality," Hot 3D Session, *High-Performance Graphics*, July 2017. Cited on p. 939

[791] Hunter, Biver, and Paul Fuqua, *Light Science and Magic: An Introduction to Photographic Lighting*, Fourth Edition, Focal Press, 2011. Cited on p. 435

[792] Hurlburt, Stephanie, "Improving Texture Compression in Games," *Game Developers Conference AMD Capsaicin & Cream Developer Sessions*, Feb. 2017. Cited on p. 870

[793] Hwu, Wen-Mei, and David Kirk, "Programming Massively Parallel Processors," Course ECE 498 AL1 Notes, Department of Electrical and Computer Engineering, University of Illinois, Fall 2007. Cited on p. 1040

[794] Igehy, Homan, Matthew Eldridge, and Kekoa Proudfoot, "Prefetching in a Texture Cache Architecture," in *Proceedings of the ACM SIGGRAPH/EUROGRAPHICS Workshop on Graphics Hardware*, ACM, pp. 133–142, Aug. 1998. Cited on p. 1017

[795] Igehy, Homan, Matthew Eldridge, and Pat Hanrahan, "Parallel Texture Caching," in *Proceedings of the ACM SIGGRAPH/EUROGRAPHICS Workshop on Graphics Hardware*, ACM, pp. 95–106, Aug. 1999. Cited on p. 1017

[796] Iglesias-Guitian, Jose A., Bochang Moon, Charalampos Koniaris, Eric Smolikowski, and Kenny Mitchell, "Pixel History Linear Models for Real-Time Temporal Filtering," *Computer Graphics Forum (Pacific Graphics 2016)*, vol. 35, no. 7, pp. 363–372, 2016. Cited on p. 143

[797] Ikits, Milan, Joe Kniss, Aaron Lefohn, and Charles Hansen, "Volume Rendering Techniques," in Randima Fernando, ed., *GPU Gems*, Addison-Wesley, pp. 667–692, 2004. Cited on p. 605, 607

[798] Iourcha, Konstantine, and Jason C. Yang, "A Directionally Adaptive Edge Anti-Aliasing Filter," in *Proceedings of the Conference on High-Performance Graphics 2009*, ACM, pp. 127–133, Aug. 2009. Cited on p. 147

[799] Isenberg, Tobias, Bert Freudenberg, Nick Halper, Stefan Schlechtweg, and Thomas Strothotte, "A Developer's Guide to Silhouette Algorithms for Polygonal Models," *IEEE Computer Graphics and Applications*, vol. 23, no. 4, pp. 28–37, July/Aug. 2003. Cited on p. 678

[800] Isenberg, M., and P. Alliez, "Compressing Polygon Mesh Geometry with Parallelogram Prediction," in *Proceedings of the Conference on Visualization '02*, IEEE Computer Society, pp. 141–146, 2002. Cited on p. 92

[801] Isensee, Pete, "C++ Optimization Strategies and Techniques," *Pete Isensee* website, 2007. Cited on p. 815

[802] Isidoro, John, Alex Vlachos, and Chris Brennan, "Rendering Ocean Water," in Wolfgang Engel, ed., *Direct3D ShaderX: Vertex & Pixel Shader Tips and Techniques*, Wordware, pp. 347–356, May 2002. Cited on p. 43

[803] Isidoro, John, "Next Generation Skin Rendering," *Game Tech Conference*, 2004. Cited on p. 635

[804] Isidoro, John, "Shadow Mapping: GPU-Based Tips and Techniques," *Game Developers Conference*, Mar. 2006. Cited on p. 250

[805] Iwanicki, Michał, "Normal Mapping with Low-Frequency Precomputed Visibility," in *SIGGRAPH 2009 Talks*, ACM, article no. 52, Aug. 2009. Cited on p. 466, 471

[806] Iwanicki, Michał, "Lighting Technology of *The Last of Us*," in *ACM SIGGRAPH 2013 Talks*, ACM, article no. 20, July 2013. Cited on p. 229, 289, 467, 476, 486, 498

[807] Iwanicki, Michał, and Angelo Pesce, "Approximate Models for Physically Based Rendering," *SIGGRAPH Physically Based Shading in Theory and Practice course*, Aug. 2015. Cited on p. 386, 387, 422, 424, 502

[808] Iwanicki, Michał, and Peter-Pike Sloan, "Ambient Dice," *Eurographics Symposium on Rendering—Experimental Ideas & Implementations*, June 2017. Cited on p. 395, 478, 488

[809] Iwanicki, Michał, and Peter-Pike Sloan, "Precomputed Lighting in *Call of Duty: Infinite Warfare*," *SIGGRAPH Advances in Real-Time Rendering in Games course*, Aug. 2017. Cited on p. 402, 471, 476, 490, 491

[810] Jakob, Wenzel, Miloš Hašan, Ling-Qi Yan, Jason Lawrence, Ravi Ramamoorthi, and Steve Marschner, "Discrete Stochastic Microfacet Models," *ACM Transactions on Graphics (SIGGRAPH 2014)*, vol. 33, no. 4, pp. 115:1–115:9, July 2014. Cited on p. 372

[811] Jakob, Wenzel, Eugene d'Eon, Otto Jakob, and Steve Marschner, "A Comprehensive Framework for Rendering Layered Materials," *ACM Transactions on Graphics (SIGGRAPH 2014)*, vol. 33, no. 4, pp. 118:1–118:14, July 2014. Cited on p. 346, 364

[812] Jakob, Wenzel, "layerlab: A Computational Toolbox for Layered Materials," *SIGGRAPH Physically Based Shading in Theory and Practice course*, Aug. 2015. Cited on p. 364

[813] James, Doug L., and Christopher D. Twigg, "Skinning Mesh Animations," *ACM Transactions on Graphics*, vol. 23, no. 3, pp. 399–407, Aug. 2004. Cited on p. 85

[814] James, Greg, "Operations for Hardware Accelerated Procedural Texture Animation," in Mark DeLoura, ed., *Game Programming Gems 2*, Charles River Media, pp. 497–509, 2001. Cited on p. 521

[815] James, Greg, and John O'Rorke, "Real-Time Glow," in Randima Fernando, ed., *GPU Gems*, Addison-Wesley, pp. 343–362, 2004. Cited on p. 517, 518, 527

[816] Jansen, Jon, and Louis Bavoil, "Fast Rendering of Opacity-Mapped Particles Using DirectX 11 Tessellation and Mixed Resolutions," NVIDIA White Paper, Feb. 2011. Cited on p. 520, 569, 570, 571, 609, 612

[817] Jarosz, Wojciech, "Fast Image Convolutions," SIGGRAPH Workshop at University of Illinois at Urbana-Champaign, 2001. Cited on p. 518

[818] Jarosz, Wojciech, *Efficient Monte Carlo Methods for Light Transport in Scattering Media*, PhD Thesis, University of California, San Diego, Sept. 2008. Cited on p. 589

[819] Jarosz, Wojciech, Nathan A. Carr, and Henrik Wann Jensen, "Importance Sampling Spherical Harmonics," *Computer Graphics Forum*, vol. 28, no. 2, pp. 577–586, 2009. Cited on p. 419

[820] Jendersie, Johannes, David Kuri, and Thorsten Grosch, "Precomputed Illuminance Composition for Real-Time Global Illumination," in *Proceedings of the 20th ACM SIGGRAPH Symposium on Interactive 3D Graphics and Games*, ACM, pp. 129–137, 2016. Cited on p. 483

[821] Jensen, Henrik Wann, Justin Legakis, and Julie Dorsey, "Rendering of Wet Materials," in *Rendering Techniques '99*, Springer, pp. 273–282, June 1999. Cited on p. 349

[822] Jensen, Henrik Wann, *Realistic Image Synthesis Using Photon Mapping*, A K Peters, Ltd., 2001. Cited on p. 630

[823] Jensen, Henrik Wann, Stephen R. Marschner, Marc Levoy, and Pat Hanrahan, "A Practical Model for Subsurface Light Transport," in *SIGGRAPH '01 Proceedings of the 28th Annual Conference on Computer Graphics and Interactive Techniques*, ACM, pp. 511–518, Aug. 2001. Cited on p. 634, 638

[824] Jeschke, Stefan, Stephan Mantler, and Michael Wimmer, "Interactive Smooth and Curved Shell Mapping," in *Rendering Techniques*, Eurographics Association, pp. 351–360, June 2007. Cited on p. 220

[825] Jiang, Yibing, "The Process of Creating Volumetric-Based Materials in *Uncharted 4*," *SIGGRAPH Advances in Real-Time Rendering in Games course*, July 2016. Cited on p. 356, 357, 358, 359

[826] Jiménez, J. J., F. R. Feito, and R. J. Segura, "Robust and Optimized Algorithms for the Point-in-Polygon Inclusion Test without Pre-processing," *Computer Graphics Forum*, vol. 28, no. 8, pp. 2264–2274, 2009. Cited on p. 970

[827] Jiménez, J. J., David Whelan, Veronica Sundstedt, and Diego Gutierrez, "Real-Time Realistic Skin Translucency," *Computer Graphics and Applications*, vol. 30, no. 4, pp. 32–41, 2010. Cited on p. 637

[828] Jimenez, Jorge, Belen Masia, Jose I. Echevarria, Fernando Navarro, and Diego Gutierrez, "Practical Morphological Antialiasing," in Wolfgang Engel, ed., *GPU Pro²*, A K Peters/CRC Press, pp. 95–113, 2011. Cited on p. 148

[829] Jimenez, Jorge, Diego Gutierrez, et al., *SIGGRAPH Filtering Approaches for Real-Time Anti-Aliasing course*, Aug. 2011. Cited on p. 147, 165

[830] Jimenez, Jorge, Jose I. Echevarria, Tiago Sousa, and Diego Gutierrez, "SMAA: Enhanced Subpixel Morphological Antialiasing," *Computer Graphics Forum*, vol. 31, no. 2, pp. 355–364, 2012. Cited on p. 146, 148

[831] Jimenez, Jorge, "Next Generation Character Rendering," *Game Developers Conference*, Mar. 2013. Cited on p. 636, 637

[832] Jimenez, Jorge, "Next Generation Post Processing in *Call of Duty Advanced Warfare*," *SIGGRAPH Advances in Real-Time Rendering in Games course*, Aug. 2014. Cited on p. 251, 527, 534, 535, 537, 540, 542, 543

[833] Jimenez, Jorge, Karoly Zsolnai, Adrian Jarabo, Christian Freude, Thomas Auzinger, Xian-Chun Wu, Javier von der Pahlen, Michael Wimmer, and Diego Gutierrez, "Separable Subsurface Scattering," *Computer Graphics Forum*, vol. 34, no. 6, pp. 188–197, 2015. Cited on p. 637

[834] Jimenez, Jorge, "Filmic SMAA: Sharp Morphological and Temporal Antialiasing," *SIGGRAPH Advances in Real-Time Rendering in Games course*, July 2016. Cited on p. 148

[835] Jimenez, Jorge, Xianchun Wu, Angelo Pesce, and Adrian Jarabo, "Practical Real-Time Strategies for Accurate Indirect Occlusion," *SIGGRAPH Physically Based Shading in Theory and Practice course*, July 2016. Cited on p. 451, 461, 462, 468, 472

[836] Jimenez, Jorge, "Dynamic Temporal Antialiasing in *Call of Duty: Infinite Warfare*," *SIGGRAPH Advances in Real-Time Rendering in Games course*, Aug. 2017. Cited on p. 142, 143, 145, 146, 148, 166, 805

[837] Jin, Shuangshuang, Robert R. Lewis, and David West, "A Comparison of Algorithms for Vertex Normal Computation," *The Visual Computer*, vol. 21, pp. 71–82, 2005. Cited on p. 695

[838] Johansson, Mikael, "Efficient Stereoscopic Rendering of Building Information Models (BIM)," *Journal of Computer Graphics Techniques*, vol. 5, no. 3, pp. 1–17, 2016. Cited on p. 927

[839] Johnson, G. S., J. Lee, C. A. Burns, and W. R. Mark, "The Irregular Z-Buffer: Hardware Acceleration for Irregular Data Structures," *ACM Transactions on Graphics*, vol. 24, no. 4, pp. 1462–1482, Oct. 2005. Cited on p. 260

[840] Johnsson, Björn, Per Ganestam, Michael Doggett, and Tomas Akenine-Möller, "Power Efficiency for Software Algorithms Running on Graphics Processors," in *Proceedings of the Fourth ACM SIGGRAPH / Eurographics Conference on High-Performance Graphics*, Eurographics Association, pp. 67–75, June 2012. Cited on p. 790

[841] Jones, James L., "Efficient Morph Target Animation Using OpenGL ES 3.0," in Wolfgang Engel, ed., *GPU Pro⁵*, CRC Press, pp. 289–295, 2014. Cited on p. 90

[842] Jönsson, Daniel, Erik Sundén, Anders Ynnerman, and Timo Ropinski, "A Survey of Volumetric Illumination Techniques for Interactive Volume Rendering," *Computer Graphics Forum*, vol. 33, no. 1, pp. 27–51, 2014. Cited on p. 605

[843] Joy, Kenneth I., *On-Line Geometric Modeling Notes*, http://graphics.idav.ucdavis.edu/education/CAGDNotes/homepage.html, 1996. Cited on p. 756

[844] Junkins, S., "The Compute Architecture of Intel Processor Graphics Gen9," Intel White Paper v1.0, Aug. 2015. Cited on p. 1006, 1007

[845] Kajiya, James T., "Anisotropic Reflection Models," *Computer Graphics (SIGGRAPH '85 Proceedings)*, vol. 19, no. 3, pp. 15–21, July 1985. Cited on p. 853

[846] Kajiya, James T., "The Rendering Equation," *Computer Graphics (SIGGRAPH '86 Proceedings)*, vol. 20, no. 4, pp. 143–150, Aug. 1986. Cited on p. 315, 437, 444

[847] Kajiya, James T., and Timothy L. Kay, "Rendering Fur with Three Dimensional Textures," *Computer Graphics (SIGGRAPH '89 Proceedings)*, vol. 17, no. 3, pp. 271–280, July 1989. Cited on p. 359, 642

[848] Kalnins, Robert D., Philip L. Davidson, Lee Markosian, and Adam Finkelstein, "Coherent Stylized Silhouettes," *ACM Transactions on Graphics (SIGGRAPH 2003)*, vol. 22, no. 3, pp. 856–861, 2003. Cited on p. 667

[849] Kämpe, Viktor, *Fast, Memory-Efficient Construction of Voxelized Shadows*, PhD Thesis, Chalmers University of Technology, 2016. Cited on p. 586

[850] Kämpe, Viktor, Erik Sintorn, Ola Olsson, and Ulf Assarsson, "Fast, Memory-Efficient Construction of Voxelized Shadows," *IEEE Transactions on Visualization and Computer Graphics*, vol. 22, no. 10, pp. 2239–2248, Oct. 2016. Cited on p. 264, 586

[851] Kaneko, Tomomichi, Toshiyuki Takahei, Masahiko Inami, Naoki Kawakami, Yasuyuki Yanagida, Taro Maeda, and Susumu Tachi, "Detailed Shape Representation with Parallax Mapping," *International Conference on Artificial Reality and Telexistence 2001*, Dec. 2001. Cited on p. 215

[852] Kang, H., H. Jang, C.-S. Cho, and J. Han, "Multi-Resolution Terrain Rendering with GPU Tessellation," *The Visual Computer*, vol. 31, no. 4, pp. 455–469, 2015. Cited on p. 567, 876

[853] Kaplan, Matthew, Bruce Gooch, and Elaine Cohen, "Interactive Artistic Rendering," in *Proceedings of the 1st International Symposium on Non-photorealistic Animation and Rendering*, ACM, pp. 67–74, June 2000. Cited on p. 670, 672

[854] Kaplanyan, Anton, "Light Propagation Volumes in CryEngine 3," *SIGGRAPH Advances in Real-Time Rendering in Games course*, Aug. 2009. Cited on p. 493

[855] Kaplanyan, Anton, and Carsten Dachsbacher, "Cascaded Light Propagation Volumes for Real-Time Indirect Illumination," in *Proceedings of the 2010 ACM SIGGRAPH Symposium on Interactive 3D Graphics and Games*, ACM, pp. 99–107, Feb. 2010. Cited on p. 494, 496

[856] Kaplanyan, Anton, "CryENGINE 3: Reaching the Speed of Light," *SIGGRAPH Advances in Real-Time Rendering in Games course*, July 2010. Cited on p. 196, 289, 290, 848, 849, 887, 892

[857] Kaplanyan, Anton, Stephen Hill, Anjul Patney, and Aaron Lefohn, "Filtering Distributions of Normals for Shading Antialiasing," in *Proceedings of High-Performance Graphics*, Eurographics Association, pp. 151–162, June 2016. Cited on p. 371

[858] Kapoulkine, Arseny, "Optimal Grid Rendering Is Not Optimal," *Bits, pixels, cycles and more* blog, July 31, 2017. Cited on p. 700, 701

[859] Karabassi, Evaggelia-Aggeliki, Georgios Papaioannou, and Theoharis Theoharis, "A Fast Depth-Buffer-Based Voxelization Algorithm," *journal of graphics tools*, vol. 4, no. 4, pp. 5–10, 1999. Cited on p. 580

[860] Karis, Brian, "Tiled Light Culling," *Graphic Rants* blog, Apr. 9, 2012. Cited on p. 113, 882

[861] Karis, Brian, "Real Shading in Unreal Engine 4," *SIGGRAPH Physically Based Shading in Theory and Practice course*, July 2013. Cited on p. 111, 113, 116, 325, 336, 340, 342, 352, 355, 383, 385, 388, 421, 423

[862] Karis, Brian, "High Quality Temporal Supersampling," *SIGGRAPH Advances in Real-Time Rendering in Games course*, Aug. 2014. Cited on p. 142, 143, 144, 620

[863] Karis, Brian, "Physically Based Hair Shading in Unreal," *SIGGRAPH Physically Based Shading in Theory and Practice course*, July 2016. Cited on p. 641, 644, 646

[864] Kass, Michael, Aaron Lefohn, and John Owens, "Interactive Depth of Field Using Simulated Diffusion on a GPU," Technical memo, Pixar Animation Studios, 2006. Cited on p. 535

[865] Kasyan, Nikolas, "Playing with Real-Time Shadows," *SIGGRAPH Efficient Real-Time Shadows course*, July 2013. Cited on p. 54, 234, 245, 251, 264, 585

[866] Kautz, Jan, Wolfgang Heidrich, and Katja Daubert, "Bump Map Shadows for OpenGL Rendering," Technical Report MPI-I-2000-4-001, Max-Planck-Institut für Informatik, Saarbrücken, Germany, Feb. 2000. Cited on p. 466

[867] Kautz, Jan, and M. D. McCool, "Approximation of Glossy Reflection with Prefiltered Environment Maps," in *Graphics Interface 2000*, Canadian Human-Computer Communications Society, pp. 119–126, May 2000. Cited on p. 423

[868] Kautz, Jan, P.-P. Vázquez, W. Heidrich, and H.-P. Seidel, "A Unified Approach to Prefiltered Environment Maps," in *Rendering Techniques 2000*, Springer, pp. 185–196, June 2000. Cited on p. 420

[869] Kautz, Jan, Peter-Pike Sloan, and John Snyder, "Fast, Arbitrary BRDF Shading for Low-Frequency Lighting Using Spherical Harmonics," in *Proceedings of the 13th Eurographics Workshop on Rendering*, Eurographics Association, pp. 291–296, June 2002. Cited on p. 401, 431

[870] Kautz, Jan, Jaakko Lehtinen, and Peter-Pike Sloan, *SIGGRAPH Precomputed Radiance Transfer: Theory and Practice course*, Aug. 2005. Cited on p. 481

[871] Kautz, Jan, "SH Light Representations," *SIGGRAPH Precomputed Radiance Transfer: Theory and Practice course*, Aug. 2005. Cited on p. 430

[872] Kavan, Ladislav, Steven Collins, Jiří Žára, and Carol O'Sullivan, "Skinning with Dual Quaternions," in *Proceedings of the 2007 Symposium on Interactive 3D Graphics and Games*, ACM, pp. 39–46, Apr.–May 2007. Cited on p. 87

[873] Kavan, Ladislav, Steven Collins, Jiří Žára, and Carol O'Sullivan, "Geometric Skinning with Approximate Dual Quaternion Blending," *ACM Transactions on Graphics*, vol. 27, no. 4, pp. 105:1–105:23, 2008. Cited on p. 87

[874] Kavan, Ladislav, Simon Dobbyn, Steven Collins, Jiří Žára, and Carol O'Sullivan, "Polypostors: 2D Polygonal Impostors for 3D Crowds," in *Proceedings of the 2008 Symposium on Interactive 3D Graphics and Games*, ACM, pp. 149–156, 2008. Cited on p. 562

[875] Kavan, Ladislav, Adam W. Bargteil, and Peter-Pike Sloan, "Least Squares Vertex Baking," *Computer Graphics Forum*, vol. 30, no. 4, pp. 1319–1326, 2011. Cited on p. 452

[876] Kay, L., "SceneJS: A WebGL-Based Scene Graph Engine," in Patrick Cozzi & Christophe Riccio, eds., *OpenGL Insights*, CRC Press, pp. 571–582, 2012. Cited on p. 829

[877] Kay, T. L., and J. T. Kajiya, "Ray Tracing Complex Scenes," *Computer Graphics (SIGGRAPH '86 Proceedings)*, vol. 20, no. 4, pp. 269–278, Aug. 1986. Cited on p. 959, 961

[878] Kelemen, Csaba, and Lázló Szirmay-Kalos, "A Microfacet Based Coupled Specular-Matte BRDF Model with Importance Sampling," in *Eurographics 2001—Short Presentations*, Eurographics Association, pp. 25–34, Sept. 2001. Cited on p. 346, 352, 419

[879] Keller, Alexander, "Instant Radiosity," in *SIGGRAPH '97: Proceedings of the 24th Annual Conference on Computer Graphics and Interactive Techniques*, ACM Press/Addison-Wesley Publishing Co., pp. 49–56, Aug. 1997. Cited on p. 491

[880] Keller, Alexander, and Wolfgang Heidrich, "Interleaved Sampling," in *Rendering Techniques 2001*, Springer, pp. 266–273, June 2001. Cited on p. 145

[881] Kemen, B., "Logarithmic Depth Buffer Optimizations & Fixes," *Outerra* blog, July 18, 2013. Cited on p. 101

[882] Kensler, Andrew, and Peter Shirley, "Optimizing Ray-Triangle Intersection via Automated Search," in *2006 IEEE Symposium on Interactive Ray Tracing*, IEEE Computer Society, pp. 33–38, 2006. Cited on p. 962

[883] Kent, James R., Wayne E. Carlson, and Richard E. Parent, "Shape Transformation for Polyhedral Objects," *Computer Graphics (SIGGRAPH '92 Proceedings)*, vol. 26, no. 2, pp. 47–54, 1992. Cited on p. 87

[884] Kershaw, Kathleen, *A Generalized Texture-Mapping Pipeline*, MSc thesis, Program of Computer Graphics, Cornell University, Ithaca, New York, 1992. Cited on p. 169, 170

[885] Kessenich, John, Graham Sellers, and Dave Shreiner, *OpenGL Programming Guide: The Official Guide to Learning OpenGL, Version 4.5 with SPIR-V*, Ninth Edition, Addison-Wesley, 2016. Cited on p. 27, 39, 41, 55, 96, 173, 174

[886] Kettlewell, Richard, "Rendering in Codemasters' GRID2 and beyond," *Game Developers Conference*, Mar. 2014. Cited on p. 258

[887] Kharlamov, Alexander, Iain Cantlay, and Yury Stepanenko, "Next-Generation SpeedTree Rendering," in Hubert Nguyen, ed., *GPU Gems 3*, Addison-Wesley, pp. 69–92, 2007. Cited on p. 207, 560, 564, 646, 856

[888] Kihl, Robert, "Destruction Masking in Frostbite 2 Using Volume Distance Fields," *SIGGRAPH Advances in Real-Time Rendering in Games course*, July 2010. Cited on p. 889, 890

[889] Kilgard, Mark J., "Realizing OpenGL: Two Implementations of One Architecture," in *Proceedings of the ACM SIGGRAPH/EUROGRAPHICS Workshop on Graphics Hardware*, ACM, pp. 45–55, Aug. 1997. Cited on p. 1007

[890] Kilgard, Mark J., "Creating Reflections and Shadows Using Stencil Buffers," *Game Developers Conference*, Mar. 1999. Cited on p. 805

[891] Kilgard, Mark J., "A Practical and Robust Bump-Mapping Technique for Today's GPUs," *Game Developers Conference*, Mar. 2000. Cited on p. 212, 214

[892] Kim, Pope, and Daniel Barrero, "Rendering Tech of Space Marine," *Korea Game Conference*, Nov. 2011. Cited on p. 892, 900, 905

[893] Kim, Pope, "Screen Space Decals in *Warhammer 40,000: Space Marine*," in *ACM SIGGRAPH 2012 Talks*, article no. 6, Aug. 2012. Cited on p. 889

[894] Kim, Tae-Yong, and Ulrich Neumann, "Opacity Shadow Maps," in *Rendering Techniques 2001*, Springer, pp. 177–182, 2001. Cited on p. 257, 570, 571, 612

[895] King, Gary, and William Newhall, "Efficient Omnidirectional Shadow Maps," in Wolfgang Engel, ed., *ShaderX³*, Charles River Media, pp. 435–448, 2004. Cited on p. 234

[896] King, Gary, "Shadow Mapping Algorithms," GPU Jackpot presentation, Oct. 2004. Cited on p. 235, 240

[897] King, Gary, "Real-Time Computation of Dynamic Irradiance Environment Maps," in Matt Pharr, ed., *GPU Gems 2*, Addison-Wesley, pp. 167–176, 2005. Cited on p. 426, 428, 430

[898] King, Yossarian, "Never Let 'Em See You Pop—Issues in Geometric Level of Detail Selection," in Mark DeLoura, ed., *Game Programming Gems*, Charles River Media, pp. 432–438, 2000. Cited on p. 861, 864

[899] King, Yossarian, "2D Lens Flare," in Mark DeLoura, ed., *Game Programming Gems*, Charles River Media, pp. 515–518, 2000. Cited on p. 524

[900] Kircher, Scott, "Lighting & Simplifying *Saints Row: The Third*," *Game Developers Conference*, Mar. 2012. Cited on p. 889, 892

[901] Kirk, David B., and Douglas Voorhies, "The Rendering Architecture of the DN-10000VS," *Computer Graphics (SIGGRAPH '90 Proceedings)*, vol. 24, no. 4, pp. 299–307, Aug. 1990. Cited on p. 185

[902] Kirk, David, ed., *Graphics Gems III*, Academic Press, 1992. Cited on p. 102, 991

[903] Kirk, David B., and Wen-mei W. Hwu, *Programming Massively Parallel Processors: A Hands-on Approach*, Third Edition, Morgan Kaufmann, 2016. Cited on p. 55, 1040

[904] Klehm, Oliver, Tobias Ritschel, Elmar Eisemann, and Hans-Peter Seidel, "Bent Normals and Cones in Screen Space," in *Vision, Modeling, and Visualization*, Eurographics Association, pp. 177–182, 2011. Cited on p. 467, 471

[905] Klein, Allison W., Wilmot Li, Michael M. Kazhdan, Wagner T. Corrêa, Adam Finkelstein, and Thomas A. Funkhouser, "Non-Photorealistic Virtual Environments," in *SIGGRAPH '00: Proceedings of the 27th Annual Conference on Computer Graphics and Interactive Techniques*, ACM Press/Addison-Wesley Publishing Co., pp. 527–534, July 2000. Cited on p. 670, 671

[906] Klein, R., G. Liebich, and W. Strasser, "Mesh Reduction with Error Control," in *Proceedings of the 7th Conference on Visualization '96*, IEEE Computer Society, pp. 311–318, 1996. Cited on p. 875

[907] Kleinhuis, Christian, "Morph Target Animation Using DirectX," in Wolfgang Engel, ed., *ShaderX⁴*, Charles River Media, pp. 39–45, 2005. Cited on p. 89

[908] Klint, Josh, "Vegetation Management in Leadwerks Game Engine 4," in Eric Lengyel, ed., *Game Engine Gems 3*, CRC Press, pp. 53–71, 2016. Cited on p. 560

[909] Kloetzli, J., "D3D11 Software Tessellation," *Game Developers Conference*, Mar. 2013. Cited on p. 879

[910] Klosowski, J. T., M. Held, J. S. B. Mitchell, H. Sowizral, and K. Zikan, "Efficient Collision Detection Using Bounding Volume Hierarchies of k-DOPs," *IEEE Transactions on Visualization and Computer Graphics*, vol. 4, no. 1, pp. 21–36, 1998. Cited on p. 979
IEEE Transactions on Visualization and Computer Graphics, vol. 6, no. 2, pp. 108–123, Apr./June 2000.

[911] Knight, Balor, Matthew Ritchie, and George Parrish, "Screen-Space Classification for Efficient Deferred Shading," Eric Lengyel, ed., *Game Engine Gems 2*, A K Peters, Ltd., pp. 55–73, 2011. Cited on p. 898

[912] Kniss, Joe, G. Kindlmann, and C. Hansen, "Multi-Dimensional Transfer Functions for Interactive Volume Rendering," *IEEE Transactions on Visualization and Computer Graphics*, vol. 8, no. 3, pp. 270–285, 2002. Cited on p. 606

[913] Kniss, Joe, S. Premoze, C.Hansen, P. Shirley, and A. McPherson, "A Model for Volume Lighting and Modeling," *IEEE Transactions on Visualization and Computer Graphics*, vol. 9, no. 2, pp. 150–162, 2003. Cited on p. 607

[914] Knowles, Pyarelal, Geoff Leach, and Fabio Zambetta, "Efficient Layered Fragment Buffer Techniques," in Patrick Cozzi & Christophe Riccio, eds., *OpenGL Insights*, CRC Press, pp. 279–292, 2012. Cited on p. 155

[915] Kobbelt, Leif, "$\sqrt{3}$-Subdivision," in *SIGGRAPH '00: Proceedings of the 27th Annual Conference on Computer Graphics and Interactive Techniques*, ACM Press/Addison-Wesley Publishing Co., pp. 103–112, July 2000. Cited on p. 756, 761

[916] Kobbelt, Leif, and Mario Botsch, "A Survey of Point-Based Techniques in Computer Graphics," *Computers & Graphics*, vol. 28, no. 6, pp. 801–814, Dec. 2004. Cited on p. 578

[917] Kochanek, Doris H. U., and Richard H. Bartels, "Interpolating Splines with Local Tension, Continuity, and Bias Control," *Computer Graphics (SIGGRAPH '84 Proceedings)*, vol. 18, no. 3, pp. 33–41, July 1984. Cited on p. 730, 731

[918] Koenderink, Jan J., Andrea J. van Doorn, and Marigo Stavridi, "Bidirectional Reflection Distribution Function Expressed in Terms of Surface Scattering Modes," *Proceedings of ECCV 2001*, vol. 2, pp. 28–39, 1996. Cited on p. 404

[919] Koenderink, Jan J., and Sylvia Pont, "The Secret of Velvety Skin," *Journal of Machine Vision and Applications*, vol. 14, no. 4, pp. 260–268, 2002. Cited on p. 356

[920] Köhler, Johan, "Practical Order Independent Transparency," Technical Report ATVI-TR-16-02, Activision Research, 2016. Cited on p. 569

[921] Kojima, Hideo, Hideki Sasaki, Masayuki Suzuki, and Junji Tago, "Photorealism Through the Eyes of a FOX: The Core of *Metal Gear Solid Ground Zeroes*," *Game Developers Conference*, Mar. 2013. Cited on p. 289

[922] Kolchin, Konstantin, "Curvature-Based Shading of Translucent Materials, such as Human Skin," in *Proceedings of the 5th International Conference on Computer Graphics and Interactive Techniques in Australia and Southeast Asia*, ACM, pp. 239–242, Dec. 2007. Cited on p. 634

[923] Koltun, Vladlen, Yiorgos Chrysanthou, and Daniel Cohen-Or, "Hardware-Accelerated From-Region Visibility Using a Dual Ray Space," in *Rendering Techniques 2001*, Springer, pp. 204–214, June 2001. Cited on p. 843

[924] Kontkanen, Janne, and Samuli Laine, "Ambient Occlusion Fields," in Wolfgang Engel, ed., *ShaderX⁴*, Charles River Media, pp. 101–108, 2005. Cited on p. 452

[925] Kontkanen, Janne, and Samuli Laine, "Ambient Occlusion Fields," in *Proceedings of the 2005 Symposium on Interactive 3D Graphics and Games*, ACM, pp. 41–48, Apr. 2005. Cited on p. 452

[926] Kontkanen, Janne, and Samuli Laine, "Sampling Precomputed Volumetric Lighting," *journal of graphics tools*, vol. 11, no. 3, pp. 1–16, 2006. Cited on p. 489, 491

[927] Koonce, Rusty, "Deferred Shading in *Tabula Rasa*," in Hubert Nguyen, ed., *GPU Gems 3*, Addison-Wesley, pp. 429–457, 2007. Cited on p. 239, 886, 887

[928] Kopta, D., T. Ize, J. Spjut, E. Brunvand, A. Davis, and A. Kensler, "Fast, Effective BVH Updates for Animated Scenes," in *Proceedings of the ACM SIGGRAPH Symposium on Interactive 3D Graphics and Games*, ACM, pp. 197–204, 2012. Cited on p. 821

[929] Kopta, D., K. Shkurko, J. Spjut, E. Brunvand, and A. Davis, "An Energy and Bandwidth Efficient Ray Tracing Architecture," *Proceedings of the 5th High-Performance Graphics Conference*, ACM, pp. 121–128, July 2013. Cited on p. 1039

[930] Kotfis, Dave, and Patrick Cozzi, "Octree Mapping from a Depth Camera," in Wolfgang Engel, ed., *GPU Pro⁷*, CRC Press, pp. 257–273, 2016. Cited on p. 573, 580, 919

[931] Kovacs, D., J. Mitchell, S. Drone, and D. Zorin, "Real-Time Creased Approximate Subdivision Surfaces with Displacements," *IEEE Transactions on Visualization and Computer Graphics*, vol. 16, no. 5, pp. 742–751, 2010. Cited on p. 777

[932] Kovalèík, Vít, and Jiří Sochor, "Occlusion Culling with Statistically Optimized Occlusion Queries," *International Conference in Central Europe on Computer Graphics, Visualization and Computer Vision (WSCG)*, Jan.–Feb. 2005. Cited on p. 845

[933] Krajcevski, P., Adam Lake, and D. Manocha, "FasTC: Accelerated Fixed-Rate Texture Encoding," in *Proceedings of the ACM SIGGRAPH Symposium on Interactive 3D Graphics and Games*, ACM, pp. 137–144, Mar. 2013. Cited on p. 870

[934] Krajcevski, P., and D. Manocha, "Fast PVRTC Compression Using Intensity Dilation," *Journal of Computer Graphics Techniques*, vol. 3, no. 4, pp. 132–145, 2014. Cited on p. 870

[935] Krajcevski, P., and D. Manocha, "SegTC: Fast Texture Compression Using Image Segmentation," in *Proceedings of High-Performance Graphics*, Eurographics Association, pp. 71–77, June 2014. Cited on p. 870

[936] Krassnigg, Jan, "A Deferred Decal Rendering Technique," in Eric Lengyel, ed., *Game Engine Gems*, Jones and Bartlett, pp. 271–280, 2010. Cited on p. 889

[937] Kraus, Martin, and Magnus Strengert, "Pyramid Filters based on Bilinear Interpolation," in *GRAPP 2007, Proceedings of the Second International Conference on Computer Graphics Theory and Applications*, INSTICC, pp. 21–28, 2007. Cited on p. 518

[938] Krishnamurthy, V., and M. Levoy, "Fitting Smooth Surfaces to Dense Polygon Meshes," in *SIGGRAPH '96: Proceedings of the 23rd Annual Conference on Computer Graphics and Interactive Techniques*, ACM, pp. 313–324, Aug. 1996. Cited on p. 765

[939] Krishnan, S., M. Gopi, M. Lin, D. Manocha, and A. Pattekar, "Rapid and Accurate Contact Determination between Spline Models Using ShellTrees," *Computer Graphics Forum*, vol. 17, no. 3, pp. 315–326, 1998. Cited on p. 718

[940] Krishnan, S., A. Pattekar, M. C. Lin, and D. Manocha, "Spherical Shell: A Higher Order Bounding Volume for Fast Proximity Queries," in *Proceedings of Third International Workshop on the Algorithmic Foundations of Robotics*, A K Peters, Ltd, pp. 122–136, 1998. Cited on p. 718

[941] Kristensen, Anders Wang, Tomas Akenine-Mller, and Henrik Wann Jensen, "Precomputed Local Radiance Transfer for Real-Time Lighting Design," *ACM Transactions on Graphics (SIGGRAPH 2005)*, vol. 24, no. 3, pp. 1208–1215, Aug. 2005. Cited on p. 481

[942] Kronander, Joel, Francesco Banterle, Andrew Gardner, Ehsan Miandji, and Jonas Unger, "Photorealistic Rendering of Mixed Reality Scenes," *Computer Graphics Forum*, vol. 34, no. 2, pp. 643–665, 2015. Cited on p. 935

[943] Kryachko, Yuri, "Using Vertex Texture Displacement for Realistic Water Rendering," in Matt Pharr, ed., *GPU Gems 2*, Addison-Wesley, pp. 283–294, 2005. Cited on p. 43

[944] Kubisch, Christoph, and Markus Tavenrath, "OpenGL 4.4 Scene Rendering Techniques," *NVIDIA GPU Technology Conference*, Mar. 2014. Cited on p. 795, 849, 851

[945] Kubisch, Christoph, "Life of a Triangle—NVIDIA's Logical Pipeline," *NVIDIA GameWorks* blog, Mar. 16, 2015. Cited on p. 32

[946] Kubisch, Christoph, "Transitioning from OpenGL to Vulkan," *NVIDIA GameWorks* blog, Feb. 11, 2016. Cited on p. 40, 41, 796, 814

[947] Kulla, Christopher, and Alejandro Conty, "Revisiting Physically Based Shading at Imageworks," *SIGGRAPH Physically Based Shading in Theory and Practice course*, Aug. 2017. Cited on p. 321, 336, 343, 346, 347, 352, 353, 358, 363, 364

[948] Kyprianidis, Jan Eric, Henry Kang, and Jürgen Döllner, "Anisotropic Kuwahara Filtering on the GPU," in Wolfgang Engel, ed., *GPU Pro*, A K Peters, Ltd., pp. 247–264, 2010. Cited on p. 665

[949] Kyprianidis, Jan Eric, John Collomosse, Tinghuai Wang, and Tobias Isenberg, "State of the 'Art': A Taxonomy of Artistic Stylization Techniques for Images and Video," *IEEE Transactions on Visualization and Computer Graphics*, vol. 19, no. 5, pp. 866–885, May 2013. Cited on p. 665, 678

[950] Lacewell, Dylan, Dave Edwards, Peter Shirley, and William B. Thompson, "Stochastic Billboard Clouds for Interactive Foliage Rendering," *journal of graphics tools*, vol. 11, no. 1, pp. 1–12, 2006. Cited on p. 563, 564

[951] Lacewell, Dylan, "Baking With OptiX," *NVIDIA GameWorks* blog, June 7, 2016. Cited on p. 452

[952] Lachambre, Sébastian, Sébastian Lagarde, and Cyril Jover, *Unity Photogrammetry Workflow*, Unity Technologies, 2017. Cited on p. 349

[953] Lacroix, Jason, "Casting a New Light on a Familiar Face: Light-Based Rendering in *Tomb Raider*," *Game Developers Conference*, Mar. 2013. Cited on p. 114, 116

[954] Lafortune, Eric P. F., Sing-Choong Foo, Kenneth E. Torrance, and Donald P. Greenberg, "Non-Linear Approximation of Reflectance Functions," in *SIGGRAPH '97: Proceedings of the 24th Annual Conference on Computer Graphics and Interactive Techniques*, ACM Press/Addison-Wesley Publishing Co., pp. 117–126, Aug. 1997. Cited on p. 424

[955] Lagae, Ares, and Philip Dutré, "An Efficient Ray-Quadrilateral Intersection Test," *journal of graphics tools*, vol. 10, no. 4, pp. 23–32, 2005. Cited on p. 967

[956] Lagae, A., S. Lefebvre, R. Cook, T. DeRose, G. Drettakis, D. S. Ebert, J. P. Lewis, K. Perlin, and M. Zwicker, "State of the Art in Procedural Noise Functions," in *Eurographics 2010—State of the Art Reports*, Eurographics Association, pp. 1–19, 2010. Cited on p. 199

[957] Lagarde, Sébastian, "Relationship Between Phong and Blinn Lighting Models," *Sébastian Lagarde* blog, Mar. 29, 2012. Cited on p. 421

[958] Lagarde, Sébastian, and Antoine Zanuttini, "Local Image-Based Lighting with Parallax-Corrected Cubemap," in *ACM SIGGRAPH 2012 Talks*, ACM, article no. 36, Aug. 2012. Cited on p. 500

[959] Lagarde, Sébastian, "Memo on Fresnel Equations," *Sébastian Lagarde* blog, Apr. 29, 2013. Cited on p. 321

[960] Lagarde, Sébastian, and Charles de Rousiers, "Moving Frostbite to Physically Based Rendering," *SIGGRAPH Physically Based Shading in Theory and Practice course*, Aug. 2014. Cited on p. 111, 113, 115, 116, 312, 325, 336, 340, 341, 354, 371, 422, 426, 435, 503, 890

[961] Lagarde, Sébastian, "IES Light Format: Specification and Reader," *Sébastian Lagarde* blog, Nov. 5, 2014. Cited on p. 116, 435

[962] Laine, Samuli, Hannu Saransaari, Janne Kontkanen, Jaakko Lehtinen, and Timo Aila, "Incremental Instant Radiosity for Real-Time Indirect Illumination," in *Proceedings of the 18th Eurographics Symposium on Rendering Techniques*, Eurographics Association, pp. 277–286, June 2007. Cited on p. 492

[963] Laine, Samuli, and Tero Karras, "'Efficient Sparse Voxel Octrees—Analysis, Extensions, and Implementation," Technical Report, NVIDIA, 2010. Cited on p. 579, 580, 586

[964] Laine, Samuli, "A Topological Approach to Voxelization," *Computer Graphics Forum*, vol. 32, no. 4, pp. 77–86, 2013. Cited on p. 581

[965] Laine, Samuli, and Tero Karras, "Apex Point Map for Constant-Time Bounding Plane Approximation," in *Eurographics Symposium on Rendering—Experimental Ideas & Implementations*, Eurographics Association, pp. 51–55, 2015. Cited on p. 980

[966] Lake, Adam, Carl Marshall, Mark Harris, and Marc Blackstein, "Stylized Rendering Techniques for Scalable Real-Time Animation," in *International Symposium on Non-Photorealistic Animation and Rendering*, ACM, pp. 13–20, June 2000. Cited on p. 670

[967] Lambert, J. H., *Photometria*, 1760. English translation by D. L. DiLaura, Illuminating Engineering Society of North America, 2001. Cited on p. 109, 389, 390, 469

[968] Lander, Jeff, "Skin Them Bones: Game Programming for the Web Generation," *Game Developer*, vol. 5, no. 5, pp. 11–16, May 1998. Cited on p. 86

[969] Lander, Jeff, "Under the Shade of the Rendering Tree," *Game Developer*, vol. 7, no. 2, pp. 17–21, Feb. 2000. Cited on p. 657, 670

[970] Lander, Jeff, "That's a Wrap: Texture Mapping Methods," *Game Developer*, vol. 7, no. 10, pp. 21–26, Oct. 2000. Cited on p. 170, 173

[971] Lander, Jeff, "Haunted Trees for Halloween," *Game Developer*, vol. 7, no. 11, pp. 17–21, Nov. 2000. Cited on p. 942

[972] Lander, Jeff, "Images from Deep in the Programmer's Cave," *Game Developer*, vol. 8, no. 5, pp. 23–28, May 2001. Cited on p. 654, 666, 672

[973] Lander, Jeff, "The Era of Post-Photorealism," *Game Developer*, vol. 8, no. 6, pp. 18–22, June 2001. Cited on p. 670

[974] Landis, Hayden, "Production-Ready Global Illumination," *SIGGRAPH RenderMan in Production course*, July 2002. Cited on p. 446, 448, 465

[975] Langlands, Anders, "Render Color Spaces," *alShaders blog*, June 23, 2016. Cited on p. 278

[976] Lanman, Douglas, and David Luebke, "Near-Eye Light Field Displays," *ACM Transactions on Graphics*, vol. 32, no. 6, pp. 220:1–220:10, Nov. 2013. Cited on p. 549, 923

[977] Lanza, Stefano, "Animation and Rendering of Underwater God Rays," in Wolfgang Engel, ed., *ShaderX⁵*, Charles River Media, pp. 315–327, 2006. Cited on p. 626, 631

[978] Lapidous, Eugene, and Guofang Jiao, "Optimal Depth Buffer for Low-Cost Graphics Hardware," in *Proceedings of the ACM SIGGRAPH/EUROGRAPHICS Workshop on Graphics Hardware*, ACM, pp. 67–73, Aug. 1999. Cited on p. 100

[979] Larsen, E., S. Gottschalk, M. Lin, and D. Manocha, "Fast Proximity Queries with Swept Sphere Volumes," Technical Report TR99-018, Department of Computer Science, University of North Carolina, 1999. Cited on p. 976

[980] Larsson, Thomas, and Tomas Akenine-Möller, "Collision Detection for Continuously Deforming Bodies," in *Eurographics 2001—Short Presentations*, Eurographics Association, pp. 325–333, Sept. 2001. Cited on p. 821

[981] Larsson, Thomas, and Tomas Akenine-Möller, "A Dynamic Bounding Volume Hierarchy for Generalized Collision Detection," *Computers & Graphics*, vol. 30, no. 3, pp. 451–460, 2006. Cited on p. 821

[982] Larsson, Thomas, Tomas Akenine-Möller, and Eric Lengyel, "On Faster Sphere-Box Overlap Testing," *journal of graphics tools*, vol. 12, no. 1, pp. 3–8, 2007. Cited on p. 977

[983] Larsson, Thomas, "An Efficient Ellipsoid-OBB Intersection Test," *journal of graphics tools*, vol. 13, no. 1, pp. 31–43, 2008. Cited on p. 978

[984] Larsson, Thomas, and Linus Källberg, "Fast Computation of Tight-Fitting Oriented Bounding Boxes," Eric Lengyel, ed., *Game Engine Gems 2*, A K Peters, Ltd., pp. 3–19, 2011. Cited on p. 951, 952

[985] Lathrop, Olin, David Kirk, and Doug Voorhies, "Accurate Rendering by Subpixel Addressing," *IEEE Computer Graphics and Applications*, vol. 10, no. 5, pp. 45–53, Sept. 1990. Cited on p. 689

[986] Latta, Lutz, "Massively Parallel Particle Systems on the GPU," in Wolfgang Engel, ed., *ShaderX³*, Charles River Media, pp. 119–133, 2004. Also presented at GDC 2004 and published as "Building a Million-Particle System," *Gamasutra*, July 28, 2004. Cited on p. 568, 571

[987] Latta, Lutz, "Everything about Particle Effects," *Game Developers Conference*, Mar. 2007. Cited on p. 568, 569, 571

[988] Lauritzen, Andrew, "Summed-Area Variance Shadow Maps," in Hubert Nguyen, ed., *GPU Gems 3*, Addison-Wesley, pp. 157–182, 2007. Cited on p. 188, 252, 253, 255

[989] Lauritzen, Andrew, and Michael McCool, "Layered Variance Shadow Maps," in *Graphics Interface 2008*, Canadian Human-Computer Communications Society, pp. 139–146, May 2008. Cited on p. 257

[990] Lauritzen, Andrew, "Deferred Rendering for Current and Future Rendering Pipelines," *SIGGRAPH Beyond Programmable Shading course*, July 2010. Cited on p. 888, 893, 895, 896, 914

[991] Lauritzen, Andrew, Marco Salvi, and Aaron Lefohn, "Sample Distribution Shadow Maps," in *Symposium on Interactive 3D Graphics and Games*, ACM, pp. 97–102, Feb. 2011. Cited on p. 54, 101, 244, 245

[992] Lauritzen, Andrew, "Intersecting Lights with Pixels: Reasoning about Forward and Deferred Rendering," *SIGGRAPH Beyond Programmable Shading course*, Aug. 2012. Cited on p. 882, 887, 896

[993] Lauritzen, Andrew, "Future Directions for Compute-for-Graphics," *SIGGRAPH Open Problems in Real-Time Rendering course*, Aug. 2017. Cited on p. 32, 812, 908

[994] LaValle, Steve, "The Latent Power of Prediction," *Oculus Developer Blog*, July 12, 2013. Cited on p. 915, 920, 936, 939

[995] LaValle, Steven M., Anna Yershova, Max Katsev, and Michael Antonov, "Head Tracking for the Oculus Rift," in *IEEE International Conference Robotics and Automation (ICRA)*, IEEE Computer Society, pp. 187–194, May–June 2014. Cited on p. 915, 916, 936

[996] Laven, Philip, *MiePlot* website and software, 2015. Cited on p. 597, 599

[997] Lax, Peter D., *Linear Algebra and Its Applications*, Second Edition, John Wiley & Sons, Inc., 2007. Cited on p. 61

[998] Lazarov, Dimitar, "Physically-Based lighting in *Call of Duty: Black Ops*," *SIGGRAPH Advances in Real-Time Rendering in Games course*, Aug. 2011. Cited on p. 340, 370, 371, 421, 476

[999] Lazarov, Dimitar, "Getting More Physical in *Call of Duty: Black Ops II*," *SIGGRAPH Physically Based Shading in Theory and Practice course*, July 2013. Cited on p. 352, 421, 502

[1000] Lazarus, F., and A. Verroust, "Three-Dimensional Metamorphosis: A Survey," *The Visual Computer*, vol. 14, no. 8, pp. 373–389, 1998. Cited on p. 87, 102

[1001] Le, Binh Huy, and Jessica K. Hodgins, "Real-Time Skeletal Skinning with Optimized Centers of Rotation," *ACM Transactions on Graphics*, vol. 35, no. 4, pp. 37:1–37:10, 2016. Cited on p. 87

[1002] Leadbetter, Richard, "The Making of *Forza Horizon 2*," *Eurogamer.net*, Oct. 11, 2014. Cited on p. 141, 900

[1003] Lecocq, Pascal, Pascal Gautron, Jean-Eudes Marvie, and Gael Sourimant, "Sub-Pixel Shadow Mapping," in *Proceedings of the 18th Meeting of the ACM SIGGRAPH Symposium on Interactive 3D Graphics and Games*, ACM, pp. 103–110, 2014. Cited on p. 259

[1004] Lecocq, Pascal, Arthur Dufay, Gael Sourimant, and Jean-Eude Marvie, "Analytic Approximations for Real-Time Area Light Shading," *IEEE Transactions on Visualization and Computer Graphics*, vol. 23, no. 5, pp. 1428–1441, 2017. Cited on p. 389

[1005] Lee, Aaron W. F., David Dobkin, Wim Sweldens, and Peter Schröder, "Multiresolution mesh morphing," in *SIGGRAPH '99: Proceedings of the 26th Annual Conference on Computer Graphics and Interactive Techniques*, ACM Press/Addison-Wesley Publishing Co., pp. 343–350, 1999. Cited on p. 87

[1006] Lee, Aaron, Henry Moreton, and Hugues Hoppe, "Displaced Subdivision Surfaces," in *SIGGRAPH '00: Proceedings of the 27th Annual Conference on Computer Graphics and Interactive Techniques*, ACM Press/Addison-Wesley Publishing Co., pp. 85–94, July 2000. Cited on p. 706, 765, 766

[1007] Lee, Aaron, "Building Your Own Subdivision Surfaces," *Gamasutra*, Sept. 8, 2000. Cited on p. 706

[1008] Lee, Hyunho, and Min-Ho Kyung, "Parallel Mesh Simplification Using Embedded Tree Collapsing," *The Visual Computer*, vol. 32, no. 6, pp. 967–976, 2016. Cited on p. 709

[1009] Lee, Hyunjun, Sungtae Kwon, and Seungyong Lee, "Real-Time Pencil Rendering," in *Proceedings of the 4th International Symposium on Non-Photorealistic Animation and Rendering*, ACM, pp. 37–45, 2006. Cited on p. 672

[1010] Lee, Jongseok, Sungyul Choe, and Seungyong Lee, "Mesh Geometry Compression for Mobile Graphics," in *2010 7th IEEE Consumer Communications and Networking Conference*, IEEE Computer Society, pp. 1–5, 2010. Cited on p. 714

[1011] Lee, Mark, "Pre-lighting in *Resistance 2*," *Game Developers Conference*, Mar. 2009. Cited on p. 892

[1012] Lee, Sungkil, and Elmar Eisemann, "Practical Real-Time Lens-Flare Rendering," *Computer Graphics Forum*, vol. 32, no. 4, pp. 1–6, 2013. Cited on p. 526

[1013] Lee, W.-J., Y. Youngsam, J. Lee, J.-W. Kim, J.-H. Nah, S. Jung, S. Lee, H.-S. Park, and T.-D. Han, "SGRT: A Mobile GPU Architecture for Real-Time Ray Tracing," in *Proceedings of the 5th High-Performance Graphics Conference*, ACM, pp. 109–119, July 2013. Cited on p. 1039

[1014] Lee, Yunjin, Lee Markosian, Seungyong Lee, and John F. Hughes, "Line Drawings via Abstracted Shading," *ACM Transactions on Graphics (SIGGRAPH 2007)*, vol. 26, no. 3, pp. 18:1–18:6, July 2007. Cited on p. 656

[1015] Lee-Steere, J., and J. Harmon, "Football at 60 FPS: The Challenges of Rendering Madden NFL 10," *Game Developers Conference*, Mar. 2010. Cited on p. 198

[1016] Lefebvre, Sylvain, and Fabrice Neyret, "Pattern Based Procedural Textures," *Proceedings of the 2003 Symposium on Interactive 3D Graphics*, ACM, pp. 203–212, 2003. Cited on p. 175

[1017] Lefebvre, Sylvain, Samuel Hornus, and Fabrice Neyret, "Octree Textures on the GPU," in Matt Pharr, ed., *GPU Gems 2*, Addison-Wesley, pp. 595–613, 2005. Cited on p. 190

[1018] Lefebvre, Sylvain, and Hugues Hoppe, "Perfect Spatial Hashing," *ACM Transactions on Graphics*, vol. 25, no. 3, pp. 579–588, July 2006. Cited on p. 190

[1019] Lehtinen, Jaakko, "A Framework for Precomputed and Captured Light Transport," *ACM Transactions on Graphics*, vol. 26, no. 4, pp. 13:1–13:22, 2007. Cited on p. 481

[1020] Lehtinen, Jaakko, *Theory and Algorithms for Efficient Physically-Based Illumination*, PhD thesis, Helsinki University of Technology, Espoo, Finland, 2007. Cited on p. 481

[1021] Lehtinen, Jaakko, Matthias Zwicker, Emmanuel Turquin, Janne Kontkanen, Frédo Durand, François Sillion, and Timo Aila, "A Meshless Hierarchical Representation for Light Transport," *ACM Transactions on Graphics*, vol. 27, no. 3, pp. 37:1–37:9, 2008. Cited on p. 484

[1022] Lengyel, Eric, "Tweaking a Vertex's Projected Depth Value," in Mark DeLoura, ed., *Game Programming Gems*, Charles River Media, pp. 361–365, 2000. Cited on p. 236, 657

[1023] Lengyel, Eric, "T-Junction Elimination and Retriangulation," in Dante Treglia, ed., *Game Programming Gems 3*, Charles River Media, pp. 338–343, 2002. Cited on p. 690

[1024] Lengyel, Eric, ed., *Game Engine Gems 2*, A K Peters, Ltd., 2011. Cited on p. 815

[1025] Lengyel, Eric, *Mathematics for 3D Game Programming and Computer Graphics*, Third Edition, Charles River Media, 2011. Cited on p. 102, 209, 210

[1026] Lengyel, Eric, "Game Math Case Studies," *Game Developers Conference*, Mar. 2015. Cited on p. 863

[1027] Lengyel, Eric, "Smooth Horizon Mapping," in Eric Lengyel, ed., *Game Engine Gems 3*, CRC Press, pp. 73–83, 2016. Cited on p. 214

[1028] Lengyel, Eric, "GPU-Friendly Font Rendering Directly from Glyph Outlines," *Journal of Computer Graphics Techniques*, vol. 6, no. 2, pp. 31–47, 2017. Cited on p. 677, 970

[1029] Lengyel, Jerome, "The Convergence of Graphics and Vision," *Computer*, vol. 31, no. 7, pp. 46–53, July 1998. Cited on p. 546

[1030] Lengyel, Jerome, "Real-Time Fur," in *Rendering Techniques 2000*, Springer, pp. 243–256, June 2000. Cited on p. 853

[1031] Lengyel, Jerome, Emil Praun, Adam Finkelstein, and Hugues Hoppe, "Real-Time Fur over Arbitrary Surfaces," in *Proceedings of the 2001 Symposium on Interactive 3D Graphics*, ACM, pp. 227–232, Mar. 2001. Cited on p. 646, 853

[1032] Lensch, Hendrik P. A., Michael Goesele, Philippe Bekaert, Jan Kautz, Marcus A. Magnor, Jochen Lang, and Hans-Peter Seidel, "Interactive Rendering of Translucent Objects," in *Pacific Conference on Computer Graphics and Applications 2002*, IEEE Computer Society, pp. 214–224, Oct. 2002. Cited on p. 635

[1033] Levoy, Marc, and Turner Whitted, "The Use of Points as a Display Primitive," Technical Report 85-022, Computer Science Department, University of North Carolina at Chapel Hill, Jan. 1985. Cited on p. 572

[1034] Levoy, Marc, and Pat Hanrahan, "Light Field Rendering," in *SIGGRAPH '96: Proceedings of the 23rd Annual Conference on Computer Graphics and Interactive Techniques*, ACM, pp. 31–42, Aug. 1996. Cited on p. 549

[1035] Levoy, Marc, Kari Pulli, Brian Curless, Szymon Rusinkiewicz, David Koller, Lucas Pereira, Matt Ginzton, Sean Anderson, James Davis, Jeremy Ginsberg, and Jonathan Shade, "The Digital Michelangelo Project: 3D Scanning of Large Statues," in *SIGGRAPH '00: Proceedings of the 27th Annual Conference on Computer Graphics and Interactive Techniques*, ACM Press/Addison-Wesley Publishing Co., pp. 131–144, July 2000. Cited on p. 573

[1036] Lévy, Bruno, Sylvain Petitjean, Nicolas Ray, and Jérome Maillot, "Least Squares Conformal Maps for Automatic Texture Atlas Generation," *ACM Transaction on Graphics*, vol. 21, no. 3, pp. 362–371, July 2002. Cited on p. 485, 486

[1037] Lewis, J. P., Matt Cordner, and Nickson Fong, "Pose Space Deformation: A Unified Approach to Shape Interpolation and Skeleton-Driven Deformation," in *SIGGRAPH '00: Proceedings of the 27th Annual Conference on Computer Graphics and Interactive Techniques*, ACM Press/Addison-Wesley Publishing Co., pp. 165–172, July 2000. Cited on p. 84, 87, 90, 102

[1038] Leyendecker, Felix, "Crafting the World of *Crysis 3*," *Game Developers Conference Europe*, Aug. 2013. Cited on p. 366

[1039] Li, Xin, "To Slerp, or Not to Slerp," *Game Developer*, vol. 13, no. 7, pp. 17–23, Aug. 2006. Cited on p. 82

[1040] Li, Xin, "iSlerp: An Incremental Approach of Slerp," *journal of graphics tools*, vol. 12, no. 1, pp. 1–6, 2007. Cited on p. 82

[1041] Licea-Kane, Bill, "GLSL: Center or Centroid? (Or When Shaders Attack!)" *The OpenGL Pipeline Newsletter*, vol. 3, 2007. Cited on p. 141

[1042] Liktor, Gábor, and Carsten Dachsbacher, "Decoupled Deferred Shading for Hardware Rasterization," in *Proceedings of the ACM SIGGRAPH Symposium on Interactive 3D Graphics and Games*, ACM, pp. 143–150, 2012. Cited on p. 910

[1043] Liktor, Gábor, and Carsten Dachsbacher, "Decoupled Deferred Shading on the GPU," in Wolfgang Engel, ed., *GPU Pro⁴*, CRC Press, pp. 81–98, 2013. Cited on p. 910

[1044] Liktor, G., M. Pan, and C. Dachsbacher, "Fractional Reyes-Style Adaptive Tessellation for Continuous Level of Detail," *Computer Graphics Forum*, vol. 33, no. 7, pp. 191–198, 2014. Cited on p. 774, 775

[1045] Liktor, G., and K. Vaidyanathan, "Bandwidth-Efficient BVH Layout for Incremental Hardware Traversal," in *Proceedings of High-Performance Graphics*, Eurographics Association, pp. 51–61, June 2016. Cited on p. 1039

[1046] Lilley, Sean, "Shadows and Cesium Implementation," *Cesium* website, Nov. 2016. Cited on p. 265

[1047] Lin, Gang, and Thomas P.-Y. Yu, "An Improved Vertex Caching Scheme for 3D Mesh Rendering," *IEEE Trans. on Visualization and Computer Graphics*, vol. 12, no. 4, pp. 640–648, 2006. Cited on p. 701

[1048] Lindbloom, Bruce, "RGB/XYZ Matrices," *Bruce Lindbloom* website, Apr. 7, 2017. Cited on p. 278

[1049] Lindholm, Erik, Mark Kilgard, and Henry Moreton, "A User-Programmable Vertex Engine," in *SIGGRAPH '01 Proceedings of the 28th Annual Conference on Computer Graphics and Interactive Techniques*, ACM, pp. 149–158, Aug. 2001. Cited on p. 15, 38

[1050] Lindholm, E., J. Nickolls, S. Oberman, and J. Montrym, "NVIDIA Tesla: A Unified Graphics and Computing Architecture," *IEEE Micro*, vol. 28, no. 2, pp. 39–55, 2008. Cited on p. 1004, 1029, 1031

[1051] Lindstrom, P., and J. D. Cohen, "On-the-Fly Decompression and Rendering of Multiresolution Terrain," in *Proceedings of the 2010 ACM SIGGRAPH Symposium on Interactive 3D Graphics and Games*, ACM, pp. 65–73, 2010. Cited on p. 879

[1052] Ling-Qi, Yan, Chi-Wei Tseng, Henrik Wann Jensen, and Ravi Ramamoorthi, "Physically-Accurate Fur Reflectance: Modeling, Measurement and Rendering," *ACM Transactions on Graphics (SIGGRAPH Asia 2015)*, vol. 34, no. 6, article no. 185, 2015. Cited on p. 640, 641, 647

[1053] Lira, Felipe, Felipe Chaves, Flávio Villalva, Jesus Sosa, Kléverson Paião, and Teófilo Dutra, "Mobile Toon Shading," in Wolfgang Engel, ed., *GPU Zen*, Black Cat Publishing, pp. 115–122, 2017. Cited on p. 659

[1054] Liu, Albert Julius, Zhao Dong, Miloš Hašan, and Steve Marschner, "Simulating the Structure and Texture of Solid Wood," *ACM Transactions on Graphics*, vol. 35, no. 6, article no. 170, 2016. Cited on p. 199

[1055] Liu, Edward, "Lens Matched Shading and Unreal Engine 4 Integration Part 3," *NVIDIA GameWorks* blog, Jan. 18, 2017. Cited on p. 930, 940

[1056] Liu, Fang, Meng-Cheng Huang, Xue-Hui Liu, and En-Hua Wu, "Efficient Depth Peeling via Bucket Sort," in *Proceedings of the Conference on High-Performance Graphics*, ACM, pp. 51–57, Aug. 2009. Cited on p. 155

[1057] Liu, Ligang, Lei Zhang, Yin Xu, Craig Gotsman, and Steven J. Gortler, "A Local/Global Approach to Mesh Parameterization," in *Proceedings of the Symposium on Geometry Processing*, Eurographics Association, pp. 1495–1504, 2008. Cited on p. 485

[1058] Liu, Songrun, Zachary Ferguson, Alec Jacobson, and Yotam Gingold, "Seamless: Seam Erasure and Seam-Aware Decoupling of Shape from Mesh Resolution," *ACM Transactions on Graphics*, vol. 36, no. 6, pp. 216:1–216:15, 2017. Cited on p. 486

[1059] Liu, Xinguo, Peter-Pike Sloan, Heung-Yeung Shum, and John Snyder, "All-Frequency Precomputed Radiance Transfer for Glossy Objects," in *Proceedings of the Fifteenth Eurographics Conference on Rendering Techniques*, Eurographics Association, pp. 337–344, June 2004. Cited on p. 432

[1060] Llopis, Noel, "High-Performance Programming with Data-Oriented Design," in Eric Lengyel, ed., *Game Engine Gems 2*, A K Peters, Ltd., pp. 251–261, 2011. Cited on p. 791, 812

[1061] Lloyd, Brandon, Jeremy Wendt, Naga Govindaraju, and Dinesh Manocha, "CC Shadow Volumes," in *Proceedings of the 15th Eurographics Workshop on Rendering Techniques*, Eurographics Association, pp. 197–206, June 2004. Cited on p. 233

[1062] Lloyd, Brandon, David Tuft, Sung-Eui Yoon, and Dinesh Manocha, "Warping and Partitioning for Low Error Shadow Maps," in *Eurographics Symposium on Rendering*, Eurographics Association, pp. 215–226, June 2006. Cited on p. 241, 242, 244

[1063] Lloyd, Brandon, *Logarithmic Perspective Shadow Maps*, PhD thesis, Dept. of Computer Science, University of North Carolina at Chapel Hill, Aug. 2007. Cited on p. 101, 241, 242

[1064] Lobanchikov, Igor A., and Holger Gruen, "GSC Game World's S.T.A.L.K.E.R: Clear Sky—A Showcase for Direct3D 10.0/1," *Game Developers Conference*, Mar. 2009. Cited on p. 252, 887, 888

[1065] Löfstedt, Marta, and Tomas Akenine-Möller, "An Evaluation Framework for Ray-Triangle Intersection Algorithms," *journal of graphics tools*, vol. 10, no. 2, pp. 13–26, 2005. Cited on p. 962

[1066] Lokovic, Tom, and Eric Veach, "Deep Shadow Maps," in *SIGGRAPH '00: Proceedings of the 27th Annual Conference on Computer Graphics and Interactive Techniques*, ACM Press/Addison-Wesley Publishing Co., pp. 385–392, July 2000. Cited on p. 257, 258, 570, 638

[1067] Loop, C., *Smooth Subdivision Based on Triangles*, MSc thesis, Department of Mathematics, University of Utah, Aug. 1987. Cited on p. 758, 759, 760, 761

[1068] Loop, Charles, and Jim Blinn, "Resolution Independent Curve Rendering Using Programmable Graphics Hardware," *ACM Transactions on Graphics*, vol. 24, no. 3, pp. 1000–1009, 2005. Cited on p. 677, 725

[1069] Loop, Charles, and Jim Blinn, "Rendering Vector Art on the GPU," in Hubert Nguyen, ed., *GPU Gems 3*, Addison-Wesley, pp. 543–561, 2007. Cited on p. 677, 725

[1070] Loop, Charles, and Scott Schaefer, "Approximating Catmull-Clark Subdivision Surfaces with Bicubic Patches," *ACM Transactions on Graphics*, vol. 27, no. 1, pp. 8:1–8:11, 2008. Cited on p. 767, 775, 776, 777, 779

[1071] Loop, Charles, Cha Zhang, and Zhengyou Zhang, "Real-Time High-Resolution Sparse Voxelization with Application to Image-Based Modeling," in *Proceedings of the 5th High-Performance Graphics Conference*, ACM, pp. 73–79, July 2013. Cited on p. 580

[1072] Loos, Bradford, and Peter-Pike Sloan, "Volumetric Obscurance," in *Proceedings of the 2010 ACM SIGGRAPH Symposium on Interactive 3D Graphics*, ACM, pp. 151–156, Feb. 2010. Cited on p. 459

[1073] Loos, Bradford J., Lakulish Antani, Kenny Mitchell, Derek Nowrouzezahrai, Wojciech Jarosz, and Peter-Pike Sloan, "Modular Radiance Transfer," *ACM Transactions on Graphics*, vol. 30, no. 6, pp. 178:1–178:10, 2011. Cited on p. 484

[1074] Lorach, Tristan, "DirectX 10 Blend Shapes: Breaking the Limits," in Hubert Nguyen, ed., *GPU Gems 3*, Addison-Wesley, pp. 53–67, 2007. Cited on p. 90

[1075] Lorach, Tristan, "Soft Particles," NVIDIA White Paper, Jan. 2007. Cited on p. 558

[1076] Lord, Kieren, and Ross Brown, "Using Genetic Algorithms to Optimise Triangle Strips," in *Proceedings of the 3rd International Conference on Computer Graphics and Interactive Techniques in Australasia and South East Asia (GRAPHITE 2005)*, ACM, pp. 169–176, 2005. Cited on p. 699

[1077] Lorensen, William E., and Harvey E. Cline, "Marching Cubes: A High Resolution 3D Surface Construction Algorithm," *Computer Graphics (SIGGRAPH '87 Proceedings)*, vol. 21, no. 4, pp. 163–169, July 1987. Cited on p. 583

[1078] Losasso, F., and H. Hoppe, "Geometry Clipmaps: Terrain Rendering Using Nested Regular Grids," *ACM Transactions on Graphics*, vol. 23, no. 3, pp. 769–776, 2004. Cited on p. 872, 873

[1079] Lottes, Timothy, "FXAA," NVIDIA White Paper, Feb. 2009. Cited on p. 148

[1080] Lottes, Timothy, "FXAA 3.11 in 15 Slides," *SIGGRAPH Filtering Approaches for Real-Time Anti-Aliasing course*, Aug. 2011. Cited on p. 148

[1081] Lottes, Timothy, "Advanced Techniques and Optimization of -HDR- VDR Color Pipelines," *Game Developers Conference*, Mar. 2016. Cited on p. 281, 286, 1010

[1082] Lottes, Timothy, "VDR Follow Up—Tonemapping for HDR Signals," *GPUOpen* website, Oct. 5, 2016. Cited on p. 281

[1083] Lottes, Timothy, "Technical Evaluation of Traditional vs New 'HDR' Encoding Crossed with Display Capability," *Timothy Lottes* blog, Oct. 12, 2016. Cited on p. 283

[1084] Lottes, Timothy, "FXAA Pixel Width Contrast Reduction," *Timothy Lottes* blog, Oct. 27, 2016. Cited on p. 148

[1085] Loviscach, Jörn, "Silhouette Geometry Shaders," in Wolfgang Engel, ed., *ShaderX³*, Charles River Media, pp. 49–56, 2004. Cited on p. 853

[1086] Loviscach, Jörn, "Care and Feeding of Normal Vectors," in Wolfgang Engel, ed., *ShaderX⁶*, Charles River Media, pp. 45–56, 2008. Cited on p. 366

[1087] Loviscach, Jörn, "Care and Feeding of Normal Vectors," *Game Developers Conference*, Mar. 2008. Cited on p. 366

[1088] Low, Kok-Lim, and Tiow-Seng Tan, "Model Simplification Using Vertex-Clustering," in *Proceedings of the 1997 Symposium on Interactive 3D Graphics*, ACM, pp. 75–81, Apr. 1997. Cited on p. 709

[1089] Ludwig, Joe, "Lessons Learned Porting *Team Fortress 2* to Virtual Reality," *Game Developers Conference*, Mar. 2013. Cited on p. 920, 932, 940

[1090] Luebke, David P., and Chris Georges, "Portals and Mirrors: Simple, Fast Evaluation of Potentially Visible Sets," in *Proceedings of the 1995 Symposium on Interactive 3D Graphics*, ACM, pp. 105–106, Apr. 1995. Cited on p. 838

[1091] Luebke, David P., "A Developer's Survey of Polygonal Simplification Algorithms," *IEEE Computer Graphics & Applications*, vol. 21, no. 3, pp. 24–35, May–June 2001. Cited on p. 706, 716

[1092] Luebke, David, *Level of Detail for 3D Graphics*, Morgan Kaufmann, 2003. Cited on p. 706, 708, 709, 716, 854, 879

[1093] Luksch, C., R. F. Tobler, T. Mühlbacher, M. Schwärzler, and M. Wimmer, "Real-Time Rendering of Glossy Materials with Regular Sampling," *The Visual Computer*, vol. 30, no. 6-8, pp. 717–727, 2014. Cited on p. 423

[1094] Lysenko, Mikola, "Meshing in a Minecraft Game," *0 FPS* blog, June 30, 2012. Cited on p. 582, 583

[1095] Ma, Wan-Chun, Tim Hawkins, Pieter Peers, Charles-Félix Chabert, Malte Weiss, and Paul Debevec, "Rapid Acquisition of Specular and Diffuse Normal Maps from Polarized Spherical Gradient Illumination," in *Proceedings of the 18th Eurographics Symposium on Rendering Techniques*, Eurographics Association, pp. 183–194, June 2007. Cited on p. 634, 635

[1096] MacDonald, J. D., and K. S. Booth, "Heuristics for Ray Tracing Using Space Subdivision," *Visual Computer*, vol. 6, no. 6, pp. 153–165, 1990. Cited on p. 953

[1097] Maciel, P., and P. Shirley, "Visual Navigation of Large Environments Using Textured Clusters," in *Proceedings of the 1995 Symposium on Interactive 3D Graphics*, ACM, pp. 96–102, 1995. Cited on p. 561, 853, 866

[1098] Macklin, Miles, "Faster Fog," *Miles Macklin* blog, June 10, 2010. Cited on p. 603

[1099] Maglo, Adrien, Guillaume Lavoué, Florent Dupont, and Céline Hudelot, "3D Mesh Compression: Survey, Comparisons, and Emerging Trends," *ACM Computing Surveys*, vol. 47, no. 3, pp. 44:1–44:41, Apr. 2015. Cited on p. 712, 714

[1100] Magnenat-Thalmann, Nadia, Richard Laperrière, and Daniel Thalmann, "Joint-Dependent Local Deformations for Hand Animation and Object Grasping," in *Graphics Interface '88*, Canadian Human-Computer Communications Society, pp. 26–33, June 1988. Cited on p. 85

[1101] Magnusson, Kenny, "Lighting You Up with *Battlefield 3*," *Game Developers Conference*, Mar. 2011. Cited on p. 482

[1102] Mah, Layla, and Stephan Hodes, "DirectCompute for Gaming: Supercharge Your Engine with Compute Shaders," *Game Developers Conference*, Mar. 2013. Cited on p. 54, 518, 535

[1103] Mah, Layla, "Powering the Next Generation Graphics: AMD GCN Architecture," *Game Developers Conference*, Mar. 2013. Cited on p. 1035

[1104] Mah, Layla, "Low Latency and Stutter-Free Rendering in VR and Graphics Applications," *Game Developers Conference*, Mar. 2015. Cited on p. 922, 928, 938, 939

[1105] Maillot, Patrick-Giles, "Using Quaternions for Coding 3D Transformations," in Andrew S. Glassner, ed., *Graphics Gems*, Academic Press, pp. 498–515, 1990. Cited on p. 77

[1106] Maillot, Jérôme, and Jos Stam, "A Unified Subdivision Scheme for Polygonal Modeling," *Computer Graphics Forum*, vol. 20, no. 3, pp. 471–479, 2001. Cited on p. 761

[1107] Maïm, Jonathan, and Daniel Thalmann, "Improved Appearance Variety for Geometry Instancing," in Wolfgang Engel, ed., *ShaderX⁶*, Charles River Media, pp. 17–28, 2008. Cited on p. 798, 800

[1108] Maïm, Jonathan, Barbara Yersin, and Daniel Thalmann, "Unique Instances for Crowds," *IEEE Computer Graphics & Applications*, vol. 29, no. 6, pp. 82–90, 2009. Cited on p. 798, 800

[1109] Malan, Hugh, "Graphics Techniques in *Crackdown*," in Wolfgang Engel, ed., *ShaderX⁷*, Charles River Media, pp. 189–215, 2009. Cited on p. 561

[1110] Malan, Hugh, "Real-Time Global Illumination and Reflections in *Dust 514*," *SIGGRAPH Advances in Real-Time Rendering in Games course*, Aug. 2012. Cited on p. 142, 143, 493

[1111] Malmer, Mattias, Fredrik Malmer, Ulf Assarsson, and Nicolas Holzschuch, "Fast Precomputed Ambient Occlusion for Proximity Shadows," *journal of graphics tools*, vol. 12, no. 2, pp. 59–71, 2007. Cited on p. 452

[1112] Malvar, Henrique S., Gary J. Sullivan, and Sridhar Srinivasan, "Lifting-Based Reversible Color Transformations for Image Compression," in *Applications of Digital Image Processing XXXI*, SPIE, 2008. Cited on p. 197

[1113] Malvar, R., "Fast Progressive Image Coding Without Wavelets," *Data Compression Conference*, Mar. 2000. Cited on p. 870

[1114] Malyshau, Dzmitry, "A Quaternion-Based Rendering Pipeline," in Wolfgang Engel, ed., *GPU Pro³*, CRC Press, pp. 265–273, 2012. Cited on p. 82, 210, 715

[1115] Mammen, Abraham, "Transparency and Antialiasing Algorithms Implemented with the Virtual Pixel Maps Technique," *IEEE Computer Graphics & Applications*, vol. 9, no. 4, pp. 43–55, July 1989. Cited on p. 139, 154

[1116] Mamou, Khaled, Titus Zaharia, and Françoise Prêteux, "TFAN: A Low Complexity 3D Mesh Compression Algorithm," *Computer Animation and Virtual Worlds*, vol. 20, pp. 1–12, 2009. Cited on p. 712

[1117] Mansencal, Thomas, "About Rendering Engines Colourspaces Agnosticism," *Colour Science* blog, Sept. 17, 2014. Cited on p. 278

[1118] Mansencal, Thomas, "About RGB Colourspace Models Performance," *Colour Science* blog, Oct. 9, 2014. Cited on p. 278

[1119] Manson, Josiah, and Scott Schaefer, "Parameterization-Aware MIP-Mapping," *Computer Graphics Forum*, vol. 31, no. 4, pp. 1455–1463, 2012. Cited on p. 191

[1120] Manson, Josiah, and Peter-Pike Sloan, "Fast Filtering of Reflection Probes," *Computer Graphics Forum*, vol. 35, no. 4, pp. 119–127, 2016. Cited on p. 420, 503, 518

[1121] Mantor, M., and M. Houston, "AMD Graphic Core Next—Low Power High Performance Graphics & Parallel Compute," *AMD Fusion Developer Summit*, June 2011. Cited on p. 1036

[1122] Mara, M., and M. McGuire, "2D Polyhedral Bounds of a Clipped, Perspective-Projected 3D Sphere," *Journal of Computer Graphics Techniques*, vol. 2, no. 2, pp. 70–83, 2013. Cited on p. 863, 886, 894

[1123] Mara, M., M. McGuire, D. Nowrouzezahrai, and D. Luebke, "Deep G-Buffers for Stable Global Illumination Approximation," in *Proceedings of High Performance Graphics*, Eurographics Association, pp. 87–98, June 2016. Cited on p. 509

[1124] Mara, Michael, Morgan McGuire, Benedikt Bitterli, and Wojciech Jarosz, "An Efficient Denoising Algorithm for Global Illumination," *High Performance Graphics*, June 2017. Cited on p. 511

[1125] Markosian, Lee, Michael A. Kowalski, Samuel J. Trychin, Lubomir D. Bourdev, Daniel Goldstein, and John F. Hughes, "Real-Time Nonphotorealistic Rendering," in *SIGGRAPH '97: Proceedings of the 24th Annual Conference on Computer Graphics and Interactive Techniques*, ACM Press/Addison-Wesley Publishing Co., pp. 415–420, Aug. 1997. Cited on p. 667

[1126] Markosian, Lee, Barbara J. Meier, Michael A. Kowalski, Loring S. Holden, J. D. Northrup, and John F. Hughes, "Art-Based Rendering with Continuous Levels of Detail," in *Proceedings of the 1st International Symposium on Non-Photorealistic Animation and Rendering*, ACM, pp. 59–66, June 2000. Cited on p. 670, 672

[1127] Marques, R., C. Bouville, M. Ribardière, L. P. Santos, and K. Bouatouch, "Spherical Fibonacci Point Sets for Illumination Integrals," *Computer Graphics Forum*, vol. 32, no. 8, pp. 134–143, 2013. Cited on p. 397

[1128] Marschner, Stephen R., Henrik Wann Jensen, Mike Cammarano, Steve Worley, and Pat Hanrahan, "Light Scattering from Human Hair Fibers," *ACM Transactions on Graphics (SIGGRAPH 2003)*, vol. 22, no. 3, pp. 780–791, 2000. Cited on p. 359, 640, 641, 642, 643, 644

[1129] Marschner, Steve, and Peter Shirley, *Fundamentals of Computer Graphics*, Fourth Edition, CRC Press, 2015. Cited on p. 102

[1130] Marshall, Carl S., "Cartoon Rendering: Real-Time Silhouette Edge Detection and Rendering," in Mark DeLoura, ed., *Game Programming Gems 2*, Charles River Media, pp. 436–443, 2001. Cited on p. 666

[1131] Martin, Sam, and Per Einarsson, "A Real-Time Radiosity Architecture for Video Game," *SIGGRAPH Advances in Real-Time Rendering in 3D Graphics and Games course*, July 2010. Cited on p. 482

[1132] Martin, Tobias, and Tiow-Seng Tan, "Anti-aliasing and Continuity with Trapezoidal Shadow Maps," in *15th Eurographics Symposium on Rendering*, Eurographics Association, pp. 153–160, June 2004. Cited on p. 241

[1133] Martinez, Adam, "Faster Photorealism in Wonderland: Physically-Based Shading and Lighting at Sony Pictures Imageworks," *SIGGRAPH Physically-Based Shading Models in Film and Game Production course*, July 2010. Cited on p. 340

[1134] Mason, Ashton E. W., and Edwin H. Blake, "Automatic Hierarchical Level of Detail Optimization in Computer Animation," *Computer Graphics Forum*, vol. 16, no. 3, pp. 191–199, 1997. Cited on p. 866

[1135] Masserann, Arnaud, "Indexing Multiple Vertex Arrays," in Patrick Cozzi & Christophe Riccio, eds., *OpenGL Insights*, CRC Press, pp. 365–374, 2012. Cited on p. 691, 699, 703

[1136] Mattausch, Oliver, Jiří Bittner, and Michael Wimmer, "CHC++: Coherent Hierarchical Culling Revisited," *Computer Graphics Forum*, vol. 27, no. 2, pp. 221–230, 2008. Cited on p. 845

[1137] Mattausch, Oliver, Jiří Bittner, Ari Silvennoinen, Daniel Scherzer, and Michael Wimmer, "Efficient Online Visibility for Shadow Maps," in Wolfgang Engel, ed., *GPU Pro³*, CRC Press, pp. 233–242, 2012. Cited on p. 247

[1138] Mattes, Ben, and Jean-Francois St-Amour, "Illustrative Rendering of *Prince of Persia*," *Game Developers Conference*, Mar. 2009. Cited on p. 658, 662

[1139] Matusik, W., C. Buehler, R. Raskar, S. J. Gortler, and L. McMillan, "Image-Based Visual Hulls," in *SIGGRAPH '00: Proceedings of the 27th Annual Conference on Computer Graphics and Interactive Techniques*, ACM Press/Addison-Wesley Publishing Co., pp. 369–374, 2000. Cited on p. 580

[1140] Maughan, Chris, "Texture Masking for Faster Lens Flare," in Mark DeLoura, ed., *Game Programming Gems 2*, Charles River Media, pp. 474–480, 2001. Cited on p. 524

[1141] Maule, Marilena, João L. D. Comba, Rafael Torchelsen, and Rui Bastos, "A Survey of Raster-Based Transparency Techniques," *Computer and Graphics*, vol. 35, no. 6, pp. 1023–1034, 2011. Cited on p. 159

[1142] Maule, Marilena, João Comba, Rafael Torchelsen, and Rui Bastos, "Hybrid Transparency," in *Proceedings of the ACM SIGGRAPH Symposium on Interactive 3D Graphics and Games*, ACM, pp. 103–118, 2013. Cited on p. 156

[1143] Mavridis, Pavlos, and Georgios Papaioannou, "High Quality Elliptical Texture Filtering on GPU," in *Symposium on Interactive 3D Graphics and Games*, ACM, pp. 23–30, Feb. 2011. Cited on p. 189

[1144] Mavridis, P., and G. Papaioannou, "The Compact YCoCg Frame Buffer," *Journal of Computer Graphics Techniques*, vol. 1, no. 1, pp. 19–35, 2012. Cited on p. 804, 805

[1145] Max, Nelson L., "Horizon Mapping: Shadows for Bump-Mapped Surfaces," *The Visual Computer*, vol. 4, no. 2, pp. 109–117, 1988. Cited on p. 460, 466

[1146] Max, Nelson L., "Weights for Computing Vertex Normals from Facet Normals," *journal of graphics tools*, vol. 4, no. 2, pp. 1–6, 1999. Also collected in [112]. Cited on p. 695

[1147] Max, Nelson, "Improved Accuracy When Building an Orthonormal Basis," *Journal of Computer Graphics Techniques*, vol. 6, no. 1, pp. 9–16, 2017. Cited on p. 75

[1148] *Maxima, a Computer Algebra System*, http://maxima.sourceforge.net/, 2017. Cited on p. 991

[1149] Mayaux, Benoit, "Real-Time Volumetric Rendering," *Revision Demo Party*, Mar.–Apr. 2013. Cited on p. 620

[1150] McAllister, David K., Anselmo A. Lastra, and Wolfgang Heidrich, "Efficient Rendering of Spatial Bi-directional Reflectance Distribution Functions," in *Graphics Hardware 2002*, Eurographics Association, pp. 79–88, Sept. 2002. Cited on p. 417, 424

[1151] McAllister, David, "Spatial BRDFs," in Randima Fernando, ed., *GPU Gems*, Addison-Wesley, pp. 293–306, 2004. Cited on p. 417, 424

[1152] McAnlis, Colt, "A Multithreaded 3D Renderer," in Eric Lengyel, ed., *Game Engine Gems*, Jones and Bartlett, pp. 149–165, 2010. Cited on p. 814

[1153] McAuley, Stephen, "Calibrating Lighting and Materials in *Far Cry 3*," *SIGGRAPH Physically Based Shading in Theory and Practice course*, Aug. 2012. Cited on p. 349

[1154] McAuley, Stephen, "Rendering the World of Far Cry 4," *Game Developers Conference*, Mar. 2015. Cited on p. 143, 146, 210, 420, 424, 453, 481, 503, 715, 864

[1155] McCabe, Dan, and John Brothers, "DirectX 6 Texture Map Compression," *Game Developer*, vol. 5, no. 8, pp. 42–46, Aug. 1998. Cited on p. 1013

[1156] McCaffrey, Jon, "Exploring Mobile vs. Desktop OpenGL Performance," in Patrick Cozzi & Christophe Riccio, eds., *OpenGL Insights*, CRC Press, pp. 337–352, 2012. Cited on p. 814

[1157] McCloud, Scott, *Understanding Comics: The Invisible Art*, Harper Perennial, 1994. Cited on p. 652, 678

[1158] McCombe, J. A., "PowerVR Graphics—Latest Developments and Future Plans," *Game Developers Conference*, Mar. 2015. Cited on p. 511, 1039, 1044

[1159] McCool, Michael D., Chris Wales, and Kevin Moule, "Incremental and Hierarchical Hilbert Order Edge Equation Polygon Rasterization," in *Graphics Hardware 2001*, Eurographics Association, pp. 65–72, Aug. 2001. Cited on p. 996, 1001

[1160] McCormack, J., R. McNamara, C. Gianos, L. Seiler, N. P. Jouppi, and Ken Corell, "Neon: A Single-Chip 3D Workstation Graphics Accelerator," in *Proceedings of the ACM SIG-GRAPH/EUROGRAPHICS Workshop on Graphics Hardware*, ACM, pp. 123–123, Aug. 1998. Cited on p. 185, 1010, 1034

[1161] McCormack, Joel, Ronald Perry, Keith I. Farkas, and Norman P. Jouppi, "Feline: Fast Elliptical Lines for Anisotropic Texture Mapping," in *SIGGRAPH '99: Proceedings of the 26th Annual Conference on Computer Graphics and Interactive Techniques*, ACM Press/Addison-Wesley Publishing Co., pp. 243–250, Aug. 1999. Cited on p. 189

[1162] McCormack, Joel, and Robert McNamara, "Tiled Polygon Traversal Using Half-Plane Edge Functions," in *Graphics Hardware 2000*, Eurographics Association, pp. 15–22, Aug. 2000. Cited on p. 22, 996, 997

[1163] McDermott, Wes, *The Comprehensive PBR Guide by Allegorithmic*, vol. 2, Allegorithmic, 2016. Cited on p. 325, 349

[1164] McDonald, J., and M. Kilgard, "Crack-Free Point-Normal Triangles Using Adjacent Edge Normals," Technical Report, NVIDIA, Dec. 2010. Cited on p. 747

[1165] McDonald, J., "Don't Throw It All Away: Efficient Buffer Management," *Game Developers Conference*, Mar. 2012. Cited on p. 117

[1166] McDonald, John, "Alpha Blending: To Pre or Not To Pre," *NVIDIA GameWorks* blog, Jan. 31, 2013. Cited on p. 208

[1167] McDonald, John, "Avoiding Catastrophic Performance Loss: Detecting CPU-GPU Sync Points," *Game Developers Conference*, Mar. 2014. Cited on p. 790, 794, 805

[1168] McEwan, Ian, David Sheets, Mark Richardson, and Stefan Gustavson, "Efficient Computational Noise in GLSL," *journal of graphics tools*, vol. 16, no. 2, pp. 85–94, 2012. Cited on p. 199

[1169] McGuire, Morgan, and John F. Hughes, "Hardware-Determined Feature Edges," in *Proceedings of the 3rd International Symposium on Non-Photorealistic Animation and Rendering*, ACM, pp. 35–47, June 2004. Cited on p. 668

[1170] McGuire, Morgan, "The SuperShader," in Wolfgang Engel, ed., *ShaderX⁴*, Charles River Media, pp. 485–498, 2005. Cited on p. 128

[1171] McGuire, Morgan, and Max McGuire, "Steep Parallax Mapping," *Symposium on Interactive 3D Graphics and Games poster*, Apr. 2005. Cited on p. 215, 216, 217, 218, 933

[1172] McGuire, Morgan, *Computer Graphics Archive*, http://graphics.cs.williams.edu/data, Aug. 2011. Cited on p. 105, 118

[1173] McGuire, Morgan, Padraic Hennessy, Michael Bukowski, and Brian Osman, "A Reconstruction Filter for Plausible Motion Blur," *Symposium on Interactive 3D Graphics and Games*, Feb. 2012. Cited on p. 537, 540, 541, 542, 543

[1174] McGuire, Morgan, Michael Mara, and David Luebke, "Scalable Ambient Obscurance," *High Performance Graphics*, June 2012. Cited on p. 459

[1175] McGuire, M., D. Evangelakos, J. Wilcox, S. Donow, and M. Mara, "Plausible Blinn-Phong Reflection of Standard Cube MIP-Maps," Technical Report CSTR201301, Department of Computer Science, Williams College, 2013. Cited on p. 419

[1176] McGuire, Morgan, and Louis Bavoil, "Weighted Blended Order-Independent Transparency," *Journal of Computer Graphics Techniques*, vol. 2, no. 2, pp. 122–141, 2013. Cited on p. 158

[1177] McGuire, Morgan, "Z-Prepass Considered Irrelevant," *Casual Effects* blog, Aug. 14, 2013. Cited on p. 803, 882

[1178] McGuire, Morgan, "The *Skylanders SWAP Force* Depth-of-Field Shader," *Casual Effects* blog, Sept. 13, 2013. Cited on p. 529, 530, 532, 533, 536

[1179] McGuire, Morgan, and Michael Mara, "Efficient GPU Screen-Space Ray Tracing," *Journal of Computer Graphics Techniques*, vol. 3, no. 4, pp. 73–85, 2014. Cited on p. 506

[1180] McGuire, Morgan, "Implementing Weighted, Blended Order-Independent Transparency," *Casual Effects* blog, Mar. 26, 2015. Cited on p. 158, 569

[1181] McGuire, Morgan, "Fast Colored Transparency," *Casual Effects* blog, Mar. 27, 2015. Cited on p. 158

[1182] McGuire, Morgan, "Peering Through a Glass, Darkly at the Future of Real-Time Transparency," *SIGGRAPH Open Problems in Real-Time Rendering course*, July 2016. Cited on p. 159, 165, 623, 649

[1183] McGuire, Morgan, "Strategies for Avoiding Motion Sickness in VR Development," *Casual Effects* blog, Aug. 12, 2016. Cited on p. 920

[1184] McGuire, Morgan, Mike Mara, Derek Nowrouzezahrai, and David Luebke, "Real-Time Global Illumination Using Precomputed Light Field Probes," in *Proceedings of the 21st ACM SIG-GRAPH Symposium on Interactive 3D Graphics and Games*, ACM, pp. 2:1–2:11, Feb. 2017. Cited on p. 490, 502

[1185] McGuire, Morgan, and Michael Mara, "Phenomenological Transparency," *IEEE Transactions of Visualization and Computer Graphics*, vol. 23, no.5, pp. 1465–1478, May 2017. Cited on p. 158, 623, 624, 629, 632, 649

[1186] McGuire, Morgan, "The Virtual Frontier: Computer Graphics Challenges in Virtual Reality & Augmented Reality," *SIGGRAPH NVIDIA talks*, July 31, 2017. Cited on p. 923, 939, 940

[1187] McGuire, Morgan, "How NVIDIA Research is Reinventing the Display Pipeline for the Future of VR, Part 2," *Road to VR* website, Nov. 30, 2017. Cited on p. 919, 940, 1046

[1188] McGuire, Morgan, *The Graphics Codex*, Edition 2.14, Casual Effects Publishing, 2018. Cited on p. 372, 512, 1047

[1189] McGuire, Morgan, "Ray Marching," in *The Graphics Codex*, Edition 2.14, Casual Effects Publishing, 2018. Cited on p. 752

[1190] McLaren, James, "The Technology of The Tomorrow Children," *Game Developers Conference*, Mar. 2015. Cited on p. 496, 504, 569

[1191] McNabb, Doug, "Sparse Procedural Volume Rendering," in Wolfgang Engel, ed., *GPU Pro⁶*, CRC Press, pp. 167–180, 2015. Cited on p. 611, 934

[1192] McReynolds, Tom, and David Blythe, *Advanced Graphics Programming Using OpenGL*, Morgan Kaufmann, 2005. Cited on p. 152, 153, 199, 200, 221, 222, 229, 538, 551, 674, 675, 678

[1193] McTaggart, Gary, "*Half-Life 2*/Valve Source Shading," *Game Developers Conference*, Mar. 2004. Cited on p. 127, 394, 402, 478, 488, 499

[1194] McVoy, Larry, and Carl Staelin, "lmbench: Portable Tools for Performance Analysis," in *Proceedings of the USENIX Annual Technical Conference*, USENIX, pp. 120–133, Jan. 1996. Cited on p. 792

[1195] Mehra, Ravish, and Subodh Kumar, "Accurate and Efficient Rendering of Detail Using Directional Distance Maps," in *Proceedings of the Eighth Indian Conference on Vision, Graphics and Image Processing*, ACM, pp. 34:1–34:8, Dec. 2012. Cited on p. 219

[1196] Melax, Stan, "A Simple, Fast, and Effective Polygon Reduction Algorithm," *Game Developer*, vol. 5, no. 11, pp. 44–49, Nov. 1998. Cited on p. 707, 860

[1197] Melax, Stan, "The Shortest Arc Quaternion," in Mark DeLoura, ed., *Game Programming Gems*, Charles River Media, pp. 214–218, 2000. Cited on p. 83

[1198] Meneveaux, Daniel, Benjamin Bringier, Emmanuelle Tauzia, Mickaël Ribardière, and Lionel Simonot, "Rendering Rough Opaque Materials with Interfaced Lambertian Microfacets," *IEEE Transactions on Visualization and Computer Graphics*, vol. 24, no. 3, pp. 1368–1380, 2018. Cited on p. 331

[1199] Meng, Johannes, Florian Simon, Johannes Hanika, and Carsten Dachsbacher, "Physically Meaningful Rendering Using Tristimulus Colours," *Computer Graphics Forum*, vol. 34, no. 4, pp. 31–40, 2015. Cited on p. 349

[1200] Merry, Bruce, "Performance Tuning for Tile-Based Architectures," in Patrick Cozzi & Christophe Riccio, eds., *OpenGL Insights*, CRC Press, pp. 323–335, 2012. Cited on p. 790, 814

[1201] Mertens, Tom, Jan Kautz, Philippe Bekaert, Hans-Peter Seidel, and Frank Van Reeth, "Efficient Rendering of Local Subsurface Scattering," in *Proceedings of the 11th Pacific Conference on Computer Graphics and Applications*, IEEE Computer Society, pp. 51–58, Oct. 2003. Cited on p. 639

[1202] Meshkin, Houman, "Sort-Independent Alpha Blending," *Game Developers Conference*, Mar. 2007. Cited on p. 156

[1203] Meyer, Alexandre, and Fabrice Neyret, "Interactive Volumetric Textures," in *Rendering Techniques '98*, Springer, pp. 157–168, July 1998. Cited on p. 565, 646

[1204] Meyer, Alexandre, Fabrice Neyret, and Pierre Poulin, "Interactive Rendering of Trees with Shading and Shadows," in *Rendering Techniques 2001*, Springer, pp. 183–196, June 2001. Cited on p. 202

[1205] Meyer, Quirin, Jochen Süßner, Gerd Sußner, Marc Stamminger, and Günther Greiner, "On Floating-Point Normal Vectors," *Computer Graphics Forum*, vol. 29, no. 4, pp. 1405–1409, 2010. Cited on p. 222

[1206] Meyers, Scott, "CPU Caches and Why You Care," *code::dive* conference, Nov. 5, 2014. Cited on p. 791, 792

[1207] Microsoft, "Coordinate Systems," *Windows Mixed Reality* website, 2017. Cited on p. 918, 932

[1208] Microsoft, "Direct3D 11 Graphics," *Windows Dev Center*. Cited on p. 42, 233, 525

[1209] Mikkelsen, Morten S., "Bump Mapping Unparametrized Surfaces on the GPU," Technical Report, Naughty Dog, 2010. Cited on p. 210

[1210] Mikkelsen, Morten S., "Fine Pruned Tiled Light Lists," in Wolfgang Engel, ed., *GPU Pro*[7], CRC Press, pp. 69–81, 2016. Cited on p. 897, 914

[1211] Miller, Gavin, "Efficient Algorithms for Local and Global Accessibility Shading," in *SIGGRAPH '94: Proceedings of the 21st Annual Conference on Computer Graphics and Interactive Techniques*, ACM, pp. 319–326, July 1994. Cited on p. 449

[1212] Miller, Gene S., and C. Robert Hoffman, "Illumination and Reflection Maps: Simulated Objects in Simulated and Real Environments," *SIGGRAPH Advanced Computer Graphics Animation course*, July 1984. Cited on p. 408, 424

[1213] Miller, Scott, "A Perceptual EOTF for Extended Dynamic Range Imagery," *SMPTE Standards Update presentation*, May 6, 2014. Cited on p. 281

[1214] Mitchell, D., and A. Netravali, "Reconstruction Filters in Computer Graphics," *Computer Graphics (SIGGRAPH '88 Proceedings)*, vol. 22, no. 4, pp. 239–246, Aug. 1988. Cited on p. 136

[1215] Mitchell, Jason L., Michael Tatro, and Ian Bullard, "Multitexturing in DirectX 6," *Game Developer*, vol. 5, no. 9, pp. 33–37, Sept. 1998. Cited on p. 200

[1216] Mitchell, Jason L., "Advanced Vertex and Pixel Shader Techniques," *European Game Developers Conference*, Sept. 2001. Cited on p. 521

[1217] Mitchell, Jason L., "Image Processing with 1.4 Pixel Shaders in Direct3D," in Wolfgang Engel, ed., *Direct3D ShaderX: Vertex & Pixel Shader Tips and Techniques*, Wordware, pp. 258–269, 2002. Cited on p. 521, 662

[1218] Mitchell, Jason L., Marwan Y. Ansari, and Evan Hart, "Advanced Image Processing with DirectX 9 Pixel Shaders," in Wolfgang Engel, ed., *ShaderX²: Shader Programming Tips and Tricks with DirectX 9*, Wordware, pp. 439–468, 2004. Cited on p. 515, 517, 521

[1219] Mitchell, Jason L., "Light Shaft Rendering," in Wolfgang Engel, ed., *ShaderX³*, Charles River Media, pp. 573–588, 2004. Cited on p. 604

[1220] Mitchell, Jason L., and Pedro V. Sander, "Applications of Explicit Early-Z Culling," *SIGGRAPH Real-Time Shading course*, Aug. 2004. Cited on p. 53, 1016

[1221] Mitchell, Jason, "Motion Blurring Environment Maps," in Wolfgang Engel, ed., *ShaderX⁴*, Charles River Media, pp. 263–268, 2005. Cited on p. 538

[1222] Mitchell, Jason, Gary McTaggart, and Chris Green, "Shading in Valve's Source Engine," *SIGGRAPH Advanced Real-Time Rendering in 3D Graphics and Games course*, Aug. 2006. Cited on p. 289, 382, 402, 499

[1223] Mitchell, Jason L., Moby Francke, and Dhabih Eng, "Illustrative Rendering in *Team Fortress 2*," *Proceedings of the 5th International Symposium on Non-Photorealistic Animation and Rendering*, ACM, pp. 71–76, Aug. 2007. Collected in [1746]. Cited on p. 678

[1224] Mitchell, Jason, " Stylization with a Purpose: The Illustrative World of *Team Fortress 2*," *Game Developers Conference*, Mar. 2008. Cited on p. 652, 654

[1225] Mitchell, Kenny, "Volumetric Light Scattering as a Post-Process," in Hubert Nguyen, ed., *GPU Gems 3*, Addison-Wesley, pp. 275–285, 2007. Cited on p. 604

[1226] Mittring, Martin, "Triangle Mesh Tangent Space Calculation," in Wolfgang Engel, ed., *ShaderX⁴*, Charles River Media, pp. 77–89, 2005. Cited on p. 210

[1227] Mittring, Martin, "Finding Next Gen—CryEngine 2," *SIGGRAPH Advanced Real-Time Rendering in 3D Graphics and Games course*, Aug. 2007. Cited on p. 43, 195, 239, 242, 255, 457, 476, 559, 856, 860, 861

[1228] Mittring, Martin, and Byran Dudash, "The Technology Behind the DirectX 11 Unreal Engine 'Samaritan' Demo," *Game Developers Conference*, Mar. 2011. Cited on p. 389, 502, 531, 641, 642

[1229] Mittring, Martin, "The Technology Behind the 'Unreal Engine 4 Elemental Demo'," *Game Developers Conference*, Mar. 2012. Cited on p. 288, 371, 383, 495, 526, 536, 571

[1230] Mohr, Alex, and Michael Gleicher, "Building Efficient, Accurate Character Skins from Examples," *ACM Transactions on Graphics (SIGGRAPH 2003)*, vol. 22, no. 3, pp. 562–568, 2003. Cited on p. 85

[1231] Möller, Tomas, and Ben Trumbore, "Fast, Minimum Storage Ray-Triangle Intersection," *journal of graphics tools*, vol. 2, no. 1, pp. 21–28, 1997. Also collected in [112]. Cited on p. 962, 965

[1232] Möller, Tomas, "A Fast Triangle-Triangle Intersection Test," *journal of graphics tools*, vol. 2, no. 2, pp. 25–30, 1997. Cited on p. 972

[1233] Möller, Tomas, and John F. Hughes, "Efficiently Building a Matrix to Rotate One Vector to Another," *journal of graphics tools*, vol. 4, no. 4, pp. 1–4, 1999. Also collected in [112]. Cited on p. 83, 84

[1234] Molnar, Steven, "Efficient Supersampling Antialiasing for High-Performance Architectures," Technical Report TR91-023, Department of Computer Science, University of North Carolina at Chapel Hill, 1991. Cited on p. 145, 547

[1235] Molnar, S., J. Eyles, and J. Poulton, "PixelFlow: High-Speed Rendering Using Image Composition," *Computer Graphics (SIGGRAPH '92 Proceedings)*, vol. 26, no. 2, pp. 231–240, July 1992. Cited on p. 883, 1022

[1236] Molnar, S., M. Cox, D. Ellsworth, and H. Fuchs, "A Sorting Classification of Parallel Rendering," *IEEE Computer Graphics and Applications*, vol. 14, no. 4, pp. 23–32, July 1994. Cited on p. 1020, 1023

[1237] Montesdeoca, S. E., H. S. Seah, and H.-M. Rall, "Art-Directed Watercolor Rendered Animation," in *Expressive 2016*, Eurographics Association, pp. 51–58, May 2016. Cited on p. 665

[1238] Morein, Steve, "ATI Radeon HyperZ Technology," *Graphics Hardware Hot3D session*, Aug. 2000. Cited on p. 1009, 1015, 1016, 1038

[1239] Moreton, Henry P., and Carlo H. Séquin, "Functional Optimization for Fair Surface Design," *Computer Graphics (SIGGRAPH '92 Proceedings)*, vol. 26, no. 2, pp. 167–176, July 1992. Cited on p. 761

[1240] Moreton, Henry, "Watertight Tessellation Using Forward Differencing," in *Graphics Hardware 2001*, Eurographics Association, pp. 25–132, Aug. 2001. Cited on p. 768, 769

[1241] Morovič, Ján, *Color Gamut Mapping*, John Wiley & Sons, 2008. Cited on p. 278

[1242] Mortenson, Michael E., *Geometric Modeling*, Third Edition, John Wiley & Sons, 2006. Cited on p. 718, 781

[1243] Morton, G. M., "A Computer Oriented Geodetic Data Base and a New Technique in File Sequencing," Technical Report, IBM, Ottawa, Ontario, Mar. 1, 1966. Cited on p. 1018

[1244] Mueller, Carl, "Architectures of Image Generators for Flight Simulators," Technical Report TR95-015, Department of Computer Science, University of North Carolina at Chapel Hill, 1995. Cited on p. 149

[1245] Mulde, Jurriaan D., Frans C. A. Groen, and Jarke J. van Wijk, "Pixel Masks for Screen-Door Transparency," in *Visualization '98*, IEEE Computer Society, pp. 351–358, Oct. 1998. Cited on p. 149

[1246] Munkberg, Jacob, and Tomas Akenine-Möller, "Backface Culling for Motion Blur and Depth of Field," *Journal of Graphics, GPU, and Game Tools*, vol. 15, no. 2, pp. 123–139, 2011. Cited on p. 835

[1247] Munkberg, Jacob, Karthik Vaidyanathan, Jon Hasselgren, Petrik Clarberg, and Tomas Akenine-Möller, "Layered Reconstruction for Defocus and Motion Blur," *Computer Graphics Forum*, vol. 33, no. 4, pp. 81–92, 2014. Cited on p. 542

[1248] Munkberg, J., J. Hasselgren, P. Clarberg, M. Andersson, and T. Akenine-Möller, "Texture Space Caching and Reconstruction for Ray Tracing," *ACM Transactions on Graphics*, vol. 35, no. 6, pp. 249:1–249:13, 2016. Cited on p. 934

[1249] Museth, Ken, "VDB: High-Resolution Sparse Volumes with Dynamic Topology," *ACM Transactions on Graphics*, vol. 32, no. 2, article no. 27, June 2013. Cited on p. 578, 584

[1250] Myers, Kevin, "Alpha-to-Coverage in Depth," in Wolfgang Engel, ed., *ShaderX⁵*, Charles River Media, pp. 69–74, 2006. Cited on p. 207

[1251] Myers, Kevin, "Variance Shadow Mapping," NVIDIA White Paper, 2007. Cited on p. 253

[1252] Myers, Kevin, Randima (Randy) Fernando, and Louis Bavoil, "Integrating Realistic Soft Shadows into Your Game Engine," NVIDIA White Paper, Feb. 2008. Cited on p. 250

[1253] Myers, Kevin, "Sparse Shadow Trees," in *ACM SIGGRAPH 2016 Talks*, ACM, article no. 14, July 2016. Cited on p. 239, 246, 263

[1254] Nagy, Gabor, "Real-Time Shadows on Complex Objects," in Mark DeLoura, ed., *Game Programming Gems*, Charles River Media, pp. 567–580, 2000. Cited on p. 229

[1255] Nagy, Gabor, "Convincing-Looking Glass for Games," in Mark DeLoura, ed., *Game Programming Gems*, Charles River Media, pp. 586–593, 2000. Cited on p. 153

[1256] Nah, J.-H., H.-J. Kwon, D.-S. Kim, C.-H. Jeong, J. Park, T.-D. Han, D. Manocha, and W.-C. Park, "RayCore: A Ray-Tracing Hardware Architecture for Mobile Devices," *ACM Transactions on Graphics*, vol. 33, no. 5, pp. 162:1–162:15, 2014. Cited on p. 1039

[1257] Naiman, Avi C., "Jagged Edges: When Is Filtering Needed?," *ACM Transactions on Graphics*, vol. 14, no. 4, pp. 238–258, 1998. Cited on p. 143

[1258] Narasimhan, Srinivasa G., Mohit Gupta, Craig Donner, Ravi Ramamoorthi, Shree K. Nayar, and Henrik Wann Jensen, "Acquiring Scattering Properties of Participating Media by Dilution," *ACM Transactions on Graphics (SIGGRAPH 2006)*, vol. 25, no. 3, pp. 1003–1012, Aug. 2006. Cited on p. 591, 592

[1259] Narkowicz, Krzysztof, *Real-Time BC6H Compression on GPU*, in Wolfgang Engel, ed., *GPU Pro^5*, CRC Press, pp. 219–230, 2014. Cited on p. 503, 870

[1260] Narkowicz, Krzysztof, "ACES Filmic Tone Mapping Curve," *Krzysztof Narkowicz* blog, Jan. 6, 2016. Cited on p. 287

[1261] Narkowicz, Krzysztof, "HDR Display—First Steps," *Krzysztof Narkowicz* blog, Aug. 31, 2016. Cited on p. 287

[1262] Nassau, Kurt, *The Physics and Chemistry of Color: The Fifteen Causes of Color*, Second Edition, John Wiley & Sons, Inc., 2001. Cited on p. 373

[1263] Navarro, Fernando, Francisco J. Serón, and Diego Gutierrez, "Motion Blur Rendering: State of the Art," *Computer Graphics Forum*, vol. 30, no. 1, pp. 3–26, 2011. Cited on p. 543

[1264] Nehab, D., P. Sander, J. Lawrence, N. Tatarchuk, and J. Isidoro, "Accelerating Real-Time Shading with Reverse Reprojection Caching," in *Graphics Hardware 2007*, Eurographics Association, pp. 25–35, Aug. 2007. Cited on p. 522, 523

[1265] Nelson, Scott R., "Twelve Characteristics of Correct Antialiased Lines," *journal of graphics tools*, vol. 1, no. 4, pp. 1–20, 1996. Cited on p. 165

[1266] Neubelt, D., and M. Pettineo, "Crafting a Next-Gen Material Pipeline for *The Order: 1886*," *SIGGRAPH Physically Based Shading in Theory and Practice course*, July 2013. Cited on p. 357, 365, 370

[1267] Neubelt, D., and M. Pettineo, "Crafting a Next-Gen Material Pipeline for *The Order: 1886*," *Game Developers Conference*, Mar. 2014. Cited on p. 365, 370, 466, 896

[1268] Neubelt, D., and M. Pettineo, "Advanced Lighting R&D at Ready At Dawn Studios," *SIGGRAPH Physically Based Shading in Theory and Practice course*, Aug. 2015. Cited on p. 398, 477, 488, 498

[1269] Ng, Ren, Ravi Ramamoorthi, and Pat Hanrahan, "All-Frequency Shadows Using Non-linear Wavelet Lighting Approximation," *ACM Transactions on Graphics (SIGGRAPH 2003)*, vol. 22, no. 3, pp. 376–281, 2003. Cited on p. 433

[1270] Ng, Ren, Ravi Ramamoorthi, and Pat Hanrahan, "Triple Product Wavelet Integrals for All-Frequency Relighting," *ACM Transactions on Graphics (SIGGRAPH 2004)*, vol. 23, no. 3, pp. 477–487, Aug. 2004. Cited on p. 402, 433, 470

[1271] Ngan, Addy, Frédo Durand, and Wojciech Matusik, "Experimental Analysis of BRDF Models," in *16th Eurographics Symposium on Rendering*, Eurographics Association, pp. 117–126, June–July 2005. Cited on p. 338, 343

[1272] Nguyen, Hubert, "Casting Shadows on Volumes," *Game Developer*, vol. 6, no. 3, pp. 44–53, Mar. 1999. Cited on p. 229

[1273] Nguyen, Hubert, "Fire in the 'Vulcan' Demo," in Randima Fernando, ed., *GPU Gems*, Addison-Wesley, pp. 87–105, 2004. Cited on p. 152, 521, 554

[1274] Nguyen, Hubert, and William Donnelly, "Hair Animation and Rendering in the 'Nalu' Demo," in Matt Pharr, ed., *GPU Gems 2*, Addison-Wesley, pp. 361–380, 2005. Cited on p. 257, 644, 719, 730

[1275] Ni, T., I. Castaño, J. Peters, J. Mitchell, P. Schneider, and V. Verma, *SIGGRAPH Efficient Substitutes for Subdivision Surfaces course*, Aug. 2009. Cited on p. 767, 781

[1276] Nichols, Christopher, "The Truth about Unbiased Rendering," *Chaosgroup Labs* blog, Sept. 29, 2016. Cited on p. 1043

[1277] Nicodemus, F. E., J. C. Richmond, J. J. Hsia, I. W. Ginsberg, and T. Limperis, "Geometric Considerations and Nomenclature for Reflectance," National Bureau of Standards (US), Oct. 1977. Cited on p. 310, 634

[1278] Nienhuys, Han-Wen, Jim Arvo, and Eric Haines, "Results of Sphere in Box Ratio Contest," *Ray Tracing News*, vol. 10, no. 1, Jan. 1997. Cited on p. 953

[1279] Nießner, M., C. Loop, M. Meyer, and T. DeRose, "Feature-Adaptive GPU Rendering of Catmull-Clark Subdivision Surfaces," *ACM Transactions on Graphics*, vol. 31, no. 1, pp. 6:1–6:11, Jan. 2012. Cited on p. 771, 774, 777, 778, 779

[1280] Nießner, M., C. Loop, and G. Greiner, "Efficient Evaluation of Semi-Smooth Creases in Catmull-Clark Subdivision Surfaces," in *Eurographics 2012—Short Papers*, Eurographics Association, pp. 41–44, May 2012. Cited on p. 777

[1281] Nießner, M., and C. Loop, "Analytic Displacement Mapping Using Hardware Tessellation," *ACM Transactions on Graphics*, vol. 32, no. 3, pp. 26:1–26:9, 2013. Cited on p. 766, 773

[1282] Nießner, M., *Rendering Subdivision Surfaces Using Hardware Tessellation*, PhD thesis, Friedrich-Alexander-Universität Erlangen-Nürnberg, 2013. Cited on p. 777, 779, 781

[1283] Nießner, M., B. Keinert, M. Fisher, M. Stamminger, C. Loop, and H. Schäfer, "Real-Time Rendering Techniques with Hardware Tessellation," *Computer Graphics Forum*, vol. 35, no. 1, pp. 113–137, 2016. Cited on p. 773, 781, 879

[1284] Nishita, Tomoyuki, Thomas W. Sederberg, and Masanori Kakimoto, "Ray Tracing Trimmed Rational Surface Patches," *Computer Graphics (SIGGRAPH '90 Proceedings)*, vol. 24, no. 4, pp. 337–345, Aug. 1990. Cited on p. 967

[1285] Nishita, Tomoyuki, Takao Sirai, Katsumi Tadamura, and Eihachiro Nakamae, "Display of the Earth Taking into Account Atmospheric Scattering," in *SIGGRAPH '93: Proceedings of the 20th Annual Conference on Computer Graphics and Interactive Techniques*, ACM, pp. 175–182, Aug. 1993. Cited on p. 614

[1286] Nöll, Tobias, and Didier Stricker, "Efficient Packing of Arbitrarily Shaped Charts for Automatic Texture Atlas Generation," in *Proceedings of the Twenty-Second Eurographics Conference on Rendering*, Eurographics Association, pp. 1309–1317, 2011. Cited on p. 191

[1287] Northrup, J. D., and Lee Markosian, "Artistic Silhouettes: A Hybrid Approach," in *Proceedings of the 1st International Symposium on Non-photorealistic Animation and Rendering*, ACM, pp. 31–37, June 2000. Cited on p. 668

[1288] Novák, J., and C. Dachsbacher, "Rasterized Bounding Volume Hierarchies," *Computer Graphics Forum*, vol. 31, no. 2, pp. 403–412, 2012. Cited on p. 565

[1289] Novosad, Justin, "Advanced High-Quality Filtering," in Matt Pharr, ed., *GPU Gems 2*, Addison-Wesley, pp. 417–435, 2005. Cited on p. 136, 517, 521

[1290] Nowrouzezahrai, Derek, Patricio Simari, and Eugene Fiume, "Sparse Zonal Harmonic Factorization for Efficient SH Rotation," *ACM Transactions on Graphics*, vol. 31, no. 3, article no. 23, 2012. Cited on p. 401

[1291] Nuebel, Markus, "Hardware-Accelerated Charcoal Rendering," in Wolfgang Engel, ed., *ShaderX³*, Charles River Media, pp. 195–204, 2004. Cited on p. 671

[1292] Nummelin, Niklas, "Frostbite on Mobile," *SIGGRAPH Moving Mobile Graphics course*, Aug. 2015. Cited on p. 903

[1293] NVIDIA Corporation, "Improve Batching Using Texture Atlases," SDK White Paper, 2004. Cited on p. 191

[1294] NVIDIA Corporation, "GPU Programming Exposed: The Naked Truth Behind NVIDIA's Demos," *SIGGRAPH Exhibitor Tech Talk*, Aug. 2005. Cited on p. 531

[1295] NVIDIA Corporation, "Solid Wireframe," White Paper, WP-03014-001_v01, Feb. 2007. Cited on p. 673, 675

[1296] NVIDIA Corporation, "NVIDIA GF100—World's Fastest GPU Delivering Great Gaming Performance with True Geometric Realism," White Paper, 2010. Cited on p. 1031

[1297] NVIDIA Corporation, "NVIDIA GeForce GTX 1080—Gaming Perfected," White Paper, 2016. Cited on p. 929, 1029, 1030, 1032, 1033

[1298] NVIDIA Corporation, "NVIDIA Tesla P100—The Most Advanced Datacenter Accelerator Ever Built," White Paper, 2016. Cited on p. 1029, 1030, 1034

[1299] *NVIDIA GameWorks DirectX Samples*, https://developer.nvidia.com/gameworks-directx -samples. Cited on p. 888, 914

[1300] *NVIDIA SDK 10*, http://developer.download.nvidia.com/SDK/10/direct3d/samples.html, 2008. Cited on p. 48, 255, 558, 647

[1301] *NVIDIA SDK 11*, https://developer.nvidia.com/dx11-samples. Cited on p. 46, 55, 150

[1302] Nystad, J., A. Lassen, A. Pomianowski, S. Ellis, and T. Olson, "Adaptive Scalable Texture Compression," in *Proceedings of the Fourth ACM SIGGRAPH / Eurographics Conference on High-Performance Graphics*, Eurographics Association, pp. 105–114, June 2012. Cited on p. 196

[1303] Oat, Chris, "A Steerable Streak Filter," in Wolfgang Engel, ed., *ShaderX³*, Charles River Media, pp. 341–348, 2004. Cited on p. 520, 524, 525

[1304] Oat, Chris, "Irradiance Volumes for Games," *Game Developers Conference*, Mar. 2005. Cited on p. 487

[1305] Oat, Chris, "Irradiance Volumes for Real-Time Rendering," in Wolfgang Engel, ed., *ShaderX⁵*, Charles River Media, pp. 333–344, 2006. Cited on p. 487

[1306] Oat, Christopher, and Pedro V. Sander, "Ambient Aperture Lighting," *SIGGRAPH Advanced Real-Time Rendering in 3D Graphics and Games course*, Aug. 2006. Cited on p. 466

[1307] Oat, Christopher, and Pedro V. Sander, "Ambient Aperture Lighting," in *Proceedings of the 2007 Symposium on Interactive 3D Graphics and Games*, ACM, pp. 61–64, Apr.–May 2007. Cited on p. 466, 467, 470

[1308] Oat, Christopher, and Thorsten Scheuermann, "Computing Per-Pixel Object Thickness in a Single Render Pass," in Wolfgang Engel, ed., *ShaderX⁶*, Charles River Media, pp. 57–62, 2008. Cited on p. 602

[1309] Obert, Juraj, J. M. P. van Waveren, and Graham Sellers, *SIGGRAPH Virtual Texturing in Software and Hardware course*, Aug. 2012. Cited on p. 867

[1310] Ochiai, H., K. Anjyo, and A. Kimura, *SIGGRAPH An Elementary Introduction to Matrix Exponential for CG course*, July 2016. Cited on p. 102

[1311] *Oculus Best Practices*, Oculus VR, LLC, 2017. Cited on p. 920, 923, 924, 925, 928, 932, 933, 935, 936, 937, 939

[1312] O'Donnell, Yuriy, and Matthäus G. Chajdas, "Tiled Light Trees," *Symposium on Interactive 3D Graphics and Games*, Feb. 2017. Cited on p. 903

[1313] O'Donnell, Yuriy, "FrameGraph: Extensible Rendering Architecture in Frostbite," *Game Developers Conference*, Feb.–Mar. 2017. Cited on p. 514, 520, 812, 814

[1314] Ofek, E., and A. Rappoport, "Interactive Reflections on Curved Objects," in *SIGGRAPH '98: Proceedings of the 25th Annual Conference on Computer Graphics and Interactive Techniques*, ACM, pp. 333–342, July 1998. Cited on p. 505

[1315] Ohlarik, Deron, "Bounding Sphere," *AGI* blog, Feb. 4, 2008. Cited on p. 950

[1316] Ohlarik, Deron, "Precisions, Precisions," *AGI* blog, Sept. 3, 2008. Cited on p. 715

[1317] Olano, M., and T. Greer, "Triangle Scan Conversion Using 2D Homogeneous Coordinates," in *Proceedings of the ACM SIGGRAPH/EUROGRAPHICS Workshop on Graphics Hardware*, ACM, pp. 89–95, Aug. 1997. Cited on p. 832, 999

[1318] Olano, Marc, Bob Kuehne, and Maryann Simmons, "Automatic Shader Level of Detail," in *Graphics Hardware 2003*, Eurographics Association, pp. 7–14, July 2003. Cited on p. 853

[1319] Olano, Marc, "Modified Noise for Evaluation on Graphics Hardware," in *Graphics Hardware 2005*, Eurographics Association, pp. 105–110, July 2005. Cited on p. 199

[1320] Olano, Marc, and Dan Baker, "LEAN Mapping," in *Proceedings of the 2010 ACM SIGGRAPH Symposium on Interactive 3D Graphics and Games*, ACM, pp. 181–188, 2010. Cited on p. 370

[1321] Olano, Marc, Dan Baker, Wesley Griffin, and Joshua Barczak, "Variable Bit Rate GPU Texture Decompression," in *Proceedings of the Twenty-Second Eurographics Symposium on Rendering Techniques*, Eurographics Association, pp. 1299–1308, June 2011. Cited on p. 871

[1322] Olick, Jon, "Segment Buffering," in Matt Pharr, ed., *GPU Gems 2*, Addison-Wesley, pp. 69–73, 2005. Cited on p. 797

[1323] Olick, Jon, "Current Generation Parallelism in Games," *SIGGRAPH Beyond Programmable Shading course*, Aug. 2008. Cited on p. 584

[1324] Oliveira, Manuel M., Gary Bishop, and David McAllister, "Relief Texture Mapping," in *SIGGRAPH '00: Proceedings of the 27th Annual Conference on Computer Graphics and Interactive Techniques*, ACM Press/Addison-Wesley Publishing Co., pp. 359–368, July 2000. Cited on p. 565

[1325] Oliveira, Manuel M., and Fabio Policarpo, "An Efficient Representation for Surface Details," Technical Report RP-351, Universidade Federal do Rio Grande do Sul, Jan. 26, 2005. Cited on p. 220

[1326] Oliveira, Manuel M., and Maicon Brauwers, "Real-Time Refraction Through Deformable Objects," in *Proceedings of the 2007 Symposium on Interactive 3D Graphics and Games*, ACM, pp. 89–96, Apr.–May 2007. Cited on p. 630

[1327] Olsson, O., and U. Assarsson, "Tiled Shading," *Journal of Graphics, GPU, and Game Tools*, vol. 15, no. 4, pp. 235–251, 2011. Cited on p. 882, 894, 895

[1328] Olsson, O., M. Billeter, and U. Assarsson, "Clustered Deferred and Forward Shading," in *High-Performance Graphics 2012*, Eurographics Association, pp. 87–96, June 2012. Cited on p. 899, 900, 901, 903

[1329] Olsson, O., M. Billeter, and U. Assarsson, "Tiled and Clustered Forward Shading: Supporting Transparency and MSAA," in *ACM SIGGRAPH 2012 Talks*, ACM, article no. 37, Aug. 2012. Cited on p. 899, 900

[1330] Olsson, Ola, Markus Billeter, and Erik Sintorn, "More Efficient Virtual Shadow Maps for Many Lights," *IEEE Transactions on Visualization and Computer Graphics*, vol. 21, no. 6, pp. 701–713, June 2015. Cited on p. 247, 882, 904

[1331] Olsson, Ola, "Efficient Shadows from Many Lights," *SIGGRAPH Real-Time Many-Light Management and Shadows with Clustered Shading course*, Aug. 2015. Cited on p. 904, 914

[1332] Olsson, Ola, "Introduction to Real-Time Shading with Many Lights," *SIGGRAPH Real-Time Many-Light Management and Shadows with Clustered Shading course*, Aug. 2015. Cited on p. 886, 892, 893, 900, 904, 905, 914, 1042

[1333] O'Neil, Sean, "Accurate Atmospheric Scattering," in Matt Pharr, ed., *GPU Gems 2*, Addison-Wesley, pp. 253–268, 2005. Cited on p. 614

[1334] van Oosten, Jeremiah, "Volume Tiled Forward Shading," *3D Game Engine Programming* website, July 18, 2017. Cited on p. 900, 914

[1335] *Open 3D Graphics Compression*, Khronos Group, 2013. Cited on p. 712

[1336] *OpenVDB*, http://openvdb.org, 2017. Cited on p. 578

[1337] Oren, Michael, and Shree K. Nayar, "Generalization of Lambert's Reflectance Model," in *SIGGRAPH '94: Proceedings of the 21st Annual Conference on Computer Graphics and Interactive Techniques*, ACM, pp. 239–246, July 1994. Cited on p. 331, 354

[1338] O'Rourke, Joseph, "Finding Minimal Enclosing Boxes," *International Journal of Computer & Information Sciences*, vol. 14, no. 3, pp. 183–199, 1985. Cited on p. 951

[1339] O'Rourke, Joseph, *Computational Geometry in C*, Second Edition, Cambridge University Press, 1998. Cited on p. 685, 686, 967

[1340] Örtegren, Kevin, and Emil Persson, "Clustered Shading: Assigning Lights Using Conservative Rasterization in DirectX 12," in Wolfgang Engel, ed., *GPU Pro⁷*, CRC Press, pp. 43–68, 2016. Cited on p. 901, 914

[1341] van Overveld, C. V. A. M., and B. Wyvill, "An Algorithm for Polygon Subdivision Based on Vertex Normals," in *Computer Graphics International '97*, IEEE Computer Society, pp. 3–12, June 1997. Cited on p. 744

[1342] van Overveld, C. V. A. M., and B. Wyvill, "Phong Normal Interpolation Revisited," *ACM Transactions on Graphics*, vol. 16, no. 4, pp. 397–419, Oct. 1997. Cited on p. 746

[1343] Ownby, John-Paul, Chris Hall, and Rob Hall, "*Toy Story 3: The Video Game*—Rendering Techniques," *SIGGRAPH Advances in Real-Time Rendering in 3D Graphics and Games course*, July 2010. Cited on p. 230, 249, 519

[1344] Paeth, Alan W., ed., *Graphics Gems V*, Academic Press, 1995. Cited on p. 102, 991

[1345] Pagán, Tito, "Efficient UV Mapping of Complex Models," *Game Developer*, vol. 8, no. 8, pp. 28–34, Aug. 2001. Cited on p. 171, 173

[1346] Palandri, Rémi, and Simon Green, "Hybrid Mono Rendering in UE4 and Unity," *Oculus Developer Blog*, Sept. 30, 2016. Cited on p. 928

[1347] Pallister, Kim, "Generating Procedural Clouds Using 3D Hardware," in Mark DeLoura, ed., *Game Programming Gems 2*, Charles River Media, pp. 463–473, 2001. Cited on p. 556

[1348] Pangerl, David, "Quantized Ring Clipping," in Wolfgang Engel, ed., *ShaderX⁶*, Charles River Media, pp. 133–140, 2008. Cited on p. 873

[1349] Pangerl, David, "Practical Thread Rendering for DirectX 9," in Wolfgang Engel, ed., *GPU Pro*, A K Peters, Ltd., pp. 541–546, 2010. Cited on p. 814

[1350] Pantaleoni, Jacopo, "VoxelPipe: A Programmable Pipeline for 3D Voxelization," in *High-Performance Graphics 2011*, Eurographics Association, pp. 99–106, Aug. 2011. Cited on p. 581

[1351] Papathanasis, Andreas, "Dragon Age II DX11 Technology," *Game Developers Conference*, Mar. 2011. Cited on p. 252, 892

[1352] Papavasiliou, D., "Real-Time Grass (and Other Procedural Objects) on Terrain," *Journal of Computer Graphics Techniques*, vol. 4, no. 1, pp. 26–49, 2015. Cited on p. 864

[1353] Parberry, Ian, "Amortized Noise," *Journal of Computer Graphics Techniques*, vol. 3, no. 2, pp. 31–47, 2014. Cited on p. 199

[1354] Parent, R., *Computer Animation: Algorithms & Techniques*, Third Edition, Morgan Kaufmann, 2012. Cited on p. 102

[1355] Paris, Sylvain, Pierre Kornprobst, Jack Tumblin, and Frédo Durand, *SIGGRAPH A Gentle Introduction to Bilateral Filtering and Its Applications course*, Aug. 2007. Cited on p. 518, 520, 543

[1356] Parker, Steven, William Martin, Peter-Pike J. Sloan, Peter Shirley, Brian Smits, and Charles Hansen, "Interactive Ray Tracing," in *Proceedings of the 1999 Symposium on Interactive 3D Graphics*, ACM, pp. 119–134, 1999. Cited on p. 431

[1357] Patney, Anjul, Marco Salvi, Joohwan Kim, Anton Kaplanyan, Chris Wyman, Nir Benty, David Luebke, and Aaron Lefohn, "Towards Foveated Rendering for Gaze-Tracked Virtual Reality," *ACM Transactions on Graphics*, vol. 35, no. 6, article no. 179, 2016. Cited on p. 143, 924, 931, 932

[1358] Patney, Anuj, *SIGGRAPH Applications of Visual Perception to Virtual Reality course*, Aug. 2017. Cited on p. 931, 940

[1359] Patry, Jasmin, "HDR Display Support in *Infamous Second Son* and *Infamous First Light* (Part 1)," *glowybits* blog, Dec. 21, 2016. Cited on p. 287

[1360] Patry, Jasmin, "HDR Display Support in *Infamous Second Son* and *Infamous First Light* (Part 2)," *glowybits* blog, Jan. 4, 2017. Cited on p. 283

[1361] Patterson, J. W., S. G. Hoggar, and J. R. Logie, "Inverse Displacement Mapping," *Computer Graphics Forum*, vol. 10 no. 2, pp. 129–139, 1991. Cited on p. 217

[1362] Paul, Richard P. C., *Robot Manipulators: Mathematics, Programming, and Control*, MIT Press, 1981. Cited on p. 73

[1363] Peercy, Mark S., Marc Olano, John Airey, and P. Jeffrey Ungar, "Interactive Multi-Pass Programmable Shading," in *SIGGRAPH '00: Proceedings of the 27th Annual Conference on Computer Graphics and Interactive Techniques*, ACM Press/Addison-Wesley Publishing Co., pp. 425–432, July 2000. Cited on p. 38

[1364] Pegoraro, Vincent, Mathias Schott, and Steven G. Parker, "An Analytical Approach to Single Scattering for Anisotropic Media and Light Distributions," in *Graphics Interface 2009*, Canadian Information Processing Society, pp. 71–77, 2009. Cited on p. 604

[1365] Pellacini, Fabio, "User-Configurable Automatic Shader Simplification," *ACM Transactions on Graphics (SIGGRAPH 2005)*, vol. 24, no. 3, pp. 445–452, Aug. 2005. Cited on p. 853

[1366] Pellacini, Fabio, Miloš Hašan, and Kavita Bala, "Interactive Cinematic Relighting with Global Illumination," in Hubert Nguyen, ed., *GPU Gems 3*, Addison-Wesley, pp. 183–202, 2007. Cited on p. 547

[1367] Pelzer, Kurt, "Rendering Countless Blades of Waving Grass," in Randima Fernando, ed., *GPU Gems*, Addison-Wesley, pp. 107–121, 2004. Cited on p. 202

[1368] Penner, E., "Shader Amortization Using Pixel Quad Message Passing," in Wolfgang Engel, ed., *GPU Pro²*, A K Peters/CRC Press, pp. 349–367, 2011. Cited on p. 1017, 1018

[1369] Penner, E., "Pre-Integrated Skin Shading," *SIGGRAPH Advances in Real-Time Rendering in Games course*, Aug. 2011. Cited on p. 634

[1370] Perlin, Ken, "An Image Synthesizer," *Computer Graphics (SIGGRAPH '85 Proceedings)*, vol. 19, no. 3, pp. 287–296, July 1985. Cited on p. 198, 199

[1371] Perlin, Ken, and Eric M. Hoffert, "Hypertexture," *Computer Graphics (SIGGRAPH '89 Proceedings)*, vol. 23, no. 3, pp. 253–262, July 1989. Cited on p. 198, 199, 618

[1372] Perlin, Ken, "Improving Noise," *ACM Transactions on Graphics (SIGGRAPH 2002)*, vol. 21, no. 3, pp. 681–682, 2002. Cited on p. 181, 198, 199

[1373] Perlin, Ken, "Implementing Improved Perlin Noise," in Randima Fernando, ed., *GPU Gems*, Addison-Wesley, pp. 73–85, 2004. Cited on p. 199, 620

[1374] Persson, Emil, "Alpha to Coverage," *Humus* blog, June 23, 2005. Cited on p. 204

[1375] Persson, Emil, "Post-Tonemapping Resolve for High-Quality HDR Anti-aliasing in D3D10," in Wolfgang Engel, ed., *ShaderX⁶*, Charles River Media, pp. 161–164, 2008. Cited on p. 142

[1376] Persson, Emil, "GPU Texture Compression," *Humus* blog, Apr. 12, 2008. Cited on p. 870

[1377] Persson, Emil, "Linearize Depth," *Humus* blog, Aug. 2, 2008. Cited on p. 601

[1378] Persson, Emil, "Performance," *Humus* blog, July 22, 2009. Cited on p. 790

[1379] Persson, Emil, "Making It Large, Beautiful, Fast, and Consistent: Lessons Learned Developing *Just Cause 2*," in Wolfgang Engel, ed., *GPU Pro*, A K Peters, Ltd., pp. 571–596, 2010. Cited on p. 114, 556, 558, 715, 882

[1380] Persson, Emil, "Volume Decals," in Wolfgang Engel, ed., *GPU Pro²*, A K Peters/CRC Press, pp. 115–120, 2011. Cited on p. 889, 890

[1381] Persson, Emil, "Creating Vast Game Worlds: Experiences from Avalanche Studios," in *ACM SIGGRAPH 2012 Talks*, ACM, article no. 32, Aug. 2012. Cited on p. 69, 210, 245, 714, 715, 796, 797

[1382] Persson, Emil, "Graphics Gems for Games: Findings from Avalanche Studios," *SIGGRAPH Advances in Real-Time Rendering in Games course*, Aug. 2012. Cited on p. 556, 797, 798

[1383] Persson, Emil, "Low-Level Thinking in High-Level Shading Languages," *Game Developers Conference*, Mar. 2013. Cited on p. 788

[1384] Persson, Emil, "Wire Antialiasing," in Wolfgang Engel, ed., *GPU Pro⁵*, CRC Press, pp. 211–218, 2014. Cited on p. 139

[1385] Persson, Emil, "Low-Level Shader Optimization for Next-Gen and DX11," *Game Developers Conference*, Mar. 2014. Cited on p. 788

[1386] Persson, Emil, "Clustered Shading," *Humus* blog, Mar. 24, 2015. Cited on p. 905, 914

[1387] Persson, Emil, "Practical Clustered Shading," *SIGGRAPH Real-Time Many-Light Management and Shadows with Clustered Shading course*, Aug. 2015. Cited on p. 883, 886, 888, 896, 897, 899, 900, 901, 914

[1388] Persson, Tobias, "Practical Particle Lighting," *Game Developers Conference*, Mar. 2012. Cited on p. 569

[1389] Pesce, Angelo, "Stable Cascaded Shadow Maps—Ideas," *C0DE517E* blog, Mar. 27, 2011. Cited on p. 245

[1390] Pesce, Angelo, "Current-Gen DOF and MB," *C0DE517E* blog, Jan. 4, 2012. Cited on p. 532, 534, 542

[1391] Pesce, Angelo, "33 Milliseconds in the Life of a Space Marine...," *SCRIBD* presentation, Oct. 8, 2012. Cited on p. 238, 245, 250, 518, 527, 542, 889

[1392] Pesce, Angelo, "Smoothen Your Functions," *C0DE517E* blog, Apr. 26, 2014. Cited on p. 200

[1393] Pesce, Angelo, "Notes on Real-Time Renderers," *C0DE517E* blog, Sept. 3, 2014. Cited on p. 882, 884, 889, 913

[1394] Pesce, Angelo, "Notes on G-Buffer Normal Encodings," *C0DE517E* blog, Jan. 24, 2015. Cited on p. 715, 887

[1395] Pesce, Angelo, "Being More Wrong: Parallax Corrected Environment Maps," *C0DE517E* blog, Mar. 28, 2015. Cited on p. 502

[1396] Pesce, Angelo, "Low-Resolution Effects with Depth-Aware Upsampling," *C0DE517E* blog, Feb. 6, 2016. Cited on p. 520

[1397] Pesce, Angelo, "The Real-Time Rendering Continuum: A Taxonomy," *C0DE517E* blog, Aug. 6, 2016. Cited on p. 913

[1398] Peters, Christoph, and Reinhard Klein, "Moment Shadow Mapping," in *Proceedings of the 19th Symposium on Interactive 3D Graphics and Games*, ACM, pp. 7–14, Feb.–Mar. 2015. Cited on p. 256

[1399] Peters, Christoph, Cedrick Münstermann, Nico Wetzstein, and Reinhard Klein, "Improved Moment Shadow Maps for Translucent Occluders, Soft Shadows and Single Scattering," *Journal of Computer Graphics Techniques*, vol. 6, no. 1, pp. 17–67, 2017. Cited on p. 257

[1400] Pettineo, Matt, "How to Fake Bokeh (and Make It Look Pretty Good)," *The Danger Zone* blog, Feb. 28, 2011. Cited on p. 536

[1401] Pettineo, Matt, "Light-Indexed Deferred Rendering," *The Danger Zone* blog, Mar. 31, 2012. Cited on p. 896, 905, 914

[1402] Pettineo, Matt, "Experimenting with Reconstruction Filters for MSAA Resolve," *The Danger Zone* blog, Oct. 28, 2012. Cited on p. 136, 142

[1403] Pettineo, Matt, "A Sampling of Shadow Techniques," *The Danger Zone* blog, Sept. 10, 2013. Cited on p. 54, 238, 245, 250, 265

[1404] Pettineo, Matt, "Shadow Sample Update," *The Danger Zone* blog, Feb. 18, 2015. Cited on p. 256, 265

[1405] Pettineo, Matt, "Rendering the Alternate History of *The Order: 1886*," *SIGGRAPH Advances in Real-Time Rendering in Games course*, Aug. 2015. Cited on p. 141, 142, 143, 245, 256, 257, 803, 896

[1406] Pettineo, Matt, "Stairway to (Programmable Sample Point) Heaven," *The Danger Zone* blog, Sept. 13, 2015. Cited on p. 142, 906

[1407] Pettineo, Matt, "Bindless Texturing for Deferred Rendering and Decals," *The Danger Zone* blog, Mar. 25, 2016. Cited on p. 192, 888, 900, 901, 907

[1408] Pettineo, Matt, "SG Series Part 6: Step into the Baking Lab," *The Danger Zone* blog, Oct. 9, 2016. Cited on p. 398, 477, 536, 540

[1409] Pfister, Hans-Peter, Matthias Zwicker, Jeroen van Barr, and Markus Gross, "Surfels: Surface Elements as Rendering Primitives," in *SIGGRAPH '00: Proceedings of the 27th Annual Conference on Computer Graphics and Interactive Techniques*, ACM Press/Addison-Wesley Publishing Co., pp. 335–342, July 2000. Cited on p. 573

[1410] Phail-Liff, Nathan, Scot Andreason, and Anthony Vitale, "Crafting Victorian London: The Environment Art and Material Pipelines of *The Order: 1886*," in *ACM SIGGRAPH 2015 Talks*, ACM, article no. 59, Aug. 2015. Cited on p. 365

[1411] Pharr, Matt, "Fast Filter Width Estimates with Texture Maps," in Randima Fernando, ed., *GPU Gems*, Addison-Wesley, pp. 417–424, 2004. Cited on p. 185

[1412] Pharr, Matt, and Simon Green, "Ambient Occlusion," in Randima Fernando, ed., *GPU Gems*, Addison-Wesley, pp. 279–292, 2004. Cited on p. 452, 465

[1413] Pharr, Matt, Wenzel Jakob, and Greg Humphreys, *Physically Based Rendering: From Theory to Implementation*, Third Edition, Morgan Kaufmann, 2016. Cited on p. 136, 144, 145, 165, 271, 442, 445, 512, 589, 623, 630

[1414] Phong, Bui Tuong, "Illumination for Computer Generated Pictures," *Communications of the ACM*, vol. 18, no. 6, pp. 311–317, June 1975. Cited on p. 118, 340, 416

[1415] Picott, Kevin P., "Extensions of the Linear and Area Lighting Models," *Computer Graphics*, vol. 18, no. 2, pp. 31–38, Mar. 1992. Cited on p. 385, 387

[1416] Piegl, Les A., and Wayne Tiller, *The NURBS Book*, Second Edition, Springer-Verlag, 1997. Cited on p. 781

[1417] Pineda, Juan, "A Parallel Algorithm for Polygon Rasterization," *Computer Graphics (SIGGRAPH '88 Proceedings)*, vol. 22, no. 4, pp. 17–20, Aug. 1988. Cited on p. 994

[1418] Pines, Josh, "From Scene to Screen," *SIGGRAPH Color Enhancement and Rendering in Film and Game Production course*, July 2010. Cited on p. 285, 289

[1419] Piponi, Dan, and George Borshukov, "Seamless Texture Mapping of Subdivision Surfaces by Model Pelting and Texture Blending," in *SIGGRAPH '00: Proceedings of the 27th Annual Conference on Computer Graphics and Interactive Techniques*, ACM Press/Addison-Wesley Publishing Co., pp. 471–478, July 2000. Cited on p. 767

[1420] Placeres, Frank Puig, "Overcoming Deferred Shading Drawbacks," in Wolfgang Engel, ed., *ShaderX^5*, Charles River Media, pp. 115–130, 2006. Cited on p. 886, 887

[1421] Pletinckx, Daniel, "Quaternion Calculus as a Basic Tool in Computer Graphics," *The Visual Computer*, vol. 5, no. 1, pp. 2–13, 1989. Cited on p. 102

[1422] Pochanayon, Adisak, "Capturing and Visualizing RealTime GPU Performance in *Mortal Kombat X*," *Game Developers Conference*, Mar. 2016. Cited on p. 790

[1423] Pohl, Daniel, Gregory S. Johnson, and Timo Bolkart, "Improved Pre-Warping for Wide Angle, Head Mounted Displays," in *Proceedings of the 19th ACM Symposium on Virtual Reality Software and Technology*, ACM, pp. 259–262, Oct. 2013. Cited on p. 628, 925, 926

[1424] Policarpo, Fabio, Manuel M. Oliveira, and João L. D. Comba, "Real-Time Relief Mapping on Arbitrary Polygonal Surfaces," in *Proceedings of the 2005 Symposium on Interactive 3D Graphics and Games*, ACM, pp. 155–162, Apr. 2005. Cited on p. 217, 218

[1425] Policarpo, Fabio, and Manuel M. Oliveira, "Relief Mapping of Non-Height-Field Surface Details," in *Proceedings of the 2006 Symposium on Interactive 3D Graphics and Games*, ACM, pp. 55–62, Mar. 2006. Cited on p. 566

[1426] Policarpo, Fabio, and Manuel M. Oliveira, "Relaxed Cone Stepping for Relief Mapping," in Hubert Nguyen, ed., *GPU Gems 3*, Addison-Wesley, pp. 409–428, 2007. Cited on p. 219

[1427] Pool, J., A. Lastra, and M. Singh, "Lossless Compression of Variable-Precision Floating-Point Buffers on GPUs," in *Proceedings of the ACM SIGGRAPH Symposium on Interactive 3D Graphics and Games*, ACM, pp. 47–54, Mar. 2012. Cited on p. 1009, 1016

[1428] Porcino, Nick, "Lost Planet Parallel Rendering," *Meshula.net* website, Oct. 2007. Cited on p. 538, 647

[1429] Porter, Thomas, and Tom Duff, "Compositing Digital Images," *Computer Graphics (SIGGRAPH '84 Proceedings)*, vol. 18, no. 3, pp. 253–259, July 1984. Cited on p. 149, 151, 153

[1430] Pötzsch, Christian, "Speeding up GPU Barrel Distortion Correction in Mobile VR," *Imagination Blog*, June 15, 2016. Cited on p. 926

[1431] Poynton, Charles, *Digital Video and HD: Algorithms and Interfaces*, Second Edition, Morgan Kaufmann, 2012. Cited on p. 161, 163, 166

[1432] Pranckevičius, Aras, "Compact Normal Storage for Small G-Buffers," *Aras' blog*, Mar. 25, 2010. Cited on p. 715

[1433] Pranckevičius, Aras, and Renaldas Zioma, "Fast Mobile Shaders," *SIGGRAPH Studio Talk*, Aug. 2011. Cited on p. 549, 803, 814

[1434] Pranckevičius, Aras, "Rough Sorting by Depth," *Aras' blog*, Jan. 16, 2014. Cited on p. 803

[1435] Pranckevičius, Aras, Jens Fursund, and Sam Martin, "Advanced Lighting Techniques in Unity," *Unity DevDay, Game Developers Conference*, Mar. 2014. Cited on p. 482

[1436] Pranckevičius, Aras, "Cross Platform Shaders in 2014," *Aras' blog*, Mar. 28, 2014. Cited on p. 129

[1437] Pranckevičius, Aras, "Shader Compilation in Unity 4.5," *Aras' blog*, May 5, 2014. Cited on p. 129

[1438] Pranckevičius, Aras, "Porting Unity to New APIs," *SIGGRAPH An Overview of Next Generation APIs course*, Aug. 2015. Cited on p. 40, 806, 814

[1439] Pranckevičius, Aras, "Every Possible Scalability Limit Will Be Reached," *Aras' blog*, Feb. 5, 2017. Cited on p. 128

[1440] Pranckevičius, Aras, "Font Rendering Is Getting Interesting," *Aras' blog*, Feb. 15, 2017. Cited on p. 677, 679

[1441] Praun, Emil, Adam Finkelstein, and Hugues Hoppe, "Lapped Textures," in *SIGGRAPH '00: Proceedings of the 27th Annual Conference on Computer Graphics and Interactive Techniques*, ACM Press/Addison-Wesley Publishing Co., pp. 465–470, July 2000. Cited on p. 671

[1442] Praun, Emil, Hugues Hoppe, Matthew Webb, and Adam Finkelstein, "Real-Time Hatching," in *SIGGRAPH '01 Proceedings of the 28th Annual Conference on Computer Graphics and Interactive Techniques*, ACM, pp. 581–586, Aug. 2001. Cited on p. 670

[1443] Preetham, Arcot J., Peter Shirley, and Brian Smitsc, "A Practical Analytic Model for Daylight," in *SIGGRAPH '99: Proceedings of the 26th Annual Conference on Computer Graphics and Interactive Techniques*, ACM Press/Addison-Wesley Publishing Co., pp. 91–100, Aug. 1999. Cited on p. 614

[1444] Preparata, F. P., and M. I. Shamos, *Computational Geometry: An Introduction*, Springer-Verlag, 1985. Cited on p. 686, 967

[1445] Preshing, Jeff, "How Ubisoft Montreal Develops Games for Multicore—Before and After C++11," *CppCon 2014*, Sept. 2014. Cited on p. 812, 815

[1446] Press, William H., Saul A. Teukolsky, William T. Vetterling, and Brian P. Flannery, *Numerical Recipes in C*, Cambridge University Press, 1992. Cited on p. 948, 951, 957

[1447] Proakis, John G., and Dimitris G. Manolakis, *Digital Signal Processing: Principles, Algorithms, and Applications*, Fourth Edition, Pearson, 2006. Cited on p. 130, 133, 135, 136

[1448] Purnomo, Budirijanto, Jonathan Bilodeau, Jonathan D. Cohen, and Subodh Kumar, "Hardware-Compatible Vertex Compression Using Quantization and Simplification," in *Graphics Hardware 2005*, Eurographics Association, pp. 53–61, July 2005. Cited on p. 713

[1449] Quidam, *Jade2 model*, published by wismo, http://www.3dvia.com/wismo, 2017. Cited on p. 653

[1450] Quílez, Íñigo, "Rendering Worlds with Two Triangles with Ray Tracing on the GPU in 4096 bytes," *NVScene*, Aug. 2008. Cited on p. 454, 594, 752

[1451] Quílez, Íñigo, "Improved Texture Interpolation," *iquilezles.org*, 2010. Cited on p. 180

[1452] Quílez, Íñigo, "Correct Frustum Culling," *iquilezles.org*, 2013. Cited on p. 986

[1453] Quílez, Íñigo, "Efficient Stereo and VR Rendering," in Wolfgang Engel, ed., *GPU Zen*, Black Cat Publishing, pp. 241–251, 2017. Cited on p. 927, 928

[1454] Ragan-Kelley, Jonathan, Charlie Kilpatrick, Brian W. Smith, and Doug Epps, "The Lightspeed Automatic Interactive Lighting Preview System," *ACM Transactions on Graphics (SIGGRAPH 2007)*, vol. 26, no. 3, 25:1–25:11, July 2007. Cited on p. 547

[1455] Ragan-Kelley, Jonathan, Jaakko Lehtinen, Jiawen Chen, Michael Doggett, and Frédo Durand, "Decoupled Sampling for Graphics Pipelines," *ACM Transactions on Graphics*, vol. 30, no. 3, pp. 17:1–17:17, May 2011. Cited on p. 910

[1456] Rákos, Daniel, "Massive Number of Shadow-Casting Lights with Layered Rendering," in Patrick Cozzi & Christophe Riccio, eds., *OpenGL Insights*, CRC Press, pp. 259–278, 2012. Cited on p. 246

[1457] Rákos, Daniel, "Programmable Vertex Pulling," in Patrick Cozzi & Christophe Riccio, eds., *OpenGL Insights*, CRC Press, pp. 293–301, 2012. Cited on p. 703

[1458] Ramamoorthi, Ravi, and Pat Hanrahan, "An Efficient Representation for Irradiance Environment Maps," in *SIGGRAPH '01 Proceedings of the 28th Annual Conference on Computer Graphics and Interactive Techniques*, ACM, pp. 497–500, Aug. 2001. Cited on p. 425, 427, 428, 429, 430

[1459] Ramamoorthi, Ravi, and Pat Hanrahan, "Frequency Space Environment Map Rendering," *ACM Transactions on Graphics*, vol. 21, no. 3, pp. 517–526, 2002. Cited on p. 431

[1460] Raskar, Ramesh, and Michael Cohen, "Image Precision Silhouette Edges," in *Proceedings of the 1999 Symposium on Interactive 3D Graphics*, ACM, pp. 135–140, 1999. Cited on p. 657, 658

[1461] Raskar, Ramesh, "Hardware Support for Non-photorealistic Rendering," in *Graphics Hardware 2001*, Eurographics Association, pp. 41–46, Aug. 2001. Cited on p. 658, 660

[1462] Raskar, Ramesh, and Jack Tumblin, *Computational Photography: Mastering New Techniques for Lenses, Lighting, and Sensors*, A K Peters, Ltd., 2007. Cited on p. 549

[1463] Rasmusson, J., J. Hasselgren, and T. Akenine-Möller, "Exact and Error-Bounded Approximate Color Buffer Compression and Decompression," in *Graphics Hardware 2007*, Eurographics Association, pp. 41–48, Aug. 2007. Cited on p. 997, 1009

[1464] Rasmusson, J., J. Ström, and T. Akenine-Möller, "Error-Bounded Lossy Compression of Floating-Point Color Buffers Using Quadtree Decomposition," *The Visual Computer*, vol. 26, no. 1, pp. 17–30, 2009. Cited on p. 1009

[1465] Ratcliff, John W., "Sphere Trees for Fast Visibility Culling, Ray Tracing, and Range Searching," in Mark DeLoura, ed., *Game Programming Gems 2*, Charles River Media, pp. 384–387, 2001. Cited on p. 821

[1466] Rauwendaal, Randall, and Mike Bailey, "Hybrid Computational Voxelization Using the Graphics Pipeline," *Journal of Computer Graphics Techniques*, vol. 2, no. 1, pp. 15–37, 2013. Cited on p. 582

[1467] Ray, Nicolas, Vincent Nivoliers, Sylvain Lefebvre, and Bruno Lévy, "Invisible Seams," in *Proceedings of the 21st Eurographics Conference on Rendering*, Eurographics Association, pp. 1489–1496, June 2010. Cited on p. 486

[1468] Reddy, Martin, *Perceptually Modulated Level of Detail for Virtual Environments*, PhD thesis, University of Edinburgh, 1997. Cited on p. 864

[1469] Reed, Nathan, "Ambient Occlusion Fields and Decals in *inFAMOUS 2*," *Game Developers Conference*, Mar. 2012. Cited on p. 452

[1470] Reed, Nathan, "Quadrilateral Interpolation, Part 1," *Nathan Reed* blog, May 26, 2012. Cited on p. 688

[1471] Reed, Nathan, and Dean Beeler, "VR Direct: How NVIDIA Technology Is Improving the VR Experience," *Game Developers Conference*, Mar. 2015. Cited on p. 928, 936, 937, 938

[1472] Reed, Nathan, "Depth Precision Visualized," *Nathan Reed* blog, July 3, 2015. Cited on p. 100, 1014

[1473] Reed, Nathan, "GameWorks VR," *SIGGRAPH*, Aug. 2015. Cited on p. 927, 928, 929

[1474] Reeves, William T., "Particle Systems—A Technique for Modeling a Class of Fuzzy Objects," *ACM Transactions on Graphics*, vol. 2, no. 2, pp. 91–108, Apr. 1983. Cited on p. 567

[1475] Reeves, William T., David H. Salesin, and Robert L. Cook, "Rendering Antialiased Shadows with Depth Maps," *Computer Graphics (SIGGRAPH '87 Proceedings)*, vol. 21, no. 4, pp. 283–291, July 1987. Cited on p. 247

[1476] Rege, Ashu, "DX11 Effects in *Metro 2033: The Last Refuge*," *Game Developers Conference*, Mar. 2010. Cited on p. 535

[1477] Reimer, Jeremy, "Valve Goes Multicore," *ars technica* website, Nov. 5, 2006. Cited on p. 812

[1478] Reinhard, Erik, Mike Stark, Peter Shirley, and James Ferwerda, "Photographic Tone Reproduction for Digital Images," *ACM Transactions on Graphics (SIGGRAPH 2002)*, vol. 21, no. 3, pp. 267–276, July 2002. Cited on p. 286, 288

[1479] Reinhard, Erik, Greg Ward, Sumanta Pattanaik, and Paul Debevec, *High Dynamic Range Imaging: Acquisition, Display, and Image-Based Lighting*, Morgan Kaufmann, 2006. Cited on p. 406, 435

[1480] Reinhard, Erik, Erum Arif Khan, Ahmet Oguz Akyüz, and Garrett Johnson, *Color Imaging: Fundamentals and Applications*, A K Peters, Ltd., 2008. Cited on p. 291

[1481] Reis, Aurelio, "Per-Pixel Lit, Light Scattering Smoke," in Wolfgang Engel, ed., *ShaderX^5*, Charles River Media, pp. 287–294, 2006. Cited on p. 569

[1482] Ren, Zhong Ren, Rui Wang, John Snyder, Kun Zhou, Xinguo Liu, Bo Sun, Peter-Pike Sloan, Hujun Bao, Qunsheng Peng, and Baining Guo, "Real-Time Soft Shadows in Dynamic Scenes Using Spherical Harmonic Exponentiation," *ACM Transactions on Graphics (SIGGRAPH 2006)*, vol. 25, no. 3, pp. 977–986, July 2006. Cited on p. 456, 458, 467

[1483] Reshetov, Alexander, "Morphological Antialiasing," in *High-Performance Graphics 2009*, Eurographics Association, pp. 109–116, Aug. 2009. Cited on p. 146

[1484] Reshetov, Alexander, "Reducing Aliasing Artifacts through Resampling," in *High-Performance Graphics 2012*, Eurographics Association, pp. 77–86, June 2012. Cited on p. 148

[1485] Reshetov, Alexander, and David Luebke, "Infinite Resolution Textures," in *High-Performance Graphics 2016*, Eurographics Association, pp. 139–150, June 2016. Cited on p. 677

[1486] Reshetov, Alexander, and Jorge Jimenez, "MLAA from 2009 to 2017," *High-Performance Graphics* research impact retrospective, July 2017. Cited on p. 143, 146, 148, 165

[1487] Reuter, Patrick, Johannes Behr, and Marc Alexa, "An Improved Adjacency Data Structure for Fast Triangle Stripping," *journal of graphics tools*, vol. 10, no. 2, pp. 41–50, 2016. Cited on p. 692

[1488] Revet, Burke, and Jon Riva, "Immense Zombie Horde Variety and Slicing," *Game Developers Conference*, Mar. 2014. Cited on p. 366

[1489] Revie, Donald, "Implementing Fur Using Deferred Shading," in Wolfgang Engel, ed., *GPU Pro^2*, A K Peters/CRC Press, pp. 57–75, 2011. Cited on p. 424

[1490] Rhodes, Graham, "Fast, Robust Intersection of 3D Line Segments," in Mark DeLoura, ed., *Game Programming Gems 2*, Charles River Media, pp. 191–204, 2001. Cited on p. 990

[1491] Ribardière, Mickaël, Benjamin Bringier, Daniel Meneveaux, and Lionel Simonot, "STD: Student's t-Distribution of Slopes for Microfacet Based BSDFs," *Computer Graphics Forum*, vol. 36, no. 2, pp. 421–429, 2017. Cited on p. 343

[1492] Rideout, Philip, "Silhouette Extraction," *The Little Grasshopper* blog, Oct. 24, 2010. Cited on p. 47, 668

[1493] Rideout, Philip, and Dirk Van Gelder, "An Introduction to Tessellation Shaders," in Patrick Cozzi & Christophe Riccio, eds., *OpenGL Insights*, CRC Press, pp. 87–104, 2012. Cited on p. 44, 46

[1494] Riguer, Guennadi, "Performance Optimization Techniques for ATI Graphics Hardware with DirectX 9.0," ATI White Paper, 2002. Cited on p. 702

[1495] Riguer, Guennadi, "LiquidVR™ Today and Tomorrow," *Game Developers Conference*, Mar. 2016. Cited on p. 928

[1496] Ring, Kevin, "Rendering the Whole Wide World on the World Wide Web," Lecture at Analytical Graphics, Inc., Dec. 2013. Cited on p. 708

[1497] Risser, Eric, Musawir Shah, and Sumanta Pattanaik, "Faster Relief Mapping Using the Secant Method," *journal of graphics tools*, vol. 12, no. 3, pp. 17–24, 2007. Cited on p. 218

[1498] Ritschel, T., T. Grosch, M. H. Kim, H.-P. Seidel, C. Dachsbacher, and J. Kautz, "Imperfect Shadow Maps for Efficient Computation of Indirect Illumination," *ACM Transactions on Graphics*, vol. 27, no. 5, pp. 129:1–129:8, 2008. Cited on p. 492, 578

[1499] Ritschel, Tobias, Thorsten Grosch, and Hans-Peter Seidel, "Approximating Dynamic Global Illumination in Image Space," in *Proceedings of the 2009 Symposium on Interactive 3D Graphics and Games*, ACM, pp. 75–82, 2009. Cited on p. 496

[1500] Ritter, Jack, "An Efficient Bounding Sphere," in Andrew S. Glassner, ed., *Graphics Gems*, Academic Press, pp. 301–303, 1990. Cited on p. 950

[1501] Robbins, Steven, and Sue Whitesides, "On the Reliability of Triangle Intersection in 3D," in *International Conference on Computational Science and Its Applications*, Springer, pp. 923–930, 2003. Cited on p. 974

[1502] Robinson, Alfred C., "On the Use of Quaternions in Simulation of Rigid-Body Motion," Technical Report 58-17, Wright Air Development Center, Dec. 1958. Cited on p. 76

[1503] Rockenbeck, Bill, "The *inFAMOUS: Second Son* Particle System Architecture," *Game Developers Conference*, Mar. 2014. Cited on p. 568, 569, 571

[1504] Rockwood, Alyn, and Peter Chambers, *Interactive Curves and Surfaces: A Multimedia Tutorial on CAGD*, Morgan Kaufmann, 1996. Cited on p. 718

[1505] Rogers, David F., *Procedural Elements for Computer Graphics*, Second Edition, McGraw-Hill, 1998. Cited on p. 685

[1506] Rogers, David F., *An Introduction to NURBS: With Historical Perspective*, Morgan Kaufmann, 2000. Cited on p. 781

[1507] Rohleder, Pawel, and Maciej Jamrozik, "Sunlight with Volumetric Light Rays," in Wolfgang Engel, ed., *ShaderX^6*, Charles River Media, pp. 325–330, 2008. Cited on p. 604

[1508] Rohlf, J., and J. Helman, "IRIS Performer: A High Performance Multiprocessing Toolkit for Real-Time 3D Graphics," in *SIGGRAPH '94: Proceedings of the 21st Annual Conference on Computer Graphics and Interactive Techniques*, ACM, pp. 381–394, July 1994. Cited on p. 807, 809, 861

[1509] Rosado, Gilberto, "Motion Blur as a Post-Processing Effect," in Hubert Nguyen, ed., *GPU Gems 3*, Addison-Wesley, pp. 575–581, 2007. Cited on p. 538

[1510] Rossignac, J., and M. van Emmerik, M., "Hidden Contours on a Frame-Buffer," in *Proceedings of the Seventh Eurographics Conference on Graphics Hardware*, Eurographics Association, pp. 188–204, Sept. 1992. Cited on p. 657

[1511] Rossignac, Jarek, and Paul Borrel, "Multi-resolution 3D Approximations for Rendering Complex Scenes," in Bianca Falcidieno & Tosiyasu L. Kunii, eds. *Modeling in Computer Graphics: Methods and Applications*, Springer-Verlag, pp. 455–465, 1993. Cited on p. 709

[1512] Rost, Randi J., Bill Licea-Kane, Dan Ginsburg, John Kessenich, Barthold Lichtenbelt, Hugh Malan, and Mike Weiblen, *OpenGL Shading Language*, Third Edition, Addison-Wesley, 2009. Cited on p. 55, 200

[1513] Roth, Marcus, and Dirk Reiners, "Sorted Pipeline Image Composition," in *Eurographics Symposium on Parallel Graphics and Visualization*, Eurographics Association, pp. 119–126, 2006. Cited on p. 1020, 1022

[1514] Röttger, Stefan, Alexander Irion, and Thomas Ertl, "Shadow Volumes Revisited," *Journal of WSCG (10th International Conference in Central Europe on Computer Graphics, Visualization and Computer Vision)*, vol. 10, no. 1–3, pp. 373–379, Feb. 2002. Cited on p. 232

[1515] Rougier, Nicolas P., "Higher Quality 2D Text Rendering," *Journal of Computer Graphics Techniques*, vol. 1, no. 4, pp. 50–64, 2013. Cited on p. 676, 677

[1516] Rougier, Nicolas P., "Shader-Based Antialiased, Dashed, Stroked Polylines," *Journal of Computer Graphics Techniques*, vol. 2, no. 2, pp. 105–121, 2013. Cited on p. 669

[1517] de Rousiers, Charles, and Matt Pettineo, "Depth of Field with Bokeh Rendering," in Patrick Cozzi & Christophe Riccio, eds., *OpenGL Insights*, CRC Press, pp. 205–218, 2012. Cited on p. 531, 536

[1518] Ruijters, Daniel, Bart M. ter Haar Romeny, and Paul Suetens, "Efficient GPU-Based Texture Interpolation Using Uniform B-Splines," *Journal of Graphics, GPU, and Game Tools*, vol. 13, no. 4, pp. 61–69, 2008. Cited on p. 180, 733, 734

[1519] Rusinkiewicz, Szymon, and Marc Levoy, "QSplat: A Multiresolution Point Rendering System for Large Meshes," in *SIGGRAPH '00: Proceedings of the 27th Annual Conference on Computer Graphics and Interactive Techniques*, ACM Press/Addison-Wesley Publishing Co., pp. 343–352, July 2000. Cited on p. 573

[1520] Rusinkiewicz, Szymon, Michael Burns, and Doug DeCarlo, "Exaggerated Shading for Depicting Shape and Detail," *ACM Transactions on Graphics*, vol. 25, no. 3, pp. 1199–1205, July 2006. Cited on p. 654

[1521] Rusinkiewicz, Szymon, Forrester Cole, Doug DeCarlo, and Adam Finkelstein, *SIGGRAPH Line Drawings from 3D Models course*, Aug. 2008. Cited on p. 656, 678

[1522] Ruskin, Elan, "Streaming Sunset Overdrive's Open World," *Game Developers Conference*, Mar. 2015. Cited on p. 871

[1523] Ryu, David, "500 Million and Counting: Hair Rendering on *Ratatouille*," Pixar Technical Memo 07-09, May 2007. Cited on p. 648

[1524] "S3TC DirectX 6.0 Standard Texture Compression," *S3 Inc.* website, 1998. Cited on p. 192

[1525] Sadeghi, Iman, Heather Pritchett, Henrik Wann Jensen, and Rasmus Tamstorf, "An Artist Friendly Hair Shading System," in *ACM SIGGRAPH 2010 Papers*, ACM, article no. 56, July 2010. Cited on p. 359, 644

[1526] Sadeghi, Iman, Oleg Bisker, Joachim De Deken, and Henrik Wann Jensen, "A Practical Microcylinder Appearance Model for Cloth Rendering," *ACM Transactions on Graphics*, vol. 32, no. 2, pp. 14:1–14:12, Apr. 2013. Cited on p. 359

[1527] Safdar, Muhammad, Guihua Cui, Youn Jin Kim, and Ming Ronnier Luo, "Perceptually Uniform Color Space for Image Signals Including High Dynamic Range and Wide Gamut," *Optics Express*, vol. 25, no. 13, pp. 15131–15151, June 2017. Cited on p. 276

[1528] Saito, Takafumi, and Tokiichiro Takahashi, "Comprehensible Rendering of 3-D Shapes," *Computer Graphics (SIGGRAPH '90 Proceedings)*, vol. 24, no. 4, pp. 197–206, Aug. 1990. Cited on p. 661, 883, 884

[1529] Salvi, Marco, "Rendering Filtered Shadows with Exponential Shadow Maps," in Wolfgang Engel, ed., *ShaderX^6*, Charles River Media, pp. 257–274, 2008. Cited on p. 256

[1530] Salvi, Marco, "Probabilistic Approaches to Shadow Maps Filtering," *Game Developers Conference*, Feb. 2008. Cited on p. 256

[1531] Salvi, Marco, Kiril Vidimče, Andrew Lauritzen, and Aaron Lefohn, "Adaptive Volumetric Shadow Maps," *Computer Graphics Forum*, vol. 29, no. 4, pp. 1289–1296, 2010. Cited on p. 258, 570

[1532] Salvi, Marco, and Karthik Vaidyanathan, "Multi-layer Alpha Blending," in *Proceedings of the 18th ACM SIGGRAPH Symposium on Interactive 3D Graphics and Games*, ACM, pp. 151–158, 2014. Cited on p. 156, 642

[1533] Salvi, Marco, "An Excursion in Temporal Supersampling," *Game Developers Conference*, Mar. 2016. Cited on p. 143

[1534] Salvi, Marco, "Deep Learning: The Future of Real-Time Rendering?," *SIGGRAPH Open Problems in Real-Time Rendering course*, Aug. 2017. Cited on p. 1043

[1535] Samet, Hanan, *Applications of Spatial Data Structures: Computer Graphics, Image Processing and GIS*, Addison-Wesley, 1989. Cited on p. 825

[1536] Samet, Hanan, *The Design and Analysis of Spatial Data Structures*, Addison-Wesley, 1989. Cited on p. 825

[1537] Samosky, Joseph, *SectionView: A System for Interactively Specifying and Visualizing Sections through Three-Dimensional Medical Image Data*, MSc thesis, Department of Electrical Engineering and Computer Science, Massachusetts Institute of Technology, 1993. Cited on p. 969

[1538] Sanchez, Bonet, Jose Luis, and Tomasz Stachowiak, "Solving Some Common Problems in a Modern Deferred Rendering Engine," *Develop* conference, July 2012. Cited on p. 570

[1539] Sander, Pedro V., Xianfeng Gu, Steven J. Gortler, Hugues Hoppe, and John Snyder, "Silhouette Clipping," in *SIGGRAPH '00: Proceedings of the 27th Annual Conference on Computer Graphics and Interactive Techniques*, ACM Press/Addison-Wesley Publishing Co., pp. 327–334, July 2000. Cited on p. 667

[1540] Sander, Pedro V., John Snyder, Steven J. Gortler, and Hugues Hoppe, "Texture Mapping Progressive Meshes," in *SIGGRAPH '01 Proceedings of the 28th Annual Conference on Computer Graphics and Interactive Techniques*, ACM, pp. 409–416, Aug. 2001. Cited on p. 710

[1541] Sander, Pedro V., David Gosselin, and Jason L. Mitchell, "Real-Time Skin Rendering on Graphics Hardware," in *ACM SIGGRAPH 2004 Sketches*, ACM, p. 148, Aug. 2004. Cited on p. 635

[1542] Sander, Pedro V., Natalya Tatarchuk, and Jason L. Mitchell, "Explicit Early-Z Culling for Efficient Fluid Flow Simulation," in Wolfgang Engel, ed., *ShaderX^5*, Charles River Media, pp. 553–564, 2006. Cited on p. 53, 1016

[1543] Sander, Pedro V., and Jason L. Mitchell, "Progressive Buffers: View-Dependent Geometry and Texture LOD Rendering," *SIGGRAPH Advanced Real-Time Rendering in 3D Graphics and Games course*, Aug. 2006. Cited on p. 860

[1544] Sander, Pedro V., Diego Nehab, and Joshua Barczak, "Fast Triangle Reordering for Vertex Locality and Reduced Overdraw," *ACM Transactions on Graphics*, vol. 26, no. 3, pp. 89:1–89:9, 2007. Cited on p. 701

[1545] Sathe, Rahul P., "Variable Precision Pixel Shading for Improved Power Efficiency," in Eric Lengyel, ed., *Game Engine Gems 3*, CRC Press, pp. 101–109, 2016. Cited on p. 814

[1546] Scandolo, Leonardo, Pablo Bauszat, and Elmar Eisemann, "Merged Multiresolution Hierarchies for Shadow Map Compression," *Computer Graphics Forum*, vol. 35, no. 7, pp. 383–390, 2016. Cited on p. 264

[1547] Schäfer, H., J. Raab, B. Keinert, M. Meyer, M. Stamminger, and M. Nießner, "Dynamic Feature-Adaptive Subdivision," in *Proceedings of the 19th Symposium on Interactive 3D Graphics and Games*, ACM, pp. 31–38, 2014. Cited on p. 779

[1548] Schander, Thomas, and Clemens Musterle, "Real-Time Path Tracing Using a Hybrid Deferred Approach," *GPU Technology Conference*, Oct. 18, 2017. Cited on p. 510

[1549] Schaufler, G., and W. Stürzlinger, "A Three Dimensional Image Cache for Virtual Reality," *Computer Graphics Forum*, vol. 15, no. 3, pp. 227–236, 1996. Cited on p. 561, 562

[1550] Schaufler, Gernot, "Nailboards: A Rendering Primitive for Image Caching in Dynamic Scenes," in *Rendering Techniques '97*, Springer, pp. 151–162, June 1997. Cited on p. 564, 565

[1551] Schaufler, Gernot, "Per-Object Image Warping with Layered Impostors," in *Rendering Techniques '98*, Springer, pp. 145–156, June–July 1998. Cited on p. 565

[1552] Scheib, Vincent, "Parallel Rendering with DirectX Command Buffers," *Beautiful Pixels* blog, July 22, 2008. Cited on p. 814

[1553] Scheiblauer, Claus, *Interactions with Gigantic Point Clouds*, PhD thesis, Vienna University of Technology, 2016. Cited on p. 575

[1554] Schertenleib, Sebastien, "A Multithreaded 3D Renderer," in Eric Lengyel, ed., *Game Engine Gems*, Jones and Bartlett, pp. 139–147, 2010. Cited on p. 814

[1555] Scherzer, Daniel, "Robust Shadow Maps for Large Environments," *Central European Seminar on Computer Graphics*, May 2005. Cited on p. 242

[1556] Scherzer, D., S. Jeschke, and M. Wimmer, "Pixel-Correct Shadow Maps with Temporal Reprojection and Shadow Test Confidence," in *Proceedings of the 18th Eurographics Symposium on Rendering Techniques*, Eurographics Association, pp. 45–50, 2007. Cited on p. 522, 523

[1557] Scherzer, D., and M. Wimmer, "Frame Sequential Interpolation for Discrete Level-of-Detail Rendering," *Computer Graphics Forum*, vol. 27, no. 4, 1175–1181, 2008. Cited on p. 856

[1558] Scherzer, Daniel, Michael Wimmer, and Werner Purgathofer, "A Survey of Real-Time Hard Shadow Mapping Methods," *Computer Graphics Forum*, vol. 30, no. 1, pp. 169–186, 2011. Cited on p. 265

[1559] Scherzer, D., L. Yang, O. Mattausch, D. Nehab, P. Sander, M. Wimmer, and E. Eisemann, "A Survey on Temporal Coherence Methods in Real-Time Rendering," *Computer Graphics Forum*, vol. 31, no. 8, pp. 2378–2408, 2011. Cited on p. 523

[1560] Scheuermann, Thorsten, "Practical Real-Time Hair Rendering and Shading," in *ACM SIGGRAPH 2004 Sketches*, ACM, p. 147, Aug. 2004. Cited on p. 641, 644, 645

[1561] Schied, Christoph, and Carsten Dachsbacher, "Deferred Attribute Interpolation for Memory-Efficient Deferred Shading," in *Proceedings of the 7th Conference on High-Performance Graphics*, ACM, pp. 43–49, Aug. 2015. Cited on p. 907

[1562] Schied, Christoph, and Carsten Dachsbacher, "Deferred Attribute Interpolation Shading," in Wolfgang Engel, ed., *GPU Pro⁷*, CRC Press, pp. 83–96, 2016. Cited on p. 907

[1563] Schied, Christoph, Anton Kaplanyan, Chris Wyman, Anjul Patney, Chakravarty R. Alla Chaitanya, John Burgess, Shiqiu Liu, Carsten Dachsbacher, and Aaron Lefohn, "Spatiotemporal Variance-Guided Filtering: Real-Time Reconstruction for Path-Traced Global Illumination," *High Performance Graphics*, July 2017. Cited on p. 511

[1564] Schilling, Andreas, G. Knittel, and Wolfgang Straßer, "Texram: A Smart Memory for Texturing," *IEEE Computer Graphics and Applications*, vol. 16, no. 3, pp. 32–41, May 1996. Cited on p. 189

[1565] Schilling, Andreas, "Antialiasing of Environment Maps," *Computer Graphics Forum*, vol. 20, no. 1, pp. 5–11, 2001. Cited on p. 372

[1566] Schlag, John, "Using Geometric Constructions to Interpolate Orientations with Quaternions," in James Arvo, ed., *Graphics Gems II*, Academic Press, pp. 377–380, 1991. Cited on p. 102

[1567] Schlag, John, "Fast Embossing Effects on Raster Image Data," in Paul S. Heckbert, ed., *Graphics Gems IV*, Academic Press, pp. 433–437, 1994. Cited on p. 211

[1568] Schlick, Christophe, "An Inexpensive BRDF Model for Physically Based Rendering," *Computer Graphics Forum*, vol. 13, no. 3, pp. 149–162, 1994. Cited on p. 320, 351

[1569] Schmalstieg, Dieter, and Robert F. Tobler, "Fast Projected Area Computation for Three-Dimensional Bounding Boxes," *journal of graphics tools*, vol. 4, no. 2, pp. 37–43, 1999. Also collected in [112]. Cited on p. 863

[1570] Schmalstieg, Dieter, and Tobias Hollerer, *Augmented Reality: Principles and Practice*, Addison-Wesley, 2016. Cited on p. 917, 940

[1571] Schmittler, J. I. Wald, and P. Slusallek, "SaarCOR: A Hardware Architecture for Ray Tracing," in *Graphics Hardware 2002*, Eurographics Association, pp. 27–36, Sept. 2002. Cited on p. 1039

[1572] Schneider, Andrew, and Nathan Vos, "*Nubis*: Authoring Realtime Volumetric Cloudscapes with the *Decima* Engine," *SIGGRAPH Advances in Real-Time Rendering in Games course*, Aug. 2017. Cited on p. 619, 620

[1573] Schneider, Jens, and Rüdiger Westermann, "GPU-Friendly High-Quality Terrain Rendering," *Journal of WSCG*, vol. 14, no. 1-3, pp. 49–56, 2006. Cited on p. 879

[1574] Schneider, Philip, and David Eberly, *Geometric Tools for Computer Graphics*, Morgan Kaufmann, 2003. Cited on p. 685, 686, 716, 950, 966, 981, 987, 991

[1575] Schollmeyer, Andre, Andrey Babanin, and Bernd Fro, "Order-Independent Transparency for Programmable Deferred Shading Pipelines," *Computer Graphics Forum*, vol. 34, no. 7, pp. 67–76, 2015. Cited on p. 887

[1576] Schorn, Peter, and Frederick Fisher, "Testing the Convexity of Polygon," in Paul S. Heckbert, ed., *Graphics Gems IV*, Academic Press, pp. 7–15, 1994. Cited on p. 686

[1577] Schott, Mathias, Vincent Pegoraro, Charles Hansen, Kévin Boulanger, and Kadi Bouatouch, "A Directional Occlusion Shading Model for Interactive Direct Volume Rendering," in *Euro-Vis'09*, Eurographics Association, pp. 855–862, 2009. Cited on p. 607

[1578] Schott, Mathias, A. V. Pascal Grosset, Tobias Martin, Vincent Pegoraro, Sean T. Smith, and Charles D. Hansen, "Depth of Field Effects for Interactive Direct Volume Rendering," *Computer Graphics Forum*, vol. 30, no. 3, pp. 941–950, 2011. Cited on p. 607

[1579] Schröder, Peter, and Wim Sweldens, "Spherical Wavelets: Efficiently Representing Functions on the Sphere," in *SIGGRAPH '95: Proceedings of the 22nd Annual Conference on Computer Graphics and Interactive Techniques*, ACM, pp. 161–172, Aug. 1995. Cited on p. 402

[1580] Schröder, Peter, "What Can We Measure?" *SIGGRAPH Discrete Differential Geometry course*, Aug. 2006. Cited on p. 954

[1581] Schroders, M. F. A., and R. V. Gulik, "Quadtree Relief Mapping," in *Graphics Hardware 2006*, Eurographics Association, pp. 61–66, Sept. 2006. Cited on p. 220

[1582] Schroeder, Tim, "Collision Detection Using Ray Casting," *Game Developer*, vol. 8, no. 8, pp. 50–56, Aug. 2001. Cited on p. 976

[1583] Schuetz, Markus, *Potree: Rendering Large Point Clouds in Web Browsers*, Diploma thesis in Visual Computing, Vienna University of Technology, 2016. Cited on p. 574, 575, 576

[1584] Schüler, Christian, "Normal Mapping without Precomputed Tangents," in Wolfgang Engel, ed., *ShaderX⁵*, Charles River Media, pp. 131–140, 2006. Cited on p. 210

[1585] Schüler, Christian, "Multisampling Extension for Gradient Shadow Maps," in Wolfgang Engel, ed., *ShaderX⁵*, Charles River Media, pp. 207–218, 2006. Cited on p. 250

[1586] Schüler, Christian, "An Efficient and Physically Plausible Real Time Shading Model," in Wolfgang Engel, ed., *ShaderX⁷*, Charles River Media, pp. 175–187, 2009. Cited on p. 325

[1587] Schüler, Christian, "An Approximation to the Chapman Grazing-Incidence Function for Atmospheric Scattering," in Wolfgang Engel, ed., *GPU Pro³*, CRC Press, pp. 105–118, 2012. Cited on p. 616

[1588] Schüler, Christian, "Branchless Matrix to Quaternion Conversion," *The Tenth Planet* blog, Aug. 7, 2012. Cited on p. 81

[1589] Schulz, Nicolas, "Moving to the Next Generation—The Rendering Technology of *Ryse*," *Game Developers Conference*, Mar. 2014. Cited on p. 371, 506, 892, 893, 904

[1590] Schulz, Nicolas, and Theodor Mader, "Rendering Techniques in *Ryse: Son of Rome*," *SIG-GRAPH Advances in Real-Time Rendering in Games course*, Aug. 2014. Cited on p. 234, 245, 246, 251, 252, 569, 864

[1591] Schulz, Nicolas, *CRYENGINE Manual*, Crytek GmbH, 2016. Cited on p. 111, 113, 631

[1592] Schumacher, Dale A., "General Filtered Image Rescaling," in David Kirk, ed., *Graphics Gems III*, Academic Press, pp. 8–16, 1992. Cited on p. 184

[1593] Schwarz, Michael, and Marc Stamminger, "Bitmask Soft Shadows," *Computer Graphics Forum*, vol. 26, no. 3, pp. 515–524, 2007. Cited on p. 252

[1594] Schwarz, Michael, and Hans-Peter Seidel, "Fast Parallel Surface and Solid Voxelization on GPUs," *ACM Transactions on Graphics*, vol. 29, no. 6, pp. 179:1–179:10, Dec. 2010. Cited on p. 581

[1595] Schwarz, Michael, "Practical Binary Surface and Solid Voxelization with Direct3D 11," in Wolfgang Engel, ed., *GPU Pro³*, CRC Press, pp. 337–352, 2012. Cited on p. 581, 582

[1596] Seetzen, Helge, Wolfgang Heidrich, Wolfgang Stuerzlinger, Greg Ward, Lorne Whitehead, Matthew Trentacoste, Abhijeet Ghosh, and Andrejs Vorozcovs, "High Dynamic Range Display Systems," *ACM Transactions on Graphics (SIGGRAPH 2004)*, vol. 23, no. 3, pp. 760–768, Aug. 2004. Cited on p. 1011

[1597] Segal, M., C. Korobkin, R. van Widenfelt, J. Foran, and P. Haeberli, "Fast Shadows and Lighting Effects Using Texture Mapping," *Computer Graphics (SIGGRAPH '92 Proceedings)*, vol. 26, no. 2, pp. 249–252, July 1992. Cited on p. 173, 221, 229

[1598] Segal, Mark, and Kurt Akeley, *The OpenGL Graphics System: A Specification (Version 4.5)*, The Khronos Group, June 2017. Editor (v1.1): Chris Frazier; Editor (v1.2–4.5): Jon Leech; Editor (v2.0): Pat Brown. Cited on p. 845, 1033

[1599] Seiler, L. D. Carmean, E. Sprangle, T. Forsyth, M. Abrash, P. Dubey, S. Junkins, A. Lake, J. Sugerman, R. Cavin, R. Espasa, E. Grochowski, T. Juan, and P. Hanrahan, "Larrabee: A Many-Core x86 Architecture for Visual Computing," *ACM Transactions on Graphics*, vol. 27, no. 3, pp. 18:1–18:15, 2008. Cited on p. 230, 996, 1017

[1600] Sekulic, Dean, "Efficient Occlusion Culling," in Randima Fernando, ed., *GPU Gems*, Addison-Wesley, pp. 487–503, 2004. Cited on p. 524, 836

[1601] Selan, Jeremy, "Using Lookup Tables to Accelerate Color Transformations," in Matt Pharr, ed., *GPU Gems 2*, Addison-Wesley, pp. 381–408, 2005. Cited on p. 289, 290

[1602] Selan, Jeremy, "Cinematic Color: From Your Monitor to the Big Screen," VES White Paper, 2012. Cited on p. 166, 283, 289, 290, 291

[1603] Selgrad, K., C. Dachsbacher, Q. Meyer, and M. Stamminger, "Filtering Multi-Layer Shadow Maps for Accurate Soft Shadows," *Computer Graphics Forum*, vol. 34, no. 1, pp. 205–215, 2015. Cited on p. 259

[1604] Selgrad, K., J. Müller, C. Reintges, and M. Stamminger, "Fast Shadow Map Rendering for Many-Lights Settings," in *Eurographics Symposium on Rendering—Experimental Ideas & Implementations*, Eurographics Association, pp. 41–47, 2016. Cited on p. 247

[1605] Sellers, Graham, Patrick Cozzi, Kevin Ring, Emil Persson, Joel da Vahl, and J. M. P. van Waveren, *SIGGRAPH Rendering Massive Virtual Worlds course*, July 2013. Cited on p. 102, 868, 874, 875, 876, 879

[1606] Sellers, Graham, Richard S. Wright Jr., and Nicholas Haemel, *OpenGL Superbible: Comprehensive Tutorial and Reference*, Seventh Edition, Addison-Wesley, 2015. Cited on p. 55

[1607] Sen, Pradeep, Mike Cammarano, and Pat Hanrahan, "Shadow Silhouette Maps," *ACM Transactions on Graphics (SIGGRAPH 2003)*, vol. 22, no. 3, pp. 521–526, 2003. Cited on p. 259

[1608] Senior, Andrew, "Facial Animation for Mobile GPUs," in Wolfgang Engel, ed., *ShaderX^7*, Charles River Media, pp. 561–570, 2009. Cited on p. 90

[1609] Senior, Andrew, "iPhone 3GS Graphics Development and Optimization Strategies," in Wolfgang Engel, ed., *GPU Pro*, A K Peters, Ltd., pp. 385–395, 2010. Cited on p. 702, 795, 804, 805

[1610] Seymour, Mike, "Manuka: Weta Digital's New Renderer," *fxguide*, Aug. 6, 2014. Cited on p. 280

[1611] Shade, J., Steven Gortler, Li-Wei He, and Richard Szeliski, "Layered Depth Images," in *SIGGRAPH '98: Proceedings of the 25th Annual Conference on Computer Graphics and Interactive Techniques*, ACM, pp. 231–242, July 1998. Cited on p. 565

[1612] Shamir, Ariel, "A survey on Mesh Segmentation Techniques," *Computer Graphics Forum*, vol. 27, no. 6, pp. 1539–1556, 2008. Cited on p. 683

[1613] Shankel, Jason, "Rendering Distant Scenery with Skyboxes," in Mark DeLoura, ed., *Game Programming Gems 2*, Charles River Media, pp. 416–420, 2001. Cited on p. 548

[1614] Shankel, Jason, "Fast Heightfield Normal Calculation," in Dante Treglia, ed., *Game Programming Gems 3*, Charles River Media, pp. 344–348, 2002. Cited on p. 695

[1615] Shanmugam, Perumaal, and Okan Arikan, "Hardware Accelerated Ambient Occlusion Techniques on GPUs," in *Proceedings of the 2007 Symposium on Interactive 3D Graphics and Games*, ACM, pp. 73–80, 2007. Cited on p. 458

[1616] Shastry, Anirudh S., "High Dynamic Range Rendering," *GameDev.net*, 2004. Cited on p. 527

[1617] Sheffer, Alla, Bruno Lévy, Maxim Mogilnitsky, and Alexander Bogomyakov, "ABF++: Fast and Robust Angle Based Flattening," *ACM Transactions on Graphics*, vol. 24, no. 2, pp. 311–330, 2005. Cited on p. 485

[1618] Shemanarev, Maxim, "Texts Rasterization Exposures," *The AGG Project*, July 2007. Cited on p. 676

[1619] Shen, Hao, Pheng Ann Heng, and Zesheng Tang, "A Fast Triangle-Triangle Overlap Test Using Signed Distances," *journals of graphics tools*, vol. 8, no. 1, pp. 17–24, 2003. Cited on p. 974

[1620] Shen, Li, Jieqing Feng, and Baoguang Yang, "Exponential Soft Shadow Mapping," *Computer Graphics Forum*, vol. 32, no. 4, pp. 107–116, 2013. Cited on p. 257

[1621] Shene, Ching-Kuang, "Computing the Intersection of a Line and a Cylinder," in Paul S. Heckbert, ed., *Graphics Gems IV*, Academic Press, pp. 353–355, 1994. Cited on p. 959

[1622] Shene, Ching-Kuang, "Computing the Intersection of a Line and a Cone," in Alan Paeth, ed., *Graphics Gems V*, Academic Press, pp. 227–231, 1995. Cited on p. 959

[1623] Sherif, Tarek, "WebGL 2 Examples," *GitHub* repository, Mar. 17, 2017. Cited on p. 122, 125

[1624] Shewchuk, Jonathan Richard, "Adaptive Precision Floating-Point Arithmetic and Fast Robust Geometric Predicates, *Discrete and Computational Geometry*, vol. 18, no. 3, pp. 305–363, Oct. 1997. Cited on p. 974

[1625] Shilov, Anton, Yaroslav Lyssenko, and Alexey Stepin, "Highly Defined: ATI Radeon HD 2000 Architecture Review," *Xbit Laboratories* website, Aug. 2007. Cited on p. 142

[1626] Shirley, Peter, *Physically Based Lighting Calculations for Computer Graphics*, PhD thesis, University of Illinois at Urbana Champaign, Dec. 1990. Cited on p. 143, 351

[1627] Shirley, Peter, Helen Hu, Brian Smits, and Eric Lafortune, "A Practitioners' Assessment of Light Reflection Models," in *Pacific Graphics '97*, IEEE Computer Society, pp. 40–49, Oct. 1997. Cited on p. 351

[1628] Shirley, Peter, *Ray Tracing in One Weekend*, Ray Tracing Minibooks Book 1, 2016. Cited on p. 512, 1047

[1629] Shirley, Peter, "New Simple Ray-Box Test from Andrew Kensler," *Pete Shirley's Graphics Blog*, Feb. 14, 2016. Cited on p. 961

[1630] Shirman, Leon A., and Salim S. Abi-Ezzi, "The Cone of Normals Technique for Fast Processing of Curved Patches," *Computer Graphics Forum*, vol. 12, no. 3, pp. 261–272, 1993. Cited on p. 833

[1631] Shishkovtsov, Oles, "Deferred Shading in *S.T.A.L.K.E.R.*," in Matt Pharr, ed., *GPU Gems 2*, Addison-Wesley, pp. 143–166, 2005. Cited on p. 216, 888

[1632] Shodhan, Shalin, and Andrew Willmott, "Stylized Rendering in *Spore*," in Wolfgang Engel, ed., *GPU Pro*, A K Peters, Ltd., pp. 549–560, 2010. Cited on p. 678

[1633] Shoemake, Ken, "Animating Rotation with Quaternion Curves," *Computer Graphics (SIGGRAPH '85 Proceedings)*, vol. 19, no. 3, pp. 245–254, July 1985. Cited on p. 73, 76, 80, 82

[1634] Shoemake, Ken, "Quaternions and 4×4 Matrices," in James Arvo, ed., *Graphics Gems II*, Academic Press, pp. 351–354, 1991. Cited on p. 80

[1635] Shoemake, Ken, "Polar Matrix Decomposition," in Paul S. Heckbert, ed., *Graphics Gems IV*, Academic Press, pp. 207–221, 1994. Cited on p. 74

[1636] Shoemake, Ken, "Euler Angle Conversion," in Paul S. Heckbert, ed., *Graphics Gems IV*, Academic Press, pp. 222–229, 1994. Cited on p. 70, 73

[1637] Shopf, J., J. Barczak, C. Oat, and N. Tatarchuk, "March of the Froblins: Simulation and Rendering of Massive Crowds of Intelligent and Details Creatures on GPU," *SIGGRAPH Advances in Real-Time Rendering in 3D Graphics and Games course*, Aug. 2008. Cited on p. 475, 848, 851

[1638] Sigg, Christian, and Markus Hadwiger, "Fast Third-Order Texture Filtering," in Matt Pharr, ed., *GPU Gems 2*, Addison-Wesley, pp. 313–329, 2005. Cited on p. 189, 517

[1639] Sikachev, Peter, Vladimir Egorov, and Sergey Makeev, "Quaternions Revisited," in Wolfgang Engel, ed., *GPU Pro^5*, CRC Press, pp. 361–374, 2014. Cited on p. 87, 210, 715

[1640] Sikachev, Peter, and Nicolas Longchamps, "Reflection System in *Thief*," *SIGGRAPH Advances in Real-Time Rendering in Games course*, Aug. 2014. Cited on p. 502

[1641] Sikachev, Peter, Samuel Delmont, Uriel Doyon, and Jean-Normand Bucci, "Next-Generation Rendering in *Thief*," in Wolfgang Engel, ed., *GPU Pro^6*, CRC Press, pp. 65–90, 2015. Cited on p. 251, 252

[1642] Sillion, François, and Claude Puech, *Radiosity and Global Illumination*, Morgan Kaufmann, 1994. Cited on p. 442, 483

[1643] Silvennoinen, Ari, and Ville Timonen, "Multi-Scale Global Illumination in Quantum Break," *SIGGRAPH Advances in Real-Time Rendering in Games course*, Aug. 2015. Cited on p. 488, 496

[1644] Silvennoinen, Ari, and Jaakko Lehtinen, "Real-Time Global Illumination by Precomputed Local Reconstruction from Sparse Radiance Probes," *ACM Transactions on Graphics (SIGGRAPH Asia 2017)*, vol. 36, no. 6, pp. 230:1–230:13, Nov. 2017. Cited on p. 484

[1645] Sintorn, Erik, Elmar Eisemann, and Ulf Assarsson, "Sample Based Visibility for Soft Shadows Using Alias-Free Shadow Maps," *Computer Graphics Forum*, vol. 27, no. 4, pp. 1285–1292, 2008. Cited on p. 261

[1646] Sintorn, Erik, and Ulf Assarsson, "Hair Self Shadowing and Transparency Depth Ordering Using Occupancy Maps," in *Proceedings of the 2009 Symposium on Interactive 3D Graphics and Games*, ACM, pp. 67–74, Feb.–Mar. 2009. Cited on p. 645

[1647] Sintorn, Erik, Viktor Kämpe, Ola Olsson, and Ulf Assarsson, "Compact Precomputed Voxelized Shadows," *ACM Transactions on Graphics*, vol. 33, no. 4, article no. 150, Mar. 2014. Cited on p. 264, 586

[1648] Sintorn, Erik, Viktor Kämpe, Ola Olsson, and Ulf Assarsson, "Per-Triangle Shadow Volumes Using a View-Sample Cluster Hierarchy," in *Proceedings of the 18th Meeting of the ACM SIGGRAPH Symposium on Interactive 3D Graphics and Games*, ACM, pp. 111–118, Mar. 2014. Cited on p. 233, 259

[1649] Skiena, Steven, *The Algorithm Design Manual*, Springer-Verlag, 1997. Cited on p. 707

[1650] Skillman, Drew, and Pete Demoreuille, "Rock Show VFX: Bringing Brütal Legend to Life," *Game Developers Conference*, Mar. 2010. Cited on p. 569, 572

[1651] Sloan, Peter-Pike, Jan Kautz, and John Snyder, "Precomputed Radiance Transfer for Real-Time Rendering in Dynamic, Low-Frequency Lighting Environments," *ACM Transactions on Graphics (SIGGRAPH 2002)*, vol. 21, no. 3, pp. 527–536, July 2002. Cited on p. 471, 479, 480

[1652] Sloan, Peter-Pike, Jesse Hall, John Hart, and John Snyder, "Clustered Principal Components for Precomputed Radiance Transfer," *ACM Transactions on Graphics (SIGGRAPH 2003)*, vol. 22, no. 3, pp. 382–391, 2003. Cited on p. 480

[1653] Sloan, Peter-Pike, Ben Luna, and John Snyder, "Local, Deformable Precomputed Radiance Transfer," *ACM Transactions on Graphics (SIGGRAPH 2005)*, vol. 24, no. 3, pp. 1216–1224, Aug. 2005. Cited on p. 431, 481

[1654] Sloan, Peter-Pike, "Normal Mapping for Precomputed Radiance Transfer," in *Proceedings of the 2006 Symposium on Interactive 3D Graphics and Games*, ACM, pp. 23–26, 2006. Cited on p. 404

[1655] Sloan, Peter-Pike, Naga K. Govindaraju, Derek Nowrouzezahrai, and John Snyder, "Image-Based Proxy Accumulation for Real-Time Soft Global Illumination," in *Pacific Graphics 2007*, IEEE Computer Society, pp. 97–105, Oct. 2007. Cited on p. 456, 467

[1656] Sloan, Peter-Pike, "Stupid Spherical Harmonics (SH) Tricks," *Game Developers Conference*, Feb. 2008. Cited on p. 395, 400, 401, 428, 429, 430, 431, 470

[1657] Sloan, Peter-Pike, "Efficient Spherical Harmonic Evaluation," *Journal of Computer Graphics Techniques*, vol. 2, no. 2, pp. 84–90, 2013. Cited on p. 400

[1658] Sloan, Peter-Pike, Jason Tranchida, Hao Chen, and Ladislav Kavan, "Ambient Obscurance Baking on the GPU," in *ACM SIGGRAPH Asia 2013 Technical Briefs*, ACM, article no. 32, Nov. 2013. Cited on p. 453

[1659] Sloan, Peter-Pike, "Deringing Spherical Harmonics," in *SIGGRAPH Asia 2017 Technical Briefs*, ACM, article no. 11, 2017. Cited on p. 401, 429

[1660] Smedberg, Niklas, and Daniel Wright, "Rendering Techniques in *Gears of War 2*," *Game Developers Conference*, Mar. 2009. Cited on p. 462

[1661] Smith, Alvy Ray, *Digital Filtering Tutorial for Computer Graphics*, Technical Memo 27, revised Mar. 1983. Cited on p. 136

[1662] Smith, Alvy Ray, and James F. Blinn, "Blue Screen Matting," in *SIGGRAPH '96: Proceedings of the 23rd Annual Conference on Computer Graphics and Interactive Techniques*, ACM, pp. 259–268, Aug. 1996. Cited on p. 159, 160

[1663] Smith, Alvy Ray, "The Stuff of Dreams," *Computer Graphics World*, vol. 21, pp. 27–29, July 1998. Cited on p. 1042

[1664] Smith, Ashley Vaughan, and Mathieu Einig, "Physically Based Deferred Shading on Mobile," in Wolfgang Engel, ed., *GPU Pro*^{7}, CRC Press, pp. 187–198, 2016. Cited on p. 903

[1665] Smith, Bruce G., "Geometrical Shadowing of a Random Rough Surface," *IEEE Transactions on Antennas and Propagation*, vol. 15, no. 5, pp. 668–671, Sept. 1967. Cited on p. 334

[1666] Smith, Ryan, "GPU Boost 3.0: Finer-Grained Clockspeed Controls," Section in "The NVIDIA GeForce GTX 1080 & GTX 1070 Founders Editions Review: Kicking Off the FinFET Generation," *AnandTech*, July 20, 2016. Cited on p. 163, 789

[1667] Smits, Brian E., and Gary W. Meyer, "Newton's Colors: Simulating Interference Phenomena in Realistic Image Synthesis," in Kadi Bouatouch & Christian Bouville, eds. *Photorealism in Computer Graphics*, Springer, pp. 185–194, 1992. Cited on p. 363

[1668] Smits, Brian, "Efficiency Issues for Ray Tracing," *journal of graphics tools*, vol. 3, no. 2, pp. 1–14, 1998. Also collected in [112]. Cited on p. 792, 961

[1669] Smits, Brian, "Reflection Model Design for *WALL-E* and *Up*," *SIGGRAPH Practical Physically Based Shading in Film and Game Production course*, Aug. 2012. Cited on p. 324

[1670] Snook, Greg, "Simplified Terrain Using Interlocking Tiles," in Mark DeLoura, ed., *Game Programming Gems 2*, Charles River Media, pp. 377–383, 2001. Cited on p. 876

[1671] Snyder, John, "Area Light Sources for Real-Time Graphics," Technical Report MSR-TR-96-11, Microsoft Research, Mar. 1996. Cited on p. 382

[1672] Snyder, John, and Jed Lengyel, "Visibility Sorting and Compositing without Splitting for Image Layer Decompositions," in *SIGGRAPH '98: Proceedings of the 25th Annual Conference on Computer Graphics and Interactive Techniques*, ACM, pp. 219–230, July 1998. Cited on p. 532, 551

[1673] Soler, Cyril, and François Sillion, "Fast Calculation of Soft Shadow Textures Using Convolution," in *SIGGRAPH '98: Proceedings of the 25th Annual Conference on Computer Graphics and Interactive Techniques*, ACM, pp. 321–332, July 1998. Cited on p. 256

[1674] Sousa, Tiago, "Adaptive Glare," in Wolfgang Engel, ed., *ShaderX*^{3}, Charles River Media, pp. 349–355, 2004. Cited on p. 288, 527

[1675] Sousa, Tiago, "Generic Refraction Simulation," in Matt Pharr, ed., *GPU Gems 2*, Addison-Wesley, pp. 295–305, 2005. Cited on p. 628

[1676] Sousa, Tiago, "Vegetation Procedural Animation and Shading in Crysis," in Hubert Nguyen, ed., *GPU Gems 3*, Addison-Wesley, pp. 373–385, 2007. Cited on p. 639

[1677] Sousa, Tiago, "Anti-Aliasing Methods in CryENGINE," *SIGGRAPH Filtering Approaches for Real-Time Anti-Aliasing course*, Aug. 2011. Cited on p. 145, 531

[1678] Sousa, Tiago, Nickolay Kasyan, and Nicolas Schulz, "Secrets of CryENGINE 3 Graphics Technology," *SIGGRAPH Advances in Real-Time Rendering in 3D Graphics and Games course*, Aug. 2011. Cited on p. 145, 234, 245, 252, 257, 262, 505

[1679] Sousa, Tiago, Nickolay Kasyan, and Nicolas Schulz, "CryENGINE 3: Three Years of Work in Review," in Wolfgang Engel, ed., *GPU Pro*^{3}, CRC Press, pp. 133–168, 2012. Cited on p. 139, 234, 238, 245, 252, 257, 542, 786, 793, 932, 937

[1680] Sousa, Tiago, Carsten Wenzel, and Chris Raine, "The Rendering Technologies of *Crysis 3*," *Game Developers Conference*, Mar. 2013. Cited on p. 887, 889, 890, 895

[1681] Sousa, Tiago, Nickolay Kasyan, and Nicolas Schulz, "CryENGINE 3: Graphics Gems," *SIGGRAPH Advances in Real-Time Rendering in 3D Graphics and Games course*, July 2013. Cited on p. 531, 535, 539, 540, 542, 604, 888, 892

[1682] Sousa, T., and J. Geoffroy, "*DOOM*: the Devil is in the Details," *SIGGRAPH Advances in Real-Time Rendering in 3D Graphics and Games course*, July 2016. Cited on p. 569, 629, 883, 901

[1683] Spencer, Greg, Peter Shirley, Kurt Zimmerman, and Donald Greenberg, "Physically-Based Glare Effects for Digital Images," in *SIGGRAPH '95: Proceedings of the 22nd Annual Conference on Computer Graphics and Interactive Techniques*, ACM, pp. 325–334, Aug. 1995. Cited on p. 524

[1684] Stachowiak, Tomasz, "Stochastic Screen-Space Reflections," *SIGGRAPH Advances in Real-Time Rendering in Games course*, Aug. 2015. Cited on p. 507, 508

[1685] Stachowiak, Tomasz, "A Deferred Material Rendering System," online article, Dec. 18, 2015. Cited on p. 907

[1686] Stam, Jos, "Multiple Scattering as a Diffusion Process," in *Rendering Techniques '95*, Springer, pp. 41–50, June 1995. Cited on p. 634

[1687] Stam, Jos, "Exact Evaluation of Catmull-Clark Subdivision Surfaces at Arbitrary Parameter Values," in *SIGGRAPH '98: Proceedings of the 25th Annual Conference on Computer Graphics and Interactive Techniques*, ACM, pp. 395–404, July 1998. Cited on p. 763

[1688] Stam, Jos, "Diffraction Shaders," in *SIGGRAPH '99: Proceedings of the 26th Annual Conference on Computer Graphics and Interactive Techniques*, ACM Press/Addison-Wesley Publishing Co., pp. 101–110, Aug. 1999. Cited on p. 361

[1689] Stam, Jos, "Real-Time Fluid Dynamics for Games," *Game Developers Conference*, Mar. 2003. Cited on p. 649

[1690] Stamate, Vlad, "Reduction of Lighting Calculations Using Spherical Harmonics," in Wolfgang Engel, ed., *ShaderX³*, Charles River Media, pp. 251–262, 2004. Cited on p. 430

[1691] Stamminger, Marc, and George Drettakis, "Perspective Shadow Maps," *ACM Transactions on Graphics (SIGGRAPH 2002)*, vol. 21, no. 3, pp. 557–562, July 2002. Cited on p. 241

[1692] St-Amour, Jean-François, "Rendering *Assassin's Creed III*," *Game Developers Conference*, Mar. 2013. Cited on p. 453

[1693] Steed, Paul, *Animating Real-Time Game Characters*, Charles River Media, 2002. Cited on p. 88

[1694] Stefanov, Nikolay, "Global Illumination in *Tom Clancy's The Division*," *Game Developers Conference*, Mar. 2016. Cited on p. 478, 483

[1695] Steinicke, Frank Steinicke, Gerd Bruder, and Scott Kuhl, "Realistic Perspective Projections for Virtual Objects and Environments," *ACM Transactions on Graphics*, vol. 30, no. 5, article no. 112, Oct. 2011. Cited on p. 554

[1696] Stemkoski, Lee, "Bubble Demo," *GitHub* repository, 2013. Cited on p. 628

[1697] Stengel, Michael, Steve Grogorick, Martin Eisemann, and Marcus Magnor, "Adaptive Image-Space Sampling for Gaze-Contingent Real-Time Rendering," *Computer Graphics Forum*, vol. 35, no. 4, pp. 129–139, 2016. Cited on p. 932

[1698] Sterna, Wojciech, "Practical Gather-Based Bokeh Depth of Field," in Wolfgang Engel, ed., *GPU Zen*, Black Cat Publishing, pp. 217–237, 2017. Cited on p. 535

[1699] Stewart, A. J., and M. S. Langer, "Towards Accurate Recovery of Shape from Shading Under Diffuse Lighting," *IEEE Trans. on Pattern Analysis and Machine Intelligence*, vol. 19, no. 9, pp. 1020–1025, Sept. 1997. Cited on p. 450

[1700] Stewart, Jason, and Gareth Thomas, "Tiled Rendering Showdown: Forward++ vs. Deferred Rendering," *Game Developers Conference*, Mar. 2013. Cited on p. 896, 897, 914

[1701] Stewart, Jason, "Compute-Based Tiled Culling," in Wolfgang Engel, ed., *GPU Pro⁶*, CRC Press, pp. 435–458, 2015. Cited on p. 894, 896, 914

[1702] Stich, Martin, Carsten Wächter, and Alexander Keller, "Efficient and Robust Shadow Volumes Using Hierarchical Occlusion Culling and Geometry Shaders," in Hubert Nguyen, ed., *GPU Gems 3*, Addison-Wesley, pp. 239–256, 2007. Cited on p. 233

[1703] Stiles, W. S., and J. M. Burch, "Interim Report to the Commission Internationale de l'Éclairage Zurich, 1955, on the National Physical Laboratory's Investigation of Colour-Matching (1955)," *Optica Acta*, vol. 2, no. 4, pp. 168–181, 1955. Cited on p. 273

[1704] Stokes, Michael, Matthew Anderson, Srinivasan Chandrasekar, and Ricardo Motta, "A Standard Default Color Space for the Internet—sRGB," Version 1.10, *International Color Consortium*, Nov. 1996. Cited on p. 278

[1705] Stone, Jonathan, "Radially-Symmetric Reflection Maps," in *SIGGRAPH 2009 Talks*, ACM, article no. 24, Aug. 2009. Cited on p. 414

[1706] Stone, Maureen, *A Field Guide to Digital Color*, A K Peters, Ltd., Aug. 2003. Cited on p. 276

[1707] Stone, Maureen, "Representing Colors as Three Numbers," *IEEE Computer Graphics and Applications*, vol. 25, no. 4, pp. 78–85, July/Aug. 2005. Cited on p. 272, 276

[1708] Storsjö, Martin, *Efficient Triangle Reordering for Improved Vertex Cache Utilisation in Real-time Rendering*, MSc thesis, Department of Information Technologies, Faculty of Technology, Åbo Akademi University, 2008. Cited on p. 701

[1709] Story, Jon, and Holger Gruen, "High Quality Direct3D 10.0 & 10.1 Accelerated Techniques," *Game Developers Conference*, Mar. 2009. Cited on p. 249

[1710] Story, Jon, "DirectCompute Accelerated Separable Filtering," *Game Developers Conference*, Mar. 2011. Cited on p. 54, 518

[1711] Story, Jon, "Advanced Geometrically Correct Shadows for Modern Game Engines," *Game Developers Conference*, Mar. 2016. Cited on p. 224, 261, 262

[1712] Story, Jon, and Chris Wyman, "HFTS: Hybrid Frustum-Traced Shadows in *The Division*," in *ACM SIGGRAPH 2016 Talks*, ACM, article no. 13, July 2016. Cited on p. 261

[1713] Strauss, Paul S., "A Realistic Lighting Model for Computer Animators," *IEEE Computer Graphics and Applications*, vol. 10, no. 6, pp. 56–64, Nov. 1990. Cited on p. 324

[1714] Ström, Jacob, and Tomas Akenine-Möller, "iPACKMAN: High-Quality, Low-Complexity Texture Compression for Mobile Phones," in *Graphics Hardware 2006*, Eurographics Association, pp. 63–70, July 2005. Cited on p. 194

[1715] Ström, Jacob, and Martin Pettersson, "ETC2: Texture Compression Using Invalid Combinations," in *Graphics Hardware 2007*, Eurographics Association, pp. 49–54, Aug. 2007. Cited on p. 194

[1716] Ström, J., P. Wennersten, J. Rasmusson, J. Hasselgren, J. Munkberg, P. Clarberg, and T. Akenine-Möller, "Floating-Point Buffer Compression in a Unified Codec Architecture," in *Graphics Hardware 2008*, Eurographics Association, pp. 75–84, June 2008. Cited on p. 1009, 1018, 1038

[1717] Ström, Jacob, and Per Wennersten, "Lossless Compression of Already Compressed Textures," in *Proceedings of the ACM SIGGRAPH/EUROGRAPHICS Conference on High-Performance Graphics*, ACM, pp. 177–182, Aug. 2011. Cited on p. 870

[1718] Ström, J., K. Åström, and T. Akenine-Möller, "Immersive Linear Algebra," http://immersivemath.com, 2015. Cited on p. 102, 1047

[1719] Strothotte, Thomas, and Stefan Schlechtweg, *Non-Photorealistic Computer Graphics: Modeling, Rendering, and Animation*, Morgan Kaufmann, 2002. Cited on p. 652, 678

[1720] Strugar, F., "Continuous Distance-Dependent Level of Detail for Rendering Heightmaps," *Journal of Graphics, GPU, and Game Tools*, vol. 14, no. 4, pp. 57–74, 2009. Cited on p. 876, 877

[1721] Sugden, B., and M. Iwanicki, "Mega Meshes: Modelling, Rendering and Lighting a World Made of 100 Billion Polygons," *Game Developers Conference*, Mar. 2011. Cited on p. 483, 868, 870

[1722] Sun, Bo, Ravi Ramamoorthi, Srinivasa Narasimhan, and Shree Nayar, "A Practical Analytic Single Scattering Model for Real Time Rendering," *ACM Transactions on Graphics (SIGGRAPH 2005)*, vol. 24, no. 3, pp. 1040–1049, 2005. Cited on p. 604

[1723] Sun, Xin, Qiming Hou, Zhong Ren, Kun Zhou, and Baining Guo, "Radiance Transfer Biclustering for Real-Time All-Frequency Biscale Rendering," *IEEE Transactions on Visualization and Computer Graphics*, vol. 17, no. 1, pp. 64–73, 2011. Cited on p. 402

[1724] Sutherland, Ivan E., Robert F. Sproull, and Robert F. Schumacker, "A Characterization of Ten Hidden-Surface Algorithms," *Computing Surveys*, vol. 6, no. 1, pp. 1–55, Mar. 1974. Cited on p. 1048

[1725] Sutter, Herb, "The Free Lunch Is Over," *Dr. Dobb's Journal*, vol. 30, no. 3, Mar. 2005. Cited on p. 806, 815

[1726] Svarovsky, Jan, "View-Independent Progressive Meshing," in Mark DeLoura, ed., *Game Programming Gems*, Charles River Media, pp. 454–464, 2000. Cited on p. 707, 711

[1727] Swoboda, Matt, "Deferred Lighting and Post Processing on PLAYSTATION 3," *Game Developers Conference*, Mar. 2009. Cited on p. 893

[1728] Swoboda, Matt, "Ambient Occlusion in Frameranger," *direct to video blog*, Jan. 15, 2010. Cited on p. 453

[1729] Szeliski, Richard, *Computer Vision: Algorithms and Applications*, Springer, 2011. Cited on p. 130, 200, 543, 549, 587, 661, 1048

[1730] Szirmay-Kalos, László, Barnabás Aszódi, István Lazányi, and Mátyás Premecz, "Approximate Ray-Tracing on the GPU with Distance Impostors," *Computer Graphics Forum*, vol. 24, no. 3, pp. 695–704, 2005. Cited on p. 502

[1731] Szirmay-Kalos, László, and Tamás Umenhoffer, "Displacement Mapping on the GPU—State of the Art," *Computer Graphics Forum*, vol. 27, no. 6, pp. 1567–1592, 2008. Cited on p. 222, 933

[1732] Szirmay-Kalos, László, Tamás Umenhoffer, Gustavo Patow, László Szécsi, and Mateu Sbert, "Specular Effects on the GPU: State of the Art," *Computer Graphics Forum*, vol. 28, no. 6, pp. 1586–1617, 2009. Cited on p. 435

[1733] Szirmay-Kalos, László, Tamás Umenhoffer, Balázs Tóth, László Szécsi, and Mateu Sbert, "Volumetric Ambient Occlusion for Real-Time Rendering and Games," *IEEE Computer Graphics and Applications*, vol. 30, no. 1, pp. 70–79, 2010. Cited on p. 459

[1734] Tabellion, Eric, and Arnauld Lamorlette, "An Approximate Global Illumination System for Computer Generated Films," *ACM Transactions on Graphics (SIGGRAPH 2004)*, vol. 23, no. 3, pp. 469–476, Aug. 2004. Cited on p. 26, 491

[1735] Tadamura, Katsumi, Xueying Qin, Guofang Jiao, and Eihachiro Nakamae, "Rendering Optimal Solar Shadows Using Plural Sunlight Depth Buffers," in *Computer Graphics International 1999*, IEEE Computer Society, pp. 166–173, June 1999. Cited on p. 242

[1736] Takayama, Kenshi, Alec Jacobson, Ladislav Kavan, and Olga Sorkine-Hornung, "A Simple Method for Correcting Facet Orientations in Polygon Meshes Based on Ray Casting," *Journal of Computer Graphics Techniques*, vol. 3, no. 4, pp. 53–63, 2014. Cited on p. 693

[1737] Takeshige, Masaya, "The Basics of GPU Voxelization," *NVIDIA GameWorks* blog, Mar. 22, 2015. Cited on p. 582

[1738] Tampieri, Filippo, "Newell's Method for the Plane Equation of a Polygon," in David Kirk, ed., *Graphics Gems III*, Academic Press, pp. 231–232, 1992. Cited on p. 685

[1739] Tanner, Christopher C., Christopher J. Migdal, and Michael T. Jones, "The Clipmap: A Virtual Mipmap," in *SIGGRAPH '98: Proceedings of the 25th Annual Conference on Computer Graphics and Interactive Techniques*, ACM, pp. 151–158, July 1998. Cited on p. 570, 867, 872

[1740] Tarini, Marco, Kai Hormann, Paolo Cignoni, and Claudio Montani, "PolyCube-Maps," *ACM Transactions on Graphics (SIGGRAPH 2004)*, vol. 23, no. 3, pp. 853–860, Aug. 2004. Cited on p. 171

[1741] Tatarchuk, Natalya, "Artist-Directable Real-Time Rain Rendering in City Environments," *SIGGRAPH Advanced Real-Time Rendering in 3D Graphics and Games course*, Aug. 2006. Cited on p. 604

[1742] Tatarchuk, Natalya, "Dynamic Parallax Occlusion Mapping with Approximate Soft Shadows," *SIGGRAPH Advanced Real-Time Rendering in 3D Graphics and Games course*, Aug. 2006. Cited on p. 217, 218, 222

[1743] Tatarchuk, Natalya, "Practical Parallax Occlusion Mapping with Approximate Soft Shadows for Detailed Surface Rendering," *SIGGRAPH Advanced Real-Time Rendering in 3D Graphics and Games course*, Aug. 2006. Cited on p. 217, 218, 222

[1744] Tatarchuk, Natalya, and Jeremy Shopf, "Real-Time Medical Visualization with FireGL," *SIGGRAPH AMD Technical Talk*, Aug. 2007. Cited on p. 607, 753

[1745] Tatarchuk, Natalya, "Real-Time Tessellation on GPU," *SIGGRAPH Advanced Real-Time Rendering in 3D Graphics and Games course*, Aug. 2007. Cited on p. 770

[1746] Tatarchuk, Natalya, Christopher Oat, Jason L. Mitchell, Chris Green, Johan Andersson, Martin Mittring, Shanon Drone, and Nico Galoppo, *SIGGRAPH Advanced Real-Time Rendering in 3D Graphics and Games course*, Aug. 2007. Cited on p. 1115

[1747] Tatarchuk, Natalya, Chris Tchou, and Joe Venzon, "*Destiny*: From Mythic Science Fiction to Rendering in Real-Time," *SIGGRAPH Advances in Real-Time Rendering in Games course*, July 2013. Cited on p. 568, 569, 892

[1748] Tatarchuk, Natalya, and Shi Kai Wang, "Creating Content to Drive *Destiny*'s Investment Game: One Solution to Rule Them All," *SIGGRAPH Production Session*, Aug. 2014. Cited on p. 366

[1749] Tatarchuk, Natalya, "Destiny's Multithreaded Rendering Architecture," *Game Developers Conference*, Mar. 2015. Cited on p. 815

[1750] Tatarchuk, Natalya, and Chris Tchou, "*Destiny* Shader Pipeline," *Game Developers Conference*, Feb.–Mar. 2017. Cited on p. 128, 129, 815

[1751] Taubin, Gabriel, André Guéziec, William Horn, and Francis Lazarus, "Progressive Forest Split Compression," in *SIGGRAPH '98: Proceedings of the 25th Annual Conference on Computer Graphics and Interactive Techniques*, ACM, pp. 123–132, July 1998. Cited on p. 706

[1752] Taylor, Philip, "Per-Pixel Lighting," *Driving DirectX* web column, Nov. 13, 2001. Cited on p. 432

[1753] Tector, C., "Streaming Massive Environments from Zero to 200MPH," *Game Developers Conference*, Mar. 2010. Cited on p. 871

[1754] Teixeira, Diogo, "Baking Normal Maps on the GPU," in Hubert Nguyen, ed., *GPU Gems 3*, Addison-Wesley, pp. 491–512, 2007. Cited on p. 853

[1755] Teller, Seth J., and Carlo H. Séquin, "Visibility Preprocessing for Interactive Walkthroughs," *Computer Graphics (SIGGRAPH '91 Proceedings)*, vol. 25, no. 4, pp. 61–69, July 1991. Cited on p. 837

[1756] Teller, Seth J., *Visibility Computations in Densely Occluded Polyhedral Environments*, PhD thesis, Department of Computer Science, University of Berkeley, 1992. Cited on p. 837

[1757] Teller, Seth, and Pat Hanrahan, "Global Visibility Algorithms for Illumination Computations," in *SIGGRAPH '94: Proceedings of the 21st Annual Conference on Computer Graphics and Interactive Techniques*, ACM, pp. 443–450, July 1994. Cited on p. 837

[1758] Teschner, Matthias, "Advanced Computer Graphics: Sampling," Course Notes, Computer Science Department, University of Freiburg, 2016. Cited on p. 144, 165

[1759] Tessman, Thant, "Casting Shadows on Flat Surfaces," *Iris Universe*, pp. 16–19, Winter 1989. Cited on p. 225

[1760] Tevs, A., I. Ihrke, and H.-P. Seidel, "Maximum Mipmaps for Fast, Accurate, and Scalable Dynamic Height Field Rendering," in *Proceedings of the 2008 Symposium on Interactive 3D Graphics and Games*, ACM, pp. 183–190, 2008. Cited on p. 220

[1761] Thibault, Aaron P., and Sean "Zoner" Cavanaugh, "Making Concept Art Real for Borderlands," *SIGGRAPH Stylized Rendering in Games course*, July 2010. Cited on p. 652, 661, 662, 664, 678

[1762] Thibieroz, Nicolas, "Deferred Shading with Multiple Render Targets," in Wolfgang Engel, ed., *ShaderX²: Introductions & Tutorials with DirectX 9*, Wordware, pp. 251–269, 2004. Cited on p. 882, 884

[1763] Thibieroz, Nicolas, "Robust Order-Independent Transparency via Reverse Depth Peeling in DirectX 10," in Wolfgang Engel, ed., *ShaderX⁶*, Charles River Media, pp. 211–226, 2008. Cited on p. 154

[1764] Thibieroz, Nicolas, "Deferred Shading with Multisampling Anti-Aliasing in DirectX 10," in Wolfgang Engel, ed., *ShaderX⁷*, Charles River Media, pp. 225–242, 2009. Cited on p. 888

[1765] Thibieroz, Nicolas, "Order-Independent Transparency Using Per-Pixel Linked Lists," in Wolfgang Engel, ed., *GPU Pro²*, A K Peters/CRC Press, pp. 409–431, 2011. Cited on p. 155

[1766] Thibieroz, Nicolas, "Deferred Shading Optimizations," *Game Developers Conference*, Mar. 2011. Cited on p. 886, 887, 892, 900

[1767] Thomas, Gareth, "Compute-Based GPU Particle Systems," *Game Developers Conference*, Mar. 2014. Cited on p. 572

[1768] Thomas, Gareth, "Advancements in Tiled-Based Compute Rendering," *Game Developers Conference*, Mar. 2015. Cited on p. 803, 894, 896, 900, 901

[1769] Thomas, Spencer W., "Decomposing a Matrix into Simple Transformations," in James Arvo, ed., *Graphics Gems II*, Academic Press, pp. 320–323, 1991. Cited on p. 72, 74

[1770] Thürmer, Grit, and Charles A. Wüthrich, "Computing Vertex Normals from Polygonal Facets," *journal of graphics tools*, vol. 3, no. 1, pp. 43–46, 1998. Also collected in [112]. Cited on p. 695

[1771] Timonen, Ville, "Line-Sweep Ambient Obscurance," *Eurographics Symposium on Rendering*, June 2013. Cited on p. 461

[1772] Toisoul, Antoine, and Abhijeet Ghosh, "Practical Acquisition and Rendering of Diffraction Effects in Surface Reflectance," *ACM Transactions on Graphics*, vol. 36, no. 5, pp. 166:1–166:16, Oct. 2017. Cited on p. 361

[1773] Toisoul, Antoine, and Abhijeet Ghosh, "Real-Time Rendering of Realistic Surface Diffraction with Low Rank Factorisation," *European Conference on Visual Media Production (CVMP)*, Dec. 2017. Cited on p. 361

[1774] Toksvig, Michael, "Mipmapping Normal Maps," *journal of graphics tools*, vol. 10, no. 3, pp. 65–71, 2005. Cited on p. 369

[1775] Tokuyoshi, Yusuke, "Error Reduction and Simplification for Shading Anti-Aliasing," Technical Report, Square Enix, Apr. 2017. Cited on p. 371

[1776] Torborg, J., and J. T. Kajiya, "Talisman: Commodity Realtime 3D Graphics for the PC," in *SIGGRAPH '96: Proceedings of the 23rd Annual Conference on Computer Graphics and Interactive Techniques*, ACM, pp. 353–363, Aug. 1996. Cited on p. 551

[1777] Torchelsen, Rafael P., João L. D. Comba, and Rui Bastos, "Practical Geometry Clipmaps for Rendering Terrains in Computer Games," in Wolfgang Engel, ed., *ShaderX⁶*, Charles River Media, pp. 103–114, 2008. Cited on p. 612, 873

[1778] Török, Balázs, and Tim Green, "The Rendering Features of *The Witcher 3: Wild Hunt*," in *ACM SIGGRAPH 2015 Talks*, ACM, article no. 7, Aug. 2015. Cited on p. 366, 420, 889

[1779] Torrance, K., and E. Sparrow, "Theory for Off-Specular Reflection from Roughened Surfaces," *Journal of the Optical Society of America*, vol. 57, no. 9, pp. 1105–1114, Sept. 1967. Cited on p. 314, 334

[1780] Toth, Robert, "Avoiding Texture Seams by Discarding Filter Taps," *Journal of Computer Graphics Techniques*, vol. 2, no. 2, pp. 91–104, 2013. Cited on p. 191

[1781] Toth, Robert, Jon Hasselgren, and Tomas Akenine-Möller, "Perception of Highlight Disparity at a Distance in Consumer Head-Mounted Displays," in *Proceedings of the 7th Conference on High-Performance Graphics*, ACM, pp. 61–66, Aug. 2015. Cited on p. 934

[1782] Toth, Robert, Jim Nilsson, and Tomas Akenine-Möller, "Comparison of Projection Methods for Rendering Virtual Reality," in *High-Performance Graphics 2016*, Eurographics Association, pp. 163–171, June 2016. Cited on p. 930

[1783] Tran, Ray, "Facetted Shadow Mapping for Large Dynamic Game Environments," in Wolfgang Engel, ed., *ShaderX⁷*, Charles River Media, pp. 363–371, 2009. Cited on p. 244

[1784] Trapp, Matthias, and Jürgen Döllner, "Automated Combination of Real-Time Shader Programs," in *Eurographics 2007—Short Papers*, Eurographics Association, pp. 53–56, Sept. 2007. Cited on p. 128

[1785] Trebilco, Damian, "Light-Indexed Deferred Rendering," in Wolfgang Engel, ed., *ShaderX⁷*, Charles River Media, pp. 243–258, 2009. Cited on p. 893

[1786] Treglia, Dante, ed., *Game Programming Gems 3*, Charles River Media, 2002. Cited on p. 1089

[1787] Trop, Oren, Ayellet Tal, and Ilan Shimshoni, "A Fast Triangle to Triangle Intersection Test for Collision Detection," *Computer Animation & Virtual Worlds*, vol. 17, no. 5, pp. 527–535, 2006. Cited on p. 974

[1788] Trowbridge, T. S., and K. P. Reitz, "Average Irregularity Representation of a Roughened Surface for Ray Reflection," *Journal of the Optical Society of America*, vol. 65, no. 5, pp. 531–536, May 1975. Cited on p. 340

[1789] Trudel, N., "Improving Geometry Culling for *Deus Ex: Mankind Divided*," *Game Developers Conference*, Mar. 2016. Cited on p. 850

[1790] Tuft, David, "Plane-Based Depth Bias for Percentage Closer Filtering," *Game Developer*, vol. 17, no. 5, pp. 35–38, May 2010. Cited on p. 249, 250

[1791] Tuft, David, "Cascaded Shadow Maps," *Windows Dev Center: DirectX Graphics and Gaming Technical Articles*, 2011. Cited on p. 244, 245, 247, 265

[1792] Tuft, David, "Common Techniques to Improve Shadow Depth Maps," *Windows Dev Center: DirectX Graphics and Gaming Technical Articles*, 2011. Cited on p. 236, 239, 240, 265

[1793] Turkowski, Ken, "Filters for Common Resampling Tasks," in Andrew S. Glassner, ed., *Graphics Gems*, Academic Press, pp. 147–165, 1990. Cited on p. 136

[1794] Turkowski, Ken, "Properties of Surface-Normal Transformations," in Andrew S. Glassner, ed., *Graphics Gems*, Academic Press, pp. 539–547, 1990. Cited on p. 68

[1795] Turkowski, Ken, "Incremental Computation of the Gaussian," in Hubert Nguyen, ed., *GPU Gems 3*, Addison-Wesley, pp. 877–890, 2007. Cited on p. 515

[1796] Ulrich, Thatcher, "Loose Octrees," in Mark DeLoura, ed., *Game Programming Gems*, Charles River Media, pp. 444–453, 2000. Cited on p. 826

[1797] Ulrich, Thatcher, "Rendering Massive Terrains Using Chunked Level of Detail Control," *SIGGRAPH Super-Size It! Scaling up to Massive Virtual Worlds course*, July 2002. Cited on p. 874, 875

[1798] Uludag, Yasin, "Hi-Z Screen-Space Tracing," in Wolfgang Engel, ed., *GPU Pro^5*, CRC Press, pp. 149–192, 2014. Cited on p. 507

[1799] Umenhoffer, Tamás, Lázló Szirmay-Kalos, and Gábor Szijártó, "Spherical Billboards and Their Application to Rendering Explosions," in *Graphics Interface 2006*, Canadian Human-Computer Communications Society, pp. 57–63, 2006. Cited on p. 559

[1800] Umenhoffer, Tamás, László Szirmay-Kalos, and Gábor Szíjártó, "Spherical Billboards for Rendering Volumetric Data," in Wolfgang Engel, ed., *ShaderX^5*, Charles River Media, pp. 275–285, 2006. Cited on p. 559

[1801] *Unity User Manual*, Unity Technologies, 2017. Cited on p. 287

[1802] *Unreal Engine 4 Documentation*, Epic Games, 2017. Cited on p. 114, 126, 128, 129, 262, 287, 364, 611, 644, 920, 923, 932, 934, 939

[1803] Upchurch, Paul, and Mathieu Desbrun, "Tightening the Precision of Perspective Rendering," *journal of graphics tools*, vol. 16, no. 1, pp. 40–56, 2012. Cited on p. 101

[1804] Upstill, S., *The RenderMan Companion: A Programmer's Guide to Realistic Computer Graphics*, Addison-Wesley, 1990. Cited on p. 37

[1805] Vaidyanathan, K., M. Salvi, R. Toth, T. Foley, T. Akenine-Möller, J. Nilsson, J. Munkberg, J. Hasselgren, M. Sugihara, P. Clarberg, T. Janczak, and A. Lefohn, "Coarse Pixel Shading," in *High Performance Graphics 2014*, Eurographics Association, pp. 9–18, June 2014. Cited on p. 924, 1013

[1806] Vaidyanathan, Karthik, Jacob Munkberg, Petrik Clarberg, and Marco Salvi, "Layered Light Field Reconstruction for Defocus Blur," *ACM Transactions on Graphics*, vol. 34, no. 2, pp. 23:1–23:12, Feb. 2015. Cited on p. 536

[1807] Vaidyanathan, K. T. Akenine-Möller, and M. Salvi, "Watertight Ray Traversal with Reduced Precision," in *High-Performance Graphics 2016*, Eurographics Association, pp. 33–40, June 2016. Cited on p. 1039

[1808] Vainio, Matt, "The Visual Effects of *inFAMOUS: Second Son*," *Game Developers Conference*, Mar. 2014. Cited on p. 572

[1809] Valient, Michal, "Deferred Rendering in *Killzone 2*," *Develop Conference*, July 2007. Cited on p. 882, 885, 886, 887

[1810] Valient, Michal, "Stable Rendering of Cascaded Shadow Maps," in Wolfgang Engel, ed., *ShaderX^6*, Charles River Media, pp. 231–238, 2008. Cited on p. 239, 245, 247

[1811] Valient, Michal, "Shadows + Games: Practical Considerations," *SIGGRAPH Efficient Real-Time Shadows course*, Aug. 2012. Cited on p. 245, 246, 252

[1812] Valient, Michal, "Taking *Killzone: Shadow Fall* Image Quality into the Next Generation," *Game Developers Conference*, Mar. 2014. Cited on p. 148, 235, 245, 490, 506, 507, 509, 523, 608, 609

[1813] Van Verth, Jim, "Doing Math with RGB (and A)," *Game Developers Conference*, Mar. 2015. Cited on p. 151, 208

[1814] Vaxman, Amir, Marcel Campen, Olga Diamanti, Daniele Panozzo, David Bommes, Klaus Hildebrandt, and Mirela Ben-Chen, "Directional Field Synthesis, Design, and Processing," *Computer Graphics Forum*, vol. 35, no. 2, pp. 545–572, 2016. Cited on p. 672

[1815] Veach, Eric, "Robust Monte Carlo Methods for Light Transport Simulation," PhD Dissertation, Stanford University, Dec. 1997. Cited on p. 445

[1816] Venkataraman, S., "Fermi Asynchronous Texture Transfers," in Patrick Cozzi & Christophe Riccio, eds., *OpenGL Insights*, CRC Press, pp. 415–430, 2012. Cited on p. 1034

[1817] Villanueva, Alberto Jaspe, Fabio Marton, and Enrico Gobbetti, "SSVDAGs: Symmetry-Aware Sparse Voxel DAGs," in *Proceedings of the 20th ACM SIGGRAPH Symposium on Interactive 3D Graphics and Games*, ACM, pp. 7–14, 2016. Cited on p. 586

[1818] *Virtual Terrain Project*,http://www.vterrain.org. Cited on p. 877

[1819] Vlachos, Alex, Jörg Peters, Chas Boyd, and Jason L. Mitchell, "Curved PN Triangles," in *Proceedings of the 2001 Symposium on Interactive 3D Graphics*, ACM, pp. 159–166, 2001. Cited on p. 744, 745, 746

[1820] Vlachos, Alex, and John Isidoro, "Smooth C^2 Quaternion-Based Flythrough Paths," in Mark DeLoura, ed., *Game Programming Gems 2*, Charles River Media, pp. 220–227, 2001. Cited on p. 102

[1821] Vlachos, Alex, "Post Processing in *The Orange Box*," *Game Developers Conference*, Feb. 2008. Cited on p. 288, 538

[1822] Vlachos, Alex, "Rendering Wounds in *Left 4 Dead 2*," *Game Developers Conference*, Mar. 2010. Cited on p. 366

[1823] Vlachos, Alex, "Advanced VR Rendering," *Game Developers Conference*, Mar. 2015. Cited on p. 371, 628, 922, 925, 926, 927, 933, 934, 939, 940, 1010

[1824] Vlachos, Alex, "Advanced VR Rendering Performance," *Game Developers Conference*, Mar. 2016. Cited on p. 784, 805, 928, 930, 931, 936, 937, 938, 940

[1825] Voorhies, Douglas, "Space-Filling Curves and a Measure of Coherence," in James Arvo, ed., *Graphics Gems II*, Academic Press, pp. 26–30, 1991. Cited on p. 1018

[1826] *Vulkan Overview*, Khronos Group, Feb. 2016. Cited on p. 806

[1827] Walbourn, Chuck, ed., *SIGGRAPH Introduction to Direct3D 10 course*, Aug. 2007. Cited on p. 798

[1828] Wald, Ingo, William R. Mark, Johannes Günther, Solomon Boulos, Thiago Ize, Warren Hunt, Steven G. Parker, and Peter Shirley, "State of the Art in Ray Tracing Animated Scenes," *Computer Graphics Forum*, vol. 28, no. 6, pp. 1691–1722, 2009. Cited on p. 953

[1829] Wald, Ingo, Sven Woop, Carsten Benthin, Gregory S. Johnsson, and Manfred Ernst, "Embree: A Kernel Framework for Efficient CPU Ray Tracing," *ACM Transactions on Graphics*, vol. 33, no. 4, pp. 143:1–143:8, 2014. Cited on p. 452, 821

[1830] Walker, R., and J. Snoeyink, "Using CSG Representations of Polygons for Practical Point-in-Polygon Tests," in *ACM SIGGRAPH '97 Visual Proceedings*, ACM, p. 152, Aug. 1997. Cited on p. 967

[1831] Wallace, Evan, "Rendering Realtime Caustics in WebGL," *Medium* blog, Jan. 7, 2016. Cited on p. 631

[1832] Walter, Bruce, Sebastian Fernandez, Adam Arbree, Kavita Bala, Michael Donikian, and Donald P. Greenberg, "Lightcuts: A Scalable Approach to Illumination," *ACM Transactions on Graphics*, vol. 24, no. 3, pp. 1098–1107, 2005. Cited on p. 431, 901

[1833] Walter, Bruce, Stephen R. Marschner, Hongsong Li, and Kenneth E. Torrance, "Microfacet Models for Refraction through Rough Surfaces," *Rendering Techniques 2007*, Eurographics Association, pp. 195–206, June 2007. Cited on p. 334, 337, 339, 340, 369, 419

[1834] Walton, Patrick, "Pathfinder, a Fast GPU-Based Font Rasterizer in Rust," *pcwalton blog*, Feb. 14, 2017. Cited on p. 676

[1835] Wan, Liang, Tien-Tsin Wong, and Chi-Sing Leung, "Isocube: Exploiting the Cubemap Hardware," *IEEE Transactions on Visualization and Computer Graphics*, vol. 13, no. 4, pp. 720–731, July 2007. Cited on p. 412

[1836] Wan, Liang, Tien-Tsin Wong, Chi-Sing Leung, and Chi-Wing Fu, "Isocube: A Cubemap with Uniformly Distributed and Equally Important Texels," in Wolfgang Engel, ed., *ShaderX^6*, Charles River Media, pp. 83–92, 2008. Cited on p. 412

[1837] Wang, Beibei, and Huw Bowles, "A Robust and Flexible Real-Time Sparkle Effect," in *Proceedings of the Eurographics Symposium on Rendering: Experimental Ideas & Implementations*, Eurographics Association, pp. 49–54, 2016. Cited on p. 372

[1838] Wang, Jiaping, Peiran Ren, Minmin Gong, John Snyder, and Baining Guo, "All-Frequency Rendering of Dynamic, Spatially-Varying Reflectance," *ACM Transactions on Graphics*, vol. 28, no. 5, pp. 133:1–133:10, 2009. Cited on p. 397, 398, 466, 472

[1839] Wang, Niniane, "Realistic and Fast Cloud Rendering," *journal of graphics tools*, vol. 9, no. 3, pp. 21–40, 2004. Cited on p. 556

[1840] Wang, Niniane, "Let There Be Clouds!" *Game Developer*, vol. 11, no. 1, pp. 34–39, Jan. 2004. Cited on p. 556

[1841] Wang, Rui, Ren Ng, David P. Luebke, and Greg Humphreys, "Efficient Wavelet Rotation for Environment Map Rendering," in *17th Eurographics Symposium on Rendering*, Eurographics Association, pp. 173–182, 2006. Cited on p. 402

[1842] Wang, R., X. Yang, Y. Yuan, Yazhen, W. Chen, K. Bala, and H. Bao, "Automatic Shader Simplification Using Surface Signal Approximation," *ACM Transactions on Graphics*, vol. 33, no. 6, pp. 226:1–226:11, 2014. Cited on p. 853

[1843] Wang, R., B. Yu, K. Marco, T. Hu, D. Gutierrez, and H. Bao, "Real-Time Rendering on a Power Budget," *ACM Transactions on Graphics*, vol. 335 no. 4, pp. 111:1–111:11, 2016. Cited on p. 866

[1844] Wang, X., X. Tong, S. Lin, S. Hu, B. Guo, and H.-Y. Shum, "Generalized Displacement Maps," in *15th Eurographics Symposium on Rendering*, Eurographics Association, pp. 227–233, June 2004. Cited on p. 219

[1845] Wang, Yulan, and Steven Molnar, "Second-Depth Shadow Mapping," Technical Report TR94-019, Department of Computer Science, University of North Carolina at Chapel Hill, 1994. Cited on p. 238

[1846] Wanger, Leonard, "The Effect of Shadow Quality on the Perception of Spatial Relationships in Computer Generated Imagery," in *Proceedings of the 1992 Symposium on Interactive 3D Graphics*, ACM, pp. 39–42, 1992. Cited on p. 225, 611

[1847] Warren, Joe, and Henrik Weimer, *Subdivision Methods for Geometric Design: A Constructive Approach*, Morgan Kaufmann, 2001. Cited on p. 718, 754, 756, 760, 761, 781

[1848] Wasson, Ben, "Maxwell's Dynamic Super Resolution Explored," *The Tech Report* website, Sept. 30, 2014. Cited on p. 139

[1849] Watson, Benjamin, and David Luebke, "The Ultimate Display: Where Will All the Pixels Come From?" *Computer*, vol. 38, no. 8, pp. 54–61, Aug. 2005. Cited on p. 1, 808, 817

[1850] Watt, Alan, and Fabio Policarpo, *Advanced Game Development with Programmable Graphics Hardware*, A K Peters, Ltd., 2005. Cited on p. 220, 222

[1851] van Waveren, J. M. P., "Real-Time Texture Streaming & Decompression," Technical Report, Id Software, Nov. 2006. Cited on p. 870

[1852] van Waveren, J. M. P., and Ignacio Castaño, "Real-Time YCoCg-DXT Decompression," Technical Report, Id Software, Sept. 2007. Cited on p. 198

[1853] van Waveren, J. M. P., and Ignacio Castaño, "Real-Time Normal Map DXT Compression," Technical Report, Id Software, Feb. 2008. Cited on p. 198

[1854] van Waveren, J. M. P., "id Tech 5 Challenges," *SIGGRAPH Beyond Programmable Shading course*, Aug. 2009. Cited on p. 812, 869

[1855] van Waveren, J. M. P., and E. Hart, "Using Virtual Texturing to Handle Massive Texture Data," *GPU Technology Conference (GTC)*, Sept. 2010. Cited on p. 868, 870

[1856] van Waveren, J. M. P., "Software Virtual Textures," Technical Report, Id Software, Feb. 2012. Cited on p. 868

[1857] van Waveren, J. M. P., "The Asynchronous Time Warp for Virtual Reality on Consumer Hardware," in *Proceedings of the 22nd ACM Conference on Virtual Reality Software and Technology*, ACM, pp. 37–46, Nov. 2016. Cited on p. 936, 937

[1858] Webb, Matthew, Emil Praun, Adam Finkelstein, and Hugues Hoppe, "Fine Tone Control in Hardware Hatching," in *Proceedings of the 2nd International Symposium on Non-Photorealistic Animation and Rendering*, ACM, pp. 53–58, June 2002. Cited on p. 671

[1859] Weber, Marco, and Peter Quayle, "Post-Processing Effects on Mobile Devices," in Wolfgang Engel, ed., *GPU Pro²*, A K Peters/CRC Press, pp. 291–305, 2011. Cited on p. 527

[1860] Wei, Li-Yi, "Tile-Based Texture Mapping," in Matt Pharr, ed., *GPU Gems 2*, Addison-Wesley, pp. 189–199, 2005. Cited on p. 175

[1861] Wei, Li-Yi, Sylvain Lefebvre, Vivek Kwatra, and Greg Turk, "State of the Art in Example-Based Texture Synthesis,' in *Eurographics 2009—State of the Art Reports*, Eurographics Association, pp. 93–117, 2009. Cited on p. 200

[1862] Weidlich, Andrea, and Alexander Wilkie, "Arbitrarily Layered Micro-Facet Surfaces," in *GRAPHITE 2007*, ACM, pp. 171–178, 2007. Cited on p. 364

[1863] Weidlich, Andrea, and Alexander Wilkie, *SIGGRAPH Asia Thinking in Layers: Modeling with Layered Materials course*, Aug. 2011. Cited on p. 364

[1864] Weier, M., M. Stengel, T. Roth, P. Didyk, E. Eisemann, M. Eisemann, S. Grogorick, A. Hinkenjann, E. Kruijff, M. Magnor, K. Myszkowski, and P. Slusallek, "Perception-Driven Accelerated Rendering," *Computer Graphics Forum*, vol. 36, no. 2, pp. 611–643, 2017. Cited on p. 587, 940

[1865] Weiskopf, D., and T. Ertl, "Shadow Mapping Based on Dual Depth Layers," *Eurographics 2003 Short Presentation*, Sept. 2003. Cited on p. 238

[1866] Welsh, Terry, "Parallax Mapping with Offset Limiting: A Per-Pixel Approximation of Uneven Surfaces," Technical Report, Infiscape Corp., Jan. 18, 2004. Also collected in [429]. Cited on p. 215, 216

[1867] Welzl, Emo, "Smallest Enclosing Disks (Balls and Ellipsoids)," in H. Maurer, ed., *New Results and New Trends in Computer Science*, LNCS 555, Springer, pp. 359–370, 1991. Cited on p. 950

[1868] Wennersten, Per, and Jacob Ström, "Table-Based Alpha Compression," *Computer Graphics Forum*, vol. 28, no. 2, pp. 687–695, 2009. Cited on p. 194

[1869] Wenzel, Carsten, "Far Cry and DirectX," *Game Developers Conference*, Mar. 2005. Cited on p. 528, 799

[1870] Wenzel, Carsten, "Real-Time Atmospheric Effects in Games," *SIGGRAPH Advanced Real-Time Rendering in 3D Graphics and Games course*, Aug. 2006. Cited on p. 559

[1871] Wenzel, Carsten, "Real-Time Atmospheric Effects in Games Revisited," *Game Developers Conference*, Mar. 2007. Cited on p. 551, 556, 601, 602, 614

[1872] Weronko, S., and S. Andreason, "Real-Time Transformations in *The Order 1886*," in *ACM SIGGRAPH 2015 Talks*, ACM, article no. 8, Aug. 2015. Cited on p. 91

[1873] Westin, Stephen H., Hongsong Li, and Kenneth E. Torrance, "A Field Guide to BRDF Models," Research Note PCG-04-01, Cornell University Program of Computer Graphics, Jan. 2004. Cited on p. 329

[1874] Westin, Stephen H., Hongsong Li, and Kenneth E. Torrance, "A Comparison of Four BRDF Models," Research Note PCG-04-02, Cornell University Program of Computer Graphics, Apr. 2004. Cited on p. 329

[1875] Wetzstein, Gordon, "Focus Cues and Computational Near-Eye Displays with Focus Cues," *SIGGRAPH Applications of Visual Perception to Virtual Reality course*, Aug. 2017. Cited on p. 549, 923

[1876] Whatley, David, "Towards Photorealism in Virtual Botany," in Matt Pharr, ed., *GPU Gems 2*, Addison-Wesley, pp. 7–45, 2005. Cited on p. 207, 858

[1877] White, John, and Colin Barré-Brisebois, "More Performance! Five Rendering Ideas from *Battlefield 3* and *Need For Speed: The Run*," *SIGGRAPH Advances in Real-Time Rendering in Games course*, Aug. 2011. Cited on p. 527, 804, 896, 898, 904

[1878] Whiting, Nick, "Integrating the Oculus Rift into Unreal Engine 4," *Gamasutra*, June 11, 2013. Cited on p. 934

[1879] Whitley, Brandon, "The Destiny Particle Architecture," *SIGGRAPH Advances in Real-Time Rendering in Games course*, Aug. 2017. Cited on p. 571

[1880] Whittinghill, David, "Nasum Virtualis: A Simple Technique for Reducing Simulator Sickness in Head Mounted VR," *Game Developers Conference*, Mar. 2015. Cited on p. 920

[1881] Widmark, M., "Terrain in *Battlefield 3*: A Modern, Complete and Scalable System," *Game Developers Conference*, Mar. 2012. Cited on p. 869, 878

[1882] Wiesendanger, Tobias, "Stingray Renderer Walkthrough," *Autodesk Stingray* blog, Feb. 1, 2017. Cited on p. 549, 803, 814

[1883] Wihlidal, Graham, "Optimizing the Graphics Pipeline with Compute," *Game Developers Conference*, Mar. 2016. Cited on p. 54, 798, 834, 837, 840, 848, 849, 851, 908, 986

[1884] Wihlidal, Graham, "Optimizing the Graphics Pipeline with Compute," in Wolfgang Engel, ed., *GPU Zen*, Black Cat Publishing, pp. 277–320, 2017. Cited on p. 54, 702, 784, 798, 812, 834, 837, 840, 848, 850, 851, 908, 986

[1885] Wihlidal, Graham, "4K Checkerboard in *Battlefield 1* and *Mass Effect Andromeda*," *Game Developers Conference*, Feb.–Mar. 2017. Cited on p. 143, 805, 906, 1042

[1886] Wiley, Abe, and Thorsten Scheuermann, "The Art and Technology of Whiteout," *SIGGRAPH AMD Technical Talk*, Aug. 2007. Cited on p. 427

[1887] Williams, Amy, Steve Barrus, R. Keith Morley, and Peter Shirley, "An Efficient and Robust Ray-Box Intersection Algorithm," *journal of graphics tools*, vol. 10, no. 1, pp. 49–54, 2005. Cited on p. 961

[1888] Williams, Lance, "Casting Curved Shadows on Curved Surfaces," *Computer Graphics (SIGGRAPH '78 Proceedings)*, vol. 12, no. 3, pp. 270–274, Aug. 1978. Cited on p. 234

[1889] Williams, Lance, "Pyramidal Parametrics," *Computer Graphics*, vol. 7, no. 3, pp. 1–11, July 1983. Cited on p. 183, 185, 408

[1890] Willmott, Andrew, "Rapid Simplification of Multi-attribute Meshes," in *Proceedings of the ACM SIGGRAPH Symposium on High-Performance Graphics*, ACM, pp. 151–158, Aug. 2011. Cited on p. 710

[1891] Wilson, Timothy, "High Performance Stereo Rendering for VR," *San Diego Virtual Reality Meetup*, Jan. 20, 2015. Cited on p. 927

[1892] Wimmer, Michael, Peter Wonka, and François Sillion, "Point-Based Impostors for Real-Time Visualization," in *Rendering Techniques 2001*, Springer, pp. 163–176, June 2001. Cited on p. 561

[1893] Wimmer, Michael, Daniel Scherzer, and Werner Purgathofer, "Light Space Perspective Shadow Maps," in *Proceedings of the Fifteenth Eurographics Conference on Rendering Techniques*, Eurographics Association, pp. 143–151, June 2004. Cited on p. 241

[1894] Wimmer, Michael, and Jiří Bittner, "Hardware Occlusion Queries Made Useful," in Matt Pharr, ed., *GPU Gems 2*, Addison-Wesley, pp. 91–108, 2005. Cited on p. 844

[1895] Wimmer, Michael, and Daniel Scherzer, "Robust Shadow Mapping with Light-Space Perspective Shadow Maps," in Wolfgang Engel, ed., *ShaderX⁴*, Charles River Media, pp. 313–330, 2005. Cited on p. 241

[1896] Winnemöller, Holger, "XDoG: Advanced Image Stylization with eXtended Difference-of-Gaussians," in *ACM SIGGRAPH/Eurographics Symposium on Non-Photorealistic Animation and Rendering*, ACM, pp. 147–156, Aug. 2011. Cited on p. 665

[1897] Wloka, Matthias, "Batch, Batch, Batch: What Does It Really Mean?" *Game Developers Conference*, Mar. 2003. Cited on p. 796

[1898] Wolff, Lawrence B., "A Diffuse Reflectance Model for Smooth Dielectric Surfaces," *Journal of the Optical Society of America*, vol. 11, no. 11, pp. 2956–2968, Nov. 1994. Cited on p. 353

[1899] Wolff, Lawrence B., Shree K. Nayar, and Michael Oren, "Improved Diffuse Reflection Models for Computer Vision," *International Journal of Computer Vision*, vol. 30, no. 1, pp. 55–71, 1998. Cited on p. 354

[1900] Woo, Andrew, "The Shadow Depth Map Revisited," in David Kirk, ed., *Graphics Gems III*, Academic Press, pp. 338–342, 1992. Cited on p. 238

[1901] Woo, Andrew, Andrew Pearce, and Marc Ouellette, "It's Really Not a Rendering Bug, You See...," *IEEE Computer Graphics and Applications*, vol. 16, no. 5, pp. 21–25, Sept. 1996. Cited on p. 688

[1902] Woo, Andrew, and Pierre Poulin, *Shadow Algorithms Data Miner*, A K Peters/CRC Press, 2011. Cited on p. 223, 265

[1903] Woodland, Ryan, "Filling the Gaps—Advanced Animation Using Stitching and Skinning," in Mark DeLoura, ed., *Game Programming Gems*, Charles River Media, pp. 476–483, 2000. Cited on p. 84, 85

[1904] Woodland, Ryan, "Advanced Texturing Using Texture Coordinate Generation," in Mark DeLoura, ed., *Game Programming Gems*, Charles River Media, pp. 549–554, 2000. Cited on p. 200, 221

[1905] Woop, Sven, Jörg Schmittler, and Philipp Slusallek, "RPU: A Programmable Ray Processing Unit for Realtime Ray Tracing," *ACM Transactions on Graphics*, vol. 24, no. 3, pp. 434–444, Aug. 2005. Cited on p. 1039

[1906] Woop, Sven, Carsten Benthin, and Ingo Wald, "Watertight Ray/Triangle Intersection," *Journal of Computer Graphics Techniques*, vol. 2, no. 1, pp. 65–82, June 2013. Cited on p. 962

[1907] Worley, Steven, "A Cellular Texture Basis Function," in *SIGGRAPH '96: Proceedings of the 23rd Annual Conference on Computer Graphics and Interactive Techniques*, ACM, pp. 291–294, 1996. Cited on p. 620

[1908] Wrenninge, Magnus, *Production Volume Rendering: Design and Implementation*, A K Peters/CRC Press, Sept. 2012. Cited on p. 582, 594, 610

[1909] Wrenninge, Magnus, Chris Kulla, and Viktor Lundqvist, "Oz: The Great and Volumetric," in *ACM SIGGRAPH 2013 Talks*, ACM, article no. 46, July 2013. Cited on p. 621

[1910] Wright, Daniel, "Dynamic Occlusion with Signed Distance Fields," *SIGGRAPH Advances in Real-Time Rendering in Games course*, Aug. 2015. Cited on p. 454, 467

[1911] Wronski, Bartlomiej, "*Assassin's Creed: Black Flag*—Road to Next-Gen Graphics," *Game Developers Conference*, Mar. 2014. Cited on p. 32, 218, 478, 571, 572, 801

[1912] Wronski, Bartlomiej, "Temporal Supersampling and Antialiasing," *Bart Wronski* blog, Mar. 15, 2014. Cited on p. 143, 540

[1913] Wronski, Bartlomiej, "GDC Follow-Up: Screenspace Reflections Filtering and Up-Sampling," *Bart Wronski* blog, Mar. 23, 2014. Cited on p. 509

[1914] Wronski, Bartlomiej, "GCN—Two Ways of Latency Hiding and Wave Occupancy," *Bart Wronski* blog, Mar. 27, 2014. Cited on p. 32, 801, 1005

[1915] Wronski, Bartlomiej, "Bokeh Depth of Field—Going Insane! Part 1," *Bart Wronski* blog, Apr. 7, 2014. Cited on p. 531

[1916] Wronski, Bartlomiej, "Temporal Supersampling pt. 2—SSAO Demonstration," *Bart Wronski* blog, Apr. 27, 2014. Cited on p. 462

[1917] Wronski, Bartlomiej, "Volumetric Fog: Unified Compute Shader-Based Solution to Atmospheric Scattering," *SIGGRAPH Advances in Real-Time Rendering in Games course*, Aug. 2014. Cited on p. 610, 611

[1918] Wronski, Bartlomiej, "Designing a Next-Generation Post-Effects Pipeline," *Bart Wronski* blog, Dec. 9, 2014. Cited on p. 514, 520, 527, 543

[1919] Wronski, Bartlomiej, "Anamorphic Lens Flares and Visual Effects," *Bart Wronski* blog, Mar. 9, 2015. Cited on p. 526

[1920] Wronski, Bartlomiej, "Fixing Screen-Space Deferred Decals," *Bart Wronski* blog, Mar. 12, 2015. Cited on p. 889, 890

[1921] Wronski, Bartlomiej, "Localized Tonemapping—Is Global Exposure and Global Tonemapping Operator Enough for Video Games?," *Bart Wronski* blog, Aug. 29, 2016. Cited on p. 286

[1922] Wronski, Bartlomiej, "Cull That Cone! Improved Cone/Spotlight Visibility Tests for Tiled and Clustered Lighting," *Bart Wronski* blog, Apr. 13, 2017. Cited on p. 901

[1923] Wronski, Bartlomiej, "Separable Disk-Like Depth of Field," *Bart Wronski* blog, Aug. 6, 2017. Cited on p. 518

[1924] Wu, Kui, and Cem Yuksel, "Real-Time Fiber-Level Cloth Rendering," *Symposium on Interactive 3D Graphics and Games*, Mar. 2017. Cited on p. 359

[1925] Wu, Kui, Nghia Truong, Cem Yuksel, and Rama Hoetzlein, "Fast Fluid Simulations with Sparse Volumes on the GPU," *Computer Graphics Forum*, vol. 37, no. 1, pp. 157–167, 2018. Cited on p. 579

[1926] Wu, Kui, and Cem Yuksel, "Real-Time Cloth Rendering with Fiber-Level Detail," *IEEE Transactions on Visualization and Computer Graphics*, to appear. Cited on p. 359

[1927] Wyman, Chris, "Interactive Image-Space Refraction of Nearby Geometry," in *GRAPHITE 2005*, ACM, pp. 205–211, Nov. 2005. Cited on p. 630, 632

[1928] Wyman, Chris, "Interactive Refractions and Caustics Using Image-Space Techniques," in Wolfgang Engel, ed., *ShaderX⁵*, Charles River Media, pp. 359–371, 2006. Cited on p. 632

[1929] Wyman, Chris, "Hierarchical Caustic Maps," in *Proceedings of the 2008 Symposium on Interactive 3D Graphics and Games*, ACM, pp. 163–172, Feb. 2008. Cited on p. 632

[1930] Wyman, C., R. Hoetzlein, and A. Lefohn, "Frustum-Traced Raster Shadows: Revisiting Irregular Z-Buffers," in *Proceedings of the 19th Symposium on Interactive 3D Graphics and Games*, ACM, pp. 15–23, Feb.–Mar. 2015. Cited on p. 261, 1001

[1931] Wyman, Chris, "Exploring and Expanding the Continuum of OIT Algorithms," in *Proceedings of High-Performance Graphics*, Eurographics Association, pp. 1–11, June 2016. Cited on p. 156, 159, 165

[1932] Wyman, Chris, Rama Hoetzlein, and Aaron Lefohn, "Frustum-Traced Irregular Z-Buffers: Fast, Sub-pixel Accurate Hard Shadows," *IEEE Transactions on Visualization and Computer Graphics*, vol. 22, no. 10, pp. 2249–2261, Oct. 2016. Cited on p. 261

[1933] Wyman, Chris, and Morgan McGuire, "Hashed Alpha Testing," *Symposium on Interactive 3D Graphics and Games*, Mar. 2017. Cited on p. 206, 208, 642

[1934] Wyszecki, Günther, and W. S. Stiles, *Color Science: Concepts and Methods, Quantitative Data and Formulae*, Second Edition, John Wiley & Sons, Inc., 2000. Cited on p. 276, 291

[1935] Xia, Julie C., Jihad El-Sana, and Amitabh Varshney, "Adaptive Real-Time Level-of-Detail-Based Rendering for Polygonal Objects," *IEEE Transactions on Visualization and Computer Graphics*, vol. 3, no. 2, pp. 171–183, June 1997. Cited on p. 772

[1936] Xiao, Xiangyun, Shuai Zhang, and Xubo Yang, "Real-Time High-Quality Surface Rendering for Large Scale Particle-Based Fluids," *Symposium on Interactive 3D Graphics and Games*, Mar. 2017. Cited on p. 572, 753

[1937] Xie, Feng, and Jon Lanz, "Physically Based Shading at DreamWorks Animation," *SIGGRAPH Physically Based Shading in Theory and Practice course*, Aug. 2017. Cited on p. 336, 359, 364

[1938] Xu, Ke, "Temporal Antialiasing in *Uncharted 4*," *SIGGRAPH Advances in Real-Time Rendering in Games course*, July 2016. Cited on p. 142, 143, 144, 492

[1939] Xu, Kun, Yun-Tao Jia, Hongbo Fu, Shimin Hu, and Chiew-Lan Tai, "Spherical Piecewise Constant Basis Functions for All-Frequency Precomputed Radiance Transfer," *IEEE Transactions on Visualization and Computer Graphics*, vol. 14, no. 2, pp. 454–467, Mar.–Apr. 2008. Cited on p. 402

[1940] Xu, Kun, Wei-Lun Sun, Zhao Dong, Dan-Yong Zhao, Run-Dong Wu, and Shi-Min Hu, "Anisotropic Spherical Gaussians," *ACM Transactions on Graphics*, vol. 32, no. 6, pp. 209:1–209:11, 2013. Cited on p. 398, 498

[1941] Yan, Ling-Qi, and Hašan, Miloš, Wenzel Jakob, Jason Lawrence, Steve Marschner, and Ravi Ramamoorthi, "Rendering Glints on High-Resolution Normal-Mapped Specular Surfaces," *ACM Transactions on Graphics (SIGGRAPH 2014)*, vol. 33, no. 4, pp. 116:1–116:9, July 2014. Cited on p. 372

[1942] Yan, Ling-Qi, Miloš Hašan, Steve Marschner, and Ravi Ramamoorthi, "Position-Normal Distributions for Efficient Rendering of Specular Microstructure," *ACM Transactions on Graphics (SIGGRAPH 2016)*, vol. 35, no. 4, pp. 56:1–56:9, July 2016. Cited on p. 372

[1943] Yang, Baoguang, Zhao Dong, Jieqing Feng, Hans-Peter Seidel, and Jan Kautz, "Variance Soft Shadow Mapping," *Computer Graphics Forum*, vol. 29, no. 7, pp. 2127–2134, 2010. Cited on p. 257, 259

[1944] Yang, Lei, Pedro V. Sander, and Jason Lawrence, "Geometry-Aware Framebuffer Level of Detail," in *Proceedings of the Nineteenth Eurographics Symposium on Rendering*, Eurographics Association, pp. 1183–1188, June 2008. Cited on p. 520

[1945] Yang, L., Y.-C. Tse, P. Sander, J. Lawrence, D. Nehab, H. Hoppe, and C. Wilkins, "Image-Space Bidirectional Scene Reprojection," *ACM Transactions on Graphics*, vol. 30, no. 6, pp. 150:1–150:10, 2011. Cited on p. 523

[1946] Yang, L., and H. Bowles, "Accelerating Rendering Pipelines Using Bidirectional Iterative Reprojection," *SIGGRAPH Advances in Real-Time Rendering in Games course*, Aug. 2012. Cited on p. 523

[1947] Ylitie, Henri, Tero Karras, and Samuli Laine, "Efficient Incoherent Ray Traversal on GPUs Through Compressed Wide BVHs," *High Performance Graphics*, July 2017. Cited on p. 511

[1948] Yoon, Sung-Eui, Peter Lindstrom, Valerio Pascucci, and Dinesh Manocha, "Cache-Oblivious Mesh Layouts," *ACM Transactions on Graphics*, vol. 24, no. 3, pp. 886–893, July 2005. Cited on p. 828

[1949] Yoon, Sung-Eui, and Dinesh Manocha, "Cache-Efficient Layouts of Bounding Volume Hierarchies," *Computer Graphics Forum*, vol. 25, no. 3, pp. 853–857, 2006. Cited on p. 828

[1950] Yoon, Sung-Eui, Sean Curtis, and Dinesh Manocha, "Ray Tracing Dynamic Scenes Using Selective Restructuring," in *18th Eurographics Symposium on Rendering*, Eurographics Association, pp. 73–84, June 2007. Cited on p. 821

[1951] Yoshida, Akiko, Matthias Ihrke, Rafał Mantiuk, and Hans-Peter Seidel, "Brightness of the Glare Illusion," *Proceeding of the 5th Symposium on Applied Perception in Graphics and Visualization*, ACM, pp. 83–90, Aug. 2008. Cited on p. 524

[1952] Yu, X., R. Wang, and J. Yu, "Real-Time Depth of Field Rendering via Dynamic Light Field Generation and Filtering," *Computer Graphics Forum*, vol. 29, no. 7, pp. 2009–2107, 2010. Cited on p. 523

[1953] Yuksel, Cem, and John Keyser, "Deep Opacity Maps," *Computer Graphics Forum*, vol. 27, no. 2, pp. 675–680, 2008. Cited on p. 257, 645, 646

[1954] Yuksel, Cem, and Sara Tariq, *SIGGRAPH Advanced Techniques in Real-Time Hair Rendering and Simulation course*, July 2010. Cited on p. 45, 642, 646, 649

[1955] Yuksel, Cem, "Mesh Color Textures," in *High Performance Graphics 2017*, Eurographics Association, pp. 17:1–17:11, 2017. Cited on p. 191

[1956] Yusov, E., "Real-Time Deformable Terrain Rendering with DirectX 11," in Wolfgang Engel, ed., *ShaderX³*, Charles River Media, pp. 13–39, 2004. Cited on p. 879

[1957] Yusov, Egor, "Outdoor Light Scattering," *Game Developers Conference*, Mar. 2013. Cited on p. 615

[1958] Yusov, Egor, "Practical Implementation of Light Scattering Effects Using Epipolar Sampling and 1D Min/Max Binary Trees," *Game Developers Conference*, Mar. 2013. Cited on p. 608

[1959] Yusov, Egor, "High-Performance Rendering of Realistic Cumulus Clouds Using Pre-computed Lighting," in *Proceedings of the Eurographics / ACM SIGGRAPH Symposium on High Performance Graphics*, Eurographics Association, pp. 127–136, Aug. 2014. Cited on p. 617, 618

[1960] Zakarin, Jordan, "How *The Jungle Book* Made Its Animals Look So Real with Groundbreaking VFX," *Inverse.com*, Apr. 15, 2016. Cited on p. 1042

[1961] Zarge, Jonathan, and Richard Huddy, "Squeezing Performance out of Your Game with ATI Developer Performance Tools and Optimization Techniques," *Game Developers Conference*, Mar. 2006. Cited on p. 713, 786, 787

[1962] Zhang, Fan, Hanqiu Sun, Leilei Xu, and Kit-Lun Lee, "Parallel-Split Shadow Maps for Large-Scale Virtual Environments," in *Proceedings of the 2006 ACM International Conference on Virtual Reality Continuum and Its Applications*, ACM, pp. 311–318, June 2006. Cited on p. 242, 244

[1963] Zhang, Fan, Hanqiu Sun, and Oskari Nyman, "Parallel-Split Shadow Maps on Programmable GPUs," in Hubert Nguyen, ed., *GPU Gems 3*, Addison-Wesley, pp. 203–237, 2007. Cited on p. 242, 243, 244

[1964] Zhang, Fan, Alexander Zaprjagaev, and Allan Bentham, "Practical Cascaded Shadow Maps," in Wolfgang Engel, ed., *ShaderX⁷*, Charles River Media, pp. 305–329, 2009. Cited on p. 242, 245

[1965] Zhang, Hansong, *Effective Occlusion Culling for the Interactive Display of Arbitrary Models*, PhD thesis, Department of Computer Science, University of North Carolina at Chapel Hill, July 1998. Cited on p. 843

[1966] Zhang, Long, Qian Sun, and Ying He, "Splatting Lines: An Efficient Method for Illustrating 3D Surfaces and Volumes," in *Proceedings of the 18th Meeting of the ACM SIGGRAPH Symposium on Interactive 3D Graphics and Games*, ACM, pp. 135–142, Mar. 2014. Cited on p. 665

[1967] Zhao, Guangyuan, and Xianming Sun, "Error Analysis of Using Henyey-Greensterin in Monte Carlo Radiative Transfer Simulations," *Electromagnetics Research Symposium*, Mar. 2010. Cited on p. 598

[1968] Zhdan, Dmitry, "Tiled Shading: Light Culling—Reaching the Speed of Light," *Game Developers Conference*, Mar. 2016. Cited on p. 894

[1969] Zhou, Kun, Yaohua Hu, Stephen Lin, Baining Guo, and Heung-Yeung Shum, "Precomputed Shadow Fields for Dynamic Scenes," *ACM Transactions on Graphics (SIGGRAPH 2005)*, vol. 24, no. 3, pp. 1196–1201, 2005. Cited on p. 466

[1970] Zhukov, Sergei, Andrei Iones, and Grigorij Kronin, "An Ambient Light Illumination Model," in *Rendering Techniques '98*, Springer, pp. 45–56, June–July 1998. Cited on p. 449, 454, 457

[1971] Zink, Jason, Matt Pettineo, and Jack Hoxley, *Practical Rendering & Computation with Direct3D 11*, CRC Press, 2011. Cited on p. 47, 54, 90, 518, 519, 520, 568, 795, 813, 814, 914

[1972] Zinke, Arno, Cem Yuksel, Weber Andreas, and John Keyser, "Dual Scattering Approximation for Fast Multiple Scattering in Hair," *ACM Transactions on Graphics (SIGGRAPH 2008)*, vol. 27, no. 3, pp. 1–10, 2008. Cited on p. 645

[1973] Zioma, Renaldas, "Better Geometry Batching Using Light Buffers," in Wolfgang Engel, ed., *ShaderX⁴*, Charles River Media, pp. 5–16, 2005. Cited on p. 893

[1974] Zirr, Tobias, and Anton Kaplanyan, "Real-Time Rendering of Procedural Multiscale Materials," *Symposium on Interactive 3D Graphics and Games*, Feb. 2016. Cited on p. 372

[1975] Zorin, Denis, Peter Schröder, and Wim Sweldens, "Interpolating Subdivision for Meshes with Arbitrary Topology," in *SIGGRAPH '96: Proceedings of the 23rd Annual Conference on Computer Graphics and Interactive Techniques*, ACM, pp. 189–192, Aug. 1996. Cited on p. 761

[1976] Zorin, Denis, *Stationary Subdivision and Multiresolution Surface Representations*, PhD thesis, CS-TR-97-32, California Institute of Technology, 1997. Cited on p. 759, 761

[1977] Zorin, Denis, Peter Schröder, Tony DeRose, Leif Kobbelt, Adi Levin, and Wim Sweldens, *SIGGRAPH Subdivision for Modeling and Animation course*, July 2000. Cited on p. 756, 760, 761, 762, 781

[1978] Zou, Ming, Tao Ju, and Nathan Carr, "An Algorithm for Triangulating Multiple 3D Polygons," *Computer Graphics Forum*, vol. 32, no. 5, pp. 157–166, 2013. Cited on p. 685

Index

For indexed terms with more than one page reference, the italicized page (or range) indicates the most significant reference.

1-ring, 759, *760*
2.5 dimensions, 531
3D printing, 578, 683, 693
3dfx Interactive, 37

A-buffer, *see under* buffer
AABB, 822, *944*, 946, 974, 976
    creation, 949
    orthographic projection, 93
AABB/object intersection, *see* intersection
        testing, AABB/AABB
Academy Color Encoding System, *see* ACES
acceleration algorithms, 14, 682, *817–879*, *see*
        also optimization
accessibility shading, 449
accommodation, 923
accumulation buffer, *see* buffer, accumulation
ACE, 1036
ACES, 287
adaptation, 285
adaptive refinement, 547
adjacency graph, 692
affinity mask, 928
Afro Samurai, 658
AHD basis, *see* basis, AHD
albedo, 314
    directional, 313
    texture, 885
aliasing, 130, *131*
    crawlies, 130
    fireflies, 132, 801
    jaggies, 130, *132*, 537
    perspective, 239
    projective, 240
    self-shadow, 236
    shadow map, 236
    temporal, 132, 182
    texture, 182, 186

alpha, *149*, 159–160, 202–208
    blending, *149–150*, 203
    channel, 24, *159*, 160, 203, 1010
    LOD, *see* level of detail, alpha
    mapping, *see* texturing
    premultiplied, 159–160
    testing, 24, 204
    unmultiplied, 160
alpha to coverage, 149, *207*
alternate frame rendering, 1013
ALU, *1002–1003*, 1029, 1036
ambient
    aperture lighting, 466
    color, 392
    cube, *394–395*, 432, 478, 488
    dice, *395*, 478, 488
    light, *see* light, ambient
ambient occlusion, 446–451
    dynamic, 453–457
    field, 452
    ground-truth, 461
    horizon-based, 460
    precomputed, 451–453
    screen-space, 457–463
    shading, 463–465
    temporal supersampling, 462
    volume, 452
    volumetric, 459
ambient/highlight/direction basis, 476
Amdahl's law, 1020
animation, 81, 85, 200, 829
    cel, 652
    impostor, 562
    particle system, 567
    sprite, 550
    subdivision, 781
    texture, *see* texturing, animation
    vertex blending, *see under* transform

anisotropic filtering, *see under* texturing, minification
anisotropic reflection, 314
anisotropic scaling, 62
anti-shadow, 227
antialiasing, 130–148
    coverage sampling, 141
    custom filter, 142
    directionally localized, 147
    distance-to-edge, 147
    enhanced quality, 141
    fast approximate, 146, 148
    FLIPQUAD, 146
    full-scene, 138
    geometry buffer, 147
    hybrid reconstruction, 146
    image-based, 147, 148
    jittering, 144, 909
    morphological, 146–148
    multisampling, *139–142*, 144–148, 155
    N-rooks, 143
    Quincunx, 145–146
    rotated grid, 143, 145, 146
    screen based, 137–148, 204–207
    subpixel morphological, 148
    subpixel reconstruction, 147
    supersampling, 138–139
        rotated grid, 1028
    temporal, *142–143*, 144–146, 148
    texture, *see* texturing, minification
aperture, 307
apex point map, 837, 980
API, 15
application stage, *see under* pipeline
arithmetic logic unit, *see* ALU
artistic rendering, *see* non-photorealistic rendering
Ashes of the Singularity, 883, 911, 913
Ashikhmin model, 357
aspect graph, *see under* spatial data structure
Assassin's Creed, 453, 539
Assassin's Creed 4: Black Flag, 478, 481
Assassin's Creed Unity, 834, 851, 905
Assimp, 716
ASTC, *see under* texturing, compression
asynchronous compute engine, *see* ACE
atan2, *8*, 72
atmosphere, 595, 596, 601, 613–616, 622–623
attenuation index, 298
augmented reality, 915–940
average cache miss ratio, 700
axis-aligned bounding box, *see* AABB
axis-aligned BSP tree, *see under* spatial data structure, BSP tree

B-spline, *see under* curves *and* surfaces
back buffer, *see* buffer, back
back plane, 93n
backface culling, *see* culling, backface
backprojection, 252
backward mapping, 532
baking, *451*, 473, 853
    least-squares, 452
balancing the pipeline, *see* pipeline
band-limited signal, 133
banding, 161, 1010
banding artifacts, 279, 1010
bandwidth, 1006
Bartleson-Breneman effect, 285
barycentric coordinates, 45, 46, 489, 673, 740, 748, 907, *963*, 998–1001
    perspective correct, 999–1001
basis, 209
    AHD, *402*, 467, 471, 484, 488, 498
    functions
        orthogonal, 398
        orthonormal, 399
    hemispherical, 402–404
    projection, 393
    spherical, 395–402
        Gaussian, *397–398*, 471–472, 477–478, 488, 498
        harmonics, *see* spherical, harmonics
        radial, 396
    standard, 8, 400
    tangent space, *209–210*, 343, 403, 766
batch, 796
batching, 795
Battlefield 1, 601
Battlefield 4, 514
BC, *see under* texturing, compression
bell curve, 515
benchmarking, 1012
bent cone, screen-space, 467
bent normal, 448, 465
Bernstein
    form, 835
        Bézier curve, 722
        Bézier patch, 737
        Bézier triangle, 740
    polynomial, *723*, 737
        Bézier triangle, 741
Bézier basis function, 723
Bézier curves, *see* curves, Bézier
Bézier patch, *see under* surfaces
Bézier triangle, *see under* surfaces
BGR color order, 1010
bias, 226
    cone, 249

normal offset, *238*, 250
receiver plane depth, 250
slope scale, *236*, 249
bidirectional reflectance distribution function,
    see BRDF
bidirectional scattering distribution function, *see*
    BSDF
bidirectional surface scattering distribution
    functions, *see* BSSRDF
bilinear interpolation, 735
billboard, 551–564, *see also* impostor
    axial, *559–560*, 568
    clouds, 563–564
    particle, 567
    screen-aligned, 553
    spherical, 559
    world-oriented, 554–559
binary space partitioning tree, *see* spatial data
    structure, BSP tree
binary tree, 820
bindless texture, 192
binormal vector, 209
biquadratic surface, 736
bitangent vector, 209, 343
blend shapes, *see* transform, morph targets
blending, 25
    additive, *151*, 527
    function, *723*, 729
        implicit surface, 752
    multi-layer alpha, 156
    operations, *see* texturing
    surfaces, *see* surfaces, implicit
Blinn lighting equation, 314
blocking, 809
bloom, 524, 604
blue-screening, 160
blur, 515–518
bokeh, *531*, 536
Boost, 793
border, 174
Borderlands, 662, 679
bottleneck, 12, *783*, 786–788, 1023
boundary representation, 581
bounded Bézier curve, *see* curves, bounded
    Bézier
bounding volume, *819*, 976
    creation, 948–953
    hierarchy, *see under* spatial data structure
    temporal, 821
bounding volume/object intersection, *see*
    intersection testing
bowtie, 684
box/object intersection, *see specific objects*
    under intersection testing

BRDF, 308–315
    anisotropic, 314
    Ashikhmin, 357
    Banks, 359
    Blinn-Phong, 314
    clear coat, 364
    cloth, 356–359
    Cook-Torrance, 314
    Disney diffuse, 354, 357
    Disney principled, 324, 340, 345, 353, 364
    Hapke model, 314
    isotropic, 310
    Kajiya-Kay, 359
    Lambertian, 313, 314
    Lommel-Seeliger model, 314
    lunar, 314
    Oren-Nayar, 354
    Phong, 314, 340
    reflectance lobe, *315*, 416
    specular lobe, *315*, 338, 416, 418
    Torrance-Sparrow, 334
    Ward, 314
    wave optics model, 359–363
Brütal Legend, 572
BSDF, 641–648
BSP tree, *see under* spatial data structure
BSSRDF, 634
buffer
    A-buffer, 155
    accumulation
        antialiasing, 139
        depth of field, 529
        motion blur, 537
        soft shadow, 228
    back, 25, 1012
    cache, 1007
    color, 24, 1009–1010
    compression, *1007–1009*, 1032–1033
    deep, 884
    double, 25, *1012*
    dynamic, 793
    framebuffer, 25
    front, 25, 1012
    G-buffer, 661, *884*
    identification, 668, *942*
    interleaved, 702
    pending, 1013
    single, 790, *1012*
    static, 794
    stencil, *24*, 53
        projection shadow, 227
        shadow volume, 230–233
    swap, 25, 1012, 1013
    triple, 1013

buffer *(continued)*
    velocity, 143, *540–541*
    visibility, 906–908, 912
    z-buffer, *24*, 53, 152, 1014–1016, 1048
        hierarchical, *see under* culling
bump mapping, 167, 208–214
    filtering
        CLEAN, 370
        LEAN, 370
        Toksvig, 369
    heightfield, 211–212
    normal map, 195, 211–214, 366, 710
    offset vector, 211
bus bandwidth, 1006
BV, *see* bounding volume
BVH, *see* spatial data structure, bounding
        volume hierarchy

C^0-continuity, *see* continuity
C^1-continuity, *see* continuity
cache
    hierarchy, 1038
    memory, 792
    post-transform, 700, 705
    pre-transform, 705
    texture, 1017–1018
    vertex, 700, 701, 703
cache-oblivious mesh, *see* mesh, cache-oblivious
CAD, 546
Call of Duty, 402, 476, 478
Call of Duty: Advanced Warfare, 286, 542, 718
Call of Duty: Black Ops, 340, 370
Call of Duty: Infinite Warfare, 325, 363–365,
        420, 902
Call of Duty: WWII, 476
camera, 307–308
camera space, 15
candela, 271
canonical view volume, 16, 94
capsule, 946
cartoon rendering, *see* shading, toon
cathode-ray tube, *see* CRT
Catmull-Clark subdivision, *see* surfaces,
        subdivision, Catmull-Clark
Catmull-Rom spline, 731
caustics, 630–632
Cel Damage, 659, 660
cel rendering, *see* shading, toon
cell, *see* culling, portal
cell-based visibility, 842
CFAA, *see* antialiasing, custom filter
character animation, *see* transform, vertex
        blending
charcoal, 652

chart, 909
checkerboard rendering, 146, 930
chroma subsampling, 804
chroma-keying, 160
chromatic aberration, 521, 628, *921*
chromaticity, 273
chrominance, 197
Chromium, 1020
CIE, 272, 273
CIE chromaticity diagram, 274–278
CIE XYZ, 273–276
CIECAM02, 278
CIELAB, 276
CIELUV, 276
ciliary corona, 524
circle of confusion, 531
Civilization V, 879
clamp, 174
Claybook, 1045
CLEAN mapping, 370
ClearType, 675
clip coordinates, 18
clipmap, 867
clipping, 19, 997–998
    guard-band, 998
    plane, 19
clock gating, 1028
clock rate, 789
CLOD, *see* level of detail, continuous
closed model, 693
clouds, 257, 556, 563–564, 598, 613, 616–620,
        622–623
clustered deferred shading, 904
clustered forward shading, 904, 907, 908, 914
clustered shading, 898–905
C^n-continuity, 728
code optimization, *see* optimization, code
CodeAnalyst, 792
coherence
    frame-to-frame, 866
    length, 362
    spatial, 837
    temporal, 866
collision detection, 14
color, 8, *272–290*
    ambient, 392
    buffer, *see* buffer, color
    grading, 289–290
    matching, 272–274
    mode, 1009
        deep color, 1010
        high color, 1009–1010
        true color, 1009–1010
    perception, 278

color appearance model, 278
color space
    ACEScg, 278
    Adobe 1998, 277
    DCI-P3, 277
    IC_TC_P, 276, 287
    Rec. 2020, 277, 281
    Rec. 709, 277, 281
    sRGB, 277, 281
    working, 278
color-matching functions, 272–273
colorimetry, 272–279
command buffer, 812–814
common-shader core, 35
communication, 1023
compositing, 159
compression
    asymmetry, 196
    buffer, *see* buffer, compression
    texture, *see* texturing, compression
    vertex, *see* vertex, compression
computational photography, 549, 573
compute shader, 14, 40, 41, 51, *54*, 245, 256,
    259, 288, 514, 518, 535, 536, 569, 578,
    582, 611, 677, 778, 784, 795, 798, 812,
    851, 879, 888, 893, 895, 896, 901, 903,
    907, 911, 912, 914, 986, 1043
compute unit, 1003, 1035
concatenation, *see* transform, concatenation of
cone tracing, 455, 467, *584*
    voxel, 495, 504
conservation of energy, 312
conservative depth, 1016
conservative rasterization, *see* rasterization,
    conservative
constructive interference, *see* light, interference,
    constructive
constructive solid geometry, 750
continuity, *see also* curves *and* surfaces
    C^0, *728*, 741, 745
    C^1, *728*, 742
    C^n, 728
    G^1, *728*, 742
    G^n, 728
continuous signal, 131
contour, 686
    edge detection, 665–669
    halo, 659
    image, 660–665
    line, 655
    loop, 667
    procedural geometry, 657–660
    shading normal, 656–657
    shell, 658–659

contouring artifacts, *see* banding artifacts
control cage, 756
control mesh, 756
control points, 720
control polygon, 754
convex hull, 950
    Bézier curve, 723
    Bézier patch, 738
    Bézier triangle, 741
    Loop, 761
convex partitioning, 684
convex polyhedron, *946*, 950
convex region, 685
convolution, 135
Cook-Torrance model, 314
cookie, 221, 230, 434
coordinate system
    left-handed, 92, *95*
    right-handed, 92
corner cutting, 753
counterclockwise vertex order, 63, 692
coverage, 995
coverage mask, A-buffer, 155
CPU-limited, 786
cracking, *689*, 769
    Bézier triangle, 747
    fractional tessellation, 769
    polygon edge, 689, 714
    quadtree, 774
    tessellation, 771
crawlies, 130
crease, 763
critical angle, 326
cross product, 7
CrossFire X, 1013
CRT, 161
Crysis, 220, 457, 458, 559
Crysis 3, 631
CSAA, *see* antialiasing, coverage sampling
CSG, 750
CSM, *see* shadow, map, cascaded
cube map, 173, 190
cube mapping, *see* environment mapping, cubic
cube texture, 190
CubeMapGen, 415
cubic convolution, 178
cubic curve, *see* curves, cubic
cuculoris, 434
CUDA, 54, 1040
culling, 830–851
    backface, 800, *831–835*
        orientation consistency, 63
    clustered backface, 833–835
    detail, 839–840

culling *(continued)*
    early-z, 53, 801, 849, 851, *1016*
    frontface, 832
    hierarchical z-buffering, 846–850
    hierarchical view frustum, 807, *835–837*, 981
    image-space, *843*, 844, 846
    object-space, 843
    occlusion, 822, *840–850*
    occlusion query, 844–845
    portal, 837–839
    ray-space, 843
    view frustum, 807, *835–837*, 981
    z, 846
    z_{max}, 1015
    z_{min}, 1015
curve segment, 729–730
curved surfaces, *see* surfaces
curves
    B-spline, *732–734*, 754, 756
    Bézier, 720–725
    bounded Bézier, 725–726
    Catmull-Rom spline, 731
    continuity, 726–728
    cubic, 721, *724*, 729
    degree, 721
    GPU rendering, 725–726
    Hermite, 729–730
    Kochanek-Bartels, 730–732
    parametric, 718–734
    piecewise, 726
    quadratic, *721*, 722–724
    quartic, 721
    S-shaped, *728*, 771
    spline, *729*, 781
    subdivision, 753–756
    tension parameter, 730

D65, *see* illuminant D65
DAG, *see* directed acyclic graph
dart, 763
data race condition, 51
data reduction, *see* simplification
data-level parallelism, 1003
data-oriented design, 791
de Casteljau
    Bézier curves, 721
    Bézier patches, 736
    Bézier triangles, 740
DEAA, *see* antialiasing, distance-to-edge
decals, 202, 888–890, 901
decimation, *see* simplification
deep color mode, 1010
deferred context, 813

deferred lighting, 892
deferred shading, 547, *883–890*, 1022, 1028
deferred texturing, 905–908
denoising, 519
dependent texture read, *see* texture, dependent read
depth
    buffer, *see* buffer, z-buffer
        reversed, 100
    complexity, *801*, 841
    peeling, 152, 154–155, 252, 625, 893
    sprite, *see under* impostor
depth of field, 523, 525, *527–536*, 835
derivative, *see* gradient of pixel
Destiny, 129, 130, 453, 815
Destiny 2, 571, 572, 1041
Destiny: The Taken King, 128
destructive interference, *see* light, interference, destructive
determinant of a matrix, 7
Deus Ex: Mankind Divided, 908
dielectric, 321
difference of Gaussians, 665
diffraction, 303, *360–361*
diffuse color, 314, 348
diffuse term, 306
diffusion, 634
    normal-map, 635
    screen-space, 636–638
    texture-space, 635
digital differential analyzer, 506
digital visual interface, 1011
dihedral angle, 654, 660, *695*
dimension reduction, 955
direct memory access, *see* DMA
Direct3D, 21n
DirectCompute, 40
directed acyclic graph, 586, 829
direction, principal, 672
directional occlusion, 465
    dynamic, 467–468
    precomputed, 466
    shading, 468–472
DirectX, 38–41
DirectX 11, 813
DirectX 12, 814
discrete geometry LOD, *see* level of detail, discrete geometry
discrete ordinate methods, 493
discrete oriented polytope, *see* k-DOP
discretized signal, 131
Disney Infinity 3.0, 372
displaced subdivision, *see* surfaces, subdivision, displaced

displacement mapping, 167, 219, 765, 770
display
    encoding, 160–165
    engine, 1011
    flare, 285
    head-mounted, 916
    interface, 1011
    list, 812
    primary, 276
    varifocal, 923
display rate, 1
display-referred, 283
DisplayPort, 1011
distance field, 677
distortion, lens, 921
distribution of normals, *see* NDF
distribution of visible normals, 333
dithering, 1010
DLAA, *see* antialiasing, directionally localized
DMA, 1034
Dolby Vision, 282
DOM, *see* discrete ordinate methods
domain, 719
    rectangular, 736
    triangular, 740
domain shader, 44
DOOM (2016), 246, 540, 629, 823, 869, 883, 901
dot product, 7
dots per inch, 817
double buffer, *see* buffer, double
downsampling, 136, *518*, 525
DRAM, 791
draw call, 35
Dreams, 577, 1045
driver, *see* graphics driver
dual paraboloid mapping, *see* environment
    mapping, parabolic
dual source-color blending, 53
dueling frusta, 242
Dust 514, 493
DVI, 1011
DXR, 1044
DXTC, *see under* texturing, compression
dynamic buffer, 793
dynamic super resolution, 139

EAC, 194
ear clipping, 685
early-*z* culling, *see under* culling
edge, *654–656*, *see also* line
    border, 654
    boundary, *654*, 661, 692, 709
    bridge, 686
    collapse, *see under* simplification

    contour, 654–656
    crease, *654*, 695, 709, 747
    detection, 661, 663
    feature, 654
    function, 994–996
    hard, 654
    join, 686
    keyholed, 686
    material, 654
    preservation, 695
    ridge, *654*, 660
    silhouette, 654–655
    stitching, 689
    suggestive contour, 655
    valley, *654*, 660
effective surface, 350
electrical optical transfer function, 161, 283
EM, *see* environment mapping
energy efficiency, 1024
Enlighten, 482
enveloping, *see* transform, vertex blending
environment mapping, 404–433
    cubic, *410–412*, 425
    irradiance, 424–433
    latitude-longitude, 406–408
    localized, 499–502
    octahedral, 413
    parabolic, 413
    prefiltered, 415–420, 471, 502, 503
    sphere, 408–410
EOTF, *see* electrical optical transfer function
EQAA, *see* antialiasing, enhanced quality
Ericsson texture compression, *see* texturing,
    compression, ETC
ESM, *see* shadow, map, exponential
ETC, *see under* texturing, compression
Euler angles, 59, *70*, 73, 82
Euler transform, *see* transform, Euler
Euler-Mascheroni constant, 802
Euler-Poincaré formula, *699*, 706
EVS, *see* exact visible set
EVSM, *see* shadow, map, exponential
EWA, 189
exact visible set, 831
execution unit, 1003
exitance, *442*, 474
explicit surface, *see* surfaces, explicit
exposure, 285, 288–289
extraordinary vertex, 758
eye space, 15
eye-dome lighting, 575

faceter, 682
fairness, 761

falloff function, 114, 381
fan, *see* triangle, fan
Far Cry, 453, 476
Far Cry 3, 478, 481
Far Cry 4, 420, 481
far plane, *93*, 99, 981
Feline, 189
fence, 938
FIFA, 616
FIFO, 808, 809, 1023
fill rate, 788
film frame rate, 536
filter, *130–137*, 515
    bilateral, 462, 518–520
    box, *134*, 165, 517, 518
    bright-pass, 527
    cross bilateral, *see* filter, joint bilateral
    disk, 518
    edge-preserving, 520
    Gaussian, 136, 189, *515*, 517, 572, 665
    joint bilateral, 249, *519*
    kernel, 517
    low-pass, 135, 136
    nearest neighbor, 134
    rotation-invariant, 515
    running-average, 523
    separable, 516, 517, 520, 532
    sinc, *135–136*, 515
    steerable, 525
    support, 517
    tent, 134
    triangle, 134
fin, 646, *668*
Final Fantasy XV, 620
fireflies, *see under* aliasing
Firewatch, 104
first principal direction, 672
fixed-function pipeline, 27
fixed-view effects, 546–547
flat shading, 120
FLIPQUAD, 146
floor, 769
flow control, 36
    dynamic, 36
    static, 36
flush, 1005
FMA, 1026, 1033
fog, 598, *600–602*, 608
force feedback, 14
form factor, 442
forward mapping, 531
forward shading, 883
forward+ shading, *see* tiled, forward shading
Forza Horizon 2, 141, 899

Forza Motorsport 7, 2, 412
foveated rendering, 931–932
FPS, 1, *13*, 789, 817
fragment, 22, *49*
fragment shader, 23, 49, 125, *see also* pixel
    shader
frame rate, 1, 808
    constant, 865
frame-to-frame coherence, 866
framebuffer, 25
frames per second, 13
FreeSync, 1011
FreeType, 676
Fresnel effect, 319
Fresnel equations, 316
Fresnel reflectance, *316–327*, 330, 331, 348, 351,
    405, 420, 421, 426, 498, 626, 631, 632,
    643, 892
    Schlick approximation, 320, 321, 326, 347,
        351, 598
front buffer, *see* buffer, front
front plane, 93n
Frostbite game engine, 111, 113, 115, 116, 287,
    290, 312, 325, 616, 804, 811, 851, 878,
    890, 893, 903
froxel, 611
frustum, 11, 17–18, *981*
    plane extraction, 983–984
    tracing, 261
frustum/object intersection, *see specific objects
        under* intersection testing
FSAA, *see* antialiasing, full-scene
full screen pass, 514
fur, 640–641, 646–649
FX Composer, 44
FXAA, *see* antialiasing, fast approximate

G-sync, 1011
G^1-continuity, *see* continuity
gamma correction, *160–165*, 184
gamut, 276, 323
    sRGB, 323
gas, ideal, 297
gather operation, 532
Gauss map, 667
Gaussian, anisotropic spherical, 398, 498
GBAA, *see* antialiasing, geometry buffer
GCN, *see under* hardware
genus, 699
geodesic curve, 81
geometric mean, 864
geometry
    clipmap, 872–873
    patch, 775

processing, *see under* pipeline
shader, 18–19, *47–48*, 647, 668, 677, 702, 786, 798
stage, *see* pipeline, geometry processing
geomorph LOD, *see* level of detail, geomorph
GigaThread engine, 1032
gimbal lock, 73
glare effects, 524
global illumination, 315, *438*
glPolygonOffset, 236, 657, 673
GLSL, 35, 39
gluLookAt, 67
gluPerspective, 99
G^n-continuity, 728
gobo, 173, 221, 230, 434
golden thread, 547
Gooch shading, *103*, 663
Gouraud shading, 118
GPA, 785
GPU, 13, *29*, *see also* hardware
computing, 54
GPU Boost, 789
GPU PerfStudio, 785
GPUView, 785
gradient of pixel, 51, 185
graftals, 672
Grand Theft Auto V, 525
graphics driver, 786, 793, 1012
graphics processing unit, *see* GPU
grayscale, conversion to, 278
great arc, 81
great circle, 81
green-screening, 160
GRID2, 258
GTX 1080, *see under* hardware
guard-band clipping, 998

H-basis, 404
hair, 257, 640–646, 649
half vector, 336
half-edge, 692
Half-Life 2, 402, 403, 476, 478, 499
Half-Life 2 basis, 403
half-space, 6, *946*
halo, 524
Halo 3, 475
haloing, 675
Halton sequence, 144
hard real time, 865
hardware
GameCube, 867
GCN, 1035–1039
GeForce 256, 29
GeForce3, 38

GTX 1080, 1029–1035
Mali architecture, 1020, 1024–1029
NVIDIA Pascal, 1029–1035
Pixel-Planes, 8n, 1026
PixelFlow, 1022
PLAYSTATION, 936
PLAYSTATION 3, 39, 700
PLAYSTATION 4, 867, 1007, 1035
Pomegranate, 1022
Talisman, 189, 551
Vega, 1035–1039
Voodoo 1, 1
Wii, 27, 39
Xbox, 1035
Xbox 360, 39
Xbox One, 867
harmonic series, 802
Hausdorff distance, 708, 875
H-basis, 475
HBM2, 1034, 1038
HDMI, 1011
HDR, 193, 271, 281–283, 405
display, 1011
HDR10, 281
head, *70*, 72
heads-up display, 561, 917, 932, 933
heat diffusion, 535
heightfield, 564–566, *see also* bump mapping
terrain, 877
Hellgate: London, 609
Helmholtz reciprocity, *312*, 351
hemisphere lighting, 431
hemispherical basis, *see* basis, hemispherical
hemispherical harmonics, 404
Henyey-Greenstein phase function, *598–599*, 620
Hermite curves, *see* curves, Hermite
Hermite interpolation, *see* interpolation, Hermite
Hertz, 13
hidden line removal, 668–669
hidden line rendering, *see* line, hidden
hierarchical image caching, *see* impostor
hierarchical spatial data structure, *see* spatial data structure
hierarchical view frustum culling, *see* culling, hierarchical view frustum
hierarchical *z*-buffering, *see under* culling
high color mode, *see* color, mode, high color
high dynamic range, *see* HDR
high-definition multimedia interface, 1011
High-Level Shading Language, *see* HLSL
highlight, 119
highlight selection, 673
histogram, 245

histogram renormalization, 196
hither, 93n
HiZ, 252, 1015, 1038
HLG, 281
HLSL, *35*, 39
homogeneous notation, 6, 58, 62, 173
homogenization, 62, 92
horizon angle, 460
horizon mapping, 460, *466*
hourglass, 684
HRAA, *see* antialiasing, hybrid reconstruction
HTC Vive, *see* Vive
HTILE, 1038
HUD, 561, 917, 932, 933
hue, 276
hull shader, 44
Hunt effect, 285
Huygens-Fresnel principle, 360
Hybrid Log-Gamma, *see* HLG
hysteresis, 861
HZB culling, *see* culling, hierarchical z-buffering

IBR, *see* image-based rendering
illuminant D65, 270, 274
image
      geometry, 566, 876
      processing, 513–522, 665
      pyramid, 846, 847
      state, 283
image-based lighting, 406, 414–424, 435
image-based rendering, 269, 545
immediate context, 813
implicit surface, *see* surfaces, implicit
importance sampling, 385, 445, 451, 503
impostor, *561–564*, 866
      depth sprite, 564–565
      layered depth image, 565
index buffer, 702–705
index of refraction, 298
      complex, 298
indirect draw command, 851
inFAMOUS Second Son, 91, 572
inflection, 728
inner product, 398
input assembler, 42
inside test, 996
instance, 15, *829*
instancing, 42, 797
instruction set architecture, 35
instruction-level parallelism, 1003
Instruments, 785, 792
integral
      double product, 464, 470
      triple product, 470

intensity, 269
interactivity, 1
interface, *see* hardware
interference, *see under* light
interleaved sampling, 145
intermediate language, 35
interpolation, 781, 998–1001
      barycentric, 963
      bicubic, 178
      bilinear, *178–180*, 182, 735–736
      centroid, 141
      Hermite, 729–732
      linear, 720
      perspective-correct, 22, 49, 1000
      quadrilinear, 189
      repeated, 740
            bilinear, 736
            linear, 720–722
      trilinear, 186
interpupillary distance, 923
intersection testing, 941–991
      AABB/AABB, 978–979
      box/plane, 970–972
      box/ray, 959–962
            ray slope, 961–962
            slabs method, 959–961
      BV/BV, 976–981
      convex polyhedron/ray, 961
      crossings test, 967–970
      dimension reduction, 955
      frustum, 981–987
      frustum/box, 986–987
      frustum/ray, 961
      frustum/sphere, 984–986
      hardware-accelerated, 942–943
      interval overlap method, 972–974
      k-DOP/k-DOP, 979–980
      k-DOP/ray, 961
      line/line, 987–990
      OBB/OBB, 980–981
      picking, 942
      plane/box, 970–972
      plane/ray, 966
      plane/sphere, 970
      polygon/ray, 966–970
      polyhedron/polyhedron, 987
      ray/box, 959–961
      rejection test, 948
      rules of thumb, 954–955
      separating axis, 946
      separating axis test, *947*, 974, 979, 980, 986–987
      sphere/box, 977–978
      sphere/ray, 955–959

sphere/sphere, 976–977
three planes, 990
triangle/box, 974–975
triangle/ray, 962–966
triangle/triangle, 972–974
interval overlap method, *see under* intersection
testing
intrinsic functions, 36
inverse displacement mapping, *see* texturing,
parallax occlusion mapping
inverse z, 100
IOR, *see* index of refraction
irradiance, *268*, 294, 425
precomputed, 474
spherical harmonics, 475
volume, 487
irradiance mapping, *see* environment mapping,
irradiance
irregular vertex, 758
isocube, 412
isosurface, 584, 682, 753
isotropic scaling, 62

$J_z a_z b_z$, 276
jaggies, *see under* aliasing
jittering, *see under* antialiasing
joint, 720, *726*, 728, 731
Jordan curve theorem, 967
judder, 935
Just Cause 2, 114, 882
Just Cause 3, 883, 899, 900

k-ary tree, 820
k-d tree, *see under* spatial data structure
k-DOP, *945–946*, 961, 976, 990
creation, 949
Kentucky Route Zero, 121
Killzone: Shadow Fall, 116, 523
Killzone 2, 885
Kite, 493
Kochanek-Bartels curves, *see* curves,
Kochanek-Bartels

LAB, 276
Lambertian shading, *see* BRDF, Lambertian
The Last of Us, 476
late depth test, 1016
late latching, 938
latency, 1, 30, 791, 807–810, 920–921, 935,
1004–1006, 1013
occlusion query, 845
Latin hypercube sampling, 143
latitude, 407, 944
layered depth image, *see under* impostor

LCD, 676
LDI, *see* impostor, layered depth image
LEAN mapping, 370
left-handed, *see under* coordinate system
lens flare, 524–526
level of detail, 44, 580, 706, 717, 807, *852–866*
alpha, 857–858
bias, 186, *see also* texturing
blend, 856
continuous, 706, 859, 860
discrete geometry, 854–856
fractional tessellation, 768
generation, 853
geomorph, 859–860
hysteresis, 861
PN triangle, 747
popping, 710, *854*, 856, 858
projected area-based, 861–864
range-based, 860–861
selection, 853, *860–864*
simplification, 710
subdivision surface, 756
switching, 853, *854–860*
time-critical, 865–866
level set, 583
LIDAR, 573
light
ambient, 391–392
attenuation mask, 230
baking, 798
bandwidth, 362
bleeding, 255
field, 269
interference
constructive, 296, 298
destructive, 296
thin-film, 361–363
inverse-square attenuation, 111
leak, 238, 255, 256
map, 484
meter, 271
monochromatic, 293
polarized, linearly, 293
polychromatic, 293
prepass, 892
probe, 414, 490, 901
propagation volumes, 493
cascaded, 494
scattering, *see* scattering
shafts, 602, 604, 608, 631
source, *106–117*, 798
area, 116–117, *224*, 228, 377–391
card, 387, 388, 427
directional, 109–110

light *(continued)*
    source *(continued)*
        disk, 379, 381, 388, 430, 435
        fill, 431
        omni, *see* light, source, point
        planar, 388
        point, 111–114
        polygonal, 389
        punctual, 110–116
        spherical, 381–384, 386, 387, 430
        spot, 114–115
        tube, 387
        volume, 224
    transport
        linearity, 438, 479
        meshless, 484
        modular, 484
        notation, 439–440
    unpolarized, 294
    velocity, phase, 294
    visible, 268
light map, 227
light-field rendering, 549
lightcuts, 431
lighting probe, 490
limit
    curve, *754*, 756
    surface, 760
line, 19, 673–675, *see also* edge
    haloing, 675
    hidden, 674–675
    integral convolution, 538
    triangle edge rendering, 673–674
line/line intersection, *see* intersection testing,
        line/line
linear blend skinning, 84
linear interpolation, 720
linear speedup, 810
linear transform, *see* transform, linear
linearly transformed cosines, 390
LiSPSM, *see* shadow, map, light space
        perspective
LittleBigPlanet, 488
load balance, 1023
lobe
    anisotropic, 422–424
    asymmetric, 422–424
local frame, 343
local illumination, 315
local lighting model, 438
LOD, *see* level of detail
log, 8
longitude, 407, 944
lookup table, 173
loop, 686

Loop subdivision, *see* surfaces, subdivision,
        Loop
loose octree, *see under* spatial data structure
lossy compression, 194
Lost Planet, 647
lozenge, 946
LPV, *see* light, propagation volumes
Lumberyard, 740, 1044
Lumigraph, 549
luminance, 197, 271, 273, 278
LUT, *see* lookup table
LUV, 276

Möbius strips, 693
Mach banding, 1010
macroscale, 208, 367
magnification, *see under* texturing
main axes, 8
Mali, *see* hardware, Mali architecture
manifold, 694
Mantle, 40
marching cubes, *583*, 683, 753
marching tetrahedra, 753
mask, 759
masked hierarchical depth buffer, 849
masking
    function, 333
    perceptual, 278
masking-shadowing function, 334, 335
material, 125
    glossy, 382–386
    instance, 126
    template, 126
matrix, *see also* transform
    adjoint, 68
    change of basis, 63, 67, 75
    column-major, 60
    determinant, 63
    orientation, 60, 70
    orthogonal, 69, 72, 80
        rotation, 70
    row-major, 60, 95
    trace, 61, 80
    transpose, 7, 63
matte, 159
mean width, 954
media, 310
mediated reality, 917
medium
    absorptive, 298
    homogeneous, 298
megatexture, 867
memory
    allocation, 793
    architecture, 1006–1007

bandwidth, 1006
    controller, 1038
    dynamic random access, 791
    hierarchy, 791
    optimization, *see* optimization, memory
    UMA, 1007
    unified, 1007
    wall, 791
merging of pixels, 24–25
merging stage, *24–25*, 53
mesh
    cache-oblivious, 700–701
    parameterization, 173
    segmentation, 683
    smoothing, 694–696
    solidity, 693–694
    triangle, 691, *699–701*
    universal, 700–701
Meshlab, 695, 716
mesoscale, 208–209, 367
message-passing architecture, *see*
            multiprocessing, message-passing
metaball, 48, 683, 751
Metal, *40*, 814
metal, 323
Metal Gear Solid V: Ground Zeroes, 289
metameric failure, 280
metamers, 273
microfacets, 331–336
microgeometry, *304*, 327–330
    masking, 328
    shadowing, 328
micropolygon, 26
microscale, 208, 367
Mie scattering, *see* scattering, Mie
Minecraft, 579, 842
minification, *see under* texturing
mipmap chain, 184
mipmapping, *see under* texturing, minification
mirror transform, *see* transform, reflection
Mirror's Edge Catalyst, 616
mixed reality, 917
MLAA, *see* antialiasing, morphological
MMU, 1024
model space, 15
modeler, 682–683
    solid, 682
    surface, 683
modified butterfly subdivision, *see* surfaces,
            subdivision
modified Gram-Schmidt, 344
Monte Carlo integration, 385, 418, 419, 423,
            444, 451, 459, 507
    noise, 445, 511
Moore's Law, 1042

morph targets, *see under* transform
morphing, *see under* transform
Morton sequence, 1018
mosaicing, *see* texturing, tiling
motion blur, *536–542*, 835
MPEG-4, 712
MRT, 50
MSAA, *see* antialiasing, multisampling
multi-view, 928
multicore, 806
multiprocessing, 805–814, 1023
    dynamic assignment, 810
    message-passing, 806
    parallel, 809–810
    pipeline, 806–809
    static assignment, 810
    symmetric, 806
    task, 811–812
    task-based, 806
multiprocessor, 1003
    shared memory, 806, 1003
    streaming, *see* streaming, multiprocessor
multisampling, *see under* antialiasing
multitexturing, *see* texturing
multum in parvo, 183

N-patch, *see* surfaces, PN triangle
N-rooks sampling, 143
nailboard, *see* impostor, depth sprite
nanogeometry, 359
NDF, 332, *337–346*, 367, 498
    anisotropic, 343–346
    Beckmann, 338
    Blinn-Phong, 339, 340
    filtering, 367–372
    generalized Trowbridge-Reitz, *see* NDF,
        GTR
    GGX, 340–342, 369
    GTR, 342
    isotropic, 338–343
    shape-invariance, 339
    Trowbridge-Reitz, *see* NDF, GGX
near plane, *93*, 99, 862, 981
nearest neighbor, *see under* filter *and* texturing,
            magnification *and* texturing,
            minification
Need for Speed, 616
Newell's formula, 685
node, 819–821
    internal, 819
    leaf, 819
    root, 819
node hierarchy, 828
noise, 872
noise function, *see* texturing, noise

non-photorealistic rendering, 651–673
noncommutativity, 65, 77
normal
    cone, 833–835
    incidence, 317
    map, *see under* bump mapping
    transform, *see* transform, normal
normal distribution function, *see* NDF
normal-masking independence, 334
normalized device coordinates, *19*, 94, 98, 100
NPR, *see* non-photorealistic rendering
NSight, 785
NURBS, 781
NVIDIA Pascal, *see under* hardware
Nyquist limit, *see under* sampling

OBB, *945*, 946, 976
OBB/object intersection, *see specific objects under* intersection testing
object-based shading, 908–912
obscurance, 449, 450, 454, 457
    volumetric, 459
occluder, 844
occluding power, 844
occlusion culling, *see* culling, occlusion
occupancy, 32, 127, 801, 886, 898, *1005*
occupancy function, 459
octahedral mapping, 413
octave, 198
octree, *see under* spatial data structure
octree texture, 190
Oculus Rift, 915, *916*, 923, 935
OETF, *see* optical electric transfer function
Okami, 653
opacity, 149
Open3DGC, 712
OpenCL, 54
OpenCTM, 712
OpenGL, 39–41
    extensions, 40
OpenGL ES, *41*, 194
OpenGL Shading Language, 35
OpenSubdiv, 777–779
optical electric transfer function, 161
optics
    geometrical, 303
    physical, 359
    wave, 359
optimization
    application stage, 790–793
    code, 790–793
    geometry processing, 798–800
    lighting, 798–800
    memory, 791–793

    merging, 805
    mobile, 814
    pipeline, 783–815
    pixel processing, 800–804
    pixel shader, 803
    rasterization, 800
The Orange Box, 288
The Order: 1886, 91, 357, 365, 370, 477, 498, 896
ordinary vertex, 758
Oren and Nayar model, 354
orientation, *see under* polygon
oriented bounding box, *see* OBB
orienting the camera, 67
over operator, *150–151*, 856
overblurring, 186
overclock, 787
overdraw, *see under* pixel

packed pixel format, 1010
padding, 792
painter's algorithm, 551, 824
painterly rendering, 652
pan, 538
parabola, 721
parabolic mapping, 413
parallax, 548
    mapping, 167, 214–220
    occlusion mapping, *see under* texturing
parallel
    architectures, 1020
    graphics, 1019
    processing, *see* multiprocessing, parallel
    projection, *see* projection, orthographic
parallelism, 810
    spatial, 806
    temporal, 806
parametric curves, *see* curves, parametric
parametric surfaces, *see* surfaces, parametric
participating media, 310
    absorption, 590
    extinction, *590*, 593, 595, 610, 616, 624, 639, 643
    optical depth, *593*, 595
    phase function, 590, 623, 626, 638, 644
        geometric, *see* scattering, geometric
        Mie, *see* scattering, Mie
        Rayleigh, *see* scattering, Rayleigh
particle
    soft, 558–559
    system, 567–572
Pascal, *see* hardware, NVIDIA Pascal
patch, 736
path tracing, 26, 444, 510, 1043, 1044

PCF, *see* percentage-closer filtering
PCI Express, 1006
Pearl Harbor, 446
pen and ink, 652
pending buffer, 1013
penumbra, *see under* shadow
per-triangle operations, 14
per-vertex operations, 14
percentage-closer filtering, 247–250, 849
perceptual quantizer, *see* PQ
performance measurement, 788–790
perp dot product, *6*, 987, 989
persistence, 935
perspective
    division, 19
    projection, *see* projection, perspective
    warping, 241
perspective-correct interpolation, *see*
    interpolation
Peter Panning, 238
Phong lighting equation, *see* BRDF, Phong
Phong shading, 118
Phong tessellation, *see under* surfaces
photogrammetry, 573, 682
photometric curve, *271, 273, 278*
photometry, 271
photopic, 271
photorealistic rendering, 545, *651*
PhyreEngine, 893
pick window, *see* intersection testing, picking
picking, *942*, 943, 957
piecewise Bézier curves, *see* curves, piecewise
ping-pong buffers, *520*, 525
pipeline, *11–27*, 783–815
    application stage, 12, *13–14*, 783
    fixed-function, 27
    flush, 1005
    functional stages, 13
    geometry processing, 12, *14–21*, 783
    parallelism, 1003
    pixel processing, 12, *22–25*, 783
    rasterization, 12, *21–22*, 783, 993–998
    software, 806
    speedup, 12
    stage, *12–13*
Pirates of the Caribbean, 454
pitch, *70, 72*
PIX, 785
pixel, 21
    local storage, 1027
    overdraw, 701, 801
    processing, *see under* pipeline
    shader, 23, 49–52
    synchronization, 156

Pixel-Planes, *see under* hardware
pixelation, 178
PixelFlow, 1022
pixels per inch, 817
pixels per second, 788
plane, 6
    axis-aligned, 8
    coordinate, 8
plane masking, 836
plane/object intersection, *see specific objects*
    under intersection testing
PLAYSTATION, *see under* hardware
point cloud, 572–578, 683
point rendering, 572–578
point-based visibility, 842
pointer indirection, 792
Poisson disk, 249
Pokémon GO, 917
polycube maps, 171
polygon
    bowtie, 684
    consolidation, 691
    contour, 686
    convex, 685
    edge cracking, *see* cracking, polygon edge
    edge stitching, 689
    hourglass, 684
    loop, 686
    merging, 691
    mesh, 691
    orientation, 691–693
    sorting, 824
    soup, 691
    star-shaped, 686
    T-vertex, 689–690
polygon-aligned BSP tree, *see* spatial data
    structure, BSP tree
polygonal techniques, 853
polygonalization, 583, 683
polymorph engine, 1031
polypostor, 562
POM, 217
popping, *see under* level of detail
port, 1006
portal culling, *see* culling, portal
pose, *921*, 924, 938
post-processing, 514
posterization, 652, 1010
potentially visible set, 831
power form, 724
power gating, 1028
PowerTune, 789
PowerVR, 196
PQ, 281

pre-lighting, 892
pre-order traversal, 835
precision, 712–715
        color, 186, 1010
        depth, 236
        floating point, 713
        mobile, 814
        subpixel, 689
precomputed radiance transfer, 471, 478, 479,
                481
        local deformable, 481
predictive rendering, 280
prefilter, 414
primitive generator, 44
primitive shader, 1037
Prince of Persia, 658
principal component analysis, 480, 484
probability, geometric, 953–954
procedural modeling, 222, 672, *682*
procedural texturing, *see* texturing, procedural
processor
        pixel, *see* pixel, shader
        vertex, *see* vertex, shader
progressive refinement, 510, 547
projection, 16–18, 92–102
        3D polygon to 2D, 966
        3D triangle to 2D, 962
        bounding volume, 861–864
        cylindrical, 172
        orthographic, 17–18, 59, *93–95*
        parallel, *see* projection, orthographic
        perspective, 17, 59, *96–102*, 1014
        planar, 172
        spherical, 172
projective texturing, *see* texturing, projective
proxy object, 819
PRT, *see* precomputed radiance transfer
PSM, *see* shadow, map, perspective
Ptex, 191
purple fringing, 628
purple line, 274
PVRTC, *see under* texturing, compression
PVS, *see* potentially visible set
PxrSurface, 343, 359, 363, 364

QEM, 708
quad, 51, 801, 994
quad overshading, 787, 853, 863, 910, *994*
quadratic curve, *see* curves, quadratic
quadratic equation, 957
quadric error metric, 708
quadtree, *see under* spatial data structure
Quake, 37, 474
Quake II, 474

Quake III, 37, 402
quantization, scalar, 714
Quantum Break, 496
quartic curve, *see* curves, quartic
quaternion, 72, 76–84
        addition, 77
        conjugate, 77, 78
        definition, 76
        dual, 87
        identity, 77
        imaginary units, 76
        inverse, 77
        laws of multiplication, 78
        logarithm, 78
        matrix conversion, 79–81
        multiplication, 77
        norm, 77, 78
        power, 78
        slerp, 81–83
        spherical linear interpolation, 81–82
        spline interpolation, 82–83
        transforms, 79–84
        unit, 78, 79
Quickhull, 950
Quincunx, *see* antialiasing, Quincunx
quintic curve, 181

radiance, *269–270*, 273, 425
        distribution, 269
        incoming, 315
radiant
        exitance, *see* exitance
        flux, 268
        intensity, 269
radiometry, 267
radiosity, 442–443
        normal mapping, 402–404
        progressive, 483
RAGE, 867
Rainbow Six Siege, 887
range-based fog, *see* fog
raster engine, 1031
raster operation, *see* ROP
rasterization, *see under* pipeline
        conservative, 22, 139, 259, 582, *1001*
                inner, 1001
                outer, 1001
                overestimated, 1001
                underestimated, 1001
rasterizer order view, *52*, 139, 156
rasterizer stage, *see* pipeline, rasterization
Ratatouille, 638
rational linear interpolation, 720

ray, 943–944
    casting, 443
        function, 437
    marching, 199, 216–220, 262, 566, 570, *594*, 607, 608, 614, 616, 618, 620–622, 639, 642, 648, 752, 753, 1048
    tracing, 26, 259, 261, *443–445*, 530, 586, 802, 953, 1006, 1044–1047
        architecture, 1039
        isosurface, 584
        voxel, 580
ray/object intersection, *see specific objects under* intersection testing
Rayleigh scattering, *see* scattering, Rayleigh
reciprocity, 312
reconstruction, 131, *133–136*
reduce, 245, 896
reflectance
    anisotropic, 328
    directional-hemispherical, 313
    equation, 311, 437
    hemispherical-directional, 313
    isotropic, 328
    spectral, 279
reflectance lobe, *see under* BRDF
reflection, 314, 315, 623, 626, 630
    environment mapping, 413
    equation, *see* reflectance, equation
    external, 317
    internal, 317, 325
        total, 326
    law of, 504
    mapping, 405
    planar, 504–505, 839
    probe, 499
        localized, 500
    proxy, 500
    screen-space, 505–509
    transform, *see* transform, reflection
refraction, 149, 302, *626–630*, 631–633, 638, 639
    image-space, 630
refractive index, 298
refresh rate, 1
    vertical, 1011
register combiners, 38
register pressure, 127, *801*, 904, 1005
regular vertex, 758
relief texture mapping, *see* texturing, relief
relighting, 547
render target, 50
RenderDoc, 785
rendering
    equation, 437–438
    spectrum, 545–546
    state, 794

RenderMan, 37, 39
repeated linear interpolation, *see* interpolation, repeated, linear
reprojection, 143, 522–523, 936
resampling, 136–137
resolve, 142
retopology, 712
retrace, vertical, 25, 1012
retroreflection, 330
reverse mapping, 532
reversed z, 100
Reyes, 908–912
RGB, 176
    color cube, 275
    color mode, *see* color, mode, true color
    to grayscale, 278
RGBA, *150*, 159, 1010
    texture, 176
RGSS, *see* antialiasing, rotated grid
right-hand rule, 692
right-handed, 92
rigid-body transform, *see* transform, rigid-body
ringing, 256, 401, 428, 570
roll, *70*, 72
ROP, 24, 25, 1010, 1032–1033
roping, 165
rotation, *see under* transform
roughness, 304
ROV, *see* rasterizer order view
RSM, *see* shadow, map, reflective

S3TC, 192
saccade, 931
SAH, *see* surface area heuristic
sample, 22
sampling, 130–137, 143, *see also* antialiasing
    band-limited signal, 133
    centroid, 141
    continuous signal, 131
    discretized signal, 131
    Nyquist limit, *133*, 182, 186
    pattern, 143
    stochastic, *145*, 149
    stratified, 144
    theorem, 133
SAT, *see* intersection testing, separating axis test
saturation, 276
SBRDF, 310
scalable link interface, 1013
scaling, *see under* transform
scan conversion, 21
scanline interleave, 1013
scatter operation, 531

scattering, 297, *589–599*
    backward, *597*, 598, 599
    forward, *597*, 598, 599, 607, 638
    geometric, 596, 599
    Mie, 298, 596, *597–599*, 614, 620
    multiple, 607, 615, 616, *621–622*, 633,
        643–646
    Rayleigh, 298, *596–597*, 613, 614
    single, *589*, 592, 610, 614, 618, 633, 638
    subsurface, *see* subsurface scattering
    Tyndall, 298
scene graph, *see under* spatial data structure
scene-referred, 283
Schlick phase function, 599
scoreboard, 1031
scotopic, 271
screen
    coordinates, 20
    mapping, 20
    space coverage, 772, *862*
scRGB, 282
SDR, 281
SDSM, *see* shadow, map, sample distribution
second-order equation, 957
sectioning, 19
segmentation, 683
semiconductor, 324
separating axis test, *see under* intersection
        testing
separating hyperplane theorem, 946
SGI algorithm, *see* triangle, strip
shade tree, 37
shader
    cores, 30
    storage buffer object, *see* unordered access
        view
    unified, *see* unified shader architecture
Shader Model, 38
Shadertoy, 199, 222, 753, 1048
shading, 16
    clustered, *see* clustered shading
    deferred, *see* deferred shading
    equation, 16
    flat, 120
    forward, 883
    Gouraud, 118
    hard, 652
    language, 35
    model, 103–106
        Lambertian, 109
    Phong, 118
    pixel, 23, *see also* pixel shader
    tiled, *see* tiled, shading
    toon, 652–654
    vertex, *see* vertex, shader

shadow, 223–265
    acne, 236
    anti-shadow, 227
    buffer, 234
    contact hardening, 251
    on curved surfaces, 229–230
    depth map, 234
    hard, 223
    map, 230, *234–252*, 594, 604
        adaptive volumetric, 258
        bias, 236–239
        cascaded, 242–247
        convolution, 255
        deep, 257–259, 638
        dual, 238
        exponential, 256–257
        filtered, 252–257
        imperfect, 492
        irregular, 259–264
        light space perspective, 241
        minmax, 252
        moment, 256
        omnidirectional, 234
        opacity, 257, 612
        parallel-split, 242
        perspective, 241
        reflective, 491, 493
        sample distribution, 245
        second-depth, 238
        sparse, 246, 263
        translucent, 639
        trapezoidal, 241
        variance, 252–255
        volumetric, 644
    penumbra, *224*, 228
    percentage-closer soft, 250–252
    planar, 225–229
        soft, 228–229
    projection, 225–227
    screen-space, 262
    soft, 224–225, 227–229, 247–252, 442
    umbra, 224
    volume, 230–233
shadowing-masking function, *see*
        masking-shadowing function
shape blending, *see* transform, morph targets
shared memory multiprocessor, *see*
        multiprocessor, shared memory
shear, *see under* transform
shell, 646
shell mapping, 220, 659
shortest arc, 81
shower door effect, 670
Shrek 2, 491
signed distance field, 454, 579, 677

signed distance function, 577, 750
    spherical, 466
silhouette, 765, 773
    loop, 667
SIMD, 31, 1003, 1005, 1035
SIMD lane, 31, 1002
simplification, *706–712*, 853
    cost function, 707–709
    edge collapse, 706–708
    level of detail, 710
    optimal placement, 707
    reversibility, 706
SIMT, 1002
simulation sickness, 920
single buffer, *see* buffer, single
skeleton-subspace deformation, *see* transform,
    vertex blending
skinning, *see* transform, vertex blending
sky, *see* atmosphere *and* clouds
skybox, *547–549*, 556, 628, 632
slab, 945
slerp, *see under* quaternion
SLI, 1013
slicemap, 581
SMAA, *see* antialiasing, subpixel morphological
small batch problem, 796
smart composition, 1028
Smith masking function, 334, 335, 339, 341–343,
    355, 358
smoothstep, 115, 181
SMOOTHVISION, 145
SMP, 806
Snell's law, *302*, 326
softbox, 388, 434
software pipelining, *see* multiprocessing
solid, 693
solid angle, 268
    differential, 311
sort, 822
    space, 1020
sort-everywhere, 1022
sort-first, 1020
sort-last, 1020, 1033
    fragment, 1021
    image, 1021, 1022
sort-middle, 1020, 1024
space subdivision, 819
space-filling curve, 1018
spacewarp, 935, 937
sparse texture, *see* texturing, sparse
sparse voxel octree, 494, 579
spatial data structure, 818–830
    aspect graph, 831
    bounding volume hierarchy, 510, *819–821*,
      942

BSP tree, 819, *822–824*
    axis-aligned, 822–823
    polygon-aligned, 823–824
    cache-aware, 827–828
    cache-oblivious, 827–828
    hierarchical, 818
    irregular, 819
    k-d tree, 822–823
    loose octree, 826–827
    octree, 819, *824–827*, 846
    quadtree, 825, 874
      restricted, 774, 877
    regular, 819
    scene graph, *828–830*, 840, 861
      LOD, 861
spatial locality, 791
spatial relationship, 438
spatialization, 830
SPD, *see* spectral power distribution
spectral power distribution, 270, 272
spectrum, 268, 274
specular
    highlight, 119
    lobe, *see under* BRDF
    term, 306
sphere, 682
    formula, 944, 956
    mapping, *see* environment mapping, sphere
sphere/object intersection, *see specific objects*
    under intersection testing
spherical
    basis, *see* basis, spherical
    coordinates, 407, *944*
    function, 392–404
    Gaussian, *see* basis, spherical, Gaussian
    harmonics, *398–401*, 427–431, 456, 480,
      488
      gradients, 488
    linear interpolation, *see under* quaternion
SPIR-V, 40
splat, 573–574
spline curves, *see* curves, spline
spline surfaces, *see* surfaces, spline
split and dice, 774–775
Split/Second, 898
Spore, 678, 710
sprite, 531, 550–551, *see also* impostor
    layered, 550–551
SRAA, *see* antialiasing, subpixel reconstruction
sRGB, *161*, 162, 165, 196, 322, 323
SSBO, *see* unordered access view
SSE, 977–979
stage
    stalling, 809
    starving, 12, 809

stalling, 809
standard dynamic range, *see* SDR
Star Ocean 4, 286
Star Wars Battlefront, 647
star-shaped polygon, 686
Starcraft II, 459
starving, *see under* stage
state
    changes, 794
    sorting, 807
static buffer, 794
stationary subdivision, *see* surfaces, subdivision,
      stationary
stencil, 759
stencil buffer, *see* buffer, stencil
steradian, 268, 269
stereo rendering, 927–931
stereo vision, 922–924
stereopsis, 922
Stevens effect, 285
stitching, 689
stream output, 19, 48–49, 571, 705
streaming, 871–872
    multiprocessor, 1003, 1029
    texture, *see* texturing, streaming
stride, 702
strip, *see* triangle, strip
stroke, 672
stylized rendering, *see* non-photorealistic
      rendering
subdivision curves, *see* curves, subdivision
subdivision surfaces, *see* surfaces, subdivision
subpixel addressing, 689
subsurface albedo, 348–349
subsurface scattering, *305–307*, 445, 607
    global, 306, 632–640
    local, 306, 347–355
subtexture, *see* texturing
summed-area table, *see under* texturing,
      minification
superscalar, 14
supershader, 128
surface area heuristic, 953
surface extraction, 583
surfaces
    acne, 236
    B-spline, *749*, 762
    Bézier patch, 735–738
    Bézier triangle, *740–741*, 745
    biquadratic, 736
    continuity, 741–742
    explicit, 944
      sphere, 944
      triangle, 944, 963

    implicit, 749–753, 944
      blending, 751
      derivatives, 751
      sphere, 956
    NURBS, 781
    parametric, 171, 734–747
    Phong tessellation, 735, 740, 748–749
    PN triangle, 46, 735, 740, *744–747*, 748, 749
    spline, 689, 761
    subdivision, 756–767
      adaptive quadtree, 718, 779–780
      approximating, 758
      Catmull-Clark, 761–763
      displaced, 765–766
      feature adaptive, 777–779
      limit position, 760
      limit surface, 760
      limit tangents, 760
      Loop, *758–761*, 763, 765–767
      mask, 759
      modified butterfly, 761
      stationary, 756
      stencil, 759
    tensor product, 735
    tessellation, 735
surfel, 573
surround, 285
SVBRDF, 310
swap buffer, *see* buffer, swap
swizzling, 1018
synchronization with monitor, 790, 1012, 1013

TAM, *see* tonal art map
tangent
    frame, 209
    map, 344
    patch, 775
    space, *see under* basis
    vector, 209, 729
TBN, 209
Team Fortress 2, 654, 677, 678, 940
tearing, 1012
technical illustration, 651, 673
temporal
    aliasing, *see* aliasing, temporal
    coherence, 866
    delay, 1
    locality, 791
temporary register, 36
tensor product surfaces, 735
terrain chunked LOD, 874–877
tessellation, 683–690, 767–780, 853
    adaptive, 770–775
    control shader, 44

domain shader, 44
evaluation shader, 44
factors, 45
fractional, 768–770, 860
hull shader, 44
levels, 45
stage, 18, *44–46*, 677
surface, 735
tessellator, 44
uniform, 767
tetrahedralization, 489
texel, 169
Texram, 189
text, 675–677, 725
texture
    array, 191
    atlas, 190
    bandwidth, 1006
    cache, *see* cache
    coordinates, 169
    cube map, 190
    dependent read, 38, 177, 220, 406
    matrix, 174n, 410
    periodicity, 175
    space, 169
    volume, 189–190
    volumetric, 646
texture processing cluster, 1031
texture-space shading, 910
texturing, 23, 167–222
    albedo color map, 201
    alpha mapping, 176, 202–208, 551
    animation, *200*, 203
    bindless, 192
    border, 174
    cellular, 199
    charts, 485
    clamp, 174
    clipmap, 867
    compression, 192–198, 486, 503
        ASTC, 196, 1029
        BC, 192–193
        DXTC, 192–193
        EAC, 194
        ETC, 194–195, 1029
        lossy, 194
        normal, 195
        PVRTC, 195–196
        S3TC, 192
    corresponder function, *169*, 174–175
    decaling, 202
    detail, 180
    diffuse color map, 201
    distortion, 687–688

image, 176–198
image size, 177
level of detail bias, 186
light mapping, 484
magnification, 177, *178–181*
    bilinear interpolation, 178
    cubic convolution, 178
    nearest neighbor, 178
minification, 177, *182–189*
    anisotropic filtering, 187–188
    bilinear interpolation, 182
    Elliptical Weighted Average, 189
    level of detail, 185
    mipmapping, 183–186
    nearest neighbor, 182
    quadrilinear interpolation, 189
    summed-area table, 186–188
    trilinear interpolation, 186
mipmapping, 485
mirror, 174
mirror once, 175
noise, 198, 549
one-dimensional, 173
parallax occlusion mapping, 167, 216–220
parameterization, 485, 486
pipeline, 169–176
procedural, 198–200
projective, 221, 688
projector function, 169–174
relief, *216–220*, 222, 565–566, 630, 646,
        853, 854
repeat, 174
seams, 486
shells, 485
sparse, 246, 263, *867–871*
streaming, 870–871
subtexture, 184
swizzling, 1018
texture coordinates, 169
tiling, 795
transcoding, 870–871
value transform function, 169
vertex, 43, 186
virtual, 867–871
wrap, 174
TFAN, 712
That Dragon, Cancer, 121
thin-film interference, *see* light, interference,
        thin-film
thread
    divergence, 32, 260
    group, *54*, 518
    shader, 31
thread-level parallelism, 1003

Threading Building Blocks, 812
three plane intersection, *see* intersection testing,
     three planes
three-dimensional printing, *see* 3D printing
three.js, *41*, 50, 189, 407, 485, 568, 628, 1048
thresholding, 656
throughput, 30, 783, 808
tile, 995
    local storage, 156
    screen, 1007, 1021
    table, 1008
    texture, 795
tiled
    caching, 1033
    deferred shading, 894, 896, 904, 914
    forward shading, 895–896, 903, 904, 914
    rasterization, *see* pipeline, rasterization
    shading, 893–898
    triangle traversal, 996
tiling, 795
time-critical rendering, 865
timer query, 785
timewarp, 935–937
timing, 955
TIN, 705, 877
Toksvig mapping, 369
Tom Clancy's The Division, 478
Tomb Raider (2013), 114, 116
Tomorrow Children, The, 496, 497
tonal art map, 671
tone mapping, 283–289
    global, 285
    local, 285
toon rendering, *see* shading, toon
top-left rule, 995
topology, 712
Torrance-Sparrow model, 334
tracking, 916, 921
transaction elimination, 1028
transcoding, *see under* texturing
transfer function, 161, 478
    volume, 605
transform, *57*, *see also* matrix
    affine, 58, 68
    angle-preserving, 66
    concatenation of, 65–66
    constraining, 73
    decomposition, 73–74
    Euler, 70–73
      extracting parameters, 72–73
      gimbal lock, 73
    feedback, 49
    inverse, 59, 61–64, 66, *69*, 75
      adjoint method, 69
      Cramer's rule, 69, 964

      Gaussian elimination, 69
      LU decomposition, 69
    length-preserving, 66
    linear, 57–58
    mirror, *see* transform, reflection
    model, 15–16
    morph targets, 89–91
    morphing, 87–91
    normal, 68–69
    orthographic, *see under* projection
    perspective, *see under* projection
    quaternion, 80
    reflection, 63, 692, 832
    rigid-body, 60, *66–67*, 74, 84
    rotation, 60–61
      about an arbitrary axis, 74–76
      from one vector to another, 83–84
      around a point, 61
    scaling, 62–63
      anisotropic, 62
      isotropic, 62
      nonuniform, 62
      uniform, 62
    shear, 63–64
    translation, 59
    vertex blending, *84–87*, 90, 102, 1006
    view, 15–16
    volume-preserving, 64
translation, 59
transparency, 148–160
    order-independent, 154–159
    screen-door, *149*, 858
    sorting, 152, 823
    stochastic, 149
    weighted average, 156–158
    weighted sum, 157
transparency adaptive antialiasing, 207
tree
    balanced, 820
    binary, 820
    k-ary tree, 820
trees (forest), 202, 559–560
triangle
    fan, 686, *696–697*
    formula, 944, 963
    list, 696
      indexed, 703
    setup, 22, 997–998
    sorting, 152–153, 802–803
    soup, 691
    strip, 697–699
      indexed, 703
      sequential, 698
    traversal, 22, 996–997
      tiled, 996

triangle/object intersection, *see specific objects under* intersection testing
triangulated irregular network, 705, 877
triangulation, 683–686
    Delaunay, 684
trilight, 432
trilinear interpolation, 186
triple buffer, 1013
tristimulus values, 273
true color mode, *see* color, mode, true color
TSM, *see* shadow, map, trapezoidal
turbulence, 198
T-vertex, *see under* polygon
TXAA, 142
Tyndall scattering, 298

UAV, *see* unordered access view
ubershader, 128
UBO, 795
UMA, *see* unified memory architecture
umbra, 224
Uncharted 2, 286, 357
Uncharted 3, 879
Uncharted 4, 290, 356–359, 492
Uncharted: Drake's Fortune, 893
under operator, 153
underclock, 787
unified memory architecture, 1007
unified shader architecture, 35, 786
uniform buffer object, 795
uniform tessellation, 767
Unity engine, 128, 287, 476, 482, 489, 740, 930
unordered access view, *51–52*, 87, 155, 192, 896, 1016
Unreal Engine, 104, 113, 114, 116, 126, 128–130, 143, 287, 325, 364, 383, 493, 495, 556, 572, 611, 740, 899, 930, 1048
up direction, 70
upsampling, 136

valence, 699, 758
Valgrind, 792
van Emde Boas layout, 827–828
VAO, 703
variance mapping, 370
VDC, *see* video display controller
vector irradiance, *379–380*, 389
vector norm, 7
Vega, *see under* hardware
vergence, 923, 932
vertex
    array, *see* vertex, buffer
    array object, 703
    blending, *see under* transform
    buffer, 701–705, 793

    cache, *see* cache, vertex
    clustering, 709
    compression, 712–715
    correspondence, 87
    pulling, 703
    shader, 15–16, *42–43*
        animation, 43
        effects, 43
        skinning, 87
    stream, 702
vertical refresh rate, 1011
vertical retrace, *see* retrace, vertical
vertical synchronization, *see* synchronization with monitor
vertices per second, 788
VGA, 1011
video display controller, 1011
video graphics array, 1011
video memory, 1006, 1011
view frustum culling, *see* culling, view frustum
view space, *15*, 26
view transform, *see* transform, view
view-independent progressive meshing, 706
VIPM, 706
virtual point light, 491
virtual reality, 523, 912, 915–940
    compositor, 924
    optics, 921–922
visibility
    buffer, *see* buffer, visibility
    cone, 470, 471
    function, 446
    test, 843
visual appearance, 103
Vive, 915, *916*, 917, 922, 925, 934
von Mises-Fisher distribution, 397
Von Neumann bottleneck, 791
voxel, 578–586
voxelization, *580–582*, 610–612, 974
VPL, *see* virtual point light
VSM, *see* shadow, map, variance
vsync, *see* synchronization with monitor
VTune, 792
Vulkan, *40*, 814

Wang tiles, 175
Ward model, 314
warp, 31
watercolor, 652, 665
watertight model, 693
watt, 268
wave
    electromagnetic, 293
    transverse, 293
wavefront, 31, 1035

wavelength, 267, 293
wavelets, 199
WebGL, *41*, 50, 122, 125, 129, 189, 201, 208,
          407, 485, 568, 628, 631, 713, 796, 805,
          829, 1048
welding vertices, 691
white point, 274
Wii, *see under* hardware
winding direction, 692
winding number, 968
window coordinates, 20
wireframe, 674, 675
The Witcher 3, 2, 263, 420, 526, 534, 873, 1049
world space, 15
wrap, *see* texturing, repeat
wrap lighting, 382, 633

Xbox, *see under* hardware
XR, 915

Y'CbCr, 892
yaw, 70n
YCoCg, *197–198*, 804–805
yon, 93n

z-buffer, *see under* buffer
z-fighting, 1014
z-prepass, *803*, 881, 882, 901, 1016
z-pyramid, 846
Zaxxon, 17
z_{max}-culling, *see* culling, z_{max}
z_{min}-culling, *see* culling, z_{min}
zonal harmonics, 401, 428, 430, 470